শ্রীচৈতন্যচরিতামৃত

Śrī Caitanya-caritāmṛta

BOOKS by
His Divine Grace
A. C. Bhaktivedanta Swami Prabhupāda

Bhagavad-gītā As It Is
Śrīmad-Bhāgavatam (18 vols., with disciples)
Śrī Caitanya-caritāmṛta (9 vols.)
The Nectar of Devotion
Kṛṣṇa, The Supreme Personality of Godhead
Teachings of Lord Caitanya
Śrī Īśopaniṣad
The Nectar of Instruction
Easy Journey to Other Planets
Kṛṣṇa Consciousness: The Topmost Yoga System
Perfect Questions, Perfect Answers
Teachings of Lord Kapila, the Son of Devahūti
Transcendental Teachings of Prahlāda Mahārāja
Dialectic Spiritualism—A Vedic View of Western Philosophy
Teachings of Queen Kuntī
Kṛṣṇa, the Reservoir of Pleasure
The Science of Self-Realization
The Path of Perfection
Search for Liberation
Life Comes from Life
The Perfection of Yoga
Beyond Birth and Death
On the Way to Kṛṣṇa
Rāja-vidyā: The King of Knowledge
Elevation to Kṛṣṇa Consciousness
Kṛṣṇa Consciousness: The Matchless Gift
The Nārada-bhakti-sūtra (with disciples)
The Mukunda-māla-stotra (with disciples)
A Second Chance
The Journey of Self-Discovery
The Laws of Nature
Wisdom Through Renunciation
Message of Godhead
Civilization and Transcendence
Geetār-gan (Bengali)
Vairāgya-vidyā (Bengali)
Buddhi-yoga (Bengali)
Bhakti-ratna-boli (Bengali)
Back to Godhead magazine (founder)

All Glories to Śrī Guru and Gaurāṅga

ŚRĪ CAITANYA-CARITĀMṚTA

of Kṛṣṇadāsa Kavirāja Gosvāmī

Ādi-līlā, Volume One
Chapters 1–7

with the original Bengali text, roman transliteration, English equivalents, translation and elaborate purports

by

HIS DIVINE GRACE
A. C. Bhaktivedanta Swami Prabhupāda
Founder-Ācārya of the International Society for Krishna Consciousness

THE BHAKTIVEDANTA BOOK TRUST
Los Angeles • Stockholm • Sydney • Hong Kong • Bombay

Readers interested in the subject matter of this book are invited by the International Society for Krishna Consciousness to correspond with its Secretary:

International Society for Krishna Consciousness
P.O. Box 262
Botany, NSW 2019
Australia

International Society for Krishna Consciousness
3764 Watseka Avenue
Los Angeles, California 90034
USA

International Society for Krishna Consciousness
P.O. Box 324
Borehamwood
Herts., WD6 1NB
United Kingdom

First Printing 1996: 3,000

Śrī Caitanya-caritāmṛta, originally published in 1975 in seventeen volumes, is now available in nine.

Library of Congress Catalog Card Number: 73-93206

ISBN 0 947259 07 4 (v. 1)
0 947259 06 6 (Set)

Printed in Australia

Presented to my friends
and devotees who like to read
my books and who approached me to request
that I render the great
Caitanya-caritāmṛta into English.

A. C. Bhaktivedanta Swami

Contents

Preface

There is no difference between the teachings of Lord Caitanya presented here and the teachings of Lord Kṛṣṇa in the *Bhagavad-gītā*. The teachings of Lord Caitanya are practical demonstrations of Lord Kṛṣṇa's teachings. Lord Kṛṣṇa's ultimate instruction in the *Bhagavad-gītā* is that everyone should surrender unto Him, Lord Kṛṣṇa. Kṛṣṇa promises to take immediate charge of such a surrendered soul. The Lord, the Supreme Personality of Godhead, is already in charge of the maintenance of this creation by virtue of His plenary expansion, Kṣīrodakaśāyī Viṣṇu, but this maintenance is not direct. However, when the Lord says that He takes charge of His pure devotee, He actually takes direct charge. A pure devotee is a soul who is forever surrendered to the Lord, just as a child is surrendered to his parents or an animal to its master. In the surrendering process, one should (1) accept things favorable for discharging devotional service, (2) reject things unfavorable, (3) always believe firmly in the Lord's protection, (4) feel exclusively dependent on the mercy of the Lord, (5) have no interest separate from the interest of the Lord, and (6) always feel oneself meek and humble.

The Lord demands that one surrender unto Him by following these six guidelines, but the unintelligent so-called scholars of the world misunderstand these demands and urge the general mass of people to reject them. At the conclusion of the Ninth Chapter of the *Bhagavad-gītā*, Lord Kṛṣṇa directly orders, "Always think of Me, become My devotee, worship Me alone, and offer obeisances unto Me alone." By so doing, the Lord says, one is sure to go to Him in His transcendental abode. But the scholarly demons misguide the masses of people by directing them to surrender not to the Personality of Godhead but rather to the impersonal, unmanifested, eternal, unborn truth. The impersonalist Māyāvādī philosophers do not accept that the ultimate aspect of the Absolute Truth is the Supreme Personality of Godhead. If one desires to understand the sun as it is, one must first face the sunshine and then the sun globe, and then, if one is able to enter into that globe, one may come face to face with the predominating deity of the sun. Due to a poor fund of knowledge, the Māyāvādī philosophers cannot go beyond the Brahman effulgence, which may be compared to the sunshine. The *Upaniṣads* confirm that one has to penetrate the dazzling effulgence of Brahman before one can see the real face of the Personality of Godhead.

Lord Caitanya therefore teaches direct worship of Lord Kṛṣṇa, who appeared as the foster child of the King of Vraja. He also teaches that the place known as Vṛndāvana is as good as Lord Kṛṣṇa because, Lord Kṛṣṇa being the Absolute Truth, there is no difference between Him and His name, qualities, form, pastimes, entourage and paraphernalia. That is the absolute nature of the Personality of Godhead. Lord Caitanya also teaches that the highest mode of worship in the highest perfectional stage is the method practiced by the damsels of Vraja. These damsels (*gopīs,* or cowherd girls) simply loved Kṛṣṇa without any motive for material or spiritual gain. Lord Caitanya also teaches that *Śrīmad-Bhāgavatam* is the spotless narration of transcendental knowledge and that the highest goal in human life is to develop unalloyed love for Kṛṣṇa, the Supreme Personality of Godhead.

Lord Caitanya's teachings are identical to those given by Lord Kapila, the original propounder of *sāṅkhya-yoga,* the *sāṅkhya* system of philosophy. This authorized system of *yoga* teaches meditation on the transcendental form of the Lord. There is no question of meditating on something void or impersonal. When one can meditate on the transcendental form of Lord Viṣṇu even without practicing involved sitting postures, such meditation is called perfect *samādhi.* That this kind of meditation is perfect *samādhi* is confirmed at the end of the Sixth Chapter of the *Bhagavad-gītā,* where Lord Kṛṣṇa says that of all *yogīs,* the greatest is the one who constantly thinks of the Lord within the core of his heart with love and devotion.

On the basis of the *sāṅkhya* philosophy of *acintya-bhedābheda-tattva,* which maintains that the Supreme Lord is simultaneously one with and different from His creation, Lord Caitanya taught that the most practical way for the mass of people to practice *sāṅkhya-yoga* meditation is simply to chant the holy name of the Lord. He taught that the holy name of the Lord is the sound incarnation of the Lord and that since the Lord is the absolute whole, there is no difference between His holy name and His transcendental form. Thus by chanting the holy name of the Lord one can directly associate with the Supreme Lord by sound vibration. As one practices chanting this sound vibration, one passes through three stages of development: the offensive stage, the clearing stage and the transcendental stage. In the offensive stage of chanting one may desire all kinds of material happiness, but in the second stage one becomes clear of all material contamination. When one is situated on the transcendental stage, one attains the most coveted position—the stage of loving God. Lord Caitanya taught that this is the highest stage of perfection for human beings.

Yoga practice is essentially meant for controlling the senses. The central controlling factor of all the senses is the mind; therefore one first has to practice controlling the mind by engaging it in Kṛṣṇa consciousness. The gross activities of the mind are expressed through the external senses, either for the acquisition of knowledge or for the functioning of the senses in accordance with the will. The subtle activities of the mind are thinking, feeling and willing, which are carried out according to one's consciousness, either polluted or clear. If one's mind is fixed on Kṛṣṇa (His name, qualities, form, pastimes, entourage and paraphernalia), all one's activities—both subtle and gross—become favorable. The *Bhagavad-gītā's* process of purifying consciousness is the process of fixing one's mind on Kṛṣṇa by talking of His transcendental activities, cleansing His temple, going to His temple, seeing the beautiful transcendental form of the Lord nicely decorated, hearing His transcendental glories, tasting food offered to Him, associating with His devotees, smelling the flowers and *tulasī* leaves offered to Him, engaging in activities for the Lord's interest, becoming angry at those who are malicious toward devotees, etc. No one can bring the activities of the mind and senses to a stop, but one can purify these activities through a change in consciousness. This change is indicated in the *Bhagavad-gītā* (2.39), where Kṛṣṇa tells Arjuna of the knowledge of *yoga* whereby one can work without fruitive results: "O son of Pṛthā, when you act in such knowledge you can free yourself from the bondage of works." A human being is sometimes restricted in sense gratification due to certain circumstances, such as disease, but such proscriptions are for the less intelligent. Without knowing the actual process by which the mind and senses can be controlled, less intelligent men may try to stop the mind and senses by force, but ultimately they give in to them and are carried away by the waves of sense gratification.

The eight principles of *sāṅkhya-yoga*—observing the regulative principles, following the rules, practicing the various sitting postures, performing the breathing exercises, withdrawing one's senses from the sense objects, etc.—are meant for those who are too much engrossed in the bodily conception of life. The intelligent man situated in Kṛṣṇa consciousness does not try to forcibly stop his senses from acting. Rather, he engages his senses in the service of Kṛṣṇa. No one can stop a child from playing by leaving him inactive; rather, the child can be stopped from engaging in nonsense by being engaged in superior activities. Similarly, the forceful restraint of sense activities by the eight principles of *yoga* is recommended for inferior men; superior men, being engaged in the superior activities of Kṛṣṇa consciousness, naturally retire from the inferior activities of material existence.

In this way Lord Caitanya teaches the science of Kṛṣṇa consciousness. That science is absolute. Dry mental speculators try to restrain themselves from material attachment, but it is generally found that the mind is too strong to be controlled and that it drags them down to sensual activities. A person in Kṛṣṇa consciousness does not run this risk. One therefore has to engage one's mind and senses in Kṛṣṇa conscious activities, and Lord Caitanya teaches one how to do this in practice.

Before accepting *sannyāsa* (the renounced order), Lord Caitanya was known as Viśvambhara. The word *viśvambhara* refers to one who maintains the entire universe and who leads all living entities. This maintainer and leader appeared as Lord Sri Kṛṣṇa Caitanya to give humanity these sublime teachings. Lord Caitanya is the ideal teacher of life's prime necessities. He is the most munificent bestower of love of Kṛṣṇa. He is the complete reservoir of all mercies and good fortune. As confirmed in *Śrīmad-Bhāgavatam,* the *Bhagavad-gītā,* the *Mahābhārata* and the *Upaniṣads,* He is the Supreme Personality of Godhead, Kṛṣṇa Himself, and He is worshipable by everyone in this age of disagreement. Everyone can join in His *saṅkīrtana* movement. No previous qualification is necessary. Just by following His teachings, anyone can become a perfect human being. If a person is fortunate enough to be attracted by Lord Caitanya, he is sure to be successful in his life's mission. In other words, those who are interested in attaining spiritual existence can easily be released from the clutches of *māyā* by the grace of Lord Caitanya. The teachings presented in this book are nondifferent from the Lord.

The conditioned soul, engrossed in the material body, increases the pages of history by all kinds of material activities. The teachings of Lord Caitanya can help the members of human society stop such unnecessary and temporary activities and be elevated to the topmost platform of spiritual activities, which begin after liberation from material bondage. Such liberated activities in Kṛṣṇa consciousness constitute the goal of human perfection. The false prestige one acquires by attempting to dominate material nature is illusory. Illuminating knowledge can be acquired by studying the teachings of Lord Caitanya, and by such knowledge one can advance in spiritual existence.

Everyone has to suffer or enjoy the fruits of his activity; no one can check the laws of material nature that govern such things. As long as one is engaged in fruitive activity, one is sure to be baffled in the attempt to attain the ultimate goal of life. I sincerely hope that by understanding the teachings of Lord Caitanya presented in this book, *Śrī Caitanya-caritāmṛta,* human society will experience a new light of spiritual life, which will open the field of activity for the pure soul.

oṁ tat sat

A. C. Bhaktivedanta Swami

March 14, 1968
The Birthday of Lord Caitanya
Śrī Śrī Rādhā-Kṛṣṇa Temple
New York, N.Y.

Foreword

Śrī Caitanya-caritāmṛta, by Śrīla Kṛṣṇadāsa Kavirāja Gosvāmī, is the principal work on the life and teachings of Śrī Kṛṣṇa Caitanya Mahāprabhu. Caitanya Mahāprabhu is the pioneer of a great social and religious movement that began in India about five hundred years ago and that has directly and indirectly influenced the subsequent course of religious and philosophical thinking not only in India but throughout the world. That Śrī Kṛṣṇa Caitanya's influence has spread so far is due in large part to the efforts of His Divine Grace A. C. Bhaktivedanta Swami Prabhupāda, the present work's translator and commentator and the founder and *ācārya* (spiritual guide) of the International Society for Krishna Consciousness.

Caitanya Mahāprabhu is thus a figure of great historical significance. However, our conventional method of historical analysis—that of seeing a man as a product of his times—fails here, for Śrī Kṛṣṇa Caitanya is a personality who transcends the limited scope of historical settings.

At a time when, in the West, man was directing his explorative spirit toward studying the structure of the physical universe and circumnavigating the world in search of new oceans and continents, Śrī Kṛṣṇa Caitanya, in the East, was inaugurating and masterminding a revolution directed inward, toward a scientific understanding of the highest knowledge of man's spiritual nature.

The chief historical sources for the life of Śrī Kṛṣṇa Caitanya are the *kadacas* (diaries) kept by Murāri Gupta and Svarūpa Dāmodara Gosvāmī. Murāri Gupta, a physician and close associate of Śrī Kṛṣṇa Caitanya's, recorded extensive notes on the first twenty-four years of His life, culminating in His initiation into the renounced order, *sannyāsa*. The events of the rest of Caitanya Mahāprabhu's forty-eight years were recorded in the diary of Svarūpa Dāmodara Gosvāmī, another of His intimate associates.

Śrī Caitanya-caritāmṛta is divided into three sections, called *līlās*, a word that literally means "pastimes"—*Ādi-līlā* (the early period),

Madhya-līlā (the middle period) and *Antya-līlā* (the final period). The notes of Murāri Gupta form the basis of the *Ādi-līlā*, and Svarūpa Dāmodara's diary provides the details for the *Madhya-* and *Antya-līlās*.

The first twelve chapters of the *Ādi-līlā* constitute the preface for the entire work. By referring to Vedic scriptural evidence, Kṛṣṇadāsa Kavirāja establishes that Caitanya Mahāprabhu is the *avatāra* (incarnation) of God for the Age of Kali—the current epoch, which began five thousand years ago and is characterized by materialism, hypocrisy and dissension. The author also proves that Caitanya Mahāprabhu is identical to Lord Kṛṣṇa and explains that He descends to liberally grant the fallen souls of this degraded age pure love of God by propagating *saṅkīrtana*—literally, "congregational glorification of God"—especially by organizing massive public chanting of the *mahā-mantra* (Great Chant for Deliverance). In addition, in the twelve-chapter preface Kṛṣṇadāsa Kavirāja reveals the esoteric purpose of Lord Caitanya's appearance in the world, describes His co-*avatāras* and principal devotees, and summarizes His teachings. In the remaining portion of the *Ādi-līlā*, chapters thirteen through seventeen, the author briefly recounts Lord Caitanya's divine birth and His life until He accepted the renounced order. This account includes His childhood miracles, schooling, marriage and early philosophical confrontations, as well as His organization of a widespread *saṅkīrtana* movement and His civil disobedience against the repression of the Muslim government.

The *Madhya-līlā*, the longest of the three divisions, narrates in detail Lord Caitanya's extensive and eventful travels throughout India as a renounced mendicant, teacher, philosopher, spiritual preceptor and mystic. During this period of six years, Śrī Caitanya Mahāprabhu transmits His teachings to His principal disciples. He debates and converts many of the renowned philosophers and theologians of His time, including Śaṅkarites, Buddhists and Muslims, and incorporates their many thousands of followers and disciples into His own burgeoning numbers. The author also includes in this section a dramatic account of Caitanya Mahāprabhu's miraculous activities at the giant Ratha-yātrā (Car Festival) in Jagannātha Purī, Orissa.

The *Antya-līlā* concerns the last eighteen years of Śrī Caitanya's manifest presence, spent in semiseclusion near the famous Jagannātha temple at Purī. During these final years, Śrī Kṛṣṇa Caitanya drifted deeper and deeper into trances of spiritual ecstasy unparalleled in all of religious and literary history, Eastern or Western. His perpetual and ever-increasing religious beatitude, graphically described in the eye-witness accounts of Svarūpa Dāmodara Gosvāmī, His constant companion during this period, clearly defy the investigative and descriptive abilities of modern psychologists and phenomenologists of religious experience.

The author of this great classic, Kṛṣṇadāsa Kavirāja Gosvāmī, born around the beginning of the sixteenth century, was a disciple of Raghunātha dāsa Gosvāmī, a confidential follower of Caitanya Mahāprabhu's. Raghunātha dāsa, a renowned ascetic saint, heard and memorized all the activities of Caitanya Mahāprabhu told to him by Svarūpa Dāmodara Gosvāmī. After the passing away of Śrī Caitanya Mahāprabhu and Svarūpa Dāmodara, Raghunātha dāsa, unable to bear the pain of separation from these objects of his complete devotion, traveled to Vṛndāvana, intending to commit suicide by jumping from Govardhana Hill. In Vṛndāvana, however, he encountered Śrīla Rūpa Gosvāmī and Śrīla Sanātana Gosvāmī, two of the most confidential disciples of Caitanya Mahāprabhu. They convinced him to give up his planned suicide and impelled him to reveal to them the spiritually inspiring events of Lord Caitanya's later life. Kṛṣṇadāsa Kavirāja Gosvāmī was also residing in Vṛndāvana at this time, and Raghunātha dāsa Gosvāmī endowed him with a full comprehension of the transcendental life of Śrī Caitanya Mahāprabhu.

By this time, contemporary and near-contemporary scholars and devotees had already written several biographical works on the life of Śrī Kṛṣṇa Caitanya. These included *Śrī Caitanya-carita*, by Murāri Gupta, *Caitanya-maṅgala*, by Locana dāsa Ṭhākura, and *Caitanya-bhāgavata*. This latter work, by Vṛndāvana dāsa Ṭhākura, who was then considered the principal authority on Śrī Caitanya's life, was highly revered. While composing his important work, Vṛndāvana dāsa, fearing that it would become too voluminous, avoided elaborately describing many of the events of Caitanya Mahāprabhu's life, particularly the later ones. Anxious to hear of these later pastimes, the devotees in Vṛndāvana requested Kṛṣṇadāsa Kavirāja Gosvāmī, whom they respected as a great saint and scholar, to compose a book narrating these episodes in detail. Upon this request, and with the permission and blessings of the Madana-mohana Deity of Vṛndāvana, he began compiling *Śrī Caitanya-caritāmṛta*, which, due to its literary excellence and philosophical thoroughness, is today universally regarded as the foremost work on the life and profound teachings of Śrī Caitanya Mahāprabhu.

Kṛṣṇadāsa Kavirāja Gosvāmī commenced work on the text at a very advanced age and in failing health, as he vividly describes in the text itself: "I have now become too old and disturbed by invalidity. While writing, my hands tremble. I cannot remember anything, nor can I see or hear properly. Still I write, and this is a great wonder." That he completed the greatest literary gem of medieval India under such debilitating conditions is surely one of the wonders of literary history.

As mentioned above, this English translation and commentary is the work of His Divine Grace A. C. Bhaktivedanta Swami Prabhupāda, the world's most distinguished teacher of Indian religious and philosophical thought. Śrīla Prabhupāda's commentary is based upon two Bengali commentaries, one by his *guru,* Śrīla Bhaktisiddhānta Sarasvatī Gosvāmī, the eminent Vedic scholar, teacher and saint who predicted, "The time will come when the people of the world will learn Bengali to read *Śrī Caitanya-caritāmṛta,*" and the other by Śrīla Bhaktisiddhānta Sarasvatī's father, Śrīla Bhaktivinoda Ṭhākura, who pioneered the propagation of Śrī Caitanya Mahāprabhu's teachings in the modern era.

Śrīla Prabhupāda is himself a disciplic descendant of Śrī Caitanya Mahāprabhu, and he is the first scholar to execute systematic English translations of the major works of Śrī Kṛṣṇa Caitanya's followers. His consummate Bengali and Sanskrit scholarship and intimate familiarity with the precepts of Śrī Kṛṣṇa Caitanya are a fitting combination that eminently qualifies him to present this important classic to the English-speaking world. The ease and clarity with which he expounds upon difficult philosophical concepts enable even a reader totally unfamiliar with Indian religious tradition to understand and appreciate this profound and monumental work.

The entire text, with commentary, presented in nine lavishly illustrated volumes by the Bhaktivedanta Book Trust, represents a contribution of major importance to the intellectual, cultural and spiritual life of contemporary man.

—The Publishers

Editor's note: Revisions in this edition are based on the transcripts of His Divine Grace A. C. Bhaktivedanta Swami Prabhupāda's original dictation of the translations, word meanings and purports of *Śrī Caitanya-caritāmṛta.*

Introduction

(Originally delivered as five morning lectures on the Caitanya-caritāmṛta*—the authoritative biography of Lord Caitanya Mahāprabhu by Kṛṣṇadāsa Kavirāja Gosvāmī—before the International Society for Krishna Consciousness, New York City, April 10–14, 1967.)*

The word *caitanya* means "living force," *carita* means "character," and *amṛta* means "immortal." As living entities we can move, but a table cannot because it does not possess living force. Movement and activity may be considered signs or symptoms of the living force. Indeed, it may be said that there can be no activity without the living force. Although the living force is present in the material condition, this condition is not *amṛta*, immortal. The words *caitanya-caritāmṛta*, then, may be translated as "the character of the living force in immortality."

But how is this living force displayed immortally? It is not displayed by man or any other creature in this material universe, for none of us are immortal in these bodies. We possess the living force, we perform activities, and we are immortal by our nature and constitution, but the material condition into which we have been put does not allow our immortality to be displayed. It is stated in the *Kaṭha Upaniṣad* that eternality and the living force belong to both ourselves and God. Although this is true in that both God and ourselves are immortal, there is a difference. As living entities, we perform many activities, but we have a tendency to fall down into material nature. God has no such tendency. Being all-powerful, He never comes under the control of material nature. Indeed, material nature is but one display of His inconceivable energies.

An analogy will help us understand the distinction between ourselves and God. From the ground we may see only clouds in the sky, but if we fly above the clouds we can see the sun shining. From the sky, skyscrapers and cities seem very tiny; similarly, from God's position this entire material creation is insignificant. The tendency of the living entity is to come down from the heights, where everything can be seen in perspective. God, however, does not have this tendency. The Supreme Lord is not subject to fall down into illusion (*māyā*) any more than the sun is subject to fall beneath the clouds. Impersonalist philosophers (Māyāvādīs) maintain that both the living entity and God Himself are under the control of *māyā* when they come into this material world. This is the fallacy of their philosophy.

Lord Caitanya Mahāprabhu should therefore not be considered one of us. He is Kṛṣṇa Himself, the supreme living entity, and as such He never comes under the cloud of *māyā*. Kṛṣṇa, His expansions and even His higher devotees never fall into the clutches of illusion. Lord Caitanya came to earth simply to preach *kṛṣṇa-bhakti*, love of Kṛṣṇa. In other words, He is Lord Kṛṣṇa Himself teaching the living entities the proper way to approach Kṛṣṇa. He is like a teacher who, seeing a student doing poorly, takes up a pencil and writes, saying, "Do it like this: A, B, C." From this one should not foolishly think that the teacher is learning his ABC's. Similarly, although Lord Caitanya appears in the guise of a devotee, we should not foolishly think He is an ordinary human being; we should always remember that Lord Caitanya is Kṛṣṇa (God) Himself teaching us how to become Kṛṣṇa conscious, and we must study Him in that light.

In the *Bhagavad-gītā* (18.66) Lord Kṛṣṇa says, "Give up all your nonsense and surrender to Me. I will protect you."

We say, "Oh, surrender? But I have so many responsibilities."

And *māyā*, illusion, says to us, "Don't do it, or you'll be out of my clutches. Just stay in my clutches, and I'll kick you."

It is a fact that we are constantly being kicked by *māyā*, just as the male ass is kicked in the face by the she-ass when he comes for sex. Similarly, cats and dogs are always fighting and whining when they have sex. Even an elephant in the jungle is caught by the use of a trained she-elephant who leads him into a pit. We should learn by observing these tricks of nature.

Māyā has many ways to entrap us, and her strongest shackle is the female. Of course, in actuality we are neither male nor female, for these designations refer only to the outer dress, the body. We are all actually Kṛṣṇa's servants. But in conditioned life we are shackled by iron chains in the form of beautiful women. Thus every male is bound by sex, and therefore one who wishes to gain liberation from the material clutches must first learn to control the sex urge. Unrestricted sex puts one fully in the clutches of illusion. Lord Caitanya Mahāprabhu officially renounced this illusion at the age of twenty-four, although His wife was sixteen and His mother seventy and He was the only male in the family. Although He was a *brāhmaṇa* and was not rich, He took *sannyāsa,* the renounced order of life, and thus extricated Himself from family entanglement.

If we wish to become fully Kṛṣṇa conscious, we have to give up the shackles of *māyā*. Or, if we remain with *māyā,* we should live in such a way that we will not be subject to illusion, as did the many householders among Lord Caitanya's closest devotees. With His followers in the renounced order, however, Lord Caitanya was very strict. He even banished Junior Haridāsa, an important *kīrtana* leader, for glancing lustfully at a woman. The Lord told him, "You are living with Me in the renounced order, and yet you are looking at a woman with lust." Other devotees of the Lord had appealed to Him to forgive Haridāsa, but He replied, "All of you can forgive him and live with him. I shall live alone." On the other hand, when the Lord learned that the wife of one of His householder devotees was pregnant, He asked that the baby be given a certain auspicious name. So while the Lord approved of householders having regulated sex, He was like a thunderbolt with those in the renounced order who tried to cheat by the method known as "drinking water under water while bathing on a fast day." In other words, He tolerated no hypocrisy among His followers.

From the *Caitanya-caritāmṛta* we learn how Lord Caitanya taught people to break the shackles of *māyā* and become immortal. Thus, as mentioned above, the title may be properly translated as "the character of the living force in immortality." The supreme living force is the Supreme Personality of Godhead. He is also the supreme entity. There are innumerable living entities, and all of them are individuals. This is very easy to understand: We are all individual in our thoughts and desires, and the Supreme Lord is also an individual person. He is different, though, in that He is the leader, the one whom no one can excel. Among the minute living entities, one being can excel another in one capacity or another. Like each of these living entities, the Lord is an individual, but He is different in that He is the supreme individual. God is also infallible, and thus in the *Bhagavad-gītā* He is addressed as Acyuta, which means "He who never falls down." This name is appropriate because in the *Bhagavad-gītā* Arjuna falls into illusion but Kṛṣṇa does not. Kṛṣṇa Himself reveals His infallibility when he says to Arjuna, "When I appear in this world, I do so by My own internal potency." (Bg. 4.6)

Thus we should not think that Kṛṣṇa is overpowered by the material potency when He is in the material world. Neither Kṛṣṇa nor His incarnations ever come under the control of material nature. They are totally free. Indeed, in *Śrīmad-Bhāgavatam* one who has a godly nature is actually defined as one who is not affected by the modes of material nature although in material nature. If even a devotee can attain this freedom, then what to speak of the Supreme Lord?

The real question is, How can we remain unpolluted by material contamination while in the material world? Śrīla Rūpa Gosvāmī explains that we can remain uncontaminated while in the world if we simply make it our ambition to serve Kṛṣṇa. One may then justifiably ask, "How can I serve?" It is not simply a matter of meditation, which is just an activity of the mind, but of performing practical work for Kṛṣṇa. In such work, we should leave no resource unused. Whatever is there, whatever we have, should be used for Kṛṣṇa. We can use everything—typewriters, automobiles, airplanes, missiles. If we simply speak to people about Kṛṣṇa consciousness, we are also rendering service. If our mind, senses, speech, money and energies are thus engaged in the service of Kṛṣṇa, then we are no longer in material nature. By virtue of spiritual consciousness, or Kṛṣṇa consciousness, we transcend the platform of material nature. It is a fact that Kṛṣṇa, His expansions and His devotees—that is, those who work for Him—are not in material nature, although people with a poor fund of knowledge think that they are.

The *Caitanya-caritāmṛta* teaches that the spirit soul is immortal and that our activities in the spiritual world are also immortal. The Māyāvādīs, who hold the view that the Absolute is impersonal and formless, contend that a realized soul has no need to talk. But the Vaiṣṇavas, devotees of Kṛṣṇa, contend that when one reaches the stage of realization, he really begins to talk. "Previously we only talked of nonsense," the Vaiṣṇava says. "Now let us begin our real talks, talks of Kṛṣṇa." In support of their view that the self-realized remain silent, the Māyāvādīs are fond of using the analogy of the waterpot, maintaining that when a pot is not filled with water it makes a sound, but that when it is filled it makes no sound. But are we waterpots? How can we be compared to them? A good analogy utilizes as many similarities between two objects as possible. A waterpot is not an active living force, but we are. Ever-silent meditation may be adequate for a waterpot, but not for us. Indeed, when a devotee realizes how much he has to say about Kṛṣṇa, twenty-four hours in a day are not sufficient. It is the fool who is celebrated as long as he does not speak, for when he breaks his silence his lack of knowledge is exposed. The *Caitanya-caritāmṛta* shows that there are many wonderful things to discover by glorifying the Supreme.

In the beginning of the *Caitanya-caritāmṛta*, Kṛṣṇadāsa Kavirāja Gosvāmī writes, "I offer my respects to my spiritual masters." He uses the plural here to indicate the disciplic succession. He offers obeisances not to his spiritual master alone but to the whole *paramparā*, the chain of disciplic succession beginning with Lord Kṛṣṇa Himself. Thus the author addresses the *guru* in the plural to show the highest respect for all his predecessor spiritual masters. After offering obeisances to the disciplic succession, the author pays obeisances to all other devotees, to the Lord Himself, to His incarnations, to the expansions of Godhead and to the manifestation of Kṛṣṇa's internal energy. Lord Caitanya Mahāprabhu (sometimes called Kṛṣṇa Caitanya) is the embodiment of all of these: He is God, *guru*, devotee, incarnation, internal energy and expansion of God. As His associate Nityānanda, He is the first expansion of God; as Advaita, He is an incarnation; as Gadādhara, He is the internal potency; and as Śrīvāsa, He is the marginal living entity in the role of a devotee. Thus Kṛṣṇa should not be thought of as being alone but should be considered as eternally existing with all His manifestations, as described by Rāmānujācārya. In the Viśiṣṭādvaita philosophy, God's energies, expansions and incarnations are considered to be oneness in diversity. In other words, God is not separate from all of these: everything together is God.

Actually, the *Caitanya-caritāmṛta* is not intended for the novice, for it is the postgraduate study of spiritual knowledge. Ideally, one begins with the *Bhagavad-gītā* and advances through *Śrīmad-Bhāgavatam* to the *Caitanya-caritāmṛta*. Although all these great scriptures are on the same absolute level, for the sake of comparative study the *Caitanya-caritāmṛta* is considered to be on the highest platform. Every verse in it is perfectly composed.

In the second verse of the *Caitanya-caritāmṛta*, the author offers his obeisances to Lord Caitanya and Lord Nityānanda. He compares them to the sun and the moon because They dissipate the darkness of the material world. In this instance the sun and the moon have risen together.

In the Western world, where the glories of Lord Caitanya are relatively unknown, one may inquire, "Who is Kṛṣṇa Caitanya?" The author of the *Caitanya-caritāmṛta*, Śrīla Kṛṣṇadāsa Kavirāja, answers that question in the third verse of his book. Generally, in the *Upaniṣads* the Supreme Absolute Truth is described in an impersonal way, but the personal aspect of the Absolute Truth is mentioned in the *Īśopaniṣad*, where we find the following verse:

hiraṇmayena pātreṇa satyasyāpihitaṁ mukham
tat tvaṁ pūṣann apāvṛṇu satya-dharmāya dṛṣṭaye

"O my Lord, sustainer of all that lives, Your real face is covered by Your dazzling effulgence. Kindly remove that covering and exhibit Yourself to Your pure devotee." (*Śrī Īśopaniṣad* 15) The impersonalists do not have the power to go beyond the effulgence of God and arrive at the Personality of Godhead, from whom this effulgence is emanating. The *Īśopaniṣad* is a hymn to that Personality of Godhead. It is not that the impersonal Brahman is denied; it is also described, but that Brahman is revealed to be the glaring effulgence of the body of Lord Kṛṣṇa. And in the *Caitanya-caritāmṛta* we learn that Lord Caitanya is Kṛṣṇa Himself. In other words, Śrī Kṛṣṇa Caitanya is the basis of the impersonal Brahman. The Paramātmā, or Supersoul, who is present within the heart of every living entity and within every atom of the universe, is but the partial representation of Lord Caitanya. Therefore Śrī Kṛṣṇa Caitanya, being the basis of both Brahman and the all-pervading Paramātmā as well, is the Supreme Personality of Godhead. As such, He is full in six opulences: wealth, fame, strength, beauty, knowledge and renunciation. In short, we should know that He is Kṛṣṇa, God, and that nothing is equal to or greater than Him. There is nothing superior to be conceived. He is the Supreme Person.

Śrīla Rūpa Gosvāmī, a confidential devotee taught for more than ten days continually by Lord Caitanya, wrote:

namo mahā-vadānyāya kṛṣṇa-prema-pradāya te
kṛṣṇāya kṛṣṇa-caitanya-nāmne gaura-tviṣe namaḥ

"I offer my respectful obeisances unto the Supreme Lord Śrī Kṛṣṇa Caitanya, who is more magnanimous than any other *avatāra,* even Kṛṣṇa Himself, because He is bestowing freely what no one else has ever given—pure love of Kṛṣṇa."

Lord Caitanya's teachings begin from the point of surrender to Kṛṣṇa. He does not pursue the paths of *karma-yoga* or *jñāna-yoga* or *haṭha-yoga* but begins at the end of material existence, at the point where one gives up all material attachment. In the *Bhagavad-gītā* Kṛṣṇa begins His teachings by distinguishing the soul from matter, and in the Eighteenth Chapter He concludes at the point where the soul surrenders to Him in devotion. The Māyāvādīs would have all talk cease there, but at that point the real discussion only begins. As the *Vedānta-sūtra* says at the very beginning, *athāto brahma-jijñāsā:* "Now let us begin to inquire about the Supreme Absolute Truth." Rūpa Gosvāmī thus praises Lord Caitanya as the most munificent incarnation of all, for He gives the greatest gift by teaching the highest form of devotional service. In other words, He answers the most important inquiries that anyone can make.

There are different stages of devotional service and God realization. Strictly speaking, anyone who accepts the existence of God is situated in devotional service. To acknowledge that God is great is something, but not much. Lord Caitanya, preaching as an *ācārya,* a great teacher, taught that we can enter into a relationship with God and actually become God's friend, parent or lover. In the *Bhagavad-gītā* Kṛṣṇa showed Arjuna His universal form because Arjuna was His very dear friend. Upon seeing Kṛṣṇa as the Lord of the universes, however, Arjuna asked Kṛṣṇa to forgive the familiarity of his friendship. Lord Caitanya goes beyond this point. Through Lord Caitanya we can become friends with Kṛṣṇa, and there will be no limit to this friendship. We can become friends of Kṛṣṇa not in awe or adoration but in complete freedom. We can even relate to God as His father or mother. This is the philosophy not only of the *Caitanya-caritāmṛta* but of *Śrīmad-Bhāgavatam* as well. There are no other scriptures in the world in which God is treated as the son of a devotee. Usually God is seen as the almighty father who supplies the demands of His sons. The great devotees, however, sometimes treat God as a son in their execution of devotional service. The son demands, and the father and mother supply, and in supplying Kṛṣṇa the devotee becomes like a father or mother. Instead of taking from God, we give to God. It was in this relationship that Kṛṣṇa's mother, Yaśodā, told the Lord, "Here, eat this or You'll die. Eat nicely." In this way Kṛṣṇa, although the proprietor of everything, depends on the mercy of His devotee. This is a uniquely high level of friendship, in which the devotee actually believes himself to be the father or mother of Kṛṣṇa.

However, Lord Caitanya's greatest gift was His teaching that Kṛṣṇa can be treated as one's lover. In this relationship the Lord becomes so much attached to His devotee that He expresses His inability to reciprocate. Kṛṣṇa was so obliged to the *gopīs,* the cowherd girls of Vṛndāvana, that He felt unable to return their love. "I cannot repay your love," He told them. "I have no more assets to give." Devotional service on this highest, most excellent platform of lover and beloved, which had never been given by any previous incarnation or *ācārya,* was given by Caitanya Mahāprabhu. Therefore Kṛṣṇadāsa Kavirāja, quoting Śrīla Rūpa Gosvāmī, writes in the fourth verse of his book, "Lord Caitanya is

Kṛṣṇa in a yellow complexion, and He is Śacīnandana, the son of mother Śacī. He is the most charitable personality because He came to deliver *kṛṣṇa-prema*, unalloyed love for Kṛṣṇa, to everyone. May you always keep Him in your hearts. It will be easy to understand Kṛṣṇa through Him."

We have often heard the phrase "love of Godhead." How far this love of Godhead can actually be developed can be learned from the Vaiṣṇava philosophy. Theoretical knowledge of love of God can be found in many places and in many scriptures, but what that love of Godhead actually is and how it is developed can be found in the Vaiṣṇava literatures. It is the unique and highest development of love of God that is given by Caitanya Mahāprabhu.

Even in this material world we can have a little sense of love. How is this possible? It is due to the presence of our original love of God. Whatever we find within our experience within this conditioned life is situated in the Supreme Lord, who is the ultimate source of everything. In our original relationship with the Supreme Lord there is real love, and that love is reflected pervertedly through material conditions. Our real love is continuous and unending, but because that love is reflected pervertedly in this material world, it lacks continuity and is inebriating. If we want real, transcendental love, we have to transfer our love to the supreme lovable object—Kṛṣṇa, the Supreme Personality of Godhead. This is the basic principle of Kṛṣṇa consciousness.

In material consciousness we are trying to love that which is not at all lovable. We give our love to cats and dogs, running the risk that at the time of death we may think of them and consequently take birth in a family of cats or dogs. Our consciousness at the time of death determines our next life. That is one reason why the Vedic scriptures stress the chastity of women: If a woman is very much attached to her husband, at the time of death she will think of him, and in the next life she will be promoted to a man's body. Generally a man's life is better than a woman's because a man usually has better facilities for understanding the spiritual science.

But Kṛṣṇa consciousness is so nice that it makes no distinction between man and woman. In the *Bhagavad-gītā* (9.32), Lord Kṛṣṇa says, "Anyone who takes shelter of Me—whether a woman, *śūdra*, *vaiśya* or anyone else of low birth—is sure to achieve My association." This is Kṛṣṇa's guarantee.

Caitanya Mahāprabhu informs us that in every country and in every scripture there is some hint of love of Godhead. But no one knows what love of Godhead actually is. The Vedic scriptures, however, are different in that they can direct the individual in the proper way to love God. Other scriptures do not give information on how one can love God, nor do they actually define or describe *what* or *who* the Godhead actually is. Although they officially promote love of Godhead, they have no idea how to execute it. But Caitanya Mahāprabhu gives a practical demonstration of how to love God in a conjugal relationship. Taking the part of Śrīmatī Rādhārāṇī, Caitanya Mahāprabhu tried to love Kṛṣṇa as Rādhārāṇī loved Him. Kṛṣṇa was always amazed by Rādhārāṇī's love. "How does Rādhārāṇī give Me such pleasure?" He would ask. In order to study Rādhārāṇī, Kṛṣṇa lived in Her role and tried to understand Himself. This is the secret of Lord Caitanya's incarnation. Caitanya Mahāprabhu is Kṛṣṇa, but He has taken the mood and role of Rādhārāṇī to show us how to love Kṛṣṇa. Thus the author writes in the fifth verse, "I offer my respectful obeisances unto the Supreme Lord, who is absorbed in Rādhārāṇī's thoughts."

This brings up the question of who Śrīmatī Rādhārāṇī is and what Rādhā-Kṛṣṇa is. Actually Rādhā-Kṛṣṇa is the exchange of love—but not ordinary love. Kṛṣṇa has immense potencies, of which three are principal: the internal, the external and the marginal potencies. In the internal potency there are three divisions: *saṁvit, hlādinī* and *sandhinī.* The *hlādinī* potency is Kṛṣṇa's pleasure potency. All living entities have this pleasure-seeking potency, for all beings are trying to have pleasure. This is the very nature of the living entity. At present we are trying to enjoy our pleasure potency by means of the body in the material condition. By bodily contact we are attempting to derive pleasure from material sense objects. But we should not entertain the nonsensical idea that Kṛṣṇa, who is always spiritual, also tries to seek pleasure on this material plane. In the *Bhagavad-gītā* Kṛṣṇa describes the material universe as a nonpermanent place full of miseries. Why, then, would He seek pleasure in matter? He is the Supersoul, the supreme spirit, and His pleasure is beyond the material conception.

To learn how Kṛṣṇa enjoys pleasure, we must study the first nine cantos of *Śrīmad-Bhāgavatam,* and then we should study the Tenth Canto, in which Kṛṣṇa's pleasure potency is displayed in His pastimes with Rādhārāṇī and the damsels of Vraja. Unfortunately, unintelligent people turn at once to the sports of Kṛṣṇa in the *Daśama-skandha,* the Tenth Canto. Kṛṣṇa's embracing Rādhārāṇī or His dancing with the cowherd girls in the *rāsa* dance are generally not understood by ordinary men, because they consider these pastimes in the light of mundane lust. They foolishly think that Kṛṣṇa is like themselves and that He embraces the *gopīs* just as an ordinary man embraces a young girl. Some people thus become interested in Kṛṣṇa because they think that His religion allows indulgence in sex. This is not *kṛṣṇa-bhakti,* love of Kṛṣṇa, but *prākṛta-sahajiyā*—materialistic lust.

To avoid such errors, we should understand what Rādhā-Kṛṣṇa actually is. Rādhā and Kṛṣṇa display Their pastimes through Kṛṣṇa's internal energy. The pleasure potency of Kṛṣṇa's internal energy is a most difficult subject matter, and unless one understands what Kṛṣṇa is, one cannot understand it. Kṛṣṇa does not take any pleasure in this material world, but He has a pleasure potency. Because we are part and parcel of Kṛṣṇa, the pleasure potency is within us also, but we are trying to exhibit that pleasure potency in matter. Kṛṣṇa, however, does not make such a vain attempt. The object of Kṛṣṇa's pleasure potency is Rādhārāṇī; Kṛṣṇa exhibits His potency as Rādhārāṇī and then engages in loving affairs with Her. In other words, Kṛṣṇa does not take pleasure in this external energy but exhibits His internal energy, His pleasure potency, as Rādhārāṇī and then enjoys with Her. Thus Kṛṣṇa manifests Himself as Rādhārāṇī in order to enjoy His internal pleasure potency. Of the many extensions, expansions and incarnations of the Lord, this pleasure potency is the foremost and chief.

It is not that Rādhārāṇī is separate from Kṛṣṇa. Rādhārāṇī is also Kṛṣṇa, for there is no difference between the energy and the energetic. Without energy, there is no meaning to the energetic, and without the energetic, there is no energy. Similarly, without Rādhā there is no meaning to Kṛṣṇa, and without Kṛṣṇa there is no meaning to Rādhā. Because of this, the Vaiṣṇava philosophy first of all pays obeisances to and worships the internal pleasure potency of the Supreme Lord. Thus the Lord and His potency are always referred to as Rādhā-Kṛṣṇa. Similarly, those who worship Nārāyaṇa first of all utter the name of Lakṣmī, as Lakṣmī-Nārāyaṇa. Similarly, those who worship Lord Rāma first of all utter the name of Sītā. In any case—Sītā-Rāma, Rādhā-Kṛṣṇa, Lakṣmī-Nārāyaṇa—the potency always comes first.

Rādhā and Kṛṣṇa are one, and when Kṛṣṇa desires to enjoy pleasure, He manifests Himself as Rādhārāṇī. The spiritual exchange of love between Rādhā and Kṛṣṇa is the actual display of Kṛṣṇa's internal pleasure potency. Although we speak of "when" Kṛṣṇa desires, just when He did desire we cannot say. We only speak in this way because in conditioned life we take it that everything has a beginning; however, in spiritual life everything is absolute, and so there is neither beginning nor end.

Yet in order to understand that Rādhā and Kṛṣṇa are one and that They also become divided, the question "When?" automatically comes to mind. When Kṛṣṇa desired to enjoy His pleasure potency, He manifested Himself in the separate form of Rādhārāṇī, and when He wanted to understand Himself through the agency of Rādhā, He united with Rādhārāṇī, and that unification is called Lord Caitanya. This is all explained by Śrīla Kṛṣṇadāsa Kavirāja in the fifth verse of the *Caitanya-caritāmṛta.*

In the next verse the author further explains why Kṛṣṇa assumed the form of Caitanya Mahāprabhu. Kṛṣṇa desired to know the glory of Rādhā's love. "Why is She so much in love with Me?" Kṛṣṇa asked. "What is My special qualification that attracts Her so? And what is the actual way in which She loves Me?" It seems strange that Kṛṣṇa, as the Supreme, should be attracted by anyone's love. A man searches after the love of a woman because he is imperfect—he lacks something. The love of a woman, that potency and pleasure, is absent in man, and therefore a man wants a woman. But this is not the case with Kṛṣṇa, who is full in Himself. Thus Kṛṣṇa expressed surprise: "Why am I attracted by Rādhārāṇī? And when Rādhārāṇī feels My love, what is She actually feeling?" To taste the essence of that loving exchange, Kṛṣṇa made His appearance in the same way that the moon appears on the horizon of the sea. Just as the moon was produced by the churning of the sea, by the churning of spiritual loving affairs the moon of Caitanya Mahāprabhu appeared. Indeed, Lord Caitanya's complexion was golden, just like the luster of the moon. Although this is figurative language, it conveys the meaning behind the appearance of Caitanya Mahāprabhu. The full significance of His appearance will be explained in later chapters.

After offering respects to Lord Caitanya, Kṛṣṇadāsa Kavirāja begins offering them to Lord Nityānanda in the seventh verse of the *Caitanya-caritāmṛta.* The author explains that Lord Nityānanda is Balarāma, who is the origin of Mahā-Viṣṇu. Kṛṣṇa's first expansion is Balarāma, a portion of whom is manifested as Saṅkarṣaṇa, who then expands as Pradyumna. In this way so many expansions take place. Although there are many expansions, Lord Śrī Kṛṣṇa is the origin, as confirmed in the *Brahma-saṁhitā.* He is like the original candle, from which many thousands and millions of candles are lit. Although any number of candles can be lit, the original candle still retains its identity as the origin. In this way Kṛṣṇa expands Himself into so many forms, and all these expansions are called *viṣṇu-tattva.* Viṣṇu is a large light, and we are small lights, but all are expansions of Kṛṣṇa.

When it is necessary to create the material universes, Viṣṇu expands Himself as Mahā-Viṣṇu. Mahā-Viṣṇu lies down in the Causal Ocean and breathes all the universes from His nostrils. Thus from Mahā-Viṣṇu and the Causal Ocean spring all the universes, and all these universes, including ours, float in the Causal Ocean. In this regard there is the story of Vāmana, who, when He took three steps, stuck His foot through the covering of this universe. Water from the Causal Ocean flowed through the hole that His foot made, and it is said that that water became the river Ganges. Therefore the Ganges is accepted as the most sacred water of Viṣṇu and is worshiped by all Hindus, from the Himalayas down to the Bay of Bengal.

Mahā-Viṣṇu is actually an expansion of Balarāma, who is Kṛṣṇa's first expansion and, in the Vṛndāvana pastimes, His brother. In the *mahā-mantra*—Hare Kṛṣṇa, Hare Kṛṣṇa, Kṛṣṇa Kṛṣṇa, Hare Hare/ Hare Rāma, Hare Rāma, Rāma Rāma, Hare Hare—the word "Rāma" refers to Balarāma. Since Lord Nityānanda is Balarāma, "Rāma" also refers to Lord Nityānanda. Thus Hare Kṛṣṇa, Hare Rāma addresses not only Kṛṣṇa and Balarāma but Lord Caitanya and Lord Nityānanda as well. The subject matter of the *Caitanya-caritāmṛta* primarily deals with what is beyond this material creation. The cosmic material expansion is called *māyā*, illusion, because it has no eternal existence. Because it is sometimes manifested and sometimes not, it is regarded as illusory. But beyond this temporary manifestation is a higher nature, as indicated in the *Bhagavad-gītā* (8.20):

paras tasmāt tu bhāvo 'nyo 'vyakto 'vyaktāt sanātanaḥ
yaḥ sa sarveṣu bhūteṣu naśyatsu na vinaśyati

"Yet there is another unmanifested nature, which is eternal and is transcendental to this manifested and unmanifested matter. It is supreme and is never annihilated. When all in this world is annihilated, that part remains as it is." The material world has a manifested state (*vyakta*) and a potential, unmanifested state (*avyakta*). The supreme nature is beyond both the manifested and the unmanifested material nature. This superior nature can be understood as the living force, which is present in the bodies of all living creatures. The body itself is composed of inferior nature, matter, but it is the superior nature that is moving the body. The symptom of that superior nature is consciousness. Thus in the spiritual world, where everything is composed of the superior nature, everything is conscious. In the material world there are inanimate objects that are not conscious, but in the spiritual world nothing is inanimate. There a table is conscious, the land is conscious, the trees are conscious—everything is conscious.

It is not possible to imagine how far this material manifestation extends. In the material world everything is calculated by imagination or by some imperfect method, but the Vedic literatures give real information of what lies beyond the material universe. Since it is not possible to obtain information of anything beyond this material nature by experimental means, those who believe only in experimental knowledge may doubt the Vedic conclusions, for such people cannot even calculate how far this universe extends, nor can they reach far into the universe itself. That which is beyond our power of conception is called *acintya,* inconceivable. It is useless to argue or speculate about the inconceivable. If something is truly inconceivable, it is not subject to speculation or experimentation. Our energy is limited, and our sense perception is limited; therefore we must rely on the Vedic conclusions regarding that subject matter which is inconceivable. Knowledge of the superior nature must simply be accepted without argument. How is it possible to argue about something to which we have no access? The method for understanding transcendental subject matter is given by Lord Kṛṣṇa Himself in the *Bhagavad-gītā,* where Kṛṣṇa tells Arjuna at the beginning of the Fourth Chapter:

imaṁ vivasvate yogaṁ proktavān aham avyayam
vivasvān manave prāha manur ikṣvākave 'bravīt

"I instructed this imperishable science of *yoga* to the sun-god, Vivasvān, and Vivasvān instructed it to Manu, the father of mankind, and Manu in turn instructed it to Ikṣvāku." (Bg. 4.1) This is the method of *paramparā,* or disciplic succession. Similarly, *Śrīmad-Bhāgavatam* explains that Kṛṣṇa imparted knowledge into the heart of Brahmā, the first created being within the universe. Brahmā imparted those lessons to his disciple Nārada, and Nārada imparted that knowledge to his disciple Vyāsadeva. Vyāsadeva imparted it to Madhvācārya, and from Madhvācārya the knowledge came down to Mādhavendra Purī and then to Īśvara Purī, and from him to Caitanya Mahāprabhu.

One may ask that if Caitanya Mahāprabhu is Kṛṣṇa Himself, then why did He need a spiritual master? Of course He did not need a spiritual master, but because He was playing the role of *ācārya* (one who teaches by example), He accepted a spiritual master. Even Kṛṣṇa

Himself accepted a spiritual master, for that is the system. In this way the Lord sets the example for men. We should not think, however, that the Lord takes a spiritual master because He is in want of knowledge. He is simply stressing the importance of accepting the disciplic succession. The knowledge of that disciplic succession actually comes from the Lord Himself, and if the knowledge descends unbroken, it is perfect. Although we may not be in touch with the original personality who first imparted the knowledge, we may receive the same knowledge through this process of transmission. In *Śrīmad-Bhāgavatam* it is stated that Kṛṣṇa, the Absolute Truth, the Personality of Godhead, transmitted transcendental knowledge into the heart of Brahmā. This, then, is one way knowledge is received—through the heart. Thus there are two processes by which one may receive knowledge: One depends directly upon the Supreme Personality of Godhead, who is situated as the Supersoul within the heart of all living entities, and the other depends upon the *guru*, or spiritual master, who is an expansion of Kṛṣṇa. Thus Kṛṣṇa transmits information both from within and from without. We simply have to receive it. If knowledge is received in this way, it doesn't matter whether it is inconceivable or not.

In *Śrīmad-Bhāgavatam* there is a great deal of information given about the Vaikuṇṭha planetary systems, which are beyond the material universe. Similarly, a great deal of inconceivable information is given in the *Caitanya-caritāmṛta*. Any attempt to arrive at this information through experimental knowledge will fail. The knowledge simply has to be accepted. According to the Vedic method, *śabda*, or transcendental sound, is regarded as evidence. Sound is very important in Vedic understanding, for, if it is pure, it is accepted as authoritative. Even in the material world we accept a great deal of information sent thousands of miles by telephone or radio. In this way we also accept sound as evidence in our daily lives. Although we cannot see the informant, we accept his information as valid on the basis of sound. Sound vibration, then, is very important in the transmission of Vedic knowledge.

The *Vedas* inform us that beyond this cosmic manifestation there are extensive planets in the spiritual sky. This material manifestation is regarded as only a small portion of the total creation. The material manifestation includes not only this universe but innumerable others as well, but all the material universes combined constitute only one fourth of the total creation. The remaining three fourths is situated in the spiritual sky. In that sky innumerable planets float, and these are called Vaikuṇṭhalokas. In every Vaikuṇṭhaloka, Nārāyaṇa presides with His four expansions: Saṅkarṣaṇa, Pradyumna, Aniruddha and Vāsudeva. This Saṅkarṣaṇa, states Kṛṣṇadāsa Kavirāja in the eighth verse of the *Caitanya-caritāmṛta*, is Lord Nityānanda.

As stated before, the material universes are manifested by the Lord in the form of Mahā-Viṣṇu. Just as a husband and wife combine to beget offspring, Mahā-Viṣṇu combines with His wife *māyā*, or material nature. This is confirmed in the *Bhagavad-gītā* (14.4), where Kṛṣṇa states:

sarva-yoniṣu kaunteya mūrtayaḥ sambhavanti yāḥ
tāsāṁ brahma mahad yonir ahaṁ bīja-pradaḥ pitā

"It should be understood that all species of life, O son of Kuntī, are made possible by birth in this material nature, and that I am the seed-giving father." Viṣṇu impregnates *māyā*, the material nature, simply by glancing at her. This is the spiritual method. Materially we are limited to impregnating by only one particular part of our body, but the Supreme Lord, Kṛṣṇa or Mahā-Viṣṇu, can impregnate by any part. Simply by glancing the Lord can conceive countless living entities in the womb of material nature. The *Brahma-saṁhitā* confirms that the spiritual body of the Supreme Lord is so powerful that any part of His body can perform the functions of any other part. We can touch only with our hands or skin, but Kṛṣṇa can touch just by glancing. We can see only with our eyes; we cannot touch or smell with them. Kṛṣṇa, however, can smell and also eat with His eyes. When food is offered to Kṛṣṇa, we do not see Him eating, but He eats simply by glancing at the food. We cannot imagine how things work in the spiritual world, where everything is spiritual. It is not that Kṛṣṇa does not eat or that we imagine that He eats; He actually eats, but His eating is different from ours. Our eating process will be similar to His when we are completely on the spiritual platform. On that platform every part of the body can act on behalf of any other part.

Viṣṇu does not require anything in order to create. He does not require the goddess Lakṣmī in order to give birth to Brahmā, for Brahmā is born from a lotus flower that grows from the navel of Viṣṇu. The goddess Lakṣmī sits at the feet of Viṣṇu and serves Him. In this material world sex is required to produce children, but in the spiritual world a man can produce as many children as he likes without having to take help from his wife. So there is no sex there. Because we have no experience with spiritual energy, we think that Brahmā's birth from the navel of Viṣṇu is simply a fictional story. We are not aware that spiritual energy is so powerful that it can do anything and everything. Material energy is dependent on certain laws, but spiritual energy is fully independent.

Countless universes reside like seeds within the skin pores of Mahā-Viṣṇu, and when He exhales, they are all manifested. In the material world we have no experience of such a thing, but we do experience a perverted reflection in the phenomenon of perspiration. We cannot imagine, however, the duration of one breath of Mahā-Viṣṇu, for within one breath all the universes are created and annihilated. This is stated in the *Brahma-saṁhitā*. Lord Brahmā lives only for the duration of one breath, and according to our time scale 4,320,000,000 years constitute only twelve hours for Brahmā, and Brahmā lives one hundred of his years. Yet the whole life of Brahmā is contained within one breath of Mahā-Viṣṇu. Thus it is not possible for us to imagine the breathing power of Mahā-Viṣṇu, who is but a partial manifestation of Lord Nityānanda. This the author of the *Caitanya-caritāmṛta* explains in the ninth verse.

In the tenth and eleventh verses Kṛṣṇadāsa Kavirāja describes Garbhodakaśāyī Viṣṇu and Kṣīrodakaśāyī Viṣṇu, successive plenary expansions of Mahā-Viṣṇu. Brahmā appears upon a lotus growing from the navel of Garbhodakaśāyī Viṣṇu, and within the stem of that lotus are so many planetary systems. Then Brahmā creates the whole of human society, animal society—everything. Kṣīrodakaśāyī Viṣṇu lies on the milk ocean within the universe, of which He is the controller and maintainer. Thus Brahmā is the creator, Viṣṇu is the maintainer, and when the time for annihilation arrives, Śiva will finish everything.

In the first eleven verses of the *Caitanya-caritāmṛta*, Kṛṣṇadāsa Kavirāja Gosvāmī thus discusses Lord Caitanya Mahāprabhu as Śrī Kṛṣṇa Himself, the Supreme Personality of Godhead, and Lord Nityānanda as Balarāma, the first expansion of Kṛṣṇa. Then in the twelfth and thirteenth verses he describes Advaitācārya, who is another principal associate of Lord Caitanya Mahāprabhu's and an incarnation of Mahā-Viṣṇu. Thus Advaitācārya is also the Lord, or, more precisely, an expansion of the Lord. The word *advaita* means "nondual," and His name is such because He is nondifferent from the Supreme Lord. He is also called *ācārya*, teacher, because He disseminated Kṛṣṇa consciousness. In this way He is just like Caitanya Mahāprabhu. Although Lord Caitanya is Śrī Kṛṣṇa Himself, He appeared as a devotee to teach people in general how to love Kṛṣṇa. Similarly, although Advaitācārya is the Lord, He appeared just to distribute the knowledge of Kṛṣṇa consciousness. Thus He is also the Lord incarnated as a devotee.

In the pastimes of Lord Caitanya, Kṛṣṇa is manifested in five different features, known as the *pañca-tattva,* to whom Śrīla Kṛṣṇadāsa Kavirāja offers his obeisances in the fourteenth verse of the *Caitanya-caritāmṛta.* Kṛṣṇa and His associates appear as devotees of the Supreme Lord in the form of Śrī Kṛṣṇa Caitanya, Śrī Nityānanda Prabhu, Śrī Advaitācārya, Śrī Gadādhara Prabhu and Śrīvāsa Prabhu. In all cases, Caitanya Mahāprabhu is the source of energy for all His devotees. Since this is the case, if we take shelter of Caitanya Mahāprabhu for the successful execution of Kṛṣṇa consciousness, we are sure to make progress. In a devotional song, Narottama dāsa Ṭhākura sings, "My dear Lord Caitanya, please have mercy upon me. There is no one who is as merciful as You. My plea is most urgent because Your mission is to deliver all fallen souls, and no one is more fallen than I. Therefore I beg priority."

With verse 15, Kṛṣṇadāsa Kavirāja Gosvāmī begins offering his obeisances directly to Kṛṣṇa Himself. Kṛṣṇadāsa Kavirāja was an inhabitant of Vṛndāvana and a great devotee. He had been living with his family in Katwa, a small town in the district of Burdwan, in Bengal. He worshiped Rādhā-Kṛṣṇa with his family, and once when there was some misunderstanding among his family members about devotional service, he was advised by Nityānanda Prabhu in a dream to leave home and go to Vṛndāvana. Although he was very old, he started out that very night and went to live in Vṛndāvana. While he was there, he met some of the Gosvāmīs, principal disciples of Lord Caitanya Mahāprabhu. He was requested to write the *Caitanya-caritāmṛta* by the devotees of Vṛndāvana. Although he began this work at a very old age, by the grace of Lord Caitanya he finished it. Today it remains the most authoritative book on Caitanya Mahāprabhu's philosophy and life.

When Kṛṣṇadāsa Kavirāja Gosvāmī was living in Vṛndāvana, there were not very many temples. At that time the three principal temples were those of Madana-mohana, Govindajī and Gopīnātha. As a resident of Vṛndāvana, Kṛṣṇadāsa Kavirāja offers his respects to the Deities in these temples and requests God's favor: "My progress in spiritual life is very slow, so I'm asking Your help." In the fifteenth verse of the *Caitanya-caritāmṛta,* Kṛṣṇadāsa offers his obeisances to the Madana-mohana *vigraha,* the Deity who can help us progress in Kṛṣṇa consciousness. In the execution of Kṛṣṇa consciousness, our first business is to know Kṛṣṇa and our relationship with Him. To know Kṛṣṇa is to know one's self, and to know one's self is to know one's relationship with

Kṛṣṇa. Since this relationship can be learned by worshiping the Madana-mohana *vigraha*, Kṛṣṇadāsa Kavirāja Gosvāmī first establishes his relationship with Him.

When this is established, in the sixteenth verse Kṛṣṇadāsa offers his obeisances to the functional Deity, Govinda. The Govinda Deity is called the functional Deity because He shows us how to serve Rādhā and Kṛṣṇa. The Madana-mohana Deity simply establishes that "I am Your eternal servant." With Govinda, however, there is actual acceptance of service. Govinda resides eternally in Vṛndāvana. In the spiritual world of Vṛndāvana the buildings are made of touchstone, the cows are known as *surabhi* cows, givers of abundant milk, and the trees are known as wish-fulfilling trees, for they yield whatever one desires. In Vṛndāvana Kṛṣṇa herds the *surabhi* cows, and He is worshiped by hundreds and thousands of *gopīs*, cowherd girls, who are all goddesses of fortune. When Kṛṣṇa descends to the material world, this same Vṛndāvana descends with Him, just as an entourage accompanies an important personage. Because when Kṛṣṇa comes His land also comes, Vṛndāvana is considered to exist beyond the material world. Therefore devotees take shelter of the Vṛndāvana in India, for it is considered to be a replica of the original Vṛndāvana. Although one may complain that no *kalpa-vṛkṣas*, wish-fulfilling trees, exist there, when the Gosvāmīs were there, *kalpa-vṛkṣas* were present. It is not that one can simply go to such a tree and make demands; one must first become a devotee. The Gosvāmīs would live under a tree for one night only, and the trees would satisfy all their desires. For the common man this may all seem very wonderful, but as one makes progress in devotional service, all this can be realized.

Vṛndāvana is actually experienced as it is by persons who have stopped trying to derive pleasure from material enjoyment. "When will my mind become cleansed of all hankering for material enjoyment so I will be able to see Vṛndāvana?" one great devotee asks. The more Kṛṣṇa conscious we become and the more we advance, the more everything is revealed as spiritual. Thus Kṛṣṇadāsa Kavirāja Gosvāmī considered the Vṛndāvana in India to be as good as the Vṛndāvana in the spiritual sky, and in the sixteenth verse of the *Caitanya-caritāmṛta* he describes Rādhārāṇī and Kṛṣṇa as seated beneath a wish-fulfilling tree in Vṛndāvana, on a throne decorated with valuable jewels. There Kṛṣṇa's dear *gopī* friends serve Rādhā and Kṛṣṇa by singing, dancing, offering betel nuts and refreshments, and decorating Their Lordships with flowers. Even today in India people decorate swinging thrones and re-create this scene during the month of July-August. Generally at that time people go to Vṛndāvana to offer their respects to the Deities there.

Finally Kṛṣṇadāsa Kavirāja Gosvāmī offers his blessings to his readers in the name of the Gopīnātha Deity, who is Kṛṣṇa as master and proprietor of the *gopīs*. When Kṛṣṇa played upon his flute, all the *gopīs*, or cowherd girls, were attracted by the sound and left their household duties, and when they came to Him, He danced with them. These activities are all described in the Tenth Canto of *Śrīmad-Bhāgavatam*. These *gopīs* were childhood friends of Kṛṣṇa, and many were married, for in India the girls are generally married by the age of twelve. The boys, however, are not married before eighteen, so Kṛṣṇa, who was fifteen or sixteen at the time, was not married. Nonetheless, He called these girls from their homes and invited them to dance with Him. That dance is called the *rāsa-līlā* dance, and it is the most elevated of all the Vṛndāvana pastimes. Kṛṣṇa is therefore called Gopīnātha because He is the beloved master of the *gopīs*.

Kṛṣṇadāsa Kavirāja Gosvāmī petitions the blessings of Lord Gopīnātha: "May that Gopīnātha, the master of the *gopīs*, Kṛṣṇa, bless you. May you become blessed by Gopīnātha." The author of the *Caitanya-caritāmṛta* prays that just as Kṛṣṇa attracted the *gopīs* by the sweet sound of His flute, He will also attract the reader's mind by that transcendental vibration.

CHAPTER ONE

The Spiritual Masters

Śrī Caitanya Mahāprabhu is none other than the combined form of Śrī Rādhā and Kṛṣṇa. He is the life of those devotees who strictly follow in the footsteps of Śrīla Rūpa Gosvāmī. Śrīla Rūpa Gosvāmī and Śrīla Sanātana Gosvāmī are the two principal followers of Śrīla Svarūpa Dāmodara Gosvāmī, who acted as the most confidential servitor of Lord Śrī Kṛṣṇa Caitanya Mahāprabhu, known as Viśvambhara in His early life. A direct disciple of Śrīla Rūpa Gosvāmī was Śrīla Raghunātha dāsa Gosvāmī. The author of *Śrī Caitanya-caritāmṛta*, Śrīla Kṛṣṇadāsa Kavirāja Gosvāmī, stands as the direct disciple of Śrīla Rūpa Gosvāmī and Śrīla Raghunātha dāsa Gosvāmī.

The direct disciple of Śrīla Kṛṣṇadāsa Kavirāja Gosvāmī was Śrīla Narottama dāsa Ṭhākura, who accepted Śrīla Viśvanātha Cakravartī as his servitor. Śrīla Viśvanātha Cakravartī Ṭhākura accepted Śrīla Jagannātha dāsa Bābājī, the spiritual master of Śrīla Bhaktivinoda Ṭhākura, who in turn accepted Śrīla Gaurakiśora dāsa Bābājī, the spiritual master of Oṁ Viṣṇupāda Śrīla Bhaktisiddhānta Sarasvatī Gosvāmī Mahārāja, the divine master of our humble self.

Since we belong to this chain of disciplic succession from Śrī Caitanya Mahāprabhu, this edition of *Śrī Caitanya-caritāmṛta* will contain nothing newly manufactured by our tiny brains, but only remnants of food originally eaten by the Lord Himself. Lord Śrī Caitanya Mahāprabhu does not belong to the mundane plane of the three qualitative modes. He belongs to the transcendental plane beyond the reach of the imperfect sense perception of a living being. Even the most erudite mundane scholar cannot approach the transcendental plane unless he submits himself to transcendental sound with a receptive mood, for in that mood only can one realize the message of Śrī Caitanya Mahāprabhu. What will be described herein, therefore, has nothing to do with the experimental thoughts created by the speculative habits of inert minds. The subject matter of this book is not a mental concoction but a factual spiritual experience that one can realize only by accepting the line of disciplic succession described above. Any deviation from that line will bewilder the reader's understanding of the mystery of *Śrī Caitanya-caritāmṛta*, which is a transcendental literature meant for the postgraduate study of one who has realized all the Vedic literatures such as the *Upaniṣads* and *Vedānta-sūtra* and their natural commentaries such as *Śrīmad-Bhāgavatam* and the *Bhagavad-gītā*.

This edition of *Śrī Caitanya-caritāmṛta* is presented for the study of sincere scholars who are really seeking the Absolute Truth. It is not the arrogant scholarship of a mental speculator but a sincere effort to serve the order of a superior authority whose service is the life and soul of this humble effort. It does not deviate even slightly from the revealed scriptures, and therefore anyone who follows in the disciplic line will be able to realize the essence of this book simply by the method of aural reception.

The First Chapter of *Śrī Caitanya-caritāmṛta* begins with fourteen Sanskrit verses that describe the Absolute Truth. Then the next three Sanskrit verses describe the principal Deities of Vṛndāvana, namely, Śrī Rādhā-Madana-mohana, Śrī Rādhā-Govindadeva and Śrī Rādhā-Gopīnāthajī. The first of the fourteen verses is a symbolic representation of the Supreme Truth, and the entire First Chapter is in actuality devoted to this single verse, which describes Lord Caitanya in His six different transcendental expansions.

The first manifestation described is the spiritual master, who appears in two plenary parts called the initiating spiritual master and instructing spiritual master. They are identical because both of them are phenomenal manifestations of the Supreme Truth. Next described are the devotees, who are divided into two classes, namely, the apprentices and the graduates. Next are the incarnations (*avatāras*) of the Lord, who are explained to be nondifferent from the Lord. These incarnations are considered in three divisions—incarnations of the potency of the Lord, incarnations of His qualities, and incarnations of His authority. In this connection, Lord Śrī Kṛṣṇa's direct manifestations and His manifestations for transcendental pastimes are discussed. Next considered are the potencies of the Lord, of which three principal manifestations are described: the consorts in the kingdom of God (Vaikuṇṭha), the queens of Dvārakā-dhāma and, highest of all, the damsels of Vrajadhāma. Finally, there is the Supreme Lord Himself, who is the fountainhead of all these manifestations.

Lord Śrī Kṛṣṇa and His plenary expansions are all in the category of the Lord Himself, the energetic Absolute Truth, whereas His devotees,

His eternal associates, are His energies. The energy and energetic are fundamentally one, but since their functions are differently exhibited, they are simultaneously different also. Thus the Absolute Truth is manifested in diversity in one unit. This philosophical truth, which is pursuant to the *Vedānta-sūtra*, is called *acintya-bhedābheda-tattva*, or the conception of simultaneous oneness and difference. In the latter portion of this chapter, the transcendental position of Śrī Caitanya Mahāprabhu and that of Śrīla Nityānanda Prabhu are described with reference to the above theistic facts.

TEXT 1

বন্দে গুরূনীশভক্তানীশমীশাবতারকান্ ।
তৎপ্রকাশাংশ্চ তচ্ছক্তীঃ কৃষ্ণচৈতন্যসংজ্ঞকম্ ॥ ১ ॥

vande gurūn īśa-bhaktān
īśam īśāvatārakān
tat-prakāśāṁś ca tac-chaktīḥ
kṛṣṇa-caitanya-saṁjñakam

vande—I offer respectful obeisances; *gurūn*—unto the spiritual masters; *īśa-bhaktān*—unto the devotees of the Supreme Lord; *īśam*—unto the Supreme Lord; *īśa-avatārakān*—unto the incarnations of the Supreme Lord; *tat*—of the Supreme Lord; *prakāśān*—unto the manifestations; *ca*—and; *tat*—of the Supreme Lord; *śaktīḥ*—unto the potencies; *kṛṣṇa-caitanya*—Śrī Kṛṣṇa Caitanya; *saṁjñakam*—named.

TRANSLATION

I offer my respectful obeisances unto the spiritual masters, the devotees of the Lord, the Lord's incarnations, His plenary portions, His energies and the primeval Lord Himself, Śrī Kṛṣṇa Caitanya.

TEXT 2

বন্দে শ্রীকৃষ্ণচৈতন্যনিত্যানন্দৌ সহোদিতৌ ।
গৌড়োদয়ে পুষ্পবন্তৌ চিত্রৌ শন্দৌ তমোনুদৌ ॥ ২ ॥

vande śrī-kṛṣṇa-caitanya-
nityānandau sahoditau
gauḍodaye puṣpavantau
citrau śan-dau tamo-nudau

vande—I offer respectful obeisances; *śrī-kṛṣṇa-caitanya*—to Lord Śrī Kṛṣṇa Caitanya; *nityānandau*—and to Lord Nityānanda; *saha-uditau*—simultaneously arisen; *gauḍa-udaye*—on the eastern horizon of Gauḍa; *puṣpavantau*—the sun and moon together; *citrau*—wonderful; *śam-dau*—bestowing benediction; *tamaḥ-nudau*—dissipating darkness.

TRANSLATION

I offer my respectful obeisances unto Śrī Kṛṣṇa Caitanya and Lord Nityānanda, who are like the sun and moon. They have arisen simultaneously on the horizon of Gauḍa to dissipate the darkness of ignorance and thus wonderfully bestow benediction upon all.

TEXT 3

যদদ্বৈতং ব্রহ্মোপনিষদি তদপ্যস্য তনুভা
য আত্মান্তর্যামী পুরুষ ইতি সোঽস্যাংশবিভবঃ ।
ষড়ৈশ্বর্যৈঃ পূর্ণো য ইহ ভগবান্ স স্বয়ময়ং
ন চৈতন্যাৎ কৃষ্ণাজ্জগতি পরতত্ত্বং পরমিহ ॥ ৩ ॥

yad advaitaṁ brahmopaniṣadi tad apy asya tanu-bhā
ya ātmāntar-yāmī puruṣa iti so 'syāṁśa-vibhavaḥ
ṣaḍ-aiśvaryaiḥ pūrṇo ya iha bhagavān sa svayam ayaṁ
na caitanyāt kṛṣṇāj jagati para-tattvaṁ param iha

yat—that which; *advaitam*—nondual; *brahma*—the impersonal Brahman; *upaniṣadi*—in the *Upaniṣads;* *tat*—that; *api*—certainly; *asya*—His; *tanu-bhā*—the effulgence of His transcendental body; *yaḥ*—who; *ātmā*—the Supersoul; *antaḥ-yāmi*—indwelling Lord; *puruṣaḥ*—supreme enjoyer; *iti*—thus; *saḥ*—He; *asya*—His; *aṁśa-vibhavaḥ*—plenary expansion; *ṣaṭ-aiśvaryaiḥ*—with all six opulences; *pūrṇaḥ*—full; *yaḥ*—who; *iha*—here; *bhagavān*—the Supreme Personality of Godhead; *saḥ*—He; *svayam*—Himself; *ayam*—this; *na*—not; *caitanyāt*—than Lord Caitanya; *kṛṣṇāt*—than Lord Kṛṣṇa; *jagati*—in the world; *para*—higher; *tattvam*—truth; *param*—another; *iha*—here.

TRANSLATION

What the Upaniṣads describe as the impersonal Brahman is but the effulgence of His body, and the Lord known as the Supersoul is but His localized plenary portion. Lord Caitanya is the Supreme

Personality of Godhead, Kṛṣṇa Himself, full with six opulences. He is the Absolute Truth, and no other truth is greater than or equal to Him.

TEXT 4

অনর্পিতচরীং চিরাৎ করুণয়াবতীর্ণঃ কলৌ
সমর্পয়িতুমুন্নতোজ্জ্বলরসাং স্বভক্তিশ্রিয়ম্ ।
হরিঃ পুরটসুন্দরদ্যুতিকদম্বসন্দীপিতঃ
সদা হৃদয়কন্দরে স্ফুরতু বঃ শচীনন্দনঃ ॥ ৪ ॥

anarpita-car īṁ cirāt karuṇayāvatīrṇaḥ kalau
samarpayitum unnatojjvala-rasāṁ sva-bhakti-śriyam
hariḥ puraṭa-sundara-dyuti-kadamba-sandīpitaḥ
sadā hṛdaya-kandare sphuratu vaḥ śacī-nandanaḥ

anarpita—not bestowed; *carīm*—having been formerly; *cirāt*—for a long time; *karuṇayā*—by causeless mercy; *avatīrṇaḥ*—descended; *kalau*—in the Age of Kali; *samarpayitum*—to bestow; *unnata*—elevated; *ujjvala-rasām*—the conjugal mellow; *sva-bhakti*—of His own service; *śriyam*—the treasure; *hariḥ*—the Supreme Lord; *puraṭa*—than gold; *sundara*—more beautiful; *dyuti*—of splendor; *kadamba*—with a multitude; *sandīpitaḥ*—lighted up; *sadā*—always; *hṛdaya-kandare*—in the cavity of the heart; *sphuratu*—let Him be manifest; *vaḥ*—your; *śacī-nandanaḥ*—the son of mother Śacī.

TRANSLATION

May the Supreme Lord who is known as the son of Śrīmatī Śacīdevī be transcendentally situated in the innermost chambers of your heart. Resplendent with the radiance of molten gold, He has appeared in the Age of Kali by His causeless mercy to bestow what no incarnation has ever offered before: the most sublime and radiant mellow of devotional service, the mellow of conjugal love.

TEXT 5

রাধা কৃষ্ণপ্রণয়বিকৃতির্হ্লাদিনীশক্তিরস্মা-
দেকাত্মানাবপি ভুবি পুরা দেহভেদং গতৌ তৌ ।
চৈতন্যাখ্যং প্রকটমধুনা তদ্দ্বয়ং চৈক্যমাপ্তং
রাধাভাবদ্যুতিসুবলিতং নৌমি কৃষ্ণস্বরূপম্ ॥ ৫ ॥

rādhā kṛṣṇa-praṇaya-vikṛtir hlādinī śaktir asmād
ekātmānāv api bhuvi purā deha-bhedaṁ gatau tau
caitanyākhyaṁ prakaṭam adhunā tad-dvayaṁ caikyam āptaṁ
rādhā-bhāva-dyuti-suvalitaṁ naumi kṛṣṇa-svarūpam

rādhā—Śrīmatī Rādhārāṇī; *kṛṣṇa*—of Lord Kṛṣṇa; *praṇaya*—of love; *vikṛtiḥ*—the transformation; *hlādinī śaktiḥ*—pleasure potency; *asmāt*—from this; *eka-ātmānau*—both the same in identity; *api*—although; *bhuvi*—on earth; *purā*—from beginningless time; *deha-bhedam*—separate forms; *gatau*—obtained; *tau*—those two; *caitanya-ākhyam*—known as Śrī Caitanya; *prakaṭam*—manifest; *adhunā*—now; *tat-dvayam*—the two of Them; *ca*—and; *aikyam*—unity; *āptam*—obtained; *rādhā*—of Śrīmatī Rādhārāṇī; *bhāva*—mood; *dyuti*—the luster; *su-valitam*—who is adorned with; *naumi*—I offer my obeisances; *kṛṣṇa-svarūpam*—to Him who is identical with Śrī Kṛṣṇa.

TRANSLATION

The loving affairs of Śrī Rādhā and Kṛṣṇa are transcendental manifestations of the Lord's internal pleasure-giving potency. Although Rādhā and Kṛṣṇa are one in Their identity, They separated Themselves eternally. Now these two transcendental identities have again united, in the form of Śrī Kṛṣṇa Caitanya. I bow down to Him, who has manifested Himself with the sentiment and complexion of Śrīmatī Rādhārāṇī although He is Kṛṣṇa Himself.

TEXT 6

শ্রীরাধায়াঃ প্রণয়মহিমা কীদৃশো বানয়ৈবা-
স্বাদ্যো যেনাদ্ভুতমধুরিমা কীদৃশো বা মদীয়ঃ ।
সৌখ্যঞ্চাস্যা মদনুভবতঃ কীদৃশং বেতি লোভা-
ত্তদ্ভাবাঢ্যঃ সমজনি শচীগর্ভসিন্ধৌ হরীন্দুঃ ॥ ৬ ॥

śrī-rādhāyāḥ praṇaya-mahimā kīdṛśo vānayaivā-
svādyo yenādbhuta-madhurimā kīdṛśo vā madīyaḥ
saukhyaṁ cāsyā mad-anubhavataḥ kīdṛśaṁ veti lobhāt
tad-bhāvāḍhyaḥ samajani śacī-garbha-sindhau harīnduḥ

śrī-rādhāyāḥ—of Śrīmatī Rādhārāṇī; *praṇaya-mahimā*—the greatness of the love; *kīdṛśaḥ*—of what kind; *vā*—or; *anayā*—by this one (Rādhā); *eva*—alone; *āsvādyaḥ*—to be relished; *yena*—by that love; *adbhuta-madhurimā*—the wonderful sweetness; *kīdṛśaḥ*—of what kind; *vā*—or; *madīyaḥ*—of Me; *saukhyam*—the happiness; *ca*—and; *asyāḥ*—Her; *mat-anubhavataḥ*—from realization of My sweetness; *kīdṛśam*—of what kind; *vā*—or; *iti*—thus; *lobhāt*—from the desire; *tat*—Her; *bhāva-āḍhyaḥ*—richly endowed with emotions; *samajani*—took birth; *śacī-garbha*—of the womb of Śrīmatī Śacī-devī; *sindhau*—in the ocean; *hari*—Lord Kṛṣṇa; *induḥ*—like the moon.

TRANSLATION

Desiring to understand the glory of Rādhārāṇī's love, the wonderful qualities in Him that She alone relishes through Her love, and the happiness She feels when She realizes the sweetness of His love, the Supreme Lord Hari, richly endowed with Her emotions, appeared from the womb of Śrīmatī Śacī-devī, as the moon appeared from the ocean.

TEXT 7

সঙ্কর্ষণঃ কারণতোয়শায়ী
গর্ভোদশায়ী চ পয়োব্ধিশায়ী ।
শেষশ্চ যস্যাংশকলাঃ স নিত্যা-
নন্দাখ্যরামঃ শরণং মমাস্তু ॥ ৭ ॥

saṅkarṣaṇaḥ kāraṇa-toya-śāyī
garbhoda-śāyī ca payobdhi-śāyī
śeṣaś ca yasyāṁśa-kalāḥ sa nityā-
nandākhya-rāmaḥ śaraṇaṁ mamāstu

saṅkarṣaṇaḥ—Mahā-Saṅkarṣaṇa in the spiritual sky; *kāraṇa-toya-śāyī*—Kāraṇodakaśāyī Viṣṇu, who lies in the Causal Ocean; *garbha-uda-śāyī*—Garbhodakaśāyī Viṣṇu, who lies in the Garbhodaka Ocean of the universe; *ca*—and; *payaḥ-abdhi-śāyī*—Kṣīrodakaśāyī Viṣṇu, who lies in the ocean of milk; *śeṣaḥ*—Śeṣa Nāga, the couch of Viṣṇu; *ca*—and; *yasya*—whose; *aṁśa*—plenary portions; *kalāḥ*—and parts of the plenary portions; *saḥ*—He; *nityānanda-ākhya*—known as Lord Nityānanda; *rāmaḥ*—Lord Balarāma; *śaraṇam*—shelter; *mama*—my; *astu*—let there be.

TRANSLATION

May Śrī Nityānanda Rāma be the object of my constant remembrance. Saṅkarṣaṇa, Śeṣa Nāga and the Viṣṇus who lie on the

Kāraṇa Ocean, Garbha Ocean and ocean of milk are His plenary portions and the portions of His plenary portions.

TEXT 8

মায়াতীতে ব্যাপিবৈকুণ্ঠলোকে
পূর্ণৈশ্বর্যে শ্রীচতুর্ব্যূহমধ্যে ।
রূপং যস্যোদ্ভাতি সঙ্কর্ষণাখ্যং
তং শ্রীনিত্যানন্দরামং প্রপদ্যে ॥ ৮ ॥

māyātīte vyāpi-vaikuṇṭha-loke
pūrṇaiśvarye śrī-catur-vyūha-madhye
rūpaṁ yasyodbhāti saṅkarṣaṇākhyaṁ
taṁ śrī-nityānanda-rāmaṁ prapadye

māyā-atīte—beyond the material creation; *vyāpi*—all-expanding; *vaikuṇṭha-loke*—in Vaikuṇṭhaloka, the spiritual world; *pūrṇa-aiśvarye*—endowed with full opulence; *śrī-catuḥ-vyūha-madhye*—in the quadruple expansions (Vāsudeva, Saṅkarṣaṇa, Pradyumna and Aniruddha); *rūpam*—form; *yasya*—whose; *udbhāti*—appears; *saṅkarṣaṇa-ākhyam*—known as Saṅkarṣaṇa; *tam*—to Him; *śrī-nityā-nanda-rāmam*—to Lord Balarāma in the form of Lord Nityānanda; *prapadye*—I surrender.

TRANSLATION

I surrender unto the lotus feet of Śrī Nityānanda Rāma, who is known as Saṅkarṣaṇa in the midst of the catur-vyūha [consisting of Vāsudeva, Saṅkarṣaṇa, Pradyumna and Aniruddha]. He possesses full opulences and resides in Vaikuṇṭhaloka, far beyond the material creation.

TEXT 9

মায়াভর্তাজাণ্ডসংঘাশ্রয়াঙ্গঃ
শেতে সাক্ষাৎ কারণাম্ভোধিমধ্যে ।
যস্যৈকাংশঃ শ্রীপুমানাদিদেব-
স্তং শ্রীনিত্যানন্দরামং প্রপদ্যে ॥ ৯ ॥

māyā-bhartājāṇḍa-saṅghāśrayāṅgaḥ
śete sākṣāt kāraṇāmbhodhi-madhye

yasyaikāṁśaḥ śrī-pumān ādi-devas
taṁ śrī-nityānanda-rāmaṁ prapadye

māyā-bhartā—the master of the illusory energy; *aja-aṇḍa-saṅgha*—of the multitude of universes; *āśraya*—the shelter; *aṅgaḥ*—whose body; *śete*—He lies; *sākṣāt*—directly; *kāraṇa-ambhodhi-madhye*—in the midst of the Causal Ocean; *yasya*—whose; *eka-aṁśaḥ*—one portion; *śrī-pumān*—the Supreme Person; *ādi-devaḥ*—the original *puruṣa* incarnation; *tam*—to Him; *śrī-nityānanda-rāmam*—to Lord Balarāma in the form of Lord Nityānanda; *prapadye*—I surrender.

TRANSLATION

I offer my full obeisances unto the feet of Śrī Nityānanda Rāma, whose partial representation called Kāraṇodakaśāyī Viṣṇu, lying on the Kāraṇa Ocean, is the original puruṣa, the master of the illusory energy, and the shelter of all the universes.

TEXT 10

যস্যাংশাংশঃ শ্রীল-গর্ভোদশায়ী
যন্নাভ্যব্জং লোকসংঘাতনালম্ ।
লোকস্রষ্টুঃ সূতিকাধামধাতু-
স্তং শ্রীনিত্যানন্দরামং প্রপদ্যে ॥ ১০ ॥

yasyāṁśāṁśaḥ śrīla-garbhoda-śāyī
yan-nābhy-abjaṁ loka-saṅghāta-nālam
loka-sraṣṭuḥ sūtikā-dhāma dhātus
taṁ śrī-nityānanda-rāmaṁ prapadye

yasya—whose; *aṁśa-aṁśaḥ*—portion of a plenary portion; *śrīla-garbha-uda-śāyī*—Garbhodakaśāyī Viṣṇu; *yat*—of whom; *nābhi-abjam*—the navel lotus; *loka-saṅghāta*—of the multitude of planets; *nālam*—having a stem that is the resting place; *loka-sraṣṭuḥ*—of Lord Brahmā, the creator of the planets; *sūtikā-dhāma*—the birthplace; *dhātuḥ*—of the creator; *tam*—to Him; *śrī-nityānanda-rāmam*—to Lord Balarāma in the form of Lord Nityānanda; *prapadye*—I surrender.

TRANSLATION

I offer my full obeisances unto the feet of Śrī Nityānanda Rāma, a partial part of whom is Garbhodakaśāyī Viṣṇu. From the navel of

Garbhodakaśāyī Viṣṇu sprouts the lotus that is the birthplace of Brahmā, the engineer of the universe. The stem of that lotus is the resting place of the multitude of planets.

TEXT 11

যস্যাংশাংশাংশঃ পরাত্মাখিলানাং
পোষ্টা বিষ্ণুর্ভাতি দুগ্ধাব্ধিশায়ী ।
ক্ষৌণীভর্তা যৎকলা সোঽপ্যনন্ত-
স্তং শ্রীনিত্যানন্দরামং প্রপদ্যে ॥ ১১ ॥

yasyāṁśāṁśāṁśaḥ parātmākhilānāṁ
poṣṭā viṣṇur bhāti dugdhābdhi-śāyī
kṣauṇī-bhartā yat-kalā so 'py anantas
taṁ śrī-nityānanda-rāmaṁ prapadye

yasya—whose; *aṁśa-aṁśa-aṁśaḥ*—a portion of a portion of a plenary portion; *para-ātmā*—the Supersoul; *akhilānām*—of all living entities; *poṣṭā*—the maintainer; *viṣṇuḥ*—Viṣṇu; *bhāti*—appears; *dugdha-abdhi-śāyī*—Kṣīrodakaśāyī Viṣṇu; *kṣauṇī-bhartā*—upholder of the earth; *yat*—whose; *kalā*—portion of a portion; *saḥ*—He; *api*—certainly; *anantaḥ*—Śeṣa Nāga; *tam*—to Him; *śrī-nityānanda-rāmam*—to Lord Balarāma in the form of Lord Nityānanda; *prapadye*—I surrender.

TRANSLATION

I offer my respectful obeisances unto the feet of Śrī Nityānanda Rāma, whose secondary part is the Viṣṇu lying in the ocean of milk. That Kṣīrodakaśāyī Viṣṇu is the Supersoul of all living entities and the maintainer of all the universes. Śeṣa Nāga is His further subpart.

TEXT 12

মহাবিষ্ণুর্জগৎকর্তা মায়য়া যঃ সৃজত্যদঃ ।
তস্যাবতার এবায়মদ্বৈতাচার্য ঈশ্বরঃ ॥ ১২ ॥

mahā-viṣṇur jagat-kartā
māyayā yaḥ sṛjaty adaḥ
tasyāvatāra evāyam
advaitācārya īśvaraḥ

His Divine Grace A. C. Bhaktivedanta Swami Prabhupāda
Founder-Ācārya of the International Society for Krishna Consciousness

Śrīla Bhaktisiddhānta Sarasvatī Gosvāmī Mahārāja
the spiritual master of
His Divine Grace A. C. Bhaktivedanta Swami Prabhupāda
and foremost scholar and devotee of his day

Śrīla Gaura-Kiśora dāsa Bābājī Mahārāja
the spiritual master of
Śrīla Bhaktisiddhānta Sarasvatī Gosvāmī
and intimate student of
Śrīla Ṭhākura Bhaktivinoda

Śrīla Ṭhākura Bhaktivinoda
the pioneer of the program
to bless the entire world with Kṛṣṇa consciousness

Śrī Pañca-tattva

ord Kṛṣṇa Caitanya surrounded (from left to right) by His avatāra *(Advaita Ācārya), lis expansion (Lord Nityānanda), His manifest internal energy (Śrī Gadādhara) and lis perfect devotee (Śrī Śrīvāsa)*

PLATE ONE: Śrī Kṛṣṇa Caitanya and Lord Nityānanda have arisen like the sun an[d] moon to dissipate the darkness of ignorance. (*p.* 24)

PLATE TWO: The *gopīs* saw their beloved Kṛṣṇa at Kurukṣetra after a long separation. (*p.* 353)

PLATE THREE: Advaita Ācārya offered *tulasī* buds in Ganges water and appealed to Śrī Kṛṣṇa to descend. (*p.* 255)

LATE FOUR: Mother Yaśodā regards Kṛṣṇa not as God but as her beloved son, and
ıus she nourishes and protects Him, thinking Him utterly helpless. (*p.* 275)

PLATE FIVE: Lord Caitanya appeared with the complexion and sentiment of Śrīma Rādhārāṇī and preached the chanting of the holy name. (*p.* 389)

LATE SIX: In Śvetadvīpa, Lord Viṣṇu can be seen sitting on a throne of Śeṣa with His
nsort, Lakṣmī. (*p.* 516)

PLATE SEVEN: In a dream Lord Balarāma appeared before Kṛṣṇadāsa Kavirāja a said, "O my dear Kṛṣṇadāsa, go to Vṛndāvana, for there you will attain all thing (p. 557)

LATE EIGHT: Lord Caitanya and His associates chanted and danced again and again
nd thus made it easier to drink nectarean love of Godhead. (*p.* 672)

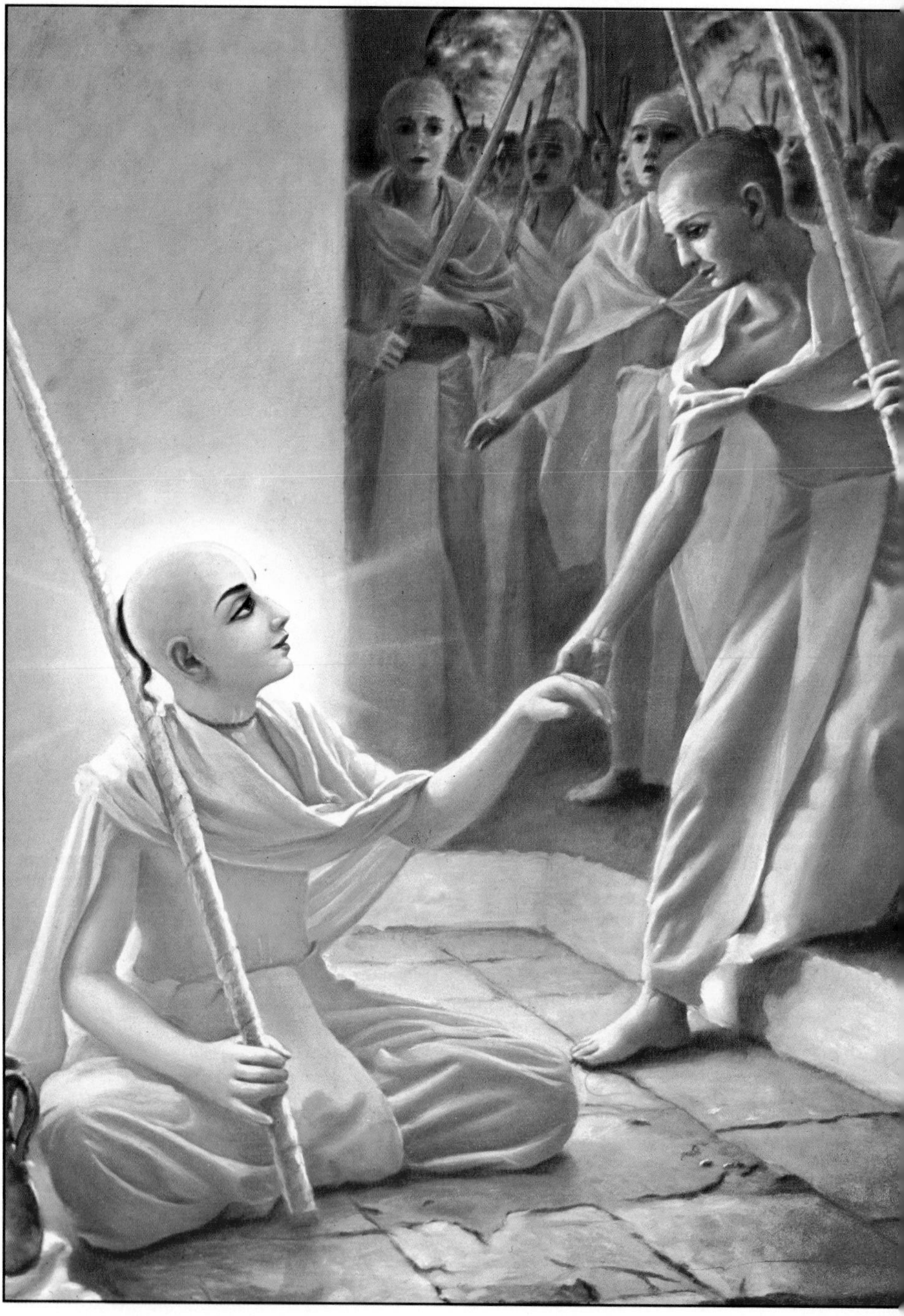

PLATE NINE: Seeing Śrī Caitanya Mahāprabhu sitting in an unclean place, Prakāśānanc
Sarasvatī caught Him by the hand and seated Him with great respect in the midst of tl
assembly. (*p.* 710)

LATE TEN: When the Māyāvādī *sannyāsīs* heard Lord Caitanya, their minds changed, ıd they began to chant the holy name of Kṛṣṇa. (*p.* 820)

PLATE ELEVEN: Whenever the crowds became too great, Śrī Caitanya Mahāprabh
would stand up, raise His hands and chant, "Hari! Hari!" All the people would th
respond, filling the land and sky with the vibration. (*p.* 828)

mahā-viṣṇuḥ—Mahā-Viṣṇu, the resting place of the efficient cause; *jagat-kartā*—the creator of the cosmic world; *māyayā*—by the illusory energy; *yaḥ*—who; *sṛjati*—creates; *adaḥ*—that universe; *tasya*—His; *avatāraḥ*—incarnation; *eva*—certainly; *ayam*—this; *advaita-ācāryaḥ*—Advaita Ācārya; *īśvaraḥ*—the Supreme Lord, the resting place of the material cause.

TRANSLATION

Lord Advaita Ācārya is the incarnation of Mahā-Viṣṇu, whose main function is to create the cosmic world through the actions of māyā.

TEXT 13

অদ্বৈতং হরিণাদ্বৈতাদাচার্যং ভক্তিশংসনাৎ ।
ভক্তাবতারমীশং তমদ্বৈতাচার্যমাশ্রয়ে ॥ ১৩ ॥

advaitaṁ hariṇādvaitād
ācāryaṁ bhakti-śaṁsanāt
bhaktāvatāram īśaṁ tam
advaitācāryam āśraye

advaitam—known as Advaita; *hariṇā*—with Lord Hari; *advaitāt*—from being nondifferent; *ācāryam*—known as Ācārya; *bhakti-śaṁsanāt*—from the propagation of devotional service to Śrī Kṛṣṇa; *bhakta-avatāram*—the incarnation as a devotee; *īśam*—to the Supreme Lord; *tam*—to Him; *advaita-ācāryam*—to Advaita Ācārya; *āśraye*—I surrender.

TRANSLATION

Because He is nondifferent from Hari, the Supreme Lord, He is called Advaita, and because He propagates the cult of devotion, He is called Ācārya. He is the Lord and the incarnation of the Lord's devotee. Therefore I take shelter of Him.

TEXT 14

পঞ্চতত্ত্বাত্মকং কৃষ্ণং ভক্তরূপস্বরূপকম্ ।
ভক্তাবতারং ভক্তাখ্যং নমামি ভক্তশক্তিকম্ ॥ ১৪ ॥

pañca-tattvātmakaṁ kṛṣṇaṁ
bhakta-rūpa-svarūpakam

bhaktāvatāraṁ bhaktākhyaṁ
namāmi bhakta-śaktikam

pañca-tattva-ātmakam—comprehending the five transcendental subject matters; *kṛṣṇam*—unto Lord Kṛṣṇa; *bhakta-rūpa*—in the form of a devotee; *sva-rūpakam*—in the expansion of a devotee; *bhakta-avatāram*—in the incarnation of a devotee; *bhakta-ākhyam*—known as a devotee; *namāmi*—I offer my obeisances; *bhakta-śaktikam*—the energy of the Supreme Personality of Godhead, who supplies energy to the devotee.

TRANSLATION

I offer my obeisances unto the Supreme Lord, Kṛṣṇa, who is non-different from His features as a devotee, devotional incarnation, devotional manifestation, pure devotee and devotional energy.

TEXT 15

জয়তাং সুরতৌ পঙ্গোর্মম মন্দমতের্গতী ।
মৎসর্বস্বপদাম্ভোজৌ রাধামদনমোহনৌ ॥ ১৫ ॥

jayatāṁ suratau paṅgor
mama manda-mater gatī
mat-sarvasva-padāmbhojau
rādhā-madana-mohanau

jayatām—all glory to; *su-ratau*—most merciful, or attached in conjugal love; *paṅgoḥ*—of one who is lame; *mama*—of me; *manda-mateḥ*—foolish; *gatī*—refuge; *mat*—my; *sarva-sva*—everything; *pada-ambhojau*—whose lotus feet; *rādhā-madana-mohanau*—Rādhārāṇī and Madana-mohana.

TRANSLATION

Glory to the all-merciful Rādhā and Madana-mohana! I am lame and ill advised, yet They are my directors, and Their lotus feet are everything to me.

TEXT 16

দীব্যদ্বৃন্দারণ্যকল্পদ্রুমাধঃ-
শ্রীমদ্রত্নাগারসিংহাসনস্থৌ ।

শ্রীমদ্‌রাধা-শ্রীলগোবিন্দদেবৌ
প্রেষ্ঠালীভিঃ সেব্যমানৌ স্মরামি ॥ ১৬ ॥

dīvyad-vṛndāraṇya-kalpa-drumādhaḥ-
śrīmad-ratnāgāra-siṁhāsana-sthau
śrīmad-rādhā-śrīla-govinda-devau
preṣṭhālībhiḥ sevyamānau smarāmi

dīvyat—shining; *vṛndā-aranya*—in the forest of Vṛndāvana; *kalpa-druma*—desire tree; *adhaḥ*—beneath; *śrīmat*—most beautiful; *ratna-āgāra*—in a temple of jewels; *siṁha-āsana-sthau*—sitting on a throne; *śrīmat*—very beautiful; *rādhā*—Śrīmatī Rādhārāṇī; *śrīla-govinda-devau*—and Śrī Govindadeva; *preṣṭha-ālībhiḥ*—by most confidential associates; *sevyamānau*—being served; *smarāmi*—I remember.

TRANSLATION

In a temple of jewels in Vṛndāvana, underneath a desire tree, Śrī Śrī Rādhā-Govinda, served by Their most confidential associates, sit upon an effulgent throne. I offer my humble obeisances unto Them.

TEXT 17

শ্রীমান্ রাসরসারম্ভী বংশীবটতটস্থিতঃ ।
কর্ষন্ বেণুস্বনৈর্গোপীর্গোপীনাথঃ শ্রিয়েঽস্তু নঃ ॥ ১৭ ॥

śrīmān rāsa-rasārambhī
vaṁśīvaṭa-taṭa-sthitaḥ
karṣan veṇu-svanair gopīr
gopī-nāthaḥ śriye 'stu naḥ

śrī-mān—most beautiful; *rāsa*—of the *rāsa* dance; *rasa*—of the mellow; *ārambhī*—the initiator; *vaṁśī-vaṭa*—Vaṁśīvaṭa; *taṭa*—on the shore; *sthitaḥ*—standing; *karṣan*—attracting; *veṇu*—of the flute; *svanaiḥ*—by the sounds; *gopīḥ*—the cowherd girls; *gopī-nāthaḥ*—Śrī Gopīnātha; *śriye*—benediction; *astu*—let there be; *naḥ*—our.

TRANSLATION

Śrī Śrīla Gopīnātha, who originated the transcendental mellow of the rāsa dance, stands on the shore in Vaṁśīvaṭa and attracts the attention of the cowherd damsels with the sound of His celebrated flute. May they all confer upon us their benediction.

TEXT 18

জয় জয় শ্রীচৈতন্য জয় নিত্যানন্দ ।
জয়াদ্বৈতচন্দ্র জয় গৌরভক্তবৃন্দ ॥ ১৮ ॥

jaya jaya śrī-caitanya jaya nityānanda
jayādvaita-candra jaya gaura-bhakta-vṛnda

jaya jaya—all glory; *śrī-caitanya*—to Śrī Caitanya; *jaya*—all glory; *nityānanda*—to Lord Nityānanda; *jaya advaita-candra*—all glory to Advaita Ācārya; *jaya*—all glory; *gaura-bhakta-vṛnda*—to the devotees of Lord Caitanya.

TRANSLATION

Glory to Śrī Caitanya and Nityānanda! Glory to Advaitacandra! And glory to all the devotees of Śrī Gaura [Lord Caitanya]!

TEXT 19

এই তিন ঠাকুর গৌড়ীয়াকে করিয়াছেন আত্মসাৎ ।
এ তিনের চরণ বন্দোঁ, তিনে মোর নাথ ॥ ১৯ ॥

ei tina ṭhākura gauḍīyāke kariyāchena ātmasāt
e tinera caraṇa vandoṅ, tine mora nātha

ei—these; *tina*—three; *ṭhākura*—Deities; *gauḍīyāke*—the Gauḍīya Vaiṣṇavas; *kariyāchena*—have done; *ātmasāt*—absorbed; *e*—these; *tinera*—of the three; *caraṇa*—lotus feet; *vandoṅ*—I worship; *tine*—these three; *mora*—my; *nātha*—Lords.

TRANSLATION

These three Deities of Vṛndāvana [Madana-mohana, Govinda and Gopīnātha] have absorbed the heart and soul of the Gauḍīya Vaiṣṇavas [followers of Lord Caitanya]. I worship Their lotus feet, for They are the Lords of my heart.

PURPORT

The author of *Śrī Caitanya-caritāmṛta* offers his respectful obeisances unto the three Deities of Vṛndāvana named Śrī Rādhā-Madana-mohana, Śrī Rādhā-Govindadeva and Śrī Rādhā-Gopīnāthajī. These three Deities are the life and soul of the Bengali Vaiṣṇavas, or Gauḍīya

Vaiṣṇavas, who have a natural aptitude for residing in Vṛndāvana. The Gauḍīya Vaiṣṇavas who follow strictly in the line of Śrī Caitanya Mahāprabhu worship the Divinity by chanting transcendental sounds meant to develop a sense of one's transcendental relationship with the Supreme Lord, a reciprocation of mellows (*rasas*) of mutual affection, and, ultimately, the achievement of the desired success in loving service. These three Deities are worshiped in three different stages of one's development. The followers of Śrī Caitanya Mahāprabhu scrupulously follow these principles of approach.

Gauḍīya Vaiṣṇavas perceive the ultimate objective in Vedic hymns composed of eighteen transcendental letters that adore Kṛṣṇa as Madana-mohana, Govinda and Gopījana-vallabha. Madana-mohana is He who charms Cupid, the god of love, Govinda is He who pleases the senses and the cows, and Gopījana-vallabha is the transcendental lover of the *gopīs*. Kṛṣṇa Himself is called Madana-mohana, Govinda, Gopījana-vallabha and countless other names as He plays in His different pastimes with His devotees.

The three Deities—Madana-mohana, Govinda and Gopījana-vallabha—have very specific qualities. Worship of Madana-mohana is on the platform of reestablishing our forgotten relationship with the Personality of Godhead. In the material world we are presently in utter ignorance of our eternal relationship with the Supreme Lord. *Paṅgoḥ* refers to one who cannot move independently by his own strength, and *manda-mateḥ* is one who is less intelligent because he is too absorbed in materialistic activities. It is best for such persons not to aspire for success in fruitive activities or mental speculation but instead simply to surrender to the Supreme Personality of Godhead. The perfection of life is simply to surrender to the Supreme. In the beginning of our spiritual life we must therefore worship Madana-mohana so that He may attract us and nullify our attachment for material sense gratification. This relationship with Madana-mohana is necessary for neophyte devotees. When one wishes to render service to the Lord with strong attachment, one worships Govinda on the platform of transcendental service. Govinda is the reservoir of all pleasures. When by the grace of Kṛṣṇa and the devotees one reaches perfection in devotional service, he can appreciate Kṛṣṇa as Gopījana-vallabha, the pleasure Deity of the damsels of Vraja.

Lord Śrī Caitanya Mahāprabhu explained this mode of devotional service in three stages, and therefore these worshipable Deities were installed in Vṛndāvana by different Gosvāmīs. They are very dear to the Gauḍīya Vaiṣṇavas there, who visit the temples at least once a day.

Besides the temples of these three Deities, many other temples have been established in Vṛndāvana, such as the temple of Rādhā-Dāmodara of Jīva Gosvāmī, the temple of Śyāmasundara of Śyāmānanda Gosvāmī, the temple of Gokulānanda of Lokanātha Gosvāmī, and the temple of Rādhā-ramaṇa of Gopāla Bhaṭṭa Gosvāmī. There are seven principal temples over four hundred years old that are the most important of the five thousand temples now existing in Vṛndāvana.

Gauḍīya indicates the part of India between the southern side of the Himalayan Mountains and the northern part of the Vindhyā Hills, which is called Āryāvarta, or the Land of the Āryans. This portion of India is divided into five parts or provinces (Pañca-gauḍadeśa): Sārasvata (Kashmir and Punjab), Kānyakubja (Uttar Pradesh, including the modern city of Lucknow), Madhya-gauḍa (Madhya Pradesh), Maithila (Bihar and part of Bengal) and Utkala (part of Bengal and the whole of Orissa). Bengal is sometimes called Gauḍadeśa, partly because it forms a portion of Maithila and partly because the capital of the Hindu king Rāja Lakṣmaṇa Sena was known as Gauḍa. This old capital later came to be known as Gauḍapura and gradually Māyāpur.

The devotees of Orissa are called Uḍiyās, the devotees of Bengal are called Gauḍīyas, and the devotees of southern India are known as Drāviḍa devotees. As there are five provinces in Āryāvarta, so Dākṣiṇātya, southern India, is also divided into five provinces, which are called Pañca-draviḍa. The four Vaiṣṇava *ācāryas* who are the great authorities of the four Vaiṣṇava disciplic successions, as well as Śrīpāda Śaṅkarācārya of the Māyāvāda school, appeared in the Pañca-draviḍa provinces. Among the four Vaiṣṇava *ācāryas*, who are all accepted by the Gauḍīya Vaiṣṇavas, Śrī Rāmānuja Ācārya appeared in the southern part of Andhra Pradesh at Mahābhūtapurī, Śrī Madhva Ācārya appeared at Pājakam (near Vimānagiri) in the district of Mangalore, Śrī Viṣṇu Svāmī appeared at Pāṇḍya, and Śrī Nimbārka appeared at Muṅgera-patana, in the extreme south.

Śrī Caitanya Mahāprabhu accepted the chain of disciplic succession from Madhva Ācārya, but the Vaiṣṇavas in His line do not accept the Tattva-vādīs, who also claim to belong to the Mādhva-sampradāya. To distinguish themselves clearly from the Tattva-vādī branch of Madhva's descendants, the Vaiṣṇavas of Bengal prefer to call themselves Gauḍīya Vaiṣṇavas. Śrī Madhva Ācārya is also known as Śrī Gauḍa-pūrṇānanda, and therefore the name Mādhva-Gauḍīya-sampradāya is quite suitable for the disciplic succession of the Gauḍīya Vaiṣṇavas. Our spiritual master, Oṁ Viṣṇupāda Śrīmad Bhaktisiddhānta Sarasvatī Gosvāmī Mahārāja, accepted initiation in the Mādhva-Gauḍīya-sampradāya.

TEXT 20

গ্রন্থের আরম্ভে করি 'মঙ্গলাচরণ' ।
গুরু, বৈষ্ণব, ভগবান্—তিনের স্মরণ ॥ ২০ ॥

granthera ārambhe kari 'maṅgalācaraṇa'
guru, vaiṣṇava, bhagavān,—tinera smaraṇa

granthera—of this book; *ārambhe*—in the beginning; *kari*—I make; *maṅgala-ācaraṇa*—auspicious invocation; *guru*—the spiritual master; *vaiṣṇava*—the devotees of the Lord; *bhagavān*—the Supreme Personality of Godhead; *tinera*—of these three; *smaraṇa*—remembering.

TRANSLATION

In the beginning of this narration, simply by remembering the spiritual master, the devotees of the Lord, and the Personality of Godhead, I have invoked their benedictions.

TEXT 21

তিনের স্মরণে হয় বিঘ্নবিনাশন ।
অনায়াসে হয় নিজ বাঞ্ছিতপূরণ ॥ ২১ ॥

tinera smaraṇe haya vighna-vināśana
anāyāse haya nija vāñchita-pūraṇa

tinera—of these three; *smaraṇe*—by remembrance; *haya*—there is; *vighna-vināśana*—the destruction of all difficulties; *anāyāse*—very easily; *haya*—there is; *nija*—our own; *vāñchita*—of the desired object; *pūraṇa*—fulfillment.

TRANSLATION

Such remembrance destroys all difficulties and very easily enables one to fulfill his own desires.

TEXT 22

সে মঙ্গলাচরণ হয় ত্রিবিধ প্রকার ।
বস্তুনির্দেশ, আশীর্বাদ, নমস্কার ॥ ২২ ॥

se maṅgalācaraṇa haya tri-vidha prakāra
vastu-nirdeśa, āśīrvāda, namaskāra

se—that; *maṅgala-ācaraṇa*—auspicious invocation; *haya*—is; *tri-vidha*—three kinds; *prakāra*—processes; *vastu-nirdeśa*—defining the object; *āśīḥ-vāda*—benedictions; *namaḥ-kāra*—obeisances.

TRANSLATION

The invocation involves three processes: defining the objective, offering benedictions and offering obeisances.

TEXT 23

প্রথম দুই শ্লোকে ইষ্টদেব-নমস্কার ।
সামান্য-বিশেষ-রূপে দুই ত' প্রকার ॥ ২৩ ॥

prathama dui śloke iṣṭa-deva-namaskāra
sāmānya-viśeṣa-rūpe dui ta' prakāra

prathama—in the first; *dui*—two; *śloke*—verses; *iṣṭa-deva*—worshipable Deity; *namaskāra*—obeisances; *sāmānya*—generally; *viśeṣa-rūpe*—and specifically; *dui*—two; *ta'*—certainly; *prakāra*—ways.

TRANSLATION

The first two verses offer respectful obeisances, generally and specifically, to the Lord, who is the object of worship.

TEXT 24

তৃতীয় শ্লোকেতে করি বস্তুর নির্দেশ ।
যাহা হইতে জানি পরতত্ত্বের উদ্দেশ ॥ ২৪ ॥

tṛtīya ślokete kari vastura nirdeśa
yāhā ha-ite jāni para-tattvera uddeśa

tṛtīya ślokete—in the third verse; *kari*—I make; *vastura*—of the object; *nirdeśa*—indication; *yāhā ha-ite*—from which; *jāni*—I understand; *para-tattvera*—of the Absolute Truth; *uddeśa*—identification.

TRANSLATION

In the third verse I indicate the Absolute Truth, who is the ultimate substance. With such a description, one can visualize the Supreme Truth.

TEXT 25

চতুর্থ শ্লোকেতে করি জগতে আশীর্বাদ ।
সর্বত্র মাগিয়ে কৃষ্ণচৈতন্য-প্রসাদ ॥ ২৫ ॥

caturtha ślokete kari jagate āśīrvāda
sarvatra māgiye kṛṣṇa-caitanya-prasāda

caturtha—fourth; *ślokete*—in the verse; *kari*—I make; *jagate*—for the world; *āśīḥ-vāda*—benediction; *sarvatra*—everywhere; *māgiye*—I am begging; *kṛṣṇa-caitanya*—of Lord Śrī Kṛṣṇa Caitanya Mahāprabhu; *prasāda*—the mercy.

TRANSLATION

In the fourth verse I have invoked the benediction of the Lord upon all the world, praying to Lord Caitanya for His mercy upon all.

TEXT 26

সেই শ্লোকে কহি বাহ্যাবতার-কারণ ।
পঞ্চ ষষ্ঠ শ্লোকে কহি মূল-প্রয়োজন ॥ ২৬ ॥

sei śloke kahi bāhyāvatāra-kāraṇa
pañca ṣaṣṭha śloke kahi mūla-prayojana

sei śloke—in that same verse; *kahi*—I tell; *bāhya*—the external; *avatāra*—for the incarnation of Lord Caitanya; *kāraṇa*—reason; *pañca*—the fifth; *ṣaṣṭha*—and the sixth; *śloke*—in the verses; *kahi*—I tell; *mūla*—the prime; *prayojana*—purpose.

TRANSLATION

In that verse I have also explained the external reason for Lord Caitanya's incarnation. But in the fifth and sixth verses I have explained the prime reason for His advent.

TEXT 27

এই ছয় শ্লোকে কহি চৈতন্যের তত্ত্ব ।
আর পঞ্চ শ্লোকে নিত্যানন্দের মহত্ত্ব ॥ ২৭ ॥

ei chaya śloke kahi caitanyera tattva
āra pañca śloke nityānandera mahattva

ei—these; *chaya*—six; *śloke*—in verses; *kahi*—I describe; *caitanyera*—of Lord Caitanya Mahāprabhu; *tattva*—truth; *āra*—further; *pañca śloke*—in five verses; *nityānandera*—of Lord Nityānanda; *mahattva*—the glory.

TRANSLATION

In these six verses I have described the truth about Lord Caitanya, whereas in the next five I have described the glory of Lord Nityānanda.

TEXT 28

আর দুই শ্লোকে অদ্বৈত-তত্ত্বাখ্যান ।
আর এক শ্লোকে পঞ্চতত্ত্বের ব্যাখ্যান ॥ ২৮ ॥

āra dui śloke advaita-tattvākhyāna
āra eka śloke pañca-tattvera vyākhyāna

āra—further; *dui śloke*—in two verses; *advaita*—of Śrī Advaita Prabhu; *tattva*—of the truth; *ākhyāna*—description; *āra*—further; *eka śloke*—in one verse; *pañca-tattvera*—of the Pañca-tattva; *vyākhyāna*—explanation.

TRANSLATION

The next two verses describe the truth of Advaita Prabhu, and the following verse describes the Pañca-tattva [the Lord, His plenary portion, His incarnation, His energies and His devotees].

TEXT 29

এই চৌদ্দ শ্লোকে করি মঙ্গলাচরণ ।
তঁহি মধ্যে কহি সব বস্তুনিরূপণ ॥ ২৯ ॥

ei caudda śloke kari maṅgalācaraṇa
taṅhi madhye kahi saba vastu-nirūpaṇa

ei caudda śloke—in these fourteen verses; *kari*—I make; *maṅgala-ācaraṇa*—auspicious invocation; *taṅhi*—therefore in that; *madhye*—within; *kahi*—I speak; *saba*—all; *vastu*—object; *nirūpaṇa*—description.

TRANSLATION

These fourteen verses, therefore, offer auspicious invocations and describe the Supreme Truth.

TEXT 30

সব শ্রোতা-বৈষ্ণবেরে করি' নমস্কার।
এই সব শ্লোকের করি অর্থ-বিচার ॥ ৩০ ॥

saba śrotā-vaiṣṇavere kari' namaskāra
ei saba ślokera kari artha-vicāra

saba—all; *śrotā*—hearers or audience; *vaiṣṇavere*—unto the Vaiṣṇavas; *kari'*—offering; *namaskāra*—obeisances; *ei saba ślokera*—of all these (fourteen) verses; *kari*—I make; *artha*—of the meaning; *vicāra*—analysis.

TRANSLATION

I offer my obeisances unto all my Vaiṣṇava readers as I begin to explain the intricacies of all these verses.

TEXT 31

সকল বৈষ্ণব, শুন করি' একমন।
চৈতন্য-কৃষ্ণের শাস্ত্র-মত-নিরূপণ ॥ ৩১ ॥

sakala vaiṣṇava, śuna kari' eka-mana
caitanya-kṛṣṇera śāstra-mata-nirūpaṇa

sakala—all; *vaiṣṇava*—O devotees of the Lord; *śuna*—please hear; *kari'*—making; *eka-mana*—rapt attention; *caitanya*—Lord Caitanya Mahāprabhu; *kṛṣṇera*—of Lord Śrī Kṛṣṇa; *śāstra*—scriptural reference; *mata*—according to; *nirūpaṇa*—decision.

TRANSLATION

I request all my Vaiṣṇava readers to read and hear with rapt attention this narration of Śrī Kṛṣṇa Caitanya as inculcated in the revealed scriptures.

PURPORT

Lord Caitanya is the Absolute Truth, Kṛṣṇa Himself. This is substantiated by evidence from the authentic spiritual scriptures. Sometimes people accept a man as God on the basis of their whimsical sentiments and without reference to the revealed scriptures, but the author of *Caitanya-caritāmṛta* proves all his statements by citing the *śāstras.* Thus he establishes that Caitanya Mahāprabhu is the Supreme Personality of Godhead.

TEXT 32

কৃষ্ণ, গুরু, ভক্ত, শক্তি, অবতার, প্রকাশ ।
কৃষ্ণ এই ছয়রূপে করেন বিলাস ॥ ৩২ ॥

kṛṣṇa, guru, bhakta, śakti, avatāra, prakāśa
kṛṣṇa ei chaya-rūpe karena vilāsa

kṛṣṇa—the Supreme Lord, Śrī Kṛṣṇa; *guru*—the spiritual masters; *bhakta*—the devotees; *śakti*—the potencies; *avatāra*—the incarnations; *prakāśa*—plenary portions; *kṛṣṇa*—Lord Kṛṣṇa; *ei chaya-rūpe*—in these six features; *karena vilāsa*—enjoys.

TRANSLATION

Lord Kṛṣṇa enjoys by manifesting Himself as the spiritual masters, the devotees, the diverse energies, the incarnations and the plenary portions. They are all six in one.

TEXT 33

এই ছয় তত্ত্বের করি চরণ বন্দন ।
প্রথমে সামান্যে করি মঙ্গলাচরণ ॥ ৩৩ ॥

ei chaya tattvera kari caraṇa vandana
prathame sāmānye kari maṅgalācaraṇa

ei—these; *chaya*—six; *tattvera*—of these expansions; *kari*—I make; *caraṇa*—the lotus feet; *vandana*—prayers; *prathame*—at first; *sāmānye*—in general; *kari*—I make; *maṅgala-ācaraṇa*—auspicious invocation.

TRANSLATION

I therefore worship the lotus feet of these six diversities of the one truth by invoking their benedictions.

TEXT 34

বন্দে গুরূনীশভক্তানীশমীশাবতারকান্ ।
তৎপ্রকাশাংশ্চ তচ্ছক্তীঃ কৃষ্ণচৈতন্যসংজ্ঞকম্ ॥ ৩৪ ॥

vande gurūn īśa-bhaktān
īśam īśāvatārakān
tat-prakāśāṁś ca tac-chaktīḥ
kṛṣṇa-caitanya-saṁjñakam

vande—I offer respectful obeisances; *gurūn*—unto the spiritual masters; *īśa-bhaktān*—unto the devotees of the Supreme Lord; *īśam*—unto the Supreme Lord; *īśa-avatārakān*—unto the incarnations of the Supreme Lord; *tat*—of the Supreme Lord; *prakāśān*—unto the manifestations; *ca*—and; *tat*—of the Supreme Lord; *śaktīḥ*—unto the potencies; *kṛṣṇa-caitanya*—Śrī Kṛṣṇa Caitanya; *saṁjñakam*—named.

TRANSLATION

I offer my respectful obeisances unto the spiritual masters, the devotees of the Lord, the Lord's incarnations, His plenary portions, His energies and the primeval Lord Himself, Śrī Kṛṣṇa Caitanya.

PURPORT

Kṛṣṇadāsa Kavirāja Gosvāmī has composed this Sanskrit verse for the beginning of his book, and now he will explain it in detail. He offers his respectful obeisances to the six principles of the Absolute Truth. *Gurūn* is plural in number because anyone who gives spiritual instructions based on the revealed scriptures is accepted as a spiritual master. Although others give help in showing the way to beginners, the *guru* who first initiates one with the *mahā-mantra* is to be known as the initiator, and the saints who give instructions for progressive advancement in Kṛṣṇa consciousness are called instructing spiritual masters. The initiating and instructing spiritual masters are equal and identical manifestations of Kṛṣṇa, although they have different dealings. Their function is to guide the conditioned souls back home, back to Godhead.

Therefore Kṛṣṇadāsa Kavirāja Gosvāmī accepted Nityānanda Prabhu and the six Gosvāmīs in the category of *guru.*

Īśa-bhaktān refers to the devotees of the Lord like Śrī Śrīvāsa and all other such followers, who are the energy of the Lord and are qualitatively nondifferent from Him. *Īśāvatārakān* refers to *ācāryas* like Advaita Prabhu, who is an *avatāra* of the Lord. *Tat-prakāśān* indicates the direct manifestation of the Supreme Personality of Godhead, Nityānanda Prabhu, and the initiating spiritual master. *Tac-chaktīḥ* refers to the spiritual energies (*śaktis*) of Śrī Caitanya Mahāprabhu. Gadādhara, Dāmodara and Jagadānanda belong to this category of internal energy.

The six principles are differently manifested but all equally worshipable. Kṛṣṇadāsa Kavirāja begins by offering his obeisances unto them to teach us the method of worshiping Lord Caitanya. The external potency of Godhead, called *māyā,* can never associate with the Lord, just as darkness cannot remain in the presence of light; yet darkness, being but an illusory and temporary covering of light, has no existence independent of light.

TEXT 35

মন্ত্রগুরু আর যত শিক্ষাগুরুগণ ।
তাঁহার চরণ আগে করিয়ে বন্দন ॥ ৩৫ ॥

mantra-guru āra yata śikṣā-guru-gaṇa
tāṅhāra caraṇa āge kariye vandana

mantra-guru—the initiating spiritual master; *āra*—and also; *yata*—as many (as there are); *śikṣā-guru-gaṇa*—all the instructing spiritual masters; *tāṅhāra*—of all of them; *caraṇa*—unto the lotus feet; *āge*—at first; *kariye*—I offer; *vandana*—respectful obeisances.

TRANSLATION

I first offer my respectful obeisances at the lotus feet of my initiating spiritual master and all my instructing spiritual masters.

PURPORT

Śrīla Jīva Gosvāmī, in his thesis *Bhakti-sandarbha* (202), has stated that uncontaminated devotional service is the objective of pure

Vaiṣṇavas and that one has to execute such service in the association of other devotees. By associating with devotees of Lord Kṛṣṇa, one develops a sense of Kṛṣṇa consciousness and thus becomes inclined toward the loving service of the Lord. This is the process of approaching the Supreme Lord by gradual appreciation in devotional service. If one desires unalloyed devotional service, one must associate with devotees of Śrī Kṛṣṇa, for by such association only can a conditioned soul achieve a taste for transcendental love and thus revive his eternal relationship with Godhead in a specific manifestation and in terms of the specific transcendental mellow (*rasa*) that one has eternally inherent in him.

If one develops love for Kṛṣṇa by Kṛṣṇa conscious activities, one can know the Supreme Absolute Truth, but he who tries to understand God simply by logical arguments will not succeed, nor will he get a taste for unalloyed devotion. The secret is that one must submissively listen to those who know perfectly the science of God, and one must begin the mode of service regulated by the preceptor. A devotee already attracted by the name, form, qualities, etc., of the Supreme Lord may be directed to his specific manner of devotional service; he need not waste time in approaching the Lord through logic. The expert spiritual master knows well how to engage his disciple's energy in the transcendental loving service of the Lord, and thus he engages a devotee in a specific devotional service according to his special tendency. A devotee must have only one initiating spiritual master because in the scriptures acceptance of more than one is always forbidden. There is no limit, however, to the number of instructing spiritual masters one may accept. Generally a spiritual master who constantly instructs a disciple in spiritual science becomes his initiating spiritual master later on.

One should always remember that a person who is reluctant to accept a spiritual master and be initiated is sure to be baffled in his endeavor to go back to Godhead. One who is not properly initiated may present himself as a great devotee, but in fact he is sure to encounter many stumbling blocks on his path of progress toward spiritual realization, with the result that he must continue his term of material existence without relief. Such a helpless person is compared to a ship without a rudder, for such a ship can never reach its destination. It is imperative, therefore, that one accept a spiritual master if he at all desires to gain the favor of the Lord. The service of the spiritual master is essential. If there is no chance to serve the spiritual master directly, a devotee should serve him by remembering his instructions. There is no difference between the spiritual master's instructions and the spiritual master himself. In his absence, therefore, his words of direction should be the pride of the disciple. If one thinks that he is above consulting anyone else, including a spiritual master, he is at once an offender at the lotus feet of the Lord. Such an offender can never go back to Godhead. It is imperative that a serious person accept a bona fide spiritual master in terms of the śāstric injunctions. Śrī Jīva Gosvāmī advises that one not accept a spiritual master in terms of hereditary or customary social and ecclesiastical conventions. One should simply try to find a genuinely qualified spiritual master for actual advancement in spiritual understanding.

TEXT 36

শ্রীরূপ, সনাতন, ভট্ট-রঘুনাথ ।
শ্রীজীব, গোপালভট্ট, দাস-রঘুনাথ ॥ ৩৬ ॥

śrī-rūpa, sanātana, bhaṭṭa-raghunātha
śrī-jīva, gopāla-bhaṭṭa, dāsa-raghunātha

śrī-rūpa—Śrīla Rūpa Gosvāmī; *sanātana*—Sanātana Gosvāmī; *bhaṭṭa-raghunātha*—Raghunātha Bhaṭṭa Gosvāmī; *śrī-jīva*—Śrīla Jīva Gosvāmī; *gopāla-bhaṭṭa*—Gopāla Bhaṭṭa Gosvāmī; *dāsa-raghunātha*—Śrīla Raghunātha dāsa Gosvāmī.

TRANSLATION

My instructing spiritual masters are Śrī Rūpa Gosvāmī, Śrī Sanātana Gosvāmī, Śrī Bhaṭṭa Raghunātha, Śrī Jīva Gosvāmī, Śrī Gopāla Bhaṭṭa Gosvāmī and Śrīla Raghunātha dāsa Gosvāmī.

TEXT 37

এই ছয় গুরু—শিক্ষাগুরু যে আমার ।
তাঁ'সবার পাদপদ্মে কোটি নমস্কার ॥ ৩৭ ॥

ei chaya guru—śikṣā-guru ye āmāra
tāṅ'-sabāra pāda-padme koṭi namaskāra

ei—these; *chaya*—six; *guru*—spiritual masters; *śikṣā-guru*—instructing spiritual masters; *ye*—who are; *āmāra*—my; *tāṅ'-sabāra*—of all of them; *pāda-padme*—unto the lotus feet; *koṭi*—ten million; *namaskāra*—respectful obeisances.

TRANSLATION

These six are my instructing spiritual masters, and therefore I offer millions of respectful obeisances unto their lotus feet.

PURPORT

By accepting the six Gosvāmīs as his instructing spiritual masters, the author specifically makes it clear that one should not be recognized as a Gauḍīya Vaiṣṇava if he is not obedient to them.

TEXT 38

ভগবানের ভক্ত যত শ্রীবাস প্রধান ।
তাঁ'সভার পাদপদ্মে সহস্র প্রণাম ॥ ৩৮ ॥

bhagavānera bhakta yata śrīvāsa pradhāna
tāṅ'-sabhāra pāda-padme sahasra praṇāma

bhagavānera—of the Supreme Personality of Godhead; *bhakta*—the devotees; *yata*—as many (as there are); *śrīvāsa pradhāna*—headed by Śrī Śrīvāsa; *tāṅ'-sabhāra*—of all of them; *pāda-padme*—unto the lotus feet; *sahasra*—thousands; *praṇāma*—respectful obeisances.

TRANSLATION

There are innumerable devotees of the Lord, of whom Śrīvāsa Ṭhākura is the foremost. I offer my respectful obeisances thousands of times unto their lotus feet.

TEXT 39

অদ্বৈত আচার্য—প্রভুর অংশ-অবতার ।
তাঁর পাদপদ্মে কোটি প্রণতি আমার ॥ ৩৯ ॥

advaita ācārya—prabhura aṁśa-avatāra
tāṅra pāda-padme koṭi praṇati āmāra

advaita ācārya—Advaita Ācārya; *prabhura*—of the Supreme Lord; *aṁśa*—partial; *avatāra*—incarnation; *tāṅra*—of Him; *pāda-padme*—unto the lotus feet; *koṭi*—ten million; *praṇati*—respectful obeisances; *āmāra*—my.

TRANSLATION

Advaita Ācārya is the Lord's partial incarnation, and therefore I offer my obeisances millions of times at His lotus feet.

TEXT 40

নিত্যানন্দরায়—প্রভুর স্বরূপপ্রকাশ ।
তাঁর পাদপদ্ম বন্দো যাঁর মুঞি দাস ॥ ৪০ ॥

nityānanda-rāya—prabhura svarūpa-prakāśa
tāṅra pāda-padma vando yāṅra muñi dāsa

nityānanda-rāya—Lord Nityānanda; *prabhura*—of the Supreme Lord; *sva-rūpa-prakāśa*—personal manifestation; *tāṅra*—of Him; *pāda-padma*—unto the lotus feet; *vando*—I offer respectful obeisances; *yāṅra*—of whom; *muñi*—I am; *dāsa*—the servant.

TRANSLATION

Śrīla Nityānanda Rāma is the plenary manifestation of the Lord, and I have been initiated by Him. I therefore offer my respectful obeisances unto His lotus feet.

TEXT 41

গদাধরপণ্ডিতাদি—প্রভুর নিজশক্তি ।
তাঁ'সবার চরণে মোর সহস্র প্রণতি ॥ ৪১ ॥

gadādhara-paṇḍitādi—prabhura nija-śakti
tāṅ'-sabāra caraṇe mora sahasra praṇati

gadādhara-paṇḍita-ādi—headed by Śrī Gadādhara Paṇḍita; *prabhura*—of the Supreme Lord; *nija-śakti*—internal potencies; *tāṅ'-sabāra*—of all of them; *caraṇe*—unto the lotus feet; *mora*—my; *sahasra*—thousands; *praṇati*—respectful obeisances.

TRANSLATION

I offer my respectful obeisances unto the internal potencies of the Lord, of whom Śrī Gadādhara Prabhu is the foremost.

TEXT 42

শ্রীকৃষ্ণচৈতন্য প্রভু স্বয়ংভগবান্ ।
তাঁহার পদারবিন্দে অনন্ত প্রণাম ॥ ৪২ ॥

śrī-kṛṣṇa-caitanya prabhu svayaṁ-bhagavān
tāṅhāra padāravinde ananta praṇāma

śrī-kṛṣṇa-caitanya—Lord Śrī Kṛṣṇa Caitanya Mahāprabhu; *prabhu*—the Supreme Lord; *svayam-bhagavān*—is the original Personality of Godhead; *tāṅhāra*—His; *pada-aravinde*—unto the lotus feet; *ananta*—innumerable; *praṇāma*—respectful obeisances.

TRANSLATION

Lord Śrī Kṛṣṇa Caitanya Mahāprabhu is the Personality of Godhead Himself, and therefore I offer innumerable prostrations at His lotus feet.

TEXT 43

সাবরণে প্রভুরে করিয়া নমস্কার ।
এই ছয় তেঁহো যৈছে—করিয়ে বিচার ॥ ৪৩ ॥

sāvaraṇe prabhure kariyā namaskāra
ei chaya teṅho yaiche—kariye vicāra

sa-āvaraṇe—along with His associates; *prabhure*—unto Lord Śrī Caitanya Mahāprabhu; *kariyā*—having made; *namaskāra*—respectful obeisances; *ei*—these; *chaya*—six; *teṅho*—He; *yaiche*—what they are like; *kariye*—I make; *vicāra*—discussion.

TRANSLATION

Having offered obeisances unto the Lord and all His associates, I shall now try to explain these six diversities in one.

PURPORT

There are many unalloyed devotees of the Supreme Personality of Godhead, all of whom are considered associates surrounding the Lord.

Kṛṣṇa should be worshiped with His devotees. The diverse principles are therefore the eternal paraphernalia through which the Absolute Truth can be approached.

TEXT 44

যদ্যপি আমার গুরু—চৈতন্যের দাস ।
তথাপি জানিয়ে আমি তাঁহার প্রকাশ ॥ ৪৪ ॥

yadyapi āmāra guru—caitanyera dāsa
tathāpi jāniye āmi tāṅhāra prakāśa

yadyapi—even though; *āmāra*—my; *guru*—spiritual master; *caitanyera*—of Lord Caitanya Mahāprabhu; *dāsa*—the servitor; *tathāpi*—still; *jāniye*—know; *āmi*—I; *tāṅhāra*—of the Lord; *prakāśa*—direct manifestation.

TRANSLATION

Although I know that my spiritual master is a servitor of Śrī Caitanya, I know Him also as a plenary manifestation of the Lord.

PURPORT

Every living entity is essentially a servant of the Supreme Personality of Godhead, and the spiritual master is also His servant. Still, the spiritual master is a direct manifestation of the Lord. With this conviction, a disciple can advance in Kṛṣṇa consciousness. The spiritual master is nondifferent from Kṛṣṇa because he is a manifestation of Kṛṣṇa.

Lord Nityānanda, who is Balarāma Himself, the first direct manifestation or expansion of Kṛṣṇa, is the original spiritual master. He helps Lord Kṛṣṇa in His pastimes, and He is a servant of the Lord.

Every living entity is eternally a servant of Śrī Kṛṣṇa Caitanya; therefore the spiritual master cannot be other than a servant of Lord Caitanya. The spiritual master's eternal occupation is to expand the service of the Lord by training disciples in a service attitude. A spiritual master never poses as the Supreme Lord Himself; he is considered a representative of the Lord. The revealed scriptures prohibit one's pretending to be God, but a bona fide spiritual master is a most faithful and confidential servant of the Lord and therefore deserves as much respect as Kṛṣṇa.

TEXT 45

গুরু কৃষ্ণরূপ হন শাস্ত্রের প্রমাণে ।
গুরুরূপে কৃষ্ণ কৃপা করেন ভক্তগণে ॥ ৪৫ ॥

guru kṛṣṇa-rūpa hana śāstrera pramāṇe
guru-rūpe kṛṣṇa kṛpā karena bhakta-gaṇe

guru—the spiritual master; *kṛṣṇa-rūpa*—as good as Kṛṣṇa; *hana*—is; *śāstrera*—of revealed scriptures; *pramāṇe*—by the evidence; *guru-rūpe*—in the form of the spiritual master; *kṛṣṇa*—Lord Śrī Kṛṣṇa; *kṛpā*—mercy; *karena*—distributes; *bhakta-gaṇe*—unto His devotees.

TRANSLATION

According to the deliberate opinion of all revealed scriptures, the spiritual master is nondifferent from Kṛṣṇa. Lord Kṛṣṇa in the form of the spiritual master delivers His devotees.

PURPORT

The relationship of a disciple with his spiritual master is as good as his relationship with the Supreme Lord. A spiritual master always represents himself as the humblest servitor of the Personality of Godhead, but the disciple must look upon him as the manifested representation of Godhead.

TEXT 46

আচার্যং মাং বিজানীয়ান্নাবমন্যেত কর্হিচিৎ ।
ন মর্ত্যবুদ্ধ্যাসূয়েত সর্বদেবময়ো গুরুঃ ॥ ৪৬ ॥

ācāryaṁ māṁ vijānīyān
nāvamanyeta karhicit
na martya-buddhyāsūyeta
sarva-deva-mayo guruḥ

ācāryam—the spiritual master; *mām*—Myself; *vijānīyāt*—one should know; *na avamanyeta*—one should never disrespect; *karhicit*—at any time; *na*—never; *martya-buddhyā*—with the idea of his being an ordinary man; *asūyeta*—one should be envious; *sarva-deva*—of all demigods; *mayaḥ*—representative; *guruḥ*—the spiritual master.

TRANSLATION

"One should know the ācārya as Myself and never disrespect him in any way. One should not envy him, thinking him an ordinary man, for he is the representative of all the demigods."

PURPORT

This is a verse from *Śrīmad-Bhāgavatam* (11.17.27) spoken by Lord Kṛṣṇa when He was questioned by Uddhava regarding the four social and spiritual orders of society. The Lord was specifically instructing how a *brahmacārī* should behave under the care of a spiritual master. A spiritual master is not an enjoyer of facilities offered by his disciples. He is like a parent. Without the attentive service of his parents, a child cannot grow to manhood; similarly, without the care of the spiritual master one cannot rise to the plane of transcendental service.

The spiritual master is also called *ācārya*, or a transcendental professor of spiritual science. The *Manu-saṁhitā* (2.140) explains the duties of an *ācārya*, describing that a bona fide spiritual master accepts charge of disciples, teaches them the Vedic knowledge with all its intricacies, and gives them their second birth. The ceremony performed to initiate a disciple into the study of spiritual science is called *upanīti*, or the function that brings one nearer to the spiritual master. One who cannot be brought nearer to a spiritual master cannot have a sacred thread, and thus he is indicated to be a *śūdra.* The sacred thread on the body of a *brāhmaṇa, kṣatriya* or *vaiśya* is a symbol of initiation by the spiritual master; it is worth nothing if worn merely to boast of high parentage. The duty of the spiritual master is to initiate a disciple with the sacred thread ceremony, and after this *saṁskāra*, or purificatory process, the spiritual master actually begins to teach the disciple about the *Vedas.* A person born a *śūdra* is not barred from such spiritual initiation, provided he is approved by the spiritual master, who is duly authorized to award a disciple the right to be a *brāhmaṇa* if he finds him perfectly qualified. In the *Vāyu Purāṇa* an *ācārya* is defined as one who knows the import of all Vedic literature, explains the purpose of the *Vedas,* abides by their rules and regulations, and teaches his disciples to act in the same way.

Only out of His immense compassion does the Personality of Godhead reveal Himself as the spiritual master. Therefore in the dealings of an *ācārya* there are no activities but those of transcendental loving service to the Lord. He is the Supreme Personality of Servitor Godhead. It is worthwhile to take shelter of such a steady devotee, who is called *āśraya-vigraha,* or the manifestation or form of the Lord of whom one must take shelter.

If one poses himself as an *ācārya* but does not have an attitude of servitorship to the Lord, he must be considered an offender, and this offensive attitude disqualifies him from being an *ācārya.* The bona fide spiritual master always engages in unalloyed devotional service to the Supreme Personality of Godhead. By this test he is known to be a direct manifestation of the Lord and a genuine representative of Śrī Nityānanda Prabhu. Such a spiritual master is known as *ācāryadeva.* Influenced by an envious temperament and dissatisfied because of an attitude of sense gratification, mundaners criticize a real *ācārya.* In fact, however, a bona fide *ācārya* is nondifferent from the Personality of Godhead, and therefore to envy such an *ācārya* is to envy the Personality of Godhead Himself. This will produce an effect subversive of transcendental realization.

As mentioned previously, a disciple should always respect the spiritual master as a manifestation of Śrī Kṛṣṇa, but at the same time one should always remember that a spiritual master is never authorized to imitate the transcendental pastimes of the Lord. False spiritual masters pose themselves as identical with Śrī Kṛṣṇa in every respect to exploit the sentiments of their disciples, but such impersonalists can only mislead their disciples, for their ultimate aim is to become one with the Lord. This is against the principles of the devotional cult.

The real Vedic philosophy is *acintya-bhedābheda-tattva,* which establishes everything to be simultaneously one with and different from the Personality of Godhead. Śrīla Raghunātha dāsa Gosvāmī confirms that this is the real position of a bona fide spiritual master and says that one should always think of the spiritual master in terms of his intimate relationship with Mukunda (Śrī Kṛṣṇa). Śrīla Jīva Gosvāmī, in his *Bhakti-sandarbha* (213), has clearly explained that a pure devotee's observation of the spiritual master and Lord Śiva as being one with the Personality of Godhead exists in terms of their being very dear to the Lord, not identical with Him in all respects. Following in the footsteps of Śrīla Raghunātha dāsa Gosvāmī and Śrīla Jīva Gosvāmī, later *ācāryas* like Śrīla Viśvanātha Cakravartī Ṭhākura have confirmed the same truths. In his prayers to the spiritual master, Śrīla Viśvanātha Cakravartī Ṭhākura confirms that all the revealed scriptures accept the spiritual master to be identical with the Personality of Godhead because he is a very dear and confidential servant of the Lord. Gauḍīya

Vaiṣṇavas therefore worship Śrīla Gurudeva (the spiritual master) in the light of his being the servitor of the Personality of Godhead. In all the ancient literatures of devotional service and in the more recent songs of Śrīla Narottama dāsa Ṭhākura, Śrīla Bhaktivinoda Ṭhākura and other unalloyed Vaiṣṇavas, the spiritual master is always considered either one of the confidential associates of Śrīmatī Rādhārāṇī or a manifested representation of Śrīla Nityānanda Prabhu.

TEXT 47

শিক্ষাগুরুকে ত' জানি কৃষ্ণের স্বরূপ ।
অন্তর্যামী, ভক্তশ্রেষ্ঠ,—এই দুই রূপ ॥ ৪৭ ॥

śikṣā-guruke ta' jāni kṛṣṇera svarūpa
antaryāmī, bhakta-śreṣṭha,—ei dui rūpa

śikṣā-guruke—the spiritual master who instructs; *ta'*—indeed; *jāni*—I know; *kṛṣṇera*—of Kṛṣṇa; *sva-rūpa*—the direct representative; *antaryāmī*—the indwelling Supersoul; *bhakta-śreṣṭha*—the best devotee; *ei*—these; *dui*—two; *rūpa*—forms.

TRANSLATION

One should know the instructing spiritual master to be the Personality of Kṛṣṇa. Lord Kṛṣṇa manifests Himself as the Supersoul and as the greatest devotee of the Lord.

PURPORT

Śrīla Kṛṣṇadāsa Kavirāja Gosvāmī states that the instructing spiritual master is a bona fide representative of Śrī Kṛṣṇa. Śrī Kṛṣṇa Himself teaches us as the instructing spiritual master from within and without. From within He teaches as Paramātmā, our constant companion, and from without He teaches from the *Bhagavad-gītā* as the instructing spiritual master. There are two kinds of instructing spiritual masters. One is the liberated person fully absorbed in meditation in devotional service, and the other is he who invokes the disciple's spiritual consciousness by means of relevant instructions. Thus the instructions in the science of devotion are differentiated in terms of the objective and subjective ways of understanding. The *ācārya* in the true sense of the term, who is authorized to deliver Kṛṣṇa, enriches the disciple with full spiritual knowledge and thus awakens him to the activities of devotional service.

When by learning from the self-realized spiritual master one actually engages himself in the service of Lord Viṣṇu, functional devotional service begins. The procedures of this devotional service are known as *abhidheya*, or actions one is dutybound to perform. Our only shelter is the Supreme Lord, and one who teaches how to approach Kṛṣṇa is the functioning form of the Personality of Godhead. There is no difference between the shelter-giving Supreme Lord and the initiating and instructing spiritual masters. If one foolishly discriminates between them, he commits an offense in the discharge of devotional service.

Śrīla Sanātana Gosvāmī is the ideal spiritual master, for he delivers one the shelter of the lotus feet of Madana-mohana. Even though one may be unable to travel on the field of Vṛndāvana due to forgetfulness of his relationship with the Supreme Personality of Godhead, he can get an adequate opportunity to stay in Vṛndāvana and derive all spiritual benefits by the mercy of Sanātana Gosvāmī. Śrī Govindajī acts exactly like the *śikṣā-guru* (instructing spiritual master) by teaching Arjuna the *Bhagavad-gītā*. He is the original preceptor, for He gives us instructions and an opportunity to serve Him. The initiating spiritual master is a personal manifestation of Śrīla Madana-mohana *vigraha*, whereas the instructing spiritual master is a personal representative of Śrīla Govindadeva *vigraha*. Both of these Deities are worshiped at Vṛndāvana. Śrīla Gopīnātha is the ultimate attraction in spiritual realization.

TEXT 48

নৈবোপযন্ত্যপচিতিং কবয়স্তবেশ
ব্রহ্মায়ুষাপি কৃতমৃদ্ধমুদঃ স্মরন্তঃ ।
যোঽন্তর্বহিস্তনুভৃতামশুভং বিধুন্ব-
ন্নাচার্য-চৈত্ত্যবপুষা স্বগতিং ব্যনক্তি ॥ ৪৮ ॥

naivopayanty apacitiṁ kavayas taveśa
brahmāyuṣāpi kṛtam ṛddha-mudaḥ smarantaḥ
yo 'ntar bahis tanu-bhṛtām aśubhaṁ vidhunvann
ācārya-caittya-vapuṣā sva-gatiṁ vyanakti

na eva—not at all; *upayanti*—are able to express; *apacitim*—their gratitude; *kavayaḥ*—learned devotees; *tava*—Your; *īśa*—O Lord; *brahma-āyuṣā*—with a lifetime equal to Lord Brahmā's; *api*—in spite of;

kṛtam—magnanimous work; *ṛddha*—increased; *mudaḥ*—joy; *smarantaḥ*—remembering; *yaḥ*—who; *antaḥ*—within; *bahiḥ*—outside; *tanu-bhṛtām*—of those who are embodied; *aśubham*—misfortune; *vidhunvan*—dissipating; *ācārya*—of the spiritual master; *caittya*—of the Supersoul; *vapuṣā*—by the forms; *sva*—own; *gatim*—path; *vyanakti*—shows.

TRANSLATION

"O my Lord! Transcendental poets and experts in spiritual science could not fully express their indebtedness to You, even if they were endowed with the prolonged lifetime of Brahmā, for You appear in two features—externally as the ācārya and internally as the Supersoul—to deliver the embodied living being by directing him how to come to You."

PURPORT

This verse from *Śrīmad-Bhāgavatam* (11.29.6) was spoken by Śrī Uddhava after he heard from Śrī Kṛṣṇa all necessary instructions about *yoga*.

TEXT 49

তেষাং সততযুক্তানাং ভজতাং প্রীতিপূর্বকম্ ।
দদামি বুদ্ধিযোগং তং যেন মামুপযান্তি তে ॥ ৪৯ ॥

teṣāṁ satata-yuktānāṁ
bhajatāṁ prīti-pūrvakam
dadāmi buddhi-yogaṁ taṁ
yena mām upayānti te

teṣām—unto them; *satata-yuktānām*—always engaged; *bhajatām*—in rendering devotional service; *prīti-pūrvakam*—in loving ecstasy; *dadāmi*—I give; *buddhi-yogam*—real intelligence; *tam*—that; *yena*—by which; *mām*—unto Me; *upayānti*—come; *te*—they.

TRANSLATION

"To those who are constantly devoted to serving Me with love, I give the understanding by which they can come to Me."

PURPORT

This verse of the *Bhagavad-gītā* (10.10) clearly states how Govindadeva instructs His bona fide devotee. The Lord declares that by enlightenment in theistic knowledge He awards attachment for Him to those who constantly engage in His transcendental loving service. This awakening of divine consciousness enthralls a devotee, who thus relishes his eternal transcendental mellow. Such an awakening is awarded only to those convinced by devotional service about the transcendental nature of the Personality of Godhead. They know that the Supreme Truth, the all-spiritual and all-powerful person, is one without a second and has fully transcendental senses. He is the fountainhead of all emanations. Such pure devotees, always merged in knowledge of Kṛṣṇa and absorbed in Kṛṣṇa consciousness, exchange thoughts and realizations as great scientists exchange their views and discuss the results of their research in scientific academies. Such exchanges of thoughts in regard to Kṛṣṇa give pleasure to the Lord, who therefore favors such devotees with all enlightenment.

TEXT 50

যথা ব্রহ্মণে ভগবান্ স্বয়মুপদিশ্যানুভাবিতবান্ ॥ ৫০ ॥

yathā brahmaṇe bhagavān
svayam upadiśyānubhāvitavān

yathā—just as; *brahmaṇe*—unto Lord Brahmā; *bhagavān*—the Supreme Lord; *svayam*—Himself; *upadiśya*—having instructed; *anubhāvitavān*—caused to perceive.

TRANSLATION

The Supreme Personality of Godhead [svayaṁ bhagavān] taught Brahmā and made him self-realized.

PURPORT

The English maxim that God helps those who help themselves is also applicable in the transcendental realm. There are many instances in the revealed scriptures of the Personality of Godhead's acting as the spiritual master from within. The Personality of Godhead was the spiritual master who instructed Brahmā, the original living being in the cosmic creation. When Brahmā was first created, he could not apply his creative energy to arrange the cosmic situation. At first there was only sound, vibrating the word *tapa,* which indicates the acceptance of hardships for spiritual realization. Refraining from sensual enjoyment, one should voluntarily accept all sorts of difficulties for spiritual realization. This is called *tapasya.* An enjoyer of the senses can never realize God, godliness or the science of theistic knowledge. Thus when Brahmā, initiated by Śrī Kṛṣṇa by the sound vibration *tapa,* engaged himself in acts of austerity, by the pleasure of Viṣṇu he was able to visualize the transcendental world, Śrī Vaikuṇṭha, through transcendental realization. Modern science can communicate using material discoveries such as radio, television and computers, but the science invoked by the austerities of Śrī Brahmā, the original father of mankind, was still more subtle. In time, material scientists may also know how we can communicate with the Vaikuṇṭha world. Lord Brahmā inquired about the potency of the Supreme Lord, and the Personality of Godhead answered his inquiry in the following six consecutive statements. These instructions, which are reproduced from *Śrīmad-Bhāgavatam* (2.9.31–36), were imparted by the Personality of Godhead, acting as the supreme spiritual master.

TEXT 51

জ্ঞানং পরমগুহ্যং মে যদ্বিজ্ঞান-সমন্বিতম্ ।
সরহস্যং তদঙ্গঞ্চ গৃহাণ গদিতং ময়া ॥ ৫১ ॥

jñānaṁ parama-guhyaṁ me
yad vijñāna-samanvitam
sa-rahasyaṁ tad-aṅgaṁ ca
gṛhāṇa gaditaṁ mayā

jñānam—knowledge; *parama*—extremely; *guhyam*—confidential; *me*—of Me; *yat*—which; *vijñāna*—realization; *samanvitam*—fully endowed with; *sa-rahasyam*—along with mystery; *tat*—of that; *aṅgam*—supplementary parts; *ca*—and; *gṛhāṇa*—just try to take up; *gaditam*—explained; *mayā*—by Me.

TRANSLATION

"Please hear attentively what I shall speak to you, for transcendental knowledge about Me is not only scientific but also full of mysteries.

PURPORT

Transcendental knowledge of Śrī Kṛṣṇa is deeper than the impersonal knowledge of Brahman, for it includes knowledge of not only His form and personality but also everything else related to Him. There is nothing in existence not related to Śrī Kṛṣṇa. In a sense, there is nothing but Śrī Kṛṣṇa, and yet nothing is Śrī Kṛṣṇa save and except His primeval personality. This knowledge constitutes a complete transcendental science, and Viṣṇu wanted to give Brahmājī full knowledge about that science. The mystery of this knowledge culminates in personal attachment to the Lord, with a resulting effect of detachment from anything "non-Kṛṣṇa." There are nine alternative transcendental means of attaining this stage: hearing, chanting, remembering, serving the lotus feet of the Lord, worshiping, praying, assisting, fraternizing with the Lord, and sacrificing everything for Him. These are different parts of the same devotional service, which is full of transcendental mystery. The Lord said to Brahmā that since He was pleased with him, by His grace the mystery was being revealed.

TEXT 52

যাবানহং যথাভাবো যদ্রূপগুণকর্মকঃ ।
তথৈব তত্ত্ববিজ্ঞানমস্তু তে মদনুগ্রহাৎ ॥ ৫২ ॥

yāvān ahaṁ yathā-bhāvo
yad-rūpa-guṇa-karmakaḥ
tathaiva tattva-vijñānam
astu te mad-anugrahāt

yāvān—as I am in My eternal form; *aham*—I; *yathā*—in whichever manner; *bhāvaḥ*—transcendental existence; *yat*—whatever; *rūpa*—various forms and colors; *guṇa*—qualities; *karmakaḥ*—activities; *tathā eva*—exactly so; *tattva-vijñānam*—factual realization; *astu*—let there be; *te*—your; *mat*—My; *anugrahāt*—by causeless mercy.

TRANSLATION

"By My causeless mercy, be enlightened in truth about My personality, manifestations, qualities and pastimes.

PURPORT

The transcendental personal forms of the Lord are a mystery, and the symptoms of these forms, which are absolutely different from anything made of mundane elements, are also mysterious. The innumerable forms of the Lord, such as Śyāmasundara, Nārāyaṇa, Rāma and Gaurasundara; the colors of these forms (white, red, yellow, cloudlike *śyāma* and others); His qualities, as the responsive Personality of Godhead to pure devotees and as impersonal Brahman to dry speculators; His uncommon activities like lifting Govardhana Hill, marrying more than sixteen thousand queens at Dvārakā, and entering the *rāsa* dance with the damsels of Vraja, expanding Himself in as many forms as there were damsels in the dance—these and innumerable other uncommon acts and attributes are all mysteries, one aspect of which is presented in the scientific knowledge of the *Bhagavad-gītā*, which is read and adored all over the world by all classes of scholars, with as many interpretations as there are empiric philosophers. The truth of these mysteries was revealed to Brahmā by the descending process, without the help of the ascending one. The Lord's mercy descends to a devotee like Brahmā and, through Brahmā, to Nārada, from Nārada to Vyāsa, from Vyāsadeva to Śukadeva and so on in the bona fide chain of disciplic succession. We cannot discover the mysteries of the Lord by our mundane endeavors; they are only revealed, by His grace, to the proper devotees. These mysteries are gradually disclosed to the various grades of devotees in proportion to the gradual development of their service attitude. In other words, impersonalists who depend upon the strength of their poor fund of knowledge and morbid speculative habits, without submission and service in the forms of hearing, chanting and the others mentioned above, cannot penetrate to the mysterious region of transcendence where the Supreme Truth is a transcendental person, free from all tinges of the material elements. Discovering the mystery of the Lord eliminates the impersonal feature realized by common spiritualists who are merely trying to enter the spiritual region from the mundane platform.

TEXT 53

অহমেবাসমেবাগ্রে নান্যদ্ যৎ সদসৎপরম্ ।
পশ্চাদহং যদেতচ্চ যোঽবশিষ্যেত সোঽস্ম্যহম্ ॥ ৫৩ ॥

aham evāsam evāgre
nānyad yat sad-asat param
paścād ahaṁ yad etac ca
yo 'vaśiṣyeta so 'smy aham

aham—I, the Personality of Godhead; *eva*—certainly; *āsam*—existed; *eva*—only; *agre*—before the creation; *na*—never; *anyat*—anything else; *yat*—which; *sat*—the effect; *asat*—the cause; *param*—the supreme; *paścāt*—at the end; *aham*—I, the Personality of Godhead; *yat*—which; *etat*—this creation; *ca*—also; *yaḥ*—who; *avaśiṣyeta*—remains; *saḥ*—that; *asmi*—am; *aham*—I, the Personality of Godhead.

TRANSLATION

"Prior to the cosmic creation, only I exist, and no phenomena exist, either gross, subtle or primordial. After creation, only I exist in everything, and after annihilation, only I remain eternally.

PURPORT

Aham means "I"; therefore the speaker who is saying *aham*, "I," must have His own personality. The Māyāvādī philosophers interpret this word *aham* as referring to the impersonal Brahman. The Māyāvādīs are very proud of their grammatical knowledge, but any person who has actual knowledge of grammar can understand that *aham* means "I" and that "I" refers to a personality. Therefore the Personality of Godhead, speaking to Brahmā, uses *aham* while describing His own transcendental form. *Aham* has a specific meaning; it is not a vague term that can be whimsically interpreted. *Aham*, when spoken by Kṛṣṇa, refers to the Supreme Personality of Godhead and nothing else.

Before the creation and after its dissolution, only the Supreme Personality of Godhead and His associates exist; there is no existence of the material elements. This is confirmed in the Vedic literature. *Vāsudevo vā idam agra āsīn na brahmā na ca śaṅkaraḥ.* The meaning of this *mantra* is that before creation there was no existence of Brahmā or Śiva, for only Viṣṇu existed. Viṣṇu exists in His abode, the Vaikuṇṭhas. There are innumerable Vaikuṇṭha planets in the spiritual sky, and on each of them Viṣṇu resides with His associates and His paraphernalia. It is also confirmed in the *Bhagavad-gītā* that although the creation is periodically dissolved, there is another abode, which is never dissolved. The word "creation" refers to the material creation because in the spiritual world everything exists eternally and there is no creation or dissolution.

The Lord indicates herein that before the material creation He existed in fullness with all transcendental opulences, including all strength, all wealth, all beauty, all knowledge, all fame and all renunciation. If one thinks of a king, he automatically thinks of his secretaries, ministers, military commanders, palaces and so on. Since a king has such opulences, one can simply try to imagine the opulences of the Supreme Personality of Godhead. When the Lord says *aham,* therefore, it is to be understood that He exists with full potency, including all opulences.

The word *yat* refers to Brahman, the impersonal effulgence of the Lord. In the *Brahma-saṁhitā* (5.40) it is said, *tad brahma niṣkalam anantam aśeṣa-bhūtam:* the Brahman effulgence expands unlimitedly. Just as the sun is a localized planet with the sunshine expanding unlimitedly from that source, so the Absolute Truth is the Supreme Personality of Godhead with His effulgence of energy, Brahman, expanding unlimitedly. From that Brahman energy the creation appears, just as a cloud appears in sunshine. From the cloud comes rain, from the rain comes vegetation, and from the vegetation come fruits and flowers, which are the basis of subsistence for many other forms of life. Similarly, the effulgent bodily luster of the Supreme Lord is the cause of the creation of infinite universes. The Brahman effulgence is impersonal, but the cause of that energy is the Supreme Personality of Godhead. From Him, in His abode, the Vaikuṇṭhas, this *brahmajyoti* emanates. He is never impersonal. Since impersonalists cannot understand the source of the Brahman energy, they mistakenly choose to think this impersonal Brahman the ultimate or absolute goal. But as stated in the *Upaniṣads,* one has to penetrate the impersonal effulgence to see the face of the Supreme Lord. If one desires to reach the source of the sunshine, he has to travel through the sunshine to reach the sun and then meet the predominating deity there. The Absolute Truth is the Supreme Person, Bhagavān, as *Śrīmad-Bhāgavatam* explains.

Sat means "effect," *asat* means "cause," and *param* refers to the ultimate truth, which is transcendental to cause and effect. The cause of the creation is called the *mahat-tattva,* or total material energy, and its effect is the creation itself. But neither cause nor effect existed in the beginning; they emanated from the Supreme Personality of Godhead, as did the energy of time. This is stated in the *Vedānta-sūtra* (*janmādy asya yataḥ*). The source of birth of the cosmic manifestation, or *mahat-tattva,* is the Personality of Godhead. This is confirmed throughout *Śrīmad-Bhāgavatam* and the *Bhagavad-gītā.* In the *Bhagavad-gītā* (10.8) the Lord says, *ahaṁ sarvasya prabhavaḥ:* "I am the fountainhead of all emanations." The material cosmos, being temporary, is sometimes manifest and sometimes unmanifest, but its energy emanates from the Supreme Absolute Lord. Before the creation there was neither cause nor effect, but the Supreme Personality of Godhead existed with His full opulence and energy.

The words *paścād aham* indicate that the Lord exists after the dissolution of the cosmic manifestation. When the material world is dissolved, the Lord still exists personally in the Vaikuṇṭhas. During the creation the Lord also exists as He is in the Vaikuṇṭhas, and He also exists as the Supersoul within the material universes. This is confirmed in the *Brahma-saṁhitā* (5.37). *Goloka eva nivasati:* although He is perfectly and eternally present in Goloka Vṛndāvana in Vaikuṇṭha, He is nevertheless all-pervading (*akhilātma-bhūtaḥ*). The all-pervading feature of the Lord is called the Supersoul. In the *Bhagavad-gītā* it is said, *ahaṁ kṛtsnasya jagataḥ prabhavaḥ:* the cosmic manifestation is a display of the energy of the Supreme Lord. The material elements (earth, water, fire, air, ether, mind, intelligence and false ego) display the inferior energy of the Lord, and the living entities are His superior energy. Since the energy of the Lord is not different from Him, in fact everything that exists is Kṛṣṇa in His impersonal feature. Sunshine, sunlight and heat are not different from the sun, and yet simultaneously they are distinct energies of the sun. Similarly, the cosmic manifestation and the living entities are energies of the Lord, and they are considered to be simultaneously one with and different from Him. The Lord therefore says, "I am everything," because everything is His energy and is therefore nondifferent from Him.

Yo 'vaśiṣyeta so 'smy aham indicates that the Lord is the balance that exists after the dissolution of the creation. The spiritual manifestation never vanishes. It belongs to the internal energy of the Supreme Lord and exists eternally. When the external manifestation is withdrawn, the spiritual activities in Goloka and the rest of the Vaikuṇṭhas continue, unrestricted by material time, which has no existence in the spiritual world. Therefore in the *Bhagavad-gītā* (15.6) it is said, *yad gatvā na nivartante tad dhāma paramaṁ mama:* "The abode from which no one returns to this material world is the supreme abode of the Lord."

TEXT 54

ঋতেঽর্থং যৎ প্রতীয়েত ন প্রতীয়েত চাত্মনি ।
তদ্বিদ্যাদাত্মনো মায়াং যথাভাসো যথা তমঃ ॥ ৫৪ ॥

ṛte 'rthaṁ yat pratīyeta
na pratīyeta cātmani

tad vidyād ātmano māyāṁ
yathābhāso yathā tamaḥ

ṛte—without; *artham*—value; *yat*—that which; *pratīyeta*—appears to be; *na*—not; *pratīyeta*—appears to be; *ca*—certainly; *ātmani*—in relation to Me; *tat*—that; *vidyāt*—you must know; *ātmanaḥ*—My; *māyām*—illusory energy; *yathā*—just as; *ābhāsaḥ*—the reflection; *yathā*—just as; *tamaḥ*—the darkness.

TRANSLATION

"What appears to be truth without Me is certainly My illusory energy, for nothing can exist without Me. It is like a reflection of a real light in the shadows, for in the light there are neither shadows nor reflections.

PURPORT

In the previous verse the Absolute Truth and its nature have been explained. One must also understand the relative truth to actually know the Absolute. The relative truth, which is called *māyā,* or material nature, is explained here. *Māyā* has no independent existence. One who is less intelligent is captivated by the wonderful activities of *māyā,* but he does not understand that behind these activities is the direction of the Supreme Lord. In the *Bhagavad-gītā* (9.10) it is said, *mayādhyakṣeṇa prakṛtiḥ sūyate sa-carācaram:* the material nature is working and producing moving and nonmoving beings only by the supervision of Kṛṣṇa.

The real nature of *māyā,* the illusory existence of the material manifestation, is clearly explained in *Śrīmad-Bhāgavatam.* The Absolute Truth is substance, and the relative truth depends upon its relationship with the Absolute for its existence. *Māyā* means energy; therefore the relative truth is explained to be the energy of the Absolute Truth. Since it is difficult to understand the distinction between the absolute and relative truths, an analogy can be given for clarification. The Absolute Truth can be compared to the sun, which is appreciated in terms of two relative truths: reflection and darkness. Darkness is the absence of sunshine, and a reflection is a projection of sunlight into darkness. Neither darkness nor reflection has an independent existence. Darkness comes when the sunshine is blocked. For example, if one stands facing the sun, his back will be in darkness. Since darkness stands in the absence of the sun, it is therefore relative to the sun. The spiritual world is compared to the real sunshine, and the material world is compared to the dark regions where the sun is not visible.

When the material manifestation appears very wonderful, this is due to a perverted reflection of the supreme sunshine, the Absolute Truth, as confirmed in the *Vedānta-sūtra.* Whatever one can see here has its substance in the Absolute. As darkness is situated far away from the sun, so the material world is also far away from the spiritual world. The Vedic literature directs us not to be captivated by the dark regions (*tamaḥ*) but to try to reach the shining regions of the Absolute (*yogi-dhāma*).

The spiritual world is brightly illuminated, but the material world is wrapped in darkness. In the material world, sunshine, moonshine or different kinds of artificial light are required to dispel darkness, especially at night, for by nature the material world is dark. Therefore the Supreme Lord has arranged for sunshine and moonshine. But in His abode, as described in the *Bhagavad-gītā* (15.6), there is no necessity for lighting by sunshine, moonshine or electricity because everything is self-effulgent.

That which is relative, temporary and far away from the Absolute Truth is called *māyā,* or ignorance. This illusion is exhibited in two ways, as explained in the *Bhagavad-gītā.* The inferior illusion is inert matter, and the superior illusion is the living entity. The living entities are called illusory in this context only because they are implicated in the illusory structures and activities of the material world. Actually the living entities are not illusory, for they are parts of the superior energy of the Supreme Lord and do not have to be covered by *māyā* if they do not want to be so. The actions of the living entities in the spiritual kingdom are not illusory; they are the actual, eternal activities of liberated souls.

TEXT 55

যথা মহান্তি ভূতানি ভূতেষূচ্চাবচেষ্বনু ।
প্রবিষ্টান্যপ্রবিষ্টানি তথা তেষু ন তেষ্বহম্ ॥ ৫৫ ॥

yathā mahānti bhūtāni
bhūteṣūccāvaceṣv anu
praviṣṭāny apraviṣṭāni
tathā teṣu na teṣv aham

yathā—as; *mahānti*—the universal; *bhūtāni*—elements; *bhūteṣu*—in the living entities; *ucca-avaceṣu*—both gigantic and minute; *anu*—

after; *praviṣṭāni*—situated internally; *apraviṣṭāni*—situated externally; *tathā*—so; *teṣu*—in them; *na*—not; *teṣu*—in them; *aham*—I.

TRANSLATION

"As the material elements enter the bodies of all living beings and yet remain outside them all, I exist within all material creations and yet am not within them.

PURPORT

The gross material elements (earth, water, fire, air and ether) combine with the subtle material elements (mind, intelligence and false ego) to construct the bodies of this material world, and yet they are beyond these bodies as well. Any material construction is nothing but an amalgamation or combination of material elements in varied proportions. These elements exist both within and beyond the body. For example, although the sky exists in space, it also enters within the body. Similarly, the Supreme Lord, who is the cause of the material energy, lives within the material world as well as beyond it. Without His presence within the material world, the cosmic body could not develop, just as without the presence of the spirit within the physical body, the body could not develop. The entire material manifestation develops and exists because the Supreme Personality of Godhead enters it as Paramātmā, or the Supersoul. The Personality of Godhead in His all-pervading feature of Paramātmā enters every entity, from the biggest to the most minute. His existence can be realized by one who has the single qualification of submissiveness and who thereby becomes a surrendered soul. The development of submissiveness is the cause of proportionate spiritual realization, by which one can ultimately meet the Supreme Lord in person, as a man meets another man face to face.

Because of his development of transcendental attachment for the Supreme Lord, a surrendered soul feels the presence of his beloved everywhere, and all his senses are engaged in the loving service of the Lord. His eyes are engaged in seeing the beautiful couple Śrī Rādhā and Kṛṣṇa sitting on a decorated throne beneath a desire tree in the transcendental land of Vṛndāvana. His nose is engaged in smelling the spiritual aroma of the lotus feet of the Lord. Similarly, his ears are engaged in hearing messages from Vaikuṇṭha, and his hands embrace the lotus feet of the Lord and His associates. Thus the Lord is manifested to a pure devotee from within and without. This is one of the mysteries of the devotional relationship in which a devotee and the Lord are bound by a tie of spontaneous love. To achieve this love should be the goal of life for every living being.

TEXT 56

এতাবদেব জিজ্ঞাস্যং তত্ত্বজিজ্ঞাসুনাত্মনঃ ।
অন্বয়-ব্যতিরেকাভ্যাং যৎ স্যাৎ সর্বত্র সর্বদা ॥ ৫৬ ॥

etāvad eva jijñāsyaṁ
tattva-jijñāsunātmanaḥ
anvaya-vyatirekābhyāṁ
yat syāt sarvatra sarvadā

etāvat—up to this; *eva*—certainty; *jijñāsyam*—to be inquired about; *tattva*—of the Absolute Truth; *jijñāsunā*—by the student; *ātmanaḥ*—of the Self; *anvaya*—directly; *vyatirekābhyām*—and indirectly; *yat*—whatever; *syāt*—it may be; *sarvatra*—everywhere; *sarvadā*—always.

TRANSLATION

"A person interested in transcendental knowledge must therefore always directly and indirectly inquire about it to know the all-pervading truth."

PURPORT

Those who are serious about the knowledge of the transcendental world, which is far beyond the material cosmic creation, must approach a bona fide spiritual master to learn the science both directly and indirectly. One must learn both the means to approach the desired destination and the hindrances to such progress. The spiritual master knows how to regulate the habits of a neophyte disciple, and therefore a serious student must learn the science in all its aspects from him.

There are different grades and standards of prosperity. The standard of comfort and happiness conceived by a common man engaged in material labor is the lowest grade of happiness, for it is in relationship with the body. The highest standard of such bodily comfort is achieved by a fruitive worker who by pious activities reaches the plane of heaven, or the kingdom of the creative gods with their delegated powers. But the conception of comfortable life in heaven is insignificant in comparison to the happiness enjoyed in the impersonal Brahman, and this *brahmānanda*, the spiritual bliss derived from impersonal Brahman, is like the water in the hoofprint of a calf compared to the ocean of love of Godhead. When one develops pure love for the Lord, he derives an ocean of transcendental happiness from the association of the Personality of Godhead. To qualify oneself to reach this stage of life is the highest perfection.

One should try to purchase a ticket to go back home, back to Godhead. The price of such a ticket is one's intense desire for it, which is not easily awakened, even if one continuously performs pious activities for thousands of lives. All mundane relationships are sure to be broken in the course of time, but once one establishes a relationship with the Personality of Godhead in a particular *rasa*, it is never to be broken, even after the annihilation of the material world.

One should understand, through the transparent medium of the spiritual master, that the Supreme Lord exists everywhere in His transcendental spiritual nature and that the living entities' relationships with the Lord are directly and indirectly existing everywhere, even in this material world. In the spiritual world there are five kinds of relationships with the Supreme Lord—*śānta*, *dāsya*, *sakhya*, *vātsalya* and *mādhurya*. The perverted reflections of these *rasas* are found in the material world. Land, home, furniture and other inert material objects are related in *śānta*, or the neutral and silent sense, whereas servants work in the *dāsya* relationship. The reciprocation between friends is called *sakhya*, the affection of a parent for a child is known as *vātsalya*, and the affairs of conjugal love constitute *mādhurya*. These five relationships in the material world are distorted reflections of the original, pure sentiments, which should be understood and perfected in relationship with the Supreme Personality of Godhead under the guidance of a bona fide spiritual master. In the material world the perverted *rasas* bring frustration. If these *rasas* are reestablished with Lord Kṛṣṇa, the result is eternal, blissful life.

From this and the preceding three verses of the *Caitanya-caritāmṛta*, which have been selected from *Śrīmad-Bhāgavatam*, the missionary activities of Lord Caitanya can be understood. *Śrīmad-Bhāgavatam* has eighteen thousand verses, which are summarized in the four verses beginning with *aham evāsam evāgre* (53) and concluding with *yat syāt sarvatra sarvadā* (56). In the first of these verses (53) the transcendental nature of Lord Kṛṣṇa, the Supreme Personality of Godhead, is explained. The second verse (54) further explains that the Lord is detached from the workings of the material energy, *māyā*. The living entities, although parts and parcels of Lord Kṛṣṇa, are prone to be controlled by the external energy; therefore, although they are spiritual, in the material world they are encased in bodies of material energy. The eternal relationship of the living entities with the Supreme Lord is explained in that verse. The next verse (55) instructs that the Supreme Personality of Godhead, by His inconceivable energies, is simultaneously one with and different from the living entities and the material energy. This knowledge is called *acintya-bhedābheda-tattva*. When an individual living entity surrenders to the Supreme Lord, Kṛṣṇa, he can then develop natural transcendental love for Him. This surrendering process should be the primary concern of a human being. In the next verse (56) it is said that a conditioned soul must ultimately approach a bona fide spiritual master and try to understand perfectly the material and spiritual worlds and his own existential position. Here the words *anvaya-vyatirekābhyām*, "directly and indirectly," suggest that one must learn the process of devotional service in its two aspects: one must directly execute the process of devotional service and indirectly avoid the impediments to progress.

TEXT 57

চিন্তামণির্জয়তি সোমগিরির্গুরুর্মে
শিক্ষাগুরুশ্চ ভগবান্ শিখিপিঞ্ছমৌলিঃ ।
যৎপাদকল্পতরুপল্লবশেখরেষু
লীলাস্বয়ম্বররসং লভতে জয়শ্রীঃ ॥ ৫৭ ॥

cintāmaṇir jayati somagirir gurur me
śikṣā-guruś ca bhagavān śikhi-piñcha-mauliḥ
yat-pāda-kalpataru-pallava-śekhareṣu
līlā-svayaṁvara-rasaṁ labhate jayaśrīḥ

cintāmaṇiḥ jayati—all glory to Cintāmaṇi; *soma-giriḥ*—Somagiri (the initiating *guru*); *guruḥ*—spiritual master; *me*—my; *śikṣā-guruḥ*—instructing spiritual master; *ca*—and; *bhagavān*—the Supreme Personality of Godhead; *śikhi-piñcha*—with peacock feathers; *mauliḥ*—whose head; *yat*—whose; *pāda*—of the lotus feet; *kalpa-taru*—like desire trees; *pallava*—like new leaves; *śekhareṣu*—at the toe nails; *līlā-svayam-vara*—of conjugal pastimes; *rasam*—the mellow; *labhate*—obtains; *jaya-śrīḥ*—Śrīmatī Rādhārāṇī.

TRANSLATION

"All glories to Cintāmaṇi and my initiating spiritual master, Somagiri. All glories to my instructing spiritual master, the Supreme Personality of Godhead, who wears peacock feathers in His crown. Under the shade of His lotus feet, which are like desire trees, Jayaśrī [Rādhārāṇī] enjoys the transcendental mellow of an eternal consort."

PURPORT

This verse is from the *Kṛṣṇa-karṇāmṛta,* which was written by a great Vaiṣṇava *sannyāsī* named Bilvamaṅgala Ṭhākura, who is also known as Līlāśuka. He intensely desired to enter into the eternal pastimes of the Lord, and he lived at Vṛndāvana for seven hundred years in the vicinity of Brahma-kuṇḍa, a still-existing bathing tank in Vṛndāvana. The history of Bilvamaṅgala Ṭhākura is given in a book called *Śrī-vallabha-digvijaya.* He appeared in the eighth century of the Śaka Era in the province of Draviḍa and was the chief disciple of Viṣṇu Svāmī. In a list of temples and monasteries kept in Śaṅkarācārya's monastery in Dvārakā, Bilvamaṅgala is mentioned as the founder of the Dvārakādhīśa temple there. He entrusted the service of his Deity to Hari Brahmacārī, a disciple of Vallabha Bhaṭṭa.

Bilvamaṅgala Ṭhākura actually entered into the transcendental pastimes of Lord Kṛṣṇa. He has recorded his transcendental experiences and appreciation in the book known as *Kṛṣṇa-karṇāmṛta.* In the beginning of that book he has offered his obeisances to his different *gurus,* and it is to be noted that he has adored them all equally. The first spiritual master mentioned is Cintāmaṇi, who was one of his instructing spiritual masters because she first showed him the spiritual path. Cintāmaṇi was a prostitute with whom Bilvamaṅgala was intimate earlier in his life. She gave him the inspiration to begin on the path of devotional service, and because she convinced him to give up material existence to try for perfection by loving Kṛṣṇa, he has first offered his respects to her. Next he offers his respects to his initiating spiritual master, Somagiri, and then to the Supreme Personality of Godhead, who was also his instructing spiritual master. He explicitly mentions Bhagavān, who has peacock feathers on His crown, because the Lord of Vṛndāvana, Kṛṣṇa the cowherd boy, used to come to Bilvamaṅgala to talk with him and supply him with milk. In his adoration of Śrī Kṛṣṇa, the Personality of Godhead, he states that Jayaśrī, the goddess of fortune, Śrīmatī Rādhārāṇī, takes shelter in the shade of His lotus feet to enjoy the transcendental *rasa* of nuptial love. The complete treatise *Kṛṣṇa-karṇāmṛta* is dedicated to the transcendental pastimes of Śrī Kṛṣṇa and Śrīmatī Rādhārāṇī. It is a book to be read and understood by the most elevated devotees of Śrī Kṛṣṇa.

TEXT 58

জীবে সাক্ষাৎ নাহি তাতে গুরু চৈত্ত্যরূপে ।
শিক্ষাগুরু হয় কৃষ্ণ মহান্তস্বরূপে ॥ ৫৮ ॥

jīve sākṣāt nāhi tāte guru caittya-rūpe
śikṣā-guru haya kṛṣṇa-mahānta-svarūpe

jīve—by the living entity; *sākṣāt*—direct experience; *nāhi*—there is not; *tāte*—therefore; *guru*—the spiritual master; *caittya-rūpe*—in the form of the Supersoul; *śikṣā-guru*—the spiritual master who instructs; *haya*—appears; *kṛṣṇa*—Kṛṣṇa, the Supreme Personality of Godhead; *mahānta*—the topmost devotee; *sva-rūpe*—in the form of.

TRANSLATION

Since one cannot visually experience the presence of the Supersoul, He appears before us as a liberated devotee. Such a spiritual master is none other than Kṛṣṇa Himself.

PURPORT

It is not possible for a conditioned soul to directly meet Kṛṣṇa, the Supreme Personality of Godhead, but if one becomes a sincere devotee and seriously engages in devotional service, Lord Kṛṣṇa sends an instructing spiritual master to show him favor and invoke his dormant propensity for serving the Supreme. The preceptor appears before the external senses of the fortunate conditioned soul, and at the same time the devotee is guided from within by the *caittya-guru,* Kṛṣṇa, who is seated as the spiritual master within the heart of the living entity.

TEXT 59

ততো দুঃসঙ্গমুৎসৃজ্য সৎসু সজ্জেত বুদ্ধিমান্ ।
সন্ত এবাস্য ছিন্দন্তি মনোব্যাসঙ্গমুক্তিভিঃ ॥ ৫৯ ॥

tato duḥsaṅgam utsṛjya
satsu sajjeta buddhi-mān
santa evāsya chindanti
mano-vyāsaṅgam uktibhiḥ

tataḥ—therefore; *duḥsaṅgam*—bad association; *utsṛjya*—giving up; *satsu*—with the devotees; *sajjeta*—one should associate; *buddhi-mān*—an intelligent person; *santaḥ*—devotees; *eva*—certainly; *asya*—one's; *chindanti*—cut off; *manaḥ-vyāsaṅgam*—opposing attachments; *uktibhiḥ*—by their instructions.

TRANSLATION

"One should therefore avoid bad company and associate only with devotees. With their realized instructions, such saints can cut the knot connecting one with activities unfavorable to devotional service."

PURPORT

This verse, which appears in *Śrīmad-Bhāgavatam* (11.26.26), was spoken by Lord Kṛṣṇa to Uddhava in the text known as the *Uddhava-gīta.* The discussion relates to the story of Purūravā and the heavenly courtesan Urvaśī. When Urvaśī left Purūravā, he was deeply affected by the separation and had to learn to overcome his grief.

It is indicated that to learn the transcendental science, it is imperative that one avoid the company of undesirable persons and always seek the company of saints and sages who are able to impart lessons of transcendental knowledge. The potent words of such realized souls penetrate the heart, thereby eradicating all misgivings accumulated through years of undesirable association. For a neophyte devotee there are two kinds of persons whose association is undesirable: (1) gross materialists who constantly engage in sense gratification and (2) unbelievers who do not serve the Supreme Personality of Godhead but serve their senses and their mental whims in terms of their speculative habits. Intelligent persons seeking transcendental realization should very scrupulously avoid their company.

TEXT 60

সতাং প্রসঙ্গান্মম বীর্যসংবিদো
ভবন্তি হৃৎকর্ণরসায়নাঃ কথাঃ ।

তজ্জোষণাদাশ্বপবর্গবর্ত্মনি
শ্রদ্ধা রতির্ভক্তিরনুক্রমিষ্যতি ॥ ৬০ ॥

satāṁ prasaṅgān mama vīrya-saṁvido
bhavanti hṛt-karṇa-rasāyanāḥ kathāḥ
taj-joṣaṇād āśv apavarga-vartmani
śraddhā ratir bhaktir anukramiṣyati

satām—of the devotees; *prasaṅgāt*—by intimate association; *mama*—of Me; *vīrya-saṁvidaḥ*—talks full of spiritual potency; *bhavanti*—appear; *hṛt*—to the heart; *karṇa*—and to the ears; *rasa-āyanāḥ*—a source of sweetness; *kathāḥ*—talks; *tat*—of them; *joṣaṇāt*—from proper cultivation; *āśu*—quickly; *apavarga*—of liberation; *vartmani*—on the path; *śraddhā*—faith; *ratiḥ*—attraction; *bhaktiḥ*—love; *anukramiṣyati*—will follow one after another.

TRANSLATION

"The spiritually powerful message of Godhead can be properly discussed only in a society of devotees, and it is greatly pleasing to hear in that association. If one hears from devotees, the way of transcendental experience quickly opens, and gradually one attains firm faith that in due course develops into attraction and devotion."

PURPORT

This verse appears in *Śrīmad-Bhāgavatam* (3.25.25), where Kapiladeva replies to the questions of His mother, Devahūti, about the process of devotional service. As one advances in devotional activities, the process becomes progressively clearer and more encouraging. Unless one gets this spiritual encouragement by following the instructions of the spiritual master, it is not possible to make advancement. Therefore, one's development of a taste for executing these instructions is the test of one's devotional service. Initially, one must develop confidence by hearing the science of devotion from a qualified spiritual master. Then, as he associates with devotees and tries to adopt the means instructed by the spiritual master in his own life, his misgivings and other obstacles are vanquished by his execution of devotional service. Strong attachment for the transcendental service of the Lord develops as he continues listening to the messages of Godhead, and if he steadfastly proceeds in this way, he is certainly elevated to spontaneous love for the Supreme Personality of Godhead.

TEXT 61

ঈশ্বরস্বরূপ ভক্ত তাঁর অধিষ্ঠান ।
ভক্তের হৃদয়ে কৃষ্ণের সতত বিশ্রাম ॥ ৬১ ॥

īśvara-svarūpa bhakta tāṅra adhiṣṭhāna
bhaktera hṛdaye kṛṣṇera satata viśrāma

īśvara—the Supreme Personality of Godhead; *svarūpa*—identical with; *bhakta*—the pure devotee; *tāṅra*—His; *adhiṣṭhāna*—abode; *bhaktera*—of the devotee; *hṛdaye*—in the heart; *kṛṣṇera*—of Lord Kṛṣṇa; *satata*—always; *viśrāma*—the resting place.

TRANSLATION

A pure devotee constantly engaged in the loving service of the Lord is identical with the Lord, who is always seated in his heart.

PURPORT

The Supreme Personality of Godhead is one without a second, and therefore He is all-powerful. He has inconceivable energies, of which three are principal. The devotee is considered to be one of these energies, never the energetic. The energetic is always the Supreme Lord. The energies are related to Him for the purpose of eternal service. A living entity in the conditioned stage can uncover his aptitude for serving the Absolute Truth by the grace of Kṛṣṇa and the spiritual master. Then the Lord reveals Himself within his heart, and he can know that Kṛṣṇa is seated in the heart of every pure devotee. Kṛṣṇa is actually situated in the heart of every living entity, but only a devotee can realize this fact.

TEXT 62

সাধবো হৃদয়ং মহ্যং সাধূনাং হৃদয়ন্ত্বহম্ ।
মদন্যত্তে ন জানন্তি নাহং তেভ্যো মনাগপি ॥ ৬২ ॥

sādhavo hṛdayaṁ mahyaṁ
sādhūnāṁ hṛdayaṁ tv aham
mad-anyat te na jānanti
nāhaṁ tebhyo manāg api

sādhavaḥ—the saints; *hṛdayam*—heart; *mahyam*—My; *sādhūnām*—of the saints; *hṛdayam*—the heart; *tu*—indeed; *aham*—I; *mat*—than Me; *anyat*—other; *te*—they; *na*—not; *jānanti*—know; *na*—nor; *aham*—I; *tebhyaḥ*—than them; *manāk*—slightly; *api*—even.

TRANSLATION

"Saints are My heart, and only I am their hearts. They do not know anyone but Me, and therefore I do not recognize anyone besides them as Mine."

PURPORT

This verse appears in *Śrīmad-Bhāgavatam* (9.4.68) in connection with a misunderstanding between Durvāsā Muni and Mahārāja Ambarīṣa. As a result of this misunderstanding, Durvāsā Muni tried to kill the king, when the Sudarśana *cakra*, the celebrated weapon of Godhead, appeared on the scene for the devoted king's protection. When the Sudarśana *cakra* attacked Durvāsā Muni, he fled in fear of the weapon and sought shelter from all the great demigods in heaven. Not one of them was able to protect him, and therefore Durvāsā Muni prayed to Lord Viṣṇu for forgiveness. Lord Viṣṇu advised him, however, that if he wanted forgiveness he had to get it from Mahārāja Ambarīṣa, not from Him. In this context Lord Viṣṇu spoke this verse.

The Lord, being full and free from problems, can wholeheartedly care for His devotees. His concern is how to elevate and protect all those who have taken shelter at His feet. The same responsibility is also entrusted to the spiritual master. The bona fide spiritual master's concern is how the devotees who have surrendered to him as a representative of the Lord may make progress in devotional service. The Supreme Personality of Godhead is always mindful of the devotees who fully engage in cultivating knowledge of Him, having taken shelter at His lotus feet.

TEXT 63

ভবদ্বিধা ভাগবতাস্তীর্থভূতাঃ স্বয়ং বিভো ।
তীর্থীকুর্বন্তি তীর্থানি স্বান্তঃস্থেন গদাভৃতা ॥ ৬৩ ॥

bhavad-vidhā bhāgavatās
tīrtha-bhūtāḥ svayaṁ vibho
tīrthī-kurvanti tīrthāni
svāntaḥ-sthena gadā-bhṛtā

bhavat—your good self; *vidhāḥ*—like; *bhāgavatāḥ*—devotees; *tīrtha*—holy places of pilgrimage; *bhūtāḥ*—existing; *svayam*—themselves; *vibho*—O almighty one; *tīrthī-kurvanti*—make into holy places of pilgrimage; *tīrthāni*—the holy places; *sva-antaḥ-sthena*—being situated in their hearts; *gadā-bhṛtā*—by the Personality of Godhead.

TRANSLATION

"Saints of your caliber are themselves places of pilgrimage. Because of their purity, they are constant companions of the Lord, and therefore they can purify even the places of pilgrimage."

PURPORT

This verse was spoken by Mahārāja Yudhiṣṭhira to Vidura in *Śrīmad-Bhāgavatam* (1.13.10). Mahārāja Yudhiṣṭhira was receiving his saintly uncle Vidura, who had been visiting sacred places of pilgrimage. Mahārāja Yudhiṣṭhira told Vidura that pure devotees like him are personified holy places because the Supreme Personality of Godhead is always with them in their hearts. By their association, sinful persons are freed from sinful reactions, and therefore wherever a pure devotee goes is a sacred place of pilgrimage. The importance of holy places is due to the presence there of such pure devotees.

TEXT 64

সেই ভক্তগণ হয় দ্বিবিধ প্রকার ।
পারিষদ্‌গণ এক, সাধকগণ আর ॥ ৬৪ ॥

sei bhakta-gaṇa haya dvi-vidha prakāra
pāriṣad-gaṇa eka, sādhaka-gaṇa āra

sei—these; *bhakta-gaṇa*—devotees; *haya*—are; *dvi-vidha*—twofold; *prakāra*—varieties; *pāriṣat-gaṇa*—factual devotees; *eka*—one; *sādhaka-gaṇa*—prospective devotees; *āra*—the other.

TRANSLATION

Such pure devotees are of two types: personal associates [pāriṣats] and neophyte devotees [sādhakas].

PURPORT

Perfect servitors of the Lord are considered His personal associates, whereas devotees endeavoring to attain perfection are called neophytes.

Among the associates, some are attracted by the opulences of the Personality of Godhead, and others are attracted by nuptial love of Godhead. The former devotees are placed in the realm of Vaikuṇṭha to render reverential devotional service, whereas the latter devotees are placed in Vṛndāvana for the direct service of Śrī Kṛṣṇa.

TEXTS 65–66

ঈশ্বরের অবতার এ-তিন প্রকার ।
অংশ-অবতার, আর গুণ-অবতার ॥ ৬৫ ॥
শক্ত্যাবেশ-অবতার—তৃতীয় এমত ।
অংশ-অবতার—পুরুষ-মৎস্যাদিক যত ॥ ৬৬ ॥

īśvarera avatāra e-tina prakāra
aṁśa-avatāra, āra guṇa-avatāra

śaktyāveśa-avatāra—tṛtīya e-mata
aṁśa-avatāra—puruṣa-matsyādika yata

īśvarera—of the Supreme Lord; *avatāra*—incarnations; *e-tina*—these three; *prakāra*—kinds; *aṁśa-avatāra*—partial incarnations; *āra*—and; *guṇa-avatāra*—qualitative incarnations; *śakti-āveśa-avatāra*—empowered incarnations; *tṛtīya*—the third; *e-mata*—thus; *aṁśa-avatāra*—partial incarnations; *puruṣa*—the three *puruṣa* incarnations; *matsya*—the fish incarnation; *ādika*—and so on; *yata*—all.

TRANSLATION

There are three categories of incarnations of Godhead: partial incarnations, qualitative incarnations and empowered incarnations. The puruṣas and Matsya are examples of partial incarnations.

TEXT 67

ব্রহ্মা, বিষ্ণু, শিব—তিন গুণাবতারে গণি ।
শক্ত্যাবেশ—সনকাদি, পৃথু, ব্যাসমুনি ॥ ৬৭ ॥

brahmā viṣṇu śiva—tina guṇāvatāre gaṇi
śakty-āveśa—sanakādi, pṛthu, vyāsa-muni

brahmā—Lord Brahmā; *viṣṇu*—Lord Viṣṇu; *śiva*—Lord Śiva; *tina*—three; *guṇa-avatāre*—among the incarnations controlling the three modes of material nature; *gaṇi*—I count; *śakti-āveśa*—empowered incarnations; *sanaka-ādi*—the four Kumāras; *pṛthu*—King Pṛthu; *vyāsa-muni*—Vyāsadeva.

TRANSLATION

Brahmā, Viṣṇu and Śiva are qualitative incarnations. Empowered incarnations are those like the Kumāras, King Pṛthu and Mahāmuni Vyāsa [the compiler of the Vedas].

TEXT 68

দুইরূপে হয় ভগবানের প্রকাশ ।
একে ত' প্রকাশ হয়, আরে ত' বিলাস ॥ ৬৮ ॥

dui-rūpe haya bhagavānera prakāśa
eke ta' prakāśa haya, āre ta' vilāsa

dui-rūpe—in two forms; *haya*—are; *bhagavānera*—of the Supreme Personality of Godhead; *prakāśa*—manifestations; *eke*—in one; *ta'*—certainly; *prakāśa*—manifestation; *haya*—is; *āre*—in the other; *ta'*—certainly; *vilāsa*—engaged in pastimes.

TRANSLATION

The Personality of Godhead exhibits Himself in two kinds of forms: prakāśa and vilāsa.

PURPORT

The Supreme Lord expands His personal forms in two primary categories. The *prakāśa* forms are manifested by Lord Kṛṣṇa for His pastimes, and their features are exactly like His. When Lord Kṛṣṇa married sixteen thousand queens in Dvārakā, He did so in sixteen thousand *prakāśa* expansions. Similarly, during the *rāsa* dance He expanded Himself in identical *prakāśa* forms to dance beside each and every *gopī* simultaneously. When the Lord manifests His *vilāsa* expansions, however, they are all somewhat different in their bodily features. Lord Balarāma is the first *vilāsa* expansion of Lord Kṛṣṇa, and the four-handed Nārāyaṇa forms in Vaikuṇṭha expand from Balarāma. There is no difference between the bodily forms of Śrī Kṛṣṇa and Balarāma except that Their bodily colors are different. Similarly, Śrī Nārāyaṇa in

Vaikuṇṭha has four hands, whereas Kṛṣṇa has only two. The expansions of the Lord who manifest such bodily differences are known as *vilāsa-vigrahas.*

TEXTS 69–70

একই বিগ্রহ যদি হয় বহুরূপ ।
আকারে ত' ভেদ নাহি, একই স্বরূপ ॥ ৬৯ ॥
মহিষী-বিবাহে, যৈছে যৈছে কৈল রাস ।
ইহাকে কহিয়ে কৃষ্ণের মুখ্য 'প্রকাশ' ॥ ৭০ ॥

eka-i vigraha yadi haya bahu-rūpa
ākāre ta' bheda nāhi, eka-i svarūpa

mahiṣī-vivāhe, yaiche yaiche kaila rāsa
ihāke kahiye kṛṣṇera mukhya 'prakāśa'

eka-i—the same one; *vigraha*—person; *yadi*—if; *haya*—becomes; *bahu-rūpa*—many forms; *ākāre*—in appearance; *ta'*—certainly; *bheda*—difference; *nāhi*—there is not; *eka-i*—one; *sva-rūpa*—identity; *mahiṣī*—with the queens of Dvārakā; *vivāhe*—in the marriage; *yaiche yaiche*—in a similar way; *kaila*—He did; *rāsa*—*rāsa* dance; *ihāke*—this; *kahiye*—I say; *kṛṣṇera*—of Kṛṣṇa; *mukhya*—principal; *prakāśa*—manifested forms.

TRANSLATION

When the Personality of Godhead expands Himself in many forms, all nondifferent in Their features, as Lord Kṛṣṇa did when He married sixteen thousand queens and when He performed His rāsa dance, such forms of the Lord are called manifested forms [prakāśa-vigrahas].

TEXT 71

চিত্রং বতৈতদেকেন বপুষা যুগপৎ পৃথক্ ।
গৃহেষু দ্ব্যষ্টসাহস্রং স্ত্রিয় এক উদাবহৎ ॥ ৭১ ॥

citraṁ bataitad ekena
vapuṣā yugapat pṛthak
gṛheṣu dvy-aṣṭa-sāhasraṁ
striya eka udāvahat

citram—wonderful; *bata*—oh; *etat*—this; *ekena*—with one; *vapuṣā*—form; *yugapat*—simultaneously; *pṛthak*—separately; *gṛheṣu*—in the houses; *dvi-aṣṭa-sāhasram*—sixteen thousand; *striyaḥ*—all the queens; *ekaḥ*—the one Śrī Kṛṣṇa; *udāvahat*—married.

TRANSLATION

"It is astounding that Lord Śrī Kṛṣṇa, who is one without a second, expanded Himself in sixteen thousand similar forms to marry sixteen thousand queens in their respective homes."

PURPORT

This verse is from *Śrīmad-Bhāgavatam* (10.69.2).

TEXT 72

রাসোৎসবঃ সংপ্রবৃত্তো গোপীমণ্ডলমণ্ডিতঃ ।
যোগেশ্বরেণ কৃষ্ণেন তাসাং মধ্যে দ্বয়োর্দ্বয়োঃ ॥ ৭২ ॥

rāsotsavaḥ sampravṛtto
gopī-maṇḍala-maṇḍitaḥ
yogeśvareṇa kṛṣṇena
tāsāṁ madhye dvayor dvayoḥ

rāsa-utsavaḥ—the festival of the *rāsa* dance; *sampravṛttaḥ*—was begun; *gopī-maṇḍala*—by groups of *gopīs; maṇḍitaḥ*—decorated; *yoga-īśvareṇa*—by the master of all mystic powers; *kṛṣṇena*—by Lord Kṛṣṇa; *tāsām*—of them; *madhye*—in the middle; *dvayoḥ dvayoḥ*—of each two.

TRANSLATION

"When Lord Kṛṣṇa, surrounded by groups of cowherd girls, began the festivities of the rāsa dance, the Lord of all mystic powers placed Himself between each two girls."

PURPORT

This verse is also quoted from *Śrīmad-Bhāgavatam* (10.33.3).

TEXTS 73–74

প্রবিষ্টেন গৃহীতানাং কণ্ঠে স্বনিকটং স্ত্রিয়ঃ ।
যং মন্যেরন্নভস্তাবদ্বিমানশতসঙ্কুলম্ ॥ ৭৩ ॥

দিবৌকসাং সদারাণামত্যৌৎসুক্যভৃতাত্মনাম্ ।
ততো দুন্দুভয়ো নেদুর্নিপেতুঃ পুষ্পবৃষ্টয়ঃ ॥ ৭৪ ॥

praviṣṭena gṛhītānāṁ
kaṇṭhe sva-nikaṭaṁ striyaḥ
yaṁ manyeran nabhas tāvad
vimāna-śata-saṅkulam

divaukasāṁ sa-dārāṇām
aty-autsukya-bhṛtātmanām
tato dundubhayo nedur
nipetuḥ puṣpa-vṛṣṭayaḥ

praviṣṭena—having entered; *gṛhītānām*—of those embracing; *kaṇṭhe*—on the neck; *sva-nikaṭam*—situated at their own side; *striyaḥ*—the *gopīs; yam*—whom; *manyeran*—would think; *nabhaḥ*—the sky; *tāvat*—at once; *vimāna*—of airplanes; *śata*—with hundreds; *saṅkulam*—crowded; *diva-okasām*—of the demigods; *sa-dārāṇām*—with their wives; *ati-autsukya*—with eagerness; *bhṛta-ātmanām*—whose minds were filled; *tataḥ*—then; *dundubhayaḥ*—kettledrums; *neduḥ*—sounded; *nipetuḥ*—fell; *puṣpa-vṛṣṭayaḥ*—showers of flowers.

TRANSLATION

"When the cowherd girls and Kṛṣṇa thus joined together, each girl thought that Kṛṣṇa was dearly embracing her alone. To behold this wonderful pastime of the Lord's, the denizens of heaven and their wives, all very eager to see the dance, flew in the sky in their hundreds of airplanes. They showered flowers and beat sweetly on drums."

PURPORT

This is another quotation from *Śrīmad-Bhāgavatam* (10.33.3–4).

TEXT 75

অনেকত্র প্রকটতা রূপস্যৈকস্য যৈকদা ।
সর্বথা তৎস্বরূপৈব স প্রকাশ ইতীর্যতে ॥ ৭৫ ॥

anekatra prakaṭatā
rūpasyaikasya yaikadā

sarvathā tat-svarūpaiva
sa prakāśa itīryate

anekatra—in many places; *prakaṭatā*—the manifestation; *rūpasya*—of form; *ekasya*—one; *yā*—which; *ekadā*—at one time; *sarvathā*—in every respect; *tat*—His; *sva-rūpa*—own form; *eva*—certainly; *saḥ*—that; *prakāśaḥ*—manifestive form; *iti*—thus; *īryate*—it is called.

TRANSLATION

"If numerous forms, all equal in their features, are displayed simultaneously, such forms are called prakāśa-vigrahas of the Lord."

PURPORT

This is a quotation from the *Laghu-bhāgavatāmṛta* (1.21), compiled by Śrīla Rūpa Gosvāmī.

TEXT 76

একই বিগ্রহ কিন্তু আকারে হয় আন ।
অনেক প্রকাশ হয়, 'বিলাস' তার নাম ॥ ৭৬ ॥

eka-i vigraha kintu ākāre haya āna
aneka prakāśa haya, 'vilāsa' tāra nāma

eka-i—one; *vigraha*—form; *kintu*—but; *ākāre*—in appearance; *haya*—is; *āna*—different; *aneka*—many; *prakāśa*—manifestations; *haya*—appear; *vilāsa*—pastime form; *tāra*—of that; *nāma*—the name.

TRANSLATION

But when the numerous forms are slightly different from one another, they are called vilāsa-vigrahas.

TEXT 77

স্বরূপমন্যাকারং যত্তস্য ভাতি বিলাসতঃ ।
প্রায়েণাত্মসমং শক্ত্যা স বিলাসো নিগদ্যতে ॥ ৭৭ ॥

svarūpam anyākāraṁ yat
tasya bhāti vilāsataḥ

prāyeṇātma-samaṁ śaktyā
sa vilāso nigadyate

sva-rūpam—the Lord's own form; *anya*—other; *ākāram*—features of the body; *yat*—which; *tasya*—His; *bhāti*—appears; *vilāsataḥ*—from particular pastimes; *prāyena*—almost; *ātma-samam*—self-similar; *śaktyā*—by His potency; *saḥ*—that; *vilāsaḥ*—the *vilāsa* (pastime) form; *nigadyate*—is called.

TRANSLATION

"When the Lord displays numerous forms with different features by His inconceivable potency, such forms are called vilāsa-vigrahas."

PURPORT

This is another quotation from the *Laghu-bhāgavatāmṛta* (1.15).

TEXT 78

যৈছে বলদেব, পরব্যোমে নারায়ণ ।
যৈছে বাসুদেব প্রদ্যুম্নাদি সঙ্কর্ষণ ॥ ৭৮ ॥

yaiche baladeva, paravyome nārāyaṇa
yaiche vāsudeva pradyumnādi saṅkarṣaṇa

yaiche—just as; *baladeva*—Baladeva; *para-vyome*—in the spiritual sky; *nārāyaṇa*—Lord Nārāyaṇa; *yaiche*—just as; *vāsudeva*—Vāsudeva; *pradyumna-ādi*—Pradyumna, etc.; *saṅkarṣaṇa*—Saṅkarṣaṇa.

TRANSLATION

Examples of such vilāsa-vigrahas are Baladeva, Nārāyaṇa in Vaikuṇṭha-dhāma, and the catur-vyūha—Vāsudeva, Saṅkarṣaṇa, Pradyumna and Aniruddha.

TEXTS 79–80

ঈশ্বরের শক্তি হয় এ-তিন প্রকার ।
এক লক্ষীগণ, পুরে মহিষীগণ আর ॥ ৭৯ ॥
ব্রজে গোপীগণ আর সভাতে প্রধান ।
ব্রজেন্দ্রনন্দন যা'তে স্বয়ং ভগবান্ ॥ ৮০ ॥

īśvarera śakti haya e-tina prakāra
eka lakṣmī-gaṇa, pure mahiṣī-gaṇa āra

vraje gopī-gaṇa āra sabhāte pradhāna
vrajendra-nandana yā'te svayaṁ bhagavān

īśvarera—of the Supreme Lord; *śakti*—energy; *haya*—is; *e-tina*—these three; *prakāra*—kinds; *eka*—one; *lakṣmī-gaṇa*—the goddesses of fortune in Vaikuṇṭha; *pure*—in Dvārakā; *mahiṣī-gaṇa*—the queens; *āra*—and; *vraje*—in Vṛndāvana; *gopī-gaṇa*—the *gopīs; āra*—and; *sabhāte*—among all of them; *pradhāna*—the chief; *vraja-indra-nandana*—Kṛṣṇa, the son of the King of Vraja; *yā'te*—because; *svayam*—Himself; *bhagavān*—the primeval Lord.

TRANSLATION

The energies [consorts] of the Supreme Lord are of three kinds: the Lakṣmīs in Vaikuṇṭha, the queens in Dvārakā and the gopīs in Vṛndāvana. The gopīs are the best of all, for they have the privilege of serving Śrī Kṛṣṇa, the primeval Lord, the son of the King of Vraja.

TEXT 81

স্বয়ংরূপ কৃষ্ণের কায়ব্যূহ—তাঁর সম ।
ভক্ত সহিতে হয় তাঁহার আবরণ ॥ ৮১ ॥

svayaṁ-rūpa kṛṣṇera kāya-vyūha—tāṅra sama
bhakta sahite haya tāṅhāra āvaraṇa

svayam-rūpa—His own original form (two-handed Kṛṣṇa); *kṛṣṇera*—of Lord Kṛṣṇa; *kāya-vyūha*—personal expansions; *tāṅra*—with Him; *sama*—equal; *bhakta*—the devotees; *sahite*—associated with; *haya*—are; *tāṅhāra*—His; *āvaraṇa*—covering.

TRANSLATION

The personal associates of the primeval Lord, Śrī Kṛṣṇa, are His devotees, who are identical with Him. He is complete with His entourage of devotees.

PURPORT

Śrī Kṛṣṇa and His various personal expansions are nondifferent in potential power. These expansions are associated with further, secondary expansions, or servitor expansions, who are called devotees.

TEXT 82

ভক্ত আদি ক্রমে কৈল সভার বন্দন ।
এ-সভার বন্দন সর্বশুভের কারণ ॥ ৮২ ॥

bhakta ādi krame kaila sabhāra vandana
e-sabhāra vandana sarva-śubhera kāraṇa

bhakta—the devotees; *ādi*—and so on; *krame*—in order; *kaila*—did; *sabhāra*—of the assembly; *vandana*—worship; *e-sabhāra*—of this assembly; *vandana*—worship; *sarva-śubhera*—of all good fortune; *kāraṇa*—the source.

TRANSLATION

Now I have worshiped all the various levels of devotees. Worshiping them is the source of all good fortune.

PURPORT

To offer prayers to the Lord, one should first offer prayers to His devotees and associates.

TEXT 83

প্রথম শ্লোকে কহি সামান্য মঙ্গলাচরণ ।
দ্বিতীয় শ্লোকেতে করি বিশেষ বন্দন ॥ ৮৩ ॥

prathama śloke kahi sāmānya maṅgalācaraṇa
dvitīya ślokete kari viśeṣa vandana

prathama—first; *śloke*—in the verse; *kahi*—I express; *sāmānya*—general; *maṅgala-ācaraṇa*—invocation of benediction; *dvitīya*—second; *ślokete*—in the verse; *kari*—I do; *viśeṣa*—particular; *vandana*—offering of prayers.

TRANSLATION

In the first verse I have invoked a general benediction, but in the second I have prayed to the Lord in a particular form.

TEXT 84

বন্দে শ্রীকৃষ্ণচৈতন্য-নিত্যানন্দৌ সহোদিতৌ ।
গৌড়োদয়ে পুষ্পবন্তৌ চিত্রৌ শন্দৌ তমোনুদৌ ॥ ৮৪ ॥

vande śrī-kṛṣṇa-caitanya-
nityānandau sahoditau
gauḍodaye puṣpavantau
citrau śan-dau tamo-nudau

vande—I offer respectful obeisances; *śrī-kṛṣṇa-caitanya*—to Lord Śrī Kṛṣṇa Caitanya; *nityānandau*—and to Lord Nityānanda; *saha-uditau*—simultaneously arisen; *gauḍa-udaye*—on the eastern horizon of Gauḍa; *puṣpavantau*—the sun and moon together; *citrau*—wonderful; *śam-dau*—bestowing benediction; *tamaḥ-nudau*—dissipating darkness.

TRANSLATION

"I offer my respectful obeisances unto Śrī Kṛṣṇa Caitanya and Lord Nityānanda, who are like the sun and moon. They have arisen simultaneously on the horizon of Gauḍa to dissipate the darkness of ignorance and thus wonderfully bestow benediction upon all."

TEXTS 85–86

ব্রজে যে বিহরে পূর্বে কৃষ্ণ-বলরাম ।
কোটীসূর্যচন্দ্র জিনি দোঁহার নিজধাম ॥ ৮৫ ॥
সেই দুই জগতেরে হইয়া সদয় ।
গৌড়দেশে পূর্ব-শৈলে করিলা উদয় ॥ ৮৬ ॥

vraje ye vihare pūrve kṛṣṇa-balarāma
koṭī-sūrya-candra jini doṅhāra nija-dhāma

sei dui jagatere ha-iyā sadaya
gauḍadeśe pūrva-śaile karilā udaya

vraje—in Vraja (Vṛndāvana); *ye*—who; *vihare*—played; *pūrve*—formerly; *kṛṣṇa*—Lord Kṛṣṇa; *balarāma*—Lord Balarāma; *koṭī*—millions; *sūrya*—suns; *candra*—moons; *jini*—overcoming; *doṅhāra*—of the two; *nija-dhāma*—the effulgence; *sei*—these; *dui*—two; *jagatere*—for the universe; *ha-iyā*—becoming; *sa-daya*—compassionate; *gauḍa-deśe*—in the country of Gauḍa; *pūrva-śaile*—on the eastern horizon; *karilā*—did; *udaya*—arise.

TRANSLATION

Śrī Kṛṣṇa and Balarāma, the Personalities of Godhead, who formerly appeared in Vṛndāvana and were millions of times more effulgent than the sun and moon, have arisen over the eastern horizon of Gauḍadeśa [West Bengal], being compassionate for the fallen state of the world.

TEXT 87

শ্রীকৃষ্ণচৈতন্য আর প্রভু নিত্যানন্দ ।
যাঁহার প্রকাশে সর্ব জগৎ আনন্দ ॥ ৮৭ ॥

śrī-kṛṣṇa-caitanya āra prabhu nityānanda
yāṅhāra prakāśe sarva jagat ānanda

śrī-kṛṣṇa-caitanya—Lord Śrī Kṛṣṇa Caitanya; *āra*—and; *prabhu nityānanda*—Lord Nityānanda; *yāṅhāra*—of whom; *prakāśe*—on the appearance; *sarva*—all; *jagat*—the world; *ānanda*—full of happiness.

TRANSLATION

The appearance of Śrī Kṛṣṇa Caitanya and Prabhu Nityānanda has surcharged the world with happiness.

TEXTS 88–89

সূর্যচন্দ্র হরে যৈছে সব অন্ধকার ।
বস্তু প্রকাশিয়া করে ধর্মের প্রচার ॥ ৮৮ ॥
এই মত দুই ভাই জীবের অজ্ঞান- ।
তমোনাশ করি' কৈল তত্ত্ববস্তু-দান ॥ ৮৯ ॥

sūrya-candra hare yaiche saba andhakāra
vastu prakāśiyā kare dharmera pracāra

ei mata dui bhāi jīvera ajñāna-
tamo-nāśa kari' kaila tattva-vastu-dāna

sūrya-candra—the sun and the moon; *hare*—drive away; *yaiche*—just as; *saba*—all; *andhakāra*—darkness; *vastu*—truth; *prakāśiyā*—manifesting; *kare*—do; *dharmera*—of inborn nature; *pracāra*—preaching; *ei mata*—like this; *dui*—two; *bhāi*—brothers; *jīvera*—of the living being; *ajñāna*—of ignorance; *tamaḥ*—of the darkness; *nāśa*—destruction; *kari'*—doing; *kaila*—made; *tattva-vastu*—of the Absolute Truth; *dāna*—gift.

TRANSLATION

As the sun and moon drive away darkness by their appearance and reveal the nature of everything, these two brothers dissipate the darkness of ignorance covering the living beings and enlighten them with knowledge of the Absolute Truth.

TEXT 90

অজ্ঞান-তমের নাম কহিয়ে 'কৈতব'।
ধর্ম-অর্থ-কাম-মোক্ষ-বাঞ্ছা আদি সব ॥ ৯০ ॥

ajñāna-tamera nāma kahiye 'kaitava'
dharma-artha-kāma-mokṣa-vāñchā ādi saba

ajñāna-tamera—of the darkness of ignorance; *nāma*—name; *kahiye*—I call; *kaitava*—cheating process; *dharma*—religiosity; *artha*—economic development; *kāma*—sense gratification; *mokṣa*—liberation; *vāñchā*—desire for; *ādi*—and so on; *saba*—all.

TRANSLATION

The darkness of ignorance is called kaitava, the way of cheating, which begins with religiosity, economic development, sense gratification and liberation.

TEXT 91

ধর্মঃ প্রোজ্ঝিতকৈতবোঽত্র পরমো নির্মৎসরাণাং সতাং
বেদ্যং বাস্তবমত্র বস্তু শিবদং তাপত্রয়োন্মূলনম্।

শ্রীমদ্ভাগবতে মহামুনিকৃতে কিংবাপরৈরীশ্বরঃ
সদ্যো হৃদ্যবরুধ্যতেহত্র কৃতিভিঃ শুশ্রূষুভিস্তৎক্ষণাৎ ॥ ৯১ ॥

dharmaḥ projjhita-kaitavo 'tra paramo nirmatsarāṇāṁ satāṁ
vedyaṁ vāstavam atra vastu śiva-daṁ tāpa-trayonmūlanam
śrīmad-bhāgavate mahā-muni-kṛte kiṁ vā parair īśvaraḥ
sadyo hṛdy avarudhyate 'tra kṛtibhiḥ śuśrūṣubhis tat-kṣaṇāt

dharmaḥ—religiosity; *projjhita*—completely rejected; *kaitavaḥ*—in which fruitive intention; *atra*—herein; *paramaḥ*—the highest; *nirmatsarāṇām*—of the one-hundred-percent pure in heart; *satām*—devotees; *vedyam*—to be understood; *vāstavam*—factual; *atra*—herein; *vastu*—substance; *śiva-dam*—giving well-being; *tāpa-traya*—of the threefold miseries; *unmūlanam*—causing uprooting; *śrīmat*—beautiful; *bhāgavate*—in the *Bhāgavata Purāṇa; mahā-muni*—by the great sage (Vyāsadeva); *kṛte*—compiled; *kim*—what; *vā*—indeed; *paraiḥ*—with others; *īśvaraḥ*—the Supreme Lord; *sadyaḥ*—at once; *hṛdi*—within the heart; *avarudhyate*—becomes confined; *atra*—herein; *kṛtibhiḥ*—by pious men; *śuśrūṣubhiḥ*—desiring to hear; *tat-kṣaṇāt*—without delay.

TRANSLATION

"The great scripture Śrīmad-Bhāgavatam, compiled by Mahāmuni Vyāsadeva from four original verses, describes the most elevated and kindhearted devotees and completely rejects the cheating ways of materially motivated religiosity. It propounds the highest principle of eternal religion, which can factually mitigate the threefold miseries of a living being and award the highest benediction of full prosperity and knowledge. Those willing to hear the message of this scripture in a submissive attitude of service can at once capture the Supreme Lord in their hearts. Therefore there is no need for any scripture other than Śrīmad-Bhāgavatam."

PURPORT

This verse appears in *Śrīmad-Bhāgavatam* (1.1.2). The words *mahā-muni-kṛte* indicate that *Śrīmad-Bhāgavatam* was compiled by the great sage Vyāsadeva, who is sometimes known as Nārāyaṇa Mahāmuni because he is an incarnation of Nārāyaṇa. Vyāsadeva, therefore, is not an ordinary man but is empowered by the Supreme Personality of

Godhead. He compiled the beautiful *Bhāgavatam* to narrate some of the pastimes of the Supreme Personality of Godhead and His devotees.

In *Śrīmad-Bhāgavatam,* a distinction between real religion and pretentious religion has been clearly made. According to this original and genuine commentation on the *Vedānta-sūtra,* there are numerous pretentious faiths that pass as religion but neglect the real essence of religion. The real religion of a living being is his natural inborn quality, whereas pretentious religion is a form of nescience that artificially covers a living entity's pure consciousness under certain unfavorable conditions. Real religion lies dormant when artificial religion dominates from the mental plane. A living being can awaken this dormant religion by hearing with a pure heart.

The path of religion prescribed by *Śrīmad-Bhāgavatam* is different from all forms of imperfect religiosity. Religion can be considered in the following three divisions: (1) the path of fruitive work, (2) the path of knowledge and mystic powers, and (3) the path of worship and devotional service.

The path of fruitive work (*karma-kāṇḍa*), even when decorated by religious ceremonies meant to elevate one's material condition, is a cheating process because it can never enable one to gain relief from material existence and achieve the highest goal. A living entity perpetually struggles hard to rid himself of the pangs of material existence, but the path of fruitive work leads him to either temporary happiness or temporary distress in material existence. By pious fruitive work one is placed in a position where he can temporarily feel material happiness, whereas vicious activities lead him to a distressful position of material want and scarcity. However, even if one is put into the most perfect situation of material happiness, he cannot in that way become free from the pangs of birth, death, old age and disease. A materially happy person is therefore in need of the eternal relief that mundane religiosity in terms of fruitive work can never award.

The paths of the culture of knowledge (*jñāna-mārga*) and of mystic powers (*yoga-mārga*) are equally hazardous, for one does not know where one will go by following these uncertain methods. An empiric philosopher in search of spiritual knowledge may endeavor most laboriously for many, many births in mental speculation, but unless and until he reaches the stage of the purest quality of goodness—in other words, until he transcends the plane of material speculation—it is not possible for him to know that everything emanates from the Personality of Godhead Vāsudeva. His attachment to the impersonal feature of the

Supreme Lord makes him unfit to rise to that transcendental stage of *vasudeva* understanding, and therefore because of his unclean state of mind he glides down again into material existence, even after having ascended to the highest stage of liberation. This falldown takes place due to his want of a *locus standi* in the service of the Supreme Lord.

As far as the mystic powers of the *yogīs* are concerned, they are also material entanglements on the path of spiritual realization. One German scholar who became a devotee of Godhead in India said that material science had already made laudable progress in duplicating the mystic powers of the *yogīs.* He therefore came to India not to learn the methods of the *yogīs'* mystic powers but to learn the path of transcendental loving service to the Supreme Lord, as mentioned in the great scripture *Śrīmad-Bhāgavatam.* Mystic powers can make a *yogī* materially powerful and thus give temporary relief from the miseries of birth, death, old age and disease, as other material sciences can also do, but such mystic powers can never be a permanent source of relief from these miseries. Therefore, according to the *Bhāgavata* school, this path of religiosity is also a method of cheating its followers. In the *Bhagavad-gītā* it is clearly defined that the most elevated and powerful mystic *yogī* is one who can constantly think of the Supreme Lord within his heart and engage in the loving service of the Lord.

The path of worship of the innumerable *devas,* or administrative demigods, is still more hazardous and uncertain than the above-mentioned processes of *karma-kāṇḍa* and *jñāna-kāṇḍa.* This system of worshiping many gods, such as Durgā, Śiva, Gaṇeśa, Sūrya and the impersonal Viṣṇu form, is accepted by persons who have been blinded by an intense desire for sense gratification. When properly executed in terms of the rites mentioned in the *śāstras,* which are now very difficult to perform in this age of want and scarcity, such worship can certainly fulfill one's desires for sense gratification, but the success obtained by such methods is certainly transient, and it is suitable only for a less intelligent person. That is the verdict of the *Bhagavad-gītā.* No sane man should be satisfied by such temporary benefits.

None of the above-mentioned three religious paths can deliver a person from the threefold miseries of material existence, namely, miseries caused by the body and mind, miseries caused by other living entities, and miseries caused by the demigods. The process of religion described in *Śrīmad-Bhāgavatam,* however, is able to give its followers permanent relief from the threefold miseries. The *Bhāgavatam* describes the highest religious form—reinstatement of the living entity in his original position of transcendental loving service to the Supreme Lord, which is free from the infections of desires for sense gratification, fruitive work, and the culture of knowledge with the aim of merging into the Absolute to become one with the Supreme Lord.

Any process of religiosity based on sense gratification, gross or subtle, must be considered a pretentious religion because it is unable to give perpetual protection to its followers. The word *projjhita* is significant. *Pra-* means "complete," and *ujjhita* indicates rejection. Religiosity in the shape of fruitive work is directly a method of gross sense gratification, whereas the process of culturing spiritual knowledge with a view to becoming one with the Absolute is a method of subtle sense gratification. All such pretentious religiosity based on gross or subtle sense gratification is completely rejected in the process of *bhāgavata-dharma*, or the transcendental religion that is the eternal function of the living being.

Bhāgavata-dharma, or the religious principle described in *Śrīmad-Bhāgavatam,* of which the *Bhagavad-gītā* is a preliminary study, is meant for liberated persons of the highest order, who attribute very little value to the sense gratification of pretentious religiosity. The first and foremost concern of fruitive workers, elevationists, empiric philosophers and salvationists is to raise their material position. But devotees of Godhead have no such selfish desires. They serve the Supreme Lord only for His satisfaction. Śrī Arjuna, wanting to satisfy his senses by becoming a so-called nonviolent and pious man, at first decided not to fight. But when he was fully situated in the principles of *bhāgavata-dharma,* culminating in complete surrender unto the will of the Supreme Lord, he changed his decision and agreed to fight for the satisfaction of the Lord. He then said:

naṣṭo mohaḥ smṛtir labdhā
tvat-prasādān mayācyuta
sthito 'smi gata-sandehaḥ
kariṣye vacanaṁ tava

"My dear Kṛṣṇa, O infallible one, my illusion is now gone. I have regained my memory by Your mercy. I am now firm and free from doubt and am prepared to act according to Your instructions." (Bg. 18.73) It is the constitutional position of the living entity to be situated in this pure consciousness. Any so-called religious process that interferes with this unadulterated spiritual position of the living being must therefore be considered a pretentious process of religiosity.

The real form of religion is spontaneous loving service to Godhead. This relationship of the living being with the Absolute Personality of Godhead in service is eternal. The Personality of Godhead is described as *vastu,* or the Substance, and the living entities are described as *vāstavas,* or the innumerable samples of the Substance in relative existence. The relationship of these substantive portions with the Supreme Substance can never be annihilated, for it is an eternal quality inherent in the living being.

By contact with material nature the living entities exhibit varied symptoms of the disease of material consciousness. To cure this material disease is the supreme object of human life. The process that treats this disease is called *bhāgavata-dharma,* or *sanātana-dharma*—real religion. This is described in the pages of *Śrīmad-Bhāgavatam.* Therefore anyone who, because of his background of pious activities in previous lives, is anxious to hear *Śrīmad-Bhāgavatam* immediately realizes the presence of the Supreme Lord within his heart and fulfills the mission of his life.

TEXT 92

তার মধ্যে মোক্ষবাঞ্ছা কৈতবপ্রধান ।
যাহা হৈতে কৃষ্ণভক্তি হয় অন্তর্ধান ॥ ৯২ ॥

tāra madhye mokṣa-vāñchā kaitava-pradhāna
yāhā haite kṛṣṇa-bhakti haya antardhāna

tāra—of them; *madhye*—in the midst; *mokṣa-vāñchā*—the desire to merge into the Supreme; *kaitava*—of cheating processes; *pradhāna*—the chief; *yāhā haite*—from which; *kṛṣṇa-bhakti*—devotion to Lord Kṛṣṇa; *haya*—becomes; *antardhāna*—disappearance.

TRANSLATION

The foremost process of cheating is to desire to achieve liberation by merging into the Supreme, for this causes the permanent disappearance of loving service to Kṛṣṇa.

PURPORT

The desire to merge into the impersonal Brahman is the subtlest type of atheism. As soon as such atheism, disguised in the dress of liberation, is encouraged, one becomes completely unable to traverse the path of devotional service to the Supreme Personality of Godhead.

TEXT 93

"প্র-শব্দেন মোক্ষাভিসন্ধিরপি নিরস্তঃ" ইতি ॥ ৯৩ ॥

"pra-śabdena mokṣābhisandhir api nirastaḥ" iti

pra-śabdena—by the prefix *pra*; *mokṣa-abhisandhiḥ*—the intention of liberation; *api*—certainly; *nirastaḥ*—nullified; *iti*—thus.

TRANSLATION

"The prefix 'pra' [in the verse from Śrīmad-Bhāgavatam] indicates that the desire for liberation is completely rejected."

PURPORT

This is an annotation by Śrīdhara Svāmī, the great commentator on *Śrīmad-Bhāgavatam.*

TEXT 94

কৃষ্ণভক্তির বাধক—যত শুভাশুভ কর্ম ।
সেহ এক জীবের অজ্ঞানতমো-ধর্ম ॥ ৯৪ ॥

kṛṣṇa-bhaktira bādhaka—yata śubhāśubha karma
seha eka jīvera ajñāna-tamo-dharma

kṛṣṇa-bhaktira—of devotional service to Kṛṣṇa; *bādhaka*—hindrance; *yata*—all; *śubha-aśubha*—auspicious or inauspicious; *karma*—activity; *seha*—that; *eka*—one; *jīvera*—of the living entity; *ajñāna-tamaḥ*—of the darkness of ignorance; *dharma*—the character.

TRANSLATION

All kinds of activities, both auspicious and inauspicious, that are detrimental to the discharge of transcendental loving service to Lord Śrī Kṛṣṇa are actions of the darkness of ignorance.

PURPORT

The poetical comparison of Lord Caitanya and Lord Nityānanda to the sun and moon is very significant. The living entities are spiritual sparks, and their constitutional position is to render devotional service to the

Supreme Lord in full Kṛṣṇa consciousness. So-called pious activities and other ritualistic performances, pious or impious, as well as the desire to escape from material existence, are all considered to be coverings of these spiritual sparks. The living entities must get free from these superfluous coverings and fully engage in Kṛṣṇa consciousness. The purpose of the appearance of Lord Caitanya and Lord Nityānanda is to dispel the darkness of the soul. Before Their appearance, all these superfluous activities of the living entities were covering Kṛṣṇa consciousness, but after the appearance of these two brothers, people's hearts are becoming cleansed, and they are again becoming situated in the real position of Kṛṣṇa consciousness.

TEXT 95

যাঁহার প্রসাদে এই তমো হয় নাশ ।
তমো নাশ করি' করে তত্ত্বের প্রকাশ ॥ ৯৫ ॥

yāṅhāra prasāde ei tamo haya nāśa
tamo nāśa kari' kare tattvera prakāśa

yāṅhāra—whose; *prasāde*—by the grace; *ei*—this; *tamaḥ*—darkness; *haya*—is; *nāśa*—destroyed; *tamaḥ*—darkness; *nāśa*—destruction; *kari'*—doing; *kare*—does; *tattvera*—of the truth; *prakāśa*—discovery.

TRANSLATION

By the grace of Lord Caitanya and Lord Nityānanda, this darkness of ignorance is removed and the truth is brought to light.

TEXT 96

তত্ত্ববস্তু—কৃষ্ণ, কৃষ্ণভক্তি, প্রেমরূপ ।
নাম-সংকীর্তন—সব আনন্দস্বরূপ ॥ ৯৬ ॥

tattva-vastu—kṛṣṇa, kṛṣṇa-bhakti, prema-rūpa
nāma-saṅkīrtana—saba ānanda-svarūpa

tattva-vastu—Absolute Truth; *kṛṣṇa*—Lord Kṛṣṇa; *kṛṣṇa-bhakti*—devotional service to Lord Kṛṣṇa; *prema-rūpa*—taking the form of love for Lord Kṛṣṇa; *nāma-saṅkīrtana*—congregational chanting of the holy name; *saba*—all; *ānanda*—of bliss; *svarūpa*—the identity.

TRANSLATION

The Absolute Truth is Śrī Kṛṣṇa, and loving devotion to Śrī Kṛṣṇa exhibited in pure love is achieved through congregational chanting of the holy name, which is the essence of all bliss.

TEXT 97

সূর্য চন্দ্র বাহিরের তমঃ সে বিনাশে ।
বহির্বস্তু ঘট-পট-আদি সে প্রকাশে ॥ ৯৭ ॥

sūrya candra bāhirera tamaḥ se vināśe
bahir-vastu ghaṭa-paṭa-ādi se prakāśe

sūrya—the sun; *candra*—the moon; *bāhirera*—of the external world; *tamaḥ*—darkness; *se*—they; *vināśe*—destroy; *bahiḥ-vastu*—external things; *ghaṭa*—waterpots; *paṭa-ādi*—plates, etc.; *se*—they; *prakāśe*—reveal.

TRANSLATION

The sun and moon dissipate the darkness of the external world and thus reveal external material objects like pots and plates.

TEXT 98

দুই ভাই হৃদয়ের ক্ষালি' অন্ধকার ।
দুই ভাগবত-সঙ্গে করান সাক্ষাৎকার ॥ ৯৮ ॥

dui bhāi hṛdayera kṣāli' andhakāra
dui bhāgavata-saṅge karāna sākṣātkāra

dui—two; *bhāi*—brothers; *hṛdayera*—of the heart; *kṣāli'*—purifying; *andhakāra*—darkness; *dui bhāgavata*—of the two *bhāgavatas; saṅge*—by the association; *karāna*—cause; *sākṣāt-kāra*—a meeting.

TRANSLATION

But these two brothers [Lord Caitanya and Lord Nityānanda] dissipate the darkness of the inner core of the heart, and thus They help one meet the two kinds of bhāgavatas [persons or things in relationship with the Personality of Godhead].

TEXT 99

এক ভাগবত বড়—ভাগবত-শাস্ত্র ।
আর ভাগবত—ভক্ত ভক্তি-রস-পাত্র ॥ ৯৯ ॥

eka bhāgavata baḍa—bhāgavata-śāstra
āra bhāgavata—bhakta bhakti-rasa-pātra

eka—one; *bhāgavata*—in relation to the Supreme Lord; *baḍa*—great; *bhāgavata-śāstra*—*Śrīmad-Bhāgavatam; āra*—the other; *bhāgavata*—in relation to the Supreme Lord; *bhakta*—pure devotee; *bhakti-rasa*—of the mellow of devotion; *pātra*—the recipient.

TRANSLATION

One of the bhāgavatas is the great scripture Śrīmad-Bhāgavatam, and the other is the pure devotee absorbed in the mellows of loving devotion.

TEXT 100

দুই ভাগবত দ্বারা দিয়া ভক্তিরস ।
তাঁহার হৃদয়ে তাঁর প্রেমে হয় বশ ॥ ১০০ ॥

dui bhāgavata dvārā diyā bhakti-rasa
tāṅhāra hṛdaye tāṅra preme haya vaśa

dui—two; *bhāgavata*—the *bhāgavatas; dvārā*—by; *diyā*—giving; *bhakti-rasa*—devotional inspiration; *tāṅhāra*—of His devotee; *hṛdaye*—in the heart; *tāṅra*—his; *preme*—by the love; *haya*—becomes; *vaśa*—under control.

TRANSLATION

Through the actions of these two bhāgavatas the Lord instills the mellows of transcendental loving service into the heart of a living being, and thus the Lord, in the heart of His devotee, comes under the control of the devotee's love.

TEXT 101

এক অদ্ভুত—সমকালে দোঁহার প্রকাশ ।
আর অদ্ভুত—চিত্তগুহার তমঃ করে নাশ ॥ ১০১ ॥

eka adbhuta—sama-kāle doṅhāra prakāśa
āra adbhuta—citta-guhāra tamaḥ kare nāśa

eka—one; *adbhuta*—wonderful thing; *sama-kāle*—at the same time; *doṅhāra*—of both; *prakāśa*—the manifestation; *āra*—the other; *adbhuta*—wonderful thing; *citta-guhāra*—of the core of the heart; *tamaḥ*—darkness; *kare*—do; *nāśa*—destruction.

TRANSLATION

The first wonder is that both brothers appear simultaneously, and the other is that They illuminate the innermost depths of the heart.

TEXT 102

এই চন্দ্র সূর্য দুই পরম সদয় ।
জগতের ভাগ্যে গৌড়ে করিলা উদয় ॥ ১০২ ॥

ei candra sūrya dui parama sadaya
jagatera bhāgye gauḍe karilā udaya

ei—these; *candra*—moon; *sūrya*—sun; *dui*—two; *parama*—very much; *sa-daya*—kind; *jagatera*—of the people of the world; *bhāgye*—for the fortune; *gauḍe*—in the land of Gauḍa; *karilā*—did; *udaya*—appearance.

TRANSLATION

These two, the sun and moon, are very kind to the people of the world. Thus for the good fortune of all, They have appeared on the horizon of Bengal.

PURPORT

The celebrated ancient capital of the Sena dynasty, which was known as Gauḍadeśa or Gauḍa, was situated in what is now the modern district of Maldah. Later this capital was transferred to the ninth or central island on the western side of the Ganges at Navadvīpa, which is now known as Māyāpur and was then called Gauḍapura. Lord Caitanya appeared there, and Lord Nityānanda came there and joined Him from the district of Birbhum. They appeared on the horizon of Gauḍadeśa to spread the science of Kṛṣṇa consciousness, and it is predicted that as the sun and moon gradually move west, the movement They began five hundred years ago will come to the Western civilizations by Their mercy.

Caitanya Mahāprabhu and Nityānanda Prabhu drive away the five kinds of ignorance of the conditioned souls. In the *Mahābhārata, Udyoga-parva,* Forty-third Chapter, these five kinds of ignorance are described. They are (1) accepting the body to be the self, (2) making material sense gratification one's standard of enjoyment, (3) being anxious due to material identification, (4) lamenting and (5) thinking that there is anything beyond the Absolute Truth. The teachings of Lord Caitanya eradicate these five kinds of ignorance. Whatever one sees or otherwise experiences one should know to be simply an exhibition of the Supreme Personality of Godhead's energy. Everything is a manifestation of Kṛṣṇa.

TEXT 103

সেই দুই প্রভুর করি চরণ বন্দন ।
যাঁহা হইতে বিঘ্ননাশ অভীষ্টপূরণ ॥ ১০৩ ॥

sei dui prabhura kari caraṇa vandana
yāṅhā ha-ite vighna-nāśa abhīṣṭa-pūraṇa

sei—these; *dui*—two; *prabhura*—of the Lords; *kari*—I do; *caraṇa*—feet; *vandana*—obeisance; *yāṅhā ha-ite*—from which; *vighna-nāśa*—destruction of obstacles; *abhīṣṭa-pūraṇa*—fulfillment of desires.

TRANSLATION

Let us therefore worship the holy feet of these two Lords. Thus one can be rid of all difficulties on the path of self-realization.

TEXT 104

এই দুই শ্লোকে কৈল মঙ্গল-বন্দন ।
তৃতীয় শ্লোকের অর্থ শুন সর্বজন ॥ ১০৪ ॥

ei dui śloke kaila maṅgala-vandana
tṛtīya ślokera artha śuna sarva-jana

ei—these; *dui*—two; *śloke*—in the verses; *kaila*—I did; *maṅgala*—auspicious; *vandana*—obeisance; *tṛtīya*—third; *ślokera*—of the verse; *artha*—meaning; *śuna*—please hear; *sarva-jana*—everyone.

TRANSLATION

I have invoked the benediction of the Lords with these two verses [texts 1 and 2 of this chapter]. Now please hear attentively the purport of the third verse.

TEXT 105

বক্তব্য-বাহুল্য, গ্রন্থ-বিস্তারের ডরে ।
বিস্তারে না বর্ণি, সারার্থ কহি অল্পাক্ষরে ॥ ১০৫ ॥

vaktavya-bāhulya, grantha-vistārera ḍare
vistāre nā varṇi, sārārtha kahi alpākṣare

vaktavya—of words to be spoken; *bāhulya*—elaboration; *grantha*—of the book; *vistārera*—of the big volume; *ḍare*—in fear; *vistāre*—in expanded form; *nā*—not; *varṇi*—I describe; *sāra-artha*—essential meaning; *kahi*—I say; *alpa-akṣare*—in few words.

TRANSLATION

I purposely avoid extensive description for fear of increasing the bulk of this book. I shall describe the essence as concisely as possible.

TEXT 106

"মিতঞ্চ সারঞ্চ বচো হি বাগ্মিতা" ইতি ॥ ১০৬ ॥

"mitaṁ ca sāraṁ ca vaco hi vāgmitā" iti

mitam—concise; *ca*—and; *sāram*—essential; *ca*—and; *vacaḥ*—speech; *hi*—certainly; *vāgmitā*—eloquence; *iti*—thus.

TRANSLATION

"Essential truth spoken concisely is true eloquence."

TEXT 107

শুনিলে খণ্ডিবে চিত্তের অজ্ঞানাদি দোষ ।
কৃষ্ণে গাঢ় প্রেম হবে, পাইবে সন্তোষ ॥ ১০৭ ॥

śunile khaṇḍibe cittera ajñānādi doṣa
kṛṣṇe gāḍha prema habe, pāibe santoṣa

śunile—on one's hearing; *khaṇḍibe*—will remove; *cittera*—of the heart; *ajñāna-ādi*—of ignorance, etc.; *doṣa*—the faults; *kṛṣṇe*—in Lord Kṛṣṇa; *gāḍha*—deep; *prema*—love; *habe*—there will be; *pāibe*—will obtain; *santoṣa*—satisfaction.

TRANSLATION

Simply hearing submissively will free one's heart from all the faults of ignorance, and thus one will achieve deep love for Kṛṣṇa. This is the path of peace.

TEXTS 108–109

শ্রীচৈতন্য-নিত্যানন্দ-অদ্বৈত-মহত্ত্ব ।
তাঁর ভক্ত-ভক্তি-নাম-প্রেম-রসতত্ত্ব ॥ ১০৮ ॥
ভিন্ন ভিন্ন লিখিয়াছি করিয়া বিচার ।
শুনিলে জানিবে সব বস্তুতত্ত্বসার ॥ ১০৯ ॥

śrī-caitanya-nityānanda-advaita-mahattva
tāṅra bhakta-bhakti-nāma-prema-rasa-tattva

bhinna bhinna likhiyāchi kariyā vicāra
śunile jānibe saba vastu-tattva-sāra

śrī-caitanya—of Lord Caitanya Mahāprabhu; *nityānanda*—of Lord Nityānanda; *advaita*—of Śrī Advaita; *mahattva*—greatness; *tāṅra*—Their; *bhakta*—devotees; *bhakti*—devotion; *nāma*—names; *prema*—love; *rasa*—mellows; *tattva*—real nature; *bhinna bhinna*—different; *likhiyāchi*—I wrote; *kariyā*—doing; *vicāra*—consideration; *śunile*—on hearing; *jānibe*—will know; *saba*—all; *vastu-tattva-sāra*—the essence of the Absolute Truth.

TRANSLATION

If one patiently hears about the glories of Śrī Caitanya Mahāprabhu, Śrī Nityānanda Prabhu and Śrī Advaita Prabhu—and Their devotees, devotional activities, names and fame, along with the mellows of Their transcendental loving exchanges—one will

learn the essence of the Absolute Truth. Therefore I have described these [in the Caitanya-caritāmṛta] with logic and discrimination.

TEXT 110

শ্রীরূপ-রঘুনাথ-পদে যার আশ ।
চৈতন্যচরিতামৃত কহে কৃষ্ণদাস ॥ ১১০ ॥

śrī-rūpa-raghunātha-pade yāra āśa
caitanya-caritāmṛta kahe kṛṣṇadāsa

śrī-rūpa—Śrīla Rūpa Gosvāmī; *raghunātha*—Śrīla Raghunātha dāsa Gosvāmī; *pade*—at the lotus feet; *yāra*—whose; *āśa*—expectation; *caitanya-caritāmṛta*—the book named *Caitanya-caritāmṛta; kahe*—describes; *kṛṣṇadāsa*—Śrīla Kṛṣṇadāsa Kavirāja Gosvāmī.

TRANSLATION

Praying at the lotus feet of Śrī Rūpa and Śrī Raghunātha, always desiring their mercy, I, Kṛṣṇadāsa, narrate Śrī Caitanya-caritāmṛta, following in their footsteps.

Thus end the Bhaktivedanta purports to Śrī Caitanya-caritāmṛta, Ādi-līlā, *First Chapter, describing the spiritual masters.*

CHAPTER TWO

Śri Caitanya Mahāprabhu, the Supreme Personality of Godhead

This chapter explains that Lord Caitanya is the Supreme Personality of Godhead Kṛṣṇa Himself. Therefore, the Brahman effulgence is the bodily luster of Lord Caitanya, and the localized Supersoul situated in the heart of every living entity is His partial representation. The *puruṣa-avatāras* are also explained in this connection. Mahā-Viṣṇu is the reservoir of all conditioned souls, but, as confirmed in the authoritative scriptures, Lord Kṛṣṇa is the ultimate fountainhead, the source of numerous plenary expansions, including Nārāyaṇa, who is generally accepted by Māyāvādī philosophers to be the Absolute Truth. The Lord's manifestation of *prābhava* and *vaibhava* expansions, as well as partial incarnations and incarnations with delegated powers, are also explained. Lord Kṛṣṇa's ages of boyhood and youth are discussed, and it is explained that His age at the beginning of youth is His eternal form.

The spiritual sky contains innumerable spiritual planets, the Vaikuṇṭhas, which are manifestations of the Supreme Lord's internal energy. Innumerable material universes are similarly exhibited by His external energy, and the living entities are manifested by His marginal energy. Because Lord Kṛṣṇa Caitanya is not different from Lord Kṛṣṇa, He is the cause of all causes; there is no cause beyond Him. He is eternal, and His form is spiritual. Lord Caitanya is directly the Supreme Lord, Kṛṣṇa, as the evidence of authoritative scriptures proves. This chapter stresses that a devotee who wishes to advance in Kṛṣṇa consciousness must have knowledge of Kṛṣṇa's personal form, His three principal energies, His pastimes and the relationship of the living entities with Him.

TEXT 1

শ্রীচৈতন্যপ্রভুং বন্দে বালোঽপি যদনুগ্রহাৎ ।
তরেন্নানমতগ্রাহব্যাপ্তং সিদ্ধান্তসাগরম্ ॥ ১ ॥

śrī-caitanya-prabhuṁ vande
bālo 'pi yad-anugrahāt
taren nānā-mata-grāha-
vyāptaṁ siddhānta-sāgaram

śrī-caitanya-prabhum—to Lord Śrī Caitanya Mahāprabhu; *vande*—I offer obeisances; *bālaḥ*—an ignorant child; *api*—even; *yat*—of whom; *anugrahāt*—by the mercy; *taret*—may cross over; *nānā*—various; *mata*—of theories; *grāha*—the crocodiles; *vyāptam*—filled with; *siddhānta*—of conclusions; *sāgaram*—the ocean.

TRANSLATION

I offer my obeisances to Sri Caitanya Mahāprabhu, by whose mercy even an ignorant child can swim across the ocean of conclusive truth, which is full of the crocodiles of various theories.

PURPORT

By the mercy of the Supreme Personality of Godhead Śrī Caitanya Mahāprabhu, even an inexperienced boy with no educational culture can be saved from the ocean of nescience, which is full of various types of philosophical doctrines that are like dangerous aquatic animals. The philosophy of the Buddha, the argumentative presentations of the *jñānīs*, the *yoga* systems of Patañjali and Gautama, and the systems of philosophers like Kaṇāda, Kapila and Dattātreya are dangerous creatures in the ocean of nescience. By the grace of Śrī Caitanya Mahāprabhu one can have real understanding of the essence of knowledge by avoiding these sectarian views and accepting the lotus feet of Kṛṣṇa as the ultimate goal of life. Let us all worship Lord Śrī Caitanya Mahāprabhu for His gracious mercy to the conditioned souls.

TEXT 2

কৃষ্ণোৎকীর্তনগাননর্তনকলাপাথোজনি-ভ্রাজিতা
সদ্ভক্তাবলিহংসচক্রমধুপশ্রেণীবিহারাস্পদম্ ।
কর্ণানন্দিকলধ্বনির্বহতু মে জিহ্বামরুপ্রাঙ্গণে
শ্রীচৈতন্যদয়ানিধে তব লসল্লীলাসুধাস্বর্ধুনী ॥ ২ ॥

kṛṣṇotkīrtana-gāna-nartana-kalā-pāthojani-bhrājitā
sad-bhaktāvali-haṁsa-cakra-madhupa-śreṇī-vihārāspadam

karṇānandi-kala-dhvanir vahatu me jihvā-maru-prāṅgaṇe
śrī-caitanya dayā-nidhe tava lasal-līlā-sudhā-svardhunī

kṛṣṇa—of the holy name of Lord Kṛṣṇa; *utkīrtana*—loud chanting; *gāna*—singing; *nartana*—dancing; *kalā*—of the other fine arts; *pāthaḥ-jani*—with lotuses; *bhrājitā*—beautified; *sat-bhakta*—of pure devotees; *āvali*—rows; *haṁsa*—of swans; *cakra*—*cakravāka* birds; *madhu-pa*—and bumble bees; *śreṇī*—like swarms; *vihāra*—of pleasure; *āspadam*—the abode; *karṇa-ānandi*—gladdening the ears; *kala*—melodious; *dhvaniḥ*—sound; *vahatu*—let it flow; *me*—my; *jihvā*—of the tongue; *maru*—desertlike; *prāṅgaṇe*—in the courtyard; *śrī-caitanya dayā-nidhe*—O Lord Caitanya, ocean of mercy; *tava*—of You; *lasat*—shining; *līlā-sudhā*—of the nectar of the pastimes; *svardhunī*—the Ganges.

TRANSLATION

O my merciful Lord Caitanya, may the nectarean Ganges waters of Your transcendental activities flow on the surface of my desertlike tongue. Beautifying these waters are the lotus flowers of singing, dancing and loud chanting of Kṛṣṇa's holy name, which are the pleasure abodes of unalloyed devotees. These devotees are compared to swans, ducks and bees. The river's flowing produces a melodious sound that gladdens their ears.

PURPORT

Our tongues always engage in vibrating useless sounds that do not help us realize transcendental peace. The tongue is compared to a desert because a desert needs a constant supply of refreshing water to make it fertile and fruitful. Water is the substance most needed in the desert. The transient pleasure derived from mundane topics of art, culture, politics, sociology, dry philosophy, poetry and so on is compared to a mere drop of water because although such topics have a qualitative feature of transcendental pleasure, they are saturated with the modes of material nature. Therefore neither collectively nor individually can they satisfy the vast requirements of the desertlike tongue. Despite crying in various conferences, therefore, the desertlike tongue continues to be parched. For this reason, people from all parts of the world must call for the devotees of Lord Śrī Caitanya Mahāprabhu, who are compared to swans swimming around the beautiful lotus feet of Śrī Caitanya Mahāprabhu or bees humming around His lotus feet in transcendental pleasure, searching for honey. The dryness of material happiness cannot be moistened by so-called philosophers who cry for Brahman, liberation and similar dry speculative objects. The urge of the soul proper is different. The soul can be solaced only by the mercy of Lord Śrī Caitanya Mahāprabhu and His many bona fide devotees, who never leave the lotus feet of the Lord to become imitation Mahāprabhus but all cling to His lotus feet like bees that never leave a honey-soaked lotus flower.

Lord Caitanya's movement of Kṛṣṇa consciousness is full of dancing and singing about the pastimes of Lord Kṛṣṇa. It is compared herein to the pure waters of the Ganges, which are full of lotus flowers. The enjoyers of these lotus flowers are the pure devotees, who are like bees and swans. They chant like the flowing of the Ganges, the river of the celestial kingdom. The author desires such sweetly flowing waves to cover his tongue. He humbly compares himself to materialistic persons who always engage in dry talk from which they derive no satisfaction. If they were to use their dry tongues to chant the holy name of the Lord—Hare Kṛṣṇa, Hare Kṛṣṇa, Kṛṣṇa Kṛṣṇa, Hare Hare/ Hare Rāma, Hare Rāma, Rāma Rāma, Hare Hare—as exemplified by Lord Caitanya, they would taste sweet nectar and enjoy life.

TEXT 3

জয় জয় শ্রীচৈতন্য জয় নিত্যানন্দ ।
জয়াদ্বৈতচন্দ্র জয় গৌরভক্তবৃন্দ ॥ ৩ ॥

jaya jaya śrī-caitanya jaya nityānanda
jayādvaita-candra jaya gaura-bhakta-vṛnda

jaya jaya—all glory; *śrī-caitanya*—to Lord Caitanya; *jaya*—all glory; *nityānanda*—to Lord Nityānanda; *jaya*—all glory; *advaita-candra*—to Advaita Ācārya; *jaya*—all glory; *gaura-bhakta-vṛnda*—to the devotees of Lord Gaurāṅga.

TRANSLATION

All glories to Lord Śrī Caitanya Mahāprabhu and Lord Śrī Nityānanda! All glories to Advaitacandra, and all glories to the devotees of Lord Gaurāṅga!

TEXT 4

তৃতীয় শ্লোকের অর্থ করি বিবরণ ।
বস্তু-নির্দেশরূপ মঙ্গলাচরণ ॥ ৪ ॥

tṛtīya ślokera artha kari vivaraṇa
vastu-nirdeśa-rūpa maṅgalācaraṇa

tṛtīya—third; *ślokera*—of the verse; *artha*—the meaning; *kari*—I do; *vivaraṇa*—description; *vastu*—of the Absolute Truth; *nirdeśa-rūpa*—in the form of delineation; *maṅgala*—auspicious; *ācaraṇa*—conduct.

TRANSLATION

Let me describe the meaning of the third verse [of the first fourteen]. It is an auspicious vibration that describes the Absolute Truth.

TEXT 5

যদদ্বৈতং ব্রহ্মোপনিষদি তদপ্যস্য তনুভা
য আত্মান্তর্যামী পুরুষ ইতি সো স্যাংশবিভবঃ।
ষড়ৈশ্বর্যৈঃ পূর্ণো য ইহ ভগবান্ স্ব স্বয়ময়ং
ন চৈতন্যাৎ কৃষ্ণাজ্জগতি পরতত্ত্বং পরমিহ ॥ ৫ ॥

yad advaitaṁ brahmopaniṣadi tad apy asya tanu-bhā
ya ātmāntar-yāmī puruṣa iti so 'syāṁśa-vibhavaḥ
ṣaḍ-aiśvaryaiḥ pūrṇo ya iha bhagavān sa svayam ayaṁ
na caitanyāt kṛṣṇāj jagati para-tattvaṁ param iha

yat—that which; *advaitam*—without a second; *brahma*—the impersonal Brahman; *upaniṣadi*—in the *Upaniṣads; tat*—that; *api*—certainly; *asya*—His; *tanu-bhā*—the effulgence of His transcendental body; *yaḥ*—who; *ātmā*—the Supersoul; *antaḥ-yāmī*—indwelling Lord ; *puruṣaḥ*—the supreme enjoyer; *iti*—thus; *saḥ*—He; *asya*—His; *aṁśa-vibhavaḥ*—expansion of a plenary portion; *ṣaṭ-aiśvaryaiḥ*—with the six opulences; *pūrṇaḥ*—full; *yaḥ*—who; *iha*—here; *bhagavān*—the Supreme Personality of Godhead; *saḥ*—He; *svayam*—Himself; *ayam*—this one; *na*—not; *caitanyāt*—than Lord Caitanya; *kṛṣṇāt*—than Lord Kṛṣṇa; *jagati*—in the world; *para*—higher; *tattvam*—truth; *param*—another; *iha*—here.

TRANSLATION

What the Upaniṣads describe as the impersonal Brahman is but the effulgence of His body, and the Lord known as the Supersoul is but His localized plenary portion. Lord Caitanya is the Supreme Personality of Godhead, Kṛṣṇa Himself, full with six opulences. He

is the Absolute Truth, and no other truth is greater than or equal to Him.

PURPORT

The compilers of the *Upaniṣads* speak very highly of the impersonal Brahman. The *Upaniṣads,* which are considered the most elevated portion of the Vedic literatures, are meant for persons who desire to get free from material association and who therefore approach a bona fide spiritual master for enlightenment. The prefix *upa-* indicates that one must receive knowledge about the Absolute Truth from a spiritual master. One who has faith in his spiritual master actually receives transcendental instruction, and as his attachment for material life slackens, he is able to advance on the spiritual path. Knowledge of the transcendental science of the *Upaniṣads* can free one from the entanglement of existence in the material world, and when thus liberated, one can be elevated to the spiritual kingdom of the Supreme Personality of Godhead by advancement in spiritual life.

The beginning of spiritual enlightenment is realization of impersonal Brahman. Such realization is effected by gradual negation of material variegatedness. Impersonal Brahman realization is the partial, distant experience of the Absolute Truth that one achieves through the rational approach. It is compared to one's seeing a hill from a distance and taking it to be a smoky cloud. A hill is not a smoky cloud, but it appears to be one from a distance because of our imperfect vision. In imperfect or smoky realization of the Absolute Truth, spiritual variegatedness is conspicuous by its absence. This experience is therefore called *advaita-vāda,* or realization of the oneness of the Absolute.

The impersonal glowing effulgence of Brahman consists only of the personal bodily rays of the Supreme Godhead, Śrī Kṛṣṇa. Since Śrī Gaurasundara, or Lord Śrī Caitanya Mahāprabhu, is identical with Śrī Kṛṣṇa Himself, the Brahman effulgence consists of the rays of His transcendental body.

Similarly, the Supersoul, which is called the Paramātmā, is a plenary representation of Caitanya Mahāprabhu. The *antar-yāmī,* the Supersoul in everyone's heart, is the controller of all living entities. This is confirmed in the *Bhagavad-gītā* (15.15), wherein Lord Kṛṣṇa says, *sarvasya cāhaṁ hṛdi sanniviṣṭaḥ:* "I am situated in everyone's heart." The *Bhagavad-gītā* (5.29) also states, *bhoktāraṁ yajña-tapasāṁ sarva-loka-maheśvaram,* indicating that the Supreme Lord, acting in His expansion as the Supersoul, is the proprietor of everything. Similarly, the *Brahma-saṁhitā* (5.35) states, *aṇḍāntara-stha-paramāṇu-cayāntara-stham.* The Lord is present everywhere, within the heart of every living entity and within each and every atom as well. Thus by this Supersoul feature the Lord is all-pervading.

Furthermore, Lord Caitanya is also the master of all wealth, strength, fame, beauty, knowledge and renunciation because He is Śrī Kṛṣṇa Himself. He is described as *pūrṇa,* or complete. In the feature of Lord Caitanya, the Lord is an ideal renouncer, just as Śrī Rāma was an ideal king. Lord Caitanya accepted the order of *sannyāsa* and exemplified exceedingly wonderful principles in His own life. No one can compare to Him in the order of *sannyāsa.* Although in Kali-yuga acceptance of the *sannyāsa* order is generally forbidden, Lord Caitanya accepted it because He is complete in renunciation. Others cannot imitate Him but can only follow in His footsteps as far as possible. Those who are unfit for this order of life are strictly forbidden by the injunctions of the *śāstras* to accept it. Lord Caitanya, however, is complete in renunciation as well as all other opulences. He is therefore the highest principle of the Absolute Truth.

By an analytical study of the truth of Lord Caitanya, one will find that He is not different from the Supreme Personality of Godhead Kṛṣṇa; no one is greater than or even equal to Him. In the *Bhagavad-gītā* (7.7) Lord Kṛṣṇa says to Arjuna, *mattaḥ parataraṁ nānyat kiñcid asti dhanañjaya:* "O conqueror of wealth [Arjuna], there is no truth superior to Me." Thus it is here confirmed that there is no truth higher than Lord Śrī Kṛṣṇa Caitanya.

The impersonal Brahman is the goal of those who cultivate the study of books of transcendental knowledge, and the Supersoul is the goal of those who perform the *yoga* practices. One who knows the Supreme Personality of Godhead surpasses realization of both Brahman and Paramātmā because Bhagavān is the ultimate platform of absolute knowledge.

The Personality of Godhead is the complete form of *sac-cid-ānanda* (full life, knowledge and bliss). By realization of the *sat* portion of the Complete Whole (unlimited existence), one realizes the impersonal Brahman aspect of the Lord. By realization of the *cit* portion of the Complete Whole (unlimited knowledge), one can realize the localized aspect of the Lord, the Paramātmā. But neither of these partial realizations of the Complete Whole can help one realize *ānanda,* or complete bliss. Without such realization of *ānanda,* knowledge of the Absolute Truth is incomplete.

This verse of the *Caitanya-caritāmṛta* by Kṛṣṇadāsa Kavirāja Gosvāmī is confirmed by a parallel statement in the *Tattva-sandarbha*, by Śrīla Jīva Gosvāmī. In the Ninth Part of the *Tattva-sandarbha* it is said that the Absolute Truth is sometimes approached as impersonal Brahman, which, although spiritual, is only a partial representation of the Absolute Truth. Nārāyaṇa, the predominating Deity in Vaikuṇṭha, is to be known as an expansion of Śrī Kṛṣṇa, but Śrī Kṛṣṇa is the Supreme Absolute Truth, the object of the transcendental love of all living entities.

TEXT 6

ব্রহ্ম, আত্মা, ভগবান্—অনুবাদ তিন ।
অঙ্গপ্রভা, অংশ, স্বরূপ—তিন বিধেয়-চিহ্ন ॥ ৬ ॥

brahma, ātmā, bhagavān—anuvāda tina
aṅga-prabhā, aṁśa, svarūpa—tina vidheya-cihna

brahma—the impersonal Brahman; *ātmā*—the localized Paramātmā; *bhagavān*—the Personality of Godhead; *anuvāda*—subjects; *tina*—three; *aṅga-prabhā*—bodily effulgence; *aṁśa*—partial manifestation; *svarūpa*—original form; *tina*—three; *vidheya-cihna*—predicates.

TRANSLATION

Impersonal Brahman, the localized Paramātmā and the Personality of Godhead are three subjects, and the glowing effulgence, the partial manifestation and the original form are their three respective predicates.

TEXT 7

অনুবাদ আগে, পাছে বিধেয় স্থাপন ।
সেই অর্থ কহি, শুন শাস্ত্র-বিবরণ ॥ ৭ ॥

anuvāda āge, pāche vidheya sthāpana
sei artha kahi, śuna śāstra-vivaraṇa

anuvāda—the subject; *āge*—first; *pāche*—afterwards; *vidheya*—the predicate; *sthāpana*—placing; *sei*—this; *artha*—the meaning; *kahi*—I speak; *śuna*—please listen; *śāstra-vivaraṇa*—to the description of the scriptures.

TRANSLATION

A predicate always follows its subject. Now I shall explain the meaning of this verse according to the revealed scriptures.

TEXT 8

স্বয়ং ভগবান্ কৃষ্ণ, বিষ্ণু-পরতত্ত্ব ।
পূর্ণজ্ঞান পূর্ণানন্দ পরম মহত্ত্ব ॥ ৮ ॥

svayaṁ bhagavān kṛṣṇa, viṣṇu-paratattva
pūrṇa-jñāna pūrṇānanda parama mahattva

svayam—Himself; *bhagavān*—the Supreme Personality of Godhead; *kṛṣṇa*—Lord Kṛṣṇa; *viṣṇu*—of all-pervading Viṣṇu; *para-tattva*—the ultimate truth; *pūrṇa-jñāna*—full knowledge; *pūrṇa-ānanda*—full bliss; *parama*—supreme; *mahattva*—greatness.

TRANSLATION

Kṛṣṇa, the original form of the Personality of Godhead, is the summum bonum of the all-pervading Viṣṇu. He is all-perfect knowledge and all-perfect bliss. He is the Supreme Transcendence.

TEXT 9

'নন্দসুত' বলি, যাঁরে ভাগবতে গাই ।
সেই কৃষ্ণ অবতীর্ণ চৈতন্যগোসাঞি ॥ ৯ ॥

'nanda-suta' bali' yāṅre bhāgavate gāi
sei kṛṣṇa avatīrṇa caitanya-gosāñi

nanda-suta—the son of Nanda Mahārāja; *bali'*—as; *yāṅre*—who; *bhāgavate*—in *Śrīmad-Bhāgavatam; gāi*—is sung; *sei*—that; *kṛṣṇa*—Lord Kṛṣṇa; *avatīrṇa*—descended; *caitanya-gosāñi*—Lord Caitanya Mahāprabhu.

TRANSLATION

He whom Śrīmad-Bhāgavatam describes as the son of Nanda Mahārāja has descended to earth as Lord Caitanya.

PURPORT

According to the rules of rhetorical arrangement for efficient composition in literature, a subject should be mentioned before its predicate. The Vedic literature frequently mentions Brahman, Paramātmā and Bhagavān, and therefore these three terms are widely known as the subjects of transcendental understanding. But it is not widely known that what is approached as the impersonal Brahman is the effulgence of Śrī Caitanya Mahāprabhu's transcendental body. Nor is it widely known that the Supersoul, or Paramātmā, is only a partial representation of Lord Caitanya, who is identical with Bhagavān Himself. Therefore the descriptions of Brahman as the effulgence of Lord Caitanya, the Paramātmā as His partial representation, and the Supreme Personality of Godhead Kṛṣṇa as identical with Lord Caitanya Mahāprabhu must be verified by evidence from authoritative Vedic literatures.

The author wants to establish first that the essence of the *Vedas* is the *viṣṇu-tattva,* the Absolute Truth, Viṣṇu, the all-pervading Godhead. The *viṣṇu-tattva* has different categories, of which the highest is Lord Kṛṣṇa, the ultimate *viṣṇu-tattva,* as confirmed in the *Bhagavad-gītā* and throughout the Vedic literature. In *Śrīmad-Bhāgavatam* the same Supreme Personality of Godhead Kṛṣṇa is described as Nandasuta, the son of King Nanda. Kṛṣṇadāsa Kavirāja Gosvāmī says that Nandasuta has again appeared as Lord Śrī Kṛṣṇa Caitanya Mahāprabhu, and he bases this statement on his understanding that the Vedic literature concludes there is no difference between Lord Kṛṣṇa and Lord Caitanya Mahāprabhu. This the author will prove. If it is thus proved that Śrī Kṛṣṇa is the origin of all *tattvas* (truths), namely Brahman, Paramātmā and Bhagavān, and that there is no difference between Śrī Kṛṣṇa and Lord Śrī Caitanya Mahāprabhu, it will not be difficult to understand that Śrī Caitanya Mahāprabhu is also the same origin of all *tattvas.* The same Absolute Truth, as He is revealed to students of different realizations, is called Brahman, Paramātmā and Bhagavān.

TEXT 10

প্রকাশবিশেষে তেঁহ ধরে তিন নাম ।
ব্রহ্ম, পরমাত্মা আর স্বয়ং-ভগবান্ ॥ ১০ ॥

prakāśa-viśeṣe teṅha dhare tina nāma
brahma, paramātmā āra svayaṁ-bhagavān

prakāśa—of manifestation; *viśeṣe*—in variety; *teṅha*—He; *dhare*—holds; *tina*—three; *nāma*—names; *brahma*—Brahman; *paramātmā*—

Paramātmā (Supersoul); *āra*—and; *svayam*—Himself; *bhagavān*—the Supreme Personality of Godhead.

TRANSLATION

In terms of His various manifestations, He is known in three features, called the impersonal Brahman, the localized Paramātmā and the original Personality of Godhead.

PURPORT

Śrīla Jīva Gosvāmī has explained the word *bhagavān* in his *Bhagavat-sandarbha.* The Personality of Godhead, being full of all conceivable and inconceivable potencies, is the absolute Supreme Whole. Impersonal Brahman is a partial manifestation of the Absolute Truth realized in the absence of such complete potencies. The first syllable of the word *bhagavān* is *bha,* which means "sustainer" and "protector." The next letter, *ga,* means "leader," "pusher" and "creator." *Va* means "dwelling" (all living beings dwell in the Supreme Lord, and the Supreme Lord dwells within the heart of every living being). Combining all these concepts, the word *bhagavān* carries the import of inconceivable potency in knowledge, energy, strength, opulence, power and influence, devoid of all varieties of inferiority. Without such inconceivable potencies, one cannot fully sustain or protect. Our modern civilization is sustained by scientific arrangements devised by many great scientific brains. We can just imagine, therefore, the gigantic brain whose arrangements sustain the gravity of the unlimited number of planets and satellites and who creates the unlimited space in which they float. If one considers the intelligence needed to orbit man-made satellites, one cannot be fooled into thinking that there is not a gigantic intelligence responsible for the arrangements of the various planetary systems. There is no reason to believe that all the gigantic planets float in space without the superior arrangement of a superior intelligence. This subject is clearly dealt with in the *Bhagavad-gītā* (15.13), where the Personality of Godhead says, "I enter into each planet, and by My energy they stay in orbit." Were the planets not held in the grip of the Personality of Godhead, they would all scatter like dust in the air. Modern scientists can only impractically explain this inconceivable strength of the Personality of Godhead.

The potencies of the syllables *bha, ga* and *va* apply in terms of many different meanings. Through His different potent agents, the Lord protects and sustains everything, but He Himself personally protects and sustains only His devotees, just as a king personally sustains and protects his own children, while entrusting the protection and sustenance of the state to various administrative agents. The Lord is the leader of His devotees, as we learn from the *Bhagavad-gītā,* which mentions that the Personality of Godhead personally instructs His loving devotees how to make certain progress on the path of devotion and thus surely approach the kingdom of God. The Lord is also the recipient of all the adoration offered by His devotees, for whom He is the objective and the goal. For His devotees the Lord creates a favorable condition for developing a sense of transcendental love of Godhead. Sometimes He does this by taking away a devotee's material attachments by force and baffling all his material protective agents, for thus the devotee must completely depend on the Lord's protection. In this way the Lord proves Himself the leader of His devotees.

The Lord is not directly attached to the creation, maintenance and destruction of the material world, for He is eternally busy in the enjoyment of transcendental bliss with paraphernalia composed of His internal potencies. Yet as the initiator of the material energy as well as the marginal potency (the living beings), He expands Himself as the *puruṣa-avatāras,* who are invested with potencies similar to His. The *puruṣa-avatāras* are also in the category of *bhagavat-tattva* because each and every one of them is identical with the original form of the Personality of Godhead. The living entities are His infinitesimal particles and are qualitatively one with Him. They are sent into this material world for material enjoyment, to fulfill their desires to be independent individuals, but still they are subject to the supreme will of the Lord. The Lord deputes Himself in the state of Supersoul to supervise the arrangements for such material enjoyment. The example of a temporary fair is quite appropriate in this connection. If the citizens of a state assemble in a fair to enjoy for a short period, the government deputes a special officer to supervise it. Such an officer is invested with all governmental power, and therefore he is identical with the government. When the fair is over, there is no need for such an officer, and he returns home. The Paramātmā is compared to such an officer.

The living beings are not all in all. They are undoubtedly parts of the Supreme Lord and are qualitatively one with Him, yet they are subject to His control. Thus they are never equal to the Lord or one with Him. The Lord who associates with the living being is the Paramātmā, or supreme living being. No one, therefore, should view the tiny living beings and supreme living being to be on an equal level.

The all-pervading truth that exists eternally during the creation, maintenance and annihilation of the material world and in which the living beings rest in trance is called the impersonal Brahman.

TEXT 11

বদন্তি তত্তত্ত্ববিদস্তত্ত্বং যজ্জ্ঞানমদ্বয়ম্ ।
ব্রহ্মেতি পরমাত্মেতি ভগবানিতি শব্দ্যতে ॥ ১১ ॥

vadanti tat tattva-vidas
tattvaṁ yaj jñānam advayam
brahmeti paramātmeti
bhagavān iti śabdyate

vadanti—they say; *tat*—that; *tattva-vidaḥ*—learned souls; *tattvam*—the Absolute Truth; *yat*—which; *jñānam*—knowledge; *advayam*—nondual; *brahma*—Brahman; *iti*—thus; *paramātmā*—Paramātmā; *iti*—thus; *bhagavān*—Bhagavān; *iti*—thus; *śabdyate*—is known.

TRANSLATION

"Learned transcendentalists who know the Absolute Truth say that it is nondual knowledge and is called impersonal Brahman, the localized Paramātmā and the Personality of Godhead."

PURPORT

This Sanskrit verse appears as the eleventh verse of the First Canto, Second Chapter, of *Śrīmad-Bhāgavatam,* where Sūta Gosvāmī answers the questions of the sages headed by Śaunaka Ṛṣi concerning the essence of all scriptural instructions. *Tattva-vidaḥ* refers to persons who have knowledge of the Absolute Truth. They can certainly understand knowledge without duality because they are on the spiritual platform. The Absolute Truth is known sometimes as Brahman, sometimes as Paramātmā and sometimes as Bhagavān. Persons who are in knowledge of the truth know that one who tries to approach the Absolute simply by mental speculation will ultimately realize the impersonal Brahman, and one who tries to approach the Absolute through *yoga* practice will be able to realize Paramātmā, but one who has complete knowledge and spiritual understanding realizes the spiritual form of Bhagavān, the Personality of Godhead.

Devotees of the Personality of Godhead know that Śrī Kṛṣṇa, the son of the King of Vraja, is the Absolute Truth. They do not discriminate between Śrī Kṛṣṇa's name, form, quality and pastimes. One who wants to separate the Lord's absolute name, form and qualities from the Lord Himself must be understood to be lacking in absolute knowledge. A pure devotee knows that when he chants the transcendental name "Kṛṣṇa," Śrī Kṛṣṇa is present as transcendental sound. He therefore chants with full respect and veneration. When he sees the forms of Śrī Kṛṣṇa, he does not see anything different from the Lord. If one sees otherwise, he must be considered untrained in absolute knowledge. This lack of absolute knowledge is called *māyā.* One who is not Kṛṣṇa conscious is ruled by the spell of *māyā* under the control of a duality in knowledge. In the Absolute, all manifestations of the Supreme Lord are nondual, just as the multifarious forms of Viṣṇu, the controller of *māyā,* are nondual. Empiric philosophers who pursue the impersonal Brahman accept only the knowledge that the personality of the living entity is not different from the personality of the Supreme Lord, and mystic *yogīs* who try to locate the Paramātmā accept only the knowledge that the pure soul is not different from the Supersoul. The absolute conception of a pure devotee, however, includes all others. A devotee does not see anything except in its relationship with Kṛṣṇa, and therefore his realization is the most perfect of all.

TEXT 12

তাঁহার অঙ্গের শুদ্ধ কিরণ-মণ্ডল ।
উপনিষৎ কহে তাঁরে ব্রহ্ম সুনির্মল ॥ ১২ ॥

tāṅhāra aṅgera śuddha kiraṇa-maṇḍala
upaniṣat kahe tāṅre brahma sunirmala

tāṅhāra—His; *aṅgera*—of the body; *śuddha*—pure; *kiraṇa*—of rays; *maṇḍala*—realm; *upaniṣat*—the *Upaniṣads; kahe*—say; *tāṅre*—unto that; *brahma*—Brahman; *su-nirmala*—transcendental.

TRANSLATION

What the Upaniṣads call the transcendental, impersonal Brahman is the realm of the glowing effulgence of the same Supreme Person.

PURPORT

Three *mantras* of the *Muṇḍaka Upaniṣad* (2.2.9–11) give information regarding the bodily effulgence of the Supreme Personality of Godhead. They state:

hiraṇmaye pare kośe virajaṁ brahma niṣkalam
tac chubhraṁ jyotiṣāṁ jyotis tad yad ātma-vido viduḥ

na tatra sūryo bhāti na candra-tārakaṁ
nemā vidyuto bhānti kuto 'yam agniḥ
tam eva bhāntam anubhāti sarvaṁ
tasya bhāsā sarvam idaṁ vibhāti

brahmaivedam amṛtaṁ purastād brahma
paścād brahma dakṣiṇataś cottareṇa
adhaś cordhvaṁ ca prasṛtaṁ brahmai-
vedaṁ viśvam idaṁ variṣṭham

"In the spiritual realm, beyond the material covering, is the unlimited Brahman effulgence, which is free from material contamination. That effulgent white light is understood by transcendentalists to be the light of all lights. In that realm there is no need of sunshine, moonshine, fire or electricity for illumination. Indeed, whatever illumination appears in the material world is only a reflection of that supreme illumination. That Brahman is in front and in back, in the north, south, east and west, and also overhead and below. In other words, that supreme Brahman effulgence spreads throughout both the material and spiritual skies."

TEXT 13

চর্মচক্ষে দেখে যৈছে সূর্য নির্বিশেষ ।
জ্ঞানমার্গে লৈতে নারে কৃষ্ণের বিশেষ ॥ ১৩ ॥

carma-cakṣe dekhe yaiche sūrya nirviśeṣa
jñāna-mārge laite nāre kṛṣṇera viśeṣa

carma-cakṣe—by the naked eye; *dekhe*—one sees; *yaiche*—just as; *sūrya*—the sun; *nirviśeṣa*—without variegatedness; *jñāna-mārge*—by the path of philosophical speculation; *laite*—to accept; *nāre*—not able; *kṛṣṇera*—of Lord Kṛṣṇa; *viśeṣa*—the variety.

TRANSLATION

As with the naked eye one cannot know the sun except as a glowing substance, merely by philosophical speculation one cannot understand Lord Kṛṣṇa's transcendental varieties.

TEXT 14

যস্য প্রভা প্রভবতো জগদণ্ডকোটি-
কোটিষ্বশেষবসুধাদিবিভূতিভিন্নম্ ।

তদ্ব্রহ্ম নিষ্কলমনন্তমশেষভূতং
গোবিন্দমাদিপুরুষং তমহং ভজামি ॥ ১৪ ॥

yasya prabhā prabhavato jagad-aṇḍa-koṭi-
koṭīṣv aśeṣa-vasudhādi-vibhūti-bhinnam
tad brahma niṣkalam anantam aśeṣa-bhūtaṁ
govindam ādi-puruṣaṁ tam ahaṁ bhajāmi

yasya—of whom; *prabhā*—the effulgence; *prabhavataḥ*—of one who excels in power; *jagat-aṇḍa*—of universes; *koṭi-koṭiṣu*—in millions and millions; *aśeṣa*—unlimited; *vasudhā-ādi*—with planets, etc.; *vibhūti*—with opulences; *bhinnam*—becoming variegated; *tat*—that; *brahma*—Brahman; *niṣkalam*—without parts; *anantam*—unlimited; *aśeṣa-bhūtam*—being complete; *govindam*—Lord Govinda; *ādi-puruṣam*—the original person; *tam*—Him; *aham*—I; *bhajāmi*—worship.

TRANSLATION

"I worship Govinda, the primeval Lord, who is endowed with great power. The glowing effulgence of His transcendental form is the impersonal Brahman, which is absolute, complete and unlimited and which displays the varieties of countless planets, with their different opulences, in millions and millions of universes."

PURPORT

This verse appears in the *Brahma-saṁhitā* (5.40). Each and every one of the countless universes is full of innumerable planets with different constitutions and atmospheres. All these come from the unlimited non-dual Brahman, or Complete Whole, which exists in absolute knowledge. The origin of that unlimited Brahman effulgence is the transcendental body of Govinda, who is offered respectful obeisances as the original and supreme Personality of Godhead.

TEXT 15

কোটী কোটী ব্রহ্মাণ্ডে যে ব্রহ্মের বিভূতি।
সেই ব্রহ্ম গোবিন্দের হয় অঙ্গকান্তি ॥ ১৫ ॥

koṭī koṭī brahmāṇḍe ye brahmera vibhūti
sei brahma govindera haya aṅga-kānti

koṭī—tens of millions; *koṭī*—tens of millions; *brahma-aṇḍe*—in universes; *ye*—which; *brahmera*—of Brahman; *vibhūti*—opulences; *sei*—that; *brahma*—Brahman; *govindera*—of Lord Govinda; *haya*—is; *aṅga-kānti*—bodily effulgence.

TRANSLATION

[Lord Brahmā said:] "The opulences of the impersonal Brahman spread throughout the millions and millions of universes. That Brahman is but the bodily effulgence of Govinda.

TEXT 16

সেই গোবিন্দ ভজি আমি, তেহোঁ মোর পতি ।
তাঁহার প্রসাদে মোর হয় সৃষ্টিশক্তি ॥ ১৬ ॥

sei govinda bhaji āmi, tehoṅ mora pati
tāṅhāra prasāde mora haya sṛṣṭi-śakti

sei—that; *govinda*—Lord Govinda; *bhaji*—worship; *āmi*—I; *tehoṅ*—He; *mora*—my; *pati*—Lord; *tāṅhāra*—His; *prasāde*—by the mercy; *mora*—my; *haya*—becomes; *sṛṣṭi*—of creation; *śakti*—power.

TRANSLATION

"I worship Govinda. He is my Lord. Only by His grace am I empowered to create the universe."

PURPORT

Although the sun is situated far away from the other planets, its rays sustain and maintain them all. Indeed, the sun diffuses its heat and light all over the universe. Similarly, the supreme sun, Govinda, diffuses His heat and light everywhere in the form of His different potencies. The sun's heat and light are nondifferent from the sun. In the same way, the unlimited potencies of Govinda are nondifferent from Govinda Himself. Therefore the all-pervasive Brahman is the all-pervasive Govinda. The *Bhagavad-gītā* (14.27) clearly mentions that the impersonal Brahman is dependent upon Govinda. That is the real conception of absolute knowledge.

TEXT 17

মুনয়ো বাতবাসনাঃ শ্রমণা ঊর্দ্ধমন্থিনঃ ।
ব্রহ্মাখ্যং ধাম তে যান্তি শান্তাঃ সন্ন্যাসিনোঽমলাঃ ॥ ১৭ ॥

munayo vāta-vāsanāḥ
śramaṇā ūrdhva-manthinaḥ
brahmākhyaṁ dhāma te yānti
śāntāḥ sannyāsino 'malāḥ

munayaḥ—saints; *vāta-vāsanāḥ*—naked; *śramanāḥ*—who perform severe physical penances; *ūrdhva*—raised up; *manthinaḥ*—whose semen; *brahma-ākhyam*—known as Brahmaloka; *dhāma*—to the abode; *te*—they; *yānti*—go; *śāntāḥ*—equipoised in Brahman; *sannyāsinaḥ*—who are in the renounced order of life; *amalāḥ*—pure.

TRANSLATION

"Naked saints and sannyāsīs who undergo severe physical penances, who can raise the semen to the brain, and who are completely equipoised in Brahman can live in the realm known as Brahmaloka."

PURPORT

In this verse from *Śrīmad-Bhāgavatam* (11.6.47), *vāta-vāsanāḥ* refers to mendicants who do not care about anything material, including clothing, but who depend wholly on nature. Such sages do not cover their bodies even in severe winter or scorching sunshine. They take great pains not to avoid any kind of bodily suffering, and they live by begging from door to door. They never discharge their semen, either knowingly or unknowingly. By such celibacy they are able to raise the semen to the brain. Thus they become most intelligent and develop very sharp memories. Their minds are never disturbed or diverted from contemplation on the Absolute Truth, nor are they ever contaminated by desire for material enjoyment. By practicing austerities under strict discipline, such mendicants attain a neutral state transcendental to the modes of nature and merge into the impersonal Brahman.

TEXT 18

আত্মান্তর্যামী যাঁরে যোগশাস্ত্রে কয় ।
সেহ গোবিন্দের অংশ বিভূতি যে হয় ॥ ১৮ ॥

ātmāntaryāmī yāṅre yoga-śāstre kaya
seha govindera aṁśa vibhūti ye haya

ātmā antaḥ-yāmī—in-dwelling Supersoul; *yāṅre*—who; *yoga-śāstre*—in the scriptures of *yoga; kaya*—is spoken; *seha*—that; *govindera*—of Govinda; *aṁśa*—plenary portion; *vibhūti*—expansion; *ye*—which; *haya*—is.

TRANSLATION

He who is described in the yoga-śāstras as the indwelling Supersoul [ātmā antar-yāmī] is also a plenary portion of Govinda's personal expansion.

PURPORT

The Supreme Personality of Godhead is by nature joyful. His enjoyments, or pastimes, are completely transcendental. He is in the fourth dimension of existence, for although the material world is measured by the limitations of length, breadth and height, the Supreme Lord is completely unlimited in His body, form and existence. He is not personally attached to any of the affairs within the material cosmos. The material world is created by the expansion of His *puruṣa-avatāras,* who direct the aggregate material energy and all the conditioned souls. By understanding the three expansions of the *puruṣa,* a living entity can transcend the position of knowing only the twenty-four elements of the material world.

One of the expansions of Mahā-Viṣṇu is Kṣīrodakaśāyī Viṣṇu, the Supersoul within every living entity. As the Supersoul of the total aggregate of living entities, or the second *puruṣa,* He is known as Garbhodakaśāyī Viṣṇu. As the creator or original cause of innumerable universes, or the first *puruṣa,* who is lying on the Causal Ocean, He is called Mahā-Viṣṇu. The three *puruṣas* direct the affairs of the material world.

The authorized scriptures direct the individual souls to revive their relationship with the Supersoul. Indeed, the system of *yoga* is the process of transcending the influence of the material elements by establishing a connection with the *puruṣa* known as Paramātmā. One who has thoroughly studied the intricacies of creation can know very easily that this Paramātmā is the plenary portion of the Supreme Being, Śrī Kṛṣṇa.

TEXT 19

অনন্ত স্ফটিকে যৈছে এক সূর্য ভাসে।
তৈছে জীবে গোবিন্দের অংশ প্রকাশে ॥ ১৯ ॥

ananta sphaṭike yaiche eka sūrya bhāse
taiche jīve govindera aṁśa prakāśe

ananta—unlimited; *sphaṭike*—in crystals; *yaiche*—just as; *eka*—one; *sūrya*—sun; *bhāse*—appears; *taiche*—just so; *jīve*—in the living entity; *govindera*—of Govinda; *aṁśa*—portion; *prakāśe*—manifests.

TRANSLATION

As the one sun appears reflected in countless jewels, so Govinda manifests Himself [as the Paramātmā] in the hearts of all living beings.

PURPORT

The sun is situated in a specific location but is reflected in countless jewels and appears in innumerable localized aspects. Similarly, the Supreme Personality of Godhead, although eternally present in His transcendental abode, Goloka Vṛndāvana, is reflected in everyone's heart as the Supersoul. In the *Upaniṣads* it is said that the *jīva* (living entity) and the Paramātmā (Supersoul) are like two birds sitting in the same tree. The Supersoul engages the living being in executing fruitive work as a result of his deeds in the past, but the Paramātmā has nothing to do with such engagements. As soon as the living being ceases to act in terms of fruitive work and takes to the service of the Lord (the Paramātmā), coming to know of His supremacy, he is immediately freed from all designations, and in that pure state he enters the kingdom of God, known as Vaikuṇṭha.

The Paramātmā, or Supersoul, the guide of the individual living beings, does not take part in fulfilling the desires of the living beings, but He arranges for their fulfillment by material nature. As soon as an individual soul becomes conscious of his eternal relationship with the Supersoul and looks only toward Him, he at once becomes free from the entanglements of material enjoyment. Christian philosophers who do not believe in the law of *karma* put forward the argument that it is absurd to say one must accept the results of past deeds of which he has no consciousness. A criminal is first reminded of his misdeeds by witnesses in a law court, and then he is punished. If death is complete forgetfulness, why should a person be punished for his past misdeeds? The conception of the Paramātmā is an invincible answer to these fallacious arguments. The Paramātmā is the witness of the past activities of the individual living being. A man may not remember what he has done in his childhood, but his father, who has seen him grow through different stages of development, certainly remembers. Similarly, the living being undergoes many changes of body through many lives, but the Supersoul is always with him and remembers all his activities, despite his evolution through different bodies.

TEXT 20

অথবা বহুনৈতেন কিং জ্ঞাতেন তবার্জুন ।
বিষ্টভ্যাহমিদং কৃৎস্নমেকাংশেন স্থিতো জগৎ ॥ ২০ ॥

atha vā bahunaitena
kiṁ jñātena tavārjuna
viṣṭabhyāham idaṁ kṛtsnam
ekāṁśena sthito jagat

atha vā—or; *bahunā*—much; *etena*—with this; *kim*—what use; *jñātena*—being known; *tava*—by you; *arjuna*—O Arjuna; *viṣṭabhya*—pervading; *aham*—I; *idam*—this; *kṛtsnam*—entire; *eka-aṁśena*—with one portion; *sthitaḥ*—situated; *jagat*—universe.

TRANSLATION

[The Personality of Godhead, Śrī Kṛṣṇa, said:] "What more shall I say to you? I live throughout this cosmic manifestation merely by My single plenary portion."

PURPORT

Describing His own potencies to Arjuna, the Personality of Godhead Śrī Kṛṣṇa spoke this verse of the *Bhagavad-gītā* (10.42).

TEXT 21

তমিমমহমজং শরীরভাজাং
হৃদি হৃদি ধিষ্ঠিতমাত্মকল্পিতানাম্ ।
প্রতিদৃশমিব নৈকধার্কমেকং
সমধিগতোহস্মি বিধূতভেদমোহঃ ॥ ২১ ॥

tam imam aham ajaṁ śarīra-bhājāṁ
hṛdi hṛdi dhiṣṭhitam ātma-kalpitānām

prati-dṛśam iva naikadhārkam ekaṁ
samadhigato 'smi vidhūta-bheda-mohaḥ

tam—Him; *imam*—this; *aham*—I; *ajam*—the unborn; *śarīra-bhājām*—of the conditioned souls endowed with bodies; *hṛdi hṛdi*—in each of the hearts; *dhiṣṭhitam*—situated; *ātma*—by themselves; *kalpitānām*—which are imagined; *prati-dṛśam*—for every eye; *iva*—like; *na eka-dhā*—not in one way; *arkam*—the sun; *ekam*—one; *samadhigataḥ*—one who has obtained; *asmi*—I am; *vidhūta*—removed; *bheda-mohaḥ*—whose misconception of duality.

TRANSLATION

[Grandfather Bhīṣma said:] "As the one sun appears differently situated to different seers, so also do You, the unborn, appear differently represented as the Paramātmā in every living being. But when a seer knows himself to be one of Your own servitors, no longer does he maintain such duality. Thus I am now able to comprehend Your eternal forms, knowing well the Paramātmā to be only Your plenary portion."

PURPORT

This verse from *Śrīmad-Bhāgavatam* (1.9.42) was spoken by Bhīṣmadeva, the grandfather of the Kurus, when he was lying on a bed of arrows at the last stage of his life. Arjuna, Kṛṣṇa and numberless friends, admirers, relatives and sages had gathered on the scene as Mahārāja Yudhiṣṭhira took moral and religious instructions from the dying Bhīṣma. Just as the final moment arrived for him, Bhīṣma spoke this verse while looking at Lord Kṛṣṇa.

Just as the one sun is the object of vision of many different persons, so the one partial representation of Lord Kṛṣṇa who lives in the heart of every living entity as the Paramātmā is a variously perceived object. One who comes intimately in touch with Lord Kṛṣṇa by engaging in His eternal service sees the Supersoul as the localized partial representation of the Supreme Personality of Godhead. Bhīṣma knew the Supersoul to be a partial expansion of Lord Kṛṣṇa, whom he understood to be the supreme, unborn transcendental form.

TEXT 22

সেইত গোবিন্দ সাক্ষাচ্চৈতন্য গোসাঞি ।
জীব নিস্তারিতে ঐছে দয়ালু আর নাই ॥ ২২ ॥

seita govinda sākṣāc caitanya gosāñi
jīva nistārite aiche dayālu āra nāi

seita—that; *govinda*—Govinda; *sākṣāt*—personally; *caitanya*—Lord Caitanya; *gosāñi*—Gosāñi; *jīva*—the fallen living entities; *nistārite*—to deliver; *aiche*—such; *dayālu*—a merciful Lord; *āra*—another; *nāi*—there is not.

TRANSLATION

That Govinda personally appears as Caitanya Gosāñi. No other Lord is as merciful in delivering the fallen souls.

PURPORT

Having described Govinda in terms of His Brahman and Paramātmā features, now the author of *Śrī Caitanya-caritāmṛta* advances his argument to prove that Lord Śrī Caitanya Mahāprabhu is the identical personality. The same Lord Śrī Kṛṣṇa, in the garb of a devotee of Śrī Kṛṣṇa, descended to this mortal world to reclaim the fallen human beings who had misunderstood the Personality of Godhead even after the explanation of the *Bhagavad-gītā.* In the *Bhagavad-gītā* the Personality of Godhead Śrī Kṛṣṇa directly instructed that the Supreme is a person, that the impersonal Brahman is His glowing effulgence, and that the Paramātmā is His partial representation. All men were therefore advised to follow the path of Śrī Kṛṣṇa, leaving aside all mundane "isms." Offenders misunderstood this instruction, however, because of their poor fund of knowledge. Thus by His causeless, unlimited mercy Śrī Kṛṣṇa came again as Śrī Caitanya Gosāñi.

The author of *Śrī Caitanya-caritāmṛta* most emphatically stresses that Lord Caitanya Mahāprabhu is Śrī Kṛṣṇa Himself. He is not an expansion of the *prakāśa* or *vilāsa* forms of Śrī Kṛṣṇa; He is the *svayaṁ-rūpa,* Govinda. Apart from the relevant scriptural evidence forwarded by Śrīla Kṛṣṇadāsa Kavirāja Gosvāmī, there are innumerable other scriptural statements regarding Lord Caitanya's being the Supreme Lord Himself. The following examples may be cited:

(1) From the *Caitanya Upaniṣad* (5): *gauraḥ sarvātmā mahā-puruṣo mahātmā mahā-yogī tri-guṇātītaḥ sattva-rūpo bhaktiṁ loke kāśyati.* "Lord Gaura, who is the all-pervading Supersoul, the Supreme Personality of Godhead, appears as a great saint and powerful mystic who is above the three modes of nature and is the emblem of transcendental activity. He disseminates the cult of devotion throughout the world."

(2) From the *Śvetāśvatara Upaniṣad* (6.7 and 3.12):

tam īśvarāṇāṁ paramaṁ maheśvaraṁ
taṁ devatānāṁ paramaṁ ca daivatam
patiṁ patīnāṁ paramaṁ parastād
vidāma devaṁ bhuvaneśam īḍyam

"O Supreme Lord, You are the Supreme Maheśvara, the worshipable Deity of all the demigods and the Supreme Lord of all lords. You are the controller of all controllers, the Personality of Godhead, the Lord of everything worshipable."

mahān prabhur vai puruṣaḥ
sattvasyaiṣa pravartakaḥ
su-nirmalām imāṁ prāptim
īśāno jyotir avyayaḥ

"The Supreme Personality of Godhead is Mahāprabhu, who disseminates transcendental enlightenment. Just to be in touch with Him is to be in contact with the indestructible *brahmajyoti.*"

(3) From the *Muṇḍaka Upaniṣad* (3.1.3):

yadā paśyaḥ paśyate rukma-varṇaṁ
kartāram īśaṁ puruṣaṁ brahma-yonim

"One who sees that golden-colored Personality of Godhead, the Supreme Lord, the supreme actor, who is the source of the Supreme Brahman, is liberated."

(4) From *Śrīmad-Bhāgavatam* (11.5.33–34 and 7.9.38):

dhyeyaṁ sadā paribhava-ghnam abhīṣṭa-dohaṁ
tīrthāspadaṁ śiva-viriñci-nutaṁ śaraṇyam
bhṛtyārti-haṁ praṇata-pāla-bhavābdhi-potaṁ
vande mahā-puruṣa te caraṇāravindam

"We offer our respectful obeisances unto the lotus feet of Him, the Lord, upon whom one should always meditate. He destroys insults to His devotees. He removes the distresses of His devotees and satisfies their desires. He, the abode of all holy places and the shelter of all sages, is worshipable by Lord Śiva and Lord Brahmā. He is the boat of the demigods for crossing the ocean of birth and death."

tyaktvā sudustyaja-surepsita-rājya-lakṣmīṁ
dharmiṣṭha ārya-vacasā yad agād araṇyam
māyā-mṛgaṁ dayitayepsitam anvadhāvad
vande mahā-puruṣa te caraṇāravindam

"We offer our respectful obeisances unto the lotus feet of the Lord, upon whom one should always meditate. He left His householder life, leaving aside His eternal consort, whom even the denizens of heaven adore. He went into the forest to deliver the fallen souls, who are put into illusion by material energy."

Prahlāda said:

itthaṁ nṛ-tiryag-ṛṣi-deva jhaṣāvatārair
lokān vibhāvayasi haṁsi jagat-pratīpān
dharmaṁ mahā-puruṣa pāsi yugānuvṛttaṁ
channaḥ kalau yad abhavas tri-yugo 'tha sa tvam

"My Lord, You kill all the enemies of the world in Your multifarious incarnations in the families of men, animals, demigods, *ṛṣis*, aquatics and so on. Thus You illuminate the worlds with transcendental knowledge. In the Age of Kali, O Mahāpuruṣa, You sometimes appear in a covered incarnation. Therefore You are known as Tri-yuga [one who appears in only three *yugas*]."

(5) From the *Kṛṣṇa-yāmala-tantra: puṇya-kṣetre nava-dvīpe bhaviṣyāmi śacī-sutaḥ.* "I shall appear in the holy land of Navadvīpa as the son of Śacī-devī."

(6) From the *Vāyu Purāṇa: kalau saṅkīrtanārambhe bhaviṣyāmi śacī-sutaḥ.* "In the Age of Kali when the *saṅkīrtana* movement is inaugurated, I shall descend as the son of Śacī-devī."

(7) From the *Brahma-yāmala-tantra:*

atha vāhaṁ dharādhāme
bhūtvā mad-bhakta-rūpa-dhṛk
māyāyāṁ ca bhaviṣyāmi
kalau saṅkīrtanāgame

"Sometimes I personally appear on the surface of the world in the garb of a devotee. Specifically, I appear as the son of Śacī in Kali-yuga to start the *saṅkīrtana* movement."

(8) From the *Ananta-saṁhitā:*

ya eva bhagavān kṛṣṇo
rādhikā-prāṇa-vallabhaḥ
sṛṣṭy ādau sa jagan-nātho
gaura āsīn maheśvari

"The Supreme Person, Śrī Kṛṣṇa Himself, who is the life of Śrī Rādhārāṇī and is the Lord of the universe in creation, maintenance and annihilation, appears as Gaura, O Maheśvarī."

TEXT 23

পরব্যোমেতে বৈসে নারায়ণ নাম ।
ষড়ৈশ্বর্যপূর্ণ লক্ষ্মীকান্ত ভগবান্ ॥ ২৩ ॥

para-vyomete vaise nārāyaṇa nāma
ṣaḍ-aiśvarya-pūrṇa lakṣmī-kānta bhagavān

para-vyomete—in the transcendental world; *vaise*—sits; *nārāyaṇa*—Lord Nārāyaṇa; *nāma*—of the name; *ṣaṭ-aiśvarya*—of six kinds of opulences; *pūrṇa*—full; *lakṣmī-kānta*—the husband of the goddess of opulence; *bhagavān*—the Supreme Personality of Godhead.

TRANSLATION

Lord Nārāyaṇa, who dominates the transcendental world, is full in six opulences. He is the Personality of Godhead, the Lord of the goddess of fortune.

TEXT 24

বেদ, ভাগবত, উপনিষৎ, আগম ।
'পূর্ণতত্ত্ব' যাঁরে কহে, নাহি যাঁর সম ॥ ২৪ ॥

veda, bhāgavata, upaniṣat, āgama
'pūrṇa-tattva' yāṅre kahe, nāhi yāṅra sama

veda—the *Vedas; bhāgavata*—*Śrīmad-Bhāgavatam*; *upaniṣat*—the *Upaniṣads; āgama*—other transcendental literatures; *pūrṇa-tattva*—full truth; *yāṅre*—unto whom; *kahe*—they say; *nāhi*—there is not; *yāṅra*—whose; *sama*—equal.

TRANSLATION

The Personality of Godhead is He who is described as the Absolute Whole in the Vedas, Bhāgavatam, Upaniṣads and other transcendental literatures. No one is equal to Him.

PURPORT

There are innumerable authoritative statements in the *Vedas* regarding the personal feature of the Absolute Truth. Some of them are as follows:

(1) From the *Ṛk-saṁhitā* (1.22.20):

tad viṣṇoḥ paramaṁ padaṁ
sadā paśyanti sūrayaḥ
divīva cakṣur ātatam

"The Personality of Godhead Viṣṇu is the Absolute Truth, whose lotus feet all the demigods are always eager to see. Like the sun-god, He pervades everything by the rays of His energy. He appears impersonal to imperfect eyes."

(2) From the *Nārāyaṇātharva-śira Upaniṣad* (1–2): *nārāyaṇād eva samutpadyante nārāyaṇāt pravartante nārāyaṇe pralīyante. . . . atha nityo nārāyaṇaḥ. . . . nārāyaṇa evedaṁ sarvaṁ yad bhūtaṁ yac ca bhavyam. . . . śuddho deva eko nārāyaṇo na dvitīyo 'sti kaścit.* "It is from Nārāyaṇa only that everything is generated, by Him only that everything is maintained, and in Him only that everything is annihilated. Therefore Nārāyaṇa is eternally existing. Everything that exists now or will be created in the future is nothing but Nārāyaṇa, who is the unadulterated Deity. There is only Nārāyaṇa and nothing else."

(3) From the *Nārāyaṇa Upaniṣad* (1.4): *yataḥ prasūtā jagataḥ prasūtī.* "Nārāyaṇa is the source from whom all the universes emanate."

(4) From the *Hayaśīrṣa Pañcarātra: paramātmā harir devaḥ.* "Hari is the Supreme Lord."

(5) From *Śrīmad-Bhāgavatam* (11.3.34–35):

nārāyaṇābhidhānasya
brahmaṇaḥ paramātmanaḥ
niṣṭhām arhatha no vaktuṁ
yūyaṁ hi brahma-vittamāḥ

"O best of the *brāhmaṇas,* please tell us of the position of Nārāyaṇa, who is also known as Brahman and Paramātmā."

sthity-udbhava-pralaya-hetur ahetur asya
yat svapna-jāgara-suṣuptiṣu sad bahiś ca
dehendriyāsu-hṛdayāni caranti yena
sañjīvitāni tad avehi paraṁ narendra

"O King, know Him who is causeless and yet is the cause of creation, maintenance and annihilation. He exists in the three states of consciousness—namely waking, dreaming and deep sleep—as well as beyond them. He enlivens the body, the senses, the breath of life, and the heart, and thus they move. Know Him to be supreme."

TEXT 25

ভক্তিযোগে ভক্ত পায় যাঁহার দর্শন ।
সূর্য যেন সবিগ্রহ দেখে দেবগণ ॥ ২৫ ॥

bhakti-yoge bhakta pāya yāṅhāra darśana
sūrya yena savigraha dekhe deva-gaṇa

bhakti-yoge—by devotional service; *bhakta*—the devotee; *pāya*—obtains; *yāṅhāra*—whose; *darśana*—sight; *sūrya*—the sun-god; *yena*—like; *sa-vigraha*—with form; *dekhe*—they see; *deva-gaṇa*—the denizens of heaven.

TRANSLATION

Through their service, devotees see that Personality of Godhead, just as the denizens of heaven see the personality of the sun.

PURPORT

The Supreme Personality of Godhead has His eternal form, which cannot be seen by material eyes or mental speculation. Only by transcendental devotional service can one understand the transcendental form of the Lord. The comparison is made here to the qualifications for viewing the personal features of the sun-god. The sun-god is a person who, although not visible to our eyes, is seen from the higher planets by the demigods, whose eyes are suitable for seeing through the glaring sunshine that surrounds him. Every planet has its own atmosphere according to the influence of the arrangement of material nature. It is therefore necessary to have a particular type of bodily construction to reach a particular planet. The inhabitants of earth may be able to reach the moon, but the inhabitants of heaven can reach even the fiery sphere called the sun. What is impossible for man on earth is easy for the demigods in heaven because of their different bodies. Similarly, to see the Supreme Lord one must have the spiritual eyes of devotional service. The Personality of Godhead is unapproachable by those who are habituated to speculation about the Absolute Truth in terms of experimental scientific thought, without reference to the transcendental vibration. The ascending approach to the Absolute Truth ends in the realization of impersonal Brahman and the localized Paramātmā but not the Supreme Transcendental Personality.

TEXT 26

জ্ঞানযোগমার্গে তাঁরে ভজে যেই সব ।
ব্রহ্ম-আত্মরূপে তাঁরে করে অনুভব ॥ ২৬ ॥

jñāna-yoga-mārge tāṅre bhaje yei saba
brahma-ātma-rūpe tāṅre kare anubhava

jñāna—of philosophical speculation; *yoga*—and of mystic *yoga; mārge*—on the paths; *tāṅre*—Him; *bhaje*—worship; *yei*—who; *saba*—all; *brahma*—of impersonal Brahman; *ātma*—and of the Supersoul (Paramātmā); *rūpe*—in the forms; *tāṅre*—Him; *kare*—do; *anubhava*—perceive.

TRANSLATION

Those who walk the paths of knowledge and yoga worship only Him, for it is Him they perceive as the impersonal Brahman and localized Paramātmā.

PURPORT

Those who are fond of mental speculation (*jñāna-mārga*) or want to meditate in mystic *yoga* to find the Absolute Truth must approach the impersonal effulgence of the Lord and His partial representation respectively. Such persons cannot realize the eternal form of the Lord.

TEXT 27

উপাসনা-ভেদে জানি ঈশ্বর-মহিমা ।
অতএব সূর্য তাঁর দিয়েত উপমা ॥ ২৭ ॥

upāsanā-bhede jāni īśvara-mahimā
ataeva sūrya tāṅra diyeta upamā

upāsanā-bhede—by the different paths of worship; *jāni*—I know; *īśvara*—of the Supreme Lord; *mahimā*—greatness; *ataeva*—therefore; *sūrya*—the sun; *tāṅra*—of Him; *diyeta*—was given; *upamā*—simile.

TRANSLATION

Thus one may understand the glories of the Lord through different modes of worship, as the analogy of the sun illustrates.

TEXT 28

সেই নারায়ণ কৃষ্ণের স্বরূপ-অভেদ ।
একই বিগ্রহ, কিন্তু আকার-বিভেদ ॥ ২৮ ॥

sei nārāyaṇa kṛṣṇera svarūpa-abheda
eka-i vigraha, kintu ākāra-vibheda

sei—that; *nārāyaṇa*—Lord Nārāyaṇa; *kṛṣṇera*—of Lord Kṛṣṇa; *svarūpa*—original form; *abheda*—not different; *eka-i*—one; *vigraha*—identity; *kintu*—but; *ākāra*—of bodily features; *vibheda*—difference.

TRANSLATION

Nārāyaṇa and Śrī Kṛṣṇa are the same Personality of Godhead, but although They are identical, Their bodily features are different.

TEXT 29

ইহোঁত দ্বিভুজ, তিঁহো ধরে চারি হাথ ।
ইহোঁ বেণু ধরে, তিঁহো চক্রাদিক সাথ ॥ ২৯ ॥

iṅhota dvi-bhuja, tiṅho dhare cāri hātha
iṅho veṇu dhare, tiṅho cakrādika sātha

iṅhota—this one; *dvi-bhuja*—two arms; *tiṅho*—He; *dhare*—manifests; *cāri*—four; *hātha*—hands; *iṅho*—this one; *veṇu*—flute; *dhare*—holds; *tiṅho*—He; *cakra-ādika*—the wheel, etc.; *sātha*—with.

TRANSLATION

This Personality of Godhead [Śrī Kṛṣṇa] has two hands and holds a flute, whereas the other [Nārāyaṇa] has four hands, with conch, wheel, mace and lotus.

PURPORT

Nārāyaṇa is identical to Śrī Kṛṣṇa. They are in fact the same person manifested differently, like a high court judge who is differently situated in his office and at home. As Nārāyaṇa the Lord is manifested with four hands, but as Kṛṣṇa He is manifested with two hands.

TEXT 30

নারায়ণস্ত্বং ন হি সর্বদেহিনা-
মাত্মাস্যধীশাখিললোকসাক্ষী ।
নারায়ণোঽঙ্গং নরভূ-জলায়না-
ত্তচ্চাপি সত্যং ন তবৈব মায়া ॥ ৩০ ॥

nārāyaṇas tvaṁ na hi sarva-dehinām
ātmāsy adhīśākhila-loka-sākṣī
nārāyaṇo 'ṅgaṁ nara-bhū-jalāyanāt
tac cāpi satyaṁ na tavaiva māyā

nārāyaṇaḥ—Lord Nārāyaṇa; *tvam*—You; *na*—not; *hi*—certainly; *sarva*—all; *dehinām*—of the embodied beings; *ātmā*—the Supersoul; *asi*—You are; *adhīśa*—O Lord; *akhila-loka*—of all the worlds; *sākṣī*—the witness; *nārāyaṇaḥ*—known as Nārāyaṇa; *aṅgam*—plenary portion; *nara*—of Nara; *bhū*—born; *jala*—in the water; *ayanāt*—due to the place of refuge; *tat*—that; *ca*—and; *api*—certainly; *satyam*—highest truth; *na*—not; *tava*—Your; *eva*—at all; *māyā*—the illusory energy.

TRANSLATION

"O Lord of lords, You are the seer of all creation. You are indeed everyone's dearest life. Are You not, therefore, my father, Nārāyaṇa? Nārāyaṇa refers to one whose abode is in the water born from Nara [Garbhodakaśāyī Viṣṇu], and that Nārāyaṇa is Your plenary portion. All Your plenary portions are transcendental. They are absolute and are not creations of māyā."

PURPORT

This statement, which is from *Śrīmad-Bhāgavatam* (10.14.14), was spoken by Lord Brahmā in his prayers to Lord Kṛṣṇa after the Lord had defeated him by displaying His mystic powers. Brahmā had tried to test Lord Kṛṣṇa to see if He were really the Supreme Personality of Godhead playing as a cowherd boy. Brahmā stole all the other boys and their calves from the pasturing grounds, but when he returned to the pastures he saw that all the boys and calves were still there, for Lord Kṛṣṇa had created them all again. When Brahmā saw this mystic power of Lord Kṛṣṇa's, he admitted defeat and offered prayers to the Lord, addressing Him as the proprietor and seer of everything in the creation and as the Supersoul who is within each and every living entity and is dear to all. That Lord Kṛṣṇa is Nārāyaṇa, the father of Brahmā, because Lord Kṛṣṇa's plenary expansion Garbhodakaśāyī Viṣṇu, after placing Himself on the Garbha Ocean, created Brahmā from His own body. Mahā-Viṣṇu in the Causal Ocean and Kṣīrodakaśāyī Viṣṇu, the Supersoul in everyone's heart, are also transcendental expansions of the Supreme Truth.

TEXT 31

শিশু বৎস হরি' ব্রহ্মা করি অপরাধ ।
অপরাধ ক্ষমাইতে মাগেন প্রসাদ ॥ ৩১ ॥

śiśu vatsa hari' brahmā kari aparādha
aparādha kṣamāite māgena prasāda

śiśu—playmates; *vatsa*—calves; *hari'*—stealing; *brahmā*—Lord Brahmā; *kari*—making; *aparādha*—offense; *aparādha*—offense; *kṣamāite*—to pardon; *māgena*—begged; *prasāda*—mercy.

TRANSLATION

After Brahmā had offended Kṛṣṇa by stealing His playmates and calves, he begged the Lord's pardon for his offensive act and prayed for the Lord's mercy.

TEXT 32

তোমার নাভিপদ্ম হৈতে আমার জন্মোদয় ।
তুমি পিতা-মাতা, আমি তোমার তনয় ॥ ৩২ ॥

tomāra nābhi-padma haite āmāra janmodaya
tumi pitā-mātā, āmi tomāra tanaya

tomāra—Your; *nābhi-padma*—lotus of the navel; *haite*—from; *āmāra*—my; *janma-udaya*—birth; *tumi*—You; *pitā*—father; *mātā*—mother; *āmi*—I; *tomāra*—Your; *tanaya*—son.

TRANSLATION

"I took birth from the lotus that grew from Your navel. Thus You are both my father and my mother, and I am Your son.

TEXT 33

পিতা মাতা বালকের না লয় অপরাধ ।
অপরাধ ক্ষম, মোরে করহ প্রসাদ ॥ ৩৩ ॥

pitā mātā bālakera nā laya aparādha
aparādha kṣama, more karaha prasāda

pitā—father; *mātā*—mother; *bālakera*—of the child; *nā*—not; *laya*—take seriously; *aparādha*—the offense; *aparādha*—the offense; *kṣama*—please pardon; *more*—unto me; *karaha*—please show; *prasāda*—mercy.

TRANSLATION

"Parents never take seriously the offenses of their children. I therefore beg Your pardon and ask for Your benediction."

TEXT 34

কৃষ্ণ কহেন—ব্রহ্মা, তোমার পিতা নারায়ণ ।
আমি গোপ, তুমি কৈছে আমার নন্দন ॥ ৩৪ ॥

kṛṣṇa kahena—brahmā, tomāra pitā nārāyaṇa
āmi gopa, tumi kaiche āmāra nandana

kṛṣṇa—Lord Kṛṣṇa; *kahena*—says; *brahmā*—O Lord Brahmā; *tomāra*—your; *pitā*—father; *nārāyaṇa*—Lord Nārāyaṇa; *āmi*—I (am); *gopa*—cowherd boy; *tumi*—you; *kaiche*—how; *āmāra*—My; *nandana*—son.

TRANSLATION

Śrī Kṛṣṇa said, "O Brahmā, your father is Nārāyaṇa. I am but a cowherd boy. How can you be My son?"

TEXT 35

ব্রহ্মা বলেন, তুমি কি না হও নারায়ণ ।
তুমি নারায়ণ—শুন তাহার কারণ ॥ ৩৫ ॥

brahmā balena, tumi ki nā hao nārāyaṇa
tumi nārāyaṇa—śuna tāhāra kāraṇa

brahmā—Lord Brahmā; *balena*—says; *tumi*—You; *ki nā hao*—are not; *nārāyaṇa*—Lord Nārāyaṇa; *tumi*—You; *nārāyaṇa*—Lord Nārāyaṇa; *śuna*—please hear; *tāhāra*—of that; *kāraṇa*—reason.

TRANSLATION

Brahmā replied, "Are You not Nārāyaṇa? You are certainly Nārāyaṇa. Please listen as I state the proofs.

TEXT 36

প্রাকৃতাপ্রাকৃত-সৃষ্ট্যে যত জীবরূপ ।
তাহার যে আত্মা তুমি মূল-স্বরূপ ॥ ৩৬ ॥

prākṛtāprākṛta-sṛṣṭye yata jīva-rūpa
tāhāra ye ātmā tumi mūla-svarūpa

prākṛta—material; *aprākṛta*—and spiritual; *sṛṣṭye*—in the creations; *yata*—as many as there are; *jīva-rūpa*—the living beings; *tāhāra*—of them; *ye*—who; *ātmā*—the Supersoul; *tumi*—You; *mūla-svarūpa*—ultimate source.

TRANSLATION

"All the living beings within the material and spiritual worlds are ultimately born of You, for You are the Supersoul of them all.

PURPORT

The cosmic manifestation is generated by the interaction of the three modes of material nature. The transcendental world has no such material modes, although it is nevertheless full of spiritual variegatedness.

In that spiritual world there are also innumerable living entities, who are eternally liberated souls engaged in transcendental loving service to Lord Kṛṣṇa. The conditioned souls, who remain within the material cosmic creation, are subjected to the threefold miseries and pangs of material nature. They exist in different species of life because they are eternally averse to transcendental loving devotion to the Supreme Lord.

Saṅkarṣaṇa is the original source of all living entities because they are all expansions of His marginal potency. Some of them are conditioned by material nature, whereas others are under the protection of the spiritual nature. The material nature is a conditional manifestation of spiritual nature, just as smoke is a conditional stage of fire. Smoke is dependent on fire, but in a blazing fire there is no place for smoke. Smoke disturbs, but fire serves. The serving spirit of the residents of the transcendental world is displayed in five varieties of relationships with the Supreme Lord, who is the central enjoyer. In the material world everyone is a self-centered enjoyer of mundane happiness and distress. One considers himself the lord of everything and tries to enjoy the illusory energy, but he is not successful because he is not independent: he is but a minute particle of the energy of Lord Saṅkarṣaṇa. All living beings exist under the control of the Supreme Lord, who is therefore called Nārāyaṇa.

TEXT 37

পৃথ্বী যৈছে ঘটকুলের কারণ আশ্রয় ।
জীবের নিদান তুমি, তুমি সর্বাশ্রয় ॥ ৩৭ ॥

pṛthvī yaiche ghaṭa-kulera kāraṇa āśraya
jīvera nidāna tumi, tumi sarvāśraya

pṛthvī—the earth; *yaiche*—just as; *ghaṭa*—of earthen pots; *kulera*—of the multitude; *kāraṇa*—the cause; *āśraya*—the shelter; *jīvera*—of the living beings; *nidāna*—root cause; *tumi*—You; *tumi*—You; *sarva-āśraya*—shelter of all.

TRANSLATION

"As the earth is the original cause and shelter of all pots made of earth, so You are the ultimate cause and shelter of all living beings.

PURPORT

As the vast earth is the source for the ingredients of all earthen pots, so the Supreme Soul is the source for the complete substance of all individual living entities. The cause of all causes, the Supreme Personality of Godhead, is the cause of the living entities. This is confirmed in the *Bhagavad-gītā* (7.10), where the Lord says, *bījaṁ māṁ sarva-bhūtānām* ("I am the seed of all living entities"), and in the *Upaniṣads*, which say, *nityo nityānāṁ cetanaś cetanānām* ("the Lord is the supreme leader among all the eternal living beings").

The Lord is the reservoir of all cosmic manifestation, animate and inanimate. The advocates of Viśiṣṭādvaita-vāda philosophy explain the *Vedānta-sūtra* by saying that although the living entity has two kinds of bodies—subtle (consisting of mind, intelligence and false ego) and gross (consisting of the five basic elements)—and although he thus lives in three bodily dimensions (gross, subtle and spiritual), he is nevertheless a spiritual soul. Similarly, the Supreme Personality of Godhead, who emanates the material and spiritual worlds, is the Supreme Spirit. As an individual spirit soul is almost identical to his gross and subtle bodies, so the Supreme Lord is almost identical to the material and spiritual worlds. The material world, full of conditioned souls trying to lord it over matter, is a manifestation of the external energy of the Supreme Lord, and the spiritual world, full of perfect servitors of the Lord, is a manifestation of His internal energy. Since all living entities are minute sparks of the Supreme Personality of Godhead, He is the Supreme Soul in both the material and spiritual worlds. The Vaiṣṇavas following Lord Caitanya stress the doctrine of *acintya-bhedābheda-tattva*, which states that the Supreme Lord, being the cause and effect of everything, is inconceivably, simultaneously one with His manifestations of energy and different from them.

TEXT 38

'নার'-শব্দে কহে সর্বজীবের নিচয় ।
'অয়ন'-শব্দেতে কহে তাহার আশ্রয় ॥ ৩৮ ॥

'nāra'-śabde kahe sarva jīvera nicaya
'ayana'-śabdete kahe tāhāra āśraya

nāra-śabde—by the word *nāra; kahe*—one means; *sarva jīvera*—of all living entities; *nicaya*—the assemblage; *ayana-śabdete*—by the word *ayana; kahe*—one means; *tāhāra*—of them; *āśraya*—the refuge.

TRANSLATION

"The word 'nāra' refers to the aggregate of all the living beings, and the word 'ayana' refers to the refuge of them all.

TEXT 39

অতএব তুমি হও মূল নারায়ণ ।
এই এক হেতু, শুন দ্বিতীয় কারণ ॥ ৩৯ ॥

ataeva tumi hao mūla nārāyaṇa
ei eka hetu, śuna dvitīya kāraṇa

ataeva—therefore; *tumi*—You; *hao*—are; *mūla*—original; *nārāyaṇa*—Nārāyaṇa; *ei*—this; *eka*—one; *hetu*—reason; *śuna*—please listen; *dvitīya*—second; *kāraṇa*—to the reason.

TRANSLATION

"You are therefore the original Nārāyaṇa. This is one reason; please listen as I state the second.

TEXT 40

জীবের ঈশ্বর—পুরুষাদি অবতার ।
তাঁহা সবা হৈতে তোমার ঐশ্বর্য অপার ॥ ৪০ ॥

jīvera īśvara—puruṣādi avatāra
tāṅhā sabā haite tomāra aiśvarya apāra

jīvera—of the living beings; *īśvara*—the Supreme Lord; *puruṣa-ādi*—*puruṣa* incarnations, etc.; *avatāra*—incarnations; *tāṅhā*—Them; *sabā*—all; *haite*—than; *tomāra*—Your; *aiśvarya*—opulences; *apāra*—boundless.

TRANSLATION

"The direct Lords of the living beings are the puruṣa incarnations. But Your opulence and power are more exalted than Theirs.

TEXT 41

অতএব অধীশ্বর তুমি সর্ব পিতা ।
তোমার শক্তিতে তাঁরা জগৎ-রক্ষিতা ॥ ৪১ ॥

ataeva adhīśvara tumi sarva pitā
tomāra śaktite tāṅrā jagat-rakṣitā

ataeva—therefore; *adhīśvara*—primeval Lord; *tumi*—You; *sarva*—of all; *pitā*—father; *tomāra*—Your; *śaktite*—by the energy; *tāṅrā*—They; *jagat*—of the cosmic creations; *rakṣitā*—protectors.

TRANSLATION

"Therefore You are the primeval Lord, the original father of everyone. They [the puruṣas] are protectors of the universes by Your power.

TEXT 42

নারের অয়ন যাতে করহ পালন ।
অতএব হও তুমি মূল নারায়ণ ॥ ৪২ ॥

nārera ayana yāte karaha pālana
ataeva hao tumi mūla nārāyaṇa

nārera—of the living beings; *ayana*—the shelters; *yāte*—those to whom; *karaha*—You give; *pālana*—protection; *ataeva*—therefore; *hao*—are; *tumi*—You; *mūla*—original; *nārāyaṇa*—Nārāyaṇa.

TRANSLATION

"Since You protect those who are the shelters of all living beings, You are the original Nārāyaṇa.

PURPORT

The controlling Deities of the living beings in the mundane worlds are the three *puruṣa-avatāras.* But the potent energy displayed by Śrī Kṛṣṇa is far more extensive than that of the *puruṣas.* Śrī Kṛṣṇa is therefore the original father and Lord who protects all creative manifestations through His various plenary portions. Since He sustains even the shelters of the collective living beings, there is no doubt that Śrī Kṛṣṇa is the original Nārāyaṇa.

TEXT 43

তৃতীয় কারণ শুন শ্রীভগবান্ ।
অনন্ত ব্রহ্মাণ্ড বহু বৈকুণ্ঠাদি ধাম ॥ ৪৩ ॥

tṛtīya kāraṇa śuna śrī-bhagavān
ananta brahmāṇḍa bahu vaikuṇṭhādi dhāma

tṛtīya—third; *kāraṇa*—reason; *śuna*—please hear; *śrī-bhagavān*—O Supreme Personality of Godhead; *ananta*—unlimited; *brahma-aṇḍa*—universes; *bahu*—many; *vaikuṇṭha-ādi*—Vaikuṇṭha, etc.; *dhāma*—planets.

TRANSLATION

"O my Lord, O Supreme Personality of Godhead! Kindly hear my third reason. There are countless universes and fathomless transcendental Vaikuṇṭhas.

TEXT 44

ইথে যত জীব, তার ত্রৈকালিক কর্ম ।
তাহা দেখ, সাক্ষী তুমি, জান সব মর্ম ॥ ৪৪ ॥

ithe yata jīva, tāra trai-kālika karma
tāhā dekha, sākṣī tumi, jāna saba marma

ithe—in these; *yata*—as many; *jīva*—living beings; *tāra*—of them; *trai-kālika*—past, present and future; *karma*—the activities; *tāhā*—that; *dekha*—You see; *sākṣi*—witness; *tumi*—You; *jāna*—You know; *saba*—of everything; *marma*—the essence.

TRANSLATION

"Both in this material world and in the transcendental world, You see all the deeds of all living beings, in the past, present and future. Since You are the witness of all such deeds, You know the essence of everything.

TEXT 45

তোমার দর্শনে সর্ব জগতের স্থিতি ।
তুমি না দেখিলে কারো নাহি স্থিতি গতি ॥ ৪৫ ॥

tomāra darśane sarva jagatera sthiti
tumi nā dekhile kāro nāhi sthiti gati

tomāra—Your; *darśane*—by the seeing; *sarva*—all; *jagatera*—of the universe; *sthiti*—maintenance; *tumi*—You; *nā dekhile*—in not seeing; *kāro*—of anyone; *nāhi*—there is not; *sthiti*—staying; *gati*—moving.

TRANSLATION

"All the worlds exist because You oversee them. None can live, move or have their being without Your supervision.

TEXT 46

নারের অয়ন যাতে কর দরশন।
তাহাতেও হও তুমি মূল নারায়ণ ॥ ৪৬ ॥

nārera ayana yāte kara daraśana
tāhāteo hao tumi mūla nārāyaṇa

nārera—of the living beings; *ayana*—the motion; *yāte*—since; *kara*—You do; *daraśana*—seeing; *tāhāteo*—therefore; *hao*—are; *tumi*—You; *mūla*—original; *nārāyaṇa*—Nārāyaṇa.

TRANSLATION

"You oversee the wanderings of all living beings. For this reason also, You are the primeval Lord Nārāyaṇa."

PURPORT

Śrī Kṛṣṇa, in His Paramātmā feature, lives in the hearts of all living beings in both the transcendental and mundane creations. As the Paramātmā, He witnesses all actions the living beings perform in all phases of time, namely past, present and future. Śrī Kṛṣṇa knows what the living beings have done for hundreds and thousands of past births, and He sees what they are doing now; therefore He knows the results of their present actions that will fructify in the future. As stated in the *Bhagavad-gītā*, the entire cosmic situation is created as soon as He glances over the material energy. Nothing can exist without His superintendence. Since He sees even the abode where the collective living beings rest, He is the original Nārāyaṇa.

TEXT 47

কৃষ্ণ কহেন—ব্রহ্মা, তোমার না বুঝি বচন।
জীব-হৃদি, জলে বৈসে সেই নারায়ণ ॥ ৪৭ ॥

kṛṣṇa kahena—brahmā, tomāra nā bujhi vacana
jīva-hṛdi, jale vaise sei nārāyaṇa

kṛṣṇa—Lord Kṛṣṇa; *kahena*—says; *brahmā*—O Brahmā; *tomāra*—your; *nā*—not; *bujhi*—I understand; *vacana*—speech; *jīva*—of the living entity; *hṛdi*—in the heart; *jale*—in the water; *vaise*—sits; *sei*—that; *nārāyaṇa*—Lord Nārāyaṇa.

TRANSLATION

Kṛṣṇa said, "Brahmā, I cannot understand what you are saying. Lord Nārāyaṇa is He who sits in the hearts of all living beings and lies down in the waters of the Kāraṇa Ocean."

TEXT 48

ব্রহ্মা কহে—জলে জীবে যেই নারায়ণ ।
সে সব তোমার অংশ—এ সত্য বচন ॥ ৪৮ ॥

brahmā kahe—jale jīve yei nārāyaṇa
se saba tomāra aṁśa—e satya vacana

brahmā—Lord Brahmā; *kahe*—says; *jale*—in the water; *jīve*—in the living being; *yei*—who; *nārāyaṇa*—Nārāyaṇa; *se*—They; *saba*—all; *tomāra*—Your; *aṁśa*—plenary part; *e*—this; *satya*—truthful; *vacana*—word.

TRANSLATION

Brahmā replied, "What I have said is true. The same Lord Nārāyaṇa who lives on the waters and in the hearts of all living beings is but a plenary portion of You.

TEXT 49

কারণাব্ধি-গর্ভোদক-ক্ষীরোদকশায়ী ।
মায়াদ্বারে সৃষ্টি করে, তাতে সব মায়ী ॥ ৪৯ ॥

kāraṇābdhi-garbhodaka-kṣīrodaka-śāyī
māyā-dvāre sṛṣṭi kare, tāte saba māyī

kāraṇa-abdhi—Kāraṇodakaśāyī Viṣṇu; *garbha-udaka*—Garbhodakaśāyī Viṣṇu; *kṣīra-udaka-śāyī*—Kṣīrodakaśāyī Viṣṇu; *māyā-dvāre*—with the material energy; *sṛṣṭi*—creation; *kare*—They do; *tāte*—therefore; *saba*—all; *māyī*—connected with *māyā.*

TRANSLATION

"The Kāraṇodakaśāyī, Garbhodakaśāyī and Kṣīrodakaśāyī forms of Nārāyaṇa all create in cooperation with the material energy. In this way They are attached to māyā.

TEXT 50

সেই তিন জলশায়ী সর্ব-অন্তর্যামী ।
ব্রহ্মাণ্ডবৃন্দের আত্মা যে পুরুষ-নামী ॥ ৫০ ॥

sei tina jala-śāyī sarva-antaryāmī
brahmāṇḍa-vṛndera ātmā ye puruṣa-nāmī

sei—these; *tina*—three; *jala-śāyī*—lying in the water; *sarva*—of all; *antaḥ yāmī*—the Supersoul; *brahma-aṇḍa*—of universes; *vṛndera*—of the multitude; *ātmā*—Supersoul; *ye*—who; *puruṣa—puruṣa; nāmī*—named.

TRANSLATION

"These three Viṣṇus lying in the water are the Supersoul of everything. The Supersoul of all the universes is known as the first puruṣa.

TEXT 51

হিরণ্যগর্ভের আত্মা গর্ভোদকশায়ী ।
ব্যষ্টিজীব-অন্তর্যামী ক্ষীরোদকশায়ী ॥ ৫১ ॥

hiraṇya-garbhera ātmā garbhodaka-śāyī
vyaṣṭi-jīva-antaryāmī kṣīrodaka-śāyī

hiraṇya-garbhera—of the total of the living entities; *ātmā*—the Supersoul; *garbha-udaka-śāyī*—Garbhodakaśāyī Viṣṇu; *vyaṣṭi*—the individual; *jīva*—of the living entity; *antaḥ-yāmī*—Supersoul; *kṣīra-udaka-śāyī*—Kṣīrodakaśāyī Viṣṇu.

TRANSLATION

"Garbhodakaśāyī Viṣṇu is the Supersoul of the aggregate of living entities, and Kṣīrodakaśāyī Viṣṇu is the Supersoul of each individual living being.

TEXT 52

এ সভার দর্শনেতে আছে মায়াগন্ধ ।
তুরীয় কৃষ্ণের নাহি মায়ার সম্বন্ধ ॥ ৫২ ॥

e sabhāra darśanete āche māyā-gandha
turīya kṛṣṇera nāhi māyāra sambandha

e—this; *sabhāra*—of the assembly; *darśanete*—in seeing; *āche*—there is; *māyā-gandha*—connection with *māyā; turīya*—the fourth; *kṛṣṇera*—of Lord Kṛṣṇa; *nāhi*—there is not; *māyāra*—of the material energy; *sambandha*—connection.

TRANSLATION

"Superficially we see that these puruṣas have a relationship with māyā, but above them, in the fourth dimension, is Lord Kṛṣṇa, who has no contact with the material energy.

PURPORT

The three *puruṣas*—Kāraṇodakaśāyī Viṣṇu, Garbhodakaśāyī Viṣṇu and Kṣīrodakaśāyī Viṣṇu—all have a relationship with the material energy, called *māyā,* because through *māyā* They create the material cosmos. These three *puruṣas,* who lie on the Kāraṇa, Garbha and Kṣīra oceans respectively, are the Supersoul of everything that be: Kāraṇodakaśāyī Viṣṇu is the Supersoul of the collective universes, Garbhodakaśāyī Viṣṇu is the Supersoul of the collective living beings, and Kṣīrodakaśāyī Viṣṇu is the Supersoul of all individual living entities. Because all of Them are somehow attracted to the affairs of the material energy, They can be said to have some affection for *māyā.* But the transcendental position of Śrī Kṛṣṇa Himself is not even slightly tinged by *māyā.* His transcendental state is called *turīya,* or the fourth-dimensional stage.

TEXT 53

বিরাড্ হিরণ্যগর্ভশ্চ কারণং চেত্যুপাধয়ঃ ।
ঈশস্য যদ্বিভির্হীনং তুরীয়ং তৎ প্রচক্ষতে ॥ ৫৩ ॥

virāḍ hiraṇya-garbhaś ca
kāraṇaṁ cety upādhayaḥ

īśasya yat tribhir hīnaṁ
turīyaṁ tat pracakṣate

virāṭ—the *virāṭ* manifestation; *hiraṇya-garbhaḥ*—the *hiraṇyagarbha* manifestation; *ca*—and; *kāraṇam*—the *kāraṇa* manifestation; *ca*—and; *iti*—thus; *upādhayaḥ*—particular designations; *īśasya*—of the Lord; *yat*—that which; *tribhiḥ*—these three; *hīnam*—without; *turīyam*—the fourth; *tat*—that; *pracakṣate*—is considered.

TRANSLATION

"In the material world the Lord is designated as virāṭ, hiraṇya-garbha and kāraṇa. But beyond these three designations, the Lord is ultimately in the fourth dimension.'

PURPORT

Virāṭ (the phenomenal manifestation of the Supreme Whole), *hiraṇya-garbha* (the numinous soul of everything), and *kāraṇa* (the cause, or causal nature) are all but designations of the *puruṣas,* who are responsible for material creation. The transcendental position surpasses these designations and is therefore called the position of the fourth dimension. This is a quotation from Śrīdhara Svāmī's commentary on the Eleventh Canto, Fifteenth Chapter, verse 16, of *Śrīmad-Bhāgavatam.*

TEXT 54

যদ্যপি তিনের মায়া লইয়া ব্যবহার ।
তথাপি তৎস্পর্শ নাহি, সভে মায়া-পার ॥ ৫৪ ॥

yadyapi tinera māyā la-iyā vyavahāra
tathāpi tat-sparśa nāhi, sabhe māyā-pāra

yadyapi—although; *tinera*—of these three; *māyā*—the material energy; *la-iyā*—taking; *vyavahāra*—the dealings; *tathāpi*—still; *tat*—of that; *sparśa*—the touch; *nāhi*—there is not; *sabhe*—all of Them; *māyā-pāra*—beyond the material energy.

TRANSLATION

"Although these three features of the Lord deal directly with the material energy, none of Them are touched by it. They are all beyond illusion.

TEXT 55

এতদীশনমীশস্য প্রকৃতিস্থোঽপি তদ্গুণৈঃ ।
ন যুজ্যতে সদাত্মস্থৈর্যথা বুদ্ধিস্তদাশ্রয়া ॥ ৫৫ ॥

etad īśanam īśasya
prakṛti-stho 'pi tad-guṇaiḥ
na yujyate sadātma-sthair
yathā buddhis tad-āśrayā

etat—this; *īśanam*—opulence; *īśasya*—of the Supreme Lord; *prakṛti-sthaḥ*—situated in the material nature; *api*—although; *tat*—of *māyā; guṇaiḥ*—by the qualities; *na*—not; *yujyate*—is affected; *sadā*—always; *ātma-sthaiḥ*—which are situated in His own energy; *yathā*—as also; *buddhiḥ*—the intelligence; *tat*—of Him; *āśrayā*—which has taken shelter.

TRANSLATION

"'This is the opulence of the Lord: Although situated in the material nature, He is never affected by the modes of nature. Similarly, those who have surrendered to Him and fixed their intelligence upon Him are not influenced by the modes of nature.'

PURPORT

This text is from *Śrīmad-Bhāgavatam* (1.11.38). Those who have taken shelter of the lotus feet of the Personality of Godhead do not identify with the material world, even while living in it. Pure devotees may deal with the three modes of material nature, but because of their transcendental intelligence in Kṛṣṇa consciousness, they are not influenced by the material qualities. The spell of material activities does not attract such devotees. Therefore, the Supreme Lord and His devotees acting under Him are always free from material contamination.

TEXT 56

সেই তিন জনের তুমি পরম আশ্রয় ।
তুমি মূল নারায়ণ—ইথে কি সংশয় ॥ ৫৬ ॥

sei tina janera tumi parama āśraya
tumi mūla nārāyaṇa—ithe ki saṁśaya

sei—these; *tina*—three; *janera*—of the plenary portions; *tumi*—You; *parama*—ultimate; *āśraya*—shelter; *tumi*—You; *mūla*—primeval; *nārāyaṇa*—Nārāyaṇa; *ithe*—in this; *ki*—what; *saṁśaya*—doubt.

TRANSLATION

"You are the ultimate shelter of these three plenary portions. Thus there is not the slightest doubt that You are the primeval Nārāyaṇa.

PURPORT

Brahmā has confirmed that Lord Kṛṣṇa is the Supreme, the source of the three manifestations known as Kṣīrodakaśāyī Viṣṇu, Garbhodakaśāyī Viṣṇu and Kāraṇodakaśāyī Viṣṇu (Mahā-Viṣṇu). For His pastimes, Lord Kṛṣṇa has four original manifestations—namely Vāsudeva, Saṅkarṣaṇa, Pradyumna and Aniruddha. The first *puruṣa-avatāra*, Mahā-Viṣṇu in the Causal Ocean, who is the creator of the aggregate material energy, is an expansion of Saṅkarṣaṇa; the second *puruṣa*, Garbhodakaśāyī Viṣṇu, is an expansion of Pradyumna; and the third *puruṣa*, Kṣīrodakaśāyī Viṣṇu, is an expansion of Aniruddha. All these are within the category of manifestations of Nārāyaṇa, who is a manifestation of Śrī Kṛṣṇa.

TEXT 57

সেই তিনের অংশী পরব্যোম-নারায়ণ ।
তেঁহ তোমার বিলাস, তুমি মূল-নারায়ণ ॥ ৫৭ ॥

sei tinera aṁśī paravyoma-nārāyaṇa
teṅha tomāra vilāsa, tumi mūla-nārāyaṇa

sei—these; *tinera*—of the three; *aṁśī*—source; *para-vyoma*—in the spiritual sky; *nārāyaṇa*—Lord Nārāyaṇa; *teṅha*—He; *tomāra*—Your; *vilāsa*—pastime expansion; *tumi*—You; *mūla*—original; *nārāyaṇa*—Nārāyaṇa.

TRANSLATION

"The source of these three features is the Nārāyaṇa in the spiritual sky. He is Your vilāsa expansion. Therefore You are the ultimate Nārāyaṇa."

TEXT 58

অতএব ব্রহ্মবাক্যে—পরব্যোম-নারায়ণ ।
তেঁহো কৃষ্ণের বিলাস—এই তত্ত্ব-বিবরণ ॥ ৫৮ ॥

ataeva brahma-vākye—paravyoma-nārāyaṇa
teṅho kṛṣṇera vilāsa—ei tattva-vivaraṇa

ataeva—therefore; *brahma*—of Lord Brahmā; *vākye*—in the speech; *para-vyoma*—in the spiritual sky; *nārāyaṇa*—Lord Nārāyaṇa; *teṅho*—He; *kṛṣṇera*—of Lord Kṛṣṇa; *vilāsa*—pastime incarnation; *ei*—this; *tattva*—of the truth; *vivaraṇa*—description.

TRANSLATION

Therefore according to the authority of Brahmā, the Nārāyaṇa who is the predominating Deity in the transcendental world is but the vilāsa feature of Kṛṣṇa. This has now been conclusively proved.

TEXT 59

এই শ্লোক তত্ত্ব-লক্ষণ ভাগবত-সার ।
পরিভাষা-রূপে ইহার সর্বত্রাধিকার ॥ ৫৯ ॥

ei śloka tattva-lakṣaṇa bhāgavata-sāra
paribhāṣā-rūpe ihāra sarvatrādhikāra

ei—this; *śloka*—verse; *tattva*—the truth; *lakṣaṇa*—indicating; *bhāgavata*—of *Śrīmad-Bhāgavatam*; *sāra*—the essence; *paribhāṣā*—of synonyms; *rūpe*—in the form; *ihāra*—of this (*Śrīmad-Bhāgavatam*); *sarvatra*—everywhere; *adhikāra*—jurisdiction.

TRANSLATION

The truth indicated in this verse [text 30] is the essence of Śrīmad-Bhāgavatam. This conclusion, through synonyms, applies everywhere.

TEXT 60

ব্রহ্ম, আত্মা, ভগবান্—কৃষ্ণের বিহার ।
এ অর্থ না জানি' মূর্খ অর্থ করে আর ॥ ৬০ ॥

brahma, ātmā, bhagavān—kṛṣṇera vihāra
e artha nā jāni' mūrkha artha kare āra

brahma—impersonal Brahman; *ātmā*—Supersoul; *bhagavān*—the Supreme Personality of Godhead; *kṛṣṇera*—of Lord Kṛṣṇa; *vihāra*—

manifestations; *e*—this; *artha*—meaning; *nā*—not; *jāni'*—knowing; *mūrkha*—fools; *artha*—meaning; *kare*—make; *āra*—other.

TRANSLATION

Not knowing that Brahman, Paramātmā and Bhagavān are all features of Kṛṣṇa, foolish scholars speculate in various ways.

TEXT 61

অবতারী নারায়ণ, কৃষ্ণ অবতার ।
তেঁহ চতুর্ভুজ, ইঁহ মনুষ্য-আকার ॥ ৬১ ॥

avatārī nārāyaṇa, kṛṣṇa avatāra
teṅha catur-bhuja, iṅha manuṣya-ākāra

avatārī—source of incarnations; *nārāyaṇa*—Lord Nārāyaṇa; *kṛṣṇa*—Lord Kṛṣṇa; *avatāra*—incarnation; *teṅha*—that; *catuḥ-bhuja*—four arms; *iṅha*—this; *manuṣya*—like a man; *ākāra*—form.

TRANSLATION

Because Nārāyaṇa has four hands whereas Kṛṣṇa looks just like a man, they say that Nārāyaṇa is the original God whereas Kṛṣṇa is but an incarnation.

PURPORT

Some scholars argue that because Nārāyaṇa has four hands whereas Śrī Kṛṣṇa has only two, Nārāyaṇa is the original Personality of Godhead and Kṛṣṇa is His incarnation. Such unintelligent scholars do not understand the features of the Absolute.

TEXT 62

এইমতে নানারূপ করে পূর্বপক্ষ ।
তাহারে নির্জিতে ভাগবত-পদ্য দক্ষ ॥ ৬২ ॥

ei-mate nānā-rūpa kare pūrva-pakṣa
tāhāre nirjite bhāgavata-padya dakṣa

ei-mate—thus; *nānā*—many; *rūpa*—forms; *kare*—takes; *pūrva-pakṣa*—the objections; *tāhāre*—them; *nirjite*—overcoming; *bhāgavata*—of *Śrīmad-Bhāgavatam; padya*—poetry; *dakṣa*—expert.

TRANSLATION

In this way their arguments appear in various forms, but the poetry of the Bhāgavatam expertly refutes them all.

TEXT 63

বদন্তি তত্তত্ত্ববিদস্তত্ত্বং যজ্জ্ঞানমদ্বয়ম্ ।
ব্রহ্মেতি পরমাত্মেতি ভগবানিতি শব্দ্যতে ॥ ৬৩ ॥

vadanti tat tattva-vidas
tattvaṁ yaj jñānam advayam
brahmeti paramātmeti
bhagavān iti śabdyate

vadanti—they say; *tat*—that; *tattva-vidaḥ*—learned souls; *tattvam*—the Absolute Truth; *yat*—which; *jñānam*—knowledge; *advayam*—non-dual; *brahma*—Brahman; *iti*—thus; *paramātmā*—Paramātmā; *iti*—thus; *bhagavān*—Bhagavān; *iti*—thus; *śabdyate*—is known.

TRANSLATION

"Learned transcendentalists who know the Absolute Truth say that it is nondual knowledge and is called impersonal Brahman, localized Paramātmā and the Personality of Godhead."

PURPORT

This text is from *Śrīmad-Bhāgavatam* (1.2.11).

TEXT 64

শুন ভাই এই শ্লোক করহ বিচার ।
এক মুখ্যতত্ত্ব, তিন তাহার প্রচার ॥ ৬৪ ॥

śuna bhāi ei śloka karaha vicāra
eka mukhya-tattva, tina tāhāra pracāra

śuna—please listen; *bhāi*—brothers; *ei*—this; *śloka*—verse; *karaha*—please give; *vicāra*—consideration; *eka*—one; *mukhya*—principal; *tattva*—truth; *tina*—three; *tāhāra*—of that; *pracāra*—manifestations.

TRANSLATION

My dear brothers, kindly listen to the explanation of this verse and consider its meaning: the one original entity is known in His three different features.

TEXT 65

অদ্বয়জ্ঞান তত্ত্ববস্তু কৃষ্ণের স্বরূপ ।
ব্রহ্ম, আত্মা, ভগবান্—তিন তাঁর রূপ ॥ ৬৫ ॥

advaya-jñāna tattva-vastu kṛṣṇera svarūpa
brahma, ātmā, bhagavān—tina tāṅra rūpa

advaya-jñāna—knowledge without duality; *tattva-vastu*—the Absolute Truth; *kṛṣṇera*—of Lord Kṛṣṇa; *sva-rūpa*—own nature; *brahma*—Brahman; *ātmā*—Paramātmā; *bhagavān*—the Supreme Personality of Godhead; *tina*—three; *tāṅra*—of Him; *rūpa*—forms.

TRANSLATION

Lord Kṛṣṇa Himself is the one undivided Absolute Truth, the ultimate reality. He manifests Himself in three features—as Brahman, Paramātmā and Bhagavān.

PURPORT

In the verse from *Śrīmad-Bhāgavatam* cited above (*Bhāg.* 1.2.11), the principal word, *bhagavān*, indicates the Personality of Godhead, and Brahman and Paramātmā are concomitants deduced from the Absolute Personality, as a government and its ministers are deductions from the supreme executive head. In other words, the principal truth is exhibited in three different phases. The Absolute Truth, the Personality of Godhead Śrī Kṛṣṇa (Bhagavān), is also known as Brahman and Paramātmā, although all these features are identical.

TEXT 66

এই শ্লোকের অর্থে তুমি হৈলা নির্বচন ।
আর এক শুন ভাগবতের বচন ॥ ৬৬ ॥

ei ślokera arthe tumi hailā nirvacana
āra eka śuna bhāgavatera vacana

ei—this; *ślokera*—of the verse; *arthe*—by the meaning; *tumi*—you; *hailā*—have become; *nirvacana*—speechless; *āra*—other; *eka*—one; *śuna*—please hear; *bhāgavatera*—of *Śrīmad-Bhāgavatam; vacana*—speech.

TRANSLATION

The import of this verse has stopped you from arguing. Now listen to another verse of Śrīmad-Bhāgavatam.

TEXT 67

এতে চাংশকলাঃ পুংসঃ কৃষ্ণস্তু ভগবান্ স্বয়ম্ ।
ইন্দ্রারি-ব্যাকুলং লোকং মৃড়য়ন্তি যুগে যুগে ॥ ৬৭ ॥

ete cāṁśa-kalāḥ puṁsaḥ
kṛṣṇas tu bhagavān svayam
indrāri-vyākulaṁ lokaṁ
mṛḍayanti yuge yuge

ete—these; *ca*—and; *aṁśa*—plenary portions; *kalāḥ*—parts of plenary portions; *puṁsaḥ*—of the *puruṣa-avatāras; kṛṣṇaḥ*—Lord Kṛṣṇa; *tu*—but; *bhagavān*—the Supreme Personality of Godhead; *svayam*—Himself; *indra-ari*—the enemies of Lord Indra; *vyākulam*—full of; *lokam*—the world; *mṛḍayanti*—make happy; *yuge yuge*—at the right time in each age.

TRANSLATION

"All these incarnations of Godhead are either plenary portions or parts of the plenary portions of the puruṣa-avatāras. But Kṛṣṇa is the Supreme Personality of Godhead Himself. In every age He protects the world through His different features when the world is disturbed by the enemies of Indra."

PURPORT

This statement of *Śrīmad-Bhāgavatam* (1.3.28) definitely negates the concept that Śrī Kṛṣṇa is an *avatāra* of Viṣṇu or Nārāyaṇa. Lord Śrī Kṛṣṇa is the original Personality of Godhead, the supreme cause of all causes. This verse clearly indicates that incarnations of the Personality of Godhead such as Śrī Rāma, Nṛsiṁha and Varāha all undoubtedly belong to the Viṣṇu group, but all of Them are either plenary portions or portions of plenary portions of the original Personality of Godhead, Lord Śrī Kṛṣṇa.

TEXT 68

সব অবতারের করি সামান্য-লক্ষণ ।
তার মধ্যে কৃষ্ণচন্দ্রের করিল গণন ॥ ৬৮ ॥

saba avatārera kari sāmānya-lakṣaṇa
tāra madhye kṛṣṇa-candrera karila gaṇana

saba—all; *avatārera*—of the incarnations; *kari*—making; *sāmānya*—general; *lakṣaṇa*—symptoms; *tāra*—of them; *madhye*—in the middle; *kṛṣṇa-candrera*—of Lord Śrī Kṛṣṇa; *karila*—did; *gaṇana*—counting.

TRANSLATION

The Bhāgavatam describes the symptoms and deeds of the incarnations in general and counts Śrī Kṛṣṇa among them.

TEXT 69

তবে সূত গোসাঞি মনে পাঞা বড় ভয়।
যার যে লক্ষণ তাহা করিল নিশ্চয় ॥ ৬৯ ॥

tabe sūta gosāñi mane pāñā baḍa bhaya
yāra ye lakṣaṇa tāhā karila niścaya

tabe—then; *sūta gosāñi*—Sūta Gosvāmī; *mane*—in the mind; *pāñā*—obtaining; *baḍa*—great; *bhaya*—fear; *yāra*—of whom; *ye*—which; *lakṣaṇa*—symptoms; *tāhā*—that; *karila*—he made; *niścaya*—certainly.

TRANSLATION

This made Sūta Gosvāmī greatly apprehensive. Therefore he distinguished each incarnation by its specific symptoms.

TEXT 70

অবতার সব—পুরুষের কলা, অংশ।
স্বয়ং-ভগবান্ কৃষ্ণ সর্ব-অবতংস ॥ ৭০ ॥

avatāra saba—puruṣera kalā, aṁśa
svayaṁ-bhagavān kṛṣṇa sarva-avataṁsa

avatāra—the incarnations; *saba*—all; *puruṣera*—of the *puruṣa-avatāras; kalā*—parts of plenary portions; *aṁśa*—plenary portions; *svayam*—Himself; *bhagavān*—the Supreme Personality of Godhead; *kṛṣṇa*—Lord Kṛṣṇa; *sarva*—of all; *avataṁsa*—crest.

TRANSLATION

All the incarnations of Godhead are plenary portions or parts of the plenary portions of the puruṣa-avatāras, but the primeval Lord is Śrī Kṛṣṇa. He is the Supreme Personality of Godhead, the fountainhead of all incarnations.

TEXT 71

পূর্বপক্ষ কহে—তোমার ভালত' ব্যাখ্যান ।
পরব্যোম-নারায়ণ স্বয়ং-ভগবান্ ॥ ৭১ ॥

pūrva-pakṣa kahe—tomāra bhāla ta' vyākhyāna
paravyoma-nārāyaṇa svayaṁ-bhagavān

pūrva-pakṣa—opposing side; *kahe*—says; *tomāra*—your; *bhāla*—nice; *ta'*—certainly; *vyākhyāna*—exposition; *para-vyoma*—situated in the spiritual sky; *nārāyaṇa*—Lord Nārāyaṇa; *svayam*—Himself; *bhagavān*—the Supreme Personality of Godhead.

TRANSLATION

An opponent may say, "This is your interpretation, but actually the Supreme Lord is Nārāyaṇa, who is in the transcendental realm.

TEXT 72

তেঁহ আসি' কৃষ্ণরূপে করেন অবতার ।
এই অর্থ শ্লোকে দেখি কি আর বিচার ॥ ৭২ ॥

teṅha āsi' kṛṣṇa-rūpe karena avatāra
ei artha śloke dekhi ki āra vicāra

teṅha—He (Nārāyaṇa); *āsi'*—coming; *kṛṣṇa-rūpe*—in the form of Lord Kṛṣṇa; *karena*—makes; *avatāra*—incarnation; *ei*—this; *artha*—meaning; *śloke*—in the verse; *dekhi*—I see; *ki*—what; *āra*—other; *vicāra*—consideration.

TRANSLATION

"He [Nārāyaṇa] incarnates as Lord Kṛṣṇa. This is the meaning of the verse as I see it. There is no need for further consideration."

TEXT 73

তারে কহে—কেনে কর কুতর্কানুমান ।
শাস্ত্রবিরুদ্ধার্থ কভু না হয় প্রমাণ ॥ ৭৩ ॥

tāre kahe—kene kara kutarkānumāna
śāstra-viruddhārtha kabhu nā haya pramāṇa

tāre—to him; *kahe*—one says; *kene*—why; *kara*—you make; *kutarka*—of a fallacious argument; *anumāna*—conjecture; *śāstra-viruddha*—contrary to scripture; *artha*—a meaning; *kabhu*—at any time; *nā*—not; *haya*—is; *pramāṇa*—evidence.

TRANSLATION

To such a misguided interpreter we may reply, "Why should you suggest such fallacious logic? An interpretation is never accepted as evidence if it opposes the principles of scripture.

TEXT 74

অনুবাদমনুক্ত্বা তু ন বিধেয়মুদীরয়েৎ ।
ন হ্যলব্ধাস্পদং কিঞ্চিৎ কুত্রচিৎ প্রতিতিষ্ঠতি ॥ ৭৪ ॥

anuvādam anuktvā tu
na vidheyam udīrayet
na hy alabdhāspadaṁ kiñcit
kutracit pratitiṣṭhati

anuvādam—the subject; *anuktvā*—not stating; *tu*—but; *na*—not; *vidheyam*—the predicate; *udīrayet*—one should speak; *na*—not; *hi*—certainly; *alabdha-āspadam*—without a secure position; *kiñcit*—something; *kutracit*—anywhere; *pratitiṣṭhati*—stands.

TRANSLATION

"'One should not state a predicate before its subject, for it cannot thus stand without proper support.'

PURPORT

This rhetorical rule appears in the *Ekādaśī-tattva*, Thirteenth Canto, in connection with the metaphorical use of words. An unknown object should not be put before the known subject because the object has no meaning if the subject is not first given.

TEXT 75

অনুবাদ না কহিয়া না কহি বিধেয় ।
আগে অনুবাদ কহি, পশ্চাদ্বিধেয় ॥ ৭৫ ॥

anuvāda nā kahiyā nā kahi vidheya
āge anuvāda kahi, paścād vidheya

anuvāda—the subject; *nā kahiyā*—not saying; *nā*—not; *kahi*—I say; *vidheya*—the predicate; *āge*—first; *anuvāda*—the subject; *kahi*—I say; *paścāt*—afterwards; *vidheya*—the predicate.

TRANSLATION

"If I do not state a subject, I do not state a predicate. First I speak the former and then I speak the latter.

TEXT 76

'বিধেয়' কহিয়ে তারে, যে বস্তু অজ্ঞাত ।
'অনুবাদ' কহি তারে, যেই হয় জ্ঞাত ॥ ৭৬ ॥

'vidheya' kahiye tāre, ye vastu ajñāta
'anuvāda' kahi tāre, yei haya jñāta

vidheya—the predicate; *kahiye*—I say; *tāre*—to him; *ye*—that; *vastu*—thing; *ajñāta*—unknown; *anuvāda*—the subject; *kahi*—I say; *tāre*—to him; *yei*—that which; *haya*—is; *jñāta*—known.

TRANSLATION

"The predicate of a sentence is what is unknown to the reader, whereas the subject is what is known to him.

TEXT 77

যৈছে কহি,—এই বিপ্র পরম পণ্ডিত ।
বিপ্র—অনুবাদ, ইহার বিধেয়—পাণ্ডিত্য ॥ ৭৭ ॥

yaiche kahi,—ei vipra parama paṇḍita
vipra—anuvāda, ihāra vidheya—pāṇḍitya

yaiche—just as; *kahi*—I say; *ei*—this; *vipra*—*brāhmaṇa; parama*—great; *paṇḍita*—learned man; *vipra*—the *brāhmaṇa; anuvāda*—subject; *ihāra*—of this; *vidheya*—predicate; *pāṇḍitya*—erudition.

TRANSLATION

"For example, we may say, 'This vipra is a greatly learned man.' In this sentence, the vipra is the subject, and the predicate is his erudition.

TEXT 78

বিপ্রত্ব বিখ্যাত তার পাণ্ডিত্য অজ্ঞাত ।
অতএব বিপ্র আগে, পাণ্ডিত্য পশ্চাত ॥ ৭৮ ॥

vipratva vikhyāta tāra pāṇḍitya ajñāta
ataeva vipra āge, pāṇḍitya paścāta

vipratva—the quality of being a *vipra; vikhyāta*—well known; *tāra*—his; *pāṇḍitya*—erudition; *ajñāta*—unknown; *ataeva*—therefore; *vipra*—the word *vipra; āge*—first; *pāṇḍitya*—erudition; *paścāta*—afterwards.

TRANSLATION

"The man's being a vipra is known, but his erudition is unknown. Therefore the person is identified first and his erudition later.

TEXT 79

তৈছে ইঁহ অবতার সব হৈল জ্ঞাত ।
কার অবতার ?—এই বস্তু অবিজ্ঞাত ॥ ৭৯ ॥

taiche iṅha avatāra saba haila jñāta
kāra avatāra?—ei vastu avijñāta

taiche—in the same way; *iṅha*—these; *avatāra*—incarnations; *saba*—all; *haila*—were; *jñāta*—known; *kāra*—whose; *avatāra*—incarnations; *ei*—this; *vastu*—thing; *avijñāta*—unknown.

TRANSLATION

"In the same way, all these incarnations were known, but whose incarnations they are was unknown.

TEXT 80

'এতে'-শব্দে অবতারের আগে অনুবাদ ।
'পুরুষের অংশ' পাছে বিধেয়-সংবাদ ॥ ৮০ ॥

'ete'-śabde avatārera āge anuvāda
'puruṣera aṁśa' pāche vidheya-saṁvāda

ete-śabde—in the word *ete* (these); *avatārera*—of the incarnations; *āge*—first; *anuvāda*—the subject; *puruṣera*—of the *puruṣa-avatāras; aṁśa*—plenary portions; *pāche*—afterwards; *vidheya*—of the predicate; *saṁvāda*—message.

TRANSLATION

"First the word 'ete' ['these'] establishes the subject [the incarnations]. Then 'plenary portions of the puruṣa-avatāras' follows as the predicate.

TEXT 81

তৈছে কৃষ্ণ অবতার-ভিতরে হৈল জ্ঞাত ।
তাঁহার বিশেষ-জ্ঞান সেই অবিজ্ঞাত ॥ ৮১ ॥

taiche kṛṣṇa avatāra-bhitare haila jñāta
tāṅhāra viśeṣa-jñāna sei avijñāta

taiche—in the same way; *kṛṣṇa*—Lord Kṛṣṇa; *avatāra-bhitare*—among the incarnations; *haila*—was; *jñāta*—known; *tāṅhāra*—of Him; *viśeṣa-jñāna*—specific knowledge; *sei*—that; *avijñāta*—unknown.

TRANSLATION

"In the same way, when Kṛṣṇa was first counted among the incarnations, specific knowledge about Him was still unknown.

TEXT 82

অতএব 'কৃষ্ণ'-শব্দ আগে অনুবাদ ।
'স্বয়ং-ভগবত্তা' পিছে বিধেয়-সংবাদ ॥ ৮২ ॥

ataeva 'kṛṣṇa'-śabda āge anuvāda
'svayaṁ-bhagavattā' piche vidheya-saṁvāda

ataeva—therefore; *kṛṣṇa-śabda*—the word *kṛṣṇa; āge*—first; *anuvāda*—the subject; *svayam-bhagavattā*—being Himself the Supreme Personality of Godhead; *piche*—afterwards; *vidheya*—of the predicate; *saṁvāda*—the message

TRANSLATION

"Therefore first the word 'kṛṣṇa' appears as the subject, followed by the predicate, describing Him as the original Personality of Godhead.

TEXT 83

কৃষ্ণের স্বয়ং-ভগবত্তা—ইহা হৈল সাধ্য ।
স্বয়ং-ভগবানের কৃষ্ণত্ব হৈল বাধ্য ॥ ৮৩ ॥

kṛṣṇera svayaṁ-bhagavattā—ihā haila sādhya
svayaṁ-bhagavānera kṛṣṇatva haila bādhya

kṛṣṇera—of Lord Kṛṣṇa; *svayam-bhagavattā*—the quality of being Himself the Supreme Personality of Godhead; *ihā*—this; *haila*—was; *sādhya*—to be established; *svayam-bhagavānera*—of the Supreme Personality of Godhead; *kṛṣṇatva*—the quality of being Lord Kṛṣṇa; *haila*—was; *bādhya*—obligatory

TRANSLATION

"This establishes that Śrī Kṛṣṇa is the original Personality of Godhead. The original Personality of Godhead is therefore necessarily Kṛṣṇa.

TEXT 84

কৃষ্ণ যদি অংশ হৈত, অংশী নারায়ণ ।
তবে বিপরীত হৈত সূতের বচন ॥ ৮৪ ॥

kṛṣṇa yadi aṁśa haita, aṁśī nārāyaṇa
tabe viparīta haita sūtera vacana

kṛṣṇa—Lord Kṛṣṇa; *yadi*—if; *aṁśa*—plenary portion; *haita*—were; *aṁśī*—the source of all expansions; *nārāyaṇa*—Lord Nārāyaṇa; *tabe*—then; *viparīta*—the reverse; *haita*—would have been; *sūtera*—of Sūta Gosvāmī; *vacana*—the statement.

TRANSLATION

"Had Kṛṣṇa been the plenary portion and Nārāyaṇa the primeval Lord, the statement of Sūta Gosvāmī would have been reversed.

TEXT 85

নারায়ণ অংশী যেই স্বয়ং-ভগবান্ ।
তেঁহ শ্রীকৃষ্ণ—ঐছে করিত ব্যাখান ॥ ৮৫ ॥

nārāyaṇa aṁśī yei svayaṁ-bhagavān
teṅha śrī-kṛṣṇa—aiche karita vyākhyāna

nārāyaṇa—Lord Nārāyaṇa; *aṁśī*—the source of all incarnations; *yei*—who; *svayam-bhagavān*—Himself the Supreme Personality of Godhead; *teṅha*—He; *śrī-kṛṣṇa*—Lord Kṛṣṇa; *aiche*—in such away; *karita*—would have made; *vyākhyāna*—explanation.

TRANSLATION

"Thus he would have said, 'Nārāyaṇa, the source of all incarnations, is the original Personality of Godhead. He has appeared as Śrī Kṛṣṇa.'

TEXT 86

ভ্রম, প্রমাদ, বিপ্রলিপ্সা, করণাপাটব ।
আর্য-বিজ্ঞবাক্যে নাহি দোষ এই সব ॥ ৮৬ ॥

bhrama, pramāda, vipralipsā, karaṇāpāṭava
ārṣa-vijña-vākye nāhi doṣa ei saba

bhrama—mistakes; *pramāda*—illusion; *vipralipsā*—cheating; *karaṇa-apāṭava*—imperfectness of the senses; *ārṣa*—of the authoritative sages; *vijña-vākye*—in the wise speech; *nāhi*—not; *doṣa*—faults; *ei*—these; *saba*—all.

TRANSLATION

"Mistakes, illusions, cheating and defective perception do not occur in the sayings of the authoritative sages.

PURPORT

Śrīmad-Bhāgavatam has listed the *avatāras,* the plenary expansions of the *puruṣa,* and Lord Kṛṣṇa appears among them. But the *Bhāgavatam* further explains Lord Kṛṣṇa's specific position as the Supreme Personality of Godhead. Since Lord Kṛṣṇa is the original Personality of Godhead, reason and argument establish that His position is always supreme.

Had Kṛṣṇa been a plenary expansion of Nārāyaṇa, the original verse would have been differently composed; indeed, its order would have been reversed. But there cannot be mistakes, illusion, cheating or imperfect perception in the words of liberated sages. Therefore there is no mistake in this statement that Lord Kṛṣṇa is the Supreme Personality of Godhead. The Sanskrit statements of *Śrīmad-Bhāgavatam* are all transcendental sounds. Śrīla Vyāsadeva revealed these statements after perfect realization, and therefore they are perfect, for liberated sages like Vyāsadeva never commit errors in their rhetorical arrangements. Unless one accepts this fact, there is no use in trying to obtain help from the revealed scriptures.

Bhrama refers to false knowledge or mistakes, such as accepting a rope as a snake or an oyster shell as gold. *Pramāda* refers to inattention or misunderstanding of reality, and *vipralipsā* is the cheating propensity. *Karaṇāpāṭava* refers to imperfectness of the material senses. There are many examples of such imperfection. The eyes cannot see that which is very distant or very small. One cannot even see his own eyelid, which is the closest thing to his eye, and if one is disturbed by a disease like jaundice, he sees everything to be yellow. Similarly, the ears cannot hear distant sounds. Since the Personality of Godhead and His plenary portions and self-realized devotees are all transcendentally situated, they cannot be misled by such deficiencies.

TEXT 87

বিরুদ্ধার্থ কহ তুমি, কহিতে কর রোষ ।
তোমার অর্থে অবিমৃষ্টবিধেয়াংশ-দোষ ॥ ৮৭ ॥

viruddhārtha kaha tumi, kahite kara roṣa
tomāra arthe avimṛṣṭa-vidheyāṁśa-doṣa

viruddha-artha—contrary meaning; *kaha*—say; *tumi*—you; *kahite*—pointing out; *kara*—you do; *roṣa*—anger; *tomāra*—your; *arthe*—in the meaning; *avimṛṣṭa-vidheya-aṁśa*—of the unconsidered predicate portion; *doṣa*—the fault.

TRANSLATION

"You say something contradictory and become angry when this is pointed out. Your explanation has the defect of a misplaced object. This is an unconsidered adjustment.

TEXT 88

যাঁর ভগবত্তা হৈতে অন্যের ভগবত্তা ।
'স্বয়ং-ভগবান্'-শব্দের তাহাতেই সত্তা ॥ ৮৮ ॥

yāṅra bhagavattā haite anyera bhagavattā
'svayaṁ-bhagavān'-śabdera tāhātei sattā

yāṅra—of whom; *bhagavattā*—the quality of being the Supreme Personality of Godhead; *haite*—from; *anyera*—of others; *bhagavattā*—the quality of being the Supreme Personality of Godhead; *svayam-bhagavān-śabdera*—of the word *svayaṁ-bhagavān*; *tāhātei*—in that; *sattā*—the presence.

TRANSLATION

"Only the Personality of Godhead, the source of all other Divinities, is eligible to be designated svayaṁ bhagavān, or the primeval Lord.

TEXT 89

দীপ হৈতে যৈছে বহু দীপের জ্বলন ।
মূল এক দীপ তাহা করিয়ে গণন ॥ ৮৯ ॥

dīpa haite yaiche bahu dīpera jvalana
mūla eka dīpa tāhā kariye gaṇana

dīpa—a lamp; *haite*—from; *yaiche*—just as; *bahu*—many; *dīpera*—of lamps; *jvalana*—lighting; *mūla*—the original; *eka*—one; *dīpa*—lamp; *tāhā*—that; *kariye*—I make; *gaṇana*—consideration

TRANSLATION

"When from one candle many others are lit, I consider that one the original.

PURPORT

The *Brahma-saṁhitā*, Chapter Five, verse 46, states that the *viṣṇu-tattva*, or the principle of the Absolute Personality of Godhead, is like a lamp because the expansions equal their origin in all respects. A burning lamp can light innumerable other lamps, and although they will not be inferior, still the lamp from which the others are lit must be considered the original. Similarly, the Supreme Personality of Godhead expands Himself in the plenary forms of the *viṣṇu-tattva,* and although they are equally powerful, the original powerful Personality of Godhead is considered the source. This analogy also explains the appearance of qualitative incarnations like Lord Śiva and Lord Brahmā. According to Śrīla Jīva Gosvāmī, *śambhos tu tamo-'dhiṣṭhānatvāt kajjalamaya-sūkṣma-dīpa-śikhā-sthānīyasya na tathā sāmyam:* "The *śambhu-tattva,* or the principle of Lord Śiva, is like a lamp covered with carbon because of his being in charge of the mode of ignorance. The illumination from such a lamp is very minute. Therefore the power of Lord Śiva cannot compare to that of the Viṣṇu principle."

TEXT 90

তৈছে সব অবতারের কৃষ্ণ সে কারণ ।
আর এক শ্লোক শুন, কুব্যাখ্যা-খণ্ডন ॥ ৯০ ॥

taiche saba avatārera kṛṣṇa se kāraṇa
āra eka śloka śuna, kuvyākhyā-khaṇḍana

taiche—in a similar way; *saba*—all; *avatārera*—of the incarnations; *kṛṣṇa*—Lord Kṛṣṇa; *se*—He; *kāraṇa*—the cause; *āra*—another; *eka*—one; *śloka*—verse; *śuna*—please hear; *ku-vyākhyā*—fallacious explanations; *khaṇḍana*—refuting.

TRANSLATION

"Kṛṣṇa, in the same way, is the cause of all causes and all incarnations. Please hear another verse to defeat all misinterpretations.

TEXTS 91–92

অত্র সর্গো বিসর্গশ্চ স্থানং পোষণমূতয়ঃ ।
মন্বন্তরেশানুকথা নিরোধো মুক্তিরাশ্রয়ঃ ॥ ৯১ ॥
দশমস্য বিশুদ্ধ্যর্থং নবানামিহ লক্ষণম্ ।
বর্ণয়ন্তি মহাত্মানঃ শ্রুতেনার্থেন চাঞ্জসা ॥ ৯২ ॥

atra sargo visargaś ca
sthānaṁ poṣaṇam ūtayaḥ
manvantareśānukathā
nirodho muktir āśrayaḥ

daśamasya viśuddhy-arthaṁ
navānām iha lakṣaṇam
varṇayanti mahātmānaḥ
śrutenārthena cāñjasā

atra—in *Śrīmad-Bhāgavatam*; *sargaḥ*—the creation of the ingredients of the universe; *visargaḥ*—the creations of Brahmā; *ca*—and; *sthānam*—the maintenance of the creation; *poṣaṇam*—the favoring of the Lord's devotees; *ūtayaḥ*—impetuses for activity; *manu-antara*—prescribed duties given by the Manus; *īśa-anukathāḥ*—a description of the incarnations of the Lord; *nirodhaḥ*—the winding up of creation; *muktiḥ*—liberation; *āśrayaḥ*—the ultimate shelter, the Supreme Personality of Godhead; *daśamasya*—of the tenth (the *āśraya*); *viśuddhi-artham*—for the purpose of perfect knowledge; *navānām*—of the nine; *iha*—here; *lakṣaṇam*—the nature; *varṇayanti*—describe; *mahā-ātmānaḥ*—the great souls; *śrutena*—by prayer; *arthena*—by explanation; *ca*—and; *añjasā*—direct.

TRANSLATION

"'Here [in Śrīmad-Bhāgavatam] ten subjects are described: (1) the creation of the ingredients of the cosmos, (2) the creations of Brahmā, (3) the maintenance of the creation, (4) special favor given to the faithful, (5) impetuses for activity, (6) prescribed duties for law-abiding men, (7) a description of the incarnations of the Lord, (8) the winding up of the creation, (9) liberation from gross and subtle material existence, and (10) the ultimate shelter, the Supreme Personality of Godhead. The tenth item is the shelter of all the others. To distinguish this ultimate shelter from the other nine subjects, the mahājanas have described these nine, directly or indirectly, through prayers or direct explanations.'

PURPORT

These verses from *Śrīmad-Bhāgavatam* (2.10.1–2) list the ten subject matters dealt with in the text of the *Bhāgavatam.* Of these, the tenth is the substance, and the other nine are categories derived from the substance. These ten subjects are listed as follows:

(1) *Sarga:* the first creation by Viṣṇu, the bringing forth of the five gross material elements, the five objects of sense perception, the ten senses, the mind, the intelligence, the false ego and the total material energy, or universal form.

(2) *Visarga:* the secondary creation, or the work of Brahmā in producing the moving and unmoving bodies in the universe (*brahmāṇḍa*).

(3) *Sthāna:* the maintenance of the universe by the Personality of Godhead, Viṣṇu. Viṣṇu's function is more important and His glory greater than Brahmā's and Lord Śiva's, for although Brahmā is the creator and Lord Śiva the destroyer, Viṣṇu is the maintainer.

(4) *Poṣaṇa:* special care and protection for devotees by the Lord. As a king maintains his kingdom and subjects but nevertheless gives special attention to the members of his family, so the Personality of Godhead gives special care to His devotees who are souls completely surrendered to Him.

(5) *Ūti:* the urge for creation, or initiative power, that is the cause of all inventions, according to the necessities of time, space and objects.

(6) *Manv-antara:* the periods controlled by the Manus, who teach regulative principles for living beings who desire to achieve perfection in human life. The rules of Manu, as described in the *Manu-saṁhitā,* guide the way to such perfection.

(7) *Īśānukathā:* scriptural information regarding the Personality of Godhead, His incarnations on earth and the activities of His devotees. Scriptures dealing with these subjects are essential for progressive human life.

(8) *Nirodha:* the winding up of all energies employed in creation. Such potencies are emanations from the Personality of Godhead who eternally lies in the Kāraṇa Ocean. The cosmic creations, manifested with His breath, are again dissolved in due course.

(9) *Mukti:* liberation of the conditioned souls encaged by the gross and subtle coverings of body and mind. When freed from all material affection, the soul, giving up the gross and subtle material bodies, can attain the spiritual sky in his original spiritual body and engage in transcendental loving service to the Lord in Vaikuṇṭhaloka or Kṛṣṇaloka. When the soul is situated in his original constitutional position of existence, he is said to be liberated. It is possible to engage in transcendental loving service to the Lord and become *jīvan-mukta,* a liberated soul, even while in the material body.

(10) *Āśraya:* the Transcendence, the summum bonum, from whom everything emanates, upon whom everything rests, and in whom everything merges after annihilation. He is the source and support of all. The *āśraya* is also called the Supreme Brahman, as in the *Vedānta-sūtra* (*athāto brahma-jijñāsā, janmādy asya yataḥ*). *Śrīmad-Bhāgavatam* especially describes this Supreme Brahman as the *āśraya.* Śrī Kṛṣṇa is this *āśraya,* and therefore the greatest necessity of life is to study the science of Kṛṣṇa.

Śrīmad-Bhāgavatam accepts Śrī Kṛṣṇa as the shelter of all manifestations because Lord Kṛṣṇa, the Supreme Personality of Godhead, is the ultimate source of everything, the supreme goal of all.

Two different principles are to be considered herein—namely *āśraya*, the object providing shelter, and *āśrita*, the dependents requiring shelter. The *āśrita* exist under the original principle, the *āśraya*. The first nine categories, described in the first nine cantos of *Śrīmad-Bhāgavatam*, from creation to liberation—including the *puruṣa-avatāras*, the incarnations, the marginal energy, or living entities, and the external energy, or material world—are all *āśrita*. The prayers of *Śrīmad-Bhāgavatam*, however, aim for the *āśraya-tattva*, the Supreme Personality of Godhead, Śrī Kṛṣṇa. The great souls expert in describing *Śrīmad-Bhāgavatam* have very diligently delineated the other nine categories, sometimes by direct narrations and sometimes by indirect narrations such as stories. The real purpose of doing this is to know perfectly the Absolute Transcendence, Śrī Kṛṣṇa, for the entire creation, both material and spiritual, rests on the body of Śrī Kṛṣṇa.

TEXT 93

আশ্রয় জানিতে কহি এ নব পদার্থ ।
এ নবের উৎপত্তি-হেতু সেই আশ্রয়ার্থ ॥ ৯৩ ॥

āśraya jānite kahi e nava padārtha
e navera utpatti-hetu sei āśrayārtha

āśraya—the ultimate shelter; *jānite*—to know; *kahi*—I discuss; *e*—these; *nava*—nine; *pada-artha*—categories; *e*—these; *navera*—of the nine; *utpatti*—of the origin; *hetu*—cause; *sei*—that; *āśraya*—of the shelter; *artha*—the meaning.

TRANSLATION

"To know distinctly the ultimate shelter of everything that be, I have described the other nine categories. The cause for the appearance of these nine is rightly called their shelter.

TEXT 94

কৃষ্ণ এক সর্বাশ্রয়, কৃষ্ণ সর্বধাম ।
কৃষ্ণের শরীরে সর্ব-বিশ্বের বিশ্রাম ॥ ৯৪ ॥

kṛṣṇa eka sarvāśraya, kṛṣṇa sarva-dhāma
kṛṣṇera śarīre sarva-viśvera viśrāma

kṛṣṇa—Lord Kṛṣṇa; *eka*—one; *sarva-āśraya*—shelter of all; *kṛṣṇa*—Lord Kṛṣṇa; *sarva-dhāma*—the abode of all; *kṛṣnera*—of Lord Kṛṣṇa; *śarīre*—in the body; *sarva-viśvera*—of all the universes; *viśrāma*—resting place.

TRANSLATION

"The Personality of Godhead Śrī Kṛṣṇa is the shelter and abode of everything. All the universes rest in His body.

TEXT 95

দশমে দশমং লক্ষ্যমাশ্রিতাশ্রয়বিগ্রহম্ ।
শ্রীকৃষ্ণাখ্যং পরং ধাম জগদ্ধাম নমামি তৎ ॥ ৯৫ ॥

daśame daśamaṁ lakṣyam
āśritāśraya-vigraham
śrī-kṛṣṇākhyaṁ paraṁ dhāma
jagad-dhāma namāmi tat

daśame—in the Tenth Canto; *daśamam*—the tenth subject matter; *lakṣyam*—to be seen; *āśrita*—of the sheltered; *āśraya*—of the shelter; *vigraham*—who is the form; *śrī-kṛṣṇa-ākhyam*—known as Lord Śrī Kṛṣṇa; *param*—supreme; *dhāma*—abode; *jagat-dhāma*—the abode of the universes; *namāmi*—I offer my obeisances; *tat*—to Him.

TRANSLATION

"'The Tenth Canto of Śrīmad-Bhāgavatam reveals the tenth object, the Supreme Personality of Godhead, who is the shelter of all surrendered souls. He is known as Śrī Kṛṣṇa, and He is the ultimate source of all the universes. Let me offer my obeisances unto Him.'

PURPORT

This quotation comes from Śrīdhara Svāmī's commentary on the first verse of the Tenth Canto, Chapter One, of *Śrīmad-Bhāgavatam.*

TEXT 96

কৃষ্ণের স্বরূপ, আর শক্তিত্রয়-জ্ঞান ।
যাঁর হয়, তাঁর নাহি কৃষ্ণেতে অজ্ঞান ॥ ৯৬ ॥

kṛṣṇera svarūpa, āra śakti-traya-jñāna
yāṅra haya, tāṅra nāhi kṛṣṇete ajñāna

kṛṣṇera—of Lord Kṛṣṇa; *sva-rūpa*—the real nature; *āra*—and; *śakti-traya*—of the three energies; *jñāna*—knowledge; *yāṅra*—whose; *haya*—there is; *tāṅra*—of him; *nāhi*—there is not; *kṛṣṇete*—in Lord Kṛṣṇa; *ajñāna*—ignorance.

TRANSLATION

"One who knows the real feature of Śrī Kṛṣṇa and His three different energies cannot remain ignorant about Him.

PURPORT

Śrīla Jīva Gosvāmī states in his *Bhagavat-sandarbha* (16) that by His potencies, which act in natural sequences beyond the scope of the speculative human mind, the Supreme Transcendence, the summum bonum, eternally and simultaneously exists in four transcendental features: His personality, His impersonal effulgence, particles of His potency (the living beings), and the principal cause of all causes. The Supreme Whole is compared to the sun, which also exists in four features, namely the personality of the sun-god, the glare of his glowing sphere, the sun rays inside the sun planet, and the sun's reflections in many other objects. The ambition to corroborate the existence of the transcendental Absolute Truth by limited conjectural endeavors cannot be fulfilled, because He is beyond the scope of our limited speculative minds. In an honest search for truth, we must admit that His powers are inconceivable to our tiny brains. The exploration of space has demanded the work of the greatest scientists of the world, yet there are countless problems regarding even fundamental knowledge of the material creation that bewilder scientists who confront them. Such material knowledge is far removed from the spiritual nature, and therefore the acts and arrangements of the Absolute Truth are, beyond all doubts, inconceivable.

The primary potencies of the Absolute Truth are mentioned to be three: internal, external and marginal. By the acts of His internal potency, the Personality of Godhead in His original form exhibits the spiritual cosmic manifestations known as the Vaikuṇṭhalokas, which exist eternally, even after the destruction of the material cosmic manifestation. By His marginal potency the Lord expands Himself as living beings who are part of Him, just as the sun distributes its rays in all directions.

By His external potency the Lord manifests the material creation, just as the sun with its rays creates fog. The material creation is but a perverse reflection of the eternal Vaikuṇṭha nature.

These three energies of the Absolute Truth are also described in the *Viṣṇu Purāṇa*, where it is said that the living being is equal in quality to the internal potency, whereas the external potency is indirectly controlled by the chief cause of all causes. *Māyā*, the illusory energy, misleads a living being as fog misleads a pedestrian by blocking off the light of the sun. Although the potency of *māyā* is inferior in quality to the marginal potency, which consists of the living beings, who are part and parcel of the Lord, it nevertheless has the power to control the living beings, just as fog can block the actions of a certain portion of the sun's rays although it cannot cover the sun. The living beings covered by the illusory energy evolve in different species of life, with bodies ranging from that of an insignificant ant to that of Brahmā, the constructor of the cosmos. The *pradhāna*, the chief cause of all causes in the impersonal vision, is none other than the Supreme Lord, whom one can see face to face in the internal potency. He takes the material all-pervasive form by His inconceivable power. Although all three potencies—namely internal, external and marginal—are essentially one in the ultimate issue, they are different in action, like electric energy, which can produce both cold and heat under different conditions. The external and marginal potencies are so called under various conditions, but in the original, internal potencies there are no such conditions, nor is it possible for the conditions of the external potency to exist in the marginal, or vice versa. One who is able to understand the intricacies of all these energies of the Supreme Lord can no longer remain an empiric impersonalist under the influence of a poor fund of knowledge.

TEXT 97

কৃষ্ণের স্বরূপের হয় ষড়্‌বিধ বিলাস ।
প্রাভব-বৈভব-রূপে দ্বিবিধ প্রকাশ ॥ ৯৭ ॥

kṛṣṇera svarūpera haya ṣaḍ-vidha vilāsa
prābhava-vaibhava-rūpe dvi-vidha prakāśa

kṛṣṇera—of Lord Kṛṣṇa; *svarūpera*—of the form; *haya*—there are; *ṣaṭ-vidha*—six kinds; *vilāsa*—pastime forms; *prābhava-vaibhava-rūpe*—in the divisions of *prābhava* and *vaibhava; dvi-vidha*—two kinds; *prakāśa*—manifestations.

TRANSLATION

"The Personality of Godhead Śrī Kṛṣṇa enjoys Himself in six primary expansions. His two manifestations are prābhava and vaibhava.

PURPORT

Now the author of *Śrī Caitanya-caritāmṛta* turns to a description of the Personality of Godhead Kṛṣṇa in His innumerable expansions. The Lord primarily expands Himself in two categories, namely *prābhava* and *vaibhava.* The *prābhava* forms are fully potent like Śrī Kṛṣṇa, and the *vaibhava* forms are partially potent. The *prābhava* forms are manifested in relation with potencies, but the *vaibhava* forms are manifested in relation with excellences. The potent *prābhava* manifestations are also of two varieties: temporary and eternal. The Mohinī, Haṁsa and Śukla forms are manifested only temporarily, in terms of a particular age. Among the other *prābhavas,* who are not very famous according to the material estimation, are Dhanvantari, Ṛṣabha, Vyāsa, Dattātreya and Kapila. Among the *vaibhava-prakāśa* forms are Kūrma, Matsya, Nara-Nārāyaṇa, Varāha, Hayagrīva, Pṛśnigarbha, Baladeva, Yajña, Vibhu, Satyasena, Hari, Vaikuṇṭha, Ajita, Vāmana, Sārvabhauma, Ṛṣabha, Viṣvaksena, Dharmasetu, Sudhāmā, Yogeśvara and Bṛhadbhānu.

TEXT 98

অংশ-শক্ত্যাবেশরূপে দ্বিবিধাবতার ।
বাল্য পৌগণ্ড ধর্ম দুই ত' প্রকার ॥ ৯৮ ॥

aṁśa-śaktyāveśa-rūpe dvi-vidhāvatāra
bālya paugaṇḍa dharma dui ta' prakāra

aṁśa—of the plenary expansion; *śakti-āveśa*—of the empowered; *rūpe*—in the forms; *dvi-vidha*—two kinds; *avatāra*—incarnations; *bālya*—childhood; *paugaṇḍa*—boyhood; *dharma*—characteristics of age; *dui*—two; *ta'*—certainly; *prakāra*—kinds

TRANSLATION

"His incarnations are of two kinds, namely partial and empowered. He appears in two ages—childhood and boyhood.

PURPORT

The *vilāsa* forms are six in number. Incarnations are of two varieties, namely *śakty-āveśa* (empowered) and *aṁśāveśa* (partial). These incarnations also come within the category of *prābhava* and *vaibhava* manifestations. Childhood and boyhood are two special features of the Personality of Godhead Śrī Kṛṣṇa, but His permanent feature is His eternal form as an adolescent youth. The original Personality of Godhead Śrī Kṛṣṇa is always worshiped in this eternal adolescent form.

TEXT 99

কিশোরস্বরূপ কৃষ্ণ স্বয়ং অবতারী ।
ক্রীড়া করে এই ছয়-রূপে বিশ্ব ভরি' ॥ ৯৯ ॥

kiśora-svarūpa kṛṣṇa svayaṁ avatārī
krīḍā kare ei chaya-rūpe viśva bhari'

kiśora-svarūpa—whose real nature is that of an adolescent; *kṛṣṇa*—Lord Kṛṣṇa; *svayam*—Himself; *avatārī*—the source of all incarnations; *krīḍā kare*—He plays; *ei*—these; *chaya-rūpe*—in six forms; *viśva*—the universes; *bhari'*—maintaining

TRANSLATION

"The Personality of Godhead Śrī Kṛṣṇa, who is eternally an adolescent, is the primeval Lord, the source of all incarnations. He expands Himself in these six categories of forms to establish His supremacy throughout the universe.

TEXT 100

এই ছয়-রূপে হয় অনন্ত বিভেদ ।
অনন্তরূপে একরূপ, নাহি কিছু ভেদ ॥ ১০০ ॥

ei chaya-rūpe haya ananta vibheda
ananta-rūpe eka-rūpa, nāhi kichu bheda

ei—these; *chaya-rūpe*—in six forms; *haya*—there are; *ananta*—unlimited; *vibheda*—varieties; *ananta-rūpe*—in unlimited forms; *eka-rūpa*—one form; *nāhi*—there is not; *kichu*—any; *bheda*—difference.

TRANSLATION

"In these six kinds of forms there are innumerable varieties. Although they are many, they are all one: there is no difference between them.

PURPORT

The Personality of Godhead manifests Himself in six different features: (1) *prābhava,* (2) *vaibhava,* (3) empowered incarnations, (4) partial incarnations, (5) childhood and (6) boyhood. The Personality of Godhead Śrī Kṛṣṇa, whose permanent feature is adolescence, enjoys His transcendental proclivities by performing pastimes in these six forms. In these six features there are unlimited divisions of the Personality of Godhead's forms. The *jīvas,* or living beings, are differentiated parts and parcels of the Lord. They are all diversities of the one without a second, the Supreme Personality of Godhead.

TEXT 101

চিচ্ছক্তি, স্বরূপশক্তি, অন্তরঙ্গা নাম ।
তাহার বৈভব অনন্ত বৈকুণ্ঠাদি ধাম ॥ ১০১॥

cic-chakti, svarūpa-śakti, antaraṅgā nāma
tāhāra vaibhava ananta vaikuṇṭhādi dhāma

cit-śakti—spiritual energy; *svarūpa-śakti*—personal energy; *antaḥ-aṅgā*—internal; *nāma*—named; *tāhāra*—of that; *vaibhava*—manifestations; *ananta*—unlimited; *vaikuṇṭha-ādi*—Vaikuṇṭha, etc.; *dhāma*—abodes.

TRANSLATION

"The cit-śakti, which is also called svarūpa-śakti or antaraṅga-śakti, displays many varied manifestations. It sustains the kingdom of God and its paraphernalia.

TEXT 102

মায়াশক্তি, বহিরঙ্গা, জগৎকারণ ।
তাহার বৈভব অনন্ত ব্রহ্মাণ্ডের গণ ॥ ১০২ ॥

māyā-śakti, bahiraṅgā, jagat-kāraṇa
tāhāra vaibhava ananta brahmāṇḍera gaṇa

māyā-śakti—the illusory energy; *bahiḥ-aṅgā*—external; *jagat-kāraṇa*—the cause of the universe; *tāhāra*—of that; *vaibhava*—manifestations; *ananta*—unlimited; *brahma-aṇḍera*—of universes; *gaṇa*—multitudes.

TRANSLATION

"The external energy, called māyā-śakti, is the cause of innumerable universes with varied material potencies.

TEXT 103

জীবশক্তি তটস্থাখ্য, নাহি যার অন্ত ।
মুখ্য তিন শক্তি, তার বিভেদ অনন্ত ॥ ১০৩ ॥

jīva-śakti taṭasthākhya, nāhi yāra anta
mukhya tina śakti, tāra vibheda ananta

jīva-śakti—the energy of the living entity; *taṭa-stha-ākhya*—known as marginal; *nāhi*—there is not; *yāra*—of which; *anta*—end; *mukhya*—principal; *tina*—three; *śakti*—energies; *tāra*—of them; *vibheda*—varieties; *ananta*—unlimited.

TRANSLATION

"The marginal potency, which is between these two, consists of the numberless living beings. These are the three principal energies, which have unlimited categories and subdivisions.

PURPORT

The internal potency of the Lord, which is called *cit-śakti* or *antaraṅga-śakti*, exhibits variegatedness in the transcendental Vaikuṇṭha cosmos. Besides ourselves, there are unlimited numbers of liberated living beings who associate with the Personality of Godhead in His innumerable features. The material cosmos displays the external energy, in which the conditioned living beings are provided all liberty to go back to the Personality of Godhead after leaving the material tabernacle. The *Śvetāśvatara Upaniṣad* (6.8) informs us:

na tasya kāryaṁ karaṇaṁ ca vidyate
na tat-samaś cābhyadhikaś ca dṛśyate

parāsya śaktir vividhaiva śrūyate
svābhāvikī jñāna-bala-kriyā ca

"The Supreme Lord is one without a second. He has nothing to do personally, nor does He have material senses. No one is equal to Him or greater than Him. He has unlimited, variegated potencies of different names, which exist within Him as autonomous attributes and provide Him full knowledge, power and pastimes."

TEXT 104

এমত স্বরূপগণ, আর তিন শক্তি ।
সভার আশ্রয় কৃষ্ণ, কৃষ্ণে সভার স্থিতি ॥ ১০৪ ॥

e-mata svarūpa-gaṇa, āra tina śakti
sabhāra āśraya kṛṣṇa, kṛṣṇe sabhāra sthiti

e-mata—in this way; *svarūpa-gaṇa*—personal forms; *āra*—and; *tina*—three; *śakti*—energies; *sabhāra*—of the whole assembly; *āśraya*—the shelter; *kṛṣṇa*—Lord Kṛṣṇa; *kṛṣṇe*—in Lord Kṛṣṇa; *sabhāra*—of the whole assembly; *sthiti*—the existence.

TRANSLATION

"These are the principal manifestations and expansions of the Personality of Godhead and His three energies. They are all emanations from Śrī Kṛṣṇa, the Transcendence. They have their existence in Him.

TEXT 105

যদ্যপি ব্রহ্মাণ্ডগণের পুরুষ আশ্রয় ।
সেই পুরুষাদি সভার কৃষ্ণ মূলাশ্রয় ॥ ১০৫ ॥

yadyapi brahmāṇḍa-gaṇera puruṣa āśraya
sei puruṣādi sabhāra kṛṣṇa mūlāśraya

yadyapi—although; *brahma-aṇḍa-gaṇera*—of the multitude of universes; *puruṣa*—the *puruṣa-avatāra; āśraya*—the shelter; *sei*—that; *puruṣa-ādi*—of the *puruṣa-avatāras,* etc.; *sabhāra*—of the assembly; *kṛṣṇa*—Lord Kṛṣṇa; *mūla-āśraya*—original source.

TRANSLATION

"Although the three puruṣas are the shelter of all the universes, Lord Kṛṣṇa is the original source of the puruṣas.

TEXT 106

স্বয়ং ভগবান্ কৃষ্ণ, কৃষ্ণ সর্বাশ্রয় ।
পরম ঈশ্বর কৃষ্ণ সর্বশাস্ত্রে কয় ॥ ১০৬ ॥

svayaṁ bhagavān kṛṣṇa, kṛṣṇa sarvāśraya
parama īśvara kṛṣṇa sarva-śāstre kaya

svayam—Himself; *bhagavān*—the Supreme Personality of Godhead; *kṛṣṇa*—Lord Kṛṣṇa; *kṛṣṇa*—Lord Kṛṣṇa; *sarva-āśraya*—the shelter of all; *parama*—Supreme; *īśvara*—Lord; *kṛṣṇa*—Lord Kṛṣṇa; *sarva-śāstre*—all scriptures; *kaya*—say.

TRANSLATION

"Thus the Personality of Godhead Śrī Kṛṣṇa is the original, primeval Lord, the source of all other expansions. All the revealed scriptures accept Śrī Kṛṣṇa as the Supreme Lord.

TEXT 107

ঈশ্বরঃ পরমঃ কৃষ্ণঃ সচ্চিদানন্দবিগ্রহ ।
অনাদিরাদির্গোবিন্দঃ সর্বকারণকারণম্ ॥ ১০৭ ॥

īśvaraḥ paramaḥ kṛṣṇaḥ
sac-cid-ānanda-vigrahaḥ
anādir ādir govindaḥ
sarva-kāraṇa-kāraṇam

īśvaraḥ—the controller; *paramaḥ*—supreme; *kṛṣṇaḥ*—Lord Kṛṣṇa; *sat*—eternal existence; *cit*—absolute knowledge; *ānanda*—absolute bliss; *vigrahaḥ*—whose form; *anādiḥ*—without beginning; *ādiḥ*—the origin; *govindaḥ*—Lord Govinda; *sarva-kāraṇa-kāraṇam*—the cause of all causes.

TRANSLATION

"'Kṛṣṇa, who is known as Govinda, is the supreme controller. He has an eternal, blissful, spiritual body. He is the origin of all. He has no other origin, for He is the prime cause of all causes.'

PURPORT

This is the first verse of the Fifth Chapter of the *Brahma-saṁhitā.*

TEXT 108

এ সব সিদ্ধান্ত তুমি জান ভালমতে ।
তবু পূর্বপক্ষ কর আমা চালাইতে ॥ ১০৮ ॥

e saba siddhānta tumi jāna bhāla-mate
tabu pūrva-pakṣa kara āmā cālāite

e—these; *saba*—all; *siddhānta*—conclusions; *tumi*—you; *jāna*—know; *bhāla-mate*—in a good way; *tabu*—still; *pūrva-pakṣa*—objection; *kara*—you make; *āmā*—to me; *cālāite*—to give useless anxiety.

TRANSLATION

"You know all the conclusions of the scriptures very well. You create these logical arguments just to agitate me."

PURPORT

A learned man who has thoroughly studied the scriptures cannot hesitate to accept Śrī Kṛṣṇa as the Supreme Personality of Godhead. If such a man argues about this matter, certainly he must be doing so to agitate the minds of his opponents.

TEXT 109

সেই কৃষ্ণ অবতারী ব্রজেন্দ্রকুমার ।
আপনে চৈতন্যরূপে কৈল অবতার ॥ ১০৯ ॥

sei kṛṣṇa avatārī vrajendra-kumāra
āpane caitanya-rūpe kaila avatāra

sei—that; *kṛṣṇa*—Lord Kṛṣṇa; *avatārī*—the source of all incarnations; *vrajendra-kumāra*—the son of the King of Vraja; *āpane*—personally; *caitanya-rūpe*—in the form of Lord Caitanya Mahāprabhu; *kaila*—made; *avatāra*—incarnation.

TRANSLATION

That same Lord Kṛṣṇa, the fountainhead of all incarnations, is known as the son of the King of Vraja. He has descended personally as Lord Śrī Caitanya Mahāprabhu.

TEXT 110

অতএব চৈতন্য গোসাঞি পরতত্ত্ব-সীমা ।
তাঁরে ক্ষীরোদশায়ী কহি, কি তাঁর মহিমা ॥ ১১০ ॥

ataeva caitanya gosāñi paratattva-sīmā
tāṅre kṣīroda-śāyī kahi, ki tāṅra mahimā

ataeva—therefore; *caitanya gosāñi*—Lord Caitanya Mahāprabhu; *para-tattva-sīmā*—the highest limit of the Absolute Truth; *tāṅre*—Him; *kṣīroda-śāyī*—Kṣīrodakaśāyī Viṣṇu; *kahi*—if I say; *ki*—what; *tāṅra*—of Him; *mahimā*—glory.

TRANSLATION

Therefore Lord Caitanya is the Supreme Absolute Truth. To call Him Kṣīrodakaśāyī Viṣṇu does not add to His glory.

TEXT 111

সেই ত' ভক্তের বাক্য নহে ব্যভিচারী ।
সকল সম্ভবে তাঁতে, যাতে অবতারী ॥ ১১১ ॥

sei ta' bhaktera vākya nahe vyabhicārī
sakala sambhave tāṅte, yāte avatārī

sei—that; *ta'*—certainly; *bhaktera*—of a devotee; *vākya*—speech; *nahe*—is not; *vyabhicārī*—deviation; *sakala*—all; *sambhave*—possibilities; *tāṅte*—in Him; *yāte*—since; *avatārī*—the source of all incarnations.

TRANSLATION

But such words from the lips of a sincere devotee cannot be false. All possibilities abide in Him, for He is the primeval Lord.

TEXT 112

অবতারীর দেহে সব অবতারের স্থিতি ।
কেহো কোনমতে কহে, যেমন যার মতি ॥ ১১২ ॥

avatārīra dehe saba avatārera sthiti
keho kona-mate kahe, yemana yāra mati

avatārīra—of the source; *dehe*—in the body; *saba*—all; *avatārera*—of the incarnations; *sthiti*—existence; *keho*—someone; *kona-mate*—in some way; *kahe*—says; *yemana*—as in the manner; *yāra*—of whom; *mati*—the opinion.

TRANSLATION

All other incarnations are situated in potential form in the original body of the primeval Lord. Thus according to one's opinion, one may address Him as any one of the incarnations.

PURPORT

It is not contradictory for a devotee to call the Supreme Lord by any one of the various names of His plenary expansions, because the original Personality of Godhead includes all such categories. Since the plenary expansions exist within the original person, one may call Him by any of these names. In *Śrī Caitanya-bhāgavata* (*Madhya* 6.95) Lord Caitanya says, "I was lying asleep in the ocean of milk, but I was awakened by the call of Nāḍā, Śrī Advaita Prabhu." Here the Lord refers to His form as Kṣīrodakaśāyī Viṣṇu.

TEXT 113

কৃষ্ণকে কহয়ে কেহ—নর-নারায়ণ ।
কেহো কহে, কৃষ্ণ হয় সাক্ষাৎ বামন ॥ ১১৩ ॥

kṛṣṇake kahaye keha—nara-nārāyaṇa
keho kahe, kṛṣṇa haya sākṣāṭ vāmana

kṛṣṇake—Lord Kṛṣṇa; *kahaye*—says; *keha*—someone; *nara-nārāyaṇa*—Nara-Nārāyaṇa; *keho*—someone; *kahe*—says; *kṛṣṇa*—Lord Kṛṣṇa; *haya*—is; *sākṣāt*—directly; *vāmana*—Lord Vāmana.

TRANSLATION

Some say that Śrī Kṛṣṇa is directly Nara-Nārāyaṇa. Others say that He is directly Vāmana.

TEXT 114

কেহো কহে, কৃষ্ণ ক্ষীরোদশায়ী অবতার ।
অসম্ভব নহে, সত্য বচন সবার ॥ ১১৪ ॥

keho kahe, kṛṣṇa kṣīroda-śāyī avatāra
asambhava nahe, satya vacana sabāra

keho—someone; *kahe*—says; *kṛṣṇa*—Lord Kṛṣṇa; *kṣīroda-śāyī*—Kṣīrodakaśāyī Viṣṇu; *avatāra*—incarnation; *asambhava*—impossible; *nahe*—is not; *satya*—true; *vacana*—speeches; *sabāra*—of all.

TRANSLATION

Some say that Kṛṣṇa is the incarnation of Kṣīrodakaśāyī Viṣṇu. None of these statements is impossible; each is as correct as the others.

PURPORT

The *Laghu-bhāgavatāmṛta* (5.383) states:

ata evā purāṇādau kecin nara-sakhātmatām
mahendrānujatāṁ kecit kecit kṣīrābdhi-śāyitām
sahasra-śīrṣatāṁ kecit kecid vaikuṇṭha-nāthatām
brūyuḥ kṛṣṇasya munayas tat-tad-vṛtty-anugāminaḥ

"According to the intimate relationships between Śrī Kṛṣṇa, the primeval Lord, and His devotees, the *Purāṇas* describe Him by various names. Sometimes He is called Nārāyaṇa; sometimes Upendra (Vāmana), the younger brother of Indra, King of heaven; and sometimes Kṣīrodakaśāyī Viṣṇu. Sometimes He is called the thousand-hooded Śeṣa Nāga, and sometimes the Lord of Vaikuṇṭha."

TEXT 115

কেহো কহে, পরব্যোমে নারায়ণ হরি ।
সকল সম্ভবে কৃষ্ণে, যাতে অবতারী ॥ ১১৫ ॥

keho kahe, para-vyome nārāyaṇa hari
sakala sambhave kṛṣṇe, yāte avatārī

keho—someone; *kahe*—says; *para-vyome*—in the transcendental world; *nārāyaṇa*—Lord Nārāyaṇa; *hari*—the Supreme Personality of Godhead; *sakala sambhave*—all possibilities; *kṛṣṇe*—in Lord Kṛṣṇa; *yāte*—since; *avatārī*—the source of all incarnations.

TRANSLATION

Some call Him Hari, or the Nārāyaṇa of the transcendental world. Everything is possible in Kṛṣṇa, for He is the primeval Lord.

TEXT 116

সব শ্রোতাগণের করি চরণ বন্দন ।
এ সব সিদ্ধান্ত শুন, করি' এক মন ॥ ১১৬ ॥

saba śrotā-gaṇera kari caraṇa vandana
e saba siddhānta śuna, kari' eka mana

saba—all; *śrotā-gaṇera*—of the hearers; *kari*—I do; *caraṇa*—to the lotus feet; *vandana*—praying; *e*—these; *saba*—all; *siddhānta*—conclusions; *śuna*—please hear; *kari'*—making; *eka*—one; *mana*—mind.

TRANSLATION

I offer my obeisances unto the feet of all who hear or read this discourse. Kindly hear with attention the conclusion of all these statements.

PURPORT

Prostrating himself at the feet of his readers, the author of *Śrī Caitanya-caritāmṛta* entreats them in all humility to hear with rapt attention these conclusive arguments regarding the Absolute Truth. One should not fail to hear such arguments, for only by such knowledge can one perfectly know Kṛṣṇa.

TEXT 117

সিদ্ধান্ত বলিয়া চিত্তে না কর অলস ।
ইহা হইতে কৃষ্ণে লাগে সুদৃঢ় মানস ॥ ১১৭ ॥

siddhānta baliyā citte nā kara alasa
ihā ha-ite kṛṣṇe lāge sudṛḍha mānasa

siddhānta—conclusion; *baliyā*—considering; *citte*—in the mind; *nā kara*—do not be; *alasa*—lazy; *ihā*—this; *ha-ite*—from; *kṛṣṇe*—in Lord Kṛṣṇa; *lāge*—becomes fixed; *su-dṛḍha*—very firm; *mānasa*—the mind.

TRANSLATION

A sincere student should not neglect the discussion of such conclusions, considering them controversial, for such discussions strengthen the mind. Thus one's mind becomes attached to Śrī Kṛṣṇa.

PURPORT

There are many students who, in spite of reading the *Bhagavad-gītā*, misunderstand Kṛṣṇa because of imperfect knowledge and conclude Him to be an ordinary historical personality. This one must not do. One should be particularly careful to understand the truth about Kṛṣṇa. If because of laziness one does not come to know Kṛṣṇa conclusively, one will be misguided about the cult of devotion, like those who declare themselves advanced devotees and imitate the transcendental symptoms sometimes observed in liberated souls. Although the use of thoughts and arguments is a most suitable process for inducing an uninitiated person to become a devotee, neophytes in devotional service must always alertly understand Kṛṣṇa through the vision of the revealed scriptures, the bona fide devotees and the spiritual master. Unless one hears about Śrī Kṛṣṇa from such authorities, one cannot make advancement in devotion to Śrī Kṛṣṇa. The revealed scriptures mention nine means of attaining devotional service, of which the first and foremost is hearing from authority. The seed of devotion cannot sprout unless watered by the process of hearing and chanting. One should submissively receive the transcendental messages from spiritually advanced sources and chant the very same messages for one's own benefit as well as the benefit of one's audience.

When Brahmā described the situation of pure devotees freed from the culture of empiric philosophy and fruitive actions, he recommended the process of hearing from persons who are on the path of devotion. Following in the footsteps of such liberated souls, who are able to vibrate real transcendental sound, can lead one to the highest stage of devotion, and thus one can become a *mahā-bhāgavata.* From the teachings of Lord Caitanya Mahāprabhu to Sanātana Gosvāmī (*Madhya* 22.65) we learn:

śāstra-yuktye sunipuṇa, dṛḍha-śraddhā yāṅra
'uttama-adhikārī' sei tāraye saṁsāra

"A person who is expert in understanding the conclusion of the revealed scriptures and who fully surrenders to the cause of the Lord is actually able to deliver others from the clutches of material existence." Śrīla

Rūpa Gosvāmī, in his *Upadeśāmṛta* (3), advises that to make rapid advancement in the cult of devotional service one should be very active and should persevere in executing the duties specified in the revealed scriptures and confirmed by the spiritual master. Accepting the path of liberated souls and the association of pure devotees enriches such activities.

Imitation devotees, who wish to advertise themselves as elevated Vaiṣṇavas and who therefore imitate the previous *ācāryas* but do not follow them in principle, are condemned in the words of *Śrīmad-Bhāgavatam* (2.3.24) as stone-hearted. Śrīla Viśvanātha Cakravartī Ṭhākura has commented on their stone-hearted condition as follows: *bahir aśru-pulakayoḥ sator api yad dhṛdayaṁ na vikriyeta tad aśma-sāram iti kaniṣṭhādhikāriṇām eva aśru-pulakādi-mattve 'pi aśma-sāra-hṛdayatayā nindaiṣā.* "Those who shed tears by practice but whose hearts have not changed are to be known as stone-hearted devotees of the lowest grade. Their imitation crying, induced by artificial practice, is always condemned." The desired change of heart referred to above is visible in the reluctance to do anything not congenial to the devotional way. To create such a change of heart, conclusive discussion about Śrī Kṛṣṇa and His potencies is absolutely necessary. False devotees may think that simply shedding tears will lead one to the transcendental plane, even if one has not had a factual change in heart, but such a practice is useless if there is no transcendental realization. False devotees, lacking the conclusion of transcendental knowledge, think that artificially shedding tears will deliver them. Similarly, other false devotees think that studying books of the previous *ācāryas* is unadvisable, like studying dry empiric philosophies. But Śrīla Jīva Gosvāmī, following the previous *ācāryas*, has inculcated the conclusions of the scriptures in the six theses called the *Ṣaṭ-sandarbhas.* False devotees who have very little knowledge of such conclusions fail to achieve pure devotion for want of zeal in accepting the favorable directions for devotional service given by self-realized devotees. Such false devotees are like impersonalists, who also consider devotional service no better than ordinary fruitive actions.

TEXT 118

চৈতন্য-মহিমা জানি এ সব সিদ্ধান্তে ।
চিত্ত দৃঢ় হঞা লাগে মহিমা-জ্ঞান হৈতে ॥ ১১৮ ॥

caitanya-mahimā jāni e saba siddhānte
citta dṛḍha hañā lāge mahimā-jñāna haite

caitanya-mahimā—the glory of Lord Caitanya Mahāprabhu; *jāni*—I know; *e*—these; *saba*—all; *siddhānte*—by the conclusions; *citta*—the mind; *dṛḍha*—firm; *hañā*—becoming; *lāge*—becomes fixed; *mahimā-jñāna*—knowledge of the greatness; *haite*—from.

TRANSLATION

By such conclusive studies I know the glories of Lord Caitanya. Only by knowing these glories can one become strong and fixed in attachment to Him.

PURPORT

One can know the glories of Śrī Caitanya Mahāprabhu only by reaching, in knowledge, a conclusive decision about Śrī Kṛṣṇa, strengthened by bona fide study of the conclusions of the *ācāryas.*

TEXT 119

চৈতন্যপ্রভুর মহিমা কহিবার তরে ।
কৃষ্ণের মহিমা কহি করিয়া বিস্তারে ॥ ১১৯ ॥

caitanya-prabhura mahimā kahibāra tare
kṛṣṇera mahimā kahi kariyā vistāre

caitanya-prabhura—of Lord Caitanya Mahāprabhu; *mahimā*—the glories; *kahibāra tare*—for the purpose of speaking; *kṛṣṇera*—of Lord Kṛṣṇa; *mahimā*—the glories; *kahi*—I speak; *kariyā*—doing; *vistāre*—in expansion.

TRANSLATION

Just to enunciate the glories of Śrī Caitanya Mahāprabhu, I have tried to describe the glories of Śrī Kṛṣṇa in detail.

TEXT 120

চৈতন্য-গোসাঞির এই তত্ত্ব-নিরূপণ ।
স্বয়ং-ভগবান্ কৃষ্ণ ব্রজেন্দ্রনন্দন ॥ ১২০ ॥

caitanya-gosāñira ei tattva-nirūpaṇa
svayaṁ-bhagavān kṛṣṇa vrajendra-nandana

caitanya-gosāñira—of Lord Caitanya Mahāprabhu; *ei*—this; *tattva*—of the truth; *nirūpaṇa*—settling; *svayam-bhagavān*—Himself the Supreme Personality of Godhead; *kṛṣṇa*—Lord Kṛṣṇa; *vrajendra-nandana*—the son of the King of Vraja.

TRANSLATION

The conclusion is that Lord Caitanya is the Supreme Personality of Godhead, Kṛṣṇa, the son of the King of Vraja.

TEXT 121

শ্রীরূপ-রঘুনাথ-পদে যার আশ ।
চৈতন্য-চরিতামৃত কহে কৃষ্ণদাস ॥ ১২১ ॥

śrī-rūpa-raghunātha-pade yāra āśa
caitanya-caritāmṛta kahe kṛṣṇadāsa

śrī-rūpa—Śrīla Rūpa Gosvāmī; *raghunātha*—Śrīla Raghunātha dāsa Gosvāmī; *pade*—at the lotus feet; *yāra*—whose; *āśa*—expectation; *caitanya-caritāmṛta*—the book named *Caitanya-caritāmṛta; kahe*—describes; *kṛṣṇa-dāsa*—Śrīla Kṛṣṇadāsa Kavirāja Gosvāmī.

TRANSLATION

Praying at the lotus feet of Śrī Rūpa and Śrī Raghunātha, always desiring their mercy, I, Kṛṣṇadāsa, narrate Śrī Caitanya-caritāmṛta, following in their footsteps.

Thus end the Bhaktivedanta purports to Śrī Caitanya-caritāmṛta, Ādi-līlā, *Second Chapter, describing Śrī Caitanya Mahāprabhu as the Supreme Personality of Godhead.*

CHAPTER THREE

The External Reasons for the Appearance of Śrī Caitanya Mahāprabhu

In this chapter the author has fully discussed the external reasons for the descent of Śrī Caitanya Mahāprabhu. The Supreme Personality of Godhead, Lord Śrī Kṛṣṇa, after displaying His pastimes as Lord Kṛṣṇa, thought it wise to make His advent in the form of a devotee to explain personally the transcendental mellows of reciprocal service and love exchanged between Himself and His servants, friends, parents and fiancees. According to the Vedic literature, the foremost occupational duty for humanity in this Age of Kali is *nāma-saṅkīrtana*, or congregational chanting of the holy name of the Lord. The incarnation for this age especially preaches this process, but only Kṛṣṇa Himself can explain the confidential loving service performed in the four principal varieties of loving affairs between the Supreme Lord and His devotees. Lord Kṛṣṇa therefore personally appeared, with His plenary portions, as Lord Caitanya. As stated in this chapter, it was for this purpose that Lord Kṛṣṇa appeared personally in Navadvīpa in the form of Śrī Kṛṣṇa Caitanya Mahāprabhu.

Kṛṣṇadāsa Kavirāja has herein presented much authentic evidence from *Śrīmad-Bhāgavatam* and other scriptures to substantiate the identity of Lord Caitanya with Śrī Kṛṣṇa Himself. He has described bodily symptoms in Lord Caitanya that are visible only in the person of the Supreme Lord, and he has proved that Lord Caitanya appeared with His personal associates—Śrī Nityānanda, Advaita, Gadādhara, Śrīvāsa and other devotees—to preach the special significance of chanting Hare Kṛṣṇa. The appearance of Lord Caitanya is both significant and confidential. He can be appreciated only by pure devotees and only through the process of devotional service. The Lord tried to conceal His identity as the Supreme Personality of Godhead by representing Himself as a devotee, but His pure devotees could recognize Him by His special features. The *Vedas* and *Purāṇas* foretell the appearance of Lord Caitanya, but still He is sometimes called, significantly, the concealed descent of the Supreme Personality of Godhead.

Advaita Ācārya was a contemporary of Lord Caitanya's father. He felt sorry for the condition of the world because even after Lord Kṛṣṇa's appearance, no one had interest in devotional service to Kṛṣṇa. This forgetfulness was so overwhelming that Advaita Prabhu was convinced that no one but Lord Kṛṣṇa Himself could enlighten people about devotional service to the Supreme Lord. Therefore Advaita requested Lord Kṛṣṇa to appear as Lord Caitanya. Offering *tulasī* leaves and Ganges water, He cried for the Lord's appearance. The Lord, being satisfied by His pure devotees, descends to satisfy them. As such, being pleased by Advaita Ācārya, Lord Caitanya appeared.

TEXT 1

শ্রীচৈতন্যপ্রভুং বন্দে যৎপাদাশ্রয়বীর্যতঃ ।
সংগৃহ্লাত্যাকরব্রাতাদজ্ঞঃ সিদ্ধান্তসন্মণীন্ ॥ ১ ॥

śrī-caitanya-prabhuṁ vande
yat-pādāśraya-vīryataḥ
saṅgṛhṇāty ākara-vrātād
ajñaḥ siddhānta-san-maṇīn

śri-caitanya-prabhum—to Lord Caitanya Mahāprabhu; *vande*—I offer my respectful obeisances; *yat*—of whom; *pāda-āśraya*—of the shelter of the lotus feet; *vīryataḥ*—from the power; *saṅgṛhṇāti*—collects; *ākara-vrātāt*—from the multitude of mines in the form of scriptures; *ajñaḥ*—a fool; *siddhānta*—of conclusion; *sat-maṇīn*—the best jewels.

TRANSLATION

I offer my respectful obeisances to Śrī Caitanya Mahāprabhu. By the potency of the shelter of His lotus feet, even a fool can collect the valuable jewels of conclusive truth from the mines of the revealed scriptures.

TEXT 2

জয় জয় শ্রীচৈতন্য জয় নিত্যানন্দ ।
জয়াদ্বৈতচন্দ্র জয় গৌরভক্তবৃন্দ ॥ ২ ॥

jaya jaya śrī-caitanya jaya nityānanda
jayādvaita-candra jaya gaura-bhakta-vṛnda

jaya jaya—all glories; *śrī-caitanya*—to Lord Caitanya Mahāprabhu; *jaya*—all glories; *nityānanda*—to Lord Nityānanda; *jaya*—all glories; *advaita-candra*—to Advaita Ācārya; *jaya*—all glories; *gaura-bhakta-vṛnda*—to all the devotees of Lord Caitanya Mahāprabhu.

TRANSLATION

All glories to Lord Caitanya! All glories to Lord Nityānanda! All glories to Advaitacandra! And all glories to all the devotees of Lord Caitanya!

TEXT 3

তৃতীয় শ্লোকের অর্থ কৈল বিবরণ ।
চতুর্থ শ্লোকের অর্থ শুন ভক্তগণ ॥ ৩ ॥

tṛtīya ślokera artha kaila vivaraṇa
caturtha ślokera artha śuna bhakta-gaṇa

tṛtīya—third; *ślokera*—of the verse; *artha*—meaning; *kaila*—there was; *vivaraṇa*—description; *caturtha*—fourth; *ślokera*—of the verse; *artha*—meaning; *śuna*—please hear; *bhakta-gaṇa*—O devotees.

TRANSLATION

I have given the purport of the third verse. Now, O devotees, please listen to the meaning of the fourth with full attention.

TEXT 4

অনর্পিতচরীং চিরাৎ করুণয়াবতীর্ণঃ কলৌ
সমর্পয়িতুমুন্নতোজ্জ্বলরসাং স্বভক্তিশ্রিয়ম্ ।
হরিঃ পুরটসুন্দরদ্যুতিকদম্বসন্দীপিতঃ
সদা হৃদয়কন্দরে স্ফুরতু বঃ শচীনন্দনঃ ॥ ৪ ॥

anarpita-carīṁ cirāt karuṇayāvatīrṇaḥ kalau
samarpayitum unnatojjvala-rasāṁ sva-bhakti-śriyam
hariḥ puraṭa-sundara-dyuti-kadamba-sandīpitaḥ
sadā hṛdaya-kandare sphuratu vaḥ śacī-nandanaḥ

anarpita—not bestowed; *carīm*—having been formerly; *cirāt*—for a long time; *karuṇayā*—by causeless mercy; *avatīrṇaḥ*—descended; *kalau*—in the Age of Kali; *samarpayitum*—to bestow; *unnata*—elevated; *ujjvala-rasām*—the conjugal mellow; *sva-bhakti*—of His own service; *śriyam*—the treasure; *hariḥ*—the Supreme Lord; *puraṭa*—than gold; *sundara*—more beautiful; *dyuti*—of splendor; *kadamba*—with a multitude; *sandīpitaḥ*—illuminated; *sadā*—always; *hṛdaya-kandare*—in the cavity of the heart; *sphuratu*—let Him be manifest; *vaḥ*—your; *śacī-nandanaḥ*—the son of mother Śacī.

TRANSLATION

"May the Supreme Lord who is known as the son of Śrīmatī Śacīdevī be transcendentally situated in the innermost core of your heart. Resplendent with the radiance of molten gold, He has descended in the Age of Kali by His causeless mercy to bestow what no incarnation has ever offered before: the most elevated mellow of devotional service, the mellow of conjugal love."

PURPORT

This is a quotation from the *Vidagdha-mādhava* (1.2), a drama compiled and edited by Śrīla Rūpa Gosvāmī.

TEXT 5

পূর্ণ ভগবান্ কৃষ্ণ ব্রজেন্দ্রকুমার ।
গোলোকে ব্রজের সহ নিত্য বিহার ॥ ৫ ॥

pūrṇa bhagavān kṛṣṇa vrajendra-kumāra
goloke vrajera saha nitya vihāra

pūrṇa—full; *bhagavān*—the Supreme Personality of Godhead; *kṛṣṇa*—Lord Kṛṣṇa; *vrajendra-kumāra*—the son of the King of Vraja; *goloke*—in Goloka; *vrajera saha*—along with Vrajadhāma; *nitya*—eternal; *vihāra*—pastimes.

TRANSLATION

Lord Kṛṣṇa, the son of the King of Vraja, is the Supreme Lord. He eternally enjoys transcendental pastimes in His eternal abode, Goloka, which includes Vrajadhāma.

PURPORT

In the previous chapter it has been established that Kṛṣṇa, the son of Vrajendra (the King of Vraja), is the Supreme Personality of Godhead, with six opulences. He eternally enjoys transcendentally variegated opulences on His planet, which is known as Goloka. The eternal pastimes of the Lord in the spiritual planet Kṛṣṇaloka are called *aprakaṭa,* or unmanifested, pastimes because they are beyond the purview of the conditioned souls. Lord Kṛṣṇa is always present everywhere, but when He is not present before our eyes, He is said to be *aprakaṭa,* or unmanifested.

TEXT 6

ব্রহ্মার এক দিনে তিহোঁ একবার ।
অবতীর্ণ হঞা করেন প্রকট বিহার ॥ ৬ ॥

brahmāra eka dine tiṅho eka-bāra
avatīrṇa hañā karena prakaṭa vihāra

brahmāra—of Lord Brahmā; *eka*—one; *dine*—in the day; *tiṅho*—He; *eka-bāra*—one time; *avatīrṇa*—descended; *hañā*—being; *karena*—performs; *prakaṭa*—manifest; *vihāra*—pastimes.

TRANSLATION

Once in a day of Brahmā, He descends to this world to manifest His transcendental pastimes.

TEXT 7

সত্য, ত্রেতা, দ্বাপর, কলি, চারিযুগ জানি ।
সেই চারিযুগে দিব্য একযুগ মানি ॥ ৭ ॥

satya, tretā, dvāpara, kali, cāri-yuga jāni
sei cāri-yuge divya eka-yuga māni

satya—Satya; *tretā*—Tretā; *dvāpara*—Dvāpara; *kali*—Kali; *cāri-yuga*—four ages; *jāni*—we know; *sei*—these; *cāri-yuge*—in the four ages; *divya*—divine; *eka-yuga*—one age; *māni*—we consider.

TRANSLATION

We know that there are four ages [yugas], namely Satya, Tretā, Dvāpara and Kali. These four together constitute one divya-yuga.

TEXT 8

একাত্তর চতুর্যুগে এক মন্বন্তর ।
চৌদ্দ মন্বন্তর ব্রহ্মার দিবস ভিতর ॥ ৮ ॥

ekāttara catur-yuge eka manv-antara
caudda manv-antara brahmāra divasa bhitara

ekāttara—seventy-one; *catuḥ-yuge*—in cycles of four ages; *eka*—one; *manu-antara*—period of a Manu; *caudda*—fourteen; *manu-antara*—periods of Manu; *brahmāra*—of Lord Brahmā; *divasa*—a day; *bhitara*—within.

TRANSLATION

Seventy-one divya-yugas constitute one manv-antara. There are fourteen manv-antaras in one day of Brahmā.

PURPORT

A *manv-antara* is the period controlled by one Manu. The reign of fourteen Manus equals the length of one day (twelve hours) in the life of Brahmā, and the night of Brahmā is of the same duration. These calculations are given in the authentic astronomy book known as the *Sūrya-siddhānta.* A Bengali translation of this book was compiled by the great professor of astronomy and mathematics Bimal Prasād Datta, later known as Bhaktisiddhānta Sarasvatī Gosvāmī, who was our merciful spiritual master. He was honored with the title Siddhānta Sarasvatī for translating the *Sūrya-siddhānta*, and the title Gosvāmī Mahārāja was added when he accepted *sannyāsa*, the renounced order of life.

TEXT 9

'বৈবস্বত'-নাম এই সপ্তম মন্বন্তর ।
সাতাইশ চতুর্যুগ তাহার অন্তর ॥ ৯ ॥

'vaivasvata'-nāma ei saptama manv-antara
sātāiśa catur-yuga tāhāra antara

vaivasvata-nāma—named Vaivasvata; *ei*—this; *saptama*—seventh; *manu-antara*—period of Manu; *sātāiśa*—twenty-seven; *catuḥ-yuga*—cycles of four ages; *tāhāra*—of that; *antara*—period.

TRANSLATION

The present Manu, who is the seventh, is called Vaivasvata [the son of Vivasvān]. Twenty-seven divya-yugas [27 X 4,320,000 solar years] of his age have now passed.

PURPORT

The names of the fourteen Manus are as follows: (1) Svāyambhuva, (2) Svārociṣa, (3) Uttama, (4) Tāmasa, (5) Raivata, (6) Cākṣuṣa, (7) Vaivasvata, (8) Sāvarṇi, (9) Dakṣa-sāvarṇi, (10) Brahma-sāvarṇi, (11) Dharma-sāvarṇi, (12) Rudraputra (Rudra-sāvarṇi), (13) Raucya, or Deva-sāvarṇi, (14) and Bhautyaka, or Indra-sāvarṇi.

TEXT 10

অষ্টাবিংশ চতুর্যুগে দ্বাপরের শেষে ।
ব্রজের সহিতে হয় কৃষ্ণের প্রকাশে ॥ ১০ ॥

aṣṭāviṁśa catur-yuge dvāparera śeṣe
vrajera sahite haya kṛṣṇera prakāśe

aṣṭāviṁśa—twenty-eighth; *catuḥ-yuge*—in the cycle of four ages; *dvāparera*—of the Dvāpara-yuga; *śeṣe*—at the end; *vrajera sahite*—along with Vraja; *haya*—is; *kṛṣṇera*—of Lord Kṛṣṇa; *prakāśe*—manifestation.

TRANSLATION

At the end of the Dvāpara-yuga of the twenty-eighth divya-yuga, Lord Kṛṣṇa appears on earth with the full paraphernalia of His eternal Vraja-dhāma.

PURPORT

Now is the term of Vaivasvata Manu, during which Lord Caitanya appears. First Lord Kṛṣṇa appears at the close of the Dvāpara-yuga of the twenty-eighth *divya-yuga,* and then Lord Caitanya appears in the Kali-yuga of the same *divya-yuga.* Lord Kṛṣṇa and Lord Caitanya appear once in each day of Brahmā, or once in fourteen *manv-antaras,* each of seventy-one *divya-yugas* in duration.

From the beginning of Brahmā's day of 4,320,000,000 years, six Manus appear and disappear before Lord Kṛṣṇa appears. Thus

1,975,320,000 years of the day of Brahmā elapse before the appearance of Lord Kṛṣṇa. This is an astronomical calculation according to solar years.

TEXT 11

দাস্য, সখ্য, বাৎসল্য, শৃঙ্গার—চারি রস ।
চারি ভাবের ভক্ত যত কৃষ্ণ তার বশ ॥ ১১ ॥

dāsya, sakhya, vātsalya, śṛṅgāra—cāri rasa
cāri bhāvera bhakta yata kṛṣṇa tāra vaśa

dāsya—servitude; *sakhya*—friendship; *vātsalya*—parental affection; *śṛṅgāra*—conjugal love; *cāri*—four; *rasa*—mellows; *cāri*—four; *bhāvera*—of the sentiments; *bhakta*—devotees; *yata*—as many as there are; *kṛṣṇa*—Lord Kṛṣṇa; *tāra*—by them; *vaśa*—subdued.

TRANSLATION

Servitude [dāsya], friendship [sakhya], parental affection [vātsalya] and conjugal love [śṛṅgāra] are the four transcendental mellows [rasas]. By the devotees who cherish these four mellows, Lord Kṛṣṇa is subdued.

PURPORT

Dāsya, sakhya, vātsalya and *śṛṅgāra* are the transcendental modes of loving service to the Lord. *Śānta-rasa,* or the neutral stage, is not mentioned in this verse because although in *śānta-rasa* one considers the Absolute Truth the sublime great, one does not go beyond that conception. *Śānta-rasa* is a very grand idea for materialistic philosophers, but such idealistic appreciation is only the beginning; it is the lowest among the relationships in the spiritual world. *Śānta-rasa* is not given much importance because as soon as there is a slight understanding between the knower and the known, active loving transcendental reciprocations and exchanges begin. *Dāsya-rasa* is the basic relationship between Kṛṣṇa and His devotees; therefore this verse considers *dāsya* the first stage of transcendental devotional service.

TEXT 12

দাস-সখা-পিতামাতা-কান্তাগণ লঞা ।
ব্রজে ক্রীড়া করে কৃষ্ণ প্রেমাবিষ্ট হঞা ॥ ১২ ॥

dāsa-sakhā-pitā-mātā-kāntā-gaṇa lañā
vraje krīḍā kare kṛṣṇa premāviṣṭa hañā

dāsa—servants; *sakhā*—friends; *pitā-mātā*—father and mother; *kāntā-gaṇa*—lovers; *lañā*—taking; *vraje*—in Vraja; *krīḍā kare*—plays; *kṛṣṇa*—Lord Kṛṣṇa; *prema-āviṣṭa*—absorbed in love; *hañā*—being.

TRANSLATION

Absorbed in such transcendental love, Lord Śrī Kṛṣṇa enjoys in Vraja with His devoted servants, friends, parents and conjugal lovers.

PURPORT

The descent of Śrī Kṛṣṇa, the Absolute Personality of Godhead, is very purposeful. In the *Bhagavad-gītā* it is said that one who knows the truth about Śrī Kṛṣṇa's descent and His various activities is at once liberated and does not have to fall again to this existence of birth and death after he leaves his present material body. In other words, one who factually understands Kṛṣṇa makes his life perfect. Imperfect life is realized in material existence, in five different relationships we share with everyone within the material world: neutrality, servitorship, friendship, filial love and amorous love between husband and wife or lover and beloved. These five enjoyable relationships within the material world are perverted reflections of relationships with the Absolute Personality of Godhead in the transcendental nature. That Absolute Personality, Śrī Kṛṣṇa, descends to revive the five eternally existing relationships. Thus He manifests His transcendental pastimes in Vraja so that people may be attracted into that sphere of activities and leave aside their imitation relationships with the mundane. Then, after fully exhibiting all such activities, the Lord disappears.

TEXT 13

যথেষ্ট বিহরি' কৃষ্ণ করে অন্তর্ধান ।
অন্তর্ধান করি' মনে করে অনুমান ॥ ১৩ ॥

yatheṣṭa vihari' kṛṣṇa kare antardhāna
antardhāna kari' mane kare anumāna

yathā-iṣṭa—as much as He wishes; *vihari'*—enjoying; *kṛṣṇa*—Lord Kṛṣṇa; *kare*—makes; *antardhāna*—disappearance; *antardhāna kari'*—

disappearing; *mane*—in the mind; *kare*—He makes; *anumāna*—consideration.

TRANSLATION

Lord Kṛṣṇa enjoys His transcendental pastimes as long as He wishes, and then He disappears. After disappearing, however, He thinks thus:

TEXT 14

চিরকাল নাহি করি প্রেমভক্তি দান ।
ভক্তিবিনা জগতের নাহি অবস্থান ॥ ১৪ ॥

cira-kāla nāhi kari prema-bhakti dāna
bhakti vinā jagatera nāhi avasthāna

cira-kāla—for a long time; *nāhi kari*—I have not done; *prema-bhakti*—loving devotional service; *dāna*—giving; *bhakti*—devotional service; *vinā*—without; *jagatera*—of the universe; *nāhi*—not; *avasthāna*—existence.

TRANSLATION

"For a long time I have not bestowed unalloyed loving service to Me upon the inhabitants of the world. Without such loving attachment, the existence of the material world is useless.

PURPORT

The Lord seldom awards pure transcendental love, but without such pure love of God, freed from fruitive activities and empiric speculation, one cannot attain perfection in life.

TEXT 15

সকল জগতে মোরে করে বিধি-ভক্তি ।
বিধি-ভক্ত্যে ব্রজভাব পাইতে নাহি শক্তি ॥ ১৫ ॥

sakala jagate more kare vidhi-bhakti
vidhi-bhaktye vraja-bhāva pāite nāhi śakti

sakala—all; *jagate*—in the universe; *more*—to Me; *kare*—they do; *vidhi-bhakti*—regulative devotional service; *vidhi-bhaktye*—by regulative devotional service; *vraja-bhāva*—the feelings of those in Vraja; *pāite*—to obtain; *nāhi*—not; *śakti*—the power.

TRANSLATION

"Everywhere in the world people worship Me according to scriptural injunctions. But simply by following such regulative principles one cannot attain the loving sentiments of the devotees in Vrajabhūmi.

TEXT 16

ঐশ্বর্যজ্ঞানেতে সব জগৎ মিশ্রিত ।
ঐশ্বর্য-শিথিল-প্রেমে নাহি মোর প্রীত ॥ ১৬ ॥

aiśvarya-jñānete saba jagat miśrita
aiśvarya-śithila-preme nāhi mora prīta

aiśvarya-jñānete—with knowledge of the opulences; *saba*—all; *jagat*—the world; *miśrita*—mixed; *aiśvarya-śithila-preme*—to love enfeebled by opulence; *nāhi*—there is not; *mora*—My; *prīta*—attraction.

TRANSLATION

"Knowing My opulences, the whole world looks upon Me with awe and veneration. But devotion made feeble by such reverence does not attract Me.

PURPORT

After His appearance, Lord Kṛṣṇa thought that He had not distributed the transcendental personal dealings with His devotees in *dāsya, sakhya, vātsalya* and *mādhurya.* One may understand the science of the Supreme Personality of Godhead from the Vedic literatures and thus become a devotee of the Lord and worship Him within the regulative principles described in the scriptures, but one will not know in this way how Kṛṣṇa is served by the residents of Vrajabhūmi. One cannot understand the dealings of the Lord in Vṛndāvana simply by executing the ritualistic regulative principles mentioned in the scriptures. By following scriptural injunctions one may enhance his appreciation for the glories of the Lord, but there is no chance for one to enter into personal dealings with Him. Giving too much attention to understanding the exalted glories of the Lord reduces the chance of one's entering into personal loving affairs with the Lord. To teach the principles of such loving dealings, the Lord decided to appear as Lord Caitanya.

TEXT 17

ঐশ্বর্যজ্ঞানে বিধি-ভজন করিয়া ।
বৈকুণ্ঠকে যায় চতুর্বিধ মুক্তি পাঞা ॥ ১৭ ॥

aiśvarya-jñāne vidhi-bhajana kariyā
vaikuṇṭhake yāya catur-vidha mukti pāñā

aiśvarya-jñāne—in knowledge of the opulences; *vidhi*—according to rules and regulations; *bhajana*—worship; *kariyā*—doing; *vaikuṇṭhake*—to Vaikuṇṭha; *yāya*—they go; *catuḥ-vidha*—four kinds; *mukti*—liberation; *pāñā*—achieving.

TRANSLATION

"By performing such regulated devotional service in awe and veneration, one may go to Vaikuṇṭha and attain the four kinds of liberation.

TEXT 18

সার্ষ্টি, সারূপ্য, আর সামীপ্য, সালোক্য ।
সাযুজ্য না লয় ভক্ত যাতে ব্রহ্ম-ঐক্য ॥ ১৮ ॥

sārṣṭi, sārūpya, āra sāmīpya, sālokya
sāyujya nā laya bhakta yāte brahma-aikya

sārṣṭi—opulences equal with the Lord's; *sārūpya*—the same form as the Lord's; *āra*—and; *sāmīpya*—personal association with the Lord; *sālokya*—residence on a Vaikuṇṭha planet; *sāyujya*—oneness with the Lord; *nā laya*—they do not accept; *bhakta*—devotees; *yāte*—since; *brahma-aikya*—oneness with Brahman.

TRANSLATION

"These liberations are sārṣṭi [achieving opulences equal to those of the Lord], sārūpya [having a form the same as the Lord's], sāmīpya

[living as a personal associate of the Lord] and sālokya [living on a Vaikuṇṭha planet]. Devotees never accept sāyujya, however, since that is oneness with Brahman.

PURPORT

Those engaged in devotional service according to the ritualistic principles mentioned in the scriptures attain these different kinds of liberation. But although such devotees can attain *sārṣṭi, sārūpya, sāmīpya* and *sālokya,* they are not concerned with these liberations, for such devotees are satisfied only in rendering transcendental loving service to the Lord. The fifth kind of liberation, *sāyujya,* is never accepted even by devotees who perform only ritualistic worship. To attain *sāyujya,* or merging into the Brahman effulgence of the Supreme Personality of Godhead, is the aspiration of the impersonalists. A devotee never cares for *sāyujya* liberation.

TEXT 19

যুগধর্ম প্রবর্তাইমু নাম-সংকীর্তন ।
চারি ভাব-ভক্তি দিয়া নাচামু ভুবন ॥ ১৯ ॥

yuga-dharma pravartāimu nāma-saṅkīrtana
cāri bhāva-bhakti diyā nācāmu bhuvana

yuga-dharma—the religion of the age; *pravartāimu*—I shall inaugurate; *nāma-saṅkīrtana*—chanting of the holy name; *cāri*—four; *bhāva*—of the moods; *bhakti*—devotion; *diyā*—giving; *nācāmu*—I shall cause to dance; *bhuvana*—the world.

TRANSLATION

"I shall personally inaugurate the religion of the age—nāma-saṅkīrtana, the congregational chanting of the holy name. I shall make the world dance in ecstasy, realizing the four mellows of loving devotional service.

TEXT 20

আপনি করিমু ভক্তভাব অঙ্গীকারে ।
আপনি আচরি' ভক্তি শিখাইমু সবারে ॥ ২০ ॥

āpani karimu bhakta-bhāva aṅgīkāre
āpani ācari' bhakti śikhāimu sabāre

āpani—personally; *karimu*—I shall make; *bhakta-bhāva*—the position of a devotee; *aṅgīkāre*—acceptance; *āpani*—personally; *ācari'*—practicing; *bhakti*—devotional service; *śikhāimu*—I shall teach; *sabāre*—to all.

TRANSLATION

"I shall accept the role of a devotee, and I shall teach devotional service by practicing it Myself.

PURPORT

When one associates with a pure devotee, he becomes so elevated that he does not aspire even for *sārṣṭi, sārūpya, sāmīpya* or *sālokya,* because he feels that such liberation is a kind of sense gratification. Pure devotees do not ask anything from the Lord for their personal benefit. Even if offered personal benefits, pure devotees do not accept them, because their only desire is to satisfy the Supreme Personality of Godhead by transcendental loving service. No one but the Lord Himself can teach this highest form of devotional service. Therefore, when the Lord took the place of the incarnation of Kali-yuga to spread the glories of chanting Hare Kṛṣṇa—the system of worship recommended in this age—He also distributed the process of devotional service performed on the platform of transcendental spontaneous love. To teach the highest principles of spiritual life, the Lord Himself appeared as a devotee in the form of Lord Caitanya.

TEXT 21

আপনে না কৈলে ধর্ম শিখান না যায় ।
এই ত' সিদ্ধান্ত গীতা-ভাগবতে গায় ॥ ২১ ॥

āpane nā kaile dharma śikhāna nā yāya
ei ta' siddhānta gītā-bhāgavate gāya

āpane—personally; *nā kaile*—if not practiced; *dharma*—religion; *śikhāna*—the teaching; *nā yāya*—does not advance; *ei*—this; *ta'*—certainly; *siddhānta*—conclusion; *gītā*—in the *Bhagavad-gītā; bhāgavate*—in *Śrīmad-Bhāgavatam; gāya*—they sing.

TRANSLATION

"Unless one practices devotional service himself, he cannot teach it to others. This conclusion is indeed confirmed throughout the Gītā and Bhāgavatam.

TEXT 22

যদা যদা হি ধর্মস্য গ্লানির্ভবতি ভারত ।
অভ্যুত্থানমধর্মস্য তদাত্মানং সৃজাম্যহম্ ॥ ২২ ॥

yadā yadā hi dharmasya
glānir bhavati bhārata
abhyutthānam adharmasya
tadātmānaṁ sṛjāmy aham

yadā yadā—whenever; *hi*—certainly; *dharmasya*—of religious principles; *glāniḥ*—decrease; *bhavati*—there is; *bhārata*—O descendant of Bharata; *abhyutthānam*—increase; *adharmasya*—of irreligion; *tadā*—then; *ātmānam*—Myself; *sṛjāmi*—manifest; *aham*—I.

TRANSLATION

"'Whenever and wherever there is a decline in religious practice, O descendant of Bharata, and a predominant rise of irreligion—at that time I descend Myself.

TEXT 23

পরিত্রাণায় সাধূনাং বিনাশায় চ দুষ্কৃতাম্ ।
ধর্মসংস্থাপনার্থায় সম্ভবামি যুগে যুগে ॥ ২৩ ॥

paritrāṇāya sādhūnāṁ
vināśāya ca duṣkṛtām
dharma-saṁsthāpanārthāya
sambhavāmi yuge yuge

paritrāṇāya—for the deliverance; *sādhūnām*—of the devotees; *vināśāya*—for the destruction; *ca*—and; *duṣkṛtām*—of the miscreants; *dharma*—religious principles; *saṁsthāpana-arthāya*—for the purpose of establishing; *sambhavāmi*—I appear; *yuge yuge*—in every age.

TRANSLATION

"'To deliver the pious and to annihilate the miscreants, as well as to reestablish the principles of religion, I Myself appear, millennium after millennium.'

PURPORT

Texts 22 and 23 were spoken by Lord Kṛṣṇa in the *Bhagavad-gītā* (4.7–8). Texts 24 and 25, which follow, are also from the *Bhagavad-gītā* (3.24, 21).

TEXT 24

উৎসীদেয়ুরিমে লোকা ন কুর্যাং কর্ম চেদহম্ ।
সঙ্করস্য চ কর্তা স্যামুপহন্যামিমাঃ প্রজাঃ ॥ ২৪ ॥

utsīdeyur ime lokā
na kuryāṁ karma ced aham
saṅkarasya ca kartā syām
upahanyām imāḥ prajāḥ

udsīdeyuḥ—would fall into ruin; *ime*—these; *lokāḥ*—worlds; *na kuryām*—did not perform; *karma*—action; *cet*—if; *aham*—I; *saṅkarasya*—of unwanted population; *ca*—and; *kartā*—the creator; *syām*—would become; *upahanyām*—would spoil; *imāḥ*—these; *prajāḥ*—living entities.

TRANSLATION

"'If I did not show the proper principles of religion, all these worlds would fall into ruin. I would be the cause of unwanted population and would spoil all these living beings.'

TEXT 25

যদ্‌যদাচরতি শ্রেষ্ঠস্তত্তদেবেতরো জনঃ ।
স যৎ প্রমাণং কুরুতে লোকস্তদনুবর্ততে ॥ ২৫ ॥

yad yad ācarati śreṣṭhas
tat tad evetaro janaḥ
sa yat pramāṇaṁ kurute
lokas tad anuvartate

yat yat—however; *ācarati*—behaves; *śreṣṭhaḥ*—the best man; *tat tat*—that; *eva*—certainly; *itaraḥ*—the lesser; *janaḥ*—man; *saḥ*—he; *yat*—which; *pramāṇam*—standard; *kurute*—shows; *lokaḥ*—the people; *tat*—that; *anuvartate*—follow.

TRANSLATION

"'Whatever actions a great man performs, common people follow. And whatever standards he sets by exemplary acts, all the world pursues.'

TEXT 26

যুগধর্ম-প্রবর্তন হয় অংশ হৈতে ।
আমা বিনা অন্যে নারে ব্রজপ্রেম দিতে ॥ ২৬ ॥

yuga-dharma-pravartana haya aṁśa haite
āmā vinā anye nāre vraja-prema dite

yuga-dharma—of the religion of the age; *pravartana*—the inauguration; *haya*—is; *aṁśa*—the plenary portion; *haite*—from; *āmā*—for Me; *vinā*—except; *anye*—another; *nāre*—is not able; *vraja-prema*—love like that of the residents of Vraja; *dite*—to bestow.

TRANSLATION

"My plenary portions can establish the principles of religion for each age. No one but Me, however, can bestow the kind of loving service performed by the residents of Vraja.

TEXT 27

সন্ত্ববতারা বহবঃ পঙ্কজনাভস্য সর্বতোভদ্রাঃ ।
কৃষ্ণাদন্যঃ কো বা লতাস্বপি প্রেমদো ভবতি ॥ ২৭ ॥

santv avatārā bahavaḥ
paṅkaja-nābhasya sarvato-bhadrāḥ
kṛṣṇād anyaḥ ko vā latāsv
api prema-do bhavati

santu—let there be; *avatārāḥ*—incarnations; *bahavaḥ*—many; *paṅkaja-nābhasya*—of the Lord, from whose navel grows a lotus flower; *sarvataḥ-bhadrāḥ*—completely auspicious; *kṛṣṇāt*—than Lord Kṛṣṇa; *anyaḥ*—other; *kaḥ vā*—who possibly; *latāsu*—on the surrendered souls; *api*—also; *prema-daḥ*—the bestower of love; *bhavati*—is.

TRANSLATION

"'There may be many all-auspicious incarnations of the Personality of Godhead, but who other than Lord Śrī Kṛṣṇa can bestow love of God upon the surrendered souls?'

PURPORT

This quotation from the writings of Bilvamaṅgala Ṭhākura is found in the *Laghu-bhāgavatāmṛta* (1.5.37).

TEXT 28

তাহাতে আপন ভক্তগণ করি' সঙ্গে ।
পৃথিবীতে অবতরি' করিমু নানা রঙ্গে ॥ ২৮ ॥

tāhāte āpana bhakta-gaṇa kari' saṅge
pṛthivīte avatari' karimu nānā raṅge

tāhāte—in that; *āpana*—My own; *bhakta-gaṇa*—with devotees; *kari'*—doing; *saṅge*—in association; *pṛthivīte*—on the earth; *avatari'*—descending; *karimu*—I shall perform; *nānā*—various; *raṅge*—colorful pastimes.

TRANSLATION

"Therefore in the company of My devotees I shall appear on earth and perform various colorful pastimes."

TEXT 29

এত ভাবি' কলিকালে প্রথম সন্ধ্যায় ।
অবতীর্ণ হৈলা কৃষ্ণ আপনি নদীয়ায় ॥ ২৯ ॥

eta bhāvi' kali-kāle prathama sandhyāya
avatīrṇa hailā kṛṣṇa āpani nadīyāya

eta—thus; *bhāvi'*—thinking; *kali-kāle*—in the Age of Kali; *prathama*—first; *sandhyāya*—in the junction; *avatīrṇa hailā*—descended; *kṛṣṇa*—Lord Kṛṣṇa; *āpani*—Himself; *nadīyāya*—in Nadia.

TRANSLATION

Thinking thus, the Personality of Godhead, Śrī Kṛṣṇa Himself, descended at Nadia early in the Age of Kali.

PURPORT

The *prathama-sandhyā* is the beginning of the age. According to astronomical calculation, the age is divided into twelve parts. The first of these twelve divisions is known as the *prathama-sandhyā.* The *prathama-sandhyā* and *śeṣa-sandhyā,* the last division of the preceding age, form the junction of the two ages. According to the *Sūrya-siddhānta,* the *prathama-sandhyā* of Kali-yuga lasts 36,000 solar years. Lord Caitanya appeared in the *prathama-sandhyā* after 4,586 solar years of Kali-yuga had passed.

TEXT 30

চৈতন্যসিংহের নবদ্বীপে অবতার ।
সিংহগ্রীব, সিংহবীর্য, সিংহের হুঙ্কার ॥ ৩০ ॥

caitanya-siṁhera navadvīpe avatāra
siṁha-grīva, siṁha-vīrya, siṁhera huṅkāra

caitanya-siṁhera—of the lionlike Lord Caitanya Mahāprabhu; *nava-dvīpe*—at Navadvīpa; *avatāra*—the incarnation; *siṁha-grīva*—having the neck of a lion; *siṁha-vīrya*—the strength of a lion; *siṁhera huṅkāra*—the roar of a lion.

TRANSLATION

Thus the lionlike Lord Caitanya has appeared in Navadvīpa. He has the shoulders of a lion, the powers of a lion, and the loud voice of a lion.

TEXT 31

সেই সিংহ বসুক্ জীবের হৃদয়-কন্দরে ।
কল্মষ-দ্বিরদ নাশে যাঁহার হুঙ্কারে ॥ ৩১ ॥

sei siṁha vasuk jīvera hṛdaya-kandare
kalmaṣa-dvirada nāśe yāṅhāra huṅkāre

sei—that; *siṁha*—lion; *vasuk*—let Him sit; *jīvera*—of the living entities; *hṛdaya*—of the heart; *kandare*—in the cavern; *kalmaṣa*—of sins; *dvi-rada*—the elephant; *nāśe*—destroys; *yāṅhāra*—of whom; *huṅkāre*—the roar.

TRANSLATION

May that lion be seated in the core of the heart of every living being. Thus with His resounding roar may He drive away one's elephantine vices.

TEXT 32

প্রথম লীলায় তাঁর 'বিশ্বম্ভর' নাম ।
ভক্তিরসে ভরিল, ধরিল ভূতগ্রাম ॥ ৩২ ॥

prathama līlāya tāṅra 'viśvambhara' nāma
bhakti-rase bharila, dharila bhūta-grāma

prathama—first; *līlāya*—in the pastimes; *tāṅra*—of Him; *viśvambhara nāma*—the name Viśvambhara; *bhakti-rase*—with the mellow of devotional service; *bharila*—He filled; *dharila*—saved; *bhūta-grāma*—all the living entities.

TRANSLATION

In His early pastimes He is known as Viśvambhara because He floods the world with the nectar of devotion and thus saves the living beings.

TEXT 33

ডুভৃঞ্ ধাতুর অর্থ—পোষণ, ধারণ ।
পুষিল, ধরিল প্রেম দিয়া ত্রিভুবন ॥ ৩৩ ॥

ḍubhṛñ dhātura artha—poṣaṇa, dhāraṇa
puṣila, dharila prema diyā tri-bhuvana

ḍubhṛñ—known as *ḍubhṛñ* (*bhṛ*); *dhātura*—of the verbal root; *artha*—the meaning; *poṣaṇa*—nourishing; *dhāraṇa*—maintaining; *puṣila*—nourished; *dharila*—maintained; *prema diyā*—distributing love of God; *tri-bhuvana*—in the three worlds.

TRANSLATION

The verbal root "ḍubhṛñ" [which is the root of the word "viśvambhara"] indicates nourishing and maintaining. He [Lord Caitanya] nourishes and maintains the three worlds by distributing love of God.

TEXT 34

শেষলীলায় ধরে নাম 'শ্রীকৃষ্ণচৈতন্য' ।
শ্রীকৃষ্ণ জানায়ে সব বিশ্ব কৈল ধন্য ॥ ৩৪ ॥

śeṣa-līlāya dhare nāma 'śrī-kṛṣṇa-caitanya'
śrī-kṛṣṇa jānāye saba viśva kaila dhanya

śeṣa-līlāya—in His final pastimes; *dhare*—He held; *nāma*—the name; *śrī-kṛṣṇa-caitanya*—Śrī Kṛṣṇa Caitanya; *śrī-kṛṣṇa*—about Lord Kṛṣṇa; *jānāye*—He taught; *saba*—all; *viśva*—the world; *kaila*—made; *dhanya*—fortunate.

TRANSLATION

In His later pastimes He is known as Lord Śrī Kṛṣṇa Caitanya. He blesses the whole world by teaching about the name and fame of Lord Śrī Kṛṣṇa.

PURPORT

Lord Caitanya remained a householder only until His twenty-fourth year had passed. Then He entered the renounced order and remained manifest in this material world until His forty-eighth year. Therefore His *śeṣa-līlā*, or the final portion of His activities, lasted twenty-four years.

Some so-called Vaiṣṇavas say that the renounced order of life was not accepted in the Vaiṣṇava *sampradāya*, or disciplic succession, until Lord Caitanya. This is not a very intelligent proposition. Śrī Caitanya Mahāprabhu took the *sannyāsa* order from Śrīpāda Keśava Bhāratī, who belonged to the Śaṅkara sect, which approves of only ten names for *sannyāsīs.* Long before the advent of Śrīpāda Śaṅkarācārya, however, the *sannyāsa* order existed in the Vaiṣṇava line of Viṣṇu Svāmī. In the Viṣṇu Svāmī Vaiṣṇava *sampradāya,* there are ten different kinds of *sannyāsa* names and 108 different names for *sannyāsīs* who accept the *tri-daṇḍa*, the triple staff of *sannyāsa.* This is approved by the Vedic rules. Therefore Vaiṣṇava *sannyāsa* was existent even before the appearance of Śaṅkarācārya, although those who know nothing about Vaiṣṇava *sannyāsa* unnecessarily declare that there is no *sannyāsa* in the Vaiṣṇava *sampradāya.*

During the time of Lord Caitanya, the influence of Śaṅkarācārya in society was very strong. People thought that one could accept *sannyāsa* only in the disciplic succession of Śaṅkarācārya. Lord Caitanya could have performed His missionary activities as a householder, but He found householder life an obstruction to His mission. Therefore He decided to accept the renounced order, *sannyāsa.* Since His acceptance of *sannyāsa* was also designed to attract public attention, Lord Caitanya, not wishing to disturb the social convention, took the renounced order of life from a *sannyāsī* in the disciplic succession of Śaṅkarācārya, although *sannyāsa* was also sanctioned in the Vaiṣṇava *sampradāya.*

In the Śaṅkara-sampradāya there are ten different names awarded to *sannyāsīs:* (1) Tīrtha, (2) Āśrama, (3) Vana, (4) Araṇya, (5) Giri, (6) Parvata, (7) Sāgara, (8) Sarasvatī, (9) Bhāratī and (10) Purī. Before one enters *sannyāsa,* he has one of the various names for a *brahmacārī,* the assistant to a *sannyāsī. Sannyāsīs* with the titles Tīrtha and Āśrama generally stay at Dvārakā, and their *brahmacārī* name is Svarūpa. Those known by the names Vana and Araṇya stay at Puruṣottama, or Jagannātha Purī, and their *brahmacārī* name is Prakāśa. Those with the names Giri, Parvata and Sāgara generally stay at Badarikāśrama, and their *brahmacārī* name is Ānanda. Those with the titles Sarasvatī, Bhāratī and Purī usually live at Śṛṅgerī in South India, and their *brahmacārī* name is Caitanya.

Śrīpāda Śaṅkarācārya established four monasteries in India, in the four directions (north, south, east and west), and he entrusted them to four *sannyāsīs* who were his disciples. Now there are hundreds of branch monasteries under these four principal monasteries, and although there is an official symmetry among them, there are many differences in their dealings. The four different sects of these monasteries are known as Ānandavāra, Bhogavāra, Kīṭavāra and Bhūmivāra, and in course of time they have developed different ideas and different slogans.

According to the regulation of the disciplic succession, one who wishes to enter the renounced order in Śaṅkara's sect must first be trained as a *brahmacārī* under a bona fide *sannyāsī.* The *brahmacārī's* name is ascertained according to the group to which the *sannyāsī* belongs. Lord Caitanya accepted *sannyāsa* from Keśava Bhāratī. When He first approached Keśava Bhāratī, He was accepted as a *brahmacārī* with the name Śrī Kṛṣṇa Caitanya Brahmacārī. After He took *sannyāsa,* He preferred to keep the name Kṛṣṇa Caitanya.

The great authorities in the disciplic succession had not offered to explain why Lord Caitanya refused to take the name Bhāratī after He took *sannyāsa* from a Bhāratī, until Śrīla Bhaktisiddhānta Sarasvatī Gosvāmī Mahārāja volunteered the explanation that because a *sannyāsī* in the Śaṅkara-sampradāya thinks that he has become the Supreme, Lord Caitanya, wanting to avoid such a misconception, kept the name Śrī Kṛṣṇa Caitanya, placing Himself as an eternal servitor. A *brahmacārī* is supposed to serve the spiritual master; therefore He did not negate that relationship of servitude to His spiritual master. Accepting such a position is favorable for the relationship between the disciple and the spiritual master.

The authentic biographies also mention that Lord Caitanya accepted the *daṇḍa* (rod) and begging pot, symbolic of the *sannyāsa* order, at the time He took *sannyāsa.*

TEXT 35

তাঁর যুগাবতার জানি' গর্গ মহাশয় ।
কৃষ্ণের নামকরণে করিয়াছে নির্ণয় ॥ ৩৫ ॥

tāṅra yugāvatāra jāni' garga mahāśaya
kṛṣṇera nāma-karaṇe kariyāche nirṇaya

tāṅra—of Him; *yuga-avatāra*—incarnation for the age; *jāni'*—knowing; *garga*—Garga Muni; *mahāśaya*—the great personality; *kṛṣṇera*—of Lord Kṛṣṇa; *nāma-karaṇe*—in the name-giving ceremony; *kariyāche*—made; *nirṇaya*—ascertainment.

TRANSLATION

Knowing Him [Lord Caitanya] to be the incarnation for Kali-yuga, Garga Muni, during the naming ceremony of Kṛṣṇa, predicted His appearance.

TEXT 36

আসন্ বর্ণাস্ত্রয়ো হ্যস্য গৃহ্নতোঽনুযুগং তনূঃ ।
শুক্লো রক্তস্তথা পীত ইদানীং কৃষ্ণতাং গতঃ ॥ ৩৬ ॥

āsan varṇās trayo hy asya
gṛhṇato 'nu-yugaṁ tanūḥ
śuklo raktas tathā pīta
idānīṁ kṛṣṇatāṁ gataḥ

āsan—were; *varṇāḥ*—colors; *trayaḥ*—three; *hi*—certainly; *asya*—of this one; *gṛhṇataḥ*—who is manifesting; *anu-yugam*—according to the age; *tanūḥ*—bodies; *śuklaḥ*—white; *raktaḥ*—red; *tathā*—thus; *pītaḥ*—yellow; *idānīm*—now; *kṛṣṇatām*—blackness; *gataḥ*—obtained.

TRANSLATION

"This boy [Kṛṣṇa] has three other colors—white, red and yellow—as He appears in different ages. Now He has appeared in a transcendental blackish color."

PURPORT

This is a verse from *Śrīmad-Bhāgavatam* (10.8.13).

TEXT 37

শুক্ল, রক্ত, পীতবর্ণ—এই তিন দ্যুতি ।
সত্য-ত্রেতা-কলিকালে ধরেন শ্রীপতি ॥ ৩৭ ॥

śukla, rakta, pīta-varṇa—ei tina dyuti
satya-tretā-kali-kāle dharena śrī-pati

śukla—white; *rakta*—red; *pīta-varṇa*—the color yellow; *ei*—these; *tina*—three; *dyuti*—lusters; *satya*—in Satya-yuga; *tretā*—in Tretā-yuga; *kali-kāle*—in the Age of Kali; *dharena*—manifests; *śrī-pati*—the husband of the goddess of fortune.

TRANSLATION

White, red and yellow—these are the three bodily lusters that the Lord, the husband of the goddess of fortune, assumes in the ages of Satya, Tretā and Kali respectively.

TEXT 38

ইদানীং দ্বাপরে তিঁহো হৈলা কৃষ্ণবর্ণ ।
এই সব শাস্ত্রাগম-পুরাণের মর্ম ॥ ৩৮ ॥

idānīṁ dvāpare tiṅho hailā kṛṣṇa-varṇa
ei saba śāstrāgama-purāṇera marma

idānīm—now; *dvāpare*—in the Dvāpara-yuga; *tiṅho*—He; *hailā*—was; *kṛṣṇa-varṇa*—blackish color; *ei*—these; *saba*—all; *śāstra-āgama*—and Vedic literatures; *purāṇera*—of the *Purāṇas; marma*—the core.

TRANSLATION

Now, in the Dvāpara-yuga, the Lord had descended in a blackish hue. This is the essence of the statements in the Purāṇas and other Vedic literatures with reference to the context.

TEXT 39

দ্বাপরে ভগবান্ শ্যামঃ পীতবাসা নিজায়ুধঃ ।
শ্রীবৎসাদিভিরঙ্কৈশ্চ লক্ষণৈরুপলক্ষিতঃ ॥ ৩৯ ॥

dvāpare bhagavān śyāmaḥ
pīta-vāsā nijāyudhaḥ
śrī-vatsādibhir aṅkaiś ca
lakṣaṇair upalakṣitaḥ

dvāpare—in the Dvāpara-yuga; *bhagavān*—the Supreme Personality of Godhead; *śyāmaḥ*—blackish; *pīta-vāsāḥ*—having yellow clothes; *nija*—own; *āyudhaḥ*—having weapons; *śrīvatsa-ādibhiḥ*—such as Śrīvatsa; *aṅkaiḥ*—by bodily markings; *ca*—and; *lakṣaṇaiḥ*—by external characteristics such as the Kaustubha jewel; *upalakṣitaḥ*—characterized.

TRANSLATION

"In the Dvāpara-yuga the Personality of Godhead appears in a blackish hue. He is dressed in yellow, He holds His own weapons, and He is decorated with the Kaustubha jewel and marks of Śrīvatsa. This is how His symptoms are described."

PURPORT

This is a verse from *Śrīmad-Bhāgavatam* (11.5.27), spoken by Saint Karabhājana, one of the nine royal mystics who explained to King Nimi the different features of the Lord in different ages.

TEXT 40

কলিযুগে যুগধর্ম—নামের প্রচার ।
তথি লাগি' পীতবর্ণ চৈতন্যাবতার ॥ ৪০ ॥

kali-yuge yuga-dharma—nāmera pracāra
tathi lāgi' pīta-varṇa caitanyāvatāra

kali-yuge—in the Age of Kali; *yuga-dharma*—the religious practice for the age; *nāmera*—of the holy name; *pracāra*—propagation; *tathi*—this; *lāgi'*—for; *pīta-varṇa*—having a yellow color; *caitanya-avatāra*—the incarnation of Lord Caitanya.

TRANSLATION

The religious practice for the Age of Kali is to broadcast the glories of the holy name. Only for this purpose has the Lord, in a yellow color, descended as Lord Caitanya.

PURPORT

In this Age of Kali the practical system of religion for everyone is the chanting of the name of Godhead. This was introduced in this age by Lord Caitanya. *Bhakti-yoga* actually begins with the chanting of the holy name, as confirmed by Madhvācārya in his commentary on the *Muṇḍaka Upaniṣad.* He quotes this verse from the *Nārāyaṇa-saṁhitā:*

dvāparīyair janair viṣṇuḥ pañcarātrais tu kevalaiḥ
kalau tu nāma-mātreṇa pūjyate bhagavān hariḥ

"In the Dvāpara-yuga people should worship Lord Viṣṇu only by the regulative principles of the *Nārada-pañcarātra* and other such authorized books. In the Age of Kali, however, people should simply chant the holy names of the Supreme Personality of Godhead." The Hare Kṛṣṇa *mantra* is specifically mentioned in many *Upaniṣads*, such as the *Kali-santaraṇa Upaniṣad*, where it is said:

hare kṛṣṇa hare kṛṣṇa kṛṣṇa kṛṣṇa hare hare
hare rāma hare rāma rāma rāma hare hare

iti ṣoḍaśakaṁ nāmnāṁ kali-kalmaṣa-nāśanaṁ
nātaḥ paratāropāyaḥ sarva-vedeṣu dṛśyate

"After searching through all the Vedic literature, one cannot find a method of religion more sublime for this age than the chanting of Hare Kṛṣṇa."

TEXT 41

তপ্তহেম-সমকান্তি, প্রকাণ্ড শরীর ।
নবমেঘ জিনি কণ্ঠধ্বনি যে গম্ভীর ॥ ৪১ ॥

tapta-hema-sama-kānti, prakāṇḍa śarīra
nava-megha jini kaṇṭha-dhvani ye gambhīra

tapta-hema—as molten gold; *sama-kānti*—same luster; *prakāṇḍa*—enormous; *śarīra*—body; *nava-megha*—new clouds; *jini*—conquering; *kaṇṭha-dhvani*—the sound of the voice; *ye*—that; *gambhīra*—deep.

TRANSLATION

The luster of His expansive body resembles molten gold. The deep sound of His voice conquers the thundering of newly assembled clouds.

TEXT 42

দৈর্ঘ্য-বিস্তারে যেই আপনার হাত ।
চারি হস্ত হয় 'মহাপুরুষ' বিখ্যাত ॥ ৪২ ॥

dairghya-vistāre yei āpanāra hāta
cāri hasta haya 'mahā-puruṣa' vikhyāta

dairghya—in length; *vistāre*—and in breadth; *yei*—who; *āpanāra*—of his own; *hāta*—hand; *cāri*—four; *hasta*—cubits; *haya*—is; *mahā-puruṣa*—as a great personality; *vikhyāta*—celebrated.

TRANSLATION

One who measures four cubits in height and in breadth by his own hand is celebrated as a great personality.

TEXT 43

'ন্যগ্রোধপরিমণ্ডল' হয় তাঁর নাম ।
ন্যগ্রোধপরিমণ্ডল-তনু চৈতন্য গুণধাম ॥ ৪৩ ॥

'nyagrodha-parimaṇḍala' haya tāṅra nāma
nyagrodha-parimaṇḍala-tanu caitanya guṇa-dhāma

nyagrodha-parimaṇḍala—*nyagrodha-parimaṇḍala; haya*—is; *tāṅra*—of him; *nāma*—the name; *nyagrodha-parimaṇḍala*—*nyagrodha-parimaṇḍala*; *tanu*—having such a body; *caitanya*—Lord Caitanya Mahāprabhu; *guṇa-dhāma*—the abode of good qualities.

TRANSLATION

Such a person is called nyagrodha-parimaṇḍala. Śrī Caitanya Mahāprabhu, who personifies all good qualities, has the body of a nyagrodha-parimaṇḍala.

PURPORT

No one other than the Supreme Lord Himself, who has engaged the conditioned souls by His own illusory energy, can possess these bodily features. These features certainly indicate an incarnation of Viṣṇu and no one else.

TEXT 44

আজানুলম্বিতভুজ কমললোচন ।
তিলফুল-জিনি-নাসা, সুধাংশু-বদন ॥ ৪৪ ॥

ājānulambita-bhuja kamala-locana
tilaphula-jini-nāsā, sudhāṁśu-vadana

ā-jānu-lambita-bhuja—arms that reach the knees; *kamala-locana*—with lotus eyes; *tila-phula*—the blossom of the sesame plant; *jini*—conquering; *nāsā*—whose nose; *sudhā-aṁśu-vadana*—whose face is like the moon.

TRANSLATION

His arms are long enough to reach His knees, His eyes are just like lotus flowers, His nose is like a sesame flower, and His face is as beautiful as the moon.

TEXT 45

শান্ত, দান্ত, কৃষ্ণভক্তি-নিষ্ঠাপরায়ণ ।
ভক্তবৎসল, সুশীল, সর্বভূতে সম ॥ ৪৫ ॥

śānta, dānta, kṛṣṇa-bhakti-niṣṭhā-parāyaṇa
bhakta-vatsala, suśīla, sarva-bhūte sama

śānta—peaceful; *dānta*—controlled; *kṛṣṇa-bhakti*—to the service of Lord Kṛṣṇa; *niṣṭhā-parāyaṇa*—fully devoted; *bhakta-vatsala*—affectionate toward the devotees; *su-śīla*—good character; *sarva-bhūte*—to all living beings; *sama*—equal.

TRANSLATION

He is peaceful, self-controlled and fully devoted to the transcendental service of Lord Śrī Kṛṣṇa. He is affectionate toward His devotees, He is gentle, and He is equally disposed toward all living beings.

TEXT 46

চন্দনের অঙ্গদ-বালা, চন্দন-ভূষণ ।
নৃত্যকালে পরি' করেন কৃষ্ণসংকীর্তন ॥ ৪৬ ॥

candanera aṅgada-bālā, candana-bhūṣaṇa
nṛtya-kāle pari' karena kṛṣṇa-saṅkīrtana

candanera—of sandalwood; *aṅgada*—and armlets; *bālā*—bangles; *candana*—of sandalwood pulp; *bhūṣaṇa*—decorations; *nṛtya-kāle*—at the time of dancing; *pari'*—putting on; *karena*—does; *kṛṣṇa-saṅkīrtana*—congregational chanting of the name of Kṛṣṇa.

TRANSLATION

He is decorated with sandalwood bangles and armlets and anointed with the pulp of sandalwood. He especially wears these decorations to dance in śrī-kṛṣṇa-saṅkīrtana.

TEXT 47

এই সব গুণ লঞা মুনি বৈশম্পায়ন ।
সহস্রনামে কৈল তাঁর নাম-গণন ॥ ৪৭ ॥

ei saba guṇa lañā muni vaiśampāyana
sahasra-nāme kaila tāṅra nāma-gaṇana

ei—these; *saba*—all; *guṇa*—qualities; *lañā*—taking; *muni*—the sage; *vaiśampāyana*—named Vaiśampāyana; *sahasra-nāme*—in the *Viṣṇu-sahasra-nāma; kaila*—did; *tāṅra*—of Him; *nāma-gaṇana*—counting of the name.

TRANSLATION

Recording all these qualities of Lord Caitanya, the sage Vaiśampāyana included His name in the Viṣṇu-sahasra-nāma.

TEXT 48

দুই লীলা চৈতন্যের—আদি আর শেষ ।
দুই লীলায় চারি চারি নাম বিশেষ ॥ ৪৮ ॥

dui līlā caitanyera—ādi āra śeṣa
dui līlāya cāri cāri nāma viśeṣa

dui—two; *līlā*—pastimes; *caitanyera*—of Lord Caitanya Mahāprabhu; *ādi*—first; *āra*—and; *śeṣa*—final; *dui*—two; *līlāya*—in pastimes; *cāri*—four; *cāri*—and four; *nāma*—names; *viśeṣa*—specific.

TRANSLATION

The pastimes of Lord Caitanya have two divisions—the early pastimes [ādi-līlā] and the later pastimes [śeṣa-līlā]. He has four names in each of these two līlās.

TEXT 49

সুবর্ণবর্ণো হেমাঙ্গো বরাঙ্গশ্চন্দনাঙ্গদী ।
সন্ন্যাসকৃচ্ছমঃ শান্তো নিষ্ঠাশান্তিপরায়ণঃ ॥ ৪৯ ॥

suvarṇa-varṇo hemāṅgo
varāṅgaś candanāṅgadī
sannyāsa-kṛc chamaḥ śānto
niṣṭhā-śānti-parāyaṇaḥ

suvarṇa—of gold; *varṇaḥ*—having the color; *hema-aṅgaḥ*—whose body was like molten gold; *vara-aṅgaḥ*—having a most beautiful body; *candana-aṅgadī*—whose body was smeared with sandalwood; *sannyāsa-kṛt*—practicing the renounced order of life; *śamaḥ*—equipoised; *śāntaḥ*—peaceful; *niṣṭhā*—devotion; *śānti*—and of peace; *parāyaṇaḥ*—the highest resort.

TRANSLATION

"In His early pastimes He appears as a householder with a golden complexion. His limbs are beautiful, and His body, smeared with the pulp of sandalwood, seems like molten gold. In His later pastimes He accepts the sannyāsa order, and He is equipoised and peaceful. He is the highest abode of peace and devotion, for He silences the impersonalist nondevotees."

PURPORT

This is a verse from the *Mahābhārata* (*Dāna-dharma, Viṣṇu-sahasra-nāma-stotra*). In his commentary on the *Viṣṇu-sahasra-nāma,* called the *Nāmārtha-sudhā,* Śrīla Baladeva Vidyābhūṣaṇa, commenting upon this verse, asserts that Lord Caitanya is the Supreme Personality of Godhead according to the evidence of the *Upaniṣads.* He explains that *suvarṇa-varṇaḥ* means a golden complexion. He also quotes the Vedic injunction *yadā paśyaḥ paśyate rukma-varṇaṁ kartāram īśaṁ puruṣaṁ brahma-yonim* (*Muṇḍaka Up.* 3.1.3). *Rukma-varṇaṁ kartāram īśam* refers to the Supreme Personality of Godhead as having a complexion the color of molten gold. *Puruṣam* means the Supreme Lord, and *brahma-yonim* indicates that He is also the Supreme Brahman. This evidence, too, proves that Lord Caitanya is the Supreme Personality of Godhead Kṛṣṇa. Another meaning of the description of the Lord as having a golden hue is that Lord Caitanya's personality is as fascinating as gold is attractive. Śrīla Baladeva Vidyābhūṣaṇa has explained that the word *varāṅga* means "exquisitely beautiful."

Lord Caitanya accepted *sannyāsa,* leaving aside His householder life, to preach His mission. He has equanimity in different senses. First, He describes the confidential truth of the Personality of Godhead, and second, He satisfies everyone by knowledge and attachment to Kṛṣṇa. He is peaceful because He renounces all topics not related to the service of Kṛṣṇa. Śrīla Baladeva Vidyābhūṣaṇa has explained that the word *niṣṭhā* indicates His being rigidly fixed in chanting the holy name of Śrī Kṛṣṇa. Lord Caitanya subdued all disturbing opponents of devotional service, especially the monists, who are actually averse to the personal feature of the Supreme Lord.

TEXT 50

ব্যক্ত করি' ভাগবতে কহে বার বার ।
কলিযুগে ধর্ম—নামসংকীর্তন সার ॥ ৫০ ॥

vyakta kari' bhāgavate kahe bāra bāra
kali-yuge dharma—nāma-saṅkīrtana sāra

vyakta—evident; *kari'*—making; *bhāgavate*—in *Śrīmad-Bhāgavatam; kahe*—they say; *bāra bāra*—time and time again; *kali-yuge*—in the Age of Kali; *dharma*—the religion; *nāma-saṅkīrtana*—congregational chanting of the holy name; *sāra*—the essence.

TRANSLATION

In Śrīmad-Bhāgavatam it is repeatedly and clearly said that the essence of religion in the Age of Kali is the chanting of the holy name of Kṛṣṇa.

TEXT 51

ইতি দ্বাপর উর্বীশ স্তুবন্তি জগদীশ্বরম্ ।
নানাতন্ত্রবিধানেন কলাবপি যথা শৃণু ॥ ৫১ ॥

iti dvāpara urv-īśa
stuvanti jagad-īśvaram
nānā-tantra-vidhānena
kalāv api yathā śṛṇu

iti—thus; *dvāpare*—in the Dvāpara Age; *uru-īśa*—O King; *stuvanti*—they praise; *jagat-īśvaram*—the Lord of the universe; *nānā*—various; *tantra*—of scriptures; *vidhānena*—by the regulations; *kalau*—in the Age of Kali; *api*—also; *yathā*—in which manner; *śṛṇu*—please hear.

TRANSLATION

"O King, in this way people in Dvāpara-yuga worshiped the Lord of the universe. In Kali-yuga they also worship the Supreme Personality of Godhead by the regulations of the revealed scriptures. Kindly now hear of that from me.

PURPORT

This verse is spoken by Saint Karabhājana in *Śrīmad-Bhāgavatam* (11.5.31).

TEXT 52

কৃষ্ণবর্ণং ত্বিষাঽকৃষ্ণং সাঙ্গোপাঙ্গাস্ত্রপার্ষদম্ ।
যজ্ঞৈঃ সংকীর্তনপ্রায়ৈর্যজন্তি হি সুমেধসঃ ॥ ৫২ ॥

kṛṣṇa-varṇaṁ tviṣākṛṣṇaṁ
sāṅgopāṅgāstra-pārṣadam
yajñaiḥ saṅkīrtana-prāyair
yajanti hi su-medhasaḥ

kṛṣṇa-varṇam—repeating the syllables *kṛṣ-ṇa; tviṣā*—with a luster; *akṛṣṇam*—not black (golden); *sa-aṅga*—along with associates; *upāṅga*—servitors; *astra*—weapons; *pārṣadam*—confidential companions; *yajñaiḥ*—by sacrifice; *saṅkīrtana-prāyaiḥ*—consisting chiefly of congregational chanting; *yajanti*—they worship; *hi*—certainly; *su-medhasaḥ*—intelligent persons.

TRANSLATION

"In the Age of Kali, intelligent persons perform congregational chanting to worship the incarnation of Godhead who constantly sings the name of Kṛṣṇa. Although His complexion is not blackish, He is Kṛṣṇa Himself. He is accompanied by His associates, servants, weapons and confidential companions."

PURPORT

This text is from *Śrīmad-Bhāgavatam* (11.5.32). Śrīla Jīva Gosvāmī has explained this verse in his commentary on the *Bhāgavatam,* known as the *Krama-sandarbha,* wherein he says that Lord Kṛṣṇa also appears with a golden complexion. That golden Lord Kṛṣṇa is Lord Caitanya, who is worshiped by intelligent men in this age. That is confirmed in *Śrīmad-Bhāgavatam* by Garga Muni, who said that although the child Kṛṣṇa was blackish, He also appears in three other colors—red, white and yellow. He exhibited His white and red complexions in the Satya and Tretā ages respectively. He did not exhibit the remaining color, yellow-gold, until He appeared as Lord Caitanya, who is known as Gaura Hari.

Śrīla Jīva Gosvāmī explains that *kṛṣṇa-varṇam* means Śrī Kṛṣṇa Caitanya. *Kṛṣṇa-varṇa* and Kṛṣṇa Caitanya are equivalent. The name Kṛṣṇa appears with both Lord Kṛṣṇa and Lord Caitanya Kṛṣṇa. Lord Śrī Caitanya Mahāprabhu is the Supreme Personality of Godhead, but He always engages in describing Kṛṣṇa and thus enjoys transcendental bliss by chanting and remembering His name and form. Lord Kṛṣṇa Himself appears as Lord Caitanya to preach the highest gospel.

Lord Caitanya always chants the holy name of Kṛṣṇa and describes it also, and because He is Kṛṣṇa Himself, whoever meets Him will automatically chant the holy name of Kṛṣṇa and later describe it to others.

He injects one with transcendental Kṛṣṇa consciousness, which merges the chanter in transcendental bliss. In all respects, therefore, He appears before everyone as Kṛṣṇa, either by personality or by sound. Simply by seeing Lord Caitanya one at once remembers Lord Kṛṣṇa. One may therefore accept Him as *viṣṇu-tattva.* In other words, Lord Caitanya is Lord Kṛṣṇa Himself.

Sāṅgopāṅgāstra-pārṣadam further indicates that Lord Caitanya is Lord Kṛṣṇa. His body is always decorated with ornaments of sandalwood and with sandalwood paste. By His superexcellent beauty He subdues all the people of the age. In other descents the Lord sometimes used weapons to defeat the demoniac, but in this age the Lord subdues them with His all-attractive figure as Caitanya Mahāprabhu. Śrīla Jīva Gosvāmī explains that His beauty is His *astra,* or weapon, to subdue the demons. Because He is all-attractive, it is to be understood that all the demigods lived with Him as His companions. His acts were uncommon and His associates wonderful. When He propagated the *saṅkīrtana* movement, He attracted many great scholars and *ācāryas,* especially in Bengal and Orissa. Lord Caitanya is always accompanied by His best associates like Lord Nityānanda, Advaita, Gadādhara and Śrīvāsa.

Śrīla Jīva Gosvāmī cites a verse from the Vedic literature which says that there is no necessity of performing sacrificial demonstrations or ceremonial functions. He comments that instead of engaging in such external, pompous exhibitions, all people, regardless of caste, color or creed, can assemble together and chant Hare Kṛṣṇa to worship Lord Caitanya. *Kṛṣṇa-varṇaṁ tviṣākṛṣṇam* indicates that prominence should be given to the name of Kṛṣṇa. Lord Caitanya taught Kṛṣṇa consciousness and chanted the name of Kṛṣṇa. Therefore, to worship Lord Caitanya, everyone should together chant the *mahā-mantra*—Hare Kṛṣṇa, Hare Kṛṣṇa, Kṛṣṇa Kṛṣṇa, Hare Hare/ Hare Rāma, Hare Rāma, Rāma Rāma, Hare Hare. To propagate worship in churches, temples or mosques is not possible, because people have lost interest in that. But anywhere and everywhere, people can chant Hare Kṛṣṇa. Thus worshiping Lord Caitanya, they can perform the highest activity and fulfill the highest religious purpose of satisfying the Supreme Lord.

Śrīla Sārvabhauma Bhaṭṭācārya, a famous disciple of Lord Caitanya, said, "The principle of transcendental devotional service having been lost, Śrī Kṛṣṇa Caitanya has appeared in order to deliver again the process of devotion. He is so kind that He is distributing love of Kṛṣṇa. Everyone should be attracted more and more to His lotus feet, as humming bees are attracted to a lotus flower."

TEXT 53

শুন, ভাই, এই সব চৈতন্য-মহিমা ।
এই শ্লোকে কহে তাঁর মহিমার সীমা ॥ ৫৩ ॥

śuna, bhāi, ei saba caitanya-mahimā
ei śloke kahe tāṅra mahimāra sīmā

śuna—please hear; *bhāi*—O brothers; *ei*—this; *saba*—all; *caitanya*—of Lord Caitanya Mahāprabhu; *mahimā*—the glories; *ei*—this; *śloke*—verse; *kahe*—says; *tāṅra*—of Him; *mahimāra*—of the glories; *sīmā*—the limit.

TRANSLATION

My dear brothers, please hear all these glories of Lord Caitanya. This verse clearly summarizes His activities and characteristics.

TEXT 54

'কৃষ্ণ' এই দুই বর্ণ সদা যাঁর মুখে ।
অথবা, কৃষ্ণকে তিহোঁ বর্ণে নিজ সুখে ॥ ৫৪ ॥

'kṛṣṇa' ei dui varṇa sadā yāṅra mukhe
athavā, kṛṣṇake tiṅho varṇe nija sukhe

kṛṣṇa—kṛṣ-ṇa; ei—these; *dui*—two; *varṇa*—syllables; *sadā*—always; *yāṅra*—of whom; *mukhe*—in the mouth; *athavā*—or else; *kṛṣṇake*—Lord Kṛṣṇa; *tiṅho*—He; *varṇe*—describes; *nija*—His own; *sukhe*—in happiness.

TRANSLATION

The two syllables "kṛṣ-ṇa" are always in His mouth; or, He constantly describes Kṛṣṇa with great pleasure.

TEXT 55

কৃষ্ণবর্ণ-শব্দের অর্থ দুই ত প্রমাণ ।
কৃষ্ণ বিনু তাঁর মুখে নাহি আইসে আন ॥ ৫৫ ॥

kṛṣṇa-varṇa-śabdera artha dui ta pramāṇa
kṛṣṇa vinu tāṅra mukhe nāhi āise āna

kṛṣṇa-varṇa-śabdera—of the word *kṛṣṇa-varṇa; artha*—the meaning; *dui*—two; *ta*—certainly; *pramāṇa*—examples; *kṛṣṇa*—Kṛṣṇa; *vinu*—except for; *tāṅra*—of Him; *mukhe*—in the mouth; *nāhi āise*—does not come; *āna*—anything else.

TRANSLATION

These are two meanings of the word "kṛṣṇa-varṇa." Indeed, nothing else but Kṛṣṇa issues from His mouth.

TEXT 56

কেহ তাঁরে বলে যদি কৃষ্ণ-বরণ ।
আর বিশেষণে তার করে নিবারণ ॥ ৫৬ ॥

keha tāṅre bale yadi kṛṣṇa-varaṇa
āra viśeṣaṇe tāra kare nivāraṇa

keha—someone; *tāṅre*—to Him; *bale*—ascribes; *yadi*—if; *kṛṣṇa*—black; *varaṇa*—the color; *āra*—another; *viśeṣaṇe*—in the adjective; *tāra*—of that; *kare*—does; *nivāraṇa*—prevention.

TRANSLATION

If someone tries to describe Him as being of blackish complexion, the next adjective [tviṣā akṛṣṇam] immediately restricts him.

TEXT 57

দেহকান্ত্যে হয় তেঁহো অকৃষ্ণবরণ ।
অকৃষ্ণবরণে কহে পীতবরণ ॥ ৫৭ ॥

deha-kāntye haya teṅho akṛṣṇa-varaṇa
akṛṣṇa-varaṇe kahe pīta-varaṇa

deha-kāntye—in the luster of the body; *haya*—is; *teṅho*—He; *akṛṣṇa*—not black; *varaṇa*—the color; *akṛṣṇa-varaṇe*—by a color that is not blackish; *kahe*—one means; *pīta*—yellow; *varaṇa*—the color.

TRANSLATION

His complexion is certainly not blackish. Indeed, His not being blackish indicates that His complexion is yellow.

TEXT 58

কলৌ যং বিদ্বাংসঃ স্ফুটমভিযজন্তে দ্যুতিভরা-
দকৃষ্ণাঙ্গং কৃষ্ণং মখবিধিভিরুৎকীর্তনময়ৈঃ ।
উপাস্যঞ্চ প্রাহুর্যমখিলচতুর্থাশ্রমজুষাং
স দেবশ্চৈতন্যাকৃতিরতিতরাং নঃ কৃপয়তু ॥ ৫৮ ॥

kalau yaṁ vidvāṁsaḥ sphuṭam abhiyajante dyuti-bharād
akṛṣṇāṅgaṁ kṛṣṇaṁ makha-vidhibhir utkīrtana-mayaiḥ
upāsyaṁ ca prāhur yam akhila-caturthāśrama-juṣāṁ
sa devaś caitanyākṛtir atitarāṁ naḥ kṛpayatu

kalau—in the Age of Kali; *yam*—Him whom; *vidvāṁsaḥ*—the learned men; *sphuṭam*—clearly manifested; *abhiyajante*—worship; *dyuti-bharāt*—due to an abundance of bodily luster; *akṛṣṇa-aṅgam*—whose body is not blackish; *kṛṣṇam*—Lord Kṛṣṇa; *makha-vidhibhiḥ*—by the performances of sacrifice; *utkīrtana-mayaiḥ*—consisting of loud chanting of the holy name; *upāsyam*—worshipable object; *ca*—and; *prāhuḥ*—they said; *yam*—whom; *akhila*—all; *caturtha-āśrama-juṣām*—of those who are in the fourth order of life (*sannyāsa*); *saḥ*—He; *devaḥ*—the Supreme Personality of Godhead; *caitanya-ākṛtiḥ*—having the form of Lord Caitanya Mahāprabhu; *atitarām*—excessively; *naḥ*—unto us; *kṛpayatu*—let Him show His mercy.

TRANSLATION

"By performing the sacrifice of congregational chanting of the holy name, learned scholars in the Age of Kali worship Lord Kṛṣṇa, who is now nonblackish because of the great upsurge of the feelings of Śrīmatī Rādhārāṇī. He is the only worshipable Deity for the paramahaṁsas, who have attained the highest stage of the fourth order [sannyāsa]. May that Supreme Personality of Godhead, Lord Caitanya, show us His great causeless mercy."

PURPORT

This verse is *Dvitīya Śrī Caitanyāṣṭaka* 1, from the *Stava-mālā* of Śrīla Rūpa Gosvāmī.

TEXT 59

প্রত্যক্ষ তাঁহার তপ্তকাঞ্চনের দ্যুতি ।
যাঁহার ছটায় নাশে অজ্ঞান-তমস্ততি ॥ ৫৯ ॥

pratyakṣa tāṅhāra tapta-kāñcanera dyuti
yāṅhāra chaṭāya nāśe ajñāna-tamastati

pratyakṣa—vivid; *tāṅhāra*—of Him; *tapta*—molten; *kāñcanera*—of gold; *dyuti*—effulgence; *yāṅhāra*—of whom; *chaṭāya*—by the luster; *nāśe*—destroys; *ajñāna*—of ignorance; *tamastati*—the extent of the darkness.

TRANSLATION

One can vividly see His glowing complexion of molten gold, which dispels the darkness of ignorance.

TEXT 60

জীবের কল্মষ-তমো নাশ করিবারে ।
অঙ্গ-উপাঙ্গ-নাম নানা অস্ত্র ধরে ॥ ৬০ ॥

jīvera kalmaṣa-tamo nāśa karibāre
aṅga-upāṅga-nāma nānā astra dhare

jīvera—of the living entity; *kalmaṣa*—of sinful activities; *tamaḥ*—the darkness; *nāśa karibāre*—for destroying; *aṅga*—associates; *upāṅga*—devotees; *nāma*—holy names; *nānā*—various; *astra*—weapons; *dhare*—He holds.

TRANSLATION

The sinful life of the living beings results from ignorance. To destroy that ignorance, He has brought various weapons, such as His plenary associates, His devotees and the holy name.

TEXT 61

ভক্তির বিরোধী কর্ম-ধর্ম বা অধর্ম ।
তাহার 'কল্মষ' নাম, সেই মহাতমঃ ॥ ৬১ ॥

bhaktira virodhī karma-dharma vā adharma
tāhāra 'kalmaṣa' nāma, sei mahā-tamaḥ

bhaktira—to devotional service; *virodhī*—averse; *karma*—activity; *dharma*—religious; *vā*—or; *adharma*—irreligious; *tāhāra*—of that; *kalmaṣa*—sin; *nāma*—the name; *sei*—this; *mahā-tamaḥ*—great darkness.

TRANSLATION

The greatest ignorance consists of activities, whether religious or irreligious, that are opposed to devotional service. They are to be known as sins [kalmaṣa].

TEXT 62

বাহু তুলি' হরি বলি' প্রেমদৃষ্ট্যে চায় ।
করিয়া কল্মষ নাশ প্রেমেতে ভাসায় ॥ ৬২ ॥

bāhu tuli' hari bali' prema-dṛṣṭye cāya
kariyā kalmaṣa nāśa premete bhāsāya

bāhu tuli'—raising the arms; *hari bali'*—chanting the holy name; *prema-dṛṣṭye*—with His glance of deep love; *cāya*—He looks; *kariyā*—causing; *kalmaṣa*—to sins; *nāśa*—destruction; *premete*—in love of God; *bhāsāya*—He floods.

TRANSLATION

Raising His arms, chanting the holy name and looking upon all with deep love, He drives away all sins and floods everyone with love of Godhead.

TEXT 63

স্মিতালোকঃ শোকং হরতি জগতাং যস্য পরিতো
গিরান্তু প্রারম্ভঃ কুশলপটলীং পল্লবয়তি ।
পদালম্ভঃ কং বা প্রণয়তি ন হি প্রেমনিবহং
স দেবশ্চৈতন্যাকৃতিরতিতরাং নঃ কৃপয়তু ॥ ৬৩ ॥

smitālokaḥ śokaṁ harati jagatāṁ yasya parito
girāṁ tu prārambhaḥ kuśala-paṭalīṁ pallavayati
padālambhaḥ kaṁ vā praṇayati na hi prema-nivahaṁ
sa devaś caitanyākṛtir atitarāṁ naḥ kṛpayatu

smita—smiling; *ālokaḥ*—glance; *śokam*—the bereavement; *harati*—takes away; *jagatām*—of the world; *yasya*—whose; *paritaḥ*—all around; *girām*—of the speech; *tu*—also; *prārambhaḥ*—the beginning; *kuśala*—of auspiciousness; *paṭalīm*—the mass; *pallavayati*—causes to blossom; *pada-ālambhaḥ*—the taking hold of the lotus feet; *kam vā*—what possibly; *praṇayati*—leads to; *na*—not; *hi*—certainly; *prema-nivaham*—quantity of love of Godhead; *saḥ*—He; *devaḥ*—the Supreme Personality of Godhead; *caitanya-ākṛtiḥ*—having the form of Lord Caitanya Mahāprabhu; *atitarām*—excessively; *naḥ*—unto us; *kṛpayatu*—may He show His mercy.

TRANSLATION

"May the Supreme Personality of Godhead in the form of Lord Śrī Caitanya bestow His causeless mercy upon us. His smiling glance at once drives away all the bereavements of the world, and His very words enliven the auspicious creepers of devotion by expanding their leaves. Taking shelter of His lotus feet invokes transcendental love of God at once."

PURPORT

This verse is *Dvitīya Śrī Caitanyāṣṭaka* 8, from the *Stava-mālā* of Śrīla Rūpa Gosvāmī.

TEXT 64

শ্রীঅঙ্গ, শ্রীমুখ যেই করে দরশন ।
তার পাপক্ষয় হয়, পায় প্রেমধন ॥ ৬৪ ॥

śrī-aṅga, śrī-mukha yei kare daraśana
tāra pāpa-kṣaya haya, pāya prema-dhana

śrī-aṅga—His body; *śrī-mukha*—His face; *yei*—anyone who; *kare*—does; *daraśana*—seeing; *tāra*—of him; *pāpa-kṣaya*—destruction of sins; *haya*—there is; *pāya*—obtains; *prema-dhana*—the wealth of love of Godhead.

TRANSLATION

Anyone who looks upon His beautiful body or beautiful face becomes freed from all sins and obtains the wealth of love of Godhead.

TEXT 65

অন্য অবতারে সব সৈন্য-শস্ত্র সঙ্গে ।
চৈতন্য-কৃষ্ণের সৈন্য অঙ্গ-উপাঙ্গে ॥ ৬৫ ॥

anya avatāre saba sainya-śastra saṅge
caitanya-kṛṣṇera sainya aṅga-upāṅge

anya—other; *avatāre*—in incarnations; *saba*—all; *sainya*—soldiers; *śastra*—and weapons; *saṅge*—along with; *caitanya-kṛṣṇera*—of Lord Kṛṣṇa as Lord Caitanya; *sainya*—soldiers; *aṅga*—plenary parts; *upāṅge*—and associates.

TRANSLATION

In other incarnations the Lord descended with armies and weapons, but in this incarnation His soldiers are His plenary parts and associates.

TEXT 66

সদোপাস্যঃ শ্রীমান্ ধৃতমনুজকায়ৈঃ প্রণয়িতাং
বহদ্ভির্গীর্বাণৈর্গিরিশ-পরমেষ্ঠি-প্রভৃতিভিঃ ।
স্বভক্তেভ্যঃ শুদ্ধাং নিজভজনমুদ্রামুপদিশন্
স চৈতন্যঃ কিং মে পুনরপি দৃশোর্যাস্যতি পদম্ ॥ ৬৬ ॥

sadopāsyaḥ śrīmān dhṛta-manuja-kāyaiḥ praṇayitāṁ
vahadbhir gīr-vāṇair giriśa-parameṣṭhi-prabhṛtibhiḥ
sva-bhaktebhyaḥ śuddhāṁ nija-bhajana-mudrām upadiśan
sa caitanyaḥ kiṁ me punar api dṛśor yāsyati padam

sadā—always; *upāsyaḥ*—worshipable; *śrīmān*—beautiful; *dhṛta*—who accepted; *manuja-kāyaiḥ*—the bodies of men; *praṇayitām*—love; *vahadbhiḥ*—who were bearing; *gīḥ-vāṇaiḥ*—by the demigods; *giriśa*—Lord Śiva; *parameṣṭhi*—Lord Brahmā; *prabhṛtibhiḥ*—headed by; *sva-bhaktebhyaḥ*—unto His own devotees; *śuddhām*—pure; *nija-bhajana*—of His own worship; *mudrām*—the mark; *upadiśan*—instructing; *saḥ*—He; *caitanyaḥ*—Lord Caitanya; *kim*—what; *me*—my; *punaḥ*—again; *api*—certainly; *dṛśoḥ*—of the two eyes; *yāsyati*—He will go; *padam*—to the abode.

TRANSLATION

"Lord Śrī Caitanya Mahāprabhu is always the most worshipable Deity of the demigods, including Lord Śiva and Lord Brahmā, who came in the garb of ordinary men, bearing love for Him. He instructs His own pure devotional service to His own devotees. Will He again be the object of my vision?"

PURPORT

This verse is *Prathama Śrī Caitanyāṣṭaka* 1, from the *Stava-mālā* of Śrīla Rūpa Gosvāmī.

TEXT 67

আঙ্গোপাঙ্গ অস্ত্র করে স্বকার্যসাধন ।
'অঙ্গ'-শব্দের অর্থ আর শুন দিয়া মন ॥ ৬৭ ॥

āṅgopāṅga astra kare sva-kārya-sādhana
'aṅga'-śabdera artha āra śuna diyā mana

āṅga-upāṅga—plenary parts and associates; *astra*—weapons; *kare*—do; *sva-kārya*—of their own business; *sādhana*—as the accomplishment; *aṅga-śabdera*—of the word *aṅga; artha*—the meaning; *āra*—another; *śuna*—please hear; *diyā*—giving; *mana*—the mind.

TRANSLATION

His plenary parts and associates perform the work of weapons as their own specific duties. Please hear from me another meaning of the word "aṅga."

TEXT 68

'অঙ্গ'-শব্দের অংশ কহে শাস্ত্র-পরমাণ ।
অঙ্গের অবয়ব 'উপাঙ্গ'-ব্যাখ্যান ॥ ৬৮ ॥

'aṅga'-śabde aṁśa kahe śāstra-paramāṇa
aṅgera avayava 'upāṅga'-vyākhyāna

aṅga-śabde—by the word *aṅga,* or limb; *aṁśa*—part; *kahe*—says; *śāstra*—of the scriptures; *paramāṇa*—the evidence; *aṅgera*—of the limb; *avayava*—the constituent part; *upāṅga-vyākhyāna*—the exposition of the word *upāṅga.*

TRANSLATION

According to the evidence of the revealed scriptures, a bodily limb [aṅga] is also called a part [aṁśa], and a part of a limb is called a partial part [upāṅga].

TEXT 69

নারায়ণস্ত্বং ন হি সর্বদেহিনা-
মাত্মাস্যধীশাখিললোকসাক্ষী ।
নারায়ণোঽঙ্গং নরভূজলায়না-
ত্তচ্চাপি সত্যং ন তবৈব মায়া ॥ ৬৯ ॥

nārāyaṇas tvaṁ na hi sarva-dehinām
ātmāsy adhīśākhila-loka-sākṣī
nārāyaṇo 'ṅgaṁ nara-bhū-jalāyanāt
tac cāpi satyaṁ na tavaiva māyā

nārāyaṇaḥ—Lord Nārāyaṇa; *tvam*—You; *na*—not; *hi*—certainly; *sarva*—all; *dehinām*—of the embodied beings; *ātmā*—the Supersoul; *asi*—You are; *adhīśa*—O Lord; *akhila-loka*—of all the worlds; *sākṣī*—the witness; *nārāyaṇaḥ*—known as Nārāyaṇa; *aṅgam*—plenary portion; *nara*—of Nara; *bhū*—born; *jala*—in the water; *ayanāt*—due to the place of refuge; *tat*—that; *ca*—and; *api*—certainly; *satyam*—highest truth; *na*—not; *tava*—Your; *eva*—at all; *māyā*—the illusory energy.

TRANSLATION

"O Lord of lords, You are the seer of all creation. You are indeed everyone's dearest life. Are You not, therefore, my father, Nārāyaṇa? 'Nārāyaṇa' refers to one whose abode is in the water born from Nara [Garbhodakaśāyī Viṣṇu], and that Nārāyaṇa is Your plenary portion. All Your plenary portions are transcendental. They are absolute and are not creations of māyā."

PURPORT

This text was spoken to Lord Kṛṣṇa by Brahmā in *Śrīmad-Bhāgavatam* (10.14.14).

TEXT 70

জলশায়ী অন্তর্যামী যেই নারায়ণ ।
সেহো তোমার অংশ, তুমি মূল নারায়ণ ॥ ৭০ ॥

jala-śāyī antar-yāmī yei nārāyaṇa
seho tomāra aṁśa, tumi mūla nārāyaṇa

jala-śāyī—lying in the water; *antaḥ-yāmī*—indwelling Supersoul; *yei*—He who; *nārāyaṇa*—Lord Nārāyaṇa; *seho*—He; *tomāra*—Your; *aṁśa*—plenary portion; *tumi*—You; *mūla*—original; *nārāyaṇa*—Nārāyaṇa.

TRANSLATION

The manifestation of the Nārāyaṇa who predominates in everyone's heart, as well as the Nārāyaṇa who lives in the waters [Kāraṇa, Garbha and Kṣīra], is Your plenary portion. You are therefore the original Nārāyaṇa.

TEXT 71

'অঙ্গ'-শব্দে অংশ কহে, সেহো সত্য হয় ।
মায়াকার্য নহে—সব চিদানন্দময় ॥ ৭১ ॥

'aṅga'-śabde aṁśa kahe, seho satya haya
māyā-kārya nahe—saba cid-ānanda-maya

aṅga-śabde—by the word *aṅga; aṁśa*—plenary portion; *kahe*—one means; *seho*—that; *satya*—the truth; *haya*—is; *māyā*—of the material energy; *kārya*—the work; *nahe*—is not; *saba*—all; *cit-ānanda-maya*—full of knowledge and bliss.

TRANSLATION

The word "aṅga" indeed refers to plenary portions. Such manifestations should never be considered products of material nature, for they are all transcendental, full of knowledge and full of bliss.

PURPORT

In the material world, if a fragment is taken from an original object, the original object is reduced by the removal of that fragment. But the Supreme Personality of Godhead is not at all affected by the actions of *māyā.* The *Īśopaniṣad* says:

oṁ pūrṇam adaḥ pūrṇam idaṁ
pūrṇāt pūrṇam udacyate
pūrṇasya pūrṇam ādāya
pūrṇam evāvaśiṣyate

"The Personality of Godhead is perfect and complete, and because He is completely perfect, all emanations from Him, such as this phenomenal world, are perfectly equipped as complete wholes. Whatever is produced of the complete whole is also complete in itself. Because He is the complete whole, even though so many complete units emanate from Him, He remains the complete balance." (*Śrī Īśopaniṣad,* Invocation)

In the realm of the Absolute, one plus one equals one, and one minus one equals one. Therefore one should not conceive of a fragment of the Supreme Lord in the material sense. In the spiritual world there is no influence of the material energy or material calculations of fragments. In the Fifteenth Chapter of the *Bhagavad-gītā,* the Lord says that the living entities are His parts and parcels. There are innumerable living entities throughout the material and spiritual universes, but still Lord Kṛṣṇa is full in Himself. To think that God has lost His personality because His many parts and parcels are distributed all over the universe is an illusion. That is a material calculation. Such calculations are possible only under the influence of the material energy, *māyā.* In the spiritual world the material energy is conspicuous only by its absence.

In the category of *viṣṇu-tattva* there is no loss of power from one expansion to the next, any more than there is a loss of illumination as one candle kindles another. Thousands of candles may be kindled by an original candle, and all will have the same candle power. In this way it is to be understood that although all the *viṣṇu-tattvas,* from Kṛṣṇa and Lord Caitanya to Rāma, Nṛsiṁha, Varāha and so on, appear with different features in different ages, all are equally invested with supreme potency.

Demigods such as Lord Brahmā and Lord Śiva come in contact with the material energy, and their power and potency are therefore of different gradations. All the incarnations of Viṣṇu, however, are equal in potency, for the influence of *māyā* cannot even approach Them.

TEXT 72

অদ্বৈত, নিত্যানন্দ—চৈতন্যের দুই অঙ্গ ।
অঙ্গের অবয়বগণ কহিয়ে উপাঙ্গ ॥ ৭২ ॥

advaita, nityānanda—caitanyera dui aṅga
aṅgera avayava-gaṇa kahiye upāṅga

advaita—Advaita Ācārya; *nityānanda*—Lord Nityānanda; *caitanyera*—of Lord Caitanya Mahāprabhu; *dui*—two; *aṅga*—limbs; *aṅgera*—of the limbs; *avayava-gaṇa*—the constituent parts; *kahiye*—I say; *upāṅga*—parts.

TRANSLATION

Śrī Advaita Prabhu and Śrī Nityānanda Prabhu are both plenary portions of Lord Caitanya. Thus They are the limbs [aṅgas] of His body. The parts of these two limbs are called the upāṅgas.

TEXT 73

অঙ্গোপাঙ্গ তীক্ষ্ণ অস্ত্র প্রভুর সহিতে ।
সেই সব অস্ত্র হয় পাষণ্ড দলিতে ॥ ৭৩ ॥

aṅgopāṅga tīkṣṇa astra prabhura sahite
sei saba astra haya pāṣaṇḍa dalite

aṅga-upāṅga—plenary portions and parts; *tīkṣṇa*—sharp; *astra*—weapons; *prabhura sahite*—along with Lord Caitanya Mahāprabhu; *sei*—these; *saba*—all; *astra*—weapons; *haya*—are; *pāṣaṇḍa*—the atheists; *dalite*—to trample.

TRANSLATION

Thus the Lord is equipped with sharp weapons in the form of His parts and plenary portions. All these weapons are competent enough to crush the faithless atheists.

PURPORT

The word *pāṣaṇḍa* is very significant here. One who compares the Supreme Personality of Godhead to the demigods is known as a *pāṣaṇḍa. Pāṣaṇḍas* try to bring the Supreme Lord down to a mundane level. Sometimes they create their own imaginary God or accept an ordinary person as God and advertise him as equal to the Supreme Personality of Godhead. They are so foolish that they present someone as the next incarnation of Lord Caitanya or Kṛṣṇa although His activities are all contradictory to those of a genuine incarnation, and thus they fool the innocent public. One who is intelligent and who studies the characteristics of the Supreme Personality of Godhead with reference to the Vedic context cannot be bewildered by the *pāṣaṇḍas.*

Pāṣaṇḍas, or atheists, cannot understand the pastimes of the Supreme Lord or transcendental loving service to the Lord. They think that devotional service is no better than ordinary fruitive activities (*karma*). As the *Bhagavad-gītā* (4.8) confirms, however, the Supreme Personality of Godhead and His devotees, saving the righteous and chastising the miscreants (*paritrāṇāya sādhūnāṁ vināśāya ca duṣkṛtām*), always curb these nonsensical atheists. Miscreants always want to deny the Supreme Personality of Godhead and put stumbling blocks in the path of devotional service. The Lord sends His bona fide representatives and appears Himself to curb this nonsense.

TEXT 74

নিত্যানন্দ গোসাঞি সাক্ষাৎ হলধর ।
অদ্বৈত আচার্য গোসাঞি সাক্ষাৎ ঈশ্বর ॥ ৭৪ ॥

nityānanda gosāñi sākṣāt haladhara
advaita ācārya gosāñi sākṣāt īśvara

nityānanda gosāñi—Lord Nityānanda Gosāñi; *sākṣāt*—directly; *haladhara*—Lord Balarāma, the holder of the plow; *advaita ācārya gosāñi*—Śrī Advaita Ācārya Gosāñi; *sākṣāt*—directly; *īśvara*—the Personality of Godhead.

TRANSLATION

Śrī Nityānanda Gosāñi is directly Haladhara [Lord Balarāma], and Advaita Ācārya is the Personality of Godhead Himself.

TEXT 75

শ্রীবাসাদি পারিষদ সৈন্য সঙ্গে লঞা ।
দুই সেনাপতি বুলে কীর্তন করিয়া ॥ ৭৫ ॥

śrīvāsādi pāriṣada sainya saṅge lañā
dui senā-pati bule kīrtana kariyā

śrīvāsa-ādi—Śrīvāsa and others; *pāriṣada*—associates; *sainya*—soldiers; *saṅge*—along with; *lañā*—taking; *dui*—two; *senā-pati*—captains; *bule*—travel; *kīrtana kariyā*—chanting the holy name.

TRANSLATION

These two captains, with Their soldiers such as Śrīvāsa Ṭhākura, travel everywhere, chanting the holy name of the Lord.

TEXT 76

পাষণ্ডদলনবানা নিত্যানন্দ রায় ।
আচার্য-হুঙ্কারে পাপ-পাষণ্ডী পলায় ॥ ৭৬ ॥

pāṣaṇḍa-dalana-vānā nityānanda rāya
ācārya-huṅkāre pāpa-pāṣaṇḍī palāya

pāṣaṇḍa-dalana—of trampling the atheists; *vānā*—having the feature; *nityānanda*—Lord Nityānanda; *rāya*—the honorable; *ācārya*—of Advaita Ācārya; *huṅkāre*—by the war cry; *pāpa*—sins; *pāṣaṇḍī*—and atheists; *palāya*—run away.

TRANSLATION

Lord Nityānanda's very features indicate that He is the subduer of the unbelievers. All sins and unbelievers flee from the loud shouts of Advaita Ācārya.

TEXT 77

সংকীর্তন-প্রবর্তক শ্রীকৃষ্ণচৈতন্য ।
সংকীর্তন-যজ্ঞে তাঁরে ভজে, সেই ধন্য ॥ ৭৭ ॥

saṅkīrtana-pravartaka śrī-kṛṣṇa-caitanya
saṅkīrtana-yajñe tāṅre bhaje, sei dhanya

saṅkīrtana-pravartaka—the initiator of congregational chanting; *śrī-kṛṣṇa-caitanya*—Lord Caitanya Mahāprabhu; *saṅkīrtana*—of congregational chanting; *yajñe*—by the sacrifice; *tāṅre*—Him; *bhaje*—worships; *sei*—he; *dhanya*—fortunate.

TRANSLATION

Lord Śrī Kṛṣṇa Caitanya is the initiator of saṅkīrtana [congregational chanting of the holy name of the Lord]. One who worships Him through saṅkīrtana is fortunate indeed.

TEXT 78

সেই ত' সুমেধা, আর কুবুদ্ধি সংসার।
সর্ব-যজ্ঞ হৈতে কৃষ্ণনামযজ্ঞ সার ॥ ৭৮ ॥

sei ta' sumedhā, āra kubuddhi saṁsāra
sarva-yajña haite kṛṣṇa-nāma-yajña sāra

sei—he; *ta'*—certainly; *su-medhā*—intelligent; *āra*—others; *ku-buddhi*—poor understanding; *saṁsāra*—in the material world; *sarva-yajña haite*—than all other sacrifices; *kṛṣṇa-nāma*—of chanting the name of Lord Kṛṣṇa; *yajña*—the sacrifice; *sāra*—the best.

TRANSLATION

Such a person is truly intelligent, whereas others, who have but a poor fund of knowledge, must endure the cycle of repeated birth and death. Of all sacrificial performances, the chanting of the Lord's holy name is the most sublime.

PURPORT

Lord Śrī Caitanya Mahāprabhu is the father and inaugurator of the *saṅkīrtana* movement. One who worships Him by sacrificing his life, money, intelligence and words for the *saṅkīrtana* movement is recognized by the Lord and endowed with His blessings. All others may be said to be foolish, for of all sacrifices in which a man may apply his energy, a sacrifice made for the *saṅkīrtana* movement is the most glorious.

TEXT 79

কোটি অশ্বমেধ এক কৃষ্ণ নাম সম।
যেই কহে, সে পাষণ্ডী, দণ্ডে তারে যম ॥ ৭৯ ॥

koṭi aśvamedha eka kṛṣṇa nāma sama
yei kahe, se pāṣaṇḍī, daṇḍe tāre yama

koṭi—ten million; *aśvamedha*—horse sacrifices; *eka*—one; *kṛṣṇa*—of Lord Kṛṣṇa; *nāma*—name; *sama*—equal to; *yei*—one who; *kahe*—says; *se*—he; *pāṣaṇḍī*—atheist; *daṇḍe*—punishes; *tāre*—him; *yama*—Yamarāja.

TRANSLATION

One who says that ten million aśvamedha sacrifices are equal to the chanting of the holy name of Lord Kṛṣṇa is undoubtedly an atheist. He is sure to be punished by Yamarāja.

PURPORT

In the list of the ten kinds of offenses in chanting the holy name of the Supreme Personality of Godhead, Hare Kṛṣṇa, the eighth offense is *dharma-vrata-tyāga-hutādi-sarva-śubha-kriyā-sāmyam api pramādaḥ.* One should never consider the chanting of the holy name of Godhead equal to pious activities like giving charity to *brāhmaṇas* or saintly persons, opening charitable educational institutions, distributing free food and so on. The results of pious activities do not equal the results of chanting the holy name of Kṛṣṇa.

The Vedic scriptures say:

go-koṭi-dānaṁ grahaṇe khagasya
prayāga-gaṅgodaka-kalpa-vāsaḥ
yajñāyutaṁ meru-suvarṇa-dānaṁ
govinda-kīrter na samaṁ śatāṁśaiḥ

"Even if one distributes ten million cows in charity during an eclipse of the sun, lives at the confluence of the Ganges and Yamunā for millions of years, or gives a mountain of gold in sacrifice to the *brāhmaṇas,* he does not earn one hundredth part of the merit derived from chanting Hare Kṛṣṇa." In other words, one who accepts the chanting of Hare Kṛṣṇa to be some kind of pious activity is completely misled. Of course, it is pious; but the real fact is that Kṛṣṇa and His name, being transcendental, are far above all mundane pious activity. Pious activity is on the material platform, but chanting of the holy name of Kṛṣṇa is completely on the spiritual plane. Therefore, although *pāṣaṇḍīs* do not understand this, pious activity can never compare to the chanting of the holy name.

TEXT 80

'ভাগবতসন্দর্ভ'-গ্রন্থের মঙ্গলাচরণে ।
এ-শ্লোক জীবগোসাঞি করিয়াছেন ব্যাখ্যানে ॥ ৮০ ॥

'bhāgavata-sandarbha'-granthera maṅgalācaraṇe
e-śloka jīva-gosāñi kariyāchena vyākhyāne

bhāgavata-sandarbha-granthera—of the book called *Bhāgavata-sandarbha; maṅgala-ācaraṇe*—in the auspicious introduction; *e-śloka*—this verse; *jīva-gosāñi*—Jīva Gosvāmī; *kariyāchena*—has made; *vyākhyāne*—in explaining.

TRANSLATION

In the auspicious introduction to the Bhāgavata-sandarbha, Śrīla Jīva Gosvāmī has given the following verse as an explanation.

TEXT 81

অন্তঃকৃষ্ণং বহির্গৌরং দর্শিতাঙ্গাদিবৈভবম্ ।
কলৌ সংকীর্তনাদ্যৈঃ স্ম কৃষ্ণচৈতন্যমাশ্রিতাঃ ॥ ৮১ ॥

antaḥ kṛṣṇaṁ bahir gauraṁ
darśitāṅgādi-vaibhavam
kalau saṅkīrtanādyaiḥ sma
kṛṣṇa-caitanyam āśritāḥ

antaḥ—internally; *kṛṣṇam*—Lord Kṛṣṇa; *bahiḥ*—externally; *gauram*—fair-colored; *darśita*—displayed; *aṅga*—limbs; *ādi*—beginning with; *vaibhavam*—expansions; *kalau*—in the Age of Kali; *saṅkīrtana-ādyaiḥ*—by congregational chanting, etc.; *sma*—certainly; *kṛṣṇa-caitanyam*—unto Lord Caitanya Mahāprabhu; *āśritāḥ*—sheltered.

TRANSLATION

"I take shelter of Lord Śrī Kṛṣṇa Caitanya Mahāprabhu, who is outwardly of a fair complexion but is inwardly Kṛṣṇa Himself. In this Age of Kali He displays His expansions [His aṅgas and upāṅgas] by performing congregational chanting of the holy name of the Lord."

PURPORT

Śrīla Jīva Gosvāmī has placed the verse from *Śrīmad-Bhāgavatam* quoted in text 52 (*kṛṣṇa-varṇaṁ tviṣākṛṣṇam*) as the auspicious introduction to his *Bhāgavata-sandarbha,* or *Ṣaṭ-sandarbha.* He has composed this text (81), which is, in effect, an explanation of the *Bhāgavatam* verse, as the second verse of the same work. The verse from *Śrīmad-Bhāgavatam* was enunciated by Karabhājana, one of the nine great sages, and it is elaborately explained by the *Sarva-saṁvādinī,* Jīva Gosvāmī's commentary on his own *Ṣaṭ-sandarbha.*

Antaḥ kṛṣṇa refers to one who is always thinking of Kṛṣṇa. This attitude is a predominant feature of Śrīmatī Rādhārāṇī. Even though many devotees always think of Kṛṣṇa, none can surpass the *gopīs,* among whom Rādhārāṇī is the leader in thinking of Kṛṣṇa. Rādhārāṇī's Kṛṣṇa consciousness surpasses that of all other devotees. Lord Caitanya accepted the position of Śrīmatī Rādhārāṇī to understand Kṛṣṇa; therefore He was always thinking of Kṛṣṇa in the same way as Rādhārāṇī. By thinking of Lord Kṛṣṇa, He always overlapped Kṛṣṇa.

Śrī Kṛṣṇa Caitanya, who was outwardly very fair, with a complexion like molten gold, simultaneously manifested His eternal associates, opulences, expansions and incarnations. He preached the process of chanting Hare Kṛṣṇa, and those who are under His lotus feet are glorious.

TEXT 82

উপপুরাণেহ শুনি শ্রীকৃষ্ণবচন।
কৃপা করি ব্যাস প্রতি করিয়াছেন কথন ॥ ৮২ ॥

upa-purāṇeha śuni śrī-kṛṣṇa-vacana
kṛpā kari vyāsa prati kariyāchena kathana

upa-purāṇeha—in the *Upapurāṇas; śuni*—we hear; *śrī-kṛṣṇa-vacana*—the words of Lord Kṛṣṇa; *kṛpā kari*—having mercy; *vyāsa prati*—toward Vyāsadeva; *kariyāchena*—He did; *kathana*—speaking.

TRANSLATION

In the Upapurāṇas we hear Śrī Kṛṣṇa showing His mercy to Vyāsadeva by speaking to him as follows.

TEXT 83

অহমেব ক্বচিদ্‌ব্রহ্মন্ সন্ন্যাসাশ্রমমাশ্রিতঃ ।
হরিভক্তিং গ্রাহয়ামি কলৌ পাপহতান্নরান্ ॥ ৮৩ ॥

aham eva kvacid brahman
sannyāsāśramam āśritaḥ
hari-bhaktiṁ grāhayāmi
kalau pāpa-hatān narān

aham—I; *eva*—certainly; *kvacit*—somewhere; *brahman*—O *brāhmaṇa; sannyāsa-āśramam*—the renounced order of life; *āśritaḥ*—taking recourse to; *hari-bhaktim*—devotional service to the Supreme Personality of Godhead; *grāhayāmi*—I shall give; *kalau*—in the Age of Kali; *pāpa-hatān*—sinful; *narān*—to men.

TRANSLATION

"O learned brāhmaṇa, sometimes I accept the renounced order of life to induce the fallen people of the Age of Kali to accept devotional service to the Lord."

TEXT 84

ভাগবত, ভারতশাস্ত্র, আগম, পুরাণ ।
চৈতন্য-কৃষ্ণ-অবতারে প্রকট প্রমাণ ॥ ৮৪ ॥

bhāgavata, bhārata-śāstra, āgama, purāṇa
caitanya-kṛṣṇa-avatāre prakaṭa pramāṇa

bhāgavata—*Śrīmad-Bhāgavatam; bhārata-śāstra*—*Mahābhārata; āgama*—Vedic literatures; *purāṇa*—the *Purāṇas; caitanya*—as Lord Caitanya Mahāprabhu; *kṛṣṇa*—of Lord Kṛṣṇa; *avatāre*—in the incarnation; *prakaṭa*—displayed; *pramāṇa*—evidence.

TRANSLATION

Śrīmad-Bhāgavatam, the Mahābhārata, the Purāṇas and other Vedic literatures all give evidence to prove that Lord Śrī Kṛṣṇa Caitanya Mahāprabhu is the incarnation of Kṛṣṇa.

TEXT 85

প্রত্যক্ষে দেখহ নানা প্রকট প্রভাব ।
অলৌকিক কর্ম, অলৌকিক অনুভাব ॥ ৮৫ ॥

pratyakṣe dekhaha nānā prakaṭa prabhāva
alaukika karma, alaukika anubhāva

pratyakṣe—directly; *dekhaha*—just see; *nānā*—various; *prakaṭa*—manifested; *prabhāva*—influence; *alaukika*—uncommon; *karma*—activities; *alaukika*—uncommon; *anubhāva*—realizations in Kṛṣṇa consciousness.

TRANSLATION

One can also directly see Lord Caitanya's manifest influence in His uncommon deeds and uncommon Kṛṣṇa conscious realization.

TEXT 86

দেখিয়া না দেখে যত অভক্তের গণ ।
উলূকে না দেখে যেন সূর্যের কিরণ ॥ ৮৬ ॥

dekhiyā nā dekhe yata abhaktera gaṇa
ulūke nā dekhe yena sūryera kiraṇa

dekhiyā—seeing; *nā dekhe*—they do not see; *yata*—all; *abhaktera*—of nondevotees; *gaṇa*—crowds; *ulūke*—the owl; *nā dekhe*—does not see; *yena*—just as; *sūryera*—of the sun; *kiraṇa*—rays.

TRANSLATION

But faithless unbelievers do not see what is clearly evident, just as owls do not see the rays of the sun.

TEXT 87

ত্বাং শীলরূপচরিতৈঃ পরমপ্রকৃষ্টৈঃ
সত্ত্বেন সাত্ত্বিকতয়া প্রবলৈশ্চ শাস্ত্রৈঃ ।
প্রখ্যাতদৈবপরমার্থবিদাং মতৈশ্চ
নৈবাসুরপ্রকৃতয়ঃ প্রভবন্তি বোদ্ধুম্ ॥ ৮৭ ॥

tvāṁ śīla-rūpa-caritaiḥ parama-prakṛṣṭaiḥ
sattvena sāttvikatayā prabalaiś ca śāstraiḥ
prakhyāta-daiva-paramārtha-vidāṁ mataiś ca
naivāsura-prakṛtayaḥ prabhavanti boddhum

tvām—You; *śīla*—character; *rūpa*—forms; *caritaiḥ*—by acts; *parama*—most; *prakṛṣṭaiḥ*—eminent; *sattvena*—by uncommon power; *sāttvikatayā*—with the quality of predominant goodness; *prabalaiḥ*—great; *ca*—and; *śāstraiḥ*—by the scriptures; *prakhyāta*—renowned; *daiva*—divine; *parama-artha-vidām*—of those who know the highest goal; *mataiḥ*—by the opinions; *ca*—and; *na*—not; *eva*—certainly; *āsura-prakṛtayaḥ*—those whose disposition is demoniac; *prabhavanti*—are able; *boddhum*—to know.

TRANSLATION

"O my Lord, those influenced by demoniac principles cannot realize You, although You are clearly the Supreme by dint of Your exalted activities, forms, character and uncommon power, which are confirmed by all the revealed scriptures in the quality of goodness and the celebrated transcendentalists in the divine nature."

PURPORT

This is a verse from the *Stotra-ratna* (12) of Yāmunācārya, the spiritual master of Rāmānujācārya. The authentic scriptures describe the transcendental activities, features, form and qualities of Kṛṣṇa, and Kṛṣṇa explains Himself in the *Bhagavad-gītā*, the most authentic scripture in the world. He is further explained in *Śrīmad-Bhāgavatam*, which is considered the explanation of the *Vedānta-sūtra*. Lord Kṛṣṇa is accepted as the Supreme Personality of Godhead by these authentic scriptures, not simply by *vox populi*. In the modern age a certain class of fools think that they can vote anyone into the position of God, as they can vote a man into the position of a political executive head. But the transcendental Supreme Personality of Godhead is perfectly described in the authentic scriptures. In the *Bhagavad-gītā* the Lord says that only fools deride Him, thinking that anyone can speak like Kṛṣṇa.

Even according to historical references, Kṛṣṇa's activities are most uncommon. Kṛṣṇa has affirmed, "I am God," and He has acted accordingly. Māyāvādīs think that everyone can claim to be God, but that is their illusion, for no one else can perform such extraordinary activities as Kṛṣṇa. When He was a child on the lap of His mother, He killed the demon Pūtanā. Then He killed the demons Tṛṇāvarta, Vatsāsura and Baka. When He was a little more grown up, He killed the demons Aghāsura and Ṛṣabhāsura. Therefore God is God from the very beginning. The idea that someone can become God by meditation is ridiculous. By hard endeavor one may realize his godly nature, but he will never become God. The *asuras,* or demons, who think that anyone can become God, are condemned.

The authentic scriptures are compiled by personalities like Vyāsadeva, Nārada, Asita and Parāśara, who are not ordinary men. All the followers of the Vedic way of life have accepted these famous personalities, whose authentic scriptures conform to the Vedic literature. Nevertheless, the demoniac do not believe their statements, and they purposely oppose the Supreme Personality of Godhead and His devotees. Today it is fashionable for common men to write whimsical words as so-called incarnations of God and be accepted as authentic by other common men. This demoniac mentality is condemned in the Seventh Chapter of the *Bhagavad-gītā,* wherein it is said that those who are miscreants and the lowest of mankind, who are fools and asses, cannot accept the Supreme Personality of Godhead because of their demoniac nature. They are compared to *ulūkas,* or owls, who cannot open their eyes in the sunlight. Because they cannot bear the sunlight, they hide themselves from it and never see it. They cannot believe that there is such illumination.

TEXT 88

আপনা লুকাইতে কৃষ্ণ নানা যত্ন করে ।
তথাপি তাঁহার ভক্ত জানয়ে তাঁহারে ॥ ৮৮ ॥

āpanā lukāite kṛṣṇa nānā yatna kare
tathāpi tāṅhāra bhakta jānaye tāṅhāre

āpanā—Himself; *lukāite*—to hide; *kṛṣṇa*—Lord Kṛṣṇa; *nānā*—various; *yatna*—efforts; *kare*—makes; *tathāpi*—still; *tāṅhāra*—His; *bhakta*—devotees; *jānaye*—know; *tāṅhāre*—Him.

TRANSLATION

Lord Śrī Kṛṣṇa tries to hide Himself in various ways, but nevertheless His pure devotees know Him as He is.

TEXT 89

উল্লংঘিতত্রিবিধসীমসমাতিশায়ি-
সম্ভাবনং তব পরিব্রঢ়িম-স্বভাবম্ ।
মায়াবলেন ভবতাপি নিগুহ্যমানং
পশ্যন্তি কেচিদনিশং ত্বদনন্যভাবাঃ ॥ ৮৯ ॥

ullaṅghita-trividha-sīma-samātiśāyi-
sambhāvanaṁ tava parivraḍhima-svabhāvam
māyā-balena bhavatāpi niguhyamānaṁ
paśyanti kecid aniśaṁ tvad-ananya-bhāvāḥ

ullaṅghita—passed over; *tri-vidha*—three kinds; *sīma*—the limitations; *sama*—of equal; *atiśāyi*—and of excelling; *sambhāvanam*—by which the adequacy; *tava*—Your; *parivraḍhima*—of supremacy; *svabhāvam*—the real nature; *māyā-balena*—by the strength of the illusory energy; *bhavatā*—Your; *api*—although; *niguhyamānam*—being hidden; *paśyanti*—they see; *kecit*—some; *aniśam*—always; *tvat*—to You; *ananya-bhāvāḥ*—those who are exclusively devoted.

TRANSLATION

"O my Lord, everything within material nature is limited by time, space and thought. Your characteristics, however, being unequaled and unsurpassed, are always transcendental to such limitations. You sometimes cover such characteristics by Your own energy, but nevertheless Your unalloyed devotees are always able to see You under all circumstances."

PURPORT

This verse is also quoted from the *Stotra-ratna* (13) of Yāmunācārya. Everything covered by the influence of *māyā* is within the limited boundaries of space, time and thought. Even the greatest manifestation we can conceive, the sky, also has limitations. From the authentic scriptures, however, it is evident that beyond the sky is a covering of seven layers, each ten times thicker than the one preceding it. The covering layers are vast, but with or without coverings, space is limited. Our power to think about space and time is also limited. Time is eternal; we may imagine billions and trillions of years, but that will still be an inadequate estimate of the extent of time. Our imperfect senses, therefore, cannot think of the greatness of the Supreme Personality of Godhead, nor can we bring Him within the limitations of time or our thinking power. His position is accordingly described by the word *ullaṅghita.* He is transcendental to space, time and thought; although He appears within them, He exists transcendentally. Even when the Lord's transcendental existence is disguised by space, time and thought, however, pure devotees of the Supreme Lord can see Him in His personal features beyond space, time and thought. In other words, even though the Lord is not visible to the eyes of ordinary men, those who are beyond the covering layers because of their transcendental devotional service can still see Him.

The sun may appear covered by a cloud, but actually it is the eyes of the tiny people below the cloud that are covered, not the sun. If those tiny people rose above the cloud in an airplane, they could then see the sunshine and the sun without impediment. Similarly, although the covering of *māyā* is very strong, Lord Kṛṣṇa says in the *Bhagavad-gītā* (7.14):

daivī hy eṣā guṇa-mayī mama māyā duratyayā
mām eva ye prapadyante māyām etāṁ taranti te

"This divine energy of Mine, consisting of the three modes of material nature, is difficult to overcome. But those who have surrendered unto Me can easily cross beyond it." To surpass the influence of the illusory energy is very difficult, but those who are determined to catch hold of the lotus feet of the Lord are freed from the clutches of *māyā*. Therefore, pure devotees can understand the Supreme Personality of Godhead, but demons, because of their miscreant behavior, cannot understand the Lord, in spite of seeing the many revealed scriptures and the uncommon activities of the Lord.

TEXT 90

অসুরস্বভাবে কৃষ্ণে কভু নাহি জানে ।
লুকাইতে নারে কৃষ্ণ ভক্তজন-স্থানে ॥ ৯০ ॥

asura-svabhāve kṛṣṇe kabhu nāhi jāne
lukāite nāre kṛṣṇa bhakta-jana-sthāne

asura-svabhāve—those whose nature is demoniac; *kṛṣṇe*—Lord Kṛṣṇa; *kabhu*—at any time; *nāhi*—not; *jāne*—know; *lukāite*—to hide; *nāre*—is not able; *kṛṣṇa*—Lord Kṛṣṇa; *bhakta-jana*—of pure devotees; *sthāne*—in a place.

TRANSLATION

Those whose nature is demoniac cannot know Kṛṣṇa at any time, but He cannot hide Himself from His pure devotees.

PURPORT

People who develop the nature of *asuras* like Rāvaṇa and Hiraṇyakaśipu can never know Kṛṣṇa, the Personality of Godhead, by challenging the authority of Godhead. But Śrī Kṛṣṇa cannot hide Himself from His pure devotees.

TEXT 91

দ্বৌ ভূতসর্গৌ লোকেঽস্মিন্ দৈব আসুর এব চ ।
বিষ্ণুভক্তঃ স্মৃতো দৈব আসুরস্তদ্বিপর্যয়ঃ ॥ ৯১ ॥

dvau bhūta-sargau loke 'smin
daiva āsura eva ca
viṣṇu-bhaktaḥ smṛto daiva
āsuras tad-viparyayaḥ

dvau—two; *bhūta*—of the living beings; *sargau*—dispositions; *loke*—in the world; *asmin*—in this; *daivaḥ*—godly; *āsuraḥ*—demoniac; *eva*—certainly; *ca*—and; *viṣṇu-bhaktaḥ*—a devotee of Lord Viṣṇu; *smṛtaḥ*—remembered; *daivaḥ*—godly; *āsuraḥ*—demoniac; *tat-viparyayaḥ*—the opposite of that.

TRANSLATION

"There are two classes of men in the created world. One consists of the demoniac and the other of the godly. The devotees of Lord Viṣṇu are the godly, whereas those who are just the opposite are called demons."

PURPORT

This is a verse from the *Padma Purāṇa*. *Viṣṇu-bhaktas*, or devotees in Kṛṣṇa consciousness, are known as *devas* (demigods). Atheists, who do not believe in God or who declare themselves God, are *asuras* (demons). *Asuras* always engage in atheistic material activities, exploring ways to utilize the resources of matter to enjoy sense gratification. The *viṣṇu-bhaktas,* Kṛṣṇa conscious devotees, are also active, but their objective is to satisfy the Supreme Personality of Godhead by devotional service. Superficially both classes may appear to work in the same way, but their purposes are completely opposite because of a difference in consciousness. *Asuras* work for personal sense gratification, whereas devotees work for the satisfaction of the Supreme Lord. Both work conscientiously, but their motives are different.

The Kṛṣṇa consciousness movement is meant for *devas,* or devotees. Demons cannot take part in Kṛṣṇa conscious activities, nor can devotees in Kṛṣṇa consciousness take part in demoniac activities or work like cats and dogs simply for sense gratification. Such activity does not appeal to those in Kṛṣṇa consciousness. Devotees accept only the bare necessities of life to keep themselves fit to act in Kṛṣṇa consciousness. The balance of their energy is used for developing Kṛṣṇa consciousness, through which one can be transferred to the abode of Kṛṣṇa by always thinking of Him, even at the point of death.

TEXT 92

আচার্য গোসাঞি প্রভুর ভক্ত-অবতার ।
কৃষ্ণ-অবতার-হেতু যাঁহার হুঙ্কার ॥ ৯২ ॥

ācārya gosāñi prabhura bhakta-avatāra
kṛṣṇa-avatāra-hetu yāṅhāra huṅkāra

ācārya gosāñi—Advaita Ācārya Gosāñi; *prabhura*—of the Lord; *bhakta-avatāra*—incarnation of a devotee; *kṛṣṇa*—of Lord Kṛṣṇa; *avatāra*—of the incarnation; *hetu*—the cause; *yāṅhāra*—whose; *huṅkāra*—loud calls.

TRANSLATION

Advaita Ācārya Gosvāmī is an incarnation of the Lord as a devotee. His loud calling was the cause for Kṛṣṇa's incarnation.

TEXT 93

কৃষ্ণ যদি পৃথিবীতে করেন অবতার ।
প্রথমে করেন গুরুবর্গের সঞ্চার ॥ ৯৩ ॥

kṛṣṇa yadi pṛthivīte karena avatāra
prathame karena guru-vargera sañcāra

kṛṣṇa—Lord Kṛṣṇa; *yadi*—if; *pṛthivīte*—on the earth; *karena*—makes; *avatāra*—incarnation; *prathame*—first; *karena*—makes; *guru-vargera*—of the group of respectable predecessors; *sañcāra*—the advent.

TRANSLATION

Whenever Śrī Kṛṣṇa desires to manifest His incarnation on earth, first He creates the incarnations of His respectable predecessors.

TEXT 94

পিতা মাতা গুরু আদি যত মান্যগণ ।
প্রথমে করেন সবার পৃথিবীতে জনম ॥ ৯৪ ॥

pitā mātā guru ādi yata mānya-gaṇa
prathame karena sabāra pṛthivīte janama

pitā—father; *mātā*—mother; *guru*—spiritual master; *ādi*—headed by; *yata*—all; *mānya-gaṇa*—respectable members; *prathame*—first; *karena*—He makes; *sabāra*—of all of them; *pṛthivīte*—on earth; *janama*—the births.

TRANSLATION

Thus respectable personalities such as His father, mother and spiritual master all take birth on earth first.

TEXT 95

মাধব-ঈশ্বর-পুরী, শচী, জগন্নাথ ।
অদ্বৈত আচার্য প্রকট হৈলা সেই সাথ ॥ ৯৫ ॥

mādhava-īśvara-purī, śacī, jagannātha
advaita ācārya prakaṭa hailā sei sātha

mādhava—Mādhavendra Purī; *īśvara-purī*—Īśvara Purī; *śacī*—Śacīmātā; *jagannātha*—Jagannātha Miśra; *advaita ācārya*—Advaita Ācārya; *prakaṭa*—manifested; *hailā*—were; *sei*—this; *sātha*—with.

TRANSLATION

Mādhavendra Purī, Īśvara Purī, Śrīmatī Śacīmātā and Śrīla Jagannātha Miśra all appeared with Śrī Advaita Ācārya.

PURPORT

Whenever the Supreme Personality of Godhead descends in His human form, He sends ahead all His devotees, who act as His father, teacher and associates in many roles. Such personalities appear before the descent of the Supreme Personality of Godhead. Before the appearance of Lord Śrī Kṛṣṇa Caitanya Mahāprabhu, there appeared His devotees like Śrī Mādhavendra Purī; His spiritual master, Śrī Īśvara Purī; His mother, Śrīmatī Śacī-devī; His father, Śrī Jagannātha Miśra; and Śrī Advaita Ācārya.

TEXT 96

প্রকটিয়া দেখে আচার্য সকল সংসার ।
কৃষ্ণভক্তিগন্ধহীন বিষয়-ব্যবহার ॥ ৯৬ ॥

prakaṭiyā dekhe ācārya sakala saṁsāra
kṛṣṇa-bhakti gandha-hīna viṣaya-vyavahāra

prakaṭiyā—manifesting; *dekhe*—He saw; *ācārya*—Advaita Ācārya; *sakala*—all; *saṁsāra*—material existence; *kṛṣṇa-bhakti*—of devotion to Lord Kṛṣṇa; *gandha-hīna*—without a trace; *viṣaya*—of the sense objects; *vyavahāra*—affairs.

TRANSLATION

Advaita Ācārya having appeared, He found the world devoid of devotional service to Śrī Kṛṣṇa because people were engrossed in material affairs.

TEXT 97

কেহ পাপে, কেহ পুণ্যে করে বিষয়-ভোগ ।
ভক্তিগন্ধ নাহি, যাতে যায় ভবরোগ ॥ ৯৭ ॥

keha pāpe, keha puṇye kare viṣaya-bhoga
bhakti-gandha nāhi, yāte yāya bhava-roga

keha—someone; *pāpe*—in sinful activities; *keha*—someone; *puṇye*—in pious activities; *kare*—do; *viṣaya*—of the sense objects; *bhoga*—enjoyment; *bhakti-gandha*—a trace of devotional service; *nāhi*—there is not; *yāte*—by which; *yāya*—goes away; *bhava-roga*—the disease of material existence.

TRANSLATION

Everyone was engaged in material enjoyment, whether sinfully or virtuously. No one was interested in the transcendental service of the Lord, which can give total relief from the repetition of birth and death.

PURPORT

Advaita Ācārya saw the entire world to be engaged in activities of material piety and impiety, without a trace of devotional service, or Kṛṣṇa consciousness, anywhere. The fact is that in this material world there is no scarcity of anything except Kṛṣṇa consciousness. Material necessities are supplied by the mercy of the Supreme Lord. We sometimes feel scarcity because of our mismanagement, but the real problem is that people are out of touch with Kṛṣṇa consciousness. Everyone is engaged in material sense gratification, but people have no plan for making an ultimate solution to their real problems, namely birth, disease, old age and death. These four material miseries are called *bhava-roga*, or material diseases. They can be cured only by Kṛṣṇa consciousness. Therefore Kṛṣṇa consciousness is the greatest benediction for human society.

TEXT 98

লোকগতি দেখি' আচার্য করুণ-হৃদয় ।
বিচার করেন, লোকের কৈছে হিত হয় ॥ ৯৮ ॥

loka-gati dekhi' ācārya karuṇa-hṛdaya
vicāra karena, lokera kaiche hita haya

loka-gati—the course of the world; *dekhi'*—seeing; *ācārya*—Advaita Ācārya; *karuṇa-hṛdaya*—compassionate heart; *vicāra karena*—considers; *lokera*—of the world; *kaiche*—how; *hita*—welfare; *haya*—there is.

TRANSLATION

Seeing the activities of the world, the Ācārya felt compassion and began to ponder how He could act for the people's benefit.

PURPORT

This sort of serious interest in the welfare of the public makes one a bona fide *ācārya.* An *ācārya* does not exploit his followers. Since the *ācārya* is a confidential servitor of the Lord, his heart is always full of compassion for humanity in its suffering. He knows that all suffering is due to the absence of devotional service to the Lord, and therefore he always tries to find ways to change people's activities, making them favorable for the attainment of devotion. That is the qualification of an *ācārya.* Although Śrī Advaita Prabhu Himself was powerful enough to do the work, as a submissive servitor He thought that without the personal appearance of the Lord, no one could improve the fallen condition of society.

In the grim clutches of *māyā,* the first-class prisoners of this material world wrongly think themselves happy because they are rich, powerful, resourceful and so on. These foolish creatures do not know that they are nothing but play dolls in the hands of material nature and that at any moment material nature's pitiless intrigues can crush to dust all their plans for godless activities. Such foolish prisoners cannot see that however they improve their position by artificial means, the calamities of repeated birth, death, disease and old age are always beyond the jurisdiction of their control. Foolish as they are, they neglect these major problems of life and busy themselves with false things that cannot help them solve their real problems. They know that they do not want to suffer death or the pangs of disease and old age, but under the influence of the illusory energy, they are grossly negligent and therefore do nothing to solve the problems. This is called *māyā.* People held in the grip of *māyā* are thrown into oblivion after death, and as a result of their *karma,* in the next life they become dogs or gods, although most of them become dogs. To become gods in the next life, they must engage in the devotional service of the Supreme Personality of Godhead; otherwise, they are sure to become dogs or hogs in terms of the laws of nature.

The third-class prisoners, being less materially opulent than the first-class prisoners, endeavor to imitate them, for they also have no information of the real nature of their imprisonment. Thus they also are misled by the illusory material nature. The function of the *ācārya,* however, is to change the activities of both the first-class and third-class prisoners for their real benefit. This endeavor makes him a very dear devotee of the Lord, who says clearly in the *Bhagavad-gītā* that no one in human society is dearer to Him than a devotee who constantly engages in His service by finding ways to preach the message of

Godhead for the real benefit of the world. The so-called *ācāryas* of the Age of Kali are more concerned with exploiting the resources of their followers than mitigating their miseries; but Śrī Advaita Prabhu, as an ideal *ācārya,* was concerned with improving the condition of the world situation.

TEXT 99

আপনি শ্রীকৃষ্ণ যদি করেন অবতার ।
আপনে আচরি' ভক্তি করেন প্রচার ॥ ৯৯ ॥

āpani śrī-kṛṣṇa yadi karena avatāra
āpane ācari' bhakti karena pracāra

āpani—Himself; *śrī-kṛṣṇa*—Lord Kṛṣṇa; *yadi*—if; *karena*—He makes; *avatāra*—incarnation; *āpane*—Himself; *ācari'*—practicing; *bhakti*—devotional service; *karena*—does; *pracāra*—propagation.

TRANSLATION

[Advaita Ācārya thought:] "If Śrī Kṛṣṇa were to appear as an incarnation, He Himself could preach devotion by His personal example.

TEXT 100

নাম বিনু কলিকালে ধর্ম নাহি আর ।
কলিকালে কৈছে হবে কৃষ্ণ অবতার ॥ ১০০ ॥

nāma vinu kali-kāle dharma nāhi āra
kali-kāle kaiche habe kṛṣṇa avatāra

nāma vinu—except for the holy name; *kali-kāle*—in the Age of Kali; *dharma*—religion; *nāhi*—there is not; *āra*—another; *kali-kāle*—in the Age of Kali; *kaiche*—how; *habe*—there will be; *kṛṣṇa*—Lord Kṛṣṇa; *avatāra*—incarnation.

TRANSLATION

"In this Age of Kali there is no religion other than the chanting of the holy name of the Lord, but how in this age will the Lord appear as an incarnation?

TEXT 101

শুদ্ধভাবে করিব কৃষ্ণের আরাধন ।
নিরন্তর সদৈন্যে করিব নিবেদন ॥ ১০১ ॥

śuddha-bhāve kariba kṛṣṇera ārādhana
nirantara sadainye kariba nivedana

śuddha-bhāve—in a purified state of mind; *kariba*—I shall do; *kṛṣṇera*—of Lord Kṛṣṇa; *ārādhana*—worship; *nirantara*—constantly; *sa-dainye*—in humility; *kariba*—I shall make; *nivedana*—request.

TRANSLATION

"I shall worship Kṛṣṇa in a purified state of mind. I shall constantly petition Him in humbleness.

TEXT 102

আনিয়া কৃষ্ণেরে করোঁ কীর্তন সঞ্চার ।
তবে সে 'অদ্বৈত' নাম সফল আমার ॥ ১০২ ॥

āniyā kṛṣṇere karoṅ kīrtana sañcāra
tabe se 'advaita' nāma saphala āmāra

āniyā—bringing; *kṛṣṇere*—Lord Kṛṣṇa; *karoṅ*—I make; *kīrtana*—chanting of the holy name; *sañcāra*—advent; *tabe*—then; *se*—this; *advaita*—nondual; *nāma*—name; *sa-phala*—fulfilled; *āmāra*—My.

TRANSLATION

"My name, 'Advaita,' will be fitting if I am able to induce Kṛṣṇa to inaugurate the movement of the chanting of the holy name."

PURPORT

The nondualist Māyāvādī philosopher who falsely believes that he is nondifferent from the Lord is unable to call Him like Advaita Prabhu. Advaita Prabhu is nondifferent from the Lord, yet in His relationship with the Lord He does not merge with Him but eternally renders service unto Him as a plenary portion. This is inconceivable for Māyāvādīs because they think in terms of mundane sense perception and therefore think that nondualism necessitates losing one's separate identity. It is clear from this verse, however, that Advaita Prabhu, although retaining His separate identity, is nondifferent from the Lord.

Śrī Caitanya Mahāprabhu preached the philosophy of inconceivable, simultaneous oneness with the Lord and difference from Him. Conceivable dualism and monism are conceptions of the imperfect senses, which are unable to reach the Transcendence because the Transcendence is beyond the conception of limited potency. The actions of Śrī Advaita Prabhu, however, give tangible proof of inconceivable nondualism. One who therefore surrenders unto Śrī Advaita Prabhu can easily follow the philosophy of inconceivable simultaneous dualism and monism.

TEXT 103

কৃষ্ণ বশ করিবেন কোন্ আরাধনে ।
বিচারিতে এক শ্লোক আইল তাঁর মনে ॥ ১০৩ ॥

kṛṣṇa vaśa karibena kon ārādhane
vicārite eka śloka āila tāṅra mane

kṛṣṇa—Lord Kṛṣṇa; *vaśa karibena*—shall propitiate; *kon ārādhane*—by what worship; *vicārite*—while considering; *eka*—one; *śloka*—verse; *āila*—came; *tāṅra*—of Him; *mane*—in the mind.

TRANSLATION

While He was thinking about how to propitiate Kṛṣṇa by worship, the following verse came to His mind.

TEXT 104

তুলসীদলমাত্রেণ জলস্য চুলুকেন বা ।
বিক্রীণীতে স্বমাত্মানং ভক্তেভ্যো ভক্তবৎসলঃ ॥ ১০৪ ॥

tulasī-dala-mātreṇa
jalasya culukena vā
vikrīṇīte svam ātmānaṁ
bhaktebhyo bhakta-vatsalaḥ

tulasī—of *tulasī; dala*—a leaf; *mātreṇa*—by only; *jalasya*—of water; *culukena*—by a palmful; *vā*—and; *vikrīṇīte*—sells; *svam*—His own;

ātmānam—self; *bhaktebhyaḥ*—unto the devotees; *bhakta-vatsalaḥ*—Lord Kṛṣṇa, who is affectionate to His devotees.

TRANSLATION

"Śrī Kṛṣṇa, who is very affectionate toward His devotees, sells Himself to a devotee who offers Him merely a tulasī leaf and a palmful of water."

PURPORT

This is a verse from the *Gautamīya-tantra.*

TEXTS 105–106

এই শ্লোকার্থ আচার্য করেন বিচারণ ।
কৃষ্ণকে তুলসীজল দেয় যেই জন ॥ ১০৫ ॥
তার ঋণ শোধিতে কৃষ্ণ করেন চিন্তন— ।
'জল-তুলসীর সম কিছু ঘরে নাহি ধন' ॥ ১০৬ ॥

ei ślokārtha ācārya karena vicāraṇa
kṛṣṇake tulasī-jala deya yei jana

tāra ṛṇa śodhite kṛṣṇa karena cintana—
'jala-tulasīra sama kichu ghare nāhi dhana'

ei—this; *śloka*—of the verse; *artha*—the meaning; *ācārya*—Advaita Ācārya; *karena*—does; *vicāraṇa*—considering; *kṛṣṇake*—to Lord Kṛṣṇa; *tulasī-jala*—*tulasī* and water; *deya*—gives; *yei jana*—that person who; *tāra*—to Him; *ṛṇa*—the debt; *śodhite*—to pay; *kṛṣṇa*—Lord Kṛṣṇa; *karena*—does; *cintana*—thinking; *jala-tulasīra sama*—equal to water and *tulasī; kichu*—any; *ghare*—in the house; *nāhi*—there is not; *dhana*—wealth.

TRANSLATION

Advaita Ācārya considered the meaning of the verse in this way: "Not finding any way to repay the debt He owes to one who offers Him a tulasī leaf and water, Lord Kṛṣṇa thinks, 'There is no wealth in My possession that is equal to a tulasī leaf and water.'

TEXT 107

তবে আত্মা বেচি' করে ঋণের শোধন ।
এত ভাবি' আচার্য করেন আরাধন ॥ ১০৭ ॥

tabe ātmā veci' kare ṛṇera śodhana
eta bhāvi' ācārya karena ārādhana

tabe—then; *ātmā*—Himself; *veci'*—selling; *kare*—does; *ṛṇera*—of the debt; *śodhana*—payment; *eta*—thus; *bhāvi'*—thinking; *ācārya*—Advaita Ācārya; *karena*—does; *ārādhana*—worshiping.

TRANSLATION

"Thus the Lord liquidates the debt by offering Himself to the devotee." Considering in this way, the Ācārya began worshiping the Lord.

PURPORT

Through devotional service one can easily please Lord Kṛṣṇa with a leaf of the *tulasī* plant and a little water. As the Lord says in the *Bhagavad-gītā* (9.26), a leaf, a flower, a fruit or some water (*patraṁ puṣpaṁ phalaṁ toyam*), when offered with devotion, very much pleases Him. He universally accepts the services of His devotees. Even the poorest of devotees in any part of the world can secure a small flower, fruit or leaf and a little water, and if these offerings, and especially *tulasī* leaves and Ganges water, are offered to Kṛṣṇa with devotion, He is very satisfied. It is said that Kṛṣṇa is so much pleased by such devotional service that He offers Himself to His devotee in exchange for it. Śrīla Advaita Ācārya knew this fact, and therefore He decided to call for the Personality of Godhead Kṛṣṇa to descend by worshiping the Lord with *tulasī* leaves and the water of the Ganges.

TEXT 108

গঙ্গাজল, তুলসীমঞ্জরী অনুক্ষণ ।
কৃষ্ণপাদপদ্ম ভাবি' করে সমর্পণ ॥ ১০৮ ॥

gaṅgā-jala, tulasī-mañjarī anukṣaṇa
kṛṣṇa-pāda-padma bhāvi' kare samarpaṇa

gaṅgā-jala—the water of the Ganges; *tulasī-mañjarī*—buds of the *tulasī* plant; *anukṣaṇa*—constantly; *kṛṣṇa*—of Lord Kṛṣṇa; *pāda-padma*—lotus feet; *bhāvi'*—thinking of; *kare*—does; *samarpaṇa*—offering.

TRANSLATION

Thinking of the lotus feet of Śrī Kṛṣṇa, He constantly offered tulasī buds in water from the Ganges.

TEXT 109

কৃষ্ণের আহ্বান করে করিয়া হুঙ্কার ।
এমতে কৃষ্ণেরে করাইল অবতার ॥ ১০৯ ॥

kṛṣṇera āhvāna kare kariyā huṅkāra
e-mate kṛṣṇere karāila avatāra

kṛṣṇera—of Lord Kṛṣṇa; *āhvāna*—invitation; *kare*—makes; *kariyā*—making; *huṅkāra*—loud shouts; *e-mate*—in this way; *kṛṣṇere*—Lord Kṛṣṇa; *karāila*—caused to make; *avatāra*—incarnation.

TRANSLATION

He appealed to Śrī Kṛṣṇa with loud calls and thus made it possible for Kṛṣṇa to appear.

TEXT 110

চৈতন্যের অবতারে এই মুখ্য হেতু ।
ভক্তের ইচ্ছায় অবতরে ধর্মসেতু ॥ ১১০ ॥

caitanyera avatāre ei mukhya hetu
bhaktera icchāya avatare dharma-setu

caitanyera—of Lord Caitanya Mahāprabhu; *avatāre*—in the incarnation; *ei*—this; *mukhya*—principal; *hetu*—cause; *bhaktera*—of the devotee; *icchāya*—by the desire; *avatare*—He descends; *dharma-setu*—protector of religion.

TRANSLATION

Therefore the principal reason for Śrī Caitanya's descent is this appeal by Advaita Ācārya. The Lord, the protector of religion, appears by the desire of His devotee.

TEXT 111

ত্বং ভক্তিযোগপরিভাবিত-হৃৎসরোজ
আস্সে শ্রুতেক্ষিতপথো ননু নাথ পুংসাম্ ।
যদ্যদ্ধিয়া ত উরুগায় বিভাবয়ন্তি
তত্তদ্বপুঃ প্রণয়সে সদনুগ্রহায় ॥ ১১১ ॥

tvaṁ bhakti-yoga-paribhāvita-hṛt-saroja
āsse śrutekṣita-patho nanu nātha puṁsām
yad yad dhiyā ta urugāya vibhāvayanti
tat tad vapuḥ praṇayase sad-anugrahāya

tvam—You; *bhakti-yoga*—by devotional service; *paribhāvita*—saturated; *hṛt*—of the heart; *saroje*—on the lotus; *āsse*—dwell; *śruta*—heard; *īkṣita*—seen; *pathaḥ*—whose path; *nanu*—certainly; *nātha*—O Lord; *puṁsām*—by the devotees; *yat yat*—whatever; *dhiyā*—by the mind; *te*—they; *uru-gāya*—O Lord, who are glorified in excellent ways; *vibhāvayanti*—contemplate upon; *tat tat*—that; *vapuḥ*—form; *praṇayase*—You manifest; *sat*—to Your devotees; *anugrahāya*—to show favor.

TRANSLATION

"O my Lord, You always dwell in the vision and hearing of Your pure devotees. You also live in their lotuslike hearts, which are purified by devotional service. O my Lord, who are glorified by exalted prayers, You show special favor to Your devotees by manifesting Yourself in the eternal forms in which they welcome You."

PURPORT

This text from *Śrīmad-Bhāgavatam* (3.9.11) is a prayer by Lord Brahmā to the Supreme Personality of Godhead Kṛṣṇa for His blessings in the work of creation. Knowledge of the Supreme Personality of Godhead can be understood from the descriptions of the Vedic scriptures. For example, the *Brahma-saṁhitā* (5.29) describes that in the abode of Lord Kṛṣṇa, which is made of *cintāmaṇi* (touchstone), the Lord, acting as a cowherd boy, is served by hundreds and thousands of goddesses of fortune. Māyāvādīs think that the devotees have imagined the form of Kṛṣṇa, but the authentic Vedic scriptures have actually described Kṛṣṇa and His various transcendental forms.

The word *śruta* in *śrutekṣita-pathaḥ* refers to the *Vedas*, and *īkṣita* indicates that the way to understand the Supreme Personality of Godhead is by proper study of the Vedic scriptures. One cannot imagine something about God or His form. Such imagination is not accepted by those who are serious about enlightenment. Here Brahmā says that one can know Kṛṣṇa through the path of properly understanding the Vedic texts. If by studying the form, name, qualities, pastimes and paraphernalia of the Supreme Godhead one is attracted to the Lord, he can execute devotional service, and the form of the Lord will be impressed in his heart and remain transcendentally situated there. Unless a devotee actually develops transcendental love for the Lord, it is not possible for him to think always of the Lord within his heart. Such constant thought of the Lord is the sublime perfection of the yogic process, as the *Bhagavad-gītā* confirms in the Sixth Chapter (47), stating that anyone absorbed in such thought is the best of all *yogīs.* Such transcendental absorption is known as *samādhi.* A pure devotee who is always thinking of the Supreme Personality of Godhead is the person qualified to see the Lord.

One cannot speak of Urugāya (the Lord, who is glorified by sublime prayers) unless one is transcendentally elevated. The Lord has innumerable forms, as the *Brahma-saṁhitā* confirms (*advaitam acyutam anādim ananta-rūpam*). The Lord expands Himself in innumerable *svāṁśa* forms. When a devotee, hearing about these innumerable forms, becomes attached to one and always thinks of Him, the Lord appears to him in that form. Lord Kṛṣṇa is especially pleasing to such devotees, in whose hearts He is always present because of their highly elevated transcendental love.

TEXT 112

এই শ্লোকের অর্থ কহি সংক্ষেপের সার ।
ভক্তের ইচ্ছায় কৃষ্ণের সর্ব অবতার ॥ ১১২ ॥

ei ślokera artha kahi saṅkṣepera sāra
bhaktera icchāya kṛṣṇera sarva avatāra

ei—this; *ślokera*—of the verse; *artha*—the meaning; *kahi*—I relate; *saṅkṣepera*—of conciseness; *sāra*—the pith; *bhaktera*—of the devotee; *icchāya*—by the desire; *kṛṣṇera*—of Lord Kṛṣṇa; *sarva*—all; *avatāra*—incarnations.

TRANSLATION

The essence of the meaning of this verse is that Lord Kṛṣṇa appears in all His innumerable eternal forms because of the desires of His pure devotees.

TEXT 113

চতুর্থ শ্লোকের অর্থ হৈল সুনিশ্চিতে ।
অবতীর্ণ হৈলা গৌর প্রেম প্রকাশিতে ॥ ১১৩ ॥

caturtha ślokera artha haila suniścite
avatīrṇa hailā gaura prema prakāśite

caturtha—fourth; *ślokera*—of the verse; *artha*—the meaning; *haila*—was; *su-niścite*—very surely; *avatīrṇa hailā*—incarnated; *gaura*—Lord Caitanya Mahāprabhu; *prema*—love of God; *prakāśite*—to manifest.

TRANSLATION

Thus I have surely determined the meaning of the fourth verse. Lord Gaurāṅga [Lord Caitanya] appeared as an incarnation to preach unalloyed love of God.

TEXT 114

শ্রীরূপ-রঘুনাথ-পদে যার আশ ।
চৈতন্যচরিতামৃত কহে কৃষ্ণদাস ॥ ১১৪ ॥

śrī-rūpa-raghunātha-pade yāra āśa
caitanya-caritāmṛta kahe kṛṣṇadāsa

śrī-rūpa—Śrīla Rūpa Gosvāmī; *raghunātha*—Śrīla Raghunātha dāsa Gosvāmī; *pade*—at the lotus feet of; *yāra*—whose; *āśa*—expectation; *caitanya-caritāmṛta*—the book named *Caitanya-caritāmṛta; kahe*—describes; *kṛṣṇa-dāsa*—Śrīla Kṛṣṇadāsa Kavirāja Gosvāmī.

TRANSLATION

Praying at the lotus feet of Śrī Rūpa and Śrī Raghunātha, always desiring their mercy, I, Kṛṣṇadāsa, narrate Śrī Caitanya-caritāmṛta, following in their footsteps.

Thus end the Bhaktivedanta purports to Śrī Caitanya-caritāmṛta, Ādi-līlā, *Third Chapter, describing the external reasons for the appearance of Śrī Caitanya Mahāprabhu.*

CHAPTER FOUR

The Confidential Reasons for the Appearance of Śrī Caitanya Mahāprabhu

In this chapter of the epic *Caitanya-caritāmṛta,* Kṛṣṇadāsa Kavirāja Gosvāmī has stressed that Lord Caitanya appeared for three principal purposes of His own. The first purpose was to relish the position of Śrīmatī Rādhārāṇī, who is the prime reciprocator of transcendental love of Śrī Kṛṣṇa. Lord Kṛṣṇa is the reservoir of transcendental loving transactions with Śrīmatī Rādhārāṇī. The subject of those loving transactions is the Lord Himself, and Rādhārāṇī is the object. Thus the subject, the Lord, wanted to relish the loving mellow in the position of the object, Rādhārāṇī.

The second reason for His appearance was to understand the transcendental mellow of Himself. Lord Kṛṣṇa is all sweetness. Rādhārāṇī's attraction for Kṛṣṇa is sublime, and to experience that attraction and understand the transcendental sweetness of Himself, He accepted the mentality of Rādhārāṇī.

The third reason that Lord Caitanya appeared was to enjoy the bliss tasted by Rādhārāṇī. The Lord thought that undoubtedly Rādhārāṇī enjoyed His company and He enjoyed the company of Rādhārāṇī, but the exchange of transcendental mellow between the spiritual couple was more pleasing to Śrīmatī Rādhārāṇī than to Śrī Kṛṣṇa. Rādhārāṇī felt more transcendental pleasure in the company of Kṛṣṇa than He could understand without taking Her position, but for Śrī Kṛṣṇa to enjoy in the position of Śrīmatī Rādhārāṇī was impossible because that position was completely foreign to Him. Kṛṣṇa is the transcendental male, and Rādhārāṇī is the transcendental female. Therefore, to know the transcendental pleasure of loving Kṛṣṇa, Lord Kṛṣṇa Himself appeared as Lord Caitanya, accepting the emotions and bodily luster of Śrīmatī Rādhārāṇī.

Lord Caitanya appeared in order to fulfill these confidential desires, and also to preach the special significance of chanting Hare Kṛṣṇa, Hare Kṛṣṇa, Kṛṣṇa Kṛṣṇa, Hare Hare/ Hare Rāma, Hare Rāma, Rāma Rāma, Hare Hare and to answer the call of Advaita Prabhu. These were secondary reasons.

Śrī Svarūpa Dāmodara Gosvāmī was the principal figure among Lord Caitanya's confidential devotees. The records of his diary have revealed these confidential purposes of the Lord. These revelations have been confirmed by the statements of Śrīla Rūpa Gosvāmī in his various prayers and poems.

This chapter also specifically describes the difference between lust and love. The transactions of Kṛṣṇa and Rādhā are completely different from material lust. Therefore the author has very clearly distinguished between them.

TEXT 1

শ্রীচৈতন্যপ্রসাদেন তদ্রূপস্য বিনির্ণয়ম্ ।
বালোঽপি কুরুতে শাস্ত্রং দৃষ্ট্বা ব্রজবিলাসিনঃ ॥ ১ ॥

śrī-caitanya-prasādena
tad-rūpasya vinirṇayam
bālo 'pi kurute śāstraṁ
dṛṣṭvā vraja-vilāsinaḥ

śrī-caitanya-prasādena—by the mercy of Lord Caitanya Mahāprabhu; *tat*—of Him; *rūpasya*—of the form; *vinirṇayam*—complete determination; *bālaḥ*—a child; *api*—even; *kurute*—makes; *śāstram*—the revealed scriptures; *dṛṣṭvā*—having seen; *vraja-vilāsinaḥ*—who enjoys the pastimes of Vraja.

TRANSLATION

By the mercy of Lord Caitanya Mahāprabhu, even a foolish child can fully describe the real nature of Lord Kṛṣṇa, the enjoyer of the pastimes of Vraja, according to the vision of the revealed scriptures.

PURPORT

One can ascertain the meaning of this Sanskrit *śloka* only when one is endowed with the causeless mercy of Lord Caitanya. Lord Śrī Kṛṣṇa, being the absolute Personality of Godhead, cannot be exposed to the mundane instruments of vision. He reserves the right not to be exposed by the intellectual feats of nondevotees. Notwithstanding this truth, even a small child can easily understand Lord Śrī Kṛṣṇa and His transcendental pastimes in the land of Vṛndāvana by the grace of Lord Caitanya Mahāprabhu.

TEXT 2

জয় জয় শ্রীচৈতন্য জয় নিত্যানন্দ ।
জয়াদ্বৈতচন্দ্র জয় গৌরভক্তবৃন্দ ॥ ২ ॥

jaya jaya śrī-caitanya jaya nityānanda
jayādvaita-candra jaya gaura-bhakta-vṛnda

jaya jaya—all glory; *śrī-caitanya*—to Lord Caitanya; *jaya*—all glory; *nityānanda*—to Lord Nityānanda; *jaya*—all glory; *advaita-candra*—to Advaita Ācārya; *jaya*—all glory; *gaura-bhakta-vṛnda*—to the devotees of Lord Caitanya Mahāprabhu.

TRANSLATION

All glory to Lord Caitanya Mahāprabhu! All glory to Lord Nityānanda! All glory to Śrī Advaita Ācārya! And all glory to all the devotees of Lord Caitanya!

TEXT 3

চতুর্থ শ্লোকের অর্থ কৈল বিবরণ ।
পঞ্চম শ্লোকের অর্থ শুন ভক্তগণ ॥ ৩ ॥

caturtha ślokera artha kaila vivaraṇa
pañcama ślokera artha śuna bhakta-gaṇa

caturtha—fourth; *ślokera*—of the verse; *artha*—the meaning; *kaila*—made; *vivaraṇa*—description; *pañcama*—fifth; *ślokera*—of the verse; *artha*—the meaning; *śuna*—please hear; *bhakta-gaṇa*—O devotees.

TRANSLATION

I have described the meaning of the fourth verse. Now, O devotees, kindly hear the explanation of the fifth verse.

TEXT 4

মূল-শ্লোকের অর্থ করিতে প্রকাশ ।
অর্থ লাগাইতে আগে কহিয়ে আভাস ॥ ৪ ॥

mūla-ślokera artha karite prakāśa
artha lāgāite āge kahiye ābhāsa

mūla—original; *ślokera*—of the verse; *artha*—the meaning; *karite*—to make; *prakāśa*—revelation; *artha*—the meaning; *lāgāite*—to touch; *āge*—first; *kahiye*—I shall speak; *ābhāsa*—hint.

TRANSLATION

Just to explain the original verse, I shall first suggest its meaning.

TEXT 5

চতুর্থ শ্লোকের অর্থ এই কৈল সার ।
প্রেম-নাম প্রচারিতে এই অবতার ॥ ৫ ॥

caturtha ślokera artha ei kaila sāra
prema-nāma pracārite ei avatāra

caturtha—fourth; *ślokera*—of the verse; *artha*—the meaning; *ei*—this; *kaila*—gave; *sāra*—essence; *prema*—love of Godhead; *nāma*—the holy name; *pracārite*—to propagate; *ei*—this; *avatāra*—incarnation.

TRANSLATION

I have given the essential meaning of the fourth verse: this incarnation [Śrī Caitanya Mahāprabhu] descends to propagate the chanting of the holy name and spread love of God.

TEXT 6

সত্য এই হেতু, কিন্তু এহো বহিরঙ্গ ।
আর এক হেতু, শুন, আছে অন্তরঙ্গ ॥ ৬ ॥

satya ei hetu, kintu eho bahiraṅga
āra eka hetu, śuna, āche antaraṅga

atya—true; *ei*—this; *hetu*—reason; *kintu*—but; *eho*—this; *bahir-nga*—external; *āra*—another; *eka*—one; *hetu*—reason; *śuna*—please ear; *āche*—is; *antaraṅga*—internal.

TRANSLATION

Although this is true, this is but the external reason for the Lord's ncarnation. Please hear one other reason—the confidential rea-on—for the Lord's appearance.

PURPORT

n the Third Chapter, fourth verse, it has been clearly said that Lord Caitanya appeared in order to distribute love of Kṛṣṇa and the chanting f His transcendental holy name, Hare Kṛṣṇa. That was the secondary purpose of Lord Caitanya's appearance. The real reason is different, as we shall see in this chapter.

TEXT 7

পূর্বে যেন পৃথিবীর ভার হরিবারে ।
কৃষ্ণ অবতীর্ণ হৈলা শাস্ত্রেতে প্রচারে ॥ ৭ ॥

pūrve yena pṛthivīra bhāra haribāre
kṛṣṇa avatīrṇa hailā śāstrete pracāre

pūrve—previously; *yena*—as; *pṛthivīra*—of the earth; *bhāra*—burden; *haribāre*—to take away; *kṛṣṇa*—Lord Kṛṣṇa; *avatīrṇa*—incarnated; *hailā*—was; *śāstrete*—the scriptures; *pracāre*—proclaim.

TRANSLATION

The scriptures proclaim that Lord Kṛṣṇa previously descended to ake away the burden of the earth.

TEXT 8

স্বয়ং-ভগবানের কর্ম নহে ভারহরণ ।
স্থিতিকর্তা বিষ্ণু করেন জগৎপালন ॥ ৮ ॥

svayaṁ-bhagavānera karma nahe bhāra-haraṇa
sthiti-kartā viṣṇu karena jagat-pālana

svayam-bhagavānera—of the original Supreme Personality of Godhead; *karma*—the business; *nahe*—is not; *bhāra-haraṇa*—taking away the burden; *sthiti-kartā*—the maintainer; *viṣṇu*—Lord Viṣṇu; *karena*—does; *jagat-pālana*—protection of the universe.

TRANSLATION

To take away this burden, however, is not the work of the Supreme Personality of Godhead. The maintainer, Lord Viṣṇu, is the one who protects the universe.

TEXT 9

কিন্তু কৃষ্ণের যেই হয় অবতার-কাল ।
ভারহরণ-কাল তাতে হইল মিশাল ॥ ৯ ॥

kintu kṛṣṇera yei haya avatāra-kāla
bhāra-haraṇa-kāla tāte ha-ila miśāla

kintu—but; *kṛṣṇera*—of Lord Kṛṣṇa; *yei*—that which; *haya*—is; *avatāra*—of incarnation; *kāla*—the time; *bhāra-haraṇa*—of taking away the burden; *kāla*—the time; *tāte*—in that; *ha-ila*—there was; *miśāla*—mixture.

TRANSLATION

But the time to lift the burden of the world mixed with the time for Lord Kṛṣṇa's incarnation.

PURPORT

We have information from the *Bhagavad-gītā* that the Lord appears at particular intervals to adjust a time-worn spiritual culture. Lord Śrī Kṛṣṇa appeared at the end of Dvāpara-yuga to regenerate the spiritual culture of human society and also to manifest His transcendental pastimes. Viṣṇu is the authorized Lord who maintains the created cosmos, and He is also the principal Deity who makes adjustments when there is improper administration in the cosmic creation. But Śrī Kṛṣṇa, being the primeval Lord, appears not in order to make such administrative adjustments but only to exhibit His transcendental pastimes and thus attract the fallen souls back home, back to Godhead.

However, the time for administrative rectification and the time for Lord Śrī Kṛṣṇa's appearance coincided at the end of the last Dvāpara-yuga. Therefore when Śrī Kṛṣṇa appeared, Viṣṇu, the Lord of maintenance, merged with Him because all the plenary portions and parts of the absolute Personality of Godhead merge with Him during His appearance.

TEXT 10

পূর্ণ ভগবান্ অবতরে যেই কালে ।
আর সব অবতার তাঁতে আসি' মিলে ॥ ১০ ॥

pūrṇa bhagavān avatare yei kāle
āra saba avatāra tāṅte āsi' mile

pūrṇa—full; *bhagavān*—the Supreme Personality of Godhead; *avatare*—incarnates; *yei*—that; *kāle*—at the time; *āra*—other; *saba*—all; *avatāra*—incarnations; *tāṅte*—in Him; *āsi'*—coming; *mile*—meet.

TRANSLATION

When the complete Supreme Personality of Godhead descends, all other incarnations of the Lord meet together within Him.

TEXTS 11–12

নারায়ণ, চতুর্ব্যূহ, মৎস্যাদ্যবতার ।
যুগ-মন্বন্তরাবতার, যত আছে আর ॥ ১১ ॥
সবে আসি' কৃষ্ণ-অঙ্গে হয় অবতীর্ণ ।
ঐছে অবতরে কৃষ্ণ ভগবান্ পূর্ণ ॥ ১২ ॥

nārāyaṇa, catur-vyūha, matsyādy-avatāra
yuga-manvantarāvatāra, yata āche āra

sabe āsi' kṛṣṇa-aṅge haya avatīrṇa
aiche avatare kṛṣṇa bhagavān pūrṇa

nārāyaṇa—Lord Nārāyaṇa; *catuḥ-vyūha*—the four expansions; *matsya-ādi*—beginning with Matsya; *avatāra*—the incarnations; *yuga-manv-antara-avatāra*—the *yuga* and *manv-antara* incarnations; *yata*—as many as; *āche*—there are; *āra*—other; *sabe*—all; *āsi'*—coming; *kṛṣṇa-aṅge*—in the body of Lord Kṛṣṇa; *haya*—are; *avatīrṇa*—incarnated; *aiche*—in this way; *avatare*—incarnates; *kṛṣṇa*—Lord Kṛṣṇa; *bhagavān*—the Supreme Personality of Godhead; *pūrṇa*—full.

TRANSLATION

Lord Nārāyaṇa, the four primary expansions [Vāsudeva, Saṅkarṣaṇa, Pradyumna and Aniruddha], Matsya and the other līlā incarnations, the yuga-avatāras, the manv-antara incarnations and as many other incarnations as there are—all descend in the body of Lord Kṛṣṇa. In this way the complete Supreme Godhead, Lord Kṛṣṇa Himself, appears.

TEXT 13

অতএব বিষ্ণু তখন কৃষ্ণের শরীরে ।
বিষ্ণুদ্বারে করে কৃষ্ণ অসুর-সংহারে ॥ ১৩ ॥

ataeva viṣṇu takhana kṛṣṇera śarīre
viṣṇu-dvāre kare kṛṣṇa asura-saṁhāre

ataeva—therefore; *viṣṇu*—Lord Viṣṇu; *takhana*—at that time; *kṛṣṇera*—of Lord Kṛṣṇa; *śarīre*—in the body; *viṣṇu-dvāre*—by Lord Viṣṇu; *kare*—does; *kṛṣṇa*—Lord Kṛṣṇa; *asura-saṁhāre*—killing the demons.

TRANSLATION

At that time, therefore, Lord Viṣṇu is present in the body of Lord Kṛṣṇa, and Lord Kṛṣṇa kills the demons through Him.

TEXT 14

আনুসঙ্গ-কর্ম এই অসুর-মারণ ।
যে লাগি' অবতার, কহি সে মূল কারণ ॥ ১৪ ॥

ānuṣaṅga-karma ei asura-māraṇa
ye lāgi' avatāra, kahi se mūla kāraṇa

ānuṣaṅga-karma—secondary work; *ei*—this; *asura*—of the demons; *māraṇa*—killing; *ye*—that; *lāgi'*—for; *avatāra*—the incarnation; *kahi*—I shall speak; *se*—the; *mūla*—root; *kāraṇa*—cause.

TRANSLATION

Thus the killing of the demons is but secondary work. I shall now speak of the main reason for the Lord's incarnation.

TEXTS 15–16

প্রেমরস-নির্যাস করিতে আস্বাদন ।
রাগমার্গ ভক্তি লোকে করিতে প্রচারণ ॥ ১৫ ॥
রসিক-শেখর কৃষ্ণ পরমকরুণ ।
এই দুই হেতু হৈতে ইচ্ছার উদ্গম ॥ ১৬ ॥

prema-rasa-niryāsa karite āsvādana
rāga-mārga bhakti loke karite pracāraṇa

rasika-śekhara kṛṣṇa parama-karuṇa
ei dui hetu haite icchāra udgama

prema-rasa—of the mellow of love of God; *niryāsa*—the essence; *karite*—to do; *āsvādana*—tasting; *rāga-mārga*—the path of spontaneous attraction; *bhakti*—devotional service; *loke*—in the world; *karite*—to do; *pracāraṇa*—propagation; *rasika-śekhara*—the supremely jubilant; *kṛṣṇa*—Lord Kṛṣṇa; *parama-karuṇa*—the most merciful; *ei*—these; *dui*—two; *hetu*—reasons; *haite*—from; *icchāra*—of desire; *udgama*—the birth.

TRANSLATION

The Lord's desire to appear was born from two reasons: the Lord wanted to taste the sweet essence of the mellows of love of God, and He wanted to propagate devotional service in the world on the platform of spontaneous attraction. Thus He is known as supremely jubilant and as the most merciful of all.

PURPORT

During the period of Lord Kṛṣṇa's appearance, the killing of *asuras* or nonbelievers such as Kaṁsa and Jarāsandha was done by Viṣṇu, who was within the person of Śrī Kṛṣṇa. Such apparent killing by Lord Śrī Kṛṣṇa took place as a matter of course and was an incidental activity for Him. But the real purpose of Lord Kṛṣṇa's appearance was to stage a dramatic performance of His transcendental pastimes at Vrajabhūmi, thus exhibiting the highest limit of transcendental mellow in the exchanges of reciprocal love between the living entity and the Supreme Lord. These reciprocal exchanges of mellows are called *rāga-bhakti,* or devotional service to the Lord in transcendental rapture. Lord Śrī Kṛṣṇa wants to make known to all the conditioned souls that He is more attracted by *rāga-bhakti* than *vidhi-bhakti*, or devotional service under scheduled regulations. It is said in the *Vedas* (*Taittirīya Up.* 2.7), *raso vai saḥ:* the Absolute Truth is the reservoir for all kinds of reciprocal exchanges of loving sentiments. He is also causelessly merciful, and He wants to bestow upon us this privilege of *rāga-bhakti.* Thus He appeared by His own internal energy. He was not forced to appear by any extraneous force.

TEXT 17

ঐশ্বর্য-জ্ঞানেতে সব জগৎ মিশ্রিত ।
ঐশ্বর্য-শিথিল-প্রেমে নাহি মোর প্রীত ॥ ১৭ ॥

aiśvarya-jñānete saba jagat miśrita
aiśvarya-śithila-preme nahi mora prīta

aiśvarya jñānete—with knowledge of majesty; *saba*—all; *jagat*—the universe; *miśrita*—mixed; *aiśvarya-śithila*—weakened by majesty; *preme*—in love; *nāhi*—there is not; *mora*—My; *prīta*—pleasure.

TRANSLATION

[Lord Kṛṣṇa thought:] "All the universe is filled with the conception of My majesty, but love weakened by that sense of majesty does not satisfy Me.

TEXT 18

আমারে ঈশ্বর মানে, আপনাকে হীন ।
তার প্রেমে বশ আমি না হই অধীন ॥ ১৮ ॥

āmāre īśvara māne, āpanāke hīna
tāra preme vaśa āmi nā ha-i adhīna

āmāre—Me; *īśvara*—the Lord; *māne*—regards; *āpanāke*—himself; *hīna*—low; *tāra*—of him; *preme*—by the love; *vaśa*—controlled; *āmi*—I; *nā ha-i*—am not; *adhīna*—subservient.

TRANSLATION

"If one regards Me as the Supreme Lord and himself as a subordinate, I do not become subservient to his love, nor can it control Me.

TEXT 19

আমাকে ত' যে যে ভক্ত ভজে যেই ভাবে।
তারে সে সে ভাবে ভজি,—এ মোর স্বভাবে ॥ ১৯ ॥

āmāke ta' ye ye bhakta bhaje yei bhāve
tāre se se bhāve bhaji,—e mora svabhāve

āmāke—Me; *ta'*—certainly; *ye ye*—whatever; *bhakta*—devotee; *bhaje*—worships; *yei*—which; *bhāve*—in the mood; *tāre*—him; *se se*—that; *bhāve*—in the mood; *bhaji*—I reciprocate; *e*—this; *mora*—My; *svabhāve*—in the nature.

TRANSLATION

"In whatever transcendental mellow My devotee worships Me, I reciprocate with him. That is My natural behavior.

PURPORT

The Lord, by His inherent nature, reveals Himself before His devotees according to their inherent devotional service. The Vṛndāvana pastimes demonstrated that although generally people worship God with reverence, the Lord is more pleased when a devotee thinks of Him as his pet son, personal friend or most dear fiance and renders service unto Him with such natural affection. The Lord becomes a subordinate object of love in such transcendental relationships. Such pure love of Godhead is unadulterated by any tinge of superfluous nondevotional desires and is not mixed with any sort of fruitive action or empiric philosophical speculation. It is pure and natural love of Godhead, spontaneously aroused in the absolute stage. This devotional service is executed in a favorable atmosphere freed from material affection.

TEXT 20

যে যথা মাং প্রপদ্যন্তে তাংস্তথৈব ভজাম্যহম্ ।
মম বর্ত্মানুবর্তন্তে মনুষ্যাঃ পার্থ সর্বশঃ ॥ ২০ ॥

ye yathā māṁ prapadyante
tāṁs tathaiva bhajāmy aham
mama vartmānuvartante
manuṣyāḥ pārtha sarvaśaḥ

ye—all who; *yathā*—as; *mām*—unto Me; *prapadyante*—surrender; *tān*—them; *tathā*—so; *eva*—certainly; *bhajāmi*—reward; *aham*—I; *mama*—My; *vartma*—path; *anuvartante*—follow; *manuṣyāḥ*—all men; *pārtha*—O son of Pṛthā; *sarvaśaḥ*—in all respects.

TRANSLATION

"'In whatever way My devotees surrender unto Me, I reward them accordingly. Everyone follows My path in all respects, O son of Pṛthā.'

PURPORT

In the Fourth Chapter of the *Bhagavad-gītā* Lord Kṛṣṇa affirms that formerly (some 120 million years before the Battle of Kurukṣetra) He explained the mystic philosophy of the *Gītā* to the sun-god. The message was received through the chain of disciplic succession, but in course of time, the chain being broken somehow or other, Lord Śrī Kṛṣṇa appeared again and taught Arjuna the truths of the *Bhagavad-gītā.* At that time the Lord spoke this verse (Bg. 4.11) to His friend Arjuna.

TEXTS 21–22

মোর পুত্র, মোর সখা, মোর প্রাণপতি ।
এইভাবে যেই মোরে করে শুদ্ধভক্তি ॥ ২১ ॥
আপনাকে বড় মানে, আমারে সম-হীন ।
সেই ভাবে হই আমি তাহার অধীন ॥ ২২ ॥

mora putra, mora sakhā, mora prāṇa-pati
ei-bhāve yei more kare śuddha-bhakti

āpanāke baḍa māne, āmāre sama-hīna
sei bhāve ha-i āmi tāhāra adhīna

mora—my; *putra*—son; *mora*—my; *sakhā*—friend; *mora*—my; *prāṇa-pati*—lord of life; *ei bhāve*—in this way; *yei*—those who; *more*—unto Me; *kare*—do; *śuddha-bhakti*—pure devotion; *āpanāke*—himself; *baḍa*—great; *māne*—he regards; *āmāre*—Me; *sama*—equal; *hīna*—or lower; *sei bhāve*—in that way; *ha-i*—am; *āmi*—I; *tāhāra*—to him; *adhīna*—subordinate.

TRANSLATION

"If one cherishes pure loving devotion to Me, thinking of Me as his son, his friend or his beloved, regarding himself as great and considering Me his equal or inferior, I become subordinate to him.

PURPORT

In the *Caitanya-caritāmṛta* three kinds of devotional service are described—namely, *bhakti* (ordinary devotional service), *śuddha-bhakti* (pure devotional service) and *viddha-bhakti* (mixed devotional service).

When devotional service is executed with some material purpose, involving fruitive activities, mental speculations or mystic *yoga*, it is called mixed or adulterated devotional service. Besides *bhakti-yoga*, the *Bhagavad-gītā* also describes *karma-yoga*, *jñāna-yoga* and *dhyāna-yoga*. *Yoga* means linking with the Supreme Lord, which is possible only through devotion. Fruitive activities ending in devotional service, philosophical speculation ending in devotional service, and the practice of mysticism ending in devotional service are known respectively as *karma-yoga*, *jñāna-yoga* and *dhyāna-yoga*. But such devotional service is adulterated by the three kinds of material activities.

For those grossly engaged in identifying the body as the self, pious activity, or *karma-yoga*, is recommended. For those who identify the mind with the self, philosophical speculation, or *jñāna-yoga*, is recommended. But devotees standing on the spiritual platform have no need of such material conceptions of adulterated devotion. Adulterated devotional service does not directly aim for love of the Supreme Personality of Godhead. Therefore service performed strictly in conformity with the revealed scriptures is better than such *viddha-bhakti* because it is free from all kinds of material contamination. It is executed in Kṛṣṇa consciousness, solely to please the Supreme Personality of Godhead.

Those who are spontaneously devoted to the Lord and have no aims for material gain are called attracted devotees. They are spontaneously attracted to the service of the Lord, and they follow in the footsteps of self-realized souls. Their pure devotion (*śuddha-bhakti*), manifested from pure love of Godhead, surpasses the regulative principles of the authoritative scriptures. Sometimes loving ecstasy transcends regulative principles; such ecstasy, however, is completely on the spiritual platform and cannot be imitated. The regulative principles help ordinary devotees rise to the stage of perfect love of Godhead. Pure love for Kṛṣṇa is the perfection of pure devotion, and pure devotional service is identical with spontaneous devotional service.

Flawless execution of regulative principles is exhibited in the Vaikuṇṭha planets. By strictly executing these principles one can be elevated to the Vaikuṇṭha planets. But spontaneous pure loving service is found in Kṛṣṇaloka alone.

TEXT 23

ময়ি ভক্তির্হি ভূতানামমৃতত্বায় কল্পতে ।
দিষ্ট্যা যদাসীন্মৎস্নেহো ভবতীনাং মদাপনঃ ॥ ২৩ ॥

mayi bhaktir hi bhūtānām
amṛtatvāya kalpate
diṣṭyā yad āsīn mat-sneho
bhavatīnāṁ mad-āpanaḥ

mayi—to Me; *bhaktiḥ*—devotional service; *hi*—certainly; *bhūtānām*—of the living beings; *amṛtatvāya*—the eternal life; *kalpate*—brings about; *diṣṭyā*—by good fortune; *yat*—which; *āsīt*—was; *mat*—for Me; *snehaḥ*—the affection; *bhavatīnām*—of all of you; *mat*—of Me; *āpanaḥ*—the obtaining.

TRANSLATION

"'Devotional service rendered to Me by the living beings revives their eternal life. O My dear damsels of Vraja, your affection for Me is your good fortune, for it is the only means by which you have obtained My favor.'

PURPORT

Pure devotional service is represented in the activities of the residents of Vrajabhūmi (Vṛndāvana). During a solar eclipse, the Lord came from Dvārakā and met the inhabitants of Vṛndāvana at Samanta-pañcaka. The meeting was intensely painful for the damsels of Vrajabhūmi because Lord Kṛṣṇa had apparently left them to reside at Dvārakā. But the Lord obligingly acknowledged the pure devotional service of the damsels of Vraja by speaking this verse (*Bhāg.* 10.82.44).

TEXT 24

মাতা মোরে পুত্রভাবে করেন বন্ধন ।
অতিহীন-জ্ঞানে করে লালন-পালন ॥ ২৪ ॥

mātā more putra-bhāve karena bandhana
atihīna-jñāne kare lālana pālana

ıātā—mother; *more*—Me; *putra-bhāve*—in the position of a son; *arena*—does; *bandhana*—binding; *ati-hīna-jñāne*—in thinking very oor; *kare*—does; *lālana*—nourishing; *pālana*—protecting.

TRANSLATION

Mother sometimes binds Me as her son. She nourishes and pro-ects Me, thinking Me utterly helpless.

TEXT 25

সখা শুদ্ধ-সখ্যে করে স্কন্ধে আরোহণ।
তুমি কোন্ বড় লোক,—তুমি আমি সম ॥ ২৫ ॥

sakhā śuddha-sakhye kare, skandhe ārohaṇa
tumi kon baḍa loka,—tumi āmi sama

akhā—the friend; *śuddha-sakhye*—in pure friendship; *kare*—does; *kandhe*—on the shoulders; *ārohaṇa*—mounting; *tumi*—You; *kon*—hat; *baḍa*—big; *loka*—person; *tumi*—You; *āmi*—I; *sama*—the same.

TRANSLATION

My friends climb on My shoulders in pure friendship, saying, What kind of big man are You? You and I are equal.'

TEXT 26

প্রিয়া যদি মান করি' করয়ে ভর্ৎসন।
বেদস্তুতি হৈতে হরে সেই মোর মন ॥ ২৬ ॥

priyā yadi māna kari' karaye bhartsana
veda-stuti haite hare sei mora mana

riyā—the lover; *yadi*—if; *māna kari'*—sulking; *karaye*—does; *bhart-ana*—rebuking; *veda-stuti*—the Vedic prayers; *haite*—from; *hare*—akes away; *sei*—that; *mora*—My; *mana*—mind.

TRANSLATION

If My beloved consort reproaches Me in a sulky mood, that steals Iy mind from the reverent hymns of the Vedas.

PURPORT

According to the *Upaniṣads*, all living entities are dependent on the supreme living entity, the Personality of Godhead. As it is said (*Kaṭha Up.* 5.3), *nityo nityānāṁ cetanaś cetanānām eko bahūnāṁ yo vidadhāti kāmān:* one eternal living entity supports all the other eternal living entities. Because the Supreme Personality of Godhead maintains all the other living entities, they remain subordinate to the Lord, even when joined with Him in the reciprocation of loving affairs.

But in the course of exchanging transcendental love of the highest purity, sometimes the subordinate devotee tries to predominate over the predominator. One who lovingly engages with the Supreme Lord as if he were His mother or father sometimes supersedes the position of the Supreme Personality of Godhead. Similarly, His fiancee or lover sometimes supersedes the position of the Lord. But such attempts are exhibitions of the highest love. Only out of pure love does the subordinate lover of the Supreme Personality of Godhead chide Him. The Lord, enjoying this chiding, takes it very nicely. The exhibition of natural love makes such activities very enjoyable. In worship of the Supreme Lord with veneration there is no manifestation of such natural love because the devotee considers the Lord his superior.

Regulative principles in devotional service are meant for those who have not invoked their natural love of Godhead. When natural love arises, all regulative methods are surpassed, and pure love is exhibited between the Lord and the devotee. Although on such a platform of love the devotee sometimes appears to predominate over the Lord or transgress regulative principles, such dealings are far more advanced than ordinary dealings through regulative principles with awe and veneration. A devotee who is actually free from all designations due to complete attachment in love for the Supreme exhibits spontaneous love for Godhead, which is always superior to the devotion of regulative principles.

The informal language used between lover and beloved is indicative of pure affection. When devotees worship their beloved as the most venerable object, spontaneous loving sentiments are observed to be lacking. A neophyte devotee who follows the Vedic instructions that regulate those who lack pure love of Godhead may superficially seem more exalted than a devotee in spontaneous love of Godhead. But in fact such spontaneous pure love is far superior to regulated devotional service. Such pure love of Godhead is always glorious in all respects, more so than reverential devotional service rendered by a less affectionate devotee.

TEXTS 27–28

এই শুদ্ধভক্ত লইয়া করিমু অবতার ।
করিব বিবিধবিধ অদ্ভুত বিহার ॥ ২৭ ॥
বৈকুণ্ঠাদ্যে নাহি যে যে লীলার প্রচার ।
সে সে লীলা করিব, যাতে মোর চমৎকার ॥ ২৮ ॥

ei śuddha-bhakta lañā karimu avatāra
kariba vividha-vidha adbhuta vihāra

vaikuṇṭhādye nāhi ye ye līlāra pracāra
se se līlā kariba, yāte mora camatkāra

ei—these; *śuddha-bhakta*—pure devotees; *lañā*—taking; *karimu*—I shall make; *avatāra*—incarnation; *kariba*—I shall do; *vividha-vidha*—various kinds; *adbhuta*—wonderful; *vihāra*—pastimes; *vaikuṇṭha-ādye*—in the Vaikuṇṭha planets, etc.; *nāhi*—not; *ye ye*—whatever; *līlāra*—of the pastimes; *pracāra*—broadcasting; *se se*—those; *līlā*—pastimes; *kariba*—I shall perform; *yāte*—in which; *mora*—My; *camatkāra*—wonder.

TRANSLATION

"Taking these pure devotees with Me, I shall descend and sport in various wonderful ways, unknown even in Vaikuṇṭha. I shall broadcast such pastimes by which even I am amazed.

PURPORT

Lord Kṛṣṇa in the form of Lord Caitanya educates His devotees to develop progressively to the stage of pure devotional service. Thus He appears periodically as a devotee to take part in various wonderful activities depicted in His sublime philosophy and teachings.

There are innumerable Vaikuṇṭha planets in the spiritual sky, and in all of them the Lord accepts the service rendered by His eternal devotees in a reverential mood. Therefore Lord Śrī Kṛṣṇa presents His most confidential pastimes as He enjoys them in His transcendental realm. Such pastimes are so attractive that they attract even the Lord, and thus He relishes them in the form of Lord Caitanya.

TEXT 29

মো-বিষয়ে গোপীগণের উপপতি-ভাবে ।
যোগমায়া করিবেক আপনপ্রভাবে ॥ ২৯ ॥

mo-viṣaye gopī-gaṇera upapati-bhāve
yoga-māyā karibeka āpana-prabhāve

mo-viṣaye—on the subject of Me; *gopī-gaṇera*—of the *gopīs; upapati*—of a paramour; *bhāve*—in the position; *yoga-māyā—yogamāyā,* Lord Kṛṣṇa's internal potency; *karibeka*—will make; *āpana*—her own; *prabhāve*—by the influence.

TRANSLATION

"The influence of yogamāyā will inspire the gopīs with the sentiment that I am their paramour.

PURPORT

Yogamāyā is the name of the internal potency that makes the Lord forget Himself and become an object of love for His pure devotee in different transcendental mellows. This *yogamāyā* potency creates a spiritual sentiment in the minds of the damsels of Vraja by which they think of Lord Kṛṣṇa as their paramour. This sentiment is never to be compared to mundane illicit sexual love. It has nothing to do with sexual psychology, although the pure love of such devotees seems to be sexual. One should know for certain that nothing can exist in this cosmic manifestation that has no real counterpart in the spiritual field. All material manifestations are emanations of the Transcendence. The erotic principles of amorous love reflected in mixed material values are perverted reflections of the reality of spirit, but one cannot understand the reality unless one is sufficiently educated in the spiritual science.

TEXT 30

আমিহ না জানি তাহা, না জানে গোপীগণ ।
দুঁহার রূপগুণে দুঁহার নিত্য হরে মন ॥ ৩০ ॥

āmiha nā jāni tāhā, nā jāne gopī-gaṇa
duṅhāra rūpa-guṇe duṅhāra nitya hare mana

āmiha—I; *nā jāni*—shall not know; *tāhā*—that; *nā jāne*—will not know; *gopī-gaṇa*—the *gopīs; duṅhāra*—of the two; *rūpa-guṇe*—the beauty and qualities; *duṅhāra*—of the two; *nitya*—always; *hare*—carry away; *mana*—the minds.

TRANSLATION

"Neither the gopīs nor I shall notice this, for our minds will always be entranced by one another's beauty and qualities.

PURPORT

In the spiritual sky the Vaikuṇṭha planets are predominated by Nārāyaṇa. His devotees have the same features He does, and the exchange of devotion there is on the platform of reverence. But above all these Vaikuṇṭha planets is Goloka, or Kṛṣṇaloka, where the original Personality of Godhead, Kṛṣṇa, fully manifests His pleasure potency in free loving affairs. Since the devotees in the material world know almost nothing about these affairs, the Lord desires to show these affairs to them.

In Goloka Vṛndāvana there is an exchange of love known as *parakīya-rasa.* It is something like the attraction of a married woman for a man other than her husband. In the material world this sort of relationship is most abominable because it is a perverted reflection of the *parakīya-rasa* in the spiritual world, where it is the highest kind of loving affair. Such feelings between the devotee and the Lord are presented by the influence of *yogamāyā.* The *Bhagavad-gītā* states that devotees of the highest grade are under the care of *daiva-māyā,* or *yogamāyā: mahātmānas tu māṁ pārtha daivīṁ prakṛtim āśritāḥ* (Bg. 9.13). Those who are actually great souls (*mahātmās*) are fully absorbed in Kṛṣṇa consciousness, always engaged in the service of the Lord. They are under the care of *daivī-prakṛti,* or *yogamāyā. Yogamāyā* creates a situation in which the devotee is prepared to transgress all regulative principles simply to love Kṛṣṇa. A devotee naturally does not like to transgress the laws of reverence for the Supreme Personality of Godhead, but by the influence of *yogamāyā* he is prepared to do anything to love the Supreme Lord better.

Those under the spell of the material energy cannot at all appreciate the activities of *yogamāyā,* for a conditioned soul can hardly understand the pure reciprocation between the Lord and His devotee. But by executing devotional service under the regulative principles, one can become very highly elevated and then begin to appreciate the dealings of pure love under the management of *yogamāyā.*

In the spiritual loving sentiment induced by the *yogamāyā* potency, both Lord Śrī Kṛṣṇa and the damsels of Vraja forget themselves in spiritual rapture. By the influence of such forgetfulness, the attractive beauty of the *gopīs* plays a prominent part in the transcendental satisfaction of the Lord, who has nothing to do with mundane sex. Because spiritual love of Godhead is above everything mundane, the *gopīs* superficially seem to transgress the codes of mundane morality. This perpetually puzzles mundane moralists. Therefore *yogamāyā* acts to cover the Lord and His pastimes from the eyes of mundaners, as confirmed in the *Bhagavad-gītā* (7.25), where the Lord says that He reserves the right of not being exposed to everyone.

The acts of *yogamāyā* make it possible for the Lord and the *gopīs*, in loving ecstasy, to sometimes meet and sometimes separate. These transcendental loving affairs of the Lord are unimaginable to empiricists involved in the impersonal feature of the Absolute Truth. Therefore the Lord Himself appears before the mundaners to bestow upon them the highest form of spiritual realization and also personally relish its essence. The Lord is so merciful that He Himself descends to take the fallen souls back home to the kingdom of Godhead, where the erotic principles of Godhead are eternally relished in their real form, distinct from the perverted sexual love so much adored and indulged in by the fallen souls in their diseased condition. The reason the Lord displays the *rāsa-līlā* is essentially to induce all the fallen souls to give up their diseased morality and religiosity, and to attract them to the kingdom of God to enjoy the reality. A person who actually understands what the *rāsa-līlā* is will certainly hate to indulge in mundane sex life. For the realized soul, hearing the Lord's *rāsa-līlā* through the proper channel will result in complete abstinence from material sexual pleasure.

TEXT 31

ধর্ম ছাড়ি' রাগে দুঁহে করয়ে মিলন ।
কভু মিলে, কভু না মিলে,—দৈবের ঘটন ॥ ৩১ ॥

dharma chāḍi' rāge duṅhe karaye milana
kabhu mile, kabhu nā mile,—daivera ghaṭana

dharma chāḍi'—giving up religious customs; *rāge*—in love; *duṅhe*—both; *karaye*—do; *milana*—meeting; *kabhu*—sometimes; *mile*—they meet; *kabhu*—sometimes; *nā mile*—they do not meet; *daivera*—of destiny; *ghaṭana*—the happening.

TRANSLATION

"Pure attachment will unite us even at the expense of moral and religious duties [dharma]. Destiny will sometimes bring us together and sometimes separate us.

PURPORT

The *gopīs* came out to meet Kṛṣṇa in the dead of night when they heard the sound of His flute. Śrīla Rūpa Gosvāmī has accordingly composed a nice verse (see *Ādi* 5.224) that describes the beautiful boy called Govinda standing by the bank of the Yamunā with His flute to His lips in the shining moonlight. Those who want to enjoy life in the materialistic way of society, friendship and love should not go to the Yamunā to see the form of Govinda. The sound of Lord Kṛṣṇa's flute is so sweet that it has made the *gopīs* forget all about their relationships with their kinsmen and flee to Kṛṣṇa in the dead of night.

By leaving home in that way, the *gopīs* transgressed the Vedic regulations of household life. This indicates that when natural feelings of love for Kṛṣṇa become fully manifest, a devotee can neglect conventional social rules and regulations. In the material world we are situated in designative positions only, but pure devotional service begins when one is freed from all designations. When love for Kṛṣṇa is awakened, the designative positions are overcome.

The spontaneous attraction of Śrī Kṛṣṇa for His dearest parts and parcels generates an enthusiasm that obliges Śrī Kṛṣṇa and the *gopīs* to meet together. To celebrate this transcendental enthusiasm, there is need of a sentiment of separation between the lover and beloved. In the condition of material tribulation, no one wants the pangs of separation. But in the transcendental form, the very same separation, being absolute in its nature, strengthens the ties of love and enhances the desire of the lover and beloved to meet. The period of separation, evaluated transcendentally, is more relishable than the actual meeting, which lacks the feelings of increasing anticipation because the lover and beloved are both present.

TEXT 32

এই সব রসনির্যাস করিব আস্বাদ ।
এই দ্বারে করিব সব ভক্তেরে প্রসাদ ॥ ৩২ ॥

ei saba rasa-niryāsa kariba āsvāda
ei dvāre kariba saba bhaktere prasāda

ei—these; *saba*—all; *rasa-niryāsa*—essence of mellows; *kariba*—I shall do; *āsvāda*—tasting; *ei dvāre*—by this; *kariba*—I shall do; *saba*—all; *bhaktere*—to the devotees; *prasāda*—favor.

TRANSLATION

"I shall taste the essence of all these rasas, and in this way I shall favor all the devotees.

TEXT 33

ব্রজের নির্মল রাগ শুনি' ভক্তগণ ।
রাগমার্গে ভজে যেন ছাড়ি' ধর্ম-কর্ম ॥ ৩৩ ॥

vrajera nirmala rāga śuni' bhakta-gaṇa
rāga-mārge bhaje yena chāḍi' dharma-karma

vrajera—of Vraja; *nirmala*—spotless; *rāga*—love; *śuni'*—hearing; *bhakta-gaṇa*—the devotees; *rāga-mārge*—on the path of spontaneous love; *bhaje*—they worship; *yena*—so that; *chāḍi'*—giving up; *dharma*—religiosity; *karma*—fruitive activity.

TRANSLATION

"Then, by hearing about the pure love of the residents of Vraja, devotees will worship Me on the path of spontaneous love, abandoning all rituals of religiosity and fruitive activity."

PURPORT

Many realized souls, such as Raghunātha dāsa Gosvāmī and King Kulaśekhara, have recommended with great emphasis that one develop this spontaneous love of Godhead, even at the risk of transgressing all the traditional codes of morality and religiosity. Śrī Raghunātha dāsa Gosvāmī, one of the six Gosvāmīs of Vṛndāvana, has written in his prayers called the *Manaḥ-śikṣā* that one should simply worship Rādhā and Kṛṣṇa with all attention. *Na dharmaṁ nādharmaṁ śruti-gaṇa-niruktaṁ kila kuru:* one should not be much interested in performing Vedic rituals or simply following rules and regulations.

King Kulaśekhara has written similarly, in his book *Mukunda-mālā-stotra* (5):

nāsthā dharme na vasu-nicaye naiva kāmopabhoge
yad bhāvyaṁ tad bhavatu bhagavan pūrva-karmānurūpam
etat prārthyaṁ mama bahu-mataṁ janma-janmāntare 'pi
tvat-pādāmbho-ruha-yuga-gatā niścalā bhaktir astu

"I have no attraction for performing religious rituals or holding any earthly kingdom. I do not care for sense enjoyments; let them appear and disappear in accordance with my previous deeds. My only desire is to be fixed in devotional service to the lotus feet of the Lord, even though I may continue to take birth here life after life."

TEXT 34

অনুগ্রহায় ভক্তানাং মানুষং দেহমাশ্রিতঃ ।
ভজতে তাদৃশীঃ ক্রীড়া যাঃ শ্রুত্বা তৎপরো ভবেৎ ॥ ৩৪ ॥

anugrahāya bhaktānāṁ
mānuṣaṁ deham āśritaḥ
bhajate tādṛśīḥ krīḍā
yāḥ śrutvā tat-paro bhavet

anugrahāya—for showing favor; *bhaktānām*—to the devotees; *mānuṣam*—humanlike; *deham*—body; *āśritaḥ*—accepting; *bhajate*—He enjoys; *tādṛśīḥ*—such; *krīḍāḥ*—pastimes; *yāḥ*—which; *śrutvā*—having heard; *tat-paraḥ*—fully intent upon Him; *bhavet*—one must become.

TRANSLATION

"Kṛṣṇa manifests His eternal humanlike form and performs His pastimes to show mercy to the devotees. Having heard such pastimes, one should engage in service to Him."

PURPORT

This text is from *Śrīmad-Bhāgavatam* (10.33.36). The Supreme Personality of Godhead has innumerable expansions of His transcendental form who eternally exist in the spiritual world. This material world is only a perverted reflection of the spiritual world, where everything is manifested without inebriety. There everything is in its original existence, free from the domination of time. Time cannot deteriorate or interfere with the conditions in the spiritual world, where different manifestations of the Supreme Personality of Godhead are the recipients of the worship of different living entities in their constitutional spiritual positions. In the spiritual world all existence is unadulterated goodness. The goodness found in the material world is contaminated by the modes of passion and ignorance.

The saying that the human form of life is the best position for devotional service has its special significance because only in this form can a living entity revive his eternal relationship with the Supreme Personality of Godhead. The human form is considered the highest state in the cycle of the species of life in the material world. If one takes advantage of this highest kind of material form, one can regain his position of devotional service to the Lord.

Incarnations of the Supreme Personality of Godhead appear in all the species of life, although this is inconceivable to the human brain. The Lord's pastimes are differentiated according to the appreciating capacity of the different types of bodies of the living entities. The Supreme Lord bestows the most merciful benediction upon human society when He appears in His human form. It is then that humanity gets the opportunity to engage in different kinds of eternal service to the Lord.

Special natural appreciation of the descriptions of a particular pastime of Godhead indicates the constitutional position of a living entity. Adoration, servitorship, friendship, parental affection and conjugal love are the five primary relationships with Kṛṣṇa. The highest perfectional stage of the conjugal relationship, enriched by many sentiments, gives the maximum relishable mellow to the devotee.

The Lord appears in different incarnations—as a fish, tortoise and boar, as Paraśurāma, Lord Rāma, Buddha and so on—to reciprocate the different appreciations of living entities in different stages of evolution. The conjugal relationship of amorous love called *parakīya-rasa* is the unparalleled perfection of love exhibited by Lord Kṛṣṇa and His devotees.

A class of so-called devotees known as *sahajiyās* try to imitate the Lord's pastimes, although they have no understanding of the amorous love in His expansions of pleasure potency. Their superficial imitation can create havoc on the path for the advancement of one's spiritual relationship with the Lord. Material sexual indulgence can never be equated with spiritual love, which is in unadulterated goodness. The activities of the *sahajiyās* simply lower one deeper into the material contamination of the senses and mind. Kṛṣṇa's transcendental pastimes display eternal servitorship to Adhokṣaja, the Supreme Lord, who is beyond all conception through material senses. Materialistic conditioned souls do not understand the transcendental exchanges of love, but they like to indulge in sense gratification in the name of devotional service. The activities of the Supreme Lord can never be understood by irresponsible persons who think the pastimes of Rādhā and Kṛṣṇa to be ordinary affairs. The *rāsa* dance is arranged by Kṛṣṇa's internal potency *yoga-māyā,* and it is beyond the grasp of the materially affected person. Trying to throw mud into transcendence with their perversity, the *sahajiyās* misinterpret the sayings *tat-paratvena nirmalam* and *tat-paro bhavet.* By misinterpreting *tādṛśīḥ krīḍāḥ,* they want to indulge in sex while pretending to imitate Lord Kṛṣṇa. But one must actually understand the imports of the words through the intelligence of the authorized *gosvāmīs.* Śrīla Narottama dāsa Ṭhākura, in his prayers to the Gosvāmīs, has explained his inability to understand such spiritual affairs:

rūpa-raghunātha-pade ha-ibe ākuti
kabe hāma bujhaba se yugala-pīriti

"When I shall be eager to understand the literature given by the Gosvāmīs, then I shall be able to understand the transcendental love affairs of Rādhā and Kṛṣṇa." In other words, unless one is trained under the disciplic succession of the Gosvāmīs, one cannot understand Rādhā and Kṛṣṇa. The conditioned souls are naturally averse to understanding the spiritual existence of the Lord, and if they try to know the transcendental nature of the Lord's pastimes while they remain absorbed in materialism, they are sure to blunder like the *sahajiyās.*

TEXT 35

'ভবেৎ' ক্রিয়া বিধিলিঙ্, সেই ইহা কয় ।
কর্তব্য অবশ্য এই, অন্যথা প্রত্যবায় ॥ ৩৫ ॥

'bhavet' kriyā vidhiliṅ, sei ihā kaya
kartavya avaśya ei, anyathā pratyavāya

bhavet—bhavet; kriyā—the verb; *vidhi-liṅ*—an injunction of the imperative mood; *sei*—that; *ihā*—here; *kaya*—says; *kartavya*—to be done; *avaśya*—certainly; *ei*—this; *anyathā*—otherwise; *pratyavāya*—detriment.

TRANSLATION

Here the use of the verb "bhavet," which is in the imperative mood, tells us that this certainly must be done. Noncompliance would be abandonment of duty.

PURPORT

This imperative is applicable to pure devotees. Neophytes will be able to understand these affairs only after being elevated by regulated devotional service under the expert guidance of the spiritual master. Then they too will be competent to hear of the love affairs of Rādhā and Kṛṣṇa.

As long as one is in material, conditioned life, strict discipline is required in the matter of moral and immoral activities. The absolute world is transcendental and free from such distinctions because there inebriety is not possible. But in this material world a sexual appetite necessitates distinction between moral and immoral conduct. There are no sexual activities in the spiritual world. The transactions between lover and beloved in the spiritual world are pure transcendental love and unadulterated bliss.

One who has not been attracted by the transcendental beauty of *rasa* will certainly be dragged down into material attraction, thus to act in material contamination and progress to the darkest region of hellish life. But by understanding the conjugal love of Rādhā and Kṛṣṇa one is freed from the grip of attraction to material so-called love between man and woman. Similarly, one who understands the pure parental love of Nanda and Yaśodā for Kṛṣṇa will be saved from being dragged into material parental affection. If one accepts Kṛṣṇa as the supreme friend, the attraction of material friendship will be finished for him, and he will not be dismayed by so-called friendship with mundane wranglers. If he is attracted by servitorship to Kṛṣṇa, he will no longer have to serve the material body in the degraded status of material existence, with the false hope of becoming master in the future. Similarly, one who sees the greatness of Kṛṣṇa in neutrality will certainly never again seek the so-called relief of impersonalist or voidist philosophy. If one is not attracted by the transcendental nature of Kṛṣṇa, one is sure to be attracted to material enjoyment, thus to become implicated in the clinging network of virtuous and sinful activities and to continue material existence by transmigrating from one material body to another. Only in Kṛṣṇa consciousness can one achieve the highest perfection of life.

TEXTS 36–37

এই বাঞ্ছা যৈছে কৃষ্ণপ্রাকট্য-কারণ ।
অসুরসংহার—আনুষঙ্গ প্রয়োজন ॥ ৩৬ ॥
এই মত চৈতন্য-কৃষ্ণ পূর্ণ ভগবান্ ।
যুগধর্মপ্রবর্তন নহে তাঁর কাম ॥ ৩৭ ॥

ei vāñchā yaiche kṛṣṇa-prākaṭya-kāraṇa
asura-saṁhāra—ānuṣaṅga prayojana

ei mata caitanya-kṛṣṇa pūrṇa bhagavān
yuga-dharma-pravartana nahe tāṅra kāma

ei—this; *vāñchā*—desire; *yaiche*—just as; *kṛṣṇa*—of Lord Kṛṣṇa; *prākaṭya*—for the manifestation; *kāraṇa*—reason; *asura-saṁhāra*—the killing of demons; *ānuṣaṅga*—secondary; *prayojana*—reason; *ei mata*—like this; *caitanya*—as Lord Caitanya Mahāprabhu; *kṛṣṇa*—Lord Kṛṣṇa; *pūrṇa*—full; *bhagavān*—the Supreme Personality of Godhead; *yuga-dharma*—the religion of the age; *pravartana*—initiating; *nahe*—is not; *tāṅra*—of Him; *kāma*—the desire.

TRANSLATION

Just as these desires are the fundamental reason for Kṛṣṇa's appearance whereas destroying the demons is only an incidental necessity, so for Śrī Kṛṣṇa Caitanya, the Supreme Personality of Godhead, promulgating the dharma of the age is incidental.

TEXT 38

কোন কারণে যবে হৈল অবতারে মন ।
যুগধর্ম-কাল হৈল সে কালে মিলন ॥ ৩৮ ॥

kona kāraṇe yabe haila avatāre mana
yuga-dharma-kāla haila se kāle milana

kona kāraṇe—by some reason; *yabe*—when; *haila*—there was; *avatāre*—in incarnation; *mana*—inclination; *yuga-dharma*—for the religion of the age; *kāla*—the time; *haila*—there was; *se kāle*—at that time; *milana*—conjunction.

TRANSLATION

When the Lord desired to appear for another reason, the time for promulgating the religion of the age also arose.

TEXT 39

দুই হেতু অবতরি' লঞা ভক্তগণ ।
আপনে আস্বাদে প্রেম-নামসংকীর্তন ॥ ৩৯ ॥

dui hetu avatari' lañā bhakta-gaṇa
āpane āsvāde prema-nāma-saṅkīrtana

dui—two; *hetu*—reasons; *avatari'*—incarnating; *lañā*—taking; *bhakta-gaṇa*—the devotees; *āpane*—Himself; *āsvāde*—tastes; *prema*—love of God; *nāma-saṅkīrtana*—and congregational chanting of the holy name.

TRANSLATION

Thus with two intentions the Lord appeared with His devotees and tasted the nectar of prema with the congregational chanting of the holy name.

TEXT 40

সেই দ্বারে আচণ্ডালে কীর্তন সঞ্চারে ।
নাম-প্রেমমালা গাঁথি' পরাইল সংসারে ॥ ৪০ ॥

sei dvāre ācaṇḍāle kīrtana sañcāre
nāma-prema-mālā gāṅthi' parāila saṁsāre

sei dvāre—by that; *ā-caṇḍāle*—even among the *caṇḍālas; kīrtana*—the chanting of the holy names; *sañcāre*—He infuses; *nāma*—of the holy names; *prema*—and of love of God; *mālā*—a garland; *gāṅthi'*—stringing together; *parāila*—He put it on; *saṁsāre*—the whole material world.

TRANSLATION

Thus He spread kīrtana even among the untouchables. He wove a wreath of the holy name and prema, with which He garlanded the entire material world.

TEXT 41

এইমত ভক্তভাব করি' অঙ্গীকার ।
আপনি আচরি' ভক্তি করিল প্রচার ॥ ৪১ ॥

ei-mata bhakta-bhāva kari' aṅgīkāra
āpani ācari' bhakti karila pracāra

ei-mata—like this; *bhakta-bhāva*—the position of a devotee; *kari'*—making; *aṅgīkāra*—acceptance; *āpani*—Himself; *ācari'*—practicing; *bhakti*—devotional service; *karila*—did; *pracāra*—propagation.

TRANSLATION

In this way, assuming the sentiment of a devotee, He preached devotional service while practicing it Himself.

PURPORT

When Rūpa Gosvāmī met Lord Śrī Caitanya Mahāprabhu at Prayāga (Allahabad), he offered his respectful obeisances by submitting that Lord Caitanya was more magnanimous than any other *avatāra* of Kṛṣṇa because He was distributing love of Kṛṣṇa. His mission was to enhance love of Godhead. In the human form of life the highest achievement is to attain the platform of love of Godhead. Lord Caitanya did not invent a system of religion, as people sometimes assume. Religious systems are meant to show the existence of God, who is then generally approached as the cosmic order-supplier. But Lord Śrī Caitanya Mahāprabhu's transcendental mission is to distribute love of Godhead to everyone. Anyone who accepts God as the Supreme can take to the process of chanting Hare Kṛṣṇa and become a lover of God. Therefore Lord Caitanya is the most magnanimous. This munificent broadcasting of devotional service is possible only for Kṛṣṇa Himself. Therefore Lord Caitanya is Kṛṣṇa.

In the *Bhagavad-gītā* Kṛṣṇa has taught the philosophy of surrender to the Supreme Personality of Godhead. One who has surrendered to the Supreme can make further progress by learning to love Him. Therefore the Kṛṣṇa consciousness movement propagated by Lord Caitanya is especially meant for those who are cognizant of the presence of the Supreme Godhead, the ultimate controller of everything. His mission is to teach people how to dovetail themselves into engagements of transcendental loving service. He is Kṛṣṇa teaching His own service from the position of a devotee. The Lord's acceptance of the role of a devotee in the eternal form of Lord Śrī Caitanya Mahāprabhu is another of the Lord's wonderful features. A conditioned soul cannot reach the absolute Personality of Godhead by his imperfect endeavor, and therefore it is wonderful that Lord Śrī Kṛṣṇa, in the form of Lord Gaurāṅga, has made it easy for everyone to approach Him.

Svarūpa Dāmodara Gosvāmī has described Lord Caitanya as Kṛṣṇa Himself with the attitude of Rādhārāṇī, or a combination of Rādhā and Kṛṣṇa. The intention of Lord Caitanya is to taste Kṛṣṇa's sweetness in transcendental love. He does not care to think of Himself as Kṛṣṇa, because He wants the position of Rādhārāṇī. We should remember this. A class of so-called devotees called the *nadīyā-nāgarīs* or *gaura-nāgarīs* pretend that they have the sentiment of *gopīs* toward Lord Caitanya, but they do not realize that He placed Himself not as the enjoyer, Kṛṣṇa, but as the enjoyed, the devotee of Kṛṣṇa. The concoctions of unauthorized persons pretending to be bona fide have not been accepted by Lord Caitanya. Presentations such as those of the *gaura-nāgarīs* are only disturbances to the sincere execution of the mission of Lord Caitanya. Lord Caitanya is undoubtedly Kṛṣṇa Himself, and He is always nondifferent from Śrīmatī Rādhārāṇī. But the emotion technically called *vipralambha-bhāva,* which the Lord adopted for confidential reasons, should not be disturbed in the name of service. A mundaner should not unnecessarily intrude into affairs of transcendence and thereby displease the Lord. One must always be on guard against this sort of devotional anomaly. A devotee is not meant to create disturbances to Kṛṣṇa. As Śrīla Rūpa Gosvāmī has explained, devotional service is *ānukūlyena,* or favorable to Kṛṣṇa. Acting unfavorably toward Kṛṣṇa is not devotion. Kaṁsa was the enemy of Kṛṣṇa. He always thought of Kṛṣṇa, but he thought of Him as an enemy. One should always avoid such unfavorable so-called service.

Lord Caitanya has accepted the role of Rādhārāṇī, and we should support that position, as Svarūpa Dāmodara did in the Gambhīrā (the room where Lord Caitanya Mahāprabhu stayed in Purī). He always reminded Lord Caitanya of Rādhā's feelings of separation as they are described in *Śrīmad-Bhāgavatam,* and Lord Caitanya appreciated his assistance. But the *gaura-nāgarīs,* who place Lord Caitanya in the position of enjoyer and themselves as His enjoyed, are not approved by Lord Caitanya or by Lord Caitanya's followers. Instead of being blessed, the foolish imitators are left completely apart. Their concoctions are against the principles of Lord Śrī Caitanya Mahāprabhu. The doctrine of transcendental enjoyment by Kṛṣṇa cannot be mixed up with the doctrine of transcendental feeling of separation from Kṛṣṇa in the role of Rādhārāṇī.

TEXT 42

দাস্য, সখ্য, বাৎসল্য, আর যে শৃঙ্গার ।
চারি প্রেম, চতুর্বিধ ভক্তই আধার ॥ ৪২ ॥

dāsya, sakhya, vātsalya, āra ye śṛṅgāra
cāri prema, catur-vidha bhakta-i ādhāra

dāsya—servitude; *sakhya*—friendship; *vātsalya*—parental affection; *āra*—and; *ye*—that; *śṛṅgāra*—conjugal love; *cāri*—four types; *prema*—

love of God; *catuḥ-vidha*—four kinds; *bhakta-i*—devotees; *ādhāra*—the containers.

TRANSLATION

Four kinds of devotees are the receptacles of the four kinds of mellows in love of God, namely servitude, friendship, parental affection and conjugal love.

TEXT 43

নিজ নিজ ভাব সবে শ্রেষ্ঠ করি' মানে ।
নিজভাবে করে কৃষ্ণসুখ আস্বাদনে ॥ ৪৩ ॥

nija nija bhāva sabe śreṣṭha kari' māne
nija-bhāve kare kṛṣṇa-sukha āsvādane

nija nija—each his own; *bhāva*—mood; *sabe*—all; *śreṣṭha kari'*—making the best; *māne*—accepts; *nija-bhāve*—in his own mood; *kare*—does; *kṛṣṇa-sukha*—happiness with Lord Kṛṣṇa; *āsvādane*—tasting.

TRANSLATION

Each kind of devotee feels that his sentiment is the most excellent, and thus in that mood he tastes great happiness with Lord Kṛṣṇa.

TEXT 44

তটস্থ হইয়া মনে বিচার যদি করি ।
সব রস হৈতে শৃঙ্গারে অধিক মাধুরী ॥ ৪৪ ॥

taṭastha ha-iyā mane vicāra yadi kari
saba rasa haite śṛṅgāre adhika mādhurī

taṭa-stha ha-iyā—becoming impartial; *mane*—in the mind; *vicāra*—consideration; *yadi*—if; *kari*—doing; *saba rasa*—all the mellows; *haite*—than; *śṛṅgāre*—in conjugal love; *adhika*—greater; *mādhurī*—sweetness.

TRANSLATION

But if we compare the sentiments in an impartial mood, we find that the conjugal sentiment is superior to all others in sweetness.

PURPORT

No one is higher or lower than anyone else in transcendental relationships with the Lord, for in the absolute realm everything is equal. But although these relationships are absolute, there are also transcendental differences between them. Thus the transcendental relationship of conjugal love is considered the highest perfection.

TEXT 45

যথোত্তরমসৌ স্বাদবিশেষোল্লাসময্যপি ।
রতির্বাসনয়া স্বাদ্বী ভাসতে কাপি কস্যচিৎ ॥ ৪৫ ॥

yathottaram asau svāda-
viśeṣollāsamayy api
ratir vāsanayā svādvī
bhāsate kāpi kasyacit

yathā-uttaram—one after another; *asau*—that; *svāda-viśeṣa*—of particular tastes; *ullāsa-mayī*—consisting of the increase; *api*—although; *ratiḥ*—love; *vāsanayā*—by the different desire; *svādvī*—sweet; *bhāsate*—exists; *kā api*—any; *kasyacit*—of someone (the devotee).

TRANSLATION

"Increasing love is experienced in various tastes, one above another. But that love which has the highest taste in the gradual succession of desire manifests itself in the form of conjugal love."

PURPORT

This is a verse from Śrīla Rūpa Gosvāmī's *Bhakti-rasāmṛta-sindhu* (2.5.38).

TEXT 46

অতএব মধুর রস কহি তার নাম ।
স্বকীয়া-পরকীয়া-ভাবে দ্বিবিধ সংস্থান ॥ ৪৬ ॥

ataeva madhura rasa kahi tāra nāma
svakīyā-parakīyā-bhāve dvi-vidha saṁsthāna

ataeva—therefore; *madhura*—sweet; *rasa*—mellow; *kahi*—I say; *tāra*—of that; *nāma*—the name; *svakīyā*—*svakīyā* (own); *parakīyā*—

and named *parakīyā* (another's); *bhāve*—in the moods; *dvi-vidha*—two types; *saṁsthāna*—positions.

TRANSLATION

Therefore I call it madhura-rasa. It has two further divisions, namely wedded and unwedded love.

TEXT 47

পরকীয়া-ভাবে অতি রসের উল্লাস ।
ব্রজ বিনা ইহার অন্যত্র নাহি বাস ॥ ৪৭ ॥

parakīyā-bhāve ati rasera ullāsa
vraja vinā ihāra anyatra nāhi vāsa

parakīyā-bhāve—in the mood of *parakīyā,* or conjugal relations outside of marriage; *ati*—very great; *rasera*—of mellow; *ullāsa*—increase; *vraja vinā*—except for Vraja; *ihāra*—of this; *anyatra*—anywhere else; *nāhi*—there is not; *vāsa*—residence.

TRANSLATION

There is a great increase of mellow in the unwedded conjugal mood. Such love is found nowhere but in Vraja.

TEXT 48

ব্রজবধূগণের এই ভাব নিরবধি ।
তার মধ্যে শ্রীরাধায় ভাবের অবধি ॥ ৪৮ ॥

vraja-vadhū-gaṇera ei bhāva niravadhi
tāra madhye śrī-rādhāya bhāvera avadhi

vraja-vadhū-gaṇera—of the young wives of Vraja; *ei*—this; *bhāva*—mood; *niravadhi*—unbounded; *tāra madhye*—among them; *śrī-rādhāya*—in Śrīmatī Rādhārāṇī; *bhāvera*—of the mood; *avadhi*—the highest limit.

TRANSLATION

This mood is unbounded in the damsels of Vraja, but among them it finds its perfection in Śrī Rādhā.

TEXT 49

প্রৌঢ় নির্মলভাব প্রেম সর্বোত্তম ।
কৃষ্ণের মাধুর্যরস-আস্বাদ-কারণ ॥ ৪৯ ॥

prauḍha nirmala-bhāva prema sarvottama
kṛṣṇera mādhurya-rasa-āsvāda-kāraṇa

prauḍha—matured; *nirmala-bhāva*—pure condition; *prema*—love; *sarva-uttama*—best of all; *kṛṣṇera*—of Lord Kṛṣṇa; *mādhurya-rasa*—of the mellow of the conjugal relationship; *āsvāda*—of the tasting; *kāraṇa*—the cause.

TRANSLATION

Her pure, mature love surpasses that of all others. Her love is the cause of Lord Kṛṣṇa's tasting the sweetness of the conjugal relationship.

TEXT 50

অতএব সেই ভাব অঙ্গীকার করি' ।
সাধিলেন নিজ বাঞ্ছা গৌরাঙ্গ-শ্রীহরি ॥ ৫০ ॥

ataeva sei bhāva aṅgīkāra kari'
sādhilena nija vāñchā gaurāṅga-śrī-hari

ataeva—therefore; *sei bhāva*—that mood; *aṅgīkāra kari'*—accepting; *sādhilena*—fulfilled; *nija*—His own; *vāñchā*—desire; *gaurāṅga*—Lord Caitanya Mahāprabhu; *śrī-hari*—the Supreme Personality of Godhead.

TRANSLATION

Therefore Lord Gaurāṅga, who is Śrī Hari Himself, accepted the sentiments of Rādhā and thus fulfilled His own desires.

PURPORT

Of the four kinds of reciprocation of loving service—*dāsya*, *sakhya*, *vātsalya* and *mādhurya*—*mādhurya* is considered the fullest. But the conjugal relationship is further divided into two varieties, namely *svakīya* and *parakīya*. *Svakīya* is the relationship with Kṛṣṇa as a formally married husband, and *parakīya* is the relationship with Kṛṣṇa as a paramour. Expert analysts have decided that the transcendental ecstasy of the *parakīya* mellow is better because it is more enthusiastic. This phase of conjugal love is found in those who have surrendered to the Lord in intense love, knowing well that such illicit love with a paramour is not morally approved in society. The risks involved in such love of Godhead make this emotion superior to the relationship in which such risk is not involved. The validity of such risk, however, is possible only in the transcendental realm. *Svakīya* and *parakīya* conjugal love of Godhead have no existence in the material world, and *parakīya* is not exhibited anywhere in Vaikuṇṭha, but only in the portion of Goloka Vṛndāvana known as Vraja.

Some devotees think that Kṛṣṇa is eternally the enjoyer in Goloka Vṛndāvana but only sometimes comes to the platform of Vraja to enjoy *parakīya-rasa.* The six Gosvāmīs of Vṛndāvana, however, have explained that Kṛṣṇa's pastimes in Vraja are eternal, like His other activities in Goloka Vṛndāvana. Vraja is a confidential part of Goloka Vṛndāvana. Kṛṣṇa exhibited His Vraja pastimes on the surface of this world, and similar pastimes are eternally exhibited in Vraja in Goloka Vṛndāvana, where *parakīya-rasa* is ever existent.

In the Third Chapter of this epic, Śrīla Kṛṣṇadāsa Kavirāja Gosvāmī has explicitly accepted the fact that Kṛṣṇa appears in this material world at the end of the Dvāpara age of the twenty-eighth *catur-yuga* of Vaivasvata Manu and brings with Him His Vrajadhāma, which is the eternal abode of His highest pastimes. As the Lord appears by His own internal potency, so He also brings all His paraphernalia by the same internal potency, without extraneous help. It is further stated here in the *Caitanya-caritāmṛta* that the *parakīya* sentiment exists only in that transcendental realm and nowhere else. This highest form of ecstasy can exist only in the most confidential part of the transcendental world, but by the causeless mercy of the Lord we can have a peep into that invisible Vraja.

The transcendental mellow relished by the *gopīs* in Vraja is superexcellently featured in Śrīmatī Rādhārāṇī. Mature assimilation of the transcendental humor of conjugal love is represented by Śrīmatī Rādhārāṇī, whose feelings are incomprehensible even to the Lord Himself. The intensity of Her loving service is the highest form of ecstasy. No one can surpass Śrīmatī Rādhārāṇī in relishing the qualities of the Lord through this supreme transcendental mellow. Therefore the Lord Himself agreed to assume the position of Rādhārāṇī in the form of Lord Śrī Gaurāṅga. He then relished the highest position of *parakīya-rasa,* as exhibited in the transcendental abode of Vraja.

TEXT 51

সুরেশানাং দুর্গং গতিরতিশয়েনোপনিষদাং
মুনীনাং সর্বস্বং প্রণতপটলীনাং মধুরিমা ।
বিনির্যাসঃ প্রেম্ণো নিখিলপশুপালাম্বুজদৃশাং
স চৈতন্যঃ কিং মে পুনরপি দৃশোর্যাস্যতি পদম্ ॥ ৫১ ॥

sureśānāṁ durgaṁ gatir atiśayenopaniṣadāṁ
munīnāṁ sarva-svaṁ praṇata-paṭalīnāṁ madhurimā
viniryāsaḥ premṇo nikhila-paśu-pālāmbuja-dṛśāṁ
sa caitanyaḥ kiṁ me punar api dṛśor yāsyati padam

sura-īśānām—of the kings of the demigods; *durgam*—fortress; *gatiḥ*—the goal; *atiśayena*—eminently; *upaniṣadām*—of the *Upaniṣads; munīnām*—of the sages; *sarva-svam*—the be-all and end-all; *praṇata-paṭalīnām*—of the groups of the devotees; *madhurimā*—the sweetness; *viniryāsaḥ*—the essence; *premṇaḥ*—of love; *nikhila*—all; *paśu-pālā*—of the cowherd women; *ambuja-dṛśām*—lotus-eyed; *saḥ*—He; *caitanyaḥ*—Lord Caitanya; *kim*—what; *me*—my; *punaḥ*—again; *api*—certainly; *dṛśoḥ*—of the two eyes; *yāsyati*—will come; *padam*—to the abode.

TRANSLATION

"Lord Caitanya is the shelter of the demigods, the goal of the Upaniṣads, the be-all and end-all of the great sages, the beautiful shelter of His devotees, and the essence of the love of the lotus-eyed gopīs. Will He again be the object of my vision?"

TEXT 52

অপারং কস্যাপি প্রণয়িজনবৃন্দস্য কুতুকী
রসস্তোমং হৃত্বা মধুরমুপভোক্তুং কমপি যঃ ।
রুচং স্বামাবব্রে দ্যুতিমিহ তদীয়াং প্রকটয়ন্
স দেবশ্চৈতন্যাকৃতিরতিতরাং নঃ কৃপয়তু ॥ ৫২ ॥

apāraṁ kasyāpi praṇayi-jana-vṛndasya kutukī
rasa-stomaṁ hṛtvā madhuram upabhoktuṁ kam api yaḥ
rucaṁ svām āvavre dyutim iha tadīyāṁ prakaṭayan
sa devaś caitanyākṛtir atitarāṁ naḥ kṛpayatu

apāram—boundless; *kasya api*—of someone; *praṇayi-jana-vṛndasya*—of the multitude of lovers; *kutukī*—one who is curious; *rasa-stomam*—

the group of mellows; *hṛtvā*—stealing; *madhuram*—sweet; *upabhoktum*—to enjoy; *kam api*—some; *yaḥ*—who; *rucam*—luster; *svām*—own; *āvavre*—covered; *dyutim*—luster; *iha*—here; *tadīyām*—related to Him; *prakaṭayan*—manifesting; *saḥ*—He; *devaḥ*—the Supreme Personality of Godhead; *caitanya-ākṛtiḥ*—having the form of Lord Caitanya Mahāprabhu; *atitarām*—greatly; *naḥ*—unto us; *kṛpayatu*—may He show His mercy.

TRANSLATION

"Lord Kṛṣṇa desired to taste the limitless nectarean mellows of the love of one of His multitude of loving damsels [Śrī Rādhā], and so He has assumed the form of Lord Caitanya. He has tasted that love while hiding His own dark complexion with Her effulgent yellow color. May that Lord Caitanya confer upon us His grace."

PURPORT

Texts 51 and 52 are, respectively, *Prathama Śrī Caitanyāṣṭaka* 2 and *Dvitīya Śrī Caitanyāṣṭaka* 3, from the *Stava-mālā* of Śrīla Rūpa Gosvāmī.

TEXT 53

ভাবগ্রহণের হেতু কৈল ধর্ম স্থাপন ।
তার মুখ্য হেতু কহি, শুন সর্বজন ॥ ৫৩ ॥

bhāva-grahaṇera hetu kaila dharma-sthāpana
tāra mukhya hetu kahi, śuna sarva-jana

bhāva-grahaṇera—of accepting the mood; *hetu*—the reason; *kaila*—did; *dharma*—religion; *sthāpana*—establishing; *tāra*—of that; *mukhya*—principal; *hetu*—reason; *kahi*—I say; *śuna*—please hear; *sarva-jana*—everyone.

TRANSLATION

To accept ecstatic love is the main reason He appeared and reestablished the religious system for this age. I shall now explain that reason. Everyone please listen.

TEXT 54

মূল হেতু আগে শ্লোকের কৈল আভাস ।
এবে কহি সেই শ্লোকের অর্থ প্রকাশ ॥ ৫৪ ॥

mūla hetu āge ślokera kaila ābhāsa
ebe kahi sei ślokera artha prakāśa

mūla hetu—the root cause; *āge*—in the beginning; *ślokera*—of the verse; *kaila*—gave; *ābhāsa*—hint; *ebe*—now; *kahi*—I shall speak; *sei*—that; *ślokera*—of the verse; *artha*—meaning; *prakāśa*—manifestation.

TRANSLATION

Having first given hints about the verse describing the principal reason why the Lord appeared, now I shall manifest its full meaning.

TEXT 55

রাধা কৃষ্ণ প্রণয়বিকৃতির্হ্লাদিনীশক্তিরস্মা-
দেকাত্মানাবপি ভুবি পুরা দেহভেদং গতৌ তৌ ।
চৈতন্যাখ্যং প্রকটমধুনা তদ্দ্বয়ঞ্চৈক্যমাপ্তং
রাধাভাবদ্যুতিসুবলিতং নৌমি কৃষ্ণস্বরূপম্ ॥ ৫৫ ॥

rādhā kṛṣṇa-praṇaya-vikṛtir hlādinī śaktir asmād
ekātmānāv api bhuvi purā deha-bhedaṁ gatau tau
caitanyākhyaṁ prakaṭam adhunā tad-dvayaṁ caikyam āptaṁ
rādhā-bhāva-dyuti-suvalitaṁ naumi kṛṣṇa-svarūpam

rādhā—Śrīmatī Rādhārāṇī; *kṛṣṇa*—of Lord Kṛṣṇa; *praṇaya*—of love; *vikṛtiḥ*—the transformation; *hlādinī śaktiḥ*—pleasure potency; *asmāt*—from this; *eka-ātmānau*—both the same in identity; *api*—although; *bhuvi*—on earth; *purā*—from beginningless time; *deha-bhedam*—separate forms; *gatau*—obtained; *tau*—these two; *caitanya-ākhyam*—known as Śrī Caitanya; *prakaṭam*—manifest; *adhunā*—now; *tat-dvayam*—the two of Them; *ca*—and; *aikyam*—unity; *āptam*—obtained; *rādhā*—of Śrīmatī Rādhārāṇī; *bhāva*—mood; *dyuti*—the luster; *suvalitam*—who is adorned with; *naumi*—I offer my obeisances; *kṛṣṇa-svarūpam*—to Him who is identical with Śrī Kṛṣṇa.

TRANSLATION

"The loving affairs of Śrī Rādhā and Kṛṣṇa are transcendental manifestations of the Lord's internal pleasure-giving potency. Although Rādhā and Kṛṣṇa are one in Their identity, They sepa-

rated Themselves eternally. Now these two transcendental identities have again united, in the form of Śrī Kṛṣṇa Caitanya. I bow down to Him, who has manifested Himself with the sentiment and complexion of Śrīmatī Rādhārāṇī although He is Kṛṣṇa Himself."

PURPORT

This text is from the diary of Śrīla Svarūpa Dāmodara Gosvāmī. It appears as the fifth of the first fourteen verses of *Śrī Caitanya-caritāmṛta.*

TEXT 56

রাধাকৃষ্ণ এক আত্মা, দুই দেহ ধরি'।
অন্যোন্যে বিলসে রস আস্বাদন করি' ॥ ৫৬ ॥

rādhā-kṛṣṇa eka ātmā, dui deha dhari'
anyonye vilase rasa āsvādana kari'

rādhā-kṛṣṇa—Rādhā and Kṛṣṇa; *eka*—one; *ātmā*—self; *dui*—two; *deha*—bodies; *dhari'*—assuming; *anyonye*—one another; *vilase*—They enjoy; *rasa*—the mellows of love; *āsvādana kari'*—tasting.

TRANSLATION

Rādhā and Kṛṣṇa are one and the same, but They have assumed two bodies. Thus They enjoy each other, tasting the mellows of love.

PURPORT

The two transcendentalists Rādhā and Kṛṣṇa are a puzzle to materialists. The above description of Rādhā and Kṛṣṇa from the diary of Śrīla Svarūpa Dāmodara Gosvāmī is a condensed explanation, but one needs great spiritual insight to understand the mystery of these two personalities. One is enjoying in two. Śrī Kṛṣṇa is the potent factor, and Śrīmatī Rādhārāṇī is the internal potency. According to Vedānta philosophy, there is no difference between the potent and the potency; they are identical. We cannot differentiate between one and the other, any more than we can separate fire from heat.

Everything in the Absolute is inconceivable in relative existence. Therefore in relative cognizance it is very difficult to assimilate this truth of the oneness between the potent and the potency. The philosophy of inconceivable oneness and difference propounded by Lord Caitanya is the only source of understanding for such intricacies of transcendence.

In fact, Rādhārāṇī is the internal potency of Śrī Kṛṣṇa, and She eternally intensifies the pleasure of Śrī Kṛṣṇa. Impersonalists cannot understand this without the help of a *mahā-bhāgavata* devotee. The very name "Rādhā" suggests that Śrīmatī Rādhārāṇī is eternally the topmost mistress of the comforts of Śrī Kṛṣṇa. As such, She is the medium transmitting the living entities' service to Śrī Kṛṣṇa. Devotees in Vṛndāvana therefore seek the mercy of Śrīmatī Rādhārāṇī in order to be recognized as loving servitors of Śrī Kṛṣṇa.

Lord Caitanya Mahāprabhu personally approaches the fallen conditioned souls of the iron age to deliver the highest principle of transcendental relationships with the Lord. The activities of Lord Caitanya are primarily in the role of the pleasure-giving portion of His internal potency.

The absolute Personality of Godhead, Śrī Kṛṣṇa, is the omnipotent form of transcendental existence, knowledge and bliss in full. His internal potency is exhibited first as *sat,* or existence—or, in other words, as the portion that expands the existence function of the Lord. When the same potency displays full knowledge it is called *cit,* or *samvit,* which expands the transcendental forms of the Lord. Finally, when the same potency plays as a pleasure-giving medium it is known as *hlādinī,* or the transcendental blissful potency. Thus the Lord manifests His internal potency in three transcendental divisions.

TEXT 57

সেই দুই এক এবে চৈতন্য গোসাঞি ।
রস আস্বাদিতে দোঁহে হৈলা একঠাঁই ॥ ৫৭ ॥

sei dui eka ebe caitanya gosāñi
rasa āsvādite doṅhe hailā eka-ṭhāñi

sei—these; *dui*—two; *eka*—one; *ebe*—now; *caitanya gosāñi*—Lord Caitanya Mahāprabhu; *rasa*—mellow; *āsvādite*—to taste; *doṅhe*—the two; *hailā*—have become; *eka-ṭhāñi*—one body.

TRANSLATION

Now, to enjoy rasa, They have appeared in one body as Lord Caitanya Mahāprabhu.

TEXT 58

ইথি লাগি' আগে করি তার বিবরণ ।
যাহা হৈতে হয় গৌরের মহিমা-কথন ॥ ৫৮ ॥

ithi lāgi' āge kari tāra vivaraṇa
yāhā haite haya gaurera mahimā-kathana

ithi lāgi'—for this; *āge*—first; *kari*—I shall do; *tāra*—of that; *vivaraṇa*—description; *yāhā haite*—from which; *haya*—there is; *gaurera*—of Lord Caitanya Mahāprabhu; *mahimā*—the glory; *kathana*—relating.

TRANSLATION

Therefore I shall first delineate the position of Rādhā and Kṛṣṇa. From that description the glory of Lord Caitanya will be known.

TEXT 59

রাধিকা হয়েন কৃষ্ণের প্রণয়-বিকার ।
স্বরূপশক্তি—'হ্লাদিনী' নাম যাঁহার ॥ ৫৯ ॥

rādhikā hayena kṛṣṇera praṇaya-vikāra
svarūpa-śakti—'hlādinī' nāma yāṅhāra

rādhikā—Śrīmatī Rādhārāṇī; *hayena*—is; *kṛṣṇera*—of Lord Kṛṣṇa; *praṇaya-vikāra*—transformation of love; *svarūpa-śakti*—personal energy; *hlādinī—hlādinī; nāma*—name; *yāṅhāra*—whose.

TRANSLATION

Śrīmatī Rādhikā is the transformation of Kṛṣṇa's love. She is His internal energy called hlādinī.

TEXT 60

হ্লাদিনী করায় কৃষ্ণে আনন্দাস্বাদন ।
হ্লাদিনীর দ্বারা করে ভক্তের পোষণ ॥ ৬০ ॥

hlādinī karāya kṛṣṇe ānandāsvādana
hlādinīra dvārā kare bhaktera poṣaṇa

hlādinī—the *hlādinī* energy; *karāya*—causes to do; *kṛṣṇe*—in Lord Kṛṣṇa; *ānanda-āsvādana*—the tasting of bliss; *hlādinīra dvārā*—by the pleasure potency; *kare*—does; *bhaktera*—of the devotee; *poṣaṇa*—nourishing.

TRANSLATION

That hlādinī energy gives Kṛṣṇa pleasure and nourishes His devotees.

PURPORT

Śrīla Jīva Gosvāmī has elaborately discussed the *hlādinī* potency in his *Prīti-sandarbha.* He says that the *Vedas* clearly state, "Only devotional service can lead one to the Personality of Godhead. Only devotional service can help a devotee meet the Supreme Lord face to face. The Supreme Personality of Godhead is attracted by devotional service, and as such the ultimate supremacy of Vedic knowledge rests in knowing the science of devotional service."

What is the particular attraction that makes the Supreme Lord enthusiastic to accept devotional service, and what is the nature of such service? The Vedic scriptures inform us that the Supreme Personality of Godhead, the Absolute Truth, is self-sufficient, and that *māyā*, nescience, can never influence Him at all. Therefore the potency that overcomes the Supreme must be purely spiritual. Such a potency cannot be anything of the material manifestation. The bliss enjoyed by the Supreme Personality of Godhead cannot be of material composition, like the impersonalist conception of the bliss of Brahman. Devotional service is reciprocation between two, and therefore it cannot be located simply within one's self. Therefore the bliss of self-realization, *brahmānanda*, cannot be equated with devotional service.

The Supreme Personality of Godhead has three kinds of internal potency, namely the *hlādinī-śakti*, or pleasure potency, the *sandhinī-śakti*, or existential potency, and the *samvit-śakti*, or cognitive potency. In the *Viṣṇu Purāṇa* (1.12.69) the Lord is addressed as follows: "O Lord, You are the support of everything. The three attributes *hlādinī*, *sandhinī* and *samvit* exist in You as one spiritual energy. But the material modes, which cause happiness, misery and mixtures of the two, do not exist in You, for You have no material qualities."

Hlādinī is the personal manifestation of the blissfulness of the Supreme Personality of Godhead, by which He enjoys pleasure. Because the pleasure potency is perpetually present in the Supreme Lord, the theory of the impersonalist that the Lord appears in the material mode of goodness cannot be accepted. The impersonalist conclusion is against the Vedic version that the Lord possesses a transcendental pleasure potency. When the pleasure potency of the Supreme Personality of Godhead is exhibited by His grace in the person of a devotee, that manifestation is called love of God. "Love of God" is an epithet for the pleasure potency of the Lord. Therefore devotional service reciprocated between the Lord and His devotee is an exhibition of the transcendental pleasure potency of the Lord.

The potency of the Supreme Personality of Godhead that always enriches Him with transcendental bliss is not material, but the Śaṅkarites have accepted it as such because they are ignorant of the identity of the Supreme Lord and His pleasure potency. Those ignorant persons cannot understand the distinction between impersonal spiritual bliss and the variegatedness of the spiritual pleasure potency. The *hlādinī* potency gives the Lord all transcendental pleasure, and the Lord bestows such a potency upon His pure devotee.

TEXT 61

সচ্চিদানন্দ, পূর্ণ, কৃষ্ণের স্বরূপ ।
একই চিচ্ছক্তি তাঁর ধরে তিন রূপ ॥ ৬১ ॥

sac-cid-ānanda, pūrṇa, kṛṣṇera svarūpa
eka-i cic-chakti tāṅra dhare tina rūpa

sat-cit-ānanda—eternity, knowledge and bliss; *pūrṇa*—full; *kṛṣṇera*—of Lord Kṛṣṇa; *sva-rūpa*—own form; *eka-i*—one; *cit-śakti*—spiritual energy; *tāṅra*—of Him; *dhare*—manifests; *tina*—three; *rūpa*—forms.

TRANSLATION

Lord Kṛṣṇa's body is eternal [sat], full of knowledge [cit] and full of bliss [ānanda]. His one spiritual energy manifests three forms.

TEXT 62

আনন্দাংশে হ্লাদিনী, সদংশে সন্ধিনী ।
চিদংশে সম্বিৎ—যারে জ্ঞান করি' মানি ॥ ৬২ ॥

ānandāṁśe hlādinī, sad-aṁśe sandhinī
cid-aṁśe saṁvit—yāre jñāna kari' māni

ānanda-aṁśe—in the bliss portion; *hlādinī*—the pleasure energy; *sat-aṁśe*—in the eternal portion; *sandhinī*—the existence-expanding energy; *cit-aṁśe*—in the cognizant portion; *samvit*—the full energy of knowledge; *yāre*—which; *jñāna kari'*—as knowledge; *māni*—I accept.

TRANSLATION

Hlādinī is His aspect of bliss; sandhinī, of eternal existence; and samvit, of cognizance, which is also accepted as knowledge.

PURPORT

In his thesis *Bhagavat-sandarbha* (103), Śrīla Jīva Gosvāmī explains the potencies of the Lord as follows: The transcendental potency of the Supreme Personality of Godhead by which He maintains His existence is called *sandhinī.* The transcendental potency by which He knows Himself and causes others to know Him is called *samvit.* The transcendental potency by which He possesses transcendental bliss and causes His devotees to have bliss is called *hlādinī.*

The total exhibition of these potencies is called *viśuddha-sattva,* and this platform of spiritual variegatedness is displayed even in the material world when the Lord appears here. The pastimes and manifestations of the Lord in the material world are therefore not at all material; they belong to the pure transcendental state. The *Bhagavad-gītā* confirms that anyone who understands the transcendental nature of the Lord's appearance, activities and disappearance becomes eligible for freedom from material bondage upon quitting the present material tabernacle. He can enter the spiritual kingdom to associate with the Supreme Personality of Godhead and reciprocate the *hlādinī* potency in transactions between him and the Lord. In the mundane mode of goodness there are tinges of passion and ignorance. Therefore mundane goodness, being mixed, is called *miśra-sattva.* But the transcendental variegatedness of *viśuddha-sattva* is completely free from all mundane qualities. *Viśuddha-sattva* is therefore the proper atmosphere in which to experience the Personality of Godhead and His transcendental pastimes. Spiritual variegatedness is eternally independent of all material conditions and is nondifferent from the Supreme Personality of Godhead, both being absolute. The Lord and His devotees simultaneously perceive the *hlādinī* potency directly by the power of the *samvit* potency.

The material modes of nature control the conditioned souls, but the Supreme Personality of Godhead is never influenced by these modes, as all Vedic literatures directly and indirectly corroborate. Lord Kṛṣṇa

Himself says in the Eleventh Canto of *Śrīmad-Bhāgavatam* (11.25.12), *sattvaṁ rajas tama iti guṇā jīvasya naiva me:* "The material modes of goodness, passion and ignorance are connected with the conditioned souls, but never with Me, the Supreme Personality of Godhead." The *Viṣṇu Purāṇa* confirms this as follows:

sattvādayo na santīśe yatra na prākṛtā guṇāḥ
sa śuddhaḥ sarva-śuddhebhyaḥ pumān ādyaḥ prasīdatu

"The Supreme Personality of Godhead, Viṣṇu, is beyond the three qualities goodness, passion and ignorance. No material qualities exist in Him. May that original person, Nārāyaṇa, who is situated in a completely transcendental position, be pleased with us." In the Tenth Canto of *Śrīmad-Bhāgavatam* (10.27.4), Indra praises Kṛṣṇa as follows:

viśuddha-sattvaṁ tava dhāma śāntaṁ
tapo-mayaṁ dhvasta-rajas-tamaskam
māyā-mayo 'yaṁ guṇa-sampravāho
na vidyate te 'grahaṇānubandhaḥ

"My dear Lord, Your abode is *viśuddha-sattva*, always undisturbed by the material qualities, and the activities there are in transcendental loving service unto Your feet. The goodness, austerity and penance of the devotees enhance such activities, which are always free from the contamination of passion and ignorance. Material qualities cannot touch You under any circumstances."

When not manifested, the modes of material nature are said to be in goodness. When they are externally manifested and active in producing the varieties of material existence, they are said to be in passion. And when there is a lack of activity and variegatedness, they are said to be in ignorance. In other words, the pensive mood is goodness, activity is passion, and inactivity is ignorance. Above all these mundane qualitative manifestations is *viśuddha-sattva*. When it is predominated by the *sandhinī* potency, it is perceivable as the existence of all that be. When predominated by the *samvit* potency, it is perceived as knowledge in transcendence. And when predominated by the *hlādinī* potency, it is perceived as the most confidential love of Godhead. *Viśuddha-sattva*, the simultaneous manifestation of these three in one, is the main feature of the kingdom of God.

The Absolute Truth is therefore the substance of reality, eternally manifest in three energies. The manifestation of the internal energy of the Lord is the inconceivably variegated spiritual world, the manifestation of the marginal energy comprises the living entities, and the manifestation of the external energy is the material cosmos. Therefore the Absolute Truth includes these four principles—the Supreme Personality of Godhead Himself, His internal energy, His marginal energy and His external energy. The form of the Lord and the expansions of His form as *svayaṁ-rūpa* and *vaibhava-prakāśa* are directly the enjoyers of the internal energy, which is the eternal exhibitor of the spiritual world, the most confidential of the manifestations of energy. The external manifestation, the material energy, provides the covering bodies of the conditioned living entities, from Brahmā down to the insignificant ant. This covering energy is manifested under the three modes of material nature and appreciated in various ways by living entities in both the higher and lower forms of life.

Each of the three divisions of the internal potency—the *sandhinī, samvit* and *hlādinī* energies—influences one of the external potencies by which the conditioned souls are conducted. Such influence manifests the three qualitative modes of material nature, proving definitely that the living entities, the marginal potency, are eternally servitors of the Lord and are therefore controlled by either the internal or the external potency.

TEXT 63

হ্লাদিনী সন্ধিনী সম্বিত্ত্বয্যেকা সর্বসংস্থিতৌ ।
হ্লাদতাপকরী মিশ্রা ত্বয়ি নো গুণবর্জিতে ॥ ৬৩ ॥

hlādinī sandhinī samvit
tvayy ekā sarva-saṁsthitau
hlāda-tāpa-karī miśrā
tvayi no guṇa-varjite

hlādinī—pleasure potency; *sandhinī*—existence potency; *samvit*—knowledge potency; *tvayi*—in You; *ekā*—one; *sarva-saṁsthitau*—who are the basis of all things; *hlāda*—pleasure; *tāpa*—and misery; *karī*—causing; *miśrā*—a mixture of the two; *tvayi*—in You; *na u*—not; *guṇa-varjite*—who are without the three modes of material nature.

TRANSLATION

"O Lord, You are the support of everything. The three attributes hlādinī, sandhinī and samvit exist in You as one spiritual energy.

But the material modes, which cause happiness, misery and mixtures of the two, do not exist in You, for You have no material qualities."

PURPORT

This text is from the *Viṣṇu Purāṇa* (1.12.69).

TEXT 64

সন্ধিনীর সার অংশ—'শুদ্ধসত্ত্ব' নাম ।
ভগবানের সত্তা হয় যাহাতে বিশ্রাম ॥ ৬৪ ॥

sandhinīra sāra aṁśa—'śuddha-sattva' nāma
bhagavānera sattā haya yāhāte viśrāma

sandhinīra—of the existence potency; *sāra*—essence; *aṁśa*—portion; *śuddha-sattva*—*śuddha-sattva* (pure existence); *nāma*—named; *bhagavānera*—of the Supreme Personality of Godhead; *sattā*—the existence; *haya*—is; *yāhāte*—in which; *viśrāma*—the resting place.

TRANSLATION

The essential portion of the sandhinī potency is śuddha-sattva. Lord Kṛṣṇa's existence rests upon it.

TEXT 65

মাতা, পিতা, স্থান, গৃহ, শয্যাসন আর ।
এসব কৃষ্ণের শুদ্ধসত্ত্বের বিকার ॥ ৬৫ ॥

mātā, pitā, sthāna, gṛha, śayyāsana āra
e-saba kṛṣṇera śuddha-sattvera vikāra

mātā—mother; *pitā*—father; *sthāna*—place; *gṛha*—house; *śayya-āsana*—beds and seats; *āra*—and; *e-saba*—all these; *kṛṣṇera*—of Lord Kṛṣṇa; *śuddha-sattvera*—of the *śuddha-sattva; vikāra*—transformations.

TRANSLATION

Kṛṣṇa's mother, father, abode, house, bedding, seats and so on are all transformations of śuddha-sattva.

PURPORT

Lord Kṛṣṇa's father, mother and household affairs are all displayed in the same *viśuddha-sattva* existence. A living entity situated in the status of pure goodness can understand the form, qualities and other features of the Supreme Personality of Godhead. Kṛṣṇa consciousness begins on the platform of pure goodness. Although there is a faint realization of Kṛṣṇa at first, Kṛṣṇa is actually realized as Vāsudeva, the absolute proprietor of omnipotence or the prime predominating Deity of all potencies. When the living entity is situated in *viśuddha-sattva*, transcendental to the three material modes of nature, he can perceive the form, quality and other features of the Supreme Personality of Godhead through his service attitude. The status of pure goodness is the platform of understanding, for the Supreme Lord is always in spiritual existence.

Kṛṣṇa is always all-spiritual. Aside from the parents of the Personality of Godhead, all the other paraphernalia of His existence are also essentially a manifestation of *sandhinī-śakti*, or a transformation of *viśuddha-sattva*. To make this more clear, it may be said that this *sandhinī-śakti* of the internal potency maintains and manifests all the variegatedness of the spiritual world. In the kingdom of God, the Lord's servants and maidservants, His consorts, His father and mother and everything else are all transformations of the spiritual existence of *sandhinī-śakti*. The existential *sandhinī-śakti* in the external potency similarly expands all the variegatedness of the material cosmos, from which we can have a glimpse of the spiritual field.

TEXT 66

সত্ত্বং বিশুদ্ধং বসুদেবশব্দিতং
যদীয়তে তত্র পুমানপাবৃতঃ ।
সত্ত্বে চ তস্মিন্ ভগবান্ বাসুদেবো
হ্যধোক্ষজো মে মনসা বিধীয়তে ॥ ৬৬ ॥

sattvaṁ viśuddhaṁ vasudeva-śabditaṁ
yad īyate tatra pumān apāvṛtaḥ
sattve ca tasmin bhagavān vāsudevo
hy adhokṣajo me manasā vidhīyate

sattvam—existence; *viśuddham*—pure; *vasudeva-śabditam*—named *vasudeva; yat*—from which; *īyate*—appears; *tatra*—in that; *pumān*—

the Supreme Personality of Godhead; *apāvṛtaḥ*—without any covering; *sattve*—in goodness; *ca*—and; *tasmin*—that; *bhagavān*—the Supreme Personality of Godhead; *vāsudevaḥ*—Vāsudeva; *hi*—certainly; *adhokṣajaḥ*—who is beyond the senses; *me*—my; *manasā*—by the mind; *vidhīyate*—is procured.

TRANSLATION

"The condition of pure goodness [śuddha-sattva], in which the Supreme Personality of Godhead is revealed without any covering, is called vasudeva. In that pure state the Supreme Godhead, who is beyond the material senses and who is known as Vāsudeva, is perceived by my mind."

PURPORT

This text from *Śrīmad-Bhāgavatam* (4.3.23), spoken by Lord Śiva when he condemned Dakṣa, the father of Satī, as an opponent of Viṣṇu, confirms beyond a doubt that Lord Kṛṣṇa, His name, His fame, His qualities and everything in connection with His paraphernalia exist in the *sandhinī-śakti* of the Lord's internal potency.

TEXT 67

কৃষ্ণে ভগবত্তা-জ্ঞান—সংবিতের সার ।
ব্রহ্মজ্ঞানাদিক সব তার পরিবার ॥ ৬৭ ॥

kṛṣṇe bhagavattā-jñāna—saṁvitera sāra
brahma-jñānādika saba tāra parivāra

kṛṣṇe—in Kṛṣṇa; *bhagavattā*—of the quality of being the original Supreme Personality of Godhead; *jñāna*—knowledge; *saṁvitera*—of the knowledge potency; *sāra*—the essence; *brahma-jñāna*—knowledge of Brahman; *ādika*—and so on; *saba*—all; *tāra*—of that; *parivāra*—dependents.

TRANSLATION

The essence of the samvit potency is knowledge that the Supreme Personality of Godhead is Lord Kṛṣṇa. All other kinds of knowledge, such as the knowledge of Brahman, are its components.

PURPORT

The activities of the *samvit-śakti* produce the effect of cognition. Both the Lord and the living entities are cognizant. Śrī Kṛṣṇa, as the Supreme Personality of Godhead, has full knowledge of everything everywhere, and therefore there are no hindrances to His cognition. He can have knowledge merely by glancing over an object, whereas innumerable impediments block the cognition of ordinary living beings. The cognition of the living beings has three divisions: direct knowledge, indirect knowledge and perverted knowledge. Sense perception of material objects by the mundane senses, such as the eye, ear, nose and hand, always produces definitely perverted knowledge. This illusion is a presentation of the material energy, which is influenced by the *samvit-śakti* in a perverted manner. Negative cognition of an object beyond the reach of sense perception is the way of indirect knowledge, which is not altogether imperfect but which produces only fragmentary knowledge in the form of impersonal spiritual realization and monism. But when the *samvit* factor of cognition is enlightened by the *hlādinī* potency of the same internal energy, they work together, and only thus can one attain knowledge of the Personality of Godhead. The *samvit-śakti* should be maintained in that state. Material knowledge and indirect spiritual knowledge are by-products of the *samvit-śakti.*

TEXT 68

হ্লাদিনীর সার 'প্রেম', প্রেমসার 'ভাব'।
ভাবের পরমকাষ্ঠা, নাম—'মহাভাব' ॥ ৬৮ ॥

hlādinīra sāra 'prema', prema-sāra 'bhāva'
bhāvera parama-kāṣṭhā, nāma—'mahā-bhāva'

hlādinīra—of the pleasure potency; *sāra*—the essence; *prema*—love for God; *prema-sāra*—the essence of such love; *bhāva*—emotion; *bhāvera*—of emotion; *parama-kāṣṭhā*—the highest limit; *nāma*—named; *mahā-bhāva—mahābhāva.*

TRANSLATION

The essence of the hlādinī potency is love of God, the essence of love of God is emotion [bhāva], and the ultimate development of emotion is mahābhāva.

PURPORT

The product of the *hlādinī-śakti* is love of Godhead, which has two divisions—namely, pure love of Godhead and adulterated love of Godhead. Only when the *hlādinī-śakti* emanates from Śrī Kṛṣṇa and is bestowed upon the living being to attract Him does the living being become a pure lover of God. But when the same *hlādinī-śakti* is adulterated by the external, material energy and emanates from the living being, it does not attract Kṛṣṇa; on the contrary, the living being becomes attracted by the glamor of the material energy. At that time instead of becoming mad with love of Godhead, the living being becomes mad after material sense enjoyment, and because of his association with the qualitative modes of material nature, he is captivated by its interactions of distressful, unhappy feelings.

TEXT 69

মহাভাবস্বরূপা শ্রীরাধা-ঠাকুরাণী ।
সর্বগুণখনি কৃষ্ণকান্তাশিরোমণি ॥ ৬৯ ॥

mahābhāva-svarūpā śrī-rādhā-ṭhākurāṇī
sarva-guṇa-khani kṛṣṇa-kāntā-śiromaṇi

mahā-bhāva—of *mahābhāva; svarūpā*—the form; *śrī-rādhā-ṭhākurāṇī*—Śrīmatī Rādhārāṇī; *sarva-guṇa*—of all good qualities; *khani*—mine; *kṛṣṇa-kāntā*—of the lovers of Lord Kṛṣṇa; *śiromaṇi*—crown jewel.

TRANSLATION

Śrī Rādhā Ṭhākurāṇī is the embodiment of mahābhāva. She is the repository of all good qualities and the crest jewel among all the lovely consorts of Lord Kṛṣṇa.

PURPORT

The unadulterated action of the *hlādinī-śakti* is displayed in the dealings of the damsels of Vraja and Śrīmatī Rādhārāṇī, who is the topmost participant in that transcendental group. The essence of the *hlādinī-śakti* is love of Godhead, the essence of love of Godhead is *bhāva*, or transcendental sentiment, and the highest pitch of that *bhāva* is called *mahābhāva*. Śrīmatī Rādhārāṇī is the personified embodiment of these three aspects of transcendental consciousness. She is therefore the highest principle in love of Godhead and is the supreme lovable object of Śrī Kṛṣṇa.

TEXT 70

তয়োরপ্যুভয়োর্মধ্যে রাধিকা সর্বথাধিকা ।
মহাভাবস্বরূপেয়ং গুণৈরতিবরীয়সী ॥ ৭০ ॥

tayor apy ubhayor madhye
rādhikā sarvathādhikā
mahābhāva-svarūpeyaṁ
guṇair ativarīyasī

tayoḥ—of them; *api*—even; *ubhayoḥ*—of both (Candrāvalī and Rādhārāṇī); *madhye*—in the middle; *rādhikā*—Śrīmatī Rādhārāṇī; *sarvathā*—in every way; *adhikā*—greater; *mahā-bhāva-svarūpā*—the form of *mahābhāva; iyam*—this one; *guṇaiḥ*—with good qualities; *ati-varīyasī*—the best of all.

TRANSLATION

"Of these two gopīs [Rādhārāṇī and Candrāvalī], Śrīmatī Rādhārāṇī is superior in all respects. She is the embodiment of mahābhāva, and She surpasses all in good qualities."

PURPORT

This is a quotation from Śrīla Rūpa Gosvāmī's *Ujjvala-nīlamaṇi* (*Rādhā-prakaraṇa* 3).

TEXT 71

কৃষ্ণপ্রেম-ভাবিত যাঁর চিত্তেন্দ্রিয়-কায় ।
কৃষ্ণ-নিজশক্তি রাধা ক্রীড়ার সহায় ॥ ৭১ ॥

kṛṣṇa-prema-bhāvita yāṅra cittendriya-kāya
kṛṣṇa-nija-śakti rādhā krīḍāra sahāya

kṛṣṇa-prema—love for Lord Kṛṣṇa; *bhāvita*—steeped in; *yāṅra*—whose; *citta*—mind; *indriya*—senses; *kāya*—body; *kṛṣṇa*—of Lord Kṛṣṇa; *nija-śakti*—His own energy; *rādhā*—Śrīmatī Rādhārāṇī; *krīḍāra*—of pastimes; *sahāya*—companion.

TRANSLATION

Her mind, senses and body are steeped in love for Kṛṣṇa. She is Kṛṣṇa's own energy, and She helps Him in His pastimes.

PURPORT

Śrīmatī Rādhārāṇī is as fully spiritual as Kṛṣṇa. No one should consider Her to be material. She is definitely not like the conditioned souls, who have material bodies, gross and subtle, covered by material senses. She is all-spiritual, and both Her body and Her mind are of the same spiritual embodiment. Because Her body is spiritual, Her senses are also spiritual. Thus Her body, mind and senses fully shine in love of Kṛṣṇa. She is the personified *hlādinī-śakti* (the pleasure-giving energy of the Lord's internal potency), and therefore She is the only source of enjoyment for Śrī Kṛṣṇa.

Śrī Kṛṣṇa cannot enjoy anything that is internally different from Him. Therefore Rādhā and Śrī Kṛṣṇa are identical. The *sandhinī* portion of Śrī Kṛṣṇa's internal potency has manifested the all-attractive form of Śrī Kṛṣṇa, and the same internal potency, in the *hlādinī* feature, has presented Śrīmatī Rādhārāṇī, who is the attraction for the all-attractive. No one can match Śrīmatī Rādhārāṇī in the transcendental pastimes of Śrī Kṛṣṇa.

TEXT 72

আনন্দচিন্ময়রসপ্রতিভাবিতাভি-
স্তাভির্য এব নিজরূপতয়া কলাভিঃ ।
গোলোক এব নিবসত্যখিলাত্মভূতো
গোবিন্দমাদিপুরুষং তমহং ভজামি ॥ ৭২ ॥

ānanda-cinmaya-rasa-pratibhāvitābhis
tābhir ya eva nija-rūpatayā kalābhiḥ
goloka eva nivasaty akhilātma-bhūto
govindam ādi-puruṣaṁ tam ahaṁ bhajāmi

ānanda—bliss; *cit*—and knowledge; *maya*—consisting of; *rasa*—mellows; *prati*—at every second; *bhāvitābhiḥ*—who are engrossed with; *tābhiḥ*—with those; *yaḥ*—who; *eva*—certainly; *nija-rūpatayā*—with His own form; *kalābhiḥ*—who are parts of portions of His pleasure potency; *goloke*—in Goloka Vṛndāvana; *eva*—certainly; *nivasati*—resides; *akhila-ātma*—as the soul of all; *bhūtaḥ*—who exists;

govindam—Lord Govinda; *ādi-puruṣam*—the original personality; *tam*—Him; *aham*—I; *bhajāmi*—worship.

TRANSLATION

"I worship Govinda, the primeval Lord, who resides in His own realm, Goloka, with Rādhā, who resembles His own spiritual figure and who embodies the ecstatic potency [hlādinī]. Their companions are Her confidantes, who embody extensions of Her bodily form and who are imbued and permeated with ever-blissful spiritual rasa."

PURPORT

This text is from the *Brahma-saṁhitā* (5.37).

TEXT 73

কৃষ্ণেরে করায় যৈছে রস আস্বাদন ।
ক্রীড়ার সহায় যৈছে, শুন বিবরণ ॥ ৭৩ ॥

kṛṣṇere karāya yaiche rasa āsvādana
krīḍāra sahāya yaiche, śuna vivaraṇa

kṛṣṇere—unto Lord Kṛṣṇa; *karāya*—causes to do; *yaiche*—how; *rasa*—the mellows; *āsvādana*—tasting; *krīḍāra*—of pastimes; *sahāya*—helper; *yaiche*—how; *śuna*—please hear; *vivaraṇa*—the description.

TRANSLATION

Now please listen to how Lord Kṛṣṇa's consorts help Him taste rasa and how they help in His pastimes.

TEXTS 74–75

কৃষ্ণকান্তাগণ দেখি ত্রিবিধ প্রকার ।
এক লক্ষ্মীগণ, পুরে মহিষীগণ আর ॥ ৭৪ ॥
ব্রজাঙ্গনা-রূপ, আর কান্তাগণ-সার ।
শ্রীরাধিকা হৈতে কান্তাগণের বিস্তার ॥ ৭৫ ॥

kṛṣṇa-kāntā-gaṇa dekhi tri-vidha prakāra
eka lakṣmī-gaṇa, pure mahiṣī-gaṇa āra

vrajāṅganā-rūpa, āra kāntā-gaṇa-sāra
śrī-rādhikā haite kāntā-gaṇera vistāra

kṛṣṇa-kāntā-gaṇa—the lovers of Lord Kṛṣṇa; *dekhi*—I see; *tri-vidha*—three; *prakāra*—kinds; *eka*—one; *lakṣmī-gaṇa*—the goddesses of fortune; *pure*—in the city; *mahiṣī-gaṇa*—the queens; *āra*—and; *vraja-aṅganā*—of the beautiful women of Vraja; *rūpa*—having the form; *āra*—another type; *kāntā-gaṇa*—of the lovers; *sāra*—the essence; *śrī-rādhikā haite*—from Śrīmatī Rādhārāṇī; *kāntā-gaṇera*—of the lovers of Kṛṣṇa; *vistāra*—the expansion.

TRANSLATION

The beloved consorts of Lord Kṛṣṇa are of three kinds: the goddesses of fortune, the queens, and the milkmaids of Vraja, who are the foremost of all. These consorts all proceed from Rādhikā.

TEXT 76

অবতারী কৃষ্ণ যৈছে করে অবতার ।
অংশিনী রাধা হৈতে তিন গণের বিস্তার ॥ ৭৬ ॥

avatārī kṛṣṇa yaiche kare avatāra
aṁśinī rādhā haite tina gaṇera vistāra

avatārī—the source of all incarnations; *kṛṣṇa*—Lord Kṛṣṇa; *yaiche*—just as; *kare*—makes; *avatāra*—incarnation; *aṁśinī*—the source of all portions; *rādhā*—Śrīmatī Rādhārāṇī; *haite*—from; *tina*—three; *gaṇera*—of the groups; *vistāra*—expansion.

TRANSLATION

Just as the fountainhead, Lord Kṛṣṇa, is the cause of all incarnations, so Śrī Rādhā is the cause of all these consorts.

TEXT 77

বৈভবগণ যেন তাঁর অঙ্গ-বিভূতি ।
বিম্ব-প্রতিবিম্ব-রূপ মহিষীর ততি ॥ ৭৭ ॥

vaibhava-gaṇa yena tāṅra aṅga-vibhūti
bimba-pratibimba-rūpa mahiṣīra tati

vaibhava-gaṇa—the expansions; *yena*—as it were; *tāṅra*—of Her; *aṅga*—of the body; *vibhūti*—powerful expansions; *bimba*—reflections; *pratibimba*—counterreflections; *rūpa*—having the form; *mahiṣīra*—of the queens; *tati*—the expansion.

TRANSLATION

The goddesses of fortune are partial manifestations of Śrīmatī Rādhikā, and the queens are reflections of Her image.

TEXT 78

লক্ষ্মীগণ তাঁর বৈভব-বিলাসাংশরূপ ।
মহিষীগণ বৈভব-প্রকাশস্বরূপ ॥ ৭৮ ॥

lakṣmī-gaṇa tāṅra vaibhava-vilāsāṁśa-rūpa
mahiṣī-gaṇa vaibhava-prakāśa-svarūpa

lakṣmī-gaṇa—the goddesses of fortune; *tāṅra*—Her; *vaibhava-vilāsa*—as *vaibhava-vilāsa; aṁśa*—of plenary portions; *rūpa*—having the form; *mahiṣī-gaṇa*—the queens; *vaibhava-prakāśa*—of *vaibhava-prakāśa; svarūpa*—having the nature.

TRANSLATION

The goddesses of fortune are Her plenary portions, and they display the forms of vaibhava-vilāsa. The queens are of the nature of Her vaibhava-prakāśa.

TEXT 79

আকার স্বভাব-ভেদে ব্রজদেবীগণ ।
কায়ব্যূহরূপ তাঁর রসের কারণ ॥ ৭৯ ॥

ākāra svabhāva-bhede vraja-devī-gaṇa
kāya-vyūha-rūpa tāṅra rasera kāraṇa

ākāra—of features; *svabhāva*—of natures; *bhede*—with differences; *vraja-devī-gaṇa*—the *gopīs; kāya*—of Her body; *vyūha*—of expansions; *rūpa*—having the form; *tāṅra*—of Her; *rasera*—of mellows; *kāraṇa*—instruments.

TRANSLATION

The Vraja-devīs have diverse bodily features. They are Her expansions and are the instruments for expanding rasa.

TEXT 80

বহু কান্তা বিনা নহে রসের উল্লাস ।
লীলার সহায় লাগি' বহুত প্রকাশ ॥ ৮০ ॥

bahu kāntā vinā nahe rasera ullāsa
līlāra sahāya lāgi' bahuta prakāśa

bahu—many; *kāntā*—lovers; *vinā*—without; *nahe*—there is not; *rasera*—of mellow; *ullāsa*—exultation; *līlāra*—of pastimes; *sahāya*—helper; *lāgi'*—for the purpose of being; *bahuta*—many; *prakāśa*—manifestations.

TRANSLATION

Without many consorts, there is not such exultation in rasa. Therefore there are many manifestations of Śrīmatī Rādhārāṇī to assist in the Lord's pastimes.

TEXT 81

তার মধ্যে ব্রজে নানা ভাব-রস-ভেদে ।
কৃষ্ণকে করায় রাসাদিক-লীলাস্বাদে ॥ ৮১ ॥

tāra madhye vraje nānā bhāva-rasa-bhede
kṛṣṇake karāya rāsādika-līlāsvāde

tāra madhye—among them; *vraje*—in Vraja; *nānā*—various; *bhāva*—of moods; *rasa*—and of mellows; *bhede*—by differences; *kṛṣṇake*—Lord Kṛṣṇa; *karāya*—cause to do; *rāsa-ādika*—beginning with the *rāsa* dance; *līlā*—of the pastimes; *āsvāde*—tasting.

TRANSLATION

Among them are various groups of consorts in Vraja who have varieties of sentiments and mellows. They help Lord Kṛṣṇa taste all the sweetness of the rāsa dance and other pastimes.

PURPORT

As already explained, Kṛṣṇa and Rādhā are one in two. They are identical. Kṛṣṇa expands Himself in multi-incarnations and plenary portions like the *puruṣas.* Similarly, Śrīmatī Rādhārāṇī expands Herself in multiforms as the goddesses of fortune, the queens and the damsels of Vraja. Such expansions from Śrīmatī Rādhārāṇī are all Her plenary portions. All these womanly forms of Kṛṣṇa are expansions corresponding to His plenary expansions of Viṣṇu forms. These expansions have been compared to reflected forms of the original form. There is no difference between the original form and the reflected forms. The female reflections of Kṛṣṇa's pleasure potency are as good as Kṛṣṇa Himself.

The plenary expansions of Kṛṣṇa's personality are called *vaibhava-vilāsa* and *vaibhava-prakāśa,* and Rādhā's expansions are similarly described. The goddesses of fortune are Her *vaibhava-vilāsa* forms, and the queens are Her *vaibhava-prakāśa* forms. The personal associates of Rādhārāṇī, the damsels of Vraja, are direct expansions of Her body. As expansions of Her personal form and transcendental disposition, they are agents of different reciprocations of love in the pastimes of Lord Kṛṣṇa, under the supreme direction of Śrīmatī Rādhārāṇī. In the transcendental realm, enjoyment is fully relished in variety. The exuberance of transcendental mellows is increased by the association of a large number of personalities similar to Rādhārāṇī, who are also known as *gopīs* or *sakhīs.* The variety of innumerable mistresses is a source of relish for Śrī Kṛṣṇa, and therefore these expansions from Śrīmatī Rādhārāṇī are necessary for enhancing the pleasure potency of Śrī Kṛṣṇa. Their transcendental exchanges of love are the superexcellent affairs of the pastimes in Vṛndāvana. By these expansions of Śrīmatī Rādhārāṇī's personal body, She helps Lord Kṛṣṇa taste the *rāsa* dance and other, similar activities. Śrīmatī Rādhārāṇī, being the central petal of the *rāsa-līlā* flower, is also known by the names found in the following verses.

TEXT 82

গোবিন্দানন্দিনী, রাধা, গোবিন্দমোহিনী ।
গোবিন্দসর্বস্ব, সর্বকান্তা-শিরোমণি ॥ ৮২ ॥

govindānandinī rādhā, govinda-mohinī
govinda-sarvasva, sarva-kāntā-śiromaṇi

govinda-ānandinī—She who gives pleasure to Govinda; *rādhā*—Śrīmatī Rādhārāṇī; *govinda-mohinī*—She who mystifies Govinda; *govinda-*

sarvasva—the be-all and end-all of Lord Govinda; *sarva-kāntā*—of all the Lord's lovers; *śiromaṇi*—the crown jewel.

TRANSLATION

Rādhā is the one who gives pleasure to Govinda, and She is also the enchantress of Govinda. She is the be-all and end-all of Govinda, and the crest jewel of all His consorts.

TEXT 83

দেবী কৃষ্ণময়ী প্রোক্তা রাধিকা পরদেবতা ।
সর্বলক্ষ্মীময়ী সর্বকান্তিঃ সম্মোহিনী পরা ॥ ৮৩ ॥

devī kṛṣṇa-mayī proktā
rādhikā para-devatā
sarva-lakṣmī-mayī sarva-
kāntiḥ sammohinī parā

devī—who shines brilliantly; *kṛṣṇa-mayī*—nondifferent from Lord Kṛṣṇa; *proktā*—called; *rādhikā*—Śrīmatī Rādhārāṇī; *para-devatā*—most worshipable; *sarva-lakṣmī-mayī*—presiding over all the goddesses of fortune; *sarva-kāntiḥ*—in whom all splendor exists; *sammohinī*—whose character completely bewilders Lord Kṛṣṇa; *parā*—the superior energy.

TRANSLATION

"The transcendental goddess Śrīmatī Rādhārāṇī is the direct counterpart of Lord Śrī Kṛṣṇa. She is the central figure for all the goddesses of fortune. She possesses all the attractiveness to attract the all-attractive Personality of Godhead. She is the primeval internal potency of the Lord."

PURPORT

This text is from the *Bṛhad-gautamīya-tantra*.

TEXT 84

'দেবী' কহি দ্যোতমানা, পরমা সুন্দরী ।
কিম্বা, কৃষ্ণপূজা-ক্রীড়ার বসতি নগরী ॥ ৮৪ ॥

'devī' kahi dyotamānā, paramā sundarī
kimvā, kṛṣṇa-pūjā-krīḍāra vasati nagarī

devī—the word *devī; kahi*—I say; *dyotamānā*—shining; *paramā*—most; *sundarī*—beautiful; *kimvā*—or; *kṛṣṇa-pūjā*—of the worship of Lord Kṛṣṇa; *krīḍāra*—and of sports; *vasati*—the abode; *nagarī*—the town.

TRANSLATION

"Devī" means "resplendent and most beautiful." Or else it means "the lovely abode of the worship and love sports of Lord Kṛṣṇa."

TEXT 85

কৃষ্ণময়ী—কৃষ্ণ যার ভিতরে বাহিরে ।
যাঁহা যাঁহা নেত্র পড়ে তাঁহা কৃষ্ণ স্ফুরে ॥ ৮৫ ॥

kṛṣṇa-mayī—kṛṣṇa yāra bhitare bāhire
yāṅhā yāṅhā netra paḍe tāṅhā kṛṣṇa sphure

kṛṣṇa-mayī—the word *kṛṣṇa-mayī; kṛṣṇa*—Lord Kṛṣṇa; *yāra*—of whom; *bhitare*—the within; *bāhire*—the without; *yāṅhā yāṅhā*—wherever; *netra*—the eyes; *paḍe*—fall; *tāṅhā*—there; *kṛṣṇa*—Lord Kṛṣṇa; *sphure*—manifests.

TRANSLATION

"Kṛṣṇa-mayī" means "one whose within and without are Lord Kṛṣṇa." She sees Lord Kṛṣṇa wherever She casts Her glance.

TEXT 86

কিম্বা, প্রেমরসময় কৃষ্ণের স্বরূপ ।
তাঁর শক্তি তাঁর সহ হয় একরূপ ॥ ৮৬ ॥

kimvā, prema-rasa-maya kṛṣṇera svarūpa
tāṅra śakti tāṅra saha haya eka-rūpa

kimvā—or; *prema-rasa*—the mellows of love; *maya*—made of; *kṛṣṇera*—of Lord Kṛṣṇa; *svarūpa*—the real nature; *tāṅra*—of Him; *śakti*—the energy; *tāṅra saha*—with Him; *haya*—there is; *eka-rūpa*—oneness.

TRANSLATION

Or "kṛṣṇa-mayī" means that She is identical with Lord Kṛṣṇa, for She embodies the mellows of love. The energy of Lord Kṛṣṇa is identical with Him.

PURPORT

Kṛṣṇa-mayī has two different imports. First, a person who always thinks of Kṛṣṇa both within and without and who always remembers only Kṛṣṇa, wherever he goes or whatever he sees, is called *kṛṣṇa-mayī.* Also, since Kṛṣṇa's personality is full of love, His loving potency, Rādhārāṇī, being nondifferent from Him, is called *kṛṣṇa-mayī.*

TEXT 87

কৃষ্ণবাঞ্ছা-পূর্তিরূপ করে আরাধনে ।
অতএব 'রাধিকা' নাম পুরাণে বাখানে ॥ ৮৭ ॥

kṛṣṇa-vāñchā-pūrti-rūpa kare ārādhane
ataeva 'rādhikā' nāma purāṇe vākhāne

kṛṣṇa-vāñchā—of the desire of Lord Kṛṣṇa; *pūrti-rūpa*—of the nature of fulfillment; *kare*—does; *ārādhane*—worship; *ataeva*—therefore; *rādhikā*—Śrīmatī Rādhikā; *nāma*—named; *purāṇe*—in the *Purāṇas;* *vākhāne*—in the description.

TRANSLATION

Her worship [ārādhana] consists of fulfilling the desires of Lord Kṛṣṇa. Therefore the Purāṇas call Her Rādhikā.

PURPORT

The name "Rādhā" is derived from the root word *ārādhana,* which means "worship." The personality who excels all in worshiping Kṛṣṇa may therefore be called Rādhikā, the greatest servitor.

TEXT 88

অনয়ারাধিতো নূনং ভগবান্ হরিরীশ্বরঃ ।
যন্নো বিহায় গোবিন্দঃ প্রীতো যামনয়দ্রহঃ ॥ ৮৮ ॥

anayārādhito nūnaṁ
bhagavān harir īśvaraḥ
yan no vihāya govindaḥ
prīto yām anayad rahaḥ

anayā—by this one; *ārādhitaḥ*—worshiped; *nūnam*—certainly; *bhagavān*—the Supreme Personality of Godhead; *hariḥ*—Lord Kṛṣṇa;

īśvaraḥ—the Supreme Lord; *yat*—from which; *naḥ*—us; *vihāya*—leaving aside; *govindaḥ*—Govinda; *prītaḥ*—pleased; *yām*—whom; *anayat*—lead; *rahaḥ*—to a lonely place.

TRANSLATION

"Truly the Personality of Godhead has been worshiped by Her. Therefore Lord Govinda, being pleased, has brought Her to a lonely spot, leaving us all behind."

PURPORT

This text is from *Śrīmad-Bhāgavatam* (10.30.28).

TEXT 89

অতএব সর্বপূজ্যা, পরম-দেবতা ।
সর্বপালিকা, সর্ব-জগতের মাতা ॥ ৮৯ ॥

ataeva sarva-pūjyā, parama-devatā
sarva-pālikā, sarva jagatera mātā

ataeva—therefore; *sarva-pūjyā*—worshipable by all; *parama*—supreme; *devatā*—goddess; *sarva-pālikā*—the protectress of all; *sarva jagatera*—of all the universes; *mātā*—the mother.

TRANSLATION

Therefore Rādhā is parama-devatā, the supreme goddess, and She is worshipable for everyone. She is the protectress of all, and She is the mother of the entire universe.

TEXT 90

'সর্বলক্ষ্মী'-শব্দ পূর্বে করিয়াছি ব্যাখ্যান ।
সর্বলক্ষ্মীগণের তিহোঁ হন অধিষ্ঠান ॥ ৯০ ॥

'sarva-lakṣmī'-śabda pūrve kariyāchi vyākhyāna
sarva-lakṣmī-gaṇera tinho hana adhiṣṭhāna

sarva-lakṣmī-śabda—the word *sarva-lakṣmī; pūrve*—previously; *kariyāchi*—I have done; *vyākhyāna*—explanation; *sarva-lakṣmī-*

gaṇera—of all the goddesses of fortune; *tiṅho*—She; *hana*—is; *adhiṣṭhāna*—abode.

TRANSLATION

I have already explained the meaning of "sarva-lakṣmī." Rādhā is the original source of all the goddesses of fortune.

TEXT 91

কিম্বা, 'সর্বলক্ষ্মী'—কৃষ্ণের ষড়্‌বিধ ঐশ্বর্য ।
তাঁর অধিষ্ঠাত্রী শক্তি—সর্বশক্তিবর্য ॥ ৯১ ॥

kimvā, 'sarva-lakṣmī'—kṛṣṇera ṣaḍ-vidha aiśvarya
tāṅra adhiṣṭhātrī śakti—sarva-śakti-varya

kimvā—or; *sarva-lakṣmī*—the word *sarva-lakṣmī; kṛṣṇera*—of Lord Kṛṣṇa; *ṣaṭ-vidha*—six kinds; *aiśvarya*—opulences; *tāṅra*—of Him; *adhiṣṭhātrī*—chief; *śakti*—energy; *sarva-śakti*—of all energies; *varya*—the best.

TRANSLATION

Or "sarva-lakṣmī" indicates that She fully represents the six opulences of Kṛṣṇa. Therefore She is the supreme energy of Lord Kṛṣṇa.

TEXT 92

সর্ব-সৌন্দর্য-কান্তি বৈসয়ে যাঁহাতে ।
সর্বলক্ষ্মীগণের শোভা হয় যাঁহা হৈতে ॥ ৯২ ॥

sarva-saundarya-kānti vaisaye yāṅhāte
sarva-lakṣmī-gaṇera śobhā haya yāṅhā haite

sarva-saundarya—of all beauty; *kānti*—the splendor; *vaisaye*—sits; *yāṅhāte*—in whom; *sarva-lakṣmī-gaṇera*—of all the goddesses of fortune; *śobhā*—the splendor; *haya*—is; *yāṅhā haite*—from whom.

TRANSLATION

The word "sarva-kānti" indicates that all beauty and luster rest in Her body. All the lakṣmīs derive their beauty from Her.

TEXT 93

কিংবা 'কান্তি'-শব্দে কৃষ্ণের সব ইচ্ছা কহে ।
কৃষ্ণের সকল বাঞ্ছা রাধাতেই রহে ॥ ৯৩ ॥

kimvā 'kānti'-śabde kṛṣṇera saba icchā kahe
kṛṣṇera sakala vāñchā rādhātei rahe

kimvā—or; *kānti-śabde*—by the word *kānti; kṛṣṇera*—of Lord Kṛṣṇa; *saba*—all; *icchā*—desires; *kahe*—says; *kṛṣṇera*—of Lord Kṛṣṇa; *sakala*—all; *vāñchā*—desires; *rādhātei*—in Śrīmatī Rādhārāṇī; *rahe*—remain.

TRANSLATION

"Kānti" may also mean "all the desires of Lord Kṛṣṇa." All the desires of Lord Kṛṣṇa rest in Śrīmatī Rādhārāṇī.

TEXT 94

রাধিকা করেন কৃষ্ণের বাঞ্ছিত পূরণ ।
'সর্বকান্তি'-শব্দের এই অর্থ বিবরণ ॥ ৯৪ ॥

rādhikā karena kṛṣṇera vāñchita pūraṇa
'sarva-kānti'-śabdera ei artha vivaraṇa

rādhikā—Śrīmatī Rādhārāṇī; *karena*—does; *kṛṣṇera*—of Lord Kṛṣṇa; *vāñchita*—desired object; *pūraṇa*—fulfilling; *sarva-kānti-śabdera*—of the word *sarva-kānti; ei*—this; *artha*—meaning; *vivaraṇa*—the description.

TRANSLATION

Śrīmatī Rādhikā fulfills all the desires of Lord Kṛṣṇa. This is the meaning of "sarva-kānti."

TEXT 95

জগৎমোহন কৃষ্ণ, তাঁহার মোহিনী ।
অতএব সমস্তের পরা ঠাকুরাণী ॥ ৯৫ ॥

jagat-mohana kṛṣṇa, tāṅhāra mohinī
ataeva samastera parā ṭhākurāṇī

jagat-mohana—enchanting the universe; *kṛṣṇa*—Lord Kṛṣṇa; *tāṅhāra*—of Him; *mohinī*—the enchantress; *ataeva*—therefore; *samastera*—of all; *parā*—foremost; *ṭhākurāṇī*—goddess.

TRANSLATION

Lord Kṛṣṇa enchants the world, but Śrī Rādhā enchants even Him. Therefore She is the supreme goddess of all.

TEXT 96

রাধা—পূর্ণশক্তি, কৃষ্ণ—পূর্ণশক্তিমান্ ।
দুই বস্তু ভেদ নাই, শাস্ত্র-পরমাণ ॥ ৯৬ ॥

rādhā—pūrṇa-śakti, kṛṣṇa—pūrṇa-śaktimān
dui vastu bheda nāi, śāstra-paramāṇa

rādhā—Śrīmatī Rādhārāṇī; *pūrṇa-śakti*—the complete energy; *kṛṣṇa*—Lord Kṛṣṇa; *pūrṇa-śaktimān*—the complete possessor of energy; *dui*—two; *vastu*—things; *bheda*—difference; *nāi*—there is not; *śāstra-paramāṇa*—the evidence of revealed scripture.

TRANSLATION

Śrī Rādhā is the full power, and Lord Kṛṣṇa is the possessor of full power. The two are not different, as evidenced by the revealed scriptures.

TEXT 97

মৃগমদ, তার গন্ধ—যৈছে অবিচ্ছেদ ।
অগ্নি, জ্বালাতে—যৈছে কভু নাহি ভেদ ॥ ৯৭ ॥

mṛgamada, tāra gandha—yaiche aviccheda
agni, jvālāte—yaiche kabhu nāhi bheda

mṛga-mada—musk; *tāra*—of that; *gandha*—fragrance; *yaiche*—just as; *aviccheda*—inseparable; *agni*—the fire; *jvālāte*—temperature; *yaiche*—just as; *kabhu*—any; *nāhi*—there is not; *bheda*—difference.

TRANSLATION

They are indeed the same, just as musk and its scent are inseparable, or as fire and its heat are nondifferent.

TEXT 98

রাধাকৃষ্ণ ঐছে সদা একই স্বরূপ ।
লীলারস আস্বাদিতে ধরে দুইরূপ ॥ ৯৮ ॥

rādhā-kṛṣṇa aiche sadā eka-i svarūpa
līlā-rasa āsvādite dhare dui-rūpa

rādhā-kṛṣṇa—Rādhā and Kṛṣṇa; *aiche*—in this way; *sadā*—always; *eka-i*—one; *svarūpa*—nature; *līlā-rasa*—the mellows of a pastime; *āsvādite*—to taste; *dhare*—manifest; *dui-rūpa*—two forms.

TRANSLATION

Thus Rādhā and Lord Kṛṣṇa are one, yet They have taken two forms to enjoy the mellows of pastimes.

TEXTS 99–100

প্রেমভক্তি শিখাইতে আপনে অবতরি ।
রাধা-ভাব-কান্তি দুই অঙ্গীকার করি' ॥ ৯৯ ॥
শ্রীকৃষ্ণচৈতন্যরূপে কৈল অবতার ।
এই ত' পঞ্চম শ্লোকের অর্থ পরচার ॥ ১০০ ॥

prema-bhakti śikhāite āpane avatari
rādhā-bhāva-kānti dui aṅgīkāra kari'

śrī-kṛṣṇa-caitanya-rūpe kaila avatāra
ei ta' pañcama ślokera artha paracāra

prema-bhakti—devotional service in love of Godhead; *śikhāite*—to teach; *āpane*—Himself; *avatari*—descending; *rādhā-bhāva*—the mood of Śrīmatī Rādhārāṇī; *kānti*—and luster; *dui*—two; *aṅgīkāra kari'*—accepting; *śrī-kṛṣṇa-caitanya*—of Lord Caitanya Mahāprabhu; *rūpe*—in the form; *kaila*—made; *avatāra*—incarnation; *ei*—this; *ta'*—certainly; *pañcama*—fifth; *ślokera*—of the verse; *artha*—meaning; *paracāra*—proclamation.

TRANSLATION

To promulgate prema-bhakti [devotional service in love of Godhead], Kṛṣṇa appeared as Śrī Kṛṣṇa Caitanya with the mood and

complexion of Śrī Rādhā. Thus I have explained the meaning of the fifth verse.

TEXT 101

ষষ্ঠ শ্লোকের অর্থ করিতে প্রকাশ ।
প্রথমে কহিয়ে সেই শ্লোকের আভাস ॥ ১০১ ॥

ṣaṣṭha ślokera artha karite prakāśa
prathame kahiye sei ślokera ābhāsa

ṣaṣṭha—sixth; *ślokera*—of the verse; *artha*—meaning; *karite*—to do; *prakāśa*—manifestation; *prathame*—first; *kahiye*—I shall speak; *sei*—that; *ślokera*—of the verse; *ābhāsa*—hint.

TRANSLATION

To explain the sixth verse, I shall first give a hint of its meaning.

TEXT 102

অবতরি' প্রভু প্রচারিল সংকীর্তন ।
এহো বাহ্য হেতু, পূর্বে করিয়াছি সূচন ॥ ১০২ ॥

avatari' prabhu pracārila saṅkīrtana
eho bāhya hetu, pūrve kariyāchi sūcana

avatari'—incarnating; *prabhu*—the Lord; *pracārila*—propagated; *saṅkīrtana*—the congregational chanting of the holy name; *eho*—this; *bāhya*—external; *hetu*—reason; *pūrve*—previously; *kariyāchi*—I have given; *sūcana*—indication.

TRANSLATION

The Lord came to propagate saṅkīrtana. That is an external purpose, as I have already indicated.

TEXT 103

অবতারের আর এক আছে মুখ্যবীজ ।
রসিকশেখর কৃষ্ণের সেই কার্য নিজ ॥ ১০৩ ॥

avatārera āra eka āche mukhya-bīja
rasika-śekhara kṛṣṇera sei kārya nija

avatārera—of the incarnation; *āra*—another; *eka*—one; *āche*—there is; *mukhya-bīja*—principal seed; *rasika-śekhara*—the foremost enjoyer of the mellows of love; *kṛṣṇera*—of Lord Kṛṣṇa; *sei*—that; *kārya*—business; *nija*—own.

TRANSLATION

There is a principal cause for Lord Kṛṣṇa's appearance. It grows from His own engagements as the foremost enjoyer of loving exchanges.

TEXT 104

অতি গূঢ় হেতু সেই ত্রিবিধ প্রকার ।
দামোদরস্বরূপ হৈতে যাহার প্রচার ॥ ১০৪ ॥

ati gūḍha hetu sei tri-vidha prakāra
dāmodara-svarūpa haite yāhāra pracāra

ati—very; *gūḍha*—esoteric; *hetu*—reason; *sei*—that; *tri-vidha*—three; *prakāra*—kinds; *dāmodara-svarūpa haite*—from Svarūpa Dāmodara; *yāhāra*—of which; *pracāra*—the proclamation.

TRANSLATION

That most confidential cause is threefold. Svarūpa Dāmodara has revealed it.

TEXT 105

স্বরূপ-গোসাঞি—প্রভুর অতি অন্তরঙ্গ ।
তাহাতে জানেন প্রভুর এসব প্রসঙ্গ ॥ ১০৫ ॥

svarūpa-gosāñi—prabhura ati antaraṅga
tāhāte jānena prabhura e-saba prasaṅga

svarūpa-gosāñi—Svarūpa Dāmodara Gosāñi; *prabhura*—of Lord Caitanya Mahāprabhu; *ati*—very; *antaraṅga*—confidential associate; *tāhāte*—by that; *jānena*—he knows; *prabhura*—of Lord Caitanya Mahāprabhu; *e-saba*—all these; *prasaṅga*—topics.

TRANSLATION

Svarūpa Gosāñi is the most intimate associate of the Lord. He therefore knows all these topics well.

PURPORT

Prior to the Lord's acceptance of the renounced order, Puruṣottama Bhaṭṭācārya, a resident of Navadvīpa, desired to enter the renounced order of life. Therefore he left home and went to Benares, where he accepted the position of *brahmacarya* from a Māyāvādī *sannyāsī.* When he became a *brahmacārī,* he was given the name Śrī Dāmodara Svarūpa. He left Benares shortly thereafter, without taking *sannyāsa,* and he came to Nilācala, Jagannātha Purī, where Lord Caitanya was staying. He met Caitanya Mahāprabhu there and dedicated his life for the service of the Lord. He became Lord Caitanya's secretary and constant companion. He used to enhance the pleasure potency of the Lord by singing appropriate songs, which were very much appreciated. Svarūpa Dāmodara could understand the secret mission of Lord Caitanya, and it was by his grace only that all the devotees of Lord Caitanya could know the real purpose of the Lord.

Svarūpa Dāmodara has been identified as Lalitā-devī, the second expansion of Rādhārāṇī. However, text 160 of Kavi-karṇapūra's authoritative *Gaura-gaṇoddeśa-dīpikā* describes Svarūpa Dāmodara as the same Viśākhā-devī who serves the Lord in Goloka Vṛndāvana. Therefore it is to be understood that Śrī Svarūpa Dāmodara is a direct expansion of Rādhārāṇī who helps the Lord experience the attitude of Rādhārāṇī.

TEXT 106

রাধিকার ভাব-মূর্তি প্রভুর অন্তর ।
সেই ভাবে সুখ-দুঃখ উঠে নিরন্তর ॥ ১০৬ ॥

rādhikāra bhāva-mūrti prabhura antara
sei bhāve sukha-duḥkha uṭhe nirantara

rādhikāra—of Śrīmatī Rādhārāṇī; *bhāva-mūrti*—the form of the emotions; *prabhura*—of Lord Caitanya Mahāprabhu; *antara*—the heart; *sei*—that; *bhāve*—in the condition; *sukha-duḥkha*—happiness and distress; *uṭhe*—arise; *nirantara*—constantly.

TRANSLATION

The heart of Lord Caitanya is the image of Śrī Rādhikā's emotions. Thus feelings of pleasure and pain arise constantly therein.

PURPORT

Lord Caitanya's heart was full of the feelings of Śrīmatī Rādhārāṇī, and His appearance resembled Hers. Svarūpa Dāmodara has explained His attitude as *rādhā-bhāva-mūrti,* the attitude of Rādhārāṇī. One who engages in sense gratification on the material platform can hardly understand *rādhā-bhāva,* but one who is freed from the demands of sense gratification can understand it. *Rādhā-bhāva* must be understood from the Gosvāmīs, those who are actually controllers of the senses. From such authorized sources it is to be known that the attitude of Śrīmatī Rādhārāṇī is the highest perfection of conjugal love, which is the highest of the five transcendental mellows, and it is the complete perfection of love of Kṛṣṇa.

These transcendental affairs can be understood on two platforms. One is called elevated, and the other is called superelevated. The loving affairs exhibited in Dvārakā are the elevated form. The superelevated position is reached in the manifestations of the pastimes of Vṛndāvana. The attitude of Lord Caitanya is certainly superelevated.

From the life of Śrī Caitanya Mahāprabhu, an intelligent person engaged in pure devotional service can understand that He always felt separation from Kṛṣṇa within Himself. In that separation He sometimes felt that He had found Kṛṣṇa and was enjoying the meeting. The significance of this separation and meeting is very specific. If someone tries to understand the exalted position of Lord Caitanya without knowing this, he is sure to misunderstand it. One must first become fully self-realized. Otherwise one may misidentify the Lord as *nāgara,* or the enjoyer of the damsels of Vraja, thus committing the mistake of *rasābhāsa,* or overlapping understanding.

TEXT 107

শেষলীলায় প্রভুর কৃষ্ণবিরহ-উন্মাদ ।
ভ্রমময় চেষ্টা, আর প্রলাপময় বাদ ॥ ১০৭ ॥

śeṣa-līlāya prabhura kṛṣṇa-viraha-unmāda
bhrama-maya ceṣṭā, āra pralāpa-maya vāda

śeṣa-līlāya—in the final pastimes; *prabhura*—of Lord Caitanya Mahāprabhu; *kṛṣṇa-viraha*—from separation from Lord Kṛṣṇa; *unmāda*—the madness; *bhrama-maya*—erroneous; *ceṣṭā*—efforts; *āra*—and; *pralāpa-maya*—delirious; *vāda*—talk.

TRANSLATION

In the final portion of His pastimes, Lord Caitanya was obsessed with the madness of separation from Lord Kṛṣṇa. He acted in erroneous ways and talked deliriously.

PURPORT

Lord Śrī Caitanya exhibited the highest stage of the feelings of a devotee in separation from the Lord. This exhibition was sublime because He was completely perfect in the feelings of separation. Materialists, however, cannot understand this. Sometimes materialistic scholars think He was diseased or crazy. Their problem is that they always engage in material sense gratification and can never understand the feelings of the devotees and the Lord. Materialists are most abominable in their ideas. They think that they can enjoy directly perceivable gross objects by their senses and that they can similarly deal with the transcendental features of Lord Caitanya. But the Lord is understood only in pursuance of the principles laid down by the Gosvāmīs, headed by Svarūpa Dāmodara. Doctrines like those of the *nadīyā-nāgarīs,* a class of so-called devotees, are never presented by authorized persons like Svarūpa Dāmodara or the six Gosvāmīs. The ideas of the *gaurāṅga-nāgarīs* are simply a mental concoction, and they are completely on the mental platform.

TEXT 108

রাধিকার ভাব যৈছে উদ্ধবদর্শনে ।
সেই ভাবে মত্ত প্রভু রহে রাত্রিদিনে ॥ ১০৮ ॥

rādhikāra bhāva yaiche uddhava-darśane
sei bhāve matta prabhu rahe rātri-dine

rādhikāra—of Śrīmatī Rādhārāṇī; *bhāva*—emotion; *yaiche*—just as; *uddhava-darśane*—in seeing Śrī Uddhava; *sei*—that; *bhāve*—in the state; *matta*—maddened; *prabhu*—Lord Caitanya Mahāprabhu; *rahe*—remains; *rātri-dine*—day and night.

TRANSLATION

Just as Rādhikā went mad at the sight of Uddhava, so Śrī Caitanya Mahāprabhu was obsessed day and night with the madness of separation.

PURPORT

Those under the shelter of the lotus feet of Śrī Caitanya Mahāprabhu can understand that His mode of worship of the Supreme Lord Kṛṣṇa in separation is the real worship of the Lord. When the feelings of separation become very intense, one attains the stage of meeting Śrī Kṛṣṇa.

So-called devotees like the *sahajiyās* cheaply imagine they are meeting Kṛṣṇa in Vṛndāvana. Such thinking may be useful, but actually meeting Kṛṣṇa is possible through the attitude of separation taught by Śrī Caitanya Mahāprabhu.

TEXT 109

রাত্রে প্রলাপ করে স্বরূপের কণ্ঠ ধরি' ।
আবেশে আপন ভাব কহয়ে উঘাড়ি' ॥ ১০৯ ॥

rātre pralāpa kare svarūpera kaṇṭha dhari'
āveśe āpana bhāva kahaye ughāḍi'

rātre—at night; *pralāpa*—delirium; *kare*—does; *svarūpera*—of Svarūpa Dāmodara; *kaṇṭha dhari'*—embracing the neck; *āveśe*—in ecstasy; *āpana*—His own; *bhāva*—mood; *kahaye*—speaks; *ughāḍi'*—exuberantly.

TRANSLATION

At night He talked incoherently in grief with His arms around Svarūpa Dāmodara's neck. He spoke out His heart in ecstatic inspiration.

TEXT 110

যবে যেই ভাব উঠে প্রভুর অন্তর ।
সেই গীতি-শ্লোকে সুখ দেন দামোদর ॥ ১১০ ॥

yabe yei bhāva uṭhe prabhura antara
sei gīti-śloke sukha dena dāmodara

yabe—when; *yei*—that; *bhāva*—mood; *uṭhe*—arises; *prabhura*—of Lord Caitanya Mahāprabhu; *antara*—in the heart; *sei*—that; *gīti*—by the song; *śloke*—or verse; *sukha*—happiness; *dena*—gives; *dāmodara*—Svarūpa Dāmodara.

TRANSLATION

Whenever a particular sentiment arose in His heart, Svarūpa Dāmodara satisfied Him by singing songs or reciting verses of the same nature.

TEXT 111

এবে কার্য নাহি কিছু এসব বিচারে ।
আগে ইহা বিবরিব করিয়া বিস্তারে ॥ ১১১ ॥

ebe kārya nāhi kichu e-saba vicāre
āge ihā vivariba kariyā vistāre

ebe—now; *kārya*—business; *nāhi*—there is not; *kichu*—any; *e-saba*—all these; *vicāre*—in the considerations; *āge*—ahead; *ihā*—this; *vivariba*—I shall describe; *kariyā*—doing; *vistāre*—in expanded detail.

TRANSLATION

To analyze these pastimes is not necessary now. Later I shall describe them in detail.

TEXT 112

পূর্বে ব্রজে কৃষ্ণের ত্রিবিধ বয়োধর্ম ।
কৌমার, পৌগণ্ড, আর কৈশোর অতিমর্ম ॥ ১১২ ॥

pūrve vraje kṛṣṇera tri-vidha vayo-dharma
kaumāra, paugaṇḍa, āra kaiśora atimarma

pūrve—previously; *vraje*—in Vraja; *kṛṣṇera*—of Lord Kṛṣṇa; *tri-vidha*—three sorts; *vayaḥ-dharma*—characteristics of age; *kaumāra*—childhood; *paugaṇḍa*—boyhood; *āra*—and; *kaiśora*—adolescence; *ati-marma*—the very core.

TRANSLATION

Formerly in Vraja Lord Kṛṣṇa displayed three ages, namely childhood, boyhood and adolescence. His adolescence is especially significant.

TEXT 113

বাৎসল্য-আবেশে কৈল কৌমার সফল ।
পৌগণ্ড সফল কৈল লঞা সখাবল ॥ ১১৩ ॥

vātsalya-āveśe kaila kaumāra saphala
paugaṇḍa saphala kaila lañā sakhāvala

vātsalya—of parental love; *āveśe*—in the attachment; *kaila*—made; *kaumāra*—childhood; *sa-phala*—fruitful; *paugaṇḍa*—boyhood; *sa-phala*—fruitful; *kaila*—made; *lañā*—taking along; *sakhā-āvala*—friends.

TRANSLATION

Parental affection made His childhood fruitful. His boyhood was successful with His friends.

TEXT 114

রাধিকাদি লঞা কৈল রাসাদি-বিলাস ।
বাঞ্ছা ভরি' আস্বাদিল রসের নির্যাস ॥ ১১৪ ॥

rādhikādi lañā kaila rāsādi-vilāsa
vāñchā bhari' āsvādila rasera niryāsa

rādhikā-ādi—Śrīmatī Rādhārāṇī and the other *gopīs; lañā*—taking along; *kaila*—did; *rāsa-ādi*—beginning with the *rāsa* dance; *vilāsa*—pastimes; *vāñchā bhari'*—fulfilling desires; *āsvādila*—He tasted; *rasera*—of mellow; *niryāsa*—the essence.

TRANSLATION

In youth He tasted the essence of rasa, fulfilling His desires in pastimes like the rāsa dance with Śrīmatī Rādhikā and the other gopīs.

TEXT 115

কৈশোর-বয়সে কাম, জগৎসকল ।
রাসাদি-লীলায় তিন করিল সফল ॥ ১১৫ ॥

kaiśora-vayase kāma, jagat-sakala
rāsādi-līlāya tina karila saphala

kaiśora-vayase—in the adolescent age; *kāma*—amorous love; *jagat-sakala*—the entire universe; *rāsa-ādi*—such as the *rāsa* dance; *līlāya*—by pastimes; *tina*—three; *karila*—made; *sa-phala*—successful.

TRANSLATION

In His youth Lord Kṛṣṇa made all three of His ages, and the entire universe, successful by His pastimes of amorous love like the rāsa dance.

TEXT 116

সোঽপি কৈশোরক-বয়ো মানয়ন্মধুসূদনঃ ।
রেমে স্ত্রীরত্নকূটস্থঃ ক্ষপাসু ক্ষপিতাহিতঃ ॥ ১১৬ ॥

so 'pi kaiśoraka-vayo
mānayan madhusūdanaḥ
reme strī-ratna-kūṭa-sthaḥ
kṣapāsu kṣapitāhitaḥ

saḥ—He; *api*—especially; *kaiśoraka-vayaḥ*—the age of adolescence; *mānayan*—honoring; *madhu-sūdanaḥ*—the killer of the Madhu demon; *reme*—enjoyed; *strī-ratna*—of the gopīs; *kūṭa*—in multitudes; *sthaḥ*—situated; *kṣapāsu*—in the autumn nights; *kṣapita-ahitaḥ*—who destroys misfortune.

TRANSLATION

"Lord Madhusūdana enjoyed His youth with pastimes on autumn nights in the midst of the jewellike milkmaids. Thus He dispelled all the misfortunes of the world."

PURPORT

This is a verse from the *Viṣṇu Purāṇa* (5.13.60).

TEXT 117

বাচা সূচিতশর্বরীরতিকলাপ্রাগল্‌ভ্যয়া রাধিকাং
ব্রীড়াকুঞ্চিতলোচনাং বিরচয়ন্নগ্রে সখীনামসৌ ।
তদ্বক্ষোরুহচিত্রকেলিমকরীপাণ্ডিত্যপারং গতঃ
কৈশোরং সফলীকরোতি কলয়ন্ কুঞ্জে বিহারং হরিঃ ॥ ১১৭ ॥

vācā sūcita-śarvarī-rati-kalā-prāgalbhyayā rādhikāṁ
vrīḍā-kuñcita-locanāṁ viracayann agre sakhīnām asau
tad-vakṣo-ruha-citra-keli-makarī-pāṇḍitya-pāraṁ gataḥ
kaiśoraṁ saphalī-karoti kalayan kuñje vihāraṁ hariḥ

vācā—by speech; *sūcita*—revealing; *śarvarī*—of the night; *rati*—in amorous pastimes; *kalā*—of the portion; *prāgalbhyayā*—the importance; *rādhikām*—Śrīmatī Rādhārāṇī; *vrīḍā*—from shame; *kuñcita-locanām*—having Her eyes closed; *viracayan*—making; *agre*—before; *sakhīnām*—Her friends; *asau*—that one; *tat*—of Her; *vakṣaḥ-ruha*—on the breasts; *citra-keli*—with variegated pastimes; *makarī*—in drawing dolphins; *pāṇḍitya*—of cleverness; *pāram*—the limit; *gataḥ*—who reached; *kaiśoram*—adolescence; *sa-phalī-karoti*—makes successful; *kalayan*—performing; *kuñje*—in the bushes; *vihāram*—pastimes; *hariḥ*—the Supreme Personality of Godhead.

TRANSLATION

"Lord Kṛṣṇa made Śrīmatī Rādhārāṇī close Her eyes in shame before Her friends by His words relating Their amorous activities on the previous night. Then He showed the highest limit of cleverness in drawing pictures of dolphins in various playful sports on Her breasts. In this way Lord Hari made His youth successful by performing pastimes in the bushes with Śrī Rādhā and Her friends."

PURPORT

This is a verse from the *Bhakti-rasāmṛta-sindhu* (2.1.231) of Śrīla Rūpa Gosvāmī.

TEXT 118

হরিরেষ ন চেদবাতরিস্যন্মথুরায়াং মধুরাক্ষি রাধিকা চ ।
অভবিষ্যদিয়ং বৃথা বিসৃষ্টির্মকরাঙ্কস্তু বিশেষতস্তদাত্র ॥ ১১৮ ॥

harir eṣa na ced avātariṣyan
mathurāyāṁ madhurākṣi rādhikā ca
abhaviṣyad iyaṁ vṛthā visṛṣṭir
makarāṅkas tu viśeṣatas tadātra

hariḥ—Lord Kṛṣṇa; *eṣaḥ*—this; *na*—not; *cet*—if; *avātariṣyat*—would have descended; *mathurāyām*—in Mathurā; *madhura-akṣi*—O lovely-eyed one (Paurṇamāsī); *rādhikā*—Śrīmatī Rādhikā; *ca*—and; *abhaviṣyat*—would have been; *iyam*—this; *vṛthā*—useless; *visṛṣṭiḥ*—the whole creation; *makara-aṅkaḥ*—the demigod of love, Cupid; *tu*—then; *viśeṣataḥ*—above all; *tadā*—then; *atra*—in this.

TRANSLATION

"O Paurṇamāsī, if Lord Hari had not descended in Mathurā with Śrīmatī Rādhārāṇī, this entire creation—and especially Cupid, the demigod of love—would have been useless."

PURPORT

This verse is spoken by Śrī Vṛndā-devī in the *Vidagdha-mādhava* (7.3) of Śrīla Rūpa Gosvāmī.

TEXTS 119–120

এই মত পূর্বে কৃষ্ণ রসের সদন ।
যদ্যপি করিল রস-নির্যাস-চর্বণ ॥ ১১৯ ॥
তথাপি নহিল তিন বাঞ্ছিত পূরণ ।
তাহা আস্বাদিতে যদি করিল যতন ॥ ১২০ ॥

ei mata pūrve kṛṣṇa rasera sadana
yadyapi karila rasa-niryāsa-carvaṇa

tathāpi nahila tina vāñchita pūraṇa
tāhā āsvādite yadi karila yatana

ei mata—like this; *pūrve*—previously; *kṛṣṇa*—Lord Kṛṣṇa; *rasera*—of mellows; *sadana*—the reservoir; *yadyapi*—even though; *karila*—did; *rasa*—of the mellows; *niryāsa*—the essence; *carvaṇa*—chewing; *tathāpi*—still; *nahila*—was not; *tina*—three; *vāñchita*—desired objects; *pūraṇa*—fulfilling; *tāhā*—that; *āsvādite*—to taste; *yadi*—though; *karila*—were made; *yatana*—efforts.

TRANSLATION

Even though Lord Kṛṣṇa, the abode of all mellows, had previously in this way chewed the essence of the mellows of love, still He was unable to fulfill three desires, although He made efforts to taste them.

TEXT 121

তাঁহার প্রথম বাঞ্ছা করিয়ে ব্যাখ্যান ।
কৃষ্ণ কহে,—'আমি হই রসের নিদান ॥ ১২১ ॥

tāṅhāra prathama vāñchā kariye vyākhyāna
kṛṣṇa kahe,—'āmi ha-i rasera nidāna

tāṅhāra—His; *prathama*—first; *vāñchā*—desire; *kariye*—I do; *vyākhyāna*—explanation; *kṛṣṇa*—Lord Kṛṣṇa; *kahe*—says; *āmi*—I; *ha-i*—am; *rasera*—of mellow; *nidāna*—primary cause.

TRANSLATION

I shall explain His first desire. Kṛṣṇa says, "I am the primary cause of all rasas.

TEXT 122

পূর্ণানন্দময় আমি চিন্ময় পূর্ণতত্ত্ব ।
রাধিকার প্রেমে আমা করায় উন্মত্ত ॥ ১২২ ॥

pūrṇānanda-maya āmi cin-maya pūrṇa-tattva
rādhikāra preme āmā karāya unmatta

pūrṇa-ānanda-maya—made of full joy; *āmi*—I; *cit-maya*—spiritual; *pūrṇa-tattva*—full of truth; *rādhikāra*—of Śrīmatī Rādhārāṇī; *preme*—the love; *āmā*—Me; *karāya*—makes; *unmatta*—maddened.

TRANSLATION

"I am the full spiritual truth and am made of full joy, but the love of Śrīmatī Rādhārāṇī drives Me mad.

TEXT 123

না জানি রাধার প্রেমে আছে কত বল ।
যে বলে আমারে করে সর্বদা বিহ্বল ॥ ১২৩ ॥

nā jāni rādhāra preme āche kata bala
ye bale āmāre kare sarvadā vihvala

nā jāni—I do not know; *rādhāra*—of Śrīmatī Rādhārāṇī; *preme*—in the love; *āche*—there is; *kata*—how much; *bala*—strength; *ye*—which;

bale—strength; *āmāre*—Me; *kare*—makes; *sarvadā*—always; *vihvala*—overwhelmed.

TRANSLATION

"I do not know the strength of Rādhā's love, with which She always overwhelms Me.

TEXT 124

রাধিকার প্রেম—গুরু, আমি—শিষ্য নট ।
সদা আমা নানা নৃত্যে নাচায় উদ্ভট ॥ ১২৪ ॥

rādhikāra prema—guru, āmi—śiṣya naṭa
sadā āmā nānā nṛtye nācāya udbhaṭa

rādhikāra—of Śrīmatī Rādhārāṇī; *prema*—the love; *guru*—teacher; *āmi*—I; *śiṣya*—disciple; *naṭa*—dancer; *sadā*—always; *āmā*—Me; *nānā*—various; *nṛtye*—in dances; *nācāya*—causes to dance; *udbhaṭa*—novel.

TRANSLATION

"The love of Rādhikā is My teacher, and I am Her dancing pupil. Her prema makes Me dance various novel dances."

TEXT 125

কস্মাদ্‌বৃন্দে প্রিয়সখি হরেঃ পাদমূলাৎ কুতোঽসৌ
কুণ্ডারণ্যে কিমিহ কুরুতে নৃত্যশিক্ষাং গুরুঃ কঃ ।
তং ত্বন্মূর্তিঃ প্রতিতরুলতং দিগ্বিদিক্ষু স্ফুরন্তী
শৈলূষীব ভ্রমতি পরিতো নর্তয়ন্তী স্ব-পশ্চাৎ ॥ ১২৫ ॥

kasmād vṛnde priya-sakhi hareḥ pāda-mūlāt kuto 'sau
kuṇḍāraṇye kim iha kurute nṛtya-śikṣāṁ guruḥ kaḥ
taṁ tvan-mūrtiḥ prati-taru-lataṁ dig-vidikṣu sphurantī
śailūṣīva bhramati parito nartayantī sva-paścāt

kasmāt—from where; *vṛnde*—O Vṛndā; *priyā-sakhi*—O dear friend; *hareḥ*—of Lord Hari; *pāda-mūlāt*—from the lotus feet; *kutaḥ*—where; *asau*—that one (Lord Kṛṣṇa); *kuṇḍa-araṇye*—in the forest on the bank of Rādhā-kuṇḍa; *kim*—what; *iha*—here; *kurute*—He does; *nṛtya-śikṣām*—dancing practice; *guruḥ*—teacher; *kaḥ*—who; *tam*—Him; *tvat-mūrtiḥ*—Your form; *prati-taru-latam*—on every tree and vine;

dik-vidikṣu—in all directions; *sphurantī*—appearing; *śailūṣī*—expert dancer; *iva*—like; *bhramati*—wanders; *paritaḥ*—all around; *nartayantī*—causing to dance; *sva-paścāt*—behind.

TRANSLATION

"O my beloved friend Vṛndā, where are you coming from?"

"I am coming from the feet of Śrī Hari."

"Where is He?"

"In the forest on the bank of Rādhā-kuṇḍa."

"What is He doing there?"

"He is learning dancing."

"Who is His master?"

"Your image, Rādhā, revealing itself in every tree and creeper in every direction, is roaming like a skillful dancer, making Him dance behind."

PURPORT

This text is from the *Govinda-līlāmṛta* (8.77) of Kṛṣṇadāsa Kavirāja Gosvāmī.

TEXT 126

নিজ-প্রেমাস্বাদে মোর হয় যে আহ্লাদ।
তাহা হ'তে কোটিগুণ রাধা-প্রেমাস্বাদ ॥ ১২৬ ॥

nija-premāsvāde mora haya ye āhlāda
tāhā ha'te koṭi-guṇa rādhā-premāsvāda

nija—own; *prema*—love; *āsvāde*—in tasting; *mora*—My; *haya*—there is; *ye*—whatever; *āhlāda*—pleasure; *tāhā ha'te*—than that; *koṭi-guṇa*—ten million times greater; *rādhā*—of Śrīmatī Rādhārāṇī; *prema-āsvāda*—the tasting of love.

TRANSLATION

"Whatever pleasure I get from tasting My love for Śrīmatī Rādhārāṇī, She tastes ten million times more than Me by Her love.

TEXT 127

আমি যৈছে পরস্পর বিরুদ্ধধর্মাশ্রয়।
রাধাপ্রেম তৈছে সদা বিরুদ্ধধর্মময় ॥ ১২৭ ॥

āmi yaiche paraspara viruddha-dharmāśraya
rādhā-prema taiche sadā viruddha-dharma-maya

āmi—I; *yaiche*—just as; *paraspara*—mutually; *viruddha-dharma*—of conflicting characteristics; *āśraya*—the abode; *rādhā-prema*—the love of Śrīmatī Rādhārāṇī; *taiche*—just so; *sadā*—always; *viruddha-dharma-maya*—consists of conflicting characteristics.

TRANSLATION

"Just as I am the abode of all mutually contradictory characteristics, so Rādha's love is always full of similar contradictions.

TEXT 128

রাধা-প্রেমা বিভু—যার বাড়িতে নাহি ঠাঞি ।
তথাপি সে ক্ষণে ক্ষণে বাড়য়ে সদাই ॥ ১২৮ ॥

rādhā-premā vibhu—yāra bāḍite nāhi ṭhāñi
tathāpi se kṣaṇe kṣaṇe bāḍaye sadāi

rādhā-premā—the love of Śrīmatī Rādhārāṇī; *vibhu*—all-pervading; *yāra*—of which; *bāḍite*—to increase; *nāhi*—there is not; *ṭhāñi*—space; *tathāpi*—still; *se*—that; *kṣaṇe kṣaṇe*—every second; *bāḍaye*—increases; *sadāi*—always.

TRANSLATION

"Rādhā's love is all-pervading, leaving no room for expansion. But still it is expanding constantly.

TEXT 129

যাহা বই গুরু বস্তু নাহি সুনিশ্চিত ।
তথাপি গুরুর ধর্ম গৌরব-বর্জিত ॥ ১২৯ ॥

yāhā va-i guru vastu nāhi suniścita
tathāpi gurura dharma gaurava-varjita

yāhā—which; *va-i*—besides; *guru*—great; *vastu*—thing; *nāhi*—there is not; *suniścita*—quite certainly; *tathāpi*—still; *gurura*—of greatness; *dharma*—characteristics; *gaurava-varjita*—devoid of pride.

TRANSLATION

"There is certainly nothing greater than Her love. But Her love is devoid of pride. That is the sign of its greatness.

TEXT 130

যাহা হৈতে সুনির্মল দ্বিতীয় নাহি আর ।
তথাপি সর্বদা বাম্য-বক্র-ব্যবহার ॥ ১৩০ ॥

yāhā haite sunirmala dvitīya nāhi āra
tathāpi sarvadā vāmya-vakra-vyavahāra

yāhā haite—than which; *su-nirmala*—very pure; *dvitīya*—second; *nāhi*—there is not; *āra*—another; *tathāpi*—still; *sarvadā*—always; *vāmya*—perverse; *vakra*—crooked; *vyavahāra*—behavior.

TRANSLATION

"Nothing is purer than Her love. But its behavior is always perverse and crooked."

TEXT 131

বিভুরপি কলয়ন্ সদাভিবৃদ্ধিং
গুরুরপি গৌরবচর্যয়া বিহীনঃ ।
মুহুরুপচিতবক্রিমাপি শুদ্ধো
জয়তি মুরদ্বিষি রাধিকানুরাগঃ ॥ ১৩১ ॥

vibhur api kalayan sadābhivṛddhiṁ
gurur api gaurava-caryayā vihīnaḥ
muhur upacita-vakrimāpi śuddho
jayati mura-dviṣi rādhikānurāgaḥ

vibhuḥ—all-pervading; *api*—although; *kalayan*—making; *sadā*—always; *abhivṛddhim*—increase; *guruḥ*—important; *api*—although; *gaurava-caryayā vihīnaḥ*—without proud behavior; *muhuḥ*—again and again; *upacita*—increased; *vakrimā*—duplicity; *api*—although; *śuddhaḥ*—pure; *jayati*—all glories to; *mura-dviṣi*—for Kṛṣṇa, the enemy of the demon Mura; *rādhikā*—of Śrīmatī Rādhārāṇī; *anu-rāgaḥ*—the love.

TRANSLATION

"All glories to Rādhā's love for Kṛṣṇa, the enemy of the demon Mura! Although it is all-pervading, it tends to increase at every moment. Although it is important, it is devoid of pride. And although it is pure, it is always beset with duplicity."

PURPORT

This is a verse from the *Dāna-keli-kaumudī* (2) of Śrīla Rūpa Gosvāmī.

TEXT 132

সেই প্রেমার শ্রীরাধিকা পরম 'আশ্রয়' ।
সেই প্রেমার আমি হই কেবল 'বিষয়' ॥ ১৩২ ॥

sei premāra śrī-rādhikā parama 'āśraya'
sei premāra āmi ha-i kevala 'viṣaya'

sei—that; *premāra*—of the love; *śrī-rādhikā*—Śrīmatī Rādhārāṇī; *parama*—highest; *āśraya*—abode; *sei*—that; *premāra*—of the love; *āmi*—I; *ha-i*—am; *kevala*—only; *viṣaya*—object.

TRANSLATION

"Śrī Rādhikā is the highest abode of that love, and I am its only object.

TEXT 133

বিষয়জাতীয় সুখ আমার আস্বাদ ।
আমা হৈতে কোটিগুণ আশ্রয়ের আহ্লাদ ॥ ১৩৩ ॥

viṣaya-jātīya sukha āmāra āsvāda
āmā haite koṭi-guṇa āśrayera āhlāda

viṣaya jātīya—relating to the object; *sukha*—happiness; *āmāra*—My; *āsvāda*—tasting; *āmā haite*—than Me; *koṭi-guṇa*—ten million times more; *āśrayera*—of the abode; *āhlāda*—pleasure.

TRANSLATION

"I taste the bliss to which the object of love is entitled. But the pleasure of Rādhā, the abode of that love, is ten million times greater.

TEXT 134

আশ্রয়জাতীয় সুখ পাইতে মন ধায় ।
যত্নে আস্বাদিতে নারি, কি করি উপায় ॥ ১৩৪ ॥

āśraya-jātiya sukha pāite mana dhāya
yatne āsvādite nāri, ki kari upāya

āśraya-jātīya—relating to the abode; *sukha*—happiness; *pāite*—to obtain; *mana*—the mind; *dhāya*—chases; *yatne*—by effort; *āsvādite*—to taste; *nāri*—I am unable; *ki*—what; *kari*—I do; *upāya*—way.

TRANSLATION

"My mind races to taste the pleasure experienced by the abode, but I cannot taste it, even by My best efforts. How may I taste it?

TEXT 135

কভু যদি এই প্রেমার হইয়ে আশ্রয় ।
তবে এই প্রেমানন্দের অনুভব হয় ॥ ১৩৫ ॥

kabhu yadi ei premāra ha-iye āśraya
tabe ei premānandera anubhava haya

kabhu—sometime; *yadi*—if; *ei*—this; *premāra*—of the love; *ha-iye*—I become; *āśraya*—the abode; *tabe*—then; *ei*—this; *prema-ānandera*—of the joy of love; *anubhava*—experience; *haya*—there is.

TRANSLATION

"If sometime I can be the abode of that love, only then may I taste its joy."

PURPORT

Viṣaya and *āśraya* are two very significant words relating to the reciprocation between Kṛṣṇa and His devotee. The devotee is called the *āśraya*, and his beloved, Kṛṣṇa, is the *viṣaya*. Different ingredients are involved in the exchange of love between the *āśraya* and *viṣaya*, which are known as *vibhāva*, *anubhāva*, *sāttvika* and *vyabhicārī*. *Vibhāva* is divided into the two categories *ālambana* and *uddīpana*. *Ālambana* may be further divided into *āśraya* and *viṣaya.* In the loving affairs of Rādhā and Kṛṣṇa, Rādhārāṇī is the *āśraya* feature and Kṛṣṇa the *viṣaya.* The transcendental consciousness of the Lord tells Him, "I am Kṛṣṇa, and I experience pleasure as the *viṣaya.* The pleasure enjoyed by Rādhārāṇī, the *āśraya,* is many times greater than the pleasure I feel." Therefore, to feel the pleasure of the *āśraya* category, Lord Kṛṣṇa appeared as Śrī Caitanya Mahāprabhu.

TEXT 136

এত চিন্তি' রহে কৃষ্ণ পরমকৌতুকী ।
হৃদয়ে বাড়য়ে প্রেম-লোভ ধক্‌ধকি ॥ ১৩৬ ॥

eta cinti' rahe kṛṣṇa parama-kautukī
hṛdaye bāḍaye prema-lobha dhakdhaki

eta cinti'—thinking this; *rahe*—remains; *kṛṣṇa*—Lord Kṛṣṇa; *parama-kautukī*—the supremely curious; *hṛdaye*—in the heart; *bāḍaye*—increases; *prema-lobha*—eager desire for love; *dhakdhaki*—blazing.

TRANSLATION

Thinking in this way, Lord Kṛṣṇa was curious to taste that love. His eager desire for that love increasingly blazed in His heart.

TEXT 137

এই এক, শুন আর লোভের প্রকার ।
স্বমাধুর্য দেখি' কৃষ্ণ করেন বিচার ॥ ১৩৭ ॥

ei eka, śuna āra lobhera prakāra
sva-mādhurya dekhi' kṛṣṇa karena vicāra

ei—this; *eka*—one; *śuna*—please hear; *āra*—another; *lobhera*—of eager desire; *prakāra*—type; *sva-mādhurya*—own sweetness; *dekhi'*—seeing; *kṛṣṇa*—Lord Kṛṣṇa; *karena*—does; *vicāra*—consideration.

TRANSLATION

That is one desire. Now please hear of another. Seeing His own beauty, Lord Kṛṣṇa began to consider.

TEXT 138

অদ্ভুত, অনন্ত, পূর্ণ মোর মধুরিমা ।
ত্রিজগতে ইহার কেহ নাহি পায় সীমা ॥ ১৩৮ ॥

adbhuta, ananta, pūrṇa mora madhurimā
tri-jagate ihāra keha nāhi pāya sīmā

adbhuta—wonderful; *ananta*—unlimited; *pūrṇa*—full; *mora*—My; *madhurimā*—sweetness; *tri-jagate*—in the three worlds; *ihāra*—of this; *keha*—someone; *nāhi*—not; *pāya*—obtains; *sīmā*—limit.

TRANSLATION

"My sweetness is wonderful, infinite and full. No one in the three worlds can find its limit.

TEXT 139

এই প্রেমদ্বারে নিত্য রাধিকা একলি ।
আমার মাধুর্যামৃত আস্বাদে সকলি ॥ ১৩৯ ॥

ei prema-dvāre nitya rādhikā ekali
āmāra mādhuryāmṛta āsvāde sakali

ei—this; *prema-dvāre*—by means of the love; *nitya*—always; *rādhikā*—Śrīmatī Rādhārāṇī; *ekali*—only; *āmāra*—of Me; *mādhurya-amṛta*—the nectar of the sweetness; *āsvāde*—tastes; *sakali*—all.

TRANSLATION

"Only Rādhikā, by the strength of Her love, tastes all the nectar of My sweetness.

TEXT 140

যদ্যপি নির্মল রাধার সৎপ্রেমদর্পণ ।
তথাপি স্বচ্ছতা তার বাঢ়ে ক্ষণে ক্ষণ ॥ ১৪০ ॥

yadyapi nirmala rādhāra sat-prema-darpaṇa
tathāpi svacchatā tāra bāḍhe kṣaṇe kṣaṇa

yadyapi—although; *nirmala*—pure; *rādhāra*—of Śrīmatī Rādhārāṇī; *sat-prema*—of real love; *darpaṇa*—the mirror; *tathāpi*—still; *svac-*

chatā—transparency; *tāra*—of that; *bāḍhe*—increases; *kṣaṇe kṣaṇa*—every moment.

TRANSLATION

"Although Rādhā's love is pure like a mirror, its purity increases at every moment.

TEXT 141

আমার মাধুর্য নাহি বাড়িতে অবকাশে ।
এ-দর্পণের আগে নব নব রূপে ভাসে ॥ ১৪১ ॥

āmāra mādhurya nāhi bāḍhite avakāśe
e-darpaṇera āge nava nava rūpe bhāse

āmāra—of Me; *mādhurya*—sweetness; *nāhi*—not; *bāḍhite*—to increase; *avakāśe*—opportunity; *e-darpaṇera āge*—in front of this mirror; *nava nava*—newer and newer; *rūpe*—in beauty; *bhāse*—shines.

TRANSLATION

"My sweetness also has no room for expansion, yet it shines before that mirror in newer and newer beauty.

TEXT 142

মন্মাধুর্য রাধার প্রেম—দোঁহে হোড় করি' ।
ক্ষণে ক্ষণে বাড়ে দোঁহে, কেহ নাহি হারি ॥ ১৪২ ॥

man-mādhurya rādhāra prema—doṅhe hoḍa kari'
kṣaṇe kṣaṇe bāḍe doṅhe, keha nāhi hāri

mat-mādhurya—My sweetness; *rādhāra*—of Śrīmatī Rādhārāṇī; *prema*—the love; *doṅhe*—both together; *hoḍa kari'*—challenging; *kṣaṇe kṣaṇe*—every second; *bāḍe*—increase; *doṅhe*—both; *keha nāhi*—no one; *hāri*—defeated.

TRANSLATION

"There is constant competition between My sweetness and the mirror of Rādhā's love. They both go on increasing, but neither knows defeat.

TEXT 143

আমার মাধুর্য নিত্য নব নব হয় ।
স্ব-স্ব-প্রেম-অনুরূপ ভক্তে আস্বাদয় ॥ ১৪৩ ॥

āmāra mādhurya nitya nava nava haya
sva-sva-prema-anurūpa bhakte āsvādaya

āmāra—of Me; *mādhurya*—the sweetness; *nitya*—always; *nava nava*—newer and newer; *haya*—is; *sva-sva-prema-anurūpa*—according to one's own love; *bhakte*—the devotee; *āsvādaya*—tastes.

TRANSLATION

"My sweetness is always newer and newer. Devotees taste it according to their own respective love.

TEXT 144

দর্পণাদ্যে দেখি' যদি আপন মাধুরী ।
আস্বাদিতে হয় লোভ, আস্বাদিতে নারি ॥ ১৪৪ ॥

darpaṇādye dekhi' yadi āpana mādhurī
āsvādite haya lobha, āsvādite nāri

darpaṇa-ādye—beginning in a mirror; *dekhi'*—seeing; *yadi*—if; *āpana*—own; *mādhurī*—sweetness; *āsvādite*—to taste; *haya*—there is; *lobha*—desire; *āsvādite*—to taste; *nāri*—I am not able.

TRANSLATION

"If I see My sweetness in a mirror, I am tempted to taste it, but nevertheless I cannot.

TEXT 145

বিচার করিয়ে যদি আস্বাদ-উপায় ।
রাধিকাস্বরূপ হইতে তবে মন ধায় ॥ ১৪৫ ॥

vicāra kariye yadi āsvāda-upāya
rādhikā-svarūpa ha-ite tabe mana dhāya

vicāra—consideration; *kariye*—I do; *yadi*—if; *āsvāda*—to taste; *upāya*—way; *rādhikā-svarūpa*—the nature of Śrīmatī Rādhārāṇī; *haite*—to become; *tabe*—then; *mana*—mind; *dhāya*—chases.

TRANSLATION

"If I deliberate on a way to taste it, I find that I hanker for the position of Rādhikā."

PURPORT

Kṛṣṇa's attractiveness is wonderful and unlimited. No one can know the end of it. Śrīmatī Rādhārāṇī alone can relish such extensiveness from Her position in the *āśraya* category. The mirror of Śrīmatī Rādhārāṇī's transcendental love is perfectly clear, yet it appears clearer and clearest in the transcendental method of understanding Kṛṣṇa. In the mirror of Rādhārāṇī's heart, the transcendental features of Kṛṣṇa appear increasingly new and fresh. In other words, the attraction of Kṛṣṇa increases in proportion to the understanding of Śrīmatī Rādhārāṇī. Each tries to supersede the other. Neither wants to be defeated in increasing the intensity of love. Desiring to understand Rādhārāṇī's attitude of increasing love, Lord Kṛṣṇa appeared as Śrī Caitanya Mahāprabhu.

TEXT 146

অপরিকলিতপূর্বঃ কশ্চমৎকারকারী
স্ফুরতি মম গরীয়ানেষ মাধুর্যপূরঃ ।
অয়মহমপি হন্ত প্রেক্ষ্য যং লুব্ধচেতাঃ
সরভসমুপভোক্তুং কাময়ে রাধিকেব ॥ ১৪৬ ॥

aparikalita-pūrvaḥ kaś camatkāra-kārī
sphurati mama garīyān eṣa mādhurya-pūraḥ
ayam aham api hanta prekṣya yaṁ lubdha-cetāḥ
sarabhasam upabhoktuṁ kāmaye rādhikeva

aparikalita—not experienced; *pūrvaḥ*—previously; *kaḥ*—who; *camatkāra-kārī*—causing wonder; *sphurati*—manifests; *mama*—My; *garīyān*—more great; *eṣaḥ*—this; *mādhurya-pūraḥ*—abundance of sweetness; *ayam*—this; *aham*—I; *api*—even; *hanta*—alas; *prekṣya*—seeing; *yam*—which; *lubdha-cetāḥ*—My mind being bewildered; *sarabhasam*—impetuously; *upabhoktum*—to enjoy; *kāmaye*—desire; *rādhikā iva*—like Śrīmatī Rādhārāṇī.

TRANSLATION

"Who manifests an abundance of sweetness greater than Mine, which has never been experienced before and which causes wonder to all? Alas, I Myself, My mind bewildered upon seeing this beauty, impetuously desire to enjoy it like Śrīmatī Rādhārāṇī."

PURPORT

This text is from the *Lalita-mādhava* (8.34) of Śrīla Rūpa Gosvāmī. It was spoken by Lord Kṛṣṇa when He saw the beauty of His own reflection in a jeweled fountain in Dvārakā.

TEXT 147

কৃষ্ণমাধুর্যের এক স্বাভাবিক বল ।
কৃষ্ণআদি নরনারী করয়ে চঞ্চল ॥ ১৪৭ ॥

kṛṣṇa-mādhuryera eka svābhāvika bala
kṛṣṇa-ādi nara-nārī karaye cañcala

kṛṣṇa—of Lord Kṛṣṇa; *mādhuryera*—of the sweetness; *eka*—one; *svābhāvika*—natural; *bala*—strength; *kṛṣṇa*—Lord Kṛṣṇa; *ādi*—beginning with; *nara-nārī*—men and women; *karaye*—makes; *cañcala*—perturbed.

TRANSLATION

The beauty of Kṛṣṇa has one natural strength: it thrills the hearts of all men and women, beginning with Lord Kṛṣṇa Himself.

TEXT 148

শ্রবণে, দর্শনে আকর্ষয়ে সর্বমন ।
আপনা আস্বাদিতে কৃষ্ণ করেন যতন ॥ ১৪৮ ॥

śravaṇe, darśane ākarṣaye sarva-mana
āpanā āsvādite kṛṣṇa karena yatana

śravaṇe—in hearing; *darśane*—in seeing; *ākarṣaye*—attracts; *sarva-mana*—all minds; *āpanā*—Himself; *āsvādite*—to taste; *kṛṣṇa*—Lord Kṛṣṇa; *karena*—makes; *yatana*—efforts.

TRANSLATION

All minds are attracted by hearing His sweet voice and flute, or by seeing His beauty. Even Lord Kṛṣṇa Himself makes efforts to taste that sweetness.

TEXT 149

এ মাধুর্যামৃত পান সদা যেই করে ।
তৃষ্ণাশান্তি নহে, তৃষ্ণা বাড়ে নিরন্তরে ॥ ১৪৯ ॥

e mādhuryāmṛta pāna sadā yei kare
tṛṣṇā-śānti nahe, tṛṣṇā bāḍhe nirantare

e—this; *mādhurya-amṛta*—nectar of sweetness; *pāna*—drinks; *sadā*—always; *yei*—that person who; *kare*—does; *tṛṣṇā-śānti*—satisfaction of thirst; *nahe*—there is not; *tṛṣṇā*—thirst; *bāḍhe*—increases; *nirantare*—constantly.

TRANSLATION

The thirst of one who always drinks the nectar of that sweetness is never satisfied. Rather, that thirst increases constantly.

TEXT 150

অতৃপ্ত হইয়া করে বিধির নিন্দন ।
অবিদগ্ধ বিধি ভাল না জানে সৃজন ॥ ১৫০ ॥

atṛpta ha-iyā kare vidhira nindana
avidagdha vidhi bhāla nā jāne sṛjana

atṛpta—unsatisfied; *ha-iyā*—being; *kare*—do; *vidhira*—of Lord Brahmā; *nindana*—blaspheming; *avidagdha*—inexperienced; *vidhi*—Lord Brahmā; *bhāla*—well; *nā jāne*—does not know; *sṛjana*—creating.

TRANSLATION

Such a person, being unsatisfied, begins to blaspheme Lord Brahmā, saying that he does not know the art of creating well and is simply inexperienced.

TEXT 151

কোটি নেত্র নাহি দিল, সবে দিল দুই ।
তাহাতে নিমেষ,—কৃষ্ণ কি দেখিব মুঞি ॥ ১৫১ ॥

koṭi netra nāhi dila, sabe dila dui
tāhāte nimeṣa,—kṛṣṇa ki dekhiba muñi

koṭi—ten million; *netra*—eyes; *nāhi dila*—did not give; *sabe*—to all; *dila*—gave; *dui*—two; *tāhāte*—in that; *nimeṣa*—a blink; *kṛṣṇa*—Lord Kṛṣṇa; *ki*—how; *dekhiba*—shall see; *muñi*—I.

TRANSLATION

He has not given millions of eyes to see the beauty of Kṛṣṇa. He has given only two eyes, and even those eyes blink. How then shall I see the lovely face of Kṛṣṇa?

TEXT 152

অটতি যদ্ভবানহ্নি কাননং, ত্রুটির্যুগায়তে ত্বামপশ্যতাম্ ।
কুটিলকুন্তলং শ্রীমুখঞ্চ তে, জড় উদীক্ষতাং পক্ষ্মকৃদ্দৃশাম্ ॥ ১৫২ ॥

aṭati yad bhavān ahni kānanaṁ
truṭir yugāyate tvām apaśyatām
kuṭila-kuntalaṁ śrī-mukhaṁ ca te
jaḍa udīkṣatāṁ pakṣma-kṛd dṛśām

aṭati—goes; *yat*—when; *bhavān*—Your Lordship; *ahni*—in the day; *kānanam*—to the forest; *truṭiḥ*—half a second; *yugāyate*—appears like a *yuga; tvām*—You; *apaśyatām*—of those not seeing; *kuṭila-kuntalam*—adorned with curled hair; *śrī-mukham*—beautiful face; *ca*—and; *te*—Your; *jaḍaḥ*—stupid; *udīkṣatām*—looking at; *pakṣma-kṛt*—the maker of eyelashes; *dṛśām*—of the eyes.

TRANSLATION

[The gopīs said:] "O Kṛṣṇa, when You go to the forest during the day and we do not see Your sweet face, which is surrounded by beautiful curling hair, half a second becomes as long as an entire age for us. And we consider the creator, who has put eyelids on the eyes we use for seeing You, to be simply a fool."

PURPORT

This verse is spoken by the *gopīs* in *Śrīmad-Bhāgavatam* (10.31.15).

TEXT 153

গোপ্যশ্চ কৃষ্ণমুপলভ্য চিরাদভীষ্টং
যৎপ্রেক্ষণে দৃশিষু পক্ষ্মকৃতং শপন্তি ।
দৃগ্‌ভির্হৃদীকৃতমলং পরিরভ্য সর্বা-
স্তদ্ভাবমাপুরপি নিত্যযুজাং দুরাপম্ ॥ ১৫৩ ॥

gopyaś ca kṛṣṇam upalabhya cirād abhīṣṭaṁ
yat-prekṣaṇe dṛśiṣu pakṣma-kṛtaṁ śapanti
dṛgbhir hṛdī-kṛtam alaṁ parirabhya sarvās
tad-bhāvam āpur api nitya-yujāṁ durāpam

gopyaḥ—the *gopīs; ca*—and; *kṛṣṇam*—Lord Kṛṣṇa; *upalabhya*—seeing; *cirāt*—after a long time; *abhīṣṭam*—desired object; *yat-prekṣaṇe*—in the seeing of whom; *dṛśiṣu*—in the eyes; *pakṣma-kṛtam*—the maker of eyelashes; *śapanti*—curse; *dṛgbhiḥ*—with the eyes; *hṛdī kṛtam*—who entered the hearts; *alam*—enough; *parirabhya*—embracing; *sarvāḥ*—all; *tat-bhāvam*—that highest stage of joy; *āpuḥ*—obtained; *api*—although; *nitya-yujām*—by perfected *yogīs; durāpam*—difficult to obtain.

TRANSLATION

"The gopīs saw their beloved Kṛṣṇa at Kurukṣetra after a long separation. They secured and embraced Him in their hearts through their eyes, and they attained a joy so intense that not even perfect yogīs can attain it. The gopīs cursed the creator for creating eyelids that interfered with their vision."

PURPORT

This text is from *Śrīmad-Bhāgavatam* (10.82.39).

TEXT 154

কৃষ্ণাবলোকন বিনা নেত্র ফল নাহি আন ।
যেই জন কৃষ্ণ দেখে, সেই ভাগ্যবান্ ॥ ১৫৪ ॥

kṛṣṇāvalokana vinā netra phala nāhi āna
yei jana kṛṣṇa dekhe, sei bhāgyavān

kṛṣṇa—Lord Kṛṣṇa; *avalokana*—looking at; *vinā*—without; *netra*—the eyes; *phala*—fruit; *nāhi*—not; *āna*—other; *yei*—who; *jana*—the person; *kṛṣṇa*—Lord Kṛṣṇa; *dekhe*—sees; *sei*—he; *bhāgyavān*—very fortunate.

TRANSLATION

There is no consummation for the eyes other than the sight of Kṛṣṇa. Whoever sees Him is most fortunate indeed.

TEXT 155

অক্ষণ্বতাং ফলমিদং ন পরং বিদামঃ
সখ্যঃ পশূননুবিবেশয়তোর্বয়স্যৈঃ ।
বক্ত্রং ব্রজেশসুতয়োরনুবেণুজুষ্টং
যৈর্বা নিপীতমনুরক্তকটাক্ষমোক্ষম্ ॥ ১৫৫ ॥

akṣaṇvatāṁ phalam idaṁ na paraṁ vidāmaḥ
sakhyaḥ paśūn anuviveśayator vayasyaiḥ
vaktraṁ vrajeśa-sutayor anuveṇu-juṣṭaṁ
yair vā nipītam anurakta-kaṭākṣa-mokṣam

akṣaṇvatām—of those who have eyes; *phalam*—the fruit; *idam*—this; *na*—not; *param*—other; *vidāmaḥ*—we know; *sakhyaḥ*—O friends; *paśūn*—the cows; *anuviveśayatoḥ*—causing to enter one forest from another; *vayasyaiḥ*—with Their friends of the same age; *vaktram*—the faces; *vraja-īśa*—of Mahārāja Nanda; *sutayoḥ*—of the two sons; *anuveṇu-juṣṭam*—possessed of flutes; *yaiḥ*—by which; *vā*—or; *nipītam*—imbibed; *anurakta*—loving; *kaṭa-akṣa*—glances; *mokṣam*—giving off.

TRANSLATION

[The gopīs said:] "O friends, those eyes that see the beautiful faces of the sons of Mahārāja Nanda are certainly fortunate. As these two sons enter the forest, surrounded by Their friends, driving the cows before Them, They hold Their flutes to Their mouths and glance lovingly upon the residents of Vṛndāvana. For those who have eyes, we think there is no greater object of vision."

PURPORT

Like the *gopīs,* one can see Kṛṣṇa continuously if one is fortunate enough. In the *Brahma-saṁhitā* it is said that sages whose eyes have been smeared with the ointment of pure love can see the form of

Śyāmasundara (Kṛṣṇa) continuously in the centers of their hearts. This text from *Śrīmad-Bhāgavatam* (10.21.7) was sung by the *gopīs* on the advent of the *śarat* season.

TEXT 156

গোপ্যস্তপঃ কিমচরন্ যদমুষ্য রূপং
লাবণ্যসারমসমোর্ধ্বমনন্যসিদ্ধম্ ।
দৃগ্ভিঃ পিবন্ত্যনুসবাভিনবং দুরাপ-
মেকান্তধাম যশসঃ শ্রিয় ঐশ্বরস্য ॥ ১৫৬ ॥

gopyas tapaḥ kim acaran yad amuṣya rūpaṁ
lāvaṇya-sāram asamordhvam ananya-siddham
dṛgbhiḥ pibanty anusavābhinavaṁ durāpam
ekānta-dhāma yaśasaḥ śriya aiśvarasya

gopyaḥ—the *gopīs; tapaḥ*—austerities; *kim*—what; *acaran*—performed; *yat*—from which; *amuṣya*—of such a one (Lord Kṛṣṇa); *rūpam*—the form; *lāvaṇya-sāram*—the essence of loveliness; *asama-ūrdhvam*—not paralleled or surpassed; *ananya-siddham*—not perfected by any other ornament (self-perfect); *dṛgbhiḥ*—by the eyes; *pibanti*—they drink; *anusava-abhinavam*—constantly new; *durāpam*—difficult to obtain; *ekānta-dhāma*—the only abode; *yaśasaḥ*—of fame; *śriyaḥ*—of beauty; *aiśvarasya*—of opulence.

TRANSLATION

[The women of Mathurā said:] "What austerities must the gopīs have performed? With their eyes they always drink the nectar of the form of Lord Kṛṣṇa, which is the essence of loveliness and is not to be equaled or surpassed. That loveliness is the only abode of beauty, fame and opulence. It is self-perfect, ever fresh and extremely rare."

PURPORT

This text from *Śrīmad-Bhāgavatam* (10.44.14) was spoken by the women of Mathurā when they saw Kṛṣṇa and Balarāma in the arena with King Kaṁsa's great wrestlers Muṣṭika and Cāṇūra.

TEXT 157

অপূর্ব মাধুরী কৃষ্ণের, অপূর্ব তার বল ।
যাহার শ্রবণে মন হয় টলমল ॥ ১৫৭ ॥

apūrva mādhurī kṛṣṇera, apūrva tāra bala
yāhāra śravaṇe mana haya ṭalamala

apūrva—unprecedented; *mādhurī*—sweetness; *kṛṣṇera*—of Lord Kṛṣṇa; *apūrva*—unprecedented; *tāra*—of that; *bala*—the strength; *yāhāra*—of which; *śravaṇe*—in hearing; *mana*—the mind; *haya*—becomes; *ṭala-mala*—unsteady.

TRANSLATION

The sweetness of Lord Kṛṣṇa is unprecedented, and its strength is also unprecedented. Simply by one's hearing of such beauty, the mind becomes unsteady.

TEXT 158

কৃষ্ণের মাধুর্যে কৃষ্ণে উপজয় লোভ ।
সম্যক্ আস্বাদিতে নারে, মনে রহে ক্ষোভ ॥ ১৫৮ ॥

kṛṣṇera mādhurye kṛṣṇe upajaya lobha
samyak āsvādite nāre, mane rahe kṣobha

kṛṣṇera—of Lord Kṛṣṇa; *mādhurye*—in the sweetness; *kṛṣṇe*—in Lord Kṛṣṇa; *upajaya*—arises; *lobha*—eager desire; *samyak*—fully; *āsvādite*—to taste; *nāre*—is not able; *mane*—in the mind; *rahe*—remains; *kṣobha*—sorrow.

TRANSLATION

Lord Kṛṣṇa's own beauty attracts Lord Kṛṣṇa Himself. But because He cannot fully enjoy it, His mind remains full of sorrow.

TEXT 159

এই ত' দ্বিতীয় হেতুর কহিল বিবরণ ।
তৃতীয় হেতুর এবে শুনহ লক্ষণ ॥ ১৫৯ ॥

ei ta' dvitīya hetura kahila vivaraṇa
tṛtīya hetura ebe śunaha lakṣaṇa

ei—this; *ta'*—certainly; *dvitīya*—second; *hetura*—of the reason; *kahila*—has been said; *vivaraṇa*—description; *tṛtīya*—the third;

hetura—of the reason; *ebe*—now; *śunaha*—please hear; *lakṣaṇa*—the characteristic.

TRANSLATION

This is a description of His second desire. Now please listen as I describe the third.

TEXT 160

অত্যন্তনিগূঢ় এই রসের সিদ্ধান্ত ।
স্বরূপগোসাঞি মাত্র জানেন একান্ত ॥ ১৬০ ॥

atyanta-nigūḍha ei rasera siddhānta
svarūpa-gosāñi mātra jānena ekānta

atyanta—extremely; *nigūḍha*—deep; *ei*—this; *rasera*—of mellow; *siddhānta*—conclusion; *svarūpa-gosāñi*—Svarūpa Dāmodara Gosvāmī; *mātra*—only; *jānena*—knows; *ekānta*—much.

TRANSLATION

This conclusion of rasa is extremely deep. Only Svarūpa Dāmodara knows much about it.

TEXT 161

যেবা কেহ অন্য জানে, সেহো তাঁহা হৈতে ।
চৈতন্যগোসাঞির তেঁহ অত্যন্ত মর্ম যাতে ॥ ১৬১ ॥

yebā keha anya jāne, seho tāṅhā haite
caitanya-gosāñira teṅha atyanta marma yāte

yebā—whoever; *keha*—someone; *anya*—other; *jāne*—knows; *seho*—he; *tāṅhā haite*—from him (Svarūpa Dāmodara); *caitanya-gosāñira*—of Lord Caitanya Mahāprabhu; *teṅha*—he; *atyanta*—extremely; *marma*—secret core; *yāte*—since.

TRANSLATION

Anyone else who claims to know it must have heard it from him, for he was the most intimate companion of Lord Caitanya Mahāprabhu.

TEXT 162

গোপীগণের প্রেমের 'রূঢ়ভাব' নাম।
বিশুদ্ধ নির্মল প্রেম, কভু নহে কাম ॥ ১৬২ ॥

gopī-gaṇera premera 'rūḍha-bhāva' nāma
viśuddha nirmala prema, kabhu nahe kāma

gopī-gaṇera—of the *gopīs; premera*—of the love; *rūḍha-bhāva*—*rūḍha-bhāva; nāma*—named; *viśuddha*—pure; *nirmala*—spotless; *prema*—love; *kabhu*—at anytime; *nahe*—is not; *kāma*—lust.

TRANSLATION

The love of the gopīs is called rūḍha-bhāva. It is pure and spotless. It is not at any time lust.

PURPORT

As already explained, the position of the *gopīs* in their loving dealings with Kṛṣṇa is transcendental. Their emotion is called *rūḍha-bhāva.* Although it is apparently like mundane sex, one should not confuse it with mundane sexual love, for it is pure and unadulterated love of Godhead.

TEXT 163

'প্রেমৈব গোপরামাণাং কাম ইত্যগমৎ প্রথাম্।'
ইত্যুদ্ধবাদয়োঽপ্যেতং বাঞ্ছন্তি ভগবৎপ্রিয়াঃ ॥ ১৬৩ ॥

premaiva gopa-rāmāṇām
kāma ity agamat prathām
ity uddhavādayo 'py etaṁ
vāñchanti bhagavat-priyāḥ

prema—love; *eva*—only; *gopa-rāmāṇām*—of the women of Vraja; *kāmaḥ*—lust; *iti*—as; *agamat*—went to; *prathām*—fame; *iti*—thus; *uddhava-ādayaḥ*—headed by Śrī Uddhava; *api*—even; *etam*—this; *vāñchanti*—desire; *bhagavat-priyāḥ*—dear devotees of the Supreme Personality of Godhead.

TRANSLATION

"The pure love of the gopīs has become celebrated by the name 'lust.' The dear devotees of the Lord, headed by Śrī Uddhava, desire to taste that love."

PURPORT

This is a verse from the *Bhakti-rasāmṛta-sindhu* (1.2.285).

TEXT 164

কাম, প্রেম,—দোঁহাকার বিভিন্ন লক্ষণ।
লৌহ আর হেম যৈছে স্বরূপে বিলক্ষণ ॥ ১৬৪ ॥

kāma, prema,—doṅhākāra vibhinna lakṣaṇa
lauha āra hema yaiche svarūpe vilakṣaṇa

kāma—lust; *prema*—love; *doṅhākāra*—of the two; *vibhinna*—separate; *lakṣaṇa*—symptoms; *lauha*—iron; *āra*—and; *hema*—gold; *yaiche*—just as; *svarūpe*—in nature; *vilakṣaṇa*—different.

TRANSLATION

Lust and love have different characteristics, just as iron and gold have different natures.

PURPORT

One should try to discriminate between sexual love and pure love, for they belong to different categories, with a gulf of difference between them. They are as different from one another as iron is from gold.

TEXT 165

আত্মেন্দ্রিয়প্রীতি-বাঞ্ছা—তারে বলি, 'কাম'।
কৃষ্ণেন্দ্রিয়প্রীতি-ইচ্ছা ধরে 'প্রেম' নাম ॥ ১৬৫ ॥

ātmendriya-prīti-vāñchā—tāre bali 'kāma'
kṛṣṇendriya-prīti-icchā dhare 'prema' nāma

ātma-indriya-prīti—for the pleasure of one's own senses; *vāñchā*—desires; *tāre*—to that; *bali*—I say; *kāma*—lust; *kṛṣṇa-indriya-prīti*—for the pleasure of Lord Kṛṣṇa's senses; *icchā*—desire; *dhare*—holds; *prema*—love; *nāma*—the name.

TRANSLATION

The desire to gratify one's own senses is kāma [lust], but the desire to please the senses of Lord Kṛṣṇa is prema [love].

PURPORT

The revealed scriptures describe pure love as follows:

sarvathā dhvaṁsa-rahitaṁ saty api dhvaṁsa-kāraṇe
yad bhāva-bandhanaṁ yūnoḥ sa premā parikīrtitaḥ

"If there is ample reason for the dissolution of a conjugal relationship and yet such a dissolution does not take place, such a relationship of intimate love is called pure."

The predominated *gopīs* were bound to Kṛṣṇa in such pure love. For them there was no question of sexual love based on sense gratification. Their only engagement in life was to see Kṛṣṇa happy in all respects, regardless of their own personal interests. They dedicated their souls only for the satisfaction of the Personality of Godhead, Śrī Kṛṣṇa. There was not the slightest tinge of sexual love between the *gopīs* and Kṛṣṇa.

The author of *Śrī Caitanya-caritāmṛta* asserts with authority that sexual love is a matter of personal sense enjoyment. All the regulative principles in the *Vedas* pertaining to desires for popularity, fatherhood, wealth and so on are different phases of sense gratification. Acts of sense gratification may be performed under the cover of public welfare, nationalism, religion, altruism, ethical codes, Biblical codes, health directives, fruitive action, bashfulness, tolerance, personal comfort, liberation from material bondage, progress, family affection or fear of social ostracism or legal punishment, but all these categories are different subdivisions of one substance—sense gratification. All such good acts are performed basically for one's own sense gratification, for no one can sacrifice his personal interest while discharging these much-advertised moral and religious principles. But above all this is a transcendental stage in which one feels himself to be only an eternal servitor of Kṛṣṇa, the absolute Personality of Godhead. All acts performed in this sense of servitude are called pure love of God because they are performed for the absolute sense gratification of Śrī Kṛṣṇa. However, any act performed for the purpose of enjoying its fruits or results is an act of sense gratification. Such actions are visible sometimes in gross and sometimes in subtle forms.

TEXT 166

কামের তাৎপর্য—নিজসম্ভোগ কেবল ।
কৃষ্ণসুখতাৎপর্য-মাত্র প্রেম ত' প্রবল ॥ ১৬৬ ॥

kāmera tātparya—nija-sambhoga kevala
kṛṣṇa-sukha-tātparya-mātra prema ta' prabala

kāmera—of lust; *tātparya*—the intent; *nija*—own; *sambhoga*—enjoyment; *kevala*—only; *kṛṣṇa-sukha*—for Lord Kṛṣṇa's happiness; *tātparya*—the intent; *mātra*—only; *prema*—love; *ta'*—certainly; *prabala*—powerful.

TRANSLATION

The object of lust is only the enjoyment of one's own senses. But love caters to the enjoyment of Lord Kṛṣṇa, and thus it is very powerful.

TEXTS 167–169

লোকধর্ম, বেদধর্ম, দেহধর্ম, কর্ম ।
লজ্জা, ধৈর্য, দেহসুখ, আত্মসুখ-মর্ম ॥ ১৬৭ ॥
দুস্ত্যজ আর্যপথ, নিজ পরিজন ।
স্বজনে করয়ে যত তাড়ন-ভর্ৎসন ॥ ১৬৮ ॥
সর্বত্যাগ করি' করে কৃষ্ণের ভজন ।
কৃষ্ণসুখহেতু করে প্রেম-সেবন ॥ ১৬৯ ॥

loka-dharma, veda-dharma, deha-dharma, karma
lajjā, dhairya, deha-sukha, ātma-sukha-marma

dustyaja ārya-patha, nija parijana
sva-jane karaye yata tāḍana-bhartsana

sarva-tyāga kari' kare kṛṣṇera bhajana
kṛṣṇa-sukha-hetu kare prema-sevana

loka-dharma—customs of the people; *veda-dharma*—Vedic injunctions; *deha-dharma*—necessities of the body; *karma*—fruitive work; *lajjā*—bashfulness; *dhairya*—patience; *deha-sukha*—the happiness of the body; *ātma-sukha*—the happiness of the self; *marma*—the essence; *dustyaja*—difficult to give up; *ārya-patha*—the path of *varṇāśrama; nija*—own; *parijana*—family members; *sva-jane*—one's own family; *karaye*—do; *yata*—all; *tāḍana*—punishment; *bhartsana*—scolding; *sarva-tyāga kari'*—giving up everything; *kare*—do; *kṛṣṇera*—of Lord Kṛṣṇa; *bhajana*—worship; *kṛṣṇa-sukha-hetu*—for the purpose of Lord Kṛṣṇa's happiness; *kare*—do; *prema*—out of love; *sevana*—service.

TRANSLATION

Social customs, scriptural injunctions, bodily demands, fruitive action, shyness, patience, bodily pleasures, self-gratification and the path of varṇāśrama-dharma, which is difficult to give up—the gopīs have forsaken all these, as well as their own relatives and their punishment and scolding, for the sake of serving Lord Kṛṣṇa. They render loving service to Him for the sake of His enjoyment.

TEXT 170

ইহাকে কহিয়ে কৃষ্ণে দৃঢ় অনুরাগ ।
স্বচ্ছ ধৌতবস্ত্রে যৈছে নাহি কোন দাগ ॥ ১৭০ ॥

ihāke kahiye kṛṣṇe dṛḍha anurāga
svaccha dhauta-vastre yaiche nāhi kona dāga

ihāke—this; *kahiye*—I say; *kṛṣṇe*—in Lord Kṛṣṇa; *dṛḍha*—strong; *anurāga*—love; *svaccha*—pure; *dhauta*—clean; *vastre*—in cloth; *yaiche*—just as; *nāhi*—not; *kona*—some; *dāga*—mark.

TRANSLATION

That is called firm attachment to Lord Kṛṣṇa. It is spotlessly pure, like a clean cloth that has no stain.

PURPORT

The author of *Śrī Caitanya-caritāmṛta* advises everyone to give up all engagements of sense gratification and, like the *gopīs*, dovetail oneself entirely with the will of the Supreme Lord. That is the ultimate instruction of Kṛṣṇa in the *Bhagavad-gītā*. We should be prepared to do anything and everything to please the Lord, even at the risk of violating the Vedic principles or ethical laws. That is the standard of love of Godhead. Such activities in pure love of Godhead are as spotless as white linen that has been completely washed. Śrīla Bhaktivinoda Ṭhākura warns us in this connection that we should not mistakenly think that the idea of giving up everything implies the renunciation of duties necessary in relation to the body and mind. Even such duties are not sense gratification if they are undertaken in a spirit of service to Kṛṣṇa.

TEXT 171

অতএব কাম-প্রেমে বহুত অন্তর ।
কাম—অন্ধতমঃ, প্রেম—নির্মল ভাস্কর ॥ ১৭১ ॥

ataeva kāma-preme bahuta antara
kāma—andha-tamaḥ, prema—nirmala bhāskara

ataeva—therefore; *kāma-preme*—in lust and love; *bahuta*—much; *antara*—space between; *kāma*—lust; *andha-tamaḥ*—blind darkness; *prema*—love; *nirmala*—pure; *bhāskara*—sun.

TRANSLATION

Therefore lust and love are quite different. Lust is like dense darkness, but love is like the bright sun.

TEXT 172

অতএব গোপীগণের নাহি কামগন্ধ ।
কৃষ্ণসুখ লাগি মাত্র, কৃষ্ণ সে সম্বন্ধ ॥ ১৭২ ॥

ataeva gopī-gaṇera nāhi kāma-gandha
kṛṣṇa-sukha lāgi mātra, kṛṣṇa se sambandha

ataeva—therefore; *gopī-gaṇera*—of the *gopīs; nāhi*—not; *kāma-gandha*—the slightest bit of lust; *kṛṣṇa-sukha*—the happiness of Lord Kṛṣṇa; *lāgi*—for; *mātra*—only; *kṛṣṇa*—Lord Kṛṣṇa; *se*—that; *sambandha*—the relationship.

TRANSLATION

Thus there is not the slightest taint of lust in the gopīs' love. Their relationship with Kṛṣṇa is only for the sake of His enjoyment.

TEXT 173

যত্তে সুজাতচরণাম্বুরুহং স্তনেষু
ভীতাঃ শনৈঃ প্রিয় দধীমহি কর্কশেষু ।
তেনাটবীমটসি তদ্ব্যথতে ন কিং স্বিৎ
কূর্পাদিভির্ভ্রমতি ধীর্ভবদায়ুষাং নঃ ॥ ১৭৩ ॥

yat te sujāta-caraṇāmburuhaṁ staneṣu
bhītāḥ śanaiḥ priya dadhīmahi karkaśeṣu
tenāṭavīm aṭasi tad vyathate na kiṁ svit
kūrpādibhir bhramati dhīr bhavad-āyuṣāṁ naḥ

yat—which; *te*—Your; *sujāta*—very fine; *caraṇa-ambu-ruham*—lotus feet; *staneṣu*—on the breasts; *bhītāḥ*—being afraid; *śanaiḥ*—gently;

priya—O dear one; *dadhīmahi*—we place; *karkaśeṣu*—rough; *tena*—with them; *aṭavīm*—the path; *aṭasi*—You roam; *tat*—they; *vyathate*—are distressed; *na*—not; *kim svit*—we wonder; *kūrpa-ādibhiḥ*—by small stones and so on; *bhramati*—flutters; *dhīḥ*—the mind; *bhavat-āyuṣām*—of those of whom Your Lordship is the very life; *naḥ*—of us.

TRANSLATION

"O dearly beloved! Your lotus feet are so soft that we place them gently on our breasts, fearing that Your feet will be hurt. Our life rests only in You. Our minds, therefore, are filled with anxiety that Your tender feet might be wounded by pebbles as You roam about on the forest path."

PURPORT

This text from *Śrīmad-Bhāgavatam* (10.31.19) was spoken by the *gopīs* when Kṛṣṇa left them in the midst of the *rāsa-līlā.*

TEXT 174

আত্ম-সুখ-দুঃখে গোপীর নাহিক বিচার ।
কৃষ্ণসুখহেতু চেষ্টা মনোব্যবহার ॥ ১৭৪ ॥

ātma-sukha-duḥkhe gopīra nāhika vicāra
kṛṣṇa-sukha-hetu ceṣṭā mano-vyavahāra

ātma-sukha-duḥkhe—in personal happiness or distress; *gopīra*—of the *gopīs; nāhika*—not; *vicāra*—consideration; *kṛṣṇa-sukha-hetu*—for the purpose of Lord Kṛṣṇa's happiness; *ceṣṭā*—activity; *manaḥ*—of the mind; *vyavahāra*—the business.

TRANSLATION

The gopīs do not care for their own pleasures or pains. All their physical and mental activities are directed toward offering enjoyment to Lord Kṛṣṇa.

TEXT 175

কৃষ্ণ লাগি' আর সব করে পরিত্যাগ ।
কৃষ্ণসুখহেতু করে শুদ্ধ অনুরাগ ॥ ১৭৫ ॥

kṛṣṇa lāgi' āra saba kare parityāga
kṛṣṇa-sukha-hetu kare śuddha anurāga

kṛṣṇa lāgi'—for Lord Kṛṣṇa; *āra*—other; *saba*—all; *kare*—do; *parityāga*—give up; *kṛṣṇa-sukha-hetu*—for the purpose of Lord Kṛṣṇa's happiness; *kare*—do; *śuddha*—pure; *anurāga*—attachments.

TRANSLATION

They renounced everything for Kṛṣṇa. They have pure attachment to giving Kṛṣṇa pleasure.

TEXT 176

এবং মদর্থোজ্‌ঝিতলোকবেদ-
স্বানাং হি বো ময্যনুবৃত্তয়েঽবলাঃ ।
ময়া পরোক্ষং ভজতা তিরোহিতং
মাসূয়িতুং মার্হথ তৎ প্রিয়ং প্রিয়াঃ ॥ ১৭৬ ॥

evaṁ mad-arthojjhita-loka-veda-
svānāṁ hi vo mayy anuvṛttaye 'balāḥ
mayā parokṣaṁ bhajatā tirohitaṁ
māsūyituṁ mārhatha tat priyaṁ priyāḥ

evam—thus; *mat-artha*—for Me; *ujjhita*—rejected; *loka*—popular customs; *veda*—Vedic injunctions; *svānām*—own families; *hi*—certainly; *vaḥ*—of you; *mayi*—Me; *anuvṛttaye*—to increase regard for; *abalāḥ*—O women; *mayā*—by Me; *parokṣam*—invisible; *bhajatā*—favoring; *tirohitam*—withdrawn from sight; *mā*—Me; *asūyitum*—to be displeased with; *mā arhatha*—you do not deserve; *tat*—therefore; *priyam*—who is dear; *priyāḥ*—O dear ones.

TRANSLATION

"O My beloved gopīs, you have renounced social customs, scriptural injunctions and your relatives for My sake. I disappeared behind you only to increase your concentration upon Me. Since I disappeared for your benefit, you should not be displeased with Me."

PURPORT

This text from *Śrīmad-Bhāgavatam* (10.32.21) was spoken by Lord Kṛṣṇa when He returned to the arena of the *rāsa-līlā*.

TEXT 177

কৃষ্ণের প্রতিজ্ঞা এক আছে পূর্ব হৈতে ।
যে যৈছে ভজে, কৃষ্ণ তারে ভজে তৈছে ॥ ১৭৭ ॥

kṛṣṇera pratijñā eka āche pūrva haite
ye yaiche bhaje, kṛṣṇa tāre bhaje taiche

kṛṣṇera—of Lord Kṛṣṇa; *pratijñā*—promise; *eka*—one; *āche*—there is; *pūrva haite*—from before; *ye*—whoever; *yaiche*—just as; *bhaje*—he worships; *kṛṣṇa*—Lord Kṛṣṇa; *tāre*—to him; *bhaje*—reciprocates; *taiche*—just so.

TRANSLATION

Lord Kṛṣṇa has a promise from before to reciprocate with His devotees according to the way they worship Him.

TEXT 178

যে যথা মাং প্রপদ্যন্তে তাংস্তথৈব ভজাম্যহম্ ।
মম বর্ত্মানুবর্তন্তে মনুষ্যাঃ পার্থ সর্বশঃ ॥ ১৭৮ ॥

ye yathā māṁ prapadyante
tāṁs tathaiva bhajāmy aham
mama vartmānuvartante
manuṣyāḥ pārtha sarvaśaḥ

ye—those who; *yathā*—as; *mām*—to Me; *prapadyante*—surrender; *tān*—them; *tathā*—so; *eva*—certainly; *bhajāmi*—reward; *aham*—I; *mama*—My; *vartma*—path; *anuvartante*—follow; *manuṣyāḥ*—men; *pārtha*—O son of Pṛthā; *sarvaśaḥ*—in all respects.

TRANSLATION

"In whatever way My devotees surrender unto Me, I reward them accordingly. Everyone follows My path in all respects, O son of Pṛthā."

PURPORT

Kṛṣṇa was never ungrateful to the *gopīs*, for as He declares to Arjuna in this verse from the *Bhagavad-gītā* (4.11), He reciprocates with His devotees in proportion to the transcendental loving service they render unto Him. Everyone follows the path that leads toward Him, but there are different degrees of progress on that path, and the Lord is realized in proportion to one's advancement. The path is one, but the progress in approaching the ultimate goal is different, and therefore the proportion of realization of this goal—namely the absolute Personality of Godhead—is also different. The *gopīs* attained the highest goal, and Lord Caitanya affirmed that there is no method of worshiping God higher than that followed by the *gopīs.*

TEXT 179

সে প্রতিজ্ঞা ভঙ্গ হৈল গোপীর ভজনে।
তাহাতে প্রমাণ কৃষ্ণ-শ্রীমুখবচনে ॥ ১৭৯ ॥

se pratijñā bhaṅga haila gopīra bhajane
tāhāte pramāṇa kṛṣṇa-śrī-mukha-vacane

se—that; *pratijñā*—promise; *bhaṅga haila*—was broken; *gopīra*—of the *gopīs; bhajane*—by the worship; *tāhāte*—in that; *pramāṇa*—the proof; *kṛṣṇa*—of Lord Kṛṣṇa; *śrī-mukha-vacane*—by the words from the mouth.

TRANSLATION

That promise has been broken by the worship of the gopīs, as Lord Kṛṣṇa Himself admits.

TEXT 180

ন পারয়েহহং নিরবদ্যসংযুজাং
স্বসাধুকৃত্যং বিবুধায়ুষাপি বঃ।
যা মাহভজন্ দুর্জয়গেহশৃঙ্খলাঃ
সংবৃশ্চ্য তদ্বঃ প্রতিযাতু সাধুনা ॥ ১৮০ ॥

na pāraye 'haṁ niravadya-saṁyujāṁ
sva-sādhu-kṛtyaṁ vibudhāyuṣāpi vaḥ
yā mābhajan durjaya-geha-śṛṅkhalāḥ
saṁvṛścya tad vaḥ pratiyātu sādhunā

na—not; *pāraye*—am able to make; *aham*—I; *niravadya-saṁyujām*—to those who are completely free from deceit; *sva-sādhu-kṛtyam*—

proper compensation; *vibudha-āyuṣā*—with a lifetime as long as that of the demigods; *api*—although; *vaḥ*—to you; *yāḥ*—who; *mā*—Me; *abhajan*—have worshiped; *durjaya-geha-śṛṅkhalāḥ*—the chains of household life, which are difficult to overcome; *saṁvṛścya*—cutting; *tat*—that; *vaḥ*—of you; *pratiyātu*—let it be returned; *sādhunā*—by the good activity itself.

TRANSLATION

"O gopīs, I am not able to repay My debt for your spotless service, even within a lifetime of Brahmā. Your connection with Me is beyond reproach. You have worshiped Me, cutting off all domestic ties, which are difficult to break. Therefore please let your own glorious deeds be your compensation."

PURPORT

This verse from *Śrīmad-Bhāgavatam* (10.32.22) was spoken by Śrī Kṛṣṇa Himself when He returned to the *gopīs* upon hearing their songs of separation.

TEXT 181

তবে যে দেখিয়ে গোপীর নিজদেহে প্রীত ।
সেহো ত' কৃষ্ণের লাগি, জানিহ নিশ্চিত ॥ ১৮১ ॥

tabe ye dekhiye gopīra nija-dehe prīta
seho ta' kṛṣṇera lāgi, jāniha niścita

tabe—now; *ye*—whatever; *dekhiye*—we see; *gopīra*—of the *gopīs; nija-dehe*—for their own bodies; *prīta*—affection; *seho*—that; *ta'*—certainly; *kṛṣṇera lāgi*—for Lord Kṛṣṇa; *jāniha*—know; *niścita*—for certain.

TRANSLATION

Now, whatever affection we see the gopīs show for their own bodies, know it for certain to be only for the sake of Lord Kṛṣṇa.

PURPORT

The selfless love of Godhead exhibited by the *gopīs* cannot have any parallel. We should not, therefore, misunderstand the carefulness of the *gopīs* in their personal decoration. The *gopīs* dressed themselves as beautifully as possible just to make Kṛṣṇa happy by seeing them. They had no ulterior desires. They dedicated their bodies, and everything they possessed, to the service of Śrī Kṛṣṇa, taking it for granted that their bodies were meant for His enjoyment. They dressed themselves with the understanding that Kṛṣṇa would be happy by seeing and touching them.

TEXT 182

'এই দেহ কৈলুঁ আমি কৃষ্ণে সমর্পণ ।
তাঁর ধন তাঁর ইহা সম্ভোগ-সাধন ॥ ১৮২ ॥

'ei deha kailuṅ āmi kṛṣṇe samarpaṇa
tāṅra dhana tāṅra ihā sambhoga-sādhana

ei—this; *deha*—body; *kailuṅ*—have done; *āmi*—I; *kṛṣṇe*—to Lord Kṛṣṇa; *samarpaṇa*—offering; *tāṅra*—of Him; *dhana*—the wealth; *tāṅra*—of Him; *ihā*—this; *sambhoga-sādhana*—brings about the enjoyment.

TRANSLATION

[The gopīs think:] "I have offered this body to Lord Kṛṣṇa. He is its owner, and it brings Him enjoyment.

TEXT 183

এদেহ-দর্শন-স্পর্শে কৃষ্ণ-সন্তোষণ' ।
এই লাগি' করে দেহের মার্জন-ভূষণ ॥ ১৮৩ ॥

e-deha-darśana-sparśe kṛṣṇa-santoṣaṇa'
ei lāgi' kare dehera mārjana-bhūṣaṇa

e-deha—of this body; *darśana*—by sight; *sparśe*—and touch; *kṛṣṇa*—of Lord Kṛṣṇa; *santoṣaṇa*—the satisfaction; *ei lāgi'*—for this; *kare*—they do; *dehera*—of the body; *mārjana*—cleaning; *bhūṣaṇa*—decorating.

TRANSLATION

"Kṛṣṇa finds joy in seeing and touching this body." It is for this reason that they cleanse and decorate their bodies.

TEXT 184

নিজাঙ্গমপি যা গোপ্যো মমেতি সমুপাসতে ।
তাভ্যঃ পরং ন মে পার্থ নিগূঢ়প্রেমভাজনম্ ॥ ১৮৪ ॥

nijāṅgam api yā gopyo
mameti samupāsate
tābhyaḥ paraṁ na me pārtha
nigūḍha-prema-bhājanam

nija-aṅgam—own body; *api*—although; *yāḥ*—who; *gopyaḥ*—the *gopīs; mama*—Mine; *iti*—thus thinking; *samupāsate*—engage in decorating; *tābhyaḥ*—than them; *param*—greater; *na*—not; *me*—for Me; *pārtha*—O Arjuna; *nigūḍha-prema*—of deep love; *bhājanam*—receptacles.

TRANSLATION

"O Arjuna, there are no greater receptacles of deep love for Me than the gopīs, who cleanse and decorate their bodies because they consider them Mine."

PURPORT

This verse is spoken by Lord Kṛṣṇa in the *Ādi Purāṇa.*

TEXT 185

আর এক অদ্ভুত গোপীভাবের স্বভাব ।
বুদ্ধির গোচর নহে যাহার প্রভাব ॥ ১৮৫ ॥

āra eka adbhuta gopī-bhāvera svabhāva
buddhira gocara nahe yāhāra prabhāva

āra—another; *eka*—one; *adbhuta*—wonderful; *gopī-bhāvera*—of the emotion of the *gopīs; svabhāva*—nature; *buddhira*—of the intelligence; *gocara*—an object of perception; *nahe*—is not; *yāhāra*—of which; *prabhāva*—the power.

TRANSLATION

There is another wonderful feature of the emotion of the gopīs. Its power is beyond the comprehension of the intelligence.

TEXT 186

গোপীগণ করে যবে কৃষ্ণ-দরশন ।
সুখবাঞ্ছা নাহি, সুখ হয় কোটিগুণ ॥ ১৮৬ ॥

gopī-gaṇa kare yabe kṛṣṇa-daraśana
sukha-vāñchā nāhi, sukha haya koṭi-guṇa

gopī-gaṇa—the *gopīs; kare*—do; *yabe*—when; *kṛṣṇa-daraśana*—seeing Lord Kṛṣṇa; *sukha-vāñchā*—desire for happiness; *nāhi*—there is not; *sukha*—the happiness; *haya*—there is; *koṭi-guṇa*—ten million times.

TRANSLATION

When the gopīs see Lord Kṛṣṇa, they derive unbounded bliss, although they have no desire for such pleasure.

TEXT 187

গোপিকা-দর্শনে কৃষ্ণের যে আনন্দ হয় ।
তাহা হৈতে কোটিগুণ গোপী আস্বাদয় ॥ ১৮৭ ॥

gopikā-darśane kṛṣṇera ye ānanda haya
tāhā haite koṭi-guṇa gopī āsvādaya

gopikā-darśane—in seeing the *gopīs; kṛṣṇera*—of Lord Kṛṣṇa; *ye*—whatever; *ānanda*—joy; *haya*—there is; *tāhā haite*—than that; *koṭi-guṇa*—ten million times more; *gopī*—the *gopīs; āsvādaya*—taste.

TRANSLATION

The gopīs taste a pleasure ten million times greater than the pleasure Lord Kṛṣṇa derives from seeing them.

PURPORT

The wonderful characteristics of the *gopīs* are beyond imagination. They have no desire for personal satisfaction, yet when Kṛṣṇa is happy by seeing them, that happiness of Kṛṣṇa makes the *gopīs* a million times more happy than Kṛṣṇa Himself.

TEXT 188

তাঁ সবার নাহি নিজসুখ-অনুরোধ ।
তথাপি বাঢ়য়ে সুখ, পড়িল বিরোধ ॥ ১৮৮ ॥

tāṅ sabāra nāhi nija-sukha-anurodha
tathāpi bāḍhaye sukha, paḍila virodha

tāṅ sabāra—of all of them; *nāhi*—not; *nija-sukha*—for their own happiness; *anurodha*—entreaty; *tathāpi*—still; *bāḍhaye*—increases; *sukha*—happiness; *paḍila*—happened; *virodha*—contradiction.

TRANSLATION

The gopīs have no inclination for their own enjoyment, and yet their joy increases. That is indeed a contradiction.

TEXT 189

এ বিরোধের এক মাত্র দেখি সমাধান ।
গোপিকার সুখ কৃষ্ণসুখে পর্যবসান ॥ ১৮৯ ॥

e virodhera eka mātra dekhi samādhāna
gopikāra sukha kṛṣṇa-sukhe paryavasāna

e—this; *virodhera*—of the contradiction; *eka*—one; *mātra*—only; *dekhi*—I see; *samādhāna*—solution; *gopikāra*—of the *gopīs; sukha*—the happiness; *kṛṣṇa-sukhe*—in the happiness of Lord Kṛṣṇa; *paryavasāna*—the conclusion.

TRANSLATION

For this contradiction I see only one solution: the joy of the gopīs lies in the joy of their beloved Kṛṣṇa.

PURPORT

The situation of the *gopīs* is perplexing, for although they did not want personal happiness, it was imposed upon them. The solution to this perplexity is that Śrī Kṛṣṇa's sense of happiness is limited by the happiness of the *gopīs.* Devotees at Vṛndāvana therefore try to serve the *gopīs,* namely Rādhārāṇī and Her associates. If one gains the favor of the *gopīs,* he easily gains the favor of Kṛṣṇa because on the recommendation of the *gopīs* Kṛṣṇa at once accepts the service of a devotee. Lord Caitanya, therefore, wanted to please the *gopīs* instead of Kṛṣṇa. But His contemporaries misunderstood Him, and for this reason Lord Caitanya renounced the order of householder life and became a *sannyāsī.*

TEXT 190

গোপিকা-দর্শনে কৃষ্ণের বাঢ়ে প্রফুল্লতা ।
সে মাধুর্য বাঢ়ে যার নাহিক সমতা ॥ ১৯০ ॥

gopikā-darśane kṛṣṇera bāḍhe praphullatā
se mādhurya bāḍhe yāra nāhika samatā

gopikā-darśane—in seeing the *gopīs; kṛṣṇera*—of Lord Kṛṣṇa; *bāḍhe*—increases; *praphullatā*—the cheerfulness; *se*—that; *mādhurya*—sweetness; *bāḍhe*—increases; *yāra*—of which; *nāhika*—there is not; *samatā*—equality.

TRANSLATION

When Lord Kṛṣṇa sees the gopīs, His joy increases, and His unparalleled sweetness increases also.

TEXT 191

আমার দর্শনে কৃষ্ণ পাইল এত সুখ ।
এই সুখে গোপীর প্রফুল্ল অঙ্গমুখ ॥ ১৯১ ॥

āmāra darśane kṛṣṇa pāila eta sukha
ei sukhe gopīra praphulla aṅga-mukha

āmāra darśane—in seeing me; *kṛṣṇa*—Lord Kṛṣṇa; *pāila*—obtained; *eta*—so much; *sukha*—happiness; *ei*—this; *sukhe*—in happiness; *gopīra*—of the *gopīs; praphulla*—full-blown; *aṅga-mukha*—bodies and faces.

TRANSLATION

[The gopīs think:] "Kṛṣṇa has obtained so much pleasure by seeing me." That thought increases the fullness and beauty of their faces and bodies.

TEXT 192

গোপী-শোভা দেখি' কৃষ্ণের শোভা বাঢ়ে যত ।
কৃষ্ণ-শোভা দেখি' গোপীর শোভা বাঢ়ে তত ॥ ১৯২ ॥

gopī-śobhā dekhi' kṛṣṇera śobhā bāḍhe yata
kṛṣṇa-śobhā dekhi' gopīra śobhā bāḍhe tata

gopī-śobhā—the beauty of the *gopīs; dekhi'*—seeing; *kṛṣṇera*—of Lord Kṛṣṇa; *śobhā*—the beauty; *bāḍhe*—increases; *yata*—as much as; *kṛṣṇa-śobhā*—the beauty of Lord Kṛṣṇa; *dekhi'*—seeing; *gopīra*—of the *gopīs; śobhā*—the beauty; *bāḍhe*—increases; *tata*—that much.

TRANSLATION

The beauty of Lord Kṛṣṇa increases at the sight of the beauty of the gopīs. And the more the gopīs see Lord Kṛṣṇa's beauty, the more their beauty increases.

TEXT 193

এইমত পরস্পর পড়ে হুড়াহুড়ি ।
পরস্পর বাড়ে, কেহ মুখ নাহি মুড়ি ॥ ১৯৩ ॥

ei-mata paraspara paḍe huḍāhuḍi
paraspara bāḍhe, keha mukha nāhi muḍi

ei mata—like this; *paraspara*—reciprocal; *paḍe*—happens; *huḍā-huḍi*—jostling; *paraspara*—mutually; *bāḍhe*—increases; *keha*—someone; *mukha*—face; *nāhi*—not; *muḍi*—covering.

TRANSLATION

In this way a competition takes place between them in which no one acknowledges defeat.

TEXT 194

কিন্তু কৃষ্ণের সুখ হয় গোপী-রূপ-গুণে ।
তাঁর সুখে সুখবৃদ্ধি হয়ে গোপীগণে ॥ ১৯৪ ॥

kintu kṛṣṇera sukha haya gopī-rūpa-guṇe
tāṅra sukhe sukha-vṛddhi haye gopī-gaṇe

kintu—but; *kṛṣṇera*—of Lord Kṛṣṇa; *sukha*—the happiness; *haya*—is; *gopī-rūpa-guṇe*—in the qualities and beauty of the *gopīs; tāṅra*—of Him; *sukhe*—in the happiness; *sukha-vṛddhi*—increase of happiness; *haye*—there is; *gopī-gaṇe*—in the *gopīs*.

TRANSLATION

Kṛṣṇa, however, derives pleasure from the beauty and good qualities of the gopīs. And when the gopīs see His pleasure, the joy of the gopīs increases.

TEXT 195

অতএব সেই সুখ কৃষ্ণ-সুখ পোষে ।
এই হেতু গোপী-প্রেমে নাহি কাম-দোষে ॥ ১৯৫ ॥

ataeva sei sukha kṛṣṇa-sukha poṣe
ei hetu gopī-preme nāhi kāma-doṣe

ataeva—therefore; *sei*—that; *sukha*—happiness; *kṛṣṇa-sukha*—the happiness of Lord Kṛṣṇa; *poṣe*—nourishes; *ei*—this; *hetu*—reason; *gopī-preme*—in the love of the *gopīs; nāhi*—there is not; *kāma-doṣe*—the fault of lust.

TRANSLATION

Therefore we find that the joy of the gopīs nourishes the joy of Lord Kṛṣṇa. For that reason the fault of lust is not present in their love.

PURPORT

By looking at the beautiful *gopīs* Kṛṣṇa becomes enlivened, and this enlivens the *gopīs,* whose youthful faces and bodies blossom. This competition of increasing beauty between the *gopīs* and Kṛṣṇa, which is without limitations, is so delicate that sometimes mundane moralists mistake these dealings to be purely amorous. But these affairs are not at all mundane, because the *gopīs'* intense desire to satisfy Kṛṣṇa surcharges the entire scene with pure love of Godhead, with not a spot of sexual indulgence.

TEXT 196

উপেত্য পথি সুন্দরীততিভিরাভিরভ্যর্চিতং
স্মিতাঙ্কুরকরম্বিতৈর্নটদপাঙ্গভঙ্গীশতৈঃ ।
স্তন-স্তবকসঞ্চরন্নয়নচঞ্চরীকাঞ্চলং
ব্রজে বিজয়িনং ভজে বিপিনদেশতঃ কেশবম্ ॥ ১৯৬ ॥

upetya pathi sundarī-tatibhir ābhir abhyarcitaṁ
smitāṅkura-karambitair naṭad-apāṅga-bhaṅgī-śataiḥ
stana-stavaka-sañcaran-nayana-cañcarīkāñcalaṁ
vraje vijayinaṁ bhaje vipina-deśataḥ keśavam

upetya—having mounted their palaces; *pathi*—on the path; *sundarī-tatibhiḥ ābhiḥ*—by the women of Vraja; *abhyarcitam*—who is worshiped; *smita-aṅkura-karambitaiḥ*—intermingled with the sprouts of gentle smiles; *naṭat*—dancing; *apāṅga*—of glances; *bhaṅgī-śataiḥ*—with a hundred manners; *stana-stavaka*—the multitude of breasts; *sañcarat*—wandering about; *nayana*—of the two eyes; *cañcarīka*—like bees; *añcalam*—Him whose corners; *vraje*—in Vraja; *vijayinam*—coming; *bhaje*—I worship; *vipina-deśataḥ*—from the forest; *keśavam*—Lord Keśava.

TRANSLATION

"I worship Lord Keśava. Coming back from the forest of Vraja, He is worshiped by the gopīs, who mount the roofs of their palaces and meet Him on the path with a hundred manners of dancing glances and gentle smiles. The corners of His eyes wander, like large black bees, around the gopīs' breasts."

PURPORT

This statement appears in the *Keśavāṣṭaka* (8) of the *Stava-mālā*, compiled by Śrīla Rūpa Gosvāmī.

TEXT 197

আর এক গোপীপ্রেমের স্বাভাবিক চিহ্ন ।
যে প্রকারে হয় প্রেম কামগন্ধহীন ॥ ১৯৭ ॥

āra eka gopī-premera svābhāvika cihna
ye prakāre haya prema kāma-gandha-hīna

āra—another; *eka*—one; *gopī-premera*—of the love of the *gopīs; svābhāvika*—natural; *cihna*—symptom; *ye*—which; *prakāre*—in the way; *haya*—is; *prema*—the love; *kāma-gandha-hīna*—without a trace of lust.

TRANSLATION

There is another natural symptom of the gopīs' love that shows it to be without a trace of lust.

TEXT 198

গোপীপ্রেমে করে কৃষ্ণমাধুর্যের পুষ্টি ।
মাধুর্যে বাঢ়ায় প্রেম হঞা মহাতুষ্টি ॥ ১৯৮ ॥

gopī-preme kare kṛṣṇa-mādhuryera puṣṭi
mādhurye bāḍhāya prema hañā mahā-tuṣṭi

gopī-preme—the love of the *gopīs; kare*—does; *kṛṣṇa-mādhuryera*—of the sweetness of Lord Kṛṣṇa; *puṣṭi*—nourishment; *mādhurye*—the sweetness; *bāḍhāya*—causes to increase; *prema*—the love; *hañā*—being; *mahā-tuṣṭi*—greatly pleased.

TRANSLATION

The love of the gopīs nourishes the sweetness of Lord Kṛṣṇa. That sweetness in turn increases their love, for they are greatly satisfied.

TEXT 199

প্রীতিবিষয়ানন্দে তদাশ্রয়ানন্দ ।
তাঁহা নাহি নিজসুখবাঞ্ছার সম্বন্ধ ॥ ১৯৯ ॥

prīti-viṣayānande tad-āśrayānanda
tāṅhā nāhi nija-sukha-vāñchāra sambandha

prīti-viṣaya-ānande—in the joy of the object of love; *tat*—of that love; *āśraya-ānanda*—the joy of the abode; *tāṅhā*—that; *nāhi*—not; *nija-sukha-vāñchāra*—of desire for one's own happiness; *sambandha*—relationship.

TRANSLATION

The happiness of the abode of love is in the happiness of the object of that love. This is not a relationship of desire for personal gratification.

TEXTS 200–201

নিরুপাধি প্রেম যাঁহা, তাঁহা এই রীতি ।
প্রীতিবিষয়সুখে আশ্রয়ের প্রীতি ॥ ২০০ ॥
নিজ প্রেমানন্দে কৃষ্ণ-সেবানন্দ বাধে ।
সে আনন্দের প্রতি ভক্তের হয় মহাক্রোধে ॥ ২০১ ॥

nirupādhi prema yāṅhā, tāṅhā ei rīti
prīti-viṣaya-sukhe āśrayera prīti

nija-premānande kṛṣṇa-sevānanda bādhe
se ānandera prati bhaktera haya mahā-krodhe

nirupādhi—without identification; *prema*—love; *yāṅhā*—which; *tāṅhā*—that; *ei*—this; *rīti*—style; *prīti-viṣaya*—of the object of love; *sukhe*—in the happiness; *āśrayera*—of the abode of that love; *prīti*—the pleasure; *nija*—one's own; *prema*—of love; *ānande*—by the joy; *kṛṣṇa*—to Lord Kṛṣṇa; *seva-ānanda*—the joy of service; *bādhe*—is obstructed; *se*—that; *ānandera prati*—toward the joy; *bhaktera*—of the devotee; *haya*—is; *mahā-krodhe*—great anger.

TRANSLATION

Whenever there is unselfish love, that is its style. The reservoir of love derives pleasure when the lovable object is pleased. When the pleasure of love interferes with the service of Lord Kṛṣṇa, the devotee becomes angry toward such ecstasy.

PURPORT

As mentioned above, the *gopīs* are the predominated lovers, and Śrī Kṛṣṇa is the predominator, the beloved. The love of the predominated nourishes the love of the predominator. The *gopīs* had no desire for selfish enjoyment. Their feeling of happiness was indirect, for it was dependent on the pleasure of Kṛṣṇa. Causeless love of Godhead is always so. Such pure love is possible only when the predominated is made happy by the happiness of the predominator. Such unadulterated love is exemplified when the lover deprecates her happiness in service that hinders her from discharging it.

TEXT 202

অঙ্গস্তম্ভারম্ভমুত্তুঙ্গয়ন্তং প্রেমানন্দং দারুকো নাভ্যনন্দৎ ।
কংসারাতের্বীজনে যেন সাক্ষাদক্ষোদীয়ানন্তরায়ো ব্যধায়ি ॥ ২০২ ॥

aṅga-stambhārambham uttuṅgayantaṁ
premānandaṁ dāruko nābhyanandat
kaṁsārāter vījane yena sākṣād
akṣodīyān antarāyo vyadhāyi

aṅga—of the limbs; *stambha-ārambham*—the beginning of stupefaction; *uttuṅgayantam*—which was causing him to reach; *prema-ānandam*—the joy of love; *dārukaḥ*—Dāruka, the Lord's chariot driver; *na*—not; *abhyanandat*—welcomed; *kaṁsa-arāteḥ*—of Lord Kṛṣṇa, the enemy of Kaṁsa; *vījane*—in fanning with a *cāmara* fan; *yena*—by which; *sākṣāt*—clearly; *akṣodīyān*—greater; *antarāyaḥ*—obstacle; *vyadhāyi*—has been created.

TRANSLATION

"Śrī Dāruka did not relish his ecstatic feelings of love, for they caused his limbs to become stunned and thus obstructed his service of fanning Lord Kṛṣṇa."

PURPORT

This verse is from the *Bhakti-rasāmṛta-sindhu* (3.2.62).

TEXT 203

গোবিন্দপ্রেক্ষণাক্ষেপি-বাষ্পপূরাভিবর্ষিণম্ ।
উচ্চৈরনিন্দদানন্দমরবিন্দবিলোচনা ॥ ২০৩ ॥

govinda-prekṣaṇākṣepi-
bāṣpa-pūrābhivarṣiṇam
uccair anindad ānandam
aravinda-vilocanā

govinda—of Lord Govinda; *prekṣaṇa*—the seeing; *ākṣepi*—hindering; *bāṣpa-pūra*—groups of tears; *abhivarṣiṇam*—which cause to rain;

uccaiḥ—powerfully; *anindat*—condemned; *ānandam*—the bliss; *aravinda-vilocanā*—the lotus-eyed Rādhārāṇī.

TRANSLATION

"The lotus-eyed Rādhārāṇī powerfully condemned the ecstatic love that caused a flow of tears that hindered Her sight of Govinda."

PURPORT

This verse is also from the *Bhakti-rasāmṛta-sindhu* (2.3.54).

TEXT 204

আর শুদ্ধভক্ত কৃষ্ণ-প্রেম-সেবা বিনে ।
স্বসুখার্থ সালোক্যাদি না করে গ্রহণে ॥ ২০৪ ॥

āra śuddha-bhakta kṛṣṇa-prema-sevā vine
sva-sukhārtha sālokyādi nā kare grahaṇe

āra—and; *śuddha-bhakta*—the pure devotee; *kṛṣṇa-prema*—out of love for Lord Kṛṣṇa; *sevā*—service; *vine*—without; *sva-sukha-artha*—for the purpose of one's own pleasure; *sālokya-ādi*—the five types of liberation, beginning from *sālokya* (residing on the same spiritual planet as the Lord); *nā kare*—do not do; *grahaṇe*—acceptance.

TRANSLATION

Furthermore, pure devotees never forsake the loving service of Lord Kṛṣṇa to aspire for their own personal pleasure through the five kinds of liberation.

PURPORT

A pure devotee of Kṛṣṇa who loves Him exclusively will flatly refuse to accept any sort of liberation, beginning from merging with the body of the Lord and extending to the other varieties of liberation, such as equality of form, opulence or abode and the opulence of living near the Lord.

TEXT 205

মদ্‌গুণশ্রুতিমাত্রেণ ময়ি সর্বগুহাশয়ে ।
মনোগতিরবিচ্ছিন্না যথা গঙ্গাম্ভসোঽম্বুধৌ ॥ ২০৫ ॥

mad-guṇa-śruti-mātreṇa
mayi sarva-guhāśaye
mano-gatir avicchinnā
yathā gaṅgāmbhaso 'mbudhau

mat—of Me; *guṇa*—of the qualities; *śruti-mātreṇa*—only by hearing; *mayi*—to Me; *sarva-guhā*—in all hearts; *āśaye*—who am situated; *manaḥ-gatiḥ*—the movement of the mind; *avicchinnā*—unobstructed; *yathā*—just as; *gaṅgā-ambhasaḥ*—of the celestial waters of the Ganges; *ambudhau*—to the ocean.

TRANSLATION

"Just as the celestial waters of the Ganges flow unobstructed into the ocean, so when My devotees simply hear of Me, their minds come to Me, who reside in the hearts of all.

TEXT 206

লক্ষণং ভক্তিযোগস্য নির্গুণস্য হ্যুদাহৃতম্ ।
অহৈতুক্যব্যবহিতা যা ভক্তিঃ পুরুষোত্তমে ॥ ২০৬ ॥

lakṣaṇaṁ bhakti-yogasya
nirguṇasya hy udāhṛtam
ahaituky avyavahitā
yā bhaktiḥ puruṣottame

lakṣaṇam—the symptom; *bhakti-yogasya*—of devotional service; *nir-guṇasya*—beyond the three modes of nature; *hi*—certainly; *udāhṛtam*—is cited; *ahaitukī*—causeless; *avyavahitā*—uninterrupted; *yā*—which; *bhaktiḥ*—devotional service; *puruṣottame*—to the Supreme Personality of Godhead.

TRANSLATION

"These are the characteristics of transcendental loving service to Puruṣottama, the Supreme Personality of Godhead: it is causeless, and it cannot be obstructed in any way.

TEXT 207

সালোক্য-সার্ষ্টি-সারূপ্য-সামীপ্যৈকত্বমপ্যুত ।
দীয়মানং ন গৃহ্নন্তি বিনা মৎসেবনং জনাঃ ॥ ২০৭ ॥

sālokya-sārṣṭi-sārūpya-
sāmīpyaikatvam apy uta
dīyamānaṁ na gṛhṇanti
vinā mat-sevanaṁ janāḥ

sālokya—being on the same planet as Me; *sārṣṭi*—having opulence equal to Mine; *sārūpya*—having the same form as Me; *sāmīpya*—having direct association with Me; *ekatvam*—oneness with Me; *api*—even; *uta*—or; *dīyamānam*—being given; *na*—not; *gṛhṇanti*—accept; *vinā*—without; *mat-sevanam*—My service; *janāḥ*—the devotees.

TRANSLATION

"My devotees do not accept sālokya, sārṣṭi, sārūpya, sāmīpya or oneness with Me—even if I offer these liberations—in preference to serving Me."

PURPORT

These three verses from *Śrīmad-Bhāgavatam* (3.29.11–13) were spoken by Lord Kṛṣṇa in the form of Kapiladeva.

TEXT 208

মৎসেবয়া প্রতীতং তে সালোক্যাদি-চতুষ্টয়ম্ ।
নেচ্ছন্তি সেবয়া পূর্ণাঃ কুতোঽন্যৎ কালবিপ্লুতম্ ॥ ২০৮ ॥

mat-sevayā pratītaṁ te
sālokyādi-catuṣṭayam
necchanti sevayā pūrṇāḥ
kuto 'nyat kāla-viplutam

mat—of Me; *sevayā*—by service; *pratītam*—obtained; *te*—they; *sālokya-ādi*—liberation, beginning *sālokya; catuṣṭayam*—four kinds of; *na icchanti*—do not desire; *sevayā*—by service; *pūrṇāḥ*—complete; *kutaḥ*—where; *anyat*—other things; *kāla-viplutam*—which are lost in time.

TRANSLATION

"My devotees, having fulfilled their desires by serving Me, do not accept the four kinds of salvation that are easily earned by such

service. Why then should they accept any pleasures that are lost in the course of time?"

PURPORT

This verse from *Śrīmad-Bhāgavatam* (9.4.67) was spoken by the Lord in connection with the characteristics of Mahārāja Ambarīṣa. Merging into the existence of the Absolute is as temporary as living in the celestial kingdom. Both of them are controlled by time; neither position is permanent.

TEXT 209

কামগন্ধহীন স্বাভাবিক গোপী-প্রেম ।
নির্মল, উজ্জ্বল, শুদ্ধ যেন দগ্ধ হেম ॥ ২০৯ ॥

kāma-gandha-hīna svābhāvika gopī-prema
nirmala, ujjvala, śuddha yena dagdha hema

kāma-gandha-hīna—without any scent of lust; *svābhāvika*—natural; *gopī-prema*—the love of the *gopīs; nirmala*—spotless; *ujjvala*—blazing; *śuddha*—pure; *yena*—like; *dagdha hema*—molten gold.

TRANSLATION

The natural love of the gopīs is devoid of any trace of lust. It is faultless, bright and pure, like molten gold.

TEXT 210

কৃষ্ণের সহায়, গুরু, বান্ধব, প্রেয়সী ।
গোপিকা হয়েন প্রিয়া শিষ্যা, সখী, দাসী ॥ ২১০ ॥

kṛṣṇera sahāya, guru, bāndhava, preyasī
gopikā hayena priyā śiṣyā, sakhī dāsī

kṛṣṇera—of Lord Kṛṣṇa; *sahāya*—helpers; *guru*—teachers; *bāndhava*—friends; *preyasī*—wives; *gopikā*—the *gopīs; hayena*—are; *priyā*—dear; *śiṣyā*—students; *sakhī*—confidantes; *dāsī*—servants.

TRANSLATION

The gopīs are the helpers, teachers, friends, wives, dear disciples, confidantes and serving maids of Lord Kṛṣṇa.

TEXT 211

সহায়া গুরবঃ শিষ্যা ভুজিষ্যা বান্ধবাঃ স্ত্রিয়ঃ ।
সত্যং বদামি তে পার্থ গোপ্যঃ কিং মে ভবন্তি ন ॥ ২১১ ॥

sahāyā guravaḥ śiṣyā
bhujiṣyā bāndhavāḥ striyaḥ
satyaṁ vadāmi te pārtha
gopyaḥ kiṁ me bhavanti na

sahāyāḥ—helpers; *guravaḥ*—teachers; *śiṣyāḥ*—students; *bhujiṣyāḥ*—servants; *bāndhavāḥ*—friends; *striyaḥ*—wives; *satyam*—truthfully; *vadāmi*—I say; *te*—unto you; *pārtha*—O Arjuna; *gopyaḥ*—the *gopīs;* *kim*—what; *me*—for Me; *bhavanti*—are; *na*—not.

TRANSLATION

"O Pārtha, I speak to you the truth. The gopīs are My helpers, teachers, disciples, servants, friends and consorts. I do not know what they are not to Me."

PURPORT

This verse was spoken by Lord Kṛṣṇa in the *Gopī-premāmṛta.*

TEXT 212

গোপিকা জানেন কৃষ্ণের মনের বাঞ্ছিত ।
প্রেমসেবা-পরিপাটী, ইষ্ট-সমীহিত ॥ ২১২ ॥

gopikā jānena kṛṣṇera manera vāñchita
prema-sevā-paripāṭī, iṣṭa-samīhita

gopikā—the *gopīs;* *jānena*—know; *kṛṣṇera*—of Lord Kṛṣṇa; *manera*—of the mind; *vāñchita*—the desired object; *prema-sevā*—of service in love; *paripāṭī*—perfection; *iṣṭa-samīhita*—achievement of the desired goal of life.

TRANSLATION

The gopīs know Kṛṣṇa's desires, and they know how to render perfect loving service for His enjoyment. They perform their service expertly for the satisfaction of their beloved.

TEXT 213

মন্মাহাত্ম্যং মৎসপর্যাং মাচ্ছ্রদ্ধাং মন্মনোগতম্ ।
জানন্তি গোপিকাঃ পার্থ নান্যে জানন্তি তত্ত্বতঃ ॥ ২১৩ ॥

man-māhātmyaṁ mat-saparyāṁ
mac-chraddhāṁ man-mano-gatam
jānanti gopikāḥ pārtha
nānye jānanti tattvataḥ

mat-māhātmyam—My greatness; *mat-saparyām*—My service; *mat-śraddhām*—respect for Me; *mat-manaḥ-gatam*—the intention of My mind; *jānanti*—they know; *gopikāḥ*—the *gopīs; pārtha*—O Arjuna; *na*—not; *anye*—others; *jānanti*—know; *tattvataḥ*—factually.

TRANSLATION

"O Pārtha, the gopīs know My greatness, My loving service, respect for Me, and My mentality. Others cannot really know these."

PURPORT

This verse was spoken by Lord Kṛṣṇa to Arjuna in the *Ādi Purāṇa.*

TEXT 214

সেই গোপীগণ-মধ্যে উত্তমা রাধিকা ।
রূপে, গুণে, সৌভাগ্যে, প্রেমে সর্বাধিকা ॥ ২১৪ ॥

sei gopī-gaṇa-madhye uttamā rādhikā
rūpe, guṇe, saubhāgye, preme sarvādhikā

sei—those; *gopī-gaṇa*—the *gopīs; madhye*—among; *uttamā*—the highest; *rādhikā*—Śrīmatī Rādhārāṇī; *rūpe*—in beauty; *guṇe*—in qualities; *saubhāgye*—in good fortune; *preme*—in love; *sarva-adhikā*—above all.

TRANSLATION

Among the gopīs, Śrīmatī Rādhikā is the foremost. She surpasses all in beauty, in good qualities, in good fortune and, above all, in love.

PURPORT

Among all the *gopīs*, Śrīmatī Rādhārāṇī is the most exalted. She is the most beautiful, the most qualified and, above all, the greatest lover of Kṛṣṇa.

TEXT 215

যথা রাধা প্রিয়া বিষ্ণোস্তস্যাঃ কুণ্ডং প্রিয়ং তথা ।
সর্বগোপীষু সৈবৈকা বিষ্ণোরত্যন্তবল্লভা ॥ ২১৫ ॥

yathā rādhā priyā viṣṇos
tasyāḥ kuṇḍaṁ priyaṁ tathā
sarva-gopīṣu saivaikā
viṣṇor atyanta-vallabhā

yathā—just as; *rādhā*—Śrīmatī Rādhārāṇī; *priyā*—very dear; *viṣṇoḥ*—to Lord Kṛṣṇa; *tasyāḥ*—Her; *kuṇḍam*—bathing place; *priyam*—very dear; *tathā*—so also; *sarva-gopīṣu*—among all the *gopīs; sā*—She; *eva*—certainly; *ekā*—alone; *viṣṇoḥ*—of Lord Kṛṣṇa; *atyanta-vallabhā*—most dear.

TRANSLATION

"Just as Rādhā is dear to Lord Kṛṣṇa, so Her bathing place [Rādhā-kuṇḍa] is dear to Him. She alone is His most beloved of all the gopīs."

PURPORT

This verse is from the *Padma Purāṇa*.

TEXT 216

ত্রৈলোক্যে পৃথিবী ধন্যা যত্র বৃন্দাবনং পুরী ।
তত্রাপি গোপিকাঃ পার্থ যত্র রাধাভিধা মম ॥ ২১৬ ॥

trai-lokye pṛthivī dhanyā
yatra vṛndāvanaṁ purī
tatrāpi gopikāḥ pārtha
yatra rādhābhidhā mama

trai-lokye—in the three worlds; *pṛthivī*—the earth; *dhanyā*—fortunate; *yatra*—where; *vṛndāvanam*—Vṛndāvana; *purī*—the town; *tatra*—

there; *api*—certainly; *gopikāḥ*—the *gopīs; pārtha*—O Arjuna; *yatra*—where; *rādhā*—Śrīmatī Rādhārāṇī; *abhidhā*—named; *mama*—My.

TRANSLATION

"O Pārtha, in all the three planetary systems, this earth is especially fortunate, for on earth is the town of Vṛndāvana. And there the gopīs are especially glorious because among them is My Śrīmatī Rādhārāṇī."

PURPORT

This verse, spoken by Lord Kṛṣṇa to Arjuna, is cited from the *Ādi Purāṇa.*

TEXT 217

রাধাসহ ক্রীড়া রস-বৃদ্ধির কারণ।
আর সব গোপীগণ রসোপকরণ ॥ ২১৭ ॥

rādhā-saha krīḍā rasa-vṛddhira kāraṇa
āra saba gopī-gaṇa rasopakaraṇa

rādhā-saha—with Śrīmatī Rādhārāṇī; *krīḍā*—pastimes; *rasa*—of mellow; *vṛddhira*—of the increase; *kāraṇa*—the cause; *āra*—the other; *saba*—all; *gopī-gaṇa*—*gopīs; rasa-upakaraṇa*—accessories of mellow.

TRANSLATION

All the other gopīs help increase the joy of Kṛṣṇa's pastimes with Rādhārāṇī. The gopīs act as the instruments of Their mutual enjoyment.

PURPORT

It is said that the *gopīs* are divided into five groups, namely the *sakhīs, nitya-sakhīs, prāṇa-sakhīs, priya-sakhīs* and *parama-preṣṭha-sakhīs.* All these fair-complexioned associates of Śrīmatī Rādhārāṇī, the Queen of Vṛndāvana-dhāma, are expert artists in evoking erotic sentiments in Kṛṣṇa. The *parama-preṣṭha-sakhīs* are eight in number, and in the ecstatic dealings of Kṛṣṇa and Rādhā they side sometimes with Kṛṣṇa and at other times with Rādhārāṇī, just to create a situation in which it appears that they favor one against the other. That makes the exchange of mellows more palatable.

TEXT 218

কৃষ্ণের বল্লভা রাধা কৃষ্ণ-প্রাণধন ।
তাঁহা বিনু সুখহেতু নহে গোপীগণ ॥ ২১৮ ॥

kṛṣṇera vallabhā rādhā kṛṣṇa-prāṇa-dhana
tāṅhā vinu sukha-hetu nahe gopī-gaṇa

kṛṣṇera—of Lord Kṛṣṇa; *vallabhā*—beloved; *rādhā*—Śrīmatī Rādhārāṇī; *kṛṣṇa-prāṇa-dhana*—the wealth of the life of Lord Kṛṣṇa; *tāṅhā*—Her; *vinu*—without; *sukha-hetu*—cause of happiness; *nahe*—are not; *gopī-gaṇa*—the *gopīs*.

TRANSLATION

Rādhā is the beloved consort of Kṛṣṇa, and She is the wealth of His life. Without Her, the gopīs cannot give Him pleasure.

TEXT 219

কংসারিরপি সংসারবাসনাবদ্ধশৃঙ্খলাম্ ।
রাধামাধায় হৃদয়ে তত্যাজ ব্রজসুন্দরীঃ ॥ ২১৯ ॥

kaṁsārir api saṁsāra-
vāsanā-baddha-śṛṅkhalām
rādhām ādhāya hṛdaye
tatyāja vraja-sundarīḥ

kaṁsa-ariḥ—Lord Kṛṣṇa, the enemy of Kaṁsa; *api*—moreover; *saṁsāra*—for the essence of enjoyment (*rāsa-līlā*); *vāsanā*—by the desire; *baddha*—tied on; *śṛṅkhalām*—who was like the chains; *rādhām*—Śrīmatī Rādhārāṇī; *ādhāya*—taking; *hṛdaye*—in the heart; *tatyāja*—left aside; *vraja-sundarīḥ*—the other *gopīs*.

TRANSLATION

"Lord Kṛṣṇa, the enemy of Kaṁsa, left aside the other gopīs during the rāsa dance and took Śrīmatī Rādhārāṇī to His heart, for She is the helper of the Lord in realizing the essence of His desires."

PURPORT

In this verse from the *Gīta-govinda* (3.1), Jayadeva Gosvāmī describes Śrī Kṛṣṇa's leaving the *rāsa-līlā* to search for Śrīmatī Rādhārāṇī.

TEXT 220

সেই রাধার ভাব লঞা চৈতন্যাবতার ।
যুগধর্ম নাম-প্রেম কৈল পরচার ॥ ২২০ ॥

sei rādhāra bhāva lañā caitanyāvatāra
yuga-dharma nāma-prema kaila paracāra

sei—that; *rādhāra*—of Śrīmatī Rādhārāṇī; *bhāva*—the emotion; *lañā*—taking; *caitanya*—of Lord Caitanya; *avatāra*—the incarnation; *yuga-dharma*—the religion of the age; *nāma-prema*—the holy name and love of Godhead; *kaila*—did; *paracāra*—preaching.

TRANSLATION

Lord Caitanya appeared with the sentiment of Rādhā. He preached the dharma of this age—the chanting of the holy name and pure love of God.

TEXT 221

সেই ভাবে নিজবাঞ্ছা করিল পূরণ ।
অবতারের এই বাঞ্ছা মূল-কারণ ॥ ২২১ ॥

sei bhāve nija-vāñchā karila pūraṇa
avatārera ei vāñchā mūla-kāraṇa

sei—that; *bhāve*—in the mood; *nija-vāñchā*—His own desires, *karila*—did; *pūraṇa*—fulfilling; *avatārera*—of the incarnation; *ei*—this; *vāñchā*—desire; *mūla*—root; *kāraṇa*—cause.

TRANSLATION

In the mood of Śrīmatī Rādhārāṇī, He also fulfilled His own desires. This is the principal reason for His appearance.

TEXT 222

শ্রীকৃষ্ণচৈতন্য গোসাঞি ব্রজেন্দ্রকুমার ।
রসময়-মূর্তি কৃষ্ণ সাক্ষাৎ শৃঙ্গার ॥ ২২২ ॥

śrī-kṛṣṇa-caitanya gosāñi vrajendra-kumāra
rasa-maya-mūrti kṛṣṇa sākṣāt śṛṅgāra

śrī-kṛṣṇa-caitanya gosāñi—Śrī Caitanya Mahāprabhu; *vrajendra-kumāra*—the child of King Nanda; *rasa-maya*—consisting of mellows; *mūrti*—the form; *kṛṣṇa*—Lord Kṛṣṇa; *sākṣāt*—directly; *śṛṅgāra*—amorous love.

TRANSLATION

Lord Śrī Kṛṣṇa Caitanya is Kṛṣṇa [Vrajendra-kumāra], the embodiment of rasas. He is amorous love personified.

TEXT 223

সেই রস আস্বাদিতে কৈল অবতার ।
আনুষঙ্গে কৈল সব রসের প্রচার ॥ ২২৩ ॥

sei rasa āsvādite kaila avatāra
ānusaṅge kaila saba rasera pracāra

sei—that; *rasa*—mellow; *āsvādite*—to taste; *kaila*—made; *avatāra*—incarnation; *ānusaṅge*—as a secondary motive; *kaila*—did; *saba*—all; *rasera*—of mellows; *pracāra*—broadcasting.

TRANSLATION

He made His appearance to taste that conjugal mellow and incidentally to broadcast all the rasas.

TEXT 224

বিশ্বেষামনুরঞ্জনেন জনয়ন্নানন্দমিন্দীবর-
শ্রেণীশ্যামলকোমলৈরুপনয়ন্নঙ্গৈরনঙ্গোৎসবম্ ।
স্বচ্ছন্দং ব্রজসুন্দরীভিরভিতঃ প্রত্যঙ্গমালিঙ্গিতঃ
শৃঙ্গারঃ সখি মূর্তিমানিব মধৌ মুগ্ধো হরিঃ ক্রীড়তি ॥ ২২৪ ॥

viśveṣām anurañjanena janayann ānandam indīvara-
śreṇī-śyāmala-komalair upanayann aṅgair anaṅgotsavam
svacchandaṁ vraja-sundarībhir abhitaḥ praty-aṅgam āliṅgitaḥ
śṛṅgāraḥ sakhi mūrtimān iva madhau mugdho hariḥ krīḍati

viśveṣām—of all the *gopīs; anurañjanena*—by the act of pleasing; *janayan*—producing; *ānandam*—the bliss; *indīvara-śreṇī*—like a row of blue lotuses; *śyāmala*—bluish black; *komalaiḥ*—and soft; *upanayan*—bringing; *aṅgaiḥ*—with His limbs; *anaṅga-utsavam*—a festival for Cupid; *svacchandam*—without restriction; *vraja-sundarī-bhiḥ*—by the young women of Vraja; *abhitaḥ*—on both sides; *prati-aṅgam*—each limb; *āliṅgitaḥ*—embraced; *śṛṅgāraḥ*—amorous love; *sakhi*—O friend; *mūrtimān*—embodied; *iva*—like; *madhau*—in the springtime; *mugdhaḥ*—perplexed; *hariḥ*—Lord Hari; *krīḍati*—plays.

TRANSLATION

"My dear friends, just see how Śrī Kṛṣṇa is enjoying the season of spring! With the gopīs embracing each of His limbs, He is like amorous love personified. With His transcendental pastimes, He enlivens all the gopīs and the entire creation. With His soft bluish-black arms and legs, which resemble blue lotus flowers, He has created a festival for Cupid."

PURPORT

This is a verse from the *Gīta-govinda* (1.11).

TEXT 225

শ্রীকৃষ্ণচৈতন্য গোসাঞি রসের সদন ।
অশেষ-বিশেষে কৈল রস আস্বাদন ॥ ২২৫ ॥

śrī-kṛṣṇa-caitanya gosāñi rasera sadana
aśeṣa-viśeṣe kaila rasa āsvādana

śrī-kṛṣṇa-caitanya gosāñi—Lord Śrī Caitanya Mahāprabhu; *rasera*—of mellow; *sadana*—the residence; *aśeṣa-viśeṣe*—unlimited varieties of enjoyment; *kaila*—did; *rasa*—mellow; *āsvādana*—tasting.

TRANSLATION

Lord Śrī Kṛṣṇa Caitanya is the abode of rasa. He Himself tasted the sweetness of rasa in endless ways.

TEXT 226

সেই দ্বারে প্রবর্তাইল কলিযুগ-ধর্ম ।
চৈতন্যের দাসে জানে এই সব মর্ম ॥ ২২৬ ॥

sei dvāre pravartāila kali-yuga-dharma
caitanyera dāse jāne ei saba marma

sei dvāre—in that way; *pravartāila*—He initiated; *kali-yuga*—of the Age of Kali; *dharma*—the religion; *caitanyera*—of Lord Caitanya Mahāprabhu; *dāse*—the servant; *jāne*—knows; *ei*—these; *saba*—all; *marma*—secrets.

TRANSLATION

Thus He initiated the dharma for the Age of Kali. The devotees of Lord Caitanya know all these truths.

PURPORT

Lord Caitanya is Śrī Kṛṣṇa Himself, the absolute enjoyer of the love of the *gopīs.* He Himself assumes the role of the *gopīs* to taste the predominated happiness of transcendental mellows. He appeared in that mode, but simultaneously He propagated the religious process for this age in a most fascinating way. Only the confidential devotees of Śrī Caitanya Mahāprabhu can understand this transcendental secret.

TEXTS 227–228

অদ্বৈত আচার্য, নিত্যানন্দ, শ্রীনিবাস ।
গদাধর, দামোদর, মুরারি, হরিদাস ॥ ২২৭ ॥
আর যত চৈতন্য-কৃষ্ণের ভক্তগণ ।
ভক্তিভাবে শিরে ধরি সবার চরণ ॥ ২২৮ ॥

advaita ācārya, nityānanda, śrīnivāsa
gadādhara, dāmodara, murāri, haridāsa

āra yata caitanya-kṛṣṇera bhakta-gaṇa
bhakti-bhāve śire dhari sabāra caraṇa

advaita ācārya—Advaita Ācārya; *nityānanda*—Lord Nityānanda; *śrīnivāsa*—Śrīvāsa Paṇḍita; *gadādhara*—Gadādhara Paṇḍita; *dāmodara*—Svarūpa Dāmodara; *murāri*—Murāri Gupta; *haridāsa*—Haridāsa Ṭhākura; *āra*—other; *yata*—all; *caitanya-kṛṣṇera*—of Śrī Kṛṣṇa Caitanya; *bhakta-gaṇa*—devotees; *bhakti-bhāve*—with a devotional attitude; *śire*—on my head; *dhari*—I take; *sabāra*—of all of them; *caraṇa*—the lotus feet.

TRANSLATION

Advaita Ācārya, Lord Nityānanda, Śrīvāsa Paṇḍita, Gadādhara Paṇḍita, Svarūpa Dāmodara, Murāri Gupta, Haridāsa Ṭhākura and all the other devotees of Śrī Kṛṣṇa Caitanya—bowing down with devotion, I hold their lotus feet on my head.

PURPORT

The author of *Śrī Caitanya-caritāmṛta* teaches us that we must offer our respectful obeisances to all such pure confidential devotees of Lord Caitanya if we indeed want to know Him in truth.

TEXT 229

যষ্ঠশ্লোকের এই কহিল আভাস।
মূল শ্লোকের অর্থ শুন করিয়ে প্রকাশ ॥ ২২৯ ॥

ṣaṣṭha-ślokera ei kahila ābhāsa
mūla ślokera artha śuna kariye prakāśa

ṣaṣṭha-ślokera—of the sixth verse; *ei*—this; *kahila*—has been spoken; *ābhāsa*—a hint; *mūla ślokera*—of the original verse; *artha*—meaning; *śuna*—please hear; *kariye prakāśa*—I am revealing.

TRANSLATION

I have given a hint of the sixth verse. Now please hear as I reveal the meaning of that original verse.

TEXT 230

শ্রীরাধায়াঃ প্রণয়মহিমা কীদৃশো বানয়ৈবা-
স্বাদ্যো যেনাদ্ভুতমধুরিমা কীদৃশো বা মদীয়ঃ।
সৌখ্যঞ্চাস্যা মদনুভবতঃ কীদৃশং বেতি লোভা-
ত্তদ্ভাবাঢ্যঃ সমজনি শচীগর্ভসিন্ধৌ হরীন্দুঃ ॥ ২৩০ ॥

śrī-rādhāyāḥ praṇaya-mahimā kīdṛśo vānayaivā-
svādyo yenādbhuta-madhurimā kīdṛśo vā madīyaḥ
saukhyaṁ cāsyā mad-anubhavataḥ kīdṛśaṁ veti lobhāt
tad-bhāvāḍhyaḥ samajani śacī-garbha-sindhau harīnduḥ

śrī-rādhāyāḥ—of Śrīmatī Rādhārāṇī; *praṇaya-mahimā*—the greatness of the love; *kīdṛśaḥ*—of what kind; *vā*—or; *anayā*—by this one (Rādhā); *eva*—alone; *āsvādyaḥ*—to be relished; *yena*—by that love; *adbhuta-madhurimā*—the wonderful sweetness; *kīdṛśaḥ*—of what kind; *vā*—or; *madīyaḥ*—of Me; *saukhyam*—the happiness; *ca*—and; *asyāḥ*—Her; *mat-anubhavataḥ*—from realization of My sweetness; *kīdṛśam*—of what kind; *vā*—or; *iti*—thus; *lobhāt*—from the desire; *tat*—Her; *bhāva-āḍhyaḥ*—richly endowed with the emotions; *samajani*—took birth; *śacī-garbha*—of the womb of Śacī-devī; *sindhau*—in the ocean; *hari*—Lord Kṛṣṇa; *induḥ*—like the moon.

TRANSLATION

"Desiring to understand the glory of Rādhārāṇī's love, the wonderful qualities in Him that She alone relishes through Her love, and the happiness She feels when She realizes the sweetness of His love, the Supreme Lord Hari, richly endowed with Her emotions, appeared from the womb of Śrīmatī Śacī-devī, as the moon appeared from the ocean."

TEXT 231

এ সব সিদ্ধান্ত গূঢ়,—কহিতে না যুয়ায় ।
না কহিলে, কেহ ইহার অন্ত নাহি পায় ॥ ২৩১ ॥

e saba siddhānta gūḍha,—kahite nā yuyāya
nā kahile, keha ihāra anta nāhi pāya

e—this; *saba*—all; *siddhānta*—conclusions; *gūḍha*—very confidential; *kahite*—to speak; *nā*—not; *yuyāya*—quite fit; *nā*—not; *kahile*—speaking; *keha*—anyone; *ihāra*—of it; *anta*—end; *nāhi*—not; *pāya*—gets.

TRANSLATION

All these conclusions are unfit to disclose in public. But if they are not disclosed, no one will understand them.

TEXT 232

অতএব কহি কিছু করিঞা নিগূঢ় ।
বুঝিবে রসিক ভক্ত, না বুঝিবে মূঢ় ॥ ২৩২ ॥

ataeva kahi kichu kariñā nigūḍha
bujhibe rasika bhakta, nā bujhibe mūḍha

ataeva—therefore; *kahi*—I speak; *kichu*—something; *kariñā*—squeezing; *nigūḍha*—essence; *bujhibe*—can understand; *rasika*—humorous; *bhakta*—devotees; *nā*—not; *bujhibe*—will understand; *mūḍha*—rascals.

TRANSLATION

Therefore I shall mention them, revealing only their essence, so that loving devotees will understand them but fools will not.

TEXT 233

হৃদয়ে ধরয়ে যে চৈতন্য-নিত্যানন্দ ।
এসব সিদ্ধান্তে সেই পাইবে আনন্দ ॥ ২৩৩ ॥

hṛdaye dharaye ye caitanya-nityānanda
e-saba siddhānte sei pāibe ānanda

hṛdaye—in the heart; *dharaye*—captures; *ye*—anyone who; *caitanya*—Śrī Caitanya Mahāprabhu; *nityānanda*—and Lord Nityānanda; *e-saba*—all these; *siddhānte*—by transcendental conclusions; *sei*—that man; *pāibe*—will get; *ānanda*—bliss.

TRANSLATION

Anyone who has captured Lord Caitanya Mahāprabhu and Lord Nityānanda Prabhu in his heart will become blissful by hearing all these transcendental conclusions.

TEXT 234

এ সব সিদ্ধান্ত হয় আম্রের পল্লব ।
ভক্তগণ-কোকিলের সর্বদা বল্লভ ॥ ২৩৪ ॥

e saba siddhānta haya āmrera pallava
bhakta-gaṇa-kokilera sarvadā vallabha

e—these; *saba*—all; *siddhānta*—transcendental conclusions; *haya*—are; *āmrera*—of mango; *pallava*—twigs; *bhakta-gaṇa*—the devotees;

kokilera—to those who are just like cuckoo birds; *sarvadā*—always; *vallabha*—pleasing.

TRANSLATION

All these conclusions are like the newly grown twigs of a mango tree; they are always pleasing to the devotees, who in this way resemble cuckoo birds.

TEXT 235

অভক্ত-উষ্ট্রের ইথে না হয় প্রবেশ ।
তবে চিত্তে হয় মোর আনন্দ-বিশেষ ॥ ২৩৫ ॥

abhakta-uṣṭrera ithe nā haya praveśa
tabe citte haya mora ānanda-viśeṣa

abhakta—nondevotee; *uṣṭrera*—of a camel; *ithe*—in this; *nā*—not; *haya*—is there; *praveśa*—entrance; *tabe*—then; *citte*—in my heart; *haya*—there is; *mora*—my; *ānanda-viśeṣa*—special jubilation.

TRANSLATION

The camellike nondevotees cannot enter into these topics. Therefore there is special jubilation in my heart.

TEXT 236

যে লাগি কহিতে ভয়, সে যদি না জানে ।
ইহা বই কিবা সুখ আছে ত্রিভুবনে ॥ ২৩৬ ॥

ye lāgi kahite bhaya, se yadi nā jāne
ihā va-i kibā sukha āche tribhuvane

ye lāgi—for the matter of which; *kahite bhaya*—afraid to speak; *se yadi nājāne*—if they do not know; *ihā va-i*—except this; *kibā*—what; *sukha*—happiness; *āche*—there is; *tri-bhuvane*—in the three worlds.

TRANSLATION

For fear of them I do not wish to speak, but if they do not understand, then what can be happier in all the three worlds?

TEXT 237

অতএব ভক্তগণে করি নমস্কার ।
নিঃশঙ্কে কহিয়ে, তার হউক্ চমৎকার ॥ ২৩৭ ॥

ataeva bhakta-gaṇe kari namaskāra
niḥśaṅke kahiye, tāra hauk camatkāra

ataeva—therefore; *bhakta-gaṇe*—unto the devotees; *kari*—I offer; *namaskāra*—obeisances; *niḥśaṅke*—without any doubt; *kahiye*—I say; *tāra*—of the devotees; *hauk*—let there be; *camatkāra*—astonishment.

TRANSLATION

Therefore after offering obeisances to the devotees, for their satisfaction I shall speak without hesitating.

TEXT 238

কৃষ্ণের বিচার এক আছয়ে অন্তরে ।
পূর্ণানন্দ-পূর্ণরসরূপ কহে মোরে ॥ ২৩৮ ॥

kṛṣṇera vicara eka āchaye antare
pūrṇānanda-pūrṇa-rasa-rūpa kahe more

kṛṣṇera—of Lord Kṛṣṇa; *vicāra*—consideration; *eka*—one; *āchaye*—is; *antare*—within the heart; *pūrṇa-ānanda*—complete transcendental bliss; *pūrṇa-rasa-rūpa*—full with transcendental mellows; *kahe more*—they say unto Me.

TRANSLATION

Once Lord Kṛṣṇa considered within His heart, "Everyone says that I am complete bliss, full of all rasas.

TEXT 239

আমা হইতে আনন্দিত হয় ত্রিভুবন ।
আমাকে আনন্দ দিবে—ঐছে কোন্ জন ॥ ২৩৯ ॥

āmā ha-ite ānandita haya tribhuvana
āmāke ānanda dibe—aiche kon jana

āmā ha-ite—from Me; *ānandita*—pleased; *haya*—becomes; *tri-bhuvana*—all the three worlds; *āmāke*—unto Me; *ānanda dibe*—will give pleasure; *aiche*—such; *kon jana*—what person.

TRANSLATION

"All the world derives pleasure from Me. Is there anyone who can give Me pleasure?

TEXT 240

আমা হৈতে যার হয় শত শত গুণ ।
সেইজন আহ্লাদিতে পারে মোর মন ॥ ২৪০ ॥

āmā haite yāra haya śata śata guṇa
sei-jana āhlādite pāre mora mana

āmā haite—than Me; *yāra*—whose; *haya*—there is; *śata śata guṇa*—hundreds of qualities more; *sei-jana*—that person; *āhlādite*—to give pleasure; *pāre*—is able; *mora*—My; *mana*—to the mind.

TRANSLATION

"One who has a hundred times more qualities than Me could give pleasure to My mind.

TEXT 241

আমা হৈতে গুণী বড় জগতে অসম্ভব ।
একলি রাধাতে তাহা করি অনুভব ॥ ২৪১ ॥

āmā haite guṇī baḍa jagate asambhava
ekali rādhāte tāhā kari anubhava

āmā haite—than Me; *guṇī*—qualified; *baḍa*—greater; *jagate*—in the world; *asambhava*—there is no possibility; *ekali*—only; *rādhāte*—in Śrīmatī Rādhārāṇī; *tāhā*—that; *kari anubhava*—I can understand.

TRANSLATION

"One more qualified than Me is impossible to find in the world. But in Rādhā alone I feel the presence of one who can give Me pleasure.

TEXTS 242–243

কোটিকাম জিনি' রূপ যদ্যপি আমার ।
অসমোর্ধ্বমাধুর্য—সাম্য নাহি যার ॥ ২৪২ ॥
মোর রূপে আপ্যায়িত হয় ত্রিভুবন ।
রাধার দর্শনে মোর জুড়ায় নয়ন ॥ ২৪৩ ॥

koṭi-kāma jini' rūpa yadyapi āmāra
asamordhva-mādhurya—sāmya nāhi yāra

mora rūpe āpyāyita haya tribhuvana
rādhāra darśane mora juḍāya nayana

koṭi-kāma—ten million Cupids; *jini'*—conquering; *rūpa*—beauty; *yadyapi*—although; *āmāra*—Mine; *asama-ūrdhva*—unequaled and unsurpassed; *mādhurya*—sweetness; *sāmya*—equality; *nāhi*—there is not; *yāra*—of whom; *mora*—My; *rūpe*—in beauty; *āpyāyita*—pleased; *haya*—becomes; *tri-bhuvana*—all three worlds; *rādhāra*—of Śrīmatī Rādhārāṇī; *darśane*—seeing; *mora*—My; *juḍāya*—satisfies; *nayana*—eyes.

TRANSLATION

"Although My beauty defeats the beauty of ten million Cupids, although it is unequaled and unsurpassed, and although it gives pleasure to the three worlds, seeing Rādhārāṇī gives pleasure to My eyes.

TEXT 244

মোর বংশী-গীতে আকর্ষয়ে ত্রিভুবন ।
রাধার বচনে হরে আমার শ্রবণ ॥ ২৪৪ ॥

mora vaṁśī-gīte ākarṣaye tri-bhuvana
rādhāra vacane hare āmāra śravaṇa

mora—My; *vaṁśī-gīte*—by the vibration of the flute; *ākarṣaye*—I attract; *tri-bhuvana*—the three worlds; *rādhāra vacane*—the words of Śrīmatī Rādhārāṇī; *hare*—conquers; *āmāra*—My; *śravaṇa*—hearing power.

TRANSLATION

"The vibration of My transcendental flute attracts the three worlds, but My ears are enchanted by the sweet words of Śrīmatī Rādhārāṇī.

TEXT 245

যদ্যপি আমার গন্ধে জগৎ সুগন্ধ ।
মোর চিত্ত-প্রাণ হরে রাধা-অঙ্গ-গন্ধ ॥ ২৪৫ ॥

yadyapi āmāra gandhe jagat sugandha
mora citta-prāṇa hare rādhā-aṅga-gandha

yadyapi—although; *āmāra*—My; *gandhe*—by the fragrance; *jagat*—the whole universe; *su-gandha*—sweet-smelling; *mora*—My; *citta-prāṇa*—mind and heart; *hare*—attracts; *rādhā*—of Śrīmatī Rādhārāṇī; *aṅga*—bodily; *gandha*—flavor.

TRANSLATION

"Although My body lends fragrance to the entire creation, the scent of Rādhārāṇī's limbs captivates My mind and heart.

TEXT 246

যদ্যপি আমার রসে জগৎ সরস ।
রাধার অধর-রস আমা করে বশ ॥ ২৪৬ ॥

yadyapi āmāra rase jagat sarasa
rādhāra adhara-rasa āmā kare vaśa

yadyapi—although; *āmāra*—of Me; *rase*—by the taste; *jagat*—the whole world; *sa-rasa*—is palatable; *rādhāra*—of Śrīmatī Rādhārāṇī; *adhara-rasa*—the taste of the lips; *āmā*—Me; *kare*—makes; *vaśa*—submissive.

TRANSLATION

"Although the entire creation is full of different tastes because of Me, I am charmed by the nectarean taste of the lips of Śrīmatī Rādhārāṇī.

TEXT 247

যদ্যপি আমার স্পর্শ কোটিন্দু-শীতল ।
রাধিকার স্পর্শে আমা করে সুশীতল ॥ ২৪৭ ॥

yadyapi āmāra sparśa koṭīndu-śītala
rādhikāra sparśe āmā kare suśītala

yadyapi—although; *āmāra*—My; *sparśa*—touch; *koṭi-indu*—like millions upon millions of moons; *śītala*—cool; *rādhikāra*—of Śrīmatī Rādhārāṇī; *sparśe*—the touch; *āmā*—Me; *kare*—makes; *su-śītala*—very, very cool.

TRANSLATION

"And although My touch is cooler than ten million moons, I am refreshed by the touch of Śrīmatī Rādhikā.

TEXT 248

এই মত জগতের সুখে আমি হেতু ।
রাধিকার রূপগুণ আমার জীবাতু ॥ ২৪৮ ॥

ei mata jagatera sukhe āmi hetu
rādhikāra rūpa-guṇa āmāra jīvātu

ei mata—in this way; *jagatera*—of the whole world; *sukhe*—in the matter of happiness; *āmi*—I am; *hetu*—the cause; *rādhikāra*—of Śrīmatī Rādhārāṇī; *rūpa-guṇa*—beauty and attributes; *āmāra*—My; *jīvātu*—life and soul.

TRANSLATION

"Thus although I am the source of happiness for the entire world, the beauty and attributes of Śrī Rādhikā are My life and soul.

TEXT 249

এই মত অনুভব আমার প্রতীত ।
বিচারি' দেখিয়ে যদি, সব বিপরীত ॥ ২৪৯ ॥

ei mata anubhava āmāra pratīta
vicāri' dekhiye yadi, saba viparīta

ei mata—in this way; *anubhava*—affectionate feelings; *āmāra*—My; *pratīta*—understood; *vicāri'*—by consideration; *dekhiye*—I see; *yadi*—if; *saba*—everything; *viparīta*—contrary.

TRANSLATION

"In this way My affectionate feelings for Śrīmatī Rādhārāṇī may be understood, but on analysis I find them contradictory.

TEXT 250

রাধার দর্শনে মোর জুড়ায় নয়ন ।
আমার দর্শনে রাধা সুখে অগেয়ান ॥ ২৫০ ॥

rādhāra darśane mora juḍāya nayana
āmāra darśane rādhā sukhe ageyāna

rādhāra—of Śrīmatī Rādhārāṇī; *darśane*—in meeting; *mora*—My; *juḍāya*—are satisfied; *nayana*—eyes; *āmāra*—of Me; *darśane*—in meeting; *rādhā*—Śrīmatī Rādhārāṇī; *sukhe*—in happiness; *ageyāna*—more advanced.

TRANSLATION

"My eyes are fully satisfied when I look upon Śrīmatī Rādhārāṇī, but by looking upon Me, She becomes even more advanced in satisfaction.

TEXT 251

পরস্পর বেণুগীতে হরয়ে চেতন ।
মোর ভ্রমে তমালেরে করে আলিঙ্গন ॥ ২৫১ ॥

paraspara veṇu-gīte haraye cetana
mora bhrame tamālere kare āliṅgana

paraspara—against each other; *veṇu-gīte*—the singing of the bamboo; *haraye*—attracts; *cetana*—consciousness; *mora*—of Me; *bhrame*—in mistake; *tamālere*—a black tree known as *tamāla; kare*—She does; *āliṅgana*—embracing.

TRANSLATION

"The flutelike murmur of the bamboos rubbing against one another steals Rādhārāṇī's consciousness, for She thinks it to be

the sound of My flute. And She embraces a tamāla tree, mistaking it for Me.

TEXT 252

কৃষ্ণ-আলিঙ্গন পাইনু, জনম সফলে ।
কৃষ্ণসুখে মগ্ন রহে বৃক্ষ করি' কোলে ॥ ২৫২ ॥

kṛṣṇa-āliṅgana pāinu, janama saphale
kṛṣṇa-sukhe magna rahe vṛkṣa kari' kole

kṛṣṇa—of Lord Kṛṣṇa; *āliṅgana*—the embrace; *pāinu*—I have gotten; *janama sa-phale*—My birth is now fulfilled; *kṛṣṇa-sukhe*—in the matter of pleasing Kṛṣṇa; *magna*—immersed; *rahe*—She remains; *vṛkṣa*—the tree; *kari'*—taking; *kole*—on the lap.

TRANSLATION

"'I have gotten the embrace of Śrī Kṛṣṇa,' She thinks, 'so now My life is fulfilled.' Thus She remains immersed in pleasing Kṛṣṇa, taking the tree in Her arms.

TEXT 253

অনুকূলবাতে যদি পায় মোর গন্ধ ।
উড়িয়া পড়িতে চাহে, প্রেমে হয় অন্ধ ॥ ২৫৩ ॥

anukūla-vāte yadi pāya mora gandha
uḍiyā paḍite cāhe, preme haya andha

anukūla-vāte—in a favorable breeze; *yadi*—if; *pāya*—there is; *mora*—My; *gandha*—fragrance; *uḍiyā*—flying; *paḍite*—to drop; *cāhe*—She wants; *preme*—in ecstatic love; *haya*—becomes; *andha*—blind.

TRANSLATION

"When a favorable breeze carries to Her the fragrance of My body, She is blinded by love and tries to fly into that breeze.

TEXT 254

তাম্বুলচর্বিত যবে করে আস্বাদনে ।
আনন্দসমুদ্রে ডুবে, কিছুই না জানে ॥ ২৫৪ ॥

tāmbūla-carvita yabe kare āsvādane
ānanda-samudre ḍube, kichui nā jāne

tāmbūla—betel nut; *carvita*—chewed; *yabe*—when; *kare*—does; *āsvādane*—tasting; *ānanda-samudre*—in an ocean of transcendental bliss; *ḍube*—drowns; *kichui*—anything; *nā*—not; *jāne*—knows.

TRANSLATION

"When She tastes the betel chewed by Me, She merges in an ocean of joy and forgets everything else.

TEXT 255

আমার সঙ্গমে রাধা পায় যে আনন্দ ।
শতমুখে বলি, তবু না পাই তার অন্ত ॥ ২৫৫ ॥

āmāra saṅgame rādhā pāya ye ānanda
śata-mukhe bali, tabu nā pāi tāra anta

āmāra—My; *saṅgame*—in association; *rādhā*—Śrīmatī Rādhārāṇī; *pāya*—gets; *ye*—whatever; *ānanda*—transcendental bliss; *śata-mukhe*—in hundreds of mouths; *bali*—if I say; *tabu*—still; *nā*—not; *pāi*—I reach; *tāra*—its; *anta*—limitation.

TRANSLATION

"Even with hundreds of mouths I could not express the transcendental pleasure She derives from My association.

TEXT 256

লীলা-অন্তে সুখে ইঁহার অঙ্গের মাধুরী ।
তাহা দেখি' সুখে আমি আপনা পাশরি ॥ ২৫৬ ॥

līlā-ante sukhe iṅhāra aṅgera mādhurī
tāhā dekhi' sukhe āmi āpanā pāśari

līlā-ante—at the end of Our pastimes; *sukhe*—in happiness; *iṅhāra*—of Śrīmatī Rādhārāṇī; *aṅgera*—of the body; *mādhurī*—sweetness; *tāhā*—that; *dekhi'*—seeing; *sukhe*—in happiness; *āmi*—I; *āpanā*—Myself; *pāśari*—forget.

TRANSLATION

"Seeing the luster of Her complexion after Our pastimes together, I forget My own identity in happiness.

TEXT 257

দোঁহার যে সমরস, ভরতমুনি মানে।
আমার ব্রজের রস সেহ নাহি জানে ॥ ২৫৭ ॥

doṅhāra ye sama-rasa, bharata-muni māne
āmāra vrajera rasa seha nāhi jāne

doṅhāra—of both; *ye*—whatever; *sama-rasa*—equal mellows; *bharata-muni*—the saintly person named Bharata Muni; *māne*—accepts; *āmāra*—My; *vrajera*—of Vṛndāvana; *rasa*—mellows; *seha*—he; *nāhi*—not; *jāne*—knows.

TRANSLATION

"The sage Bharata has said that the mellows of lover and beloved are equal. But he does not know the mellows of My Vṛndāvana.

PURPORT

According to expert sexologists like Bharata Muni, the male and the female enjoy equally in material sexual pleasure. But in the spiritual world the relationships are different, although this is unknown to mundane experts.

TEXT 258

অন্যের সঙ্গমে আমি যত সুখ পাই।
তাহা হৈতে রাধা-সুখ শত অধিকাই ॥ ২৫৮ ॥

anyera saṅgame āmi yata sukha pāi
tāhā haite rādhā-sukha śata adhikāi

anyera—others; *saṅgame*—by meeting; *āmi*—I; *yata*—all; *sukha*—happiness; *pāi*—get; *tāhā haite*—than that; *rādhā-sukha*—happiness by association with Rādhārāṇī; *śata*—one hundred times; *adhikāi*—increased.

TRANSLATION

"The happiness I feel when meeting Rādhārāṇī is a hundred times greater than the happiness I get from meeting others.

TEXT 259

নির্ধূতামৃতমাধুরীপরিমলঃ কল্যাণি বিম্বাধরো
বক্ত্রং পঙ্কজসৌরভং কুহরিতশ্লাঘাভিদস্তে গিরঃ ।
অঙ্গং চন্দনশীতলং তনুরিয়ং সৌন্দর্যসর্বস্বভাক্
ত্বামাসাদ্য মমেদমিন্দ্রিয়কুলং রাধে মুহুর্মোদতে ॥ ২৫৯ ॥

nirdhūtāmṛta-mādhurī-parimalaḥ kalyāṇi bimbādharo
vaktraṁ paṅkaja-saurabhaṁ kuharita-ślāghā-bhidas te giraḥ
aṅgaṁ candana-śītalaṁ tanur iyaṁ saundarya-sarvasva-bhāk
tvām āsādya mamedam indriya-kulaṁ rādhe muhur modate

nirdhūta—defeats; *amṛta*—of nectar; *mādhurī*—the sweetness; *parimalaḥ*—whose flavor; *kalyāṇi*—O most auspicious one; *bīmba-adharaḥ*—red lips; *vaktram*—face; *paṅkaja-saurabham*—which smells like a lotus flower; *kuharita*—of the sweet sounds made by the cuckoos; *ślāghā*—the pride; *bhidaḥ*—which defeat; *te*—Your; *giraḥ*—words; *aṅgam*—limbs; *candana-śītalam*—as cool as sandalwood pulp; *tanuḥ*—body; *iyam*—this; *saundarya*—of beauty; *sarva-sva-bhāk*—which displays the all-in-all; *tvām*—You; *āsādya*—tasting; *mama*—My; *idam*—this; *indriya-kulam*—all the senses; *rādhe*—O Śrīmatī Rādhārāṇī; *muhuḥ*—again and again; *modate*—become pleased.

TRANSLATION

"'My dear auspicious Rādhārāṇī, Your body is the source of all beauty. Your red lips are softer than the sense of immortal sweetness, Your face bears the aroma of a lotus flower, Your sweet words defeat the vibrations of the cuckoo, and Your limbs are cooler than the pulp of sandalwood. All My transcendental senses are overwhelmed in ecstatic pleasure by tasting You, who are completely decorated by beautiful qualities.'

PURPORT

This verse, spoken by Lord Kṛṣṇa to Rādhā, is recorded in the *Lalita-mādhava* (9.9) of Śrīla Rūpa Gosvāmī.

TEXT 260

রূপে কংসহরস্য লুব্ধনয়নাং স্পর্শেঽতিহৃষ্যত্ত্বচং
বাণ্যামুৎকলিতশ্রুতিং পরিমলে সংহৃষ্টনাসাপুটাম্ ।
আরজ্যদ্রসনাং কিলাধরপুটে ন্যঞ্চন্মুখাম্ভোরুহাং
দম্ভোদ্গীর্ণমহাধৃতিং বহিরপি প্রোদ্যদ্বিকারাকুলাম্ ॥ ২৬০ ॥

rūpe kaṁsa-harasya lubdha-nayanāṁ sparśe 'tihṛṣyat-tvacaṁ
vāṇyām utkalita-śrutiṁ parimale saṁhṛṣṭa-nāsā-puṭām
ārajyad-rasanāṁ kilādhara-puṭe nyañcan-mukhāmbho-ruhāṁ
dambhodgīrṇa-mahā-dhṛtiṁ bahir api prodyad-vikārākulām

rūpe—in the beauty; *kaṁsa-harasya*—of Kṛṣṇa, the enemy of Kaṁsa; *lubdha*—captivated; *nayanām*—whose eyes; *sparśe*—in the touch; *ati-hṛṣyat*—very jubilant; *tvacam*—whose skin; *vāṇyām*—in the vibration of the words; *utkalita*—very eager; *śrutim*—whose ear; *parimale*—in the fragrance; *saṁhṛṣṭa*—stolen by happiness; *nāsā-puṭām*—whose nostrils; *ārajyat*—being completely attracted; *rasanām*—whose tongue; *kila*—what to speak of; *adhara-puṭe*—to the lips; *nyañcat*—bending down; *mukha*—whose face; *ambhaḥ-ruhām*—like a lotus flower; *dambha*—by pride; *udgīrṇa*—manifesting; *mahā-dhṛtim*—great patience; *bahiḥ*—externally; *api*—although; *prodyat*—manifesting; *vikāra*—transformations; *ākulām*—overwhelmed.

TRANSLATION

"'Her eyes are enchanted by the beauty of Lord Kṛṣṇa, the enemy of Kaṁsa. Her body thrills in pleasure at His touch. Her ears are always attracted to His sweet voice, Her nostrils are enchanted by His fragrance, and Her tongue hankers for the nectar of His soft lips. She hangs down her lotuslike face, exercising self-control only by pretense, but She cannot help showing the external signs of Her spontaneous love for Lord Kṛṣṇa.'

PURPORT

Thus Śrīla Rūpa Gosvāmī describes the countenance of Rādhārāṇī.

TEXT 261

তাতে জানি, মোতে আছে কোন এক রস ।
আমার মোহিনী রাধা, তারে করে বশ ॥ ২৬১ ॥

tāte jāni, mote āche kona eka rasa
āmāra mohinī rādhā, tāre kare vaśa

tāte—thereupon; *jāni*—I can understand; *mote*—in Me; *āche*—there is; *kona*—some; *eka*—one; *rasa*—transcendental mellow; *āmāra*—My; *mohinī*—captivator; *rādhā*—Śrīmatī Rādhārāṇī; *tāre*—Her; *kare vaśa*—subdues.

TRANSLATION

"Considering this, I can understand that some unknown mellow in Me controls the entire existence of My captivator, Śrīmatī Rādhārāṇī.

TEXT 262

আমা হৈতে রাধা পায় যে জাতীয় সুখ ।
তাহা আস্বাদিতে আমি সদাই উন্মুখ ॥ ২৬২ ॥

āmā haite rādhā pāya ye jātīya sukha
tāhā āsvādite āmi sadāi unmukha

āmā haite—from Me; *rādhā*—Śrīmatī Rādhārāṇī; *pāya*—gets; *ye*—whatever; *jātīya*—types of; *sukha*—happiness; *tāhā*—that; *āsvādite*—to taste; *āmi*—I; *sadāi*—always; *unmukha*—very eager.

TRANSLATION

"I am always eager to taste the joy that Rādhārāṇī derives from Me.

TEXT 263

নানা যত্ন করি আমি, নারি আস্বাদিতে ।
সেই সুখমাধুর্য-ঘ্রাণে লোভ বাঢ়ে চিত্তে ॥ ২৬৩ ॥

nānā yatna kari āmi, nāri āsvādite
sei sukha-mādhurya-ghrāṇe lobha bāḍhe citte

nānā—various; *yatna*—attempts; *kari*—do; *āmi*—I; *nāri*—I am not able; *āsvādite*—to taste; *sei*—that; *sukha*—of the happiness; *mādhurya*—the sweetness; *ghrāṇe*—by smelling; *lobha*—desire; *bāḍhe*—increases; *citte*—in the mind.

TRANSLATION

"In spite of various efforts, I have not been able to taste it. But My desire to relish that pleasure increases as I smell its sweetness.

TEXT 264

রস আস্বাদিতে আমি কৈল অবতার ।
প্রেমরস আস্বাদিল বিবিধ প্রকার ॥ ২৬৪ ॥

rasa āsvādite āmi kaila avatāra
prema-rasa āsvādila vividha prakāra

rasa—mellows; *āsvādite*—to taste; *āmi*—I; *kaila*—made; *avatāra*—incarnation; *prema-rasa*—transcendental mellows of love; *āsvādila*—I tasted; *vividha prakāra*—different varieties of.

TRANSLATION

"Formerly I appeared in the world to taste mellows, and I tasted the mellows of pure love in various ways.

TEXT 265

রাগমার্গে ভক্ত ভক্তি করে যে প্রকারে ।
তাহা শিখাইল লীলা-আচরণ-দ্বারে ॥ ২৬৫ ॥

rāga-mārge bhakta bhakti kare ye prakāre
tāhā śikhāila līlā-ācaraṇa-dvāre

rāga-mārge—on the path of spontaneous love; *bhakta*—the devotee; *bhakti*—devotional service; *kare*—does; *ye prakāre*—in what way; *tāhā*—that; *śikhāila*—I taught; *līlā*—pastimes; *ācaraṇa-dvāre*—by means of practical demonstration.

TRANSLATION

"I taught devotional service that springs from the devotees' spontaneous love by demonstrating it with My pastimes.

TEXT 266

এই তিন তৃষ্ণা মোর নহিল পূরণ ।
বিজাতীয়-ভাবে নহে তাহা আস্বাদন ॥ ২৬৬ ॥

ei tina tṛṣṇā mora nahila pūraṇa
vijātīya-bhāve nahe tāhā āsvādana

ei—these; *tina*—three; *tṛṣṇā*—desires; *mora*—My; *nahila*—were not; *pūraṇa*—satisfied; *vijātīya*—of the opposite partner of a relationship; *bhāve*—in ecstasy; *nahe*—is not possible; *tāhā*—that; *āsvādana*—tasting.

TRANSLATION

"But these three desires of Mine were not satisfied, for one cannot enjoy them in a contrary position.

TEXT 267

রাধিকার ভাবকান্তি অঙ্গীকার বিনে ।
সেই তিন সুখ কভু নহে আস্বাদনে ॥ ২৬৭ ॥

rādhikāra bhāva-kānti aṅgīkāra vine
sei tina sukha kabhu nahe āsvādane

rādhikāra—of Śrīmatī Rādhārāṇī; *bhāva-kānti*—luster of ecstatic love; *aṅgīkāra*—accepting; *vine*—without; *sei*—those; *tina*—three; *sukha*—happiness; *kabhu*—at any time; *nahe*—is not possible; *āsvādane*—tasting.

TRANSLATION

"Unless I accept the luster of the ecstatic love of Śrī Rādhikā, these three desires cannot be fulfilled.

TEXT 268

রাধাভাব অঙ্গীকরি' ধরি' তার বর্ণ ।
তিনসুখ আস্বাদিতে হব অবতীর্ণ ॥ ২৬৮ ॥

rādhā-bhāva aṅgīkari' dhari' tāra varṇa
tina-sukha āsvādite haba avatīrṇa

rādhā-bhāva—the moods of Rādhārāṇī; *aṅgīkari'*—accepting; *dhari'*—taking; *tāra varṇa*—Her bodily complexion; *tina*—three; *sukha*—happiness; *āsvādite*—to taste; *haba*—I shall; *avatīrṇa*—descend as an incarnation.

TRANSLATION

"Therefore, assuming Rādhārāṇī's sentiments and bodily complexion, I shall descend to fulfill these three desires."

TEXT 269

সর্বভাবে কৈল কৃষ্ণ এই ত' নিশ্চয় ।
হেনকালে আইল যুগাবতার-সময় ॥ ২৬৯ ॥

sarva-bhāve kaila kṛṣṇa ei ta' niścaya
hena-kāle āila yugāvatāra-samaya

sarva-bhāve—in all respects; *kaila*—made; *kṛṣṇa*—Lord Kṛṣṇa; *ei*—this; *ta'*—certainly; *niścaya*—decision; *hena-kāle*—at this time; *āila*—came; *yuga-avatāra*—of the incarnation according to the age; *samaya*—the time.

TRANSLATION

In this way Lord Kṛṣṇa came to a decision. Simultaneously, the time came for the incarnation of the age.

TEXT 270

সেইকালে শ্রীঅদ্বৈত করেন আরাধন ।
তাঁহার হুঙ্কারে কৈল কৃষ্ণে আকর্ষণ ॥ ২৭০ ॥

sei-kāle śrī-advaita karena ārādhana
tāṅhāra huṅkāre kaila kṛṣṇe ākarṣaṇa

sei-kāle—at that time; *śrī-advaita*—Advaita Ācārya; *karena*—performs; *ārādhana*—worship; *tāṅhāra*—of Him; *huṅkāre*—by the tumultuous call; *kaila*—did; *kṛṣṇe*—to Lord Kṛṣṇa; *ākarṣaṇa*—attraction.

TRANSLATION

At that time Śrī Advaita was earnestly worshiping Him. Advaita attracted Him with His loud calls.

TEXTS 271–272

পিতামাতা, গুরুগণ, আগে অবতারি' ।
রাধিকার ভাব-বর্ণ অঙ্গীকার করি' ॥ ২৭১ ॥
নবদ্বীপে শচীগর্ভ-শুদ্ধদুগ্ধসিন্ধু ।
তাহাতে প্রকট হৈলা কৃষ্ণ পূর্ণ ইন্দু ॥ ২৭২ ॥

pitā-mātā, guru-gaṇa, āge avatāri'
rādhikāra bhāva-varṇa aṅgīkāra kari'

nava-dvīpe śacī-garbha-śuddha-dugdha-sindhu
tāhāte prakaṭa hailā kṛṣṇa pūrṇa indu

pitā-mātā—parents; *guru-gaṇa*—teachers; *āge*—first; *avatāri'*—descending; *rādhikāra*—of Śrīmatī Rādhārāṇī; *bhāva-varṇa*—the luster of transcendental ecstasy; *aṅgīkāra kari'*—accepting; *navadvīpe*—in Navadvīpa; *śacī-garbha*—the womb of Śacī; *śuddha*—pure; *dugdha-sindhu*—the ocean of milk; *tāhāte*—in that; *prakaṭa*—manifested; *hailā*—became; *kṛṣṇa*—Lord Kṛṣṇa; *pūrṇa indu*—full moon.

TRANSLATION

First Lord Kṛṣṇa made His parents and elders appear. Then Kṛṣṇa Himself, with the sentiments and complexion of Rādhikā, appeared in Navadvīpa, like the full moon, from the womb of mother Śacī, which is like an ocean of pure milk.

TEXT 273

এই ত' করিলুঁ ষষ্ঠশ্লোকের ব্যাখ্যান ।
শ্রীরূপ-গোসাঞির পাদপদ্ম করি' ধ্যান ॥ ২৭৩ ॥

ei ta' kariluṅ ṣaṣṭha ślokera vyākhyāna
śrī-rūpa-gosāñira pāda-padma kari' dhyāna

ei ta'—thus; *kariluṅ*—I have made; *ṣaṣṭha ślokera*—of the sixth verse; *vyākhyāna*—explanation; *śrī-rūpa*—Śrīla Rūpa Gosvāmī; *gosāñira*—of the master; *pāda-padma*—lotus feet; *kari'*—doing; *dhyāna*—meditation.

TRANSLATION

Meditating on the lotus feet of Śrī Rūpa Gosvāmī, I have thus explained the sixth verse.

TEXT 274

এই দুই শ্লোকের আমি যে করিল অর্থ।
শ্রীরূপ-গোসাঞির শ্লোক প্রমাণ সমর্থ ॥ ২৭৪ ॥

ei dui ślokera āmi ye karila artha
śrī-rūpa-gosāñira śloka pramāṇa samartha

ei—these; *dui*—two; *ślokera*—of the verses; *āmi*—I; *ye*—whatever; *karila*—gave; *artha*—the meanings; *śrī-rūpa-gosāñira*—of Śrī Rūpa Gosvāmī; *śloka*—verse; *pramāṇa*—evidence; *samartha*—competent.

TRANSLATION

I can support the explanation of these two verses [verses 5 and 6 of the First Chapter] with a verse by Śrī Rūpa Gosvāmī.

TEXT 275

অপারং কস্যাপি প্রণয়িজনবৃন্দস্য কুতুকী
রসস্তোমং হৃত্বা মধুরমুপভোক্তুং কমপি যঃ।
রুচং স্বামাবব্রে দ্যুতিমিহ তদীয়াং প্রকটয়ন্
স দেবশ্চৈতন্যাকৃতিরতিতরাং নঃ কৃপয়তু ॥ ২৭৫ ॥

apāraṁ kasyāpi praṇayi-jana-vṛndasya kutukī
rasa-stomaṁ hṛtvā madhuram upabhoktuṁ kam api yaḥ
rucaṁ svāṁ āvavre dyutim iha tadīyāṁ prakaṭayan
sa devaś caitanyākṛtir atitarāṁ naḥ kṛpayatu

apāram—boundless; *kasya api*—of someone; *praṇayi-jana-vṛndasya*—of the multitude of lovers; *kutukī*—one who is curious; *rasa-stomam*—the group of mellows; *hṛtvā*—stealing; *madhuram*—sweet; *upabhoktum*—to enjoy; *kam api*—some; *yaḥ*—who; *rucam*—luster; *svām*—own; *āvavre*—covered; *dyutim*—luster; *iha*—here; *tadīyām*—related to Him; *prakaṭayan*—manifesting; *saḥ*—He; *devaḥ*—the Supreme Personality of Godhead; *caitanya-ākṛtiḥ*—having the form of Lord Caitanya Mahāprabhu; *atitarām*—greatly; *naḥ*—unto us; *kṛpayatu*—may He show His mercy.

TRANSLATION

"Lord Kṛṣṇa desired to taste the limitless nectarean mellows of the love possessed by one of His multitude of loving damsels [Śrī

Rādhā], and so He has assumed the form of Lord Caitanya. He has tasted that love while hiding His own dark complexion with Her effulgent yellow color. May that Lord Caitanya confer upon us His grace."

PURPORT

This is the third verse of the second *Caitanyāṣṭaka* of Śrīla Rūpa Gosvāmī's *Stava-mālā.*

TEXT 276

মঙ্গলাচরণং কৃষ্ণচৈতন্য-তত্ত্বলক্ষণম্ ।
প্রয়োজনঞ্চাবতারে শ্লোকষট্কৈর্নিরূপিতম্ ॥ ২৭৬ ॥

maṅgalācaraṇaṁ kṛṣṇa-
caitanya-tattva-lakṣaṇam
prayojanaṁ cāvatāre
śloka-ṣaṭkair nirūpitam

maṅgala-ācaraṇam—invoking auspiciousness; *kṛṣṇa-caitanya*—of Lord Kṛṣṇa Caitanya Mahāprabhu; *tattva-lakṣaṇam*—symptoms of the truth; *prayojanam*—necessity; *ca*—also; *avatāre*—in the matter of His incarnation; *śloka*—verses; *ṣaṭkaiḥ*—by six; *nirūpitam*—ascertained.

TRANSLATION

Thus the auspicious invocation, the essential nature of the truth of Lord Caitanya, and the need for His appearance have been set forth in six verses.

TEXT 277

শ্রীরূপ-রঘুনাথ-পদে যার আশ ।
চৈতন্যচরিতামৃত কহে কৃষ্ণদাস ॥ ২৭৭ ॥

śrī-rūpa-raghunātha-pade yāra āśa
caitanya-caritāmṛta kahe kṛṣṇadāsa

śrī-rūpa—Śrīla Rūpa Gosvāmī; *raghunātha*—Śrīla Raghunātha dāsa Gosvāmī; *pade*—at the lotus feet; *yāra*—whose; *āśa*—expectation; *caitanya-caritāmṛta*—the book named *Caitanya-caritāmṛta; kahe*—describes; *kṛṣṇa-dāsa*—Śrīla Kṛṣṇadāsa Kavirāja Gosvāmī.

TRANSLATION

Praying at the lotus feet of Śrī Rūpa and Śrī Raghunātha, always desiring their mercy, I, Kṛṣṇadāsa, narrate Śrī Caitanya-caritāmṛta, following in their footsteps.

Thus end the Bhaktivedanta purports to Śrī Caitanya-caritāmṛta, Ādi-līlā, *Fourth Chapter, describing the confidential reasons for the appearance of Lord Caitanya.*

CHAPTER FIVE

The Glories of Lord Nityānanda Balarāma

This chapter is chiefly devoted to describing the essential nature and glories of Śrī Nityānanda Prabhu. Lord Śrī Kṛṣṇa is the absolute Personality of Godhead, and His first expansion in a form for pastimes is Śrī Balarāma.

Beyond the limitation of this material world is the spiritual sky, *paravyoma,* which has many spiritual planets, the supreme of which is called Kṛṣṇaloka. Kṛṣṇaloka, the abode of Kṛṣṇa, has three divisions, which are known as Dvārakā, Mathurā and Gokula. In that abode the Personality of Godhead expands Himself into four plenary portions—Kṛṣṇa, Balarāma, Pradyumna (the transcendental Cupid) and Aniruddha. They are known as the original quadruple forms.

In Kṛṣṇaloka is a transcendental place known as Śvetadvīpa or Vṛndāvana. Below Kṛṣṇaloka in the spiritual sky are the Vaikuṇṭha planets. On each Vaikuṇṭha planet a four-handed Nārāyaṇa, expanded from the first quadruple manifestation, is present. The Personality of Godhead known as Śrī Balarāma in Kṛṣṇaloka is the original Saṅkarṣaṇa (attracting Deity), and from this Saṅkarṣaṇa expands another Saṅkarṣaṇa, called Mahā-saṅkarṣaṇa, who resides in one of the Vaikuṇṭha planets. By His internal potency, Mahā-saṅkarṣaṇa maintains the transcendental existence of all the planets in the spiritual sky, where all the living beings are eternally liberated souls. The influence of the material energy is conspicuous there by its absence. On those planets the second quadruple manifestation is present.

Outside of the Vaikuṇṭha planets is the impersonal manifestation of Śrī Kṛṣṇa, which is known as Brahmaloka. On the other side of Brahmaloka is the spiritual *kāraṇa-samudra,* or Causal Ocean. The material energy exists on the other side of the Causal Ocean, without touching it. In the Causal Ocean is Mahā-Viṣṇu, the original *puruṣa* expansion from Saṅkarṣaṇa. Mahā-Viṣṇu places His glance over the material energy, and by a reflection of His transcendental body He amalgamates Himself within the material elements.

As the source of the material elements, the material energy is known as *pradhāna*, and as the source of the manifestations of the material energy it is known as *māyā*. But material nature is inert in that she has no independent power to do anything. She is empowered to make the cosmic manifestation by the glance of Mahā-Viṣṇu. Therefore the material energy is not the original cause of the material manifestation. Rather, the transcendental glance of Mahā-Viṣṇu over material nature produces that cosmic manifestation.

Mahā-Viṣṇu again enters every universe as the reservoir of all living entities, Garbhodakaśāyī Viṣṇu. From Garbhodakaśāyī Viṣṇu expands Kṣīrodakaśāyī Viṣṇu, the Supersoul of every living entity. Garbhodakaśāyī Viṣṇu also has His own Vaikuṇṭha planet in every universe, where He lives as the Supersoul or supreme controller of the universe. Garbhodakaśāyī Viṣṇu reclines in the midst of the watery portion of the universe and generates the first living creature of the universe, Brahmā. The imaginary universal form is a partial manifestation of Garbhodakaśāyī Viṣṇu.

On the Vaikuṇṭha planet in every universe is an ocean of milk, and within that ocean is an island called Śvetadvīpa, where Lord Viṣṇu lives. Therefore this chapter describes two Śvetadvīpas—one in the abode of Kṛṣṇa and the other in the ocean of milk in every universe. The Śvetadvīpa in the abode of Kṛṣṇa is identical with Vṛndāvana-dhāma, which is the place where Kṛṣṇa appears Himself to display His loving pastimes. In the Śvetadvīpa within every universe is a Śeṣa form of Godhead who serves Viṣṇu by assuming the form of His umbrella, slippers, couch, pillows, garments, residence, sacred thread, throne and so on.

Lord Baladeva in Kṛṣṇaloka is Nityānanda Prabhu. Therefore Nityānanda Prabhu is the original Saṅkarṣaṇa, and Mahā-saṅkarṣaṇa and His expansions as the *puruṣas* in the universes are plenary expansions of Nityānanda Prabhu.

In this chapter the author has described the history of his leaving home for a personal pilgrimage to Vṛndāvana and his achieving all success there. In this description it is revealed that the author's original paternal home and birthplace were in the district of Katwa, in the village of Jhāmaṭapura, which is near Naihāṭī. Kṛṣṇadāsa Kavirāja's brother invited Śrī Mīnaketana Rāmadāsa, a great devotee of Lord Nityānanda, to his home, but a priest named Guṇārṇava Miśra did not receive him well, and Kṛṣṇadāsa Kavirāja Gosvāmī's brother, not recognizing the glories of Lord Nityānanda, also took sides with the priest. Therefore Rāmadāsa became sorry, broke his flute and went away. This was a great disaster for the brother of Kṛṣṇadāsa Kavirāja Gosvāmī. But on that very night Lord Nityānanda Prabhu Himself graced Kṛṣṇadāsa Kavirāja Gosvāmī in a dream and ordered him to leave on the next day for Vṛndāvana.

TEXT 1

বন্দেঽনন্তাদ্ভুতৈশ্বর্যং শ্রীনিত্যানন্দমীশ্বরম্ ।
যস্যেচ্ছয়া তৎস্বরূপমজ্ঞেনাপি নিরূপ্যতে ॥ ১ ॥

vande 'nantādbhutaiśvaryaṁ
śrī-nityānandam īśvaram
yasyecchayā tat-svarūpam
ajñenāpi nirūpyate

vande—let me offer my obeisances; *ananta*—unlimited; *adbhuta*—and wonderful; *aiśvaryam*—whose opulence; *śrī-nityānandam*—unto Lord Nityānanda; *īśvaram*—the Supreme Personality of Godhead; *yasya*—whose; *icchayā*—by the will; *tat-svarūpam*—His identity; *ajñena*—by the ignorant; *api*—even; *nirūpyate*—can be ascertained.

TRANSLATION

Let me offer my obeisances to Lord Śrī Nityānanda, the Supreme Personality of Godhead, whose opulence is wonderful and unlimited. By His will, even a fool can understand His identity.

TEXT 2

জয় জয় শ্রীচৈতন্য জয় নিত্যানন্দ ।
জয়াদ্বৈতচন্দ্র জয় গৌরভক্তবৃন্দ ॥ ২ ॥

jaya jaya śrī-caitanya jaya nityānanda
jayādvaita-candra jaya gaura-bhakta-vṛnda

jaya jaya—all glories; *śrī-caitanya*—to Śrī Caitanya Mahāprabhu; *jaya nityānanda*—all glories to Lord Nityānanda; *jaya advaita-candra*—all glories to Advaita Ācārya; *jaya gaura-bhakta-vṛnda*—all glories to the devotees of Lord Śrī Caitanya Mahāprabhu.

TRANSLATION

All glories to Śrī Caitanya Mahāprabhu! All glories to Lord Nityānanda! All glories to Advaita Ācārya! And all glories to all the devotees of Lord Caitanya Mahāprabhu!

TEXT 3

এই ষট্‌শ্লোকে কহিল কৃষ্ণচৈতন্য-মহিমা।
পঞ্চশ্লোকে কহি নিত্যানন্দতত্ত্ব-সীমা ॥ ৩ ॥

ei ṣaṭ-śloke kahila kṛṣṇa-caitanya-mahimā
pañca-śloke kahi nityānanda-tattva-sīmā

ei—this; *ṣaṭ-śloke*—in six verses; *kahila*—described; *kṛṣṇa-caitanya-mahimā*—the glories of Lord Śrī Caitanya Mahāprabhu; *pañca-śloke*—in five verses; *kahi*—let me explain; *nityānanda*—of Lord Nityānanda; *tattva*—of the truth; *sīmā*—the limitation.

TRANSLATION

I have described the glory of Śrī Kṛṣṇa Caitanya in six verses. Now, in five verses I shall describe the glory of Lord Nityānanda.

TEXT 4

সর্ব-অবতারী কৃষ্ণ স্বয়ং ভগবান্।
তাঁহার দ্বিতীয় দেহ শ্রীবলরাম ॥ ৪ ॥

sarva-avatārī kṛṣṇa svayaṁ bhagavān
tāṅhāra dvitīya deha śrī-balarāma

sarva-avatārī—the source of all incarnations; *kṛṣṇa*—Lord Kṛṣṇa; *svayam*—personally; *bhagavān*—the Supreme Personality of Godhead; *tāṅhāra*—His; *dvitīya*—second; *deha*—expansion of the body; *śrī-balarāma*—Lord Balarāma.

TRANSLATION

The Supreme Personality of Godhead, Kṛṣṇa, is the fountainhead of all incarnations. Lord Balarāma is His second body.

PURPORT

Lord Śrī Kṛṣṇa, the absolute Personality of Godhead, is the primeval Lord, the original form of Godhead, and His first expansion is Śrī Balarāma. The Personality of Godhead can expand Himself in innumerable forms. The forms that have unlimited potency are called *svāṁśa*, and forms that have limited potencies (the living entities) are called *vibhinnāṁśa.*

TEXT 5

একই স্বরূপ দোঁহে, ভিন্নমাত্র কায় ।
আদ্য কায়ব্যূহ, কৃষ্ণলীলার সহায় ॥ ৫ ॥

eka-i svarūpa doṅhe, bhinna-mātra kāya
ādya kāya-vyūha, kṛṣṇa-līlāra sahāya

eka-i—one; *svarūpa*—identity; *doṅhe*—both of Them; *bhinna-mātra kāya*—only two different bodies; *ādya*—original; *kāya-vyūha*—quadruple expansions; *kṛṣṇa-līlāra*—in the pastimes of Lord Kṛṣṇa; *sahāya*—assistance.

TRANSLATION

These two are one and the same identity. They differ only in form. Lord Balarāma is the first bodily expansion of Kṛṣṇa, and He assists in Lord Kṛṣṇa's transcendental pastimes.

PURPORT

Balarāma is a *svāṁśa* expansion of the Lord, and therefore there is no difference in potency between Kṛṣṇa and Balarāma. The only difference is in Their bodily structure. As the first expansion of Godhead, Balarāma is the chief Deity among the first quadruple forms, and He is the foremost assistant of Śrī Kṛṣṇa in His transcendental activities.

TEXT 6

সেই কৃষ্ণ—নবদ্বীপে শ্রীচৈতন্যচন্দ্র ।
সেই বলরাম—সঙ্গে শ্রীনিত্যানন্দ ॥ ৬ ॥

sei kṛṣṇa—navadvīpe śrī-caitanya-candra
sei balarāma—saṅge śrī-nityānanda

sei kṛṣṇa—that original Kṛṣṇa; *navadvīpe*—at Navadvīpa; *śrī-caitanya-candra*—Lord Śrī Caitanya Mahāprabhu; *sei balarāma*—that Lord Balarāma; *saṅge*—with Him; *śrī-nityānanda*—Lord Nityānanda.

TRANSLATION

That original Lord Kṛṣṇa appeared in Navadvīpa as Lord Caitanya, and Balarāma appeared with Him as Lord Nityānanda.

TEXT 7

সঙ্কর্ষণঃ কারণতোয়শায়ী গর্ভোদশায়ী চ পয়োঽব্ধিশায়ী ।
শেষশ্চ যস্যাংশকলাঃ স নিত্যানন্দাখ্যরামঃ শরণং মমাস্তু ॥ ৭ ॥

saṅkarṣaṇaḥ kāraṇa-toya-śāyī
garbhoda-śāyī ca payobdhi-śāyī
śeṣaś ca yasyāṁśa-kalāḥ sa nityā-
nandākhya-rāmaḥ śaraṇaṁ mamāstu

saṅkarṣaṇaḥ—Mahā-saṅkarṣaṇa in the spiritual sky; *kāraṇa-toya-śāyī*—Kāraṇodakaśāyī Viṣṇu, who lies in the Causal Ocean; *garbha-uda-śāyī*—Garbhodakaśāyī Viṣṇu, who lies in the Garbhodaka Ocean of the universe; *ca*—and; *payaḥ-abdhi-śāyī*—Kṣīrodakaśāyī Viṣṇu, who lies in the ocean of milk; *śeṣaḥ*—Śeṣa Nāga, the couch of Viṣṇu; *ca*—and; *yasya*—whose; *aṁśa*—plenary portions; *kalāḥ*—and parts of the plenary portions; *saḥ*—He; *nityānanda-ākhya*—known as Lord Nityānanda; *rāmaḥ*—Lord Balarāma; *śaraṇam*—shelter; *mama*—my; *astu*—let there be.

TRANSLATION

May Śrī Nityānanda Rāma be the object of my constant remembrance. Saṅkarṣaṇa, Śeṣa Nāga and the Viṣṇus who lie on the Kāraṇa Ocean, Garbha Ocean and ocean of milk are His plenary portions and the portions of His plenary portions.

PURPORT

Śrī Svarūpa Dāmodara Gosvāmī has recorded this verse in his diary to offer his respectful obeisances to Lord Nityānanda Prabhu. This verse also appears as the seventh of the first fourteen verses of *Śrī Caitanya-caritāmṛta.*

TEXT 8

শ্রীবলরাম গোসাঞি মূল-সঙ্কর্ষণ ।
পঞ্চরূপ ধরি' করেন কৃষ্ণের সেবন ॥ ৮ ॥

śrī-balarāma gosāñi mūla-saṅkarṣaṇa
pañca-rūpa dhari' karena kṛṣṇera sevana

śrī-balarāma—Balarāma; *gosāñi*—the Lord; *mūla-saṅkarṣaṇa*—the original Saṅkarṣaṇa; *pañca-rūpa dhari'*—accepting five bodies; *karena*—does; *kṛṣṇera*—of Lord Kṛṣṇa; *sevana*—service.

TRANSLATION

Lord Balarāma is the original Saṅkarṣaṇa. He assumes five other forms to serve Lord Kṛṣṇa.

TEXT 9

আপনে করেন কৃষ্ণলীলার সহায় ।
সৃষ্টিলীলা-কার্য করে ধরি' চারি কায় ॥ ৯ ॥

āpane karena kṛṣṇa-līlāra sahāya
sṛṣṭi-līlā-kārya kare dhari' cāri kāya

āpane—personally; *karena*—performs; *kṛṣṇa-līlāra sahāya*—assistance in the pastimes of Lord Kṛṣṇa; *sṛṣṭi-līlā*—of the pastimes of creation; *kārya*—the work; *kare*—does; *dhari'*—accepting; *cāri kāya*—four bodies.

TRANSLATION

He Himself helps in the pastimes of Lord Kṛṣṇa, and He does the work of creation in four other forms.

TEXT 10

সৃষ্ট্যাদিক সেবা,—তাঁর আজ্ঞার পালন ।
'শেষ'-রূপে করে কৃষ্ণের বিবিধ সেবন ॥ ১০ ॥

sṛṣṭy-ādika sevā,—tāṅra ājñāra pālana
'śeṣa'-rūpe kare kṛṣṇera vividha sevana

sṛṣṭi-ādika sevā—service in the matter of creation; *tāṅra*—His; *ājñāra*—of the order; *pālana*—execution; *śeṣa-rūpe*—the form of Lord Śeṣa; *kare*—does; *kṛṣṇera*—of Lord Kṛṣṇa; *vividha sevana*—varieties of service.

TRANSLATION

He executes the orders of Lord Kṛṣṇa in the work of creation, and in the form of Lord Śeṣa He serves Kṛṣṇa in various ways.

PURPORT

According to expert opinion, Balarāma, as the chief of the original quadruple forms, is also the original Saṅkarṣaṇa. Balarāma, the first expansion of Kṛṣṇa, expands Himself in five forms: (1) Mahā-saṅkarṣaṇa, (2) Kāraṇābdhiśāyī, (3) Garbhodakaśāyī, (4) Kṣīrodaka-śāyī, and (5) Śeṣa. These five plenary portions are responsible for both the spiritual and material cosmic manifestations. In these five forms Lord Balarāma assists Lord Kṛṣṇa in His activities. The first four of these forms are responsible for the cosmic manifestations, whereas Śeṣa is responsible for personal service to the Lord. Śeṣa is called Ananta, or unlimited, because He assists the Personality of Godhead in His unlimited expansions by performing an unlimited variety of services. Śrī Balarāma is the servitor Godhead who serves Lord Kṛṣṇa in all affairs of existence and knowledge. Lord Nityānanda Prabhu, who is the same servitor Godhead, Balarāma, performs the same service to Lord Gaurāṅga by constant association.

TEXT 11

সর্বরূপে আস্বাদয়ে কৃষ্ণ-সেবানন্দ ।
সেই বলরাম—গৌরসঙ্গে নিত্যানন্দ ॥ ১১ ॥

sarva-rūpe āsvādaye kṛṣṇa-sevānanda
sei balarāma—gaura-saṅge nityānanda

sarva-rūpe—in all these forms; *āsvādaye*—tastes; *kṛṣṇa-sevā-ānanda*—the transcendental bliss of serving Kṛṣṇa; *sei balarāma*—that Lord Balarāma; *gaura-saṅge*—with Gaurasundara; *nityānanda*—Lord Nityānanda.

TRANSLATION

In all the forms He tastes the transcendental bliss of serving Kṛṣṇa. That same Balarāma is Lord Nityānanda, the companion of Lord Gaurasundara.

TEXT 12

সপ্তম শ্লোকের অর্থ করি চারিশ্লোকে ।
যাতে নিত্যানন্দতত্ত্ব জানে সর্বলোকে ॥ ১২ ॥

saptama ślokera artha kari cāri-śloke
yāte nityānanda-tattva jāne sarva-loke

saptama ślokera—of the seventh verse; *artha*—the meaning; *kari*—I do; *cāri-śloke*—in four verses; *yāte*—in which; *nityānanda-tattva*—the truth of Lord Nityānanda; *jāne*—one knows; *sarva-loke*—all over the world.

TRANSLATION

I have explained the seventh verse in four subsequent verses. By these verses all the world can know the truth about Lord Nityānanda.

TEXT 13

মায়াতীতে ব্যাপিবৈকুণ্ঠলোকে
পূর্ণৈশ্বর্যে শ্রীচতুর্ব্যূহমধ্যে ।
রূপং যস্যোদ্ভাতি সঙ্কর্ষণাখ্যং
তং শ্রীনিত্যানন্দরামং প্রপদ্যে ॥ ১৩ ॥

māyātīte vyāpi-vaikuṇṭha-loke
pūrṇaiśvarye śrī-catur-vyūha-madhye
rūpaṁ yasyodbhāti saṅkarṣaṇākhyaṁ
taṁ śrī-nityānanda-rāmaṁ prapadye

māyā-atīte—beyond the material creation; *vyāpi*—all-expanding; *vaikuṇṭha-loke*—in Vaikuṇṭhaloka, the spiritual world; *pūrṇa-aiśvarye*—endowed with full opulence; *śrī-catuḥ-vyūha-madhye*—in the quadruple expansions (Vāsudeva, Saṅkarṣaṇa, Pradyumna and

Aniruddha); *rūpam*—form; *yasya*—whose; *udbhāti*—appears; *saṅkarṣaṇa-ākhyam*—known as Saṅkarṣaṇa; *tam*—to Him; *śrī-nityānanda-rāmam*—to Lord Balarāma in the form of Lord Nityānanda; *prapadye*—I surrender.

TRANSLATION

I surrender unto the lotus feet of Śrī Nityānanda Rāma, who is known as Saṅkarṣaṇa in the midst of the catur-vyūha [consisting of Vāsudeva, Saṅkarṣaṇa, Pradyumna and Aniruddha]. He possesses full opulences and resides in Vaikuṇṭhaloka, far beyond the material creation.

PURPORT

This is a verse from Śrī Svarūpa Dāmodara Gosvāmī's diary. It appears as the eighth of the first fourteen verses of *Śrī Caitanya-caritāmṛta.*

TEXT 14

প্রকৃতির পার 'পরব্যোম'-নামে ধাম।
কৃষ্ণবিগ্রহ যৈছে বিভূত্যাদি-গুণবান্ ॥ ১৪ ॥

prakṛtira pāra 'paravyoma'-nāme dhāma
kṛṣṇa-vigraha yaiche vibhūty-ādi-guṇavān

prakṛtira—the material nature; *pāra*—beyond; *para-vyoma*—the spiritual sky; *nāme*—in name; *dhāma*—the place; *kṛṣṇa-vigraha*—the form of Lord Kṛṣṇa; *yaiche*—just as; *vibhūti-ādi*—like the six opulences; *guṇa-vān*—full with transcendental attributes.

TRANSLATION

Beyond the material nature lies the realm known as paravyoma, the spiritual sky. Like Lord Kṛṣṇa Himself, it possesses all transcendental attributes, such as the six opulences.

PURPORT

According to Sāṅkhya philosophy, the material cosmos is composed of twenty-four elements: the five gross material elements, the three subtle material elements, the five knowledge-acquiring senses, the five active senses, the five objects of sense pleasure, and the *mahat-tattva* (the total material energy). Empiric philosophers, unable to go beyond these elements, speculate that anything beyond them must be *avyakta*, or inexplicable. But the world beyond the twenty-four elements is not inexplicable, for it is explained in the *Bhagavad-gītā* as the eternal (*sanātana*) nature. Beyond the manifested and unmanifested existence of material nature (*vyaktāvyakta*) is the *sanātana* nature, which is called the *paravyoma*, or the spiritual sky. Since that nature is spiritual in quality, there are no qualitative differences there: everything there is spiritual, everything is good, and everything possesses the spiritual form of Śrī Kṛṣṇa Himself. That spiritual sky is the manifested internal potency of Śrī Kṛṣṇa; it is distinct from the material sky, manifested by His external potency.

The all-pervading Brahman, composed of the impersonal glowing rays of Śrī Kṛṣṇa, exists in the spiritual world with the Vaikuṇṭha planets. We can get some idea of that spiritual sky by a comparison to the material sky, for the rays of the sun in the material sky can be compared to the *brahmajyoti*, the glowing rays of the Personality of Godhead. In the *brahmajyoti* there are unlimited Vaikuṇṭha planets, which are spiritual and therefore self-luminous, with a glow many times greater than that of the sun. The Personality of Godhead Śrī Kṛṣṇa, His innumerable plenary portions and the portions of His plenary portions dominate each Vaikuṇṭha planet. In the highest region of the spiritual sky is the planet called Kṛṣṇaloka, which has three divisions, namely Dvārakā, Mathurā and Goloka, or Gokula.

To a gross materialist this kingdom of God, Vaikuṇṭha, is certainly a mystery. But to an ignorant man everything is a mystery for want of sufficient knowledge. The kingdom of God is not a myth. Even the material planets, which float over our heads in the millions and billions, are still a mystery to the ignorant. Material scientists are now attempting to penetrate this mystery, and a day may come when the people of this earth will be able to travel in outer space and see the variegatedness of these millions of planets with their own eyes. In every planet there is as much material variegatedness as we find in our own planet.

This planet earth is but an insignificant spot in the cosmic structure. Yet foolish men, puffed up by a false sense of scientific advancement, have concentrated their energy in the pursuit of so-called economic development on this planet, not knowing of the variegated economic facilities available on other planets. According to modern astronomy, the gravity of the moon is different from that of earth. Therefore one who goes to the moon will be able to pick up large weights and jump vast distances. In the *Rāmāyaṇa,* Hanumān is described as being able to lift huge weights as heavy as hills and jump over the ocean. Modern astronomy has confirmed that this is indeed possible.

The disease of the modern civilized man is his disbelief of everything in the revealed scriptures. Faithless nonbelievers cannot make progress in spiritual realization, for they cannot understand the spiritual potency. The small fruit of a banyan contains hundreds of seeds, and in each seed is the potency to produce another banyan tree with the potency to produce millions more of such fruits. This law of nature is visible before us, although how it works is beyond our understanding. This is but an insignificant example of the potency of Godhead; there are many similar phenomena that no scientist can explain.

Everything, in fact, is inconceivable, for the truth is revealed only to the proper persons. Although there are varieties of personalities, from Brahmā down to the insignificant ant, all of whom are living beings, their development of knowledge is different. Therefore we have to gather knowledge from the right source. Indeed, in reality we can get knowledge only from the Vedic sources. The four *Vedas,* with their supplementary *Purāṇas,* the *Mahābhārata,* the *Rāmāyaṇa* and their corollaries, which are known as *smṛtis,* are all authorized sources of knowledge. If we are at all to gather knowledge, we must gather it from these sources without hesitation.

Revealed knowledge may in the beginning be unbelievable because of our paradoxical desire to verify everything with our tiny brains, but the speculative means of attaining knowledge is always imperfect. The perfect knowledge propounded in the revealed scriptures is confirmed by the great *ācāryas,* who have left ample commentations upon them; none of these *ācāryas* has disbelieved in the *śāstras.* One who disbelieves in the *śāstras* is an atheist, and we should not consult an atheist, however great he may be. A staunch believer in the *śāstras,* with all their diversities, is the right person from whom to gather real knowledge. Such knowledge may seem inconceivable in the beginning, but when put forward by the proper authority its meaning is revealed, and then one no longer has any doubts about it.

TEXT 15

সর্বগ, অনন্ত, বিভু— বৈকুণ্ঠাদি ধাম ।
কৃষ্ণ, কৃষ্ণ-অবতারের তাহাঞি বিশ্রাম ॥ ১৫ ॥

sarvaga, ananta, vibhu—vaikuṇṭhādi dhāma
kṛṣṇa, kṛṣṇa-avatārera tāhāñi viśrāma

sarva-ga—all-pervading; *ananta*—unlimited; *vibhu*—greatest; *vaikuṇṭha-ādi dhāma*—all the places known as Vaikuṇṭhaloka; *kṛṣṇa*—of Lord Kṛṣṇa; *kṛṣṇa-avatārera*—of the incarnations of Lord Kṛṣṇa; *tāhāñi*—there; *viśrāma*—the residence.

TRANSLATION

That Vaikuṇṭha region is all-pervading, infinite and supreme. It is the residence of Lord Kṛṣṇa and His incarnations.

TEXT 16

তাহার উপরিভাগে 'কৃষ্ণলোক'-খ্যাতি ।
দ্বারকা-মথুরা-গোকুল—ত্রিবিধত্বে স্থিতি ॥ ১৬ ॥

tāhāra upari-bhāge 'kṛṣṇa-loka'-khyāti
dvārakā-mathurā-gokula—tri-vidhatve sthiti

tāhāra—of all of them; *upari-bhāge*—on the top; *kṛṣṇa-loka-khyāti*—the planet known as Kṛṣṇaloka; *dvārakā-mathurā-gokula*—the three places known as Dvārakā, Mathurā and Vṛndāvana; *tri-vidhatve*—in three departments; *sthiti*—situated.

TRANSLATION

In the highest region of that spiritual sky is the spiritual planet called Kṛṣṇaloka. It has three divisions—Dvārakā, Mathurā and Gokula.

TEXT 17

সর্বোপরি শ্রীগোকুল—ব্রজলোক-ধাম ।
শ্রীগোলোক, শ্বেতদ্বীপ, বৃন্দাবন নাম ॥ ১৭ ॥

sarvopari śrī-gokula—vrajaloka-dhāma
śrī-goloka, śvetadvīpa, vṛndāvana nāma

sarva-upari—above all of them; *śrī-gokula*—the place known as Gokula; *vraja-loka-dhāma*—the place of Vraja; *śrī-goloka*—the place named Goloka; *śveta-dvīpa*—the white island; *vṛndāvana nāma*—also named Vṛndāvana.

TRANSLATION

Śrī Gokula, the highest of all, is also called Vraja, Goloka, Śvetadvīpa and Vṛndāvana.

TEXT 18

সর্বগ, অনন্ত, বিভু, কৃষ্ণতনুসম ।
উপর্যধো ব্যাপিয়াছে, নাহিক নিয়ম ॥ ১৮ ॥

sarvaga, ananta, vibhu, kṛṣṇa-tanu-sama
upary-adho vyāpiyāche, nāhika niyama

sarva-ga—all-pervading; *ananta*—unlimited; *vibhu*—the greatest; *kṛṣṇa-tanu-sama*—exactly like the transcendental body of Kṛṣṇa; *upari-adhaḥ*—up and down; *vyāpiyāche*—expanded; *nāhika*—there is no; *niyama*—regulation.

TRANSLATION

Like the transcendental body of Lord Kṛṣṇa, Gokula is all-pervading, infinite and supreme. It expands both above and below, without any restriction.

PURPORT

Śrīla Jīva Gosvāmī, the great authority and philosopher in the line of Śrī Caitanya Mahāprabhu, has discussed the abode of Kṛṣṇa in his *Kṛṣṇa-sandarbha.* In the *Bhagavad-gītā* the Lord refers to "My abode." Śrīla Jīva Gosvāmī, examining the nature of Kṛṣṇa's abode, refers to the *Skanda Purāṇa*, which states:

yā yathā bhuvi vartante puryo bhagavataḥ priyāḥ
tās tathā santi vaikuṇṭhe tat-tal-līlārtham ādṛtāḥ

"The abodes of Godhead in the material world, such as Dvārakā, Mathurā and Gokula, are facsimiles representing the abodes of Godhead in the kingdom of God, Vaikuṇṭha-dhāma." The unlimited spiritual atmosphere of that Vaikuṇṭha-dhāma is far above and beyond the material cosmos. This is confirmed in the *Svāyambhuva-tantra,* in a discussion between Lord Śiva and Pārvatī regarding the effect of chanting the *mantra* of fourteen syllables. There it is stated:

nānā-kalpa-latākīrṇaṁ vaikuṇṭhaṁ vyāpakaṁ smaret
adhaḥ sāmyaṁ guṇānāṁ ca prakṛtiḥ sarva-kāraṇam

"While chanting the *mantra,* one should always remember the spiritual world, which is very extensive and full of desire trees that can yield anything one desires. Below that Vaikuṇṭha region is the potential material energy, which causes the material manifestation." The places of the pastimes of Lord Kṛṣṇa, such as Dvārakā, Mathurā and Vṛndāvana, eternally and independently exist in Kṛṣṇaloka. They are the actual abodes of Lord Kṛṣṇa, and there is no doubt that they are situated above the material cosmic manifestation.

The abode known as Vṛndāvana or Gokula is also known as Goloka. The *Brahma-saṁhitā* states that Gokula, the highest region of the kingdom of God, resembles a lotus flower with thousands of petals. The outer portion of that lotuslike planet is a square place known as Śvetadvīpa. In the inner portion of Gokula there is an elaborate arrangement for Śrī Kṛṣṇa's residence with His eternal associates such as Nanda and Yaśodā. That transcendental abode exists by the energy of Śrī Baladeva, who is the original whole of Śeṣa, or Ananta. The *tantras* also confirm this description by stating that the abode of Śrī Anantadeva, a plenary portion of Baladeva, is called the kingdom of God. Vṛndāvana-dhāma is the innermost abode within the quadrangular realm of Śvetadvīpa, which lies outside of the boundary of Gokula Vṛndāvana.

According to Jīva Gosvāmī, Vaikuṇṭha is also called Brahmaloka. The *Nārada-pañcarātra,* in a statement concerning the mystery of Vijaya, describes:

tat sarvopari goloke tatra lokopari svayam
viharet paramānandī govindo 'tula-nāyakaḥ

"The predominator of the *gopīs,* Govinda, the principal Deity of Gokula, always enjoys Himself in a place called Goloka, in the topmost part of the spiritual sky."

From the authoritative evidence cited by Jīva Gosvāmī we may conclude that Kṛṣṇaloka is the supreme planet in the spiritual sky, which is far beyond the material cosmos. For the enjoyment of transcendental variety, the pastimes of Kṛṣṇa there have three divisions, and these pastimes are performed in the three abodes Dvārakā, Mathurā and Gokula. When Kṛṣṇa descends to this universe, He enjoys the pastimes in places of the same name. These places on earth are nondifferent from those original abodes, for they are facsimiles of those original holy places in the transcendental world. They are as good as Śrī Kṛṣṇa Himself and are equally worshipable. Lord Caitanya declared that Lord Kṛṣṇa, who presents Himself as the son of the King of Vraja, is worshipable, and that Vṛndāvana-dhāma is equally worshipable.

TEXT 19

ব্রহ্মাণ্ডে প্রকাশ তার কৃষ্ণের ইচ্ছায় ।
একই স্বরূপ তার, নাহি দুই কায় ॥ ১৯ ॥

brahmāṇḍe prakāśa tāra kṛṣṇera icchāya
eka-i svarūpa tāra, nāhi dui kāya

brahmāṇḍe—within the material world; *prakāśa*—manifestation; *tāra*—of it; *kṛṣṇera icchāya*—by the supreme will of Lord Kṛṣṇa; *eka-i*—it is the same; *svarūpa*—identity; *tāra*—of it; *nāhi*—not; *dui*—two; *kāya*—bodies.

TRANSLATION

That abode is manifested within the material world by the will of Lord Kṛṣṇa. It is identical to that original Gokula; they are not two different bodies.

PURPORT

The above-mentioned *dhāmas* are movable, by the omnipotent will of Lord Kṛṣṇa. When Śrī Kṛṣṇa appears on the face of the earth, He can also make His *dhāmas* appear, without changing their original structure. One should not discriminate between the *dhāmas* on the earth and those in the spiritual sky, thinking those on earth to be material and the original abodes to be spiritual. All of them are spiritual. Only for us, who cannot experience anything beyond matter in our present conditioned state, do the *dhāmas* and the Lord Himself, in His *arcā* form, appear before us resembling matter to give us the facility to see spirit with material eyes. In the beginning this may be difficult for a neophyte to understand, but in due course, when one is advanced in devotional service, it will be easier, and he will appreciate the Lord's presence in these tangible forms.

TEXT 20

চিন্তামণিভূমি, কল্পবৃক্ষময় বন ।
চর্মচক্ষে দেখে তারে প্রপঞ্চের সম ॥ ২০ ॥

cintāmaṇi-bhūmi, kalpa-vṛkṣa-maya vana
carma-cakṣe dekhe tāre prapañcera sama

cintāmaṇi-bhūmi—the land of touchstone; *kalpa-vṛkṣa-maya*—full of desire trees; *vana*—forests; *carma-cakṣe*—the material eyes; *dekhe*—see; *tāre*—it; *prapañcera sama*—equal to the material creation.

TRANSLATION

The land there is touchstone [cintāmaṇi], and the forests abound with desire trees. Material eyes see it as an ordinary place.

PURPORT

By the grace of the Lord His *dhāmas* and He Himself can all be present simultaneously, without losing their original importance. Only when one fully develops in affection and love of Godhead can one see those *dhāmas* in their original appearance.

Śrīla Narottama dāsa Ṭhākura, a great *ācārya* in the preceptorial line of Lord Śrī Caitanya Mahāprabhu, has said for our benefit that one can perfectly see the *dhāmas* only when one completely gives up the mentality of lording it over material nature. One's spiritual vision develops proportionately to one's giving up the debased mentality of unnecessarily enjoying matter. A diseased person who has become diseased because of a certain bad habit must be ready to follow the advice of the physician, and as a natural sequence he must attempt to give up the cause of the disease. The patient cannot indulge in the bad habit and at the same time expect to be cured by the physician. Modern materialistic civilization, however, is maintaining a diseased atmosphere. The living being is a spiritual spark, as spiritual as the Lord Himself. The only difference is that the Lord is great and the living being is small. Qualitatively they are one, but quantitatively they are different. Therefore, since the living being is spiritual in constitution, he can be happy only in the spiritual sky, where there are unlimited spiritual spheres called Vaikuṇṭhas. A spiritual being conditioned by a material body must therefore try to get rid of his disease instead of developing the cause of the disease.

Foolish persons engrossed in their material assets are unnecessarily proud of being leaders of the people, but they ignore the spiritual value of man. Such illusioned leaders make plans covering any number of years, but they can hardly make humanity happy in a state conditioned by the threefold miseries inflicted by material nature. One cannot control the laws of nature by any amount of struggling. One must at last be subject to death, nature's ultimate law. Death, birth, old age and illness are symptoms of the diseased condition of the living being. The highest aim of human life should therefore be to get free from these miseries and go back home, back to Godhead.

TEXT 21

প্রেমনেত্রে দেখে তার স্বরূপ-প্রকাশ ।
গোপ-গোপীসঙ্গে যাঁহা কৃষ্ণের বিলাস ॥ ২১ ॥

prema-netre dekhe tāra svarūpa-prakāśa
gopa-gopī-saṅge yāṅhā kṛṣṇera vilāsa

prema-netre—with the eyes of love of Godhead; *dekhe*—one sees; *tāra*—its; *svarūpa-prakāśa*—manifestation of identity; *gopa*—cowherd boys; *gopī-saṅge*—with the cowherd damsels; *yāṅhā*—where; *kṛṣṇera vilāsa*—the pastimes of Lord Kṛṣṇa.

TRANSLATION

But with the eyes of love of Godhead one can see its real identity as the place where Lord Kṛṣṇa performs His pastimes with the cowherd boys and cowherd girls.

TEXT 22

চিন্তামণিপ্রকরসদ্মসু কল্পবৃক্ষ-
লক্ষাবৃতেষু সুরভীরভিপালয়ন্তম্ ।
লক্ষ্মীসহস্রশতসম্ভ্রমসেব্যমানং
গোবিন্দমাদিপুরুষং তমহং ভজামি ॥ ২২ ॥

cintāmaṇi-prakara-sadmasu kalpa-vṛkṣa-
lakṣāvṛteṣu surabhīr abhipālayantam
lakṣmī-sahasra-śata-sambhrama-sevyamānaṁ
govindam ādi-puruṣaṁ tam ahaṁ bhajāmi

cintāmaṇi—touchstone; *prakara*—groups made of; *sadmasu*—in abodes; *kalpa-vṛkṣa*—of desire trees; *lakṣa*—by millions; *āvṛteṣu*—surrounded; *surabhīḥ*—*surabhi* cows; *abhipālayantam*—tending; *lakṣmī*—of goddesses of fortune; *sahasra*—of thousands; *śata*—by hundreds; *sambhrama*—with great respect; *sevyamānam*—being served; *govindam*—Govinda; *ādi-puruṣam*—the original person; *tam*—Him; *aham*—I; *bhajāmi*—worship.

TRANSLATION

"I worship Govinda, the primeval Lord, the first progenitor, who is tending cows yielding all desires in abodes built with spiritual gems and surrounded by millions of purpose trees. He is always served with great reverence and affection by hundreds and thousands of goddesses of fortune."

PURPORT

This is a verse from the *Brahma-saṁhitā* (5.29). This description of the abode of Kṛṣṇa gives us definite information of the transcendental place where not only is life eternal, blissful and full of knowledge, but there are ample vegetables, milk, jewels, and beautiful homes and gardens tended by lovely damsels who are all goddesses of fortune. Kṛṣṇaloka is the topmost planet in the spiritual sky, and below it are innumerable spheres, a description of which can be found in *Śrīmad-Bhāgavatam.* In the beginning of Lord Brahmā's self-realization he was shown a transcendental vision of the Vaikuṇṭha spheres by the grace of Nārāyaṇa. Later, by the grace of Kṛṣṇa, he was shown a transcendental vision of Kṛṣṇaloka. This transcendental vision is like the reception of television from the moon via a mechanical system for receiving modulated waves, but it is achieved by penance and meditation within oneself.

Śrīmad-Bhāgavatam (Second Canto) states that in Vaikuṇṭhaloka the material modes of nature, represented by the qualities of goodness, passion and ignorance, have no influence. In the material world the highest qualitative manifestation is goodness, which is characterized by truthfulness, mental equilibrium, cleanliness, control of the senses, simplicity, essential knowledge, faith in God, scientific knowledge and so on. Nevertheless, all these qualities are mixed with passion and imperfection. But the qualities in Vaikuṇṭha are a manifestation of God's internal potency, and therefore they are purely spiritual and transcendental, with no trace of material infection. No material planet, even Satyaloka, is comparable in quality to the spiritual planets, where the five inherent qualities of the material world—namely ignorance, misery, egoism, anger and envy—are completely absent.

In the material world, everything is a creation. Anything we can think of within our experience, including even our own bodies and minds, was created. This process of creation began with the life of Brahmā, and the creative principle is prevalent all over the material universe because of the quality of passion. But since the quality of passion is conspicuous by its absence in the Vaikuṇṭha planets, nothing there is created; everything there is eternally existent. And because there is no mode of ignorance, there is also no question of annihilation or destruction. In the material world one may try to make everything permanent by developing the above-mentioned qualities of goodness, but because the goodness in the material world is mixed with passion and ignorance, nothing here can exist permanently, despite all the good plans of the best scientific brains. Therefore in the material world we have no experience of eternity, bliss and fullness of knowledge. But in the spiritual world, because of the complete absence of the qualitative modes, everything is eternal, blissful and cognizant. Everything can speak, everything can move, everything can hear, and everything can see in fully blessed existence for eternity. The situation being so, naturally space and time, in the forms of past, present and future, have no influence there. In the spiritual sky there is no change because time has no influence. Consequently, the influence of *māyā*, the total external energy, which induces us to become more and more materialistic and forget our relationship with God, is also absent there.

As spiritual sparks of the beams emanating from the transcendental body of the Lord, we are all permanently related with Him and equal to Him in quality. The material energy is a covering of the spiritual spark, but in the absence of that material covering, the living beings in Vaikuṇṭhaloka are never forgetful of their identities: they are eternally cognizant of their relationship with God in their constitutional position of rendering transcendental loving service to the Lord. Because they constantly engage in the transcendental service of the Lord, it is natural to conclude that their senses are also transcendental, for one cannot serve the Lord with material senses. The inhabitants of Vaikuṇṭhaloka do not possess material senses with which to lord it over material nature.

Persons with a poor fund of knowledge conclude that a place void of material qualities must be some sort of formless nothingness. In reality, however, there are qualities in the spiritual world, but they are different from the material qualities because everything there is eternal, unlimited and pure. The atmosphere there is self-illuminating, and thus there is no need of a sun, a moon, fire, electricity and so on. One who can reach that abode does not come back to the material world with a material body. There is no difference between atheists and the faithful in the Vaikuṇṭha planets because all who settle there are freed from the material qualities, and thus *suras* and *asuras* become equally obedient loving servitors of the Lord.

The residents of Vaikuṇṭha have brilliantly black complexions much more fascinating and attractive than the dull white and black complexions found in the material world. Their bodies, being spiritual, have no equals in the material world. The beauty of a bright cloud when lightning flashes on it merely hints at their beauty. Generally the inhabitants of Vaikuṇṭha dress in yellow clothing. Their bodies are delicate and attractively built, and their eyes are like the petals of lotus flowers. Like Lord Viṣṇu, the residents of Vaikuṇṭha have four hands decorated with a conchshell, wheel, club and lotus flower. Their chests are beautifully broad and fully decorated with necklaces of a brilliant diamondlike metal surrounded by costly jewels never to be found in the material world. The residents of Vaikuṇṭha are always powerful and effulgent. Some of them have complexions like red coral cat's eyes and lotus flowers, and each of them has earrings of costly jewels. On their heads they wear flowery crowns resembling garlands.

In the Vaikuṇṭhas there are airplanes, but they make no tumultuous sounds. Material airplanes are not at all safe: they can fall down and crash at any time, for matter is imperfect in every respect. In the spiritual sky, however, the airplanes are also spiritual, and they are spiritually brilliant and bright. These airplanes do not fly business executives, politicians or planning commissions as passengers, nor do they carry cargo or postal bags, for these are all unknown there. These planes are for pleasure trips only, and the residents of Vaikuṇṭha fly in them with their heavenly, beautiful, fairylike consorts. Therefore these airplanes, full of residents of Vaikuṇṭha, both male and female, increase the beauty of the spiritual sky. We cannot imagine how beautiful they are, but their beauty may be compared to the clouds in the sky accompanied by silver branches of electric lightning. The spiritual sky of Vaikuṇṭhaloka is always decorated in this way.

The full opulence of the internal potency of Godhead is always resplendent in Vaikuṇṭhaloka, where goddesses of fortune are ever-increasingly attached to serving the lotus feet of the Personality of Godhead. These goddesses of fortune, accompanied by their friends, always create a festive atmosphere of transcendental mirth. Always singing the glories of the Lord, they are not silent even for a moment.

There are unlimited Vaikuṇṭha planets in the spiritual sky, and the ratio of these planets to the material planets in the material sky is three to one. Thus the poor materialist is busy making political adjustments on a planet that is most insignificant in God's creation. To say nothing of this planet earth, the whole universe, with innumerable planets throughout the galaxies, is comparable to a single mustard seed in a bag full of mustard seeds. But the poor materialist makes plans to live comfortably here and thus wastes his valuable human energy in something that is doomed to frustration. Instead of wasting his time with business speculations, he should seek the life of plain living and high spiritual thinking and thus save himself from perpetual materialistic unrest.

Even if a materialist wants to enjoy developed material facilities, he can transfer himself to planets where he can experience material pleasures much more advanced than those available on earth. The best plan is to prepare oneself to return to the spiritual sky after leaving the body. However, if one is intent on enjoying material facilities, one can transfer himself to other planets in the material sky by utilizing yogic powers. The playful spaceships of the astronauts are but childish entertainments and are of no use for this purpose. The *aṣṭāṅga-yoga* system is a materialistic art of controlling air by transferring it from the stomach to the navel, from the navel to the heart, from the heart to the collarbone, from there to the eyeballs, from there to the cerebellum and from there to any desired planet. The velocities of air and light are taken into consideration by the material scientist, but he has no information of the velocity of the mind and intelligence. We have some limited experience of the velocity of the mind because in a moment we can transfer our minds to places hundreds of thousands of miles away. Intelligence is even finer. Finer than intelligence is the soul, which is not matter like mind and intelligence but is spirit, or antimatter. The soul is hundreds of thousands of times finer and more powerful than intelligence. We can thus only imagine the velocity of the soul in its traveling from one planet to another. Needless to say, the soul travels by its own strength and not with the help of any kind of material vehicle.

The bestial civilization of eating, sleeping, fearing and sense-gratifying has misled modern man into forgetting how powerful a soul he has. As we have already described, the soul is a spiritual spark many, many times more illuminating, dazzling and powerful than the sun, moon or electricity. Human life is spoiled when man does not realize his real identity with his soul. Lord Caitanya appeared with Lord Nityānanda to save man from this type of misleading civilization.

Śrīmad-Bhāgavatam also describes how *yogīs* can travel to all the planets in the universe. When the vital force is lifted to the cerebellum, there is every chance that this force will burst out from the eyes, nose, ears, etc., as these are places that are known as the seventh orbit of the vital force. But the *yogīs* can block these holes by complete suspension of air. The *yogī* then concentrates the vital force in the middle position, that is, between the eyebrows. At this position, the *yogī* can think of the planet to which he wants to go after leaving the body. He can then decide whether he wants to go to the abode of Kṛṣṇa in the transcendental Vaikuṇṭhas, from which he will not be required to descend into the material world, or to travel to higher planets in the material universe. The perfect *yogī* is at liberty to do either.

For the perfect *yogī* who has attained success in the method of leaving his body in perfect consciousness, transferring from one planet to another is as easy as an ordinary man's walking to the grocery store. As already discussed, the material body is just a covering of the spiritual soul. Mind and intelligence are the undercoverings, and the gross body of earth, water, air and so on is the overcoating of the soul. As such, any advanced soul who has realized himself by the yogic process, who knows the relationship between matter and spirit, can leave the gross dress of the soul in perfect order and as he desires. By the grace of God, we have complete freedom. Because the Lord is kind to us, we can live anywhere—either in the spiritual sky or in the material sky, upon whichever planet we desire. However, misuse of this freedom causes one to fall down into the material world and suffer the threefold miseries of conditioned life. The living of a miserable life in the material world by dint of the soul's choice is nicely illustrated by Milton in *Paradise Lost.* Similarly, by choice the soul can regain paradise and return home, back to Godhead.

At the critical time of death, one can place the vital force between the two eyebrows and decide where he wants to go. If he is reluctant to maintain any connection with the material world, he can, in less than a second, reach the transcendental abode of Vaikuṇṭha and appear there completely in his spiritual body, which will be suitable for him in the spiritual atmosphere. He has simply to desire to leave the material world both in finer and in grosser forms and then move the vital force to the topmost part of the skull and leave the body from the hole in the skull called the *brahma-randhra.* This is easy for one perfect in the practice of *yoga.*

Of course, man is endowed with free will, and as such if he does not want to free himself from the material world he may enjoy the life of *brahma-pada* (occupation of the post of Brahmā) and visit Siddhaloka, the planets of materially perfect beings, who have full capacities to control gravity, space and time. To visit these higher planets in the material universe, one need not give up his mind and intelligence (finer matter), but need only give up grosser matter (the material body).

Each and every planet has its particular atmosphere, and if one wants to travel to any particular planet within the material universe, one has to adapt his material body to the climatic condition of that planet. For instance, if one wants to go from India to Europe, where the climatic condition is different, one has to change his dress accordingly. Similarly, a complete change of body is necessary if one wants to go to the transcendental planets of Vaikuṇṭha. However, if one wants to go to the higher material planets, he can keep his finer dress of mind, intelligence and ego, but has to leave his gross dress (body) made of earth, water, fire, etc.

When one goes to a transcendental planet, it is necessary to change both the finer and gross bodies, for one has to reach the spiritual sky completely in a spiritual form. This change of dress will take place automatically at the time of death if one so desires.

The *Bhagavad-gītā* confirms that one will attain his next material body according to his desires at the time he leaves his body. The desire of the mind carries the soul to a suitable atmosphere as the wind carries aromas from one place to another. Unfortunately, those who are not *yogīs* but gross materialists, who throughout their lives indulge in sense gratification, are puzzled by the disarrangement of the bodily and mental condition at the time of death. Such gross sensualists, encumbered by the main ideas, desires and associations of the lives they have led, desire something against their interest and thus foolishly take on new bodies that perpetuate their material miseries.

Systematic training of the mind and intelligence is therefore needed so that at the time of death one may consciously desire a suitable body, either on this planet or another material planet or even a transcendental planet. A civilization that does not consider the progressive advancement of the immortal soul merely fosters a bestial life of ignorance.

It is foolish to think that every soul that passes away goes to the same place. Either the soul goes to a place he desires at the time of death, or upon leaving his body he is forced to accept a position according to his acts in his previous life. The difference between the materialist and the *yogī* is that a materialist cannot determine his next body, whereas a *yogī* can consciously attain a suitable body for enjoyment in the higher planets. Throughout his life, the gross materialist who is constantly after sense gratification spends all day earning his livelihood to maintain his family, and at night he wastes his energy in sex enjoyment or else goes to sleep thinking about all he has done in the daytime. That is the monotonous life of the materialist. Although differently graded as businessmen, lawyers, politicians, professors, judges, coolies, pickpockets, laborers and so on, materialists all simply engage in eating, sleeping, fearing and sense gratification and thus spoil their valuable lives pursuing luxury and neglecting to perfect their lives through spiritual realization.

Yogīs, however, try to perfect their lives, and therefore the *Bhagavad-gītā* enjoins that everyone should become a *yogī*. *Yoga* is the system for linking the soul in the service of the Lord. Only under superior guidance can one practice such *yoga* in his life without changing his social position. As already described, a *yogī* can go anywhere he desires without mechanical help, for a *yogī* can place his mind and intelligence within the air circulating inside his body, and by practicing the art of breath control he can mix that air with the air that blows all over the universe outside his body. With the help of this universal air, a *yogī* can travel to any planet and get a body suitable for its atmosphere. We can understand this process by comparing it to the electronic transmission of radio messages. With radio transmitters, sound waves produced at a certain station can travel all over the earth in seconds. But sound is produced from the ethereal sky, and as already explained, subtler than the ethereal sky is the mind, and finer than the mind is the intelligence. Spirit is still finer than the intelligence, and by nature it is completely different from matter. Thus we can just imagine how quickly the spirit soul can travel through the universal atmosphere.

To come to the stage of manipulating finer elements like mind, intelligence and spirit, one needs appropriate training, an appropriate mode of life and appropriate association. Such training depends upon sincere prayers, devotional service, achievement of success in mystic perfection, and the successful merging of oneself in the activities of the soul and Supersoul. A gross materialist, whether he be an empiric philosopher, a scientist, a psychologist or whatever, cannot attain such success through blunt efforts and word jugglery.

Materialists who perform *yajñas*, or great sacrifices, are comparatively better than grosser materialists who do not know anything beyond laboratories and test tubes. The advanced materialists who perform such sacrifices can reach the planet called Vaiśvānara, a fiery planet similar to the sun. On this planet, which is situated on the way to Brahmaloka, the topmost planet in the universe, such an advanced materialist can free himself from all traces of vice and its effects. When such a materialist is purified, he can rise to the orbit of the pole star (Dhruvaloka). Within this orbit, which is called the Śiśumāra-cakra, are situated the Āditya-lokas and the Vaikuṇṭha planet within this universe.

A purified materialist who has performed many sacrifices, undergone severe penances and given the major portion of his wealth in charity can reach such planets as Dhruvaloka, and if he becomes still more qualified there, he can penetrate still higher orbits and pass through the navel of the universe to reach the planet Maharloka, where sages like Bhṛgu Muni live. In Maharloka one can live even to the time of the partial annihilation of the universe. This annihilation begins when Anantadeva, from the lowest position in the universe, produces a great blazing fire. The heat of this fire reaches even Maharloka, and then the residents of Maharloka travel to Brahmaloka, which exists for twice the duration of *parārdha* time.

In Brahmaloka there is an unlimited number of airplanes that are controlled not by *yantra* (machine) but by *mantra* (psychic action). Because of the existence of the mind and intelligence on Brahmaloka, its residents have feelings of happiness and distress, but there is no cause of lamentation from old age, death, fear or distress. They feel sympathy, however, for the suffering living beings who are consumed in the fire of annihilation. The residents of Brahmaloka do not have gross material bodies to change at death, but they transform their subtle bodies into spiritual bodies and thus enter the spiritual sky. The residents of Brahmaloka can attain perfection in three different ways. Virtuous persons who reach Brahmaloka by dint of their pious work become masters of various planets after the resurrection of Brahmā, those who have worshiped Garbhodakaśāyī Viṣṇu are liberated with Brahmā, and those who are pure devotees of the Personality of Godhead at once push through the covering of the universe and enter the spiritual sky.

The numberless universes exist together in foamlike clusters, and so only some of them are surrounded by the water of the Causal Ocean. When agitated by the glance of Kāraṇodakaśāyī Viṣṇu, material nature produces the total elements, which are eight in number and which gradually evolve from finer to gross. A part of ego is the sky, a part of which is air, a part of which is fire, a part of which is water, a part of which is earth. Thus one universe inflates to an area of four billion miles in diameter. A *yogī* who desires gradual liberation must penetrate all the different coverings of the universe, including the subtle coverings of the three qualitative modes of material nature. One who does this never has to return to this mortal world.

According to Śukadeva Gosvāmī, the above description of the material and spiritual skies is neither imaginary nor utopian. The actual facts are recorded in the Vedic hymns, and Lord Vāsudeva disclosed them to Lord Brahmā when Brahmā satisfied Him. One can achieve the perfection of life only when he has a definite idea of Vaikuṇṭha and the Supreme Godhead. One should always think about and describe the Supreme Personality of Godhead, for this is recommended in both the *Bhagavad-gītā* and the *Bhāgavata Purāṇa*, which are two authorized commentaries upon the *Vedas*. Lord Caitanya has made all these subject matters easier for the fallen people of this age to accept, and *Śrī Caitanya-caritāmṛta* has therefore presented them for the easy understanding of all concerned.

TEXT 23

মথুরা-দ্বারকায় নিজরূপ প্রকাশিয়া ।
নানারূপে বিলসয়ে চতুর্ব্যূহ হৈঞা ॥ ২৩ ॥

mathurā-dvārakāya nija-rūpa prakāśiyā
nānā-rūpe vilasaye catur-vyūha haiñā

mathurā—in Mathurā; *dvārakāya*—in Dvārakā; *nija-rūpa*—personal body; *prakāśiyā*—manifesting; *nānā-rūpe*—in various ways; *vilasaye*—enjoys pastimes; *catuḥ-vyūha haiñā*—expanding into four wonderful forms.

TRANSLATION

Lord Kṛṣṇa manifests His own form in Mathurā and Dvārakā. He enjoys pastimes in various ways by expanding into the quadruple forms.

TEXT 24

বাসুদেব-সঙ্কর্ষণ-প্রদ্যুম্নানিরুদ্ধ ।
সর্বচতুর্ব্যূহ-অংশী, তুরীয়, বিশুদ্ধ ॥ ২৪ ॥

vāsudeva-saṅkarṣaṇa-pradyumnāniruddha
sarva-catur-vyūha-aṁśī, turīya, viśuddha

vāsudeva—Lord Vāsudeva; *saṅkarṣaṇa*—Lord Saṅkarṣaṇa; *pradyumna*—Lord Pradyumna; *aniruddha*—and Lord Aniruddha; *sarva-catuḥ-vyūha*—of all other quadruple expansions; *aṁśī*—source; *turīya*—transcendental; *viśuddha*—pure.

TRANSLATION

Vāsudeva, Saṅkarṣaṇa, Pradyumna and Aniruddha are the primary quadruple forms, from whom all other quadruple forms are manifested. They are all purely transcendental.

TEXT 25

এই তিন লোকে কৃষ্ণ কেবল-লীলাময় ।
নিজগণ লঞা খেলে অনন্ত সময় ॥ ২৫ ॥

ei tina loke kṛṣṇa kevala-līlā-maya
nija-gaṇa lañā khele ananta samaya

ei—these; *tina*—three; *loke*—in the locations; *kṛṣṇa*—Lord Kṛṣṇa; *kevala*—only; *līlā-maya*—consisting of pastimes; *nija-gaṇa lañā*—with His personal associates; *khele*—He plays; *ananta samaya*—unlimited time.

TRANSLATION

Only in these three places [Dvārakā, Mathurā and Gokula] does the all-sporting Lord Kṛṣṇa perform His endless pastimes with His personal associates.

TEXT 26

পরব্যোম-মধ্যে করি' স্বরূপ প্রকাশ ।
নারায়ণরূপে করেন বিবিধ বিলাস ॥ ২৬ ॥

para-vyoma-madhye kari' svarūpa prakāśa
nārāyaṇa-rūpe karena vividha vilāsa

para-vyoma-madhye—within the spiritual sky; *kari'*—making; *svarūpa prakāśa*—manifesting His identity; *nārāyaṇa-rūpe*—the form of Lord Nārāyaṇa; *karena*—performs; *vividha vilāsa*—varieties of pastimes.

TRANSLATION

In the Vaikuṇṭha planets of the spiritual sky the Lord manifests His identity as Nārāyaṇa and performs pastimes in various ways.

TEXTS 27–28

স্বরূপবিগ্রহ কৃষ্ণের কেবল দ্বিভুজ ।
নারায়ণরূপে সেই তনু চতুর্ভুজ ॥ ২৭ ॥
শঙ্খ-চক্র-গদা-পদ্ম, মহৈশ্বর্যময় ।
শ্রী-ভূ-নীলা-শক্তি যাঁর চরণ সেবয় ॥ ২৮ ॥

svarūpa-vigraha kṛṣṇera kevala dvi-bhuja
nārāyaṇa-rūpe sei tanu catur-bhuja

śaṅkha-cakra-gadā-padma, mahaiśvarya-maya
śrī-bhū-nīlā-śakti yāṅra caraṇa sevaya

svarūpa-vigraha—personal form; *kṛṣṇera*—of Lord Kṛṣṇa; *kevala*—only; *dvi-bhuja*—two hands; *nārāyaṇa-rūpe*—in the form of Lord Nārāyaṇa; *sei*—that; *tanu*—body; *catuḥ-bhuja*—four-handed; *śaṅkha-cakra*—conchshell and disc; *gadā*—club; *padma*—lotus flower; *mahā*—very great; *aiśvarya-maya*—full of opulence; *śrī*—named *śrī; bhū*—named *bhū; nīlā*—named *nīlā; śakti*—energies; *yāṅra*—whose; *caraṇa sevaya*—serve the lotus feet.

TRANSLATION

Kṛṣṇa's own form has only two hands, but in the form of Lord Nārāyaṇa He has four hands. Lord Nārāyaṇa holds a conchshell, disc, club and lotus flower, and He is full of great opulence. The śrī, bhū and nīlā energies serve at His lotus feet.

PURPORT

In the Rāmānuja and Madhva sects of Vaiṣṇavism there are extensive descriptions of the *śrī, bhū* and *nīlā* energies. In Bengal the *nīlā* energy is sometimes called the *līlā* energy. These three energies are employed in the service of four-handed Nārāyaṇa in Vaikuṇṭha. Relating how three of the Ālvārs, namely Bhūta-yogī, Sara-yogī and Bhrānta-yogī, saw Nārāyaṇa in person when they took shelter at the house of a *brāhmaṇa* in the village of Gehalī, the *Prapannāmṛta* of the Śrī-sampradāya describes Nārāyaṇa as follows:

tārkṣyādhirūḍhaṁ taḍid-ambudābhaṁ
lakṣmī-dharaṁ vakṣasi paṅkajākṣam
hasta-dvaye śobhita-śaṅkha-cakraṁ
viṣṇuṁ dadṛśur bhagavantam ādyam

ā-jānu-bāhuṁ kamanīya-gātraṁ
pārśva-dvaye śobhita-bhūmi-nīlam
pītāmbaraṁ bhūṣaṇa-bhūṣitāṅgaṁ
catur-bhujaṁ candana-ruṣitāṅgam

"They saw the lotus-eyed Lord Viṣṇu, the Supreme Personality of Godhead, mounted on Garuḍa and holding Lakṣmī, the goddess of fortune, to His chest. He resembled a bluish rain cloud with flashing lightning, and in two of His four hands He held a conchshell and disc. His arms stretched down to His knees, and all His beautiful limbs were smeared with sandalwood and decorated with glittering ornaments. He wore yellow clothes, and by either side stood His energies Bhūmi and Nīlā."

There is the following reference to the *śrī, bhū* and *nīlā* energies in the *Sītopaniṣad: mahā-lakṣmīr deveśasya bhinnābhinna-rūpā cetanācetanātmikā. sā devī tri-vidhā bhavati, śakty-ātmanā icchā-śaktiḥ kriyā-śaktiḥ sākṣāc-chaktir iti. icchā-śaktis tri-vidhā bhavati, śrī-bhūmi-nīlātmikā.* "Mahā-Lakṣmī, the supreme energy of the Lord, is experienced in different ways. She is divided into material and spiritual potencies, and in both features she acts as the willing energy, creative energy and the internal energy. The willing energy is again divided into three, namely *śrī, bhū* and *nīlā.*"

Quoting from the revealed scriptures in his commentary on the *Bhagavad-gītā* (4.6), Madhvācārya has stated that mother material nature, which is conceived of as the illusory energy, Durgā, has three divisions, namely *śrī, bhū* and *nīlā.* She is the illusory energy for those who are weak in spiritual strength because such energies are created energies of Lord Viṣṇu. Although each energy has no direct relationship with the unlimited, they are subordinate to the Lord because the Lord is the master of all energies.

In his *Bhagavat-sandarbha* (Text 23), Śrīla Jīva Gosvāmī Prabhu states, "The *Padma Purāṇa* refers to the eternally auspicious abode of Godhead, which is full in all opulences, including the energies *śrī, bhū* and *nīlā.* The *Mahā-saṁhitā,* which discusses the transcendental name and form of Godhead, also mentions Durgā as the potency of the Supersoul in relationship with the living entities. The internal potency acts in relation with His personal affairs, and the material potency manifests the three modes." Quoting elsewhere from the revealed scriptures, he states that *śrī* is the energy of Godhead that maintains the cosmic manifestation, *bhū* is the energy that creates the cosmic manifestation, and *nīlā,* Durgā, is the energy that destroys the creation. All these energies act in relation with the living beings, and thus they are together called *jīva-māyā.*

TEXT 29

যদ্যপি কেবল তাঁর ক্রীড়ামাত্র ধর্ম ।
তথাপি জীবেরে কৃপায় করে এক কর্ম ॥ ২৯ ॥

yadyapi kevala tāṅra krīḍā-mātra dharma
tathāpi jīvere kṛpāya kare eka karma

yadyapi—although; *kevala*—only; *tāṅra*—His; *krīḍā-mātra*—pastime only; *dharma*—characteristic function; *tathāpi*—still; *jīvere*—to the fallen souls; *kṛpāya*—by the causeless mercy; *kare*—does; *eka*—one; *karma*—activity.

TRANSLATION

Although His pastimes are His only characteristic functions, by His causeless mercy He performs one activity for the fallen souls.

TEXT 30

সালোক্য-সামীপ্য-সার্ষ্টি-সারূপ্যপ্রকার ।
চারি মুক্তি দিয়া করে জীবের নিস্তার ॥ ৩০ ॥

sālokya-sāmīpya-sārṣṭi-sārūpya-prakāra
cāri mukti diyā kare jīvera nistāra

sālokya—the liberation called *sālokya; sāmīpya*—the liberation called *sāmīpya; sārṣṭi*—the liberation called *sārṣṭi; sārūpya*—the liberation called *sārūpya; prakāra*—varieties; *cāri*—four; *mukti*—liberation; *diyā*—giving; *kare*—does; *jīvera*—of the fallen souls; *nistāra*—deliverance.

TRANSLATION

He delivers the fallen living entities by offering them the four kinds of liberation—sālokya, sāmīpya, sārṣṭi and sārūpya.

PURPORT

There are two kinds of liberated souls—those who are liberated by the favor of the Lord and those who are liberated by their own effort. One who gets liberation by his own effort is called an impersonalist, and he merges into the glaring effulgence of the Lord, the *brahmajyoti.* But devotees of the Lord who qualify themselves for liberation by devotional service are offered four kinds of liberation, namely *sālokya* (status equal to that of the Lord), *sāmīpya* (constant association with the Lord), *sārṣṭi* (opulence equal to that of the Lord) and *sārūpya* (features like those of the Lord).

TEXT 31

ব্রহ্মসাযুজ্য-মুক্তের তাহা নাহি গতি ।
বৈকুণ্ঠ-বাহিরে হয় তা'সবার স্থিতি ॥ ৩১ ॥

brahma-sāyujya-muktera tāhā nāhi gati
vaikuṇṭha-bāhire haya tā'-sabāra sthiti

brahma-sāyujya—of merging into the Supreme Brahman; *muktera*—of the liberation; *tāhā*—there (in Vaikuṇṭha); *nāhi*—not; *gati*—entrance; *vaikuṇṭha-bāhire*—outside the Vaikuṇṭha planets; *haya*—there is; *tā'-sabāra sthiti*—the residence of all of them.

TRANSLATION

Those who attain brahma-sāyujya liberation cannot gain entrance into Vaikuṇṭha; their residence is outside the Vaikuṇṭha planets.

TEXT 32

বৈকুণ্ঠ-বাহিরে এক জ্যোতির্ময় মণ্ডল ।
কৃষ্ণের অঙ্গের প্রভা, পরম উজ্জ্বল ॥ ৩২ ॥

vaikuṇṭha-bāhire eka jyotir-maya maṇḍala
kṛṣṇera aṅgera prabhā, parama ujjvala

vaikuṇṭha-bāhire—outside the Vaikuṇṭhalokas; *eka*—one; *jyotiḥ-maya maṇḍala*—the atmosphere of the glowing effulgence; *kṛṣṇera*—of Lord Kṛṣṇa; *aṅgera*—of the body; *prabhā*—rays; *parama*—supremely; *ujjvala*—bright.

TRANSLATION

Outside the Vaikuṇṭha planets is the atmosphere of the glowing effulgence, which consists of the supremely bright rays of the body of Lord Kṛṣṇa.

TEXT 33

'সিদ্ধলোক' নাম তার প্রকৃতির পার ।
চিৎস্বরূপ, তাঁহা নাহি চিচ্ছক্তি-বিকার ॥ ৩৩ ॥

'siddha-loka' nāma tāra prakṛtira pāra
cit-svarūpa, tāṅhā nāhi cic-chakti vikāra

'siddha-loka'—the region of the Siddhas; *nāma*—named; *tāra*—of the effulgent atmosphere; *prakṛtira pāra*—beyond this material nature; *cit-svarūpa*—full of knowledge; *tāṅhā*—there; *nāhi*—there is not; *cit-śakti-vikāra*—change of the spiritual energy.

TRANSLATION

That region is called Siddhaloka, and it is beyond the material nature. Its essence is spiritual, but it does not have spiritual varieties.

TEXT 34

সূর্যমণ্ডল যেন বাহিরে নির্বিশেষ ।
ভিতরে সূর্যের রথ-আদি সবিশেষ ॥ ৩৪ ॥

sūrya-maṇḍala yena bāhire nirviśeṣa
bhitare sūryera ratha-ādi saviśeṣa

sūrya-maṇḍala—the sun globe; *yena*—like; *bāhire*—externally; *nirviśeṣa*—with out varieties; *bhitare*—within; *sūryera*—of the sun-god; *ratha-ādi*—opulences like chariots and other things; *sa-viśeṣa*—full of varieties.

TRANSLATION

It is like the homogeneous effulgence around the sun. But inside the sun are the chariots, horses and other opulences of the sun-god.

PURPORT

Outside of Vaikuṇṭha, the abode of Kṛṣṇa, which is called *paravyoma,* is the glaring effulgence of Kṛṣṇa's bodily rays. This is called the *brahma-jyoti.* The transcendental region of that effulgence is called Siddhaloka or Brahmaloka. When impersonalists achieve liberation, they merge into that Brahmaloka effulgence. This transcendental region is undoubtedly spiritual, but it contains no manifestations of spiritual activities or variegatedness. It is compared to the glow of the sun. Within the sun's glow is the sphere of the sun, where one can experience all sorts of varieties.

TEXT 35

কামাদ্দ্বেষাদ্ ভয়াৎ স্নেহাদ্ যথা ভক্ত্যেশ্বরে মনঃ ।
আবেশ্য তদঘং হিত্বা বহবস্তদ্গতিং গতাঃ ॥ ৩৫ ॥

kāmād dveṣād bhayāt snehād
yathā bhaktyeśvare manaḥ
āveśya tad aghaṁ hitvā
bahavas tad gatiṁ gatāḥ

kāmāt—influenced by lusty desire; *dveṣāt*—by envy; *bhayāt*—by fear; *snehāt*—or by affection; *yathā*—as; *bhaktyā*—by devotion; *īśvare*—in the Supreme Personality of Godhead; *manaḥ*—the mind; *āveśya*—fully absorbing; *tat*—that; *agham*—sinful activity; *hitvā*—giving up; *bahavaḥ*—many; *tat*—that; *gatim*—destination; *gatāḥ*—achieved.

TRANSLATION

"As through devotion to the Lord one can attain His abode, many have attained that goal by abandoning their sinful activities and absorbing their minds in the Lord through lust, envy, fear or affection."

PURPORT

As the powerful sun, by its glowing rays, can purify all kinds of impurities, so the all-spiritual Personality of Godhead can purify all material qualities in a person He attracts. Even if one is attracted by Godhead in he mode of material lust, such attraction is converted into spiritual love of Godhead by His grace. Similarly, if one is related to the Lord in fear and animosity, he also becomes purified by the spiritual attraction of the Lord. Although God is great and the living entity small, they are spiritual individuals, and therefore as soon as there is a reciprocal exchange by the living entity's free will, at once the great spiritual being attracts the small living entity, thus freeing him from all material bondage. This is a verse from *Śrīmad-Bhāgavatam* (7.1.30).

TEXT 36

যদরীণাং প্রিয়াণাঞ্চ প্রাপ্যমেকমিবোদিতম্ ।
তদ্ব্রহ্মকৃষ্ণয়োরৈক্যাৎ কিরণার্কোপমাজুষোঃ ॥ ৩৬ ॥

yad arīṇāṁ priyāṇāṁ ca
prāpyam ekam ivoditam
tad brahma-kṛṣṇayor aikyāt
kiraṇārkopamā-juṣoḥ

yat—that; *arīṇām*—of the enemies of the Supreme Personality of Godhead; *priyāṇām*—of the devotees, who are very dear to the Supreme Personality of Godhead; *ca*—and; *prāpyam*—destination; *ekam*—one only; *iva*—thus; *uditam*—said; *tat*—that; *brahma*—of impersonal Brahman; *kṛṣṇayoḥ*—and of Kṛṣṇa, the Supreme Personality of Godhead; *aikyāt*—due to the oneness; *kiraṇa*—the sunshine; *arka*—and the sun; *upamā*—the comparison; *juṣoḥ*—which is understood by.

TRANSLATION

"Where it has been stated that the Lord's enemies and devotees attain the same destination, this refers to the ultimate oneness of Brahman and Lord Kṛṣṇa. This may be understood by the analogy of the sun and the sunshine, in which Brahman is like the sunshine and Kṛṣṇa Himself is like the sun."

PURPORT

This verse is from the *Bhakti-rasāmṛta-sindhu* (1.2.278) of Śrīla Rūpa Gosvāmī, who further discusses this same topic in his *Laghu-bhāgavatāmṛta* (*Pūrva* 5.41). There he refers to the *Viṣṇu Purāṇa* (4.15.1), where Maitreya Muni asked Parāśara, in regard to Jaya and Vijaya, how it was that Hiraṇyakaśipu next became Rāvaṇa and enjoyed more material happiness than the demigods but did not attain salvation, although when he became Śiśupāla, quarreled with Kṛṣṇa and was killed, he attained salvation and merged into the body of Lord Kṛṣṇa. Parāśara replied that Hiraṇyakaśipu failed to recognize Lord Nṛsiṁhadeva as Lord Viṣṇu. He thought that Nṛsiṁhadeva was some living entity who had acquired such opulence by various pious activities. Being overcome by the mode of passion, he considered Lord Nṛsiṁhadeva an ordinary living entity, not understanding His form. Nevertheless, because Hiraṇyakaśipu was killed by the hands of Lord Nṛsiṁhadeva, in his next life he became Rāvaṇa and had proprietorship of unlimited opulence. As Rāvaṇa, with unlimited material enjoyment, he could not accept Lord Rāma as the Personality of Godhead. Therefore even though he was killed by Rāma, he did not attain *sāyujya,* or oneness with the body of the Lord. In his Rāvaṇa body he was too much attracted to Rāma's wife, Jānakī, and because of that attraction he was able to see Lord Rāma. But instead of accepting Lord Rāma as an incarnation of Viṣṇu, Rāvaṇa thought Him an ordinary living being. When killed by the hands of Rāma, therefore, he got the privilege of taking birth as Śiśupāla, who had such immense opulence that he could think himself a competitor to Kṛṣṇa. Although Śiśupāla was always envious of Kṛṣṇa, he frequently uttered the name of Kṛṣṇa and always thought of the beautiful features of Kṛṣṇa. Thus by constantly thinking and chanting of Kṛṣṇa, even unfavorably, he was cleansed of the contamination of his sinful activities. When Śiśupāla was killed by the Sudarśana *cakra* of Kṛṣṇa as an enemy, his constant remembrance of Kṛṣṇa dissolved the reactions of his vices, and he attained salvation by becoming one with the body of the Lord.

From this incident one can understand that even a person who thinks of Kṛṣṇa as an enemy and is killed by Him may be liberated by becoming one with the body of Kṛṣṇa. What then must be the destination of devotees who always think favorably of Kṛṣṇa as their master or friend? These devotees must attain a situation better than Brahmaloka, the impersonal bodily effulgence of Kṛṣṇa. Devotees cannot be situated in the impersonal Brahman effulgence, into which impersonalists desire to merge. The devotees are placed in Vaikuṇṭhaloka or Kṛṣṇaloka.

This discussion between Maitreya Muni and Parāśara Muni centered on whether devotees come down into the material world in every millennium like Jaya and Vijaya, who were cursed by the Kumāras to that effect. In the course of these instructions to Maitreya about Hiraṇyakaśipu, Rāvaṇa and Śiśupāla, Parāśara did not say that these demons were formerly Jaya and Vijaya. He simply described the transmigration through three lives. It is not necessary for the Vaikuṇṭha associates of the Supreme Personality of Godhead to come to take the roles of His enemies in all the millenniums in which He appears. The "falldown" of Jaya and Vijaya occurred in a particular millennium; Jaya and Vijaya do not come down in every millennium to act as demons. To think that some associates of the Lord fall down from Vaikuṇṭha in every millennium to become demons is totally incorrect.

The Supreme Personality of Godhead has all the tendencies that may be found in the living entity, for He is the chief living entity. Therefore it is natural that sometimes Lord Viṣṇu wants to fight. Just as He has the tendencies to create, to enjoy, to be a friend, to accept a mother and father, and so on, He also has the tendency to fight. Sometimes important landlords and kings keep wrestlers with whom they practice mock fighting, and Viṣṇu makes similar arrangements. The demons who fight with the Supreme Personality of Godhead in the material world are sometimes His associates. When there is a scarcity of demons and the Lord wants to fight, He instigates some of His associates of Vaikuṇṭha to come and play as demons. When it is said that Śiśupāla merged into the body of Kṛṣṇa, it should be noted that in this case he was not Jaya or Vijaya: he was actually a demon.

In his *Bṛhad-bhāgavatāmṛta*, Śrīla Sanātana Gosvāmī has explained that the attainment of salvation by merging into the Brahman effulgence of the Lord cannot be accepted as the highest success in life, because demons like Kaṁsa, who were famous for killing *brāhmaṇas* and cows, attained that salvation. For devotees such salvation is abominable. Devotees are actually in a transcendental position, whereas nondevotees are candidates for hellish conditions of life. There is always a difference between the life of a devotee and the life of a demon, and their realizations are as different as heaven and hell.

Demons are always accustomed to being malicious toward devotees and to killing *brāhmaṇas* and cows. For demons, merging into the Brahman effulgence may be very glorious, but for devotees it is hellish. A devotee's aim in life is to attain perfection in loving the Supreme Personality of Godhead. Those who aspire to merge into the Brahman effulgence are as abominable as demons. Devotees who aspire to associate with the Supreme Lord to render Him transcendental loving service are far superior.

TEXT 37

তৈছে পরব্যোমে নানা চিচ্ছক্তিবিলাস ।
নির্বিশেষ জ্যোতির্বিম্ব বাহিরে প্রকাশ ॥ ৩৭ ॥

taiche para-vyome nānā cic-chakti-vilāsa
nirviśeṣa jyotir-bimba bāhire prakāśa

taiche—in that way; *para-vyome*—in the spiritual sky; *nānā*—varieties; *cit-śakti-vilāsa*—pastimes of spiritual energy; *nirviśeṣa*—impersonal; *jyotiḥ*—of the effulgence; *bimba*—reflection; *bāhire*—externally; *prakāśa*—manifested.

TRANSLATION

Thus in the spiritual sky there are varieties of pastimes within the spiritual energy. Outside the Vaikuṇṭha planets appears the impersonal reflection of light.

TEXT 38

নির্বিশেষ-ব্রহ্ম সেই কেবল জ্যোতির্ময় ।
সাযুজ্যের অধিকারী তাঁহা পায় লয় ॥ ৩৮ ॥

nirviśeṣa-brahma sei kevala jyotir-maya
sāyujyera adhikārī tāṅhā pāya laya

nirviśeṣa-brahma—the impersonal Brahman effulgence; *sei*—that; *kevala*—only; *jyotiḥ-maya*—effulgent rays; *sāyujyera*—the liberation called *sāyujya* (oneness with the Supreme); *adhikārī*—one who is fit for; *tāṅhā*—there (in the impersonal Brahman effulgence); *pāya*—gets; *laya*—merging.

TRANSLATION

That impersonal Brahman effulgence consists only of the effulgent rays of the Lord. Those fit for sāyujya liberation merge into that effulgence.

TEXT 39

সিদ্ধলোকস্তু তমসঃ পারে যত্র বসন্তি হি ।
সিদ্ধা ব্রহ্মসুখে মগ্না দৈত্যাশ্চ হরিণা হতাঃ ॥ ৩৯ ॥

siddha-lokas tu tamasaḥ
pāre yatra vasanti hi
siddhā brahma-sukhe magnā
daityāś ca hariṇā hatāḥ

siddha-lokaḥ—Siddhaloka, or impersonal Brahman; *tu*—but; *tamasaḥ*—of darkness; *pāre*—beyond the jurisdiction; *yatra*—where; *vasanti*—reside; *hi*—certainly; *siddhāḥ*—the spiritually perfect; *brahma-sukhe*—in the transcendental bliss of becoming one with the Supreme; *magnāḥ*—absorbed; *daityāḥ ca*—as well as the demons; *hariṇā*—by the Supreme Personality of Godhead; *hatāḥ*—killed.

TRANSLATION

"Beyond the region of ignorance [the material cosmic manifestation] lies the realm of Siddhaloka. The Siddhas reside there, absorbed in the bliss of Brahman. Demons killed by the Lord also attain that realm."

PURPORT

Tamas means darkness. The material world is dark, and beyond the material world is light. In other words, after passing through the entire material atmosphere, one can come to the luminous spiritual sky, whose impersonal effulgence is known as Siddhaloka. Māyāvādī philosophers who aspire to merge with the body of the Supreme Personality of Godhead, as well as demoniac persons who are killed by Kṛṣṇa, such as Kaṁsa and Śiśupāla, enter that Brahman effulgence. *Yogīs* who attain oneness through meditation according to the Patañjali *yoga* system also reach Siddhaloka. This is a verse from the *Brahmāṇḍa Purāṇa.*

TEXT 40

সেই পরব্যোমে নারায়ণের চারি পাশে ।
দ্বারকা-চতুর্ব্যূহের দ্বিতীয় প্রকাশে ॥ ৪০ ॥

sei para-vyome nārāyaṇera cāri pāśe
dvārakā-catur-vyūhera dvitīya prakāśe

sei—that; *para-vyome*—in the spiritual sky; *nārāyaṇera*—of Lord Nārāyaṇa; *cāri pāśe*—on four sides; *dvārakā*—Dvārakā; *catur-vyūhera*—of the quadruple expansions; *dvitīya*—the second; *prakāśe*—manifestation.

TRANSLATION

In that spiritual sky, on the four sides of Nārāyaṇa, are the second expansions of the quadruple expansions of Dvārakā.

PURPORT

Within the spiritual sky is a second manifestation of the quadruple forms of Dvārakā from the abode of Kṛṣṇa. Among these forms, which are all spiritual and immune to the material modes, Śrī Baladeva is represented as Mahā-saṅkarṣaṇa.

The activities in the spiritual sky are manifested by the internal potency in pure spiritual existence. They expand in six transcendental opulences, which are all manifestations of Mahā-saṅkarṣaṇa, who is the ultimate reservoir and objective of all living entities. Although belonging to the marginal potency, known as *jīva-śakti,* the spiritual sparks known as the living entities are subjected to the conditions of material energy. It is because these sparks are related with both the internal and external potencies of the Lord that they are known as belonging to the marginal potency.

In considering the quadruple forms of the absolute Personality of Godhead, known as Vāsudeva, Saṅkarṣaṇa, Pradyumna and Aniruddha, the impersonalists, headed by Śrīpāda Śaṅkarācārya, have interpreted the aphorisms of the *Vedānta-sūtra* in a way suitable for the impersonalist school. To provide the intrinsic import of such aphorisms, however, Śrīla Rūpa Gosvāmī, the leader of the six Gosvāmīs of Vṛndāvana, has properly replied to the impersonalists in his *Laghu-bhāgavatāmṛta,* which is a natural commentary on the aphorisms of the *Vedānta-sūtra.*

The *Padma Purāṇa,* as quoted by Śrīla Rūpa Gosvāmī in his *Laghu-bhāgavatāmṛta,* describes that in the spiritual sky there are four directions, corresponding to east, west, north and south, in which Vāsudeva, Saṅkarṣaṇa, Aniruddha and Pradyumna are situated. The same forms are also situated in the material sky. The *Padma Purāṇa* also describes a place in the spiritual sky known as Vedavatī-pura, where Vāsudeva resides. In Viṣṇuloka, which is above Satyaloka, Saṅkarṣaṇa resides. Mahā-saṅkarṣaṇa is another name of Saṅkarṣaṇa. Pradyumna lives in Dvārakā-pura, and Aniruddha lies on the eternal bed of Śeṣa, generally known as *ananta-śayyā,* on the island called Śvetadvīpa, in the ocean of milk.

TEXT 41

বাসুদেব-সঙ্কর্ষণ-প্রদ্যুম্নানিরুদ্ধ ।
'দ্বিতীয় চতুর্ব্যূহ' এই—তুরীয়, বিশুদ্ধ ॥ ৪১ ॥

vāsudeva-saṅkarṣaṇa-pradyumnāniruddha
'dvitīya catur-vyūha' ei—turīya, viśuddha

vāsudeva—the expansion named Vāsudeva; *saṅkarṣaṇa*—the expansion named Saṅkarṣaṇa; *pradyumna*—the expansion named Pradyumna; *aniruddha*—the expansion named Aniruddha; *dvitīya catuḥ-vyūha*—the second quadruple expansion; *ei*—this; *turīya*—transcendental; *viśuddha*—free from all material contamination.

TRANSLATION

Vāsudeva, Saṅkarṣaṇa, Pradyumna and Aniruddha constitute this second quadruple. They are purely transcendental.

PURPORT

Śrīpāda Śaṅkarācārya has misleadingly explained the quadruple form (*catur-vyūha*) in his interpretation of the forty-second aphorism of Chapter Two of the second *khaṇḍa* of the *Vedānta-sūtra* (*utpatty-asambhavāt*). In verses 41 through 47 of this chapter of *Śrī Caitanya-caritāmṛta*, Śrīla Kṛṣṇadāsa Kavirāja Gosvāmī answers Śrīpāda Śaṅkarācārya's misleading objections to the personal feature of the Absolute Truth.

The Supreme Personality of Godhead, the Absolute Truth, is not like a material object that can be known by experimental knowledge or sense perception. In the *Nārada-pañcarātra* this fact has been explained by Nārāyaṇa Himself to Lord Śiva. But Śaṅkarācārya, the incarnation of Śiva, under the order of Nārāyaṇa, his master, had to mislead the monists, who favor ultimate extinction. In the conditioned stage of existence, all living entities have four basic defects, of which one is the cheating propensity. Śaṅkarācārya has carried this cheating propensity to the extreme to mislead the monists.

Actually, the explanation of the quadruple forms in the Vedic literature cannot be understood by the speculation of a conditioned soul. The quadruple forms should therefore be accepted just as They are described. The authority of the *Vedas* is such that even if one does not understand something by his limited perception, he should accept the Vedic injunction and not create interpretations to suit his imperfect understanding. In his *Śārīraka-bhāṣya*, however, Śaṅkarācārya has increased the misunderstanding of the monists.

The quadruple forms have a spiritual existence that can be realized in *vasudeva-sattva* (*śuddha-sattva*), or unqualified goodness, which accompanies complete absorption in the understanding of Vāsudeva. The quadruple forms, who are full in the six opulences of the Supreme Personality of Godhead, are the enjoyers of the internal potency.

Thinking the absolute Personality of Godhead to be poverty-stricken or to have no potency—or, in other words, to be impotent—is simply rascaldom. This rascaldom is the profession of the conditioned soul, and it increases his bewilderment. One who cannot understand the distinctions between the spiritual world and the material world has no qualification to examine or know the situation of the transcendental quadruple forms. In his commentary on *Vedānta-sūtra* 2.2.42–45, His Holiness Śrīpāda Śaṅkarācārya has made a futile attempt to nullify the existence of these quadruple forms in the spiritual world.

Śaṅkarācārya says (*sūtra* 42) that devotees think the Supreme Personality of Godhead Vāsudeva, Śrī Kṛṣṇa, to be one, to be free from material qualities and to have a transcendental body full of bliss and eternal existence. He is the ultimate goal of the devotees, who believe that the Supreme Personality of Godhead expands Himself into four other eternal transcendental forms—Vāsudeva, Saṅkarṣaṇa, Pradyumna and Aniruddha. From Vāsudeva, who is the primary expansion, come Saṅkarṣaṇa, Pradyumna and Aniruddha in that order. Another name of Vāsudeva is Paramātmā, another name of Saṅkarṣaṇa is *jīva* (the living entity), another name of Pradyumna is mind, and another name of Aniruddha is *ahaṅkāra* (false ego). Among these expansions, Vāsudeva is considered the origin of the material nature. Therefore Śaṅkarācārya says that Saṅkarṣaṇa, Pradyumna and Aniruddha must be creations of that original cause.

Great souls assert that Nārāyaṇa, who is known as the Paramātmā, or Supersoul, is beyond material nature, and this is in accordance with the statements of the Vedic literature. Māyāvādīs also agree that Nārāyaṇa can expand Himself in various forms. Śaṅkara says that he does not attempt to argue that portion of the devotees' understanding, but he must protest the idea that Saṅkarṣaṇa is produced from Vāsudeva, Pradyumna is produced from Saṅkarṣaṇa, and Aniruddha is produced from Pradyumna, for if Saṅkarṣaṇa is understood to represent the living entities created from the body of Vāsudeva, the living entities would have to be noneternal. The living entities are supposed to be freed from material contamination by engaging in prolonged temple worship of the Supreme Personality of Godhead, reading Vedic literature and performing *yoga* and pious activities to attain the Supreme Lord. But if the living entities had been created from material nature at a certain point, they would be noneternal and would have no chance to be liberated and associate with the Supreme Personality of Godhead. When a cause is nullified, its results are nullified. In the second chapter of the *Vedānta-*

sūtra's second *khaṇḍa*, Ācārya Vedavyāsa has also refuted the conception that the living beings were ever born (*nātmā śruter nityatvāc ca tābhyaḥ*). Because there is no creation for the living entities, they must be eternal.

Śaṅkarācārya says (*sūtra* 43) that devotees think that Pradyumna, who is considered to represent the senses, has sprung from Saṅkarṣaṇa, who is considered to represent the living entities. But we cannot actually experience that a person can produce senses. Devotees also say that from Pradyumna has sprung Aniruddha, who is considered to represent the ego. But Śaṅkarācārya says that unless the devotees can show how ego and the means of knowledge can generate from a person, such an explanation of the *Vedānta-sūtra* cannot be accepted, for no other philosophers accept the *sūtras* in that way.

Śaṅkarācārya also says (*sūtra* 44) that he cannot accept the devotees' idea that Saṅkarṣaṇa, Pradyumna and Aniruddha are equally as powerful as the absolute Personality of Godhead, full in the six opulences of knowledge, wealth, strength, fame, beauty and renunciation, and free from the flaw of generation at a certain point. Even if They are full expansions, the flaw of generation remains. Vāsudeva, Saṅkarṣaṇa, Pradyumna and Aniruddha, being distinct individual persons, cannot be one. Therefore if They are accepted as absolute, full and equal, there would have to be many Personalities of Godhead. But there is no need to accept that there are many Personalities of Godhead, because acceptance of one omnipotent God is sufficient for all purposes. The acceptance of more than one God is contradictory to the conclusion that Lord Vāsudeva, the absolute Personality of Godhead, is one without a second. Even if we agree to accept that the quadruple forms of Godhead are all identical, we cannot avoid the incongruous flaw of noneternity. Unless we accept that there are some differences among the personalities, there is no meaning to the idea that Saṅkarṣaṇa is an expansion of Vāsudeva, Pradyumna is an expansion of Saṅkarṣaṇa, and Aniruddha is an expansion of Pradyumna. There must be a distinction between cause and effect. For example, a pot is distinct from the earth from which it is made, and therefore we can ascertain that the earth is the cause and the pot is the effect. Without such distinctions, there is no meaning to cause and effect. Furthermore, the followers of the Pañcarātric principles do not accept any differences in knowledge and qualities between Vāsudeva, Saṅkarṣaṇa, Pradyumna and Aniruddha. The devotees accept all these expansions to be one, but why should they restrict oneness to these quadruple expansions? Certainly we should not do so, for all living entities, from Brahmā to the insignificant ant, are expansions of Vāsudeva, as accepted in all the *śrutis* and *smṛtis*.

Śaṅkarācārya also says (*sūtra* 45) that the devotees who follow the *Pañcarātra* state that God's qualities and God Himself, as the owner of the qualities, are the same. But how can the *Bhāgavata* school state that the six opulences—wisdom, wealth, strength, fame, beauty and renunciation—are identical with Lord Vāsudeva? This is impossible.

In his *Laghu-bhāgavatāmṛta* (*Pūrva* 5.165–193), Śrīla Rūpa Gosvāmī has refuted the charges directed against the devotees by Śrīpāda Śaṅkarācārya regarding their explanation of the quadruple forms Vāsudeva, Saṅkarṣaṇa, Pradyumna and Aniruddha. Rūpa Gosvāmī says that these four expansions of Nārāyaṇa are present in the spiritual sky, where They are famous as Mahāvastha. Among Them, Vāsudeva is worshiped within the heart by meditation because He is the predominating Deity of the heart, as explained in *Śrīmad-Bhāgavatam* (4.3.23).

Saṅkarṣaṇa, the second expansion, is Vāsudeva's personal expansion for pastimes, and since He is the reservoir of all living entities, He is sometimes called *jīva*. The beauty of Saṅkarṣaṇa is greater than that of innumerable full moons radiating light beams. He is worshipable as the principle of ego. He has invested Anantadeva with all the potencies of sustenance. For the dissolution of the creation, He also exhibits Himself as the Supersoul in Rudra, in Adharma (the personality of irreligion), in *sarpa* (snakes), in Antaka (Yamarāja, the lord of death) and in the demons.

Pradyumna, the third manifestation, appears from Saṅkarṣaṇa. Those who are especially intelligent worship this Pradyumna expansion of Saṅkarṣaṇa as the principle of the intelligence. The goddess of fortune always chants the glories of Pradyumna in the place known as *Ilāvṛta-varṣa,* and she always serves Him with great devotion. His complexion appears sometimes golden and sometimes bluish like new monsoon clouds in the sky. He is the origin of the creation of the material world, and He has invested His creative principle in Cupid. It is by His direction only that all men and demigods and other living entities function with energy for regeneration.

Aniruddha, the fourth of the quadruple expansions, is worshiped by great sages and psychologists as the principle of the mind. His complexion is similar to the bluish hue of a blue cloud. He engages in the maintenance of the cosmic manifestation and is the Supersoul of Dharma (the deity of religiosity), the Manus (the progenitors of mankind) and the *devatās* (demigods). The *Mokṣa-dharma* Vedic scripture indicates that Pradyumna is the Deity of the total mind, whereas Aniruddha is the Deity of the total ego, but previous statements regarding the quadruple forms are confirmed in the *Pañcarātra tantras* in all respects.

In the *Laghu-bhāgavatāmṛta* (*Pūrva* 5.86–100), there is a lucid explanation of the inconceivable potencies of the Supreme Personality of Godhead. Negating Śaṅkarācārya's statements, the *Mahā-varāha Purāṇa* declares:

sarve nityāḥ śāśvatāś ca dehās tasya parātmanaḥ
hānopādāna-rahitā naiva prakṛti-jāḥ kvacit

"All the varied expansions of the Personality of Godhead are transcendental and eternal, and all of them repeatedly descend to all the different universes of the material creation. Their bodies, composed of eternity, bliss and knowledge, are everlasting; there is no chance of their decaying, for they are not creations of the material world. Their forms are concentrated spiritual existence, always complete with all spiritual qualities and devoid of material contamination."

Confirming these statements, the *Nārada-pañcarātra* asserts:

maṇir yathā vibhāgena nīla-pītādibhir yutaḥ
rūpa-bhedam avāpnoti dhyāna-bhedāt tathācyutaḥ

"The infallible Personality of Godhead can manifest His body in different ways according to different modes of worship, just as the *vaidūrya* gem can manifest itself in various colors, such as blue and yellow." Each incarnation is distinct from all the others. This is possible by the Lord's inconceivable potency, by which He can simultaneously represent Himself as one, as various partial forms and as the origin of these partial forms. Nothing is impossible for His inconceivable potencies.

Kṛṣṇa is one without a second, but He manifests Himself in different bodies, as stated by Nārada in the Tenth Canto of *Śrīmad-Bhāgavatam:*

citraṁ bataitad ekena vapuṣā yugapat pṛthak
gṛheṣu dvy-aṣṭa-sāhasraṁ striya eka udāvahat

"It is wonderful indeed that one Kṛṣṇa has simultaneously become different Kṛṣṇas in 16,000 palaces to accept 16,000 queens as His wives." (*Bhāg.* 10.69.2) The *Padma Purāṇa* also explains:

sa devo bahudhā bhūtvā nirguṇaḥ puruṣottamaḥ
ekī-bhūya punaḥ śete nirdoṣo harir ādi-kṛt

"The same Personality of Godhead, Puruṣottama, the original person, who is always devoid of material qualities and contamination, can exhibit Himself in various forms and at the same time lie down in one form."

In the Tenth Canto of *Śrīmad-Bhāgavatam* it is said, *yajanti tvan-mayās tvāṁ vai bahu-mūrty-eka-mūrtikam:* "O my Lord, although You manifest Yourself in varieties of forms, You are one without a second. Therefore pure devotees concentrate upon You and worship only You." (*Bhāg.* 10.40.7) In the *Kūrma Purāṇa* it is said:

asthūlaś cānaṇuś caiva sthūlo 'ṇuś caiva sarvataḥ
avarṇaḥ sarvataḥ proktaḥ śyāmo raktānta-locanaḥ

"The Lord is personal although impersonal, He is atomic although great, and He is blackish and has red eyes although He is colorless." By material calculation all this may appear contradictory, but if we understand that the Supreme Personality of Godhead has inconceivable potencies, we can accept these facts as eternally possible in Him. In our present condition we cannot understand the spiritual activities and how they occur, but although they are inconceivable in the material context, we should not disregard such contradictory conceptions.

Although it is apparently inconceivable, it is quite possible for the Absolute to reconcile all opposing elements. *Śrīmad-Bhāgavatam* establishes this in the Sixth Canto (6.9.34–37):

"O my Lord, Your transcendental pastimes and enjoyments all appear inconceivable because they are not limited by the causal and effective actions of material thought. You can do everything without performing bodily work. The *Vedas* say that the Absolute Truth has multifarious potencies and does not need to do anything personally. My dear Lord, You are entirely devoid of material qualities. Without anyone's help, You can create, maintain and dissolve the entire qualitative material manifestation, yet in all such activities You do not change. You do not accept the results of Your activities, unlike ordinary demons and demigods, who suffer or enjoy the reactions of their activities in the material world. Unaffected by the reactions of work, You eternally exist with Your full spiritual potency. This we cannot fully understand.

"Because You are unlimited in Your six opulences, no one can count Your transcendental qualities. Philosophers and other thoughtful persons are overwhelmed by the contradictory manifestations of the physical world and the propositions of logical arguments and judgments.

Because they are bewildered by word jugglery and disturbed by the different calculations of the scriptures, their theories cannot touch You, who are the ruler and controller of everyone and whose glories are beyond conception.

"Your inconceivable potency keeps You unattached to the mundane qualities. Surpassing all conceptions of material contemplation, Your pure transcendental knowledge keeps You beyond all speculative processes. By Your inconceivable potency, there is nothing contradictory in You.

"People may sometimes think of You as impersonal or personal, but You are one. For persons who are confused or bewildered, a rope may appear to manifest itself as different kinds of snakes. For similar confused persons who are uncertain about You, You create various philosophical methods in pursuance of their uncertain positions."

We should always remember the differences between spiritual and material actions. The Supreme Lord, being all-spiritual, can perform any act without extraneous help. In the material world, if we want to manufacture an earthen pot, we need the ingredients, a machine and also a laborer. But we should not extend this idea to the actions of the Supreme Lord, for He can create anything in a moment without that which appears necessary in our own conception. When the Lord appears as an incarnation to fulfill a particular purpose, this does not indicate that He is unable to fulfill it without appearing. He can do anything simply by His will, but by His causeless mercy He appears to be dependent upon His devotees. He appears as the son of Yaśodāmātā not because He is dependent on her care but because He accepts such a role by His causeless mercy. When He appears for the protection of His devotees, He naturally accepts trials and tribulations on their behalf.

In the *Bhagavad-gītā* it is said that the Lord, being equally disposed toward every living being, has no enemies and no friends but that He has special affection for a devotee who always thinks of Him in love. Therefore neutrality and partiality are both among the transcendental qualities of the Lord, and they are properly adjusted by His inconceivable energy. The Lord is Parabrahman, or the source of the impersonal Brahma, which is His all-pervading feature of neutrality. In His personal feature, however, as the owner of all transcendental opulences, the Lord displays His partiality by taking the side of His devotees. Partiality, neutrality and all such qualities are present in God; otherwise they could not be experienced in the creation. Since He is the total existence, all things are properly adjusted in the Absolute. In the relative world such qualities are displayed in a perverted manner, and therefore we experience non-duality as a perverted reflection. Because there is no logic to explain how things happen in the realm of spirit, the Lord is sometimes described as being beyond the range of experience. But if we simply accept the Lord's inconceivability, we can then adjust all things in Him. Nondevotees cannot understand the Lord's inconceivable energy, and consequently for them it is said that He is beyond the range of conceivable expression. The author of the *Brahma-sūtras* accepts this fact and says, *śrutes tu śabda-mūlatvāt:* the Supreme Personality of Godhead, being inconceivable to an ordinary man, can be understood only through the evidence of the Vedic injunctions. The *Skanda Purāṇa* confirms, *acintyāḥ khalu ye bhāvā na tāṁs tarkeṇa yojayet:* "Matters inconceivable to a common man should not be a subject for argument." We find very wonderful qualities even in such material things as jewels and drugs. Indeed, their qualities often appear inconceivable. Therefore if we do not attribute inconceivable potencies to the Supreme Personality of Godhead, we cannot establish His supremacy. It is because of these inconceivable potencies that the glories of the Lord have always been accepted as difficult to understand.

Ignorance and the jugglery of words are very common in human society, but they do not help one understand the inconceivable energies of the Supreme Personality of Godhead. If we accept such ignorance and word jugglery, we cannot accept the Supreme Lord's perfection in six opulences. For example, one of the opulences of the Supreme Lord is complete knowledge. Therefore, how could ignorance be conceivable in Him? Vedic instructions and sensible arguments establish that the Lord's maintaining the cosmic manifestation and simultaneously being indifferent to the activities of its maintenance cannot be contradictory, because of His inconceivable energies. To a person who is always absorbed in the thought of snakes, a rope always appears to be a snake, and similarly to a person bewildered by material qualities and devoid of knowledge of the Absolute, the Supreme Personality of Godhead appears according to diverse bewildered conclusions.

Someone might argue that the Absolute would be affected by duality if He were both all-cognizance (Brahman) and the Personality of Godhead with six opulences in full (Bhagavān). To refute such an argument, the aphorism *svarūpa-dvayam īkṣyate* declares that in spite of appearances, there is no chance of duality in the Absolute, for He is but one in diverse manifestations. Understanding that the Absolute displays varied pastimes by the influence of His energies at once removes the apparent incongruity of His inconceivably opposite energies. *Śrīmad-*

Bhāgavatam (3.4.16) gives the following description of the inconceivable potency of the Lord:

karmāṇy anīhasya bhavo 'bhavasya te
durgāśrayo 'thāri-bhayāt palāyanam
kālātmano yat pramadā-yutāśrayaḥ
svātman-rateḥ khidyati dhīr vidām iha

"Although the Supreme Personality of Godhead has nothing to do, He nevertheless acts; although He is always unborn, He nevertheless takes birth; although He is time, fearful to everyone, He flees Mathurā in fear of His enemy to take shelter in a fort; and although He is self-sufficient, He marries 16,000 women. These pastimes seem like bewildering contradictions, even to the most intelligent." Had these activities of the Lord not been a reality, sages would not have been puzzled by them. Therefore such activities should never be considered imaginary. Whenever the Lord desires, His inconceivable energy (*yogamāyā*) serves Him in creating and performing such pastimes.

The scriptures known as the *Pañcarātra-śāstras* are recognized Vedic scriptures that have been accepted by the great *ācāryas*. These scriptures are not products of the modes of passion and ignorance. Learned scholars and *brāhmaṇas* therefore always refer to them as *sātvata-saṁhitās*. The original speaker of these scriptures is Nārāyaṇa, the Supreme Personality of Godhead. This is especially mentioned in the *Mokṣa-dharma* (349.68), which is part of the *Śānti-parva* of the *Mahābhārata*. Liberated sages like Nārada and Vyāsa, who are free from the four defects of conditioned souls, are the propagators of these scriptures. Śrī Nārada Muni is the original speaker of the *Pañcarātra-śāstra*. *Śrīmad-Bhāgavatam* is also considered a *sātvata-saṁhitā*. Indeed, Śrī Caitanya Mahāprabhu declared, *śrīmad-bhāgavataṁ purāṇam amalam:* "*Śrīmad-Bhāgavatam* is a spotless *Purāṇa*." Malicious editors and scholars who attempt to misrepresent the *Pañcarātra-śāstras* to refute their regulations are most abominable. In the modern age, such malicious scholars have even commented misleadingly upon the *Bhagavad-gītā*, which was spoken by Kṛṣṇa, to prove that there is no Kṛṣṇa. How the Māyāvādīs have misrepresented the *pāñcarātrika-vidhi* will be shown below.

(1) In commenting on *Vedānta-sūtra* 2.2.42, Śrīpāda Śaṅkarācārya has claimed that Saṅkarṣaṇa is a *jīva*, an ordinary living entity, but there is no evidence in any Vedic scripture that devotees of the Lord have ever said that Saṅkarṣaṇa is an ordinary living entity. He is an

infallible plenary expansion of the Supreme Personality of Godhead in the Viṣṇu category, and He is beyond the creation of material nature. He is the original source of the living entities. The *Upaniṣads* declare, *nityo nityānāṁ cetanaś cetanānām:* "He is the supreme living entity among all the living entities." Therefore He is *vibhu-caitanya,* the greatest. He is directly the cause of the cosmic manifestation and the infinitesimal living beings. He is the infinite living entity, and ordinary living entities are infinitesimal. Therefore He is never to be considered an ordinary living being, for that would be against the conclusion of the authorized scriptures. The living entities are also beyond the limitations of birth and death. This is the version of the *Vedas,* and it is accepted by those who follow scriptural injunctions and who have actually descended in the disciplic succession.

(2) In answer to Śaṅkarācārya's commentary on *Vedānta-sūtra* 2.2.43, it must be said that the original Viṣṇu of all the Viṣṇu categories, which are distributed in several ways, is Mūla-saṅkarṣaṇa. *Mūla* means "the original." Saṅkarṣaṇa is also Viṣṇu, but from Him all other Viṣṇus expand. This is confirmed in the *Brahma-saṁhitā* (5.46), wherein it is said that just as a flame transferred from another flame acts like the original, so the Viṣṇus who emanate from Mūlasaṅkarṣaṇa are as good as the original Viṣṇu. One should worship that Supreme Personality of Godhead, Govinda, who thus expands Himself.

(3) In reply to the commentary of Śaṅkarācārya on the forty-fourth aphorism, it may be said that no pure devotees strictly following the principles of the *Pañcarātra* will ever accept the statement that all the expansions of Viṣṇu are different identities, for this idea is completely false. Even Śrīpāda Śaṅkarācārya, in his commentary on the forty-second aphorism, has accepted that the Personality of Godhead can automatically expand Himself variously. Therefore his commentary on the forty-second aphorism and his commentary on the forty-fourth aphorism are contradictory. It is a defect of Māyāvāda commentaries that they make one statement in one place and a contradictory statement in another place as a tactic to refute the Bhāgavata school. Thus Māyāvādī commentators do not even follow regulative principles. It should be noted that the Bhāgavata school accepts the quadruple forms of Nārāyaṇa, but that does not mean that it accepts many Gods. Devotees know perfectly well that the Absolute Truth, the Supreme Personality of Godhead, is one without a second. They are never pantheists, worshipers of many Gods, for this is against the injunction of the *Vedas*. Devotees completely believe, with strong faith, that Nārāyaṇa is transcendental and has inconceivable proprietorship of various tran-

scendental potencies. We therefore recommend that scholars consult the *Laghu-bhāgavatāmṛta* of Śrīla Rūpa Gosvāmī, where these ideas are explicitly stated. Śrīpāda Śaṅkarācārya has tried to prove that Vāsudeva, Saṅkarṣaṇa, Pradyumna and Aniruddha expand through cause and effect. He has compared Them with earth and earthen pots. That is completely ignorant, however, for there is no such thing as cause and effect in Their expansions (*nānyad yat sad-asat-param*). The *Kūrma Purāṇa* also confirms, *deha-dehi-vibhedo 'yaṁ neśvare vidyate kvacit:* "There is no difference between body and soul in the Supreme Personality of Godhead." Cause and effect are material. For example, it is seen that a father's body is the cause of a son's body, but the soul is neither cause nor effect. On the spiritual platform there are none of the differences we find in cause and effect. Since all the forms of the Supreme Personality of Godhead are spiritually supreme, They are equally controllers of material nature. Standing on the fourth dimension, They are predominating figures on the transcendental platform. There is no trace of material contamination in Their expansions because material laws cannot influence Them. There is no such rule as cause and effect outside of the material world. Therefore the understanding of cause and effect cannot approach the full, transcendental, complete expansions of the Supreme Personality of Godhead. The Vedic literature proves this:

oṁ pūrṇam adaḥ pūrṇam idaṁ pūrṇāt pūrṇam udacyate
pūrṇasya pūrṇam ādāya pūrṇam evāvaśiṣyate

"The Personality of Godhead is perfect and complete, and because He is completely perfect, all emanations from Him, such as this phenomenal world, are perfectly equipped as complete wholes. Whatever is produced of the complete whole is also complete by itself. Because He is the complete whole, even though so many complete units emanate from Him, He remains the complete balance." (*Bṛhad-āraṇyaka Upaniṣad* 5.1) It is most apparent that nondevotees violate the rules and regulations of devotional service to equate the whole cosmic manifestation, which is the external feature of Viṣṇu, with the Supreme Personality of Godhead, who is the controller of *māyā*, or with His quadruple expansions. Equating *māyā* with spirit, or *māyā* with the Lord, is a sign of atheism. The cosmic creation, which manifests life in forms from Brahmā to the ant, is the external feature of the Supreme Lord. It comprises one fourth of the Lord's energy, as confirmed in the *Bhagavad-gītā* (*ekāṁśena sthito jagat*). The cosmic manifestation of the illusory energy is material nature, and everything within material nature is made of matter. Therefore, one should not try to compare the expansions of material nature to the *catur-vyūha,* the quadruple expansions of the Personality of Godhead, but unfortunately the Māyāvādī school unreasonably attempts to do this.

(4) To answer Śaṅkarācārya's commentary on *Vedānta-sūtra* 2.2.45, the substance of the transcendental qualities and their spiritual nature is described in the *Laghu-bhāgavatāmṛta* (*Pūrva* 5.208–214) as follows: "Some say that transcendence must be void of all qualities because qualities are manifested only in matter. According to them, all qualities are like temporary, flickering mirages. But this is not acceptable. Since the Supreme Personality of Godhead is absolute, His qualities are nondifferent from Him. His form, name, qualities and everything else pertaining to Him are as spiritual as He is. Every qualitative expansion of the absolute Personality of Godhead is identical with Him. Since the Absolute Truth, the Personality of Godhead, is the reservoir of all pleasure, all the transcendental qualities that expand from Him are also reservoirs of pleasure. This is confirmed in the scripture known as *Brahma-tarka,* which states that the Supreme Lord Hari is qualified by Himself, and therefore Viṣṇu and His pure devotees and their transcendental qualities cannot be different from their persons. In the *Viṣṇu Purāṇa* Lord Viṣṇu is worshiped in the following words: 'Let the Supreme Personality of Godhead be merciful toward us. His existence is never infected by material qualities.' In the same *Viṣṇu Purāṇa* it is also said that all the qualities attributed to the Supreme Lord, such as knowledge, opulence, beauty, strength and influence, are known to be nondifferent from Him. This is also confirmed in the *Padma Purāṇa,* which explains that whenever the Supreme Lord is described as having no qualities, this should be understood to indicate that He is devoid of material qualities. In the First Chapter of *Śrīmad-Bhāgavatam* (1.16.29) it is said, 'O Dharma, protector of religious principles, all noble and sublime qualities are eternally manifested in the person of Kṛṣṇa, and devotees and transcendentalists who aspire to become faithful also desire to possess such transcendental qualities.'" It is therefore to be understood that Lord Śrī Kṛṣṇa, the transcendental form of absolute bliss, is the fountainhead of all pleasurable transcendental qualities and inconceivable potencies. In this connection we may recommend references to *Śrīmad-Bhāgavatam,* Third Canto, Chapter Twenty-six, verses 21, 25, 27 and 28.

Śrīpāda Rāmānujācārya has also refuted the arguments of Śaṅkara in his own commentary on the *Vedānta-sūtra,* which is known as the

Śrī-bhāṣya: "Śrīpāda Śaṅkarācārya has tried to equate the *Pañcarātras* with the philosophy of the atheist Kapila, and thus he has tried to prove that the *Pañcarātras* contradict the Vedic injunctions. The *Pañcarātras* state that the personality of *jīva* called Saṅkarṣaṇa has emerged from Vāsudeva, the supreme cause of all causes, that Pradyumna, the mind, has come from Saṅkarṣaṇa, and that Aniruddha, the ego, has come from Pradyumna. But one cannot say that the living entity (*jīva*) takes birth or is created, for such a statement is against the injunction of the *Vedas*. As stated in the *Kaṭha Upaniṣad* (2.18), living entities, as individual spiritual souls, can have neither birth nor death. All Vedic literature declares that the living entities are eternal. Therefore when it is said that Saṅkarṣaṇa is *jīva*, this indicates that He is the predominating Deity of the living entities. Similarly, Pradyumna is the predominating Deity of the mind, and Aniruddha is the predominating Deity of the ego.

"It has been said that Pradyumna, the mind, was produced from Saṅkarṣaṇa. But if Saṅkarṣaṇa were a living entity, this could not be accepted, because a living entity cannot be the cause of the mind. The Vedic injunctions state that everything—including life, mind and the senses—comes from the Supreme Personality of Godhead. It is impossible for the mind to be produced by a living entity, for the *Vedas* state that everything comes from the Absolute Truth, the Supreme Lord.

"Saṅkarṣaṇa, Pradyumna and Aniruddha have all the potent features of the absolute Personality of Godhead, according to the revealed scriptures, which contain undeniable facts that no one can refute. Therefore these members of the quadruple manifestation are never to be considered ordinary living beings. Each of Them is a plenary expansion of the Absolute Godhead, and thus each is identical with the Supreme Lord in knowledge, opulence, energy, influence, prowess and potencies. The evidence of the *Pañcarātras* cannot be neglected. Only untrained persons who have not genuinely studied the *Pañcarātras* think that the *Pañcarātras* contradict the *śrutis* regarding the birth or beginning of the living entity. In this connection, we must accept the verdict of *Śrīmad-Bhāgavatam*, which says, 'The absolute Personality of Godhead, who is known as Vāsudeva and who is very affectionate toward His surrendered devotees, expands Himself in quadruple forms who are subordinate to Him and at the same time identical with Him in all respects.' The *Pauṣkara-saṁhitā* states, 'The scriptures that recommend that *brāhmaṇas* worship the quadruple forms of the Supreme Personality of Godhead are called *āgamas* [authorized Vedic literatures].' In all Vaiṣṇava literature it is said that worshiping these quadruple forms is as good as worshiping the Supreme Personality of Godhead Vāsudeva, who in His different expansions, complete in six opulences, can accept offerings from His devotees of the results of their prescribed duties. Worshiping the expansions for pastimes, such as Nṛsiṁha, Rāma, Śeṣa and Kūrma, promotes one to the worship of the Saṅkarṣaṇa quadruple. From that position one is raised to the platform of worshiping Vāsudeva, the Supreme Brahman. In the *Pauṣkara-saṁhitā* it is said, 'If one fully worships according to the regulative principles, one can attain the Supreme Personality of Godhead, Vāsudeva.' It is to be accepted that Saṅkarṣaṇa, Pradyumna and Aniruddha are as good as Lord Vāsudeva, for They all have inconceivable power and can accept transcendental forms like Vāsudeva. Saṅkarṣaṇa, Pradyumna and Aniruddha are never born, but They can manifest Themselves in various incarnations before the eyes of pure devotees. This is the conclusion of all Vedic literature. That the Lord can manifest Himself before His devotees by His inconceivable power is not against the teaching of the *Pañcarātras.* Since Saṅkarṣaṇa, Pradyumna and Aniruddha are, respectively, the predominating Deities of all living entities, the total mind and the total ego, the designation of Saṅkarṣaṇa, Pradyumna and Aniruddha as '*jīva,*' 'mind' and 'ego' are never contradictory to the statements of the scriptures. These terms identify these Deities, just as the terms 'sky' and 'light' sometimes identify the Absolute Brahman.

"The scriptures completely deny the birth or production of the living entity. In the *Parama-saṁhitā* it is described that material nature, which is used for others' purposes, is factually inert and always subject to transformation. The field of material nature is the arena of the activities of fruitive actors, and since the material field is externally related with the Supreme Personality of Godhead, it is also eternal. In every *saṁhitā*, the *jīva* (living entity) has been accepted as eternal, and in the *Pañcarātras* the birth of the *jīva* is completely denied. Anything that is produced must also be annihilated. Therefore if we accept the birth of the living entity, we also have to accept his annihilation. But since the Vedic literatures say that the living entity is eternal, one should not think the living being to be produced at a certain time. In the beginning of the *Parama-saṁhitā* it is definitely stated that the face of material nature is constantly changeable. Therefore 'beginning,' 'annihilation' and all such terms are applicable only in the material nature.

"Considering all these points, one should understand that Śaṅkarācārya's statement that Saṅkarṣaṇa is born as a *jīva* is completely against the Vedic statements. His assertions are completely refuted by the above arguments. In this connection the commentary of Śrīdhara Svāmī on *Śrīmad-Bhāgavatam* (3.1.34) is very helpful."

For a detailed refutation of Śaṅkarācārya's arguments attempting to prove Saṅkarṣaṇa an ordinary living being, one may refer to Śrīmat Sudarśanācārya's commentary on the *Śrī-bhāṣya,* which is known as the *Śruta-prakāśikā.*

The original quadruple forms—Kṛṣṇa, Baladeva, Pradyumna and Aniruddha—expand into another quadruple, which is present in the Vaikuṇṭha planets of the spiritual sky. Therefore the quadruple forms in the spiritual sky are the second manifestation of the original quadruple in Dvārakā. As explained above, Vāsudeva, Saṅkarṣaṇa, Pradyumna and Aniruddha are all changeless, transcendental plenary expansions of the Supreme Lord who have no relation to the material modes. The Saṅkarṣaṇa form in the second quadruple is not only a representation of Balarāma but also the original cause of the Causal Ocean, where Kāraṇodakaśāyī Viṣṇu lies asleep, breathing out the seeds of innumerable universes.

In the spiritual sky there is a spiritual creative energy technically called *śuddha-sattva,* which is a pure spiritual energy that sustains all the Vaikuṇṭha planets with the full opulences of knowledge, wealth, prowess, etc. All these actions of *śuddha-sattva* display the potencies of Mahā-saṅkarṣaṇa, who is the ultimate reservoir of all individual living entities who are suffering in the material world. When the cosmic creation is annihilated, the living entities, who are indestructible by nature, rest in the body of Mahā-saṅkarṣaṇa. Saṅkarṣaṇa is therefore sometimes called the total *jīva.* As spiritual sparks, the living entities have the tendency to be inactive in the association of the material energy, just as sparks of a fire have the tendency to be extinguished as soon as they leave the fire. The spiritual nature of the living being can be rekindled, however, in association with the Supreme Being. Because the living being can appear either in matter or in spirit, the *jīva* is called the marginal potency.

Saṅkarṣaṇa is the origin of Kāraṇa Viṣṇu, who is the original form who creates the universes, and that Saṅkarṣaṇa is but a plenary expansion of Śrī Nityānanda Rāma.

TEXT 42

তাঁহা যে রামের রূপ—মহাসঙ্কর্ষণ ।
চিচ্ছক্তি-আশ্রয় তিহোঁ, কারণের কারণ ॥ ৪২ ॥

tāṅhā ye rāmera rūpa—mahā-saṅkarṣaṇa
cic-chakti-āśraya tiṅho, kāraṇera kāraṇa

tāṅhā—there; *ye*—which; *rāmera rūpa*—the personal feature of Balarāma; *mahā-saṅkarṣaṇa*—Mahā-saṅkarṣaṇa; *cit-śakti-āśraya*—the shelter of the spiritual potency; *tiṅho*—He; *kāraṇera kāraṇa*—the cause of all causes.

TRANSLATION

There [in the spiritual sky] the personal feature of Balarāma called Mahā-saṅkarṣaṇa is the shelter of the spiritual energy. He is the primary cause, the cause of all causes.

TEXT 43

চিচ্ছক্তি-বিলাস এক—'শুদ্ধসত্ত্ব' নাম ।
শুদ্ধসত্ত্বময় যত বৈকুণ্ঠাদি-ধাম ॥ ৪৩ ॥

cic-chakti-vilāsa eka—'śuddha-sattva' nāma
śuddha-sattva-maya yata vaikuṇṭhādi-dhāma

cit-śakti-vilāsa—pastimes in the spiritual energy; *eka*—one; *śuddha-sattva nāma*—named *śuddha-sattva,* pure existence, free from material contamination; *śuddha-sattva-maya*—of purely spiritual existence; *yata*—all; *vaikuṇṭha-ādi-dhāma*—the spiritual planets, known as Vaikuṇṭhas.

TRANSLATION

One variety of the pastimes of the spiritual energy is described as pure goodness [viśuddha-sattva]. It comprises all the abodes of Vaikuṇṭha.

TEXT 44

ষড়্‌বিধৈশ্বর্য তাঁহা সকল চিন্ময় ।
সঙ্কর্ষণের বিভূতি সব, জানিহ নিশ্চয় ॥ ৪৪ ॥

ṣaḍ-vidhaiśvarya tāṅhā sakala cinmaya
saṅkarṣaṇera vibhūti saba, jāniha niścaya

ṣaṭ-vidha-aiśvarya—six kinds of opulences; *tāṅhā*—there; *sakala cit-maya*—everything spiritual; *saṅkarṣaṇera*—of Lord Saṅkarṣaṇa; *vibhūti saba*—all different opulences; *jāniha niścaya*—know certainly.

TRANSLATION

The six attributes are all spiritual. Know for certain that they are all manifestations of the opulence of Saṅkarṣaṇa.

TEXT 45

'জীব'-নাম তটস্থাখ্য এক শক্তি হয় ।
মহাসঙ্কর্ষণ—সব জীবের আশ্রয় ॥ ৪৫ ॥

'jīva'-nāma taṭasthākhya eka śakti haya
mahā-saṅkarṣaṇa—saba jīvera āśraya

jīva—the living entity; *nāma*—named; *taṭa-sthā-ākhya*—known as the marginal potency; *eka*—one; *śakti*—energy; *haya*—is; *mahā-saṅkarṣaṇa*—Mahā-saṅkarṣaṇa; *saba*—all; *jīvera*—of living entities; *āśraya*—the shelter.

TRANSLATION

There is one marginal potency, known as the jīva. Mahā-saṅkarṣaṇa is the shelter of all jīvas.

TEXT 46

যাঁহা হৈতে বিশ্বোৎপত্তি, যাঁহাতে প্রলয় ।
সেই পুরুষের সঙ্কর্ষণ সমাশ্রয় ॥ ৪৬ ॥

yāṅhā haite viśvotpatti, yāṅhāte pralaya
sei puruṣera saṅkarṣaṇa samāśraya

yāṅhā haite—from whom; *viśva-utpatti*—the creation of the material cosmic manifestation; *yāṅhāte*—in whom; *pralaya*—merging; *sei puruṣera*—of that Supreme Personality of Godhead; *saṅkarṣaṇa*—Saṅkarṣaṇa; *samāśraya*—the original shelter.

TRANSLATION

Saṅkarṣaṇa is the original shelter of the puruṣa, from whom this world is created and in whom it is dissolved.

TEXT 47

সর্বাশ্রয়, সর্বাদ্ভুত, ঐশ্বর্য অপার ।
'অনন্ত' কহিতে নারে মহিমা যাঁহার ॥ ৪৭ ॥

sarvāśraya, sarvādbhuta, aiśvarya apāra
'ananta' kahite nāre mahimā yāṅhāra

sarva-āśraya—the shelter of everything; *sarva-adbhuta*—wonderful in every respect; *aiśvarya*—opulences; *apāra*—unfathomed; *ananta*—Ananta Śeṣa; *kahite nāre*—cannot speak; *mahimā yāṅhāra*—the glories of whom.

TRANSLATION

He [Saṅkarṣaṇa] is the shelter of everything. He is wonderful in every respect, and His opulences are infinite. Even Ananta cannot describe His glory.

TEXT 48

তুরীয়, বিশুদ্ধসত্ত্ব, 'সঙ্কর্ষণ' নাম ।
তিঁহো যাঁর অংশ, সেই নিত্যানন্দ-রাম ॥ ৪৮ ॥

turīya, viśuddha-sattva, 'saṅkarṣaṇa' nāma
tiṅho yāṅra aṁśa, sei nityānanda-rāma

turīya—transcendental; *viśuddha-sattva*—pure existence; *saṅkarṣaṇa nāma*—named Saṅkarṣaṇa; *tiṅho yāṅra aṁśa*—of whom that Saṅkarṣaṇa is also a partial expansion; *sei nityānanda-rāma*—that person is known as Balarāma or Nityānanda.

TRANSLATION

That Saṅkarṣaṇa, who is transcendental pure goodness, is a partial expansion of Nityānanda Balarāma.

TEXT 49

অষ্টম শ্লোকের কৈল সংক্ষেপে বিবরণ ।
নবম শ্লোকের অর্থ শুন দিয়া মন ॥ ৪৯ ॥

aṣṭama ślokera kaila saṅkṣepe vivaraṇa
navama ślokera artha śuna diyā mana

aṣṭama—eighth; *ślokera*—of the verse; *kaila*—I have done; *saṅkṣepe*—in brief; *vivaraṇa*—description; *navama*—the ninth; *ślokera*—of the verse; *artha*—the meaning; *śuna*—please hear; *diyā mana*—with mental attention.

TRANSLATION

I have briefly explained the eighth verse. Now please listen with attention as I explain the ninth verse.

TEXT 50

মায়াভর্তাজাণ্ডসঙ্ঘাশ্রয়াঙ্গঃ
শেতে সাক্ষাৎ কারণাম্ভোধি-মধ্যে ।
যস্যৈকাংশঃ শ্রীপুমানাদিদেব-
স্তং শ্রীনিত্যানন্দরামং প্রপদ্যে ॥ ৫০ ॥

māyā-bhartājāṇḍa-saṅghāśrayāṅgaḥ
śete sākṣāt kāraṇāmbhodhi-madhye
yasyaikāṁśaḥ śrī-pumān ādi-devas
taṁ śrī-nityānanda-rāmaṁ prapadye

māyā-bhartā—the master of the illusory energy; *aja-aṇḍa-saṅgha*—of the multitude of universes; *āśraya*—the shelter; *aṅgaḥ*—whose body; *śete*—He lies; *sākṣāt*—directly; *kāraṇa-ambhodhi-madhye*—in the midst of the Causal Ocean; *yasya*—whose; *eka-aṁśaḥ*—one portion; *śrī-pumān*—the Supreme Person; *ādi-devaḥ*—the original *puruṣa* incarnation; *tam*—to Him; *śrī-nityānanda-rāmam*—to Lord Balarāma in the form of Lord Nityānanda; *prapadye*—I surrender.

TRANSLATION

I offer my full obeisances unto the feet of Śrī Nityānanda Rāma, whose partial representation called Kāraṇodakaśāyī Viṣṇu, lying on the Kāraṇa Ocean, is the original puruṣa, the master of the illusory energy, and the shelter of all the universes.

TEXT 51

বৈকুণ্ঠ-বাহিরে যেই জ্যোতির্ময় ধাম ।
তাহার বাহিরে 'কারণার্ণব' নাম ॥ ৫১ ॥

vaikuṇṭha-bāhire yei jyotir-maya dhāma
tāhāra bāhire 'kāraṇārṇava' nāma

vaikuṇṭha-bāhire—outside the Vaikuṇṭha planets; *yei*—that; *jyotiḥ-maya dhāma*—impersonal Brahman effulgence; *tāhāra bāhire*—outside that effulgence; *kāraṇa-arṇava nāma*—an ocean called Kāraṇa.

TRANSLATION

Outside the Vaikuṇṭha planets is the impersonal Brahman effulgence, and beyond that effulgence is the Kāraṇa Ocean, or Causal Ocean.

PURPORT

The impersonal glowing effulgence known as impersonal Brahman is the outer space of the Vaikuṇṭha planets in the spiritual sky. Beyond that impersonal Brahman is the great Causal Ocean, which lies between the material and spiritual skies. The material nature is a by-product of this Causal Ocean.

Kāraṇodakaśāyī Viṣṇu, who lies on the Causal Ocean, creates the universes merely by glancing upon material nature. Therefore Kṛṣṇa personally has nothing to do with the material creation. The *Bhagavad-gītā* confirms that the Lord glances over material nature and thus she produces the many material universes. Neither Kṛṣṇa in Goloka nor Nārāyaṇa in Vaikuṇṭha comes directly in contact with the material creation. They are completely aloof from the material energy.

It is the function of Mahā-saṅkarṣaṇa in the form of Kāraṇodakaśāyī Viṣṇu to glance over the material creation, which is situated beyond the limits of the Causal Ocean. Material nature is connected with the Personality of Godhead by His glance over her and nothing more. It is said that she is impregnated by the energy of His glance. The material energy, *māyā,* never even touches the Causal Ocean, for the Lord's glance focuses upon her from a great distance away.

The glancing power of the Lord agitates the entire cosmic energy, and thus its actions begin at once. This indicates that matter, however powerful she may be, has no power by herself. Her activity begins by the grace of the Lord, and then the entire cosmic creation is manifested in a systematic way. The analogy of a woman's conception can help us understand this subject to a certain extent. The mother is passive, but the father puts his energy within the mother, and thus she conceives. She supplies the ingredients for the birth of the child in her womb. Similarly, the Lord activates material nature, which then supplies the ingredients for cosmic development.

Material nature has two different phases. The aspect called *pradhāna* supplies the material ingredients for cosmic development, and the aspect called *māyā* causes the manifestation of her ingredients, which are temporary, like foam in the ocean. In reality, the temporary manifestations of material nature are originally caused by the spiritual glance of the Lord. The Personality of Godhead is the direct, or remote, cause of creation, and material nature is the indirect, or immediate, cause. Materialistic scientists, puffed-up by the magical changes their so-called inventions have brought about, cannot see the real potency of Godhead behind matter. Therefore the jugglery of science is gradually leading people to a godless civilization at the cost of the goal of human life. Having missed the goal of life, materialists run after self-sufficiency, not knowing that material nature is already self-sufficient by the grace of God. Thus creating a colossal hoax in the name of civilization, they create an imbalance in the natural self-sufficiency of material nature.

To think of material nature as all in all, not knowing the original cause, is ignorance. Lord Caitanya appeared in order to dissipate this darkness of ignorance by igniting the spark of spiritual life that can, by His causeless mercy, enlighten the entire world.

To explain how *māyā* acts by Kṛṣṇa's power, the author of *Śrī Caitanya-caritāmṛta* gives the analogy of an iron rod in a fire: although the rod is not fire, it becomes red-hot and acts like fire itself. Similarly, all the actions and reactions of material nature are not actually the work of material nature but are actions and reactions of the energy of the Supreme Lord manifested through matter. The power of electricity is transmitted through the medium of copper, but this does not mean that the copper is electricity. The power is generated at a powerhouse under the control of an expert living being. Similarly, behind all the jugglery of the natural laws is a great living being, who is a person like the mechanical engineer in the powerhouse. It is by His intelligence that the entire cosmic creation moves in a systematic way.

The modes of nature, which directly cause material actions, are also originally activated by Nārāyaṇa. A simple analogy will explain how this is so: When a potter manufactures a pot from clay, the potter's wheel, his tools and the clay are the immediate causes of the pot, but the potter is the chief cause. Similarly, Nārāyaṇa is the chief cause of all material creations, and the material energy supplies the ingredients of matter. Therefore without Nārāyaṇa, all other causes are useless, just as the potter's wheel and tools are useless without the potter himself. Since materialistic scientists ignore the Personality of Godhead, it is as if they were concerned with the potter's wheel and its rotation, the potter's tools and the ingredients for the pots, but had no knowledge of the potter himself. Therefore modern science has created an imperfect, godless civilization that is in gross ignorance of the ultimate cause. Scientific advancement should have a great goal to attain, and that great goal should be the Personality of Godhead. In the *Bhagavad-gītā* it is said that after conducting research for many, many births, great men of knowledge who stress the importance of experimental thought can know the Personality of Godhead, who is the cause of all causes. When one knows Him perfectly, one surrenders unto Him and then becomes a *mahātmā*.

TEXT 52

বৈকুণ্ঠ বেড়িয়া এক আছে জলনিধি ।
অনন্ত, অপার—তার নাহিক অবধি ॥ ৫২ ॥

vaikuṇṭha beḍiyā eka āche jala-nidhi
ananta, apāra—tāra nāhika avadhi

vaikuṇṭha—the spiritual planets of Vaikuṇṭha; *beḍiyā*—surrounding; *eka*—one; *āche*—there is; *jala-nidhi*—ocean of water; *ananta*—unlimited; *apāra*—unfathomed; *tāra*—of that; *nāhika*—no; *avadhi*—limitation.

TRANSLATION

Surrounding Vaikuṇṭha is a mass of water that is endless, unfathomed and unlimited.

TEXT 53

বৈকুণ্ঠের পৃথিব্যাদি সকল চিন্ময় ।
মায়িক ভূতের তথি জন্ম নাহি হয় ॥ ৫৩ ॥

vaikuṇṭhera pṛthivy-ādi sakala cinmaya
māyika bhūtera tathi janma nāhi haya

vaikuṇṭhera—of the spiritual world; *pṛthivī-ādi*—earth, water, etc.; *sakala*—all; *cit-maya*—spiritual; *māyika*—material; *bhūtera*—of elements; *tathi*—there; *janma*—generation; *nāhi haya*—there is not.

TRANSLATION

The earth, water, fire, air and ether of Vaikuṇṭha are all spiritual. Material elements are not found there.

TEXT 54

চিন্ময়-জল সেই পরম কারণ ।
যার এক কণা গঙ্গা পতিতপাবন ॥ ৫৪ ॥

cinmaya-jala sei parama kāraṇa
yāra eka kaṇā gaṅgā patita-pāvana

cit-maya—spiritual; *jala*—water; *sei*—that; *parama kāraṇa*—original cause; *yāra*—of which; *eka*—one; *kaṇā*—drop; *gaṅgā*—the sacred Ganges; *patita-pāvana*—the deliverer of fallen souls.

TRANSLATION

The water of the Kāraṇa Ocean, which is the original cause, is therefore spiritual. The sacred Ganges, which is but a drop of it, purifies the fallen souls.

TEXT 55

সেই ত' কারণার্ণবে সেই সঙ্কর্ষণ ।
আপনার এক অংশে করেন শয়ন ॥ ৫৫ ॥

sei ta' kāraṇārṇave sei saṅkarṣaṇa
āpanāra eka aṁśe karena śayana

sei—that; *ta'*—certainly; *kāraṇa-arṇave*—in the ocean of cause, or Causal Ocean; *sei*—that; *saṅkarṣaṇa*—Lord Saṅkarṣaṇa; *āpanāra*—of His own; *eka*—one; *aṁśe*—by the part; *karena śayana*—lies down.

TRANSLATION

In that ocean lies a plenary portion of Lord Saṅkarṣaṇa.

TEXT 56

মহৎস্রষ্টা পুরুষ, তিঁহো জগৎ-কারণ ।
আদ্য-অবতার করে মায়ায় ঈক্ষণ ॥ ৫৬ ॥

mahat-sraṣṭā puruṣa, tiṅho jagat-kāraṇa
ādya-avatāra kare māyāya īkṣaṇa

mahat-sraṣṭā—the creator of the total material energy; *puruṣa*—the person; *tiṅho*—He; *jagat-kāraṇa*—the cause of the material cosmic manifestation; *ādya*—original; *avatāra*—incarnation; *kare*—does; *māyāya*—over the material energy; *īkṣaṇa*—glance.

TRANSLATION

He is known as the first puruṣa, the creator of the total material energy. He, the cause of the universes, the first incarnation, casts His glance over māyā.

TEXT 57

মায়াশক্তি রহে কারণাব্ধির বাহিরে ।
কারণ-সমুদ্র মায়া পরশিতে নারে ॥ ৫৭ ॥

māyā-śakti rahe kāraṇābdhira bāhire
kāraṇa-samudra māyā paraśite nāre

māyā-śakti—material energy; *rahe*—remains; *kāraṇa-abdhira*—to the Causal Ocean; *bāhire*—external; *kāraṇa-samudra*—the Causal Ocean; *māyā*—material energy; *paraśite nāre*—cannot touch.

TRANSLATION

Māyā-śakti resides outside the Kāraṇa Ocean. Māyā cannot touch its waters.

TEXT 58

সেই ত' মায়ার দুইবিধ অবস্থিতি ।
জগতের উপাদান 'প্রধান', প্রকৃতি ॥ ৫৮ ॥

sei ta' māyāra dui-vidha avasthiti
jagatera upādāna 'pradhāna', prakṛti

sei—that; *ta'*—certainly; *māyāra*—of the material energy; *dui-vidha*—two varieties; *avasthiti*—existence; *jagatera*—of the material world; *upādāna*—the ingredients; *pradhāna*—named *pradhāna; prakṛti*—material nature.

TRANSLATION

Māyā has two varieties of existence. One is called pradhāna or prakṛti. It supplies the ingredients of the material world.

PURPORT

Māyā, the external energy of the Supreme Personality of Godhead, is divided into two parts. *Māyā* is both the cause of the cosmic manifestation and the agent who supplies its ingredients. As the cause of the cosmic manifestation she is known as *māyā*, and as the agent supplying the ingredients of the cosmic manifestation she is known as *pradhāna*. An explicit description of these divisions of the external energy is given in *Śrīmad-Bhāgavatam* (11.24.1–4). Elsewhere in *Śrīmad-Bhāgavatam* (10.63.26) the ingredients and cause of the material cosmic manifestation are described as follows:

kālo daivaṁ karma jīvaḥ svabhāvo
dravyaṁ kṣetraṁ prāṇa ātmā vikāraḥ
tat-saṅghāto bīja-roha-pravāhas
tvan-māyaiṣā tan-niṣedhaṁ prapadye

"O my Lord! Time, activity, providence and nature are four parts of the causal aspect [*māyā*] of the external energy. The conditioned vital force, the subtle material ingredients called the *dravya*, and material nature (which is the field of activity where the false ego acts as the soul), as well as the eleven senses and five elements (earth, water, fire, air and ether), which are the sixteen ingredients of the body—these are the ingredient aspect of *māyā*. The body is generated from activity, and activity is generated from the body, just as a tree is generated from a seed that is generated from a tree. This reciprocal cause and effect is called *māyā*. My dear Lord, You can save me from this cycle of cause and effect. I worship Your lotus feet."

Although the living entity is primarily related to the causal portion of *māyā*, he is nevertheless conducted by the ingredients of *māyā*. Three forces work in the causal portion of *māyā:* knowledge, desire and activity. The material ingredients are a manifestation of *māyā* as *pradhāna*. In other words, when the three qualities of *māyā* are in a dormant stage, they exist as *prakṛti*, *avyakta* or *pradhāna*. The word *avyakta*, referring to the nonmanifested, is another name of *pradhāna*. In the *avyakta* stage, material nature is without varieties. Varieties are manifested by the *pradhāna* portion of *māyā*. The word *pradhāna* is therefore more important than *avyakta* or *prakṛti*.

TEXT 59

জগৎকারণ নহে প্রকৃতি জড়রূপা ।
শক্তি সঞ্চারিয়া তারে কৃষ্ণ করে কৃপা ॥ ৫৯ ॥

jagat-kāraṇa nahe prakṛti jaḍa-rūpā
śakti sañcāriyā tāre kṛṣṇa kare kṛpā

jagat—of the material world; *kāraṇa*—the cause; *nahe*—cannot be; *prakṛti*—the material nature; *jaḍa-rūpā*—dull, without action; *śakti*—energy; *sañcāriyā*—infusing; *tāre*—unto the dull material nature; *kṛṣṇa*—Lord Kṛṣṇa; *kare*—shows; *kṛpā*—mercy.

TRANSLATION

Because prakṛti is dull and inert, it cannot actually be the cause of the material world. But Lord Kṛṣṇa shows His mercy by infusing His energy into the dull, inert material nature.

TEXT 60

কৃষ্ণশক্ত্যে প্রকৃতি হয় গৌণ কারণ ।
অগ্নিশক্ত্যে লৌহ যৈছে করয়ে জারণ ॥ ৬০ ॥

kṛṣṇa-śaktye prakṛti haya gauṇa kāraṇa
agni-śaktye lauha yaiche karaye jāraṇa

kṛṣṇa-śaktye—by the energy of Kṛṣṇa; *prakṛti*—the material nature; *haya*—becomes; *gauṇa*—indirect; *kāraṇa*—cause; *agni-śaktye*—by the energy of fire; *lauha*—iron; *yaiche*—just as; *karaye*—becomes; *jāraṇa*—powerful or red-hot.

TRANSLATION

Thus prakṛti, by the energy of Lord Kṛṣṇa, becomes the secondary cause, just as iron becomes red-hot by the energy of fire.

TEXT 61

অতএব কৃষ্ণ মূল-জগৎকারণ ।
প্রকৃতি—কারণ যৈছে অজাগলস্তন ॥ ৬১ ॥

ataeva kṛṣṇa mūla-jagat-kāraṇa
prakṛti—kāraṇa yaiche ajā-gala-stana

ataeva—therefore; *kṛṣṇa*—Lord Kṛṣṇa; *mūla*—original; *jagat-kāraṇa*—the cause of the cosmic manifestation; *prakṛti*—material nature; *kāraṇa*—cause; *yaiche*—exactly like; *ajā-gala-stana*—nipples on the neck of a goat.

TRANSLATION

Therefore Lord Kṛṣṇa is the original cause of the cosmic manifestation. Prakṛti is like the nipples on the neck of a goat, for they cannot give any milk.

PURPORT

The external energy, composed of *pradhāna* or *prakṛti* as the ingredient-supplying portion and *māyā* as the causal portion, is known as *māyā-śakti.* Inert material nature is not the actual cause of the material manifestation, for Kāraṇārṇavaśāyī, Mahā-Viṣṇu, the plenary expansion of Kṛṣṇa, activates all the ingredients. It is in this way that material nature has the power to supply the ingredients. The analogy given is that iron has no power to heat or burn, but after coming in contact with fire the iron becomes red-hot and can then diffuse heat and burn other things. Material nature is like iron, for it has no independence to act without the touch of Viṣṇu, who is compared to fire. Lord Viṣṇu activates material nature by the power of His glance, and then the ironlike material nature becomes a material-supplying agent just as iron made red-hot becomes a burning agent. Material nature cannot independently become an agent for supplying the material ingredients. This is more clearly explained by Śrī Kapiladeva, an incarnation of Godhead, in *Śrīmad-Bhāgavatam* (3.28.40):

> *yatholmukād visphuliṅgād dhūmād vāpi sva-sambhavāt*
> *apy ātmatvenābhimatād yathāgniḥ pṛthag ulmukāt*

"Although smoke, flaming wood, and sparks are all considered together as ingredients of a fire, the flaming wood is nevertheless different from the fire, and the smoke is different from the flaming wood." The material elements (earth, water, fire, etc.) are like smoke, the living entities are like sparks, and material nature as *pradhāna* is like the flaming wood. But all of them together are recipients of power from the Supreme Personality of Godhead and are thus able to manifest their individual capacities. In other words, the Supreme Personality of Godhead is the origin of all manifestations. Material nature can supply only when it is activated by the glance of the Supreme Personality of Godhead.

Just as a woman can deliver a child after being impregnated by the semen of a man, so material nature can supply the material elements after being glanced upon by Mahā-Viṣṇu. Therefore *pradhāna* cannot be independent of the superintendence of the Supreme Personality of Godhead. This is confirmed in the *Bhagavad-gītā* (9.10): *mayā-dhyakṣeṇa prakṛtiḥ sūyate sa-carācaram. Prakṛti,* the total material energy, works under the superintendence of the Lord. The original source of the material elements is Kṛṣṇa. Therefore the attempt of the atheistic Sāṅkhya philosophers to consider material nature the source of these elements, forgetting Kṛṣṇa, is useless, like trying to get milk from the nipplelike bumps of skin hanging on the neck of a goat.

TEXT 62

মায়া-অংশে কহি তারে নিমিত্ত-কারণ ।
সেহ নহে, যাতে কর্তা-হেতু—নারায়ণ ॥ ৬২ ॥

māyā-aṁśe kahi tāre nimitta-kāraṇa
seha nahe, yāte kartā-hetu—nārāyaṇa

māyā-aṁśe—to the other portion of the material nature; *kahi*—I say; *tāre*—unto her; *nimitta-kāraṇa*—immediate cause; *seha nahe*—that cannot be; *yāte*—because; *kartā-hetu*—the original cause; *nārāyaṇa*—Lord Nārāyaṇa.

TRANSLATION

The māyā aspect of material nature is the immediate cause of the cosmic manifestation. But it cannot be the real cause, for the original cause is Lord Nārāyaṇa.

TEXT 63

ঘটের নিমিত্ত-হেতু যৈছে কুম্ভকার ।
তৈছে জগতের কর্তা—পুরুষাবতার ॥ ৬৩ ॥

ghaṭera nimitta-hetu yaiche kumbhakāra
taiche jagatera kartā—puruṣāvatāra

ghaṭera—of the earthen pot; *nimitta-hetu*—original cause; *yaiche*—just as; *kumbhakāra*—the potter; *taiche*—similarly; *jagatera kartā*—the creator of the material world; *puruṣa-avatāra*—the *puruṣa* incarnation, or Kāraṇārṇavaśāyī Viṣṇu.

TRANSLATION

Just as the original cause of an earthen pot is the potter, so the creator of the material world is the first puruṣa incarnation [Kāraṇārṇavaśāyī Viṣṇu].

TEXT 64

কৃষ্ণ—কর্তা, মায়া তাঁর করেন সহায় ।
ঘটের কারণ—চক্র-দণ্ডাদি উপায় ॥ ৬৪ ॥

kṛṣṇa—kartā, māyā tāṅra karena sahāya
ghaṭera kāraṇa—cakra-daṇḍādi upāya

kṛṣṇa—Lord Kṛṣṇa; *kartā*—the creator; *māyā*—material energy; *tāṅra*—His; *karena*—does; *sahāya*—assistance; *ghaṭera kāraṇa*—the cause of the earthen pot; *cakra-daṇḍa-ādi*—the wheel, the rod, and so on; *upāya*—instruments.

TRANSLATION

Lord Kṛṣṇa is the creator, and māyā only helps Him as an instrument, just like the potter's wheel and other instruments, which are the instrumental causes of a pot.

TEXT 65

দূর হৈতে পুরুষ করে মায়াতে অবধান ।
জীবরূপ বীর্য তাতে করেন আধান ॥ ৬৫ ॥

dūra haite puruṣa kare māyāte avadhāna
jīva-rūpa vīrya tāte karena ādhāna

dūra haite—from a distance; *puruṣa*—the Supreme Personality of Godhead; *kare*—does; *māyāte*—unto the material energy; *avadhāna*—glancing over; *jīva-rūpa*—the living entities; *vīrya*—seed; *tāte*—in her; *karena*—does; *ādhāna*—impregnation.

TRANSLATION

The first puruṣa casts His glance at māyā from a distance, and thus He impregnates her with the seed of life in the form of the living entities.

TEXT 66

এক অঙ্গাভাসে করে মায়াতে মিলন।
মায়া হৈতে জন্মে তবে ব্রহ্মাণ্ডের গণ ॥ ৬৬ ॥

eka aṅgābhāse kare māyāte milana
māyā haite janme tabe brahmāṇḍera gaṇa

eka—one; *aṅga-ābhāse*—bodily reflection; *kare*—does; *māyāte*—in the material energy; *milana*—mixture; *māyā*—the material energy; *haite*—from; *janme*—grows; *tabe*—then; *brahma-aṇḍera gaṇa*—the groups of universes.

TRANSLATION

The reflected rays of His body mix with māyā, and thus māyā gives birth to myriad universes.

PURPORT

The Vedic conclusion is that the cosmic manifestation visible to the eyes of the conditioned soul is caused by the Absolute Truth, the Personality of Godhead, through the exertion of His specific energies, although in the conclusion of atheistic deliberations this manifested cosmic exhibition is attributed to material nature. The energy of the Absolute Truth is exhibited in three ways: spiritual, material and marginal. The Absolute Truth is identical with His spiritual energy. Only when contacted by the spiritual energy can the material energy work and the temporary material manifestations thus appear active. In the conditioned state the living entities of the marginal energy are a mixture of spiritual and material energies. The marginal energy is originally under the control of the spiritual energy, but, under the control of the material energy, the living entities have been wandering in forgetfulness within the material world since time immemorial.

The conditioned state is caused by misuse of the individual independence of the spiritual platform, for this separates the living entity from the association of the spiritual energy. But when the living entity is enlightened by the grace of the Supreme Lord or His pure devotee and becomes inclined to revive his original state of loving service, he is on the most auspicious platform of eternal bliss and knowledge. The marginal *jīva*, or living entity, misuses his independence and becomes averse to the eternal service attitude when he independently thinks he is not energy but the energetic. This misconception of his own existence leads him to the attitude of lording it over material nature.

Material nature appears to be just the opposite of the spiritual energy. The fact is that the material energy can work only when in contact with the spiritual energy. Originally the energy of Kṛṣṇa is spiritual, but it works in diverse ways, like electrical energy, which can exhibit the functions of refrigerating or heating through its manifestations in different ways. The material energy is spiritual energy covered by a cloud of illusion, or *māyā*. Therefore, the material energy is not self-sufficient in working. Kṛṣṇa invests His spiritual energy into material energy, and then it can act, just as iron can act like fire after being heated by fire. The material energy can act only when empowered by the spiritual energy.

When covered by the cloud of material energy, the living entity, who is also a spiritual energy of the Supreme Personality of Godhead, forgets about the activities of the spiritual energy and considers all that happens in the material manifestation to be wonderful. But a person who is engaged in devotional service in full Kṛṣṇa consciousness and who is therefore already situated in the spiritual energy can understand that the material energy has no independent powers: whatever actions are going on are due to the help of the spiritual energy. The material energy, which is a perverted form of the spiritual energy, presents everything pervertedly, thus causing misconceptions and duality. Material scientists and philosophers conditioned by the spell of material nature suppose that material energy acts automatically, and therefore they are frustrated, like an illusioned person who tries to get milk from the nipple-like bunches of skin on the neck of a goat. As there is no possibility of getting milk from these bunches of skin, there is similarly no possibility that anyone will be successful in understanding the original cause of creation by putting forward theories produced by the material energy. Such an attempt is a manifestation of ignorance.

The material energy of the Supreme Personality of Godhead is called *māyā*, or illusion, because in two capacities (by supplying the material elements and by causing the material manifestation) it makes the conditioned soul unable to understand the real truth of creation. However, when a living entity is liberated from the conditioned life of matter, he can understand the two different activities of material nature, namely covering and bewildering.

The origin of creation is the Supreme Personality of Godhead. As confirmed in the *Bhagavad-gītā* (9.10), the cosmic manifestation is working under the direction of the Supreme Lord, who invests the material energy with three material qualities. Agitated by these qualities, the elements supplied by the material energy produce varieties of things, just as an artist produces varieties of pictures by mixing the three colors red, yellow and blue. Yellow represents the quality of goodness, red represents passion, and blue represents ignorance. Therefore the colorful material creation is but an interaction of these three qualities, represented in eighty-one varieties of mixtures (3 X 3 equaling 9, 9 X 9 thus equaling 81). Deluded by material energy, the conditioned soul, enamored by these eighty-one varieties of manifestations, wants to lord it over material energy, just as a moth wants to enjoy a fire. This illusion is the net result of the conditioned soul's forgetfulness of his eternal relationship with the Supreme personality of Godhead. When conditioned, the soul is impelled by the material energy to engage in sense gratification, whereas one enlightened by the spiritual energy engages himself in the service of the Supreme Lord in his eternal relationship.

Kṛṣṇa is the original cause of the spiritual world, and He is the covered cause of the material manifestation. He is also the original cause of the marginal potency, the living entities. He is both the leader and maintainer of the living entities, who are called the marginal potency because they can act under the protection of the spiritual energy or under the cover of the material energy. With the help of the spiritual energy we can understand that independence is visible only in Kṛṣṇa, who by His inconceivable energy is able to act in any way He likes.

The Supreme Personality of Godhead is the Absolute Whole, and the living entities are parts of the Absolute Whole. This relationship of the Supreme Personality of Godhead and the living entities is eternal. One should never mistakenly think that the spiritual whole can be divided into small parts by the small material energy. The *Bhagavad-gītā* does not support this Māyāvāda theory. Rather, it clearly states that the living entities are eternally small fragments of the supreme spiritual whole. As a part can never be equal with the whole, so a living entity, as a minute fragment of the spiritual whole, cannot be equal at any time to the Supreme Whole, the absolute Personality of Godhead. Although the Supreme Lord and the living entities are quantitatively related as the whole and the parts, the parts are nevertheless qualitatively one with the whole. Thus the living entities, although always qualitatively one with the Supreme Lord, are in a relative position. The Supreme Personality of Godhead is the controller of everything, and the living entities are always controlled, either by the spiritual energy or by the material energy. Therefore a living entity can never become the controller of material or spiritual energies. The natural position of the living being is always as a subordinate of the Supreme Personality of Godhead. When one agrees to act in such a position, he attains perfection in life, but if one rebels against this principle, he is in the conditioned state.

TEXT 67

অগণ্য, অনন্ত যত অণ্ড-সন্নিবেশ ।
ততরূপে পুরুষ করে সবাতে প্রকাশ ॥ ৬৭ ॥

agaṇya, ananta yata aṇḍa-sanniveśa
tata-rūpe puruṣa kare sabāte prakāśa

agaṇya—innumerable; *ananta*—unlimited; *yata*—all; *aṇḍa*—universes; *sanniveśa*—groups; *tata-rūpe*—in as many forms; *puruṣa*—the Lord; *kare*—does; *sabāte*—in every one of them; *prakāśa*—manifestation.

TRANSLATION

The puruṣa enters each and every one of the countless universes. He manifests Himself in as many separate forms as there are universes.

TEXT 68

পুরুষ-নাসাতে যবে বাহিরায় শ্বাস ।
নিশ্বাস সহিতে হয় ব্রহ্মাণ্ড-প্রকাশ ॥ ৬৮ ॥

puruṣa-nāsāte yabe bāhirāya śvāsa
niśvāsa sahite haya brahmāṇḍa-prakāśa

puruṣa-nāsāte—in the nostrils of the Lord; *yabe*—when; *bāhirāya*—expels; *śvāsa*—breath; *niśvāsa sahite*—with that exhalation; *haya*—there is; *brahmāṇḍa-prakāśa*—manifestation of universes.

TRANSLATION

When the puruṣa exhales, the universes are manifested with each outward breath.

TEXT 69

পুনরপি শ্বাস যবে প্রবেশে অন্তরে ।
শ্বাস-সহ ব্রহ্মাণ্ড পৈশে পুরুষ-শরীরে ॥ ৬৯ ॥

punarapi śvāsa yabe praveśe antare
śvāsa-saha brahmāṇḍa paiśe puruṣa-śarīre

punarapi—thereafter; *śvāsa*—breath; *yabe*—when; *praveśe*—enters; *antare*—within; *śvāsa-saha*—with that inhaled breath; *brahmāṇḍa*—universes; *paiśe*—enter; *puruṣa-śarīre*—within the body of the Lord.

TRANSLATION

Thereafter, when He inhales, all the universes again enter His body.

PURPORT

In His form as Kāraṇodakaśāyī Viṣṇu the Lord impregnates material nature by His glance. The transcendental molecules of that glance are particles of spirit, or spiritual atoms, which appear in different species of life according to the seeds of their individual *karma* from the previous cosmic manifestation. And the Lord Himself, by His partial representation, creates a body of innumerable universes and again enters each of those universes as Garbhodakaśāyī Viṣṇu. His coming in contact with *māyā* is explained in the *Bhagavad-gītā* by a comparison between air and the sky. The sky enters everything material, yet it is far away from us.

TEXT 70

গবাক্ষের রন্ধ্রে যেন ত্রসরেণু চলে ।
পুরুষের লোপকূপে ব্রহ্মাণ্ডের জালে ॥ ৭০ ॥

gavākṣera randhre yena trasareṇu cale
puruṣera loma-kūpe brahmāṇḍera jāle

gavākṣera—of windows of a room; *randhre*—within the holes; *yena*—like; *trasareṇu*—six atoms together; *cale*—moves; *puruṣera*—of the Lord; *loma-kūpe*—in the holes of the hair; *brahmāṇḍera*—of universes; *jāle*—a network.

TRANSLATION

Just as atomic particles of dust pass through the openings of a window, so the networks of universes pass through the pores of the skin of the puruṣa.

TEXT 71

যস্যৈকনিশ্বসিত-কালমথাবলম্ব্য
জীবন্তি লোমবিলজা জগদণ্ডনাথাঃ ।
বিষ্ণুর্মহান্ স ইহ যস্য কলাবিশেষো
গোবিন্দমাদিপুরুষং তমহং ভজামি ॥ ৭১ ॥

yasyaika-niśvasita-kālam athāvalambya
jīvanti loma-vila-jā jagad-aṇḍa-nāthāḥ
viṣṇur mahān sa iha yasya kalā-viśeṣo
govindam ādi-puruṣaṁ tam ahaṁ bhajāmi

yasya—whose; *eka*—one; *niśvasita*—of breath; *kālam*—time; *atha*—thus; *avalambya*—taking shelter of; *jīvanti*—live; *loma-vila-jāḥ*—grown from the hair holes; *jagat-aṇḍa-nāthāḥ*—the masters of the universes (the Brahmās); *viṣṇuḥ mahān*—the Supreme Lord, Mahā-Viṣṇu; *saḥ*—that; *iha*—here; *yasya*—whose; *kalā-viśeṣaḥ*—particular plenary portion or expansion; *govindam*—Lord Govinda; *ādi-puruṣam*—the original person; *tam*—Him; *aham*—I; *bhajāmi*—worship.

TRANSLATION

"The Brahmās and other lords of the mundane worlds appear from the pores of Mahā-Viṣṇu and remain alive for the duration of His one exhalation. I adore the primeval Lord, Govinda, of whom Mahā-Viṣṇu is a portion of a plenary portion."

PURPORT

This description of the Lord's creative energy is from the *Brahma-saṁhitā* (5.48), which Lord Brahmā compiled after his personal realization. When Mahā-Viṣṇu exhales, the spiritual seeds of the universes emanate from Him in the form of molecular particles like those that are visible, three times the size of an atom, when sunlight is diffused through a small hole. In these days of atomic research it will be a worthwhile engagement for atomic scientists to learn from this statement how the entire creation develops from the spiritual atoms emanating from the body of the Lord.

TEXT 72

ক্বাহং তমো-মহদহং-খ-চরাগ্নিবার্ভূ-
সংবেষ্টিতাণ্ডঘট-সপ্তবিতস্তিকায়ঃ ।
ক্বেদৃগ্বিধাঽবিগণিতাণ্ডপরাণুচর্যা-
বাতাধ্বরোমবিবরস্য চ তে মহিত্বম্ ॥ ৭২ ॥

kvāhaṁ tamo-mahad-ahaṁ-kha-carāgni-vār-bhū-
saṁveṣṭitāṇḍa-ghaṭa-sapta-vitasti-kāyaḥ
kvedṛg-vidhāvigaṇitāṇḍa-parāṇu-caryā-
vātādhva-roma-vivarasya ca te mahitvam

kva—where; *aham*—I; *tamaḥ*—material nature; *mahat*—the total material energy; *aham*—false ego; *kha*—ether; *cara*—air; *agni*—fire; *vāḥ*—water; *bhū*—earth; *saṁveṣṭita*—surrounded by; *aṇḍa-ghaṭa*—a potlike universe; *sapta-vitasti*—seven *vitastis; kāyaḥ*—body; *kva*—where; *īdṛk*—such; *vidha*—like; *avigaṇita*—unlimited; *aṇḍa*—universes; *para-aṇu-caryā*—moving like the atomic dust; *vāta-adhva*—air holes; *roma*—of hair on the body; *vivarasya*—of the holes; *ca*—also; *te*—Your; *mahitvam*—greatness.

TRANSLATION

"Where am I, a small creature of seven spans the measure of my own hand? I am enclosed in the universe composed of material nature, the total material energy, false ego, ether, air, water and earth. And what is Your glory? Unlimited universes pass through the pores of Your body just like particles of dust passing through the opening of a window."

PURPORT

When Lord Brahmā, after having stolen all Kṛṣṇa's calves and cowherd boys, returned and saw that the calves and boys were still roaming with Kṛṣṇa, he offered this prayer (*Bhāg.* 10.14.11) in his defeat. A conditioned soul, even one so great as Brahmā, who manages the affairs of the entire universe, cannot compare to the Personality of Godhead, for He can produce numberless universes simply by the spiritual rays emanating from the pores of His body. Material scientists should take lessons from the utterances of Śrī Brahmā regarding our insignificance in comparison to God. In these prayers of Brahmā there is much to learn for those who are falsely puffed up by the accumulation of power.

TEXT 73

অংশের অংশ যেই, 'কলা' তার নাম ।
গোবিন্দের প্রতিমূর্তি শ্রীবলরাম ॥ ৭৩ ॥

aṁśera aṁśa yei, 'kalā' tāra nāma
govindera pratimūrti śrī-balarāma

aṁśera—of the part; *aṁśa*—part; *yei*—that which; *kalā*—a *kalā*, or part of the plenary portion; *tāra*—its; *nāma*—name; *govindera*—of Lord Govinda; *prati-mūrti*—counterform; *śrī-balarāma*—Lord Balarāma.

TRANSLATION

A part of a part of a whole is called a kalā. Śrī Balarāma is the counterform of Lord Govinda.

TEXT 74

তাঁর এক স্বরূপ—শ্রীমহাসঙ্কর্ষণ ।
তাঁর অংশ 'পুরুষ' হয় কলাতে গণন ॥ ৭৪ ॥

tāṅra eka svarūpa—śrī-mahā-saṅkarṣaṇa
tāṅra aṁśa 'puruṣa' haya kalāte gaṇana

tāṅra—His; *eka*—one; *svarūpa*—manifestation; *śrī-mahā-saṅkarṣaṇa*—the great Lord Mahā-saṅkarṣaṇa; *tāṅra*—His; *aṁśa*—part; *puruṣa*—the Mahā-Viṣṇu incarnation; *haya*—is; *kalāte gaṇana*—counted as a *kalā*.

TRANSLATION

Balarāma's own expansion is called Mahā-saṅkarṣaṇa, and His fragment, the puruṣa, is counted as a kalā, or a part of a plenary portion.

TEXT 75

যাঁহাকে ত' কলা কহি, তিঁহো মহাবিষ্ণু ।
মহাপুরুষাবতারী তেঁহো সর্বজিষ্ণু ॥ ৭৫ ॥

yāṅhāke ta' kalā kahi, tiṅho mahā-viṣṇu
mahā-puruṣāvatārī teṅho sarva-jiṣṇu

yāṅhāke—unto whom; ta'—certainly; *kalā kahi*—I say *kalā; tiṅho*—He; *mahā-viṣṇu*—Lord Mahā-Viṣṇu; *mahā-puruṣāvatārī*—Mahā-Viṣṇu, the source of other *puruṣa* incarnations; *teṅho*—He; *sarva—jiṣṇu*—all-pervading.

TRANSLATION

I say that this kalā is Mahā-Viṣṇu. He is the Mahā-puruṣa, who is the source of the other puruṣas and who is all-pervading.

TEXT 76

গর্ভোদ-ক্ষীরোদশায়ী দোঁহে 'পুরুষ' নাম ।
সেই দুই, যাঁর অংশ,—বিষ্ণু, বিশ্বধাম ॥ ৭৬ ॥

garbhoda-kṣīroda-śāyī doṅhe 'puruṣa' nāma
sei dui, yāṅra aṁśa,—viṣṇu, viśva-dhāma

garbha-uda—in the ocean known as Garbhodaka within the universe; *kṣīra-uda-śāyī*—one who lies in the ocean of milk; *doṅhe*—both of Them; *puruṣa nāma*—known as *puruṣa,* Lord Viṣṇu; *sei*—those; *dui*—two; *yāṅra aṁśa*—whose plenary portions; *viṣṇu viśva-dhāma*—Lord Viṣṇu, the abode of the total universes.

TRANSLATION

Garbhodaśāyī and Kṣīrodaśāyī are both called puruṣas. They are plenary portions of Kāraṇodaśāyī Viṣṇu, the first puruṣa, who is the abode of all the universes.

PURPORT

The symptoms of the *puruṣa* are described in the *Laghu-bhāgavatāmṛta.* While describing the incarnations of the Supreme personality of Godhead, the author has quoted from the *Viṣṇu Purāṇa*

(6.8.59), where it is said, "Let me offer my respectful obeisances unto Puruṣottama, Lord Kṛṣṇa, who is always free from the contamination of the six material dualities; whose plenary expansion, Mahā-Viṣṇu, glances over matter to create the cosmic manifestation; who expands Himself in various transcendental forms, all of which are one and the same; who is the master of all living entities; who is always free and liberated from the contamination of material energy; and who, when He appears in this material world, seems one of us, although He has an eternally spiritual, blissful, transcendental form." In summarizing this statement, Rūpa Gosvāmī has concluded that the plenary expansion of the Supreme Personality of Godhead who acts in cooperation with the material energy is called the *puruṣa.*

TEXT 77

বিষ্ণোস্তু ত্রীণি রূপাণি পুরুষাখ্যান্যথো বিদুঃ ।
একন্তু মহতঃ স্রষ্টৃ দ্বিতীয়ং ত্বণ্ডসংস্থিতম্ ।
তৃতীয়ং সর্বভূতস্থং তানি জ্ঞাত্বা বিমুচ্যতে ॥ ৭৭ ॥

viṣṇos tu trīṇi rūpāṇi
puruṣākhyāny atho viduḥ
ekaṁ tu mahataḥ sraṣṭṛ
dvitīyaṁ tv aṇḍa-saṁsthitam
tṛtīyaṁ sarva-bhūta-sthaṁ
tāni jñātvā vimucyate

viṣṇoḥ—of Lord Viṣṇu; *tu*—certainly; *trīṇi*—three; *rūpāṇi*—forms; *puruṣa-ākhyāni*—celebrated as the *puruṣa; atho*—how; *viduḥ*—they know; *ekam*—one of them; *tu*—but; *mahataḥ sraṣṭṛ*—the creator of the total material energy; *dvitīyam*—the second; *tu*—but; *aṇḍa-saṁsthitam*—situated within the universe; *tṛtīyam*—the third; *sarva-bhūta-stham*—within the hearts of all living entities; *tāni*—these three; *jñātvā*—knowing; *vimucyate*—one becomes liberated.

TRANSLATION

"Viṣṇu has three forms called puruṣas. The first, Mahā-Viṣṇu, is the creator of the total material energy [mahat], the second is Garbhodaśāyī, who is situated within each universe, and the third is Kṣīrodaśāyī, who lives in the heart of every living being. He who knows these three becomes liberated from the clutches of māyā."

PURPORT

This verse appears in the *Laghu-bhāgavatāmṛta* (*Pūrva* 2.9), where it has been quoted from the *Sātvata-tantra.*

TEXT 78

যদ্যপি কহিয়ে তাঁরে কৃষ্ণের 'কলা' করি ।
মৎস্য-কূর্মাদ্যবতারের তিঁহো অবতারী ॥ ৭৮ ॥

yadyapi kahiye tāṅre kṛṣṇera 'kalā' kari
matsya-kūrmādy-avatārera tiṅho avatārī

yadyapi—although; *kahiye*—I say; *tāṅre*—to Him; *kṛṣṇera*—of Lord Kṛṣṇa; *kalā*—part of the part; *kari*—making; *matsya*—the fish incarnation; *kūrma-ādi*—the tortoise incarnation and others; *avatārera*—of all these incarnations; *tiṅho*—He; *avatārī*—the original source.

TRANSLATION

Although Kāraṇodaśāyī Viṣṇu is called a kalā of Lord Kṛṣṇa, He is the source of Matsya, Kūrma and the other incarnations.

TEXT 79

এতে চাংশকলাঃ পুংসঃ কৃষ্ণস্তু ভগবান্ স্বয়ম্ ।
ইন্দ্রারি-ব্যাকুলং লোকং মৃড়য়ন্তি যুগে যুগে ॥ ৭৯ ॥

ete cāṁśa-kalāḥ puṁsaḥ
kṛṣṇas tu bhagavān svayam
indrāri-vyākulaṁ lokaṁ
mṛḍayanti yuge yuge

ete—all these; *ca*—also; *aṁśa-kalāḥ*—part or part of the part; *puṁsaḥ*—of the Supreme Person; *kṛṣṇaḥ tu*—but Lord Kṛṣṇa; *bhagavān*—the original Personality of Godhead; *svayam*—Himself; *indra-ari*—the demons; *vyākulam*—disturbed; *lokam*—all the planets; *mṛḍayanti*—makes them happy; *yuge yuge*—in different millenniums.

TRANSLATION

"All these incarnations of Godhead are either plenary portions or parts of the plenary portions of the puruṣa-avatāras. But Kṛṣṇa is the Supreme Personality of Godhead Himself. In every age He pro-

tects the world through His different features when the world is disturbed by the enemies of Indra."

PURPORT

This quotation is from *Śrīmad-Bhāgavatam* (1.3.28).

TEXT 80

সেই পুরুষ সৃষ্টি-স্থিতি-প্রলয়ের কর্তা ।
নানা অবতার করে, জগতের ভর্তা ॥ ৮০ ॥

sei puruṣa sṛṣṭi-sthiti-pralayera kartā
nānā avatāra kare, jagatera bhartā

sei—that; *puruṣa*—the Personality of Godhead; *sṛṣṭi-sthiti-pralayera*—of creation, maintenance and annihilation; *kartā*—creator; *nānā*—various; *avatāra*—incarnations; *kare*—makes; *jagatera*—of the material world; *bhartā*—maintainer.

TRANSLATION

That puruṣa [Kāraṇodakaśāyī Viṣṇu] is the performer of creation, maintenance and destruction. He manifests Himself in many incarnations, for He is the maintainer of the world.

TEXT 81

সৃষ্ট্যাদি-নিমিত্তে যেই অংশের অবধান ।
সেই ত' অংশেরে কহি 'অবতার' নাম ॥ ৮১ ॥

sṛṣṭy-ādi-nimitte yei aṁśera avadhāna
sei ta' aṁśere kahi 'avatāra' nāma

sṛṣṭi-ādi-nimitte—for the cause of creation, maintenance and annihilation; *yei*—which; *aṁśera avadhāna*—manifestation of the part; *sei ta'*—that certainly; *aṁśere kahi*—I speak about that plenary expansion; *avatāra nāma*—by the name "incarnation."

TRANSLATION

That fragment of the Supreme Lord, known as the Mahā-puruṣa, appears for the purpose of creation, maintenance and annihilation and is called an incarnation.

TEXT 82

আদ্যাবতার, মহাপুরুষ, ভগবান্ ।
সর্ব-অবতার-বীজ, সর্বাশ্রয়-ধাম ॥ ৮২ ॥

ādyāvatāra, mahā-puruṣa, bhagavān
sarva-avatāra-bīja, sarvāśraya-dhāma

ādya-avatāra—the original incarnation; *mahā-puruṣa*—Lord Mahā-Viṣṇu; *bhagavān*—the Personality of Godhead; *sarva-avatāra-bīja*—the seed of all different kinds of incarnations; *sarva-āśraya-dhāma*—the shelter of everything.

TRANSLATION

That Mahā-puruṣa is identical with the Personality of Godhead. He is the original incarnation, the seed of all others, and the shelter of everything.

TEXT 83

আদ্যোঽবতারঃ পুরুষঃ পরস্য
কালঃ স্বভাবঃ সদসন্মনশ্চ ।
দ্রব্যং বিকারো গুণ ইন্দ্রিয়াণি
বিরাট্ স্বরাট্ স্থাস্নু চরিষ্ণু ভূম্নঃ ॥ ৮৩ ॥

ādyo 'vatāraḥ puruṣaḥ parasya
kālaḥ svabhāvaḥ sad-asan manaś ca
dravyaṁ vikāro guṇa indriyāṇi
virāṭ svarāṭ sthāsnu cariṣṇu bhūmnaḥ

ādyaḥ avatāraḥ—the original incarnation; *puruṣaḥ*—Mahā-Viṣṇu; *parasya*—of the Supreme Lord; *kālaḥ*—time; *svabhāvaḥ*—nature; *sat-asat*—cause and effect; *manaḥ ca*—as well as the mind; *dravyam*—the five elements; *vikāraḥ*—transformation or the false ego; *guṇaḥ*—modes of nature; *indriyāṇi*—senses; *virāṭ*—the universal form; *svarāṭ*—complete independence; *sthāsnu*—immovable; *cariṣṇu*—movable; *bhūmnaḥ*—of the Supreme Personality of Godhead.

TRANSLATION

"The puruṣa [Mahā-Viṣṇu] is the primary incarnation of the Supreme Personality of Godhead. Time, nature, prakṛti (as cause

and effect), the mind, the material elements, false ego, the modes of nature, the senses, the universal form, complete independence and the moving and nonmoving beings appear subsequently as His opulences."

PURPORT

Describing the incarnations and their symptoms, the *Laghu-bhāgavatāmṛta* has stated that when Lord Kṛṣṇa descends to conduct the creative affairs of the material manifestation, He is an *avatāra,* or incarnation. The two categories of *avatāras* are empowered devotees and *tad-ekātma-rūpa* (the Lord Himself). An example of *tad-ekātma-rūpa* is Śeṣa, and an example of a devotee is Vasudeva, the father of Lord Kṛṣṇa. Śrīla Baladeva Vidyābhūṣaṇa has commented that the material cosmic manifestation is a partial kingdom of God where God must sometimes come to execute a specific function. The plenary portion of the Lord through whom Lord Kṛṣṇa executes such actions is called Mahā-Viṣṇu, who is the primal beginning of all incarnations. Inexperienced observers presume that the material energy provides both the cause and the elements of the cosmic manifestation and that the living entities are the enjoyers of material nature. But the devotees of the Bhāgavata school, which has scrutinizingly examined the entire situation, can understand that material nature can independently be neither the supplier of the material elements nor the cause of the material manifestation. Material nature gets the power to supply the material elements from the glance of the supreme *puruṣa,* Mahā-Viṣṇu, and when empowered by Him she is called the cause of the material manifestation. Both features of material nature, as the cause of the material creation and as the source of its elements, exist due to the glance of the Supreme Personality of Godhead. The various expansions of the Supreme Lord who act to empower the material energy are known as plenary expansions or incarnations. As illustrated by the analogy of many flames lit from one flame, all these plenary expansions and incarnations are as good as Viṣṇu Himself; nevertheless, because of their activities in controlling *māyā,* sometimes they are known as *māyika,* or having a relationship with *māyā.* This is a verse from *Śrīmad-Bhāgavatam* (2.6.42).

TEXT 84

জগৃহে পৌরুষং রূপং ভগবান্মহদাদিভিঃ ।
সম্ভূতং ষোড়শকলমাদৌ লোকসিসৃক্ষয়া ॥ ৮৪ ॥

jagṛhe pauruṣaṁ rūpaṁ
bhagavān mahad-ādibhiḥ
sambhūtaṁ ṣoḍaśa-kalam
ādau loka-sisṛkṣayā

jagṛhe—accepted; *pauruṣam*—the *puruṣa* incarnation; *rūpam*—the form; *bhagavān*—the Supreme Personality of Godhead; *mahat-ādibhiḥ*—by the total material energy etc.; *sambhūtam*—created; *ṣoḍaśa*—sixteen; *kalam*—energies; *ādau*—originally; *loka*—the material worlds; *sisṛkṣayā*—with the desire to create.

TRANSLATION

"In the beginning of the creation, the Lord expanded Himself in the form of the puruṣa incarnation, accompanied by all the ingredients of material creation. First He created the sixteen principal energies suitable for creation. This was for the purpose of manifesting the material universes."

PURPORT

This is a verse from *Śrīmad-Bhāgavatam* (1.3.1). The commentary of Madhva on *Śrīmad-Bhāgavatam* mentions that the following sixteen spiritual energies are present in the spiritual world: (1) *śrī,* (2) *bhū,* (3) *līlā,* (4) *kānti,* (5) *kīrti,* (6) *tuṣṭi,* (7) *gīr,* (8) *puṣṭi,* (9) *satyā* (10) *jñānājñānā,* (11) *jayā utkarṣiṇī,* (12) *vimalā,* (13) *yogamāyā,* (14) *prahvī,* (15) *īśānā* and (16) *anugrahā.* In his commentary on the *Laghu-bhāgavatāmṛta,* Śrī Baladeva Vidyābhūṣaṇa has said that the above energies are also known by nine names: (1) *vimalā,* (2) *utkarṣiṇī* (3) *jñānā,* (4) *kriyā,* (5) *yogā,* (6) *prahvī,* (7) *satyā,* (8) *īśānā* and (9) *anugrahā.* In the *Bhagavat-sandarbha* of Śrīla Jīva Gosvāmī (text 103) they are described as *śrī, puṣṭi, gīr, kānti, kīrti, tuṣṭi, ilā, jaya; vidyāvidyā, māyā, samvit, sandhinī, hlādinī, bhakti, mūrti, vimalā, yogā, prahvī, īśānā, anugrahā,* etc. All these energies act in different spheres of the Lord's supremacy.

TEXT 85

যদ্যপি সর্বাশ্রয় তিঁহো, তাঁহাতে সংসার ।
অন্তরাত্মা-রূপে তিঁহো জগৎ-আধার ॥ ৮৫ ॥

yadyapi sarvāśraya tiṅho, tāṅhāte saṁsāra
antarātmā-rūpe tiṅho jagat-ādhāra

yadyapi—although; *sarva-āśraya*—the shelter of everything; *tiṅho*—He (the Lord); *tāṅhāte*—in Him; *saṁsāra*—the material creation; *antaḥ-ātmā-rūpe*—in the form of the Supersoul; *tiṅho*—He; *jagat-ādhāra*—the support of the whole creation.

TRANSLATION

Although the Lord is the shelter of everything and although all the universes rest in Him, He, as the Supersoul, is also the support of everything.

TEXT 86

প্রকৃতি-সহিতে তাঁর উভয় সম্বন্ধ ।
তথাপি প্রকৃতি-সহ নাহি স্পর্শগন্ধ ॥ ৮৬ ॥

prakṛti-sahite tāṅra ubhaya sambandha
tathāpi prakṛti-saha nāhi sparśa-gandha

prakṛti-sahite—with the material energy; *tāṅra*—His; *ubhaya sambandha*—both relationships; *tathāpi*—still; *prakṛti-saha*—with the material nature; *nāhi*—there is not; *sparśa-gandha*—even the slightest contact.

TRANSLATION

Although He is thus connected with the material energy in two ways, He does not have the slightest contact with it.

PURPORT

In the *Laghu-bhāgavatāmṛta*, Śrīla Rūpa Gosvāmī, commenting upon the Lord's transcendental position beyond the material qualities, says that Viṣṇu, as the controller and superintendent of material nature, has a connection with the material qualities. That connection is called *yoga.* However, the person who directs a prison is not also a prisoner. Similarly, although the Supreme Personality of Godhead Viṣṇu directs or supervises the qualitative nature, He has no connection with the material modes of nature. The expansions of Lord Viṣṇu always retain their supremacy; they are never connected with the material qualities. One may argue that Mahā-Viṣṇu cannot have any connection with the material qualities, because if He were so connected, *Śrīmad-Bhāgavatam* would not state that material nature, ashamed of her thankless task of acting to induce the living entities to become averse to the Supreme Lord, remains behind the Lord in shyness. In answer to this argument, it may be said that the word *guṇa* means "regulation." Lord Viṣṇu, Lord Brahmā and Lord Śiva are situated within this universe as the directors of the three modes, and their connection with the modes is known as *yoga.* This does not indicate, however, that these personalities are bound by the qualities of nature. Lord Viṣṇu specifically is always the controller of the three qualities. There is no question of His coming under their control.

Although the causal and element-supplying features exist in material nature by dint of the glance of the Supreme Personality of Godhead, the Lord is never affected by glancing over the material qualities. By the will of the Supreme Lord the different qualitative changes in the material world take place, but there is no possibility of material affection, change or contamination for Lord Viṣṇu.

TEXT 87

এতদীশনমীশস্য প্রকৃতিস্থোঽপি তদ্‌গুণৈঃ ।
ন যুজ্যতে সদাত্মস্থৈর্যথা বুদ্ধিস্তদাশ্রয়া ॥ ৮৭ ॥

etad īśanam īśasya
prakṛti-stho 'pi tad-guṇaiḥ
na yujyate sadātma-sthair
yathā buddhis tad-āśrayā

etat—this is; *īśanam*—opulence; *īśasya*—of the Lord; *prakṛti-sthaḥ*—within this material world; *api*—although; *tat-guṇaiḥ*—by the material qualities; *na yujyate*—never affected; *sadā*—always; *ātma-sthaiḥ*—situated in His own energy; *yathā*—as also; *buddhiḥ*—intelligence; *tat*—His; *āśrayā*—devotees.

TRANSLATION

"This is the opulence of the Lord. Although situated within the material nature, He is never affected by the modes of nature. Similarly, those who have surrendered to Him and have fixed their intelligence upon Him are not influenced by the modes of nature."

PURPORT

This is a verse from *Śrīmad-Bhāgavatam* (1.11.38).

TEXT 88

এই মত গীতাতেহ পুনঃ পুনঃ কয় ।
সর্বদা ঈশ্বর-তত্ত্ব অচিন্ত্যশক্তি হয় ॥ ৮৮ ॥

ei mata gītāteha punaḥ punaḥ kaya
sarvadā īśvara-tattva acintya-śakti haya

ei mata—in this way; *gītāteha*—in the *Bhagavad-gītā; punaḥ punaḥ*—again and again; *kaya*—it is said; *sarvadā*—always; *īśvara-tattva*—the truth of the Absolute Truth; *acintya-śakti haya*—is inconceivable.

TRANSLATION

Thus the Bhagavad-gītā also states again and again that the Absolute Truth always possesses inconceivable power.

TEXT 89

আমি ত' জগতে বসি, জগৎ আমাতে ।
না আমি জগতে বসি, না আমা জগতে ॥ ৮৯ ॥

āmi ta' jagate vasi, jagat āmāte
nā āmi jagate vasi, nā āmā jagate

āmi—I; *ta'*—certainly; *jagate*—in the material world; *vasi*—situated; *jagat*—the whole material creation; *āmāte*—in Me; *nā*—not; *āmi*—I; *jagate*—within the material world; *vasi*—situated; *nā*—nor; *āmā*—in Me; *jagate*—the material world.

TRANSLATION

[Lord Kṛṣṇa said:] "I am situated in the material world, and the world rests in Me. But at the same time I am not situated in the material world, nor does it rest in Me in truth.

PURPORT

Nothing in existence is possible unless energized by the will of the Lord. The entire manifested creation is therefore resting on the energy of the Lord, but one should not therefore presume that the material manifestation is identical with the Supreme Personality of Godhead. A cloud may rest in the sky, but that does not mean that the sky and the cloud are one and the same. Similarly, the qualitative material nature and its products are never identical with the Supreme Lord. The tendency to lord it over material nature, or *māyā,* cannot be a feature of the Supreme Personality of Godhead. When He descends to the material world, He maintains His transcendental nature, unaffected by the material qualities. In both the spiritual and material worlds, He is always the controller of all energies. The uncontaminated spiritual nature always exists within Him. The Lord appears and disappears in the material world in different features for His pastimes, yet He is the origin of all cosmic manifestations.

The material manifestation cannot exist separate from the Supreme Lord, yet Lord Viṣṇu, the Supreme Personality of Godhead, in spite of His connection with the material nature, cannot be subordinate to nature's influence. His original form of eternal bliss and knowledge is never subordinate to the three qualities of material nature. This is a specific feature of the Supreme Lord's inconceivable potencies.

TEXT 90

অচিন্ত্য ঐশ্বর্য এই জানিহ আমার ।
এই ত' গীতার অর্থ কৈল পরচার ॥ ৯০ ॥

acintya aiśvarya ei jāniha āmāra
ei ta' gītāra artha kaila paracāra

acintya—inconceivable; *aiśvarya*—opulence; *ei*—this; *jāniha*—you must know; *āmāra*—of Me; *ei ta'*—this; *gītāra artha*—the meaning of the *Bhagavad-gītā; kaila paracāra*—Lord Kṛṣṇa propagated.

TRANSLATION

"O Arjuna, you should know this as My inconceivable opulence." This is the meaning propagated by Lord Kṛṣṇa in the Bhagavad-gītā.

TEXT 91

সেই ত' পুরুষ যাঁর 'অংশ' ধরে নাম ।
চৈতন্যের সঙ্গে সেই নিত্যানন্দ-রাম ॥ ৯১ ॥

sei ta' puruṣa yāṅra 'aṁśa' dhare nāma
caitanyera saṅge sei nityānanda-rāma

sei ta'—that; *puruṣa*—Supreme Person; *yāṅra*—of whom; *aṁśa*—as part; *dhare nāma*—is known; *caitanyera saṅge*—with Śrī Caitanya Mahāprabhu; *sei*—that; *nityānanda-rāma*—Lord Nityānanda or Balarāma.

TRANSLATION

That Mahā-puruṣa [Kāraṇodakaśāyī Viṣṇu] is known as a plenary part of Him who is Lord Nityānanda Balarāma, the favorite associate of Lord Caitanya.

TEXT 92

এই ত' নবম শ্লোকের অর্থ-বিবরণ ।
দশম শ্লোকের অর্থ শুন দিয়া মন ॥ ৯২ ॥

ei ta' navama ślokera artha-vivaraṇa
daśama ślokera artha śuna diyā mana

ei ta'—thus; *navama ślokera*—of the ninth verse; *artha-vivaraṇa*—description of the meaning; *daśama ślokera*—of the tenth verse; *artha*—meaning; *śuna*—hear; *diyā mana*—with attention.

TRANSLATION

I have thus explained the ninth verse, and now I shall explain the tenth. Please listen with rapt attention.

TEXT 93

যস্যাংশাংশঃ শ্রীল-গর্ভোদশায়ী
যন্নাভ্যব্জং লোকসংঘাতনালম্ ।
লোকস্রষ্টুঃ সূতিকাধাম ধাতু-
স্তং শ্রীনিত্যানন্দরামং প্রপদ্যে ॥ ৯৩ ॥

yasyāṁśāṁśaḥ śrīla-garbhoda-śāyī
yan-nābhy-abjaṁ loka-saṅghāta-nālam
loka-sraṣṭuḥ sūtikā-dhāma dhātus
taṁ śrī-nityānanda-rāmaṁ prapadye

yasya—whose; *aṁśa-aṁśaḥ*—portion of a plenary portion; *śrīla-garbha-uda-śāyī*—Garbhodakaśāyī Viṣṇu; *yat*—of whom; *nābhi-abjam*—the navel lotus; *loka-saṅghāta*—of the multitude of planets;

nālam—having a stem that is the resting place; *loka-sraṣṭuḥ*—of Lord Brahmā, creator of the planets; *sūtikā-dhāma*—the birthplace; *dhātuḥ*—of the creator; *tam*—to Him; *śrī-nityānanda-rāmam*—to Lord Balarāma in the form of Lord Nityānanda; *prapadye*—I surrender.

TRANSLATION

I offer my full obeisances unto the feet of Śrī Nityānanda Rāma, a partial part of whom is Garbhodakaśāyī Viṣṇu. From the navel of Garbhodakaśāyī Viṣṇu sprouts the lotus that is the birthplace of Brahmā, the engineer of the universe. The stem of that lotus is the resting place of the multitude of planets.

PURPORT

In the *Mahābhārata, Śānti-parva,* it is said that He who is Pradyumna is also Aniruddha. He is also the father of Brahmā. Thus Garbhodaka-śāyī Viṣṇu and Kṣīrodakaśāyī Viṣṇu are identical plenary expansions of Pradyumna, the original Deity of Brahmā, who is born from the lotus flower. It is Pradyumna who gives Brahmā direction for cosmic management. A full description of Brahmā's birth is given in *Śrīmad-Bhāgavatam* (3.8.15–16).

Describing the features of the three *puruṣas,* the *Laghu-bhāgavatāmṛta* says that Garbhodakaśāyī Viṣṇu has a four-handed form, and when He Himself enters the hollow of the universe and lies down in the ocean of milk He is known as Kṣīrodakaśāyī Viṣṇu, who is the Supersoul of all living entities, including the demigods. In the *Sātvata-tantra* it is said that the third *puruṣa* incarnation, Kṣīro-dakaśāyī Viṣṇu, is situated as the Supersoul in everyone's heart. He is an expansion of Garbhodakaśāyī Viṣṇu for pastimes.

TEXT 94

সেই ত' পুরুষ অনন্তব্রহ্মাণ্ড সৃজিয়া ।
সব অণ্ডে প্রবেশিলা বহু-মূর্তি হঞা ॥ ৯৪ ॥

sei ta' puruṣa ananta-brahmāṇḍa sṛjiyā
saba aṇḍe praveśilā bahu-mūrti hañā

sei—that; *ta'*—certainly; *puruṣa*—incarnation; *ananta-brahmāṇḍa*—innumerable universes; *sṛjiyā*—creating; *saba*—all; *aṇḍe*—in the egg-like universes; *praveśilā*—entered; *bahu-mūrti hañā*—taking multifarious forms.

TRANSLATION

After creating millions of universes, the first puruṣa entered into each of them in a separate form, as Śrī Garbhodakaśāyī.

TEXT 95

ভিতরে প্রবেশি' দেখে সব অন্ধকার ।
রহিতে নাহিক স্থান করিল বিচার ॥ ৯৫ ॥

bhitare praveśi' dekhe saba andhakāra
rahite nāhika sthāna karila vicāra

bhitare—within the universe; *praveśi'*—entering; *dekhe*—He sees; *saba*—all; *andhakāra*—darkness; *rahite*—to stay; *nāhika*—there is not; *sthāna*—place; *karila vicāra*—considered.

TRANSLATION

Entering the universe, He found only darkness, with no place in which to reside. Thus He began to consider.

TEXT 96

নিজাঙ্গ-স্বেদজল করিল সৃজন ।
সেই জলে কৈল অর্ধ-ব্রহ্মাণ্ড ভরণ ॥ ৯৬ ॥

nijāṅga-sveda-jala karila sṛjana
sei jale kaila ardha-brahmāṇḍa bharaṇa

nija-aṅga—of His own body; *sveda-jala*—water from perspiration; *karila*—did; *sṛjana*—creation; *sei jale*—with that water; *kaila*—did; *ardha-brahmāṇḍa*—half of the universe; *bharaṇa*—filling.

TRANSLATION

Then He created water from the perspiration of His own body and with that water filled half the universe.

TEXT 97

ব্রহ্মাণ্ড-প্রমাণ পঞ্চাশৎকোটি-যোজন ।
আয়াম, বিস্তার, দুই হয় এক সম ॥ ৯৭ ॥

brahmāṇḍa-pramāṇa pañcāśat-koṭi-yojana
āyāma, vistāra, dui haya eka sama

brahmāṇḍa-pramāṇa—measurement of the universe; *pañcāśat*—fifty; *koṭi*—ten millions; *yojana*—lengths of eight miles; *āyāma*—length; *vistāra*—breadth; *dui*—both of them; *haya*—are; *eka sama*—one and the same.

TRANSLATION

The universe measures five hundred million yojanas. Its length and breadth are one and the same.

TEXT 98

জলে ভরি' অর্ধ তাঁহা কৈল নিজ-বাস ।
আর অর্ধে কৈল চৌদ্দভুবন প্রকাশ ॥ ৯৮ ॥

jale bhari' ardha tāṅhā kaila nija-vāsa
āra ardhe kaila caudda-bhuvana prakāśa

jale—with water; *bhari'*—filling; *ardha*—half; *tāṅhā*—there; *kaila*—made; *nija-vāsa*—own residence; *āra*—other; *ardhe*—in the half; *kaila*—did; *caudda-bhuvana*—fourteen worlds; *prakāśa*—manifestation.

TRANSLATION

After filling half the universe with water, He made His own residence therein and manifested the fourteen worlds in the other half.

PURPORT

The fourteen worlds are enumerated in *Śrīmad-Bhāgavatam,* Second Canto, Fifth Chapter. The upper planetary systems are (1) Bhū, (2) Bhuvar, (3) Svar, (4) Mahar, (5) Janas, (6) Tapas and (7) Satya. The seven lower planetary systems are (1) Tala, (2) Atala, (3) Vitala, (4) Nitala, (5) Talātala, (6) Mahātala and (7) Sutala. The lower planets as a whole are called Pātāla. Among the upper planetary systems, Bhū, Bhuvar and Svar constitute Svargaloka, and the rest are called Martya. The entire universe is thus known as Triloka.

TEXT 99

তাঁহাই প্রকট কৈল বৈকুণ্ঠ নিজ-ধাম ।
শেষ-শয়ন-জলে করিল বিশ্রাম ॥ ৯৯ ॥

tāṅhāi prakaṭa kaila vaikuṇṭha nija-dhāma
śeṣa-śayana-jale karila viśrāma

tāṅhāi—there; *prakaṭa*—manifestation; *kaila*—did; *vaikuṇṭha*—the spiritual world; *nija-dhāma*—His own abode; *śeṣa*—of Lord Śeṣa; *śayana*—on the bed; *jale*—on the water; *karila*—did; *viśrāma*—rest.

TRANSLATION

There He manifested Vaikuṇṭha as His own abode and rested in the waters on the bed of Lord Śeṣa.

TEXTS 100–101

অনন্তশয্যাতে তাঁহা করিল শয়ন ।
সহস্র মস্তক তাঁর সহস্র বদন ॥ ১০০ ॥
সহস্র-চরণ-হস্ত, সহস্র-নয়ন ।
সর্ব-অবতার-বীজ, জগৎ-কারণ ॥ ১০১ ॥

ananta-śayyāte tāṅhā karila śayana
sahasra mastaka tāṅra sahasra vadana

sahasra-caraṇa-hasta, sahasra-nayana
sarva-avatāra-bīja, jagat-kāraṇa

ananta-śayyāte—on Lord Ananta as a bed; *tāṅhā*—there; *karila śayana*—lay down; *sahasra*—thousands; *mastaka*—heads; *tāṅra*—His; *sahasra vadana*—thousands of faces; *sahasra*—thousands; *caraṇa*—legs; *hasta*—hands; *sahasra-nayana*—thousands of eyes; *sarva-avatāra-bīja*—the seed of all incarnations; *jagat-kāraṇa*—the cause of the material world.

TRANSLATION

He lay there with Ananta as His bed. Lord Ananta is a divine serpent having thousands of heads, thousands of faces, thousands of

eyes and thousands of hands and feet. He is the seed of all incarnations and is the cause of the material world.

PURPORT

In the reservoir of water first created by the perspiration of Garbhodakaśāyī Viṣṇu, the Lord lies on the Śeṣa plenary expansion of Viṣṇu, who is described in *Śrīmad-Bhāgavatam* and in the four *Vedas* as follows:

sahasra-śīrṣā puruṣaḥ sahasrākṣaḥ sahasra-pāt
sa bhūmiṁ viśvato vṛtvātyatiṣṭhad daśāṅgulam

The Viṣṇu form called Ananta-śayana has thousands of hands and legs and thousands of eyes, and He is the active generator of all the incarnations within the material world.

TEXT 102

তাঁর নাভিপদ্ম হৈতে উঠিল এক পদ্ম ।
সেই পদ্মে হৈল ব্রহ্মার জন্ম-সদ্ম ॥ ১০২ ॥

tāṅra nābhi-padma haite uṭhila eka padma
sei padme haila brahmāra janma-sadma

tāṅra—His; *nābhi-padma*—lotus navel; *haite*—from; *uṭhila*—grew; *eka*—one; *padma*—lotus flower; *sei padme*—on that lotus; *haila*—there was; *brahmāra*—of Lord Brahmā; *janma-sadma*—the place of birth.

TRANSLATION

From His navel grew a lotus flower, which became the birthplace of Lord Brahmā.

TEXT 103

সেই পদ্মনালে হৈল চৌদ্দভুবন ।
তেঁহো ব্রহ্মা হঞা সৃষ্টি করিল সৃজন ॥ ১০৩ ॥

sei padma-nāle haila caudda-bhuvana
teṅho brahmā hañā sṛṣṭi karila sṛjana

sei padma-nāle—within the stem of that lotus flower; *haila*—were; *caudda-bhuvana*—the fourteen worlds; *teṅho*—He Himself; *brahmā hañā*—appearing as Brahmā; *sṛṣṭi*—the creation; *karila sṛjana*—created.

TRANSLATION

Within the stem of that lotus were the fourteen worlds. Thus the Supreme Lord, as Brahmā, created the entire creation.

TEXT 104

বিষ্ণুরূপ হঞা করে জগৎ পালনে ।
গুণাতীত-বিষ্ণু স্পর্শ নাহি মায়া-গুণে ॥ ১০৪ ॥

viṣṇu-rūpa hañā kare jagat pālane
guṇātīta-viṣṇu sparśa nāhi māyā-guṇe

viṣṇu-rūpa—the form of Lord Viṣṇu; *hañā*—becoming; *kare*—does; *jagat pālane*—maintenance of the material world; *guṇa-atīta*—beyond the material qualities; *viṣṇu*—Lord Viṣṇu; *sparśa*—touch; *nāhi*—not; *māyā-guṇe*—in the material qualities.

TRANSLATION

And as Lord Viṣṇu He maintains the entire world. Lord Viṣṇu, being beyond all material attributes, has no touch with the material qualities.

PURPORT

Śrī Baladeva Vidyābhūṣaṇa says that although Viṣṇu is the predominating Deity of the quality of goodness in the material world, He is never affected by the quality of goodness, for He directs that quality simply by His supreme will. It is said that all living entities can derive all good fortune from the Lord simply by His will. In the *Vāmana Purāṇa* it is said that the same Viṣṇu expands Himself as Brahmā and Śiva to direct the different qualities.

Because Lord Viṣṇu expands the quality of goodness, He has the name Sattvatanu. The multifarious incarnations of Kṣīrodakaśāyī Viṣṇu are known as Sattvatanu. Therefore in all Vedic scriptures Viṣṇu has been described as being free from all material qualities. In the Tenth Canto of *Śrīmad-Bhāgavatam* it is said:

harir hi nirguṇaḥ sākṣāt puruṣaḥ prakṛteḥ paraḥ
sa sarva-dṛg upadraṣṭā taṁ bhajan nirguṇo bhavet

"The Supreme Personality of Godhead, Hari, is always uncontaminated by the modes of material nature, for He is beyond the material manifestation. He is the source of the knowledge of all the demigods, headed by Lord Brahmā, and He is the witness of everything. Therefore one who worships the Supreme Lord Viṣṇu also attains freedom from the contamination of material nature." (*Bhāg.* 10.88.5) One can attain freedom from the contamination of material nature by worshiping Viṣṇu, and therefore He is called Sattvatanu, as described above.

TEXT 105

রুদ্ররূপ ধরি' করে জগৎ সংহার ।
সৃষ্টি-স্থিতি-প্রলয়—ইচ্ছায় যাঁহার ॥ ১০৫ ॥

rudra-rūpa dhari' kare jagat saṁhāra
sṛṣṭi-sthiti-pralaya—icchāya yāṅhāra

rudra-rūpa—the form of Lord Śiva; *dhari'*—accepting; *kare*—does; *jagat saṁhāra*—annihilation of the material world; *sṛṣṭi-sthiti-pralaya*—creation, maintenance and annihilation; *icchāya*—by the will; *yāṅhāra*—of whom.

TRANSLATION

Assuming the form of Rudra, He destroys the creation. Thus creation, maintenance and dissolution are created by His will.

PURPORT

Maheśvara, or Lord Śiva, is not an ordinary living being, nor is he equal to Lord Viṣṇu. Effectively comparing Lord Viṣṇu and Lord Śiva, the *Brahma-saṁhitā* says that Viṣṇu is like milk, whereas Śiva is like yogurt. Yogurt is nothing like milk, but nevertheless it is milk also.

TEXT 106

হিরণ্যগর্ভ, অন্তর্যামী, জগৎ-কারণ ।
ঙ্ঘাঁর অংশ করি' করে বিরাট-কল্পন ॥ ১০৬ ॥

hiraṇya-garbha, antaryāmī, jagat-kāraṇa
yāṅra aṁśa kari' kare virāṭa-kalpana

hiraṇya-garbha—Hiraṇyagarbha; *antaḥ-yāmī*—the Supersoul; *jagat-kāraṇa*—the cause of the material world; *yāṅra aṁśa kari'*—taking as His expansion; *kare*—does; *virāṭa-kalpana*—conception of the universal form.

TRANSLATION

He is the Supersoul, Hiraṇyagarbha, the cause of the material world. The universal form is conceived as His expansion.

TEXT 107

হেন নারায়ণ,—যাঁর অংশের অংশ ।
সেই প্রভু নিত্যানন্দ—সর্ব-অবতংস ॥ ১০৭ ॥

hena nārāyaṇa,—yāṅra aṁśera aṁśa
sei prabhu nityānanda—sarva-avataṁsa

hena—such; *nārāyaṇa*—Lord Nārāyaṇa; *yāṅra*—of whom; *aṁśera*—of the plenary part; *aṁśa*—apart; *sei*—that; *prabhu*—the Lord; *nityānanda*—Nityānanda; *sarva-avataṁsa*—the source of all incarnations.

TRANSLATION

That Lord Nārāyaṇa is a part of a plenary part of Lord Nityānanda Balarāma, who is the source of all incarnations.

TEXT 108

দশম শ্লোকের অর্থ কৈল বিবরণ ।
একাদশ শ্লোকের অর্থ শুন দিয়া মন ॥ ১০৮ ॥

daśama ślokera artha kaila vivaraṇa
ekādaśa ślokera artha śuna diyā mana

daśama—tenth; *ślokera*—of the verse; *artha*—meaning; *kaila*—have done; *vivaraṇa*—description; *ekādaśa*—eleventh; *ślokera*—of the verse; *artha*—meaning; *śuna*—please hear; *diyā mana*—with the mind.

TRANSLATION

I have thus explained the tenth verse. Now please listen to the meaning of the eleventh verse with all your mind.

TEXT 109

যস্যাংশাংশাংশঃ পরাত্মাখিলানাং
পোষ্টা বিষ্ণুর্ভাতি দুগ্ধাব্ধিশায়ী ।
ক্ষৌণীভর্তা যৎকলা সোঽপ্যনন্ত-
স্তং শ্রীনিত্যানন্দরামং প্রপদ্যে ॥ ১০৯ ॥

yasyāṁśāṁśāṁśaḥ parātmākhilānāṁ
poṣṭā viṣṇur bhāti dugdhābdhi-śāyī
kṣauṇī-bhartā yat-kalā so 'py anantas
taṁ śrī-nityānanda-rāmaṁ prapadye

yasya—whose; *aṁśa-aṁśa-aṁśaḥ*—a portion of a portion of a plenary portion; *para-ātmā*—the Supersoul; *akhilānām*—of all living entities; *poṣṭā*—the maintainer; *viṣṇuḥ*—Viṣṇu; *bhāti*—appears; *dugdha-abdhi-śāyī*—Kṣīrodakaśāyī Viṣṇu; *kṣauṇī-bhartā*—upholder of the earth; *yat*—whose; *kalā*—portion of a portion; *saḥ*—He; *api*—certainly; *anantaḥ*—Śeṣa Nāga; *tam*—to Him; *śrī-nityānanda-rāmam*—to Lord Balarāma in the form of Lord Nityānanda; *prapadye*—I surrender.

TRANSLATION

I offer my respectful obeisances unto the feet of Śrī Nityānanda Rāma, whose secondary part is the Viṣṇu lying in the ocean of milk. That Kṣīrodakaśāyī Viṣṇu is the Supersoul of all living entities and the maintainer of all the universes. Śeṣa Nāga is His further subpart.

TEXT 110

নারায়ণের নাভিনাল-মধ্যেতে ধরণী ।
ধরণীর মধ্যে সপ্ত সমুদ্র যে গণি ॥ ১১০ ॥

nārāyaṇera nābhi-nāla-madhyete dharaṇī
dharaṇīra madhye sapta samudra ye gaṇi

nārāyaṇera—of Lord Nārāyaṇa; *nābhi-nāla*—the stem from the navel; *madhyete*—within; *dharaṇī*—the material planets; *dharaṇīra madhye*—among the material planets; *sapta*—seven; *samudra*—oceans; *ye gaṇi*—they count.

TRANSLATION

The material planets rest within the stem that grows from the lotus navel of Lord Nārāyaṇa. Among these planets are seven oceans.

TEXT 111

তাঁহা ক্ষীরোদধি-মধ্যে 'শ্বেতদ্বীপ' নাম ।
পালয়িতা বিষ্ণু,—তাঁর সেই নিজ ধাম ॥ ১১১ ॥

tāṅhā kṣīrodadhi-madhye 'śvetadvīpa' nāma
pālayitā viṣṇu,—tāṅra sei nija dhāma

tāṅhā—within that; *kṣīra-udadhi-madhye*—in part of the ocean known as the ocean of milk; *śvetadvīpa nāma*—the island named Śvetadvīpa; *pālayitā viṣṇu*—the maintainer, Lord Viṣṇu; *tāṅra*—of Him; *sei*—that; *nija dhāma*—own residential quarters.

TRANSLATION

There, in part of the ocean of milk, lies Śvetadvīpa, the abode of the sustainer, Lord Viṣṇu.

PURPORT

In the *Siddhānta-śiromaṇi*, an astrological text, the different oceans are described as follows: (1) the ocean of salt water, (2) the ocean of milk, (3) the ocean of yogurt, (4) the ocean of clarified butter, (5) the ocean of sugarcane juice, (6) the ocean of liquor and (7) the ocean of sweet water. On the southern side of the ocean of salt water is the ocean of milk, where Lord Kṣīrodakaśāyī Viṣṇu resides. He is worshiped there by demigods like Brahmā.

TEXT 112

সকল জীবের তিঁহো হয়ে অন্তর্যামী ।
জগৎ-পালক তিঁহো জগতের স্বামী ॥ ১১২ ॥

sakala jīvera tiṅho haye antaryāmī
jagat-pālaka tiṅho jagatera svāmī

sakala—all; *jīvera*—of the living entities; *tiṅho*—He; *haye*—is; *antaḥ-yāmī*—the Supersoul; *jagat-pālaka*—the maintainer of the material world; *tiṅho*—He; *jagatera svāmī*—the Lord of the material world.

TRANSLATION

He is the Supersoul of all living entities. He maintains this material world, and He is its Lord.

PURPORT

The *Laghu-bhāgavatāmṛta* (*Pūrva* 2.36–42) gives the following description of the Viṣṇuloka within this universe, quoted from the *Viṣṇu-dharmottara:* "Above Rudraloka, the planet of Lord Śiva, is the planet called Viṣṇuloka, 400,000 miles in circumference, which is inaccessible to any mortal living being. Above that Viṣṇuloka and east of the Sumeru Hill is a golden island called Mahā-Viṣṇuloka, in the ocean of salt water. Lord Brahmā and other demigods sometimes go there to meet Lord Viṣṇu. Lord Viṣṇu lies there with the goddess of fortune, and it is said that during the four months of the rainy season He enjoys sleeping on that Śeṣa Nāga bed. East of Sumeru is the ocean of milk, in which there is a white city on a white island where the Lord can be seen sitting with His consort, Lakṣmījī, on a throne of Śeṣa. That feature of Viṣṇu also enjoys sleeping during the four months of the rainy season. The Śveta-dvīpa in the milk ocean is situated just south of the ocean of salt water. It is calculated that the area of Śvetadvīpa is 200,000 square miles. This transcendentally beautiful island is decorated with desire trees to please Lord Viṣṇu and His consort." There are references to Śvetadvīpa in the *Brahmāṇḍa Purāṇa*, *Viṣṇu Purāṇa*, *Mahābhārata* and *Padma Purāṇa*, and there is the following reference in *Śrīmad-Bhāgavatam* (11.15.18).

śvetadvīpa-patau cittaṁ śuddhe dharma-maye mayi
dhārayañ chvetatāṁ yāti ṣaḍ-ūrmi-rahito naraḥ

"My dear Uddhava, you may know that My transcendental form of Viṣṇu in Śvetadvīpa is identical with Me in divinity. Anyone who places this Lord of Śvetadvīpa within his heart can surpass the pangs of the six material tribulations: hunger, thirst, birth, death, lamentation and illusion. Thus one can attain his original, transcendental form."

TEXT 113

যুগ-মন্বন্তরে ধরি' নানা অবতার ।
ধর্ম সংস্থাপন করে, অধর্ম সংহার ॥ ১১৩ ॥

yuga-manvantare dhari' nānā avatāra
dharma saṁsthāpana kare, adharma saṁhāra

yuga-manu-antare—in the ages and millenniums of Manu; *dhari'*—accepting; *nānā*—various; *avatāra*—incarnations; *dharma saṁsthāpana kare*—establishes the principles of religion; *adharma saṁhāra*—vanquishing irreligious principles.

TRANSLATION

In the ages and millenniums of Manu, He appears as different incarnations to establish the principles of real religion and vanquish the principles of irreligion.

PURPORT

The Lord Viṣṇu who lies in the ocean of milk incarnates Himself in various forms to maintain the laws of the cosmos and annihilate the causes of disturbance. Such incarnations are visible in every *manv-antara* (i.e., in the course of the reign of each Manu, who lives for 71 x 4,320,000 years). Fourteen such Manus take their birth and die, to yield a place for the next, during one day of Brahmā.

TEXT 114

দেবগণে না পায় যাঁহার দরশন ।
ক্ষীরোদকতীরে যাই' করেন স্তবন ॥ ১১৪ ॥

deva-gaṇe nā pāya yāṅhāra daraśana
kṣīrodaka-tīre yāi' karena stavana

deva-gaṇe—the demigods; *nā*—not; *pāya*—get; *yāṅhāra*—whose; *daraśana*—sight; *kṣīra-udaka-tīre*—on the shore of the ocean of milk; *yāi'*—go; *karena stavana*—offer prayers.

TRANSLATION

Unable to see Him, the demigods go to the shore of the ocean of milk and offer prayers to Him.

PURPORT

The denizens of heaven, who live in the planetary systems beginning from Svarloka, cannot even see Lord Viṣṇu in Śvetadvīpa. Unable to reach the island, they can simply approach the beach of the milk ocean to offer transcendental prayers to the Lord, appealing to Him on special occasions to appear as an incarnation.

TEXT 115

তবে অবতরি' করে জগৎ পালন ।
অনন্ত বৈভব তাঁর নাহিক গণন ॥ ১১৫ ॥

tabe avatari' kare jagat pālana
ananta vaibhava tāṅra nāhika gaṇana

tabe—at that time; *avatari'*—descending; *kare*—does; *jagat pālana*—maintenance of the material world; *ananta*—unlimited; *vaibhava*—the opulences; *tāṅra*—of Him; *nāhika*—there is not; *gaṇana*—counting.

TRANSLATION

He then descends to maintain the material world. His unlimited opulences cannot be counted.

TEXT 116

সেই বিষ্ণু হয় যাঁর অংশাংশের অংশ ।
সেই প্রভু নিত্যানন্দ—সর্ব-অবতংস ॥ ১১৬ ॥

sei viṣṇu haya yāṅra aṁśāṁśera aṁśa
sei prabhu nityānanda—sarva-avataṁsa

sei—that; *viṣṇu*—Lord Viṣṇu; *haya*—is; *yāṅra*—whose; *aṁśa-aṁśera*—of the part of the plenary part; *aṁśa*—part; *sei*—that; *prabhu*—Lord; *nityānanda*—Nityānanda; *sarva-avataṁsa*—the source of all incarnations.

TRANSLATION

That Lord Viṣṇu is but a part of a part of a plenary portion of Lord Nityānanda, who is the source of all incarnations.

PURPORT

The Lord of Śvetadvīpa has immense potency for creation and destruction. Śrī Nityānanda Prabhu, being Baladeva Himself, the original form of Saṅkarṣaṇa, is the original form of the Lord of Śvetadvīpa.

TEXT 117

সেই বিষ্ণু 'শেষ'-রূপে ধরেন ধরণী।
কাঁহা আছে মহী, শিরে, হেন নাহি জানি ॥ ১১৭ ॥

sei viṣṇu 'śeṣa'-rūpe dharena dharaṇī
kāṅhā āche mahī, śire, hena nāhi jāni

sei—that; *viṣṇu*—Lord Viṣṇu; *śeṣa-rūpe*—in form of Lord Śeṣa; *dharena*—carries; *dharaṇī*—the planets; *kāṅhā*—where; *āche*—are; *mahī*—the planets; *śire*—on the head; *hena nāhi jāni*—I cannot understand.

TRANSLATION

That same Lord Viṣṇu, in the form of Lord Śeṣa, holds the planets upon His heads, although He does not know where they are, for He cannot feel their existence upon His heads.

TEXT 118

সহস্র বিস্তীর্ণ যাঁর ফণার মণ্ডল।
সূর্য জিনি' মণিগণ করে ঝলমল ॥ ১১৮ ॥

sahasra vistīrṇa yāṅra phaṇāra maṇḍala
sūrya jini' maṇi-gaṇa kare jhala-mala

sahasra—thousands; *vistīrṇa*—spread; *yāṅra*—whose; *phaṇāra*—of the hoods; *maṇḍala*—group; *sūrya*—the sun; *jini'*—conquering; *maṇi-gaṇa*—jewels; *kare*—do; *jhala-mala*—glittering.

TRANSLATION

His thousands of extended hoods are adorned with dazzling jewels surpassing the sun.

TEXT 119

পঞ্চাশৎকোটি-যোজন পৃথিবী-বিস্তার ।
যাঁর একফণে রহে সর্ষপ-আকার ॥ ১১৯ ॥

pañcāśat-koṭi-yojana pṛthivī-vistāra
yāṅra eka-phaṇe rahe sarṣapa-ākāra

pañcāśat—fifty; *koṭi*—ten millions; *yojana*—eight miles; *pṛthivī*—of the universe; *vistāra*—breadth; *yāṅra*—whose; *eka-phaṇe*—on one of the hoods; *rahe*—stays; *sarṣapa-ākāra*—like a mustard seed.

TRANSLATION

The universe, which measures five hundred million yojanas in diameter, rests on one of His hoods like a mustard seed.

PURPORT

The Lord of Śvetadvīpa expands Himself as Śeṣa Nāga, who sustains all the planets upon His innumerable hoods. These huge global spheres are compared to grains of mustard resting on the spiritual hoods of Śeṣa Nāga. The scientists' law of gravity is a partial explanation of Lord Saṅkarṣaṇa's energy. The name "Saṅkarṣaṇa" has an etymological relationship to the idea of gravity. There is a reference to Śeṣa Nāga in *Śrīmad-Bhāgavatam* (5.17.21), where it is said:

yam āhur asya sthiti janma-saṁyamaṁ
tribhir vihīnaṁ yam anantam ṛṣayaḥ
na veda siddārtham iva kvacit sthitaṁ
bhū-maṇḍalaṁ mūrdha-sahasra-dhāmasu

"O my Lord, the hymns of the *Vedas* proclaim that You are the effective cause for the creation, maintenance and destruction. But in fact You are transcendental to all limitations and are therefore known as unlimited. On Your thousands of hoods rest the innumerable global spheres, like grains of mustard so insignificant that You have no perception of their weight." The *Bhāgavatam* further says (5.25.2):

yasyedaṁ kṣiti-maṇḍalaṁ bhagavato 'nanta-mūrteḥ sahasra-śirasa ekasminn eva śīrṣaṇi dhriyamāṇaṁ siddhārtha iva lakṣyate.

"Lord Anantadeva has thousands of hoods. Each sustains a global sphere that appears like a grain of mustard."

TEXT 120

সেই ত' 'অনন্ত' 'শেষ'—ভক্ত-অবতার ।
ঈশ্বরের সেবা বিনা নাহি জানে আর ॥ ১২০ ॥

sei ta' 'ananta' 'śeṣa'—bhakta-avatāra
īśvarera sevā vinā nāhi jāne āra

sei ta'—that; *ananta*—Lord Ananta; *śeṣa*—the incarnation Śeṣa; *bhakta-avatāra*—incarnation of a devotee; *īśvarera sevā*—the service of the Lord; *vinā*—without; *nāhi*—not; *jāne*—knows; *āra*—anything else.

TRANSLATION

That Ananta Śeṣa is the devotee incarnation of Godhead. He knows nothing but service to Lord Kṛṣṇa.

PURPORT

Śrīla Jīva Gosvāmī, in his *Kṛṣṇa-sandarbha,* has described Śeṣa Nāga as follows: "Śrī Anantadeva has thousands of faces and is fully independent. Always ready to serve the Supreme Personality of Godhead, He waits upon Him constantly. Saṅkarṣaṇa is the first expansion of Vāsudeva, and because He appears by His own will, He is called *svarāṭ,* fully independent. He is therefore infinite and transcendental to all limits of time and space. He Himself appears as the thousand-headed Śeṣa." In the *Skanda Purāṇa,* in the *Ayodhyā-māhātmya* chapter, the demigod Indra requested Lord Śeṣa, who was standing before him as Lakṣmaṇa, "Please go to Your eternal abode, Viṣṇuloka, where Your expansion Śeṣa, with His serpentine hoods, is also present." After thus dispatching Lakṣmaṇa to the regions of Pātāla, Lord Indra returned to his abode. This quotation indicates that the Saṅkarṣaṇa of the quadruple form descends with Lord Rāma as Lakṣmaṇa. When Lord Rāma disappears, Śeṣa again separates Himself from the personality of Lakṣmaṇa. Śeṣa then returns to His own abode in the Pātāla regions, and Lakṣmaṇa returns to His abode in Vaikuṇṭha.

The *Laghu-bhāgavatāmṛta* gives the following description: "The Saṅkarṣaṇa of the second group of quadruple forms appears as Rāma, taking with Him Śeṣa, who bears the global spheres. There are two features of Śeṣa. One is the bearer of the globes, and the other is the bedstead servitor. The Śeṣa who bears the globes is a potent incarnation of Saṅkarṣaṇa, and therefore He is sometimes also called Saṅkarṣaṇa. The bedstead feature of Śeṣa always presents himself as an eternal servitor of the Lord."

TEXT 121

সহস্র বদনে করে কৃষ্ণগুণ গান ।
নিরবধি গুণ গা'ন, অন্ত নাহি পা'ন ॥ ১২১ ॥

sahasra-vadane kare kṛṣṇa-guṇa gāna
niravadhi guṇa gā'na, anta nāhi pā'na

sahasra-vadane—in thousands of mouths; *kare*—does; *kṛṣṇa-guṇa gāna*—chanting of the holy attributes of Kṛṣṇa; *niravadhi*—continuously; *guṇa gā'na*—chanting of the transcendental qualities; *anta nāhi pā'na*—does not reach the end.

TRANSLATION

With His thousands of mouths He sings the glories of Lord Kṛṣṇa, but although He always sings in that way, He does not find an end to the qualities of the Lord.

TEXT 122

সনকাদি ভাগবত শুনে যাঁর মুখে ।
ভগবানের গুণ কহে, ভাসে প্রেমসুখে ॥ ১২২ ॥

sanakādi bhāgavata śune yāṅra mukhe
bhagavānera guṇa kahe, bhāse prema-sukhe

sanaka-ādi—the great sages headed by Sanaka, Sananda, etc.; *bhāgavata—Śrīmad-Bhāgavatam; śune*—hear; *yāṅra mukhe*—from whose mouth; *bhagavānera*—of the Personality of Godhead; *guṇa*—attributes; *kahe*—say; *bhāse*—float; *prema-sukhe*—in the transcendental bliss of love of Godhead.

TRANSLATION

The four Kumāras hear Śrīmad-Bhāgavatam from His lips, and they in turn repeat it in the transcendental bliss of love of Godhead.

TEXT 123

ছত্র, পাদুকা, শয্যা, উপাধান, বসন ।
আরাম, আবাস, যজ্ঞসূত্র, সিংহাসন ॥ ১২৩ ॥

chatra, pādukā, śayyā, upādhāna, vasana
ārāma, āvāsa, yajña-sūtra, siṁhāsana

chatra—umbrella; *pādukā*—slippers; *śayyā*—bed; *upādhāna*—pillow; *vasana*—garments; *ārāma*—resting chair; *āvāsa*—residence; *yajña-sūtra*—sacred thread; *siṁha-āsana*—throne.

TRANSLATION

He serves Lord Kṛṣṇa, assuming all the following forms: umbrella, slippers, bedding, pillow, garments, resting chair, residence, sacred thread and throne.

TEXT 124

এত মূর্তিভেদ করি' কৃষ্ণসেবা করে ।
কৃষ্ণের শেষতা পাঞা 'শেষ' নাম ধরে ॥ ১২৪ ॥

eta mūrti-bheda kari' kṛṣṇa-sevā kare
kṛṣṇera śeṣatā pāñā 'śeṣa' nāma dhare

eta—so many; *mūrti-bheda*—different forms; *kari'*—taking; *kṛṣṇa-sevā kare*—serves Lord Kṛṣṇa; *kṛṣṇera*—of Lord Kṛṣṇa; *śeṣatā*—ultimate end; *pāñā*—having reached; *śeṣa nāma dhare*—assumes the name Śeṣa Nāga.

TRANSLATION

He is thus called Lord Śeṣa, for He has attained the ultimate end of servitude to Kṛṣṇa. He takes many forms for the service of Kṛṣṇa, and thus He serves the Lord.

TEXT 125

সেই ত' অনন্ত, যাঁর কহি এক কলা ।
হেন প্রভু নিত্যানন্দ, কে জানে তাঁর খেলা ॥ ১২৫ ॥

sei ta' ananta, yāṅra kahi eka kalā
hena prabhu nityānanda, ke jāne tāṅra khelā

sei ta'—that; *ananta*—Lord Ananta; *yāṅra*—of whom; *kahi*—I say; *eka kalā*—one part of the part; *hena*—such; *prabhu nityānanda*—Lord Nityānanda Prabhu; *ke*—who; *jāne*—knows; *tāṅra*—His; *khelā*—pastimes.

TRANSLATION

That person of whom Lord Ananta is a kalā, or part of a plenary part, is Lord Nityānanda Prabhu. Who, therefore, can know the pastimes of Lord Nityānanda?

TEXT 126

এসব প্রমাণে জানি নিত্যানন্দতত্ত্বসীমা ।
তাঁহাকে 'অনন্ত' কহি, কি তাঁর মহিমা ॥ ১২৬ ॥

e-saba pramāṇe jāni nityānanda-tattva-sīmā
tāṅhāke 'ananta' kahi, ki tāṅra mahimā

e-saba—all these; *pramāṇe*—by the evidences; *jāni*—I know; *nityānanda-tattva-sīmā*—the limit of the truth of Lord Nityānanda; *tāṅhāke*—to Him (Lord Nityānanda, Balarāma); *ananta*—Lord Ananta; *kahi*—if I say; *ki tāṅre mahimā*—what glory do I speak about Him.

TRANSLATION

From these conclusions we can know the limit of the truth of Lord Nityānanda. But what glory is there in calling Him Ananta?

TEXT 127

অথবা ভক্তের বাক্য মানি সত্য করি' ।
সকল সম্ভবে তাঁতে, যাতে অবতারী ॥ ১২৭ ॥

athavā bhaktera vākya māni satya kari'
sakala sambhave tāṅte, yāte avatārī

athavā—otherwise; *bhaktera vākya*—anything spoken by a pure devotee; *māni*—I accept; *satya kari'*—as truth; *sakala*—everything; *sambhave*—possible; *tāṅte*—in Him; *yāte*—since; *avatārī*—the original source of all incarnations.

TRANSLATION

But I accept it as the truth because it has been said by devotees. Since He is the source of all incarnations, everything is possible in Him.

TEXT 128

অবতার-অবতারী—অভেদ, যে জানে ।
পূর্বে যৈছে কৃষ্ণকে কেহো কাহো করি' মানে ॥ ১২৮ ॥

avatāra-avatārī—abheda, ye jāne
pūrve yaiche kṛṣṇake keho kāho kari' māne

avatāra-avatārī—an incarnation and the source of all incarnations; *abheda*—identical; *ye jāne*—anyone who knows; *pūrve*—formerly; *yaiche*—just as; *kṛṣṇake*—unto Lord Kṛṣṇa; *keho*—somebody; *kāho*—somewhere; *kari'*—making; *māne*—accepts.

TRANSLATION

They know that there is no difference between the incarnation and the source of all incarnations. Previously Lord Kṛṣṇa was regarded in the light of different principles by different people.

TEXT 129

কেহো কহে, কৃষ্ণ সাক্ষাৎ নরনারায়ণ ।
কেহো কহে, কৃষ্ণ হয় সাক্ষাৎ বামন ॥ ১২৯ ॥

keho kahe, kṛṣṇa sākṣāt nara-nārāyaṇa
keho kahe, kṛṣṇa haya sākṣāt vāmana

keho kahe—someone says; *kṛṣṇa*—Lord Kṛṣṇa; *sākṣāt*—directly; *nara-nārāyaṇa*—Lord Nara-Nārāyaṇa; *keho kahe*—someone says; *kṛṣṇa haya*—Kṛṣṇa is; *sākṣāt vāmana*—Lord Vāmanadeva.

TRANSLATION

Some said that Kṛṣṇa was directly Lord Nara-Nārāyaṇa, and some called Him Lord Vāmanadeva incarnate.

TEXT 130

কেহো কহে, কৃষ্ণ ক্ষীরোদশায়ী অবতার ।
অসম্ভব নহে, সত্য বচন সবার ॥ ১৩০ ॥

keho kahe, kṛṣṇa kṣīroda-śāyī avatāra
asambhava nahe, satya vacana sabāra

keho kahe—someone says; *kṛṣṇa*—Lord Kṛṣṇa; *kṣīroda-śāyī avatāra*—an incarnation of Lord Viṣṇu lying in the ocean of milk; *asambhava nahe*—there is not impossibility; *satya*—true; *vacana sabāra*—everyone's statement.

TRANSLATION

Some called Lord Kṛṣṇa an incarnation of Lord Kṣīrodakaśāyī. All these names are true; nothing is impossible.

TEXT 131

কৃষ্ণ যবে অবতরে সর্বাংশ-আশ্রয় ।
সর্বাংশ আসি' তবে কৃষ্ণেতে মিলয় ॥ ১৩১ ॥

kṛṣṇa yabe avatare sarvāṁśa-āśraya
sarvāṁśa āsi' tabe kṛṣṇete milaya

kṛṣṇa—Lord Kṛṣṇa; *yabe*—when; *avatare*—descends; *sarva-aṁśa-āśraya*—the shelter of all other *viṣṇu-tattvas; sarva-aṁśa*—all plenary portions; *āsi'*—coming; *tabe*—at that time; *kṛṣṇete*—in Kṛṣṇa; *milaya*—join.

TRANSLATION

When the Supreme Personality of Godhead Kṛṣṇa appears, He is the shelter of all plenary parts. Thus at that time all His plenary portions join in Him.

TEXT 132

যেই যেই রূপে জানে, সেই তাহা কহে ।
সকল সম্ভবে কৃষ্ণে, কিছু মিথ্যা নহে ॥ ১৩২ ॥

yei yei rūpe jāne, sei tāhā kahe
sakala sambhave kṛṣṇe, kichu mithyā nahe

yei yei—whatever; *rūpe*—in the form; *jāne*—one knows; *sei*—he; *tāhā*—that; *kahe*—says; *sakala sambhave kṛṣṇe*—everything is possible in Kṛṣṇa; *kichu mithyā nahe*—there is no falsity.

TRANSLATION

In whatever form one knows the Lord, one speaks of Him in that way. In this there is no falsity, since everything is possible in Kṛṣṇa.

PURPORT

In this connection we may mention an incident that took place between two of our *sannyāsīs* while we were preaching the Hare Kṛṣṇa *mahā-mantra* in Hyderabad. One of them stated that "Hare Rāma" refers to Śrī Balarāma, and the other protested that "Hare Rāma" means Lord Rāma. Ultimately the controversy came to me, and I gave the decision that if someone says that the "Rāma" in "Hare Rāma" is Lord Rāmacandra and someone else says that the "Rāma" in "Hare Rāma" is Śrī Balarāma, both are correct because there is no difference between Śrī Balarāma and Lord Rāma. Here in *Śrī Caitanya-caritāmṛta* we find that Kṛṣṇadāsa Kavirāja Gosvāmī has stated the same conclusion:

yei yei rūpe jāne, sei tāhā kahe
sakala sambhave kṛṣṇe, kichu mithyā nahe

If someone calls Lord Rāmacandra by the vibration Hare Rāma, understanding it to mean "O Lord Rāmacandra!" he is quite right. Similarly, if one says that Hare Rāma means "O Śrī Balarāma!" he is also right. Those who are aware of the *viṣṇu-tattva* do not fight over all these details.

In the *Laghu-bhāgavatāmṛta* Śrīla Rūpa Gosvāmī has explained Kṛṣṇa's being both Kṣīrodakaśāyī Viṣṇu and Nārāyaṇa in the spiritual sky and expanding in the quadruple forms known as Vāsudeva, Saṅkarṣaṇa, Pradyumna and Aniruddha. He has refuted the idea that Kṛṣṇa is an incarnation of Nārāyaṇa. Some devotees think that Nārāyaṇa is the original Personality of Godhead and that Kṛṣṇa is an incarnation. Even Śaṅkarācārya, in his commentary on the *Bhagavad-gītā,* has accepted Nārāyaṇa as the transcendental Personality of Godhead who appeared as Kṛṣṇa, the son of Devakī and Vasudeva. Therefore this matter may be difficult to understand. But the Gauḍīya Vaiṣṇava-sampradāya, headed by Rūpa Gosvāmī, has established the principle of the *Bhagavad-gītā* that everything emanates from Kṛṣṇa, who says in the *Bhagavad-gītā, ahaṁ sarvasya prabhavaḥ:* "I am the original source of everything." "Everything" includes Nārāyaṇa. Therefore Rūpa Gosvāmī, in his *Laghu-bhāgavatāmṛta*, has established that Kṛṣṇa, not Nārāyaṇa, is the original Personality of Godhead.

In this connection he has quoted a verse from *Śrīmad-Bhāgavatam* (3.2.15) that states:

sva-śānta-rūpeṣv itaraiḥ svarūpair
abhyardyamāneṣv anukampitātmā
parāvareśo mahad-aṁśa-yukto
hy ajo 'pi jāto bhagavān yathāgniḥ

"When pure devotees of the Lord like Vasudeva are greatly disturbed by dangerous demons like Kaṁsa, Lord Kṛṣṇa joins with all His pastime expansions, such as the Lord of Vaikuṇṭha, and, although unborn, becomes manifest, just as fire becomes manifest by the friction of *araṇi* wood." *Araṇi* wood is used to ignite a sacrificial fire without matches or any other flame. Just as fire appears from *araṇi* wood, the Supreme Lord appears when there is friction between devotees and nondevotees. When Kṛṣṇa appears, He appears in full, including within Himself all His expansions, such as Nārāyaṇa, Vāsudeva, Saṅkarṣaṇa, Aniruddha and Pradyumna. Kṛṣṇa is always integrated with His other incarnations, like Nṛsiṁhadeva, Varāha, Vāmana, Nara-Nārāyaṇa, Hayagrīva and Ajita. In Vṛndāvana Lord Kṛṣṇa sometimes exhibits the functions of such incarnations.

In the *Brahmāṇḍa Purāṇa* it is said, "The same Personality of Godhead who is known in Vaikuṇṭha as the four-handed Nārāyaṇa, the friend of all living entities, and in the milk ocean as the Lord of Śvetadvīpa, and who is the best of all *puruṣas*, appeared as the son of Nanda. In a fire there are many sparks of different dimensions; some of them are very big, and some are small. The small sparks are compared to the living entities, and the large sparks are compared to the Viṣṇu expansions of Lord Kṛṣṇa. All the incarnations emanate from Kṛṣṇa, and after the end of their pastimes they again merge with Kṛṣṇa."

Therefore in the various *Purāṇas* Kṛṣṇa is described sometimes as Nārāyaṇa, sometimes as Kṣīrodakaśāyī Viṣṇu, sometimes as Garbhodakaśāyī Viṣṇu and sometimes as Vaikuṇṭhanātha, the Lord of Vaikuṇṭha. Because Kṛṣṇa is always full, Mūla-saṅkarṣaṇa is in Kṛṣṇa, and since all incarnations are manifested from Mūla-saṅkarṣaṇa, it should be understood that He can manifest different incarnations by His supreme will, even in the presence of Kṛṣṇa. Great sages have therefore glorified the Lord by different names. Thus when the original person, the source of all incarnations, is sometimes described as an incarnation, there is no discrepancy.

TEXT 133

অতএব শ্রীকৃষ্ণচৈতন্য গোসাঞি ।
সর্ব অবতার-লীলা করি' সবারে দেখাই ॥ ১৩৩ ॥

ataeva śrī-kṛṣṇa-caitanya gosāñi
sarva avatāra-līlā kari' sabāre dekhāi

ataeva—therefore; *śrī-kṛṣṇa-caitanya*—Lord Śrī Caitanya Mahāprabhu; *gosāñi*—the Lord; *sarva*—all; *avatāra-līlā*—the pastimes of different incarnations; *kari'*—exhibiting; *sabāre*—to everyone; *dekhāi*—He showed.

TRANSLATION

Therefore Lord Caitanya Mahāprabhu has exhibited to everyone all the pastimes of all the various incarnations.

TEXT 134

এইরূপে নিত্যানন্দ 'অনন্ত'-প্রকাশ ।
সেইভাবে—কহে মুঞি চৈতন্যের দাস ॥ ১৩৪ ॥

ei-rūpe nityānanda 'ananta'-prakāśa
sei-bhāve—kahe muñi caitanyera dāsa

ei-rūpe—in this way; *nityānanda*—Lord Nityānanda; *ananta-prakāśa*—unlimited manifestations; *sei-bhāve*—in that transcendental emotion; *kahe*—He says; *muñi*—I; *caitanyera dāsa*—the servant of Lord Caitanya.

TRANSLATION

Thus Lord Nityānanda has unlimited incarnations. In transcendental emotion He calls Himself a servant of Lord Caitanya.

TEXT 135

কভু গুরু, কভু সখা, কভু ভৃত্য-লীলা ।
পূর্বে যেন তিনভাবে ব্রজে কৈল খেলা ॥ ১৩৫ ॥

kabhu guru, kabhu sakhā, kabhu bhṛtya-līlā
pūrve yena tina-bhāve vraje kaila khelā

kabhu—sometimes; *guru*—spiritual master; *kabhu*—sometimes; *sakhā*—friend; *kabhu*—sometimes; *bhṛtya-līlā*—pastimes as a servant; *pūrve*—formerly; *yena*—as; *tina-bhāve*—in three different moods; *vraje*—in Vṛndāvana; *kaila khelā*—plays with Kṛṣṇa.

TRANSLATION

Sometimes He serves Lord Caitanya as His guru, sometimes as His friend and sometimes as His servant, just as Lord Balarāma played with Lord Kṛṣṇa in these three different moods in Vraja.

TEXT 136

বৃষ হঞা কৃষ্ণসনে মাথামাথি রণ ।
কভু কৃষ্ণ করে তাঁর পাদ-সম্বাহন ॥ ১৩৬ ॥

vṛṣa hañā kṛṣṇa-sane māthā-māthi raṇa
kabhu kṛṣṇa kare tāṅra pāda-saṁvāhana

vṛṣa hañā—becoming a bull; *kṛṣṇa-sane*—with Kṛṣṇa; *māthā-māthi raṇa*—fighting head to head; *kabhu*—sometimes; *kṛṣṇa*—Kṛṣṇa; *kare*—does; *tāṅra*—His; *pāda-saṁvāhana*—massaging the feet.

TRANSLATION

Playing like a bull, Lord Balarāma fights with Kṛṣṇa head to head. And sometimes Lord Kṛṣṇa massages the feet of Lord Balarāma.

TEXT 137

আপনাকে ভৃত্য করি' কৃষ্ণে প্রভু জানে ।
কৃষ্ণের কলার কলা আপনাকে মানে ॥ ১৩৭ ॥

āpanāke bhṛtya kari' kṛṣṇe prabhu jāne
kṛṣṇera kalāra kalā āpanāke māne

āpanāke—Himself; *bhṛtya kari'*—considering a servant; *kṛṣṇa*—Kṛṣṇa; *prabhu*—master; *jāne*—He knows; *kṛṣṇera*—of Lord Kṛṣṇa; *kalāra kalā*—as a plenary portion of a plenary portion; *āpanāke*—Himself; *māne*—He accepts.

TRANSLATION

He considers Himself a servant and knows Kṛṣṇa to be His master. Thus He regards Himself as a fragment of His plenary portion.

TEXT 138

বৃষায়মাণৌ নর্দন্তৌ যুযুধাতে পরস্পরম্ ।
অনুকৃত্য রুতৈর্জন্তূংশ্চেরতুঃ প্রাকৃতৌ যথা ॥ ১৩৮ ॥

vṛṣāyamāṇau nardantau
yuyudhāte parasparam
anukṛtya rutair jantūṁś
ceratuḥ prākṛtau yathā

vṛṣāyamāṇau—becoming like bulls; *nardantau*—making roaring sounds; *yuyudhāte*—both used to fight; *parasparam*—each other; *anukṛtya*—imitating; *rutaiḥ*—with cries; *jantūn*—the animals; *ceratuḥ*—used to play; *prākṛtau*—ordinary boys; *yathā*—just like.

TRANSLATION

"Acting just like ordinary boys, They played like roaring bulls as They fought each other, and They imitated the calls of various animals."

PURPORT

This and the following quotation are from the *Bhāgavatam* (10.11.40 and 10.15.14).

TEXT 139

ক্বচিৎ ক্রীড়া-পরিশ্রান্তং গোপোৎসঙ্গোপবর্হণম ।
স্বয়ং বিশ্রাময়ত্যার্যং পাদসম্বাহনাদিভিঃ ॥ ১৩৯ ॥

kvacit krīḍā-pariśrāntaṁ
gopotsaṅgopabarhaṇam
svayaṁ viśrāmayaty āryaṁ
pāda-saṁvāhanādibhiḥ

kvacit—sometimes; *krīḍā*—playing; *pariśrāntam*—very much fatigued; *gopa-utsaṅga*—the lap of a cowherd boy; *upabarhaṇam*—whose pillow; *svayam*—personally Lord Kṛṣṇa; *viśrāmayati*—causing to rest; *āryam*—His elder brother; *pāda-saṁvāhana-ādibhiḥ*—by massaging His feet, etc.

TRANSLATION

"Sometimes when Lord Kṛṣṇa's elder brother, Lord Balarāma, felt tired after playing and lay His head on the lap of a cowherd boy, Lord Kṛṣṇa Himself served Him by massaging His feet."

TEXT 140

কেয়ং বা কুত আয়াতা দৈবী বা নার্যুতাসুরী ।
প্রায়ো মায়াস্তু মে ভর্তুর্নান্যা মেহপি বিমোহিনী ॥ ১৪০ ॥

keyaṁ vā kuta āyātā
daivī vā nāry utāsurī
prāyo māyāstu me bhartur
nānyā me 'pi vimohinī

kā—who; *iyam*—this; *vā*—or; *kutaḥ*—from where; *āyātā*—has come; *daivī*—whether demigod; *vā*—or; *nārī*—woman; *uta*—or; *āsurī*—demoness; *prāyaḥ*—in most cases; *māyā*—illusory energy; *astu*—she must be; *me*—My; *bhartuḥ*—of the master, Lord Kṛṣṇa; *na*—not; *anyā*—any other; *me*—My; *api*—certainly; *vimohinī*—bewilderer.

TRANSLATION

"Who is this mystic power, and where has she come from? Is she a demigod or a demoness? She must be the illusory energy of My master, Lord Kṛṣṇa, for who else can bewilder Me?"

PURPORT

The playful pastimes of the Lord caused suspicion in the mind of Lord Brahmā, and therefore Lord Brahmā, to test Kṛṣṇa's Lordship, stole all the Lord's calves and cowherd boys with his own mystic power. Śrī Kṛṣṇa responded, however, by replacing all the calves and boys in the field. Lord Balarāma's thoughts of astonishment at such wonderful retaliation are recorded in this verse (*Bhāg*. 10.13.37).

TEXT 141

যস্যাঙ্ঘ্রিপঙ্কজারজো ঽখিললোক-পালৈ-
র্মৌল্যুত্তমৈর্ধৃতমুপাসিত-তীর্থতীর্থম্ ।
ব্রহ্মা ভবোঽহমপি যস্য কলাঃ কলায়াঃ
শ্রীশ্চোদ্বহেম চিরমস্য নৃপাসনং ক্ব ? ॥ ১৪১ ॥

yasyāṅghri-paṅkaja-rajo 'khila-loka-pālair
mauly-uttamair dhṛtam upāsita-tīrtha-tīrtham
brahmā bhavo 'ham api yasya kalāḥ kalāyāḥ
śrīś codvahema ciram asya nṛpāsanaṁ kva

yasya—whose; *aṅghri-paṅkaja*—lotuslike feet; *rajaḥ*—the dust; *akhila-loka*—of the universal planetary systems; *pālaiḥ*—by the masters; *mauli-uttamaiḥ*—with valuable turbans on their heads; *dhṛtam*—accepted; *upāsita*—worshiped; *tīrtha-tīrtham*—the sanctifier of the holy places; *brahmā*—Lord Brahmā; *bhavaḥ*—Lord Śiva; *aham api*—even I; *yasya*—of whom; *kalāḥ*—portions; *kalāyāḥ*—of a plenary portion; *śrīḥ*—the goddess of fortune; *ca*—and; *udvahema*—we carry; *ciram*—eternally; *asya*—of Him; *nṛpa-āsanam*—the throne of a king; *kva*—where.

TRANSLATION

"What is the value of a throne to Lord Kṛṣṇa? The masters of the various planetary systems accept the dust of His lotus feet on their crowned heads. That dust makes the holy places sacred, and even Lord Brahmā, Lord Śiva, Lakṣmī and I Myself, who are all portions of His plenary portion, eternally carry that dust on our heads."

PURPORT

When the Kauravas, to flatter Baladeva so that He would become their ally, spoke ill of Śrī Kṛṣṇa, Lord Baladeva became angry and spoke this verse (*Bhāg.* 10.68.37).

TEXT 142

একলে ঈশ্বর কৃষ্ণ, আর সব ভৃত্য ।
যারে যৈছে নাচায়, সে তৈছে করে নৃত্য ॥ ১৪২ ॥

ekale īśvara kṛṣṇa, āra saba bhṛtya
yāre yaiche nācāya, se taiche kare nṛtya

ekale—alone; *īśvara*—the Supreme Personality of Godhead; *kṛṣṇa*—Kṛṣṇa; *āra*—others; *saba*—all; *bhṛtya*—servants; *yāre*—unto whom; *yaiche*—as; *nācāya*—He causes to dance; *se*—He; *taiche*—in that way; *kare nṛtya*—dances.

TRANSLATION

Lord Kṛṣṇa alone is the supreme controller, and all others are His servants. They dance as He makes them do so.

TEXT 143

এই মত চৈতন্যগোসাঞি একলে ঈশ্বর ।
আর সব পারিষদ, কেহ বা কিঙ্কর ॥ ১৪৩ ॥

ei mata caitanya-gosāñi ekale īśvara
āra saba pāriṣada, keha vā kiṅkara

ei mata—in this way; *caitanya-gosāñi*—Lord Śrī Caitanya Mahāprabhu; *ekale*—alone; *īśvara*—the Supreme Personality of Godhead; *āra saba*—all others; *pāriṣada*—associates; *keha*—someone; *vā*—or; *kiṅkara*—servants.

TRANSLATION

Thus Lord Caitanya is also the only controller. All others are His associates or servants.

TEXTS 144–145

গুরুবর্গ,—নিত্যানন্দ, অদ্বৈত আচার্য ।
শ্রীবাসাদি, আর যত—লঘু, সম, আর্য ॥ ১৪৪ ॥
সবে পারিষদ, সবে লীলার সহায় ।
সবা লঞা নিজ-কার্য সাধে গৌর-রায় ॥ ১৪৫ ॥

guru-varga,—nityānanda, advaita ācārya
śrīvāsādi, āra yata—laghu, sama, ārya

sabe pāriṣada, sabe līlāra sahāya
sabā lañā nija-kārya sādhe gaura-rāya

guru-varga—elders; *nityānanda*—Lord Nityānanda; *advaita ācārya*—and Advaita Ācārya; *śrīvāsa-ādi*—Śrīvāsa Ṭhākura and others; *āra*—others; *yata*—all; *laghu, sama, ārya*—junior, equal or superior; *sabe*—everyone; *pāriṣada*—associates; *sabe*—everyone; *līlāra sahāya*—helpers in the pastimes; *sabā lañā*—taking all of them; *nija-kārya*—His own aims; *sādhe*—executes; *gaura-rāya*—Lord Śrī Caitanya Mahāprabhu.

TRANSLATION

His elders such as Lord Nityānanda, Advaita Ācārya and Śrīvāsa Ṭhākura, as well as His other devotees—whether His juniors, equals or superiors—are all His associates who help Him in His pastimes. Lord Gaurāṅga fulfills His aims with their help.

TEXT 146

অদ্বৈত আচার্য, নিত্যানন্দ,—দুই অঙ্গ ।
দুইজন লঞা প্রভুর যত কিছু রঙ্গ ॥ ১৪৬ ॥

advaita ācārya, nityānanda,—dui aṅga
dui-jana lañā prabhura yata kichu raṅga

advaita ācārya—Śrī Advaita Ācārya; *nityānanda*—Lord Nityānanda; *dui aṅga*—two limbs of the Lord; *dui-jana lañā*—taking the two of Them; *prabhura*—of Lord Śrī Caitanya Mahāprabhu; *yata*—all; *kichu*—some; *raṅga*—playful activities.

TRANSLATION

Śrī Advaita Ācārya and Śrīla Nityānanda Prabhu, who are plenary parts of the Lord, are His principal associates. With these two the Lord performs His pastimes in various ways.

TEXT 147

অদ্বৈত-আচার্য গোসাঞি সাক্ষাৎ ঈশ্বর ।
প্রভু গুরু করি' মানে, তিঁহো ত' কিঙ্কর ॥ ১৪৭ ॥

advaita-ācārya-gosāñi sākṣāt īśvara
prabhu guru kari' māne, tiṅho ta' kiṅkara

advaita-ācārya—Advaita Ācārya; *gosāñi*—the Lord; *sākṣāt īśvara*—directly the Supreme Personality of Godhead; *prabhu*—Lord Śrī

Caitanya Mahāprabhu; *guru kari' māne*—accepts Him as His teacher; *tinho ta' kinkara*—but He is the servant.

TRANSLATION

Lord Advaita Ācārya is directly the Supreme Personality of Godhead. Although Lord Caitanya accepts Him as His preceptor, Advaita Ācārya is a servant of the Lord.

PURPORT

Lord Caitanya always offered respects to Advaita Prabhu as He would to His father because Advaita was even older than His father; yet Advaita Prabhu always considered Himself a servant of Lord Caitanya. Śrī Advaita Prabhu and Īśvara Purī, Lord Caitanya's spiritual master, were both disciples of Mādhavendra Purī, who was also the spiritual master of Nityānanda Prabhu. Thus Advaita Prabhu, as Lord Caitanya's spiritual uncle, was always to be respected because one should respect one's spiritual master's Godbrothers as one respects one's spiritual master. Because of all these considerations, Śrī Advaita Prabhu was superior to Lord Caitanya, yet Advaita Prabhu considered Himself Lord Caitanya's subordinate.

TEXT 148

আচার্য-গোসাঞির তত্ত্ব না যায় কথন ।
কৃষ্ণ অবতারি যেঁহো তারিল ভুবন ॥ ১৪৮ ॥

ācārya-gosāñira tattva nā yāya kathana
kṛṣṇa avatāri yenho tārila bhuvana

ācārya-gosāñira—of Advaita Ācārya; *tattva*—the truth; *nā yāya kathana*—cannot be described; *kṛṣṇa*—Lord Kṛṣṇa; *avatāri*—making descend; *yenho*—who; *tārila*—delivered; *bhuvana*—all the world.

TRANSLATION

I cannot describe the truth of Advaita Ācārya. He has delivered the entire world by making Lord Kṛṣṇa descend.

TEXT 149

নিত্যানন্দ-স্বরূপ পূর্বে হইয়া লক্ষ্মণ ।
লঘুভ্রাতা হৈয়া করে রামের সেবন ॥ ১৪৯ ॥

nityānanda-svarūpa pūrve ha-iyā lakṣmaṇa
laghu-bhrātā haiyā kare rāmera sevana

nityānanda-svarūpa—Lord Nityānanda Svarūpa; *pūrve*—formerly; *ha-iyā*—becoming; *lakṣmaṇa*—Lakṣmaṇa, Lord Rāmacandra's younger brother; *laghu-bhrātrā haiyā*—becoming the younger brother; *kare*—does; *rāmera sevana*—service to Lord Rāmacandra.

TRANSLATION

Lord Nityānanda Svarūpa formerly appeared as Lakṣmaṇa and served Lord Rāmacandra as His younger brother.

PURPORT

Among the *sannyāsīs* of the Śaṅkara-sampradāya there are different names for *brahmacārīs.* Each *sannyāsī* has some assistants, known as *brahmacārīs,* who are called by different names according to the names of the *sannyāsī.* Among such *brahmacārīs* there are four names: Svarūpa, Ānanda, Prakāśa and Caitanya. Nityānanda Prabhu maintained Himself as a *brahmacārī;* He never took *sannyāsa.* As a *brahmacārī* His name was Nityānanda Svarūpa, and therefore the *sannyāsī* under whom He was living must have been from the *tīrthas* or *āśramas* of the Śaṅkara-sampradāya, because one of the names for the assistant *brahmacārī* of such a *sannyāsī* is Svarūpa.

TEXT 150

রামের চরিত্র সব,—দুঃখের কারণ ।
স্বতন্ত্র লীলায় দুঃখ সহেন লক্ষ্মণ ॥ ১৫০ ॥

rāmera caritra saba,—duḥkhera kāraṇa
svatantra līlāya duḥkha sahena lakṣmaṇa

rāmera caritra saba—all the activities of Lord Rāmacandra; *duḥkhera kāraṇa*—causes of suffering; *sva-tantra*—although independent; *līlāya*—in the pastimes; *duḥkha*—unhappiness; *sahena lakṣmaṇa*—Lakṣmaṇa tolerates.

TRANSLATION

The activities of Lord Rāma were full of suffering, but Lakṣmaṇa, of His own accord, tolerated that suffering.

TEXT 151

নিষেধ করিতে নারে, যাতে ছোট ভাই ।
মৌন ধরি' রহে লক্ষ্মণ মনে দুঃখ পাই' ॥ ১৫১ ॥

niṣedha karite nāre, yāte choṭa bhāi
mauna dhari' rahe lakṣmaṇa mane duḥkha pāi'

niṣedha karite nāre—unable to prohibit Lord Rāmacandra; *yāte*—because; *choṭa bhāi*—younger brother; *mauna dhari'*—becoming silent; *rahe*—remains; *lakṣmaṇa*—Lakṣmaṇa; *mane*—in the mind; *duḥkha*—unhappiness; *pāi'*—getting.

TRANSLATION

As a younger brother He could not stop Lord Rāma from His resolution, and so He remained silent, although unhappy in His mind.

TEXT 152

কৃষ্ণ-অবতারে জ্যেষ্ঠ হৈলা সেবার কারণ ।
কৃষ্ণকে করাইল নানা সুখ আস্বাদন ॥ ১৫২ ॥

kṛṣṇa-avatāre jyeṣṭha hailā sevāra kāraṇa
kṛṣṇake karāila nānā sukha āsvādana

kṛṣṇa-avatāre—in the incarnation of Lord Kṛṣṇa; *jyeṣṭha hailā*—He became the elder brother; *sevāra kāraṇa*—for the purpose of service; *kṛṣṇake*—to Kṛṣṇa; *karāila*—made; *nānā*—various; *sukha*—happinesses; *āsvādana*—tasting.

TRANSLATION

When Lord Kṛṣṇa appeared, He [Balarāma] became His elder brother to serve Him to His heart's content and make Him enjoy all sorts of happiness.

TEXT 153

রাম-লক্ষ্মণ—কৃষ্ণ-রামের অংশবিশেষ ।
অবতার-কালে দোঁহে দোঁহাতে প্রবেশ ॥ ১৫৩ ॥

rāma-lakṣmaṇa—kṛṣṇa-rāmera aṁśa-viśeṣa
avatāra-kāle doṅhe doṅhāte praveśa

rāma-lakṣmaṇa—Rāmacandra and Lakṣmaṇa; *kṛṣṇa-rāmera aṁśa-viśeṣa*—particular expansions of Lord Kṛṣṇa and Lord Balarāma; *avatāra-kāle*—at the time of incarnation; *doṅhe*—both of Them (Rāma and Lakṣmaṇa); *doṅhāte praveśa*—entered into Them both (Kṛṣṇa and Balarāma).

TRANSLATION

Śrī Rāma and Śrī Lakṣmaṇa, who are plenary portions of Lord Kṛṣṇa and Lord Balarāma respectively, entered into Them at the time of Kṛṣṇa's and Balarāma's appearance.

PURPORT

With reference to the *Viṣṇu-dharmottara,* the *Laghu-bhāgavatāmṛta* explains that Rāma is an incarnation of Vāsudeva, Lakṣmaṇa is an incarnation of Saṅkarṣaṇa, Bharata is an incarnation of Pradyumna, and Śatrughna is an incarnation of Aniruddha. The *Padma Purāṇa* describes that Rāmacandra is Nārāyaṇa and that Lakṣmaṇa, Bharata and Śatrughna are respectively Śeṣa, Cakra and Śaṅkha (the conchshell in the hand of Nārāyaṇa). In the *Rāma-gīta* of the *Skanda Purāṇa,* Lakṣmaṇa, Bharata and Śatrughna have been described as the triple attendants of Lord Rāma.

TEXT 154

সেই অংশ লঞা জ্যেষ্ঠ-কনিষ্ঠাভিমান ।
অংশাংশি-রূপে শাস্ত্রে করয়ে ব্যাখ্যান ॥ ১৫৪ ॥

sei aṁśa lañā jyeṣṭha-kaniṣṭhābhimāna
aṁśāṁśi-rūpe śāstre karaye vyākhyāna

sei aṁśa lañā—taking that plenary portion; *jyeṣṭha-kaniṣṭha-abhimāna*—considering Themselves the elder or younger; *aṁśa-aṁśi-rūpe*—as the expansion and the original Supreme Personality of Godhead; *śāstre*—in the revealed scriptures; *karaye*—does; *vyākhyāna*—explanation.

TRANSLATION

Kṛṣṇa and Balarāma present Themselves as younger brother and elder brother, but in the scriptures They are described as the original Supreme Personality of Godhead and His expansion.

TEXT 155

রামাদিমূর্তিষু কলানিয়মেন তিষ্ঠন্
নানাবতারমকরোদ্ভুবনেষু কিন্তু ।
কৃষ্ণঃ স্বয়ং সমভবৎ পরমঃ পুমান্ যো
গোবিন্দমাদিপুরুষং তমহং ভজামি ॥ ১৫৫ ॥

rāmādi-mūrtiṣu kalā-niyamena tiṣṭhan
nānāvatāram akarod bhuvaneṣu kintu
kṛṣṇaḥ svayaṁ samabhavat paramaḥ pumān yo
govindam ādi-puruṣaṁ tam ahaṁ bhajāmi

rāma-ādi—the incarnation of Lord Rāma, etc.; *mūrtiṣu*—in different forms; *kalā-niyamena*—by the order of plenary portions; *tiṣṭhan*—existing; *nānā*—various; *avatāram*—incarnations; *akarot*—executed; *bhuvaneṣu*—within the worlds; *kintu*—but; *kṛṣṇaḥ*—Lord Kṛṣṇa; *svayam*—personally; *samabhavat*—appeared; *paramaḥ*—the supreme; *pumān*—person; *yaḥ*—who; *govindam*—unto Lord Govinda; *ādi-puruṣam*—the original person; *tam*—unto Him; *aham*—I; *bhajāmi*—offer obeisances.

TRANSLATION

"I worship Govinda, the primeval Lord, who by His various plenary portions appears in the world in different forms and incarnations such as Lord Rāma, but who personally appears in His supreme original form as Lord Kṛṣṇa."

PURPORT

This is a quotation from *Brahma-saṁhitā* (5.39).

TEXT 156

শ্রীচৈতন্য—সেই কৃষ্ণ, নিত্যানন্দ—রাম ।
নিত্যানন্দ পূর্ণ করে চৈতন্যের কাম ॥ ১৫৬ ॥

śrī-caitanya—sei kṛṣṇa, nityānanda—rāma
nityānanda pūrṇa kare caitanyera kāma

śrī-caitanya—Lord Śrī Caitanya; *sei kṛṣṇa*—that original Kṛṣṇa; *nityānanda*—Lord Nityānanda; *rāma*—Balarāma; *nityānanda*—Lord

Nityānanda; *pūrṇa kare*—fulfills; *caitanyera kāma*—all the desires of Lord Śrī Caitanya Mahāprabhu.

TRANSLATION

Lord Caitanya is the same Lord Kṛṣṇa, and Lord Nityānanda is Lord Balarāma. Lord Nityānanda fulfills all of Lord Caitanya's desires.

TEXT 157

নিত্যানন্দ-মহিমা-সিন্ধু অনন্ত, অপার ।
এক কণা স্পর্শি মাত্র,—সে কৃপা তাঁহার ॥ ১৫৭ ॥

nityānanda-mahimā-sindhu ananta, apāra
eka kaṇā sparśi mātra,—se kṛpā tāṅhāra

nityānanda-mahimā—of the glories of Lord Nityānanda; *sindhu*—the ocean; *ananta*—unlimited; *apāra*—unfathomed; *eka kaṇā*—one fragment; *sparśi*—I touch; *mātra*—only; *se*—that; *kṛpā*—mercy; *tāṅhāra*—His.

TRANSLATION

The ocean of Lord Nityānanda's glories is infinite and unfathomable. Only by His mercy can I touch even a drop of it.

TEXT 158

আর এক শুন তাঁর কৃপার মহিমা ।
অধম জীবেরে চঢ়াইল ঊর্ধ্বসীমা ॥ ১৫৮ ॥

āra eka śuna tāṅra kṛpāra mahimā
adhama jīvere caḍhāila ūrdhva-sīmā

āra—another; *eka*—one; *śuna*—please hear; *tāṅra kṛpāra mahimā*—glory of His mercy; *adhama jīvere*—the downtrodden living being; *caḍhāila*—He elevated; *ūrdhva-sīmā*—to the topmost limit.

TRANSLATION

Please listen to another glory of His mercy. He made a fallen living entity climb to the highest limit.

TEXT 159

বেদগুহ্য কথা এই অযোগ্য কহিতে ।
তথাপি কহিয়ে তাঁর কৃপা প্রকাশিতে ॥ ১৫৯ ॥

veda-guhya kathā ei ayogya kahite
tathāpi kahiye tāṅra kṛpā prakāśite

veda—like the *Vedas; guhya*—very confidential; *kathā*—incident; *ei*—this; *ayogya kahite*—not fit to disclose; *tathāpi*—still; *kahiye*—I speak; *tāṅra*—His; *kṛpā*—mercy; *prakāśite*—to manifest.

TRANSLATION

To disclose it is not proper, for it should be kept as confidential as the Vedas, yet I shall speak of it to make His mercy known to all.

TEXT 160

উল্লাস-উপরি লেখোঁ তোমার প্রসাদ ।
নিত্যানন্দ প্রভু, মোর ক্ষম অপরাধ ॥ ১৬০ ॥

ullāsa-upari lekhoṅ tomāra prasāda
nityānanda prabhu, mora kṣama aparādha

ullāsa-upari—on account of great ecstasy; *lekhoṅ*—I write; *tomāra prasāda*—Your mercy; *nityānanda prabhu*—Lord Nityānanda; *mora*—my; *kṣama*—please excuse; *aparādha*—offenses.

TRANSLATION

O Lord Nityānanda, I write of Your mercy out of great exultation. Please forgive me for my offenses.

TEXT 161

অবধূত গোসাঞির এক ভৃত্য প্রেমধাম ।
মীনকেতন রামদাস হয় তাঁর নাম ॥ ১৬১ ॥

avadhūta gosāñira eka bhṛtya prema-dhāma
mīnaketana rāmadāsa haya tāṅra nāma

avadhūta—the mendicant; *gosāñira*—of Lord Nityānanda; *eka*—one; *bhṛtya*—servant; *prema-dhāma*—reservoir of love; *mīnaketana*—Mīnaketana; *rāma-dāsa*—Rāmadāsa; *haya*—is; *tāṅra*—his; *nāma*—name.

TRANSLATION

Lord Nityānanda Prabhu had a servant named Śrī Mīnaketana Rāmadāsa, who was a reservoir of love.

TEXT 162

আমার আলয়ে অহোরাত্র-সংকীর্তন ।
তাহাতে আইলা তেঁহো পাঞা নিমন্ত্রণ ॥ ১৬২ ॥

āmāra ālaye aho-rātra-saṅkīrtana
tāhāte āilā teṅho pāñā nimantraṇa

āmāra ālaye—at my house; *ahaḥ-rātra*—day and night; *saṅkīrtana*—chanting the Hare Kṛṣṇa *mantra; tāhāte*—on account of this; *āilā*—came; *teṅho*—he; *pāñā nimantraṇa*—getting an invitation.

TRANSLATION

At my house there was saṅkīrtana day and night, and therefore he visited there, having been invited.

TEXT 163

মহাপ্রেমময় তিঁহো বসিলা অঙ্গনে ।
সকল বৈষ্ণব তাঁর বন্দিলা চরণে ॥ ১৬৩ ॥

mahā-prema-maya tiṅho vasilā aṅgane
sakala vaiṣṇava tāṅra vandilā caraṇe

mahā-prema-maya—absorbed in emotional love; *tiṅho*—he; *vasilā*—sat; *aṅgane*—in the courtyard; *sakala vaiṣṇava*—all other Vaiṣṇavas; *tāṅra*—his; *vandilā*—worshiped; *caraṇe*—lotus feet.

TRANSLATION

Absorbed in emotional love, he sat in my courtyard, and all the Vaiṣṇavas bowed down at his feet.

TEXT 164

নমস্কার করিতে, কা'র উপরেতে চড়ে ।
প্রেমে কা'রে বংশী মারে, কাহাকে চাপড়ে ॥ ১৬৪ ॥

namaskāra karite, kā're uparete caḍe
preme kā're vaṁśī māre, kāhāke cāpaḍe

namaskāra karite—while offering obeisances, bowing down; *kā'ra*—of someone; *uparete*—on the body; *caḍe*—gets up; *preme*—in ecstatic love; *kā're*—someone; *vaṁśī*—the flute; *māre*—strikes; *kāhāke*—someone; *cāpaḍe*—slaps.

TRANSLATION

In a joyful mood of love of God he sometimes climbed upon the shoulder of someone offering obeisances, and sometimes he struck others with his flute or mildly slapped them.

TEXT 165

যে নয়ন দেখিতে অশ্রু হয় মনে যার ।
সেই নেত্রে অবিচ্ছিন্ন বহে অশ্রুধার ॥ ১৬৫ ॥

ye nayana dekhite aśru haya mane yāra
sei netre avicchinna vahe aśru-dhāra

ye—his; *nayana*—eyes; *dekhite*—seeing; *aśru*—tears; *haya*—appear; *mane*—from the mind; *yāra*—of someone; *sei netre*—in his eyes; *avicchinna*—continuously; *vahe*—flows; *aśru-dhāra*—a shower of tears.

TRANSLATION

When someone saw the eyes of Mīnaketana Rāmadāsa, tears would automatically flow from his own eyes, for a constant shower of tears flowed from the eyes of Mīnaketana Rāmadāsa.

TEXT 166

কভু কোন অঙ্গে দেখি পুলক-কদম্ব ।
এক অঙ্গে জাড্য তাঁর, আর অঙ্গে কম্প ॥ ১৬৬ ॥

kabhu kona aṅge dekhi pulaka-kadamba
eka aṅge jāḍya tāṅra, āra aṅge kampa

kabhu—sometimes; *kona*—some; *aṅge*—in parts of the body; *dekhi*—I see; *pulaka-kadamba*—eruptions of ecstasy like *kadamba* flowers; *eka aṅge*—in one part of the body; *jāḍya*—stunned; *tāṅra*—his; *āra aṅge*—in another limb; *kampa*—trembling.

TRANSLATION

Sometimes there were eruptions of ecstasy like kadamba flowers on some parts of his body, and sometimes one limb would be stunned while another would be trembling.

TEXT 167

নিত্যানন্দ বলি' যবে করেন হুঙ্কার ।
তাহা দেখি' লোকের হয় মহা-চমৎকার ॥ ১৬৭ ॥

nityānanda bali' yabe karena huṅkāra
tāhā dekhi' lokera haya mahā-camatkāra

nityānanda—the name Nityānanda; *bali'*—saying; *yabe*—whenever; *karena huṅkāra*—makes a great sound; *tāhā dekhi'*—seeing that; *lokera*—of the people; *haya*—there is; *mahā-camatkāra*—great wonder and astonishment.

TRANSLATION

Whenever he shouted aloud the name Nityānanda, the people around him were filled with great wonder and astonishment.

TEXT 168

গুণার্ণব মিশ্র নামে এক বিপ্র আর্য ।
শ্রীমূর্তি-নিকটে তেঁহো করে সেবা-কার্য ॥ ১৬৮ ॥

guṇārṇava miśra nāme eka vipra ārya
śrī-mūrti-nikaṭe teṅho kare sevā-kārya

guṇārṇava miśra—of Guṇārṇava Miśra; *nāme*—by the name; *eka*—one; *vipra*—*brāhmaṇa; ārya*—very respectable; *śrī-mūrti-nikaṭe*—by the side of the Deity; *teṅho*—he; *kare*—does; *sevā-kārya*—activities in devotion.

TRANSLATION

One respectable brāhmaṇa named Śrī Guṇārṇava Miśra was serving the Deity.

TEXT 169

অঙ্গনে আসিয়া তেঁহো না কৈল সম্ভাষ ।
তাহা দেখি' ক্রুদ্ধ হঞা বলে রামদাস ॥ ১৬৯ ॥

aṅgane āsiyā teṅho nā kaila sambhāṣa
tāhā dekhi' kruddha hañā bale rāmadāsa

aṅgane—to the courtyard; *āsiyā*—coming; *teṅho*—he; *nā*—not; *kaila*—did; *sambhāṣa*—address; *tāhā dekhi'*—seeing this; *kruddha hañā*—becoming angry; *bale*—says; *rāma-dāsa*—Śrī Rāmadāsa.

TRANSLATION

When Mīnaketana was seated in the yard, this brāhmaṇa did not offer him respect. Seeing this, Śrī Rāmadāsa became angry and spoke.

TEXT 170

'এই ত' দ্বিতীয় সূত রোমহরষণ ।
বলদেব দেখি' যে না কৈল প্রত্যুদগম' ॥ ১৭০ ॥

'ei ta' dvitīya sūta romaharaṣaṇa
baladeva dekhi' ye nā kaila pratyudgama'

ei ta'—this; *dvitīya*—second; *sūta romaharaṣaṇa*—Romaharṣaṇa-sūta; *baladeva dekhi'*—seeing Lord Balarāma; *ye*—who; *nā*—not; *kaila*—did; *pratyudgama*—stand up.

TRANSLATION

"Here I find the second Romaharṣaṇa-sūta, who did not stand to show honor when he saw Lord Balarāma."

TEXT 171

এত বলি' নাচে গায়, করয়ে সন্তোষ ।
কৃষ্ণকার্য করে বিপ্র—না করিল রোষ ॥ ১৭১ ॥

eta bali' nāce gāya, karaye santoṣa
kṛṣṇa-kārya kare vipra—nā karila roṣa

eta bali'—saying this; *nāce*—he dances; *gāya*—chants; *karaye santoṣa*—becomes satisfied; *kṛṣṇa-kārya*—the duties of Deity worship; *kare*—performs; *vipra*—the *brāhmaṇa; nā karila*—did not become; *roṣa*—angry.

TRANSLATION

After saying this, he danced and sang to his heart's content, but the brāhmaṇa did not become angry, for he was then serving Lord Kṛṣṇa.

PURPORT

Mīnaketana Rāmadāsa was a great devotee of Lord Nityānanda. When he entered the house of Kṛṣṇadāsa Kavirāja, Guṇārṇava Miśra, the priest who was worshiping the Deity installed in the house, did not receive him very well. A similar event occurred when Romaharṣaṇa-sūta was speaking to the great assembly of sages at Naimiṣāraṇya. Lord Baladeva entered that great assembly, but since Romaharṣaṇa-sūta was on the *vyāsāsana,* he did not get down to offer respect to Lord Baladeva. The behavior of Guṇārṇava Miśra indicated that he had no great respect for Lord Nityānanda, and this idea was not at all palatable to Mīnaketana Rāmadāsa. For this reason the mentality of Mīnaketana Rāmadāsa is never deprecated by devotees.

TEXT 172

উৎসবান্তে গেলা তিঁহো করিয়া প্রসাদ ।
মোর ভ্রাতা-সনে তাঁর কিছু হৈল বাদ ॥ ১৭২ ॥

utsavānte gelā tiṅho kariyā prasāda
mora bhrātā-sane tāṅra kichu haila vāda

utsava-ante—after the festival; *gelā*—went away; *tiṅho*—he; *kariyā prasāda*—showing mercy; *mora*—of me; *bhrātā-sane*—with the brother; *tāṅra*—of him; *kichu*—some; *haila*—there was; *vāda*—controversy.

TRANSLATION

At the end of the festival Mīnaketana Rāmadāsa went away, offering his blessings to everyone. At that time he had some controversy with my brother.

TEXT 173

শ্রীচৈতন্যপ্রভুতে তাঁর সুদৃঢ় বিশ্বাস।
নিত্যানন্দ-প্রতি তাঁর বিশ্বাস-আভাস ॥ ১৭৩ ॥

śrī-caitanya-prabhute tāṅra sudṛḍha viśvāsa
nityānanda-prati tāṅra viśvāsa-ābhāsa

śrī-caitanya-prabhute—unto Lord Caitanya; *tāṅra*—his; *su-dṛḍha*—fixed; *viśvāsa*—faith; *nityānanda-prati*—unto Lord Nityānanda; *tāṅra*—his; *viśvāsa-ābhāsa*—dim reflection of faith.

TRANSLATION

My brother had firm faith in Lord Caitanya but only a dim glimmer of faith in Lord Nityānanda.

TEXT 174

ইহা জানি' রামদাসের দুঃখ হইল মনে।
তবে ত' ভ্রাতারে আমি করিনু ভর্ৎসনে ॥ ১৭৪ ॥

ihā jāni' rāmadāsera duḥkha ha-ila mane
tabe ta' bhrātāre āmi karinu bhartsane

ihā—this; *jāni'*—knowing; *rāma-dāsera*—of the saint Rāmadāsa; *duḥkha*—unhappiness; *ha-ila*—there was; *mane*—in the mind; *tabe*—at that time; *ta'*—certainly; *bhrātāre*—to my brother; *āmi*—I; *karinu*—did; *bhartsane*—chastisement.

TRANSLATION

Knowing this, Śrī Rāmadāsa felt unhappy in his mind. I then rebuked my brother.

TEXT 175

দুই ভাই একতনু—সমান-প্রকাশ ।
নিত্যানন্দ না মান, তোমার হবে সর্বনাশ ॥ ১৭৫ ॥

dui bhāi eka-tanu—samāna-prakāśa
nityānanda nā māna, tomāra habe sarva-nāśa

dui bhāi—two brothers; *eka-tanu*—one body; *samāna-prakāśa*—equal manifestation; *nityānanda*—Lord Nityānanda; *nā māne*—you do not believe; *tomāra*—your; *habe*—that will be; *sarva-nāśa*—downfall.

TRANSLATION

"These two brothers," I told him, "are like one body; They are identical manifestations. If you do not believe in Lord Nityānanda, you will fall down.

TEXT 176

একেতে বিশ্বাস, অন্যে না কর সম্মান ।
"অর্ধকুক্কুটী-ন্যায়" তোমার প্রমাণ ॥ ১৭৬ ॥

ekete viśvāsa, anye nā kara sammāna
"ardha-kukkuṭī-nyāya" tomāra pramāṇa

ekete viśvāsa—faith in one; *anye*—in the other; *nā*—not; *kara*—do; *sammāna*—respect; *ardha-kukkuṭī-nyāya*—the logic of accepting half of a hen; *tomāra*—your; *pramāṇa*—evidence.

TRANSLATION

"If you have faith in one but disrespect the other, your logic is like the logic of accepting half a hen.*

TEXT 177

কিংবা, দোঁহা না মানিঞা হও ত' পাষণ্ড ।
একে মানি' আরে না মানি,—এইমত ভণ্ড ॥ ১৭৭ ॥

---

*A foolish farmer once thought he would save money by cutting off his hen's head, which he had to feed, and leaving its tail, which produced the eggs. Hence the term *ardha-kukkuṭī-nyāya,* literally "half-hen logic."

kiṁvā, doṅhā nā māniñā hao ta' pāṣaṇḍa
eke māni' āre nā māni,—ei-mata bhaṇḍa

kiṁvā—otherwise; *doṅhā*—both of Them; *nā*—not; *māniñā*—accepting; *hao*—you become; *ta'*—certainly; *pāṣaṇḍa*—atheist; *eke*—one of Them; *māni'*—accepting; *āre*—the other; *nā māni*—not accepting; *ei-mata*—this kind of faith; *bhaṇḍa*—hypocrisy.

TRANSLATION

"It would be better to be an atheist by slighting both brothers than a hypocrite by believing in one and slighting the other."

TEXT 178

ক্রুদ্ধ হৈয়া বংশী ভাঙ্গি' চলে রামদাস ।
তৎকালে আমার ভ্রাতার হৈল সর্বনাশ ॥ ১৭৮ ॥

kruddha haiyā vaṁśī bhāṅgi' cale rāmadāsa
tat-kāle āmāra bhrātāra haila sarva-nāśa

kruddha haiyā—being very angry; *vaṁśī*—the flute; *bhāṅgi'*—breaking; *cale*—departs; *rāma-dāsa*—Rāmadāsa; *tat-kāle*—at that time; *āmāra*—my; *bhrātāra*—of the brother; *haila*—there was; *sarva-nāśa*—downfall.

TRANSLATION

Thus Śrī Rāmadāsa broke his flute in anger and went away, and at that time my brother fell down.

TEXT 179

এই ত' কহিল তাঁর সেবক-প্রভাব ।
আর এক কহি তাঁর দয়ার স্বভাব ॥ ১৭৯ ॥

ei ta' kahila tāṅra sevaka-prabhāva
āra eka kahi tāṅra dayāra svabhāva

ei ta'—thus; *kahila*—explained; *tāṅra*—of Him; *sevaka-prabhāva*—the power of the servant; *āra*—other; *eka*—one; *kahi*—I say; *tāṅra*—His; *dayāra*—of mercy; *svabhāva*—characteristic.

TRANSLATION

I have thus described the power of the servants of Lord Nityānanda. Now I shall describe another characteristic of His mercy.

TEXT 180

ভাইকে ভর্ৎসিনু মুঞি, লঞা এই গুণ ।
সেই রাত্রে প্রভু মোরে দিলা দরশন ॥ ১৮০ ॥

bhāike bhartsinu muñi, lañā ei guṇa
sei rātre prabhu more dilā daraśana

bhāike—my brother; *bhartsinu*—chastised; *muñi*—I; *lañā*—taking; *ei*—this; *guṇa*—as a good quality; *sei rātre*—on that night; *prabhu*—my Lord; *more*—unto me; *dilā*—gave; *daraśana*—appearance.

TRANSLATION

That night Lord Nityānanda appeared to me in a dream because of my good quality in chastising my brother.

TEXT 181

নৈহাটি নিকটে 'ঝামটপুর' নামে গ্রাম ।
তাঁহা স্বপ্নে দেখা দিলা নিত্যানন্দ-রাম ॥ ১৮১ ॥

naihāṭi-nikaṭe 'jhāmaṭapura' nāme grāma
tāṅhā svapne dekhā dilā nityānanda-rāma

naihāṭi-nikaṭe—near the village Naihāṭi; *jhāmaṭapura*—Jhāmaṭapura; *nāme*—by the name; *grāma*—village; *tāṅhā*—there; *svapne*—in a dream; *dekhā*—appearance; *dilā*—gave; *nityānanda-rāma*—Lord Nityānanda Balarāma.

TRANSLATION

In the village of Jhāmaṭapura, which is near Naihāṭi, Lord Nityānanda appeared to me in a dream.

PURPORT

There is now a railway line to Jhāmaṭapura. If one wants to go there, he can take a train on the Katwa railway line and go directly to the station known as Sālāra. From that station one can go directly to Jhāmaṭapura.

TEXT 182

দণ্ডবৎ হৈয়া আমি পড়িনু পায়েতে ।
নিজপাদপদ্ম প্রভু দিলা মোর মাথে ॥ ১৮২ ॥

daṇḍavat haiyā āmi paḍinu pāyete
nija-pāda-padma prabhu dilā mora māthe

daṇḍavat haiyā—offering obeisances; *āmi*—I; *paḍinu*—fell down; *pāyete*—at His lotus feet; *nija-pāda-padma*—His own lotus feet; *prabhu*—the Lord; *dilā*—placed; *mora*—my; *māthe*—on the head.

TRANSLATION

I fell at His feet, offering my obeisances, and He then placed His own lotus feet upon my head.

TEXT 183

'উঠ', 'উঠ' বলি' মোরে বলে বার বার ।
উঠি' তাঁর রূপ দেখি' হৈনু চমৎকার ॥ ১৮৩ ॥

'uṭha', 'uṭha' bali' more bale bāra bāra
uṭhi' tāṅra rūpa dekhi' hainu camatkāra

uṭha uṭha—get up, get up; *bali'*—saying; *more*—unto me; *bale*—says; *bāra bāra*—again and again; *uṭhi'*—getting up; *tāṅra*—His; *rūpa dekhi'*—seeing the beauty; *hainu*—became; *camatkāra*—astonished.

TRANSLATION

"Arise! Get up!" He told me again and again. Upon rising, I was greatly astonished to see His beauty.

TEXT 184

শ্যাম-চিক্কণ কান্তি, প্রকাণ্ড শরীর ।
সাক্ষাৎ কন্দর্প, যৈছে মহামল্ল-বীর ॥ ১৮৪ ॥

śyāma-cikkaṇa kānti, prakāṇḍa śarīra
sākṣāt kandarpa, yaiche mahā-malla-vīra

śyāma—blackish; *cikkaṇa*—glossy; *kānti*—luster; *prakāṇḍa*—heavy; *śarīra*—body; *sākṣāt*—directly; *kandarpa*—Cupid; *yaiche*—like; *mahā-malla*—very stout and strong; *vīra*—hero.

TRANSLATION

He had a glossy blackish complexion, and His tall, strong, heroic stature made Him seem like Cupid himself.

TEXT 185

সুবলিত হস্ত, পদ, কমল-নয়ান ।
পট্টবস্ত্র শিরে, পট্টবস্ত্র পরিধান ॥ ১৮৫ ॥

suvalita hasta, pada, kamala-nayāna
paṭṭa-vastra śire, paṭṭa-vastra paridhāna

suvalita—well-formed; *hasta*—hands; *pada*—legs; *kamala-nayāna*—eyes like lotus flowers; *paṭṭa-vastra*—silk cloth; *śire*—on the head; *paṭṭa-vastra*—silk garments; *paridhāna*—wearing.

TRANSLATION

He had beautifully formed hands, arms and legs, and eyes like lotus flowers. He wore a silk cloth, with a silk turban on His head.

TEXT 186

সুবর্ণ-কুণ্ডল কর্ণে, স্বর্ণাঙ্গদ-বালা ।
পায়েতে নূপুর বাজে, কণ্ঠে পুষ্পমালা ॥ ১৮৬ ॥

suvarṇa-kuṇḍala karṇe, svarṇāṅgada-vālā
pāyete nūpura bāje, kaṇṭhe puṣpa-mālā

suvarṇa-kuṇḍala—gold earrings; *karṇe*—on the ears; *svarṇa-aṅgada*—golden armlets; *vālā*—and bangles; *pāyete*—on the feet; *nūpura*—ankle bells; *bāje*—tinkle; *kaṇṭhe*—on the neck; *puṣpa-mālā*—flower garland.

TRANSLATION

He wore golden earrings on His ears, and golden armlets and bangles. He wore tinkling anklets on His feet and a garland of flowers around His neck.

TEXT 187

চন্দনলেপিত-অঙ্গ, তিলক সুঠাম।
মত্তগজ জিনি' মদ-মন্থর পয়ান ॥ ১৮৭ ॥

candana-lepita-aṅga, tilaka suṭhāma
matta-gaja jini' mada-manthara payāna

candana—with sandalwood pulp; *lepita*—smeared; *aṅga*—body; *tilaka suṭhāma*—nicely decorated with *tilaka; matta-gaja*—a mad elephant; *jini'*—surpassing; *mada-manthara*—maddened by drinking; *payāna*—movement.

TRANSLATION

His body was anointed with sandalwood pulp, and He was nicely decorated with tilaka. His movements surpassed those of a maddened elephant.

TEXT 188

কোটিচন্দ্র জিনি' মুখ উজ্জ্বল-বরণ।
দাড়িম্ব-বীজ-সম দন্ত তাম্বূল-চর্বণ ॥ ১৮৮ ॥

koṭi-candra jini' mukha ujjvala-varaṇa
dāḍimba-bīja-sama danta tāmbūla-carvaṇa

koṭi-candra—millions upon millions of moons; *jini'*—surpassing; *mukha*—face; *ujjvala-varaṇa*—bright and brilliant; *dāḍimba-bīja*—pomegranate seeds; *sama*—like; *danta*—teeth; *tāmbūla-carvaṇa*—chewing betel nut.

TRANSLATION

His face was more beautiful than millions upon millions of moons, and His teeth were like pomegranate seeds because of His chewing betel.

TEXT 189

প্রেমে মত্ত অঙ্গ ডাহিনে-বামে দোলে।
'কৃষ্ণ' 'কৃষ্ণ' বলিয়া গম্ভীর বোল বলে ॥ ১৮৯ ॥

preme matta aṅga ḍāhine-vāme dole
'kṛṣṇa' 'kṛṣṇa' baliyā gambhīra bola bale

preme—in ecstasy; *matta*—absorbed; *aṅga*—the whole body; *ḍāhine*—to the right side; *vāme*—to the left side; *dole*—moves; *kṛṣṇa kṛṣṇa*—Kṛṣṇa, Kṛṣṇa; *baliyā*—saying; *gambhīra*—deep; *bola*—words; *bale*—was uttering.

TRANSLATION

His body moved to and fro, right and left, for He was absorbed in ecstasy. He chanted "Kṛṣṇa, Kṛṣṇa" in a deep voice.

TEXT 190

রাঙ্গা-যষ্টি হস্তে দোলে যেন মত্ত সিংহ ।
চারিপাশে বেড়ি আছে চরণেতে ভৃঙ্গ ॥ ১৯০ ॥

rāṅgā-yaṣṭi haste dole yena matta siṁha
cāri-pāśe veḍi āche caraṇete bhṛṅga

rāṅgā-yaṣṭi—a red stick; *haste*—in the hand; *dole*—moves; *yena*—like; *matta*—mad; *siṁha*—lion; *cāri-pāśe*—all around; *veḍi*—surrounding; *āche*—there is; *caraṇete*—at the lotus feet; *bhṛṅga*—bumblebees.

TRANSLATION

His red stick moving in His hand, He seemed like a maddened lion. All around the four sides of His feet were bumblebees.

TEXT 191

পারিষদগণে দেখি' সব গোপ-বেশে ।
'কৃষ্ণ' 'কৃষ্ণ' কহে সবে সপ্রেম আবেশে ॥ ১৯১ ॥

pāriṣada-gaṇe dekhi' saba gopa-veśe
'kṛṣṇa' 'kṛṣṇa' kahe sabe saprema āveśe

pāriṣada-gaṇe—associates; *dekhi'*—seeing; *saba*—all; *gopa-veśe*—in the dress of cowherd boys; *kṛṣṇa kṛṣṇa*—Kṛṣṇa, Kṛṣṇa; *kahe*—says; *sabe*—all; *sa-prema*—of ecstatic love; *āveśe*—in absorption.

TRANSLATION

His devotees, dressed like cowherd boys, surrounded His feet like so many bees and also chanted "Kṛṣṇa, Kṛṣṇa," absorbed in ecstatic love.

TEXT 192

শিঙ্গা বাঁশী বাজায় কেহ, কেহ নাচে গায় ।
সেবক যোগায় তাম্বূল, চামর ঢুলায় ॥ ১৯২ ॥

śiṅgā vāṁśī bājāya keha, keha nāce gāya
sevaka yogāya tāmbūla, cāmara ḍhulāya

śiṅgā vāṁśī—horns and flutes; *bājāya*—play; *keha*—some; *keha*—some of them; *nāce*—dance; *gāya*—sing; *sevaka*—a servant; *yogāya*—supplies; *tāmbūla*—betel nut; *cāmara*—fan; *ḍhulāya*—moves.

TRANSLATION

Some of them played horns and flutes, and others danced and sang. Some of them offered betel nuts, and others waved cāmara fans about Him.

TEXT 193

নিত্যানন্দ-স্বরূপের দেখিয়া বৈভব ।
কিবা রূপ, গুণ, লীলা—অলৌকিক সব ॥ ১৯৩ ॥

nityānanda-svarūpera dekhiyā vaibhava
kibā rūpa, guṇa, līlā—alaukika saba

nityānanda-svarūpera—of Lord Nityānanda Svarūpa; *dekhiyā*—seeing; *vaibhava*—the opulence; *kibā rūpa*—what a wonderful form; *guṇa*—qualities; *līlā*—pastimes; *alaukika*—uncommon; *saba*—all.

TRANSLATION

Thus I saw such opulence in Lord Nityānanda Svarūpa. His wonderful form, qualities and pastimes are all transcendental.

TEXT 194

আনন্দে বিহ্বল আমি, কিছু নাহি জানি ।
তবে হাসি' প্রভু মোরে কহিলেন বাণী ॥ ১৯৪ ॥

ānande vihvala āmi, kichu nāhi jāni
tabe hāsi' prabhu more kahilena vāṇī

ānande—in transcendental ecstasy; *vihvala*—overwhelmed; *āmi*—I; *kichu*—anything; *nāhi*—not; *jāni*—know; *tabe*—at that time; *hāsi'*—smiling; *prabhu*—the Lord; *more*—unto me; *kahilena*—says; *vāṇī*—some words.

TRANSLATION

I was overwhelmed with transcendental ecstasy, not knowing anything else. Then Lord Nityānanda smiled and spoke to me as follows.

TEXT 195

আরে আরে কৃষ্ণদাস, না করহ ভয় ।
বৃন্দাবনে যাহ,—তাঁহা সর্ব লভ্য হয় ॥ ১৯৫ ॥

āre āre kṛṣṇadāsa, nā karaha bhaya
vṛndāvane yāha,—tāṅhā sarva labhya haya

āre āre—O! O!; *kṛṣṇa-dāsa*—Kṛṣṇadāsa; *nā*—not; *karaha*—make; *bhaya*—fear; *vṛndāvane yāha*—go to Vṛndāvana; *tāṅhā*—there; *sarva*—everything; *labhya*—available; *haya*—is.

TRANSLATION

"O my dear Kṛṣṇadāsa, do not be afraid. Go to Vṛndāvana, for there you will attain all things."

TEXT 196

এত বলি' প্রেরিলা মোরে হাতসানি দিয়া ।
অন্তর্ধান কৈল প্রভু নিজগণ লঞা ॥ ১৯৬ ॥

eta bali' prerilā more hātasāni diyā
antardhāna kaila prabhu nija-gaṇa lañā

eta bali'—saying this; *prerilā*—dispatched; *more*—me; *hātasāni*—indication of the hand; *diyā*—giving; *antardhāna kaila*—disappeared; *prabhu*—my Lord; *nija-gaṇa lañā*—taking His personal associates.

TRANSLATION

After saying this, He directed me toward Vṛndāvana by waving His hand. Then He disappeared with His associates.

TEXT 197

মূর্চ্ছিত হইয়া মুঞি পড়িনু ভূমিতে ।
স্বপ্নভঙ্গ হৈল, দেখি, হঞাছে প্রভাতে ॥ ১৯৭ ॥

mūrcchita ha-iyā muñi paḍinu bhūmite
svapna-bhaṅga haila, dekhi, hañāche prabhāte

mūrcchita ha-iyā—fainting; *muñi*—I; *paḍinu*—fell; *bhūmite*—on the ground; *svapna-bhaṅga*—breaking of the dream; *haila*—there was; *dekhi*—I saw; *hañāche*—there was; *prabhāte*—morning light.

TRANSLATION

I fainted and fell to the ground, my dream broke, and when I regained consciousness I saw that morning had come.

TEXT 198

কি দেখিনু কি শুনিনু, করিয়ে বিচার ।
প্রভু-আজ্ঞা হৈল বৃন্দাবন যাইবার ॥ ১৯৮ ॥

ki dekhinu ki śuninu, kariye vicāra
prabhu-ājñā haila vṛndāvana yāibāra

ki dekhinu—what did I see; *ki śuninu*—what did I hear; *kariye vicāra*—I began to consider; *prabhu-ājñā*—the order of my Lord; *haila*—there was; *vṛndāvana*—to Vṛndāvana; *yāibāra*—to go.

TRANSLATION

I thought about what I had seen and heard and concluded that the Lord had ordered me to proceed to Vṛndāvana at once.

TEXT 199

সেইক্ষণে বৃন্দাবনে করিনু গমন ।
প্রভুর কৃপাতে সুখে আইনু বৃন্দাবন ॥ ১৯৯ ॥

sei kṣaṇe vṛndāvane karinu gamana
prabhura kṛpāte sukhe āinu vṛndāvana

sei kṣaṇe—that very second; *vṛndāvane*—toward Vṛndāvana; *karinu*—I did; *gamana*—starting; *prabhura kṛpāte*—by the mercy of Lord Nityānanda; *sukhe*—in great happiness; *āinu*—arrived; *vṛndāvana*—at Vṛndāvana.

TRANSLATION

That very second I started for Vṛndāvana, and by His mercy I reached there in great happiness.

TEXT 200

জয় জয় নিত্যানন্দ, নিত্যানন্দ-রাম ।
যাঁহার কৃপাতে পাইনু বৃন্দাবন-ধাম ॥ ২০০ ॥

jaya jaya nityānanda, nityānanda-rāma
yāṅhāra kṛpāte pāinu vṛndāvana-dhāma

jaya jaya—all glories; *nityānanda*—to Lord Nityānanda; *nityānanda-rāma*—to Lord Balarāma, who appeared as Nityānanda; *yāṅhāra kṛpāte*—by whose mercy; *pāinu*—I got; *vṛndāvana-dhāma*—shelter at Vṛndāvana.

TRANSLATION

All glory, all glory to Lord Nityānanda Balarāma, by whose mercy I have attained shelter in the transcendental abode of Vṛndāvana!

TEXT 201

জয় জয় নিত্যানন্দ, জয় কৃপাময় ।
যাঁহা হৈতে পাইনু রূপ-সনাতনাশ্রয় ॥ ২০১ ॥

jaya jaya nityānanda, jaya kṛpā-maya
yāṅhā haite pāinu rūpa-sanātanāśraya

jaya jaya—all glories; *nityānanda*—to Lord Nityānanda; *jaya kṛpā-maya*—all glories to the most merciful Lord; *yāṅhā haite*—from whom; *pāinu*—I got; *rūpa-sanātana-āśraya*—shelter at the lotus feet of Rūpa Gosvāmī and Sanātana Gosvāmī.

TRANSLATION

All glory, all glory to the merciful Lord Nityānanda, by whose mercy I have attained shelter at the lotus feet of Śrī Rūpa and Śrī Sanātana!

TEXT 202

যাঁহা হৈতে পাইনু রঘুনাথ-মহাশয় ।
যাঁহা হৈতে পাইনু শ্রীস্বরূপ-আশ্রয় ॥ ২০২ ॥

yāṅhā haite pāinu raghunātha-mahāśaya
yāṅhā haite pāinu śrī-svarūpa-āśraya

yāṅhā haite—from whom; *pāinu*—I got; *raghunātha-mahā-āśaya*—the shelter of Raghunātha dāsa Gosvāmī; *yāṅhā haite*—from whom; *pāinu*—I got; *śrī-svarūpa-āśraya*—shelter at the feet of Svarūpa Dāmodara Gosvāmī.

TRANSLATION

By His mercy I have attained the shelter of the great personality Śrī Raghunātha dāsa Gosvāmī, and by His mercy I have found the refuge of Śrī Svarūpa Dāmodara.

PURPORT

Anyone desiring to become expert in the service of Śrī Śrī Rādhā and Kṛṣṇa should always aspire to be under the guidance of Svarūpa Dāmodara Gosvāmī, Rūpa Gosvāmī, Sanātana Gosvāmī and Raghunātha dāsa Gosvāmī. To come under the protection of the Gosvāmīs, one must get the mercy and grace of Nityānanda Prabhu. The author has tried to explain this fact in these two verses.

TEXT 203

সনাতন-কৃপায় পাইনু ভক্তির সিদ্ধান্ত ।
শ্রীরূপ-কৃপায় পাইনু ভক্তিরসপ্রান্ত ॥ ২০৩ ॥

sanātana-kṛpāya pāinu bhaktira siddhānta
śrī-rūpa-kṛpāya pāinu bhakti-rasa-prānta

sanātana-kṛpāya—by the mercy of Sanātana Gosvāmī; *pāinu*—I got; *bhaktira siddhānta*—the conclusions of devotional service; *śrī-rūpa-*

kṛpāya—by the mercy of Śrīla Rūpa Gosvāmī; *pāinu*—I got; *bhakti-rasa-prānta*—the limit of the mellows of devotional service.

TRANSLATION

By the mercy of Sanātana Gosvāmī I have learned the final conclusions of devotional service, and by the grace of Śrī Rūpa Gosvāmī I have tasted the highest nectar of devotional service.

PURPORT

Śrī Sanātana Gosvāmī Prabhu, the teacher of the science of devotional service, wrote several books, of which the *Bṛhad-bhāgavatāmṛta* is very famous; anyone who wants to know about the subject matter of devotees, devotional service and Kṛṣṇa must read this book. Sanātana Gosvāmī also wrote a special commentary on the Tenth Canto of *Śrīmad-Bhāgavatam* known as the *Daśama-ṭippanī*, which is so excellent that by reading it one can understand very deeply the pastimes of Kṛṣṇa in His exchanges of loving activities. Another famous book by Sanātana Gosvāmī is the *Hari-bhakti-vilāsa*, which states the rules and regulations for all divisions of Vaiṣṇavas, namely, Vaiṣṇava householders, Vaiṣṇava *brahmacārīs*, Vaiṣṇava *vānaprasthas* and Vaiṣṇava *sannyāsīs*. This book was especially written, however, for Vaiṣṇava householders. Śrīla Raghunātha dāsa Gosvāmī has described Sanātana Gosvāmī in his prayer *Vilāpa-kusumāñjali*, verse six, where he has expressed his obligation to Sanātana Gosvāmī in the following words:

vairāgya-yug-bhakti-rasaṁ prayatnair
apāyayan mām anabhīpsum andham
kṛpāmbudhir yaḥ para-duḥkha-duḥkhī
sanātanas taṁ prabhum āśrayāmi

"I was unwilling to drink the nectar of devotional service possessed of renunciation, but Sanātana Gosvāmī, out of his causeless mercy, made me drink it, even though I was otherwise unable to do so. Therefore he is an ocean of mercy. He is very compassionate to fallen souls like me, and thus it is my duty to offer my respectful obeisances unto his lotus feet." Kṛṣṇadāsa Kavirāja Gosvāmī also, in the last section of the *Caitanya-caritāmṛta*, specifically mentions the names of Rūpa Gosvāmī, Sanātana Gosvāmī and Śrīla Jīva Gosvāmī and offers his respectful obeisances unto the lotus feet of these three spiritual masters, as well as Raghunātha dāsa. Śrīla Raghunātha dāsa Gosvāmī also accepted Sanātana Gosvāmī as the teacher of the science of devotional service. Śrīla Rūpa Gosvāmī is described as the *bhakti-rasācārya,* or one who knows the essence of devotional service. His famous book *Bhakti-rasāmṛta-sindhu* is the science of devotional service, and by reading this book one can understand the meaning of devotional service. Another of his famous books is the *Ujjvala-nīlamaṇi.* In this book he elaborately explains the loving affairs and transcendental activities of Lord Kṛṣṇa and Rādhārāṇī.

TEXT 204

জয় জয় নিত্যানন্দ-চরণারবিন্দ ।
যাঁহা হৈতে পাইনু শ্রীরাধাগোবিন্দ ॥ ২০৪ ॥

jaya jaya nityānanda-caraṇāravinda
yāṅhā haite pāinu śrī-rādhā-govinda

jaya jaya—all glories to; *nityānanda*—of Lord Nityānanda; *caraṇa-aravinda*—the lotus feet; *yāṅhā haite*—from whom; *pāinu*—I got; *śrī-rādhā-govinda*—the shelter of Śrī Rādhā and Govinda.

TRANSLATION

All glory, all glory to the lotus feet of Lord Nityānanda, by whose mercy I have attained Śrī Rādhā-Govinda!

PURPORT

Śrīla Narottama dāsa Ṭhākura, who is famous for his poetic composition known as *Prārthanā,* has lamented in one of his prayers, "When will Lord Nityānanda be merciful upon me so that I will forget all material desires?" Śrīla Narottama dāsa Ṭhākura confirms that unless one is freed from material desires to satisfy the needs of the body and senses, one cannot understand the transcendental abode of Lord Kṛṣṇa, Vṛndāvana. He also confirms that one cannot understand the loving affairs of Rādhā and Kṛṣṇa without going through the direction of the six Gosvāmīs. In another verse Narottama dāsa Ṭhākura has stated that without the causeless mercy of Nityānanda Prabhu, one cannot enter into the affairs of Rādhā and Kṛṣṇa.

TEXT 205

জগাই মাধাই হৈতে মুঞি সে পাপিষ্ঠ ।
পুরীষের কীট হৈতে মুঞি সে লঘিষ্ঠ ॥ ২০৫ ॥

jagāi mādhāi haite muñi se pāpiṣṭha
purīṣera kīṭa haite muñi se laghiṣṭha

jagāi mādhāi—the two brothers Jagāi and Mādhāi; *haite*—than; *muñi*—I; *se*—that; *pāpiṣṭha*—more sinful; *purīṣera*—in stool; *kīṭa*—the worms; *haite*—than; *muñi*—I am; *se*—that; *laghiṣṭha*—lower.

TRANSLATION

I am more sinful than Jagāi and Mādhāi and even lower than the worms in the stool.

TEXT 206

মোর নাম শুনে যেই তার পুণ্য ক্ষয় ।
মোর নাম লয় যেই তার পাপ হয় ॥ ২০৬ ॥

mora nāma śune yei tāra puṇya kṣaya
mora nāma laya yei tāra pāpa haya

mora nāma—my name; *śune*—hears; *yei*—anyone who; *tāra*—his; *puṇya kṣaya*—destruction of piety; *mora nāma*—my name; *laya*—takes; *yei*—anyone; *tāra*—his; *pāpa*—sin; *haya*—is.

TRANSLATION

Anyone who hears my name loses the results of his pious activities. Anyone who utters my name becomes sinful.

TEXT 207

এমন নির্ঘৃণ মোরে কেবা কৃপা করে ।
এক নিত্যানন্দ বিনু জগৎ ভিতরে ॥ ২০৭ ॥

emana nirghṛṇa more kebā kṛpā kare
eka nityānanda vinu jagat bhitare

emana—such; *nirghṛṇa*—abominable; *more*—unto me; *kebā*—who; *kṛpā*—mercy; *kare*—shows; *eka*—one; *nityānanda*—Lord Nityānanda; *vinu*—but; *jagat*—world; *bhitare*—within.

TRANSLATION

Who in this world but Nityānanda could show His mercy to such an abominable person as me?

TEXT 208

প্রেমে মত্ত নিত্যানন্দ কৃপা-অবতার ।
উত্তম, অধম, কিছু না করে বিচার ॥ ২০৮ ॥

preme matta nityānanda kṛpā-avatāra
uttama, adhama, kichu nā kare vicāra

preme—in ecstatic love; *matta*—mad; *nityānanda*—Lord Nityānanda; *kṛpā*—merciful; *avatāra*—incarnation; *uttama*—good; *adhama*—bad; *kichu*—any; *nā*—not; *kare*—makes; *vicāra*—consideration.

TRANSLATION

Because He is intoxicated by ecstatic love and is an incarnation of mercy, He does not distinguish between the good and the bad.

TEXT 209

যে আগে পড়য়ে, তারে করয়ে নিস্তার ।
অতএব নিস্তারিলা মো-হেন দুরাচার ॥ ২০৯ ॥

ye āge paḍaye, tāre karaye nistāra
ataeva nistārilā mo-hena durācāra

ye—whoever; *āge*—in front; *paḍaye*—falls down; *tāre*—unto him; *karaye*—does; *nistāra*—deliverance; *ataeva*—therefore; *nistārilā*—delivered; *mo*—as me; *hena*—such; *durācāra*—sinful and fallen person.

TRANSLATION

He delivers all those who fall down before Him. Therefore He has delivered such a sinful and fallen person as me.

TEXT 210

মো-পাপিষ্ঠে আনিলেন শ্রীবৃন্দাবন ।
মো-হেন অধমে দিলা শ্রীরূপ-চরণ ॥ ২১০ ॥

mo-pāpiṣṭhe ānilena śrī-vṛndāvana
mo-hena adhame dilā śrī-rūpa-caraṇa

mo-pāpiṣṭhe—unto me, who am so sinful; *ānilena*—He brought; *śrī-vṛndāvana*—to Vṛndāvana; *mo-hena*—such as me; *adhame*—to the lowest of mankind; *dilā*—delivered; *śrī-rūpa-caraṇa*—the lotus feet of Rūpa Gosvāmī.

TRANSLATION

Although I am sinful and I am the most fallen, He has conferred upon me the lotus feet of Śrī Rūpa Gosvāmī.

TEXT 211

শ্রীমদনগোপাল-শ্রীগোবিন্দ-দরশন ।
কহিবার যোগ্য নহে এসব কথন ॥ ২১১ ॥

śrī-madana-gopāla-śrī-govinda-daraśana
kahibāra yogya nahe e-saba kathana

śrī-madana-gopāla—Lord Madana Gopāla; *śrī-govinda*—Lord Rādhā-Govinda; *daraśana*—visiting; *kahibāra*—to speak; *yogya*—fit; *nahe*—not; *e-saba kathana*—all these confidential words.

TRANSLATION

I am not fit to speak all these confidential words about my visiting Lord Madana Gopāla and Lord Govinda.

TEXT 212

বৃন্দাবন-পুরন্দর শ্রীমদনগোপাল ।
রাসবিলাসী সাক্ষাৎ ব্রজেন্দ্রকুমার ॥ ২১২ ॥

vṛndāvana-purandara śrī-madana-gopāla
rāsa-vilāsī sākṣāt vrajendra-kumāra

vṛndāvana-purandara—the chief Deity of Vṛndāvana; *śrī-madana-gopāla*—Lord Madana Gopāla; *rāsa-vilāsī*—the enjoyer of the *rāsa* dance; *sākṣāt*—directly; *vrajendra-kumāra*—the son of Nanda Mahārāja.

TRANSLATION

Lord Madana Gopāla, the chief Deity of Vṛndāvana, is the enjoyer of the rāsa dance and is directly the son of the King of Vraja.

TEXT 213

শ্রীরাধা-ললিতা-সঙ্গে রাস-বিলাস ।
মন্মথ-মন্মথরূপে যাঁহার প্রকাশ ॥ ২১৩ ॥

śrī-rādhā-lalitā-saṅge rāsa-vilāsa
manmatha-manmatha-rūpe yāṅhāra prakāśa

śrī-rādhā—Śrīmatī Rādhārāṇī; *lalitā*—Her personal associate named Lalitā; *saṅge*—with; *rāsa-vilāsa*—enjoyment of the *rāsa* dance; *manmatha*—of Cupid; *manmatha-rūpe*—in the form of Cupid; *yāṅhāra*—of whom; *prakāśa*—manifestation.

TRANSLATION

He enjoys the rāsa dance with Śrīmatī Rādhārāṇī, Śrī Lalitā and others. He manifests Himself as the Cupid of Cupids.

TEXT 214

তাসামাবিরভূচ্ছৌরিঃ স্ময়মানমুখাম্বুজঃ ।
পীতাম্বরধরঃ স্রগ্বী সাক্ষান্মন্মথমন্মথঃ ॥ ২১৪ ॥

tāsām āvirabhūc chauriḥ
smayamāna-mukhāmbujaḥ
pītāmbara-dharaḥ sragvī
sākṣān manmatha-manmathaḥ

tāsām—among them; *āvirabhūt*—appeared; *śauriḥ*—Lord Kṛṣṇa; *smayamāna*—smiling; *mukha-ambujaḥ*—lotus face; *pīta-ambara-dharaḥ*—dressed with yellow garments; *sragvī*—decorated with a flower garland; *sākṣāt*—directly; *manmatha*—of Cupid; *manmathaḥ*—Cupid.

TRANSLATION

"Wearing yellow garments and decorated with a flower garland, Lord Kṛṣṇa, appearing among the gopīs with His smiling lotus face, looked directly like the charmer of the heart of Cupid."

PURPORT

This is a quotation from *Śrīmad-Bhāgavatam* (10.32.2).

TEXT 215

স্বমাধুর্যে লোকের মন করে আকর্ষণ ।
দুই পাশে রাধা ললিতা করেন সেবন ॥ ২১৫ ॥

sva-mādhurye lokera mana kare ākarṣaṇa
dui pāśe rādhā lalitā karena sevana

sva-mādhurye—in His own sweetness; *lokera*—of all people; *mana*—the minds; *kare*—does; *ākarṣaṇa*—attracting; *dui pāśe*—on two sides; *rādhā*—Śrīmatī Rādhārāṇī; *lalitā*—and Her associate Lalitā; *karena*—do; *sevana*—service.

TRANSLATION

With Rādhā and Lalitā serving Him on His two sides, He attracts the hearts of all by His own sweetness.

TEXT 216

নিত্যানন্দ-দয়া মোরে তাঁরে দেখাইল ।
শ্রীরাধা-মদনমোহনে প্রভু করি' দিল ॥২১৬ ॥

nityānanda-dayā more tāṅre dekhāila
śrī-rādhā-madana-mohane prabhu kari' dila

nityānanda-dayā—the mercy of Lord Nityānanda; *more*—unto me; *tāṅre*—Madana-mohana; *dekhāila*—showed; *śrī-rādhā-madana-mohane*—Rādhā-Madana-mohana; *prabhu kari' dila*—gave as my Lord and master.

TRANSLATION

The mercy of Lord Nityānanda showed me Śrī Madana-mohana and gave me Śrī Madana-mohana as my Lord and master.

TEXT 217

মো-অধমে দিল শ্রীগোবিন্দ দরশন ।
কহিবার কথা নহে অকথ্য-কথন ॥ ২১৭ ॥

mo-adhame dila śrī-govinda daraśana
kahibāra kathā nahe akathya-kathana

mo-adhame—to one as abominable as me; *dila*—delivered; *śrī-govinda daraśana*—the audience of Lord Śrī Govinda; *kahibāra*—to speak this; *kathā*—words; *nahe*—there are not; *akathya*—unspeakable; *kathana*—narration.

TRANSLATION

He granted to one as low as me the sight of Lord Govinda. Words cannot describe this, nor is it fit to be disclosed.

TEXTS 218–219

বৃন্দাবনে যোগপীঠে কল্পতরু বনে ।
রত্নমণ্ডপ, তাহে রত্নসিংহাসনে ॥ ২১৮ ॥
শ্রীগোবিন্দ বসিয়াছেন ব্রজেন্দ্রনন্দন ।
মাধুর্য প্রকাশি' করেন জগৎ মোহন ॥ ২১৯ ॥

vṛndāvane yoga-pīṭhe kalpa-taru-vane
ratna-maṇḍapa, tāhe ratna-siṁhāsane

śrī-govinda vasiyāchena vrajendra-nandana
mādhurya prakāśi' karena jagat mohana

vṛndāvane—at Vṛndāvana; *yoga-pīṭhe*—at the principal temple; *kalpa-taru-vane*—in the forest of desire trees; *ratna-maṇḍapa*—an altar made of gems; *tāhe*—upon it; *ratna-siṁha-āsane*—on the throne of gems; *śrī-govinda*—Lord Govinda; *vasiyāchena*—was sitting; *vrajendra-nandana*—the son of Nanda Mahārāja; *mādhurya prakāśi'*—manifesting His sweetness; *karena*—does; *jagat mohana*—enchantment of the whole world.

TRANSLATION

On an altar made of gems in the principal temple of Vṛndāvana, amidst a forest of desire trees, Lord Govinda, the son of the King of Vraja, sits upon a throne of gems and manifests His full glory and sweetness, thus enchanting the entire world.

TEXT 220

বাম-পার্শ্বে শ্রীরাধিকা সখীগণ-সঙ্গে ।
রাসাদিক-লীলা প্রভু করে কত রঙ্গে ॥ ২২০ ॥

vāma-pārśve śrī-rādhikā sakhī-gaṇa-saṅge
rāsādika-līlā prabhu kare kata raṅge

vāma-pārśve—on the left side; *śrī-rādhikā*—Śrīmatī Rādhārāṇī; *sakhī-gaṇa-saṅge*—with Her personal friends; *rāsa-ādika-līlā*—pastimes like the *rāsa* dance; *prabhu*—Lord Kṛṣṇa; *kare*—performs; *kata raṅge*—in many ways.

TRANSLATION

By His left side is Śrīmatī Rādhārāṇī and Her personal friends. With them Lord Govinda enjoys the rāsa-līlā and many other pastimes.

TEXT 221

যাঁর ধ্যান নিজ-লোকে করে পদ্মাসন ।
অষ্টাদশাক্ষর-মন্ত্রে করে উপাসন ॥ ২২১ ॥

yāṅra dhyāna nija-loke kare padmāsana
aṣṭādaśākṣara-mantre kare upāsana

yāṅra—of whom; *dhyāna*—the meditation; *nija-loke*—in his own abode; *kare*—does; *padma-āsana*—Lord Brahmā; *aṣṭādaśa-akṣara-mantre*—by the hymn composed of eighteen letters; *kare*—does; *upāsana*—worshiping.

TRANSLATION

Lord Brahmā, sitting on his lotus seat in his own abode, always meditates on Him and worships Him with the mantra consisting of eighteen syllables.

PURPORT

In his own planet, Lord Brahmā, with the inhabitants of that planet, worships the form of Lord Govinda, Kṛṣṇa, by the *mantra* of eighteen syllables, *klīṁ kṛṣṇāya govindāya gopī-jana-vallabhāya svāhā.* Those who are initiated by a bona fide spiritual master and who chant the Gāyatrī *mantra* three times a day know this *aṣṭādaśākṣara* (eighteen-syllable) *mantra.* The inhabitants of Brahmaloka and the planets below Brahmaloka worship Lord Govinda by meditating with this *mantra.*

There is no difference between meditating and chanting, but in the present age meditation is not possible on this planet. Therefore loud chanting of a *mantra* like the *mahā-mantra*, Hare Kṛṣṇa, with soft chanting of the *aṣṭādaśākṣara*, the *mantra* of eighteen syllables, is recommended.

Lord Brahmā lives in the highest planetary system, known as Brahmaloka or Satyaloka. In every planet there is a predominating deity. As the predominating deity in Satyaloka is Lord Brahmā, so in the heavenly planets Indra is the predominating deity, and on the sun, the sun-god, Vivasvān, is the predominating deity. The inhabitants and predominating deities of every planet are all recommended to worship Govinda either by meditation or by chanting.

TEXT 222

চৌদ্দভুবনে যাঁর সবে করে ধ্যান।
বৈকুণ্ঠাদি-পুরে যাঁর লীলাগুণ গান ॥ ২২২ ॥

caudda-bhuvane yāṅra sabe kare dhyāna
vaikuṇṭhādi-pure yāṅra līlā-guṇa gāna

caudda-bhuvane—within the fourteen worlds; *yāṅra*—of whom; *sabe*—all; *kare dhyāna*—perform meditation; *vaikuṇṭha-ādi-pure*—in the abodes of the Vaikuṇṭha planets; *yāṅra*—of whom; *līlā-guṇa*—attributes and pastimes; *gāna*—chanting.

TRANSLATION

Everyone in the fourteen worlds meditates upon Him, and all the denizens of Vaikuṇṭha sing of His qualities and pastimes.

TEXT 223

যাঁর মাধুরীতে করে লক্ষ্মী আকর্ষণ।
রূপগোসাঞি করিয়াছেন সে-রূপ বর্ণন ॥ ২২৩ ॥

yāṅra mādhurīte kare lakṣmī ākarṣaṇa
rūpa-gosāñi kariyāchena se-rūpa varṇana

yāṅra—of whom; *mādhurīte*—by the sweetness; *kare*—does; *lakṣmī*—the goddess of fortune; *ākarṣaṇa*—attraction; *rūpa-gosāñi*—Śrīla Rūpa Gosvāmī; *kariyāchena*—has done; *se*—that; *rūpa*—of the beauty; *varṇana*—enunciation.

TRANSLATION

The goddess of fortune is attracted by His sweetness, which Śrīla Rūpa Gosvāmī has described in this way:

PURPORT

Śrīla Rūpa Gosvāmī, in his *Laghu-bhāgavatāmṛta*, has quoted from the *Padma Purāṇa*, where it is stated that Lakṣmī-devī, the goddess of fortune, after seeing the attractive features of Lord Kṛṣṇa, was attracted to Him, and to get the favor of Lord Kṛṣṇa she engaged herself in meditation. When asked by Kṛṣṇa why she engaged in meditation with austerity, Lakṣmī-devī answered, "I want to be one of Your associates like the *gopīs* in Vṛndāvana." Hearing this, Lord Śrī Kṛṣṇa replied that it was quite impossible. Lakṣmī-devī then said that she wanted to remain just like a golden line on the chest of the Lord. The Lord granted the request, and since then Lakṣmī has always been situated on the chest of Lord Kṛṣṇa as a golden line. The austerity and meditation of Lakṣmī-devī are also mentioned in *Śrīmad-Bhāgavatam* (10.16.36), where the Nāga-patnīs, the wives of the serpent Kāliya, in the course of their prayers to Kṛṣṇa, said that the goddess of fortune, Lakṣmī, also wanted His association as a *gopī* and desired the dust of His lotus feet.

TEXT 224

স্মেরাং ভঙ্গীত্রয়পরিচিতাং সাচিবিস্তীর্ণদৃষ্টিং
বংশীন্যস্তাধরকিশলয়ামুজ্জ্বলাং চন্দ্রকেণ ।
গোবিন্দাখ্যাং হরিতনুমিতঃ কেশিতীর্থোপকণ্ঠে
মা প্রেক্ষিষ্ঠাস্তব যদি সখে বন্ধুসঙ্গেঽস্তি রঙ্গঃ ॥ ২২৪ ॥

smerāṁ bhaṅgī-traya-paricitāṁ sāci-vistīrṇa-dṛṣṭiṁ
vaṁśī-nyastādhara-kiśalayām ujjvalāṁ candrakeṇa
govindākhyāṁ hari-tanum itaḥ keśi-tīrthopakaṇṭhe
mā prekṣiṣṭhās tava yadi sakhe bandhu-saṅge 'sti raṅgaḥ

smerām—smiling; *bhaṅgī-traya-paricitām*—bent in three places, namely the neck, waist and knees; *sāci-vistīrṇa-dṛṣṭim*—with a broad sideways glance; *vaṁśī*—on the flute; *nyasta*—placed; *adhara*—lips; *kiśalayām*—newly blossomed; *ujjvalām*—very bright; *candrakeṇa*—by the moonshine; *govinda-ākhyām*—named Lord Govinda; *hari-tanum*—the transcendental body of the Lord; *itaḥ*—here; *keśi-tīrtha-upakaṇṭhe*—on the bank of the Yamunā in the neighborhood of

Keśīghāṭa; *mā*—do not; *prekṣiṣṭhāḥ*—glance over; *tava*—your; *yadi*—if; *sakhe*—O dear friend; *bandhu-saṅge*—to worldly friends; *asti*—there is; *raṅgaḥ*—attachment.

TRANSLATION

"My dear friend, if you are indeed attached to your worldly friends, do not look at the smiling face of Lord Govinda as He stands on the bank of the Yamunā at Keśīghāṭa. Casting sidelong glances, He places His flute to His lips, which seem like newly blossomed twigs. His transcendental body, bending in three places, appears very bright in the moonlight."

PURPORT

This is a verse quoted from the *Bhakti-rasāmṛta-sindhu* (1.2.239) in connection with practical devotional service. Generally people in their conditioned life engage in the pleasure of society, friendship and love. This so-called love is lust, not love. But people are satisfied with such a false understanding of love. Vidyāpati, a great and learned poet of Mithilā, has said that the pleasure derived from friendship, society and family life in the material world is like a drop of water, but our hearts desire pleasure like an ocean. Thus the heart is compared to a desert of material existence that requires the water of an ocean of pleasure to satisfy its dryness. If there is a drop of water in the desert, one may indeed say that it is water, but such a minute quantity of water has no value. Similarly, in this material world no one is satisfied in the dealings of society, friendship and love. Therefore if one wants to derive real pleasure within his heart, he must seek the lotus feet of Govinda. In this verse Rūpa Gosvāmī indicates that if one wants to be satisfied in the pleasure of society, friendship and love, he need not seek shelter at the lotus feet of Govinda, for if one takes shelter under His lotus feet he will forget that minute quantity of so-called pleasure. One who is not satisfied with that so-called pleasure may seek the lotus feet of Govinda, who stands on the shore of the Yamunā at Keśītīrtha, or Keśīghāṭa, in Vṛndāvana and attracts all the *gopīs* to His transcendental loving service.

TEXT 225

সাক্ষাৎ ব্রজেন্দ্রসুত ইথে নাহি আন।
যেবা অজ্ঞে করে তাঁরে প্রতিমা-হেন জ্ঞান ॥ ২২৫ ॥

sākṣāt vrajendra-suta ithe nāhi āna
yebā ajñe kare tāṅre pratimā-hena jñāna

sākṣāt—directly; *vrajendra-suta*—the son of Nanda Mahārāja; *ithe*—in this matter; *nāhi*—there is not; *āna*—any exception; *yebā*—whatever; *ajñe*—a foolish person; *kare*—does; *tāṅre*—unto Him; *pratimā-hena*—as a statue; *jñāna*—such a consideration.

TRANSLATION

Without a doubt He is directly the son of the King of Vraja. Only a fool considers Him a statue.

TEXT 226

সেই অপরাধে তার নাহিক নিস্তার ।
ঘোর নরকেতে পড়ে, কি বলিব আর ॥ ২২৬ ॥

sei aparādhe tāra nāhika nistāra
ghora narakete paḍe, ki baliba āra

sei aparādhe—by that offense; *tāra*—his; *nāhika*—there is not; *nistāra*—deliverance; *ghora*—terrible; *narakete*—in a hellish condition; *paḍe*—falls down; *ki baliba*—what will I say; *āra*—more.

TRANSLATION

For that offense, he cannot be liberated. Rather, he will fall into a terrible hellish condition. What more should I say?

PURPORT

In his *Bhakti-sandarbha* Jīva Gosvāmī has stated that those who are actually very serious about devotional service do not differentiate between the form of the Lord made of clay, metal, stone or wood and the original form of the Lord. In the material world a person and his photograph, picture or statue are different. But the statue of Lord Kṛṣṇa and Kṛṣṇa Himself, the Supreme Personality of Godhead, are not different, because the Lord is absolute. What we call stone, wood and metal are energies of the Supreme Lord, and energies are never separate from the energetic. As we have several times explained, no one can separate the sunshine energy from the energetic sun. Therefore material energy may appear separate from the Lord, but transcendentally it is nondifferent from the Lord.

The Lord can appear anywhere and everywhere because His diverse energies are distributed everywhere like sunshine. We should therefore understand whatever we see to be the energy of the Supreme Lord and should not differentiate between the Lord and His *arcā* form made from clay, metal, wood or paint. Even if one has not developed this consciousness, one should accept it theoretically from the instructions of the spiritual master and should worship the *arcā-mūrti,* or form of the Lord in the temple, as nondifferent from the Lord.

The *Padma Purāṇa* specifically mentions that anyone who thinks the form of the Lord in the temple to be made of wood, stone or metal is certainly in a hellish condition. Impersonalists are against the worship of the Lord's form in the temple, and there is even a group of people who pass as Hindus but condemn such worship. Their so-called acceptance of the *Vedas* has no meaning, for all the *ācāryas,* even the impersonalist Śaṅkarācārya, have recommended the worship of the transcendental form of the Lord. Impersonalists like Śaṅkarācārya recommend the worship of five forms, known as *pañcopāsanā,* which include Lord Viṣṇu. Vaiṣṇavas, however, worship the forms of Lord Viṣṇu in His varied manifestations, such as Rādhā-Kṛṣṇa, Lakṣmī-Nārāyaṇa, Sītā-Rāma and Rukmiṇī-Kṛṣṇa. Māyāvādīs admit that worship of the Lord's form is required in the beginning, but they think that in the end everything is impersonal. Therefore, since they are ultimately against worship of the Lord's form, Lord Śrī Caitanya Mahāprabhu has described them as offenders.

Śrīmad-Bhāgavatam has condemned those who think the body to be the self as *bhauma ijya-dhīḥ. Bhauma* means earth, and *ijya-dhīḥ* means worshiper. There are two kinds of *bhauma ijya-dhīḥ:* those who worship the land of their birth, such as nationalists, who make many sacrifices for the motherland, and those who condemn the worship of the form of the Lord. One should not worship the planet earth or land of his birth, nor should one condemn the form of the Lord, which is manifested in metal or wood for our facility. Material things are also the energy of the Supreme Lord.

TEXT 227

হেন যে গোবিন্দ প্রভু, পাইনু যাঁহা হৈতে ।
তাঁহার চরণ-কৃপা কে পারে বর্ণিতে ॥ ২২৭ ॥

hena ye govinda prabhu, pāinu yāṅhā haite
tāṅhāra caraṇa-kṛpā ke pāre varṇite

hena—thus; *ye govinda*—this Lord Govinda; *prabhu*—master; *pāinu*—I got; *yāṅhā haite*—from whom; *tāṅhāra*—His; *caraṇa-kṛpā*—mercy of the lotus feet; *ke*—who; *pāre*—is able; *varṇite*—to describe.

TRANSLATION

Therefore who can describe the mercy of the lotus feet of Him [Lord Nityānanda] by whom I have attained the shelter of this Lord Govinda?

TEXT 228

বৃন্দাবনে বৈসে যত বৈষ্ণব-মণ্ডল ।
কৃষ্ণনাম-পরায়ণ, পরম-মঙ্গল ॥ ২২৮ ॥

vṛndāvane vaise yata vaiṣṇava-maṇḍala
kṛṣṇa-nāma-parāyaṇa, parama-maṅgala

vṛndāvane—in Vṛndāvana; *vaise*—there are; *yata*—all; *vaiṣṇava-maṇḍala*—groups of devotees; *kṛṣṇa-nāma-parāyaṇa*—addicted to the name of Lord Kṛṣṇa; *parama-maṅgala*—all-auspicious.

TRANSLATION

All the groups of Vaiṣṇavas who live in Vṛndāvana are absorbed in chanting the all-auspicious name of Kṛṣṇa.

TEXT 229

যাঁর প্রাণধন—নিত্যানন্দ-শ্রীচৈতন্য ।
রাধাকৃষ্ণ-ভক্তি বিনে নাহি জানে অন্য ॥ ২২৯ ॥

yāṅra prāṇa-dhana—nityānanda-śrī-caitanya
rādhā-kṛṣṇa-bhakti vine nāhi jāne anya

yāṅra—whose; *prāṇa-dhana*—life and soul; *nityānanda-śrī-caitanya*—Lord Nityānanda and Śrī Caitanya Mahāprabhu; *rādhā-kṛṣṇa*—to Kṛṣṇa and Rādhārāṇī; *bhakti*—devotional service; *vine*—except; *nāhi jāne anya*—do not know anything else.

TRANSLATION

Lord Caitanya and Lord Nityānanda are the life and soul of those Vaiṣṇavas, who do not know anything but devotional service to Śrī Śrī Rādhā-Kṛṣṇa.

TEXT 230

সে বৈষ্ণবের পদরেণু, তার পদছায়া ।
অধমেরে দিল প্রভু-নিত্যানন্দ-দয়া ॥ ২৩০ ॥

se vaiṣṇavera pada-reṇu, tāra pada-chāyā
adhamere dila prabhu-nityānanda-dayā

se vaiṣṇavera—of all those Vaiṣṇavas; *pada-reṇu*—the dust of the feet; *tāra*—their; *pada-chāyā*—the shade of the feet; *adhamere*—unto this fallen soul; *dila*—gave; *prabhu-nityānanda-dayā*—the mercy of Lord Nityānanda Prabhu.

TRANSLATION

The dust and shade of the lotus feet of the Vaiṣṇavas have been granted to this fallen soul by the mercy of Lord Nityānanda.

TEXT 231

'তাঁহা সর্ব লভ্য হয়'—প্রভুর বচন ।
সেই সূত্র—এই তার কৈল বিবরণ ॥ ২৩১ ॥

'tāṅhā sarva labhya haya'—prabhura vacana
sei sūtra—ei tāra kaila vivaraṇa

tāṅhā—at that place; *sarva*—everything; *labhya*—obtainable; *haya*—is; *prabhura*—of the Lord; *vacana*—the word; *sei sūtra*—that synopsis; *ei*—this; *tāra*—His; *kaila vivaraṇa*—has been described.

TRANSLATION

Lord Nityānanda said, "In Vṛndāvana all things are possible." Here I have explained His brief statement in detail.

TEXT 232

সে সব পাইনু আমি বৃন্দাবনে আয় ।
সেই সব লভ্য এই প্রভুর কৃপায় ॥ ২৩২ ॥

se saba pāinu āmi vṛndāvane āya
sei saba labhya ei prabhura kṛpāya

se saba—all this; *pāinu*—got; *āmi*—I; *vṛndāvane*—to Vṛndāvana; *āya*—coming; *sei saba*—all this; *labhya*—obtainable; *ei*—this; *prabhura kṛpāya*—by the mercy of Lord Nityānanda.

TRANSLATION

I have attained all this by coming to Vṛndāvana, and this was made possible by the mercy of Lord Nityānanda.

PURPORT

All the inhabitants of Vṛndāvana are Vaiṣṇavas. They are all-auspicious because somehow or other they always chant the holy name of Kṛṣṇa. Even though some of them do not strictly follow the rules and regulations of devotional service, on the whole they are devotees of Kṛṣṇa and chant His name directly or indirectly. Purposely or without purpose, even when they pass on the street they are fortunate enough to exchange greetings by saying the name of Rādhā or Kṛṣṇa. Thus directly or indirectly they are auspicious.

The present city of Vṛndāvana has been established by the Gauḍīya Vaiṣṇavas since the six Gosvāmīs went there and directed the construction of their different temples. Of all the temples in Vṛndāvana, ninety percent belong to the Gauḍīya Vaiṣṇava sect, the followers of the teachings of Lord Caitanya Mahāprabhu and Nityānanda, and seven temples are very famous. The inhabitants of Vṛndāvana do not know anything but the worship of Rādhā and Kṛṣṇa. In recent years some unscrupulous so-called priests known as caste *gosvāmīs* have introduced the worship of demigods privately, but no genuine and rigid Vaiṣṇavas participate in this. Those who are serious about the Vaiṣṇava method of devotional activities do not take part in such worship of demigods.

The Gauḍīya Vaiṣṇavas never differentiate between Rādhā-Kṛṣṇa and Lord Caitanya. They say that since Lord Caitanya is the combined form of Rādhā-Kṛṣṇa, He is not different from Rādhā and Kṛṣṇa. But some misled people try to prove that they are greatly elevated by saying that they like to chant the holy name of Lord Gaura instead of the names of Rādhā and Kṛṣṇa. Thus they purposely differentiate between Lord Caitanya and Rādhā-Kṛṣṇa. According to them, the system of *nadīyā-nāgarī*, which they have recently invented in their fertile brains, is the worship of Gaura, Lord Caitanya, but they do not like to worship Rādhā and Kṛṣṇa. They put forward the argument that since Lord Caitanya Himself appeared as Rādhā and Kṛṣṇa combined, there is no necessity of worshiping Rādhā and Kṛṣṇa. Such differentiation by so-called devotees of Lord Caitanya Mahāprabhu is considered disruptive by pure devotees. Anyone who differentiates between Rādhā-Kṛṣṇa and Gaurāṅga is to be considered a plaything in the hands of *māyā*.

There are others who are against the worship of Caitanya Mahāprabhu, thinking Him mundane. But any sect that differentiates between Lord Caitanya Mahāprabhu and Rādhā-Kṛṣṇa, either by worshiping Rādhā-Kṛṣṇa as distinct from Lord Caitanya or by worshiping Lord Caitanya but not Rādhā-Kṛṣṇa, is in the group of *prākṛta-sahajiyās*.

Śrīla Kṛṣṇadāsa Kavirāja Gosvāmī, the author of *Śrī Caitanya-caritāmṛta*, predicts in verses 225 and 226 that in the future those who manufacture imaginary methods of worship will gradually give up the worship of Rādhā-Kṛṣṇa, and although they will call themselves devotees of Lord Caitanya, they will also give up the worship of Caitanya Mahāprabhu and fall down into material activities. For the real worshipers of Lord Caitanya, the ultimate goal of life is to worship Śrī Śrī Rādhā and Kṛṣṇa.

TEXT 233

আপনার কথা লিখি নির্লজ্জ হইয়া ।
নিত্যানন্দগুণে লেখায় উন্মত্ত করিয়া ॥ ২৩৩ ॥

āpanāra kathā likhi nirlajja ha-iyā
nityānanda-guṇe lekhāya unmatta kariyā

āpanāra—personal; *kathā*—description; *likhi*—I write; *nirlajja ha-iyā*—being shameless; *nityānanda-guṇe*—the attributes of Nityānanda; *lekhāya*—cause to write; *unmatta kariyā*—making like a madman.

TRANSLATION

I have described my own story without reservations. The attributes of Lord Nityānanda, making me like a madman, force me to write these things.

TEXT 234

নিত্যানন্দ-প্রভুর গুণ-মহিমা অপার ।
'সহস্রবদনে' শেষ নাহি পায় যাঁর ॥ ২৩৪ ॥

nityānanda-prabhura guṇa-mahimā apāra
'sahasra-vadane' śeṣa nāhi pāya yāṅra

nityānanda-prabhura—of Lord Nityānanda; *guṇa-mahimā*—glories of transcendental attributes; *apāra*—unfathomable; *sahasra-vadane*—in thousands of mouths; *śeṣa*—ultimate end; *nāhi*—does not; *pāya*—get; *yāṅra*—whose.

TRANSLATION

The glories of Lord Nityānanda's transcendental attributes are unfathomable. Even Lord Śeṣa, with His thousands of mouths, cannot find their limit.

TEXT 235

শ্রীরূপ-রঘুনাথ-পদে যার আশ ।
চৈতন্যচরিতামৃত কহে কৃষ্ণদাস ॥ ২৩৫ ॥

śrī-rūpa-raghunātha-pade yāra āśa
caitanya-caritāmṛta kahe kṛṣṇadāsa

śrī-rūpa—Śrīla Rūpa Gosvāmī; *raghunātha*—Śrīla Raghunātha dāsa Gosvāmī; *pade*—at the lotus feet; *yāra*—whose; *āśa*—expectation; *caitanya-caritāmṛta*—the book named *Caitanya-caritāmṛta; kahe*—describes; *kṛṣṇa-dāsa*—Śrīla Kṛṣṇadāsa Kavirāja Gosvāmī.

TRANSLATION

Praying at the lotus feet of Śrī Rūpa and Śrī Raghunātha, always desiring their mercy, I, Kṛṣṇadāsa, narrate Śrī Caitanya-caritāmṛta, following in their footsteps.

Thus end the Bhaktivedanta purports to Śrī Caitanya-caritāmṛta, Ādi-līlā, *Fifth Chapter, describing the glories of Lord Nityānanda Balarāma.*

CHAPTER SIX

The Glories of Śrī Advaita Ācārya

The truth of Advaita Ācārya has been described in two verses. It is said that material nature has two features, namely the material cause and the efficient cause. The efficient causal activities are caused by Mahā-Viṣṇu, and the material causal activities are caused by another form of Mahā-Viṣṇu, known as Advaita. That Advaita, the superintendent of the cosmic manifestation, has descended in the form of Advaita Ācārya to associate with Lord Caitanya. When He is addressed as the servitor of Lord Caitanya, His glories are magnified because unless one is invigorated by this mentality of servitorship one cannot understand the mellows derived from devotional service to the Supreme Lord, Kṛṣṇa.

TEXT 1

বন্দে তং শ্রীমদদ্বৈতাচার্যমদ্ভুতচেষ্টিতম্ ।
যস্য প্রসাদাদজ্ঞোঽপি তৎস্বরূপং নিরূপয়েৎ ॥ ১ ॥

vande taṁ śrīmad-advaitā-
cāryam adbhuta-ceṣṭitam
yasya prasādād ajño 'pi
tat-svarūpaṁ nirūpayet

vande—I offer my respectful obeisances; *tam*—unto Him; *śrīmat*—with all opulences; *advaita-ācāryam*—Śrī Advaita Ācārya; *adbhuta-ceṣṭitam*—whose activities are wonderful; *yasya*—of whom; *prasādāt*—by the mercy; *ajñaḥ api*—even a foolish person; *tat-svarūpam*—His characteristics; *nirūpayet*—may describe.

TRANSLATION

I offer my respectful obeisances to Śrī Advaita Ācārya, whose activities are all wonderful. By His mercy, even a foolish person can describe His characteristics.

TEXT 2

জয় জয় শ্রীচৈতন্য জয় নিত্যানন্দ ।
জয়াদ্বৈতচন্দ্র জয় গৌরভক্তবৃন্দ ॥ ২ ॥

jaya jaya śrī-caitanya jaya nityānanda
jayādvaita-candra jaya gaura-bhakta-vṛnda

jaya jaya—all glories; *śrī-caitanya*—to Lord Śrī Caitanya Mahāprabhu; *jaya*—all glories; *nityānanda*—to Lord Nityānanda; *jaya advaita-candra*—all glories to Advaita Ācārya; *jaya gaura-bhakta-vṛnda*—all glories to the devotees of Śrī Caitanya Mahāprabhu.

TRANSLATION

All glories to Lord Śrī Caitanya Mahāprabhu! All glories to Lord Nityānanda! All glories to Advaita Ācārya! And all glories to all the devotees of Lord Śrī Caitanya Mahāprabhu!

TEXT 3

পঞ্চ শ্লোকে কহিল শ্রীনিত্যানন্দ-তত্ত্ব ।
শ্লোকদ্বয়ে কহি অদ্বৈতাচার্যের মহত্ত্ব ॥ ৩ ॥

pañca śloke kahila śrī-nityānanda-tattva
śloka-dvaye kahi advaitācāryera mahattva

pañca śloke—in five verses; *kahila*—described; *śrī-nityānanda-tattva*—the truth of Śrī Nityānanda; *śloka-dvaye*—in two verses; *kahi*—I describe; *advaita-ācāryera*—of Advaita Ācārya; *mahattva*—the glories.

TRANSLATION

In five verses I have described the principle of Lord Nityānanda. Then in the following two verses I describe the glories of Śrī Advaita Ācārya.

TEXT 4

মহাবিষ্ণুর্জগৎকর্তা মায়য়া যঃ সৃজত্যদঃ ।
তস্যাবতার এবায়মদ্বৈতাচার্য ঈশ্বরঃ ॥ ৪ ॥

mahā-viṣṇur jagat-kartā
māyayā yaḥ sṛjaty adaḥ
tasyāvatāra evāyam
advaitācārya īśvaraḥ

mahā-viṣṇuḥ—Mahā-Viṣṇu, the resting place of the efficient cause; *jagat-kartā*—the creator of the cosmic world; *māyayā*—by the illusory energy; *yaḥ*—who; *sṛjati*—creates; *adaḥ*—that universe; *tasya*—His; *avatāraḥ*—incarnation; *eva*—certainly; *ayam*—this; *advaita-ācāryaḥ*—Advaita Ācārya; *īśvaraḥ*—the Supreme Lord, the resting place of the material cause.

TRANSLATION

Lord Advaita Ācārya is the incarnation of Mahā-Viṣṇu, whose main function is to create the cosmic world through the actions of māyā.

TEXT 5

অদ্বৈতং হরিণাদ্বৈতাদাচার্যং ভক্তিশংসনাৎ ।
ভক্তাবতারমীশং তমদ্বৈতাচার্যমাশ্রয়ে ॥ ৫ ॥

advaitaṁ hariṇādvaitād
ācāryaṁ bhakti-śaṁsanāt
bhaktāvatāram īśaṁ tam
advaitācāryam āśraye

advaitam—known as Advaita; *hariṇā*—with Lord Hari; *advaitāt*—from being nondifferent; *ācāryam*—known as Ācārya; *bhakti-śaṁsanāt*—from the propagation of devotional service to Śrī Kṛṣṇa; *bhakta-avatāram*—the incarnation as a devotee; *īśam*—to the Supreme Lord; *tam*—to Him; *advaita-ācāryam*—to Advaita Ācārya; *āśraye*—I surrender.

TRANSLATION

Because He is nondifferent from Hari, the Supreme Lord, He is called Advaita, and because He propagates the cult of devotion, He is called Ācārya. He is the Lord and the incarnation of the Lord's devotee. Therefore I take shelter of Him.

TEXT 6

অদ্বৈত-আচার্য গোসাঞি সাক্ষাৎ ঈশ্বর ।
যাঁহার মহিমা নহে জীবের গোচর ॥ ৬ ॥

advaita-ācārya gosāñi sākṣāt īśvara
yāṅhāra mahimā nahe jīvera gocara

advaita-ācārya—Advaita Ācārya; *gosāñi*—the Lord; *sākṣāt īśvara*—directly the Supreme Personality of Godhead; *yāṅhāra mahimā*—whose glories; *nahe*—not; *jīvera gocara*—within the reach of the understanding of ordinary living beings.

TRANSLATION

Śrī Advaita Ācārya is indeed directly the Supreme Personality of Godhead Himself. His glory is beyond the conception of ordinary living beings.

TEXT 7

মহাবিষ্ণু সৃষ্টি করেন জগদাদি কার্য ।
তাঁর অবতার সাক্ষাৎ অদ্বৈত আচার্য ॥ ৭ ॥

mahā-viṣṇu sṛṣṭi karena jagad-ādi kārya
tāṅra avatāra sākṣāt advaita ācārya

mahā-viṣṇu—the original Viṣṇu; *sṛṣṭi*—creation; *karena*—does; *jagat-ādi*—the material world; *kārya*—the occupation; *tāṅra*—His; *avatāra*—incarnation; *sākṣāt*—directly; *advaita ācārya*—Prabhu Advaita Ācārya.

TRANSLATION

Mahā-Viṣṇu performs all the functions for the creation of the universes. Śrī Advaita Ācārya is His direct incarnation.

TEXT 8

যে পুরুষ সৃষ্টি-স্থিতি করেন মায়ায় ।
অনন্ত ব্রহ্মাণ্ড সৃষ্টি করেন লীলায় ॥ ৮ ॥

ye puruṣa sṛṣṭi-sthiti karena māyāya
ananta brahmāṇḍa sṛṣṭi karena līlāya

ye puruṣa—that personality who; *sṛṣṭi-sthiti*—creation and maintenance; *karena*—performs; *māyāya*—through the external energy; *ananta brahmāṇḍa*—unlimited universes; *sṛṣṭi*—creation; *karena*—does; *līlāya*—by pastimes.

TRANSLATION

That puruṣa creates and maintains with His external energy. He creates innumerable universes in His pastimes.

TEXT 9

ইচ্ছায় অনন্ত মূর্তি করেন প্রকাশ ।
এক এক মূর্তে করেন ব্রহ্মাণ্ডে প্রবেশ ॥ ৯ ॥

icchāya ananta mūrti karena prakāśa
eka eka mūrte karena brahmāṇḍe praveśa

icchāya—by His will; *ananta mūrti*—unlimited forms; *karena*—does; *prakāśa*—manifestation; *eka eka*—each and every; *mūrte*—form; *karena*—does; *brahmāṇḍe*—within the universe; *praveśa*—entrance.

TRANSLATION

By His will He manifests Himself in unlimited forms, in which He enters each and every universe.

TEXT 10

সে পুরুষের অংশ—অদ্বৈত, নাহি কিছু ভেদ ।
শরীর-বিশেষ তাঁর,—নাহিক বিচ্ছেদ ॥ ১০ ॥

se puruṣera aṁśa—advaita, nāhi kichu bheda
śarīra-viśeṣa tāṅra—nāhika viccheda

se—that; *puruṣera*—of the Lord; *aṁśa*—part; *advaita*—Advaita Ācārya; *nāhi*—not; *kichu*—any; *bheda*—difference; *śarīra-viśeṣa*—another specific transcendental body; *tāṅra*—of Him; *nāhika viccheda*—there is no separation.

TRANSLATION

Śrī Advaita Ācārya is a plenary part of that puruṣa and so is not different from Him. Indeed, Śrī Advaita Ācārya is not separate but is another form of that puruṣa.

TEXT 11

সহায় করেন তাঁর লইয়া 'প্রধান'।
কোটি ব্রহ্মাণ্ড করেন ইচ্ছায় নির্মাণ ॥ ১১ ॥

sahāya karena tāṅra la-iyā 'pradhāna'
koṭi brahmāṇḍa karena icchāya nirmāṇa

sahāya karena—He helps; *tāṅra*—His; *lā-iyā*—with; *pradhāna*—the material energy; *koṭi-brahmāṇḍa*—millions of universes; *karena*—does; *icchāya*—only by the will; *nirmāṇa*—creation.

TRANSLATION

He [Advaita Ācārya] helps in the pastimes of the puruṣa, with whose material energy and by whose will He creates innumerable universes.

TEXT 12

জগৎ-মঙ্গল অদ্বৈত, মঙ্গল-গুণধাম।
মঙ্গল-চরিত্র সদা, 'মঙ্গল' যাঁর নাম ॥ ১২ ॥

jagat-maṅgala advaita, maṅgala-guṇa-dhāma
maṅgala-caritra sadā, 'maṅgala' yāṅra nāma

jagat-maṅgala—all-auspicious for the world; *advaita*—Advaita Ācārya; *maṅgala-guṇa-dhāma*—the reservoir of all auspicious attributes; *maṅgala-caritra*—all characteristics are auspicious; *sadā*—always; *maṅgala*—auspicious; *yāṅra nāma*—whose name.

TRANSLATION

Being a reservoir of all auspicious attributes, Śrī Advaita Ācārya is all-auspicious for the world. His characteristics, activities and name are always auspicious.

PURPORT

Śrī Advaita Prabhu, who is an incarnation of Mahā-Viṣṇu, is an *ācārya*, or teacher. All His activities and all the other activities of Viṣṇu are auspicious. Anyone who can view the all-auspiciousness in the pastimes of Lord Viṣṇu also becomes auspicious simultaneously. Therefore, since Lord Viṣṇu is the fountainhead of auspiciousness, anyone who is attracted by the devotional service of Lord Viṣṇu can render the greatest service to human society. Rejected persons of the material world who refuse to understand pure devotional service as the eternal function of the living entities, and as actual liberation of the living being from conditioned life, become bereft of all devotional service because of their poor fund of knowledge.

In the teachings of Advaita Prabhu there is no question of fruitive activities or impersonal liberation. Bewildered by the spell of the material energy, however, persons who could not understand that Advaita Prabhu is nondifferent from Viṣṇu wanted to follow Him with their impersonal conceptions. The attempt of Advaita Prabhu to punish them is also auspicious. Lord Viṣṇu and His activities can bestow all good fortune, directly and indirectly. In other words, being favored by Lord Viṣṇu and being punished by Lord Viṣṇu are one and the same because all the activities of Viṣṇu are absolute. According to some, Maṅgala was another name of Advaita Prabhu. As the causal incarnation, or Lord Viṣṇu's incarnation for a particular occasion, He is the supply agent or ingredient in material nature. However, He is never to be considered material. All His activities are spiritual. Anyone who hears about and glorifies Him becomes glorified himself, for such activities free one from all kinds of misfortune. One should not invest any material contamination or impersonalism in the Viṣṇu form. Everyone should try to understand the real identity of Lord Viṣṇu, for by such knowledge one can attain the highest stage of perfection.

TEXT 13

কোটি অংশ, কোটি শক্তি, কোটি অবতার ।
এত লঞা সৃজে পুরুষ সকল সংসার ॥ ১৩ ॥

koṭi aṁśa, koṭi śakti, koṭi avatāra
eta lañā sṛje puruṣa sakala saṁsāra

koṭi aṁśa—millions of parts and parcels; *koṭi śakti*—millions and millions of energies; *koṭi avatāra*—millions upon millions of incarnations; *eta*—all this; *lañā*—taking; *sṛje*—creates; *puruṣa*—the original person, Mahā-Viṣṇu; *sakala saṁsāra*—all the material world.

TRANSLATION

Mahā-Viṣṇu creates the entire material world with millions of His parts, energies and incarnations.

TEXTS 14–15

মায়া যৈছে দুই অংশ—'নিমিত্ত', 'উপাদান'।
মায়া—'নিমিত্ত'-হেতু, উপাদান—'প্রধান' ॥ ১৪ ॥
পুরুষ ঈশ্বর ঐছে দ্বিমূর্তি হইয়া।
বিশ্ব-সৃষ্টি করে 'নিমিত্ত' 'উপাদান' লঞা ॥ ১৫ ॥

māyā yaiche dui aṁśa—'nimitta', 'upādāna'
māyā—'nimitta'-hetu, upādāna—'pradhāna'

puruṣa īśvara aiche dvi-mūrti ha-iyā
viśva-sṛṣṭi kare 'nimitta' 'upādāna' lañā

māyā—the external energy; *yaiche*—as; *dui aṁśa*—two parts; *nimitta*—the cause; *upādāna*—the ingredients; *māyā*—the material energy; *nimitta-hetu*—original cause; *upādāna*—ingredients; *pradhāna*—immediate cause; *puruṣa*—the person Lord Viṣṇu; *īśvara*—the Supreme Personality of Godhead; *aiche*—in that way; *dvi-mūrti ha-iyā*—taking two forms; *viśva-sṛṣṭi kare*—creates this material world; *nimitta*—the original cause; *upādāna*—the material cause; *lañā*—with.

TRANSLATION

Just as the external energy consists of two parts—the efficient cause [nimitta] and the material cause [upādāna], māyā being the efficient cause and pradhāna the material cause—so Lord Viṣṇu, the Supreme Personality of Godhead, assumes two forms to create the material world with the efficient and material causes.

PURPORT

There are two kinds of research to find the original cause of creation. One conclusion is that the Supreme Personality of Godhead, the all-blissful, eternal, all knowing form, is indirectly the cause of this cosmic manifestation and directly the cause of the spiritual world, where there are innumerable spiritual planets known as Vaikuṇṭhas, as well as His personal abode, known as Goloka Vṛndāvana. In other words, there are two manifestations—the material cosmos and the spiritual world. As in the material world there are innumerable planets and universes, so in the spiritual world there are also innumerable spiritual planets and universes, including the Vaikuṇṭhas and Goloka. The Supreme Lord is the cause of both the material and spiritual worlds. The other conclusion, of course, is that this cosmic manifestation is caused by an inexplicable unmanifested void. This argument is meaningless.

The first conclusion is accepted by the Vedānta philosophers, and the second is supported by the atheistic philosophical system of the Sāṅkhya *smṛti,* which directly opposes the Vedāntic philosophical conclusion. Material scientists cannot see any cognizant spiritual substance that might be the cause of the creation. Such atheistic Sāṅkhya philosophers think that the symptoms of knowledge and living force visible in the innumerable living creatures are caused by the three qualities of the cosmic manifestation. Therefore the Sāṅkhyites are against the conclusion of Vedānta regarding the original cause of creation.

Factually, the supreme absolute spirit soul is the cause of every kind of manifestation, and He is always complete, both as the energy and as the energetic. The cosmic manifestation is caused by the energy of the Supreme Absolute Person, in whom all energies are conserved. Philosophers who are subjectively engaged in the cosmic manifestation can appreciate only the wonderful energies of matter. Such philosophers accept the conception of God only as a product of the material energy. According to their conclusions, the source of the energy is also a product of the energy. Such philosophers wrongly observe that the living creatures within the cosmic manifestation are caused by the material energy, and they think that the supreme absolute conscious being must similarly be a product of the material energy.

Since materialistic philosophers and scientists are too much engaged with their imperfect senses, naturally they conclude that the living force is a product of a material combination. But the actual fact is just the opposite. Matter is a product of spirit. According to the *Bhagavad-gītā,* the supreme spirit, the Personality of Godhead, is the source of all energies. When one advances in research work by studying a limited substance within the limits of space and time, one is amazed by the various wonderful cosmic manifestations, and naturally one goes on hypnotically accepting the path of research work or the inductive method. Through the deductive way of understanding, however, one accepts the Supreme Absolute Person, the Personality of Godhead, as the cause of all causes, who is full with diverse energies and who is neither impersonal nor void. The impersonal manifestation of the Supreme Person is another display of His energy. Therefore the conclusion that matter is the original cause of creation is completely different from the real truth. The material manifestation is caused by the glance of the Supreme Personality of Godhead, who is inconceivably potent. Material nature is electrified by the supreme authority, and the conditioned soul, within the limits of time and space, is trapped by awe of the material manifestation. In other words, the Supreme Personality of Godhead is actually realized in the vision of a material philosopher and scientist through the manifestations of His material energy. For one who does not understand the power of the Supreme Personality of Godhead or His diverse energies because of not knowing the relationship between the source of the energies and the energies themselves, there is always a chance of error, which is known as *vivarta.* As long as materialistic scientists and philosophers do not come to the right conclusion, certainly they will hover above the material field, bereft of proper understanding of the Absolute Truth.

The great Vaiṣṇava philosopher Śrīla Baladeva Vidyābhūṣaṇa has very nicely explained the materialistic conclusion in his *Govinda-bhāṣya,* a commentary on the *Vedānta-sūtra.* He writes as follows:

"The Sāṅkhya philosopher Kapila has connected the different elementary truths according to his own opinion. Material nature, according to him, consists of the equilibrium of the three material qualities—goodness, passion and ignorance. Material nature produces the material energy, known as *mahat,* and *mahat* produces the false ego. The ego produces the five objects of sense perception, which produce the ten senses (five for acquiring knowledge and five for working), the mind and the five gross elements. Counting the *puruṣa,* or the enjoyer, with these twenty-four elements, there are twenty-five different truths. The non-manifested stage of these twenty-five elementary truths is called *prakṛti,* or material nature. The qualities of material nature can associate in three different stages, namely as the cause of happiness, the cause of distress and the cause of illusion. The quality of goodness is the cause of material happiness, the quality of passion is the cause of material distress, and the quality of ignorance is the cause of illusion. Our material experience lies within the boundaries of these three manifestations of happiness, distress and illusion. For example, a beautiful woman is certainly a cause of material happiness for one who possesses her as a wife, but the same beautiful woman is a cause of distress to a man whom she rejects or who is the cause of her anger, and if she leaves a man she becomes the cause of illusion.

"The two kinds of senses are the ten external senses and the one internal sense, the mind. Thus there are eleven senses. According to Kapila, material nature is eternal and all-powerful. Originally there is no spirit, and matter has no cause. Matter itself is the chief cause of everything. It is the all-pervading cause of all causes. The Sāṅkhya philosophy regards the total energy (*mahat-tattva*), the false ego and the five objects of sense perception as the seven diverse manifestations of material nature, which has two features, known as the material cause and efficient cause. The *puruṣa,* the enjoyer, is without transformation, whereas material nature is always subject to transformation. But although material nature is inert, it is the cause of enjoyment and salvation for many living creatures. Its activities are beyond the conception of sense perception, but still one may guess at them by superior intelligence. Material nature is one, but because of the interaction of the three qualities, it can produce the total energy and the wonderful cosmic manifestation. Such transformations divide material nature into two features, namely the efficient and material causes. The *puruṣa,* the enjoyer, is inactive and without material qualities, although at the same time He is the master, existing separately in each and every body as the emblem of knowledge. By understanding the material cause, one can guess that the *puruṣa,* the enjoyer, being without activity, is aloof from all kinds of enjoyment or superintendence. Sāṅkhya philosophy, after describing the nature of *prakṛti* (material nature) and *puruṣa* (the enjoyer), asserts that the creation is only a product of their unification or proximity to one another. With such unification the living symptoms are visible in material nature, but one can guess that in the person of the enjoyer, the *puruṣa,* there are powers of control and enjoyment. When the *puruṣa* is illusioned for want of sufficient knowledge, He feels Himself to be the enjoyer, and when He is in full knowledge He is liberated. In the Sāṅkhya philosophy the *puruṣa* is described to be always indifferent to the activities of *prakṛti.*

"The Sāṅkhya philosopher accepts three kinds of evidences, namely direct perception, hypothesis and traditional authority. When such evidence is complete, everything is perfect. The process of comparison is within such perfection. Beyond such evidence there is no proof. There is not much controversy regarding direct perceptional evidence or authorized traditional evidence. The Sāṅkhya system of philosophy identifies three kinds of procedures—namely, *pariṇāmāt* (transformation), *samanvayāt* (adjustment) and *śaktitaḥ* (performance of energies)—as the causes of the cosmic manifestation."

Śrīla Baladeva Vidyābhūṣaṇa, in his commentary on the *Vedānta-sūtra,* has tried to nullify this conclusion because he thinks that discrediting these so-called causes of the cosmic manifestation will nullify the entire Sāṅkhya philosophy. Materialistic philosophers accept matter to be the material and efficient cause of creation; for them, matter is the cause of every type of manifestation. Generally they give the example of a waterpot and clay. Clay is the cause of the waterpot, but the clay can be found as both cause and effect. The waterpot is the effect and clay itself is the cause, but clay is visible everywhere. A tree is matter, but a tree produces fruit. Water is matter, but water flows. In this way, say the Sāṅkhyites, matter is the cause of movements and production. As such, matter can be considered the material and efficient cause of everything in the cosmic manifestation. Śrīla Baladeva Vidyābhūṣaṇa has therefore enunciated the nature of *pradhāna* as follows:

"Material nature is inert, and as such it cannot be the cause of matter, neither as the material nor as the efficient cause. Seeing the wonderful arrangement and management of the cosmic manifestation generally suggests that a living brain is behind this arrangement, for without a living brain such an arrangement could not exist. One should not imagine that such an arrangement can exist without conscious direction. In our practical experience we never see that inert bricks can themselves construct a big building.

"The example of the waterpot cannot be accepted because a waterpot has no perception of pleasure and distress. Such perception is within. Therefore the covering body, or the waterpot, cannot be synchronized with it.

"Sometimes the material scientist suggests that trees grow from the earth automatically, without assistance from a gardener, because that is a tendency of matter. They also consider the intuition of living creatures from birth to be material. But such material tendencies as bodily intuition cannot be accepted as independent, for they suggest the existence of a spirit soul within the body. Actually, neither the tree nor any other body of a living creature has any tendency or intuition; the tendency and intuition exist because the soul is present within the body. In this connection, the example of a car and driver may be given very profitably. The car has a tendency to turn right and left, but one cannot say that the car itself, as matter, turns right and left without the direction of a driver. A material car has neither tendencies nor intuitions independent of the intentions of the driver within the car. The same principle applies for the automatic growth of trees in the forest. The growth takes place because of the soul's presence within the tree.

"Sometimes foolish people take it for granted that because scorpions are born from heaps of rice, the rice has produced the scorpions. The real fact, however, is that the mother scorpion lays eggs within the rice and by the proper fermentation of the rice the eggs give birth to several baby scorpions, which in due course come out. This does not mean that the rice gives birth to the scorpions. Similarly, sometimes bugs are seen to come from dirty beds. This does not mean, however, that the beds give birth to the bugs. It is the living soul that comes forth, taking advantage of the dirty condition of the bed. There are different kinds of living creatures. Some of them come from embryos, some from eggs and some from the fermentation of perspiration. Different living creatures have different sources of appearance, but one should not conclude that matter produces such living creatures.

"The example cited by materialists that trees automatically come from the earth follows the same principle. Taking advantage of a certain condition, a living entity comes from the earth. According to the *Bṛhad-āraṇyaka Upaniṣad,* every living being is forced by divine superintendence to take a certain type of body according to his past deeds. There are many varieties of bodies, and because of a divine arrangement a living entity takes bodies of different shapes.

"When a person thinks 'I am doing this,' the 'I am' does not refer to the body. It refers to something more than the body, or within the body. As such, the body as it is has neither tendencies nor intuition; the tendencies and intuition belong to the soul within the body. Material scientists sometimes suggest that the tendencies of male and female bodies cause their union and that this is the cause of the birth of the child. But since the *puruṣa,* according to Sāṅkhya philosophy, is always unaffected, where does the tendency to give birth come from?

"Sometimes material scientists give the example that milk turns into curd automatically and that distilled water pouring from the clouds falls down to earth, produces different kinds of trees, and enters different kinds of flowers and fruits with different fragrances and tastes. Therefore, they say, matter produces varieties of material things on its own. In reply to this argument, the same proposition of the *Bṛhad-āraṇyaka Upaniṣad*—that different kinds of living creatures are put into different kinds of bodies by the management of a superior power—is repeated. Under superior superintendence, various souls, according to their past activities, are given the chance to take a particular type of body, such as that of a tree, animal, bird or beast, and thus their different tendencies develop under these circumstances. The *Bhagavad-gītā* (13.22) also further affirms:

puruṣaḥ prakṛti-stho hi bhuṅkte prakṛti-jān guṇān
kāraṇaṁ guṇa-saṅgo 'sya sad-asad-yoni-janmasu

'The living entity in material nature thus follows the ways of life, enjoying the three modes of nature. This is due to his association with that material nature. Thus he meets with good and evil among various species.' The soul is given different types of bodies. For example, were souls not given varieties of tree bodies, the different varieties of fruits and flowers could not be produced. Each class of tree produces a particular kind of fruit and flower; it is not that there is no distinction between the different classes. An individual tree does not produce flowers of different colors or fruits of different tastes. There are demarcated classes, as we find them among humans, animals, birds and other species. There are innumerable living entities, and their activities, performed in the material world according to the different qualities of the material modes of nature, give them the chance to have different kinds of lives.

"Thus one should understand that *pradhāna,* matter, cannot act unless impelled by a living creature. The materialistic theory that matter independently acts cannot, therefore, be accepted. Matter is called *prakṛti,* which refers to female energy. A woman is *prakṛti,* a female. A female cannot produce a child without the association of a *puruṣa,* a man. The *puruṣa* causes the birth of a child because the man injects the soul, which is sheltered in the semen, into the womb of the woman. The woman, as the material cause, supplies the body of the soul, and as the efficient cause she gives birth to the child. But although the woman appears to be the material and efficient cause of the birth of a child, originally the *puruṣa,* the male, is the cause of the child. Similarly, this material world gives rise to varieties of manifestations due to the entrance of Garbhodakaśāyī Viṣṇu within the universe. He is present not only within the universe but within the bodies of all living creatures, as well as within the atom. We understand from the *Brahma-saṁhitā* that the Supersoul is present within the universe, within the atom and within the heart of every living creature. Therefore the theory that matter is the cause of the entire cosmic manifestation cannot be accepted by any man with sufficient knowledge of matter and spirit.

"Materialists sometimes give the argument that as straw eaten by a cow produces milk automatically, so material nature, under different circumstances, produces varieties of manifestations. Thus originally matter is the cause. In refuting this argument, we may say that an animal of the same species as the cow—namely, the bull—also eats straw like the cow but does not produce milk. Under the circumstances, it cannot be said that straw in connection with a particular species produces milk. The conclusion should be that there is superior management, as confirmed in the *Bhagavad-gītā* (9.10), where the Lord says, *mayā-dhyakṣeṇa prakṛtiḥ sūyate sa-carācaram:* 'This material nature is working under My direction, O son of Kuntī, and it is producing all moving and unmoving beings.' The Supreme Lord says, *mayā-dhyakṣeṇa* ('under My superintendence'). When He desires that the cow produce milk by eating straw, there is milk, and when He does not so desire it, the mixture of such straw cannot produce milk. If the way of material nature had been that straw produced milk, a stack of straw could also produce milk. But that is not possible. And the same straw given to a human female also cannot produce milk. That is the meaning of the *Bhagavad-gītā's* statement that only under superior orders does anything take place. Matter itself has no power to produce independently. The conclusion, therefore, is that matter, which has no self-knowledge, cannot be the cause of the material creation. The ultimate creator is the Supreme Personality of Godhead.

"If matter were accepted as the original cause of creation, all the authorized scriptures in the world would be useless, for in every scripture, especially the Vedic scriptures like the *Manu-smṛti,* the Supreme Personality of Godhead is said to be the ultimate creator. The *Manu-smṛti* is considered the highest Vedic direction to humanity. Manu is the giver of law to mankind, and in the *Manu-smṛti* it is clearly stated that before the creation the entire universal space was darkness, without information and without variety, and was in a state of complete suspension, like a dream. Everything was darkness. The Supreme Personality of Godhead then entered the universal space, and although He is invisible, He created the visible cosmic manifestation. In the material world the Supreme Personality of Godhead is not manifested by His personal presence, but the presence of the cosmic manifestation in different varieties is the proof that everything has been created under His direction. He entered the universe with all creative potencies, and thus He removed the darkness of the unlimited space.

"The form of the Supreme Personality of Godhead is described to be transcendental, very subtle, eternal, all-pervading, inconceivable and therefore nonmanifested to the material senses of a conditioned living creature. He desired to expand Himself into many living entities, and with such a desire He first created a vast expanse of water within the universal space and then impregnated that water with living entities. By that process of impregnation a massive body appeared, blazing like a thousand suns, and in that body was the first creative principle,

Brahmā. The great Parāśara Ṛṣi has confirmed this in the *Viṣṇu Purāṇa.* He says that the cosmic manifestation visible to us is produced from Lord Viṣṇu and sustained under His protection. He is the principal maintainer and destroyer of the universal form.

"This cosmic manifestation is one of the diverse energies of the Supreme Personality of Godhead. As a spider secretes saliva and weaves a web by its own movements but at the end winds up the web within its body, so Lord Viṣṇu produces this cosmic manifestation from His transcendental body and at the end winds it up within Himself. All the great sages of the Vedic understanding have accepted that the Supreme Personality of Godhead is the original creator.

"It is sometimes claimed that the impersonal speculations of great philosophers are meant for the advancement of knowledge without religious ritualistic principles. But the religious ritualistic principles are actually meant for the advancement of spiritual knowledge. By performance of religious rituals one ultimately reaches the supreme goal of knowledge by understanding that Vāsudeva, the Supreme Personality of Godhead, is the cause of everything. It is clearly stated in the *Bhagavad-gītā* that even those who are advocates of knowledge alone, without any religious ritualistic processes, advance in knowledge after many, many lifetimes of speculation and thus come to the conclusion that Vāsudeva is the supreme cause of everything that be. As a result of this achievement of the goal of life, such an advanced learned scholar or philosopher surrenders unto the Supreme Personality of Godhead. Religious ritualistic performances are actually meant to cleanse the contaminated mind in the material world, and the special feature of this Age of Kali is that one can easily execute the process of cleansing the mind of contamination by chanting the holy names of God—Hare Kṛṣṇa, Hare Kṛṣṇa, Kṛṣṇa Kṛṣṇa, Hare Hare/ Hare Rāma, Hare Rāma, Rāma Rāma, Hare Hare.

"A Vedic injunction states, *sarve vedā yat padam āmananti* (*Kaṭha Up.* 1.2.15): all Vedic knowledge is searching after the Supreme Personality of Godhead. Similarly, another Vedic injunction states, *nārāyaṇa-parā vedāḥ:* the *Vedas* are meant for understanding Nārāyaṇa, the Supreme Lord. Similarly, the *Bhagavad-gītā* also confirms, *vedaiś ca sarvair aham eva vedyaḥ:* by all the *Vedas,* Kṛṣṇa is to be known. Therefore, the main purpose of understanding the *Vedas,* performing Vedic sacrifices and speculating on the *Vedānta-sūtra* is to understand Kṛṣṇa. Accepting the impersonalist view of voidness or the nonexistence of the Supreme Personality of Godhead negates all study of the *Vedas.*

Impersonal speculation aims at disproving the conclusion of the *Vedas.* Therefore any impersonal speculative presentation should be understood to be against the principles of the *Vedas,* or standard scriptures. Since the speculation of the impersonalists does not follow the principles of the *Vedas,* their conclusion must be considered to be against the Vedic principles. Anything not supported by the Vedic principles must be considered imaginary and lacking in standard proof. Therefore no impersonalist explanation of any Vedic literature can be accepted.

"If one tries to nullify the conclusions of the *Vedas* by accepting an unauthorized scripture or so-called scripture, it will be very hard for him to come to the right conclusion about the Absolute Truth. The system for adjusting two contradictory scriptures is to refer to the *Vedas,* for references from the *Vedas* are accepted as final judgments. When we refer to a particular scripture, it must be authorized, and for this authority it must strictly follow the Vedic injunctions. If someone presents an alternative doctrine he himself has manufactured, that doctrine will prove itself useless, for any doctrine that tries to prove that Vedic evidence is meaningless immediately proves itself meaningless. The followers of the *Vedas* unanimously accept the authority of Manu and Parāśara in the disciplic succession. Their statements, however, do not support the atheistic Kapila, because the Kapila mentioned in the *Vedas* is a different Kapila, the son of Kardama and Devahūti. The atheist Kapila is a descendant of the dynasty of Agni and is one of the conditioned souls. But the Kapila who is the son of Kardama Muni is accepted as an incarnation of Vāsudeva. The *Padma Purāṇa* gives evidence that the Supreme Personality of Godhead Vāsudeva takes birth in the incarnation of Kapila and, by His expansion of theistic Sāṅkhya philosophy, teaches all the demigods and a *brāhmaṇa* of the name Āsuri. In the doctrine of the atheist Kapila there are many statements directly against the Vedic principles. The atheist Kapila does not accept the Supreme Personality of Godhead. He says that the living entity is himself the Supreme Lord and that no one is greater than him. His conceptions of so-called conditioned and liberated life are materialistic, and he refuses to accept the importance of immortal time. All such statements are against the principles of the *Vedānta-sūtra.*"

TEXT 16

আপনে পুরুষ—বিশ্বের 'নিমিত্ত'-কারণ ।
অদ্বৈত-রূপে 'উপাদান' হন নারায়ণ ॥ ১৬ ॥

āpane puruṣa—viśvera 'nimitta'-kāraṇa
advaita-rūpe 'upādāna' hana nārāyaṇa

āpane—personally; *puruṣa*—Lord Viṣṇu; *viśvera*—of the entire material world; *nimitta kāraṇa*—the original cause; *advaita-rūpe*—in the form of Advaita; *upādāna*—the material cause; *hana*—becomes; *nārāyaṇa*—Lord Nārāyaṇa.

TRANSLATION

Lord Viṣṇu Himself is the efficient [nimitta] cause of the material world, and Nārāyaṇa in the form of Śrī Advaita is the material cause [upādāna].

TEXT 17

'নিমিত্তাংশে' করে তেঁহো মায়াতে ঈক্ষণ ।
'উপাদান' অদ্বৈত করেন ব্রহ্মাণ্ড-সৃজন ॥ ১৭ ॥

'nimittāṁśe' kare teṅho māyāte īkṣaṇa
'upādāna' advaita karena brahmāṇḍa-sṛjana

nimitta-aṁśe—in the portion as the original cause; *kare*—does; *teṅho*—He; *māyāte*—in the external energy; *īkṣaṇa*—glancing; *upādāna*—the material cause; *advaita*—Advaita Ācārya; *karena*—does; *brahmāṇḍa-sṛjana*—creation of the material world.

TRANSLATION

Lord Viṣṇu, in His efficient aspect, glances over the material energy, and Śrī Advaita, as the material cause, creates the material world.

TEXT 18

যদ্যপি সাংখ্য মানে, 'প্রধান'—কারণ ।
জড় হইতে কভু নহে জগৎ-সৃজন ॥ ১৮ ॥

yadyapi sāṅkhya māne, 'pradhāna'—kāraṇa
jaḍa ha-ite kabhu nahe jagat-sṛjana

yadyapi—although; *sāṅkhya*—Sāṅkhya philosophy; *māne*—accepts; *pradhāna*—ingredients; *kāraṇa*—cause; *jaḍa ha-ite*—from matter;

kabhu—at any time; *nahe*—there is not; *jagat-sṛjana*—the creation of the material world.

TRANSLATION

Although the Sāṅkhya philosophy accepts that the material ingredients are the cause, the creation of the world never arises from dead matter.

TEXT 19

নিজ সৃষ্টিশক্তি প্রভু সঞ্চারে প্রধানে ।
ঈশ্বরের শক্ত্যে তবে হয়ে ত' নির্মাণে ১৯ ॥

nija sṛṣṭi-śakti prabhu sañcāre pradhāne
īśvarera śaktye tabe haye ta' nirmāṇe

nija—own; *sṛṣṭi-śakti*—power for creation; *prabhu*—the Lord; *sañcāre*—infuses; *pradhāne*—in the ingredients; *īśvarera śaktye*—by the power of the Lord; *tabe*—then; *haye*—there is; *ta'*—certainly; *nirmāṇe*—the beginning of creation.

TRANSLATION

The Lord infuses the material ingredients with His own creative potency. Then, by the power of the Lord, creation takes place.

TEXT 20

অদ্বৈতরূপে করে শক্তি-সঞ্চারণ ।
অতএব অদ্বৈত হয়েন মুখ্য কারণ ॥ ২০ ॥

advaita-rūpe kare śakti-sañcāraṇa
ataeva advaita hayena mukhya kāraṇa

advaita-rūpe—in the form of Advaita Ācārya; *kare*—does; *śakti-sañcāraṇa*—infusion of the energy; *ataeva*—therefore; *advaita*—Advaita Ācārya; *hayena*—is; *mukhya kāraṇa*—the original cause.

TRANSLATION

In the form of Advaita He infuses the material ingredients with creative energy. Therefore, Advaita is the original cause of creation.

TEXT 21

অদ্বৈত-আচার্য—কোটিব্রহ্মাণ্ডের কর্তা ।
আর এক এক মূর্ত্যে ব্রহ্মাণ্ডের ভর্তা ॥ ২১ ॥

advaita-ācārya koṭi-brahmāṇḍera kartā
āra eka eka mūrtye brahmāṇḍera bhartā

advaita-ācārya—Advaita Ācārya; *koṭi-brahmāṇḍera kartā*—the creator of millions and millions of universes; *āra*—and; *eka eka*—each and every; *mūrtye*—by expansions; *brahmāṇḍera bhartā*—maintainer of the universe.

TRANSLATION

Śrī Advaita Ācārya is the creator of millions and millions of universes, and by His expansions [as Garbhodakaśāyī Viṣṇu] He maintains each and every universe.

TEXT 22

সেই নারায়ণের মুখ্য অঙ্গ,—অদ্বৈত ।
'অঙ্গ'-শব্দে অংশ করি' কহে ভাগবত ॥ ২২ ॥

sei nārāyaṇera mukhya aṅga,—advaita
'aṅga'-śabde aṁśa kari' kahe bhāgavata

sei—that; *nārāyaṇera*—of Lord Nārāyaṇa; *mukhya aṅga*—the primary part; *advaita*—Advaita Ācārya; *aṅga-śabde*—by the word *aṅga; aṁśa kari'*—taking as a plenary portion; *kahe*—says; *bhāgavata—Śrīmad-Bhāgavatam.*

TRANSLATION

Śrī Advaita is the principal limb [aṅga] of Nārāyaṇa. Śrīmad-Bhāgavatam speaks of "limb" [aṅga] as "a plenary portion" [aṁśa] of the Lord.

TEXT 23

নারায়ণস্ত্বং ন হি সর্বদেহিনামাত্মাস্যধীশাখিল-লোকসাক্ষী ।
নারায়ণোঽঙ্গং নর-ভূ-জলায়নাত্তচ্চাপি সত্যং ন তবৈব মায়া ॥ ২৩ ॥

nārāyaṇas tvaṁ na hi sarva-dehinām
ātmāsy adhīśākhila-loka-sākṣī
nārāyaṇo 'ṅgaṁ nara-bhū-jalāyanāt
tac cāpi satyaṁ na tavaiva māyā

nārāyaṇaḥ—Lord Nārāyaṇa; *tvam*—You; *na*—not; *hi*—certainly; *sarva*—all; *dehinām*—of the embodied beings; *ātmā*—the Supersoul; *asi*—You are; *adhīśa*—O Lord; *akhila-loka*—of all the worlds; *sākṣī*—the witness; *nārāyaṇaḥ*—known as Nārāyaṇa; *aṅgam*—plenary portion; *nara*—of Nara; *bhū*—born; *jala*—in the water; *ayanāt*—due to the place of refuge; *tat*—that; *ca*—and; *api*—certainly; *satyam*—highest truth; *na*—not; *tava*—Your; *eva*—at all; *māyā*—the illusory energy.

TRANSLATION

"O Lord of lords, You are the seer of all creation. You are indeed everyone's dearest life. Are You not, therefore, my father, Nārāyaṇa? 'Nārāyaṇa' refers to one whose abode is in the water born from Nara [Garbhodakaśāyī Viṣṇu], and that Nārāyaṇa is Your plenary portion. All Your plenary portions are transcendental. They are absolute and are not creations of māyā."

PURPORT

This text is from *Śrīmad-Bhāgavatam* (10.14.14).

TEXT 24

ঈশ্বরের 'অঙ্গ' অংশ—চিদানন্দময় ।
মায়ার সম্বন্ধ নাহি' এই শ্লোকে কয় ॥ ২৪ ॥

īśvarera 'aṅga' aṁśa—cid-ānanda-maya
māyāra sambandha nāhi' ei śloke kaya

īśvarera—of the Lord; *aṅga*—limb; *aṁśa*—part; *cit-ānanda-maya*—all-spiritual; *māyāra*—of the material energy; *sambandha*—relationship; *nāhi'*—there is not; *ei śloke*—this verse; *kaya*—says.

TRANSLATION

This verse describes that the limbs and plenary portions of the Lord are all spiritual; They have no relationship with the material energy.

TEXT 25

'অংশ' না কহিয়া, কেনে কহ তাঁরে 'অঙ্গ'।
'অংশ' হৈতে 'অঙ্গ', যাতে হয় অন্তরঙ্গ ॥ ২৫ ॥

'aṁśa' nā kahiyā, kene kaha tāṅre 'aṅga'
'aṁśa' haite 'aṅga,' yāte haya antaraṅga

aṁśa—part; *nā kahiyā*—not saying; *kene*—why; *kaha*—you say; *tāṅre*—Him; *aṅga*—limb; *aṁśa haite*—than a part; *aṅga*—limb; *yāte*—because; *haya*—is; *antaraṅga*—more.

TRANSLATION

Why has Śrī Advaita been called a limb and not a part? The reason is that "limb" implies greater intimacy.

TEXT 26

মহাবিষ্ণুর অংশ—অদ্বৈত গুণধাম।
ঈশ্বরে অভেদ, তেঞি 'অদ্বৈত' পূর্ণ নাম ॥ ২৬ ॥

mahā-viṣṇura aṁśa—advaita guṇa-dhāma
īśvare abheda, teñi 'advaita' pūrṇa nāma

mahā-viṣṇura—of Lord Mahā-Viṣṇu; *aṁśa*—part; *advaita*—Advaita Ācārya; *guṇa-dhāma*—reservoir of all attributes; *īśvare*—from the Lord; *abheda*—nondifferent; *teñi*—therefore; *advaita*—nondifferent; *pūrṇa nāma*—full name.

TRANSLATION

Śrī Advaita, who is a reservoir of virtues, is the main limb of Mahā-Viṣṇu. His full name is Advaita, for He is identical in all respects with that Lord.

TEXT 27

পূর্বে যৈছে কৈল সর্ব-বিশ্বের সৃজন।
অবতরি' কৈল এবে ভক্তি-প্রবর্তন ॥ ২৭ ॥

pūrve yaiche kaila sarva-viśvera sṛjana
avatari' kaila ebe bhakti-pravartana

pūrve—formerly; *yaiche*—as; *kaila*—performed; *sarva*—all; *viśvera*—of the universes; *sṛjana*—creation; *avatari'*—taking incarnation; *kaila*—did; *ebe*—now; *bhakti-pravartana*—inauguration of the *bhakti* cult.

TRANSLATION

As He had formerly created all the universes, now He descended to introduce the path of bhakti.

TEXT 28

জীব নিস্তারিল কৃষ্ণভক্তি করি' দান ।
গীতা-ভাগবতে কৈল ভক্তির ব্যাখ্যান ॥ ২৮ ॥

jīva nistārila kṛṣṇa-bhakti kari' dāna
gītā-bhāgavate kaila bhaktira vyākhyāna

jīva—the living entities; *nistārila*—delivered; *kṛṣṇa-bhakti*—devotional service to Lord Kṛṣṇa; *kari'*—making; *dāna*—gift; *gītā-bhāgavate*—in the *Bhagavad-gītā* and *Śrīmad-Bhāgavatam; kaila*—performed; *bhaktira vyākhyāna*—explanation of devotional service.

TRANSLATION

He delivered all living beings by offering the gift of kṛṣṇa-bhakti. He explained the Bhagavad-gītā and Śrīmad-Bhāgavatam in the light of devotional service.

PURPORT

Although Śrī Advaita Prabhu is an incarnation of Viṣṇu, for the welfare of the conditioned souls He manifested Himself as a servitor of the Supreme Personality of Godhead, and throughout all His activities He showed Himself to be an eternal servitor. Lord Caitanya and Lord Nityānanda also manifested the same principle, although They also belong to the category of Viṣṇu. If Lord Caitanya, Lord Nityānanda and Advaita Prabhu had exhibited Their all-powerful Viṣṇu potencies within this material world, people would have become greater impersonalists, monists and self-worshipers than they had already become under the spell of this age. Therefore the Personality of Godhead and His different incarnations and forms played the parts of devotees to instruct the conditioned souls how to approach the transcendental stage of devotional service. Advaita Ācārya especially intended to teach the conditioned souls about devotional service. The word *ācārya* means "teacher." The special function of such a teacher is to make people Kṛṣṇa conscious. A bona fide teacher following in the footsteps of Advaita Ācārya has no other business than to spread the principles of Kṛṣṇa consciousness all over the world. The real qualification of an *ācārya* is that he presents himself as a servant of the Supreme. Such a bona fide *ācārya* can never support the demoniac activities of atheistic men who present themselves as God. It is the main business of an *ācārya* to defy such imposters posing as God before the innocent public.

TEXT 29

ভক্তি-উপদেশ বিনু তাঁর নাহি কার্য ।
অতএব নাম হৈল 'অদ্বৈত আচার্য' ॥ ২৯ ॥

bhakti-upadeśa vinu tāṅra nāhi kārya
ataeva nāma haila 'advaita ācārya'

bhakti-upadeśa—instruction of devotional service; *vinu*—without; *tāṅra*—His; *nāhi*—there is not; *kārya*—occupation; *ataeva*—therefore; *nāma*—the name; *haila*—became; *advaita ācārya*—the supreme teacher (*ācārya*) Advaita Prabhu.

TRANSLATION

Since He has no other occupation than to teach devotional service, His name is Advaita Ācārya.

TEXT 30

বৈষ্ণবের গুরু তেঁহো জগতের আর্য ।
দুইনাম-মিলনে হৈল 'অদ্বৈত-আচার্য' ॥ ৩০ ॥

vaiṣṇavera guru teṅho jagatera ārya
dui-nāma-milane haila 'advaita-ācārya'

vaiṣṇavera—of the devotees; *guru*—spiritual master; *teṅho*—He; *jagatera ārya*—the most respectable personality in the world; *dui-nāma-milane*—by combining the two names; *haila*—there was; *advaita-ācārya*—the name Advaita Ācārya.

TRANSLATION

He is the spiritual master of all devotees and is the most revered personality in the world. By a combination of these two names, His name is Advaita Ācārya.

PURPORT

Śrī Advaita Ācārya is the prime spiritual master of the Vaiṣṇavas, and He is worshipable by all Vaiṣṇavas. Vaiṣṇavas must follow in the footsteps of Advaita Ācārya, for by so doing one can actually engage in the devotional service of the Lord.

TEXT 31

কমল-নয়নের তেঁহো, যাতে 'অঙ্গ', 'অংশ' ।
'কমলাক্ষ' করি ধরে নাম অবতংস ॥ ৩১ ॥

kamala-nayanera teṅho, yāte 'aṅga' 'aṁśa'
'kamalākṣa' kari dhare nāma avataṁsa

kamala-nayanera—of the lotus-eyed; *teṅho*—He; *yāte*—since; *aṅga*—limb; *aṁśa*—part; *kamala-akṣa*—the lotus-eyed; *kari'*—accepting that; *dhare*—takes; *nāma*—the name; *avataṁsa*—partial expansion.

TRANSLATION

Since He is a limb or part of the lotus-eyed Supreme Lord, He also bears the name Kamalākṣa.

TEXT 32

ঈশ্বরসারূপ্য পায় পারিষদগণ ।
চতুর্ভুজ, পীতবাস, যৈছে নারায়ণ ॥ ৩২ ॥

īśvara-sārūpya pāya pāriṣada-gaṇa
catur-bhuja, pīta-vāsa, yaiche nārāyaṇa

īśvara-sārūpya—the same bodily features as the Lord; *pāya*—gets; *pāriṣada-gaṇa*—the associates; *catur-bhuja*—four hands; *pīta-vāsa*—yellow dress; *yaiche*—just as; *nārāyaṇa*—Lord Nārāyaṇa.

TRANSLATION

His associates have the same bodily features as the Lord. They all have four arms and are dressed in yellow garments like Nārāyaṇa.

TEXT 33

অদ্বৈত-আচার্য—ঈশ্বরের অংশবর্য ।
তাঁর তত্ত্ব-নাম-গুণ, সকলি আশ্চর্য ॥ ৩৩ ॥

advaita-ācārya—īśvarera aṁśa-varya
tāṅra tattva-nāma-guṇa, sakali āścarya

advaita-ācārya—Advaita Ācārya Prabhu; *īśvarera*—of the Supreme Lord; *aṁśa-varya*—principal part; *tāṅra*—His; *tattva*—truths; *nāma*—names; *guṇa*—attributes; *sakali*—all; *āścarya*—wonderful.

TRANSLATION

Śrī Advaita Ācārya is the principal limb of the Supreme Lord. His truths, names and attributes are all wonderful.

TEXT 34

যাঁহার তুলসীজলে, যাঁহার হুঙ্কারে ।
স্বগণ সহিতে চৈতন্যের অবতারে ॥ ৩৪ ॥

yāṅhāra tulasī-jale, yāṅhāra huṅkāre
sva-gaṇa sahite caitanyera avatāre

yāṅhāra—whose; *tulasī-jale*—by *tulasī* leaves and Ganges water; *yāṅhāra*—of whom; *huṅkāre*—by the loud voice; *sva-gaṇa*—His personal associates; *sahite*—accompanied by; *caitanyera*—of Lord Śrī Caitanya Mahāprabhu; *avatāre*—in the incarnation.

TRANSLATION

He worshiped Kṛṣṇa with tulasī leaves and water of the Ganges and called for Him in a loud voice. Thus Lord Caitanya Mahāprabhu appeared on earth, accompanied by His personal associates.

TEXT 35

যাঁর দ্বারা কৈল প্রভু কীর্তন প্রচার ।
যাঁর দ্বারা কৈল প্রভু জগৎ নিস্তার ॥ ৩৫ ॥

yāṅra dvārā kaila prabhu kīrtana pracāra
yāṅra dvārā kaila prabhu jagat nistāra

yāṅra dvārā—by whom; *kaila*—did; *prabhu*—Lord Śrī Caitanya Mahāprabhu; *kīrtana pracāra*—spreading of the *saṅkīrtana* movement; *yāṅra dvārā*—by whom; *kaila*—did; *prabhu*—Śrī Caitanya Mahāprabhu; *jagat nistāra*—deliverance of the entire world.

TRANSLATION

It is through Him [Advaita Ācārya] that Lord Caitanya spread the saṅkīrtana movement and through Him that He delivered the world.

TEXT 36

আচার্য গোসাঞির গুণ-মহিমা অপার ।
জীবকীট কোথায় পাইবেক তার পার ॥ ৩৬ ॥

ācārya gosāñira guṇa-mahimā apāra
jīva-kīṭa kothāya pāibeka tāra pāra

ācārya gosāñira—of Advaita Ācārya; *guṇa-mahimā*—the glory of the attributes; *apāra*—unfathomable; *jīva-kīṭa*—a living being who is just like a worm; *kothāya*—where; *pāibeka*—will get; *tāra*—of that; *pāra*—the other side.

TRANSLATION

The glory and attributes of Advaita Ācārya are unlimited. How can the insignificant living entities fathom them?

TEXT 37

আচার্য গোসাঞি চৈতন্যের মুখ্য অঙ্গ ।
আর এক অঙ্গ তাঁর প্রভু নিত্যানন্দ ॥ ৩৭ ॥

ācārya gosāñi caitanyera mukhya aṅga
āra eka aṅga tāṅra prabhu nityānanda

ācārya gosāñi—Advaita Ācārya; *caitanyera*—of Lord Śrī Caitanya Mahāprabhu; *mukhya*—primary; *aṅga*—part; *āra*—another; *eka*—one; *aṅga*—part; *tāṅra*—of Lord Caitanya Mahāprabhu; *prabhu nityā-nanda*—Lord Nityānanda.

TRANSLATION

Śrī Advaita Ācārya is a principal limb of Lord Caitanya. Another limb of the Lord is Nityānanda Prabhu.

TEXT 38

প্রভুর উপাঙ্গ—শ্রীবাসাদি ভক্তগণ ।
হস্তমুখনেত্র-অঙ্গ চক্রাদ্যস্ত্র-সম ॥ ৩৮ ॥

prabhura upāṅga—śrīvāsādi bhakta-gaṇa
hasta-mukha-netra-aṅga cakrādy-astra-sama

prabhura upāṅga—Lord Caitanya's smaller parts; *śrīvāsa-ādi*—headed by Śrīvāsa; *bhakta-gaṇa*—the devotees; *hasta*—hands; *mukha*—face; *netra*—eyes; *aṅga*—parts of the body; *cakra-ādi*—the disc; *astra*—weapons; *sama*—like.

TRANSLATION

The devotees headed by Śrīvāsa are His smaller limbs. They are like His hands, face and eyes and His disc and other weapons.

TEXT 39

এসব লইয়া চৈতন্যপ্রভুর বিহার ।
এসব লইয়া করেন বাঞ্ছিত প্রচার ॥ ৩৯ ॥

e-saba la-iyā caitanya-prabhura vihāra
e-saba la-iyā karena vāñchita pracāra

e-saba—all these; *la-iyā*—taking; *caitanya-prabhura*—of Śrī Caitanya Mahāprabhu; *vihāra*—pastimes; *e-saba*—all of them; *la-iyā*—taking; *karena*—does; *vāñchita pracāra*—spreading His mission.

TRANSLATION

With all of them Lord Caitanya performed His pastimes, and with them He spread His mission.

TEXT 40

মাধবেন্দ্রপুরীর ইঁহো শিষ্য, এই জ্ঞানে ।
আচার্য-গোসাঞিরে প্রভু গুরু করি' মানে ॥ ৪০ ॥

mādhavendra-purīra iṅho śiṣya, ei jñāne
ācārya-gosāñire prabhu guru kari' māne

mādhavendra-purīra—of Mādhavendra Purī; *iṅho*—Advaita Ācārya; *śiṣya*—disciple; *ei jñāne*—by this consideration; *ācārya-gosāñire*—unto Advaita Ācārya; *prabhu*—Śrī Caitanya Mahāprabhu; *guru*—spiritual master; *kari'*—taking as; *māne*—obeys Him.

TRANSLATION

Thinking "He [Śrī Advaita Ācārya] is a disciple of Śrī Mādhavendra Purī," Lord Caitanya obeys Him, respecting Him as His spiritual master.

PURPORT

Śrī Mādhavendra Purī is one of the *ācāryas* in the disciplic succession from Madhvācārya. Mādhavendra Purī had two principal disciples, Īśvara Purī and Śrī Advaita Prabhu. Therefore the Gauḍīya Vaiṣṇava-sampradāya is a disciplic succession from Madhvācārya. This fact has been accepted in the authorized books known as *Gaura-gaṇoddeśa-dīpikā* and *Prameya-ratnāvalī*, as well as by Gopāla Guru Gosvāmī. The *Gaura-gaṇoddeśa-dīpikā* (22) clearly states the disciplic succession of the Gauḍīya Vaiṣṇavas as follows: "Lord Brahmā is the direct disciple of Viṣṇu, the Lord of the spiritual sky. His disciple is Nārada, Nārada's disciple is Vyāsa, and Vyāsa's disciples are Śukadeva Gosvāmī and Madhvācārya. Padmanābha Ācārya is the disciple of Madhvācārya, and Narahari is the disciple of Padmanābha Ācārya. Mādhava is the disciple of Narahari, Akṣobhya is the direct disciple of Mādhava, and Jayatīrtha is the disciple of Akṣobhya. Jayatīrtha's disciple is Jñānasindhu, and his disciple is Mahānidhi. Vidyānidhi is the disciple of Mahānidhi, and Rājendra is the disciple of Vidyānidhi. Jayadharma is the disciple of Rājendra. Puruṣottama is the disciple of Jayadharma. Śrīmān Lakṣmīpati is the disciple of Vyāsatīrtha, who is the disciple of Puruṣottama. And Mādhavendra Purī is the disciple of Lakṣmīpati."

TEXT 41

লৌকিক-লীলাতে ধর্মমর্যাদা-রক্ষণ ।
স্তুতি-ভক্ত্যে করেন তাঁর চরণ বন্দন ॥ ৪১ ॥

laukika-līlāte dharma-maryādā-rakṣaṇa
stuti-bhaktye karena tāṅra caraṇa vandana

laukika—popular; *līlāte*—in pastimes; *dharma-maryādā*—etiquette of religious principles; *rakṣaṇa*—observing; *stuti*—prayers; *bhaktye*—by devotion; *karena*—He does; *tāṅra*—of Advaita Ācārya; *caraṇa*—lotus feet; *vandana*—worshiping.

TRANSLATION

To maintain the proper etiquette for the principles of religion, Lord Caitanya bows down at the lotus feet of Śrī Advaita Ācārya with reverential prayers and devotion.

TEXT 42

চৈতন্যগোসাঞিকে আচার্য করে 'প্রভু'-জ্ঞান ।
আপনাকে করেন তাঁর 'দাস'-অভিমান ॥ ৪২ ॥

caitanya-gosāñike ācārya kare 'prabhu'-jñāna
āpanāke karena tāṅra 'dāsa'-abhimāna

caitanya-gosāñike—unto Śrī Caitanya Mahāprabhu; *ācārya*—Advaita Ācārya; *kare*—does; *prabhu-jñāna*—considering His master; *āpanāke*—unto Himself; *karena*—does; *tāṅra*—of Śrī Caitanya Mahāprabhu; *dāsa*—as a servant; *abhimāna*—conception.

TRANSLATION

Śrī Advaita Ācārya, however, considers Lord Caitanya Mahāprabhu His master, and He thinks of Himself as a servant of Lord Caitanya Mahāprabhu.

PURPORT

The *Bhakti-rasāmṛta-sindhu* of Rūpa Gosvāmī explains the superexcellent quality of devotional service as follows:

brahmānando bhaved eṣa cet parārdha-guṇī-kṛtaḥ
naiti bhakti-sukhāmbhodheḥ paramāṇu-tulām api

"If multiplied billions of times, the transcendental pleasure derived from impersonal Brahman realization still could not compare to even an atomic portion of the ocean of *bhakti,* or transcendental service." *(B.r.s.* 1.1.38) Similarly, the *Bhāvārtha-dīpikā* states:

tvat-kathāmṛta-pāthodhau viharanto mahā-mudaḥ
kurvanti kṛtinaḥ kecic catur-vargaṁ tṛṇopamam

"For those who take pleasure in the transcendental topics of the Supreme Personality of Godhead, the four progressive realizations of religiosity, economic development, sense gratification and liberation, all combined together, cannot compare, any more than a straw could, to the happiness derived from hearing about the transcendental activities of the Lord." Those who engage in the transcendental service of the lotus feet of Kṛṣṇa, being relieved of all material enjoyment, have no attraction to topics of impersonal monism. In the *Padma Purāṇa,* in connection with the glorification of the month of Kārttika, it is stated that devotees pray:

varaṁ deva mokṣaṁ na mokṣāvadhiṁ vā
na cānyaṁ vṛṇe 'haṁ vareśād apīha
idaṁ te vapur nātha gopāla-bālaṁ
sadā me manasy āvirāstāṁ kim anyaiḥ

kuverātmajau baddha-mūrtyaiva yadvat
tvayā mocitau bhakti-bhājau kṛtau ca
tathā prema-bhaktiṁ svakāṁ me prayaccha
na mokṣe graho me 'sti dāmodareha

"Dear Lord, always remembering Your childhood pastimes at Vṛndāvana is better for us than aspiring to merge into the impersonal Brahman. During Your childhood pastimes You liberated the two sons of Kuvera and made them great devotees of Your Lordship. Similarly, I wish that instead of giving me liberation You may award me such devotion unto You." In the *Hayaśīrṣīya-śrī-nārāyaṇa-vyūha-stava,* in the chapter called *Nārāyaṇa-stotra,* it is stated:

na dharmaṁ kāmam arthaṁ vā
mokṣaṁ vā vara-deśvara
prārthaye tava pādābje
dāsyam evābhikāmaye

"My dear Lord, I do not wish to become a man of religion or a master of economic development or sense gratification, nor do I wish for liberation. Although I can have all these from You, the supreme bestower of benedictions, I do not pray for any of these. I simply pray that I may always be engaged as a servant of Your lotus feet." Nṛsiṁhadeva offered Prahlāda Mahārāja all kinds of benedictions, but Prahlāda Mahārāja did not accept any of them, for he simply wanted to engage in the service of the lotus feet of the Lord. Similarly, a pure devotee wishes to be blessed like Mahārāja Prahlāda by being thus endowed with devotional service. Devotees also offer their respects to Hanumān, who always remained a servant of Lord Rāma. The great devotee Hanumān prayed:

bhava-bandha-cchide tasyai spṛhayāmi na muktaye
bhavān prabhur ahaṁ dāsa iti yatra vilupyate

"I do not wish to take liberation or to merge in the Brahman effulgence, where the conception of being a servant of the Lord is completely lost." Similarly, in the *Nārada-pañcarātra* it is stated:

dharmārtha-kāma-mokṣeṣu necchā mama kadācana
tvat-pāda-paṅkajasyādho jīvitaṁ dīyatāṁ mama

"I do not want any one of the four desirable stations. I simply want to engage as a servant of the lotus feet of the Lord." King Kulaśekhara, in his very famous book *Mukunda-mālā-stotra,* prays:

nāhaṁ vande tava caraṇayor dvandvam advandva-hetoḥ
kumbhī-pākaṁ gurum api hare nārakaṁ nāpanetum
ramyā-rāmā-mṛdu-tanu-latā-nandane nābhirantuṁ
bhāve bhāve hṛdaya-bhavane bhāvayeyaṁ bhavantam

"My Lord, I do not worship You to be liberated from this material entanglement, nor do I wish to save myself from the hellish condition of material existence, nor do I ever pray for a beautiful wife to enjoy in a nice garden. I wish only that I may always be in full ecstasy with the pleasure of serving Your Lordship." (*M.m.s.* 4) In *Śrīmad-Bhāgavatam* also there are many instances in the Third and Fourth cantos in which devotees pray to the Lord simply to be engaged in His service, and nothing else (*Bhāg.* 3.4.15, 3.25.34, 3.25.36, 4.8.22, 4.9.10 and 4.20.24).

TEXT 43

সেই অভিমান-সুখে আপনা পাসরে ।
'কৃষ্ণদাস' হও—জীবে উপদেশ করে ॥ ৪৩ ॥

sei abhimāna-sukhe āpanā pāsare
'kṛṣṇa-dāsa' hao—jīve upadeśa kare

sei—that; *abhimāna-sukhe*—in the happiness of that conception; *āpanā*—Himself; *pāsare*—He forgets; *kṛṣṇa-dāsa hao*—You are servants of Lord Kṛṣṇa; *jīve*—the living beings; *upadeśa kare*—He instructs.

TRANSLATION

He forgets Himself in the joy of that conception and teaches all living entities, "You are servants of Śrī Caitanya Mahāprabhu."

PURPORT

The transcendental devotional service of the Supreme Personality of Godhead is so ecstatic that even the Lord Himself plays the part of a devotee. Forgetting Himself to be the Supreme, He personally teaches the whole world how to render service to the Supreme Personality of Godhead.

TEXT 44

কৃষ্ণদাস-অভিমানে যে আনন্দসিন্ধু ।
কোটী-ব্রহ্মসুখ নহে তার এক বিন্দু ॥ ৪৪ ॥

kṛṣṇa-dāsa-abhimāne ye ānanda-sindhu
koṭī-brahma-sukha nahe tāra eka bindu

kṛṣṇa-dāsa-abhimāne—under this impression of being a servant of Kṛṣṇa; *ye*—that; *ānanda-sindhu*—ocean of transcendental bliss; *koṭī-brahma-sukha*—ten million times the transcendental bliss of becoming one with the Absolute; *nahe*—not; *tāra*—of the ocean of transcendental bliss; *eka*—one; *bindu*—drop.

TRANSLATION

The conception of servitude to Śrī Kṛṣṇa generates such an ocean of joy in the soul that even the joy of oneness with the Absolute, if multiplied ten million times, could not compare to a drop of it.

TEXT 45

মুঞি যে চৈতন্যদাস, আর নিত্যানন্দ ।
দাস-ভাব-সম নহে অন্যত্র আনন্দ ॥ ৪৫ ॥

muñi ye caitanya-dāsa āra nityānanda
dāsa-bhāva-sama nahe anyatra ānanda

muñi—I; *ye*—that; *caitanya-dāsa*—servant of Lord Caitanya; *āra*—and; *nityānanda*—of Lord Nityānanda; *dāsa-bhāva*—the emotion of being a servant; *sama*—equal to; *nahe*—not; *anyatra*—anywhere else; *ānanda*—transcendental bliss.

TRANSLATION

He says, "Nityānanda and I are servants of Lord Caitanya." Nowhere else is there such joy as that which is tasted in this emotion of servitude.

TEXT 46

পরমপ্রেয়সী লক্ষ্মী হৃদয়ে বসতি ।
তেঁহো দাস্য-সুখ মাগে করিয়া মিনতি ॥ ৪৬ ॥

parama-preyasī lakṣmī hṛdaye vasati
teṅho dāsya-sukha māge kariyā minati

parama-preyasī—the most beloved; *lakṣmī*—the goddess of fortune; *hṛdaye*—on the chest; *vasati*—residence; *teṅho*—she; *dāsya-sukha*—the happiness of being a maidservant; *māge*—begs; *kariyā*—offering; *minati*—prayers.

TRANSLATION

The most beloved goddess of fortune resides on the chest of Śrī Kṛṣṇa, yet she too, earnestly praying, begs for the joy of service at His feet.

TEXT 47

দাস্য-ভাবে আনন্দিত পারিষদগণ ।
বিধি, ভব, নারদ আর শুক, সনাতন ॥ ৪৭ ॥

dāsya-bhāve ānandita pāriṣada-gaṇa
vidhi, bhava, nārada āra śuka, sanātana

dāsya-bhāve—in the conception of being a servant; *ānandita*—very pleased; *pāriṣada-gaṇa*—all the associates; *vidhi*—Lord Brahmā;

bhava—Lord Śiva; *nārada*—the great sage Nārada; *āra*—and; *śuka*—Śukadeva Gosvāmī; *sanātana*—and Sanātana Kumāra.

TRANSLATION

All the associates of Lord Kṛṣṇa, such as Brahmā, Śiva, Nārada, Śuka and Sanātana Kumāra, are very pleased in the sentiment of servitude.

TEXT 48

নিত্যানন্দ অবধূত সবাতে আগল ।
চৈতন্যের দাস্য-প্রেমে হইলা পাগল ॥ ৪৮ ॥

nityānanda avadhūta sabāte āgala
caitanyera dāsya-preme ha-ilā pāgala

nityānanda avadhūta—the mendicant Lord Nityānanda; *sabāte*—among all; *āgala*—foremost; *caitanyera dāsya-preme*—in the emotional ecstatic love of being a servant of Śrī Caitanya Mahāprabhu; *ha-ilā pāgala*—became mad.

TRANSLATION

Śrī Nityānanda, the wandering mendicant, is the foremost of all the associates of Lord Caitanya. He became mad in the ecstasy of service to Lord Caitanya.

TEXTS 49–50

শ্রীবাস, হরিদাস, রামদাস, গদাধর ।
মুরারি, মুকুন্দ, চন্দ্রশেখর, বক্রেশ্বর ॥ ৪৯ ॥
এসব পণ্ডিতলোক পরম-মহত্ত্ব ।
চৈতন্যের দাস্যে সবায় করয়ে উন্মত্ত ॥ ৫০ ॥

śrīvāsa, haridāsa, rāmadāsa, gadādhara
murāri, mukunda, candraśekhara, vakreśvara

e-saba paṇḍita-loka parama-mahattva
caitanyera dāsye sabāya karaye unmatta

śrīvāsa—Śrīvāsa Ṭhākura; *haridāsa*—Haridāsa Ṭhākura; *rāmadāsa*—Rāmadāsa; *gadādhara*—Gadādhara; *murāri*—Murāri; *mukunda*—

Mukunda; *candraśekhara*—Candraśekhara; *vakreśvara*—Vakreśvara; *e-saba*—all of them; *paṇḍita-loka*—very learned scholars; *parama-mahattva*—very much glorified; *caitanyera*—of Śrī Caitanya Mahāprabhu; *dāsye*—the servitude; *sabāya*—all of them; *karaye unmatta*—makes mad.

TRANSLATION

Śrīvāsa, Haridāsa, Rāmadāsa, Gadādhara, Murāri, Mukunda, Candraśekhara and Vakreśvara are all glorious and are all learned scholars, but the sentiment of servitude to Lord Caitanya makes them mad in ecstasy.

TEXT 51

এই মত গায়, নাচে, করে অট্টহাস ।
লোকে উপদেশে,—'হও চৈতন্যের দাস' ॥ ৫১ ॥

ei mata gāya, nāce, kare aṭṭahāsa
loke upadeśe,—'hao caitanyera dāsa'

ei mata—in this way; *gāya*—chant; *nāce*—dance; *kare*—do; *aṭṭa-hāsa*—laughing like madmen; *loke*—unto the people in general; *upadeśe*—instruct; *hao*—just become; *caitanyera dāsa*—servants of Śrī Caitanya.

TRANSLATION

Thus they dance, sing and laugh like madmen, and they instruct everyone, "Just be loving servants of Lord Caitanya."

TEXT 52

চৈতন্যগোসাঞি মোরে করে গুরু-জ্ঞান ।
তথাপিহ মোর হয় দাস-অভিমান ॥ ৫২ ॥

caitanya-gosāñi more kare guru jñāna
tathāpiha mora haya dāsa-abhimāna

caitanya-gosāñi—Lord Śrī Caitanya Mahāprabhu; *more*—unto Me; *kare*—does; *guru-jñāna*—consideration as a spiritual master; *tathā-piha*—still; *mora*—My; *haya*—there is; *dāsa-abhimāna*—the conception of being His servant.

TRANSLATION

Śrī Advaita Ācārya thinks, "Lord Caitanya considers Me His spiritual master, yet I feel Myself to be only His servant."

TEXT 53

কৃষ্ণপ্রেমের এই এক অপূর্ব প্রভাব।
গুরু-সম-লঘুকে করায় দাস্যভাব ॥ ৫৩ ॥

kṛṣṇa-premera ei eka apūrva prabhāva
guru-sama-laghuke karāya dāsya-bhāva

kṛṣṇa-premera—of love of Kṛṣṇa; *ei*—this; *eka*—one; *apūrva prabhāva*—unprecedented influence; *guru*—to those on the level of the spiritual master; *sama*—equal level; *laghuke*—unto the less important; *karāya*—makes; *dāsya-bhāva*—the conception of being a servant.

TRANSLATION

Love for Kṛṣṇa has this one unique effect: it imbues superiors, equals and inferiors with the spirit of service to Lord Kṛṣṇa.

PURPORT

There are two kinds of devotional service: the way of *pāñcarātrika* regulative principles and the way of *bhāgavata* transcendental loving service. The love of Godhead of those engaged in *pāñcarātrika* regulative principles depends more or less on the opulent and reverential platform, but the worship of Rādhā and Kṛṣṇa is purely on the platform of transcendental love. Even persons who play as the superiors of Kṛṣṇa also take the chance to offer transcendental loving service to the Lord. The service attitude of the devotees who play the parts of superiors of the Lord is very difficult to understand, but it can be very plainly understood in connection with the superexcellence of their particular service to Lord Kṛṣṇa. A vivid example is the service of mother Yaśodā to Kṛṣṇa, which is distinct. In the feature of Nārāyaṇa, the Lord can accept services only from His associates who play parts in which they are equal to or less than Him, but in the feature of Lord Kṛṣṇa He accepts service very plainly from His fathers, teachers and other elders who are His superiors, as well as from His equals and His subordinates. This is very wonderful.

TEXT 54

ইহার প্রমাণ শুন—শাস্ত্রের ব্যাখ্যান ।
মহদনুভব যাতে সুদৃঢ় প্রমাণ ॥ ৫৪ ॥

ihāra pramāṇa śuna—śāstrera vyākhyāna
mahad-anubhava yāte sudṛḍha pramāṇa

ihāra—of this; *pramāṇa*—evidence; *śuna*—please hear; *śāstrera vyākhyāna*—the description in the revealed scriptures; *mahat-anubhava*—the conception of great souls; *yāte*—by which; *su-dṛḍha*—strong; *pramāṇa*—evidence.

TRANSLATION

For evidence, please listen to the examples described in the revealed scriptures, which are corroborated by the realization of great souls.

TEXTS 55–56

অন্যের কা কথা, ব্রজে নন্দ মহাশয় ।
তার সম 'গুরু' কৃষ্ণের আর কেহ নয় ॥ ৫৫ ॥
শুদ্ধবাৎসল্যে ঈশ্বর-জ্ঞান নাহি তার ।
তাহাকেই প্রেমে করায় দাস্য-অনুকার ॥ ৫৬ ॥

anyera kā kathā, vraje nanda mahāśaya
tāra sama 'guru' kṛṣṇera āra keha naya

śuddha-vātsalye īśvara-jñāna nāhi tāra
tāhākei preme karāya dāsya-anukāra

anyera—of others; *kā*—what; *kathā*—to speak; *vraje*—in Vṛndāvana; *nanda mahāśaya*—Nanda Mahārāja; *tāra sama*—like him; *guru*—a superior; *kṛṣṇera*—of Lord Kṛṣṇa; *āra*—another; *keha*—anyone; *naya*—not; *śuddha-vātsalye*—in transcendental paternal love; *īśvara-jñāna*—conception of the Supreme Lord; *nāhi*—not; *tāra*—his; *tāhākei*—unto him; *preme*—ecstatic love; *karāya*—makes; *dāsya-anukāra*—the conception of being a servant.

TRANSLATION

Although no one is a more respected elder for Kṛṣṇa than Nanda Mahārāja in Vraja, who in transcendental paternal love has no

knowledge that his son is the Supreme Personality of Godhead, still ecstatic love makes him, what to speak of others, feel himself to be a servant of Lord Kṛṣṇa.

TEXT 57

তেঁহো রতি-মতি মাগে কৃষ্ণের চরণে ।
তাহার শ্রীমুখবাণী তাহাতে প্রমাণে ॥ ৫৭ ॥

teṅho rati-mati māge kṛṣṇera caraṇe
tāhāra śrī-mukha-vāṇī tāhāte pramāṇe

teṅho—he also; *rati-mati*—affection and attraction; *māge*—begs; *kṛṣṇera caraṇe*—unto the lotus feet of Kṛṣṇa; *tāhāra*—his; *śrī-mukha-vāṇī*—words from his mouth; *tāhāte*—in that; *pramāṇe*—evidence.

TRANSLATION

He too prays for attachment and devotion to the lotus feet of Lord Kṛṣṇa, as the words from his own mouth give evidence.

TEXTS 58–59

শুন উদ্ধব, সত্য, কৃষ্ণ—আমার তনয় ।
তেঁহো ঈশ্বর—হেন যদি তোমার মনে লয় ॥ ৫৮ ॥
তথাপি তাঁহাতে রহু মোর মনোবৃত্তি ।
তোমার ঈশ্বর-কৃষ্ণে হউক মোর মতি ॥ ৫৯ ॥

śuna uddhava, satya, kṛṣṇa—āmāra tanaya
teṅho īśvara—hena yadi tomāra mane laya

tathāpi tāṅhāte rahu mora mano-vṛtti
tomāra īśvara-kṛṣṇe hauka mora mati

śuna uddhava—my dear Uddhava, please hear me; *satya*—the truth; *kṛṣṇa*—Lord Kṛṣṇa; *āmāra tanaya*—my son; *teṅho*—He; *īśvara*—the Supreme Personality of Godhead; *hena*—thus; *yadi*—if; *tomāra*—your; *mane*—the mind; *laya*—takes; *tathāpi*—still; *tāṅhāte*—unto Him; *rahu*—let there be; *mora*—my; *manaḥ-vṛtti*—mental functions; *tomāra*—your; *īśvara-kṛṣṇe*—to Kṛṣṇa, the Supreme Lord; *hauka*—let there be; *mora*—my; *mati*—attention.

TRANSLATION

"My dear Uddhava, please hear me. In truth Kṛṣṇa is my son, but even if you think that He is God, I would still bear toward Him my own feelings for my son. May my mind be attached to your Lord Kṛṣṇa.

TEXT 60

মনসো বৃত্তয়ো নঃ স্যুঃ কৃষ্ণপাদাম্বুজাশ্রয়াঃ ।
বাচোঽভিধায়িনীর্নাম্নাং কায়স্তৎপ্রহ্বণাদিষু ॥ ৬০ ॥

manaso vṛttayo naḥ syuḥ
kṛṣṇa-pādāmbujāśrayāḥ
vāco 'bhidhāyinīr nāmnāṁ
kāyas tat-prahvaṇādiṣu

manasaḥ—of the mind; *vṛttayaḥ*—activities (thinking, feeling and willing); *naḥ*—of us; *syuḥ*—let there be; *kṛṣṇa*—of Lord Kṛṣṇa; *pāda-ambuja*—the lotus feet; *āśrayāḥ*—those sheltered by; *vācaḥ*—the words; *abhidhāyinīḥ*—speaking; *nāmnām*—of His holy names; *kāyaḥ*—the body; *tat*—to Him; *prahvaṇa-ādiṣu*—bowing down to Him, etc.

TRANSLATION

"May our minds be attached to the lotus feet of your Lord Kṛṣṇa, may our tongues chant His holy names, and may our bodies lie prostrate before Him.

TEXT 61

কর্মভির্ভ্রাম্যমাণানাং যত্র ক্বাপীশ্বরেচ্ছয়া ।
মঙ্গলাচরিতৈর্দানৈ রতির্নঃ কৃষ্ণ ঈশ্বরে ॥ ৬১ ॥

karmabhir bhrāmyamāṇānāṁ
yatra kvāpīśvarecchayā
maṅgalācaritair dānai
ratir naḥ kṛṣṇa īśvare

karmabhiḥ—by the activities; *bhrāmyamāṇānām*—of those wandering within the material universe; *yatra*—wherever; *kva api*—anywhere;

īśvara-icchayā—by the supreme will of the Personality of Godhead; *maṅgala-ācaritaiḥ*—by auspicious activities; *dānaiḥ*—like charity and philanthropy; *ratiḥ*—the attraction; *naḥ*—our; *kṛṣṇe*—in Kṛṣṇa; *īśvare*—the Supreme Personality of Godhead.

TRANSLATION

"Wherever we wander in the material universe under the influence of karma by the will of the Lord, may our auspicious activities cause our attraction to Lord Kṛṣṇa to increase."

PURPORT

These verses from *Śrīmad-Bhāgavatam* (10.47.66–67) were spoken by the denizens of Vṛndāvana, headed by Mahārāja Nanda and his associates, to Uddhava, who had come from Mathurā.

TEXT 62

শ্রীদামাদি ব্রজে যত সখার নিচয় ।
ঐশ্বর্য-জ্ঞান-হীন, কেবল-সখ্যময় ॥ ৬২ ॥

śrīdāmādi vraje yata sakhāra nicaya
aiśvarya-jñāna-hīna, kevala-sakhya-maya

śrīdāmā-ādi—Kṛṣṇa's friends, headed by Śrīdāmā; *vraje*—in Vṛndāvana; *yata*—all; *sakhāra*—of the friends; *nicaya*—the group; *aiśvarya*—of opulence; *jñāna*—knowledge; *hīna*—without; *kevala*—purely; *sakhya-maya*—fraternal affection.

TRANSLATION

Lord Kṛṣṇa's friends in Vṛndāvana, headed by Śrīdāmā, have pure fraternal affection for Lord Kṛṣṇa and have no idea of His opulences.

TEXT 63

কৃষ্ণসঙ্গে যুদ্ধ করে, স্কন্ধে আরোহণ ।
তারা দাস্যভাবে করে চরণ-সেবন ॥ ৬৩ ॥

kṛṣṇa-saṅge yuddha kare, skandhe ārohaṇa
tārā dāsya-bhāve kare caraṇa-sevana

kṛṣṇa-saṅge—with Kṛṣṇa; *yuddha kare*—fight; *skandhe*—on His shoulders; *ārohaṇa*—getting up; *tārā*—they; *dāsya-bhāve*—in the conception of being Lord Kṛṣṇa's servants; *kare*—do; *caraṇa-sevana*—worship the lotus feet.

TRANSLATION

Although they fight with Him and climb upon His shoulders, they worship His lotus feet in a spirit of servitude.

TEXT 64

পাদসংবাহনং চক্রুঃ কেচিত্তস্য মহাত্মনঃ ।
অপরে হতপাপ্মানো ব্যজনৈঃ সমবীজয়ন্ ॥ ৬৪ ॥

pāda-saṁvāhanaṁ cakruḥ
kecit tasya mahātmanaḥ
apare hata-pāpmāno
vyajanaiḥ samavījayan

pāda-saṁvāhanam—massaging the feet; *cakruḥ*—performed; *kecit*—some of them; *tasya*—of Lord Kṛṣṇa; *mahā-ātmanaḥ*—of the Supreme Personality of Godhead; *apare*—others; *hata*—destroyed; *pāpmānaḥ*—whose resultant actions of sinful life; *vyajanaiḥ*—with hand-held fans; *samavījayan*—fanned very pleasingly.

TRANSLATION

"Some of the friends of Śrī Kṛṣṇa, the Supreme Personality of Godhead, massaged His feet, and others whose sinful reactions had been destroyed fanned Him with hand-held fans."

PURPORT

This verse, quoted from *Śrīmad-Bhāgavatam* (10.15.17), describes how Lord Kṛṣṇa and Lord Balarāma were playing with the cowherd boys after killing Dhenukāsura in Tālavana.

TEXTS 65–66

কৃষ্ণের প্রেয়সী ব্রজে যত গোপীগণ ।
যাঁর পদধূলি করে উদ্ধব প্রার্থন ॥ ৬৫ ॥

যাঁ-সবার উপরে কৃষ্ণের প্রিয় নাহি আন ।
তাঁহারা আপনাকে করে দাসী-অভিমান ॥ ৬৬ ॥

kṛṣṇera preyasī vraje yata gopī-gaṇa
yāṅra pada-dhūli kare uddhava prārthana

yāṅ-sabāra upare kṛṣṇera priya nāhi āna
tāṅhārā āpanāke kare dāsī-abhimāna

kṛṣṇera—of Lord Kṛṣṇa; *preyasī*—the beloved girls; *vraje*—in Vṛndāvana; *yata*—all; *gopī-gaṇa*—the *gopīs; yāṅra*—of whom; *pada-dhūli*—the dust of the feet; *kare*—does; *uddhava*—Uddhava; *prārthana*—desiring; *yāṅ-sabāra*—all of them; *upare*—beyond; *kṛṣṇera*—of Lord Kṛṣṇa; *priya*—dear; *nāhi*—there is not; *āna*—anyone else; *tāṅhārā*—all of them; *āpanāke*—to themselves; *kare*—do; *dāsī-abhimāna*—the conception of being maidservants.

TRANSLATION

Even the beloved girlfriends of Lord Kṛṣṇa in Vṛndāvana, the gopīs, the dust of whose feet was desired by Śrī Uddhava and who are more dear to Kṛṣṇa than anyone else, regard themselves as Kṛṣṇa's maidservants.

TEXT 67

ব্রজজনার্তিহন্ বীর যোষিতাং নিজ-জনস্ময়ধ্বংসনস্মিত ।
ভজ সখে ভবৎকিঙ্করীঃ স্ম নো জলরুহাননং চারু দর্শয় ॥ ৬৭ ॥

vraja-janārti-han vīra yoṣitāṁ
nija-jana-smaya-dhvaṁsana-smita
bhaja sakhe bhavat-kiṅkarīḥ sma no
jala-ruhānanaṁ cāru darśaya

vraja-jana-ārti-han—O one who diminishes all the painful conditions of the inhabitants of Vṛndāvana; *vīra*—O hero; *yoṣitām*—of women; *nija*—personal; *jana*—of the associates; *smaya*—the pride; *dhvaṁ-sana*—destroying; *smita*—whose smile; *bhaja*—worship; *sakhe*—O dear friend; *bhavat-kiṅkarīḥ*—Your servants; *sma*—certainly; *naḥ*—unto us; *jala-ruha-ānanam*—a face exactly like a lotus flower; *cāru*—attractive; *darśaya*—please show.

TRANSLATION

"O Lord, remover of the afflictions of the inhabitants of Vṛndāvana! O hero of all women! O Lord who destroy the pride of Your devotees by Your sweet, gentle smile! O friend! We are Your maidservants. Please fulfill our desires and show us Your attractive lotus face."

PURPORT

This verse in connection with the *rāsa* dance of Kṛṣṇa with the *gopīs* is quoted from *Śrīmad-Bhāgavatam* (10.31.6). When Kṛṣṇa disappeared from His companions in the course of dancing, the *gopīs* sang like this in separation from Kṛṣṇa.

TEXT 68

অপি বত মধুপুর্য্যামার্যপুত্রোঽধুনাস্তে
স্মরতি স পিতৃগেহান্ সৌম্য বন্ধূংশ্চ গোপান্ ।
ক্বচিদপি স কথাং নঃ কিঙ্করীণাং গৃণীতে
ভুজমগুরুসুগন্ধং মূর্দ্ধ্যধাস্যৎ কদা নু ॥ ৬৮ ॥

api bata madhu-puryām ārya-putro 'dhunāste
smarati sa pitṛ-gehān saumya bandhūṁś ca gopān
kvacid api sa kathāṁ naḥ kiṅkarīṇāṁ gṛṇīte
bhujam aguru-sugandhaṁ mūrdhny adhāsyat kadā nu

api—certainly; *bata*—regrettable; *madhu-puryām*—in the city of Mathurā; *ārya-putraḥ*—the son of Nanda Mahārāja; *adhunā*—now; *āste*—resides; *smarati*—remembers; *saḥ*—He; *pitṛ-gehān*—the household affairs of His father; *saumya*—O great soul (Uddhava); *bandhūn*—His many friends; *ca*—and; *gopān*—the cowherd boys; *kvacit*—sometimes; *api*—or; *saḥ*—He; *kathām*—talks; *naḥ*—of us; *kiṅkarīṇām*—of the maidservants; *gṛṇīte*—relates; *bhujam*—hand; *aguru-su-gandham*—having the fragrance of *aguru; mūrdhni*—on the head; *adhāsyat*—will keep; *kadā*—when; *nu*—may be.

TRANSLATION

"O Uddhava! It is indeed regrettable that Kṛṣṇa resides in Mathurā. Does He remember His father's household affairs and His friends, the cowherd boys? O great soul! Does He ever talk

about us, His maidservants? When will He lay on our heads His aguru-scented hand?"

PURPORT

This verse appears in *Śrīmad-Bhāgavatam* (10.47.21), in the section known as the *Bhramara-gītā.* When Uddhava came to Vṛndāvana, Śrīmatī Rādhārāṇī, in complete separation from Kṛṣṇa, sang like this.

TEXTS 69–70

তাঁ-সবার কথা রহু,—শ্রীমতী রাধিকা ।
সবা হৈতে সকলাংশে পরম-অধিকা ॥ ৬৯ ॥
তেঁহো যাঁর দাসী হৈঞা সেবেন চরণ ।
যাঁর প্রেমগুণে কৃষ্ণ বদ্ধ অনুক্ষণ ॥ ৭০ ॥

tāṅ-sabāra kathā rahu,—śrīmatī rādhikā
sabā haite sakalāṁśe parama-adhikā

teṅho yāṅra dāsī haiñā sevena caraṇa
yāṅra prema-guṇe kṛṣṇa baddha anukṣaṇa

tāṅ-sabāra—of the *gopīs; kathā*—talk; *rahu*—let alone; *śrīmatī rādhikā*—Śrīmatī Rādhārāṇī; *sabā haite*—than all of them; *sakala-aṁśe*—in every respect; *parama-adhikā*—highly elevated; *teṅho*—She also; *yāṅra*—whose; *dāsī*—maidservant; *haiñā*—becoming; *sevena*—worships; *caraṇa*—the lotus feet; *yāṅra*—whose; *prema-guṇe*—because of loving attributes; *kṛṣṇa*—Lord Kṛṣṇa; *baddha*—obliged; *anukṣaṇa*—always.

TRANSLATION

What to speak of the other gopīs, even Śrī Rādhikā, who in every respect is the most elevated of them all and who has bound Śrī Kṛṣṇa forever by Her loving attributes, serves His feet as His maidservant.

TEXT 71

হা নাথ রমণ প্রেষ্ঠ ক্বাসি ক্বাসি মহাভুজ ।
দাস্যাস্তে কৃপণায়া মে সখে দর্শয় সন্নিধিম্ ॥ ৭১ ॥

hā nātha ramaṇa preṣṭha
kvāsi kvāsi mahā-bhuja
dāsyās te kṛpaṇāyā me
sakhe darśaya sannidhim

hā—O; *nātha*—My Lord; *ramaṇa*—O My husband; *preṣṭha*—O My most dear one; *kva asi kva asi*—where are You, where are You; *mahā-bhuja*—O mighty-armed one; *dāsyāḥ*—of the maidservant; *te*—You; *kṛpaṇāyāḥ*—very much aggrieved by Your absence; *me*—to Me; *sakhe*—O My friend; *darśaya*—show; *sannidhim*—nearness to You.

TRANSLATION

"O My Lord, O My husband, O most dearly beloved! O mighty-armed Lord! Where are You? Where are You? O My friend, reveal Yourself to Your maidservant, who is very much aggrieved by Your absence."

PURPORT

This verse is quoted from *Śrīmad-Bhāgavatam* (10.30.39). When the *rāsa* dance was going on in full swing, Kṛṣṇa left all the *gopīs* and took only Śrīmatī Rādhārāṇī with Him. At that time all the *gopīs* lamented, and Śrīmatī Rādhārāṇī, being proud of Her position, requested Kṛṣṇa to carry Her wherever He liked. Then Kṛṣṇa immediately disappeared from the scene, and Śrīmatī Rādhārāṇī began to lament.

TEXT 72

দ্বারকাতে রুক্মিণ্যাদি যতেক মহিষী ।
তাঁহারাও আপনাকে মানে কৃষ্ণদাসী ॥ ৭২ ॥

dvārakāte rukmiṇy-ādi yateka mahiṣī
tāṅhārāo āpanāke māne kṛṣṇa-dāsī

dvārakāte—in Dvārakā-dhāma; *rukmiṇī-ādi*—headed by Rukmiṇī; *yateka*—all of them; *mahiṣī*—the queens; *tāṅhārāo*—all of them also; *āpanāke*—themselves; *māne*—consider; *kṛṣṇa-dāsī*—maidservants of Kṛṣṇa.

TRANSLATION

In Dvārakā-dhāma, all the queens, headed by Rukmiṇī, also consider themselves maidservants of Lord Kṛṣṇa.

TEXT 73

চৈদ্যায় মার্পয়িতুমুদ্যত-কার্মুকেষু
রাজস্বজেয়-ভটশেখরিতাঙ্ঘ্রিরেণুঃ ।
নিন্যে মৃগেন্দ্র ইব ভাগমজাবিযূথা-
ত্তচ্ছ্রীনিকেত-চরণোঽস্তু মমার্চনায় ॥ ৭৩ ॥

caidyāya mārpayitum udyata-kārmukeṣu
rājasv ajeya-bhaṭa-śekharitāṅghri-reṇuḥ
ninye mṛgendra iva bhāgam ajāvi-yūthāt
tac chrī-niketa-caraṇo 'stu mamārcanāya

caidyāya—unto Śiśupāla; *mā*—me; *arpayitum*—to deliver or to give in charity; *udyata*—upraised; *kārmukeṣu*—whose bows and arrows; *rājasu*—among the kings headed by Jarāsandha; *ajeya*—unconquerable; *bhaṭa*—of the soldiers; *śekharita-aṅghri-reṇuḥ*—the dust of whose lotus feet is the crown; *ninye*—forcibly took; *mṛga-indraḥ*—the lion; *iva*—like; *bhāgam*—the share; *aja*—of the goats; *avi*—and sheep; *yūthāt*—from the midst; *tat*—that; *śrī-niketa*—of the shelter of the goddess of fortune; *caraṇaḥ*—the lotus feet; *astu*—let there be; *mama*—my; *arcanāya*—for worshiping .

TRANSLATION

"When Jarāsandha and other kings, bows and arrows upraised, stood ready to deliver me in charity to Śiśupāla, He forcibly took me from their midst, as a lion takes its share of goats and sheep. The dust of His lotus feet is therefore the crown of unconquerable soldiers. May those lotus feet, which are the shelter of the goddess of fortune, be the object of my worship."

PURPORT

This verse from *Śrīmad-Bhāgavatam* (10.83.8) was spoken by Queen Rukmiṇī.

TEXT 74

তপশ্চরন্তীমাজ্ঞায় স্বপাদস্পর্শনাশয়া ।
সখ্যোপেত্যাগ্রহীৎ পাণিং সাহং তদ্গৃহমার্জনী ॥ ৭৪ ॥

tapaś carantīm ājñāya
sva-pāda-sparśanāśayā

sakhyopetyāgrahīt pāṇiṁ
sāhaṁ tad-gṛha-mārjanī

tapaḥ—austerity; *carantīm*—performing; *ājñāya*—knowing; *sva-pāda-sparśana*—of touching His feet; *āśayā*—with the desire; *sakhyā*—with His friend Arjuna; *upetya*—coming; *agrahīt*—accepted; *pāṇim*—my hand; *sā*—that woman; *aham*—I; *tat*—His; *gṛha-mārjanī*—keeper of the home.

TRANSLATION

"Knowing me to be performing austerities with the desire to touch His feet, He came with His friend Arjuna and accepted my hand. Yet I am but a maidservant engaged in sweeping the floor of the house of Śrī Kṛṣṇa."

PURPORT

Like the previous verse, this verse appears in *Śrīmad-Bhāgavatam* (10.83.11) in connection with the meeting of the family ladies of the Kuru and Yadu dynasties at Samanta-pañcaka. At the time of that meeting, the queen of Kṛṣṇa named Kālindī spoke to Draupadī in this way.

TEXT 75

আত্মারামস্য তস্যেমা বয়ং বৈ গৃহদাসিকাঃ ।
সর্বসঙ্গনিবৃত্ত্যাদ্ধা তপসা চ বভূবিম ॥ ৭৫ ॥

ātmārāmasya tasyemā
vayaṁ vai gṛha-dāsikāḥ
sarva-saṅga-nivṛttyāddhā
tapasā ca babhūvima

ātmārāmasya—of the Supreme Personality of Godhead, who is satisfied in Himself; *tasya*—His; *imāḥ*—all; *vayam*—we; *vai*—certainly; *gṛha-dāsikāḥ*—the maidservants of the home; *sarva*—all; *saṅga*—association; *nivṛttyā*—fully bereft of; *addhā*—directly; *tapasā*—on account of austerity; *ca*—also; *babhūvima*—we have become.

TRANSLATION

"Through austerity and through renunciation of all attachments, we have become maidservants in the home of the Supreme Personality of Godhead, who is satisfied in Himself."

PURPORT

During the same incident, this verse, quoted from *Śrīmad-Bhāgavatam* (10.83.39), was spoken to Draupadī by a queen of Kṛṣṇa's named Lakṣmaṇā.

TEXT 76

আনের কি কথা, বলদেব মহাশয় ।
যাঁর ভাব—শুদ্ধসখ্য-বাৎসল্যাদিময় ॥ ৭৬ ॥

ānera ki kathā, baladeva mahāśaya
yāṅra bhāva—śuddha-sakhya-vātsalyādi-maya

ānera—of others; *ki kathā*—what to speak; *baladeva*—Lord Baladeva; *mahāśaya*—the Supreme Personality; *yāṅra*—His; *bhāva*—emotion; *śuddha-sakhya*—pure friendship; *vātsalya-ādi-maya*—with a touch of paternal love.

TRANSLATION

What to speak of others, even Lord Baladeva, the Supreme Personality of Godhead, is full of emotions like pure friendship and paternal love.

PURPORT

Although Lord Baladeva appeared before the birth of Lord Kṛṣṇa and is therefore Kṛṣṇa's worshipable elder brother, He used to act as Kṛṣṇa's eternal servitor. In the spiritual sky all the Vaikuṇṭha planets are predominated by the quadruple expansions of Kṛṣṇa known as the *catur-vyūha.* They are direct expansions from Baladeva. It is the singularity of the Supreme Lord that everyone in the spiritual sky thinks himself a servitor of the Lord. According to social convention one may be superior to Kṛṣṇa, but factually everyone engages in His service. Therefore in the spiritual sky or the material sky, in all the different planets, no one is able to supersede Lord Kṛṣṇa or demand service from Him. On the contrary, everyone engages in the service of Lord Kṛṣṇa. As such, the more a person engages in the service of the Lord, the more he is important; and, conversely, the more one is bereft of the transcendental service of Kṛṣṇa, the more he invites the bad fortune of material contamination. In the material world, although materialists want to become one with God or compete with God, everyone directly or indirectly engages in the service of the Lord. The more one is forgetful of the service of Kṛṣṇa, the more he is considered to be dying. Therefore, when one develops pure Kṛṣṇa consciousness, he immediately develops his eternal servitorship to Kṛṣṇa.

TEXT 77

তেঁহো আপনাকে করেন দাস-ভাবনা ।
কৃষ্ণদাস-ভাব বিনু আছে কোন জনা ॥ ৭৭ ॥

teṅho āpanāke karena dāsa-bhāvanā
kṛṣṇa-dāsa-bhāva vinu āche kona janā

teṅho—He also; *āpanāke*—Himself; *karena*—does; *dāsa-bhāvanā*—considering a servant; *kṛṣṇa-dāsa-bhāva*—the conception of being a servant of Kṛṣṇa; *vinu*—without; *āche*—is; *kona*—what; *janā*—person.

TRANSLATION

He also considers Himself a servant of Lord Kṛṣṇa. Indeed, who is there who does not have this conception of being a servant of Lord Kṛṣṇa?

TEXT 78

সহস্র-বদনে যেঁহো শেষ-সঙ্কর্ষণ ।
দশ দেহ ধরি' করে কৃষ্ণের সেবন ॥ ৭৮ ॥

sahasra-vadane yeṅho śeṣa-saṅkarṣaṇa
daśa deha dhari' kare kṛṣṇera sevana

sahasra-vadane—with thousands of mouths; *yeṅho*—one who; *śeṣa-saṅkarṣaṇa*—Lord Śeṣa, the incarnation of Saṅkarṣaṇa; *daśa*—ten; *deha*—bodies; *dhari'*—accepting; *kare*—does; *kṛṣṇera*—of Lord Kṛṣṇa; *sevana*—service.

TRANSLATION

He who is Śeṣa, Saṅkarṣaṇa, with His thousands of mouths, serves Śrī Kṛṣṇa by assuming ten forms.

TEXT 79

অনন্ত ব্রহ্মাণ্ডে রুদ্র—সদাশিবের অংশ ।
গুণাবতার তেঁহো, সর্বদেব-অবতংস ॥ ৭৯ ॥

ananta brahmāṇḍe rudra—sadāśivera aṁśa
guṇāvatāra teṅho, sarva-deva-avataṁsa

ananta—unlimited; *brahmāṇḍe*—in the universes; *rudra*—Lord Śiva; *sadāśivera aṁśa*—part and parcel of Sadāśiva; *guṇa-avatāra*—an incarnation of a quality; *teṅho*—he also; *sarva-deva-avataṁsa*—the ornament of all the demigods.

TRANSLATION

Rudra, who is an expansion of Sadāśiva and who appears in unlimited universes, is also a guṇāvatāra [qualitative incarnation] and is the ornament of all the demigods in the endless universes.

PURPORT

There are eleven expansions of Rudra, or Lord Śiva. They are as follows: Ajaikapāt, Ahibradhna, Virūpākṣa, Raivata, Hara, Bahurūpa, Devaśreṣṭha Tryambaka, Sāvitra, Jayanta, Pināki and Aparājita. Besides these expansions there are eight forms of Rudra called earth, water, fire, air, sky, the sun, the moon and *soma-yājī.* Generally all these Rudras have five faces, three eyes and ten arms. Sometimes it is found that Rudra is compared to Brahmā and considered a living entity. But when Rudra is explained to be a partial expansion of the Supreme Personality of Godhead, he is compared to Śeṣa. Lord Śiva is therefore simultaneously an expansion of Lord Viṣṇu and, in his capacity for annihilating the creation, one of the living entities. As an expansion of Lord Viṣṇu he is called Hara, and he is transcendental to the material qualities, but when he is in touch with *tamo-guṇa* he appears contaminated by the material modes of nature. This is explained in *Śrīmad-Bhāgavatam* and the *Brahma-saṁhitā.* In *Śrīmad-Bhāgavatam,* Tenth Canto, it is stated that Lord Rudra is always associated with the material nature when she is in the neutral, unmanifested stage, but when the modes of material nature are agitated he associates with material nature from a distance. In the *Brahma-saṁhitā* the relationship between Viṣṇu and Lord Śiva is compared to that between milk and yogurt. Milk is converted into yogurt by certain additives, but although milk and yogurt have the same ingredients, they have different functions. Similarly, Lord Śiva is an expansion of Lord Viṣṇu, yet because of his taking part in the annihilation of the cosmic manifestation, he is considered to be changed, like milk converted into yogurt. In the *Purāṇas* it is found that Śiva appears sometimes from the heads of Brahmā and sometimes from the head of

Viṣṇu. The annihilator, Rudra, is born from Saṅkarṣaṇa and the ultimate fire to burn the whole creation. In the *Vāyu Purāṇa* there is a description of Sadāśiva in one of the Vaikuṇṭha planets. That Sadāśiva is a direct expansion of Lord Kṛṣṇa's form for pastimes. It is said that Sadāśiva (Lord Śambhu) is an expansion from the Sadāśiva in the Vaikuṇṭha planets (Lord Viṣṇu) and that his consort, Mahāmāyā, is an expansion of Ramā-devī, or Lakṣmī. Mahāmāyā is the origin or birthplace of material nature.

TEXT 80

তেঁহো করেন কৃষ্ণের দাস্য-প্রত্যাশ ।
নিরন্তর কহে শিব, 'মুঞি কৃষ্ণদাস' ॥ ৮০ ॥

teṅho karena kṛṣṇera dāsya-pratyāśa
nirantara kahe śiva, 'muñi kṛṣṇa-dāsa'

teṅho—he; *karena*—does; *kṛṣṇera*—of Lord Kṛṣṇa; *dāsya-pratyāśa*—expectation of being a servant; *nirantara*—constantly; *kahe*—says; *śiva*—Lord Śiva; *muñi*—I; *kṛṣṇa-dāsa*—a servant of Kṛṣṇa.

TRANSLATION

He also desires only to be a servant of Lord Kṛṣṇa. Śrī Sadāśiva always says, "I am a servant of Lord Kṛṣṇa."

TEXT 81

কৃষ্ণপ্রেমে উন্মত্ত, বিহ্বল দিগম্বর ।
কৃষ্ণ-গুণ-লীলা গায়, নাচে নিরন্তর ॥ ৮১ ॥

kṛṣṇa-preme unmatta, vihvala digambara
kṛṣṇa-guṇa-līlā gāya, nāce nirantara

kṛṣṇa-preme—in ecstatic love of Kṛṣṇa; *unmatta*—almost mad; *vihvala*—overwhelmed; *digambara*—without any dress; *kṛṣṇa*—of Lord Kṛṣṇa; *guṇa*—attributes; *līlā*—pastimes; *gāya*—chants; *nāce*—dances; *nirantara*—constantly.

TRANSLATION

Intoxicated by ecstatic love for Lord Kṛṣṇa, he becomes overwhelmed and incessantly dances without clothing and sings about Lord Kṛṣṇa's qualities and pastimes.

TEXT 82

পিতা-মাতা-গুরু-সখা-ভাব কেনে নয় ।
কৃষ্ণপ্রেমের স্বভাবে দাস্য-ভাব সে করয় ॥ ৮২ ॥

pitā-mātā-guru-sakhā-bhāva kene naya
kṛṣṇa-premera svabhāve dāsya-bhāva se karaya

pitā—father; *mātā*—mother; *guru*—superior teacher; *sakhā*—friend; *bhāva*—the emotion; *kene naya*—let it be; *kṛṣṇa-premera*—of love of Kṛṣṇa; *svabhāve*—in a natural inclination; *dāsya bhāva*—the emotion of becoming a servant; *se*—that; *karaya*—does.

TRANSLATION

All the emotions, whether those of father, mother, teacher or friend, are full of sentiments of servitude. That is the nature of love of Kṛṣṇa.

TEXT 83

এক কৃষ্ণ—সর্বসেব্য, জগৎ-ঈশ্বর ।
আর যত সব,—তাঁর সেবকানুচর ॥ ৮৩ ॥

eka kṛṣṇa—sarva-sevya, jagat-īśvara
āra yata saba,—tāṅra sevakānucara

eka kṛṣṇa—one Lord Kṛṣṇa; *sarva-sevya*—worthy of being served by all; *jagat-īśvara*—the Lord of the universe; *āra yata saba*—all others; *tāṅra*—His; *sevaka-anucara*—servants of the servants.

TRANSLATION

Lord Kṛṣṇa, the one master and the Lord of the universe, is worthy of being served by everyone. Indeed, everyone is but a servant of His servants.

TEXT 84

সেই কৃষ্ণ অবতীর্ণ—চৈতন্য-ঈশ্বর ।
অতএব আর সব,—তাঁহার কিঙ্কর ॥ ৮৪ ॥

sei kṛṣṇa avatīrṇa—caitanya-īśvara
ataeva āra saba,—tāṅhāra kiṅkara

sei—that; *kṛṣṇa*—Lord Kṛṣṇa; *avatīrṇa*—descended; *caitanya-īśvara*—Lord Caitanya, the Supreme Personality of Godhead; *ataeva*—therefore; *āra*—others; *saba*—all; *tāṅhāra kiṅkara*—His servants.

TRANSLATION

That same Lord Kṛṣṇa has descended as Lord Caitanya, the Supreme Personality of Godhead. Everyone, therefore, is His servant.

TEXT 85

কেহ মানে, কেহ না মানে, সব তাঁর দাস।
যে না মানে, তার হয় সেই পাপে নাশ ॥ ৮৫ ॥

keha māne, keha nā māne, saba tāṅra dāsa
ye nā māne, tāra haya sei pāpe nāśa

keha māne—someone accepts; *keha nā māne*—someone does not accept; *saba tāṅra dāsa*—all His servants; *ye nā māne*—one who does not accept; *tāra*—of him; *haya*—there is; *sei*—that; *pāpe*—in sinful activity; *nāśa*—annihilation.

TRANSLATION

Some accept Him whereas others do not, yet everyone is His servant. One who does not accept Him, however, will be ruined by his sinful activities.

PURPORT

When a living entity forgets his constitutional position, he prepares himself to be an enjoyer of the material resources. Sometimes he is also misguided by the thought that service to the Supreme Personality of Godhead is not absolute engagement. In other words, he thinks that there are many other engagements for a living entity besides the service of the Lord. Such a foolish person does not know that in any position he either directly or indirectly engages in activities of service to the Supreme Lord. Actually, if a person does not engage in the service of the Lord, all inauspicious activities encumber him because service to the Supreme Lord, Lord Caitanya, is the constitutional position of the infinitesimal living entities. Because the living entity is infinitesimal, the allurement of material enjoyment attracts him, and he tries to enjoy matter, forgetting his constitutional position. But when his dormant Kṛṣṇa consciousness is awakened, he no longer engages in the service of matter but engages in the service of the Lord. In other words, when one is forgetful of his constitutional position, he appears in the position of the lord of material nature. Even at that time he remains a servant of the Supreme Lord, but in an unqualified or contaminated state.

TEXT 86

চৈতন্যের দাস মুঞি, চৈতন্যের দাস ।
চৈতন্যের দাস মুঞি, তাঁর দাসের দাস ॥ ৮৬ ॥

caitanyera dāsa muñi, caitanyera dāsa
caitanyera dāsa muñi, tāṅra dāsera dāsa

caitanyera—of Lord Śrī Caitanya Mahāprabhu; *dāsa*—servant; *muñi*—I; *caitanyera dāsa*—a servant of Lord Caitanya; *caitanyera dāsa muñi*—I am a servant of Caitanya Mahāprabhu; *tāṅra dāsera dāsa*—a servant of His servant.

TRANSLATION

"I am a servant of Lord Caitanya, a servant of Lord Caitanya. I am a servant of Lord Caitanya, and a servant of His servants."

TEXT 87

এত বলি' নাচে, গায়, হুঙ্কার গম্ভীর ।
ক্ষণেকে বসিলা আচার্য হৈঞা সুস্থির ॥ ৮৭ ॥

eta bali' nāce, gāya, huṅkāra gambhīra
kṣaṇeke vasilā ācārya haiñā susthira

eta bali'—saying this; *nāce*—dances; *gāya*—sings; *huṅkāra*—loud vibrations; *gambhīra*—deep; *kṣaṇeke*—in a moment; *vasilā*—sits down; *ācārya*—Advaita Ācārya; *haiñā su-sthira*—being very patient.

TRANSLATION

Saying this, Advaita Prabhu dances and loudly sings. Then at the next moment He quietly sits down.

TEXT 88

ভক্ত-অভিমান মূল শ্রীবলরামে ।
সেই ভাবে অনুগত তাঁর অংশগণে ॥ ৮৮ ॥

bhakta-abhimāna mūla śrī-balarāme
sei bhāve anugata tāṅra aṁśa-gaṇe

bhakta-abhimāna—to think oneself a devotee; *mūla*—original; *śrī-balarāme*—in Lord Balarāma; *sei bhāve*—in that ecstasy; *anugata*—followers; *tāṅra aṁśa-gaṇe*—all His parts and parcels.

TRANSLATION

The source of the sentiment of servitude is indeed Lord Balarāma. The plenary expansions who follow Him are all influenced by that ecstasy.

TEXT 89

তাঁর অবতার এক শ্রীসঙ্কর্ষণ ।
ভক্ত বলি' অভিমান করে সর্বক্ষণ ॥ ৮৯ ॥

tāṅra avatāra eka śrī-saṅkarṣaṇa
bhakta bali' abhimāna kare sarva-kṣaṇa

tāṅra avatāra—His incarnation; *eka*—one; *śrī-saṅkarṣaṇa*—Lord Saṅkarṣaṇa; *bhakta bali'*—as a devotee; *abhimāna*—conception; *kare*—does; *sarva-kṣaṇa*—always.

TRANSLATION

Lord Saṅkarṣaṇa, who is one of His incarnations, always considers Himself a devotee.

TEXT 90

তাঁর অবতার আন শ্রীযুত লক্ষ্মণ ।
শ্রীরামের দাস্য তিঁহো কৈল অনুক্ষণ ॥ ৯০ ॥

tāṅra avatāra āna śrī-yuta lakṣmaṇa
śrī-rāmera dāsya tiṅho kaila anukṣaṇa

tāṅra avatāra—His incarnation; *āna*—another; *śrī-yuta*—with all beauty and opulence; *lakṣmaṇa*—Lord Lakṣmaṇa; *śrī-rāmera*—of Rāmacandra; *dāsya*—servitude; *tiṅho*—He; *kaila*—did; *anukṣaṇa*—always.

TRANSLATION

Another of His incarnations, Lakṣmaṇa, who is very beautiful and opulent, always serves Lord Rāma.

TEXT 91

সঙ্কর্ষণ-অবতার কারণাব্ধিশায়ী ।
তাঁহার হৃদয়ে ভক্তভাব অনুযায়ী ॥ ৯১ ॥

saṅkarṣaṇa-avatāra kāraṇābdhi-śāyī
tāṅhāra hṛdaye bhakta-bhāva anuyāyī

saṅkarṣaṇa-avatāra—an incarnation of Lord Saṅkarṣaṇa; *kāraṇa-abdhi-śāyī*—Lord Viṣṇu lying on the Causal Ocean; *tāṅhāra*—His; *hṛdaye*—in the heart; *bhakta-bhāva*—the emotion of being a devotee; *anuyāyī*—accordingly.

TRANSLATION

The Viṣṇu who lies on the Causal Ocean is an incarnation of Lord Saṅkarṣaṇa, and, accordingly, the emotion of being a devotee is always present in His heart.

TEXT 92

তাঁহার প্রকাশ-ভেদ, অদ্বৈত-আচার্য ।
কায়মনোবাক্যে তাঁর ভক্তি সদা কার্য ॥ ৯২ ॥

tāṅhāra prakāśa-bheda, advaita-ācārya
kāya-mano-vākye tāṅra bhakti sadā kārya

tāṅhāra—His; *prakāśa-bheda*—separate expansion; *advaita-ācārya*—Advaita Ācārya; *kāya-manaḥ-vākye*—by His body, mind and words; *tāṅra*—His; *bhakti*—devotion; *sadā*—always; *kārya*—occupational duty.

TRANSLATION

Advaita Ācārya is a separate expansion of Him. He always engages in devotional service with His thoughts, words and actions.

TEXT 93

বাক্যে কহে, 'মুঞি চৈতন্যের অনুচর'।
মুঞি তাঁর ভক্ত—মনে ভাবে নিরন্তর ॥ ৯৩ ॥

vākye kahe, 'muñi caitanyera anucara'
muñi tāṅra bhakta—mane bhāve nirantara

vākye—by words; *kahe*—He says; *muñi*—I am; *caitanyera anucara*—a follower of Lord Śrī Caitanya Mahāprabhu; *muñi*—I; *tāñra*—His; *bhakta*—devotee; *mane*—in His mind; *bhāve*—in this condition; *nirantara*—always.

TRANSLATION

By His words He declares, "I am a servant of Lord Caitanya." Thus with His mind He always thinks, "I am His devotee."

TEXT 94

জল-তুলসী দিয়া করে কায়াতে সেবন।
ভক্তি প্রচারিয়া সব তারিলা ভুবন ॥ ৯৪ ॥

jala-tulasī diyā kare kāyāte sevana
bhakti pracāriyā saba tārilā bhuvana

jala-tulasī—Ganges water and *tulasī* leaves; *diyā*—offering together; *kare*—does; *kāyāte*—with the body; *sevana*—worship; *bhakti*—the cult of devotional service; *pracāriyā*—preaching; *saba*—all; *tārilā*—delivered; *bhuvana*—the universe.

TRANSLATION

With His body He worshiped the Lord by offering Ganges water and tulasī leaves, and by preaching devotional service He delivered the entire universe.

TEXT 95

পৃথিবী ধরেন যেই শেষ-সঙ্কর্ষণ ।
কায়ব্যূহ করি' করেন কৃষ্ণের সেবন ॥ ৯৫ ॥

pṛthivī dharena yei śeṣa-saṅkarṣaṇa
kāya-vyūha kari' karena kṛṣṇera sevana

pṛthivī—planets; *dharena*—holds; *yei*—that one who; *śeṣa-saṅkarṣaṇa*—Lord Śeṣa Saṅkarṣaṇa; *kāya-vyūha kari'*—expanding Himself in different bodies; *karena*—does; *kṛṣṇera sevana*—service to Lord Kṛṣṇa.

TRANSLATION

Śeṣa Saṅkarṣaṇa, who holds all the planets on His heads, expands Himself in different bodies to render service to Lord Kṛṣṇa.

TEXT 96

এই সব হয় শ্রীকৃষ্ণের অবতার ।
নিরন্তর দেখি সবার ভক্তির আচার ॥ ৯৬ ॥

ei saba haya śrī-kṛṣṇera avatāra
nirantara dekhi sabāra bhaktira ācāra

ei saba—all of them; *haya*—are; *śrī-kṛṣṇera avatāra*—incarnations of Lord Kṛṣṇa; *nirantara*—constantly; *dekhi*—I see; *sabāra*—of all; *bhaktira ācāra*—behavior as devotees.

TRANSLATION

These are all incarnations of Lord Kṛṣṇa, yet we always find that they act as devotees.

TEXT 97

এ-সবাকে শাস্ত্রে কহে 'ভক্ত-অবতার' ।
'ভক্ত-অবতার'-পদ উপরি সবার ॥ ৯৭ ॥

e-sabāke śāstre kahe 'bhakta-avatāra'
'bhakta-avatāra'-pada upari sabāra

e-sabāke—all of them; *śāstre*—the scriptures; *kahe*—say; *bhakta-avatāra*—incarnations as devotees; *bhakta-avatāra*—of such an incarnation as a devotee; *pada*—the position; *upari sabāra*—above all other positions.

TRANSLATION

The scriptures call them incarnations as devotees [bhakta-avatāra]. The position of being such an incarnation is above all others.

PURPORT

The Supreme Personality of Godhead appears in different incarnations, but His appearance in the role of a devotee is more beneficial to the conditioned souls than the other incarnations, with all their opulences. Sometimes a conditioned soul is bewildered when he tries to understand the incarnation of Godhead with full opulence. Lord Kṛṣṇa appeared and performed many uncommon activities, and some materialists misunderstood Him, but in His appearance as Lord Caitanya He did not show much of His opulences, and therefore fewer conditioned souls were bewildered. Misunderstanding the Lord, many fools consider themselves incarnations of the Supreme Personality of Godhead, but the result is that after leaving the material body they enter the species of jackals. Persons who cannot understand the real significance of an incarnation must attain such lower species of life as punishment. Conditioned souls who are puffed up by false egoism and who try to become one with the Supreme Lord become Māyāvādīs.

TEXT 98

একমাত্র 'অংশী'—কৃষ্ণ' 'অংশ'—অবতার ।
অংশী অংশে দেখি জ্যেষ্ঠ-কনিষ্ঠ-আচার ॥ ৯৮ ॥

eka-mātra 'aṁśī'—kṛṣṇa, 'aṁśa'—avatāra
aṁśī aṁśe dekhi jyeṣṭha-kaniṣṭha-ācāra

eka-mātra—only one; *aṁśī*—source of all incarnations; *kṛṣṇa*—Lord Kṛṣṇa; *aṁśa*—of the part; *avatāra*—incarnations; *aṁśī*—is the source of all incarnations; *aṁśe*—in the incarnation; *dekhi*—we can see; *jyeṣṭha*—as superior; *kaniṣṭha*—and inferior; *ācāra*—behavior.

TRANSLATION

Lord Kṛṣṇa is the source of all incarnations, and all others are His parts or partial incarnations. We find that the whole and the part behave as superior and inferior.

TEXT 99

জ্যেষ্ঠ-ভাবে অংশীতে হয় প্রভু-জ্ঞান ।
কনিষ্ঠ-ভাবে আপনাতে ভক্ত-অভিমান ॥ ৯৯ ॥

jyeṣṭha-bhāve aṁśite haya prabhu-jñāna
kaniṣṭha-bhāve āpanāte bhakta-abhimāna

jyeṣṭha-bhāve—in the emotion of being superior; *aṁśīte*—in the original source of all incarnations; *haya*—there is; *prabhu-jñāna*—knowledge as master; *kaniṣṭha-bhāve*—in an inferior conception; *āpanāte*—in Himself; *bhakta-abhimāna*—the conception of being a devotee.

TRANSLATION

The source of all incarnations has the emotions of a superior when He considers Himself the master, and He has the emotions of an inferior when He considers Himself a devotee.

PURPORT

A fraction of a particular thing is called a part, and that from which the fraction is distinguished is called the whole. Therefore the fraction, or part, is included within the whole. The Lord is the whole, and the devotee is the part or fractional part. That is the relationship between the Lord and the devotee. There are also gradations of devotees, who are calculated as greater or lesser. When a devotee is great he is called *prabhu*, and when he is lesser he is called *bhakta*, or a devotee. The supreme whole is Kṛṣṇa, and Baladeva and all Viṣṇu incarnations are His fractions. Lord Kṛṣṇa is therefore conscious of His superior position, and all Viṣṇu incarnations are conscious of Their positions as devotees.

TEXT 100

কৃষ্ণের সমতা হৈতে বড় ভক্তপদ ।
আত্মা হৈতে কৃষ্ণের ভক্ত হয় প্রেমাস্পদ ॥ ১০০ ॥

kṛṣṇera samatā haite baḍa bhakta-pada
ātmā haite kṛṣṇera bhakta haya premāspada

kṛṣṇera—with Lord Kṛṣṇa; *samatā*—equality; *haite*—than this; *baḍa*—greater; *bhakta-pada*—the position of a devotee; *ātmā haite*—than His own self; *kṛṣṇera*—of Lord Kṛṣṇa; *bhakta*—a devotee; *haya*—is; *prema-āspada*—the object of love.

TRANSLATION

The position of being a devotee is higher than that of equality with Lord Kṛṣṇa, for the devotees are dearer to Lord Kṛṣṇa than His own self.

PURPORT

The conception of oneness with the Supreme Personality of Godhead is inferior to that of eternal service to the Lord because Lord Kṛṣṇa is more affectionate to devotees than to His personal self. In *Śrīmad-Bhāgavatam* (9.4.68) the Lord clearly says:

sādhavo hṛdayaṁ mahyaṁ sādhūnāṁ hṛdayaṁ tv aham
mad anyat te na jānanti nāhaṁ tebhyo manāg api

"The devotees are My heart, and I am the heart of My devotees. My devotees do not know anyone but Me; similarly, I do not know anyone but My devotees." This is the intimate relationship between the Lord and His devotees.

TEXT 101

আত্মা হৈতে কৃষ্ণ ভক্তে বড় করি' মানে ।
ইহাতে বহুত শাস্ত্র-বচন প্রমাণে ॥ ১০১ ॥

ātmā haite kṛṣṇa bhakte baḍa kari' māne
ihāte bahuta śāstra-vacana pramāṇe

ātmā haite—than His own self; *kṛṣṇa*—Lord Kṛṣṇa; *bhakte*—His devotee; *baḍa kari' māne*—accepts as greater; *ihāte*—in this connection; *bahuta*—many; *śāstra-vacana*—quotations from revealed scripture; *pramāṇe*—evidences.

TRANSLATION

Lord Kṛṣṇa considers His devotees greater than Himself. In this connection the scriptures provide an abundance of evidence.

TEXT 102

ন তথা মে প্রিয়তম আত্মযোনির্ন শঙ্করঃ ।
ন চ সঙ্কর্ষণো ন শ্রীর্নৈবাত্মা চ যথা ভবান্ ॥ ১০২ ॥

na tathā me priya-tama
ātma-yonir na śaṅkaraḥ
na ca saṅkarṣaṇo na śrīr
naivātmā ca yathā bhavān

na tathā—not so much; *me*—My; *priya-tamaḥ*—dearmost; *ātma-yoniḥ*—Lord Brahmā; *na śaṅkaraḥ*—nor Śaṅkara (Lord Śiva); *na ca*—nor; *saṅkarṣaṇaḥ*—Lord Saṅkarṣaṇa; *na*—nor; *śrīḥ*—the goddess of fortune; *na*—nor; *eva*—certainly; *ātmā*—My self; *ca*—and; *yathā*—as; *bhavān*—you.

TRANSLATION

"O Uddhava! Neither Brahmā, nor Śaṅkara, nor Saṅkarṣaṇa, nor Lakṣmī, nor even My own self is as dear to Me as you."

PURPORT

This text is from *Śrīmad-Bhāgavatam* (11.14.15).

TEXT 103

কৃষ্ণসাম্যে নহে তাঁর মাধুর্যাস্বাদন ।
ভক্তভাবে করে তাঁর মাধুর্য চর্বণ ॥ ১০৩ ॥

kṛṣṇa-sāmye nahe tāṅra mādhuryāsvādana
bhakta-bhāve kare tāṅra mādhurya carvaṇa

kṛṣṇa-sāmye—on an equal level with Kṛṣṇa; *nahe*—not; *tāṅra*—His; *mādhurya-āsvādana*—relishing the sweetness; *bhakta-bhāve*—as a devotee; *kare*—does; *tāṅra*—His; *mādhurya carvaṇa*—chewing of the sweetness.

TRANSLATION

The sweetness of Lord Kṛṣṇa is not to be tasted by those who consider themselves equal to Kṛṣṇa. It is to be tasted only through the sentiment of servitude.

TEXT 104

শাস্ত্রের সিদ্ধান্ত এই,—বিজ্ঞের অনুভব ।
মূঢ়লোক নাহি জানে ভাবের বৈভব ॥ ১০৪ ॥

śāstrera siddhānta ei,—vijñera anubhava
mūḍha-loka nāhi jāne bhāvera vaibhava

śāstrera—of the revealed scriptures; *siddhānta*—conclusion; *ei*—this; *vijñera anubhava*—realization by experienced devotees; *mūḍha-loka*—fools and rascals; *nāhi jāne*—do not know; *bhāvera vaibhava*—devotional opulences.

TRANSLATION

This conclusion of the revealed scriptures is also the realization of experienced devotees. Fools and rascals, however, cannot understand the opulences of devotional emotions.

PURPORT

When a person is liberated in the *sārūpya* form of liberation, having a spiritual form exactly like Viṣṇu, it is not possible for him to relish the relationship of Kṛṣṇa's personal associates in their exchanges of mellows. The devotees of Kṛṣṇa, however, in their loving relationships with Kṛṣṇa, sometimes forget their own identities; sometimes they think themselves one with Kṛṣṇa and yet relish still greater transcendental mellow in that way. People in general, because of their foolishness only, try to become masters of everything, forgetting the transcendental mellow of servitorship to the Lord. When a person is actually advanced in spiritual understanding, however, he can accept the transcendental servitorship of the Lord without hesitation.

TEXTS 105–106

ভক্তভাব অঙ্গীকরি' বলরাম, লক্ষ্মণ ।
অদ্বৈত, নিত্যানন্দ, শেষ, সঙ্কর্ষণ ॥ ১০৫ ॥
কৃষ্ণের মাধুর্যরসামৃত করে পান ।
সেই সুখে মত্ত, কিছু নাহি জানে আন ॥ ১০৬ ॥

bhakta-bhāva aṅgīkari' balarāma, lakṣmaṇa
advaita, nityānanda, śeṣa, saṅkarṣaṇa

kṛṣṇera mādhurya-rasāmṛta kare pāna
sei sukhe matta, kichu nāhi jāne āna

bhakta-bhāva—the conception of being a devotee; *aṅgīkari'*—accepting; *balarāma*—Lord Balarāma; *lakṣmaṇa*—Lord Lakṣmaṇa; *advaita*—Advaita Ācārya; *nityānanda*—Lord Nityānanda; *śeṣa*—Lord Śeṣa; *saṅkarṣaṇa*—Lord Saṅkarṣaṇa; *kṛṣṇera*—of Lord Kṛṣṇa; *mādhurya*—transcendental bliss; *rasa-amṛta*—the nectar of such a taste; *kare pāna*—They drink; *sei sukhe*—in such happiness; *matta*—mad; *kichu*—anything; *nāhi*—do not; *jāne*—know; *āna*—else.

TRANSLATION

Baladeva, Lakṣmaṇa, Advaita Ācārya, Lord Nityānanda, Lord Śeṣa and Lord Saṅkarṣaṇa taste the nectarean mellows of the transcendental bliss of Lord Kṛṣṇa by recognizing Themselves as being His devotees and servants. They are all mad with that happiness, and They know nothing else.

TEXT 107

অন্যের আছুক্ কার্য, আপনে শ্রীকৃষ্ণ ।
আপন-মাধুর্য-পানে হইলা সতৃষ্ণ ॥ ১০৭ ॥

anyera āchuk kārya, āpane śrī-kṛṣṇa
āpana-mādhurya-pāne ha-ilā satṛṣṇa

anyera—of others; *āchuk*—let be; *kārya*—the business; *āpane*—personally; *śrī-kṛṣṇa*—Lord Śrī Kṛṣṇa; *āpana-mādhurya*—personal sweetness; *pāne*—in drinking; *ha-ilā*—became; *sa-tṛṣṇa*—very eager.

TRANSLATION

What to speak of others, even Lord Kṛṣṇa Himself becomes thirsty to taste His own sweetness.

TEXT 108

স্বমাধুর্য আস্বাদিতে করেন যতন ।
ভক্তভাব বিনু নহে তাহা আস্বাদন ॥ ১০৮ ॥

svā-mādhurya āsvādite karena yatana
bhakta-bhāva vinu nahe tāhā āsvādana

svā-mādhurya—the sweetness of Himself; *āsvādite*—to taste; *karena yatana*—makes endeavors; *bhakta-bhāva*—the emotion of being a devotee; *vinu*—without; *nahe*—there is not; *tāhā*—that; *āsvādana*—tasting.

TRANSLATION

He tries to taste His own sweetness, but He cannot do so without accepting the emotions of a devotee.

PURPORT

Lord Śrī Kṛṣṇa wanted to relish the transcendental mellow of a devotee, and therefore He accepted the role of a devotee by appearing as Śrī Kṛṣṇa Caitanya Mahāprabhu.

TEXT 109

ভক্তভাব অঙ্গীকরি' হৈলা অবতীর্ণ ।
শ্রীকৃষ্ণচৈতন্যরূপে সর্বভাবে পূর্ণ ॥ ১০৯ ॥

bhakta-bhāva aṅgīkari' hailā avatīrṇa
śrī-kṛṣṇa-caitanya-rūpe sarva-bhāve pūrṇa

bhakta-bhāva—the ecstasy of being a devotee; *aṅgīkari'*—accepting; *hailā*—became; *avatīrṇa*—incarnated; *śrī-kṛṣṇa-caitanya-rūpe*—in the form of Lord Śrī Kṛṣṇa Caitanya; *sarva-bhāve pūrṇa*—complete in every respect.

TRANSLATION

Therefore Lord Kṛṣṇa accepted the position of a devotee and descended in the form of Lord Caitanya, who is complete in every respect.

TEXT 110

নানা-ভক্তভাবে করেন স্বমাধুর্য পান ।
পূর্বে করিয়াছি এই সিদ্ধান্ত ব্যাখ্যান ॥ ১১০ ॥

nānā-bhakta-bhāve karena sva-mādhurya pāna
pūrve kariyāchi ei siddhānta vyākhyāna

nānā-bhakta-bhāve—various emotions of a devotee; *karena*—does; *sva-mādhurya pāna*—drinking the sweetness of Himself; *pūrve*—formerly; *kariyāchi*—I discussed; *ei*—this; *siddhānta*—conclusion; *vyākhyāna*—the explanation.

TRANSLATION

He tastes His own sweetness through the various emotions of a devotee. I have formerly explained this conclusion.

PURPORT

Lord Caitanya, who is known as Śrī Gaurahari, is complete in relishing all the different mellows, namely neutrality, servitorship, fraternity, parental affection and conjugal love. By accepting the ecstasy of different grades of devotees, He is complete in relishing all the mellows of these relationships.

TEXT 111

অবতারগণের ভক্তভাবে অধিকার ।
ভক্তভাব হৈতে অধিক সুখ নাহি আর ॥ ১১১ ॥

avatāra-gaṇera bhakta-bhāve adhikāra
bhakta-bhāva haite adhika sukha nāhi āra

avatāra-gaṇera—of all the incarnations; *bhakta-bhāve*—in the emotion of a devotee; *adhikāra*—there is the right; *bhakta-bhāva*—the emotion of being a devotee; *haite*—than; *adhika*—greater; *sukha*—happiness; *nāhi*—not; *āra*—any other.

TRANSLATION

All the incarnations are entitled to the emotions of devotees. There is no higher bliss than this.

PURPORT

All the different incarnations of Lord Viṣṇu have the right to play the roles of servitors of Lord Kṛṣṇa by descending as devotees. When an incarnation gives up the understanding of His Godhood and plays the part of a servitor, He enjoys a greater taste of transcendental mellows than when He plays the part of the Supreme Personality of Godhead.

TEXT 112

মূল ভক্ত-অবতার শ্রীসঙ্কর্ষণ ।
ভক্ত-অবতার তঁহি অদ্বৈতে গণন ॥ ১১২ ॥

mūla bhakta-avatāra śrī-saṅkarṣaṇa
bhakta-avatāra taṅhi advaite gaṇana

mūla—original; *bhakta*—of a devotee; *avatāra*—incarnation; *śrī-saṅkarṣaṇa*—Lord Śrī Saṅkarṣaṇa; *bhakta-avatāra*—the incarnation of a devotee; *taṅhi*—as that; *advaite*—Advaita Ācārya; *gaṇana*—counting.

TRANSLATION

The original bhakta-avatāra is Saṅkarṣaṇa. Śrī Advaita is counted among such incarnations.

PURPORT

Although Śrī Advaita Prabhu belongs to the Viṣṇu category, He displays servitorship to Lord Caitanya Mahāprabhu as one of His associates. When Lord Viṣṇu appears as a servitor, He is called an incarnation of a devotee of Lord Kṛṣṇa. Śrī Saṅkarṣaṇa, who is an incarnation of Viṣṇu in the spiritual sky known as the greater Vaikuṇṭha, is the chief of the quadruple incarnations and is the original incarnation of a devotee. Lord Mahā-Viṣṇu, who is lying on the Causal Ocean, is a manifestation of Saṅkarṣaṇa. He is the original Personality of Godhead who glances over the material and efficient causes of the cosmic manifestation. Advaita Prabhu is accepted as an incarnation of Mahā-Viṣṇu. All the plenary manifestations of Saṅkarṣaṇa are indirect expansions of Lord

Kṛṣṇa. That consideration also makes Advaita Prabhu an eternal servitor of Gaura Kṛṣṇa. Therefore He is accepted as a devotee incarnation.

TEXT 113

অদ্বৈত-আচার্য গোসাঞির মহিমা অপার ।
যাঁহার হুঙ্কারে কৈল চৈতন্যাবতার ॥ ১১৩ ॥

advaita-ācārya gosāñira mahimā apāra
yāṅhāra huṅkāre kaila caitanyāvatāra

advaita-ācārya—Advaita Ācārya; *gosāñira*—of the Lord; *mahimā apāra*—unlimited glories; *yāṅhāra*—of whom; *huṅkāre*—by the vibration; *kaila*—brought; *caitanya-avatāra*—the incarnation of Lord Caitanya.

TRANSLATION

The glories of Śrī Advaita Ācārya are boundless, for His sincere vibrations brought about Lord Caitanya's descent upon this earth.

TEXT 114

সংকীর্তন প্রচারিয়া সব জগৎ তারিল ।
অদ্বৈত-প্রসাদে লোক প্রেমধন পাইল ॥ ১১৪ ॥

saṅkīrtana pracāriyā saba jagat tārila
advaita-prasāde loka prema-dhana pāila

saṅkīrtana pracāriyā—by preaching the cult of *saṅkīrtana; saba*—all; *jagat*—the universe; *tārila*—delivered; *advaita-prasāde*—by the mercy of Advaita Ācārya; *loka*—all people; *prema-dhana pāila*—received the treasure of loving God.

TRANSLATION

He liberated the universe by preaching saṅkīrtana. Thus the people of the world received the treasure of love of Godhead through the mercy of Śrī Advaita.

TEXT 115

অদ্বৈত-মহিমা অনন্ত কে পারে কহিতে ।
সেই লিখি, যেই শুনি মহাজন হৈতে ॥ ১১৫ ॥

advaita-mahimā ananta ke pāre kahite
sei likhi, yei śuni mahājana haite

advaita-mahimā—the glories of Advaita Ācārya; *ananta*—unlimited; *ke*—who; *pāre*—is able; *kahite*—to say; *sei*—that; *likhi*—I write; *yei*—whatever; *śuni*—I hear; *mahājana haite*—from authority.

TRANSLATION

Who can describe the unlimited glories of Advaita Ācārya? I write here as much as I have known from great authorities.

TEXT 116

আচার্য-চরণে মোর কোটি নমস্কার ।
ইথে কিছু অপরাধ না লবে আমার ॥ ১১৬ ॥

ācārya-caraṇe mora koṭi namaskāra
ithe kichu aparādha nā labe āmāra

ācārya-caraṇe—at the lotus feet of Advaita Ācārya; *mora*—my; *koṭi namaskāra*—offering obeisances ten million times; *ithe*—in this connection; *kichu*—some; *aparādha*—offense; *nā labe*—please do not take; *āmāra*—my.

TRANSLATION

I offer my obeisances ten million times to the lotus feet of Śrī Advaita Ācārya. Please do not take offense at this.

TEXT 117

তোমার মহিমা—কোটিসমুদ্র অগাধ ।
তাহার ইয়ত্তা কহি,—এ বড় অপরাধ ॥ ১১৭ ॥

tomāra mahimā—koṭi-samudra agādha
tāhāra iyattā kahi,—e baḍa aparādha

tomāra mahimā—Your glories; *koṭi-samudra agādha*—as unfathomable as the millions of seas and oceans; *tāhāra*—of that; *iyattā*—the measure; *kahi*—I say; *e*—this; *baḍa*—great; *aparādha*—offense.

TRANSLATION

Your glories are as fathomless as millions of oceans and seas. Speaking of its measure is a great offense indeed.

TEXT 118

জয় জয় জয় শ্রীঅদ্বৈত আচার্য।
জয় জয় শ্রীচৈতন্য, নিত্যানন্দ আর্য ॥ ১১৮ ॥

jaya jaya jaya śrī-advaita ācārya
jaya jaya śrī-caitanya, nityānanda ārya

jaya jaya—all glories; *jaya*—all glories; *śrī-advaita ācārya*—to Śrī Advaita Ācārya; *jaya jaya*—all glories; *śrī-caitanya*—to Lord Śrī Caitanya Mahāprabhu; *nityānanda*—Lord Nityānanda; *ārya*—the superior.

TRANSLATION

All glories, all glories to Śrī Advaita Ācārya! All glories to Lord Caitanya Mahāprabhu and the superior Lord Nityānanda!

TEXT 119

দুই শ্লোকে কহিল অদ্বৈত-তত্ত্বনিরূপণ।
পঞ্চতত্ত্বের বিচার কিছু শুন, ভক্তগণ ॥ ১১৯ ॥

dui śloke kahila advaita-tattva-nirūpaṇa
pañca-tattvera vicāra kichu śuna, bhakta-gaṇa

dui śloke—in two verses; *kahila*—described; *advaita*—Advaita; *tattva-nirūpaṇa*—ascertaining the truth; *pañca-tattvera*—of the five truths; *vicāra*—consideration; *kichu*—something; *śuna*—please hear; *bhakta-gaṇa*—O devotees.

TRANSLATION

Thus in two verses I have described the truth concerning Advaita Ācārya. Now, O devotees, please hear about the five truths [pañca-tattva].

TEXT 120

শ্রীরূপ-রঘুনাথ-পদে যার আশ ।
চৈতন্যচরিতামৃত কহে কৃষ্ণদাস ॥ ১২০ ॥

śrī-rūpa-raghunātha-pade yāra āśa
caitanya-caritāmṛta kahe kṛṣṇadāsa

śrī-rūpa—Śrīla Rūpa Gosvāmī; *raghunātha*—Śrīla Raghunātha dāsa Gosvāmī; *pade*—at the lotus feet; *yāra*—whose; *āśa*—expectation; *caitanya-caritāmṛta*—the book named *Caitanya-caritāmṛta; kahe*—describes; *kṛṣṇa-dāsa*—Śrīla Kṛṣṇadāsa Kavirāja Gosvāmī.

TRANSLATION

Praying at the lotus feet of Śrī Rūpa and Śrī Raghunātha, always desiring their mercy, I, Kṛṣṇadāsa, narrate Śrī Caitanya-caritāmṛta, following in their footsteps.

Thus end the Bhaktivedanta purports to Śrī Caitanya-caritāmṛta, Ādi-līlā, *Sixth Chapter, describing the glories of Śrī Advaita Ācārya.*

CHAPTER SEVEN

Lord Caitanya in Five Features

TEXT 1

অগত্যেকগতিং নত্বা হীনার্থাধিকসাধকম্ ।
শ্রীচৈতন্যং লিখ্যতেঽস্য প্রেমভক্তিবদান্যতা ॥ ১ ॥

agaty-eka-gatiṁ natvā
hīnārthādhika-sādhakam
śrī-caitanyaṁ likhyate 'sya
prema-bhakti-vadānyatā

agati—of the most fallen; *eka*—the only one; *gatim*—destination; *natvā*—after offering obeisances; *hīna*—inferior; *artha*—interest; *adhika*—greater than that; *sādhakam*—who can render; *śrī-caitanyam*—unto Lord Śrī Caitanya; *likhyate*—is being written; *asya*—of the Lord, Śrī Caitanya Mahāprabhu; *prema*—love; *bhakti*—devotional service; *vadānyatā*—magnanimity.

TRANSLATION

Let me first offer my respectful obeisances unto Lord Caitanya Mahāprabhu, who is the ultimate goal of life for one bereft of all possessions in this material world and is the only meaning for one advancing in spiritual life. Thus let me write about His magnanimous contribution of devotional service in love of God.

PURPORT

A person in the conditioned stage of material existence is in an atmosphere of helplessness, but the conditioned soul, under the illusion of *māyā*, or the external energy, thinks that he is completely protected by his country, society, friendship and love, not knowing that at the time of death none of these can save him. The laws of material nature are so strong that none of our material possessions can save us from the cruel hands of death. In the *Bhagavad-gītā* (13.9) it is stated, *janma-mṛtyu-jarā-vyādhi-duḥkha-doṣānudarśanam:* one who is actually advancing must always consider the four principles of miserable life, namely, birth, death, old age and disease. One cannot be saved from all these miseries unless he takes shelter of the lotus feet of the Lord. Śrī Caitanya Mahāprabhu is therefore the only shelter for all conditioned souls. An intelligent person, therefore, does not put his faith in any material possessions, but completely takes shelter of the lotus feet of the Lord. Such a person is called *akiñcana,* or one who does not possess anything in this material world. The Supreme Personality of Godhead is also known as Akiñcana-gocara, for He can be achieved by a person who does not put his faith in material possessions. Therefore, for the fully surrendered soul who has no material possessions on which to depend, Lord Śrī Caitanya Mahāprabhu is the only shelter.

Everyone depends upon *dharma* (religiosity), *artha* (economic development), *kāma* (sense gratification) and ultimately *mokṣa* (salvation), but Śrī Caitanya Mahāprabhu, due to His magnanimous character, can give more than salvation. Therefore in this verse the words *hīnārthādhika-sādhakam* indicate that although by material estimation salvation is of a quality superior to the inferior interests of religiosity, economic development and sense gratification, above salvation there is the position of devotional service and transcendental love for the Supreme Personality of Godhead. Śrī Caitanya Mahāprabhu is the bestower of this great benediction. Śrī Caitanya Mahāprabhu said, *premā pum-artho mahān:* "Love of Godhead is the ultimate benediction for all human beings." Śrīla Kṛṣṇadāsa Kavirāja Gosvāmī, the author of *Śrī Caitanya-caritāmṛta,* therefore first offers his respectful obeisances unto Lord Caitanya Mahāprabhu before describing His magnanimity in bestowing love of Godhead.

TEXT 2

জয় জয় মহাপ্রভু শ্রীকৃষ্ণচৈতন্য ।
তাঁহার চরণাশ্রিত, সেই বড় ধন্য ॥ ২ ॥

jaya jaya mahāprabhu śrī-kṛṣṇa-caitanya
tāṅhāra caraṇāśrita, sei baḍa dhanya

jaya—all glories; *jaya*—all glories; *mahāprabhu*—unto the Supreme Lord; *śrī-kṛṣṇa-caitanya*—Śrī Kṛṣṇa Caitanya; *tāṅhāra*—of His; *caraṇa-āśrita*—one who has taken shelter of the lotus feet; *sei*—he; *baḍa*—is very much; *dhanya*—glorified.

TRANSLATION

Let me offer glorification to the Supreme Lord Śrī Caitanya Mahāprabhu. One who has taken shelter of His lotus feet is the most glorified person.

PURPORT

Prabhu means master. Śrī Caitanya Mahāprabhu is the supreme master of all masters; therefore He is called Mahāprabhu. Any person who takes shelter of Śrī Kṛṣṇa Caitanya Mahāprabhu is most glorified because by the mercy of Śrī Caitanya Mahāprabhu he is able to get promotion to the platform of loving service to the Lord, which is transcendental to salvation.

TEXT 3

পূর্বে গুর্বাদি ছয় তত্ত্বে কৈল নমস্কার ।
গুরুতত্ত্ব কহিয়াছি, এবে পাঁচের বিচার ॥ ৩ ॥

pūrve gurv-ādi chaya tattve kaila namaskāra
guru-tattva kahiyāchi, ebe pāñcera vicāra

pūrve—in the beginning; *guru-ādi*—the spiritual master and others; *chaya*—six; *tattve*—in the subjects of; *kaila*—I have done; *namaskāra*—obeisances; *guru-tattva*—the truth in understanding the spiritual master; *kahiyāchi*—I have already described; *ebe*—now; *pāñcera*—of the five; *vicāra*—consideration.

TRANSLATION

In the beginning I have discussed the truth about the spiritual master. Now I shall try to explain the Pañca-tattva.

PURPORT

In the First Chapter of the *Caitanya-caritāmṛta, Ādi-līlā*, the author, Śrīla Kṛṣṇadāsa Kavirāja Gosvāmī, has described the initiator spiritual master and the instructor spiritual master in the verse beginning with the words *vande gurūn īśa-bhaktān īśam īśāvatārakān.* In that verse there are six transcendental subject matters, of which the truth regarding the spiritual master has already been described. Now the author will describe the other five *tattvas* (truths), namely, *īśa-tattva* (the Supreme Lord), His expansion *tattva,* His incarnation *tattva,* His energy *tattva* and His devotee *tattva.*

TEXT 4

পঞ্চতত্ত্ব অবতীর্ণ চৈতন্যের সঙ্গে ।
পঞ্চতত্ত্ব লঞা করেন সংকীর্তন রঙ্গে ॥ ৪ ॥

pañca-tattva avatīrṇa caitanyera saṅge
pañca-tattva lañā karena saṅkīrtana raṅge

pañca-tattva—these five *tattvas; avatīrṇa*—advented; *caitanyera*—with Caitanya Mahāprabhu; *saṅge*—in company with; *pañca-tattva*—the same five subjects; *lañā*—taking with Himself; *karena*—He does; *saṅkīrtana*—the *saṅkīrtana* movement; *raṅge*—in great pleasure.

TRANSLATION

These five tattvas incarnate with Lord Caitanya Mahāprabhu, and thus the Lord executes His saṅkīrtana movement with great pleasure.

PURPORT

In *Śrīmad-Bhāgavatam* (11.5.32) there is the following statement regarding Śrī Caitanya Mahāprabhu:

kṛṣṇa-varṇaṁ tviṣākṛṣṇaṁ sāṅgopāṅgāstra-pārṣadam
yajñaiḥ saṅkīrtana-prāyair yajanti hi su-medhasaḥ

"In the Age of Kali, people who are endowed with sufficient intelligence will worship the Lord, who is accompanied by His associates, by performance of the *saṅkīrtana-yajña.*" Śrī Caitanya Mahāprabhu is always accompanied by His plenary expansion Śrī Nityānanda Prabhu, His incarnation Śrī Advaita Prabhu, His internal potency Śrī Gadādhara Prabhu and His marginal potency Śrīvāsa Prabhu. He is in the midst of them as the Supreme Personality of Godhead. One should know that Śrī

Caitanya Mahāprabhu is always accompanied by these other *tattvas.* Therefore our obeisances to Śrī Caitanya Mahāprabhu are complete when we say *śrī-kṛṣṇa-caitanya prabhu-nityānanda śrī-advaita gadādhara śrīvāsādi-gaura-bhakta-vṛnda.* As preachers of the Kṛṣṇa consciousness movement, we first offer our obeisances to Śrī Caitanya Mahāprabhu by chanting this Pañca-tattva *mantra;* then we say Hare Kṛṣṇa, Hare Kṛṣṇa, Kṛṣṇa Kṛṣṇa, Hare Hare/ Hare Rāma, Hare Rāma, Rāma Rāma, Hare Hare. There are ten offenses in the chanting of the Hare Kṛṣṇa *mahā-mantra,* but these are not considered in the chanting of the Pañca-tattva *mantra,* namely, *śrī-kṛṣṇa-caitanya prabhu-nityānanda śrī-advaita gadādhara śrīvāsādi-gaura-bhakta-vṛnda.* Śrī Caitanya Mahāprabhu is known as *mahā-vadānyāvatāra,* the most magnanimous incarnation, for He does not consider the offenses of the fallen souls. Thus to derive the full benefit of the chanting of the *mahā-mantra* (Hare Kṛṣṇa, Hare Kṛṣṇa, Kṛṣṇa Kṛṣṇa, Hare Hare/ Hare Rāma, Hare Rāma, Rāma Rāma, Hare Hare), we must first take shelter of Śrī Caitanya Mahāprabhu, learn the Pañca-tattva *mahā-mantra,* and then chant the Hare Kṛṣṇa *mahā-mantra.* That will be very effective.

Taking advantage of Śrī Caitanya Mahāprabhu, many unscrupulous devotees manufacture a *mahā-mantra* of their own. Sometimes they sing *bhaja nitāi gaura rādhe śyāma hare kṛṣṇa hare rāma* or *śrī-kṛṣṇa-caitanya prabhu-nityānanda hare kṛṣṇa hare rāma śrī-rādhe govinda.* Actually, however, one should chant the names of the full Pañca-tattva (*śrī-kṛṣṇa-caitanya prabhu-nityānanda śrī-advaita gadādhara śrīvāsādi-gaura-bhakta-vṛnda*) and then the sixteen words Hare Kṛṣṇa, Hare Kṛṣṇa, Kṛṣṇa Kṛṣṇa, Hare Hare/ Hare Rāma, Hare Rāma, Rāma Rāma, Hare Hare. But these unscrupulous, less intelligent men confuse the entire process. Of course, since they are also devotees they can express their feelings in that way, but the method prescribed by Śrī Caitanya Mahāprabhu's pure devotees is to first chant the full Pañca-tattva *mantra* and then chant the *mahā-mantra*—Hare Kṛṣṇa, Hare Kṛṣṇa, Kṛṣṇa Kṛṣṇa, Hare Hare/ Hare Rāma, Hare Rāma, Rāma Rāma, Hare Hare.

TEXT 5

পঞ্চতত্ত্ব—একবস্তু, নাহি কিছু ভেদ।
রস আস্বাদিতে তবু বিবিধ বিভেদ ॥ ৫ ॥

pañca-tattva—eka-vastu, nāhi kichu bheda
rasa āsvādite tabu vividha vibheda

pañca-tattva—the five subjects; *eka-vastu*—they are one in five; *nāhi*—there is not; *kichu*—anything; *bheda*—difference; *rasa*—mellows; *āsvādite*—to taste; *tabu*—yet; *vividha*—varieties; *vibheda*—differences.

TRANSLATION

Spiritually there are no differences between these five tattvas, for on the transcendental platform everything is absolute. Yet there are also varieties in the spiritual world, and in order to taste these spiritual varieties one should distinguish between them.

PURPORT

In his *Anubhāṣya* commentary Śrī Bhaktisiddhānta Sarasvatī Ṭhākura describes the Pañca-tattva as follows: The supreme energetic, the Personality of Godhead, manifesting in order to enjoy five kinds of pastimes, appears as the members of the Pañca-tattva. Actually there is no difference between them because they are situated on the absolute platform, but they manifest different spiritual varieties as a challenge to the impersonalists to taste different kinds of spiritual humors (*rasas*). In the *Vedas* it is said, *parāsya śaktir vividhaiva śrūyate:* "The varieties of energy of the Supreme Personality of Godhead are differently known." From this statement of the *Vedas* one can understand that there are eternal varieties of humors, or tastes, in the spiritual world. Śrī Gaurāṅga, Śrī Nityānanda, Śrī Advaita, Śrī Gadādhara and Śrīvāsa Ṭhākura are all on the same platform, but in spiritually distinguishing between them one should understand that Śrī Caitanya Mahāprabhu is the form of a devotee, Nityānanda Prabhu appears in the form of a devotee's spiritual master, Advaita Prabhu is the form of a *bhakta* (devotee) incarnation, Gadādhara Prabhu is the energy of a *bhakta*, and Śrīvāsa Ṭhākura is a pure devotee. Thus there are spiritual distinctions between them. The *bhakta-rūpa* (Śrī Caitanya Mahāprabhu), the *bhakta-svarūpa* (Śrī Nityānanda Prabhu) and the *bhakta-avatāra* (Śrī Advaita Prabhu) are described as the Supreme Personality of Godhead Himself, His immediate manifestation and His plenary expansion, and They all belong to the Viṣṇu category. Although the spiritual and marginal energies of the Supreme Personality of Godhead are nondifferent from the Supreme Personality of Godhead Viṣṇu, they are predominated subjects, whereas Lord Viṣṇu is the predominator. As such, although they are on the same platform, they have appeared differently in order to facilitate tasting of transcendental mellows. Actually, however, there is no possibility of one being different from the other, for the worshiper and the worshipable cannot be separated at any stage. On the absolute platform, one cannot be understood without the other.

TEXT 6

পঞ্চতত্ত্বাত্মকং কৃষ্ণং ভক্তরূপ-স্বরূপকম্ ।
ভক্তাবতারং ভক্তাখ্যং নমামি ভক্তশক্তিকম্ ॥ ৬ ॥

pañca-tattvātmakaṁ kṛṣṇaṁ
bhakta-rūpa-svarūpakam
bhaktāvatāraṁ bhaktākhyaṁ
namāmi bhakta-śaktikam

pañca-tattva-ātmakam—comprehending the five transcendental subject matters; *kṛṣṇam*—unto Lord Kṛṣṇa; *bhakta-rūpa*—in the form of a devotee; *svarūpakam*—in the expansion of a devotee; *bhakta-avatāram*—in the incarnation of a devotee; *bhakta-ākhyam*—known as a devotee; *namāmi*—I offer my obeisances; *bhakta-śaktikam*—the energy of the Supreme Personality of Godhead.

TRANSLATION

Let me offer my obeisances unto Lord Śrī Kṛṣṇa, who has manifested Himself in five as a devotee, expansion of a devotee, incarnation of a devotee, pure devotee and devotional energy.

PURPORT

Śrī Nityānanda Prabhu is the immediate expansion of Śrī Caitanya Mahāprabhu as His brother. He is the personified spiritual bliss of *sac-cid-ānanda-vigraha.* His body is transcendental and full of ecstasy in devotional service. Śrī Caitanya Mahāprabhu is therefore called *bhakta-rūpa* (the form of a devotee), and Śrī Nityānanda Prabhu is called *bhakta-svarūpa* (the expansion of a devotee). Śrī Advaita Prabhu, the incarnation of a devotee, is *viṣṇu-tattva* and belongs to the same category. There are also different types of *bhaktas,* or devotees, on the platforms of neutrality, servitude, friendship, parenthood and conjugal love. Devotees like Śrī Dāmodara, Śrī Gadādhara and Śrī Rāmānanda are different energies. This confirms the Vedic *sūtra parāsya śaktir vividhaiva śrūyate.* All these *bhakta* subjects taken together constitute Śrī Caitanya Mahāprabhu, who is Kṛṣṇa Himself.

TEXT 7

স্বয়ং ভগবান্ কৃষ্ণ একলে ঈশ্বর ।
অদ্বিতীয়, নন্দাত্মজ, রসিক-শেখর ॥ ৭ ॥

svayaṁ bhagavān kṛṣṇa ekale īśvara
advitīya, nandātmaja, rasika-śekhara

svayam—Himself; *bhagavān*—the Supreme Personality of Godhead; *kṛṣṇa*—Lord Kṛṣṇa; *ekale*—the only one; *īśvara*—the supreme controller; *advitīya*—without a second; *nanda-ātmaja*—appeared as the son of Mahārāja Nanda; *rasika*—enjoyer of mellows; *śekhara*—summit.

TRANSLATION

Kṛṣṇa, the reservoir of all pleasure, is the Supreme Personality of Godhead Himself, the supreme controller. No one is greater than or equal to Śrī Kṛṣṇa, yet He appears as the son of Mahārāja Nanda.

PURPORT

In this verse Kavirāja Gosvāmī gives an accurate description of Lord Kṛṣṇa, the Supreme Personality of Godhead, by stating that although no one is equal to or greater than Him and He is the reservoir of all spiritual pleasure, He nevertheless appears as the son of Mahārāja Nanda and Yaśodāmayī.

TEXT 8

রাসাদি-বিলাসী, ব্রজললনা-নাগর ।
আর যত সব দেখ,—তাঁর পরিকর ॥ ৮ ॥

rāsādi-vilāsī, vrajalalanā-nāgara
āra yata saba dekha,—tāṅra parikara

rāsa-ādi—the *rāsa* dance; *vilāsī*—the enjoyer; *vraja-lalanā*—the damsels of Vṛndāvana; *nāgara*—the leader; *āra*—others; *yata*—all; *saba*—everyone; *dekha*—must know; *tāṅra*—His; *parikara*—associates.

TRANSLATION

Lord Śrī Kṛṣṇa, the Supreme Personality of Godhead, is the supreme enjoyer in the rāsa dance. He is the leader of the damsels of Vraja, and all others are simply His associates.

PURPORT

The word *rāsādi-vilāsī* ("the enjoyer of the *rāsa* dance") is very important. The *rāsa* dance can be enjoyed only by Śrī Kṛṣṇa because He is the supreme leader and chief of the damsels of Vṛndāvana. All others are His devotees and associates. Although no one can compare with Śrī Kṛṣṇa, the Supreme Personality of Godhead, there are many unscrupulous rascals who imitate the *rāsa* dance of Śrī Kṛṣṇa. They are Māyāvādīs, and people should be wary of them. The *rāsa* dance can be performed only by Śrī Kṛṣṇa and no one else.

TEXT 9

সেই কৃষ্ণ অবতীর্ণ শ্রীকৃষ্ণচৈতন্য ।
সেই পরিকরগণ সঙ্গে সব ধন্য ॥ ৯ ॥

sei kṛṣṇa avatīrṇa śrī-kṛṣṇa-caitanya
sei parikara-gaṇa saṅge saba dhanya

sei kṛṣṇa—that very Lord Kṛṣṇa; *avatīrṇa*—has advented; *śrī-kṛṣṇa-caitanya*—in the form of Lord Caitanya Mahāprabhu; *sei*—those; *parikara-gaṇa*—associates; *saṅge*—with Him; *saba*—all; *dhanya*—glorious.

TRANSLATION

The selfsame Lord Kṛṣṇa advented Himself as Śrī Caitanya Mahāprabhu with all His eternal associates, who are also equally glorious.

TEXT 10

একলে ঈশ্বর-তত্ত্ব চৈতন্য ঈশ্বর ।
ভক্তভাবময় তাঁর শুদ্ধ কলেবর ॥ ১০ ॥

ekale īśvara-tattva caitanya-īśvara
bhakta-bhāvamaya tāṅra śuddha kalevara

ekale—only one person; *īśvara-tattva*—the supreme controller; *caitanya*—the supreme living force; *īśvara*—controller; *bhakta-bhāvamaya*—in the ecstasy of a devotee; *tāṅra*—His; *śuddha*—transcendental; *kalevara*—body.

TRANSLATION

Śrī Caitanya Mahāprabhu, who is the supreme controller, the one Personality of Godhead, has ecstatically become a devotee, yet His body is transcendental and not materially tinged.

PURPORT

There are different *tattvas,* or truths, including *īśa-tattva, jīva-tattva* and *śakti-tattva. Īśa-tattva* refers to the Supreme Personality of Godhead Viṣṇu, who is the supreme living force. In the *Kaṭha Upaniṣad* it is said, *nityo nityānāṁ cetanaś cetanānām:* the Supreme Personality of Godhead is the supreme eternal and the supreme living force. The living entities are also eternal and are also living forces, but they are very minute in quantity, whereas the Supreme Lord is the supreme living force and the supreme eternal. The supreme eternal never accepts a body of a temporary material nature, whereas the living entities, who are part and parcel of the supreme eternal, are prone to do so. Thus according to the Vedic *mantras* the Supreme Lord is the supreme master of innumerable living entities.

The Māyāvādī philosophers, however, try to equate the minute living entities with the supreme living entity. Because they recognize no distinctions between them, their philosophy is called Advaita-vāda, or monism. Factually, however, there is a distinction. This verse is especially meant to impart to the Māyāvādī philosopher the understanding that the Supreme Personality of Godhead is the supreme controller. The supreme controller, the Personality of Godhead, is Kṛṣṇa Himself, but as a transcendental pastime He has accepted the form of a devotee, Lord Caitanya Mahāprabhu.

As stated in the *Bhagavad-gītā,* when the Supreme Personality of Godhead Kṛṣṇa comes to this planet exactly like a human being, some rascals consider Him to be one of the ordinary humans. One who thinks in that mistaken way is described as *mūḍha,* or foolish. Therefore one should not foolishly consider Caitanya Mahāprabhu to be an ordinary human being. He has accepted the ecstasy of a devotee, but He is the Supreme Personality of Godhead. Since the time of Caitanya Mahāprabhu, there have been many imitation incarnations of Kṛṣṇa who cannot understand that Caitanya Mahāprabhu is Kṛṣṇa Himself and not an ordinary human being. Less intelligent men create their own "Gods" by advertising a human being as God. This is their mistake. Therefore here the words *tāṅra śuddha kalevara* warn that Caitanya Mahāprabhu's body is not material but purely spiritual. One should not, therefore, accept Caitanya Mahāprabhu as an ordinary devotee, although He has assumed the form of a devotee. Yet one must certainly know that although Caitanya Mahāprabhu is the Supreme Personality of Godhead, because He accepted the ecstasy of a devotee one should not misunderstand His pastimes and place Him in exactly the same position as Kṛṣṇa. It is for this reason only that when Śrī Kṛṣṇa Caitanya Mahāprabhu was addressed as Kṛṣṇa or Viṣṇu He blocked His ears, not wanting to hear Himself addressed as the Supreme Personality of Godhead. There is a class of devotees called Gaurāṅga-nāgarī, who stage plays of Kṛṣṇa's pastimes using a *vigraha*, or form, of Caitanya Mahāprabhu. This is a mistake that is technically called *rasābhāsa.* While Caitanya Mahāprabhu is trying to enjoy as a devotee, one should not disturb Him by addressing Him as the Supreme Personality of Godhead.

TEXT 11

কৃষ্ণমাধুর্যের এক অদ্ভুত স্বভাব ।
আপনা আস্বাদিতে কৃষ্ণ করে ভক্তভাব ॥ ১১ ॥

kṛṣṇa-mādhuryera eka adbhuta svabhāva
āpanā āsvādite kṛṣṇa kare bhakta-bhāva

kṛṣṇa-mādhuryera—the supreme pleasure potency of Kṛṣṇa; *eka*—is one; *adbhuta*—wonderful; *svabhāva*—nature; *āpanā*—Himself; *āsvādite*—to taste; *kṛṣṇa*—the Supreme Personality of Godhead; *kare*—does; *bhakta-bhāva*—accept the form of a devotee.

TRANSLATION

The transcendental mellow of conjugal love of Kṛṣṇa is so wonderful that Kṛṣṇa Himself accepts the form of a devotee to relish and taste it fully.

PURPORT

Although Kṛṣṇa is the reservoir of all pleasure, He has a special intention to taste Himself by accepting the form of a devotee. It is to be concluded that although Lord Caitanya is present in the form of a devotee, He is Kṛṣṇa Himself. Therefore Vaiṣṇavas sing, *śrī-kṛṣṇa-caitanya rādhā-kṛṣṇa nahe anya:* "Rādhā and Kṛṣṇa combined together are Śrī

Kṛṣṇa Caitanya Mahāprabhu." And as Śrī Svarūpa Dāmodara Gosvāmī has said, *caitanyākhyaṁ prakaṭam adhunā tad-dvayaṁ caikyam āptam:* Rādhā and Kṛṣṇa assumed oneness in the form of Śrī Caitanya Mahāprabhu.

TEXT 12

ইথে ভক্তভাব ধরে চৈতন্য গোসাঞি ।
'ভক্তস্বরূপ' তাঁর নিত্যানন্দ-ভাই ॥ ১২ ॥

ithe bhakta-bhāva dhare caitanya gosāñi
'bhakta-svarūpa' tāṅra nityānanda-bhāi

ithe—for this reason; *bhakta-bhāva*—the ecstasy of a devotee; *dhare*—accepts; *caitanya*—Lord Caitanya Mahāprabhu; *gosāñi*—the transcendental teacher; *bhakta-svarūpa*—exactly like a pure devotee; *tāṅra*—His; *nityānanda*—Lord Nityānanda; *bhāi*—brother.

TRANSLATION

For this reason Śrī Caitanya Mahāprabhu, the supreme teacher, accepts the form of a devotee and accepts Lord Nityānanda as His elder brother.

TEXT 13

'ভক্ত-অবতার' তাঁর আচার্য-গোসাঞি ।
এই তিন তত্ত্ব সবে প্রভু করি' গাই ॥ ১৩ ॥

'bhakta-avatāra' tāṅra ācārya-gosāñi
ei tina tattva sabe prabhu kari' gāi

bhakta-avatāra—incarnation as a devotee; *tāṅra*—His; *ācārya-gosāñi*—the supreme teacher, Advaita Ācārya Prabhu; *ei*—all these; *tina*—three; *tattva*—truths; *sabe*—all; *prabhu*—the predominator; *kari'*—by such understanding; *gāi*—we sing.

TRANSLATION

Śrī Advaita Ācārya is Lord Caitanya's incarnation as a devotee. Therefore these three tattvas [Caitanya Mahāprabhu, Nityānanda Prabhu and Advaita Gosāñi] are the predominators, or masters.

PURPORT

Gosāñi means *gosvāmī.* A person who has full control over the senses and mind is called a *gosvāmī* or *gosāñi.* One who does not have such control is called a *godāsa,* or a servant of the senses, and cannot become a spiritual master. A spiritual master who actually has control over the mind and senses is called Gosvāmī. Although the Gosvāmī title has become a hereditary designation for unscrupulous men, actually the title Gosāñi, or Gosvāmī, began from Śrī Rūpa Gosvāmī, who presented himself as an ordinary *gṛhastha* and minister in government service but became a *gosvāmī* when he was actually elevated by the instruction of Lord Caitanya Mahāprabhu. Therefore Gosvāmī is not a hereditary title but refers to one's qualifications. When one is highly elevated in spiritual advancement, regardless of wherefrom he comes, he may be called Gosvāmī. Śrī Caitanya Mahāprabhu, Śrī Nityānanda Prabhu and Śrī Advaita Gosāñi Prabhu are natural *gosvāmīs* because They belong to the *viṣṇu-tattva* category. As such, all of Them are *prabhus* ("predominators" or "masters"), and They are sometimes called Caitanya Gosāñi, Nityānanda Gosāñi and Advaita Gosāñi. Unfortunately, Their so-called descendants who do not have the qualifications of *gosvāmīs* have accepted this title as a hereditary designation or a professional degree. That is not in accord with the śāstric injunctions.

TEXT 14

এক মহাপ্রভু, আর প্রভু দুইজন ।
দুই প্রভু সেবে মহাপ্রভুর চরণ ॥ ১৪ ॥

eka mahāprabhu, āra prabhu duijana
dui prabhu seve mahāprabhura caraṇa

eka mahāprabhu—one Mahāprabhu, or the supreme predominator; *āra prabhu duijana*—and the other two (Nityānanda and Advaita) are two *prabhus* (masters); *dui prabhu*—the two *prabhus* (Nityānanda and Advaita Gosāñi); *seve*—serve; *mahāprabhura*—of the supreme predominator, Lord Caitanya Mahāprabhu; *caraṇa*—the lotus feet.

TRANSLATION

One of Them is Mahāprabhu, and the other two are prabhus. These two prabhus serve the lotus feet of Mahāprabhu.

PURPORT

Although Śrī Caitanya Mahāprabhu, Śrī Nityānanda Prabhu and Śrī Advaita Prabhu all belong to the same Viṣṇu category, Śrī Caitanya Mahāprabhu is nevertheless accepted as the Supreme, and the other two *prabhus* engage in His transcendental loving service to teach ordinary living entities that every one of us is subordinate to Śrī Caitanya Mahāprabhu. In another place in the *Caitanya-caritāmṛta* (*Ādi* 5.142) it is said, *ekale īśvara kṛṣṇa, āra saba bhṛtya:* the only supreme master is Kṛṣṇa, and all others, both *viṣṇu-tattva* and *jīva-tattva,* engage in the service of the Lord. Both the *viṣṇu-tattva* (as Nityānanda Prabhu and Advaita) and the *jīva-tattva* (*śrīvāsādi-gaura-bhakta-vṛnda*) engage in the service of the Lord, but one must distinguish between the *viṣṇu-tattva* servitors and the *jīva-tattva* servitors. The *jīva-tattva* servitor, the spiritual master, is actually the servitor God. As explained in previous verses, in the absolute world there are no such differences, yet one must observe these differences in order to distinguish the Supreme from His subordinates.

TEXT 15

এই তিন তত্ত্ব,—'সর্বারাধ্য' করি মানি ।
চতুর্থ যে ভক্ততত্ত্ব,—'আরাধক' জানি ॥ ১৫ ॥

ei tina tattva,—'sarvārādhya' kari māni
caturtha ye bhakta-tattva,—'ārādhaka' jāni

ei tina tattva—all three of these truths; *sarva-ārādhya*—worshipable by all living entities; *kari māni*—accepting such; *caturtha*—fourth; *ye*—who is; *bhakta-tattva*—in the category of devotees; *ārādhaka*—worshiper; *jāni*—I understand.

TRANSLATION

The three predominators [Caitanya Mahāprabhu, Nityānanda Prabhu and Advaita Prabhu] are worshipable by all living entities, and the fourth principle [Śrī Gadādhara Prabhu] is to be understood as Their worshiper.

PURPORT

In his *Anubhāṣya,* Śrī Bhaktisiddhānta Sarasvatī Ṭhākura, describing the truth about the Pañca-tattva, explains that we should understand that Lord Śrī Caitanya Mahāprabhu is the supreme predominator and that Nityānanda Prabhu and Advaita Prabhu are His subordinates but are also predominators. Lord Śrī Caitanya Mahāprabhu is the Supreme Lord, and Nityānanda Prabhu and Advaita Prabhu are manifestations of the Supreme Lord. All of Them are *viṣṇu-tattva,* the Supreme, and are therefore worshipable by the living entities. Although the other two *tattvas* within the category of Pañca-tattva—namely, *śakti-tattva* and *jīva-tattva,* represented by Gadādhara and Śrīvāsa—are worshipers of the Supreme Lord, they are in the same category because they eternally engage in the transcendental loving service of the Lord.

TEXT 16

শ্রীবাসাদি যত কোটি কোটি ভক্তগণ ।
'শুদ্ধভক্ত'-তত্ত্বমধ্যে তাঁ-সবার গণন ॥ ১৬ ॥

śrīvāsādi yata koṭi koṭi bhakta-gaṇa
'śuddha-bhakta'-tattva-madhye tāṅ-sabāra gaṇana

śrīvāsa-ādi—devotees headed by Śrīvāsa Ṭhākura; *yata*—all others; *koṭi koṭi*—innumerable; *bhakta-gaṇa*—devotees; *śuddha-bhakta*—pure devotees; *tattva-madhye*—in the truth; *tāṅ-sabāra*—all of them; *gaṇana*—counted.

TRANSLATION

There are innumerable pure devotees of the Lord, headed by Śrīvāsa Ṭhākura, who are known as unalloyed devotees.

TEXT 17

গদাধর-পণ্ডিতাদি প্রভুর 'শক্তি'-অবতার ।
'অন্তরঙ্গ-ভক্ত' করি' গণন যাঁহার ॥ ১৭ ॥

gadādhara-paṇḍitādi prabhura 'śakti'-avatāra
'antaraṅga-bhakta' kari' gaṇana yāṅhāra

gadādhara—Gadādhara; *paṇḍita*—of the learned scholar; *ādi*—headed by; *prabhura*—of the Lord; *śakti*—potency; *avatāra*—incarnation; *antaraṅga*—very confidential; *bhakta*—devotee; *kari'*—accepting; *gaṇana*—counting; *yāṅhāra*—of whom.

TRANSLATION

The devotees headed by Gadādhara Paṇḍita are to be considered incarnations of the internal potency of the Lord. They are confidential devotees engaged in the service of the Lord.

PURPORT

In connection with verses 16 and 17, Śrī Bhaktisiddhānta Sarasvatī Ṭhākura explains in his *Anubhāṣya:* "There are specific symptoms by which the internal devotees and the unalloyed or pure devotees are to be known. All unalloyed devotees are *śakti-tattvas,* or potencies of the Lord. Some of them are situated in conjugal love and others in filial affection, fraternity and servitude. Certainly all of them are devotees, but by making a comparative study it is found that the devotees or potencies who are engaged in conjugal love are better situated than the others. Thus devotees who are in a relationship with the Supreme Personality of Godhead in conjugal love are considered to be the most confidential devotees of Lord Śrī Caitanya Mahāprabhu. Those who engage in the service of Lord Nityānanda Prabhu and Lord Advaita Prabhu generally have relationships of parental love, fraternity, servitude and neutrality. When such devotees develop great attachment for Śrī Caitanya Mahāprabhu, they too become situated within the intimate circle of devotees in conjugal love." This gradual development of devotional service is described by Śrī Narottama dāsa Ṭhākura as follows:

gaurāṅga balite habe pulaka śarīra
hari hari balite nayane ba'be nīra

āra kabe nitāicāṅda karuṇā karibe
saṁsāra-vāsanā mora kabe tuccha habe

viṣaya chāḍiyā kabe śuddha habe mana
kabe hāma heraba śrī-vṛndāvana

rūpa-raghunātha-pade ha-ibe ākuti
kabe hāma bujhaba śrī-yugala-pirīti

"When will there be eruptions on my body as soon as I chant the name of Lord Caitanya, and when will there be incessant torrents of tears as soon as I chant the holy names Hare Kṛṣṇa? When will Lord Nityānanda be merciful toward me and free me from all desires for material enjoyment? When will my mind be completely freed from all contamination of desires for material pleasure? Only at that time will it be possible for me to understand Vṛndāvana. Only if I become attached to the instructions given by the six Gosvāmīs, headed by Rūpa Gosvāmī and Raghunātha dāsa Gosvāmī, will it be possible for me to understand the conjugal love of Rādhā and Kṛṣṇa." By attachment to the devotional service of Lord Caitanya Mahāprabhu, one immediately comes to the ecstatic position. When he develops his love for Nityānanda Prabhu he is freed from all attachment to the material world, and at that time he becomes eligible to understand the Lord's pastimes in Vṛndāvana. In that condition, when one develops his love for the six Gosvāmīs, he can understand the conjugal love between Rādhā and Kṛṣṇa. These are the different stages of a pure devotee's promotion to conjugal love in the service of Rādhā and Kṛṣṇa in an intimate relationship with Śrī Caitanya Mahāprabhu.

TEXTS 18–19

যাঁ-সবা লঞা প্রভুর নিত্য বিহার ।
যাঁ-সবা লঞা প্রভুর কীর্তন-প্রচার ॥ ১৮ ॥
যাঁ-সবা লঞা করেন প্রেম আস্বাদন ।
যাঁ-সবা লঞা দান করে প্রেমধন ॥ ১৯ ॥

yāṅ-sabā lañā prabhura nitya vihāra
yāṅ-sabā lañā prabhura kīrtana-pracāra

yāṅ-sabā lañā karena prema āsvādana
yāṅ-sabā lañā dāna kare prema-dhana

yāṅ-sabā—all; *lañā*—taking company; *prabhura*—of the Lord; *nitya*—eternal; *vihāra*—pastime; *yāṅ-sabā*—all those who are; *lañā*—taking company; *prabhura*—of the Lord; *kīrtana—saṅkīrtana; pracāra*—movement; *yāṅ-sabā*—persons with whom; *lañā*—in accompaniment; *karena*—He does; *prema*—love of God; *āsvādana*—taste; *yāṅ-sabā*—those who are; *lañā*—in accompaniment; *dāna kare*—gives in charity; *prema-dhana*—love of Godhead.

TRANSLATION

The internal devotees or potencies are all eternal associates in the pastimes of the Lord. Only with them does the Lord advent to propound the saṅkīrtana movement, only with them does the Lord

taste the mellow of conjugal love, and only with them does He distribute this love of God to people in general.

PURPORT

Distinguishing between pure devotees and internal or confidential devotees, Śrī Rūpa Gosvāmī, in his book *Upadeśāmṛta,* traces the following gradual process of development. Out of many thousands of *karmīs,* one is better when he is situated in perfect Vedic knowledge. Out of many such learned scholars and philosophers, one who is actually liberated from material bondage is better, and out of many such persons who are actually liberated, one who is a devotee of the Supreme Personality of Godhead is considered to be the best. Among the many such transcendental lovers of the Supreme Personality of Godhead, the *gopīs* are the best, and among the *gopīs* Śrīmatī Rādhikā is the best. Śrīmatī Rādhikā is very dear to Lord Kṛṣṇa, and similarly Her ponds, namely, Śyāma-kuṇḍa and Rādhā-kuṇḍa, are also very dear to the Supreme Personality of Godhead.

Śrīla Bhaktisiddhānta Sarasvatī Ṭhākura comments in his *Anubhāṣya* that among the five *tattvas,* two are energies (*śakti-tattva*) and the three others are energetic (*śaktimān tattva*). Unalloyed and internal devotees are both engaged in the favorable culture of Kṛṣṇa consciousness untinged by philosophical speculation or fruitive activities. They are all understood to be pure devotees, and those among them who simply engage in conjugal love are called *mādhurya-bhaktas,* or internal devotees. The loving services in parental love, fraternity and servitude are included in conjugal love of God. In conclusion, therefore, every confidential devotee is a pure devotee of the Lord.

Śrī Caitanya Mahāprabhu enjoys His pastimes with His immediate expansion Nityānanda Prabhu. His pure devotees and His three *puruṣa* incarnations, namely, Kāraṇodakaśāyī Viṣṇu, Garbhodakaśāyī Viṣṇu and Kṣīrodakaśāyī Viṣṇu, always accompany the Supreme Lord to propound the *saṅkīrtana* movement.

TEXTS 20–21

সেই পঞ্চতত্ত্ব মিলি' পৃথিবী আসিয়া ।
পূর্ব-প্রেমভাণ্ডারের মুদ্রা উঘাড়িয়া ॥ ২০ ॥
পাঁচে মিলি' লুটে প্রেম, করে আস্বাদন ।
যত যত পিয়ে, তৃষ্ণা বাঢ়ে অনুক্ষণ ॥ ২১ ॥

sei pañca-tattva mili' pṛthivī āsiyā
pūrva-premabhāṇḍārera mudrā ughāḍiyā

pāṅce mili' luṭe prema, kare āsvādana
yata yata piye, tṛṣṇā bāḍhe anukṣaṇa

sei—those; *pañca-tattva*—five truths; *mili'*—combined together; *pṛthivī*—on this earth; *āsiyā*—descending; *pūrva*—original; *prema-bhāṇḍārera*—the store of transcendental love; *mudrā*—seal; *ughāḍiyā*—opening; *pāṅce mili'*—mixing together all these five; *luṭe*—plunder; *prema*—love of Godhead; *kare āsvādana*—taste; *yata yata*—as much as; *piye*—drink; *tṛṣṇā*—thirst; *bāḍhe*—increases; *anukṣaṇa*—again and again.

TRANSLATION

The characteristics of Kṛṣṇa are understood to be a storehouse of transcendental love. Although that storehouse of love certainly came with Kṛṣṇa when He was present, it was sealed. But when Śrī Caitanya Mahāprabhu came with His associates of the Pañca-tattva, they broke the seal and plundered the storehouse to taste transcendental love of Kṛṣṇa. The more they tasted it, the more their thirst for it grew.

PURPORT

Śrī Caitanya Mahāprabhu is called *mahā-vadānyāvatāra* because although He is Śrī Kṛṣṇa Himself, He is even more favorably disposed to the poor fallen souls than Lord Śrī Kṛṣṇa. When Lord Śrī Kṛṣṇa Himself was personally present, He demanded that everyone surrender unto Him and promised that He would then give one all protection, but when Śrī Caitanya Mahāprabhu came to this earth with His associates, He simply distributed transcendental love of God without discrimination. Śrī Rūpa Gosvāmī, therefore, could understand that Lord Caitanya was none other than Śrī Kṛṣṇa Himself, for no one but the Supreme Personality of Godhead can distribute confidential love of the Supreme Person.

TEXT 22

পুনঃ পুনঃ পিয়াইয়া হয় মহামত্ত ।
নাচে, কান্দে, হাসে, গায়, যৈছে মদমত্ত ॥ ২২ ॥

punaḥ punaḥ piyāiyā haya mahāmatta
nāce, kānde, hāse, gāya, yaiche mada-matta

punaḥ punaḥ—again and again; *piyāiyā*—causing to drink; *haya*—becomes; *mahā-matta*—highly ecstatic; *nāce*—dances; *kānde*—cries; *hāse*—laughs; *gāya*—chants; *yaiche*—as if; *mada-matta*—one is drunk.

TRANSLATION

Śrī Pañca-tattva themselves danced again and again and thus made it easier to drink nectarean love of Godhead. They danced, cried, laughed and chanted like madmen, and in this way they distributed love of Godhead.

PURPORT

People generally cannot understand the actual meaning of chanting and dancing. Describing the Gosvāmīs, Śrī Śrīnivāsa Ācārya stated, *kṛṣṇotkīrtana-gāna-nartana-parau:* not only did Lord Caitanya Mahāprabhu and His associates demonstrate this chanting and dancing, but the six Gosvāmīs also followed in the next generation. The present Kṛṣṇa consciousness movement follows the same principle, and therefore simply by chanting and dancing we have received good responses all over the world. It is to be understood, however, that this chanting and dancing do not belong to this material world. They are actually transcendental activities, for the more one engages in chanting and dancing, the more he can taste the nectar of transcendental love of Godhead.

TEXT 23

পাত্রাপাত্র-বিচার নাহি, নাহি স্থানাস্থান ।
যেই যাঁহা পায়, তাঁহা করে প্রেমদান ॥ ২৩ ॥

pātrāpātra-vicāra nāhi, nāhi sthānāsthāna
yei yāṅhā pāya, tāṅhā kare prema-dāna

pātra—recipient; *apātra*—not a recipient; *vicāra*—consideration; *nāhi*—there is none; *nāhi*—there is none; *sthāna*—favorable place; *asthāna*—unfavorable place; *yei*—anyone; *yāṅhā*—wherever; *pāya*—gets the opportunity; *tāṅhā*—there only; *kare*—does; *prema-dāna*—distribution of love of Godhead.

TRANSLATION

In distributing love of Godhead, Caitanya Mahāprabhu and His associates did not consider who was a fit candidate and who was not, nor where such distribution should or should not take place. They made no conditions. Wherever they got the opportunity, the members of the Pañca-tattva distributed love of Godhead.

PURPORT

There are some rascals who dare to speak against the mission of Lord Caitanya by criticizing the Kṛṣṇa consciousness movement for accepting Europeans and Americans as *brāhmaṇas* and offering them *sannyāsa.* But here is an authoritative statement that in distributing love of Godhead one should not consider whether the recipients are Europeans, Americans, Hindus, Muslims, etc. The Kṛṣṇa consciousness movement should be spread wherever possible, and one should accept those who thus become Vaiṣṇavas as being greater than *brāhmaṇas,* Hindus or Indians. Śrī Caitanya Mahāprabhu desired that His name be spread in each and every town and village on the surface of the globe. Therefore, when the cult of Caitanya Mahāprabhu is spread all over the world, should those who embrace it not be accepted as Vaiṣṇavas, *brāhmaṇas* and *sannyāsīs*? These foolish arguments are sometimes raised by envious rascals, but Kṛṣṇa conscious devotees do not care about them. We strictly follow the principles set down by the Pañca-tattva.

TEXT 24

লুটিয়া, খাইয়া, দিয়া, ভাণ্ডার উজাড়ে ।
আশ্চর্য ভাণ্ডার, প্রেম শতগুণ বাড়ে ॥ ২৪ ॥

luṭiyā, khāiyā, diyā, bhāṇḍāra ujāḍe
āścarya bhāṇḍāra, prema śata-guṇa bāḍe

luṭiyā—plundering; *khāiyā*—eating; *diyā*—distributing; *bhāṇḍāra*—store; *ujāḍe*—emptied; *āścarya*—wonderful; *bhāṇḍāra*—store; *prema*—love of Godhead; *śata-guṇa*—one hundred times; *bāḍe*—increases.

TRANSLATION

Although the members of the Pañca-tattva plundered the storehouse of love of Godhead and ate and distributed its contents, there was no scarcity, for this wonderful storehouse is so complete that as the love is distributed, the supply increases hundreds of times.

PURPORT

A pseudo incarnation of Kṛṣṇa once told his disciple that he had emptied himself by giving him all knowledge and was thus spiritually bankrupt. Such bluffers speak in this way to cheat the public, but actual spiritual consciousness is so perfect that the more it is distributed, the more it increases. Bankruptcy is a term that applies in the material world, but the storehouse of love of Godhead in the spiritual world can never be depleted. Kṛṣṇa is providing for millions and trillions of living entities by supplying all their necessities, and even if all the innumerable living entities wanted to become Kṛṣṇa conscious, there would be no scarcity of love of Godhead, nor would there be insufficiency in providing for their maintenance. Our Kṛṣṇa consciousness movement was started single-handedly, and no one provided for our livelihood, but at present we are spending hundreds and thousands of dollars all over the world, and the movement is increasing more and more. Thus there is no question of scarcity. Although jealous persons may be envious, if we stick to our principles and follow in the footsteps of the Pañca-tattva, this movement will go on unchecked by imitation *svāmīs, sannyāsīs,* religionists, philosophers or scientists, for it is transcendental to all material considerations. Therefore those who propagate the Kṛṣṇa consciousness movement should not be afraid of such rascals and fools.

TEXT 25

উছলিল প্রেমবন্যা চৌদিকে বেড়ায় ।
স্ত্রী, বৃদ্ধ, বালক, যুবা, সবারে ডুবায় ॥ ২৫ ॥

uchalila prema-vanyā caudike veḍāya
strī, vṛddha, bālaka, yuvā, sabāre ḍubāya

uchalila—became agitated; *prema-vanyā*—the inundation of love of Godhead; *caudike*—in all directions; *veḍāya*—surrounding; *strī*—women; *vṛddha*—old men; *bālaka*—children; *yuvā*—young men; *sabāre*—all of them; *ḍubāya*—merged into.

TRANSLATION

The flood of love of Godhead swelled in all directions, and thus young men, old men, women and children were all immersed in that inundation.

PURPORT

When the contents of the storehouse of love of Godhead is thus distributed, there is a powerful inundation that covers the entire land. In Śrīdhāma Māyāpur there is sometimes a great flood after the rainy season. This is an indication that from the birthplace of Lord Caitanya the inundation of love of Godhead should be spread all over the world, for this will help everyone, including old men, young men, women and children. The Kṛṣṇa consciousness movement of Śrī Caitanya Mahāprabhu is so powerful that it can inundate the entire world and interest all classes of men in the subject of love of Godhead.

TEXT 26

সজ্জন, দুর্জন, পঙ্গু, জড়, অন্ধগণ ।
প্রেমবন্যায় ডুবাইল জগতের জন ॥ ২৬ ॥

saj-jana, durjana, paṅgu, jaḍa, andha-gaṇa
prema-vanyāya ḍubāila jagatera jana

sat-jana—gentle men; *durjana*—rogues; *paṅgu*—lame; *jaḍa*—invalid; *andha-gaṇa*—blind men; *prema-vanyāya*—in the inundation of love of Godhead; *ḍubāila*—drowned; *jagatera*—all over the world; *jana*—people.

TRANSLATION

The Kṛṣṇa consciousness movement will inundate the entire world and drown everyone, whether one be a gentleman, a rogue or even lame, invalid or blind.

PURPORT

Here again it may be emphasized that although jealous rascals protest that Europeans and Americans cannot be given the sacred thread or *sannyāsa*, there is no need even to consider whether one is a gentleman or a rogue because this is a spiritual movement which is not concerned with the external body of skin and bones. Because it is being properly conducted under the guidance of the Pañca-tattva, strictly following the regulative principles, it has nothing to do with external impediments.

TEXT 27

জগৎ ডুবিল, জীবের হৈল বীজ নাশ।
তাহা দেখি' পাঁচ জনের পরম উল্লাস ॥ ২৭ ॥

jagat ḍubila, jīvera haila bīja nāśa
tāhā dekhi' pāñca janera parama ullāsa

jagat—the whole world; *ḍubila*—drowned; *jīvera*—of the living entities; *haila*—it so became; *bīja*—the seed; *nāśa*—completely finished; *tāhā*—then; *dekhi'*—by seeing; *pāñca*—five; *janera*—of the persons; *parama*—highest; *ullāsa*—happiness.

TRANSLATION

When the five members of the Pañca-tattva saw the entire world drowned in love of Godhead and the seed of material enjoyment in the living entities completely destroyed, they all became exceedingly happy.

PURPORT

In this connection, Śrīla Bhaktisiddhānta Sarasvatī Ṭhākura writes in his *Anubhāṣya* that since the living entities all belong to the marginal potency of the Lord, each and every living entity has a natural tendency to become Kṛṣṇa conscious, although at the same time the seed of material enjoyment is undoubtedly within him. The seed of material enjoyment, watered by the course of material nature, fructifies to become a tree of material entanglement that endows the living entity with all kinds of material enjoyment. To enjoy such material facilities is to be afflicted with the three material miseries. However, when by nature's law there is a flood, the seeds within the earth become inactive. Similarly, as the inundation of love of Godhead spreads all over the world, the seeds of material enjoyment become impotent. Thus the more the Kṛṣṇa consciousness movement spreads, the more the desire for material enjoyment decreases. The seed of material enjoyment automatically becomes impotent with the increase of the Kṛṣṇa consciousness movement.

Instead of being envious that Kṛṣṇa consciousness is spreading all over the world by the grace of Lord Caitanya, those who are jealous should be happy, as indicated here by the words *parama ullāsa*. But because they are *kaniṣṭha-adhikārīs* or *prākṛta-bhaktas* (materialistic devotees who are not advanced in spiritual knowledge), they are envious instead of happy, and they try to find faults in the Kṛṣṇa consciousness movement. Yet Śrīmat Prabodhānanda Sarasvatī writes in his *Caitanya-candrāmṛta* that when influenced by Lord Caitanya's Kṛṣṇa consciousness movement, materialists become averse to talking about their wives and children, supposedly learned scholars give up their tedious studies of Vedic literature, *yogīs* give up their impractical practices of mystic *yoga,* ascetics give up their austere activities of penance and austerity, and *sannyāsīs* give up their study of Sāṅkhya philosophy. Thus they are all attracted by the *bhakti-yoga* practices of Lord Caitanya and cannot relish a mellow superior to that of Kṛṣṇa consciousness.

TEXT 28

যত যত প্রেমবৃষ্টি করে পঞ্চজনে ।
তত তত বাঢ়ে জল, ব্যাপে ত্রিভুবনে ॥ ২৮ ॥

yata yata prema-vṛṣṭi kare pañca-jane
tata tata bāḍhe jala, vyāpe tri-bhuvane

yata—as many; *yata*—so many; *prema-vṛṣṭi*—showers of love of Godhead; *kare*—causes; *pañca-jane*—the five members of the Pañca-tattva; *tata tata*—as much as; *bāḍhe*—increases; *jala*—water; *vyāpe*—spreads; *tri-bhuvane*—all over the three worlds.

TRANSLATION

The more the five members of the Pañca-tattva cause the rains of love of Godhead to fall, the more the inundation increases and spreads all over the world.

PURPORT

The Kṛṣṇa consciousness movement is not stereotyped or stagnant. It will spread all over the world in spite of all objections by fools and rascals that European and American *mlecchas* cannot be accepted as *brāhmaṇas* or *sannyāsīs.* Here it is indicated that this process will spread and inundate the entire world with Kṛṣṇa consciousness.

TEXTS 29–30

মায়াবাদী, কর্মনিষ্ঠ কুতার্কিকগণ ।
নিন্দক, পাষণ্ডী, যত পড়ুয়া অধম ॥ ২৯ ॥
সেই সব মহাদক্ষ ধাঞা পলাইল ।
সেই বন্যা তা-সবারে ছুঁইতে নারিল ॥ ৩০ ॥

māyāvādī, karma-niṣṭha kutārkika-gaṇa
nindaka, pāsaṇḍī yata paḍuyā adhama

sei saba mahādakṣa dhāñā palāila
sei vanyā tā-sabāre chuṅite nārila

māyāvādī—the impersonalist philosophers; *karma-niṣṭha*—the fruitive workers; *kutārkika-gaṇa*—the false logicians; *nindaka*—the blasphemers; *pāṣaṇḍī*—nondevotees; *yata*—all; *paḍuyā*—students; *adhama*—the lowest class; *sei saba*—all of them; *mahā-dakṣa*—they are very expert; *dhāñā*—running; *palāila*—went away; *sei vanyā*—that inundation; *tā-sabāre*—all of them; *chuṅite*—touching; *nārila*—could not.

TRANSLATION

The impersonalists, fruitive workers, false logicians, blasphemers, nondevotees and lowest among the student community are very expert in avoiding the Kṛṣṇa consciousness movement, and therefore the inundation of Kṛṣṇa consciousness cannot touch them.

PURPORT

Like Māyāvādī philosophers in the past such as Prakāśānanda Sarasvatī of Benares, modern impersonalists are not interested in Lord Caitanya's Kṛṣṇa consciousness movement. They do not know the value of this material world; they consider it false and cannot understand how the Kṛṣṇa consciousness movement can utilize it. They are so absorbed in impersonal thought that they take it for granted that all spiritual variety is material. Because they do not know anything beyond their misconception of the *brahmajyoti,* they cannot understand that Kṛṣṇa, the Supreme Personality of Godhead, is spiritual and therefore beyond the conception of material illusion. Whenever Kṛṣṇa incarnates personally or as a devotee, these Māyāvādī philosophers accept Him as an ordinary human being. This is condemned in the *Bhagavad-gītā* (9.11):

avajānanti māṁ mūḍhā mānuṣīṁ tanum āśritam
paraṁ bhāvam ajānanto mama bhūta-maheśvaram

"Fools deride Me when I descend in the human form. They do not know My transcendental nature as the Supreme Lord of all that be."

There are also other unscrupulous persons who exploit the Lord's appearance by posing as incarnations to cheat the innocent public. An incarnation of God should pass the tests of the statements of the *śāstras* and also perform uncommon activities. One should not accept a rascal as an incarnation of God but should test his ability to act as the Supreme Personality of Godhead. For example, Kṛṣṇa taught Arjuna in the *Bhagavad-gītā,* and Arjuna also accepted Him as the Supreme Personality of Godhead, but for our understanding Arjuna requested the Lord to manifest His universal form, thus testing whether He was actually the Supreme Lord. Similarly, one must test a so-called incarnation of Godhead according to the standard criteria. To avoid being misled by an exhibition of mystic powers, it is best to examine a so-called incarnation of God in the light of the statements of the *śāstras.* Caitanya Mahāprabhu is described in the *śāstras* as an incarnation of Kṛṣṇa; therefore if one wants to imitate Lord Caitanya and claim to be an incarnation, he must show evidence from the *śāstras* about his appearance to substantiate his claim.

TEXTS 31–32

তাহা দেখি' মহাপ্রভু করেন চিন্তন ।
জগৎ ডুবাইতে আমি করিলুঁ যতন ॥ ৩১ ॥
কেহ কেহ এড়াইল, প্রতিজ্ঞা হইল ভঙ্গ ।
তা-সবা ডুবাইতে পাতিব কিছু রঙ্গ ॥ ৩২ ॥

tāhā dekhi' mahāprabhu karena cintana
jagat ḍubāite āmi kariluṅ yatana

keha keha eḍāila, pratijñā ha-ila bhaṅga
tā-sabā ḍubaite pātiba kichu raṅga

tāhā dekhi'—observing this advancement; *mahāprabhu*—Lord Śrī Caitanya Mahāprabhu; *karena*—does; *cintana*—thinking; *jagat*—the whole world; *ḍubāite*—to drown; *āmi*—I; *kariluṅ*—endeavored; *yatana*—attempts; *keha keha*—some of them; *eḍāila*—escaped; *pratijñā*—promise; *ha-ila*—became; *bhaṅga*—broken; *tā-sabā*—all of them;

ḍubāite—to make them drown; *pātiba*—shall devise; *kichu*—some; *raṅga*—trick.

TRANSLATION

Seeing that the Māyāvādīs and others were fleeing, Lord Caitanya thought, "I wanted everyone to be immersed in this inundation of love of Godhead, but some of them have escaped. Therefore I shall devise a trick to drown them also."

PURPORT

Here is an important point. Lord Caitanya Mahāprabhu wanted to invent a way to capture the Māyāvādīs and others who did not take interest in the Kṛṣṇa consciousness movement. This is the symptom of an *ācārya.* An *ācārya* who comes for the service of the Lord cannot be expected to conform to a stereotype, for he must find the ways and means by which Kṛṣṇa consciousness may be spread. Sometimes jealous persons criticize the Kṛṣṇa consciousness movement because it engages equally both boys and girls in distributing love of Godhead. Not knowing that boys and girls in countries like Europe and America mix very freely, these fools and rascals criticize the boys and girls in Kṛṣṇa consciousness for intermingling. But these rascals should consider that one cannot suddenly change a community's social customs. However, since both the boys and the girls are being trained to become preachers, those girls are not ordinary girls but are as good as their brothers who are preaching Kṛṣṇa consciousness. Therefore, to engage both boys and girls in fully transcendental activities is a policy intended to spread the Kṛṣṇa consciousness movement. These jealous fools who criticize the intermingling of boys and girls will simply have to be satisfied with their own foolishness because they cannot think of how to spread Kṛṣṇa consciousness by adopting ways and means that are favorable for this purpose. Their stereotyped methods will never help spread Kṛṣṇa consciousness. Therefore, what we are doing is perfect by the grace of Lord Caitanya Mahāprabhu, for it is He who proposed to invent a way to capture those who strayed from Kṛṣṇa consciousness.

TEXT 33

এত বলি' মনে কিছু করিয়া বিচার ।
সন্ন্যাস-আশ্রম প্রভু কৈলা অঙ্গীকার ॥ ৩৩ ॥

eta bali' mane kichu kariyā vicāra
sannyāsa-āśrama prabhu kailā aṅgīkāra

eta bali'—saying this; *mane*—within the mind; *kichu*—something; *kariyā*—doing; *vicāra*—consideration; *sannyāsa-āśrama*—the renounced order of life; *prabhu*—the Lord; *kailā*—did; *aṅgīkāra*—accept.

TRANSLATION

Thus the Lord accepted the sannyāsa order of life after full consideration.

PURPORT

There was no need for Lord Śrī Caitanya Mahāprabhu to accept *sannyāsa,* for He is God Himself and therefore has nothing to do with the material bodily concept of life. Śrī Caitanya Mahāprabhu did not identify Himself with any of the eight *varṇas* and *āśramas,* namely, *brāhmaṇa, kṣatriya, vaiśya, śūdra, brahmacārī, gṛhastha, vānaprastha* and *sannyāsa.* He identified Himself as the Supreme Spirit. Śrī Caitanya Mahāprabhu, or for that matter any pure devotee, never identifies with these social and spiritual divisions of life, for a devotee is always transcendental to these different gradations of society. Nevertheless, Lord Caitanya decided to accept *sannyāsa* on the grounds that when He became a *sannyāsī* everyone would show Him respect and in that way be favored. Although there was actually no need for Him to accept *sannyāsa,* He did so for the benefit of those who might think Him an ordinary human being. The main purpose of His accepting *sannyāsa* was to deliver the Māyāvādī *sannyāsīs.* This will be evident later in this chapter.

Śrīla Bhaktisiddhānta Sarasvatī Ṭhākura has explained the term "Māyāvādī" as follows: "The Supreme Personality of Godhead is transcendental to the material conception of life. A Māyāvādī is one who considers the body of the Supreme Personality of Godhead Kṛṣṇa to be made of *māyā* and who also considers the abode of the Lord and the process of approaching Him, devotional service, to be *māyā.* The Māyāvādī considers all the paraphernalia of devotional service to be *māyā.*" *Māyā* refers to material existence, which is characterized by the reactions of fruitive activities. Māyāvādīs consider devotional service to be among such fruitive activities. According to them, when *bhāgavatas* (devotees) are purified by philosophical speculation, they will come to the real point of liberation. Those who speculate in this way regarding devotional service are called *kutārkikas* (false logicians), and those who consider devotional service to be fruitive activity are called *karmaniṣṭhas.* Those who criticize devotional service are called *nindakas* (blasphemers). Similarly, nondevotees who consider devotional activities to be material are called *pāṣaṇḍīs,* and scholars with a similar viewpoint are called *adhama paḍuyās.*

The *kutārkikas, nindakas, pāṣaṇḍīs* and *adhama paḍuyās* all avoided the benefit of Śrī Caitanya Mahāprabhu's movement of developing love of Godhead. Śrī Caitanya Mahāprabhu felt compassion for them, and it is for this reason that He decided to accept the *sannyāsa* order, for by seeing Him as a *sannyāsī* they would offer Him respects. The *sannyāsa* order is still respected in India. Indeed, the very dress of a *sannyāsī* still commands respect from the Indian public. Therefore Śrī Caitanya Mahāprabhu accepted *sannyāsa* to facilitate preaching His devotional cult, although otherwise He had no need to accept the fourth order of spiritual life.

TEXT 34

চব্বিশ বৎসর ছিলা গৃহস্থ-আশ্রমে ।
পঞ্চবিংশতি বর্ষে কৈল যতিধর্মে ॥ ৩৪ ॥

cabbiśa vatsara chilā gṛhastha-āśrame
pañca-viṁśati varṣe kaila yati-dharme

cabbiśa—twenty-four; *vatsara*—years; *chilā*—He remained; *gṛhastha*—householder life; *āśrame*—the order of; *pañca*—five; *viṁśati*—twenty; *varṣe*—in the year; *kaila*—did; *yati-dharme*—accepted the *sannyāsa* order.

TRANSLATION

Śrī Caitanya Mahāprabhu remained in householder life for twenty-four years, and on the verge of His twenty-fifth year He accepted the sannyāsa order.

PURPORT

There are four orders of spiritual life, namely, *brahmacarya, gṛhastha, vānaprastha* and *sannyāsa,* and in each of these *āśramas* there are four divisions. The divisions of the *brahmacarya-āśrama* are *sāvitrya, prājāpatya, brāhma* and *bṛhat,* and the divisions of the *gṛhasthāśrama* are *vārtā* (professionals), *sañcaya* (accumulators), *śālīna* (those who do not ask anything from anyone) and *śiloñchana* (those who collect grains from the paddy fields). Similarly, the divisions of the *vānaprastha-*

āśrama are *vaikhānasa, vālakhilya, auḍumbara* and *pheṇapa,* and the divisions of *sannyāsa* are *kuṭīcaka, bahūdaka, haṁsa* and *niṣkriya.* There are two kinds of *sannyāsīs,* who are called *dhīras* and *narottamas,* as stated in *Śrīmad-Bhāgavatam* (1.13.26–27). At the end of the month of January in the year 1432 *śakābda* (A.D. 1510), Śrī Caitanya Mahāprabhu accepted the *sannyāsa* order from Keśava Bhāratī, who belonged to the Śaṅkara-sampradāya.

TEXT 35

সন্ন্যাস করিয়া প্রভু কৈলা আকর্ষণ ।
যতেক পালাঞাছিল তার্কিকাদিগণ ॥ ৩৫ ॥

sannyāsa kariyā prabhu kailā ākarṣaṇa
yateka pālāñāchila tārkikādigaṇa

sannyāsa—the *sannyāsa* order; *kariyā*—accepting; *prabhu*—the Lord; *kailā*—did; *ākarṣaṇa*—attract; *yateka*—all; *pālāñāchila*—fled; *tārkika-ādi-gaṇa*—all persons, beginning with the logicians.

TRANSLATION

After accepting the sannyāsa order, Śrī Caitanya Mahāprabhu attracted the attention of all those who had evaded Him, beginning with the logicians.

TEXT 36

পড়ুয়া, পাষণ্ডী, কর্মী, নিন্দকাদি যত ।
তারা আসি' প্রভু-পায় হয় অবনত ॥ ৩৬ ॥

paḍuyā, pāṣaṇḍī, karmī, nindakādi yata
tārā āsi' prabhu-pāya haya avanata

paḍuyā—students; *pāṣaṇḍī*—material adjusters; *karmī*—fruitive actors; *nindaka-ādi*—critics; *yata*—all; *tārā*—they; *āsi'*—coming; *prabhu*—the Lord's; *pāya*—lotus feet; *haya*—became; *avanata*—surrendered.

TRANSLATION

Thus the students, infidels, fruitive workers and critics all came to surrender unto the lotus feet of the Lord.

TEXT 37

অপরাধ ক্ষমাইল, ডুবিল প্রেমজলে ।
কেবা এড়াইবে প্রভুর প্রেম-মহাজালে ॥ ৩৭ ॥

aparādha kṣamāila, ḍubila prema-jale
kebā eḍāibe prabhura prema-mahājāle

aparādha—offense; *kṣamāila*—excused; *ḍubila*—merged into; *prema-jale*—in the ocean of love of Godhead; *kebā*—who else; *eḍāibe*—will go away; *prabhura*—the Lord's; *prema*—loving; *mahā-jāle*—network.

TRANSLATION

Lord Caitanya excused them all, and they merged into the ocean of devotional service, for no one can escape the unique loving network of Śrī Caitanya Mahāprabhu.

PURPORT

Śrī Caitanya Mahāprabhu was an ideal *ācārya.* An *ācārya* is an ideal teacher who knows the purpose of the revealed scriptures, behaves exactly according to their injunctions and teaches his students to adopt these principles also. As an ideal *ācārya,* Śrī Caitanya Mahāprabhu devised ways to capture all kinds of atheists and materialists. Every *ācārya* has a specific means of propagating his spiritual movement with the aim of bringing men to Kṛṣṇa consciousness. Therefore, the method of one *ācārya* may be different from that of another, but the ultimate goal is never neglected. Śrīla Rūpa Gosvāmī recommends:

tasmāt kenāpy upāyena manaḥ kṛṣṇe niveśayet
sarve vidhi-niṣedhā syur etayor eva kiṅkarāḥ

An *ācārya* should devise a means by which people may somehow or other come to Kṛṣṇa consciousness. First they should become Kṛṣṇa conscious, and all the prescribed rules and regulations may later gradually be introduced. In our Kṛṣṇa consciousness movement we follow this policy of Lord Śrī Caitanya Mahāprabhu. For example, since boys and girls in the Western countries freely intermingle, special concessions regarding their customs and habits are necessary to bring them to Kṛṣṇa consciousness. The *ācārya* must devise a means to bring them to devotional service. Therefore, although I am a *sannyāsī* I sometimes take part in getting boys and girls married, although in the history of *sannyāsa* no *sannyāsī* has personally taken part in marrying his disciples.

TEXT 38

সবা নিস্তারিতে প্রভু কৃপা-অবতার ।
সবা নিস্তারিতে করে চাতুরী অপার ॥ ৩৮ ॥

sabā nistārite prabhu kṛpā-avatāra
sabā nistārite kare cāturī apāra

sabā—all; *nistārite*—to deliver; *prabhu*—the Lord; *kṛpā*—mercy; *avatāra*—incarnation; *sabā*—all; *nistārite*—to deliver; *kare*—did; *cāturī*—devices; *apāra*—unlimited.

TRANSLATION

Śrī Caitanya Mahāprabhu appeared in order to deliver all the fallen souls. Therefore He devised many methods to liberate them from the clutches of māyā.

PURPORT

It is the concern of the *ācārya* to show mercy to the fallen souls. In this connection, *deśa-kāla-pātra* (the place, the time and the object) should be taken into consideration. Since the European and American boys and girls in our Kṛṣṇa consciousness movement preach together, less intelligent men criticize that they are mingling without restriction. In Europe and America boys and girls mingle unrestrictedly and have equal rights; therefore it is not possible to completely separate the men from the women. However, we are thoroughly instructing both men and women how to preach, and actually they are preaching wonderfully. Of course, we very strictly prohibit illicit sex. Boys and girls who are not married are not allowed to sleep together or live together, and there are separate arrangements for boys and girls in every temple. *Gṛhasthas* live outside the temple, for in the temple we do not allow even husband and wife to live together. The results of this are wonderful. Both men and women are preaching the gospel of Lord Caitanya Mahāprabhu and Lord Kṛṣṇa with redoubled strength. In this verse the words *sabā nistārite kare cāturī apāra* indicate that Śrī Caitanya Mahāprabhu wanted to deliver one and all. Therefore it is a principle that a preacher must strictly follow the rules and regulations laid down in the *śāstras* yet at the same time devise a means by which the preaching work to reclaim the fallen may go on with full force.

TEXT 39

তবে নিজ ভক্ত কৈল যত ম্লেচ্ছ আদি ।
সবে এড়াইল মাত্র কাশীর মায়াবাদী ॥ ৩৯ ॥

tabe nija bhakta kaila yata mleccha ādi
sabe eḍāila mātra kāśīra māyāvādī

tabe—thereafter; *nija*—own; *bhakta*—devotee; *kaila*—converted; *yata*—all; *mleccha*—one who does not follow the Vedic principles; *ādi*—heading the list; *sabe*—all those; *eḍāila*—escaped; *mātra*—only; *kāśīra*—of Vārāṇasī; *māyāvādī*—impersonalists.

TRANSLATION

All were converted into devotees of Lord Caitanya, even the mlecchas and yavanas. Only the impersonalist followers of Śaṅkarācārya evaded Him.

PURPORT

In this verse it is clearly indicated that although Lord Caitanya Mahāprabhu converted Muslims and other *mlecchas* into devotees, the impersonalist followers of Śaṅkarācārya could not be converted. After accepting the renounced order of life, Caitanya Mahāprabhu converted many *karma-niṣṭhas* who were addicted to fruitive activities, many great logicians like Sārvabhauma Bhaṭṭācārya, *nindakas* (blasphemers) like Prakāśānanda Sarasvatī, *pāṣaṇḍīs* (nondevotees) like Jagāi and Mādhāi, and *adhama paḍuyās* (degraded students) like Mukunda and his friends. All of them gradually became devotees of the Lord, even the Pāṭhāns (Muslims), but the worst offenders, the impersonalists, were extremely difficult to convert, for they very tactfully escaped the devices of Lord Caitanya Mahāprabhu.

In describing the Kāśīra Māyāvādīs, Śrīla Bhaktisiddhānta Sarasvatī Ṭhākura has explained that persons who are bewildered by empiric knowledge or direct sensual perception, and who thus consider that even this limited material world can be gauged by their material estimations, conclude that anything that one can discern by direct sense perception is but *māyā*, or illusion. They maintain that although the Absolute Truth is beyond the range of sense perception, it includes no spiritual variety or enjoyment. According to the Kāśīra Māyāvādīs, the spiritual world is simply void. They do not believe in the Personality of the Absolute Truth or in His varieties of activities in the spiritual world. Although they have their own arguments, which are not very strong, they have no conception of the variegated activities of the Absolute Truth. These impersonalists, who are followers of Śaṅkarācārya, are generally known as Kāśīra Māyāvādīs (impersonalists residing in Vārāṇasī).

Near Vārāṇasī there is another group of impersonalists, who are known as Saranātha Māyāvādīs. Outside the city of Vārāṇasī is a place known as Saranātha, where there is a big Buddhist *stūpa*. Many followers of Buddhist philosophy live there, and they are known as Saranātha Māyāvādīs. The impersonalists of Saranātha differ from those of Vārāṇasī, for the Vārāṇasī impersonalists propagate the idea that the impersonal Brahman is truth whereas material varieties are false, but the Saranātha impersonalists do not even believe that the Absolute Truth, or Brahman, can be understood as the opposite of *māyā*, or illusion. According to their vision, materialism is the only manifestation of the Absolute Truth.

Factually both the Kāśīra and the Saranātha Māyāvādīs, as well as any other philosophers who have no knowledge of the spirit soul, are advocates of utter materialism. None of them have clear knowledge regarding the Absolute or the spiritual world. Philosophers like the Saranātha Māyāvādīs who do not believe in the spiritual existence of the Absolute Truth but consider material varieties to be everything do not believe that there are two kinds of nature, inferior (material) and superior (spiritual), as described in the *Bhagavad-gītā*. Actually, neither the Vārāṇasī nor Saranātha Māyāvādīs accept the principles of the *Bhagavad-gītā*, due to a poor fund of knowledge.

Since these impersonalists who do not have perfect spiritual knowledge cannot understand the principles of *bhakti-yoga*, they must be classified among the nondevotees who are against the Kṛṣṇa consciousness movement. We sometimes feel inconvenienced by the hindrances offered by these impersonalists, but we do not care about their so-called philosophy, for we are propagating our own philosophy as presented in *Bhagavad-gītā As It Is* and getting successful results. Theorizing as if devotional service were subject to their mental speculation, both kinds of Māyāvādī impersonalists conclude that the subject matter of *bhakti-yoga* is a creation of *māyā* and that Kṛṣṇa, devotional service and the devotee are also *māyā*. Therefore, as stated by Śrī Caitanya Mahāprabhu, *māyāvādī kṛṣṇe aparādhī:* "All the Māyāvādīs are offenders to Lord Kṛṣṇa." (Cc. *Madhya* 17.129) It is not possible for them to understand the Kṛṣṇa consciousness movement; therefore we do not value their philosophical conclusions. However expert such quarrelsome impersonalists are in putting forward their so-called logic, we defeat them in every respect and go forward with our Kṛṣṇa consciousness movement. Their imaginative mental speculation cannot deter the progress of the Kṛṣṇa consciousness movement, which is completely spiritual and is never under the control of such Māyāvādīs.

TEXT 40

বৃন্দাবন যাইতে প্রভু রহিলা কাশীতে ।
মায়াবাদিগণ তাঁরে লাগিল নিন্দিতে ॥ ৪০ ॥

vṛndāvana yāite prabhu rahilā kāśīte
māyāvādi-gaṇa tāṅre lāgila nindite

vṛndāvana—the holy place called Vṛndāvana; *yāite*—while going there; *prabhu*—Lord Śrī Caitanya Mahāprabhu; *rahilā*—remained; *kāśīte*—at Vārāṇasī; *māyāvādi-gaṇa*—the Māyāvādī philosophers; *tāṅre*—unto Him; *lagila*—began; *nindite*—to speak against Him.

TRANSLATION

While Lord Caitanya Mahāprabhu was passing through Vārāṇasī on His way to Vṛndāvana, the Māyāvādī sannyāsī philosophers blasphemed against Him in many ways.

PURPORT

While preaching Kṛṣṇa consciousness with full vigor, Śrī Caitanya Mahāprabhu faced many Māyāvādī philosophers. Similarly, we are also facing opposing *svāmīs, yogīs,* impersonalists, scientists, philosophers and other mental speculators, and by the grace of Lord Kṛṣṇa we successfully defeat all of them without difficulty.

TEXT 41

সন্ন্যাসী হইয়া করে গায়ন, নাচন ।
না করে বেদান্ত-পাঠ, করে সংকীর্তন ॥ ৪১ ॥

sannyāsī ha-iyā kare gāyana, nācana
nā kare vedānta-pāṭha, kare saṅkīrtana

sannyāsī—a person in the renounced order of life; *ha-iyā*—accepting such a position; *kare*—does; *gāyana*—singing; *nācana*—dancing; *nā kare*—does not practice; *vedānta-pāṭha*—study of the Vedānta philosophy; *kare saṅkīrtana*—but simply engages in *saṅkīrtana*.

TRANSLATION

[The blasphemers said:] "Although a sannyāsī, He does not take interest in the study of Vedānta but instead always engages in chanting and dancing in saṅkīrtana.

PURPORT

Fortunately or unfortunately, we also meet such Māyāvādīs who criticize our method of chanting and accuse us of not being interested in study. They do not know that we have translated volumes and volumes of books into English and that the students in our temples regularly study them in the morning, afternoon and evening. We are writing and printing books, and our students study them and distribute them all over the world. No Māyāvādī school can present as many books as we have; nevertheless, they accuse us of not being fond of study. Such accusations are completely false. But although we study, we do not study the nonsense of the Māyāvādīs.

Māyāvādī *sannyāsīs* neither chant nor dance. Their technical objection is that this method of chanting and dancing is called *tauryatrika*, which indicates that a *sannyāsī* should completely avoid such activities and engage his time in the study of Vedānta. Actually, such men do not understand what is meant by Vedānta. In the *Bhagavad-gītā* (15.15) Kṛṣṇa says, *vedaiś ca sarvair aham eva vedyo vedānta-kṛd veda-vid eva cāham:* "By all the *Vedas* I am to be known; indeed I am the compiler of Vedānta, and I am the knower of the *Vedas*." Lord Kṛṣṇa is the actual compiler of Vedānta, and whatever He speaks is Vedānta philosophy. Although they are lacking the knowledge of Vedānta presented by the Supreme Personality of Godhead in the transcendental form of *Śrīmad-Bhāgavatam*, the Māyāvādīs are very proud of their study. Foreseeing the bad effects of their presenting Vedānta philosophy in a perverted way, Śrīla Vyāsadeva compiled *Śrīmad-Bhāgavatam* as a commentary on the *Vedānta-sūtra*. *Śrīmad-Bhāgavatam* is *bhāṣyo 'yaṁ brahma-*

sūtrāṇām; in other words, all the Vedānta philosophy in the aphorisms of the *Brahma-sūtra* is thoroughly described in the pages of *Śrīmad-Bhāgavatam.* Thus the factual propounder of Vedānta philosophy is a Kṛṣṇa conscious person who always engages in reading and understanding the *Bhagavad-gītā* and *Śrīmad-Bhāgavatam* and teaching the purport of these books to the entire world. The Māyāvādīs are very proud of having monopolized the Vedānta philosophy, but devotees have their own commentaries on Vedānta, such as *Śrīmad-Bhāgavatam* and others written by the *ācāryas.* The commentary of the Gauḍīya Vaiṣṇavas is the *Govinda-bhāṣya.*

The Māyāvādīs' accusation that devotees do not study Vedānta is false. The Māyāvādīs do not know that chanting, dancing and preaching the principles of *Śrīmad-Bhāgavatam,* called *bhāgavata-dharma,* are the same as studying Vedānta. Since they think that reading Vedānta philosophy is the only function of a *sannyāsī* and they did not find Caitanya Mahāprabhu engaged in such direct study, they criticized the Lord. Śrīpāda Śaṅkarācārya has given special stress to the study of Vedānta philosophy: *vedānta-vākyeṣu sadā ramantaḥ kaupīnavantaḥ khalu bhāgyavantaḥ.* "A *sannyāsī,* accepting the renounced order very strictly and wearing nothing more than a loincloth, should always enjoy the philosophical statements in the *Vedānta-sūtra.* Such a person in the renounced order is to be considered very fortunate." The Māyāvādīs in Vārāṇasī blasphemed Lord Caitanya because His behavior did not follow these principles. Lord Caitanya, however, bestowed His mercy upon these Māyāvādī *sannyāsīs* and delivered them by means of His Vedānta discourses with Prakāśānanda Sarasvatī and Sārvabhauma Bhaṭṭācārya.

TEXT 42

মূর্খ সন্ন্যাসী নিজ-ধর্ম নাহি জানে ।
ভাবুক হইয়া ফেরে ভাবুকের সনে ॥ ৪২ ॥

mūrkha sannyāsī nija-dharma nāhi jane
bhāvuka ha-iyā phere bhāvukera sane

mūrkha—illiterate; *sannyāsī*—one in the renounced order of life; *nija-dharma*—own duty; *nāhi*—does not; *jāne*—know; *bhāvuka*—in ecstasy; *ha-iyā*—becoming; *phere*—wanders; *bhāvukera*—with another ecstatic person; *sane*—with.

TRANSLATION

"This Caitanya Mahāprabhu is an illiterate sannyāsī and therefore does not know His real function. Guided only by His sentiments, He wanders about in the company of other sentimentalists."

PURPORT

Foolish Māyāvādīs, not knowing that the Kṛṣṇa consciousness movement is based on a solid philosophy of transcendental science, superficially conclude that those who dance and chant do not have philosophical knowledge. Those who are Kṛṣṇa conscious actually have full knowledge of the essence of Vedānta philosophy, for they study the real commentary on the Vedānta philosophy, *Śrīmad-Bhāgavatam,* and follow the actual words of the Supreme Personality of Godhead as found in *Bhagavad-gītā As It Is.* After understanding the Bhāgavata philosophy, or *bhāgavata-dharma,* they become fully spiritually conscious or Kṛṣṇa conscious, and therefore their chanting and dancing is not material but is on the spiritual platform. Although everyone admires the ecstatic chanting and dancing of the devotees, who are therefore popularly known as "the Hare Kṛṣṇa people," Māyāvādīs cannot appreciate these activities because of their poor fund of knowledge.

TEXT 43

এ সব শুনিয়া প্রভু হাসে মনে মনে ।
উপেক্ষা করিয়া কারো না কৈল সম্ভাষণে ॥ ৪৩ ॥

e saba śuniyā prabhu hāse mane mane
upekṣā kariyā kāro nā kaila sambhāṣaṇe

e saba—all these; *śuniyā*—after hearing; *prabhu*—the Lord; *hāse*—smiled; *mane mane*—within His mind; *upekṣā*—rejection; *kariyā*—doing so; *kāro*—with anyone; *na*—did not; *kaila*—make; *sambhāṣaṇe*—conversation.

TRANSLATION

Hearing all this blasphemy, Lord Caitanya Mahāprabhu merely smiled to Himself, rejected all these accusations and did not talk with the Māyāvādīs.

PURPORT

As Kṛṣṇa conscious devotees, we do not like to converse with Māyāvādī philosophers simply to waste valuable time, but whenever there is an opportunity we impress our philosophy upon them with great vigor and success.

TEXT 44

উপেক্ষা করিয়া কৈল মথুরা গমন ।
মথুরা দেখিয়া পুনঃ কৈল আগমন ॥ ৪৪ ॥

upekṣā kariyā kaila mathurā gamana
mathurā dekhiyā punaḥ kaila āgamana

upekṣā—neglecting them; *kariyā*—doing so; *kaila*—did; *mathurā*—the town named Mathurā; *gamana*—traveling; *mathurā*—Mathurā; *dekhiyā*—after seeing it; *punaḥ*—again; *kaila āgamana*—came back.

TRANSLATION

Thus neglecting the blasphemy of the Vārāṇasī Māyāvādīs, Lord Caitanya Mahāprabhu proceeded to Mathurā, and after visiting Mathurā He returned to meet the situation.

PURPORT

Lord Caitanya Mahāprabhu did not talk with the Māyāvādī philosophers when He first visited Vārāṇasī, but He returned there from Mathurā to convince them of the real purpose of Vedānta.

TEXT 45

কাশীতে লেখক শূদ্র-শ্রীচন্দ্রশেখর ।
তাঁর ঘরে রহিলা প্রভু স্বতন্ত্র ঈশ্বর ॥ ৪৫ ॥

kāśīte lekhaka śūdra-śrīcandraśekhara
tāṅra ghare rahilā prabhu svatantra īśvara

kāśīte—in Vārāṇasī; *lekhaka*—writer; *śūdra*—born of a *śūdra* family; *śrī-candraśekhara*—Candraśekhara; *tāṅra ghare*—in his house; *rahilā*—remained; *prabhu*—the Lord; *svatantra*—independent; *īśvara*—the supreme controller.

TRANSLATION

This time Lord Caitanya stayed at the house of Candraśekhara, although he was regarded as a śūdra or kāyastha, for the Lord, as the Supreme Personality of Godhead, is completely independent.

PURPORT

Lord Caitanya stayed at the house of Candraśekhara, a clerk, although a *sannyāsī* is not supposed to reside in a *śūdra's* house. Five hundred years ago, especially in Bengal, it was the system that persons who were born in the families of *brāhmaṇas* were accepted as *brāhmaṇas*, and all those who took birth in other families—even the higher castes, namely, the *kṣatriyas* and *vaiśyas*—were considered *śūdra* non-*brāhmaṇas*. Therefore although Śrī Candraśekhara was a clerk from a *kāyastha* family in upper India, he was considered a *śūdra*. Similarly, *vaiśyas*, especially those of the *suvarṇa-vaṇik* community, were accepted as *śūdras* in Bengal, and even the *vaidyas*, who were generally physicians, were also considered *śūdras*. Lord Caitanya Mahāprabhu, however, did not accept this artificial principle, which was introduced in society by self-interested men, and later the *kāyasthas*, *vaidyas* and *vaṇiks* all began to accept the sacred thread, despite objections from the so-called *brāhmaṇas*.

Before the time of Caitanya Mahāprabhu, the *suvarṇa-vaṇik* class was condemned by Ballāl Sen, who was then the King of Bengal, due to a personal grudge. In Bengal the *suvarṇa-vaṇik* class are always very rich, for they are bankers and dealers in gold and silver. Therefore, Ballāl Sen used to borrow money from a *suvarṇa-vaṇik* banker. Ballāl Sen's bankruptcy later obliged the *suvarṇa-vaṇik* banker to stop advancing money to him, and thus Ballāl Sen became angry and condemned the entire *suvarṇa-vaṇik* society as belonging to the *śūdra* community. He tried to induce the *brāhmaṇas* not to accept the *suvarṇa-vaṇiks* as followers of the instructions of the *Vedas* under the brahminical directions, but although some *brāhmaṇas* approved of Ballāl Sen's actions, others did not. Thus the *brāhmaṇas* also became divided amongst themselves, and those who supported the *suvarṇa-vaṇik* class were rejected from the *brāhmaṇa* community. At the present day the same biases are still being followed.

There are many Vaiṣṇava families in Bengal whose members, although not actually born *brāhmaṇas*, act as *ācāryas* by initiating disciples and offering the sacred thread as enjoined in the Vaiṣṇava *tantras*. For example, in the families of Ṭhākura Raghunandana Ācārya, Ṭhākura Kṛṣṇadāsa, Navanī Hoḍa and Rasikānanda-deva (a disciple of

Śyāmānanda Prabhu), the sacred thread ceremony is performed, as it is for the caste Gosvāmīs, and this system has continued for the past three to four hundred years. Accepting disciples born in *brāhmaṇa* families, they are bona fide spiritual masters who have the facility to worship the *śālagrāma-śilā*, which is worshiped with the Deity. As of this writing, *śālagrāma-śilā* worship has not yet been introduced in our Kṛṣṇa consciousness movement, but soon it will be introduced in all our temples as an essential function of *arcana-mārga* (Deity worship).

TEXT 46

তপন-মিশ্রের ঘরে ভিক্ষা-নির্বাহণ ।
সন্ন্যাসীর সঙ্গে নাহি মানে নিমন্ত্রণ ॥ ৪৬ ॥

tapana-miśrera ghare bhikṣā-nirvāhaṇa
sannyāsīra saṅge nāhi māne nimantraṇa

tapana-miśrera—of Tapana Miśra; *ghare*—in the house; *bhikṣā*—accepting food; *nirvāhaṇa*—regularly executed; *sannyāsīra*—with other Māyāvādī *sannyāsīs; saṅge*—in company with them; *nāhi*—never; *māne*—accepted; *nimantraṇa*—invitation.

TRANSLATION

As a matter of principle, Lord Caitanya regularly accepted His food at the house of Tapana Miśra. He never mixed with other sannyāsīs, nor did He accept invitations from them.

PURPORT

This exemplary behavior of Lord Caitanya definitely proves that a Vaiṣṇava *sannyāsī* cannot accept invitations from Māyāvādī *sannyāsīs* or intimately mix with them.

TEXT 47

সনাতন গোসাঞি আসি' তাঁহাই মিলিলা ।
তাঁর শিক্ষা লাগি' প্রভু দু-মাস রহিলা ॥ ৪৭ ॥

sanātana gosāñi āsi' tāṅhāi mililā
tāṅra śikṣā lāgi' prabhu du-māsa rahilā

sanātana—Sanātana; *gosāñi*—a great devotee; *āsi'*—coming there; *tāṅhai*—there at Vārāṇasī; *milila*—visited Him; *tāṅra*—His; *śikṣā*—instruction; *lāgi'*—for the matter of; *prabhu*—Lord Caitanya Mahāprabhu; *du-māsa*—two months; *rahilā*—remained there.

TRANSLATION

When Sanātana Gosvāmī came from Bengal, he met Lord Caitanya at the house of Tapana Miśra, where Lord Caitanya remained continuously for two months to teach him devotional service.

PURPORT

Lord Caitanya taught Sanātana Gosvāmī in the line of disciplic succession. Sanātana Gosvāmī was a very learned scholar in Sanskrit and other languages, but until instructed by Lord Caitanya Mahāprabhu he did not write anything about Vaiṣṇava behavior. His very famous book *Hari-bhakti-vilāsa,* which gives directions for Vaiṣṇava candidates, was written completely in compliance with the instructions of Śrī Caitanya Mahāprabhu. In the *Hari-bhakti-vilāsa* Śrī Sanātana Gosvāmī gives definite instructions that by proper initiation by a bona fide spiritual master one can immediately become a *brāhmaṇa.* In this connection he says:

yathā kāñcanatāṁ yāti kāṁsyaṁ rasa-vidhānataḥ
tathā dīkṣā-vidhānena dvijatvaṁ jāyate nṛṇām

"As bell metal is turned to gold when mixed with mercury in an alchemical process, so one who is properly trained and initiated by a bona fide spiritual master immediately becomes a *brāhmaṇa.*" Sometimes those born in *brāhmaṇa* families protest this, but they have no strong arguments against this principle. By the grace of Kṛṣṇa and His devotee, one's life can change. This is confirmed in *Śrīmad-Bhāgavatam* by the words *jahāti bandham* and *śudhyanti. Jahāti bandham* indicates that a living entity is conditioned by a particular type of body. The body is certainly an impediment, but one who associates with a pure devotee and follows his instructions can avoid this impediment and become a regular *brāhmaṇa* by initiation under his strict guidance. Śrīla Jīva Gosvāmī states how a non-*brāhmaṇa* can be turned into a *brāhmaṇa* by the association of a pure devotee. *Prabhaviṣṇave namaḥ:* Lord Viṣṇu is so powerful that He can do .anything He likes. Therefore it is not difficult for Viṣṇu to change the body of a devotee who is under the guidance of a pure devotee of the Lord.

TEXT 48

তাঁরে শিখাইলা সব বৈষ্ণবের ধর্ম ।
ভাগবত-আদি শাস্ত্রের যত গূঢ় মর্ম ॥ ৪৮ ॥

tāṅre śikhāilā saba vaiṣṇavera dharma
bhāgavata-ādi śāstrera yata gūḍha marma

tāṅre—unto him (Sanātana Gosvāmī); *śikhāilā*—the Lord taught him; *saba*—all; *vaiṣṇavera*—of the devotees; *dharma*—regular activities; *bhāgavata*—*Śrīmad-Bhāgavatam; ādi*—beginning with; *śāstrera*—of the revealed scriptures; *yata*—all; *gūḍha*—confidential; *marma*—purpose.

TRANSLATION

On the basis of scriptures like Śrīmad-Bhāgavatam, which reveal these confidential directions, Śrī Caitanya Mahāprabhu instructed Sanātana Gosvāmī regarding all the regular activities of a devotee.

PURPORT

In the *paramparā* system, the instructions taken from the bona fide spiritual master must also be based on revealed Vedic scriptures. One who is in the line of disciplic succession cannot manufacture his own way of behavior. There are many so-called followers of the Vaiṣṇava cult in the line of Caitanya Mahāprabhu who do not scrupulously follow the conclusions of the *śāstras,* and therefore they are considered to be *apa-sampradāya,* which means "outside of the *sampradāya.*" Some of these groups are known as *āula, bāula, kartābhajā, neḍā, daraveśa, sāṅi sahajiyā, sakhībhekī, smārta, jāta-gosāñi, ativāḍī, cūḍādhārī* and *gaurāṅga-nāgarī.* In order to follow strictly the disciplic succession of Lord Caitanya Mahāprabhu, one should not associate with these *apa-sampradāya* communities.

One who is not taught by a bona fide spiritual master cannot understand the Vedic literature. To emphasize this point, Lord Kṛṣṇa, while instructing Arjuna, clearly said that it was because Arjuna was His devotee and confidential friend that he could understand the mystery of the *Bhagavad-gītā.* It is to be concluded, therefore, that one who wants to understand the mystery of revealed scriptures must approach a bona fide spiritual master, hear from him very submissively and render service to him. Then the import of the scriptures will be revealed. It is stated in the *Vedas* (*Śvetāśvatara Up.* 6.23):

yasya deve parā bhaktir yathā deve tathā gurau
tasyaite kathitā hy arthā prakāśante mahātmanaḥ

"The real import of the scriptures is revealed to one who has unflinching faith in both the Supreme Personality of Godhead and the spiritual master." Śrīla Narottama dāsa Ṭhākura advises, *sādhu-śāstra-guru-vākya, hṛdaye kariyā aikya.* The meaning of this instruction is that one must consider the instructions of the *sādhu,* the revealed scriptures and the spiritual master in order to understand the real purpose of spiritual life. Neither a *sādhu* (saintly person or Vaiṣṇava) nor a bona fide spiritual master says anything that is beyond the scope of the sanction of the revealed scriptures. Thus the statements of the revealed scriptures correspond to those of the bona fide spiritual master and saintly persons. One must therefore act with reference to these three important sources of understanding.

TEXT 49

ইতিমধ্যে চন্দ্রশেখর, মিশ্র-তপন ।
দুঃখী হঞা প্রভু-পায় কৈল নিবেদন ॥ ৪৯ ॥

itimadhye candraśekhara, miśra-tapana
duḥkhī hañā prabhu-pāya kaila nivedana

iti-madhye—in the meantime; *candraśekhara*—the clerk of the name Candraśekhara; *miśra-tapana*—as well as Tapana Miśra; *duḥkhī hañā*—becoming very unhappy; *prabhu-pāya*—at the lotus feet of the Lord; *kaila*—made; *nivedana*—an appeal.

TRANSLATION

While Lord Caitanya Mahāprabhu was instructing Sanātana Gosvāmī, both Candraśekhara and Tapana Miśra became very unhappy. Therefore they submitted an appeal unto the lotus feet of the Lord.

TEXT 50

কতেক শুনিব প্রভু তোমার নিন্দন ।
না পারি সহিতে, এবে ছাড়িব জীবন ॥ ৫০ ॥

kateka śuniba prabhu tomāra nindana
nā pāri sahite, ebe chāḍiba jīvana

kateka—how much; *śuniba*—shall we hear; *prabhu*—O Lord; *tomāra*—Your; *nindana*—blasphemy; *nā pāri*—we are not able; *sahite*—to tolerate; *ebe*—now; *chāḍiba*—give up; *jīvana*—life.

TRANSLATION

"How long can we tolerate the blasphemy by Your critics against Your conduct? We should give up our lives rather than hear such blasphemy.

PURPORT

One of the most important instructions by Śrī Caitanya Mahāprabhu regarding regular Vaiṣṇava behavior is that a Vaiṣṇava should be tolerant like a tree and submissive like grass.

tṛṇād api su-nīcena taror iva sahiṣṇunā
amāninā māna-dena kīrtanīyaḥ sadā hariḥ

"One should chant the holy name of the Lord in a humble state of mind, thinking oneself lower than the straw in the street; one should be more tolerant than a tree, devoid of all sense of false prestige and ready to offer all respect to others. In such a state of mind one can chant the holy name of the Lord constantly." Nevertheless, the author of these instructions, Lord Caitanya Mahāprabhu, did not tolerate the misbehavior of Jagāi and Mādhāi. When they harmed Lord Nityānanda Prabhu, He immediately became angry and wanted to kill them, and it was only by the mercy of Lord Nityānanda Prabhu that they were saved. One should be very meek and humble in his personal transactions, and if insulted a Vaiṣṇava should be tolerant and not angry. But if there is blasphemy against one's *guru* or another Vaiṣṇava, one should be as angry as fire. This was exhibited by Lord Caitanya Mahāprabhu. One should not tolerate blasphemy against a Vaiṣṇava but should immediately take one of three actions. If someone blasphemes a Vaiṣṇava, one should stop him with arguments and higher reason. If one is not expert enough to do this he should give up his life on the spot, and if he cannot do this, he must go away. While Caitanya Mahāprabhu was in Benares or Kāśī, the Māyāvādī *sannyāsīs* blasphemed Him in many ways because although He was a *sannyāsī* He was indulging in chanting and dancing. Tapana Miśra and Candraśekhara heard this criticism, and it was intolerable for them because they were great devotees of Lord Caitanya. They could not stop it, however, and therefore they appealed to Lord Caitanya Mahāprabhu because this blasphemy was so intolerable that they had decided to give up their lives.

TEXT 51

তোমারে নিন্দয়ে যত সন্ন্যাসীর গণ ।
শুনিতে না পারি, ফাটে হৃদয়-শ্রবণ ॥ ৫১ ॥

tomāre nindaye yata sannyāsīra gaṇa
śunite nā pāri, phāṭe hṛdaya-śravaṇa

tomāre—unto You; *nindaye*—blasphemes; *yata*—all; *sannyāsīra gaṇa*—the Māyāvādī *sannyāsīs; śunite*—to hear; *nā*—cannot; *pāri*—tolerate; *phāṭe*—it breaks; *hṛdaya*—our hearts; *śravaṇa*—while hearing such blasphemy.

TRANSLATION

"The Māyāvādī sannyāsīs are all criticizing Your Holiness. We cannot tolerate hearing such criticism, for this blasphemy breaks our hearts."

PURPORT

This is a manifestation of real love for Kṛṣṇa and Lord Caitanya Mahāprabhu. There are three categories of Vaiṣṇavas: *kaniṣṭha-adhikārīs, madhyama-adhikārīs* and *uttama-adhikārīs.* The *kaniṣṭha-adhikārī*, or the devotee in the lowest stage of Vaiṣṇava life, has firm faith but is not familiar with the conclusions of the *śāstras.* The devotee in the second stage, the *madhyama-adhikārī*, is completely aware of the śāstric conclusion and has firm faith in his *guru* and the Lord. He, therefore, avoiding nondevotees, preaches to the innocent. However, the *mahā-bhāgavata* or *uttama-adhikārī*, the devotee in the highest stage of devotional life, does not see anyone as being against the Vaiṣṇava principles, for he regards everyone as a Vaiṣṇava but himself. This is the essence of Caitanya Mahāprabhu's instruction that one be more tolerant than a tree and think oneself lower than the straw in the street (*tṛṇād api su-nīcena taror iva sahiṣṇunā*). However, even if a devotee is in the *uttama-bhāgavata* status he must come down to the second status of life, *madhyama-adhikārī,* to be a preacher, for a preacher should not tolerate blasphemy against another Vaiṣṇava. Although a *kaniṣṭha-adhikārī* also cannot tolerate such blasphemy, he is not competent to stop it by citing śāstric evidences. Therefore Tapana Miśra and Candraśekhara are understood to be *kaniṣṭha-adhikārīs* because they could not refute the arguments of the *sannyāsīs* in Benares. They appealed to Lord Caitanya Mahāprabhu to take action, for they felt that they could not tolerate such criticism although they also could not stop it.

TEXT 52

ইহা শুনি রহে প্রভু ঈষৎ হাসিয়া ।
সেই কালে এক বিপ্র মিলিল আসিয়া ॥ ৫২ ॥

ihā śuni rahe prabhu īṣat hāsiyā
sei kāle eka vipra milila āsiyā

ihā—this; *śuni*—hearing; *rahe*—remained; *prabhu*—Lord Caitanya Mahāprabhu; *īṣat*—slightly; *hāsiyā*—smiling; *sei kāle*—at that time; *eka*—one; *vipra*—*brāhmaṇa; milila*—met; *āsiyā*—coming there.

TRANSLATION

While Tapana Miśra and Candraśekhara were thus talking with Śrī Caitanya Mahāprabhu, He only smiled slightly and remained silent. At that time a brāhmaṇa came there to meet the Lord.

PURPORT

Because the blasphemy was cast against Śrī Caitanya Mahāprabhu Himself, He did not feel sorry, and therefore He was smiling. This is ideal Vaiṣṇava behavior. One should not become angry upon hearing criticism of himself, but if other Vaiṣṇavas are criticized one must be prepared to act as previously suggested. Śrī Caitanya Mahāprabhu was very compassionate for His pure devotees Tapana Miśra and

Candraśekhara; therefore by His grace this *brāhmaṇa* immediately came to Him. By His omnipotence the Lord created this situation for the happiness of His devotees.

TEXT 53

আসি' নিবেদন করে চরণে ধরিয়া।
এক বস্তু মাগোঁ, দেহ প্রসন্ন হইয়া ॥ ৫৩ ॥

āsi' nivedana kare caraṇe dhariyā
eka vastu māgoṅ, deha prasanna ha-iyā

āsi'—coming there; *nivedana*—submissive statement; *kare*—made; *caraṇe*—unto the lotus feet; *dhariyā*—capturing; *eka*—one; *vastu*—thing; *māgoṅ*—beg from You; *deha*—kindly give it to me; *prasanna*—being pleased; *ha-iyā*—becoming so.

TRANSLATION

The brāhmaṇa immediately fell at the lotus feet of Caitanya Mahāprabhu and requested Him to accept his proposal in a joyful mood.

PURPORT

The Vedic injunctions state, *tad viddhi praṇipātena paripraśnena sevayā:* one must approach a superior authority in humbleness (Bg. 4.34). One cannot challenge a superior authority, but with great submission one can submit his proposal for acceptance by the spiritual master or spiritual authorities. Śrī Caitanya Mahāprabhu is an ideal teacher by His personal behavior, and so also are all His disciples. Thus this *brāhmaṇa*, being purified in association with Caitanya Mahāprabhu, followed these principles in submitting his request to the higher authority. He fell down at the lotus feet of Śrī Caitanya Mahāprabhu and then spoke as follows.

TEXT 54

সকল সন্ন্যাসী মুঞি কৈনু নিমন্ত্রণ।
তুমি যদি আইস, পূর্ণ হয় মোর মন ॥ ৫৪ ॥

sakala sannyāsī muñi kainu nimantraṇa
tumi yadi āisa, pūrṇa haya mora mana

sakala—all; *sannyāsī*—renouncers; *muñi*—I; *kainu*—made; *nimantraṇa*—invited; *tumi*—Your good self; *yadi*—if; *āisa*—come; *pūrṇa*—fulfillment; *haya*—becomes; *mora*—my; *mana*—mind.

TRANSLATION

"My dear Lord, I have invited all the sannyāsīs of Benares to my home. My desires will be fulfilled if You also accept my invitation.

PURPORT

This *brāhmaṇa* knew that Caitanya Mahāprabhu was the only Vaiṣṇava *sannyāsī* in Benares at that time and all the others were Māyāvādīs. It is the duty of a *gṛhastha* to sometimes invite *sannyāsīs* to take food at his home. This *gṛhastha-brāhmaṇa* wanted to invite all the *sannyāsīs* to his house, but he also knew that it would be very difficult to induce Lord Caitanya Mahāprabhu to accept such an invitation because the Māyāvādī *sannyāsīs* would be present. Therefore he fell down at His feet and fervently appealed to the Lord to be compassionate and grant his request. Thus he humbly submitted his desire.

TEXT 55

না যাহ সন্ন্যাসি-গোষ্ঠী, ইহা আমি জানি ।
মোরে অনুগ্রহ কর নিমন্ত্রণ মানি' ॥ ৫৫ ॥

nā yāha sannyāsi-goṣṭhī, ihā āmi jāni
more anugraha kara nimantraṇa māni'

nā—not; *yāha*—You go; *sannyāsi-goṣṭhī*—the association of Māyāvādī *sannyāsīs; ihā*—this; *āmi*—I; *jāni*—know; *more*—unto me; *anugraha*—merciful; *kara*—become; *nimantraṇa*—invitation; *māni'*—accepting.

TRANSLATION

"My dear Lord, I know that You never mix with other sannyāsīs, but please be merciful unto me and accept my invitation."

PURPORT

An *ācārya*, or great personality of the Vaiṣṇava school, is very strict in his principles, but although he is as hard as a thunderbolt, sometimes he is as soft as a rose. Thus actually he is independent. He follows all the rules and regulations strictly, but sometimes he slackens this policy. It was known that Lord Caitanya never mixed with the Māyāvādī *sannyāsīs,* yet He conceded to the request of the *brāhmaṇa,* as stated in the next verse.

TEXT 56

প্রভু হাসি' নিমন্ত্রণ কৈল অঙ্গীকার ।
সন্ন্যাসীরে কৃপা লাগি' এ ভঙ্গী তাঁহার ॥ ৫৬ ॥

prabhu hāsi' nimantraṇa kaila aṅgīkāra
sannyāsīre kṛpā lāgi' e bhaṅgī tāṅhāra

prabhu—the Lord; *hāsi'*—smiling; *nimantraṇa*—invitation; *kaila*—made; *aṅgīkāra*—acceptance; *sannyāsīre*—unto the Māyāvādī *sannyāsīs; kṛpā*—to show them mercy; *lāgi'*—for the matter of; *e*—this; *bhaṅgī*—gesture; *tāṅhāra*—His.

TRANSLATION

Lord Caitanya smiled and accepted the invitation of the brāhmaṇa. He made this gesture to show His mercy to the Māyāvādī sannyāsīs.

PURPORT

Tapana Miśra and Candraśekhara appealed to the lotus feet of the Lord regarding their grief at the criticism of Him by the *sannyāsīs* in Benares. Caitanya Mahāprabhu merely smiled, yet He wanted to fulfill the desires of His devotees, and the opportunity came when the *brāhmaṇa* came to request Him to accept his invitation to be present in the midst of the other *sannyāsīs.* This coincidence was made possible by the omnipotence of the Lord.

TEXT 57

সে বিপ্র জানেন প্রভু না যা'ন কা'র ঘরে ।
তাঁহার প্রেরণায় তাঁরে অত্যাগ্রহ করে ॥ ৫৭ ॥

se vipra jānena prabhu nā yā'na kā'ra ghare
tāṅhāra preraṇāya tāṅre atyāgraha kare

se—that; *vipra*—*brāhmaṇa; jānena*—knew it; *prabhu*—Lord Caitanya Mahāprabhu; *nā*—never; *yā'na*—goes; *kā'ra*—anyone's; *ghare*—house; *taṅhāra*—His; *preraṇāya*—by inspiration; *tāṅre*—unto Him; *atyāgraha kare*—strongly urging to accept the invitation.

TRANSLATION

The brāhmaṇa knew that Lord Caitanya Mahāprabhu never went to anyone else's house, yet due to inspiration from the Lord he earnestly requested Him to accept this invitation.

TEXT 58

আর দিনে গেলা প্রভু সে বিপ্র-ভবনে ।
দেখিলেন, বসিয়াছেন সন্ন্যাসীর গণে ॥ ৫৮ ॥

āra dine gelā prabhu se vipra-bhavane
dekhilena, vasiyāchena sannyāsīra gaṇe

āra—next; *dine*—day; *gelā*—went; *prabhu*—the Lord; *se*—that; *vipra*—*brāhmaṇa; bhavane*—in the house of; *dekhilena*—He saw; *vasiyāchena*—there were sitting; *sannyāsīra*—all the *sannyāsīs; gaṇe*—in a group.

TRANSLATION

The next day, when Lord Śrī Caitanya Mahāprabhu went to the house of that brāhmaṇa, He saw all the sannyāsīs of Benares sitting there.

TEXT 59

সবা নমস্করি' গেলা পাদ-প্রক্ষালনে ।
পাদ প্রক্ষালন করি বসিলা সেই স্থানে ॥ ৫৯ ॥

sabā namaskari' gelā pāda-prakṣālane
pāda prakṣālana kari vasilā sei sthāne

sabā—to all; *namaskari'*—offering obeisances; *gelā*—went; *pāda*—foot; *prakṣālane*—for washing; *pāda*—foot; *prakṣālana*—washing; *kari*—finishing; *vasilā*—sat down; *sei*—in that; *sthāne*—place.

TRANSLATION

As soon as Śrī Caitanya Mahāprabhu saw the sannyāsīs He immediately offered obeisances, and then He went to wash His feet. After washing His feet, He sat down by the place where He had done so.

PURPORT

By offering His obeisances to the Māyāvādī *sannyāsīs,* Śrī Caitanya Mahāprabhu very clearly exhibited His humbleness to everyone. Vaiṣṇavas must not be disrespectful to anyone, to say nothing of a *sannyāsī.* Śrī Caitanya Mahāprabhu teaches, *amāninā māna-dena:* one should always be respectful to others but should not demand respect for himself. A *sannyāsī* should always walk barefoot, and therefore when he enters a temple or a society of devotees he should first wash his feet and then sit down in a proper place. In India it is still the prevalent custom that one put his shoes in a specified place and then enter the temple barefoot after washing his feet. Śrī Caitanya Mahāprabhu is an ideal *ācārya,* and those who follow in His footsteps should practice the methods of devotional life that He teaches us.

TEXT 60

বসিয়া করিলা কিছু ঐশ্বর্য প্রকাশ ।
মহাতেজোময় বপু কোটিসূর্যাভাস ॥ ৬০ ॥

vasiyā karilā kichu aiśvarya prakāśa
mahātejomaya vapu koṭi-sūryābhāsa

vasiyā—after sitting; *karilā*—exhibited; *kichu*—some; *aiśvarya*—mystic power; *prakāśa*—manifested; *mahā-tejo-maya*—very brilliantly; *vapu*—body; *koṭi*—millions; *sūrya*—sun; *ābhāsa*—reflection.

TRANSLATION

After sitting on the ground, Caitanya Mahāprabhu exhibited His mystic power by manifesting an effulgence as brilliant as the illumination of millions of suns.

PURPORT

Śrī Caitanya Mahāprabhu, as the Supreme Personality of Godhead Kṛṣṇa, is full of all potencies. Therefore it is not remarkable for Him to manifest the illumination of millions of suns. Lord Śrī Kṛṣṇa is known as Yogeśvara, the master of all mystic powers. Śrī Kṛṣṇa Caitanya Mahāprabhu is Lord Kṛṣṇa Himself; therefore He can exhibit any mystic power.

TEXT 61

প্রভাবে আকর্ষিল সব সন্ন্যাসীর মন ।
উঠিল সন্ন্যাসী সব ছাড়িয়া আসন ॥ ৬১ ॥

prabhāve ākarṣila saba sannyāsīra mana
uṭhila sannyāsī saba chāḍiyā āsana

prabhāve—by such illumination; *ākarṣila*—He attracted; *saba*—all; *sannyāsīra*—the Māyāvādī *sannyāsīs; mana*—mind; *uṭhila*—stood up; *sannyāsī*—all the Māyāvādī *sannyāsīs*; *saba*—all; *chāḍiyā*—giving up; *āsana*—sitting places.

TRANSLATION

When the sannyāsīs saw the brilliant illumination of the body of Śrī Caitanya Mahāprabhu, their minds were attracted, and they all immediately gave up their sitting places and stood in respect.

PURPORT

To draw the attention of common men, sometimes saintly persons, *ācāryas* and teachers exhibit extraordinary opulences. This is necessary to attract the attention of fools, but a saintly person should not misuse such power for personal sense gratification like false saints who declare themselves to be God. Even a magician can exhibit extraordinary feats that are not understandable to common men, but this does not mean that the magician is God. It is a most sinful activity to attract attention by exhibiting mystic powers and then to utilize this opportunity to declare oneself to be God. A real saintly person never declares himself to be God but always places himself in the position of a servant of God. For a servant of God there is no need to exhibit mystic powers, and he does not like to do so, but on behalf of the Supreme Personality of Godhead a humble servant of God performs his activities in such a wonderful way that no common man can dare try to act like him. Yet a saintly person never takes credit for such actions because he knows very well that when wonderful things are done on his behalf by the grace of the Supreme Lord, all credit goes to the master and not to the servant.

TEXT 62

প্রকাশানন্দ-নামে সর্ব সন্ন্যাসী-প্রধান ।
প্রভুকে কহিল কিছু করিয়া সম্মান ॥ ৬২ ॥

prakāśānanda-nāme sarva sannyāsi-pradhāna
prabhuke kahila kichu kariyā sammāna

prakāśānanda—Prakāśānanda; *nāme*—of the name; *sarva*—all; *sannyāsi-pradhāna*—chief of the Māyāvādī *sannyāsīs*; *prabhuke*—unto the Lord; *kahila*—said; *kichu*—something; *kariyā*—showing Him; *sammāna*—respect.

TRANSLATION

The leader of all the Māyāvādī sannyāsīs present was named Prakāśānanda Sarasvatī, and after standing up he addressed Lord Caitanya Mahāprabhu as follows with great respect.

PURPORT

As Lord Śrī Caitanya Mahāprabhu showed respect to all the Māyāvādī *sannyāsīs*, similarly the leader of the Māyāvādī *sannyāsīs*, Prakāśānanda, also showed his respects to the Lord.

TEXT 63

ইহাঁ আইস, ইহাঁ আইস, শুনহ শ্রীপাদ ।
অপবিত্র স্থানে বৈস, কিবা অবসাদ ॥ ৬৩ ॥

ihāṅ āisa, ihāṅ āisa, śunaha śrīpāda
apavitra sthāne vaisa, kibā avasāda

ihāṅ āisa—come here; *ihāṅ āisa*—come here; *śunaha*—kindly hear; *śrīpāda*—Your Holiness; *apavitra*—unholy; *sthāne*—place; *vaisa*—You are sitting; *kibā*—what is that; *avasāda*—lamentation.

TRANSLATION

"Please come here. Please come here, Your Holiness. Why do You sit in that unclean place? What has caused Your lamentation?"

PURPORT

Here is the distinction between Lord Caitanya Mahāprabhu and Prakāśānanda Sarasvatī. In the material world everyone wants to introduce himself as very important and great, but Caitanya Mahāprabhu introduced Himself very humbly and meekly. The Māyāvādīs were sitting in an exalted position, and Caitanya Mahāprabhu sat in a place that was not even clean. Therefore the Māyāvādī *sannyāsīs* thought that He must have been aggrieved for some reason, and Prakāśānanda Sarasvatī inquired about the cause for His lamentation.

TEXT 64

প্রভু কহে,—আমি হই হীন-সম্প্রদায় ।
তোমা-সবার সভায় বসিতে না যুয়ায় ॥ ৬৪ ॥

prabhu kahe,—āmi ha-i hīna-sampradāya
tomā-sabāra sabhāya vasite nā yuyāya

prabhu kahe—the Lord replied; *āmi*—I; *ha-i*—am; *hīna-sampradāya*—belonging to a lower spiritual school; *tomā-sabāra*—of all of you; *sabhāya*—in the assembly; *vasite*—to sit down; *nā*—never; *yuyāya*—I can dare.

TRANSLATION

The Lord replied, "I belong to a lower order of sannyāsīs. Therefore I do not deserve to sit with you."

PURPORT

Māyāvādī *sannyāsīs* are always very puffed up because of their knowledge of Sanskrit and because they belong to the Śaṅkara-sampradāya. They are always under the impression that unless one is a *brāhmaṇa* and a very good Sanskrit scholar, especially in grammar, one cannot accept the renounced order of life or become a preacher. Māyāvādī *sannyāsīs* always misinterpret all the *śāstras* with their word jugglery and grammatical compositions, yet Śrīpāda Śaṅkarācārya himself condemned such jugglery of words in the verse *prāpte sannihite kāle na hi na hi rakṣati ḍukṛñ karaṇe. Ḍukṛñ* refers to suffixes and prefixes in Sanskrit grammar. Śaṅkarācārya warned his disciples that if they concerned themselves only with the principles of grammar, not worshiping Govinda, they were fools who would never be saved. Yet in spite of Śrīpāda Śaṅkarācārya's instructions, foolish Māyāvādī *sannyāsīs* are always busy juggling words on the basis of strict Sanskrit grammar.

Māyāvādī *sannyāsīs* are very puffed up if they hold the elevated *sannyāsa* title Tīrtha, Āśrama or Sarasvatī. Even among Māyāvādīs, those who belong to other *sampradāyas* and hold other titles, such as Vana, Araṇya or Bhāratī, are considered to be lower-grade *sannyāsīs.* Śrī Caitanya Mahāprabhu accepted *sannyāsa* from the Bhāratī-sampradāya, and thus He considered Himself a lower *sannyāsī* than Prakāśānanda Sarasvatī. To remain distinct from Vaiṣṇava *sannyāsīs,* the *sannyāsīs* of the Māyāvādi-sampradāya always think themselves to be situated in a very much elevated spiritual order, but Lord Śrī Caitanya Mahāprabhu, in order to teach them how to become humble and meek, accepted Himself as belonging to a lower *sampradāya* of *sannyāsīs.* Thus He wanted to point out clearly that a *sannyāsī* is one who is advanced in spiritual knowledge. One who is advanced in spiritual knowledge should be accepted as occupying a better position than those who lack such knowledge.

The Māyāvādi-sampradāya *sannyāsīs* are generally known as Vedāntīs, as if Vedānta were their monopoly. Actually, however, Vedāntī refers to a person who perfectly knows Kṛṣṇa. As confirmed in the *Bhagavad-gītā* (15.15), *vedaiś ca sarvair aham eva vedyaḥ:* By all the *Vedas* it is Kṛṣṇa who is to be known. The so-called Māyāvādī Vedāntīs do not know who Kṛṣṇa is; therefore their title of Vedāntī, or "knower of Vedānta philosophy," is simply a pretension. Māyāvādī *sannyāsīs* always think of themselves as real *sannyāsīs* and consider *sannyāsīs* of the Vaiṣṇava order to be *brahmacārīs.* A *brahmacārī* is supposed to engage in the service of a *sannyāsī* and accept him as his *guru.* Māyāvādī *sannyāsīs* therefore declare themselves to be not only *gurus* but *jagad-gurus,* or the spiritual masters of the entire world, although, of course, they cannot see the entire world. Sometimes they dress gorgeously and travel on the backs of elephants in processions, and thus they are always puffed up, accepting themselves as *jagad-gurus.* Śrīla Rūpa Gosvāmī, however, has explained that *jagad-guru* properly refers to one who is the controller of his tongue, mind, words, belly, genitals and anger. *Pṛthivīṁ sa śiṣyāt:* such a *jagad-guru* is completely fit to make disciples all over the world. Due to false prestige, Māyāvādī *sannyāsīs* who do not have these qualifications sometimes harass and blaspheme a Vaiṣṇava *sannyāsī* who humbly engages in the service of the Lord.

TEXT 65

আপনে প্রকাশানন্দ হাতেতে ধরিয়া ।
বসাইলা সভামধ্যে সম্মান করিয়া ॥ ৬৫ ॥

āpane prakāśānanda hātete dhariyā
vasāilā sabhā-madhye sammāna kariyā

āpane—personally; *prakāśānanda*—Prakāśānanda; *hātete*—by His hand; *dhariyā*—capturing; *vasāilā*—made Him sit; *sabhā-madhye*—in the assembly of; *sammāna*—with great respect; *kariyā*—offering Him.

TRANSLATION

Prakāśānanda Sarasvatī, however, caught Śrī Caitanya Mahāprabhu personally by the hand and seated Him with great respect in the midst of the assembly.

PURPORT

The respectful behavior of Prakāśānanda Sarasvatī toward Śrī Caitanya Mahāprabhu is very much to be appreciated. Such behavior is calculated to be *ajñāta-sukṛti,* or pious activities that one executes unknowingly. Thus Śrī Caitanya Mahāprabhu very tactfully gave Prakāśānanda Sarasvatī an opportunity to advance in *ajñāta-sukṛti* so that in the future he might actually become a Vaiṣṇava *sannyāsī.*

TEXT 66

পুছিল, তোমার নাম 'শ্রীকৃষ্ণচৈতন্য' ।
কেশব-ভারতীর শিষ্য, তাতে তুমি ধন্য ॥ ৬৬ ॥

puchila, tomāra nāma 'śrī-kṛṣṇa-caitanya'
keśava-bhāratīra śiṣya, tāte tumi dhanya

puchila—inquired; *tomāra*—Your; *nāma*—name; *śrī-kṛṣṇa-caitanya*—the name Śrī Kṛṣṇa Caitanya; *keśava-bhāratīra śiṣya*—You are a disciple of Keśava Bhāratī; *tāte*—in that connection; *tumi*—You are; *dhanya*—glorious.

TRANSLATION

Prakāśānanda Sarasvatī then said, "I understand that Your name is Śrī Kṛṣṇa Caitanya. You are a disciple of Śrī Keśava Bhāratī, and therefore You are glorious.

TEXT 67

সাম্প্রদায়িক সন্ন্যাসী তুমি, রহ এই গ্রামে ।
কি কারণে আমা-সবার না কর দর্শনে ॥ ৬৭ ॥

sāmpradāyika sannyāsī tumi, raha ei grāme
ki kāraṇe āmā-sabāra nā kara darśane

sāmpradāyika—of the community; *sannyāsī*—Māyāvādī *sannyāsī; tumi*—You are; *raha*—live; *ei*—this; *grāme*—in Vārāṇasī; *ki kāraṇe*—for what reason; *āmā-sabāra*—with us; *nā*—do not; *kara*—endeavor; *darśane*—to mix.

TRANSLATION

"You belong to our Śaṅkara-sampradāya and live in our village, Vārāṇasī. Why then do You not associate with us? Why is it that You avoid even seeing us?

PURPORT

A Vaiṣṇava *sannyāsī* or a Vaiṣṇava in the second stage of advancement in spiritual knowledge can understand four principles—namely, the Supre.me Personality of Godhead, the devotees, the innocent and the jealous—and he behaves differently with each. He tries to increase his love for Godhead, make friendship with devotees and preach Kṛṣṇa consciousness among the innocent, but he avoids the jealous who are envious of the Kṛṣṇa consciousness movement. Lord Caitanya Mahāprabhu Himself exemplified such behavior, and this is why Prakāśānanda Sarasvatī inquired why He did not associate or even talk with them. Caitanya Mahāprabhu confirmed by example that a preacher of the Kṛṣṇa consciousness movement generally should not waste his time talking with Māyāvādī *sannyāsīs,* but when there are arguments on the basis of *śāstra,* a Vaiṣṇava must come forward to talk and defeat them in philosophy.

According to Māyāvādī *sannyāsīs,* only one who takes *sannyāsa* in the disciplic succession from Śaṅkarācārya is a Vedic *sannyāsī.* Sometimes it is challenged that the *sannyāsīs* who are preaching in the Kṛṣṇa consciousness movement are not genuine because they do not belong to *brāhmaṇa* families, for Māyāvādīs do not offer *sannyāsa* to one who does not belong to a *brāhmaṇa* family by birth. Unfortunately, however, they do not know that at present everyone is born a *śūdra* (*kalau śūdra-sambhavaḥ*). It is to be understood that there are no *brāhmaṇas* in this age because those who claim to be *brāhmaṇas* simply on the basis of birthright do not have the brahminical qualifications. However, even if one is born in a non-*brāhmaṇa* family, if he has the brahminical qualifications he should be accepted as a *brāhmaṇa,* as confirmed by Śrīla Nārada Muni and the great saint Śrīdhara Svāmī. This is also stated in *Śrīmad-Bhāgavatam.* Both Nārada and Śrīdhara Svāmī completely agree that one cannot be a *brāhmaṇa* by birthright but must possess the qualities of a *brāhmaṇa.* Thus in our Kṛṣṇa consciousness movement we never offer the *sannyāsa* order to a person whom we do not find to be qualified in terms of the prescribed brahminical principles. Although it is a fact that unless one is a *brāhmaṇa* he cannot become a *sannyāsī,* it is not a valid principle that an unqualified man who is born in a *brāhmaṇa* family is a *brāhmaṇa* whereas a brahminically qualified person born in a non-*brāhmaṇa* family cannot be accepted. The Kṛṣṇa consciousness movement strictly follows the injunctions of *Śrīmad-Bhāgavatam,* avoiding misleading heresy and manufactured conclusions.

TEXT 68

সন্ন্যাসী হইয়া কর নর্তন-গায়ন ।
ভাবুক সব সঙ্গে লঞা কর সংকীর্তন ॥ ৬৮ ॥

sannyāsī ha-iyā kara nartana-gāyana
bhāvuka saba saṅge lañā kara saṅkīrtana

sannyāsī—the renounced order of life; *ha-iyā*—accepting; *kara*—You do; *nartana-gāyana*—dancing and chanting; *bhāvuka*—fanatics;

saba—all; *saṅge*—in Your company; *lañā*—accepting them; *kara*—You do; *saṅkīrtana*—chanting of the holy name of the Lord.

TRANSLATION

"You are a sannyāsī. Why then do You indulge in chanting and dancing, engaging in Your saṅkīrtana movement in the company of fanatics?

PURPORT

This is a challenge by Prakāśānanda Sarasvatī to Śrī Caitanya Mahāprabhu. Śrīla Bhaktisiddhānta Sarasvatī Ṭhākura writes in his *Anubhāṣya* that Śrī Caitanya Mahāprabhu, who is the object of Vedānta philosophical research, has very kindly determined who is an appropriate candidate for study of Vedānta philosophy. The first qualification of such a candidate is expressed by Śrī Caitanya Mahāprabhu in His *Śikṣāṣṭaka:*

tṛṇād api su-nīcena taror iva sahiṣṇunā
amāninā māna-dena kīrtanīyaḥ sadā hariḥ

This statement indicates that one can hear or speak about Vedānta philosophy through the disciplic succession. One must be very humble and meek, more tolerant than a tree and more humble than the grass. One should not claim respect for himself but should be prepared to give all respect to others. One must have these qualifications to be eligible to understand Vedic knowledge.

TEXT 69

বেদান্ত-পঠন, ধ্যান,—সন্ন্যাসীর ধর্ম ।
তাহা ছাড়ি' কর কেনে ভাবুকের কর্ম ॥ ৬৯ ॥

vedānta-paṭhana, dhyāna,—sannyāsīra dharma
tāhā chāḍi' kara kene bhāvukera karma

vedānta-paṭhana—studying Vedānta philosophy; *dhyāna*—meditation; *sannyāsīra*—of a *sannyāsī; dharma*—duties; *tāhā chāḍi'*—giving them up; *kara*—You do; *kene*—why; *bhāvukera*—of the fanatics; *karma*—activities.

TRANSLATION

"Meditation and the study of Vedānta are the sole duties of a sannyāsī. Why do You abandon these to dance with fanatics?

PURPORT

As explained in regard to verse 41, Māyāvādī *sannyāsīs* do not approve of chanting and dancing. Prakāśānanda Sarasvatī, like Sārvabhauma Bhaṭṭācārya, misunderstood Śrī Caitanya Mahāprabhu to be a misled young *sannyāsī,* and therefore he asked Him why He indulged in the association of fanatics instead of executing the duty of a *sannyāsī.*

TEXT 70

প্রভাবে দেখিয়ে তোমা সাক্ষাৎ নারায়ণ ।
হীনাচার কর কেনে, ইথে কি কারণ ॥ ৭০ ॥

prabhāve dekhiye tomā sākṣāt nārāyaṇa
hīnācāra kara kene, ithe ki kāraṇa

prabhāve—in Your opulence; *dekhiye*—I see; *tomā*—You; *sākṣāt*—directly; *nārāyaṇa*—the Supreme Personality of Godhead; *hīna-ācāra*—lower-class behavior; *kara*—You do; *kene*—why; *ithe*—in this; *ki*—what is; *kāraṇa*—reason.

TRANSLATION

"You look as brilliant as if You were Nārāyaṇa Himself. Will You kindly explain the reason that You have adopted the behavior of lower-class people?"

PURPORT

Due to renunciation, Vedānta study, meditation and the strict regulative principles of their daily routine, Māyāvādī *sannyāsīs* are certainly in a position to execute pious activities. Thus Prakāśānanda Sarasvatī, on account of his piety, could understand that Caitanya Mahāprabhu was not an ordinary person but the Supreme Personality of Godhead. *Sākṣāt nārāyaṇa:* he considered Him to be Nārāyaṇa Himself. Māyāvādī *sannyāsīs* address one another as Nārāyaṇa because they think that they are all going to be Nārāyaṇa or merge with Nārāyaṇa in the next life.

Prakāśānanda Sarasvatī appreciated that Caitanya Mahāprabhu had already directly become Nārāyaṇa and did not need to wait until His next life. One difference between the Vaiṣṇava and Māyāvādī philosophies is that Māyāvādī philosophers think that after giving up their bodies they are going to become Nārāyaṇa by merging with His body, whereas Vaiṣṇava philosophers understand that after the body dies they are going to have a transcendental, spiritual body in which to associate with Nārāyaṇa.

TEXT 71

প্রভু কহে—শুন, শ্রীপাদ, ইহার কারণ ।
গুরু মোরে মূর্খ দেখি' করিল শাসন ॥ ৭১ ॥

prabhu kahe—śuna, śrīpāda, ihāra kāraṇa
guru more mūrkha dekhi' karila śāsana

prabhu kahe—the Lord replied; *śuna*—kindly hear; *śrīpāda*—Your Holiness; *ihāra*—of this; *kāraṇa*—reason; *guru*—My spiritual master; *more*—Me; *mūrkha*—fool; *dekhi'*—understanding; *karila*—he did; *śāsana*—chastisement.

TRANSLATION

Śrī Caitanya Mahāprabhu replied to Prakāśānanda Sarasvatī, "My dear sir, kindly hear the reason. My spiritual master considered Me a fool, and therefore he chastised Me.

PURPORT

When Prakāśānanda Sarasvatī inquired from Lord Caitanya Mahāprabhu why He neither studied Vedānta nor performed meditation, Lord Caitanya presented Himself as a number one fool in order to indicate that the present age, Kali-yuga, is an age of fools and rascals in which it is not possible to obtain perfection simply by reading Vedānta philosophy and meditating. The *śāstras* strongly recommend:

harer nāma harer nāma harer nāmaiva kevalam
kalau nāsty eva nāsty eva nāsty eva gatir anyathā

"In this age of quarrel and hypocrisy the only means of deliverance is the chanting of the holy names of the Lord. There is no other way. There is no other way. There is no other way." People in general in Kali-yuga are so fallen that it is not possible for them to obtain perfection simply by studying the *Vedānta-sūtra.* One should therefore seriously take to the constant chanting of the holy name of the Lord.

TEXT 72

মূর্খ তুমি, তোমার নাহিক বেদান্তাধিকার ।
'কৃষ্ণমন্ত্র' জপ' সদা,—এই মন্ত্রসার ॥ ৭২ ॥

mūrkha tumi, tomāra nāhika vedāntādhikāra
'kṛṣṇa-mantra' japa sadā,—ei mantra-sāra

mūrkha tumi—You are a fool; *tomāra*—Your; *nāhika*—there is not; *vedānta*—Vedānta philosophy; *adhikāra*—qualification to study; *kṛṣṇa-mantra*—the hymn of Kṛṣṇa (Hare Kṛṣṇa); *japa*—chant; *sadā*—always; *ei*—this; *mantra*—hymn; *sāra*—essence of all Vedic knowledge.

TRANSLATION

"'You are a fool,' he said. 'You are not qualified to study Vedānta philosophy, and therefore You must always chant the holy name of Kṛṣṇa. This is the essence of all mantras, or Vedic hymns.

PURPORT

Śrī Bhaktisiddhānta Sarasvatī Gosvāmī Mahārāja comments in this connection, "One can become perfectly successful in the mission of his life if he acts exactly according to the words he hears from the mouth of his spiritual master." This acceptance of the words of the spiritual master is called *śrauta-vākya,* which indicates that the disciple must carry out the spiritual master's instructions without deviation. Śrīla Viśvanātha Cakravartī Ṭhākura remarks in this connection that a disciple must accept the words of his spiritual master as his life and soul. Śrī Caitanya Mahāprabhu here confirms this by saying that since His spiritual master ordered Him only to chant the holy name of Kṛṣṇa, He always chanted the Hare Kṛṣṇa *mahā-mantra* according to this direction (*'kṛṣṇa-mantra' japa sadā,—ei mantra-sāra*).

Kṛṣṇa is the origin of everything. Therefore when a person is fully Kṛṣṇa conscious it is to be understood that his relationship with Kṛṣṇa has been fully confirmed. Lacking Kṛṣṇa consciousness, one is only partially related with Kṛṣṇa and is therefore not in his constitutional position. Although Śrī Caitanya Mahāprabhu is the Supreme Personality of Godhead Kṛṣṇa, the spiritual master of the entire universe, He nevertheless took the position of a disciple in order to teach by example how a devotee should strictly follow the orders of a spiritual master in executing the duty of always chanting the Hare Kṛṣṇa *mahā-mantra.* One who is very much attracted to the study of Vedānta philosophy must take lessons from Śrī Caitanya Mahāprabhu. In this age, no one is actually competent to study Vedānta, and therefore it is better that one chant the holy name of the Lord, which is the essence of all Vedic knowledge, as Kṛṣṇa Himself confirms in the *Bhagavad-gītā* (15.15):

vedaiś ca sarvair aham eva vedyo
vedānta-kṛd veda-vid eva cāham

"By all the *Vedas,* I am to be known. Indeed, I am the compiler of *Vedānta,* and I am the knower of the *Vedas.*"

Only fools give up the service of the spiritual master and think themselves advanced in spiritual knowledge. In order to check such fools, Caitanya Mahāprabhu Himself presented the perfect example of how to be a disciple. A spiritual master knows very well how to engage each disciple in a particular duty, but if a disciple, thinking himself more advanced than his spiritual master, gives up his orders and acts independently, he checks his own spiritual progress. Every disciple must consider himself completely unaware of the science of Kṛṣṇa and must always be ready to carry out the orders of the spiritual master to become competent in Kṛṣṇa consciousness. A disciple should always remain a fool before his spiritual master. Therefore sometimes pseudo spiritualists accept a spiritual master who is not even fit to become a disciple because they want to keep him under their control. This is useless for spiritual realization.

One who imperfectly knows Kṛṣṇa consciousness cannot know Vedānta philosophy. A showy display of Vedānta study without Kṛṣṇa consciousness is a feature of the external energy, *māyā,* and as long as one is attracted by the inebrieties of this ever-changing material energy, he deviates from devotion to the Supreme Personality of Godhead. An actual follower of Vedānta philosophy is a devotee of Lord Viṣṇu, who is the greatest of the great and the maintainer of the entire universe. Unless one surpasses the field of activities in service to the limited, one cannot reach the unlimited. Knowledge of the unlimited is actual *brahma-*

jñāna, or knowledge of the Supreme. Those who are addicted to fruitive activities and speculative knowledge cannot understand the value of the holy name of Lord Kṛṣṇa, which is always completely pure, eternally liberated and full of spiritual bliss. One who has taken shelter of the holy name of the Lord, which is identical with the Lord, does not have to study Vedānta philosophy, for he has already completed all such study.

One who is unfit to chant the holy name of Kṛṣṇa but thinks that the holy name is different from Kṛṣṇa and thus takes shelter of Vedānta study in order to understand Him must be considered a number one fool, as confirmed by Caitanya Mahāprabhu by His personal behavior, and philosophical speculators who want to make Vedānta philosophy an academic career are also considered to be within the material energy. A person who always chants the holy name of the Lord, however, is already beyond the ocean of nescience, and thus even a person born in a low family who engages in chanting the holy name of the Lord is considered to be beyond the study of Vedānta philosophy. In this connection *Śrīmad-Bhāgavatam* (3.33.7) states:

aho bata śva-paco 'to garīyān
yaj-jihvāgre vartate nāma tubhyam
tepus tapas te juhuvuḥ sasnur āryā
brahmānūcur nāma gṛṇanti ye te

"If a person born in a family of dog-eaters takes to the chanting of the holy name of Kṛṣṇa, it is to be understood that in his previous life he must have executed all kinds of austerities and penances and performed all the Vedic *yajñas.*" Another quotation states:

ṛg-vedo 'tha yajur-vedaḥ sāma-vedo 'py atharvaṇaḥ
adhītās tena yenoktaṁ harir ity akṣara-dvayam

"A person who chants the two syllables *ha-ri* has already studied the four *Vedas—Sāma, Ṛg, Yajur* and *Atharva.*"

Taking advantage of these verses, there are some *sahajiyās* who, taking everything very cheaply, consider themselves elevated Vaiṣṇavas but do not care even to touch the *Vedānta-sūtra* or Vedānta philosophy. A real Vaiṣṇava should, however, study Vedānta philosophy, but if after studying Vedānta one does not adopt the chanting of the holy name of the Lord, he is no better than a Māyāvādī. Therefore, one should not be a Māyāvādī, yet one should not be unaware of the subject matter of

Vedānta philosophy. Indeed, Caitanya Mahāprabhu exhibited His knowledge of Vedānta in His discourses with Prakāśānanda Sarasvatī. Thus it is to be understood that a Vaiṣṇava should be completely conversant with Vedānta philosophy, yet he should not think that studying Vedānta is all in all and therefore be unattached to the chanting of the holy name. A devotee must know the importance of simultaneously understanding Vedānta philosophy and chanting the holy names. If by studying Vedānta one becomes an impersonalist, he has not been able to understand Vedānta. This is confirmed in the *Bhagavad-gītā* (15.15). *Vedānta* means "the end of knowledge." The ultimate end of knowledge is knowledge of Kṛṣṇa, who is identical with His holy name. Cheap Vaiṣṇavas (*sahajiyās*) do not care to study the Vedānta philosophy as commented upon by the four *ācāryas.* In the Gauḍīya-sampradāya there is a Vedānta commentary called the *Govinda-bhāṣya,* but the *sahajiyās* consider such commentaries to be untouchable philosophical speculation, and they consider the *ācāryas* to be mixed devotees. Thus they clear their way to hell.

TEXT 73

কৃষ্ণমন্ত্র হৈতে হবে সংসার-মোচন ।
কৃষ্ণনাম হৈতে পাবে কৃষ্ণের চরণ ॥ ৭৩ ॥

kṛṣṇa-mantra haite habe saṁsāra-mocana
kṛṣṇa-nāma haite pābe kṛṣṇera caraṇa

kṛṣṇa-mantra—the chanting of the Hare Kṛṣṇa *mahā-mantra*; *haite*—from; *habe*—it will be; *saṁsāra*—material existence; *mocana*—deliverance; *kṛṣṇa-nāma*—the holy name of Lord Kṛṣṇa; *haite*—from; *pābe*—one will get; *kṛṣṇera*—of Lord Kṛṣṇa; *caraṇa*—lotus feet.

TRANSLATION

"Simply by chanting the holy name of Kṛṣṇa one can obtain freedom from material existence. Indeed, simply by chanting the Hare Kṛṣṇa mantra one will be able to see the lotus feet of the Lord.

PURPORT

In his *Anubhāṣya,* Śrī Bhaktisiddhānta Sarasvatī Gosvāmī says that the actual effect that will be visible as soon as one achieves transcendental knowledge is that he will immediately become free from the clutches of *māyā* and fully engage in the service of the Lord. Unless one serves the Supreme Personality of Godhead Mukunda, one cannot become free from fruitive activities under the external energy. However, when one chants the holy name of the Lord offenselessly, one can realize a transcendental position that is completely aloof from the material conception of life. Rendering service to the Lord, a devotee relates to the Supreme Personality of Godhead in one of five relationships—namely, *śānta, dāsya, sakhya, vātsalya* or *mādhurya*—and thus he relishes transcendental bliss in that relationship. Such a relationship certainly transcends the body and mind. When one realizes that the holy name of the Lord is identical with the Supreme Person, he becomes completely eligible to chant the holy name of the Lord. Such an ecstatic chanter and dancer must be considered to have a direct relationship with the Lord.

According to the Vedic principles, there are three stages of spiritual advancement, namely, *sambandha-jñāna, abhidheya* and *prayojana. Sambandha-jñāna* refers to establishing one's original relationship with the Supreme Personality of Godhead, *abhidheya* refers to acting according to that constitutional relationship, and *prayojana* is the ultimate goal of life, which is to develop love of Godhead (*premā pum-artho mahān*). If one adheres to the regulative principles under the order of the spiritual master, he very easily achieves the ultimate goal of his life. A person who is addicted to the chanting of the Hare Kṛṣṇa *mantra* very easily gets the opportunity to serve the Supreme Personality of Godhead directly. There is no need for such a person to understand the grammatical jugglery in which Māyāvādī *sannyāsīs* generally indulge. Śrī Śaṅkarācārya also stressed this point: *na hi na hi rakṣati ḍukṛñ karaṇe.* "Simply by juggling grammatical suffixes and prefixes one cannot save himself from the clutches of death." The grammatical word jugglers cannot bewilder a devotee who engages in chanting the Hare Kṛṣṇa *mahā-mantra.* Simply addressing the energy of the Supreme Lord as Hare and the Lord Himself as Kṛṣṇa very soon situates the Lord within the heart of the devotee. By thus addressing Rādhā and Kṛṣṇa, one directly engages in His Lordship's service. The essence of all revealed scriptures and all knowledge is present when one addresses the Lord and His energy by the Hare Kṛṣṇa *mantra,* for this transcendental vibration can completely liberate a conditioned soul and directly engage him in the service of the Lord.

Śrī Caitanya Mahāprabhu presented Himself as a grand fool, yet He maintained that all the words that He had heard from His spiritual master strictly followed the principles stated by Vyāsadeva in *Śrīmad-Bhāgavatam* (1.7.6).

anarthopaśamaṁ sākṣād bhakti-yogam adhokṣaje
lokasyājānato vidvāṁś cakre sātvata-saṁhitām

"The material miseries of a living entity, which are superfluous to him, can be directly mitigated by the linking process of devotional service. But the mass of people do not know this, and therefore the learned Vyāsadeva compiled this Vedic literature [*Śrīmad-Bhāgavatam*], which is in relation to the Supreme Truth." One can overcome all misconceptions and entanglement in the material world by practicing *bhakti-yoga*, and therefore Vyāsadeva, acting on the instruction of Śrī Nārada, has very kindly introduced *Śrīmad-Bhāgavatam* to relieve the conditioned souls from the clutches of *māyā*. Lord Caitanya's spiritual master instructed Him, therefore, that one must read *Śrīmad-Bhāgavatam* regularly and with scrutiny to gradually become attached to the chanting of the Hare Kṛṣṇa *mahā-mantra*.

The holy name and the Lord are identical. One who is completely free from the clutches of *māyā* can understand this fact. This knowledge, which is achieved by the mercy of the spiritual master, places one on the supreme transcendental platform. Śrī Caitanya Mahāprabhu presented Himself as a fool because prior to accepting the shelter of a spiritual master He could not understand that simply by chanting one can be relieved from all material conditions. But as soon as He became a faithful servant of His spiritual master and followed his instructions, He very easily saw the path of liberation. Śrī Caitanya Mahāprabhu's chanting of the Hare Kṛṣṇa *mantra* must be understood to be devoid of all offenses. The ten offenses against the holy name are as follows: (1) to blaspheme a devotee of the Lord, (2) to consider the Lord and the demigods to be on the same level or to think that there are many gods, (3) to neglect the orders of the spiritual master, (4) to minimize the authority of scriptures (*Vedas*), (5) to interpret the holy name of God, (6) to commit sins on the strength of chanting, (7) to instruct the glories of the Lord's name to the unfaithful, (8) to compare the chanting of the holy name with material piety, (9) to be inattentive while chanting the holy name, and (10) to be attached to material things in spite of chanting the holy name.

TEXT 74

নাম বিনু কলিকালে নাহি আর ধর্ম ।
সর্বমন্ত্রসার নাম, এই শাস্ত্রমর্ম ॥ ৭৪ ॥

nāma vinu kali-kāle nāhi āra dharma
sarva-mantra-sāra nāma, ei śāstra-marma

nāma—the holy name; *vinu*—without; *kali-kāle*—in this Age of Kali; *nāhi*—there is none; *āra*—or any alternative; *dharma*—religious principle; *sarva*—all; *mantra*—hymns; *sāra*—essence; *nāma*—the holy name; *ei*—this is; *śāstra*—revealed scriptures; *marma*—purport.

TRANSLATION

"'In this Age of Kali there is no religious principle other than the chanting of the holy name, which is the essence of all Vedic hymns. This is the purport of all scriptures.'

PURPORT

The principles of the *paramparā* system were strictly honored in previous ages—Satya-yuga, Tretā-yuga and Dvāpara-yuga—but in the present age, Kali-yuga, people neglect the importance of this system of *śrauta-paramparā*, or receiving knowledge by disciplic succession. In this age, people are prepared to argue that they can understand that which is beyond their limited knowledge and perception through so-called scientific observations and experiments, not knowing that actual truth comes down to man from authorities. This argumentative attitude is against the Vedic principles, and it is very difficult for one who adopts it to understand that the holy name of Kṛṣṇa is as good as Kṛṣṇa Himself. Since Kṛṣṇa and His holy name are identical, the holy name is eternally pure and beyond material contamination. It is the Supreme Personality of Godhead as a transcendental vibration. The holy name is completely different from material sound, as confirmed by Narottama dāsa Ṭhākura: *golokera prema-dhana, hari-nāma-saṅkīrtana.* The transcendental vibration of *hari-nāma-saṅkīrtana* is imported from the spiritual world. Thus although materialists who are addicted to experimental knowledge and the so-called "scientific method" cannot place their faith in the chanting of the Hare Kṛṣṇa *mahā-mantra,* it is a fact that simply by chanting the Hare Kṛṣṇa *mantra* offenselessly one can be freed from all subtle and gross material conditions. The spiritual world is called Vaikuṇṭha, which means "without anxiety." In the material world everything is full of anxiety (*kuṇṭha*), whereas in the spiritual world (Vaikuṇṭha) everything is free from anxiety. Therefore those who are afflicted by a combination of anxieties cannot understand the Hare Kṛṣṇa *mantra*, which is free from all anxiety. In the present age the vibration of the Hare Kṛṣṇa *mahā-mantra* is the only process that is in a transcendental position, beyond material contamination. Since the holy name can deliver a conditioned soul, it is explained here to be *sarva-mantra-sāra*, the essence of all Vedic hymns.

A name that represents an object of this material world may be subjected to arguments and experimental knowledge, but in the absolute world a name and its owner, the fame and the famous, are identical, and similarly the qualities, pastimes and everything else pertaining to the Absolute are also absolute. Although Māyāvādīs profess monism, they differentiate between the holy name of the Supreme Lord and the Lord Himself. For this offense of *nāmāparādha* they gradually glide down from their exalted position of *brahma-jñāna*, as confirmed in *Śrīmad-Bhāgavatam* (10.2.32):

āruhya kṛcchreṇa paraṁ padaṁ tataḥ
patanty adho 'nādṛta-yuṣmad-aṅghrayaḥ

Although by severe austerities they rise to the exalted position of *brahma-jñāna*, they nevertheless fall down due to imperfect knowledge of the Absolute Truth. Although they profess to understand the Vedic *mantra sarvaṁ khalv idaṁ brahma* (*Chāndogya Up.* 3.14.1), which means "Everything is Brahman," they are unable to understand that the holy name is also Brahman. If they regularly chant the *mahā-mantra*, however, they can be relieved from this misconception. Unless one properly takes shelter of the holy name, he cannot be relieved from the offensive stage in chanting the holy name.

TEXT 75

এত বলি' এক শ্লোক শিখাইল মোরে ।
কণ্ঠে করি' এই শ্লোক করিহ বিচারে ॥ ৭৫ ॥

eta bali' eka śloka śikhāila more
kaṇṭhe kari' ei śloka kariha vicāre

eta bali'—saying this; *eka śloka*—one verse; *śikhāila*—taught; *more*—Me; *kaṇṭhe*—in the throat; *kari'*—keeping; *ei*—this; *śloka*—verse; *kariha*—You should do; *vicāre*—in consideration.

TRANSLATION

"After describing the potency of the Hare Kṛṣṇa mahā-mantra, My spiritual master taught Me another verse, advising Me to always keep it within My throat.

TEXT 76

হরের্নাম হরের্নাম হরের্নামৈব কেবলম্ ।
কলৌ নাস্ত্যেব নাস্ত্যেব নাস্ত্যেব গতিরন্যথা ॥ ৭৬ ॥

harer nāma harer nāma
harer nāmaiva kevalam
kalau nāsty eva nāsty eva
nāsty eva gatir anyathā

hareḥ nāma—the holy name of the Lord; *hareḥ nāma*—the holy name of the Lord; *hareḥ nāma*—the holy name of the Lord; *eva*—certainly; *kevalam*—only; *kalau*—in this Age of Kali; *na asti*—there is none; *eva*—certainly; *na asti*—there is none; *eva*—certainly; *na asti*—there is none; *eva*—certainly; *gatiḥ*—progress; *anyathā*—otherwise.

TRANSLATION

"'For spiritual progress in this Age of Kali, there is no alternative, there is no alternative, there is no alternative to the holy name, the holy name, the holy name of the Lord.'

PURPORT

For progress in spiritual life, the *śāstras* recommend meditation in Satya-yuga, sacrifice for the satisfaction of Lord Viṣṇu in Tretā-yuga and gorgeous worship of the Lord in the temple in Dvāpara-yuga, but in the Age of Kali one can achieve spiritual progress only by chanting the holy name of the Lord. This is confirmed in various scriptures. In *Śrīmad-Bhāgavatam* there are many references to this fact. In the Twelfth Canto (3.51) it is said:

kaler doṣa-nidhe rājann asti hy eko mahān guṇaḥ
kīrtanād eva kṛṣṇasya mukta-saṅgaḥ paraṁ vrajet

In the Age of Kali there are many faults, for people are subjected to many miserable conditions, yet in this age there is one great benediction—simply by chanting the Hare Kṛṣṇa *mantra* one can be freed from all material contamination and thus be elevated to the spiritual world. The *Nārada-pañcarātra* also praises the Hare Kṛṣṇa *mahā-mantra* as follows:

trayo vedāḥ ṣaḍ-aṅgāni chandāṁsi vividhāḥ surāḥ
sarvam aṣṭākṣarāntaḥ-sthaṁ yac cānyad api vāṅ-mayam
sarva-vedānta-sārārthaḥ saṁsārārṇava-tāraṇaḥ

"The essence of all Vedic knowledge—comprehending the three kinds of Vedic activity [*karma-kāṇḍa, jñāna-kāṇḍa* and *upāsanā-kāṇḍa*], the *chandas,* or Vedic hymns, and the processes for satisfying the demigods—is included in the eight syllables Hare Kṛṣṇa, Hare Kṛṣṇa. This is the reality of all Vedānta. The chanting of the holy name is the only means to cross the ocean of nescience." Similarly, the *Kali-santaraṇa Upaniṣad* states, "Hare Kṛṣṇa, Hare Kṛṣṇa, Kṛṣṇa Kṛṣṇa, Hare Hare/ Hare Rāma, Hare Rāma, Rāma Rāma, Hare Hare—these sixteen names composed of thirty-two syllables are the only means to counteract the evil effects of Kali-yuga. In all the *Vedas* it is seen that to cross the ocean of nescience there is no alternative to the chanting of the holy name." Similarly, Śrī Madhvācārya, while commenting upon the *Muṇḍaka Upaniṣad,* has quoted the following verse from the *Nārāyaṇa-saṁhitā:*

dvāparīyair janair viṣṇuḥ pañcarātrais tu kevalaiḥ
kalau tu nāma-mātreṇa pūjyate bhagavān hariḥ

"In Dvāpara-yuga one could satisfy Kṛṣṇa or Viṣṇu only by worshiping Him gorgeously according to the *pāñcarātrikī* system, but in the Age of Kali one can satisfy and worship the Supreme Personality of Godhead Hari simply by chanting the holy name." In his *Bhakti-sandarbha* (text 284), Śrīla Jīva Gosvāmī strongly emphasizes the chanting of the holy name of the Lord as follows:

nanu bhagavan-nāmātmakā eva mantrāḥ, tatra viśeṣeṇa namaḥ-śabdādy-alaṅkṛtāḥ śrī-bhagavatā śrīmad-ṛṣibhiś cāhita-śakti-viśeṣāḥ, śrī-bhagavatā samam ātma-sambandha-viśeṣa-pratipādakāś ca tatra kevalāni śrī-bhagavan-nāmāny api nirapekṣāṇy eva parama-puruṣārtha-phala-paryanta-dāna-samarthāni tato mantreṣu nāmato 'py adhika-sāmarthye labdhe kathaṁ dīkṣādy-apekṣā. ucyate—yady api svarūpato nāsti, tathāpi prāyaḥ svabhāvato dehādi-sambandhena kadarya-śīlānāṁ vikṣipta-cittānāṁ janānāṁ tat-saṅkocī-karaṇāya śrīmad-ṛṣi-prabhṛtibhir atrārcana-mārge kvacit kvacit kācit kācin maryādā sthāpitāsti.

Śrīla Jīva Gosvāmī states that the substance of all the Vedic *mantras* is the chanting of the holy name of the Lord. Every *mantra* begins with the prefix *nama oṁ* and eventually addresses by name the Supreme Personality of Godhead. By the supreme will of the Lord there is a specific potency in each and every *mantra* chanted by great sages like Nārada Muni and other *ṛṣis.* Chanting the holy name of the Lord immediately renovates the transcendental relationship of the living being with the Supreme Lord.

To chant the holy name of the Lord, one need not depend upon other paraphernalia, for one can immediately get all the desired results of linking with the Supreme Personality of Godhead. It may therefore be questioned why there is a necessity for initiation or further spiritual activities in devotional service for one who engages in the chanting of the holy name of the Lord. The answer is that although it is correct that one who fully engages in chanting the holy name need not depend upon the process of initiation, generally a devotee is addicted to many abominable material habits due to material contamination from his previous life. In order to get quick relief from all these contaminations, it is required that one engage in the worship of the Lord in the temple. The worship of the Deity in the temple is essential to reduce one's restlessness due to the contaminations of conditioned life. Thus Nārada, in his *pāñcarātrikī-vidhi*, and other great sages have sometimes stressed that since every conditioned soul has a bodily concept of life aimed at sense enjoyment, to restrict this sense enjoyment the rules and regulations for worshiping the Deity in the temple are essential. Śrīla Rūpa Gosvāmī has described that the holy name of the Lord can be chanted by liberated souls, but almost all the souls we have to initiate are conditioned. It is advised that one chant the holy name of the Lord without offenses and according to the regulative principles, yet due to their past bad habits they violate these rules and regulations. Thus the regulative principles for worship of the Deity are also simultaneously essential.

TEXT 77

এই আজ্ঞা পাঞা নাম লই অনুক্ষণ ।
নাম লৈতে লৈতে মোর ভ্রান্ত হৈল মন ॥ ৭৭ ॥

ei ājñā pāñā nāma la-i anukṣaṇa
nāma laite laite mora bhrānta haila mana

ei—this; *ājñā*—order; *pāñā*—receiving; *nāma*—the holy name; *la-i*—chant; *anukṣaṇa*—always; *nāma*—the holy name; *laite*—accepting; *laite*—accepting; *mora*—My; *bhrānta*—bewilderment; *haila*—taking place; *mana*—in the mind.

TRANSLATION

"Since I received this order from My spiritual master, I always chant the holy name, but I thought that by chanting and chanting the holy name I had been bewildered.

TEXT 78

ধৈর্য ধরিতে নারি, হৈলাম উন্মত্ত ।
হাসি, কান্দি, নাচি, গাই, যৈছে মদমত্ত ॥ ৭৮ ॥

dhairya dharite nāri, hailāma unmatta
hāsi, kāndi, nāci, gāi, yaiche madamatta

dhairya—patience; *dharite*—capturing; *nāri*—unable to take; *hailāma*—I have become; *unmatta*—mad after it; *hāsi*—laugh; *kāndi*—cry; *nāci*—dance; *gāi*—sing; *yaiche*—as much as; *madamatta*—madman.

TRANSLATION

"While chanting the holy name of the Lord in pure ecstasy, I lose myself, and thus I laugh, cry, dance and sing just like a madman.

TEXT 79

তবে ধৈর্য ধরি' মনে করিলুঁ বিচার ।
কৃষ্ণনামে জ্ঞানাচ্ছন্ন হইল আমার ॥ ৭৯ ॥

tabe dhairya dhari' mane karilun̐ vicāra
kṛṣṇa-nāme jñānācchanna ha-ila āmāra

tabe—thereafter; *dhairya*—patience; *dhari'*—accepting; *mane*—in the mind; *karilun̐*—I did; *vicāra*—consideration; *kṛṣṇa-nāme*—in the holy name of Kṛṣṇa; *jñāna ācchanna*—covering of My knowledge; *ha-ila*—has become; *āmāra*—of Me.

TRANSLATION

"Collecting My patience, therefore, I began to consider that chanting the holy name of Kṛṣṇa had covered all My spiritual knowledge.

PURPORT

Śrī Caitanya Mahāprabhu hints in this verse that to chant the holy name of Kṛṣṇa one does not need to speculate on the philosophical aspects of the science of God, for one automatically becomes ecstatic and without consideration immediately chants, dances, laughs, cries and sings just like a madman.

TEXT 80

পাগল হইলাঙ আমি, ধৈর্য নাহি মনে ।
এত চিন্তি' নিবেদিলুঁ গুরুর চরণে ॥ ৮০ ॥

pāgala ha-ilān̐ āmi, dhairya nāhi mane
eta cinti' nivedilun̐ gurura caraṇe

pāgala—madman; *ha-ilān̐*—I have become; *āmi*—I; *dhairya*—patience; *nāhi*—not; *mane*—in the mind; *eta*—thus; *cinti'*—considering; *nivedilun̐*—I submitted; *gurura*—of the spiritual master; *caraṇe*—at his lotus feet.

TRANSLATION

"I saw that I had become mad by chanting the holy name, and I immediately submitted this at the lotus feet of my spiritual master.

PURPORT

Śrī Caitanya Mahāprabhu, as an ideal teacher, shows us how a disciple should deal with his spiritual master. Whenever there is doubt regarding any point, he should refer the matter to his spiritual master for clarification. Śrī Caitanya Mahāprabhu said that while chanting and dancing He had developed the kind of mad ecstasy that is possible only for a liberated soul. Yet even in His liberated position, He referred everything to His spiritual master whenever there were doubts. Thus in any condition, even when liberated, we should never think ourselves independent of the spiritual master, but must refer to him as soon as there is some doubt regarding our progressive spiritual life.

TEXT 81

কিবা মন্ত্র দিলা, গোসাঞি, কিবা তার বল ।
জপিতে জপিতে মন্ত্র করিল পাগল ॥ ৮১ ॥

kibā mantra dilā, gosāñi, kibā tāra bala
japite japite mantra karila pāgala

kibā—what kind of; *mantra*—hymn; *dilā*—you have given; *gosāñi*—My lord; *kibā*—what is; *tāra*—its; *bala*—strength; *japite*—chanting; *japite*—chanting; *mantra*—the hymn; *karila*—has made Me; *pāgala*—madman.

TRANSLATION

"'My dear lord, what kind of mantra have you given Me? I have become mad simply by chanting this mahā-mantra!

PURPORT

Śrī Caitanya Mahāprabhu prays in His *Śikṣāṣṭaka:*

yugāyitaṁ nimeṣeṇa cakṣuṣā prāvṛṣāyitam
śūnyāyitaṁ jagat sarvaṁ govinda-viraheṇa me

"O Govinda! Feeling Your separation, I am considering a moment to be like twelve years or more. Tears are flowing from my eyes like torrents of rain, and I am feeling all vacant in the world in Your absence." It is the aspiration of a devotee that while he chants the Hare Kṛṣṇa *mahā-mantra* his eyes will fill with tears, his voice falter and his heart throb. These are good signs in chanting the holy name of the Lord. In ecstasy, one should feel the entire world to be vacant without the presence of Govinda. This is a sign of separation from Govinda. In material life we are all separated from Govinda and are absorbed in material sense gratification. Therefore, when one comes to his senses on the spiritual platform he becomes so eager to meet Govinda that without Govinda the entire world becomes a vacant place.

TEXT 82

হাসায়, নাচায়, মোরে করায় ক্রন্দন ।
এত শুনি' গুরু হাসি বলিলা বচন ॥ ৮২ ॥

hāsāya, nācāya, more karāya krandana
eta śuni' guru hāsi balilā vacana

hāsāya—it causes Me to laugh; *nācāya*—it causes Me to dance; *more*—unto Me; *karāya*—it causes; *krandana*—crying; *eta*—thus; *śuni'*—hearing; *guru*—My spiritual master; *hāsi*—smiling; *balilā*—said; *vacana*—words.

TRANSLATION

"'Chanting the holy name in ecstasy causes Me to dance, laugh and cry.' When My spiritual master heard all this, he smiled and then began to speak.

PURPORT

When a disciple very perfectly makes progress in spiritual life, this gladdens the spiritual master, who then also smiles in ecstasy, thinking, "How successful my disciple has become!" He feels so glad that he smiles as he enjoys the progress of the disciple, just as a smiling parent enjoys the activities of a child who is trying to stand up or crawl perfectly.

TEXT 83

কৃষ্ণনাম-মহামন্ত্রের এই ত' স্বভাব ।
যেই জপে, তার কৃষ্ণে উপজয়ে ভাব ॥ ৮৩ ॥

kṛṣṇa-nāma-mahā-mantrera ei ta' svabhāva
yei jape, tāra kṛṣṇe upajaye bhāva

kṛṣṇa-nāma—the holy name of Kṛṣṇa; *mahā-mantrera*—of the supreme hymn; *ei ta'*—this is its; *svabhāva*—nature; *yei*—anyone; *jape*—chants; *tāra*—his; *kṛṣṇe*—unto Kṛṣṇa; *upajaye*—develops; *bhāva*—ecstasy.

TRANSLATION

"'It is the nature of the Hare Kṛṣṇa mahā-mantra that anyone who chants it immediately develops his loving ecstasy for Kṛṣṇa.

PURPORT

In this verse it is explained that one who chants the Hare Kṛṣṇa *mantra* develops *bhāva,* ecstasy, which is the point at which revelation begins. It is the preliminary stage in developing one's original love for God. Lord Kṛṣṇa mentions this *bhāva* stage in the *Bhagavad-gītā* (10.8):

ahaṁ sarvasya prabhavo mattaḥ sarvaṁ pravartate
iti matvā bhajante māṁ budhā bhāva-samanvitāḥ

"I am the source of all spiritual and material worlds. Everything emanates from Me. The wise who know this perfectly engage in My devotional service and worship Me with all their hearts." A neophyte disciple begins by hearing and chanting, associating with devotees and practicing the regulative principles, and thus he vanquishes all of his unwanted bad habits. In this way he develops attachment for Kṛṣṇa and cannot forget Kṛṣṇa even for a moment. *Bhāva* is the almost successful stage of spiritual life.

A sincere student aurally receives the holy name from the spiritual master, and after being initiated he follows the regulative principles given by the spiritual master. When the holy name is properly served in this way, automatically the spiritual nature of the holy name spreads; in other words, the devotee becomes qualified in offenselessly chanting the holy name. When one is completely fit to chant the holy name in this way, he is eligible to make disciples all over the world, and he actually becomes *jagad-guru.* Then the entire world, under his influence, begins to chant the holy names of the Hare Kṛṣṇa *mahā-mantra.* Thus all the disciples of such a spiritual master increase in attachment for Kṛṣṇa, and therefore he sometimes cries, sometimes laughs, sometimes dances and sometimes chants. These symptoms are very prominently manifest in the body of a pure devotee. Sometimes when our students of the Kṛṣṇa consciousness movement chant and dance, even in India people are astonished to see how these foreigners have learned to chant and dance in this ecstatic fashion. As explained by Caitanya Mahāprabhu, however, actually this is not due to practice, for without extra endeavor these symptoms become manifest in anyone who sincerely chants the Hare Kṛṣṇa *mahā-mantra.*

Many fools, not knowing the transcendental nature of the Hare Kṛṣṇa *mahā-mantra,* sometimes impede our loudly chanting this *mantra,* yet one who is actually advanced in the fulfillment of chanting the Hare Kṛṣṇa *mahā-mantra* induces others to chant also. Kṛṣṇadāsa Kavirāja Gosvāmī explains, *kṛṣṇa-śakti vinā nahe tāra pravartana:* unless one receives special power of attorney from the Supreme Personality of Godhead, he cannot preach the glories of the Hare Kṛṣṇa *mahā-mantra.* As devotees propagate the Hare Kṛṣṇa *mahā-mantra,* the general population of the entire world gets the opportunity to understand the glories of the holy name. While chanting and dancing or hearing the holy name of the Lord, one automatically remembers the Supreme Personality of Godhead, and because there is no difference between the holy name and Kṛṣṇa, the chanter is immediately linked with Kṛṣṇa. Thus connected, a devotee develops his original attitude of service to the Lord. In this attitude of constantly serving Kṛṣṇa, which is called *bhāva,* he always thinks of Kṛṣṇa in many different ways. One who has attained this *bhāva* stage is no longer under the clutches of the illusory energy. When other spiritual ingredients, such as trembling, perspiration and tears, are added to this *bhāva* stage, the devotee gradually attains love of Kṛṣṇa.

The holy name of Kṛṣṇa is called the *mahā-mantra.* Other *mantras* mentioned in the *Nārada-pañcarātra* are known simply as *mantras,* but the chanting of the holy name of the Lord is called the *mahā-mantra.*

TEXT 84

কৃষ্ণবিষয়ক প্রেমা—পরম পুরুষার্থ ।
যার আগে তৃণতুল্য চারি পুরুষার্থ ॥ ৮৪ ॥

kṛṣṇa-viṣayaka premā—parama puruṣārtha
yāra āge tṛṇa-tulya cāri puruṣārtha

kṛṣṇa-viṣayaka—in the subject of Kṛṣṇa; *premā*—love; *parama*—the highest; *puruṣa-artha*—achievement of the goal of life; *yāra*—whose; *āge*—before; *tṛṇa-tulya*—like the grass in the street; *cāri*—four; *puruṣa-artha*—achievements.

TRANSLATION

"Religiosity, economic development, sense gratification and liberation are known as the four goals of life, but before love of Godhead, the fifth and highest goal, these appear as insignificant as straw in the street.

PURPORT

While chanting the holy name of the Lord, one should not desire the material advancements represented by religiosity, economic development, sense gratification and ultimately liberation from the material world. As stated by Caitanya Mahāprabhu, the highest perfection in life is to develop one's love for Kṛṣṇa (*premā pum-artho mahān śrī-caitanya-mahāprabhor matam idam*). When we compare love of Godhead with religiosity, economic development, sense gratification and liberation, we can understand that these achievements may be desirable objectives for *bubhukṣus,* or those who desire to enjoy this material world, and *mumukṣus,* or those who desire liberation from it, but they are very insignificant in the eyes of a pure devotee who has developed *bhāva,* the preliminary stage of love of Godhead.

Dharma (religiosity), *artha* (economic development), *kāma* (sense gratification) and *mokṣa* (liberation) are the four principles of religion that pertain to the material world. Therefore in the beginning of *Śrīmad-Bhāgavatam* it is declared, *dharmaḥ projjhita-kaitavo 'tra:* cheating religious systems in terms of these four material principles are completely discarded from *Śrīmad-Bhāgavatam,* for *Śrīmad-Bhāgavatam* teaches only how to develop one's dormant love of God. The *Bhagavad-gītā* is the preliminary study of *Śrīmad-Bhāgavatam,* and therefore it ends with the words *sarva-dharmān parityajya mām ekaṁ śaraṇaṁ vraja:* "Abandon all varieties of religion and just surrender unto Me." (Bg. 18.66) To adopt this means, one should reject all ideas of religiosity, economic development, sense gratification and liberation and fully engage in the service of the Lord, which is transcendental to these four principles. Love of Godhead is the original function of the spirit soul, and it is as eternal as the soul and the Supreme Personality of Godhead. This eternity is called *sanātana.* When a devotee revives his loving service to the Supreme Personality of Godhead, it should be understood that he has been successful in achieving the desired goal of his life. At that time everything is automatically done by the mercy of the holy name, and the devotee automatically advances in his spiritual progress.

TEXT 85

পঞ্চম পুরুষার্থ—প্রেমানন্দামৃতসিন্ধু ।
মোক্ষাদি আনন্দ যার নহে এক বিন্দু ॥ ৮৫ ॥

pañcama puruṣārtha—premānandāmṛta-sindhu
mokṣādi ānanda yāra nahe eka bindu

pañcama—fifth; *puruṣa-artha*—goal of life; *prema-ānanda*—the spiritual bliss of love of Godhead; *amṛta*—eternal; *sindhu*—ocean; *mokṣa-ādi*—liberation and other principles of religiosity; *ānanda*—pleasures derived from them; *yāra*—whose; *nahe*—never comparable; *eka*—one; *bindu*—drop.

TRANSLATION

"'For a devotee who has actually developed bhāva, the pleasure derived from dharma, artha, kāma and mokṣa appears like a drop in the presence of the sea.

TEXT 86

কৃষ্ণনামের ফল—'প্রেমা', সর্বশাস্ত্রে কয় ।
ভাগ্যে সেই প্রেমা তোমায় করিল উদয় ॥ ৮৬ ॥

kṛṣṇa-nāmera phala—'premā', sarva-śāstre kaya
bhāgye sei premā tomāya karila udaya

kṛṣṇa-nāmera—of the holy name of the Lord; *phala*—result; *premā*—love of Godhead; *sarva*—in all; *śāstre*—revealed scriptures; *kaya*—describe; *bhāgye*—fortunately; *sei*—that; *premā*—love of Godhead; *tomāya*—Your; *karila*—has done; *udaya*—arisen.

TRANSLATION

"'The conclusion of all revealed scriptures is that one should awaken his dormant love of Godhead. You are greatly fortunate to have already done so.

TEXT 87

প্রেমার স্বভাবে করে চিত্ত-তনু ক্ষোভ ।
কৃষ্ণের চরণ-প্রাপ্ত্যে উপজায় লোভ ॥ ৮৭ ॥

premāra svabhāve kare citta-tanu kṣobha
kṛṣṇera caraṇa-prāptye upajāya lobha

premāra—out of love of Godhead; *svabhāve*—by nature; *kare*—it induces; *citta*—the consciousness; *tanu*—the body; *kṣobha*—agitated; *kṛṣṇera*—of Lord Kṛṣṇa; *caraṇa*—lotus feet; *prāptye*—to obtain; *upajāya*—it so becomes; *lobha*—aspiration.

TRANSLATION

"'It is a characteristic of love of Godhead that by nature it induces transcendental symptoms in one's body and makes one more and more greedy to achieve the shelter of the lotus feet of the Lord.

TEXT 88

প্রেমার স্বভাবে ভক্ত হাসে, কান্দে, গায় ।
উন্মত্ত হইয়া নাচে, ইতি-উতি ধায় ॥ ৮৮ ॥

premāra svabhāve bhakta hāse, kānde, gāya
unmatta ha-iyā nāce, iti-uti dhāya

premāra—by such love of Godhead; *svabhāve*—by nature; *bhakta*—the devotee; *hāse*—laughs; *kānde*—cries; *gāya*—chants; *unmatta*—mad; *ha-iyā*—becoming; *nāce*—dances; *iti*—here; *uti*—there; *dhāya*—moves.

TRANSLATION

"'When one actually develops love of Godhead, he naturally sometimes cries, sometimes laughs, sometimes chants and sometimes runs here and there just like a madman.

PURPORT

In this connection Bhaktisiddhānta Sarasvatī Gosvāmī says that sometimes persons who have no love of Godhead at all display ecstatic bodily symptoms. Artificially they sometimes laugh, cry and dance just like madmen, but this cannot help one progress in Kṛṣṇa consciousness. Rather, such artificial agitation of the body is to be given up when one naturally develops the necessary bodily symptoms. Actual blissful life, manifested in genuine spiritual laughing, crying and dancing, is the symptom of real advancement in Kṛṣṇa consciousness, which can be achieved by a person who always voluntarily engages in the transcendental loving service of the Lord. If one who is not yet developed imitates such symptoms artificially, he creates chaos in the spiritual life of human society.

TEXTS 89–90

স্বেদ, কম্প, রোমাঞ্চাশ্রু, গদ্গদ, বৈবর্ণ্য ।
উন্মাদ, বিষাদ, ধৈর্য, গর্ব, হর্ষ, দৈন্য ॥ ৮৯ ॥

এত ভাবে প্রেমা ভক্তগণেরে নাচায় ।
কৃষ্ণের আনন্দামৃতসাগরে ভাসায় ॥ ৯০ ॥

sveda, kampa, romāñcāśru, gadgada, vaivarṇya
unmāda, viṣāda, dhairya, garva, harṣa, dainya

eta bhāve premā bhaktagaṇere nācāya
kṛṣṇera ānandāmṛta-sāgare bhāsāya

sveda—perspiration; *kampa*—trembling; *romāñca*—standing of the hairs on the body; *aśru*—tears; *gadgada*—faltering; *vaivarṇya*—changing of bodily color; *unmāda*—madness; *viṣāda*—melancholy; *dhairya*—patience; *garva*—pride; *harṣa*—joyfulness; *dainya*—humbleness; *eta*—in many ways; *bhāve*—in ecstasy; *premā*—love of Godhead; *bhakta-gaṇere*—unto the devotees; *nācāya*—causes to dance; *kṛṣṇera*—of Lord Kṛṣṇa; *ānanda*—transcendental bliss; *amṛta*—nectar; *sāgare*—in the ocean; *bhāsāya*—floats.

TRANSLATION

"'Perspiration, trembling, standing on end of one's bodily hairs, tears, faltering voice, fading complexion, madness, melancholy, patience, pride, joy and humility—these are various natural symptoms of ecstatic love of Godhead, which causes a devotee to dance and float in an ocean of transcendental bliss while chanting the Hare Kṛṣṇa mantra.

PURPORT

Śrīla Jīva Gosvāmī, in his *Prīti-sandarbha* (66), explains this stage of love of Godhead: *bhagavat-prīti-rūpā vṛttir māyādi-mayī na bhavati. kiṁ tarhi, svarūpa-śakty-ānanda-rūpā, yad-ānanda-parādhīnaḥ śrī-bhagavān apīti.* Similarly, in the 69th text he offers further explanation: *tad evaṁ prīter lakṣaṇaṁ citta-dravas tasya ca roma-harṣādikam. kathañcij jāte 'pi citta-drave roma-harṣādike vā na ced āśaya-śuddhis tadāpi na bhakteḥ samyag-āvirbhāva iti jñāpitam. āśaya-śuddhir nāma cānya-tātparya-parityāgaḥ prīti-tātparyaṁ ca. ata evānimittā svābhāvikī ceti tad viśeṣaṇam.* Transcendental love of Godhead is not under the jurisdiction of the material energy, for it is the transcendental bliss and pleasure potency of the Supreme Personality of Godhead. Since the Supreme Lord is also under the influence of transcendental bliss, when one comes in touch with such bliss in love of Godhead, one's heart melts, and the symptoms of this are standing of the hairs on end, etc. Sometimes a person thus melts and manifests these transcendental symptoms yet at the same time is not well behaved in his personal transactions. This indicates that he has not yet reached complete perfection in devotional life. In other words, a devotee who dances in ecstasy but after dancing and crying appears to be attracted to material affairs has not yet reached the perfection of devotional service, which is called *āśaya-śuddhi*, or the perfection of existence. One who attains the perfection of existence is completely averse to material enjoyment and engrossed in transcendental love of Godhead. It is therefore to be concluded that the ecstatic symptoms of *āśaya-śuddhi* are visible when a devotee's service has no material cause and is purely spiritual in nature. These are characteristics of transcendental love of Godhead, as stated in *Śrīmad-Bhāgavatam* (1.2.6):

sa vai puṁsāṁ paro dharmo yato bhaktir adhokṣaje
ahaituky apratihatā yayātmā suprasīdati

"That religion is best which causes its followers to become ecstatic in love of God that is unmotivated and free from material impediments, for this alone can completely satisfy the self."

TEXT 91

ভাল হৈল, পাইলে তুমি পরমপুরুষার্থ ।
তোমার প্রেমেতে আমি হৈলাঙ কৃতার্থ ॥ ৯১ ॥

bhāla haila, pāile tumi parama-puruṣārtha
tomāra premete āmi hailāṅ kṛtārtha

bhāla haila—let it be good; *pāile*—You have gotten; *tumi*—You; *parama-puruṣārtha*—superexcellent goal of life; *tomāra*—Your; *premete*—by development in love of Godhead; *āmi*—I; *hailāṅ*—become; *kṛta-artha*—very much obliged.

TRANSLATION

"'It is very good, my dear child, that You have attained the supreme goal of life by developing love of Godhead. Thus You have pleased me very much, and I am very much obliged to You.

PURPORT

According to the revealed scriptures, if a spiritual master can convert even one soul into a perfectly pure devotee, his mission in life is fulfilled. Śrīla Bhaktisiddhānta Sarasvatī Ṭhākura always used to say, "Even at the expense of all the properties, temples and *maṭhas* that I have, if I could convert even one person into a pure devotee, my mission would be fulfilled." It is very difficult, however, to understand the science of Kṛṣṇa, what to speak of developing love of Godhead. Therefore if by the grace of Lord Caitanya and the spiritual master a disciple attains the standard of pure devotional service, the spiritual master is very happy. The spiritual master is not actually happy if the disciple brings him money, but when he sees that a disciple is following the regulative principles and advancing in spiritual life, he is very glad and feels obliged to such an advanced disciple.

TEXT 92

নাচ, গাও, ভক্তসঙ্গে কর সংকীর্তন ।
কৃষ্ণনাম উপদেশি' তার' সর্বজন ॥ ৯২ ॥

nāca, gāo, bhakta-saṅge kara saṅkīrtana
kṛṣṇa-nāma upadeśi' tāra' sarva-jana

nāca—go on dancing; *gāo*—chant; *bhakta-saṅge*—in the society of devotees; *kara*—continue; *saṅkīrtana*—chanting of the holy name in assembly; *kṛṣṇa-nāma*—the holy name of Kṛṣṇa; *upadeśi'*—by instructing; *tāra'*—deliver; *sarva-jana*—all fallen souls.

TRANSLATION

"'My dear child, continue dancing, chanting and performing saṅkīrtana in association with devotees. Furthermore, go out and preach the value of chanting kṛṣṇa-nāma, for by this process You will be able to deliver all fallen souls.'

PURPORT

It is another ambition of the spiritual master to see his disciples not only chant, dance and follow the regulative principles but also preach the *saṅkīrtana* movement to others in order to deliver them, for the Kṛṣṇa consciousness movement is based on the principle that one should become as perfect as possible in devotional service oneself and also preach the cult for others' benefit. There are two classes of unalloyed devotees—namely, *goṣṭhy-ānandīs* and *bhajanānandīs. Bhajanānandī* refers to one who is satisfied to cultivate devotional service for himself, and *goṣṭhy-ānandī* is one who is not satisfied simply to become perfect himself but wants to see others also take advantage of the holy name of the Lord and advance in spiritual life. The outstanding example is Prahlāda Mahārāja. When he was offered a benediction by Lord Nṛsiṁhadeva, Prahlāda Mahārāja said:

naivodvije para duratyaya-vaitaraṇyās
tvad-vīrya-gāyana-mahāmṛta-magna-cittaḥ
śoce tato vimukha-cetasa indriyārtha-
māyā-sukhāya bharam udvahato vimūḍhān

"My dear Lord, I have no problems and want no benediction from You because I am quite satisfied to chant Your holy name. This is sufficient for me because whenever I chant I immediately merge in an ocean of transcendental bliss. I only lament to see others bereft of Your love. They are rotting in material activities for transient material pleasure and spoiling their lives toiling all day and night simply for sense gratification, with no attachment for love of Godhead. I am simply lamenting for them and devising various plans to deliver them from the clutches of *māyā*." (*Bhāg.* 7.9.43)

Śrīla Bhaktisiddhānta Sarasvatī Ṭhākura explains in his *Anubhāṣya*, "A person who has attracted the attention of the spiritual master by his sincere service likes to dance and chant with similarly developed Kṛṣṇa conscious devotees. The spiritual master authorizes such a devotee to deliver fallen souls in all parts of the world. Those who are not advanced prefer to chant the Hare Kṛṣṇa *mantra* in a solitary place." Such activities constitute, in the language of Śrīla Bhaktisiddhānta Sarasvatī Ṭhākura, a type of cheating process in the sense that they imitate the activities of exalted personalities like Haridāsa Ṭhākura. One should not attempt to imitate such exalted devotees. Rather, everyone should endeavor to preach the cult of Śrī Caitanya Mahāprabhu in all parts of the world and thus become successful in spiritual life. One who is not very expert in preaching may chant in a secluded place, avoiding bad association, but for one who is actually advanced, preaching and meeting people who are not engaged in devotional service are not disadvantages. A devotee gives the nondevotees his association but is not affected by their misbehavior. Thus by the activities of a pure devotee even those who are bereft of love of Godhead get a chance to become devotees of the Lord one day. In this connection Śrīla Bhaktisiddhānta Sarasvatī Ṭhākura advises that one discuss the verse in *Śrīmad-Bhāgavatam* beginning *naitat samācarej jātu manasāpi hy anīśvaraḥ* (10.33.30), and the following verse in *Bhakti-rasāmṛta-sindhu* (1.2.255):

anāsaktasya viṣayān yathārham upayuñjataḥ
nirbandhaḥ kṛṣṇa-sambandhe yuktaṁ vairāgyam ucyate

One should not imitate the activities of great personalities. One should be detached from material enjoyment and should accept everything in connection with Kṛṣṇa's service.

TEXT 93

এত বলি' এক শ্লোক শিখাইল মোরে ।
ভাগবতের সার এই—বলে বারে বারে ॥ ৯৩ ॥

eta bali' eka śloka śikhāila more
bhāgavatera sāra ei—bale vāre vāre

eta bali'—saying this; *eka*—one; *śloka*—verse; *śikhāila*—has taught; *more*—unto Me; *bhāgavatera*—of *Śrīmad-Bhāgavatam; sāra*—essence; *ei*—this is; *bale*—he said; *vāre vāre*—again and again.

TRANSLATION

"Saying this, My spiritual master taught Me a verse from Śrīmad-Bhāgavatam. It is the essence of all the Bhāgavatam's instructions; therefore he recited this verse again and again.

PURPORT

This verse from *Śrīmad-Bhāgavatam* (11.2.40) was spoken by Śrī Nārada Muni to Vasudeva to teach him about *bhāgavata-dharma.* Vasudeva had already achieved the result of *bhāgavata-dharma* because Lord Kṛṣṇa appeared in his house as his son, yet in order to teach others, he desired to hear from Śrī Nārada Muni to be enlightened in the process of *bhāgavata-dharma.* This is the humbleness of a great devotee.

TEXT 94

এবংব্রতঃ স্বপ্রিয়নামকীর্ত্যা
জাতানুরাগো দ্রুতচিত্ত উচ্চৈঃ ।
হসত্যথো রোদিতি রৌতি গায়-
ত্যুন্মাদবন্নৃত্যতি লোকবাহ্যঃ ॥ ৯৪ ॥

evaṁ-vrataḥ sva-priya-nāma-kīrtyā
jātānurāgo druta-citta uccaiḥ
hasaty atho roditi rauti gāyaty
unmāda-van nṛtyati loka-bāhyaḥ

evam-vrataḥ—when one thus engages in the vow to chant and dance; *sva*—own; *priya*—very dear; *nāma*—holy name; *kīrtyā*—by chanting; *jāta*—in this way develops; *anurāgaḥ*—attachment; *druta-cittaḥ*—very eagerly; *uccaiḥ*—loudly; *hasati*—laughs; *atho*—also; *roditi*—cries; *rauti*—becomes agitated; *gāyati*—chants; *unmāda-vat*—like a madman; *nṛtyati*—dancing; *loka-bāhyaḥ*—without caring for outsiders.

TRANSLATION

"'When a person is actually advanced and takes pleasure in chanting the holy name of the Lord, who is very dear to him, he is agitated and loudly chants the holy name. He also laughs, cries, becomes agitated and chants just like a madman, not caring for outsiders.'

TEXTS 95–96

এই তাঁর বাক্যে আমি দৃঢ় বিশ্বাস ধরি' ।
নিরন্তর কৃষ্ণনাম সংকীর্তন করি ॥ ৯৫ ॥
সেই কৃষ্ণনাম কভু গাওয়ায়, নাচায় ।
গাহি, নাচি নাহি আমি আপন-ইচ্ছায় ॥ ৯৬ ॥

ei tāṅra vākye āmi dṛḍha viśvāsa dhari'
nirantara kṛṣṇa-nāma saṅkīrtana kari

sei kṛṣṇa-nāma kabhu gāoyāya, nācāya
gāhi, nāci nāhi āmi āpana-icchāya

ei—this; *tāṅra*—his (My spiritual master's); *vākye*—in the words of; *āmi*—I; *dṛḍha*—firm; *viśvāsa*—faith; *dhari'*—depend; *nirantara*—

always; *kṛṣṇa-nāma*—the holy name of Lord Kṛṣṇa; *saṅkīrtana*—chanting; *kari*—continue; *sei*—that; *kṛṣṇa-nāma*—the holy name of Lord Kṛṣṇa; *kabhu*—sometimes; *gāoyāya*—causes Me to chant; *nācāya*—causes Me to dance; *gāhi*—by chanting; *nāci*—dancing; *nāhi*—not; *āmi*—Myself; *āpana*—own; *icchāya*—will.

TRANSLATION

"I firmly believe in these words of My spiritual master, and therefore I always chant the holy name of the Lord, alone and in the association of devotees. That holy name of Lord Kṛṣṇa sometimes causes Me to chant and dance, and therefore I chant and dance. Please do not think that I intentionally do it. I do it automatically.

PURPORT

A person who cannot keep his faith in the words of his spiritual master but acts independently never receives the authority to chant the holy name of the Lord. It is said in the *Vedas* (*Śvetāśvatara Up.* 6.23):

yasya deve parā bhaktir yathā deve tathā gurau
tasyaite kathitā hy arthāḥ prakāśante mahātmanaḥ

"Only unto those great souls who have implicit faith in both the Lord and the spiritual master are all the imports of Vedic knowledge automatically revealed." This Vedic injunction is very important, and Śrī Caitanya Mahāprabhu supported it by His personal behavior. Believing in the words of His spiritual master, He introduced the *saṅkīrtana* movement, just as the present Kṛṣṇa consciousness movement was started with belief in the words of our spiritual master. He wanted to preach, we believed in his words and tried somehow or other to fulfill them, and now this movement has become successful all over the world. Therefore faith in the words of the spiritual master and in the Supreme Personality of Godhead is the secret of success. Śrī Caitanya Mahāprabhu never disobeyed the orders of His spiritual master and stopped propagating the *saṅkīrtana* movement. Śrī Bhaktisiddhānta Sarasvatī Gosvāmī, at the time of his passing away, ordered all his disciples to work conjointly to preach the mission of Caitanya Mahāprabhu all over the world. Later, however, some self-interested, foolish disciples disobeyed his orders. Each one of them wanted to become head of the mission, and they fought in the courts, neglecting the order of the spiritual master, and the entire mission was defeated. We are not proud of this;

however, the truth must be explained. We believed in the words of our spiritual master and started in a humble way—in a helpless way—but due to the spiritual force of the order of the supreme authority, this movement has become successful.

It is to be understood that when Śrī Caitanya Mahāprabhu chanted and danced, He did so by the influence of the pleasure potency of the spiritual world. Śrī Caitanya Mahāprabhu never considered the holy name of the Lord to be a material vibration, nor does any pure devotee mistake the chanting of the Hare Kṛṣṇa *mantra* to be a material musical manifestation. Lord Caitanya never tried to be the master of the holy name; rather He taught us how to be servants of the holy name. If one chants the holy name of the Lord just to make a show, not knowing the secret of success, he may increase his bile secretion, but he will never attain perfection in chanting the holy name. Śrī Caitanya Mahāprabhu presented himself in this way: "I am a great fool and do not have knowledge of right and wrong. In order to understand the real meaning of the *Vedānta-sūtra*, I never followed the explanation of the Śaṅkara-sampradāya or Māyāvādī *sannyāsīs*. I'm very much afraid of the illogical arguments of the Māyāvādī philosophers. Therefore I think I have no authority regarding their explanations of the *Vedānta-sūtra*. I firmly believe that simply chanting the holy name of the Lord can remove all misconceptions of the material world. I believe that simply by chanting the holy name of the Lord one can attain the shelter of the lotus feet of the Lord. In this age of quarrel and disagreement, the chanting of the holy names is the only way to liberation from the material clutches.

"By chanting the holy name," Lord Caitanya continued, "I became almost mad. However, after inquiring from My spiritual master I have come to the conclusion that instead of striving for achievement in the four principles of religiosity [*dharma*], economic development [*artha*], sense gratification [*kāma*] and liberation [*mokṣa*], it is better if somehow or other one develops transcendental love of Godhead. That is the greatest success in life. One who has attained love of Godhead chants and dances by his nature, not caring for the public." This stage of life is known as *bhāgavata-jīvana*, or the life of a devotee.

Śrī Caitanya Mahāprabhu continued, "I never chanted and danced to make an artificial show. I dance and chant because I firmly believe in the words of My spiritual master. Although the Māyāvādī philosophers do not like this chanting and dancing, I nevertheless perform it on the strength of his words. Therefore it is to be concluded that I deserve very little credit for these activities of chanting and dancing, for they are being done automatically by the grace of the Supreme Personality of Godhead."

TEXT 97

কৃষ্ণনামে যে আনন্দসিন্ধু-আস্বাদন ।
ব্রহ্মানন্দ তার আগে খাতোদক-সম ॥ ৯৭ ॥

kṛṣṇa-nāme ye ānanda-sindhu-āsvādana
brahmānanda tāra āge khātodaka-sama

kṛṣṇa-nāme—in the holy name of the Lord; *ye*—which; *ānanda*—transcendental bliss; *sindhu*—ocean; *āsvādana*—tasting; *brahma-ānanda*—the transcendental bliss of impersonal understanding; *tāra*—its; *āge*—in front; *khāta-udaka*—shallow water in the canals; *sama*—like.

TRANSLATION

"Compared to the ocean of transcendental bliss that one tastes by chanting the Hare Kṛṣṇa mantra, the pleasure derived from impersonal Brahman realization [brahmānanda] is like the shallow water in a canal.

PURPORT

In the *Bhakti-rasāmṛta-sindhu* (1.1.38) it is stated:

brahmānando bhaved eṣa cet parārdha-guṇī-kṛtaḥ
naiti bhakti-sukhāmbhodheḥ paramāṇu-tulām api

"If *brahmānanda*, the transcendental bliss derived from understanding impersonal Brahman, were multiplied a million times, such a quantity of *brahmānanda* could not compare with even an atomic portion of the pleasure relished in pure devotional service."

TEXT 98

ত্বৎসাক্ষাৎকরণাহ্লাদ-বিশুদ্ধাব্ধিস্থিতস্য মে ।
সুখানি গোষ্পদায়ন্তে ব্রাহ্মাণ্যপি জগদ্গুরো ॥ ৯৮ ॥

tvat-sākṣāt-karaṇāhlāda-
viśuddhābdhi-sthitasya me

sukhāni goṣpadāyante
brāhmāṇy api jagad-guro

tvat—Your; *sākṣāt*—meeting; *karaṇa*—such action; *āhlāda*—pleasure; *viśuddha*—spiritually purified; *abdhi*—ocean; *sthitasya*—being situated; *me*—by me; *sukhāni*—happiness; *goṣpadāyante*—a small hole created by the hoof of a calf; *brāhmaṇi*—the pleasure derived from impersonal Brahman understanding; *api*—also; *jagat-guro*—O master of the universe.

TRANSLATION

"'My dear Lord, O master of the universe, since I have directly seen You, my transcendental bliss has taken the shape of a great ocean. Being situated in that ocean, I now realize all other so-called happiness to be like the water contained in the hoofprint of a calf.'"

PURPORT

The transcendental bliss enjoyed in pure devotional service is like an ocean, whereas material happiness and even the happiness to be derived from the realization of impersonal Brahman are just like the water in the hoofprint of a calf. This is a verse from the *Hari-bhakti-sudhodaya* (14.36).

TEXT 99

প্রভুর মিষ্টবাক্য শুনি' সন্ন্যাসীর গণ ।
চিত্ত ফিরি' গেল, কহে মধুর বচন ॥ ৯৯ ॥

prabhura miṣṭa-vākya śuni' sannyāsīra gaṇa
citta phiri' gela, kahe madhura vacana

prabhura—of the Lord; *miṣṭa-vākya*—sweet words; *śuni'*—after hearing; *sannyāsīra gaṇa*—all the groups of *sannyāsīs; citta*—consciousness; *phiri'*—moved; *gela*—went; *kahe*—said; *madhura*—pleasing; *vacana*—words.

TRANSLATION

After hearing Lord Śrī Caitanya Mahāprabhu, all the Māyāvādī sannyāsīs were moved. Their minds changed, and thus they spoke with pleasing words.

PURPORT

The Māyāvādī *sannyāsīs* met Caitanya Mahāprabhu at Vārāṇasī to criticize the Lord regarding His participation in the *saṅkīrtana* movement, which they did not like. This demonic nature of opposition to the *saṅkīrtana* movement perpetually exists. As it existed in the time of Śrī Caitanya Mahāprabhu, similarly it existed long before that, even in the time of Prahlāda Mahārāja. He used to chant in *saṅkīrtana* although his father did not like it, and that was the reason for the misunderstanding between the father and son. In the *Bhagavad-gītā* (7.15) the Lord says:

na māṁ duṣkṛtino mūḍhāḥ prapadyante narādhamāḥ
māyayāpahṛta-jñānā āsuraṁ bhāvam āśritāḥ

"Those miscreants who are grossly foolish, who are lowest among mankind, whose knowledge is stolen by illusion, and who partake of the atheistic nature of demons do not surrender unto Me." The Māyāvādī *sannyāsīs* are *āsuraṁ bhāvam āśritāḥ,* which means that they have taken the path of the *asuras* (demons), who do not believe in the existence of the form of the Lord. The Māyāvādīs say that the ultimate source of everything is impersonal, and in this way they deny the existence of God. Saying that there is no God is direct denial of God, and saying that God exists but has no head, legs or hands and cannot speak, hear or eat is a negative way of denying His existence. A person who cannot see is called blind, one who cannot walk is called lame, one who has no hands is called helpless, one who cannot speak is called dumb, and one who cannot hear is called deaf. The Māyāvādīs' proposition that God has no legs, no eyes, no ears and no hands is an indirect way of insulting Him by defining Him as blind, deaf, dumb, lame, helpless, etc. Therefore although they present themselves as great Vedāntists, they are factually *māyayāpahṛta-jñāna;* in other words, they seem to be very learned scholars, but the essence of their knowledge has been taken away.

Impersonalist Māyāvādīs always try to defy Vaiṣṇavas because Vaiṣṇavas accept the Supreme Personality as the supreme cause and want to serve Him, talk with Him and see Him, just as the Lord is also eager to see His devotees and talk, eat and dance with them. These personal exchanges of love do not appeal to the Māyāvādī *sannyāsīs.* Therefore the original purpose of the Māyāvādī *sannyāsīs* of Benares in meeting Caitanya Mahāprabhu was to defeat His personal conception of God. Śrī Caitanya Mahāprabhu, however, as a preacher, turned the minds of the Māyāvādī *sannyāsīs.* They were melted by the sweet words of Śrī Caitanya Mahāprabhu and thus became friendly and spoke to Him also in sweet words. Similarly, all preachers will have to meet opponents, but they should not make them more inimical. They are already enemies, and if we talk with them harshly or impolitely their enmity will merely increase. We should therefore follow in the footsteps of Lord Caitanya Mahāprabhu as far as possible and try to convince the opposition by quoting from the *śāstras* and presenting the conclusion of the *ācāryas.* It is in this way that we should try to defeat all the enemies of the Lord.

TEXT 100

যে কিছু কহিলে তুমি, সব সত্য হয় ।
কৃষ্ণপ্রেমা সেই পায়, যার ভাগ্যোদয় ॥ ১০০ ॥

ye kichu kahile tumi, saba satya haya
kṛṣṇa-premā sei pāya, yāra bhāgyodaya

ye—all; *kichu*—that; *kahile*—You spoke; *tumi*—You; *saba*—everything; *satya*—truth; *haya*—becomes; *kṛṣṇa-premā*—love of Godhead; *sei*—anyone; *pāya*—achieves; *yāra*—whose; *bhāgya-udaya*—fortune is now awakened.

TRANSLATION

"Dear Śrī Caitanya Mahāprabhu, what You have said is all true. Only one who is favored by fortune attains love of Godhead.

PURPORT

One who is actually very fortunate can begin Kṛṣṇa consciousness, as stated by Caitanya Mahāprabhu to Śrīla Rūpa Gosvāmī:

brahmāṇḍa bhramite kona bhāgyavān jīva
guru-kṛṣṇa-prasāde pāya bhakti-latā-bīja
(Cc. *Madhya* 19.151)

There are millions of living entities who have become conditioned by the laws of material nature, and they are wandering throughout the planetary systems of this universe in different bodily forms. Among them, one who is fortunate meets a bona fide spiritual master by the grace of Kṛṣṇa and comes to understand the meaning of devotional service. By discharging devotional service under the direction of the bona fide spiritual master, or *ācārya,* he develops love of Godhead. One whose love of Godhead (*kṛṣṇa-prema*) is awakened and who thus becomes a devotee of the inconceivable Supreme Personality of Godhead is to be considered extremely fortunate. The Māyāvādī *sannyāsīs* admitted this fact to Śrī Caitanya Mahāprabhu. It is not easy for one to become a Kṛṣṇa conscious person, but by the mercy of Śrī Caitanya Mahāprabhu it can be possible, as will be proven in the course of this narration.

TEXT 101

কৃষ্ণে ভক্তি কর—ইহার সবার সন্তোষ ।
বেদান্ত না শুন কেনে, তার কিবা দোষ ॥ ১০১ ॥

kṛṣṇe bhakti kara—ihāya sabāra santoṣa
vedānta nā śuna kene, tāra kibā doṣa

kṛṣṇe—unto Kṛṣṇa; *bhakti*—devotional service; *kara*—do; *ihāya*—in this matter; *sabāra*—of everyone; *santoṣa*—there is satisfaction; *vedānta*—the philosophy of the *Vedānta-sūtra; nā*—do not; *śuna*—hear; *kene*—why; *tāra*—of the philosophy; *kibā*—what is; *doṣa*—fault.

TRANSLATION

"Dear Sir, there is no objection to Your being a great devotee of Lord Kṛṣṇa. Everyone is satisfied with this. But why do You avoid discussion on the Vedānta-sūtra? What is the fault in it?"

PURPORT

Śrīla Bhaktisiddhānta Sarasvatī Ṭhākura comments in this connection, "Māyāvādī *sannyāsīs* accept that the commentary by Śrī Śaṅkarācārya known as *Śārīraka-bhāṣya* gives the real meaning of the *Vedanta-sūtra.* In other words, Māyāvādī *sannyāsīs* accept the meanings expressed in the explanations of the *Vedānta-sūtra* by Śaṅkarācārya, which are based on monism. Thus they explain the *Vedānta-sūtra,* the *Upaniṣads* and all such Vedic literatures in their own impersonal way." The great Māyāvādī *sannyāsī* Sadānanda Yogīndra has written a book known as *Vedānta-sāra,* in which he writes, *vedānto nāma upaniṣat-pramāṇam. tad-upakāriṇi śārīraka-sūtrādīni ca.* According to Sadānanda Yogīndra, the *Vedānta-sūtra* and *Upaniṣads,* as presented by Śrī Śaṅkarācārya in his *Śārīraka-bhāṣya* commentary, are the only sources of Vedic evidence. Actually, however, *Vedānta* refers to the essence of Vedic knowledge, and it is not a fact that there is nothing more than Śaṅkarācārya's *Śārīraka-bhāṣya.* There are other *Vedānta* commentaries, written by Vaiṣṇava *ācāryas,* none of whom follow Śrī Śaṅkarācārya or accept the imaginative commentary of his school. Their commentaries are based on the philosophy of duality. Monist philosophers like Śaṅkarācārya and his followers want to establish that God and the living entity are one, and instead of worshiping the Supreme Personality of Godhead they present themselves as God. They want to be worshiped as God by others. Such persons do not accept the philosophies of the Vaiṣṇava *ācāryas,* which are known as *śuddhādvaita* (purified monism), *śuddha-dvaita* (purified dualism), *viśiṣṭādvaita* (specific monism), *dvaitādvaita* (monism and dualism) and *acintya-bhedābheda* (inconceivable oneness and difference). Māyāvādīs do not discuss these philosophies, for they are firmly convinced of their own philosophy of *kevalādvaita,* exclusive monism. Accepting this system of philosophy as the pure understanding of the *Vedānta-sūtra,* they believe that Kṛṣṇa has a body made of material elements and that the activities of loving service to Kṛṣṇa are sentimentality. They are known as Māyāvādīs because according to their opinion Kṛṣṇa has a body made of *māyā* and the loving service of the Lord executed by devotees is also *māyā.* They consider such devotional service to be an aspect of fruitive activities (*karma-kāṇḍa*). According to their view, *bhakti* consists of mental speculation or sometimes meditation. This is the difference between the Māyāvādī and Vaiṣṇava philosophies.

TEXT 102

এত শুনি' হাসি' প্রভু বলিলা বচন ।
দুঃখ না মানহ যদি, করি নিবেদন ॥ ১০২ ॥

eta śuni' hāsi' prabhu balilā vacana
duḥkha nā mānaha yadi, kari nivedana

eta—thus; *śuni'*—hearing; *hāsi'*—smiling; *prabhu*—Lord Caitanya Mahāprabhu; *balilā*—said; *vacana*—His words; *duḥkha*—unhappy; *nā*—do not; *mānaha*—take it; *yadi*—if; *kari*—I say; *nivedana*—something unto you.

TRANSLATION

After hearing the Māyāvādī sannyāsīs speak in that way, Lord Caitanya Mahāprabhu smiled slightly and said, "My dear sirs, if you don't mind I can say something to you regarding Vedānta philosophy."

PURPORT

The Māyāvādī *sannyāsīs*, appreciating Lord Caitanya Mahāprabhu, inquired from Him why He did not discuss Vedānta philosophy. Actually, however, the entire system of Vaiṣṇava activities is based on Vedānta philosophy. Vaiṣṇavas do not neglect Vedānta, but they do not care to understand Vedānta on the basis of the *Śārīraka-bhāṣya* commentary. Therefore, to clarify the situation, Lord Śrī Caitanya Mahāprabhu, with the permission of the Māyāvādī *sannyāsīs*, wanted to speak regarding Vedānta philosophy.

The Vaiṣṇavas are by far the greatest philosophers in the world, and the greatest among them was Śrīla Jīva Gosvāmī Prabhu, whose philosophy was again presented less than four hundred years later by Śrīla Bhaktisiddhānta Sarasvatī Ṭhākura Mahārāja. Therefore one must know very well that Vaiṣṇava philosophers are not sentimentalists or cheap devotees like the *sahajiyās*. All the Vaiṣṇava *ācāryas* were vastly learned scholars who understood Vedānta philosophy fully, for unless one knows Vedānta philosophy he cannot be an *ācārya*. To be accepted as an *ācārya* among Indian transcendentalists who follow the Vedic principles, one must become a vastly learned scholar in Vedānta philosophy, either by studying it or hearing it.

Bhakti develops in pursuance of Vedānta philosophy. This is stated in *Śrīmad-Bhāgavatam* (1.2.12):

tac chraddadhānā munayo jñāna-vairāgya-yuktayā
paśyanty ātmani cātmānaṁ bhaktyā śruta-gṛhītayā

The words *bhaktyā śruta-gṛhītayā* in this verse are very important, for they indicate that *bhakti* must be based upon the philosophy of the *Upaniṣads* and *Vedānta-sūtra*. Śrīla Rūpa Gosvāmī said:

śruti-smṛti-purāṇādi-pañcarātra-vidhiṁ vinā
aikāntikī harer bhaktir utpātāyaiva kalpate

"Devotional service performed without reference to the *Vedas, Purāṇas, Pañcarātras,* etc., must be considered sentimentalism, and it causes nothing but disturbance to society." There are different grades of Vaiṣṇavas (*kaniṣṭha-adhikārī, madhyama-adhikārī* and *uttama-adhikārī*), but to be a *madhyama-adhikārī* preacher one must be a learned scholar in the *Vedānta-sūtra* and other Vedic literatures because when *bhakti-yoga* develops on the basis of Vedānta philosophy it is factual and steady. In this connection we may quote the translation and purport of the verse mentioned above (*Bhāg.* 1.2.12):

TRANSLATION

The seriously inquisitive student or sage, well equipped with knowledge and detachment, realizes that Absolute Truth by rendering devotional service in terms of what he has heard from the Vedānta-śruti.

PURPORT

The Absolute Truth is realized in full by the process of devotional service to the Lord, Vāsudeva, or the Personality of Godhead, who is the full-fledged Absolute Truth. Brahman is His transcendental bodily effulgence, and Paramātmā is His partial representation. As such, Brahman or Paramātmā realization of the Absolute Truth is but a partial realization. There are four different types of human beings—the *karmīs,* the *jñānīs,* the *yogīs* and the devotees. The *karmīs* are materialistic, whereas the other three are transcendental. The first-class transcendentalists are the devotees who have realized the Supreme Person. The second-class transcendentalists are those who have partially realized the plenary portion of the absolute person. And the third-class transcendentalists are those who have barely realized the spiritual focus of the absolute person. As stated in the *Bhagavad-gītā* and other Vedic literatures, the Supreme Person is realized by devotional service which is backed by full knowledge and detachment from material association. We have already discussed the point that devotional service is followed by knowledge and detachment from material association. As Brahman and Paramātmā realization are imperfect realizations of the Absolute Truth, so the means of realizing Brahman and Paramātmā, i.e., the paths of *jñāna* and *yoga,* are also imperfect means of realizing the Absolute Truth. Devotional service which is based on the foreground of full knowledge combined with detachment from material association, and which is fixed by dint of the aural reception of the *Vedānta-śruti,* is the only perfect method by which the seriously inquisitive student can realize the Absolute Truth. Devotional service is not, therefore, meant for the less intelligent class of transcendentalists.

There are three classes of devotees, namely, first, second and third class. The third-class devotees, or the neophytes, who have no knowledge and are not detached from material association, but who are simply attracted by the preliminary process of worshiping the Deity in the temple, are called material devotees. Material devotees are more attached to material benefit than transcendental profit. Therefore, one has to make definite progress from the position of material devotional service to the second-class devotional position. In the second-class position, the devotee can see four principles in the devotional line, namely, the Personality of Godhead, His devotees, the ignorant and the envious. One has to raise himself at least to the stage of a second-class devotee and thus become eligible to know the Absolute Truth.

A third-class devotee, therefore, has to receive the instructions of devotional service from the authoritative sources of *Bhāgavata*. The number one *Bhāgavata* is the established personality of devotee, and the other *Bhāgavata* is the message of Godhead. The third-class devotee therefore has to go to the personality of devotee in order to learn the instructions of devotional service. Such a personality of devotee is not a professional man who earns his livelihood by the business of the *Bhāgavatam*. Such a devotee must be a representative of Śukadeva Gosvāmī, like Sūta Gosvāmī, and must preach the cult of devotional service for the all-around benefit of all people. A neophyte devotee has very little taste for hearing from the authorities. Such a neophyte devotee makes a show of hearing from the professional man to satisfy his senses. This sort of hearing and chanting has spoiled the whole thing, so one should be very careful about the faulty process. The holy messages of Godhead, as inculcated in the *Bhagavad-gītā* or in *Śrīmad-Bhāgavatam*, are undoubtedly transcendental subjects, but even though they are so, such transcendental matters are not to be received from the professional man, who spoils them as the serpent spoils milk simply by the touch of his tongue.

A sincere devotee must, therefore, be prepared to hear the Vedic literature like the *Upaniṣads*, *Vedānta-sūtra* and other literatures left by the previous authorities, or Gosvāmīs, for the benefit of his progress. Without hearing such literatures, one cannot make actual progress. And without hearing and following the instructions, the show of devotional service becomes worthless and therefore a sort of disturbance in the path of devotional service. Unless, therefore, devotional service is established on the principles of *śruti, smṛti, Purāṇa* and *Pañcarātra* authorities, the make-show of devotional service should at once be rejected. An unauthorized devotee should never be recognized as a pure devotee. By assimilation of such messages from the Vedic literatures, one can see the all-pervading localized aspect of the Personality of Godhead within his own self constantly. This is called *samādhi*.

TEXT 103

ইহা শুনি' বলে সর্ব সন্ন্যাসীর গণ ।
তোমাকে দেখিয়ে যৈছে সাক্ষাৎ নারায়ণ ॥ ১০৩ ॥

ihā śuni' bale sarva sannyāsīra gaṇa
tomāke dekhiye yaiche sākṣāt nārāyaṇa

ihā—this; *śuni'*—hearing; *bale*—spoke; *sarva*—all; *sannyāsīra*—of the Māyāvādī *sannyāsīs; gaṇa*—group; *tomāke*—unto You; *dekhiye*—we see; *yaiche*—exactly like; *sākṣāt*—directly; *nārāyaṇa*—the Supreme Personality of Godhead.

TRANSLATION

Hearing this, the Māyāvādī sannyāsīs became somewhat humble and addressed Caitanya Mahāprabhu as Nārāyaṇa Himself, who they all agreed He was.

PURPORT

Māyāvādī *sannyāsīs* address each other as Nārāyaṇa. Whenever they see another *sannyāsī,* they offer him respect by calling *oṁ namo nārāyaṇāya* ("I offer my respect unto you, Nārāyaṇa"), although they know perfectly well what kind of Nārāyaṇa he is. Nārāyaṇa has four hands, but although they are puffed up with the idea of being Nārāyaṇa, they cannot exhibit more than two. Since their philosophy declares that Nārāyaṇa and an ordinary human being are on the same level, they sometimes use the term *daridra-nārāyaṇa* ("poor Nārāyaṇa"), which was invented by a so-called *svāmī* who did not know anything about Vedānta philosophy. Therefore although all these Māyāvādī *sannyāsīs* who called themselves Nārāyaṇa were actually unaware of the position of Nārāyaṇa, due to their austerities Lord Caitanya Mahāprabhu enabled them to understand Him to be Nārāyaṇa Himself. Lord Caitanya is certainly the Supreme Personality of Godhead Nārāyaṇa appearing as a devotee of Nārāyaṇa, and thus the Māyāvādī *sannyāsīs,* understanding that He was directly Nārāyaṇa Himself whereas they were false, puffed-up Nārāyaṇas, spoke to Him as follows.

TEXT 104

তোমার বচন শুনি' জুড়ায় শ্রবণ ।
তোমার মাধুরী দেখি' জুড়ায় নয়ন ॥ ১০৪ ॥

tomāra vacana śuni' juḍāya śravaṇa
tomāra mādhurī dekhi' juḍāya nayana

tomāra—Your; *vacana*—speeches; *śuni'*—hearing; *juḍāya*—very much satisfied; *śravaṇa*—aural reception; *tomāra*—Your; *mādhurī*—nectar; *dekhi'*—seeing; *juḍāya*—satisfies; *nayana*—our eyes.

TRANSLATION

"Dear Caitanya Mahāprabhu," they said, "to tell You the truth, we are greatly pleased to hear Your words, and furthermore Your bodily features are so pleasing that we feel extraordinary satisfaction in seeing You.

PURPORT

In the *śāstras* it is said:

ataḥ śrī-kṛṣṇa-nāmādi na bhaved grāhyam indriyaiḥ
sevonmukhe hi jihvādau svayam eva sphuraty adaḥ

"With one's materially contaminated senses one cannot understand the Supreme Personality of Godhead or His name, form, qualities or paraphernalia, but if one renders service unto Him, the Lord reveals Himself." (*Bhakti-rasāmṛta-sindhu* 1.2.234) Here one can see the effect of the Māyāvādī *sannyāsīs'* service toward Nārāyaṇa. Because the Māyāvādīs offered a little respect to Śrī Caitanya Mahāprabhu and because they were pious and actually followed the austere rules and regulations of *sannyāsa,* they had some understanding of Vedānta philosophy, and by the grace of Lord Caitanya Mahāprabhu they could appreciate that He was none other than the Supreme Personality of Godhead, who is endowed with all six opulences. One of these opulences is His beauty. By His extraordinarily beautiful bodily features, the Māyāvādī *sannyāsīs* recognized Śrī Caitanya Mahāprabhu as Nārāyaṇa Himself. He was not a farcical Nārāyaṇa like the *daridra-nārāyaṇas* invented by so-called *sannyāsīs.*

TEXT 105

তোমার প্রভাবে সবার আনন্দিত মন ।
কভু অসঙ্গত নহে তোমার বচন ॥ ১০৫ ॥

tomāra prabhāve sabāra ānandita mana
kabhu asaṅgata nahe tomāra vacana

tomāra—Your; *prabhāve*—by influence; *sabāra*—of everyone; *ānandita*—joyful; *mana*—mind; *kabhu*—at anytime; *asaṅgata*—unreasonable; *nahe*—does not; *tomāra*—Your; *vacana*—speeches.

TRANSLATION

"Dear Sir, by Your influence our minds are greatly satisfied, and we believe that Your words will never be unreasonable. Therefore You may speak on the Vedānta-sūtra."

PURPORT

In this verse the words *tomāra prabhāve* ("Your influence") are very important. Unless one is spiritually advanced he cannot influence an audience. Bhaktivinoda Ṭhākura has sung, *śuddha-bhakata-caraṇa-reṇu, bhajana-anukūla.* "Unless one associates with a pure devotee, he cannot be influenced to understand devotional service." These Māyāvādī *sannyāsīs* were fortunate enough to meet the Supreme Personality of Godhead in the form of a devotee, and certainly they were greatly influenced by the Lord. They knew that since a perfectly advanced spiritualist never says anything false, all his words are reasonable and agree with the Vedic version. A highly realized person never says anything that has no meaning. Māyāvādī philosophers claim to be the Supreme Personality of Godhead, and this has no meaning, but Śrī Caitanya Mahāprabhu never uttered such nonsense. The Māyāvādī *sannyāsīs* were convinced about His personality, and therefore they wanted to hear the purport of Vedānta philosophy from Him.

TEXT 106

প্রভু কহে, বেদান্ত-সূত্র ঈশ্বর-বচন ।
ব্যাসরূপে কৈল যাহা শ্রীনারায়ণ ॥ ১০৬ ॥

prabhu kahe, vedānta-sūtra īśvara-vacana
vyāsa-rūpe kaila yāhā śrī-nārāyaṇa

prabhu kahe—the Lord began to speak; *vedānta-sūtra*—the philosophy of *Vedanta-sūtra; īśvara-vacana*—spoken by the Supreme Personality of Godhead; *vyāsa-rūpe*—in the form of Vyāsadeva; *kaila*—He has made; *yāhā*—whatever; *śrī-nārāyaṇa*—the Supreme Personality of Godhead.

TRANSLATION

The Lord said, "Vedānta philosophy consists of words spoken by the Supreme Personality of Godhead Nārāyaṇa in the form of Vyāsadeva.

PURPORT

The *Vedānta-sūtra*, which consists of aphorisms revealing the method of understanding Vedic knowledge, is the concise form of all Vedic knowledge. It begins with the words *athāto brahma-jijñāsā:* "Now is the time to inquire about the Absolute Truth." The human form of life is especially meant for this purpose, and therefore the *Vedānta-sūtra* very concisely explains the human mission. This is confirmed by the words of the *Vāyu* and *Skanda Purāṇas*, which define a *sūtra* as follows:

alpākṣaram asandigdhaṁ sāra-vat viśvato-mukham
astobham anavadyaṁ ca sūtraṁ sūtra-vido viduḥ

"A *sūtra* is a compilation of aphorisms that expresses the essence of all knowledge in a minimum of words. It must be universally applicable and faultless in its linguistic presentation." Anyone familiar with such *sūtras* must be aware of the *Vedānta-sūtra*, which is well known among scholars by the following additional names: (1) *Brahma-sūtra*, (2) *Śārīraka*, (3) *Vyāsa-sūtra*, (4) *Bādarāyaṇa-sūtra*, (5) *Uttara-mīmāṁsā* and (6) *Vedānta-darśana*.

There are four chapters (*adhyāyas*) in the *Vedānta-sūtra*, and there are four divisions (*pādas*) in each chapter. Therefore the *Vedānta-sūtra* may be referred to as *ṣoḍaśa-pāda*, or sixteen divisions of aphorisms. The theme of each and every division is fully described in terms of five different subject matters (*adhikaraṇas*), which are technically called *pratijñā, hetu, udāharaṇa, upanaya* and *nigamana*. Every theme must necessarily be explained with reference to *pratijñā*, or a solemn declaration of the purpose of the treatise. The solemn declaration given in the beginning of the *Vedānta-sūtra* is *athāto brahma-jijñāsā*, which indicates that this book was written with the solemn declaration to inquire about the Absolute Truth. Similarly, reasons must be expressed (*hetu*), examples must be given in terms of various facts (*udāharaṇa*), the theme must gradually be brought nearer for understanding (*upanaya*), and finally it must be supported by authoritative quotations from the Vedic *śāstras* (*nigamana*).

According to the great dictionary compiler Hemacandra, also known as Koṣakāra, Vedānta refers to the purport of the *Upaniṣads* and the *Brāhmaṇa* portion of the *Vedas.* Professor Apte, in his dictionary, describes the *Brāhmaṇa* portion of the *Vedas* as that portion which states the rules for employment of hymns at various sacrifices and gives detailed explanations of their origin, sometimes with lengthy illustrations in the form of legends and stories. It is distinct from the *mantra* portion of the *Vedas.* Hemacandra says that the supplement of the *Vedas* is called the *Vedānta-sūtra. Veda* means knowledge, and *anta* means the end. In other words, proper understanding of the ultimate purpose of the *Vedas* is called Vedānta knowledge. Such knowledge, as given in the aphorisms of the *Vedānta-sūtra,* must be supported by the *Upaniṣads.*

According to learned scholars, there are three different sources of knowledge, which are called *prasthāna-traya.* According to these scholars, Vedānta is one of such sources, for it presents Vedic knowledge on the basis of logic and sound arguments. In the *Bhagavad-gītā* (13.5) the Lord says, *brahma-sūtra-padaiś caiva hetumadbhir viniścitaiḥ:* "Understanding of the ultimate goal of life is ascertained in the *Brahma-sūtra* by legitimate logic and argument concerning cause and effect." Therefore the *Vedānta-sūtra* is known as *nyāya-prasthāna,* the *Upaniṣads* are known as *śruti-prasthāna,* and the *Gītā, Mahābhārata* and *Purāṇas* are known as *smṛti-prasthāna.* All scientific knowledge of transcendence must be supported by *śruti, smṛti* and a sound logical basis.

It is said that both the Vedic knowledge and the supplement of the *Vedas* called the *Sātvata-pañcarātra* emanated from the breathing of Nārāyaṇa, the Supreme Personality of Godhead. The *Vedānta-sūtra* aphorisms were compiled by Śrīla Vyāsadeva, a powerful incarnation of Śrī Nārāyaṇa, although it is sometimes said that they were compiled by a great sage named Apāntaratamā. The *Pañcarātra* and *Vedānta-sūtra,* however, express the same opinions. Śrī Caitanya Mahāprabhu therefore confirms that there is no difference in opinion between the two, and He declares that because the *Vedānta-sūtra* was compiled by Śrīla Vyāsadeva, it may be understood to have emanated from the breathing of Śrī Nārāyaṇa. Śrīla Bhaktisiddhānta Sarasvatī Ṭhākura comments that while Vyāsadeva was compiling the *Vedānta-sūtra,* seven of his great saintly contemporaries were also engaged in similar work. These saints were Ātreya Ṛṣi, Āśmarathya, Auḍulomi, Kārṣṇājini, Kāśakṛtsna, Jaimini and Bādarī. In addition, it is stated that Pārāśarī and Karmandībhikṣu also discussed the *Vedānta-sūtra* aphorisms before Vyāsadeva.

As mentioned above, the *Vedānta-sūtra* consists of four chapters. The first two chapters discuss the relationship of the living entity with the Supreme Personality of Godhead. This is known as *sambandha-jñāna*, or knowledge of the relationship. The third chapter describes how one can act in his relationship with the Supreme Personality of Godhead. This is called *abhidheya-jñāna.* The relationship of the living entity with the Supreme Lord is described by Śrī Caitanya Mahāprabhu: *jīvera 'svarūpa' haya kṛṣṇera 'nitya-dāsa'.* "The living entity is an eternal servant of Kṛṣṇa, the Supreme God." (Cc. *Madhya* 20.108) Therefore, to act in that relationship one must perform *sādhana-bhakti*, or the prescribed duties of service to the Supreme Personality of Godhead. This is called *abhidheya-jñāna.* The fourth chapter describes the result of such devotional service (*prayojana-jñāna*). This ultimate goal of life is to go back home, back to Godhead. The words *anāvṛttiḥ śabdāt* in the *Vedānta-sūtra* indicate this ultimate goal.

Śrīla Vyāsadeva, a powerful incarnation of Nārāyaṇa, compiled the *Vedānta-sūtra*, and in order to protect it from unauthorized commentaries, he personally composed *Śrīmad-Bhāgavatam* on the instruction of his spiritual master, Nārada Muni, as the original commentary on the *Vedānta-sūtra.* Besides *Śrīmad-Bhāgavatam*, there are commentaries on the *Vedānta-sūtra* composed by all the major Vaiṣṇava *ācāryas*, and in each of them devotional service to the Lord is described very explicitly. Only those who follow Śaṅkara's commentary have described the *Vedānta-sūtra* in an impersonal way, without reference to *viṣṇu-bhakti*, or devotional service to the Lord, Viṣṇu. Generally people very much appreciate this *Śārīraka-bhāṣya*, or impersonal description of the *Vedānta-sūtra*, but all commentaries that are devoid of devotional service to Lord Viṣṇu must be considered to differ in purpose from the original *Vedānta-sūtra.* In other words, Lord Caitanya definitely confirmed that the commentaries, or *bhāṣyas*, written by the Vaiṣṇava *ācāryas* on the basis of devotional service to Lord Viṣṇu, and not the *Śārīraka-bhāṣya* of Śaṅkarācārya, give the actual explanation of the *Vedānta-sūtra.*

TEXT 107

ভ্রম, প্রমাদ, বিপ্রলিপ্সা, করণাপাটব ।
ঈশ্বরের বাক্যে নাহি দোষ এই সব ॥ ১০৭ ॥

bhrama, pramāda, vipralipsā, karaṇāpāṭava
īśvarera vākye nāhi doṣa ei saba

bhrama—mistake; *pramāda*—illusion; *vipralipsā*—cheating purposes; *karaṇa-apāṭava*—inefficiency of the material senses; *īśvarera*—of the Lord; *vākye*—in the speech; *nāhi*—there is not; *doṣa*—fault; *ei saba*—all this.

TRANSLATION

"The material defects of mistakes, illusions, cheating and sensory inefficiency do not exist in the words of the Supreme Personality of Godhead.

PURPORT

A mistake is the acceptance of an object to be different from what it is or the acceptance of false knowledge. For example, one may see a rope in the dark and think it to be a serpent, or one may see a glittering oyster shell and think it to be gold. These are mistakes. Similarly, an illusion is a misunderstanding that arises from inattention while hearing, and cheating is the transmission of such defective knowledge to others. Materialistic scientists and philosophers generally use such words as "maybe" and "perhaps" because they do not have actual knowledge of complete facts. Therefore their instructing others is an example of cheating. The final defect of the materialistic person is his inefficient senses. Although our eyes, for example, have the power to see, they cannot see that which is situated at a distance, nor can they see the eyelid, which is the object nearest to the eye. To our untrained eyes the sun appears to be just like a plate, and to the eyes of one who is suffering from jaundice everything appears to be yellow. Therefore we cannot rely on the knowledge acquired through such imperfect eyes. The ears are equally imperfect. We cannot hear a sound vibrated a long distance away unless we put a telephone to our ear. Similarly, if we analyze all our senses in this way, we will find them all to be imperfect. Therefore it is useless to acquire knowledge through the senses. The Vedic process is to hear from authority. In the *Bhagavad-gītā* (4.2) the Lord says, *evaṁ paramparā-prāptam imaṁ rājarṣayo viduḥ:* "The supreme science was thus received through the chain of disciplic succession, and the saintly kings understood it in that way." We have to hear not from a telephone but from an authorized person, for it is he who has real knowledge.

TEXT 108

উপনিষৎ-সহিত সূত্র কহে যেই তত্ত্ব ।
মুখ্যবৃত্ত্যে সেই অর্থ পরম মহত্ত্ব ॥ ১০৮ ॥

upaniṣat-sahita sūtra kahe yei tattva
mukhya-vṛttye sei artha parama mahattva

upaniṣat—the authorized Vedic version; *sahita*—along with; *sūtra*—the *Vedānta-sūtra; kahe*—it is said; *yei*—the subject matter; *tattva*—in truth; *mukhya-vṛttye*—by direct understanding; *sei*—that truth; *artha*—meaning; *parama*—ultimate; *mahattva*—glory.

TRANSLATION

"The Absolute Truth is described in the Upaniṣads and Brahma-sūtra, but one must understand the verses as they are. That is the supreme glory in understanding.

PURPORT

It has become fashionable since the time of Śaṅkarācārya to explain everything regarding the *śāstras* in an indirect way. Scholars take pride in explaining everything in their own way, and they declare that one can understand the Vedic scriptures in any way he likes. This "any way you like" method is foolishness, and it has created havoc in the Vedic culture. One cannot accept scientific knowledge in his own whimsical way. In the science of mathematics, for example, two plus two equals four, and one cannot make it equal three or five. Yet although it is not possible to alter real knowledge, people have taken to the fashion of understanding Vedic knowledge in any way they like. It is for this reason that we have presented *Bhagavad-gītā As It Is.* We do not create meanings by concoction. Sometimes commentators say that the word *kurukṣetra* in the first verse of the *Bhagavad-gītā* refers to one's body, but we do not accept this. We understand that Kurukṣetra is a place that still exists, and according to the Vedic version it is a *dharma-kṣetra,* or a place of pilgrimage. People still go there to perform Vedic sacrifices. Foolish commentators, however, say that *kurukṣetra* means the body and that *pañca-pāṇḍava* refers to the five senses. In this way they distort the meaning, and people are misled. Here Śrī Caitanya Mahāprabhu confirms that all Vedic literatures, including the *Upaniṣads, Brahma-sūtra* and others, whether *śruti, smṛti* or *nyāya*, must be understood according to their original statements. To describe the direct meaning of the Vedic literatures is glorious, but to describe them in one's own way, using imperfect senses and imperfect knowledge, is a disastrous blunder. Śrī Caitanya Mahāprabhu fully deprecated the attempt to describe the *Vedas* in this way.

Regarding the *Upaniṣads*, the following eleven *Upaniṣads* are considered to be the topmost: *Īśa, Kena, Kaṭha, Praśna, Muṇḍaka, Māṇḍūkya, Taittirīya, Aitareya, Chāndogya, Bṛhad-āraṇyaka* and *Śvetāśvatara*. However, in the *Muktikopaniṣad*, verses 30–39, there is a description of 108 *Upaniṣads*. They are as follows: (1) *Īśopaniṣad*, (2) *Kenopaniṣad*, (3) *Kaṭhopaniṣad*, (4) *Praśnopaniṣad*, (5) *Muṇḍakopaniṣad*, (6) *Māṇḍūkyopaniṣad*, (7) *Taittirīyopaniṣad*, (8) *Aitareyopaniṣad*, (9) *Chāndogyopaniṣad*, (10) *Bṛhad-āraṇyakopaniṣad*, (11) *Brahmopaniṣad*, (12) *Kaivalyopaniṣad*, (13) *Jābālopaniṣad*, (14) *Śvetāśvataropaniṣad*, (15) *Haṁsopaniṣad*, (16) *Āruṇeyopaniṣad*, (17) *Garbhopaniṣad*, (18) *Nārāyaṇopaniṣad*, (19) *Paramahaṁsopaniṣad*, (20) *Amṛta-bindūpaniṣad*, (21) *Nāda-bindūpaniṣad*, (22) *Śiropaniṣad*, (23) *Atharva-śikhopaniṣad*, (24) *Maitrāyaṇy-upaniṣad*, (25) *Kauṣītaky-upaniṣad*, (26) *Bṛhaj-jābālopaniṣad*, (27) *Nṛsiṁha-tāpanīyopaniṣad*, (28) *Kālāgni-rudropaniṣad*, (29) *Maitreyy-upaniṣad*, (30) *Subālopaniṣad*, (31) *Kṣurikopaniṣad*, (32) *Mantrikopaniṣad*, (33) *Sarva-sāropaniṣad*, (34) *Nirālambopaniṣad*, (35) *Śuka-rahasyopaniṣad*, (36) *Vajra-sūcikopaniṣad*, (37) *Tejo-bindūpaniṣad*, (38) *Nāda-bindūpaniṣad*, (39) *Dhyāna-bindūpaniṣad*, (40) *Brahma-vidyopaniṣad*, (41) *Yoga-tattvopaniṣad*, (42) *Ātma-bodhopaniṣad*, (43) *Nārada-parivrājakopaniṣad*, (44) *Triśikhy-upaniṣad*, (45) *Sītopaniṣad*, (46) *Yoga-cūḍāmaṇy-upaniṣad* (47) *Nirvāṇopaniṣad*, (48) *Maṇḍala-brāhmaṇopaniṣad*, (49) *Dakṣiṇā-mūrty-upaniṣad*, (50) *Śarabhopaniṣad*, (51) *Skandopaniṣad*, (52) *Mahānārāyaṇopaniṣad*, (53) *Advaya-tārakopaniṣad*, (54) *Rāma-rahasyopaniṣad*, (55) *Rāma-tāpaṇy-upaniṣad*, (56) *Vāsudevopaniṣad*, (57) *Mudgalopaniṣad*, (58) *Śāṇḍilyopaniṣad*, (59) *Paiṅgalopaniṣad*, (60) *Bhikṣūpaniṣad*, (61) *Mahad-upaniṣad*, (62) *Śārīrakopaniṣad*, (63) *Yoga-śikhopaniṣad*, (64) *Turīyātītopaniṣad*, (65) *Sannyāsopaniṣad*, (66) *Paramahaṁsa-parivrājakopaniṣad*, (67) *Mālikopaniṣad*, (68) *Avyaktopaniṣad*, (69) *Ekākṣaropaniṣad*, (70) *Pūrṇopaniṣad*, (71) *Sūryopaniṣad*, (72) *Akṣy-upaniṣad*, (73) *Adhyātmopaniṣad*, (74) *Kuṇḍikopaniṣad*, (75) *Sāvitry-upaniṣad*, (76) *Ātmopaniṣad*, (77) *Pāśupatopaniṣad*, (78) *Param-brahmopaniṣad*, (79) *Avadhūtopaniṣad*, (80) *Tripurātapanopaniṣad*, (81) *Devy-upaniṣad*, (82) *Tripuropaniṣad*, (83) *Kaṭha-rudropaniṣad*, (84) *Bhāvanopaniṣad*, (85) *Hṛdayopaniṣad*, (86) *Yoga-kuṇḍaliny-upaniṣad*, (87) *Bhasmopaniṣad*, (88) *Rudrākṣopaniṣad*, (89) *Gaṇopaniṣad*, (90) *Darśanopaniṣad*, (91) *Tāra-sāropaniṣad*, (92) *Mahā-vākyopaniṣad*, (93) *Pañca-brahmopaniṣad*, (94) *Prāṇāgni-hotropaniṣad*, (95) *Gopāla-tāpany-upaniṣad*, (96) *Kṛṣṇopaniṣad*, (97) *Yājñavalkyopaniṣad*, (98) *Varāhopaniṣad*, (99) *Śāṭyāyany-upaniṣad*, (100) *Hayagrīvopaniṣad*, (101) *Dattātreyopaniṣad*, (102) *Gāruḍo-*

panișad, (103) *Kaly-upanișad,* (104) *Jābāly-upanișad,* (105) *Saubhāgyopanișad,* (106) *Sarasvatī-rahasyopanișad,* (107) *Bahvṛcopanișad* and (108) *Muktikopanișad.* Thus there are 108 generally accepted *Upanișads,* of which eleven are the most important, as previously stated.

TEXT 109

গৌণ-বৃত্ত্যে যেবা ভাষ্য করিল আচার্য ।
তাহার শ্রবণে নাশ হয় সর্ব কার্য ॥ ১০৯ ॥

gauṇa-vṛttye yebā bhāṣya karila ācārya
tāhāra śravaṇe nāśa haya sarva kārya

gauṇa-vṛttye—by indirect meanings; *yebā*—which; *bhāṣya*—commentary; *karila*—prepared; *ācārya*—Śaṅkarācārya; *tāhāra*—its; *śravaṇe*—hearing; *nāśa*—destruction; *haya*—becomes; *sarva*—all; *kārya*—business.

TRANSLATION

"Śrīpāda Śaṅkarācārya has described all the Vedic literatures in terms of indirect meanings. One who hears such explanations is ruined.

TEXT 110

তাঁহার নাহিক দোষ, ঈশ্বর-আজ্ঞা পাঞা ।
গৌণার্থ করিল মুখ্য অর্থ আচ্ছাদিয়া ॥ ১১০ ॥

tāṅhāra nāhika doṣa, īśvara-ājñā pāñā
gauṇārtha karila mukhya artha ācchādiyā

tāṅhāra—of Śrī Śaṅkarācārya; *nāhika*—there is none; *doṣa*—fault; *īśvara*—the Supreme Lord; *ājñā*—order; *pāñā*—receiving; *gauṇa-artha*—indirect meaning; *karila*—make; *mukhya*—direct; *artha*—meaning; *ācchādiyā*—covering.

TRANSLATION

"Śaṅkarācārya is not at fault, for it is under the order of the Supreme Personality of Godhead that he has covered the real purpose of the Vedas.

PURPORT

The Vedic literature is to be considered a source of real knowledge, but if one does not take it as it is, one will be misled. For example, the *Bhagavad-gītā* is an important Vedic literature that has been taught for many years, but because it was commented upon by unscrupulous rascals, people derived no benefit from it, and no one came to the conclusion of Kṛṣṇa consciousness. Since the purpose of the *Bhagavad-gītā* is now being presented as it is, however, within four or five short years thousands of people all over the world have become Kṛṣṇa conscious. That is the difference between direct and indirect explanations of the Vedic literature. Therefore Śrī Caitanya Mahāprabhu said, *mukhya-vṛttye sei artha parama mahattva:* "To teach the Vedic literature according to its direct meaning, without false commentary, is glorious." Unfortunately, Śrī Śaṅkarācārya, by the order of the Supreme Personality of Godhead, compromised between atheism and theism in order to cheat the atheists and bring them to theism, and to do so he gave up the direct method of Vedic knowledge and tried to present a meaning which is indirect. It is with this purpose that he wrote his *Śārīraka-bhāṣya* commentary on the *Vedānta-sūtra.*

One should not, therefore, attribute very much importance to the *Śārīraka-bhāṣya.* In order to understand Vedānta philosophy, one must study *Śrīmad-Bhāgavatam,* which begins with the words *oṁ namo bhagavate vāsudevāya, janmādy asya yato 'nvayād itarataś cārtheṣv abhijñaḥ sva-rāṭ:* "I offer my obeisances unto Lord Śrī Kṛṣṇa, son of Vasudeva, who is the Supreme All-pervading Personality of Godhead. I meditate upon Him, the transcendent reality, who is the primeval cause of all causes, from whom all manifested universes arise, in whom they dwell and by whom they are destroyed. I meditate upon that eternally effulgent Lord, who is directly and indirectly conscious of all manifestations and yet is fully independent." (*Bhāg.* 1.1.1) *Śrīmad-Bhāgavatam* is the real commentary on the *Vedānta-sūtra.* Unfortunately, if one is attracted to Śrī Śaṅkarācārya's commentary, *Śārīraka-bhāṣya,* his spiritual life is doomed.

One may argue that since Śaṅkarācārya is an incarnation of Lord Śiva, how is it that he cheated people in this way? The answer is that he did so on the order of his master, the Supreme Personality of Godhead. This is confirmed in the *Padma Purāṇa,* in the words of Lord Śiva himself:

māyāvādam asac chāstraṁ pracchannaṁ bauddham ucyate
mayaiva kalpitaṁ devi kalau brāhmaṇa-rūpiṇā

brahmaṇaś cāparaṁ rūpaṁ nirguṇaṁ vakṣyate mayā
sarva-svaṁ jagato 'py asya mohanārthaṁ kalau yuge

vedānte tu mahā-śāstre māyāvādam avaidikam
mayaiva vakṣyate devi jagatāṁ nāśa-kāraṇāt

"The Māyāvāda philosophy," Lord Śiva informed his wife Pārvatī, "is impious [*asac chāstra*]. It is covered Buddhism. My dear Pārvatī, in Kali-yuga I assume the form of a *brāhmaṇa* and teach this imagined Māyāvāda philosophy. In order to cheat the atheists, I describe the Supreme Personality of Godhead to be without form and without qualities. Similarly, in explaining Vedānta I describe the same Māyāvāda philosophy in order to mislead the entire population toward atheism by denying the personal form of the Lord." In the *Śiva Purāṇa* the Supreme Personality of Godhead told Lord Śiva:

dvāparādau yuge bhūtvā kalayā mānuṣādiṣu
svāgamaiḥ kalpitais tvaṁ ca janān mad-vimukhān kuru

"In Kali-yuga, mislead the people in general by propounding imaginary meanings for the *Vedas* to bewilder them." These are the descriptions of the *Purāṇas.*

Śrīla Bhaktisiddhānta Sarasvatī Ṭhākura comments that *mukhya-vṛtti* ("the direct meaning") is *abhidhā-vṛtti,* or the meaning that one can understand immediately from the statements of dictionaries, whereas *gauṇa-vṛtti* ("the indirect meaning") is a meaning that one imagines without consulting the dictionary. For example, one politician has said that Kurukṣetra refers to the body, but in the dictionary there is no such definition. Therefore this imaginary meaning is *gauṇa-vṛtti,* whereas the direct meaning found in the dictionary is *mukhya-vṛtti* or *abhidhā-vṛtti.* This is the distinction between the two. Śrī Caitanya Mahāprabhu recommends that one understand the Vedic literature in terms of *abhidhā-vṛtti,* and the *gauṇa-vṛtti* He rejects. Sometimes, however, as a matter of necessity, the Vedic literature is described in terms of the *lakṣaṇā-vṛtti* or *gauṇa-vṛtti,* but one should not accept such explanations as permanent truths.

The purpose of the discussions in the *Upaniṣads* and *Vedānta-sūtra* is to philosophically establish the personal feature of the Absolute Truth. The impersonalists, however, in order to establish their philosophy, accept these discussions in terms of *lakṣaṇā-vṛtti,* or indirect meanings. Thus instead of being *tattva-vāda,* or in search of the Absolute Truth, they become Māyāvāda, or illusioned by the material energy. When Śrī Viṣṇu Svāmī, one of the four *ācāryas* of the Vaiṣṇava cult, presented his thesis on the subject matter of *śuddhādvaita-vāda,* immediately the Māyāvādīs took advantage of this philosophy and tried to establish their *advaita-vāda* or *kevalādvaita-vāda.* To defeat this *kevalādvaita-vāda,* Śrī Rāmānujācārya presented his philosophy as *viśiṣṭādvaita-vāda,* and Śrī Madhvācārya presented his philosophy of *tattva-vāda,* both of which are stumbling blocks to the Māyāvādīs because they defeat their philosophy in scrupulous detail. Students of Vedic philosophy know very well how strongly Śrī Rāmānujācārya's *viśiṣṭādvaita-vāda* and Śrī Madhvācārya's *tattva-vāda* contest the impersonal Māyāvāda philosophy. Śrī Caitanya Mahāprabhu, however, accepted the direct meaning of the Vedānta philosophy and thus defeated the Māyāvāda philosophy immediately. He opined in this connection that anyone who follows the principles of the *Śārīraka-bhāṣya* is doomed. This is confirmed in the *Padma Purāṇa,* where Lord Śiva tells Pārvatī:

śṛṇu devi pravakṣyāmi tāmasāni yathā-kramam
yeṣāṁ śravaṇa-mātreṇa pātityaṁ jñāninām api

apārthaṁ śruti-vākyānāṁ darśayal loka-garhitam
karma-svarūpa-tyājyatvam atra ca pratipādyate

sarva-karma-paribhraṁśān naiṣkarmyaṁ tatra cocyate
parātma-jīvayor aikyaṁ mayātra pratipādyate

"My dear wife, hear my explanations of how I have spread ignorance through Māyāvāda philosophy. Simply by hearing it, even an advanced scholar will fall down. In this philosophy, which is certainly very inauspicious for people in general, I have misrepresented the real meaning of the *Vedas* and recommended that one give up all activities in order to achieve freedom from *karma.* In this Māyāvāda philosophy I have described the *jīvātmā* and Paramātmā to be one and the same." How the Māyāvāda philosophy was condemned by Śrī Caitanya Mahāprabhu and His followers is described in *Śrī Caitanya-caritāmṛta, Antya-līlā,* Second Chapter, verses 94 through 99, where Svarūpa-dāmodara Gosvāmī says that anyone who is eager to understand the Māyāvāda philosophy must be considered insane. This especially applies to a Vaiṣṇava who reads the *Śārīraka-bhāṣya* and considers himself to be one with God. The Māyāvādī philosophers have presented their arguments in such attractive, flowery language that hearing Māyāvāda philosophy may sometimes change the mind of even a *mahā-bhāgavata,* or very advanced devotee. An actual Vaiṣṇava cannot tolerate any philosophy that claims God and the living being to be one and the same.

TEXT 111

'ব্রহ্ম'-শব্দে মুখ্য অর্থে কহে—'ভগবান' ।
চিদৈশ্বর্য-পরিপূর্ণ, অনূর্ধ্ব-সমান ॥ ১১১ ॥

'brahma'-śabde mukhya arthe kahe—'bhagavān'
cid-aiśvarya-paripūrṇa, anūrdhva-samāna

brahma—the Absolute Truth; *śabde*—by this word; *mukhya*—direct; *arthe*—meaning; *kahe*—says; *bhagavān*—the Supreme Personality of Godhead; *cit-aiśvarya*—spiritual opulence; *paripūrṇa*—full of; *anūrdhva*—unsurpassed by anyone; *samāna*—not equaled by anyone.

TRANSLATION

"According to direct understanding, the Absolute Truth is the Supreme Personality of Godhead, who has all spiritual opulences. No one can be equal to or greater than Him.

PURPORT

This statement by Śrī Caitanya Mahāprabhu is confirmed in *Śrīmad-Bhāgavatam* (1.2.11):

vadanti tat tattva-vidas tattvaṁ yaj jñānam advayam
brahmeti paramātmeti bhagavān iti śabdyate

"Learned transcendentalists who know the Absolute Truth call this nondual substance Brahman, Paramātmā or Bhagavān." The Absolute Truth is ultimately understood as Bhagavān, partially understood as Paramātmā and vaguely understood as the impersonal Brahman. Bhagavān, or the Supreme Personality of Godhead, is opulent in all excellence; no one can be equal to or greater than Him. This is also confirmed in the *Bhagavad-gītā* (7.7), where the Lord says, *mattaḥ parataraṁ nānyat kiñcid asti dhanañjaya:* "O conqueror of wealth [Arjuna], there is no truth superior to Me." There are many other verses which prove that the Absolute Truth in the ultimate sense is understood to be the Supreme Personality of Godhead, Kṛṣṇa.

TEXT 112

তাঁহার বিভূতি, দেহ,—সব চিদাকার ।
চিদ্বিভূতি আচ্ছাদি' তাঁরে কহে 'নিরাকার' ॥ ১১২ ॥

tāṅhāra vibhūti, deha,—saba cid-ākāra
cid-vibhūti ācchādi' tāṅre kahe 'nirākāra'

tāṅhāra—His (the Supreme Personality of Godhead's); *vibhūti*—spiritual power; *deha*—body; *saba*—everything; *cit-ākāra*—spiritual form; *cit-vibhūti*—spiritual opulence; *ācchādi'*—covering; *tāṅre*—Him; *kahe*—says; *nirākāra*—without form.

TRANSLATION

"Everything about the Supreme Personality of Godhead is spiritual, including His body, opulence and paraphernalia. Māyāvāda philosophy, however, covering His spiritual opulence, advocates the theory of impersonalism.

PURPORT

It is stated in the *Brahma-saṁhitā, īśvaraḥ paramaḥ kṛṣṇaḥ sac-cid-ānanda-vigrahaḥ:* "The Supreme Personality of Godhead, Kṛṣṇa, has a spiritual body which is full of knowledge, eternity and bliss." In this material world everyone's body is just the opposite—temporary, full of ignorance and full of misery. Therefore when the Supreme Personality of Godhead is sometimes described as *nirākāra*, this is to indicate that He does not have a material body like us.

Māyāvādī philosophers do not know how it is that the Supreme Personality of Godhead is formless. The Supreme Lord does not have a form like ours but has a spiritual form. Not knowing this, Māyāvādī philosophers simply advocate the onesided view that the Supreme Godhead, or Brahman, is formless (*nirākāra*). In this connection Śrīla Bhaktivinoda Ṭhākura offers many quotes from the Vedic literature. If one accepts the real or direct meaning of these Vedic statements, one can understand that the Supreme Personality of Godhead has a spiritual body (*sac-cid-ānanda-vigraha*).

In the *Bṛhad-āraṇyaka Upaniṣad* (5.1.1) it is said, *pūrṇam adaḥ pūrṇam idaṁ pūrṇāt pūrṇam udacyate.* This indicates that the body of the Supreme Personality of Godhead is spiritual, for even though He expands in many ways, He remains the same. In the *Bhagavad-gītā*

(10.8) the Lord says, *ahaṁ sarvasya prabhavo mattaḥ sarvaṁ pravartate:* "I am the origin of all. Everything emanates from Me." Māyāvādī philosophers materialistically think that if the Supreme Truth expands Himself in everything, He must lose His original form. Thus they think that there cannot be any form other than the expansive gigantic body of the Lord. But the *Bṛhad-āraṇyaka Upaniṣad* confirms, *pūrṇam idaṁ pūrṇāt pūrṇam udacyate:* "Although He expands in many ways, He keeps His original personality. His original spiritual body remains as it is." Similarly, elsewhere it is stated, *vicitra-śaktiḥ puruṣaḥ purāṇaḥ:* "The Supreme Personality of Godhead, the original person [*puruṣa*], has multifarious energies." And the *Śvetāśvatara Upaniṣad* declares, *sa vṛkṣa-kālākṛtibhiḥ paro 'nyo yasmāt prapañcaḥ parivartate 'yaṁ dharmāvahaṁ pāpanudaṁ bhageśam:* "He is the origin of material creation, and it is due to Him only that everything changes. He is the protector of religion and annihilator of all sinful activities. He is the master of all opulences." (*Śvet. Up.* 6.6) *Vedāham etaṁ puruṣaṁ mahāntam āditya-varṇaṁ tamasaḥ parastāt:* "Now I understand the Supreme Personality of Godhead to be the greatest of the great. He is effulgent like the sun and is beyond this material world." (*Śvet. Up.* 3.8) *Patiṁ patīnāṁ paramaṁ parastāt:* "He is the master of all masters, the superior of all superiors." (*Śvet. Up.* 6.7) *Mahān prabhur vai puruṣaḥ:* "He is the supreme master and supreme person." (*Śvet. Up.* 3.12) *Parāsya śaktir vividhaiva śrūyate:* "We can understand His opulences in different ways." (*Śvet. Up.* 6.8) Similarly, in the *Ṛg Veda* it is stated, *tad viṣṇoḥ paramaṁ padaṁ sadā paśyanti sūrayaḥ:* "Viṣṇu is the Supreme, and those who are actually learned think only of His lotus feet." In the *Praśna Upaniṣad* (6.3) it is said, *sa īkṣāṁ cakre:* "He glanced over the material creation." In the *Aitareya Upaniṣad* (1.1.1–2) it is said, *sa aikṣata*—"He glanced over the material creation"—and *sa imāl̐ lokān asṛjata*—"He created this entire material world."

Thus many verses can be quoted from the *Upaniṣads* and *Vedas* which prove that the Supreme Godhead is not impersonal. In the *Kaṭha Upaniṣad* (2.2.13) it is also said, *nityo nityānāṁ cetanaś cetanānām eko bahūnāṁ yo vidadhāti kāmān:* "He is the supreme eternally conscious person, who maintains all other living entities." From all these Vedic references one can understand that the Absolute Truth is a person and that no one can equal or excel Him. Although there are many foolish Māyāvādī philosophers who think that they are even greater than Kṛṣṇa, Kṛṣṇa is *asamaurdhva:* no one is equal to or above Him.

As stated in the *Śvetāśvatara Upaniṣad* (3.19), *apāṇi-pādo javano grahītā.* This verse describes the Absolute Truth as having no legs or hands. Although this is an impersonal description, it does not mean that the Absolute Personality of Godhead has no form. He has a spiritual form that is distinct from the forms of matter. In this verse Caitanya Mahāprabhu clarifies this distinction.

TEXT 113

চিদানন্দ—তেঁহো, তাঁর স্থান, পরিবার।
তাঁরে কহে—প্রাকৃত-সত্ত্বের বিকার ॥ ১১৩ ॥

cid-ānanda—teṅho, tāṅra sthāna, parivāra
tāṅre kahe—prākṛta-sattvera vikāra

cit-ānanda—spiritual bliss; *teṅho*—He is personally; *tāṅra*—His; *sthāna*—abode; *parivāra*—entourage; *tāṅre*—unto Him; *kahe*—someone says; *prākṛta*—material; *sattvera*—goodness; *vikāra*—transformation.

TRANSLATION

"The Supreme Personality of Godhead is full of spiritual potencies. Therefore His body, name, fame and entourage are all spiritual. The Māyāvādī philosopher, due to ignorance, says that these are all merely transformations of the material mode of goodness.

PURPORT

In the Seventh Chapter of the *Bhagavad-gītā* the Supreme Personality of Godhead has classified His energies in two distinct divisions—namely, *prākṛta* and *aprākṛta*, or *parā-prakṛti* and *aparā-prakṛti.* In the *Viṣṇu Purāṇa* the same distinction is made. The Māyāvādī philosophers cannot understand these two *prakṛtis*, or natures—material and spiritual—but one who is actually intelligent can understand them. Considering the many varieties and activities in material nature, why should the Māyāvādī philosophers deny the spiritual varieties of the spiritual world? The *Bhāgavatam* (10.2.32) says:

ye 'nye 'ravindākṣa vimukta-māninas
tvayy asta-bhāvād aviśuddha-buddhayaḥ

The intelligence of those who think themselves liberated but have no information of the spiritual world is not yet clear. In this verse the term *aviśuddha-buddhayaḥ* refers to unclean intelligence. Due to unclean intelligence or a poor fund of knowledge, the Māyāvādī philosophers cannot understand the distinction between material and spiritual varieties; therefore they cannot even think of spiritual varieties because they take it for granted that all variety is material.

Śrī Caitanya Mahāprabhu, therefore, explains in this verse that Kṛṣṇa—the Supreme Personality of Godhead, or the Absolute Truth—has a spiritual body that is distinct from material bodies, and thus His name, abode, entourage and qualities are all spiritual. The material mode of goodness has nothing to do with spiritual varieties. Māyāvādī philosophers, however, cannot clearly understand spiritual varieties; therefore they imagine a negation of the material world to be the spiritual world. The material qualities of goodness, passion and ignorance cannot act in the spiritual world, which is therefore called *nirguṇa,* as clearly indicated in the *Bhagavad-gītā* (*trai-guṇya-viṣayā vedā nistraiguṇyo bhavārjuna*). The material world is a manifestation of the three modes of material nature, but one has to become free from these modes to come to the spiritual world, where their influence is completely absent. Now Lord Śrī Caitanya Mahāprabhu will disassociate Lord Śiva from Māyāvāda philosophy in the following verse.

TEXT 114

তাঁর দোষ নাহি, তেঁহো আজ্ঞাকারী দাস ।
আর যেই শুনে তার হয় সর্বনাশ ॥ ১১৪ ॥

tāṅra doṣa nāhi, teṅho ājñā-kārī dāsa
āra yei śune tāra haya sarva-nāśa

tāṅra—his (Lord Śiva's); *doṣa*—fault; *nāhi*—there is none; *teṅho*—he; *ājñā-kārī*—obedient order-carrier; *dāsa*—servant; *āra*—others; *yei*—anyone; *śune*—hears (the Māyāvāda philosophy); *tāra*—of him; *haya*—becomes; *sarva-nāśa*—everything lost

TRANSLATION

"Śaṅkarācārya, who is an incarnation of Lord Śiva, is faultless because he is a servant carrying out the orders of the Lord. But those who follow his Māyāvādī philosophy are doomed. They will lose all their advancement in spiritual knowledge.

PURPORT

Māyāvādī philosophers are very proud of exhibiting their Vedānta knowledge through grammatical jugglery, but in the *Bhagavad-gītā* Lord Śrī Kṛṣṇa certifies that they are *māyayāpahṛta-jñāna*, bereft of real knowledge due to *māyā*. *Māyā* has two potencies with which to execute her two functions—the *prakṣepātmikā-śakti*, the power to throw the living entity into the ocean of material existence, and the *āvaraṇātmikā-śakti*, the power to cover the knowledge of the living entity. The function of the *āvaraṇātmikā-śakti* is explained in the *Bhagavad-gītā* by the word *māyayāpahṛta-jñānāḥ*.

Why the *daivī-māyā*, or illusory energy of Kṛṣṇa, takes away the knowledge of the Māyāvādī philosophers is also explained in the *Bhagavad-gita* by the use of the words *āsuraṁ bhāvam āśritāḥ*, which refer to a person who does not agree to the existence of the Lord. The Māyāvādīs, who are not in agreement with the existence of the Lord, can be classified in two groups, exemplified by the impersonalist Śaṅkarites of Vārāṇasī and the Buddhists of Saranātha. Both groups are Māyāvādīs, and Kṛṣṇa takes away their knowledge due to their atheistic philosophies. Neither group agrees to accept the existence of a personal God. The Buddhist philosophers clearly deny both the soul and God, and although the Śaṅkarites do not openly deny God, they say that the Absolute is *nirākāra*, or formless. Thus both the Buddhists and the Śaṅkarites are *aviśuddha-buddhayaḥ*, or imperfect and unclean in their knowledge and intelligence.

The most prominent Māyāvādī scholar, Sadānanda Yogīndra, has written a book called *Vedānta-sāra*, in which he expounds the philosophy of Śaṅkarācārya, and all the followers of Śaṅkara's philosophy attribute great importance to his statements. In this *Vedānta-sāra* Sadānanda Yogīndra defines Brahman as *sac-cid-ānanda* combined with knowledge and without duality, and he defines ignorance (*jaḍa*) as knowledge distinct from that of *sat* and *asat*. This is almost inconceivable, but it is a product of the three material qualities. Thus he considers anything other than pure knowledge to be material. The center of ignorance is considered to be sometimes all-pervading and sometimes individual. Thus according to his opinion both the all-pervading Viṣṇu and the individual living entities are products of ignorance.

In simple language, it is the opinion of Sadānanda Yogīndra that since everything is *nirākāra* (formless), the conception of Viṣṇu and the conception of the individual soul are both products of ignorance. He also explains that the *viśuddha-sattva* conception of the Vaiṣṇavas is nothing but *pradhāna,* or the chief principle of creation. He maintains that when all-pervading knowledge is contaminated by the *viśuddha-sattva,* which consists of a transformation of the quality of goodness, there arises the conception of the Supreme Personality of Godhead, who is the omnipotent, omniscient supreme ruler, the Supersoul, the cause of all causes, the supreme *īśvara,* etc. According to Sadānanda Yogīndra, because *īśvara,* the Supreme Lord, is the reservoir of all ignorance, He may be called *sarva-jña,* or omniscient, but one who denies the existence of the omnipotent Supreme Personality of Godhead is more than *īśvara,* or the Lord. His conclusion, therefore, is that the Supreme Personality of Godhead (*īśvara*) is a transformation of material ignorance and that the living entity (*jīva*) is covered by ignorance. Thus he describes both collective and individual existence in darkness. According to Māyāvādī philosophers, the Vaiṣṇava conception of the Lord as the Supreme Personality of Godhead and of the *jīva,* or individual soul, as His eternal servant is a manifestation of ignorance. If we accept the judgment of Lord Kṛṣṇa in the *Bhagavad-gītā,* however, the Māyāvādīs are to be considered *māyayāpahṛta-jñāna,* or bereft of all knowledge, because they do not recognize the existence of the Supreme Personality of Godhead or they claim that His existence is a product of the material conception (*māyā*). These are characteristics of *asuras,* or demons.

Lord Śrī Caitanya Mahāprabhu, in His discourses with Sārvabhauma Bhaṭṭācārya, said:

jīvera nistāra lāgi' sūtra kaila vyāsa
māyāvādi-bhāṣya śunile haya sarva-nāśa
(Cc. *Madhya* 6.169)

Vyāsadeva composed the *Vedānta-sūtra* to deliver the conditioned souls from this material world, but Śaṅkarācārya, by presenting the *Vedānta-sūtra* in his own way, has clearly done a great disservice to human society, for one who follows his Māyāvāda philosophy is doomed. In the *Vedanta-sūtra,* devotional service is clearly indicated, but the Māyāvādī philosophers refuse to accept the spiritual body of the Supreme Absolute Person and refuse to accept that the living entity has an individual existence separate from that of the Supreme Lord. Thus they have created atheistic havoc all over the world, for such a conclusion is against the very nature of the transcendental process of pure devotional service. The Māyāvādī philosophers' unrealizable ambition to become one with the Supreme through denying the existence of the Personality of Godhead results in a most calamitous misrepresentation of spiritual knowledge, and one who follows this philosophy is doomed to remain perpetually in this material world. Therefore the Māyāvādīs are called *aviśuddha-buddhayaḥ*, or unclean in knowledge. Because they are unclean in knowledge, all their austerities and penances end in frustration. Thus although they may be honored at first as very learned scholars, ultimately they descend to physical activities of politics, social work, etc. Instead of becoming one with the Supreme Lord, they again become one with these material activities. This is explained in *Śrīmad-Bhāgavatam*(10.2.32):

āruhya kṛcchreṇa paraṁ padaṁ tataḥ
patanty adho 'nādṛta-yuṣmad-aṅghrayaḥ

In actuality the Māyāvādī philosophers very strictly follow the austerities and penances of spiritual life and in this way are elevated to the impersonal Brahman platform, but due to their negligence of the lotus feet of the Lord they again fall down to material existence.

TEXT 115

প্রাকৃত করিয়া মানে বিষ্ণু-কলেবর ।
বিষ্ণুনিন্দা আর নাহি ইহার উপর ॥ ১১৫ ॥

prākṛta kariyā māne viṣṇu-kalevara
viṣṇu-nindā āra nāhi ihāra upara

prākṛta—material; *kariyā*—taking it to be so; *māne*—accepts; *viṣṇu*—Lord Viṣṇu's; *kalevara*—body; *viṣṇu-nindā*—defaming or blaspheming Lord Viṣṇu; *āra*—beyond this; *nāhi*—none; *ihāra*—of this; *upara*—above.

TRANSLATION

"One who considers the transcendental body of Lord Viṣṇu to be made of material nature is the greatest offender at the lotus feet of the Lord. There is no greater blasphemy against the Supreme Personality of Godhead.

PURPORT

Śrī Bhaktisiddhānta Sarasvatī Gosvāmī explains that the variegated personal feature of the Absolute Truth is the *viṣṇu-tattva* and that the material energy, which creates this cosmic manifestation, is the energy of Lord Viṣṇu. The creative force is merely the energy of the Lord, but the foolish conclude that because the Lord has distributed Himself in an impersonal form He has no separate existence. The impersonal Brahman, however, cannot possess energies, nor do the Vedic literatures state that *māyā* (the illusory energy) is covered by another *māyā.* There are hundreds and thousands of references, however, to *viṣṇu-māyā* (*parāsya śaktiḥ*), or the energy of Lord Viṣṇu. In the *Bhagavad-gītā* (7.14) Kṛṣṇa refers to *mama māyā* ("My energy"). *Māyā* is controlled by the Supreme Personality of Godhead; it is not that He is covered by *māyā.* Therefore Lord Viṣṇu cannot be a product of the material energy. In the beginning of the *Vedānta-sūtra* it is said, *janmādy asya yataḥ,* indicating that the material energy is also an emanation of the Supreme Brahman. How then could He be covered by the material energy? If that were possible, material energy would be greater than the Supreme Brahman. Even these simple arguments, however, cannot be understood by the Māyāvādī philosophers, and therefore the term *māyayāpahṛta-jñāna,* which is applied to them in the *Bhagavad-gītā,* is extremely appropriate. Anyone who thinks that Lord Viṣṇu is a product of the material energy, as explained by Sadānanda Yogīndra, should immediately be understood to be insane, for his knowledge has been stolen by the illusory energy.

Lord Viṣṇu cannot be placed within the category of the demigods. Those who are actually bewildered by the Māyāvāda philosophy and are still in the darkness of ignorance consider Lord Viṣṇu to be a demigod, in defiance of the Ṛg-vedic *mantra oṁ tad viṣṇoḥ paramaṁ padam* ("Viṣṇu is always in a superior position"). This *mantra* is confirmed in the *Bhagavad-gītā: mattaḥ parataraṁ nānyat*—there is no truth superior to Lord Kṛṣṇa, or Viṣṇu. Thus only those whose knowledge has been bewildered consider Lord Viṣṇu to be a demigod and therefore suggest that one may worship either Lord Viṣṇu, the goddess Kālī (Durgā) or whomever one likes and achieve the same result. This is an ignorant conclusion that is not accepted in the *Bhagavad-gītā* (9.25), which distinctly says, *yānti deva-vratā devān . . . yānti mad-yājino 'pi mām:* The worshipers of the demigods will be promoted to the respective planets of the demigods, but devotees of the Supreme Lord will go back home, back to Godhead. Lord Kṛṣṇa explains very clearly in the *Bhagavad-gītā* (7.14) that His material energy is very difficult to overcome: *daivī hy eṣā guṇa-mayī mama māyā duratyayā. Māyā's* influence is so strong that even learned scholars and spiritualists are also covered by *māyā* and think themselves to be as good as the Supreme Personality of

Godhead. Actually, however, to free oneself from the influence of *māyā* one must surrender to the Supreme Personality of Godhead, as Kṛṣṇa also states in the *Bhagavad-gītā* (7.14): *mām eva ye prapadyante māyām etāṁ taranti te.* It is to be concluded, therefore, that Lord Viṣṇu does not belong to this material creation but to the spiritual world. To misconceive Lord Viṣṇu to have a material body or to equate Him with the demigods is the most offensive blasphemy against Lord Viṣṇu, and offenders against the lotus feet of Lord Viṣṇu cannot advance in spiritual knowledge. They are called *māyayāpahṛta-jñāna*, or those whose knowledge has been stolen by the influence of illusion.

One who thinks that there is a difference between Lord Viṣṇu's body and His soul dwells in the darkest region of ignorance. There is no difference between Lord Viṣṇu's body and Viṣṇu's soul, for they are *advaya-jñāna*, one knowledge. In this world there is a difference between the material body and the spiritual soul, but in the spiritual world everything is spiritual and there are no such differences. The greatest offense of the Māyāvādī philosophers is to consider Lord Viṣṇu and the living entities to be one and the same. In this connection the *Padma Purāṇa* states, *arcye viṣṇau śilā-dhir guruṣu nara-matir vaiṣṇave jāti-buddhiḥ . . . yasya vā nārakī saḥ:* "One who considers the *arcā-mūrti*, the worshipable Deity of Lord Viṣṇu, to be stone, the spiritual master to be an ordinary human being, and a Vaiṣṇava to belong to a particular caste or creed is possessed of hellish intelligence." One who follows such conclusions is doomed.

TEXT 116

ঈশ্বরের তত্ত্ব—যেন জ্বলিত জ্বলন ।
জীবের স্বরূপ—যৈছে স্ফুলিঙ্গের কণ ॥ ১১৬ ॥

īśvarera tattva—yena jvalita jvalana
jīvera svarūpa—yaiche sphuliṅgera kaṇa

īśvarera tattva—the truth of the Supreme Personality of Godhead; *yena*—is like; *jvalita*—blazing; *jvalana*—fire; *jīvera*—of the living entities; *svarūpa*—identity; *yaiche*—is like; *sphuliṅgera*—of the spark; *kaṇa*—particle.

TRANSLATION

"The Lord is like a great blazing fire, and the living entities are like small sparks of that fire.

PURPORT

Although sparks and a big fire are both fire and both have the power to burn, the burning power of the fire and that of the spark are not the same. Why should one artificially try to become like a big fire although by constitution he is like a small spark? It is due to ignorance. One should therefore understand that neither the Supreme Personality of Godhead nor the small sparklike living entities have anything to do with matter, but when the spiritual spark comes in contact with the material world his fiery quality is extinguished. That is the position of the conditioned souls. Because they are in touch with the material world, their spiritual quality is almost dead, but because these spiritual sparks are all Kṛṣṇa's parts and parcels, as the Lord states in the *Bhagavad-gītā* (*mamaivāṁśaḥ*), they can revive their original position by getting free from material contact. This is pure philosophical understanding. In the *Bhagavad-gītā* the spiritual sparks are declared to be *sanātana* (eternal); therefore the material energy, *māyā*, cannot affect their constitutional position.

Someone may argue, "Why is there a need to create the spiritual sparks?" The answer can be given in this way: Since the Absolute Personality of Godhead is omnipotent, He has both unlimited and limited potencies. This is the meaning of omnipotent. To be omnipotent, He must have not only unlimited potencies but limited potencies also. Thus to exhibit His omnipotence He displays both. The living entities are endowed with limited potency although they are part of the Lord. The Lord displays the spiritual world by His unlimited potencies, whereas by His limited potencies the material world is displayed. In the *Bhagavad-gītā* (7.5) the Lord says:

apareyam itas tv anyāṁ prakṛtiṁ viddhi me parām
jīva-bhūtāṁ mahā-bāho yayedaṁ dhāryate jagat

"Besides these inferior energies, O mighty-armed Arjuna, there is another, superior energy of Mine, which comprises all living entities who are exploiting the resources of this material, inferior nature." The *jīva-bhūta,* the living entities, control this material world with their limited potencies. Generally, people are bewildered by the activities of scientists and technologists. Due to *māyā* they think that there is no need of God and that they can do everything and anything, but actually they cannot. Since this cosmic manifestation is limited, their existence is also limited.

Everything in this material world is limited, and for this reason there is creation, sustenance and dissolution. However, in the world of unlimited energy, the spiritual world, there is neither creation nor destruction.

If the Personality of Godhead did not possess both limited and unlimited energies, He could not be called omnipotent. *Aṇor aṇīyān mahato mahīyān:* "The Lord is greater than the greatest and smaller than the smallest." He is smaller than the smallest in the form of the living entities and greater than the greatest in His form of Kṛṣṇa. If there were no one to control, there would be no meaning to the conception of the supreme controller (*īśvara*), just as there is no meaning to a king without his subjects. If all the subjects became king, there would be no distinction between the king and an ordinary citizen. Thus for the Lord to be the supreme controller there must be a creation to control. The basic principle for the existence of the living entities is called *cid-vilāsa,* or spiritual pleasure. The omnipotent Lord displays His pleasure potency as the living entities. The Lord is described in the *Vedānta-sūtra* (1.1.12) as *ānanda-mayo 'bhyāsāt.* He is by nature the reservoir of all pleasures, and because He wants to enjoy pleasure, there must be energies to give Him pleasure or supply Him the impetus for pleasure. This is the perfect philosophical understanding of the Absolute Truth.

TEXT 117

জীবতত্ত্ব—শক্তি, কৃষ্ণতত্ত্ব—শক্তিমান্ ।
গীতা-বিষ্ণুপুরাণাদি তাহাতে প্রমাণ ॥ ১১৭ ॥

jīva-tattva—śakti, kṛṣṇa-tattva—śaktimān
gītā-viṣṇupurāṇādi tāhāte pramāṇa

jīva-tattva—the truth of the living entities; *śakti*—energy; *kṛṣṇa-tattva*—the truth of the Supreme Personality of Godhead; *śakti-mān*—the possessor of the energies; *gītā*—the *Bhagavad-gītā; viṣṇu-purāṇa-ādi—Viṣṇu Purāṇa* and other *Purāṇas; tāhāte*—in them; *pramāṇa*—there are evidences.

TRANSLATION

"The living entities are energies, not the energetic. The energetic is Kṛṣṇa. This is very vividly described in the Bhagavad-gītā, the Viṣṇu Purāṇa and other Vedic literatures.

PURPORT

As already explained, there are three *prasthānas* on the path of advancement in spiritual knowledge—namely, *nyāya-prasthāna* (Vedānta philosophy), *śruti-prasthāna* (the *Upaniṣads* and Vedic *mantras*) and *smṛti-prasthāna* (the *Bhagavad-gītā*, *Mahābhārata*, *Purāṇas*, etc.). Unfortunately, Māyāvādī philosophers do not accept the *smṛti-prasthāna*. *Smṛti* refers to the conclusions drawn from the Vedic evidence. Sometimes Māyāvādī philosophers do not accept the authority of the *Bhagavad-gītā* and the *Purāṇas*, and this is called *ardha-kukkuṭī-nyāya*, "the logic of half a hen" (see *Ādi-līlā* 5.176). If one believes in the Vedic literatures, one must accept all the Vedic literatures recognized by the great *ācāryas*, but the Māyāvādī philosophers accept only the *nyāya-prasthāna* and *śruti-prasthāna*, rejecting the *smṛti-prasthāna*. Here, however, Śrī Caitanya Mahāprabhu cites evidence from the *Gītā*, *Viṣṇu Purāṇa*, etc., which are *smṛti-prasthāna*. No one can avoid the Personality of Godhead in the statements of the *Bhagavad-gītā* and other Vedic literatures such as the *Mahābhārata* and the *Purāṇas*. Lord Caitanya therefore quotes a passage from the *Bhagavad-gītā* (7.5).

TEXT 118

অপরেয়মিতস্ত্বন্যাং প্রকৃতিং বিদ্ধি মে পরাম্ ।
জীবভূতাং মহাবাহো যয়েদং ধার্যতে জগৎ ॥ ১১৮ ॥

apareyam itas tv anyāṁ
prakṛtiṁ viddhi me parām
jīva-bhūtāṁ mahā-bāho
yayedaṁ dhāryate jagat

aparā—inferior energy; *iyam*—this material world; *itaḥ*—beyond this; *tu*—but; *anyām*—another; *prakṛtim*—energy; *viddhi*—you must know; *me*—of Me; *parām*—which is superior energy; *jīva-bhūtām*—they are the living entities; *mahā-bāho*—O mighty-armed; *yayā*—by which; *idam*—this material world; *dhāryate*—is being conducted; *jagat*—the cosmic manifestation.

TRANSLATION

"Besides these inferior energies, O mighty-armed Arjuna, there is another, superior energy of Mine, which comprises the living

entities who are exploiting the resources of this material, inferior nature.'

PURPORT

In the *Bhagavad-gītā* it is explained that the five elements earth, water, fire, air and ether constitute the gross energy of the Absolute Truth and that there are also three subtle energies, namely, the mind, intelligence and false ego, or identification with the phenomenal world. Thus the entire cosmic manifestation is divided into eight energies, all of which are inferior. As explained in the *Bhagavad-gītā* (*mama māyā duratyayā*), the inferior energy, known as *māyā,* is so strong that although the living entity does not belong to this energy, due to the superior strength of the inferior energy the living entity (*jīva-bhūta*) forgets his real position and identifies with it. Kṛṣṇa says distinctly that beyond the material energy there is a superior energy which is known as the *jīva-bhūta,* or living entities. When in contact with the material energy, this superior energy conducts all the activities of the entire material, phenomenal world.

The supreme cause is Kṛṣṇa (*janmādy asya yataḥ*), who is the origin of all energies, which work variously. The Supreme Personality of Godhead has both inferior and superior energies, and the difference between them is that the superior energy is factual whereas the inferior energy is a reflection of the superior. A reflection of the sun in a mirror or on water appears to be the sun but is not. Similarly, the material world is but a reflection of the spiritual world. Although it appears to be factual, it is not; it is only a temporary reflection, whereas the spiritual world is a factual reality. The material world, with its gross and subtle forms, is merely a reflection of the spiritual world.

The living entity is not a product of the material energy; he is spiritual energy, but in contact with matter he forgets his identity. Thus the living entity identifies himself with matter and enthusiastically engages in material activities in the guises of a technologist, scientist, philosopher, etc. He does not know that he is not at all a material product but is spiritual. His real identity thus being lost, he struggles very hard in the material world, and the Hare Kṛṣṇa movement, or Kṛṣṇa consciousness movement, is trying to revive his original consciousness. His activities in manufacturing big skyscrapers are evidence of intelligence, but this kind of intelligence is not at all advanced. He should know that his only real concern is how to get free from material contact, for by absorbing his mind in material activities he takes material bodies again and again, and although he falsely claims to be very intelligent, in material consciousness he is not at all intelligent. When we speak about the Kṛṣṇa consciousness movement, which is meant to make people intelligent, the conditioned living entity therefore misunderstands it. He is so engrossed in the material concept of life that he does not think there can be any activities that are actually based on intelligence beyond the construction of skyscrapers and big roads and the manufacturing of cars. This is proof of *māyayāpahṛta-jñāna,* or loss of all intelligence due to the influence of *māyā.* When a living entity is freed from such misconceptions, he is called liberated. When one is actually liberated he no longer identifies with the material world. The symptom of *mukti* (liberation) is that one engages in spiritual activities instead of falsely engaging in material activities.

Transcendental loving devotional service is the spiritual activity of the spirit soul. Māyāvādī philosophers confuse such spiritual activity with material activity, but the *Bhagavad-gītā* (14.26) confirms:

māṁ ca yo 'vyabhicāreṇa bhakti-yogena sevate
sa guṇān samatītyaitān brahma-bhūyāya kalpate

One who engages in the spiritual activities of unalloyed devotional service (*avyabhicāriṇī-bhakti*) is immediately elevated to the transcendental platform, and he is to be considered *brahma-bhūta,* which indicates that he is no longer in the material world but is in the spiritual world. Devotional service is enlightenment, or awakening. When the living entity perfectly performs spiritual activities under the direction of the spiritual master, he becomes perfect in knowledge and understands that he is not God but a servant of God. As explained by Caitanya Mahāprabhu, *jīvera 'svarūpa' haya—kṛṣṇera 'nitya-dāsa':* the real identity of the living entity is that he is an eternal servant of the Supreme (Cc. *Madhya* 20.108). As long as one does not come to this conclusion, he must be in ignorance. This is also confirmed by the Lord in the *Bhagavad-gītā* (7.19): *bahūnāṁ janmanām ante jñānavān māṁ prapadyate . . . sa mahātmā su-durlabhaḥ.* "After many births of struggling for existence and cultivating knowledge, when one comes to the point of real knowledge he surrenders unto Me. Such an advanced *mahātmā,* or great soul, is very rarely to be seen." Thus although the Māyāvādī philosophers appear to be very much advanced in knowledge, they are not yet perfect. To come to the point of perfection they must voluntarily surrender to Kṛṣṇa.

TEXT 119

বিষ্ণুশক্তিঃ পরা প্রোক্তা ক্ষেত্রজ্ঞাখ্যা তথাপরা ।
অবিদ্যাকর্মসংজ্ঞান্যা তৃতীয়া শক্তিরিষ্যতে ॥ ১১৯ ॥

viṣṇu-śaktiḥ parā proktā
kṣetra-jñākhyā tathā parā
avidyā-karma-saṁjñānyā
tṛtīyā śaktir iṣyate

viṣṇu-śaktiḥ—the potency of Lord Viṣṇu; *parā*—spiritual; *proktā*—it is said; *kṣetra-jña-ākhyā*—the potency known as *kṣetra-jña; tathā*—as well as; *parā*—spiritual; *avidyā*—ignorance; *karma*—fruitive activities; *saṁjñā*—known as; *anyā*—other; *tṛtīyā*—third; *śaktiḥ*—potency; *iṣyate*—known thus.

TRANSLATION

"'The potency of Lord Viṣṇu is summarized in three categories—namely, the spiritual potency, the living entities and ignorance. The spiritual potency is full of knowledge; the living entities, although belonging to the spiritual potency, are subject to bewilderment; and the third energy, which is full of ignorance, is always visible in fruitive activities.'

PURPORT

This is a quotation from the *Viṣṇu Purāṇa* (6.7.61).

In the previous verse, quoted from the *Bhagavad-gītā*, it has been established that the living entities are to be categorized among the Lord's potencies. The Lord is potent, and there are varieties of potencies (*parāsya śaktir vividhaiva śrūyate*). Now, in this quotation from the *Viṣṇu Purāṇa*, this is further confirmed. There are varieties of potencies, and they have been divided into three categories—namely, spiritual, marginal and external.

The spiritual potency is manifested in the spiritual world. Kṛṣṇa's form, qualities, activities and entourage are all spiritual. This is confirmed in the *Bhagavad-gītā* (4.5):

ajo 'pi sann avyayātmā bhūtānām īśvaro 'pi san
prakṛtiṁ svām adhiṣṭhāya sambhavāmy ātma-māyayā

"Although I am unborn and My transcendental body never deteriorates, and although I am the Lord of all living entities, by My spiritual potency I still appear in every millennium in My original transcendental form." *Ātma-māyā* refers to the spiritual potency. When Kṛṣṇa comes to this or any other universe, He does so with His spiritual potency. We take birth by the force of the material potency, but as stated here with reference to the *Viṣṇu Purāṇa*, the *kṣetra-jña*, or living entity, belongs to the spiritual potency; thus when we free ourselves from the clutches of the material potency we can also enter the spiritual world.

The material potency is the energy of darkness, or complete ignorance of spiritual activities. In the material potency, the living entity engages himself in fruitive activities, thinking that he can be happy through expansion in terms of material energy. This fact is prominently manifest in this Age of Kali because human society, not understanding the spiritual nature, is busily expanding in material activities. The men of the present day are almost unaware of their spiritual identity. They think that they are products of the elements of the material world and that everything will end with the annihilation of the body. Therefore they conclude that as long as one has a material body consisting of material senses, one should enjoy the senses as much as possible. Since they are atheists, they do not care whether there is a next life. Such activities are described in this verse as *avidyā-karma-saṁjñānyā.*

The material energy is separated from the spiritual energy of the Supreme Personality of Godhead. Thus although it is originally created by the Supreme Lord, He is not actually present within it. The Lord also confirms in the *Bhagavad-gītā* (9.4), *mat-sthāni sarva-bhūtāni:* "Everything is resting on Me." This indicates that everything is resting on His own energy. For example, the planets are resting within outer space, which is the separated energy of Kṛṣṇa. The Lord explains in the *Bhagavad-gītā* (7.4):

bhūmir āpo 'nalo vāyuḥ khaṁ mano buddhir eva ca
ahaṅkāra itīyaṁ me bhinnā prakṛtir aṣṭadhā

"Earth, water, fire, air, ether, mind, intelligence and false ego—all together these eight constitute My separated material energies." The separated energy acts as if it were independent, but here it is said that although such energies are certainly factual, they are not independent but merely separated.

The separated energy can be understood from a practical example. I compose books by speaking into a dictaphone, and when the dictaphone is replayed, it appears that I am speaking personally, but actually I am not. I spoke personally, but then the dictaphone tape, which is separate from me, acts exactly like me. Similarly, the material energy originally emanates from the Supreme Personality of Godhead, but it acts separately, although the energy is supplied by the Lord. This is also explained in the *Bhagavad-gītā* (9.10): *mayādhyakṣeṇa prakṛtiḥ sūyate sa-carācaram.* "This material nature is working under My direction, O son of Kuntī, and it is producing all moving and unmoving beings." Under the guidance or superintendence of the Supreme Personality of Godhead, the material energy works as if independent, although it is not actually independent.

In this verse from the *Viṣṇu Purāṇa* the total energy of the Supreme Personality of Godhead is classified in three divisions—namely, the spiritual or internal potency of the Lord, the marginal potency, or *kṣetra-jña* (the living entity), and the material potency, which is separated from the Supreme Personality of Godhead and appears to act independently. When Śrīla Vyāsadeva, by meditation and self-realization, saw the Supreme Personality of Godhead, he also saw the separated energy of the Lord standing behind Him (*apaśyat puruṣaṁ pūrṇaṁ māyāṁ ca tad-apāśrayam*). Vyāsadeva also realized that it is this separated energy of the Lord, the material energy, that covers the knowledge of the living entities (*yayā sammohito jīva ātmānaṁ tri-guṇātmakam*). The separated, material energy bewilders the living entities (*jīvas*), and thus they work very hard under its influence, not knowing that they are not fulfilling their mission in life. Unfortunately, most of them think that they are the body and should therefore enjoy the material senses irresponsibly since when death comes everything will be finished. This atheistic philosophy also flourished in India, where it was sometimes propagated by Cārvāka Muni, who said:

ṛṇaṁ kṛtvā ghṛtaṁ pibet yāvaj jīvet sukhaṁ jīvet
bhasmī-bhūtasya dehasya kutaḥ punar āgamano bhavet

His theory was that as long as one lives one should eat as much ghee as possible. In India, ghee (clarified butter) is a basic ingredient in preparing many varieties of food. Since everyone wants to enjoy nice food, Cārvāka Muni advised that one eat as much ghee as possible. One may say, "I have no money. How shall I purchase ghee?" Cārvāka Muni, however, says, "If you have no money, then beg, borrow or steal, but in some way secure ghee and enjoy life." For one who further objects that he will be held accountable for such unauthorized activities as begging, borrowing and stealing, Cārvāka Muni replies, "You will not be held responsible. As soon as your body is burned to ashes after death, everything is finished."

This is called ignorance. From the *Bhagavad-gītā* it is understood that one does not die with the annihilation of his body (*na hanyate hanyamāne śarīre*). The annihilation of one body involves changing to another (*tathā dehāntara-prāptiḥ*). Therefore, to perform irresponsible activities in the material world is very dangerous. Without knowledge of the spirit soul and its transmigration, people are allured by the material energy to engage in many such activities, as if one could become happy simply by dint of material knowledge, without reference to spiritual existence. Therefore the entire material world and its activities are referred to as *avidyā-karma-saṁjñānyā.*

In order to dissipate the ignorance of the human beings who work under the material energy, which is separated from the Supreme Personality of Godhead, the Lord comes down to revive their original nature of spiritual activities (*yadā yadā hi dharmasya glānir bhavati bhārata*). As soon as they deviate from their original nature, the Lord comes to teach them, *sarva-dharmān parityajya mām ekaṁ śaraṇaṁ vraja:* "My dear living entities, give up all material activities and simply surrender unto Me for protection." (Bg. 18.66)

It is the statement of Cārvāka Muni that one should beg, borrow or steal money to purchase ghee and enjoy life (*ṛṇaṁ kṛtvā ghṛtaṁ pibet*). Thus even the greatest atheist of India recommends that one eat ghee, not meat. No one could conceive of human beings' eating meat like tigers and dogs, but men have become so degraded that they are just like animals and can no longer claim to have a human civilization.

TEXT 120

হেন জীবতত্ত্ব লঞা লিখি' পরতত্ত্ব ।
আচ্ছন্ন করিল শ্রেষ্ঠ ঈশ্বর-মহত্ত্ব ॥ ১২০ ॥

hena jīva-tattva lañā likhi' para-tattva
ācchanna karila śreṣṭha īśvara-mahattva

hena—such degraded; *jīva-tattva*—the living entities; *lañā*—taking them; *likhi'*—having written; *para-tattva*—as the Supreme; *ācchanna*—covering; *karila*—did; *śreṣṭha*—the Supreme Personality of Godhead; *īśvara*—the Lord's; *mahattva*—glories.

TRANSLATION

"The Māyāvāda philosophy is so degraded that it has taken the insignificant living entities to be the Lord, the Supreme Truth, thus covering the glory and supremacy of the Absolute Truth with monism.

PURPORT

Śrīla Bhaktivinoda Ṭhākura comments in this connection that in all Vedic scriptures the *jīva-tattva,* the truth of the living entities, is mentioned to be one of the energies of the Lord. If one does not accept the living entity to be a minute, infinitesimal spark of the Supreme but equates the *jīva-tattva* with the Supreme Brahman or Supreme Personality of Godhead, it must be understood that his entire philosophy is based on a misunderstanding. Unfortunately, Śrīpāda Śaṅkarācārya purposely claimed the *jīva-tattva,* or living entities, to be equal to the Supreme God. Therefore his entire philosophy is based on a misunderstanding, and it misguides people to become atheists, whose mission in life is unfulfilled. The mission of human life, as described in the *Bhagavad-gītā,* is to surrender unto the Supreme Lord and become His devotee, but the Māyāvāda philosophy misleads one to defy the existence of the Supreme Personality of Godhead and pose oneself as the Supreme Lord. Thus it has misguided hundreds of thousands of innocent men.

In the *Vedānta-sūtra,* Vyāsadeva has described that the Supreme Personality of Godhead is potent and that everything, material or spiritual, is but an emanation of His energy. The Lord, the Supreme Brahman, is the origin or source of everything (*janmādy asya yataḥ*), and all other manifestations are emanations of different energies of the Lord. This is also confirmed in the *Viṣṇu Purāṇa:*

ekadeśa-sthitasyāgner jyotsnā vistāriṇī yathā
parasya brahmaṇaḥ śaktis tathedam akhilaṁ jagat

"Whatever we see in this world is simply an expansion of different energies of the Supreme Personality of Godhead, who is exactly like a fire that spreads illumination for a long distance although it is situated in one place." This is a very vivid analogy. Similarly, it is stated that just as everything in the material world exists in the sunshine, which is the energy of the sun, so everything exists on the basis of the spiritual and material energies of the Supreme Personality of Godhead. Thus although Kṛṣṇa is situated in His own abode (*goloka eva nivasaty akhilātma-bhūtaḥ*), where He enjoys His transcendental pastimes with the cowherd boys and *gopīs,* He is nevertheless present everywhere, even within the atoms of this universe (*aṇḍāntara-stha-paramāṇu-cayāntara-stham*). This is the verdict of the Vedic literature.

Unfortunately, the Māyāvāda philosophy, misguiding people by claiming the living entity to be the Lord, has created havoc throughout the entire world and led almost everyone to godlessness. By thus covering the glories of the Supreme Lord, the Māyāvādī philosophers have done the greatest disservice to human society. It is to counteract these most abominable activities of the Māyāvādī philosophers that Lord Caitanya has introduced the Hare Kṛṣṇa *mahā-mantra.*

harer nāma harer nāma harer nāmaiva kevalam
kalau nāsty eva nāsty eva nāsty eva gatir anyathā

"In this age of quarrel and hypocrisy, the only means of deliverance is chanting the holy name of the Lord. There is no other way. There is no other way. There is no other way." People should simply engage in the chanting of the Hare Kṛṣṇa *mahā-mantra,* for thus they will gradually come to understand that they are not the Supreme Personality of Godhead, as they have been taught by the Māyāvādī philosophers, but are eternal servants of the Lord. As soon as one engages himself in the transcendental service of the Lord, he becomes free.

māṁ ca yo 'vyabhicāreṇa bhakti-yogena sevate
sa guṇān samatītyaitān brahma-bhūyāya kalpate

"One who engages in full devotional service, unfailing in all circumstances, at once transcends the modes of material nature and thus comes to the level of Brahman." (Bg. 14.26) Therefore the Hare Kṛṣṇa movement, or Kṛṣṇa consciousness movement, is the only light for the foolish living entities who think either that there is no God or that if God exists He is formless and they themselves are also God. These misconceptions are very dangerous, and the only way to counteract them is to spread the Hare Kṛṣṇa movement.

TEXT 121

ব্যাসের সূত্রেতে কহে 'পরিণাম'-বাদ ।
'ব্যাস ভ্রান্ত'—বলি' তার উঠাইল বিবাদ ॥ ১২১ ॥

vyāsera sūtrete kahe 'pariṇāma'-vāda
'vyāsa bhrānta'—bali' tāra uṭhāila vivāda

vyāsera—of Śrīla Vyāsadeva; *sūtrete*—in the aphorisms; *kahe*—describes; *pariṇāma*—transformation; *vāda*—philosophy; *vyāsa*—Śrīla Vyāsadeva; *bhrānta*—mistaken; *bali'*—accusing him; *tāra*—his; *uṭhāila*—raised; *vivāda*—opposition.

TRANSLATION

"In his Vedānta-sūtra Śrīla Vyāsadeva has described that everything is but a transformation of the energy of the Lord. Śaṅkarācārya, however, has misled the world by commenting that Vyāsadeva was mistaken. Thus he has raised great opposition to theism throughout the entire world.

PURPORT

Śrīla Bhaktivinoda Ṭhākura explains, "In the *Vedanta-sūtra* of Śrīla Vyāsadeva it is definitely stated that all cosmic manifestations result from transformations of various energies of the Lord. Śaṅkarācārya, however, not accepting the energy of the Lord, thinks that it is the Lord who is transformed. He has taken many clear statements from the Vedic literature and twisted them to try to prove that if the Lord, or the Absolute Truth, were transformed, His oneness would be disturbed. Thus he has accused Śrīla Vyāsadeva of being mistaken. In developing his philosophy of monism, therefore, he has established *vivarta-vāda*, or the Māyāvāda theory of illusion."

In the *Brahma-sūtra*, Second Chapter, the first aphorism is as follows: *tad-ananyatvam ārambhaṇa-śabdādibhyaḥ.* Commenting on this *sūtra* in his *Śārīraka-bhāṣya,* Śaṅkarācārya has introduced the statement *vācārambhaṇaṁ vikāro nāmadheyam* from the *Chāndogya Upaniṣad* (6.1.4) to try to prove that acceptance of the transformation of the energy of the Supreme Lord is faulty. He has tried to defy this transformation of energy in a misguided way, which will be explained later. Since his conception of God is impersonal, he does not believe that the entire cosmic manifestation is a transformation of the energies of the Lord, for as soon as one accepts the various energies of the Absolute Truth, one must immediately accept the Absolute Truth to be personal, not impersonal. A person can create many things by the transformation of his energy. For example, a businessman transforms his energy by establishing many big factories or business organizations, yet he remains a person although his energy has been transformed into these many factories or business concerns. The Māyāvādī philosophers do not understand this simple fact. Their tiny brains and poor fund of knowledge cannot afford them sufficient enlightenment to realize that when a man's energy is transformed, the man himself is not transformed but remains the same person.

Not believing in the fact that the energy of the Absolute Truth is transformed, Śaṅkarācārya has propounded his theory of illusion. This theory states that although the Absolute Truth is never transformed, we think that it is transformed, which is an illusion. Śaṅkarācārya does not believe in the transformation of the energy of the Absolute Truth, for he claims that everything is one and that the living entity is therefore also one with the Supreme. This is the Māyāvāda theory.

Śrīla Vyāsadeva has explained that the Absolute Truth is a person who has different potencies. Merely by His desire that there be creation and by His glance (*sa aikṣata*), He created this material world (*sa asṛjata*). After creation, He remains the same person: He is not transformed into everything. One should accept that the Lord has inconceivable energies and that it is by His order and will that varieties of manifestations have come into existence. In the Vedic literature it is said, *sa-tattvato 'nyathā-buddhir vikāra ity udāhṛtaḥ.* This *mantra* indicates that from one fact another fact is generated. For example, a father is one fact, and a son generated from the father is a second fact. Thus both of them are truths, although one is generated from the other. This generation of a second, independent truth from a first truth is called *vikāra,* or transformation resulting in a by-product. The Supreme Brahman is the Absolute Truth, and the energies that have emanated from Him and are existing separately, such as the living entities and the cosmic manifestation, are also truths. This is an example of transformation, which is called *vikāra* or *pariṇāma.* To give another example of *vikāra,* milk is a truth, but the same milk may be transformed into yogurt. Thus yogurt is a transformation of milk, although the ingredients of yogurt and milk are the same.

In the *Chāndogya Upaniṣad* there is the following *mantra: aitad-ātmyam idaṁ sarvam.* This *mantra* indicates without a doubt that the entire world is Brahman. The Absolute Truth has inconceivable energies, as confirmed in the *Śvetāśvatara Upaniṣad* (*parāsya śaktir vividhaiva śrūyate*), and the entire cosmic manifestation is evidence of these different energies of the Supreme Lord. The Supreme Lord is a fact, and therefore whatever is created by the Supreme Lord is also factual.

Everything is true and complete (*pūrṇam*), but the original *pūrṇam*, the complete Absolute Truth, always remains the same. *Pūrṇāt pūrṇam udacyate pūrṇasya pūrṇam ādāya.* The Absolute Truth is so perfect that although innumerable energies emanate from Him and manifest creations which appear to be different from Him, He nevertheless maintains His personality. He never deteriorates under any circumstances.

It is to be concluded that the entire cosmic manifestation is a transformation of the energy of the Supreme Lord, not of the Supreme Lord or Absolute Truth Himself, who always remains the same. The material world and the living entities are transformations of the energy of the Lord, the Absolute Truth or Brahman, who is the original source. In other words, the Absolute Truth, Brahman, is the original ingredient, and the other manifestations are transformations of this ingredient. This is also confirmed in the *Taittirīya Upaniṣad* (3.1): *yato vā imāni bhūtāni jāyante.* "This entire cosmic manifestation is made possible by the Absolute Truth, the Supreme Personality of Godhead." In this verse it is indicated that Brahman, the Absolute Truth, is the original cause and that the living entities (*jīvas*) and the cosmic manifestation are effects of this cause. The cause being a fact, the effects are also factual. They are not illusion. Śaṅkarācārya has inconsistently tried to prove that it is an illusion to accept the material world and the *jīvas* as by-products of the Supreme Lord because (in his conception) the existence of the material world and the *jīvas* is different and separate from that of the Absolute Truth. With this jugglery of understanding, Māyāvādī philosophers have propagated the slogan *brahma satyaṁ jagan mithyā*, which declares that the Absolute Truth is fact but the cosmic manifestation and the living entities are simply illusions, or that all of them are in fact the Absolute Truth and that the material world and living entities do not separately exist.

It is therefore to be concluded that Śaṅkarācārya, in order to present the Supreme Lord, the living entities and the material nature as indivisible and ignorant, tries to cover the glories of the Supreme Personality of Godhead. He maintains that the material cosmic manifestation is *mithyā*, or false, but this is a great blunder. If the Supreme Personality of Godhead is a fact, how can His creation be false? Even in ordinary dealings, one cannot think the material cosmic manifestation to be false. Therefore Vaiṣṇava philosophers say that the cosmic creation is not false but temporary. It is separated from the Supreme Personality of Godhead, but since it is wonderfully created by the energy of the Lord, to say that it is false is blasphemous.

Nondevotees factually appreciate the wonderful creation of material nature, but they cannot appreciate the intelligence and energy of the Supreme Personality of Godhead, who is behind this material creation. Śrīpāda Rāmānujācārya, however, refers to a *sūtra* from the *Aitareya Upaniṣad* (1.1.1), *ātmā vā idam agra āsīt,* which points out that the supreme *ātmā,* the Absolute Truth, existed before the creation. One may argue, "If the Supreme Personality of Godhead is completely spiritual, how is it possible for Him to be the origin of creation and have within Himself both material and spiritual energies?" To answer this challenge, Śrīpāda Rāmānujācārya quotes a *mantra* from the *Taittirīya Upaniṣad* (3.1) that states:

yato vā imāni bhūtāni jāyante
yena jātāni jīvanti
yat prayanty abhisaṁviśanti

This *mantra* confirms that the entire cosmic manifestation emanates from the Absolute Truth, rests upon the Absolute Truth and after annihilation again reenters the body of the Absolute Truth, the Supreme Personality of Godhead. The living entity is originally spiritual, and when he enters the spiritual world or the body of the Supreme Lord, he still retains his identity as an individual soul. In this connection Śrīpāda Rāmānujācārya gives the analogy that when a green bird enters a green tree it does not become one with the tree: it retains its identity as a bird, although it appears to merge with the greenness of the tree. To give another analogy, an animal that enters a forest keeps its individuality, although apparently the beast merges with the forest. Similarly, in material existence, both the material energy and the living entities of the marginal potency maintain their individuality. Thus although the energies of the Supreme Personality of Godhead interact within the cosmic manifestation, each keeps its separate individual existence. Merging with the material or spiritual energies, therefore, does not involve loss of individuality. According to Śrī Rāmānujapāda's theory of Viśiṣṭādvaita, although all the energies of the Lord are one, each keeps its individuality (*vaiśiṣṭya*).

Śrīpāda Śaṅkarācārya has tried to mislead the readers of the *Vedānta-sūtra* by misinterpreting the words *ānanda-mayo 'bhyāsāt,* and he has even tried to find fault with Vyāsadeva. All the aphorisms of the *Vedānta-sūtra* need not be examined here, however, since we intend to present the *Vedānta-sūtra* in a separate volume.

TEXT 122

পরিণাম-বাদে ঈশ্বর হয়েন বিকারী ।
এত কহি' 'বিবর্ত'-বাদ স্থাপনা যে করি ॥ ১২২ ॥

pariṇāma-vāde īśvara hayena vikārī
eta kahi' 'vivarta'-vāda sthāpanā ye kari

pariṇāma-vāde—by accepting the theory of transformation of energy; *īśvara*—the Supreme Lord; *hayena*—becomes; *vikārī*—transformed; *eta kahi'*—saying this; *vivarta*—illusion; *vāda*—theory; *sthāpanā*—establishing; *ye*—what; *kari*—do.

TRANSLATION

"According to Śaṅkarācārya, by accepting the theory of the transformation of the energy of the Lord, one creates an illusion by indirectly accepting that the Absolute Truth is transformed.

PURPORT

Śrīla Bhaktivinoda Ṭhākura comments that if one does not clearly understand the meaning of *pariṇāma-vāda,* or transformation of energy, one is sure to misunderstand the truth regarding this material cosmic manifestation and the living entities. In the *Chāndogya Upaniṣad* (6.8.4) it is said, *san-mūlāḥ saumyemāḥ prajāḥ sad-āyatanāḥ sat-pratiṣṭhāḥ.* The material world and the living entities are separate beings, and they are eternally true, not false. Śaṅkarācārya, however, unnecessarily fearing that by *pariṇāma-vāda* (transformation of energy) Brahman would be transformed (*vikārī*), has imagined both the material world and the living entities to be false and to have no individuality. By word jugglery he has tried to prove that the individual identities of the living entities and the material world are illusory, and he has cited the analogies of mistaking a rope for a snake or an oyster shell for gold. Thus he has most abominably cheated people in general.

The analogy of misunderstanding a rope to be a snake is mentioned in the *Māṇḍūkya Upaniṣad,* but it is meant to explain the error of identifying the body with the soul. Since the soul is actually a spiritual particle, as confirmed in the *Bhagavad-gītā* (*mamaivāṁśo jīva-loke*), it is due to illusion (*vivarta-vāda*) that a human being, like an animal, identifies the body with the self. This is a proper example of *vivarta,* or illusion. The verse *atattvato 'nyathā-buddhir vivarta ity udāhṛtaḥ* describes such an illusion. To not know actual facts and thus to mistake one thing for another (as, for example, to accept the body as oneself) is called *vivarta-vāda.* Every conditioned living entity who considers the body to be the soul is deluded by this *vivarta-vāda.* One can be attacked by this *vivarta-vāda* philosophy when he forgets the inconceivable power of the omnipotent Personality of Godhead.

How the Supreme Personality of Godhead remains as He is, never changing, is explained in the *Īśopaniṣad: pūrṇasya pūrṇam ādāya pūrṇam evāvaśiṣyate.* God is complete. Even if a complete manifestation is taken away from Him, He continues to be complete. The material creation is manifested by the energy of the Lord, but He is still the same person. His form, entourage, qualities and so on never deteriorate. Śrīla Jīva Gosvāmī, in his *Paramātma-sandarbha,* comments regarding the *vivarta-vāda* as follows: "Under the spell of *vivarta-vāda* one imagines the separate entities, namely the cosmic manifestation and the living entities, to be one with Brahman. This is due to complete ignorance regarding the actual fact. The Absolute Truth, or Parabrahman, is always one and always the same. He is completely free from all other conceptions of existence. He is completely free from false ego, for He is the full spiritual identity. It is absolutely impossible for Him to be subjected to ignorance and fall under the spell of a misconception (*vivarta-vāda*). The Absolute Truth is beyond our conception. One must admit that He has unblemished qualities that He does not share with every living entity. He is never tainted in the slightest degree by the flaws of ordinary living beings. Everyone must therefore understand the Absolute Truth to possess inconceivable potencies."

TEXT 123

বস্তুতঃ পরিণাম-বাদ—সেই সে প্রমাণ ।
দেহে আত্মবুদ্ধি—এই বিবর্তের স্থান ॥ ১২৩ ॥

vastutaḥ pariṇāma-vāda—sei se pramāṇa
dehe ātma-buddhi—ei vivartera sthāna

vastutaḥ—factually; *pariṇāma-vāda*—transformation of the energy; *sei*—that; *se*—only; *pramāṇa*—proof; *dehe*—in the body; *ātma-buddhi*—concept of self; *ei*—this; *vivartera*—of illusion; *sthāna*—place.

TRANSLATION

"Transformation of energy is a proven fact. It is the false bodily conception of the self that is an illusion.

PURPORT

The *jīva,* or living entity, is a spiritual spark who is part of the Supreme Personality of Godhead. Unfortunately, he thinks the body to be the self, and that misunderstanding is called *vivarta,* or acceptance of untruth to be truth. The body is not the self, but animals and foolish people think that it is. *Vivarta* (illusion) does not, however, denote a change in the identity of the spirit soul; it is the misconception that the body is the self that is an illusion. Similarly, the Supreme Personality of Godhead does not change when His external energy, consisting of the eight gross and subtle material elements listed in the *Bhagavad-gītā* (*bhūmir āpo 'nalo vāyuḥ,* etc.), acts and reacts in different phases.

TEXT 124

অবিচিন্ত্য-শক্তিযুক্ত শ্রীভগবান্ ।
ইচ্ছায় জগদ্‌রূপে পায় পরিণাম ॥ ১২৪ ॥

avicintya-śakti-yukta śrī-bhagavān
icchāya jagad-rūpe pāya pariṇāma

avicintya—inconceivable; *śakti*—potency; *yukta*—possessed of; *śrī*—the affluent; *bhagavān*—Personality of Godhead; *icchāya*—by His wish; *jagat-rūpe*—in the form of the cosmic manifestation; *pāya*—becomes; *pariṇāma*—transformed by His energy.

TRANSLATION

"The Supreme Personality of Godhead is opulent in all respects. Therefore by His inconceivable energies He has transformed the material cosmic manifestation.

TEXT 125

তথাপি অচিন্ত্যশক্ত্যে হয় অবিকারী ।
প্রাকৃত চিন্তামণি তাহে দৃষ্টান্ত যে ধরি ॥ ১২৫ ॥

tathāpi acintya-śaktye haya avikārī
prākṛta cintāmaṇi tāhe dṛṣṭānta ye dhari

tathāpi—yet; *acintya-śaktye*—by inconceivable potency; *haya*—remains; *avikārī*—without change; *prākṛta*—material; *cintāmaṇi*—touchstone; *tāhe*—in that respect; *dṛṣṭānta*—; *ye*—which; *dhari*—we accept.

TRANSLATION

"Using the example of a touchstone, which by its energy turns iron to gold and yet remains the same, we can understand that although the Supreme Personality of Godhead transforms His innumerable energies, He remains unchanged.

TEXT 126

নানা রত্নরাশি হয় চিন্তামণি হৈতে ।
তথাপিহ মণি রহে স্বরূপে অবিকৃতে ॥ ১২৬ ॥

nānā ratna-rāśi haya cintāmaṇi haite
tathāpiha maṇi rahe svarūpe avikṛte

nānā—varieties; *ratna-rāśi*—valuable jewels; *haya*—become possible; *cintāmaṇi*—the touchstone; *haite*—from; *tathāpiha*—still, certainly; *maṇi*—the touchstone; *rahe*—remains; *svarūpe*—in its original form; *avikṛte*—without change.

TRANSLATION

"Although a touchstone produces many varieties of valuable jewels, it nevertheless remains the same. It does not change its original form.

TEXT 127

প্রাকৃত-বস্তুতে যদি অচিন্ত্যশক্তি হয় ।
ঈশ্বরের অচিন্ত্যশক্তি,—ইথে কি বিস্ময় ॥ ১২৭ ॥

prākṛta-vastute yadi acintya-śakti haya
īśvarera acintya-śakti,—ithe ki vismaya

prākṛta-vastute—in material things; *yadi*—if; *acintya*—inconceivable; *śakti*—potency; *haya*—becomes possible; *īśvarera*—of the Supreme Lord; *acintya*—inconceivable; *śakti*—potency; *ithe*—in this; *ki*—what; *vismaya*—wonderful.

TRANSLATION

"If there is such inconceivable potency in material objects, why should we not believe in the inconceivable potency of the Supreme Personality of Godhead?

PURPORT

The argument of Śrī Caitanya Mahāprabhu described in this verse can be very easily understood even by a common man if he simply thinks of the activities of the sun, which has been giving off unlimited amounts of heat and light since time immemorial and yet has not even slightly decreased in power. Modern science believes that it is by sunshine that the entire cosmic manifestation is maintained, and actually one can see how the actions and reactions of sunshine maintain order throughout the universe. The growth of vegetables and even the rotation of the planets take place due to the heat and light of the sun. Sometimes, therefore, modern scientists consider the sun to be the original cause of creation, not knowing that the sun is only a medium, for it is also created by the supreme energy of the Supreme Personality of Godhead. Aside from the sun and the touchstone, there are many other material things that transform their energy in different ways and yet remain as they are. It is not necessary, therefore, for the original cause, the Supreme Personality of Godhead, to change due to the changes or transformations of His different energies.

The falsity of Śrīpāda Śaṅkarācārya's explanation of *vivarta-vāda* and *pariṇāma-vāda* has been detected by the Vaiṣṇava *ācāryas,* especially Jīva Gosvāmī, whose opinion is that actually Śaṅkara did not understand the *Vedānta-sūtra.* In Śaṅkara's explanation of one *sūtra, ānanda-mayo 'bhyāsāt,* he has interpreted the affix *mayaṭ* with such word jugglery that this very explanation proves that he had little knowledge of the *Vedānta-sūtra* but simply wanted to support his impersonalism through the aphorisms of the Vedānta philosophy. Actually, however, he failed to do so because he could not put forward strong arguments. In this connection, Śrīla Jīva Gosvāmī cites the phrase *brahma puccham pratiṣṭhā* (*Taittirīya Up.* 2.5), which gives Vedic evidence that Brahman is the origin of everything. In explaining this verse, Śrīpāda Śaṅkarācārya interpreted various Sanskrit words in such a way that he implied, according to Jīva Gosvāmī, that Vyāsadeva had very little knowledge of higher logic. Such unscrupulous deviation from the real meaning of the *Vedānta-sūtra* has created a class of men who by word jugglery try to derive various indirect meanings from the Vedic literatures, especially the *Bhagavad-gītā.* One of them has even explained that the word *kurukṣetra* refers to the body. Such interpretations imply, however, that neither Lord Kṛṣṇa nor Vyāsadeva had a proper sense of word usage or etymological adjustment. They lead one to assume that since Lord Kṛṣṇa could not personally sense the meaning of what He was speaking and Vyāsadeva did not know the meaning of what he was writing, Lord Kṛṣṇa left His book to be explained later by the Māyāvādīs. Such interpretations merely prove, however, that their proponents have very little philosophical sense.

Instead of wasting one's time falsely deriving such indirect meanings from the *Vedānta-sūtra* and other Vedic literatures, one should accept the words of these books as they are. In presenting *Bhagavad-gītā As It Is,* therefore, we have not changed the meaning of the original words. Similarly, if one studies the *Vedānta-sūtra* as it is, without whimsical and capricious adulteration, one can understand the *Vedanta-sūtra* very easily. Śrīla Vyāsadeva therefore explains the *Vedānta-sūtra,* beginning from the first *sūtra, janmādy asya yataḥ,* in his *Śrīmad-Bhāgavatam* (1.1.1):

janmādy asya yato 'nvayād itaratas cārtheṣv abhijñaḥ sva-rāṭ

"I meditate upon Him [Lord Śrī Kṛṣṇa], the transcendent reality, who is the primeval cause of all causes, from whom all manifested universes arise, in whom they dwell, and by whom they are destroyed. I meditate upon that eternally effulgent Lord, who is directly and indirectly conscious of all manifestations and yet is fully independent." The Supreme Personality of Godhead knows very well how to do everything perfectly. He is *abhijña,* always fully conscious. The Lord therefore says in the *Bhagavad-gītā* (7.26) that He knows everything, past, present and future, but that no one but a devotee knows Him as He is. Therefore, the Absolute Truth, the Personality of Godhead, is at least partially understood by devotees of the Lord, but the Māyāvādī philosophers, who unnecessarily speculate to understand the Absolute Truth, simply waste their time.

TEXT 128

'প্রণব' সে মহাবাক্য—বেদের নিদান ।
ঈশ্বরস্বরূপ প্রণব সর্ববিশ্ব-ধাম ॥ ১২৮ ॥

'praṇava' se mahāvākya—vedera nidāna
īśvara-svarūpa praṇava sarva-viśva-dhāma

praṇava—the *oṁkāra; se*—that; *mahā-vākya*—transcendental sound vibration; *vedera*—of the *Vedas; nidāna*—basic principle; *īśvara-svarūpa*—direct representation of the Supreme Personality of Godhead; *praṇava*—*oṁkāra; sarva-viśva*—of all universes; *dhāma*—is the reservoir.

TRANSLATION

"The Vedic sound vibration oṁkāra, the principal word in the Vedic literatures, is the basis of all Vedic vibrations. Therefore one should accept oṁkāra as the sound representation of the Supreme Personality of Godhead and the reservoir of the cosmic manifestation.

PURPORT

In the *Bhagavad-gītā* (8.13) the glories of *oṁkāra* are described as follows:

oṁ ity ekākṣaraṁ brahma vyāharan mām anusmaran
yaḥ prayāti tyajan dehaṁ sa yāti paramāṁ gatim

This verse indicates that *oṁkāra*, or *praṇava*, is a direct representation of the Supreme Personality of Godhead. Therefore if at the time of death one simply remembers *oṁkāra*, he remembers the Supreme Personality of Godhead and is therefore immediately transferred to the spiritual world. *Oṁkāra* is the basic principle of all Vedic *mantras*, for it is a representation of Lord Kṛṣṇa, understanding of whom is the ultimate goal of the *Vedas*, as stated in the *Bhagavad-gītā* (*vedaiś ca sarvair aham eva vedyaḥ*). Māyāvādī philosophers cannot understand these simple facts explained in the *Bhagavad-gītā*, and yet they are very proud of being Vedāntīs. Sometimes, therefore, we refer to the Vedāntī philosophers as Vidantīs, those who have no teeth (*vi* means "without," and *dantī* means "possessing teeth"). The statements of the Śaṅkara philosophy, which are the teeth of the Māyāvādī philosopher, are always broken by the strong arguments of Vaiṣṇava philosophers such as the great *ācāryas*, especially Rāmānujācārya. Śrīpāda Rāmānujācārya and Madhvācārya break the teeth of the Māyāvādī philosophers, who can therefore be called Vidantīs, "toothless."

As mentioned above, the transcendental vibration *oṁkāra* is explained in the *Bhagavad-gītā*, Chapter Eight, verse thirteen:

oṁ ity ekākṣaraṁ brahma vyāharan mām anusmaran
yaḥ prayāti tyajan dehaṁ sa yāti paramāṁ gatim

"After being situated in this *yoga* practice and vibrating the sacred syllable *oṁ*, the supreme combination of letters, if one thinks of the Supreme Personality of Godhead and quits his body, he will certainly reach the spiritual planets." If one actually understands that *oṁkāra* is the sound representation of the Supreme Personality of Godhead, whether he chants *oṁkāra* or the Hare Kṛṣṇa *mantra*, the result is certainly the same.

The transcendental vibration of *oṁkāra* is further explained in the *Bhagavad-gītā*, Chapter Nine, verse seventeen:

pitāham asya jagato mātā dhātā pitāmahaḥ
vedyaṁ pavitram oṁkāra ṛk sāma yajur eva ca

"I am the father of this universe, the mother, the support and the grandsire. I am the object of knowledge, the purifier and the syllable *oṁ*. I am also the *Ṛg*, the *Sāma* and the *Yajur Vedas*."

Similarly, the transcendental sound *oṁ* is further explained in the *Bhagavad-gītā*, Chapter Seventeen, verse twenty-three:

oṁ tat sad iti nirdeśo brahmaṇas tri-vidhaḥ smṛtaḥ
brāhmaṇās tena vedāś ca yajñāś ca vihitāḥ purā

"From the beginning of creation, the three syllables *oṁ tat sat* have been used to indicate the Supreme Absolute Truth [Brahman]. They were uttered by *brāhmaṇas* while chanting Vedic hymns and during sacrifices for the satisfaction of the Supreme."

Throughout all the Vedic literatures the glories of *oṁkāra* are specifically mentioned. Śrīla Jīva Gosvāmī, in his thesis *Bhagavat-sandarbha*, says that in the Vedic literature *oṁkāra* is considered to be the sound vibration of the holy name of the Supreme Personality of Godhead. Only this vibration of transcendental sound can deliver a conditioned soul from the clutches of *māyā.* Sometimes *oṁkāra* is also called the deliverer (*tāra*). *Śrīmad-Bhāgavatam* begins with the *oṁkāra* vibration: *oṁ namo bhagavate vāsudevāya.* Therefore *oṁkāra* has been described by the great commentator Śrīdhara Svāmī as *tārāṅkura,* the seed of deliverance from the material world. Since the Supreme Godhead is absolute, His holy name and His sound vibration *oṁkāra* are as good as He Himself. Caitanya Mahāprabhu says that the holy name, or *oṁkāra,* the transcendental representation of the Supreme Personality of Godhead, has all the potencies of the Personality of Godhead.

nāmnām akāri bahudhā nija-sarva-śaktis
tatrārpitā niyamitaḥ smaraṇe na kālaḥ

All potencies are invested in the holy vibration of the holy name of the Lord. There is no doubt that the holy name of the Lord, or *oṁkāra,* is the Supreme Personality of Godhead Himself. In other words, anyone who chants *oṁkāra* and the holy name of the Lord, Hare Kṛṣṇa, immediately meets the Supreme Lord directly in His sound form. In the *Nārada-pañcarātra* it is clearly said that the Supreme Personality of Godhead Nārāyaṇa personally appears before the chanter who engages in chanting the *aṣṭākṣara,* or eight-syllable *mantra, oṁ namo nārāyaṇāya.* A similar statement in the *Māṇḍūkya Upaniṣad* declares that whatever one sees in the spiritual world is all an expansion of the spiritual potency of *oṁkāra.*

On the basis of all the *Upaniṣads,* Śrīla Jīva Gosvāmī says that *oṁkāra* is the Supreme Absolute Truth and is accepted as such by all the *ācāryas* and authorities. *Oṁkāra* is beginningless, changeless, supreme and free from deterioration and external contamination. *Oṁkāra* is the origin, middle and end of everything, and any living entity who thus understands *oṁkāra* attains the perfection of spiritual identity in *oṁkāra. Oṁkāra,* being situated in everyone's heart, is *īśvara,* the Supreme Personality of Godhead, as confirmed in the *Bhagavad-gītā* (18.61): *īśvaraḥ sarva-bhūtānāṁ hṛd-deśe 'rjuna tiṣṭhati. Oṁkāra* is as good as Viṣṇu because *oṁkāra* is as all-pervasive as Viṣṇu. One who knows *oṁkāra* and Lord Viṣṇu to be identical no longer has to lament or hanker. One who chants *oṁkāra* no longer remains a *śūdra* but immediately comes to the position of a *brāhmaṇa.* Simply by chanting *oṁkāra* one can understand the whole creation to be one unit, or an expansion of the energy of the Supreme Lord: *idaṁ hi viśvaṁ bhagavān ivetaro yato jagat-sthāna-nirodha-sambhavāḥ.* "The Supreme Lord Personality of Godhead is Himself this cosmos, and still He is aloof from it. From Him only this cosmic manifestation has emanated, in Him it rests, and unto Him it enters after annihilation." (*Bhāg.* 1.5.20) Although one who does not understand concludes otherwise, *Śrīmad-Bhāgavatam* states that the entire cosmic manifestation is but an expansion of the energy of the Supreme Lord. Realization of this is possible simply by chanting the holy name of the Lord, *oṁkāra.*

One should not, however, foolishly conclude that because the Supreme Personality of Godhead is omnipotent, we have manufactured a combination of letters—*a, u* and *m*—to represent Him. Factually the transcendental sound *oṁkāra,* although a combination of the three letters *a, u* and *m,* has transcendental potency, and one who chants *oṁkāra* will very soon realize *oṁkāra* and Lord Viṣṇu to be nondifferent. Kṛṣṇa declares, *praṇavaḥ sarva-vedeṣu:* "I am the syllable *oṁ* in the Vedic *mantras.*" (Bg. 7.8) One should therefore conclude that among the many incarnations of the Supreme Personality of Godhead, *oṁkāra* is the sound incarnation. All the *Vedas* accept this thesis. One should always remember that the holy name of the Lord and the Lord Himself are always identical (*abhinnatvān nāma-nāminoḥ*). Since *oṁkāra* is the basic principle of all Vedic knowledge, it is uttered before one begins to chant any Vedic hymn. Without *oṁkāra,* no Vedic *mantra* is successful. The Gosvāmīs therefore declare that *praṇava* (*oṁkāra*) is the complete representation of the Supreme Personality of Godhead, and they have analyzed *oṁkāra* in terms of its alphabetical constituents as follows:

a-kāreṇocyate kṛṣṇaḥ sarva-lokaika-nāyakaḥ
u-kāreṇocyate rādhā ma-kāro jīva-vācakaḥ

Oṁkāra is a combination of the letters *a, u* and *m. A-kāreṇocyate kṛṣṇaḥ:* the letter *a* (*a-kāra*) refers to Kṛṣṇa, who is *sarva-lokaika-nāyakaḥ,* the master of all living entities and planets, material and spiritual. *Nāyaka* means "leader." He is the supreme leader (*nityo nityānāṁ cetanaś cetanānām*). The letter *u* (*u-kāra*) indicates Śrīmatī Rādhārāṇī, the pleasure potency of Kṛṣṇa, and *m* (*ma-kāra*) indicates the living entities (*jīvas*). Thus *oṁ* is the complete combination of Kṛṣṇa, His potency and His eternal servitors. In other words, *oṁkāra* represents Kṛṣṇa, His name, fame, pastimes, entourage, expansions, devotees, potencies and everything else pertaining to Him. As Caitanya Mahāprabhu states in the present verse of *Śrī Caitanya-caritāmṛta, sarva-*

viśva-dhāma: oṁkāra is the resting place of everything, just as Kṛṣṇa is the resting place of everything (*brahmaṇo hi pratiṣṭhāham*).

The Māyāvādī philosophers consider many Vedic *mantras* to be the *mahā-vākya,* or principal Vedic *mantra,* such as *tat tvam asi* (*Chāndogya Upaniṣad* 6.8.7), *idaṁ sarvaṁ yad ayam ātmā* and *brahmedaṁ sarvam* (*Bṛhad-āraṇyaka Upaniṣad* 2.5.1), *ātmaivedaṁ sarvam* (*Chāndogya Upaniṣad* 7.25.2) and *neha nānāsti kiñcana* (*Kaṭha Upaniṣad* 2.1.11). That is a great mistake. Only *oṁkāra* is the *mahā-vākya.* All these other *mantras* that the Māyāvādīs accept as the *mahā-vākya* are only incidental. They cannot be taken as the *mahā-vākya,* or *mahā-mantra.* The *mantra tat tvam asi* indicates only a partial understanding of the *Vedas,* unlike *oṁkāra,* which represents the full understanding of the *Vedas.* Therefore the transcendental sound that includes all Vedic knowledge is *oṁkāra* (*praṇava*).

Aside from *oṁkāra,* none of the words uttered by the followers of Śaṅkarācārya can be considered the *mahā-vākya.* They are merely passing remarks. Śaṅkarācārya, however, has never stressed chanting of the *mahā-vākya oṁkāra;* he has accepted only *tat tvam asi* as the *mahā-vākya.* Imagining the living entity to be God, he has misrepresented all the *mantras* of the *Vedānta-sūtra* with the motive of proving that there is no separate existence of the living entities and the Supreme Absolute Truth. This is similar to the politician's attempt to prove nonviolence from the *Bhagavad-gītā.* Kṛṣṇa is violent to demons, and to attempt to prove that Kṛṣṇa is not violent is ultimately to deny Kṛṣṇa. As such explanations of the *Bhagavad-gītā* are absurd, so also is Śaṅkarācārya's explanation of the *Vedānta-sūtra,* and no sane and reasonable man will accept it. At present, however, the *Vedānta-sūtra* is misrepresented not only by the so-called Vedāntīs but also by other unscrupulous persons who are so degraded that they even recommend that *sannyāsīs* eat meat, fish and eggs. In this way, the so-called followers of Śaṅkara, the impersonalist Māyāvādīs, are sinking lower and lower. How can these degraded men explain the *Vedānta-sūtra,* which is the essence of all Vedic literature?

Lord Śrī Caitanya Mahāprabhu has declared, *māyāvādi-bhāṣya śunile haya sarva-nāśa:* "Anyone who hears commentary on the *Vedānta-sūtra* from the Māyāvāda school is completely doomed." As explained in the *Bhagavad-gītā* (15.15), *vedaiś ca sarvair aham eva vedyaḥ:* all Vedic literature aims at understanding Kṛṣṇa. Māyāvāda philosophy, however, has deviated everyone from Kṛṣṇa. Therefore there is a great need for the Kṛṣṇa consciousness movement all over the world to save the world from degradation. Every intelligent and sane man must abandon the philosophical explanation of the Māyāvādīs and accept the explanation of Vaiṣṇava *ācāryas.* One should read *Bhagavad-gītā As It Is* to try to understand the real purpose of the *Vedas.*

TEXT 129

সর্বাশ্রয় ঈশ্বরের প্রণব উদ্দেশ ।
'তত্ত্বমসি'-বাক্য হয় বেদের একদেশ ॥ ১২৯ ॥

sarvāśraya īśvarera praṇava uddeśa
'tat tvam asi'—vākya haya vedera ekadeśa

sarva-āśraya—the reservoir of everything; *īśvarera*—of the Supreme Personality of Godhead; *praṇava—oṁkāra; uddeśa*—purpose; *tat tvam asi*—the Vedic *mantra tat tvam asi* ("you are the same"); *vākya*—statement; *haya*—becomes; *vedera*—of the Vedic literature; *eka-deśa*—partial understanding.

TRANSLATION

"It is the purpose of the Supreme Personality of Godhead to present praṇava [oṁkāra] as the reservoir of all Vedic knowledge. The words 'tat tvam asi' are only a partial explanation of the Vedic knowledge.

PURPORT

Tat tvam asi means "you are the same spiritual identity."

TEXT 130

'প্রণব, মহাবাক্য—তাহা করি' আচ্ছাদন ।
মহাবাক্যে করি 'তত্ত্বমসি'র স্থাপন ॥ ১৩০ ॥

'praṇava, mahā-vākya—tāhā kari' ācchādana
mahāvākye kari 'tat tvam asi'ra sthāpana

praṇava—oṁkāra; mahā-vākya—principal *mantra; tāhā*—that; *kari'*—making; *ācchādana*—covered; *mahā-vākye*—in place of the principal *mantra; kari*—I do; *'tat tvam asi'ra sthāpana*—establishment of the statement *tat tvam asi.*

TRANSLATION

"Praṇava [oṁkāra] is the mahā-vākya [mahā-mantra] in the Vedas. Śaṅkarācārya's followers cover this to stress without authority the mantra tat tvam asi.

PURPORT

The Māyāvādī philosophers stress the statements *tat tvam asi, so 'ham,* etc., but they do not stress the real *mahā-mantra, praṇava* (*oṁkāra*). Therefore, because they misrepresent Vedic knowledge, they are the greatest offenders to the lotus feet of the Lord. Caitanya Mahāprabhu says clearly, *māyāvādī kṛṣṇe aparādhī:* "Māyāvādī philosophers are the greatest offenders to Lord Kṛṣṇa." Lord Kṛṣṇa declares:

tān ahaṁ dviṣataḥ krūrān saṁsāreṣu narādhamān
kṣipāmy ajasram aśubhān āsurīṣv eva yoniṣu

"Those who are envious and mischievous, who are the lowest among mankind, I perpetually cast into the ocean of material existence, into various demoniac species of life." (Bg. 16.19) Life in demoniac species awaits the Māyāvādī philosophers after death because they are envious of Kṛṣṇa. When Kṛṣṇa says in the *Bhagavad-gītā* (9.34) *man-manā bhava mad-bhakto mad-yājī māṁ namaskuru* ("Engage your mind always in thinking of Me, become My devotee, offer obeisances to Me and worship Me"), one demoniac scholar says that it is not Kṛṣṇa to whom one must surrender. This scholar is already suffering in this life, and he will have to suffer again in the next if in this life he does not complete his prescribed suffering. One should be very careful not to be envious of the Supreme Personality of Godhead. In the next verse, therefore, Śrī Caitanya Mahāprabhu clearly states the purpose of the *Vedas.*

TEXT 131

সর্ববেদসূত্রে করে কৃষ্ণের অভিধান ।
মুখ্যবৃত্তি ছাড়ি' কৈল লক্ষণা-ব্যাখ্যান ॥ ১৩১ ॥

sarva-veda-sūtre kare kṛṣṇera abhidhāna
mukhya-vṛtti chāḍi' kaila lakṣaṇā-vyākhyāna

sarva-veda-sūtre—in all the aphorisms of the *Vedānta-sūtra; kare*—establishes; *kṛṣṇera*—of Lord Kṛṣṇa; *abhidhāna*—explanation; *mukhya-vṛtti*—direct interpretation; *chāḍi'*—giving up; *kaila*—made; *lakṣaṇā*—indirect; *vyākhyāna*—explanation.

TRANSLATION

"In all the Vedic sūtras and literatures, it is Lord Kṛṣṇa who is to be understood, but the followers of Śaṅkarācārya have covered the real meaning of the Vedas with indirect explanations.

PURPORT

It is said:

vede rāmāyaṇe caiva purāṇe bhārate tathā
ādāv ante ca madhye ca hariḥ sarvatra gīyate

"In the Vedic literature, including the *Rāmāyaṇa, Purāṇas* and *Mahābhārata,* from the very beginning (*ādau*) to the end (*ante ca*), as well as within the middle (*madhye ca*), only Hari, the Supreme Personality of Godhead, is explained."

TEXT 132

স্বতঃপ্রমাণ বেদ প্রমাণ-শিরোমণি ।
লক্ষণা করিলে স্বতঃপ্রমাণতা-হানি ॥ ১৩২ ॥

svataḥ-pramāṇa veda—pramāṇa-śiromaṇi
lakṣaṇā karile svataḥ-pramāṇatā-hāni

svataḥ-pramāṇa—self-evident; *veda*—the Vedic literatures; *pramāṇa*—evidence; *śiromaṇi*—topmost; *lakṣaṇā*—interpretation; *karile*—doing; *svataḥ-pramāṇatā*—self-evidence; *hāni*—lost.

TRANSLATION

"The self-evident Vedic literatures are the highest evidence of all, but if these literatures are interpreted, their self-evident nature is lost.

PURPORT

We quote Vedic evidence to support our statements, but if we interpret it according to our own judgment, the authority of the Vedic literature is rendered imperfect or useless. In other words, by interpreting the Vedic version one minimizes the value of Vedic evidence. When one quotes from Vedic literature, it is understood that the quotations are authoritative. How can one bring the authority under his own control? That is a case of *principiis obsta.*

TEXT 133

এই মত প্রতিসূত্রে সহজার্থ ছাড়িয়া ।
গৌণার্থ ব্যাখ্যা করে কল্পনা করিয়া ॥ ১৩৩ ॥

ei mata pratisūtre sahajārtha chāḍiyā
gauṇārtha vyākhyā kare kalpanā kariyā

ei mata—like this; *prati-sūtre*—in every *sūtra,* or aphorism, of the *Vedānta-sūtra; sahaja-artha*—the clear, simple meaning; *chāḍiyā*—giving up; *gauṇa-artha*—indirect meaning; *vyākhyā*—explanation; *kare*—he makes; *kalpanā kariyā*—by imagination.

TRANSLATION

"To prove their philosophy, the members of the Māyāvāda school have given up the real, easily understood meaning of the Vedic literature and introduced indirect meanings based on their imaginative powers."

PURPORT

Unfortunately, the Śaṅkarite interpretation has covered almost the entire world. Therefore there is a great need to present the original, easily understood natural import of the Vedic literature. We have therefore begun by presenting *Bhagavad-gītā As It Is,* and we propose to present all the Vedic literature in terms of the direct meaning of its words.

TEXT 134

এই মতে প্রতিসূত্রে করেন দূষণ ।
শুনি' চমৎকার হৈল সন্ন্যাসীর গণ ॥ ১৩৪ ॥

ei mate pratisūtre karena dūṣaṇa
śuni' camatkāra haila sannyāsīra gaṇa

ei mate—in this way; *prati-sūtre*—in each and every aphorism; *karena*—shows; *dūṣaṇa*—defects; *śuniyā*—hearing; *camatkāra*—

struck with wonder; *haila*—they became; *sannyāsīra*—of all the Māyāvādīs; *gaṇa*—the group.

TRANSLATION

When Śrī Caitanya Mahāprabhu thus showed for each and every sūtra the defects in Śaṅkarācārya's explanations, all the assembled Māyāvādī sannyāsīs were struck with wonder.

TEXT 135

সকল সন্ন্যাসী কহে,—'শুনহ শ্রীপাদ ।
তুমি যে খণ্ডিলে অর্থ, এ নহে বিবাদ ॥ ১৩৫ ॥

sakala sannyāsī kahe,—'śunaha śrīpāda
tumi ye khaṇḍile artha, e nahe vivāda

sakala—all; *sannyāsī*—the Māyāvādī *sannyāsīs; kahe*—say; *śunaha*—please hear; *śrīpāda*—Your Holiness; *tumi*—You; *ye*—that; *khaṇḍile*—refuted; *artha*—meaning; *e*—this; *nahe*—not; *vivāda*—quarrel.

TRANSLATION

All the Māyāvādī sannyāsīs said, "Your Holiness, kindly know from us that we actually have no quarrel with Your refutation of these meanings, for You have given a clear understanding of the sūtras.

TEXT 136

আচার্য-কল্পিত অর্থ,—ইহা সভে জানি ।
সম্প্রদায়-অনুরোধে তবু তাহা মানি ॥ ১৩৬ ॥

ācārya-kalpita artha,—ihā sabhe jāni
sampradāya-anurodhe tabu tāhā māni

ācārya—Śaṅkarācārya; *kalpita*—imaginative; *artha*—meaning; *ihā*—this; *sabhe*—all of us; *jāni*—know; *sampradāya-anurodhe*—but for the sake of our party; *tabu*—still; *tāhā*—that; *māni*—we accept.

TRANSLATION

"We know that all this word jugglery springs from the imagination of Śaṅkarācārya, and yet because we belong to his sect, we accept it although it does not satisfy us.

TEXT 137

মুখ্যার্থ ব্যাখ্যা কর, দেখি তোমার বল ।'
মুখ্যার্থে লাগাল প্রভু সূত্রসকল ॥ ১৩৭ ॥

mukhyārtha vyākhyā kara, dekhi tomāra bala'
mukhyārthe lāgāla prabhu sūtra-sakala

mukhya-artha—direct meaning; *vyākhyā*—explanation; *kara*—You do; *dekhi*—let us see; *tomāra*—Your; *bala*—strength; *mukhya-arthe*—direct meaning; *lāgāla*—began; *prabhu*—the Lord; *sūtra-sakala*—all the aphorisms of the *Vedānta-sūtra.*

TRANSLATION

"Now let us see," the Māyāvādī sannyāsīs continued, "how well You can describe the sūtras in terms of their direct meaning." Hearing this, Lord Caitanya Mahāprabhu began His direct explanation of the Vedānta-sūtra.

TEXT 138

বৃহদ্বস্তু 'ব্রহ্ম' কহি—'শ্রীভগবান্' ।
ষড়্বিধৈশ্বর্যপূর্ণ, পরতত্ত্বধাম ॥ ১৩৮ ॥

bṛhad-vastu 'brahma' kahi—'śrī-bhagavān'
ṣaḍ-vidhaiśvarya-pūrṇa, para-tattva-dhāma

bṛhat-vastu—the substance, which is greater than the greatest; *brahma*—called by the name Brahman; *kahi*—we call; *śrī-bhagavān*—the Supreme Personality of Godhead; *ṣaṭ*—six; *vidha*—varieties; *aiś-varya*—opulences; *pūrṇa*—full; *para-tattva*—Absolute Truth; *dhāma*—reservoir.

TRANSLATION

"Brahman, who is greater than the greatest, is the Supreme Personality of Godhead. He is full in six opulences, and therefore He is the reservoir of ultimate truth and absolute knowledge.

PURPORT

In *Śrīmad-Bhāgavatam* it is said that the Absolute Truth is understood in three phases of realization: the impersonal Brahman, the localized

Paramātmā and ultimately the Supreme Personality of Godhead. The impersonal Brahman and localized Paramātmā are expansions of the potency of the Supreme Personality of Godhead, who is complete in six opulences, namely wealth, fame, strength, beauty, knowledge and renunciation. Since He possesses His six opulences, the Personality of Godhead is the ultimate truth in absolute knowledge.

TEXT 139

স্বরূপ-ঐশ্বর্যে তাঁর নাহি মায়াগন্ধ ।
সকল বেদের হয় ভগবান্ সে 'সম্বন্ধ' ॥ ১৩৯ ॥

svarūpa-aiśvarye tāṅra nāhi māyā-gandha
sakala vedera haya bhagavān se 'sambandha'

svarūpa—in His original form; *aiśvarye*—opulence; *tāṅra*—His; *nāhi*—there is none; *māyā-gandha*—contamination of the material world; *sakala*—in all; *vedera*—*Vedas; haya*—it is so; *bhagavān*—the Supreme Personality of Godhead; *se*—that; *sambandha*—relationship.

TRANSLATION

"In His original form the Supreme Personality of Godhead is full with transcendental opulences, which are free from the contamination of the material world. It is to be understood that in all Vedic literature the Supreme Personality of Godhead is the ultimate goal.

TEXT 140

তাঁরে 'নির্বিশেষ' কহি, চিচ্ছক্তি না মানি ।
অর্ধ স্বরূপ না মানিলে পূর্ণতা হয় হানি ॥ ১৪০ ॥

tāṅre 'nirviśeṣa' kahi, cic-chakti nā māni
ardha-svarūpa nā mānile pūrṇatā haya hāni

tāṅre—unto Him; *nirviśeṣa*—impersonal; *kahi*—we say; *cit-śakti*—spiritual energy; *nā*—do not; *māni*—accept; *ardha*—half; *svarūpa*—form; *nā*—not; *mānile*—accepting; *pūrṇatā*—fullness; *haya*—becomes; *hāni*—defective.

TRANSLATION

"When we speak of the Supreme as impersonal, we deny His spiritual potencies. Logically, if you accept half of the truth, you cannot understand the whole.

PURPORT

In the *Upaniṣads* it is said:

> *oṁ pūrṇam adaḥ pūrṇam idaṁ pūrṇāt pūrṇam udacyate*
> *pūrṇasya pūrṇam ādāya pūrṇam evāvaśiṣyate*

This verse, which is mentioned in the *Īśopaniṣad, Bṛhad-āraṇyaka Upaniṣad* and many other *Upaniṣads,* indicates that the Supreme Personality of Godhead is full in six opulences. His position is unique, for He possesses all riches, strength, influence, beauty, knowledge and renunciation. Brahman means the greatest, but the Supreme Personality of Godhead is greater than the greatest, just as the sun globe is greater than the sunshine, which is all-pervading in the universe. Although the sunshine that spreads all over the universes appears very great to the less knowledgeable, greater than the sunshine is the sun itself, and greater than the sun is the sun-god. Similarly, impersonal Brahman is not the greatest, although it appears to be so. Impersonal Brahman is only the bodily effulgence of the Supreme Personality of Godhead, but the transcendental form of the Lord is greater than both the impersonal Brahman and localized Paramātmā. Therefore whenever the word "Brahman" is used in the Vedic literature, it is understood to refer to the Supreme Personality of Godhead.

In the *Bhagavad-gītā* the Lord is also addressed as Parabrahman. Māyāvādīs and others sometimes misunderstand Brahman because every living entity is also Brahman. Therefore Kṛṣṇa is referred to as Parabrahman (the Supreme Brahman). In the Vedic literature, whenever the words "Brahman" or "Parabrahman" are used, they are to be understood to refer to the Supreme Personality of Godhead, Kṛṣṇa. This is their real meaning. Since the entire Vedic literature deals with the subject of Brahman, Kṛṣṇa is therefore the ultimate goal of Vedic understanding. The impersonal *brahmajyoti* rests on the personal form of the Lord. Therefore although the impersonal effulgence, the *brahmajyoti,* is the first realization, one must enter into it, as mentioned in the *Īśopaniṣad,* to find the Supreme Person, and then one's knowledge is perfect. The *Bhagavad-gītā* (7.19) also confirms this: *bahūnāṁ janmanām ante jñānavān māṁ prapadyate.* One's search for the Absolute Truth by dint of speculative knowledge is complete when one comes to the point of understanding Kṛṣṇa and surrenders unto Him. That is the real point of perfectional knowledge.

Partial realization of the Absolute Truth as impersonal Brahman denies the complete opulences of the Lord. This is a hazardous understanding of the Absolute Truth. Unless one accepts all the features of the Absolute Truth—namely impersonal Brahman, localized Paramātmā and ultimately the Supreme Personality of Godhead—one's knowledge is imperfect. Śrīpāda Rāmānujācārya, in his *Vedārtha-saṅgraha*, says, *jñānena dharmeṇa svarūpam api nirūpitam, na tu jñāna-mātraṁ brahmeti katham idam avagamyate.* He thus indicates that the real identity of the Absolute Truth must be understood in terms of both His knowledge and His characteristics. Simply to understand the Absolute Truth to be full of knowledge is not sufficient. In the Vedic literature (*Muṇḍaka Up.* 1.1.9) we find the statement *yaḥ sarva-jñaḥ sarva-vit,* which means that the Absolute Truth knows everything perfectly, but we also learn from the Vedic description *parāsya śaktir vividhaiva śrūyate* that not only does He know everything, but He also acts accordingly by utilizing His different energies. Thus to understand that Brahman, the Supreme, is conscious is not sufficient. One must know how He consciously acts through His different energies. Māyāvāda philosophy simply informs us of the consciousness of the Absolute Truth but does not give us information of how He acts with His consciousness. That is the defect of that philosophy.

TEXT 141

ভগবান্-প্রাপ্তিহেতু যে করি উপায় ।
শ্রবণাদি ভক্তি—কৃষ্ণ-প্রাপ্তির সহায় ॥ ১৪১ ॥

bhagavān-prāpti-hetu ye kari upāya
śravaṇādi bhakti—kṛṣṇa-prāptira sahāya

bhagavān—the Supreme Personality of Godhead; *prāpti-hetu*—the means by which He can be approached; *ye*—what; *kari*—I do; *upāya*—means; *śravaṇa-ādi*—devotional service, beginning with hearing; *bhakti*—devotional service; *kṛṣṇa*—the Supreme Lord; *prāptira*—to approach Him; *sahāya*—means.

TRANSLATION

"It is only by devotional service, beginning with hearing, that one can approach the Supreme Personality of Godhead. That is the only means to approach Him.

PURPORT

Māyāvādī philosophers are satisfied simply to understand Brahman to be the sum total of knowledge, but Vaiṣṇava philosophers not only know in detail about the Supreme Personality of Godhead but also know how to approach Him directly. The method for this is described by Śrī Caitanya Mahāprabhu as nine kinds of devotional service, beginning with hearing:

śravaṇaṁ kīrtanaṁ viṣṇoḥ smaraṇaṁ pāda-sevanam
arcanaṁ vandanaṁ dāsyaṁ sakhyam ātma-nivedanam
(*Bhāg.* 7.5.23)

The nine kinds of devotional service are hearing about Kṛṣṇa, chanting about Him, remembering Him, offering service to His lotus feet, offering Him worship in the temple, offering prayers to Him, working as His servant, making friendship with Him and unreservedly surrendering to Him. One can directly approach the Supreme Personality of Godhead simply by executing these nine kinds of devotional service, of which hearing about the Lord is the most important (*śravaṇādi*). Śrī Caitanya Mahāprabhu has very favorably stressed the importance of this process of hearing. According to His method, if people are simply given a chance to hear about Kṛṣṇa, certainly they will gradually develop their dormant awareness, or love of Godhead. *Śravaṇādi-śuddha-citte karaye udaya* (Cc. *Madhya* 22.107). Love of God is dormant in everyone, and if one is given a chance to hear about the Lord, certainly that love develops. Our Kṛṣṇa consciousness movement acts on this principle. We simply give people the chance to hear about the Supreme Personality of Godhead and give them *prasādam* to eat, and the actual result is that all over the world people are responding to this process and becoming pure devotees of Lord Kṛṣṇa. We have opened hundreds of centers all over the world just to give people in general a chance to hear about Kṛṣṇa and accept Kṛṣṇa's *prasādam.* These two processes can be accepted by anyone, even a child. It doesn't matter whether one is poor or rich, learned or foolish, black or white, old or still a child—anyone who simply hears about the Supreme Personality of Godhead and takes *prasādam* is certainly elevated to the transcendental position of devotional service.

TEXT 142

সেই সর্ববেদের 'অভিধেয়' নাম ।
সাধনভক্তি হৈতে হয় প্রেমের উদগম ॥ ১৪২ ॥

sei sarva-vedera 'abhidheya' nāma
sādhana-bhakti haite haya premera udgama

sei sarva-vedera—that is the essence of all Vedic literature; *abhidheya nāma*—the process called *abhidheya*, or devotional activities; *sādhana-bhakti*—another name of this process, "devotional service in practice"; *haite*—from this; *haya*—there is; *premera*—of love of Godhead; *udgama*—awakening.

TRANSLATION

"By practicing this regulated devotional service under the direction of the spiritual master, certainly one awakens his dormant love of Godhead. This process is called abhidheya.

PURPORT

By the practice of devotional service, beginning with hearing and chanting, the impure heart of a conditioned soul is purified, and thus he can understand his eternal relationship with the Supreme personality of Godhead. That eternal relationship is described by Śrī Caitanya Mahāprabhu: *jīvera 'svarūpa' haya kṛṣṇera 'nitya-dāsa.'* "The living entity is an eternal servitor of the Supreme Personality of Godhead." When one is convinced about this relationship, which is called *sambandha*, he then acts accordingly. That is called *abhidheya.* The next step is *prayojana-siddhi*, or fulfillment of the ultimate goal of one's life. If one can understand his relationship with the Supreme Personality of Godhead and act accordingly, automatically his mission in life is fulfilled. The Māyāvādī philosophers miss even the first stage in self-realization because they have no conception of God's being personal. He is the master of all, and He is the only person who can accept the service of all living entities, but since this knowledge is lacking in Māyāvāda philosophy, Māyāvādīs do not have knowledge even of their relationship with God. They wrongly think that everyone is God or that everyone is equal to God. Therefore, since the real position of the living entity is not clear to them, how can they advance further? Although they are very much puffed up at being liberated, Māyāvādī philosophers very shortly fall down again to material activities due to their neglecting the lotus feet of the Lord. That is called *patanty adhaḥ:*

ye 'nye 'ravindākṣa vimukta-māninas
tvayy asta-bhāvād aviśuddha-buddhayaḥ

āruhya kṛcchreṇa paraṁ padaṁ tataḥ
patanty adho 'nādṛta-yuṣmad-aṅghrayaḥ
(*Bhāg.* 10.2.32)

Here it is said that persons who think themselves liberated but do not execute devotional service, not knowing their relationship with the Lord, are certainly misled. One must know his relationship with the Lord and act accordingly. Then the fulfillment of his life's mission will be possible.

TEXT 143

কৃষ্ণের চরণে হয় যদি অনুরাগ ।
কৃষ্ণ বিনু অন্যত্র তার নাহি রহে রাগ ॥ ১৪৩ ॥

kṛṣṇera caraṇe haya yadi anurāga
kṛṣṇa vinu anyatra tāra nāhi rahe rāga

kṛṣṇera—of Kṛṣṇa; *caraṇe*—at the lotus feet; *haya*—becomes; *yadi*—if; *anurāga*—attachment; *kṛṣṇa*—the Supreme Personality of Godhead; *vinu*—without; *anyatra*—anywhere else; *tāra*—his; *nāhi*—there does not; *rahe*—remain; *rāga*—attachment.

TRANSLATION

"If one develops his love of Godhead and becomes attached to the lotus feet of Kṛṣṇa, gradually he loses his attachment to everything else.

PURPORT

This is a test of advancement in devotional service. As stated in *Śrīmad-Bhāgavatam* (11.2.42), *bhaktir pareśānubhavo viraktir anyatra ca:* in *bhakti,* a devotee's only attachment is Kṛṣṇa; he no longer wants to maintain his attachments to many other things. Although Māyāvādī philosophers are supposed to be very much advanced on the path of liberation, we see that after some time they descend to politics and philanthropic activities. Many big *sannyāsīs* who were supposedly liberated and very advanced have come down again to materialistic activities, although they left this world as *mithyā* (false). When a devotee develops in devotional service, however, he no longer has attachments to such philanthropic activities. He is simply inspired to serve the Lord, and he engages his entire life in such service. This is the difference between Vaiṣṇava and Māyāvādī philosophers. Devotional service, therefore, is practical, whereas Māyāvāda philosophy is merely mental speculation.

TEXT 144

পঞ্চম পুরুষার্থ সেই প্রেম-মহাধন ।
কৃষ্ণের মাধুর্য-রস করায় আস্বাদন ॥ ১৪৪ ॥

pañcama puruṣārtha sei prema-mahādhana
kṛṣṇera mādhurya-rasa karāya āsvādana

pañcama—fifth; *puruṣa-artha*—goal of life; *sei*—that; *prema*—love of God; *mahā-dhana*—foremost wealth; *kṛṣṇera*—of Lord Kṛṣṇa; *mādhurya*—conjugal love; *rasa*—mellow; *karāya*—causes; *āsvādana*—taste.

TRANSLATION

"Love of Godhead is so exalted that it is considered to be the fifth goal of human life. By awakening one's love of Godhead, one can attain the platform of conjugal love, tasting it even during the present span of life.

PURPORT

The Māyāvādī philosophers consider the highest goal of perfection to be liberation (*mukti*), which is the fourth perfectional platform. Generally people are aware of four principal goals of life—religiosity (*dharma*), economic development (*artha*), sense gratification (*kāma*) and ultimately liberation (*mokṣa*)—but devotional service is situated on the platform above liberation. In other words, when one is actually liberated (*mukta*) he can understand the meaning of love of Godhead (*kṛṣṇa-prema*). While teaching Rūpa Gosvāmī, Śrī Caitanya Mahāprabhu stated, *koṭi-mukta-madhye 'durlabha' eka kṛṣṇa-bhakta:* "Out of millions of liberated persons, one may become a devotee of Lord Kṛṣṇa."

The most elevated Māyāvādī philosopher can rise to the platform of liberation, but *kṛṣṇa-bhakti*, devotional service to Kṛṣṇa, is transcendental to such liberation. Śrīla Vyāsadeva explains this fact in *Śrīmad-Bhāgavatam* (1.1.2):

dharmaḥ projjhita-kaitavo 'tra paramo nirmatsarāṇāṁ satāṁ
vedyaṁ vāstavam atra vastu śiva-daṁ tāpa-trayonmūlanam

"Completely rejecting all religions which are materially motivated, the *Bhāgavata Purāṇa* propounds the highest truth, which is understandable by those devotees who are pure in heart. The highest truth is reality distinguished from illusion for the welfare of all. Such truth uproots the threefold miseries." *Śrīmad-Bhāgavatam,* the explanation of the *Vedānta-sūtra,* is meant for *paramo nirmatsarāṇām,* those who are completely aloof from jealousy. Māyāvādī philosophers are jealous of the existence of the Personality of Godhead. Therefore the *Vedānta-sūtra* is not actually meant for them. They unnecessarily poke their noses into the *Vedanta-sūtra,* but they have no ability to understand it because, as the author of the *Vedānta-sūtra* writes in his commentary, *Śrīmad-Bhāgavatam,* it is meant for those who are pure in heart (*paramo nirmatsarāṇām*). If one is envious of Kṛṣṇa, how can he understand the *Vedānta-sūtra* or *Śrīmad-Bhāgavatam*? The Māyāvādīs' primary occupation is to offend the Supreme Personality of Godhead, Kṛṣṇa. For example, although Kṛṣṇa demands our surrender in the *Bhagavad-gītā,* the greatest scholar and so-called philosopher in modern India has protested that it is "not to Kṛṣṇa" that we have to surrender. Therefore, he is envious. Since Māyāvādīs of all different descriptions are envious of Kṛṣṇa, they have no scope for understanding the meaning of the *Vedānta-sūtra.* Even if they were on the liberated platform, as they falsely claim, love of Kṛṣṇa is beyond the state of liberation—a fact stated by Śrī Caitanya Mahāprabhu and repeated here by Kṛṣṇadāsa Kavirāja Gosvāmī.

TEXT 145

প্রেমা হৈতে কৃষ্ণ হয় নিজ ভক্তবশ ।
প্রেমা হৈতে পায় কৃষ্ণের সেবা-সুখরস ॥ ১৪৫ ॥

premā haite kṛṣṇa haya nija bhakta-vaśa
premā haite pāya kṛṣṇera sevā-sukha-rasa

premā—love of Kṛṣṇa; *haite*—from; *kṛṣṇa*—the Supreme Personality of Godhead; *haya*—becomes; *nija*—His own; *bhakta-vaśa*—submissive to devotees; *premā*—love of God; *haite*—from; *pāya*—he gets; *kṛṣṇera*—of Lord Kṛṣṇa; *sevā-sukha-rasa*—the mellow of devotional service.

TRANSLATION

"The Supreme Lord, who is greater than the greatest, becomes submissive to even a very insignificant devotee because of his devotional service. It is the beautiful and exalted nature of devotional service that the infinite Lord becomes submissive to the infinitesimal living entity because of it. In reciprocal devotional activities with the Lord, the devotee actually enjoys the transcendental mellow of devotional service.

PURPORT

Becoming one with the Supreme Personality of Godhead is not very important for a devotee. *Muktiḥ svayaṁ mukulitāñjali sevate 'smān* (*Kṛṣṇa-karṇāmṛta* 107). Speaking from his actual experience, Śrīla Bilvamaṅgala Ṭhākura says that if one develops love of Godhead, *mukti* (liberation) becomes subservient and unimportant to him. *Mukti* stands before the devotee and is prepared to render all kinds of services. The Māyāvādī philosophers' standard of *mukti* is very insignificant for a devotee, for by devotional service even the Supreme Personality of Godhead becomes subordinate to him. An actual example is that the Supreme Lord Kṛṣṇa became the chariot driver of Arjuna, and when Arjuna asked Him to draw his chariot between the two armies (*senayor ubhayor madhye rathaṁ sthāpaya me 'cyuta*), Kṛṣṇa executed his order. Such is the relationship between the Supreme Lord and a devotee that although the Lord is greater than the greatest, He is prepared to render service to the insignificant devotee by dint of his sincere and unalloyed devotional service.

TEXT 146

সম্বন্ধ, অভিধেয়, প্রয়োজন নাম ।
এই তিন অর্থ সর্বসূত্রে পর্যবসান ॥ ১৪৬ ॥

sambandha, abhidheya, prayojana nāma
ei tina artha sarva-sūtre paryavasāna

sambandha—relationship; *abhidheya*—functional duties; *prayojana*—the goal of life; *nāma*—name; *ei*—there; *tina*—three; *artha*—purport; *sarva*—all; *sūtre*—in the aphorisms of the *Vedānta; paryavasāna*—culmination.

TRANSLATION

"One's relationship with the Supreme Personality of Godhead, activities in terms of that relationship, and the ultimate goal of life [to develop love of God]—these three subjects are explained in every aphorism of the Vedānta-sūtra, for they form the culmination of the entire Vedānta philosophy."

PURPORT

In *Śrīmad-Bhāgavatam* (5.5.5) it is said:

parābhavas tāvad abodha-jāto
yāvan na jijñāsata ātma-tattvam

"A human being is defeated in all his activities as long as he does not know the goal of life, which can be understood when one is inquisitive about Brahman." It is such inquiry that begins the *Vedānta-sūtra: athāto brahma-jijñāsā.* A human being should be inquisitive to know who he is, what the universe is, what God is, and what the relationship is between himself, God and the material world. Such questions cannot be asked by cats and dogs, but they must arise in the heart of a real human being. Knowledge of these four items—namely oneself, the universe, God, and their internal relationship—is called *sambandha-jñāna*, or the knowledge of one's relationship. When one's relationship with the Supreme Lord is established, the next program is to act in that relationship. This is called *abhidheya*, or activity in relationship with the Lord. After executing such prescribed duties, when one attains the highest goal of life, love of Godhead, he achieves *prayojana-siddhi*, or the fulfillment of his human mission. In the *Brahma-sūtra*, or *Vedānta-sūtra*, these subjects are very carefully explained. Therefore one who does not understand the *Vedānta-sūtra* in terms of these principles is simply wasting his time. This is the version of *Śrīmad-Bhāgavatam* (1.2.8):

dharmaḥ sv-anuṣṭhitaḥ puṁsāṁ viṣvaksena-kathāsu yaḥ
notpādayed yadi ratiṁ śrama eva hi kevalam

One may be a very learned scholar and execute his prescribed duty very nicely, but if he does not ultimately become inquisitive about the Supreme Personality of Godhead and is indifferent to *śravaṇaṁ kīrtanam* (hearing and chanting), all that he has done is but a waste of time. Māyāvādī philosophers, who do not understand the relationship between themselves, the cosmic manifestation and the Supreme Personality of Godhead, are simply wasting their time, and their philosophical speculation has no value.

TEXT 147

এইমত সর্বসূত্রের ব্যাখ্যান শুনিয়া ।
সকল সন্ন্যাসী কহে বিনয় করিয়া ॥ ১৪৭ ॥

ei-mata sarva-sūtrera vyākhyāna śuniyā
sakala sannyāsī kahe vinaya kariyā

ei-mata—in this way; *sarva-sūtrera*—of all the aphorisms of the *Vedānta-sūtra; vyākhyāna*—explanation; *śuniyā*—by hearing; *sakala*—all; *sannyāsī*—the groups of Māyāvādī *sannyāsīs; kahe*—said; *vinaya*—humbly; *kariyā*—doing so.

TRANSLATION

When all the Māyāvādī sannyāsīs thus heard the explanation of Caitanya Mahāprabhu on the basis of sambandha, abhidheya and prayojana, they spoke very humbly.

PURPORT

Everyone who actually desires to understand the Vedānta philosophy must certainly accept the explanation of Lord Caitanya Mahāprabhu and the Vaiṣṇava *ācāryas* who have also commented on the *Vedānta-sūtra* according to the principles of *bhakti-yoga.* After hearing the explanation of the *Vedānta-sūtra* from Śrī Caitanya Mahāprabhu, all the *sannyāsīs,* headed by Prakāśānanda Sarasvatī, became very humble and obedient to the Lord, and they spoke as follows.

TEXT 148

বেদময়-মূর্তি তুমি,—সাক্ষাৎ নারায়ণ ।
ক্ষম অপরাধ,—পূর্বে যে কৈলুঁ নিন্দন ॥ ১৪৮ ॥

vedamaya-mūrti tumi,—sākṣāt nārāyaṇa
kṣama aparādha,—pūrve ye kailuṅ nindana

veda-maya—transformation of the Vedic knowledge; *mūrti*—form; *tumi*—You; *sākṣāt*—directly; *nārāyaṇa*—the Supreme Personality of Godhead; *kṣama*—excuse; *aparādha*—offense; *pūrve*—before; *ye*—that; *kailuṅ*—we have done; *nindana*—criticism.

TRANSLATION

"Dear Sir, You are Vedic knowledge personified and are directly Nārāyaṇa Himself. Kindly excuse us for the offenses we previously committed by criticizing You."

PURPORT

The complete path of *bhakti-yoga* is based upon the process of becoming humble and submissive. By the grace of Lord Caitanya Mahāprabhu, all the Māyāvādī *sannyāsīs* were very humble and submissive after hearing His explanation of the *Vedānta-sūtra*, and they begged to be pardoned for the offenses they had committed by criticizing the Lord for simply chanting and dancing and not taking part in the study of the *Vedānta-sūtra.* We are propagating the Kṛṣṇa consciousness movement simply by following in the footsteps of Lord Caitanya Mahāprabhu. We may not be very well versed in the *Vedānta-sūtra* aphorisms and may not understand their meaning, but we follow in the footsteps of the *ācāryas,* and because of our strictly and obediently following in the footsteps of Lord Caitanya Mahāprabhu, it is to be understood that we know everything regarding the *Vedānta-sūtra.*

TEXT 149

সেই হৈতে সন্ন্যাসীর ফিরি গেল মন ।
'কৃষ্ণ' 'কৃষ্ণ' নাম সদা করয়ে গ্রহণ ॥ ১৪৯ ॥

sei haite sannyāsīra phiri gela mana
'kṛṣṇa' 'kṛṣṇa' nāma sadā karaye grahaṇa

sei haite—from that time; *sannyāsīra*—all the Māyāvādī *sannyāsīs; phiri*—turn; *gela*—became; *mana*—mind; *kṛṣṇa kṛṣṇa*—the holy name of the Supreme Personality of Godhead, Kṛṣṇa; *nāma*—name; *sadā*—always; *karaye*—do; *grahaṇa*—accept.

TRANSLATION

From that moment when the Māyāvādī sannyāsīs heard the explanation of the Vedānta-sūtra from the Lord, their minds changed, and on the instruction of Caitanya Mahāprabhu, they too chanted "Kṛṣṇa! Kṛṣṇa!" always.

PURPORT

In this connection it may be mentioned that sometimes the *sahajiyā* class of devotees opine that Prakāśānanda Sarasvatī and Prabodhānanda Sarasvatī are the same man. Prabodhānanda Sarasvatī was a great Vaiṣṇava devotee of Lord Caitanya Mahāprabhu, but Prakāśānanda Sarasvatī, the head of the Māyāvādī *sannyāsīs* in Benares, was a different person. Prabodhānanda Sarasvatī belonged to the Rāmānuja-sampradāya, whereas Prakāśānanda Sarasvatī belonged to the Śaṅkarācārya-sampradāya. Prabodhānanda Sarasvatī wrote a number of books, among which are the *Caitanya-candrāmṛta, Rādhā-rasa-sudhā-nidhi, Saṅgīta-mādhava, Vṛndāvana-śataka* and *Navadvīpa-śataka.* While traveling in southern India, Caitanya Mahāprabhu met Prabodhānanda Sarasvatī, who had two brothers, Veṅkaṭa Bhaṭṭa and Tirumalaya Bhaṭṭa, who were Vaiṣṇavas of the Rāmānuja-sampradāya. Gopāla Bhaṭṭa Gosvāmī was the nephew of Prabodhānanda Sarasvatī. From historical records it is found that Śrī Caitanya Mahāprabhu traveled in South India in the year 1433 Śakābda (A.D. 1511) during the Cāturmāsya period, and it was at that time that He met Prabodhānanda, who belonged to the Rāmānuja-sampradāya. How then could the same person meet Him as a member of the Śaṅkara-sampradāya in 1435 Śakābda, two years later? It is to be concluded that the guess of the *saha-jiyā-sampradāya* that Prabodhānanda Sarasvatī and Prakāśānanda Sarasvatī were the same man is a mistaken idea.

TEXT 150

এইমতে তাঁ-সবার ক্ষমি' অপরাধ ।
সবাকারে কৃষ্ণ নাম করিলা প্রসাদ ॥ ১৫০ ॥

ei-mate tāṅ-sabāra kṣami' aparādha
sabākāre kṛṣṇa-nāma karilā prasāda

ei-mate—in this way; *tāṅ-sabāra*—of all the *sannyāsīs; kṣami'*—excusing; *aparādha*—offense; *sabākāre*—all of them; *kṛṣṇa-nāma*—the holy name of Kṛṣṇa; *karilā*—gave; *prasāda*—as mercy.

TRANSLATION

Thus Lord Caitanya excused all the offenses of the Māyāvādī sannyāsīs and very mercifully blessed them with kṛṣṇa-nāma.

PURPORT

Śrī Caitanya Mahāprabhu is the mercy incarnation of the Supreme Personality of Godhead. He is addressed by Śrīla Rūpa Gosvāmī as *mahā-vadānyāvatāra,* or the most magnanimous incarnation. Śrīla Rūpa Gosvāmī also says, *karuṇayāvatīrṇaḥ kalau:* it is only by His mercy that He has descended in this Age of Kali. Here this is exemplified. Śrī Caitanya Mahāprabhu did not like to see Māyāvādī *sannyāsīs* because He thought of them as offenders to the lotus feet of Kṛṣṇa, but here He excuses them (*tāṅ-sabāra kṣami' aparādha*). This is an example in preaching. *Āpani ācari' bhakti śikhāimu sabāre.* Śrī Caitanya Mahāprabhu teaches us that those whom preachers meet are almost all offenders who are opposed to Kṛṣṇa consciousness, but it is a preacher's duty to convince them of the Kṛṣṇa consciousness movement and then induce them to chant the Hare Kṛṣṇa *mahā-mantra.* Our propagation of the *saṅkīrtana* movement is continuing, despite many opponents, and people are taking up this chanting process even in remote parts of the world like Africa. By inducing the offenders to chant the Hare Kṛṣṇa *mantra,* Lord Caitanya Mahāprabhu exemplified the success of the Kṛṣṇa consciousness movement. We should follow very respectfully in the footsteps of Lord Caitanya, and there is no doubt that we shall be successful in our attempts.

TEXT 151

তবে সব সন্ন্যাসী মহাপ্রভুকে লৈয়া ।
ভিক্ষা করিলেন সভে, মধ্যে বসাইয়া ॥ ১৫১ ॥

tabe saba sannyāsī mahāprabhuke laiyā
bhikṣā karilena sabhe, madhye vasāiyā

tabe—after this; *saba*—all; *sannyāsī*—the Māyāvādī *sannyāsīs; mahāprabhuke*—Caitanya Mahāprabhu; *laiyā*—taking Him; *bhikṣā karilena*—took *prasādam,* or took lunch; *sabhe*—all together; *madhye*—in the middle; *vasāiyā*—seating Him.

TRANSLATION

After this, all the sannyāsīs took the Lord into their midst, and thus they all took their meal together.

PURPORT

Previously Śrī Caitanya Mahāprabhu had neither mixed nor talked with the Māyāvādī *sannyāsīs,* but now He took lunch with them. It is to be concluded that when Lord Caitanya induced them to chant Hare Kṛṣṇa and excused them for their offenses, they were purified, and therefore there was no objection to taking lunch, or *bhagavat-prasādam,* with them, although Śrī Caitanya Mahāprabhu knew that the food was not offered to the Deity. Māyāvādī *sannyāsīs* do not worship the Deity, or if they do so they generally worship the deity of Lord Śiva or the *pañco-pāsanā* (Lord Viṣṇu, Lord Śiva, Durgā-devī, Gaṇeśa and Sūrya). Here we do not find any mention of the demigods or Viṣṇu, and yet Caitanya Mahāprabhu accepted food in the midst of the *sannyāsīs* on the basis that they had chanted the Hare Kṛṣṇa *mahā-mantra* and that He had excused their offenses.

TEXT 152

ভিক্ষা করি' মহাপ্রভু আইলা বাসাঘর।
হেন চিত্র-লীলা করে গৌরাঙ্গ-সুন্দর ॥ ১৫২ ॥

bhikṣā kari' mahāprabhu āilā vāsāghara
hena citra-līlā kare gaurāṅga-sundara

bhikṣā—accepting food from others; *kari'*—accepting; *mahāprabhu*—Lord Caitanya; *āilā*—returned; *vāsāghara*—to His residence; *hena*—thus; *citra-līlā*—wonderful pastimes; *kare*—does; *gaurāṅga*—Lord Śrī Caitanya Mahāprabhu; *sundara*—very beautiful.

TRANSLATION

After taking lunch among the Māyāvādī sannyāsīs, Śrī Caitanya

Mahāprabhu, who is known as Gaurasundara, returned to His residence. Thus the Lord performs His wonderful pastimes.

TEXT 153

চন্দ্রশেখর, তপন মিশ্র, আর সনাতন ।
শুনি' দেখি' আনন্দিত সবাকার মন ॥ ১৫৩ ॥

candraśekhara, tapana miśra, āra sanātana
śuni' dekhi' ānandita sabākāra mana

candraśekhara—Candraśekhara; *tapana miśra*—Tapana Miśra; *āra*—and; *sanātana*—Sanātana; *śuni'*—hearing; *dekhi'*—seeing; *ānandita*—very pleased; *sabākāra*—all of them; *mana*—minds.

TRANSLATION

Hearing the arguments of Śrī Caitanya Mahāprabhu and seeing His victory, Candraśekhara, Tapana Miśra and Sanātana Gosvāmī were all extremely pleased.

PURPORT

Here is an example of how a *sannyāsī* should preach. When Śrī Caitanya Mahāprabhu went to Vārāṇasī, He went there alone, not with a big party. Locally, however, He made friendships with Candraśekhara and Tapana Miśra, and Sanātana Gosvāmī also came to see Him. Therefore, although He did not have many friends there, due to His sound preaching and His victory in arguing with the local *sannyāsīs* on the Vedānta philosophy, He became greatly famous in that part of the country, as explained in the next verse.

TEXT 154

প্রভুকে দেখিতে আইসে সকল সন্ন্যাসী ।
প্রভুর প্রশংসা করে সব বারাণসী ॥ ১৫৪ ॥

prabhuke dekhite āise sakala sannyāsī
prabhura praśaṁsā kare saba vārāṇasī

prabhuke—unto Lord Caitanya Mahāprabhu; *dekhite*—to see; *āise*—they came; *sakala*—all; *sannyāsī*—the Māyāvādī *sannyāsīs; prabhura*—

of Lord Caitanya Mahāprabhu; *praśaṁsā*—praise; *kare*—they do; *saba*—all; *vārāṇasī*—the city of Vārāṇasī.

TRANSLATION

Many Māyāvādī sannyāsīs of Vārāṇasī came to see the Lord after this incident, and the entire city praised Him.

TEXT 155

বারাণসীপুরী আইলা শ্রীকৃষ্ণচৈতন্য ।
পুরীসহ সর্বলোক হৈল মহাধন্য ॥ ১৫৫ ॥

vārāṇasī-purī āilā śrī-kṛṣṇa-caitanya
purī-saha sarva-loka haila mahā-dhanya

vārāṇasī—of the name Vārāṇasī; *purī*—city; *āilā*—came; *śrī-kṛṣṇa-caitanya*—Lord Śrī Caitanya Mahāprabhu; *purī*—city; *saha*—with; *sarva-loka*—all the people; *haila*—became; *mahā-dhanya*—thankful.

TRANSLATION

Śrī Caitanya Mahāprabhu visited the city of Vārāṇasī, and all of its people were very thankful.

TEXT 156

লক্ষ লক্ষ লোক আইসে প্রভুকে দেখিতে ।
মহাভিড় হৈল দ্বারে, নারে প্রবেশিতে ॥ ১৫৬ ॥

lakṣa lakṣa loka āise prabhuke dekhite
mahā-bhiḍa haila dvāre, nāre praveśite

lakṣa lakṣa—hundreds of thousands; *loka*—people; *āise*—came; *prabhuke*—unto the Lord; *dekhite*—to see; *mahā-bhiḍa*—a great crowd; *haila*—there happened; *dvāre*—at the door; *nāre*—may not; *praveśite*—to enter.

TRANSLATION

The crowd at the door of His residence was so great that it numbered hundreds of thousands.

TEXT 157

প্রভু যবে যা'ন বিশ্বেশ্বর-দরশনে ।
লক্ষ লক্ষ লোক আসি' মিলে সেই স্থানে ॥ ১৫৭ ॥

prabhu yabe yā'na viśveśvara-daraśane
lakṣa lakṣa loka āsi' mile sei sthāne

prabhu—Lord Caitanya Mahāprabhu; *yabe*—when; *yā'na*—goes; *viśveśvara*—the deity of Vārāṇasī; *daraśane*—to visit; *lakṣa lakṣa*—hundreds of thousands; *loka*—people; *āsi'*—come; *mile*—meet; *sei*—that; *sthāne*—on the place.

TRANSLATION

When the Lord went to visit the temple of Viśveśvara, hundreds of thousands of people assembled to see Him.

PURPORT

The important point in this verse is that Śrī Caitanya Mahāprabhu regularly visited the temple of Viśveśvara (Lord Śiva) at Vārāṇasī. Vaiṣṇavas generally do not visit a demigod's temple, but here we see that Śrī Caitanya Mahāprabhu regularly visited the temple of Viśveśvara, who was the predominating deity of Vārāṇasī. Generally Māyāvādī *sannyāsīs* and worshipers of Lord Śiva live in Vārāṇasī, but how is it that Caitanya Mahāprabhu, who took the part of a Vaiṣṇava *sannyāsī*, also visited the Viśveśvara temple? The answer is that a Vaiṣṇava does not behave impudently toward the demigods. A Vaiṣṇava gives proper respect to all, although he never accepts a demigod to be as good as the Supreme Personality of Godhead.

In the *Brahma-saṁhitā* there are *mantras* offering obeisances to Lord Śiva, Lord Brahmā, the sun-god and Lord Gaṇeśa, as well as Lord Viṣṇu, all of whom are worshiped by the impersonalists as *pañcopāsanā.* In their temples impersonalists install deities of Lord Viṣṇu, Lord Śiva, the sun-god, goddess Durgā and sometimes Lord Brahmā also, and this system is continuing at present in India under the guise of the Hindu religion. Vaiṣṇavas can also worship all these demigods, but only on the principles of the *Brahma-saṁhitā,* which is recommended by Śrī Caitanya Mahāprabhu. We may note in this connection the *mantras* for worshiping Lord Śiva, Lord Brahmā, goddess Durgā, the sun-god and Gaṇeśa, as described in the *Brahma-saṁhitā.*

sṛṣṭi-sthiti-pralaya-sādhana-śaktir ekā
chāyeva yasya bhuvanāni bibharti durgā
icchānurūpam api yasya ca ceṣṭate sā
govindam ādi-puruṣaṁ tam ahaṁ bhajāmi

"The external potency, *māyā,* who is of the nature of the shadow of the *cit* [spiritual] potency, is worshiped by all people as Durgā, the creating, preserving and destroying agency of this mundane world. I adore the primeval Lord, Govinda, in accordance with whose will Durgā conducts herself." (Bs. 5.44)

kṣīraṁ yathā dadhi vikāra-viśeṣa-yogāt
sañjāyate na hi tataḥ pṛthag asti hetoḥ
yaḥ śambhutām api tathā samupaiti kāryād
govindam ādi-puruṣaṁ tam ahaṁ bhajāmi

"Milk is transformed into curd by the actions of acids, yet the effect, curd, is neither the same as nor different from its cause, viz., milk. I adore the primeval Lord, Govinda, of whom the state of Śambhu is a similar transformation for the performance of the work of destruction." (Bs. 5.45)

bhāsvān yathāśma-śakaleṣu nijeṣu tejaḥ
svīyaṁ kiyat prakaṭayaty api tadvad atra
brahmā ya eṣa jagad-aṇḍa-vidhāna-kartā
govindam ādi-puruṣaṁ tam ahaṁ bhajāmi

"I adore the primeval Lord, Govinda, from whom the separated subjective portion Brahmā receives his power for the regulation of the mundane world, just as the sun manifests a portion of his own light in all the effulgent gems that bear such names as *sūrya-kānta.*" (Bs. 5.49)

yat-pāda-pallava-yugaṁ vinidhāya kumbha-
dvandve praṇāma-samaye sa gaṇādhirājaḥ
vighnān vihantum alam asya jagat-trayasya
govindam ādi-puruṣaṁ tam ahaṁ bhajāmi

"I worship the primeval Lord, Govinda. Gaṇeśa always holds His lotus feet upon the pair of *tumuli* protruding from his elephant head in order to obtain power for his function of destroying all obstacles on the path of progress in the three worlds." (Bs. 5.50)

yac cakṣur eṣa savitā sakala-grahāṇāṁ
rājā samasta-sura-mūrtir aśeṣa-tejāḥ
yasyājñayā bhramati sambhṛta-kāla-cakro
govindam ādi-puruṣaṁ tam ahaṁ bhajāmi

"The sun, full of infinite effulgence, who is the king of all the planets and the image of the good soul, is like the eye of this world. I adore the primeval Lord, Govinda, in pursuance of whose order the sun performs his journey, mounting the wheel of time." (Bs. 5.52)

All the demigods are servants of Kṛṣṇa; they are not equal with Kṛṣṇa. Therefore even if one goes to a temple of the *pañcopāsanā,* as mentioned above, one should not accept the deities as they are accepted by the impersonalists. All of them are to be accepted as personal demigods, but they all serve the order of the Supreme Personality of Godhead. Śaṅkarācārya, for example, is understood to be an incarnation of Lord Śiva, as described in the *Padma Purāṇa.* He propagated the Māyāvāda philosophy under the order of the Supreme Lord. We have already discussed this point in text 114 of this chapter: *tāṅra doṣa nāhi, teṅho ājñā-kārī dāsa.* "Śaṅkarācārya is not at fault, for he has thus covered the real purpose of the *Vedas* under the order of the Supreme Personality of Godhead." Although Lord Śiva, in the form of a *brāhmaṇa* (Śaṅkarācārya), preached the false philosophy of Māyāvāda, Śrī Caitanya Mahāprabhu nevertheless said that since he did it on the order of the Supreme Personality of Godhead, there was no fault on his part (*tāṅra doṣa nāhi*).

We must offer proper respects to all the demigods. If one can offer respects even to an ant, why not to the demigods? One must always know, however, that no demigod is equal to or above the Supreme Lord. *Ekale īśvara kṛṣṇa, āra saba bhṛtya:* "Only Kṛṣṇa is the Supreme Personality of Godhead, and all others, including the demigods such as Lord Śiva, Lord Brahmā, goddess Durgā and Ganeśa, are His servants." Everyone serves the purpose of the Supreme Godhead, and what to speak of such small and insignificant living entities as ourselves? We are surely eternal servants of the Lord. The Māyāvāda philosophy maintains that the demigods, the living entities and the Supreme Personality of Godhead are all equal. It is therefore a most foolish misrepresentation of Vedic knowledge.

TEXT 158

স্নান করিতে যবে যা'ন গঙ্গাতীরে ।
তাহাঞি সকল লোক হয় মহাভিড়ে ॥ ১৫৮ ॥

snāna karite yabe yā'na gaṅgā-tīre
tāhāñi sakala loka haya mahā-bhiḍe

snāna—bath; *karite*—taking; *yabe*—when; *yā'na*—goes; *gaṅgā*—Ganges; *tīre*—bank; *tāhāñi*—then and there; *sakala*—all; *loka*—people; *haya*—assembled; *mahā-bhiḍe*—in great crowds.

TRANSLATION

Whenever Lord Caitanya went to the banks of the Ganges to take His bath, big crowds of many hundreds of thousands of people assembled there.

TEXT 159

বাহু তুলি' প্রভু বলে,—বল হরি হরি ।
হরিধ্বনি করে লোক স্বর্গমর্ত্য ভরি' ॥ ১৫৯ ॥

bāhu tuli' prabhu bale,—bala hari hari
hari-dhvani kare loka svarga-martya bhari'

bāhu tuli'—raising the arms; *prabhu*—Lord Śrī Caitanya Mahāprabhu; *bale*—speaks; *bala*—all of you chant; *hari hari*—the holy name of Lord Kṛṣṇa (Hari); *hari-dhvani*—the sound vibration of Hari; *kare*—does; *loka*—all people; *svarga-martya*—in heaven, the sky and the land; *bhari'*—completely filling.

TRANSLATION

Whenever the crowds were too great, Śrī Caitanya Mahāprabhu stood up, raised His hands and chanted, "Hari! Hari!" to which all the people responded, filling both the land and sky with the vibration.

TEXT 160

লোক নিস্তারিয়া প্রভুর চলিতে হৈল মন ।
বৃন্দাবনে পাঠাইলা শ্রীসনাতন ॥ ১৬০ ॥

loka nistāriyā prabhura calite haila mana
vṛndāvane pāṭhāilā śrī-sanātana

loka—people; *nistāriyā*—delivering; *prabhura*—of the Lord; *calite*—to leave; *haila*—became; *mana*—mind; *vṛndāvane*—toward Vṛndāvana; *pāṭhāilā*—sent; *śrī-sanātana*—Sanātana Gosvāmī.

TRANSLATION

After thus delivering the people in general, the Lord desired to leave Vārāṇasī. After instructing Śrī Sanātana Gosvāmī, He sent him toward Vṛndāvana.

PURPORT

The actual purpose of Lord Caitanya's stay at Vārāṇasī after coming back from Vṛndāvana was to meet Sanātana Gosvāmī and teach him. Sanātana Gosvāmī met Śrī Caitanya Mahāprabhu after the Lord's return to Vārāṇasī, where the Lord taught him for two months about the intricacies of Vaiṣṇava philosophy and Vaiṣṇava activities. After completely instructing him, He sent him to Vṛndāvana to execute His orders. When Sanātana Gosvāmī went to Vṛndāvana, there were no temples. The city was lying vacant like an open field. Sanātana Gosvāmī sat down on the bank of the Yamunā, and after some time he gradually constructed the first temple; then other temples were constructed, and now the city is full of temples, numbering about five thousand.

TEXT 161

রাত্রি-দিবসে লোকের শুনি' কোলাহল ।
বারাণসী ছাড়ি' প্রভু আইলা নীলাচল ॥ ১৬১ ॥

rātri-divase lokera śuni' kolāhala
vārāṇasī chāḍi' prabhu āilā nīlācala

rātri—night; *divase*—day; *lokera*—of the people in general; *śuni*—hearing; *kolāhala*—tumult; *vārāṇasī*—the city of Benares; *chāḍi'*—leaving; *prabhu*—the Lord; *āilā*—returned; *nīlācala*—to Purī.

TRANSLATION

Because the city of Vārāṇasī was always full of tumultuous crowds,

Śrī Caitanya Mahāprabhu, after sending Sanātana to Vṛndāvana, returned to Jagannātha Purī.

TEXT 162

এই লীলা কহিব আগে বিস্তার করিয়া ।
সংক্ষেপে কহিলাঙ ইহাঁ প্রসঙ্গ পাইয়া ॥ ১৬২ ॥

ei līlā kahiba āge vistāra kariyā
saṅkṣepe kahilāṅ ihāṅ prasaṅga pāiyā

ei—these; *līlā*—pastimes; *kahiba*—I shall speak; *āge*—later on; *vistāra*—vivid description; *kariyā*—making; *saṅkṣepe*—in short; *kahilāṅ*—I have spoken; *ihāṅ*—in this place; *prasaṅga*—topics; *pāiyā*—taking advantage of.

TRANSLATION

I have here given a brief account of these pastimes of Lord Caitanya, but later I shall describe them in an extensive way.

TEXT 163

এই পঞ্চতত্ত্বরূপে শ্রীকৃষ্ণচৈতন্য ।
কৃষ্ণ-নাম-প্রেম দিয়া বিশ্ব কৈলা ধন্য ॥ ১৬৩ ॥

ei pañca-tattva-rūpe śrī-kṛṣṇa-caitanya
kṛṣṇa-nāma-prema diyā viśva kailā dhanya

ei—this; *pañca-tattva-rūpe*—the Lord in His five forms; *śrī-kṛṣṇa-caitanya*—Lord Śrī Caitanya Mahāprabhu; *kṛṣṇa-nāma*—the holy name of Lord Kṛṣṇa; *prema*—love of Kṛṣṇa; *diyā*—delivering; *viśva*—the whole world; *kailā*—made; *dhanya*—thankful.

TRANSLATION

Śrī Kṛṣṇa Caitanya Mahāprabhu and His associates of the Pañca-tattva distributed the holy name of the Lord to invoke love of Godhead throughout the universe, and thus the entire universe was thankful.

PURPORT

Here it is said that Lord Caitanya made the entire universe thankful to Him for propagating the *saṅkīrtana* movement with His associates. Lord Caitanya Mahāprabhu has already sanctified the entire universe by His presence five hundred years ago, and therefore anyone who attempts to serve Śrī Caitanya Mahāprabhu sincerely by following in His footsteps and following the instructions of the *ācāryas* will successfully be able to preach the holy names of the Hare Kṛṣṇa *mahā-mantra* all over the universe. There are some foolish critics who say that Europeans and Americans cannot be offered *sannyāsa,* but here we find that Śrī Caitanya Mahāprabhu wanted to preach the *saṅkīrtana* movement all over the universe. For preaching work, *sannyāsīs* are essential. These critics think that only Indians or Hindus should be offered *sannyāsa* to preach, but their knowledge is practically nil. Without *sannyāsīs,* the preaching work will be impeded. Therefore, under the instruction of Lord Caitanya and with the blessings of His associates, there should be no discrimination in this matter, but people in all parts of the world should be trained to preach and given *sannyāsa* so that the cult of Śrī Caitanya Mahāprabhu's *saṅkīrtana* movement will expand boundlessly. We do not care about the criticism of fools. We shall go on with our work and simply depend on the blessings of Lord Caitanya Mahāprabhu and His associates, the Pañca-tattva.

TEXT 164

মথুরাতে পাঠাইল রূপ-সনাতন ।
দুই সেনাপতি কৈল ভক্তি প্রচারণ ॥ ১৬৪ ॥

mathurāte pāṭhāila rūpa-sanātana
dui senā-pati kaila bhakti pracāraṇa

mathurāte—toward Mathurā; *pāṭhāila*—sent; *rūpa-sanātana*—the two brothers Rūpa Gosvāmī and Sanātana Gosvāmī; *dui*—both of them; *senā-pati*—as commanders in chief; *kaila*—He made them; *bhakti*—devotional service; *pracāraṇa*—to broadcast.

TRANSLATION

Lord Caitanya dispatched the two generals Rūpa Gosvāmī and Sanātana Gosvāmī to Vṛndāvana to preach the bhakti cult.

PURPORT

When Rūpa Gosvāmī and Sanātana Gosvāmī went to Vṛndāvana, there was not a single temple, but by their preaching they were gradually able to construct various temples. Sanātana Gosvāmī constructed the Madana-mohana temple, and Rūpa Gosvāmī constructed the Govindajī temple. Similarly, their nephew Jīva Gosvāmī constructed the Rādhā-Dāmodara temple, Śrī Gopāla Bhaṭṭa Gosvāmī constructed the Rādhā-ramaṇa temple, Śrī Lokanātha Gosvāmī constructed the Gokulānanda temple, and Śyāmānanda Gosvāmī constructed the Śyāmasundara temple. In this way, many temples were gradually constructed. For preaching, construction of temples is also necessary. The Gosvāmīs not only engaged in writing books but also constructed temples because both are needed for preaching work. Śrī Caitanya Mahāprabhu wanted the cult of His *saṅkīrtana* movement to spread all over the world. Now that the International Society for Krishna Consciousness has taken up this task of preaching the cult of Lord Caitanya, its members should not only construct temples in every town and village of the globe but also distribute the books that have already been written and further increase the number of books. Both distribution of books and construction of temples must continue side by side in parallel lines.

TEXT 165

নিত্যানন্দ-গোসাঞে পাঠাইলা গৌড়দেশে ।
তেঁহো ভক্তি প্রচারিলা অশেষ-বিশেষে ॥ ১৬৫ ॥

nityānanda-gosāñe pāṭhāilā gauḍa-deśe
teṅho bhakti pracārilā aśeṣa-viśeṣe

nityānanda—Lord Nityānanda; *gosāñe*—the *ācārya; pāṭhāilā*—was sent; *gauḍa-deśe*—in Bengal; *teṅho*—He; *bhakti*—devotional cult; *pracārilā*—preached; *aśeṣa-viśeṣe*—in a very extensive way.

TRANSLATION

As Rūpa Gosvāmī and Sanātana Gosvāmī were sent toward Mathurā, so Nityānanda Prabhu was sent to Bengal to preach extensively the cult of Caitanya Mahāprabhu.

PURPORT

The name of Lord Nityānanda is very famous in Bengal. Of course, anyone who knows Lord Nityānanda knows Śrī Caitanya Mahāprabhu also, but there are some misguided devotees who stress the importance of Lord Nityānanda more than that of Śrī Caitanya Mahāprabhu. This is not good. Nor should Śrī Caitanya Mahāprabhu be stressed more than Lord Nityānanda. The author of the *Caitanya-caritāmṛta*, Kṛṣṇadāsa Kavirāja Gosvāmī, left his home because of his brother's stressing the importance of Śrī Caitanya Mahāprabhu over that of Nityānanda Prabhu. Actually, one should offer respect to the Pañca-tattva without such foolish discrimination, not considering Nityānanda Prabhu to be greater, Caitanya Mahāprabhu to be greater or Advaita Prabhu to be greater. The respect should be offered equally: *śrī-kṛṣṇa-caitanya prabhu-nityānanda śrī-advaita gadādhara śrīvāsādi-gaura-bhakta-vṛnda.* All devotees of Lord Caitanya or Nityānanda are worshipable persons.

TEXT 166

আপনে দক্ষিণ দেশ করিলা গমন ।
গ্রামে গ্রামে কৈলা কৃষ্ণনাম প্রচারণ ॥ ১৬৬ ॥

āpane dakṣiṇa deśa karilā gamana
grāme grāme kailā kṛṣṇa-nāma pracāraṇa

āpane—personally; *dakṣiṇa deśa*—South India; *karilā*—went; *gamana*—traveling; *grāme grāme*—in each and every village; *kailā*—He did; *kṛṣṇa-nāma*—the holy name of Lord Kṛṣṇa; *pracāraṇa*—broadcasting.

TRANSLATION

Śrī Caitanya Mahāprabhu personally went to South India, and He broadcast the holy name of Lord Kṛṣṇa in every village and town.

TEXT 167

সেতুবন্ধ পর্যন্ত কৈলা ভক্তির প্রচার ।
কৃষ্ণপ্রেম দিয়া কৈলা সবার নিস্তার ॥ ১৬৭ ॥

setubandha paryanta kailā bhaktira pracāra
kṛṣṇa-prema diyā kailā sabāra nistāra

setubandha—the place where Lord Rāmacandra constructed His bridge; *paryanta*—up to that place; *kailā*—did; *bhaktira*—of the cult of devotional service; *pracāra*—broadcast; *kṛṣṇa-prema*—love of Kṛṣṇa; *diyā*—delivering; *kailā*—did; *sabāra*—everyone; *nistāra*—deliverance.

TRANSLATION

Thus the Lord went to the southernmost tip of the Indian peninsula, known as Setubandha [Cape Comorin]. Everywhere He distributed the bhakti cult and love of Kṛṣṇa, and in this way He delivered everyone.

TEXT 168

এই ত' কহিল পঞ্চতত্ত্বের ব্যাখ্যান ।
ইহার শ্রবণে হয় চৈতন্যতত্ত্ব-জ্ঞান ॥ ১৬৮ ॥

ei ta' kahila pañca-tattvera vyākhyāna
ihāra śravaṇe haya caitanya-tattva jñāna

ei ta'—this; *kahila*—described; *pañca-tattvera*—of the Pañca-tattva; *vyākhyāna*—explanation; *ihāra*—of this; *śravaṇe*—hearing; *haya*—becomes; *caitanya-tattva*—the truth of Śrī Caitanya Mahāprabhu; *jñāna*—knowledge.

TRANSLATION

I have thus explained the truth of the Pañca-tattva. One who hears this explanation increases in knowledge of Śrī Caitanya Mahāprabhu.

PURPORT

The Pañca-tattva is a very important factor in understanding Śrī Caitanya Mahāprabhu. There are *sahajiyās* who, not knowing the importance of the Pañca-tattva, concoct their own slogans, such as *bhaja nitāi gaura, rādhe śyāma, japa hare kṛṣṇa hare rāma* or *śrī-kṛṣṇa-caitanya prabhu-nityānanda hare kṛṣṇa hare rāma śrī-rādhe govinda.* Such chants may be good poetry, but they cannot help us to go forward in devotional service. In such chants there are also many discrepancies, which need not be discussed here. Strictly speaking, when chanting the names of the Pañca-tattva, one should fully offer his obeisances: *śrī-kṛṣṇa-caitanya prabhu-nityānanda śrī-advaita gadādhara śrīvāsādi-gaura-bhakta-vṛnda.* By such chanting one is blessed with the competency to chant the Hare Kṛṣṇa *mahā-mantra* without offense. When chanting the Hare Kṛṣṇa *mahā-mantra,* one should also chant it fully: Hare Kṛṣṇa, Hare Kṛṣṇa, Kṛṣṇa Kṛṣṇa, Hare Hare/ Hare Rāma, Hare Rāma, Rāma Rāma, Hare Hare. One should not foolishly adopt any of the slogans concocted by imaginative devotees. If one actually wants to derive the effects of chanting, one must strictly follow the great *ācāryas.* This is confirmed in the *Mahābhārata: mahā-jano yena gataḥ sa panthāḥ.* "The real path of progress is that which is traversed by great *ācāryas* and authorities."

TEXT 169

শ্রীচৈতন্য, নিত্যানন্দ, অদ্বৈত,—তিন জন ।
শ্রীবাস-গদাধর-আদি যত ভক্তগণ ॥ ১৬৯ ॥

śrī-caitanya, nityānanda, advaita,—tina jana
śrīvāsa-gadādhara-ādi yata bhakta-gaṇa

śrī-caitanya, nityānanda, advaita—Śrī Caitanya Mahāprabhu, Nityānanda Prabhu and Advaita Prabhu; *tina*—these three; *jana*—personalities; *śrīvāsa-gadādhara*—Śrīvāsa and Gadādhara; *ādi*—etc.; *yata*—all; *bhakta-gaṇa*—the devotees.

TRANSLATION

While chanting the Pañca-tattva mahā-mantra, one must chant the names of Śrī Caitanya, Nityānanda, Advaita, Gadādhara and Śrīvāsa with their many devotees. This is the process.

TEXT 170

সবাকার পাদপদ্মে কোটি নমস্কার ।
যৈছে তৈছে কহি কিছু চৈতন্য-বিহার ॥ ১৭০ ॥

sabākāra pādapadme koṭi namaskāra
yaiche taiche kahi kichu caitanya-vihāra

sabākāra—all of them; *pāda-padme*—on the lotus feet; *koṭi*—countless; *namaskāra*—obeisances; *yaiche taiche*—somehow or other; *kahi*—I speak; *kichu*—something; *caitanya-vihāra*—about the pastimes of Lord Caitanya Mahāprabhu.

TRANSLATION

I again and again offer obeisances unto the Pañca-tattva. Thus I think that I will be able to describe something about the pastimes of Lord Caitanya Mahāprabhu.

TEXT 171

শ্রীরূপ-রঘুনাথ-পদে যার আশ ।
চৈতন্যচরিতামৃত কহে কৃষ্ণদাস ॥ ১৭১ ॥

śrī-rūpa-raghunātha-pade yāra āśa
caitanya-caritāmṛta kahe kṛṣṇadāsa

śrī-rūpa—Śrīla Rūpa Gosvāmī; *raghunātha*—Śrīla Raghunātha dāsa Gosvāmī; *pade*—at the lotus feet; *yāra*—whose; *āśa*—expectation; *caitanya-caritāmṛta*—the book named *Caitanya-caritāmṛta; kahe*—describes; *kṛṣṇa-dāsa*—Śrīla Kṛṣṇadāsa Kavirāja Gosvāmī.

TRANSLATION

Praying at the lotus feet of Śrī Rūpa and Śrī Raghunātha, always desiring their mercy, I, Kṛṣṇadāsa, narrate Śrī Caitanya-caritāmṛta, following in their footsteps.

PURPORT

Śrī Caitanya Mahāprabhu wanted to preach the *saṅkīrtana* movement of love of Kṛṣṇa throughout the entire world, and therefore during His presence He inspired the *saṅkīrtana* movement. Specifically, He sent Rūpa Gosvāmī and Sanātana Gosvāmī to Vṛndāvana and Nityānanda to Bengal and personally went to South India. In this way He kindly left the task of preaching His cult in the rest of the world to the International Society for Krishna Consciousness. The members of this Society must always remember that if they stick to the regulative principles and preach sincerely according to the instructions of the *ācāryas*, surely they will have the profound blessings of Lord Caitanya Mahāprabhu, and their preaching work will be successful everywhere throughout the world.

Thus end the Bhaktivedanta purports to Śrī Caitanya-caritāmṛta, Ādi-līlā, *Seventh Chapter, describing Lord Caitanya in five features.*

Appendixes

The Author

His Divine Grace A. C. Bhaktivedanta Swami Prabhupāda appeared in this world in 1896 in Calcutta, India. He first met his spiritual master, Śrīla Bhaktisiddhānta Sarasvatī Gosvāmī, in Calcutta in 1922. Bhaktisiddhānta Sarasvatī, a prominent religious scholar and the founder of sixty-four Gauḍīya Maṭhas (Vedic institutes), liked this educated young man and convinced him to dedicate his life to teaching Vedic knowledge. Śrīla Prabhupāda became his student and, in 1933, his formally initiated disciple.

At their first meeting, in 1922, Śrīla Bhaktisiddhānta Sarasvatī requested Śrīla Prabhupāda to broadcast Vedic knowledge in English. In the years that followed, Śrīla Prabhupāda wrote a commentary on the *Bhagavad-gītā,* assisted the Gauḍīya Maṭha in its work and, in 1944, started *Back to Godhead,* an English fortnightly magazine. Single-handedly, Śrīla Prabhupāda edited it, typed the manuscripts, checked the galley proofs and even distributed the individual copies. The magazine is now being continued by his disciples in the West.

In 1950 Śrīla Prabhupāda retired from married life, adopting the *vānaprastha* (retired) order to devote more time to his studies and writing. He traveled to the holy city of Vṛndāvana, where he lived in humble circumstances in the historic temple of Rādhā-Dāmodara. There he engaged for several years in deep study and writing. He accepted the renounced order of life (*sannyāsa*) in 1959. At Rādhā-Dāmodara, Śrīla Prabhupāda began work on his life's masterpiece: a multivolume commentated translation of the eighteen-thousand-verse *Śrīmad-Bhāgavatam* (*Bhāgavata Purāṇa*). He also wrote *Easy Journey to Other Planets.*

After publishing three volumes of the *Bhāgavatam,* Śrīla Prabhupāda came to the United States, in September 1965, to fulfill the mission of his spiritual master. Subsequently, His Divine Grace wrote more than fifty volumes of authoritative commentated translations and summary studies of the philosophical and religious classics of India.

When he first arrived by freighter in New York City, Śrīla Prabhupāda was practically penniless. Only after almost a year of great difficulty did he establish the International Society for Krishna Consciousness, in July of 1966. Before he passed away on November 14, 1977, he had guided the Society and seen it grow to a worldwide confederation of more than one hundred *āśramas*, schools, temples, institutes and farm communities.

In 1972 His Divine Grace introduced the Vedic system of primary and secondary education in the West by founding the *gurukula* school in Dallas, Texas. Since then his disciples have established similar schools throughout the United States and the rest of the world.

Śrīla Prabhupāda also inspired the construction of several large international cultural centers in India. The center at Śrīdhāma Māyāpur is the site for a planned spiritual city, an ambitions project for which construction will extend over many years to come. In Vṛndāvana are the magnificent Kṛṣṇa-Balarāma Temple and International Guesthouse, *gurukula* school, and Śrīla Prabhupāda Memorial and Museum. There is also a major cultural and educational center in Bombay. Other centers are planned in a dozen important locations on the Indian subcontinent.

Śrīla Prabhupāda's most significant contribution, however, is his books. Highly respected by scholars for their authority, depth and clarity, they are used as textbooks in numerous college courses. His writings have been translated into over fifty languages. The Bhaktivedanta Book Trust, established in 1972 to publish the works of His Divine Grace, has thus become the world's largest publisher of books in the field of Indian religion and philosophy.

In just twelve years, from his arrival in America in 1965 till his passing away in Vṛndāvana in 1977, despite his advanced age Śrīla Prabhupāda circled the globe fourteen times on lecture tours that took him to six continents. Notwithstanding such a vigorous schedule, Śrīla Prabhupāda continued to write prolifically. His writings constitute a veritable library of Vedic philosophy, religion, literature and culture.

References

The purports of *Śrī Caitanya-caritāmṛta* are all confirmed by standard Vedic authorities. The following scriptures are cited in this volume. For specific page references, consult the general index.

Ādi Purāṇa
Aitareya Upaniṣad
Ananta-saṁhitā
Anubhāṣya
Bhagavad-gītā
Bhagavat-sandarbha
Bhakti-rasāmṛta-sindhu
Bhakti-sandarbha
Bhāvārtha-dīpikā
Brahmāṇḍa Purāṇa
Brahma-saṁhitā
Brahma-tarka
Brahma-yāmala
Bṛhad-āraṇyaka Upaniṣad
Bṛhad-bhāgavatāmṛta
Bṛhad-gautamīya-tantra
Caitanya-bhāgavata
Caitanya-caritāmṛta
Caitanya Upaniṣad
Chāndogya Upaniṣad
Dāna-keli-kaumudī
Gaura-gaṇoddeśa-dīpikā
Gopī-premāmṛta
Govinda-līlāmṛta
Hari-bhakti-sudhodaya
Hari-bhakti-vilāsa
Hayaśīrṣa-pañcarātra
Hayaśīrṣa-śrī-nārāyaṇa-vyūha-stava
Īśopaniṣad
Kalisantaraṇa Upaniṣad
Kaṭha Upaniṣad
Krama-sandarbha
Kṛṣṇa-sandarbha
Kṛṣṇa-yāmala
Kūrma Purāṇa
Laghu-bhāgavatāmṛta
Lalita-mādhava
Mahābhārata
Mahā-saṁhitā

Mahā-varāha Purāṇa
Māṇḍūkya Upaniṣad
Manu-smṛti
Mukunda-mālā-stotra
Muṇḍaka Upaniṣad
Nārada-pañcarātra
Nārāyaṇa-saṁhitā
Nārāyaṇātharva-śira Upaniṣad
Nārāyaṇa Upaniṣad
Nāmārtha-sudhābhidha
Padma Purāṇa
Parama-saṁhitā
Paramātma-sandarbha
Pauṣkara-saṁhitā
Prameya-ratnāvalī
Praśna Upaniṣad
Ṛg Veda
Ṛk-saṁhitā
Sātvata Tantra
Sītopaniṣad
Śiva Purāṇa
Skanda Purāṇa
Śrīmad-Bhāgavatam
Stava-mālā
Stotra-ratna
Svāyambhuva-tantra
Śvetāśvatara Upaniṣad
Taittirīya Upaniṣad
Tattva-sandarbha
Ujjvala-nīlamalni
Upadeśāmṛta
Upaniṣads
Vāmana Purāṇa
Vāyu Purāṇa
Vedārtha-saṅgraha
Vidaghdha-mādhava
Viṣṇu Purāṇa

Glossary

A

Abhidheya—action one is duty-bound to perform according to one's constitutional relationship with God.
Ācārya—an authorized teacher who teaches by his example.
Acintya—inconceivable.
Acintya-bhedābheda-tattva—the philosophy which maintains that the Lord is simultaneously one with and different from His energies.
Acyuta—the name of Kṛṣṇa meaning "He who never falls down."
Adhama paḍuyās—degraded scholars who consider devotional activities material.
Adhokṣaja—the Supreme Lord, who is beyond material sense perception.
Advaita-vāda—the philosophy of monism, which claims to teach realization of the oneness of the Absolute.
Advaita—nondual.
Āgamas—authorized Vedic literatures; also, specifically the *Pañcarātras.*
Ajñāta-sukṛti—pious activities executed unknowingly.
Akiñcana—one who possesses nothing in the material world.
Amṛta—immortal.
Aṁśāveśa—partial incarnations of God.
Ānanda—complete transcendental bliss.
Ananta—unlimited.
Aparā prakṛti—material energy.
Aprakaṭa—unmanifested.
Arcā-mūrti—the form of the Lord in the temple.
Arcana-mārga—Deity worship.
Artha—economic development.
Āśraya—the Transcendence, who is the source and support of all.
Āśraya-vigraha—the manifestation of the Lord of whom one must take shelter.

Aṣṭāṅga-yoga—the eightfold system of mystic *yoga*, meant for realizing the presence of Paramātmā, the Lord in the heart.
Asuras—demons.
Avyakta—unmanifested.

B

Bhagavān—the name of Kṛṣṇa meaning "the possessor of all opulences in full."
Bhāgavata-dharma—the transcendental religion that is the eternal function of the living being.
Bhāgavata jīvana—the life of a devotee.
Bhāgavatas—persons or things in relationship with the Lord.
Bhajanānandī—devotee who is satisfied to cultivate devotional service for himself.
Bhakta—a devotee of the Lord; one who performs devotional service (*bhakti*).
Bhakta-avatāra—an incarnation of God as a devotee.
Bhakti—devotional service.
Bhakti-rasācārya—one who knows and teaches the essence of devotional service.
Bhāva—the stage of transcendental love experienced after transcendental affection.
Bhava-roga—material miseries or diseases.
Bhrama—false knowledge or mistakes.
Bhū—the creative energy of the cosmic creation.
Brahma-bhūta—stage of liberation from material entanglement when one becomes joyous beyond any hankering or lamentation and gains a universal vision.
Brahma-jñāna—knowledge of the Supreme.
Brahmajyoti—the impersonal effulgence of Kṛṣṇa's body.
Brahman—the Lord's all-pervading feature of neutrality.
Brahmānanda—the spiritual bliss derived from impersonal Brahman realization.
Brahmāṇḍa—the universe.
Brahma-randhra—the hole in the skull through which the perfected *yogī* quits his body .
Bubhukṣus—those who desire to enjoy the material world.

C

Caitanya—living force.
Caitanya-caritāmṛta—the character of the living force in immortality; the title of this book.
Caitya-guru—Kṛṣṇa who is seated as the spiritual master within the heart of the living being.
Catur-vyūha—the quadruple expansions of Kṛṣṇa who predominate over the Vaikuṇṭha planets.
Cid-vilāsa—spiritual pleasure.
Cintāmaṇi—touchstone; when applied to a metal transforms it into gold.
Cit—unlimited knowledge.
Cit-śakti—the internal potency of the Lord.
Cupid—the demigod of love, Kāmadeva.

D

Daivī prakṛti—*See: Yogamāyā.*
Dāsya-rasa—the relationship with the Lord as His servant.
Devas—administrative demigods.
Dhāma—abode.
Dharma—religion; duty, especially everyone's eternal service nature.

G

Gauḍīya Vaiṣṇavas—followers of Lord Caitanya.
Gopījana-vallabha—the name of Kṛṣṇa meaning "the transcendental lover of the *gopīs*."
Godāsa—servant of senses.
Gopīs—pure devotees of Kṛṣṇa who relate to Him as His cowherd girl-friends.
Gosāñi—*See: Gosvāmī.*
Goṣṭhy-ānandī—devotees who desire to preach glories of holy name.
Gosvāmī—one who has control over mind and senses.
Govinda—the name of Kṛṣṇa meaning "He who pleases the senses and the cows."
Guru—spiritual master.

H

Hlādinī—Kṛṣṇa's pleasure potency.

I

Īśānukathā—scriptural information about the Lord and His devotees.
Īśa-tattva—the Supreme Lord.
Īśvara—the supreme controller.

J

Jīva-bhūta—*See: Jīvas*
Jīvas—souls, the atomic living beings.
Jīva-tattva—*See: Jīvas*
Jñāna—transcendental knowledge.
Jñāna-mārga—the path of culturing knowledge by empirical philosophical speculation.

K

Kalmaṣa—sin.
Kalpa-vṛkṣa—wish-fulfilling trees.
Kāma—lust, the desire to gratify one's own senses.
Kaniṣṭha-adhikārī—devotee in lowest stage of Vaiṣṇava life.
KaraṇāpāṭavaKāraṇāpāṭava—imperfection of the material senses.
Karma—(1) material action performed according to scriptural regulations; (2) action pertaining to the development of the material body; (3) any material action which will incur a subsequent reaction; (4) the material reaction one incurs due to fruitive activities.
Karma-kāṇḍa—the part of the *Vedas* outlining the path of fruitive work, or such work itself.
Karma-niṣṭhas—those who consider devotional service to be fruitive activities.
Keśava—the name of Kṛṣṇa meaning "He who has long, black curling hair."

Kṛṣṇa-bhakti—love of Kṛṣṇa.
Kṛṣṇa-prema—*See: Kṛṣṇa-bhakti*
Kṣetrajña—the living entity.
Kutārkikas—false logicians.

M

Madana-mohana—the name of Kṛṣṇa meaning "He who charms Cupid."
Mādhurya-bhaktas—devotees engaged only in conjugal love.
Mādhurya-rasa—relationship with Kṛṣṇa in conjugal love.
Madhusūdana—the name of Kṛṣṇa meaning "the killer of the Madhu demon."
Madhyama-adhikārī—devotee with firm faith who preaches to innocent and avoids atheists.
Mahā-bhāgavata—a devotee in the highest stage of devotional life.
Mahābhāva—the highest pitch of transcendental sentiment.
Mahājanas—the twelve authorized agents of the Lord whose duty is to preach the cult of devotional service to the people in general.
Mahāprabhu—supreme master of all masters.
Mahā-vadānyāvatāra—Lord Caitanya, the most magnanimous incarnation.
Manu—a demigod son of Brahmā who is the forefather and lawgiver of the human race.
Manvantara—a period controlled by a Manu.
Māyā—the external illusory energy of the Lord.
Māyā-śakti—*See: Māyā.*
Miśra-sattva—mundane goodness.
Mokṣa—liberation.
Mukti—liberation of a conditioned soul from material consciousness.
Mūḍha—fool, rascal.
Mukunda—the name of Kṛṣṇa meaning "the giver of liberation."
Mumukṣus—those who desire liberation from the material world.

N

Nāmāparādha—offense against the holy names.

Nāma-saṅkīrtana—congregational chanting of the holy names.
Nīlā—the Lord's energy that destroys the creation.
Nindakas—blasphemers.
Nirguṇa—without material qualities.
Nirodha—the winding up of all energies employed in creation.

P

Pāñcarātrika—the system of regulations for devotional service of the Lord.
Pañca-tattva—the Lord, His plenary portion, His incarnation, His energy and His devotee; Śrī Caitanya Mahāprabhu, Nityānanda Prabhu, Advaita Prabhu, Gadādhara Prabhu and Śrīvāsa Ṭhākura.
Parakīya-rasa—relationship with Kṛṣṇa as His paramour.
Paramahaṁsas—the topmost class of God-realized devotees.
Paramparā—disciplic succession.
Parā-prakṛti—spiritual energy.
Paravyoma—the spiritual sky.
Pāriṣats—devotees who are personal associates of the Lord.
Pāṣaṇḍa—a nonbeliever; one who compares the Supreme Lord to the demigods or who considers devotional activities to be material.
Poṣaṇa—the Lord's special care and protection for His devotees.
Prabhu—master.
Pradhāna—the chief principle of creation.
Prakāśa-vigrahas—forms of the Lord manifested for His pastimes.
Prākṛta-bhaktas—materialistic devotees not advanced in spiritual knowledge.
Prākṛta-sahajiyā—a pseudo devotee of Kṛṣṇa.
Pramāda—inattention or misunderstanding of reality.
Prayojana—the ultimate goal of life, to develop love of God.
Prema—real love of God, the highest perfectional stage of life.

R

Rādhā-bhāva-mūrti—the mood of Rādhārāṇī.
Rādhā-kuṇḍa—the bathing place of Śrīmatī Rādhārāṇī.
Rāga-bhakti—devotional service in transcendental rapture.
Rasa—spiritual relationship.

Rasābhāsa—an incompatible mixture of *rasas*.
Rāsādi-vilāsī—the enjoyer of the *rāsa* dance and other pastimes.
Rāsa-līlā—Kṛṣṇa's pastime of dancing with the *gopīs*.
Rūḍha-bhāva—the love of the *gopīs*.

S

Śabda—transcendental sound.
Sac-cid-ānanda—full life, knowledge and bliss.
Sādhakas—neophyte devotees.
Sādhu—a saintly person or Vaiṣṇava.
Sahajiyās—a class of so-called devotees who, considering God cheap, ignore the scriptural injunctions and try to imitate the Lord's pastimes.
Sakhya-rasa—relationship with Kṛṣṇa in friendship.
Śaktyāveśa-jīvas—souls empowered as incarnations of God.
Samādhi—trance, or absorption in the service of the Lord; also, the place where a God-realized soul has passed away or is interred.
Sambandha-jñāna—establishing one's original relationship with the Lord.
Śambhu-tattva—the principle of Lord Śiva.
Sāmīpya—liberation of living as a personal associate of the Lord.
Samvit—the knowledge potency of the Lord.
Sanātana-dharma—*See: Bhāgavata-dharma.*
Sandhinī—the existence potency of the Lord.
Saṅkīrtana—congregational chanting of the holy name of the Lord.
Śānta-rasa—relationship with Kṛṣṇa in neutral appreciation.
Sarga—the first creation by Viṣṇu.
Sārṣṭi—the liberation of achieving opulences equal to those of the Lord.
Sārūpya-mukti—the liberation of having the same bodily features as the Lord's.
Sarva-jña—omniscient.
Śāstras—revealed scriptures.
Sat—unlimited existence.
Sattvatanu—Viṣṇu who expands the quality of goodness.
Sātvata-saṁhitās—scriptures in the mode of goodness.
Sāyujya-mukti—the liberation of merging into the Brahman effulgence.
Siddhaloka—the planets of materially perfect beings.

Śikṣā-guru—an instructing spiritual master.
Śiśumāra-cakra—the orbit of the polestar.
Śrauta-vākya—acceptance of the words of the revealed scripture and of the spiritual master.
Śravaṇaṁ kīrtanam—hearing and chanting about the Lord.
Śrī—the energy of Godhead that maintains the cosmic manifestation.
Śṛṅgāra—conjugal love of God.
Sthāna—the maintenance of the universe by Viṣṇu.
Śuddha-bhakti—pure devotional service.
Śuddha-sattva—the condition of pure goodness.
Surabhi cows—the cows in the spiritual world, who can give unlimited milk.
Sūtra—an aphorism expressing essential knowledge in minimum words; a book of such aphorisms.
Svakīyā—relationship with Kṛṣṇa as a formally married wife.
Svāṁśa—forms of God having unlimited potencies.
Svarāṭ—fully independent.
Śyāmasundara—the name of Kṛṣṇa meaning "He who has a very beautiful blackish form."

T

Tamo-guṇa—the mode of ignorance.
Tapaḥ—the acceptance of hardships for spiritual realization.

U

Urugāya—the name of the Lord meaning "He who is glorified with sublime prayers."
Ūti—the urge for creation that is the cause of all inventions.
Uttama-adhikārī—a devotee in highest stage of devotional life.

V

Vaikuṇṭha—the spiritual world (lit. "without anxiety").

Vaikuṇṭha-nātha—the Lord of Vaikuṇṭha.
Vātsalya-rasa—the relationship with Kṛṣṇa as His parent.
Vedāntī—a person who knows *Vedānta,* i.e., who perfectly knows Kṛṣṇa.
Vibhinnāṁśa—the living beings, all of whom have limited potencies.
Viddha-bhakti—mixed devotional service.
Vidhi-bhakti—devotional service under scheduled regulations.
Vilāsa-vigrahas—expansions of the Lord who manifest bodily differences.
Vipralipsā—the cheating propensity.
Visarga—the secondary creation by Brahmā.
Viṣṇu-bhaktas—devotees in Kṛṣṇa consciousness.
Viṣṇu-tattva—a primary expansion of Kṛṣṇa having full status as Godhead.
Viśvambhara—one who maintains the entire universe and who leads all living beings; the name of Lord Caitanya before He entered the renounced order.
Vivarta—illusion.
Vrajendra-kumāra—Kṛṣṇa, the child of King Nanda.

Y

Yajñas—sacrifices.
Yoga—linking one's consciousness with the Supreme Lord.
Yoga-mārga—the path of developing mystic powers.
Yogamāyā—the internal potency of the Lord.
Yogeśvara—master of all mystic powers, Kṛṣṇa.

Bengali Pronunciation Guide

BENGALI DIACRITICAL EQUIVALENTS AND PRONUNCIATION

Vowels

অ a আ ā ই i ঈ ī উ u ঊ ū ঋ ṛ

ৠ ṝ এ e ঐ ai ও o ঔ au

ং ṁ (*anusvāra*) ঁ ṅ (*candra-bindu*) ঃ ḥ (*visarga*)

Consonants

Gutturals:	ক ka	খ kha	গ ga	ঘ gha	ঙ ṅa
Palatals:	চ ca	ছ cha	জ ja	ঝ jha	ঞ ña
Cerebrals:	ট ṭa	ঠ ṭha	ড ḍa	ঢ ḍha	ণ ṇa
Dentals:	ৎ,ত ta	থ tha	দ da	ধ dha	ন ṇa
Labials:	প pa	ফ pha	ব ba	ভ bha	ম ma
Semivowels:	য়,য ya	র ra	ল la	ব va	ড় ḍa
Sibilants:	শ śa	ষ ṣa	স sa	হ ha	ঢ় ḍha

Vowel Symbols

The vowels are written as follows after a consonant:

া ā ি i ী ī ু u ূ ū ৃ ṛ ৄ ṝ ে e ৈ ai ো o ৌ au

For example: কা kā কি ki কী kī কু ku কূ kū কৃ kṛ

কৄ kṝ কে ke কৈ kai কো ko কৌ kau

The letter **a** is implied after a consonant with no vowel symbol.

The symbol *virāma* (্) indicates that there is no final vowel. ক্ k

The letters on the previous page should be pronounced as follows:

a — like the **a** in **a**lone; sometimes like the **o** in g**o**; final **a** is usually silent.
ā — like the **a** in f**a**r.
i, ī — like the **ee** in m**ee**t.
u, ū — like the **u** in r**u**le.
ṛ — like the **ri** in **ri**m.
ṝ — like the **ree** in **ree**d.
e — like the **ai** in p**ai**n; rarely like the **e** in b**e**t.
ei — like the **ai** in p**ai**n.
ai — like the **oi** in b**oi**l.
o — like the **o** in g**o**.
au — like the **o** in g**o**.
ṁ — (*anusvāra*) like the **ng** in so**ng**.
ḥ — (*visarga*) a final **h** sound like in A**h**.
ṅ (ঁ)— (*candra-bindu*) a nasal **n** sound like in the French word *bon;* almost silent.
ñ — like **n** above.
k — like the **k** in **k**ite.
kh — like the **kh** in Ec**kh**art.
g — like the **g** in **g**ot.
gh — like the **gh** in bi**g-h**ouse.
ṅ — like the **n** in ba**n**k.
c — like the **ch** in **ch**alk.
ch — like the **chh** in mu**ch-h**aste.
j — like the **j** in **j**oy.
jh — like the **geh** in colle**ge-h**all.
ṭ — like the **t** in **t**alk, but with the tip of the tongue against the roof of the mouth.
ṭh — like the **th** in ho**t-h**ouse, but with the tip of the tongue against the roof of the mouth.
ḍ — like the **d** in **d**awn, but with the tip of the tongue against the roof of the mouth.
ḍh — like the **dh** in goo**d-h**ouse, but with the tip of the tongue against the roof of the mouth.
ṇ — like the **n** in g**n**aw, but with the tip of the tongue against the roof of the mouth.
t — as in **t**alk, but with the tongue against the teeth.
th — as in ho**t-h**ouse, but with the tongue against the teeth.
d — as in **d**awn, but with the tongue against the teeth.
dh — as in goo**d-h**ouse, but with the tongue against the teeth.
n — as in **n**or, but with the tongue against the teeth.
p — like the **p** in **p**ine.
ph — like the **ph** in **ph**ilosopher.
b — like the **b** in **b**ird.
bh — like the **bh** in ru**b h**ard.
m — like the **m** in **m**other.
y (য)— like the **j** in **j**aw.
y (য়)— like the **y** in **y**ear.
r — like the **r** in **r**un.
l — like the **l** in **l**aw.
v — like the **b** in **b**ird or the **w** in d**w**arf.
ś, ṣ — like the **sh** in **sh**op.
s — like the **s** in **s**un.
h — like the **h** in **h**ome.

This is a general guide to Bengali pronunciation. The Bengali transliterations in this book accurately show the original Bengali spelling of the text. One should note, however, that in Bengali, as in English, spelling is not always a true indication of how a word is pronounced. Audiocassettes of His Divine Grace A. C. Bhaktivedanta Swami Prabhupāda chanting the original Bengali verses are available from the International Society for Krishna Consciousness.

Index of Bengali and Sanskrit Verses

his index constitutes a complete listing of the first and second lines of the two-
ıe texts and the first and third lines of the four-line texts in this volume of *Śrī
aitanya-caritāmṛta.* The references are to chapter and verse.

A

General Index

The references are to chapter and verse. Numbers in boldface type refer to translations of the texts of *Śrī Caitanya-caritāmṛta.* Numbers in parentheses indicate the approximate page of long purports.

B

Conditioned souls (*continued*)
independence misused by, 5.66
Lord delivers, 4.30
Lord's descent &, 4.9, 6.97
māyā covers, 3.98, 5.66
modes of nature control, 4.62
suffering by, 2.36
Consciousness, three states of, 2.24
Cowherd boys, **4.25, 6.62–64**
Creation
Aniruddha &, 5.41 (3)
atheistic conceptions of, 6.14–15 (1–6)
Balarāma and, **5.9–10**
Lord cause of, 6.14–15 (5), **6.16–21,** 7.121 (2)
Pradyumna &, 5.41 (3)
Sāṅkhya philosophy &, 6.14–15 (2–3), **6.18**
Cupid, 1.19, 5.41 (3)

D

Dakṣa, 4.66
Dākṣiṇātya, 1.19
Dāna-keli-kaumudī, **4.131**
Daridra-nārāyaṇa, 7.103
Dāruka, **4.202**
Daśama-ṭippanī, 5.203
Dattātreya, Lord, 2.10, 2.97
Defects, four material, **7.107**
Deity form(s) of Lord
devotees worship, 5.226
Gopīnātha, **1.17, 1.19,** 1.47
Govindajī, **1.16, 1.19,** 1.47
impersonalists &, 5.226
Lord nondifferent from, **5.225–26**
Madana-mohana, **1.15, 1.19,** 1.47
Māyāvādīs & worship to, 7.151
as mercy for conditioned souls, 5.19
misconception about, 7.115
spiritual progress &, 7.76
Demigods
Aniruddha &, 5.41 (3)
Caitanya &, 3.52, **3.66, 4.51**
caste *gosvāmīs* &, 5.232
chanting Lord's name &, 7.76
devotees & worship to, 7.157
Demigods (*continued*)
Kṛṣṇa served by, 7.157
Lord superior to, 7.115
potency of, 3.71
rāsa dance witnessed by, **1.73–74**
Viṣṇu approached by, **5.114**
worship to, 1.91 (2), 5.226, 7.115, 7.157
Demons
atheists as, 3.91
becoming God &, 3.87
defined, **3.91**
Kṛṣṇa consciousness movement &, 3.91
Kṛṣṇa unknown to, 3.89–**90**
Kṛṣṇa's childhood &, 3.87
Kṛṣṇa's descent &, **4.13–14,** 4.15–16
liberation of, **5.36**
Siddhaloka attained by, **5.39**
Viṣṇu kills, **4.13,** 4.15–16
Devahūti, 1.60, 6.14–15 (8)
Devaśreṣṭha Tryambaka, 6.79
Devī defined, **4.84**
Devotee(s) of Lord
Advaita incarnates as, **7.13**
association with, 1.35, **1.59, 1.60**
attachments of, 7.143
attracted, 4.21–22
blasphemy &, 7.50, 7.51
Caitanya incarnates as, 4.41, 6.28, 7.5, **7.10–12**
Caitanya shelter of, **4.51**
Caitanya's intimate glories &, **4.233–34**
categories of, three, 7.51
compared to cuckoo birds, **4.234**
compared to Ganges, **4.205**
demigod worship &, 7.157
dualistic philosophy by, 7.101
as godly, **3.91**
hearing from, 2.117
imitation, 2.117
Kṛṣṇa's reciprocation with, 2.91–92, **4.177–80**
liberation &, **3.17–18, 4.207–8,** 5.30, 5.36
Lord controlled by, **1.100**
Lord leader of, 2.10
Lord seen by, **2.25**

J

Kṛṣṇa (*continued*)
Mahā-Viṣṇu &, 5.76
as master of all, **6.83–85,** 7.14, 7.157
material creation &, 5.51
material energy separate from, **2.52–53**
material nature energized by, **5.59–61**
Māyāvādīs envious of, 7.130
meeting, separation &, 4.108
Nārāyaṇa compared with, **2.28–29**
nondual nature of, 2.11
as origin, **2.107**
pleasure of, **4.239–48**
plenary portions of, **3.69, 6.23–24**
prābhava expansions of, **2.97**
prakāśa expansions of, **1.68–75**
preacher dear to, 3.98
primary relationships with, 4.34
protection by, **2.67**
pure devotees know, **3.88–90**
qualities of, as unlimited, **5.121**
queens of, **6.72–75**
quoted on spiritual master, **1.46**
Rādhārāṇī &. *See under:* Rādhārāṇī
rāsa dance enjoyed by, **5.220, 7.8**
rasas &, **3.11–12, 4.21–22, 4.121**
remembrance of, 3.91
sandhinī potency &, 4.71
satisfaction of, **3.104**
scriptures describe, 3.111
seeing, **4.151–55**
as shelter, 2.91–92, **2.93–95**
Śiśupāla &, 5.36
Śiva &, **6.80,** 7.157
as source
of energies, **7.117,** 7.118
of everything, 7.83
of happiness, **4.248**
of incarnations, **2.67, 2.70, 2.75–86, 2.89–90, 5.4**
of Mahā-Viṣṇu, **5.71**
of material elements, 5.61
of Nārāyaṇa, 2.5
of *puruṣa-avatāras,* **2.105, 3.70**
of Supersoul, **2.5, 2.8**
of universes, **2.95**
sun-god &, 7.157
"superiors" of, 6.53, **6.55–61,** 6.76

Kṛṣṇa (*continued*)
as Supersoul, **2.36**
as supreme controller, **5.142, 7.7**
as Supreme Lord, **2.106–7, 7.7**
as supreme whole, 6.99
sweetness of
attractiveness of, **5.215, 5.224**
Caitanya's descent &, **6.109–10**
devotees' taste, **4.144**
goddess of fortune &, **5.223**
gopīs &, **4.190, 4.198**
hearing about, **4.157**
Kṛṣṇa desires to taste, **4.144–46, 6.107–10**
Rādhārāṇī &, **4.139, 1.142–43**
servitude sentiment &, **6.103**
as unlimited, **4.138, 1.142–43**
touch of, **4.247**
understanding, **2.13**, 4.1
universal form of, 7.30
vaibhava expansions of, **2.97**
Vedas &, 6.14–15 (7), 7.41, 7.64, 7.72 (1), 7.128 (2, 5)
Vedic scriptures describe, 3.87
vilāsa expansions of, **1.68, 1.76–78**
as witness, **2.44–46**
See also: Caitanya Mahāprabhu
Kṛṣṇa consciousness, 3.97, 4.35, 7.27
Kṛṣṇa consciousness movement
avoidance of, **7.30**
book distribution &, 7.164
brāhmaṇas in, 7.67
Caitanya followed by, 7.148
chanting & dancing in, 7.22, 7.83
compared to Ganges, 2.2
concessions in, 7.37
criticism of, 7.23, 7.31–32
demons &, 3.91
effect of, 7.27
faith in *guru* &, 7.95–96
gender comparison in, 7.31–32
hearing process &, 7.141
holy name spread by, 7.83
impersonalists &, 7.39
living entities' illusion &, 7.118
maintenance of, 7.24
male-female association &, 7.31–32, 7.37, 7.38

L

N

R

S

T

U

Y